Strategic Management Model

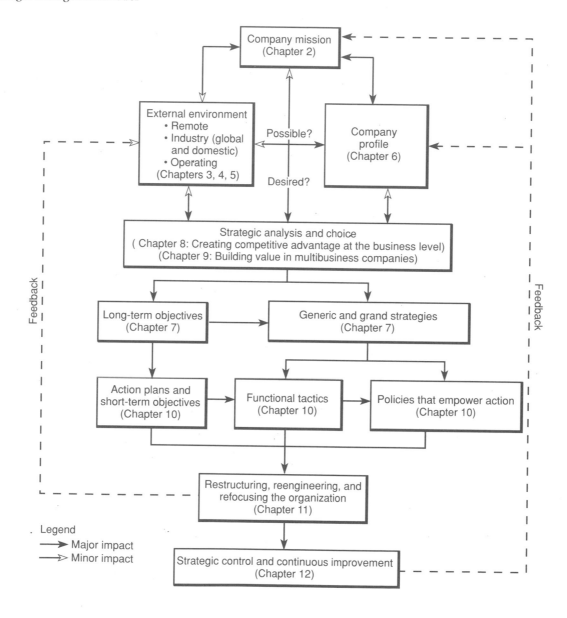

STRATEGIC MANAGEMENT
FORMULATION, IMPLEMENTATION, AND CONTROL

STRATEGIC MANAGEMENT
FORMULATION, IMPLEMENTATION, AND CONTROL

JOHN A. PEARCE II

College of Commerce and Finance
Villanova University

RICHARD B. ROBINSON, JR.

College of Business Administration
University of South Carolina

Sixth Edition

Boston, Massachusetts   Burr Ridge, Illinios   Dubuque, Iowa
Madison, Wisconsin   New York, New York   San Francisco, California   St. Louis, Missouri

Irwin/McGraw-Hill

A Division of The McGraw·Hill Companies

Irwin Book Team

Publisher: *Rob Zwettler*
Executive editor: *Craig S. Beytien*
Developmental editor: *Jennifer R. Boxell*
Marketing manager: *Michael Campbell*
Project editor: *Gladys True*
Production supervisor: *Dina L. Genovese*
Graphics supervisor: *Bethany Stubbe*
Director, Prepress Purchasing: *Kimberly Meriwether David*
Compositor: *Weimer Graphics, Inc., Division of Shepard Poorman Communications Corp.*
Typeface: *10/12 Times Roman*
Printer: *Quebecor Printing/Dubuque*

Library of Congress Cataloging-in-Publication Data

Pearce, John A.
    Strategic management : formulation, implementation, and control /
John A. Pearce, II, Richard B. Robinson, Jr. — 6th ed.
     p.   cm.
    Includes index.
    ISBN 0-256-15478-3
    1. Strategic planning.   I. Robinson, Richard B. (Richard Braden),
1947-   . II. Title.
HD30.28.P3395   1997
658.4′012—dc20   96-9674

Printed in the United States of America
   4 5 6 7 8 9 0 QD 3 2 1 0 9 8

To Susan McCartney Pearce,
David Donham Pearce, Mark McCartney Pearce,
Josephine Elizabeth Robinson,
Katherine Elizabeth Robinson, John Braden Robinson—
for the love, joy, and vitality that they give to our lives.

PREFACE

This sixth edition of *Strategic Management: Formulation, Implementation, and Control* is both the culmination of almost 20 years of work by many people and a major revision designed to fit the 21st century needs of strategy students. We were pleased that the fifth edition was used by more teachers and students than any previous edition. This preface describes what we have done to make the sixth edition even more effective and relevant in preparing students for the exciting global economy they are about to enter. It also gives us the opportunity to recognize many outstanding contributors.

The sixth edition of *Strategic Management: Formulation, Implementation, and Control* provides a thoroughly revised, state-of-the-art treatment of the critical business skills needed to plan and manage strategic activities. We have divided the text into 12 chapters filled with many real-world business examples. Sensitivity to the 21st century strategic ramifications of topics like the global economy, entrepreneurship, ethics, restructuring, continuous improvement, integrated operations and manufacturing, virtual organization, and cultural diversity are evident throughout this major revision of the text. A newly revised and exciting cohesion case on the world's most successful global business, The Coca-Cola Company, is included based on the popular reaction to the use of Coca-Cola in the 5th edition. Coca-Cola remains large but still entrepreneurial, innovative, growing, and cleverly managed—a collection of thousands of locally focused operations in every corner of the globe. It provides an extraordinarily useful example that students will find beneficial, recognizable, and motivational in their study of strategic management, entrepreneurship, and global business.

Contemporary research in strategic management, with an emphasis on conceptual tools and skills created by value-adding scholars and practitioners in the field, will be evident throughout the 12 chapters in this edition. While the text retains its solid academic connection, we have endeavored to create text material that is practical, skills oriented, and applicable on the job.

We have selected 41 cases for this edition—all new! A special relationship with IN-SEAD has ensured a contemporary, global flavor to our case selections. The tireless cooperation of some of the world's best case writers has been a major contribution, ensuring a good sampling of companies by size, formulation versus implementation issues, and industry versus business-unit level of analysis.

We are pleased to maintain our strategic alliance with Halcyon's Office Profit. Office Profit provides a one-stop, comprehensive software tool for examining the financial and operating data of a firm to assess its capabilities and options relative to industry standards and historical performance. Some of our cases can be examined via financial data already loaded on the disk available with this book.

Other components of our teaching package include a totally revised, comprehensive intructor's manual, a set of two-color transparencies, packaged with PowerPoint presentation slides, a computerized test bank, and two videos. These elements are coordinated and backed by Irwin's outstanding customer support capabilities.

Changes to Our Text Material

The literature and research comprising the strategic management field has been developing at a rapid pace in recent years both in the academic literature and the business press. We have endeavored to create an edition that incorporates major developments from both sources while keeping our focus centered on a straightforward and logical framework through which students can grasp the complexity and essence of strategic management. Some of the revisions that deserve particular note are:

· The text went from 11 chapters in the fifth edition to 12 chapters in this edition. The reason was to provide a treatment of strategic analysis and choice over two chapters instead of one chapter as in previous editions. A new Chapter 8 focuses on tools and techniques for strategic analysis at the business level—single- or dominant-product/service companies. A new Chapter 9 covers strategic analysis in multibusiness companies and covers behavioral considerations shaping strategic choice.

· Previous adopters will note a revised model of the strategic management process. Covered in Chapter 1, our revisions sought to reflect strategic analysis at different organizational levels while also portraying the role of action plans, continuous improvement, and employee empowerment within the strategic management process. While the model has been revised, we went to great efforts to keep the useful attributes mentioned by so many previous adopters as being a key distinctive competence present in our book: a logical flow, distinct elements, and easy-to-understand guide to strategic management.

· The role of the CEO and the board of directors has received prominent attention in Chapter 1. We have developed the exciting examples of Saturn and Nissan to explain company philosophy. Complementing this material, Chapter 2 has also increased its attention to customer influences on strategy, customer-driven organizations, and the essence of quality as a part of mission development.

· Our three-chapter set examining the environment has undergone considerable revision. Some key highlights include adding a major section on ecological issues; examining issues of regulation and innovation-friendly regulation as entry barriers; and highlighting techniques and concepts to create meaningful customer profiles and unique customer segmentation early on in strategic management.

· Globalization is certainly a defining theme in environmental analysis, and we have added important new examples and a discussion of factors that drive global companies. Forecasting competitive behavior and the creation of early warning systems when confronting competitive or environmental problems received new coverage in Chapter 5. Accompanying these new developments is a revised, three-chapter core replete with dynamic examples and contemporary discussion linking them to the field's most important concepts in a breadth of coverage (three chapters) that continues to be one of the most expansive available.

· Attention to value chain analysis as a framework for examining a firm's strengths and weaknesses was expanded along with a major new discussion of benchmarking as a means to leverage the use of value chain analysis and other techniques for understanding firm capabilities. New examples—an exciting global female entrepreneur at England's Laura Ashley, Avery Dennison's global benchmarking, and the dramatic changes in the global PC industry—illustrate these topics.

· Our discussion of strategic alternatives in Chapter 7 was expanded in two ways. First, we sought to help students understand the linkage between strategic intent and corporate purpose—the big picture. Second, we added significantly to our discussion of market development as a grand strategy while expanding the coverage of strategic alliances and outsourcing as strategy elements—all changes intended to emphasis the focus and partnering trends among the best businesses around the globe.

· Already mentioned above, our treatment of strategic analysis and choice has been expanded from one large chapter to two chapters of more modest length. Our major concern here was to create a more user-friendly coverage of strategic analysis in the somewhat distinct venues of single- or dominant-product businesses and multibusiness companies. Chapter 8 seeks to focus on the single-product business by discussing techniques and concepts managers use to examine business strategy alternatives—identifying and choosing the best way to build sustainable competitive advantage. The chapter emphasizes speed and market focus, as well as the traditional cost leadership and differentiation sources of competitive advantage. Strategic analysis focused on identifying sources of each type of competitive advantage along with organizational resources required to support and sustain them form the basis for strategic analysis and choice at the business level.

· Strategic analysis and choice facing managers of multibusiness companies as they seek to maximize long-term shareholder value is the focus of a new Chapter 9. Rationalizing diversification, and examining opportunities for sharing in frastructure and capabilities are developed as key conceptual "tools" to make corporate strategic decisions. This chapter also retains a revised, reduced coverage of portfolio techniques and a focused coverage of key behavioral considerations in strategic choice.

· The three chapters on implementation and strategic control underwent major revision. Creating value activities provides a current, integrating theme for Chapter 10's material on action plans and functional tactics. Major revisions include coverage of flexible manufacturing systems, JIT, SPC, and outsourcing as operating tactical options; marketing responses to diversity, the decreasing importance of size, and HRM in a downsized, outsourcing environment; and a major emphasis on the use of policies as a source of employee empowerment.

· New material in Chapter 11 examines (1) guidelines to match structure to strategy emphasizing restructuring to support strategically critical activities, (2) business process engineering as a means to do the restructuring, and (3) downsizing, outsourcing, and self-managing work teams as ways to truly redefine the way an organization's "work" or strategically critical activities get done with speed, quality, and cost effectiveness. The discussion of leadership and culture has been reworked to place embracing change through three fundamental means as a central theme. Examples from prominent companies that have visibly restructured themselves in the 1990s provide many useful strategy-in-action examples.

· Chapter 12's well-received coverage of strategic control was revised to include updated literature on strategic control and to add significant new material on continuous improvement. The emphasis was placed on strategic control; operational control and budgets were given reduced, yet focused coverage; and a new section was added on continuous improvement to build customer value, replete with how-to guidelines and current examples.

Overall, we found ourselves reenergized by the challenge to "continuously improve" on well-received text material. A lot has changed during the 1990s—changes that have revitalized and redefined the nature and focus of strategic management. The challenge and result for us has been a major revitalization and revision of our book while keeping a structured, student-friendly flow an overriding requirement.

We have updated, increased, and improved our *Strategy in Action* capsules. The fundamental idea behind them remains the same—provide interesting, separate examples that enrich text material and engage students as they read the text. The 12 chapters contain 42 of these illustration vignettes, 36 of which are completely new to the sixth edition. Each Strategy in Action provides a contemporary business example of a key chapter topic designed to enhance student interest and aid learning.

We also have 14 *Global Strategy in Action* capsules in this edition, with at least one in every chapter. These capsules are introduced to help students appreciate how strategic managers worldwide meet global competition, and we are excited about the interesting, all-new set assembled for this edition. They are more diverse, personal, and educational, taking students into a variety of surprising businesses around the world. They also offer North American student users the chance in a sense to "benchmark" companies most familiar to them with several best-practice companies across a variety of industries throughout the global economy.

We have responded to adopters' positive response to the introduction of The Coca-Cola Company as our cohesion case in the last edition by retaining the company as the cohesion case for this edition. While the company is the same, users of the cohesion case will be pleased to see a virtually totally rewritten coverage of strategic management at Coca-Cola. This company has made incredible progress since 1995. It has refined and built sustainable competitive advantages based on speed, market focus, differentiation, and cost leadership. Its strategies are specific, varied, and very educational. Numerous visual as well as narrative illustrations of each aspect of strategic management at Coca-Cola around the globe have been provided to help students learn strategic management from one of, if not the best global business system in the history of world commerce.

Our survey of adopters told us to continue to inform students about what they need to do in preparing a case—and to maintain a strategic point of view while doing so. We have included a major section at the end of Chapter 12 that is solely intended to aid students in understanding case method pedagogy and to prepare them to analyze a case, prepare it for class, and participate in class discussion. Additional support for this is included in the instructor's manual, providing instructors with the discretion to increase case preparation assistance for students. The case method section along with the cohesion case provide two proven learning aids that ensure that students understand and benefit from the case method pedagogy.

Five supplements accompany or are available to accompany our text to increase readers' ability to enhance their competence in the practice of strategic management: A guide to industry information sources follows Chapter 5. Students will find it helpful in rapidly orienting them to where and how to get company and industry data.

Also following Chapter 5 is a supplement on strategic planning tools and techniques for forecasting. It offers a practical assessment of each of 20 planning aids as well as source information on these detailed how-to materials.

A revised guide to financial analysis is provided following Chapter 6. It provides a thorough, easty-to-use guide to the quantitative analysis of financial and operating information, which will help refamiliarize students with previously learned techniques and introduce them to others.

Halcyon's Office Profit software is also available to accompany this sixth edition. It has been thoroughly updated for Windows 95 use, can be disk- or CD-ROM–based, and includes excellent industry comparative data from Robert Morris Associates. It has become an industry standard among commercial lenders, and the software choice in all SBA and SBDC offices. It allows quick and thorough financial and operating analysis, projections, and a variety of analyses that will have students focusing on strategic interpretation, not simple calculation. We have data from some of the cases in the sixth edition already preloaded on the Halcyon disk. Students can, however, use it on all cases as well as in their future managerial or entrepreneurial careers.

Cases in the Sixth Edition

We are truly excited about the 41 cases and industry notes assembled in this sixth edition. First, we have crafted a special relationship with INSEAD in Europe to provide 10 cases and industry notes distributed exclusively through them. These cases have undergone thorough class testing, are written by some of the world's best case writers, and take students into a variety of companies around the world. Following the INSEAD initiative, we have endeavored to ensure a strong global feel to our sixth edition case selection. The result means that over two-thirds of our cases involve companies either located or doing business outside North America.

Second, all 41 cases are new to this edition of *Strategic Management: Formulation, Implementation, and Control*. They all involve issues addressed in the 1990s, with a major emphasis on strategy implementation issues versus offerings most commonly found in strategy texts. We have a good mixture of small and large firms, global and domestic market commitments, and service, retail, technology, and manufacturing activities.

We are particularly pleased to organize the cases into three "kinds" of cases. First, we have 30 individual cases to let students explore separate companies in great detail. Then we assemble two industry case sets that examine two industries and two players within each industry. This way students can explore two industry settings in great detail while also viewing the industry from the perspective of the management teams of two significant industry participants. Finally, to further refine student skills in industry analysis, we have assembled five industry notes that let them examine a variety of industry settings with which they are likely familiar as a customer or a potential employee.

Acknowledgments

We have benefited from the help of many people in the evolution of this book over six editions. Students, adopters, colleagues, reviewers, and business contacts have provided hundreds of insightful comments, suggestions, and contributions that have progressively enhanced this book. We are indebted to the researchers, writers, and practicing managers who have accelerated the development of the literature on strategic management.

We are likewise indebted to the talented case researchers who have produced the cases used in this book, as well as the growing network of case authors dedicated to the revitalization of case research as an important academic endeavor. The discipline of strategic management is eminently more teachable when current, well-written and well-researched cases are available. We encourage every opportunity to properly recognize and reward first-class case research—it is a major avenue through which top strategic management scholars should be recognized.

The following strategic management scholars have provided the results of their case research in the creation of this sixth edition of *Strategic Management: Formulation, Implementation, and Control:*

Mary Ackenhusen
INSEAD

A. J. Almaney
DePaul University

James Almeida
University of South Carolina

Katherine A. Auer
The Pennsylvania State University

Amy Beekman
University of South Carolina

Patricia Bilafer
Bentley College

Eric Brown
George Mason University

Robert F. Bruner
INSEAD

Neil Churchill
INSEAD

Philippe Demigne
INSEAD

Jean–Christopher Donck
INSEAD

Yves Doz
INSEAD

Julie Driscoll
Bentley College

Soumitra Dutta
INSEAD

Harold Dyck
California State University

Mary Fandel
Bentley College

Bertrand George
INSEAD

Barbara Gottfried
Bentley College

Sue Greenfeld
California State University

Jean M. Hanebury
Texas A&M University

Karen Hare
Bentley College

Earl Harper
Grand Valley State University

Alan N. Hoffman
Bentley College

Phyllis G. Holland
Valdosta State University

Mel Horwitch
Theseus

Stephen Jenner
California State University

Kevin Kaiser
INSEAD

James A. Kidney
Southern Connecticut State University

Jeffrey A. Krug
The University of Memphis

Joseph Lampel
New York University

Sharon Ungar Lane
Bentley College

Roland Larose
Bentley College

Michael Levy
INSEAD

Charles C. Manz
Arizona State University

Linda Merrill
Bentley College

Carol Rugg
Bentley College

W. Kent Moore
Valdosta State University

Uri Savoray
INSEAD

Jaideep Motwani
Grand Valley State University

Frank M. Shipper
Salisbury State University

Karen Mullen
Bentley College

Bonnie Silvieria
Bentley College

Daniel Muzyka
INSEAD

Glenda Smith
Villanova University

Carlos de Pommes
Theseus

Romuald A. Stone
James Madison University

H. Lee Remmers
INSEAD

Ram Subramanian
Grand Valley State University

Linda Riesenman
Villanova University

Chris Taubman
INSEAD

George C. Rubenson
Salisbury State University

James Teboul
INSEAD

Alison Rude
Bentley College

S. David Young
INSEAD

We have personally ensured that the dean at each of the case author's respective institutions is aware of the value that his or her case research efforts have added to professionals' ability to teach strategic management.

The development of this book through six editions has been greatly enhanced by the generous time, energy, and ideas from the following people (we apologize if the affiliation has changed):

A. J. Almaney
DePaul University

Jeff Bracker
University of Louisville

B. Alpert
San Francisco State University

Dorothy Brawley
Kennesaw State College

Alan Amason
University of Georgia

James W. Bronson
Washington State University

Sonny Aries
University of Toledo

William Burr
University of Oregon

Amy Vernberg Beekman
University of South Carolina

Gene E. Burton
California State University–Fresno

Robert Earl Bolick
Metropolitan State University

Edgar T. Busch
Western Kentucky University

Bill Boulton
Auburn University

Charles M. Byles
Virginia Commonwealth University

Charles Boyd
Southwest Missouri State University

Gerard A. Cahill

Jim Callahan
University of LaVerne

James W. Camerius
Northern Michigan University

Richard Castaldi
San Diego State University

Gary J. Castogiovanni
Louisiana State University

Jafor Chowdbury
University of Scranton

James J. Chrisman
University of South Carolina

J. Carl Clamp
University of South Carolina

Earl D. Cooper
Florida Institute of Technology

Louis Coraggio
Troy State University

Jeff Covin
Georgia Institute of Technology

John P. Cragin
Oklahoma Baptist University

Larry Cummings
Northwestern University

Peter Davis
Memphis State University

William Davis
Auburn University

Julio DeCastro
University of Colorado

D. Keith Denton
Southwest Missouri State University

F. Derakhshan
*California State University–
San Bernardino*

Brook Dobni
University of Saskatchewan

Mark Dollinger
Indiana University

Max E. Douglas
Indiana State University

Derrick Dsouza
University of North Texas

Thomas J. Dudley
Pepperdine University

John Dunkelberg
Wake Forest University

Norbert Esser
Central Wesleyan College

Forest D. Etheredge
Aurora University

Liam Fahey

Mark Fiegener
Oregon State University

Calvin D. Fowler
Embry–Riddle Aeronautical University

Debbie Francis
Auburn University–Montgomery

Elizabeth Freeman
Southern Methodist University

Mahmound A. Gaballa
Mansfield University

Donna M. Gallo
Boston College

Diane Garsombke
University of Maine

Betsy Gatewood
University of Houston

Michael Geringer
Southern Methodist University

Manton C. Gibbs
Indiana University of Pennsylvania

Nicholas A. Glaskowsky, Jr.
University of Miami

Tom Goho
Wake Forest University

Jon Goodman
University of Southern California

Pradeep Gopalakrishna
Hofstra University

R. H. Gordon
Hofstra University

Barbara Gottfried
Bentley College

Peter Goulet
University of Northern Iowa

Walter E. Greene
University of Texas–Pan American

Sue Greenfeld
*California State University–
San Bernardino*

David W. Grigsby
Clemson University

Daniel E. Hallock
St. Edward's University

Don Hambrick
Columbia University

Barry Hand
Indiana State University

Samuel Hazen
Tarleton State University

W. Harvey Hegarty
Indiana University

Edward A. Hegner
*California State University–
Sacramento*

Marilyn M. Helms
University of Tennessee–Chattanooga

Lanny Herron
University of Baltimore

D. Higginbothan
University of Missouri

Roger Higgs
Western Carolina University

William H. Hinkle
Johns Hopkins University

Charles T. Hofer
University of Georgia

Alan N. Hoffman
Bentley College

Richard Hoffman
College of William and Mary

Eileen Hogan
George Mason University

Gary L. Holman
St. Martin's College

Don Hopkins
Temple University

Cecil Horst
*Keller Graduate School of
Management*

Henry F. House
Auburn University–Montgomery

William C. House
University of Arkansas–Fayetteville

Frank Hoy
University of Texas–El Paso

Warren Huckabay

Eugene H. Hunt
Virginia Commonwealth University

Tammy G. Hunt
*University of North Carolina–
Wilmington*

John W. Huonker
University of Arizona

Stephen R. Jenner
California State University

Shailendra Jha
Wilfrid Laurier University–Ontario

C. Boyd Johnson
California State University–Fresno

Troy Jones
University of Central Florida

Jon Kalinowski
Mankato State University

Al Kayloe
Lake Erie College

Michael J. Keefe
Southwest Texas State University

Kay Keels
Louisiana State University

James A. Kidney
Southern Connecticut State University

John D. King
Embry-Riddle Aeronautical University

Raymond M. Kinnunen
Northeastern University

John B. Knauff
University of St. Thomas

Rose Knotts
University of North Texas

Dan Kopp
Southwest Missouri State University

Michael Koshuta
Valparaiso University

Myroslaw Kyj
Widener University of Pennsylvania

Dick LaBarre
Ferris State University

Ryan Lancaster
The University of Phoenix

Anne T. Lawrence
San Jose State University

Joseph Leonard
Miami University–Ohio

Robert Letovsky
Saint Michael's College

Benjamin Litt
Lehigh University

Frank S. Lockwood
University of South Carolina

John Logan
University of South Carolina

Sandra Logan
Newberry College

Jean M. Lundin
Lake Superior State University

Rodney H. Mabry
Clemson University

Donald C. Malm
University of Missouri–St. Louis

Charles C. Manz
Arizona State University

John Maurer
Wayne State University

Denise Mazur
Aquinas College

Edward McClelland
Roanoke College

Bob McDonald
Central Wesleyan College

Patricia P. McDougall
Georgia Institute of Technology

S. Mehta
San Jose State University

Ralph Melaragno
Pepperdine University

Richard Merner
University of Delaware

Timothy Mescon
Kennesaw State College

Philip C. Micka
Park College

Bill J. Middlebrook
Southwest Texas State University

James F. Molly, Jr.
Northeastern University

Cynthia Montgomery
Harvard University

Robert Mookler
St. John's University

Gary W. Muller
Hofstra University

Terry Muson
Northern Montana College

Stephanie Newell
Bowling Green State University

Michael E. Nix
Trinity College of Vermont

Kenneth Olm
University of Texas–Austin

Benjamin M. Oviatt
Georgia State University

Joseph Paolillo
University of Mississippi

Gerald Parker
St. Louis University

Paul J. Patinka
University of Colorado

James W. Pearce
Western Carolina University

Michael W. Pitts
Virginia Commonwealth University

Douglas Polley
St. Cloud State University

Valerie J. Porciello
Bentley College

Mark S. Poulous
St. Edward's University

John B. Pratt
Saint Joseph's College

Oliver Ray Price
West Coast University

John Primus
Golden Gate University

Norris Rath
Shepard College

Paula Rechner
University of Illinois

Richard Reed
Washington State University

J. Bruce Regan
University of St. Thomas

F. A. Ricci
Georgetown University

Keith Robbins
George Mason University

Gary Roberts
Kennesaw State College

Lloyd E. Roberts
Mississippi College

John K. Ross III
Southwest Texas State University

Les Rue
Georgia State University

J. A. Ruslyk
Memphis State University

Ronald J. Salazar
Idaho State University

Jack Scarborough
Barry University

Paul J. Schlachter
Florida International University

John Seeger
Bentley College

Martin Shapiro
Iona College

Arthur Sharplin
McNeese State University

Frank Shipper
Salisbury State University

Rodney C. Shrader
Georgia State University

Lois Shufeldt
Southwest Missouri State University

F. Bruce Simmons III
The University of Akron

Mark Simon
Georgia State University

Michael Skipton
Memorial University

Fred Smith
Western Illinois University

Scott Snell
Michigan State University

Coral R. Snodgrass
Canisius College

Rudolph P. Snowadzky
University of Maine

Neil Snyder
University of Virginia

Melvin J. Stanford
Mankato State University

Warren S. Stone
Virginia Commonwealth University

Ram Subramanian
Grand Valley State University

Paul M. Swiercz
Georgia State University

Robert L. Swinth
Montana State University

Russell Teasley
University of South Carolina

George H. Tompson
University of South Carolina

Jody Tompson
University of New Zealand

Melanie Trevino
University of Texas–El Paso

Howard Tu
Memphis State University

Craig Tunwall
Ithaca College

Elaine M. Tweedy
University of Scranton

Arieh A. Ullmann
SUNY–Binghamton

P. Veglahn
James Madison University

George Vozikis
The Citadel

William Waddell
*California State University–
Los Angeles*

Bill Warren
College of William and Mary

Kirby Warren
Columbia University

Steven J. Warren
Rutgers University

Michael White
University of Tulsa

Randy White
Auburn University

Sam E. White
Portland State University

Frank Winfrey
Kent State University

Joseph Wolfe
University of Tulsa

Robley Wood
Virginia Commonwealth University

Edward D. Writh, Jr.
Florida Institute of Technology

John Young
University of Colorado

Jan Zahrly
Old Dominion University

Alan Zeiber
Portland State University

The valuable ideas, recommendations, and support of these outstanding scholars and teachers have added quality to this book.

Because we are affiliated with two separate universities, we have two sets of co-workers to thank.

As the Endowed Chair holder of the College of Commerce and Finance at Villanova University, Jack is able to combine his scholarly and teaching activities with his co-authorship of this text. He is grateful to Villanova University and his colleagues for the support and encouragement that they provide.

Richard deeply appreciates the support and assistance of strategy colleagues Alan Bauerschmidt, Carl Clamp, John Logan, Michael Leiblein, Harry Sapienza, Bill Sandberg, and David Schweiger at USC. Doctoral candidates James Almeida, Amy Beeckman, and Jim Bloodgood made major contributions to the development, class testing, and refinement of selected business case studies. Susie VanHuss, Program Director, Dean David Shrock, and Associate Deans Bob Markland and Randy Martin provided much appreciated encouragement, recognition, and support. A special thanks goes to Cheryl Fowler, Susie Gorsage, and Sandy Bennett for their clerical and logistical support.

None of this would have been possible without the outstanding Irwin organization. We thank Gerald Saykes for getting us started over 20 years ago and continuing to support this project. Craig Beytein's editorial leadership is outstanding. His team including Jenny Boxell, Gladys True, Kim Kanakes, and Harriet Stockanes continue the Irwin legacy of professionalism and excellence. The Irwin field organization deserves special recognition for six successful editions. And John Black's leadership through much strategic change has been a calming force that kept us focused.

In using this text, we hope that you will share our enthusiasm both for the rich subject of strategic management and for the learning approach that we have taken. We value your recommendations and thoughts about our material. Please contact Jack or Richard at the following addresses:

Dr. John A. Pearce II
College of Commerce & Finance
Villanova University
Vollanova, PN 19085-1678
610-519-4332
Jpearce@email.vill.edu

Dr. Richard Robinson
College of Business Administration
University of South Carolina
Columbia, SC 29205
803-777-5961
Robinson@darla.badm.sc.edu

We wish you the very best as you advance your knowledge in the exciting and rewarding field of strategic management.

Jack Pearce
Richard Robinson

About the Authors

John A. Pearce II, Ph.D., is the endowed chair holder of the College of Commerce and Finance at Villanova University. Previously, Dr. Pearce was holder of the Eakin Endowed Chair in Strategic Management at George Mason University and was a State of Virginia Eminent Scholar. In 1994, he received the Fulbright U.S. Professional Award for service in Malaysia. Professor Pearce has taught at Penn State, West Virginia University, the University of Malta where as a Fulbright Senior Professor in International Management he served as the Head of Business Faculties, and at the University of South Carolina where he was Director of Ph.D. Programs in Strategic Management. He received a Ph.D. degree in Business Administration from the Pennsylvania State University.

Professor Pearce is coauthor of 24 books that have been used to help educate more than 1,000,000 students and managers. He has also authored more than 165 articles and professional papers. These have been published in journals that include the *Academy of Management Journal*, *California Management Review*, *Journal of Applied Psychology*, *Journal of Business Venturing*, *Sloan Management Review*, and *Strategic Management Journal*. Several of these publications have resulted from Professor Pearce's work as a principal on research projects funded for more than $2 million. He is a recognized expert in the field of strategic management, with special accomplishments in the areas of strategy formulation, implementation, and control, management during recessions, mission statement development, competitive assessment, industry analysis, joint ventures, and tools for strategy evaluation and design.

A frequent leader of executive development programs and an active consultant to business and industry, Dr. Pearce's client list includes domestic and multinational firms engaged in manufacturing, service, and nonprofit industries.

Richard B. Robinson, Jr., Ph.D., is Professor of Strategy and Entrepreneurship and is a Business Partnership Foundation Fellow in the College of Business Administration at the University of South Carolina. Professor Robinson recently returned to USC after serving for three years as president and CEO of a rapidly growing hazardous waste management company.

Professor Robinson has published numerous articles and professional papers in preeminent journals and associations dedicated to improving the practice of strategic management and the art of entrepreneurship. He has coauthored 26 texts, proceedings, and supplements for book publishers that include Richard D. Irwin, McGraw-Hill, Random House, and the Academy of Management.

Professor Robinson is the recipient of several awards in recognition of his work in strategic management and entrepreneurship. He also has held offices in the Academy of Management, the Southern Management Association, and the International Council of Small Business.

Professor Robinson currently serves on the investment advisory committee of two venture capital funds.

CONTENTS

I OVERVIEW OF STRATEGIC MANAGEMENT *1*

1 Strategic Management *2*
The Nature and Value of Strategic Management *3*
Dimensions of Strategic Decisions *4*
   Three Levels of Strategy 5
   Characteristics of Strategic Management Decisions 6
Formality in Strategic Management *9*
   The Strategy Makers 9
   Benefits of Strategic Management 10
   Risks of Strategic Management 11
   Executives' Views of Strategic Management 12
The Strategic Management Process *12*
Components of the Strategic Management Model *13*
   Company Mission 13
   Company Profile 14
   External Environment 15
   Strategic Analysis and Choice 15
   Long-Term Objectives 15
   Generic and Grand Strategies 15
   Action Plans and Short-Term Objectives 16
   Functional Tactics 16
   Policies that Empower Action 16
   Restructuring, Reengineering, and Refocusing the Organization 16
   Strategic Control and Continuous Improvement 17
Strategic Management as a Process *17*
   Changes in the Process 18

Summary   *19*
Cohesion Case: The Coca-Cola Company   *22*

II   STRATEGY FORMULATION   *27*

2   Defining the Company Mission   *28*
What Is a Company Mission?   *29*
   The Need for an Explicit Mission   29
Formulating a Mission   *29*
   Basic Product or Service: Primary Market; Principal Technology   31
   Company Goals: Survival, Growth, Profitability   32
   Company Philosophy   34
   Public Image   35
   Company Self-Concept   37
   Newest Trends in Mission Components   39
Overseeing the Strategy Makers   *42*
   Board Success Factors   44
The Stakeholder Approach to Company Responsibility   *45*
   Social Responsibility   47
   Guidelines for a Socially Responsible Firm   49
Summary   *51*
Cohesion Case: Company Mission at The Coca-Cola Company   *57*

3   The External Environment   *61*
Remote Environment   *62*
   1. Economic Factors   62
   2. Social Factors   64
   3. Political Factors   65
   4. Technological Factors   66
   5. Ecological Factors   67
Industry Environment   *73*
Overview   *74*
How Competitive Forces Shape Strategy   *74*
Contending Forces   *75*
   A. Threat of Entry   76
   B. Powerful Suppliers   77
   C. Powerful Buyers   79
   D. Substitute Products   80
   E. Jockeying for Position   80
Industry Analysis and Competitive Analysis   *81*
Industry Boundaries   *81*
   Problems in Defining Industry Boundaries   82
   Developing a Realistic Industry Definition   83

Industry Structure   *84*
   Concentration   84
   Economies of Scale   84
   Product Differentiation   85
   Barriers to Entry   85
Competitive Analysis   *86*
   How to Identify Competitors   86
   Common Mistakes in Identifying Competitors   87
Operating Environment   *88*
   1. Competitive Position   88
   2. Customer Profiles   89
   3. Suppliers   92
   4. Creditors   93
   5. Human Resources: Nature of the Labor Market   93
Emphasis on Environmental Factors   *94*
Summary   *95*
Cohesion Case: Assessing the External Environment at The Coca-Cola Company   *99*

4   The Global Environment: Strategic Considerations for Multinational Firms   *103*
Development of a Global Corporation   *106*
Why Firms Globalize   *107*
Considerations Prior to Globalization   *109*
Complexity of the Global Environment   *111*
Control Problems of the Global Firm   *112*
Global Strategic Planning   *113*
   Multidomestic Industries and Global Industries   113
   The Multinational Challenge   116
   International Strategy Options   117
Globalization of the Company Mission   *118*
   Components of the Company Mission Revisited   120
   Product or Service, Market, and Technology   120
   Company Goals: Survival, Growth, and Profitability   121
   Company Philosophy   121
   Self-Concept   122
   Public Image   122
Competitive Strategies for U.S. Firms in Foreign Markets   *122*
   Niche Market Exporting   123
   Licensing/Contract Manufacturing   123
   Joint Ventures   124
   Foreign Branching   125
   Foreign Subsidiaries   125
Summary   *126*
Appendix: Components of the Multinational Environment   *129*
Cohesion Case: The Global Environment and The Coca-Cola Company   *131*

5   Environmental Forecasting   *136*

Importance of Forecasting   *137*

Select Critical Environmental Variables   *137*

    Who Selects the Key Variables?   140

    What Variables Should Be Selected?   141

Select Sources of Significant Environmental Information   *141*

Evaluate Forecasting Techniques   *141*

    Techniques Available   143

Integrate Forecast Results into the Strategic Management Process   *151*

Monitor the Critical Aspects of Managing Forecasts   *153*

Summary   *155*

Appendix 5-A: Sources for Environmental Forecasts   *158*

Appendix 5-B: Strategic Planning Forecasting Tools and Techniques   *162*

Cohesion Case: Forecasting and The Coca-Cola Company   *164*

6   Internal Analysis   *168*

Traditional Approaches to Internal Analysis   *169*

    SWOT Analysis   170

    The Functional Approach   173

    Value Chain Analysis   176

Internal Analysis: Making Meaningful Comparisons   *181*

    Comparison with Past Performance   181

    Stage of Industry Evolution   181

    Benchmarking—Comparison with Competitors   185

    Comparison with Success Factors in the Industry   188

Summary   *189*

Appendix: Using Financial Analysis   *191*

Cohesion Case: Internal Analysis at The Coca-Cola Company   *203*

7   Formulating Long-Term Objectives and Grand Strategies   *210*

Long-Term Objectives   *211*

    Qualities of Long-Term Objectives   214

Generic Strategies   *216*

Grand Strategies   *217*

    Concentrated Growth   218

    Market Development   222

    Product Development   225

    Innovation   226

    Horizontal Integration   227

    Vertical Integration   228

    Concentric Diversification   229

    Conglomerate Diversification   230

    Turnaround   231

Divestiture   234

Liquidation   235

Corporate Combinations   *235*

Joint Ventures   236

Strategic Alliances   237

Consortia, Keiretsus, and Chaebols   239

Selection of Long-Term Objectives and Grand Strategy Sets   *240*

Sequence of Objectives and Strategy Selection   *241*

Summary   *241*

Cohesion Case: Formulating Long-Term Objective and Grand Strategies at The Coca-Cola Company   *244*

8   Strategic Analysis and Choice in Single- or Dominant-Product Businesses: Building Sustainable Competitive Advantages   247

Evaluating and Choosing Business Strategies: Seeking Sustained Competitive Advantage   *248*

Evaluating Cost Leadership Opportunities   249

Evaluating Differentiation Opportunities   251

Evaluating Speed as a Competitive Advantage   254

Evaluating Market Focus as a Way to Competitive Advantage   257

Selected Industry Environments and Business Strategy Choices   *259*

Competitive Advantage in Emerging Industries   259

Competitive Advantage in the Transition to Industry Maturity   260

Competitive Advantage in Mature and Declining Industries   262

Competitive Advantage in Fragmented Industries   262

Competitive Advantage in Global Industries   263

Dominant-Product/Service Business: Evaluating and Choosing to Diversify to Build Value   *264*

Grand Strategy Selection Matrix   265

Model of Grand Strategy Selection Clusters   267

Opportunities for Building Value as a Basis for Choosing Diversification or Integration   270

Summary   *271*

Cohesion Case: Building Sustainable Competitive Advantages at Coca-Cola   *273*

9   Strategic Analysis and Choice in the Multibusiness Company: Rationalizing Diversification and Building Shareholder Value   276

Rationalizing Diversification and Integration   *277*

Are Opportunities for Sharing Infrastructure and Capabilities Forthcoming?   278

Are We Capitalizing on Our Core Competencies?   281

Does the Company's Business Portfolio Balance Financial Resources?   282

Does Our Business Portfolio Achieve Appropriate Levels of Risk and Growth?   291

Behavioral Considerations Affecting Strategic Choice   *292*

Role of the Current Strategy   292

Degree of the Firm's External Dependence   292

Attitudes toward Risk   *293*

Internal Political Considerations   *293*

Timing   *294*

Competitive Reaction   *294*

Summary   *295*

Cohesion Case: Building Stockholder Value as a Multibusiness Company
  at Coca-Cola   *297*

III   STRATEGY/IMPLEMENTATION   *301*

---

10   Implementing Strategy through Action Plans, Functional Tactics, and Employee Empowerment   *303*

Action Plans and Short-Term Objectives   *304*

  Qualities of Effective Short-Term Objectives   *306*

  The Value-Added Benefits of Action Plans and Short-Term Objectives   *308*

Functional Tactics that Implement Business Strategies   *309*

  Differences between Business Strategies and Functional Tactics   *310*

  Functional Tactics in Production/Operations   *311*

  Functional Tactics in Marketing   *313*

  Functional Tactics in Accounting and Finance   *315*

  Functional Tactics in Research and Development   *316*

  Functional Tactics in Human Resource Management (HRM)   *318*

Empowering Operating Personnel: The Role of Policies   *320*

  Creating Policies that Empower   *322*

Summary   *325*

Cohesion Case: Implementing Strategy through the Business Functions at Coca-Cola   *328*

11   Implementing Strategy through Restructuring and Reengineering the Company's Structure, Leadership, Culture, and Rewards   *338*

Structuring an Effective Organization   *339*

  Primary Organizational Structures and Their Strategy-Related Pros and Cons   *340*

  Guidelines to Match Structure to Strategy   *346*

Organizational Leadership   *352*

  Strategic Leadership: Embracing Change   *353*

  Assignment of Key Managers   *355*

Organizational Culture   *356*

  Managing the Strategy-Culture Relationship   *358*

Reward Systems: Motivating Strategy Execution   *361*

  Guidelines for Structuring Effective Reward Systems   *362*

Summary   *366*

Cohesion Case: Implementing Strategy by Restructuring and Reengineering Coca-Cola's
  Organizational Structure, Leadership, Culture, and Rewards   *370*

12   Strategic Control and Continuous Improvement   *379*

Establishing Strategic Controls   *380*
  Premise Control   381
  Implementation Control   383
  Strategic Surveillance   386
  Special Alert Control   387
Operational Control Systems   *388*
  Budgets   389
  Scheduling   389
  Key Success Factors   390
Using Operational Control Systems: Monitoring Performance and Evaluating Deviations   *390*
The Quality Imperative: Continuous Improvement to Build Customer Value   *393*
Summary   *397*
Cohesion Case: Strategic Control and Continuous Improvement at Coca-Cola   *400*

Guide to Strategic Management Case Analysis   *G-1*

The Case Method   *G-1*
Preparing for Case Discussion   *G-1*
  Suggestions for Effective Preparation   G-1
Participating in Class   *G-2*
  The Student as Active Learner   G-2
  Your Professor as Discussion Leader   G-3
Assignments   *G-3*
  Written Assignments   G-3
  Oral Presentations   G-4
  Working as a Team Member   G-4
Summary   *G-5*

IV   CASES   *C-1*

Section A   Company Cases   *1-1*

  1   NTN Communications, Inc.—Interactive Television: The Future is Now   *1-1*
  2   Liz Claiborne, 1993: Troubled Times for the Woman's Retail Giant   *2-1*
  3   Perdue Farms, Inc.—1994   *3-1*
  4   Friends Provident: Reengineering Customer Services   *4-1*
  5   Mobil Chemical and the VPP   *5-1*
  6   TQM and Mobil Chemical's Washington, New Jersey, Facility   *6-1*
  7   Perrigo Company   *7-1*
  8   Ben & Jerry's Homemade, Inc.   *8-1*
  9   Snapple Beverage Corporation   *9-1*
  10   Eastman Kodak Company   *10-1*
  11   Diesel Technology Company   *11-1*

12   Merrill Electronics Corporation (A)   *12-1*

13   Merrill Electronics Corporation (B)   *13-1*

14   Videoton (A)   *14-1*

15   Videoton (B)   *15-1*

16   The 3M Company: Integrating Europe (A)   *16-1*

17   The 3M Company: Integrating Europe (B)   *17-1*

18   W. L. Gore & Associates, Inc.   *18-1*

19   Hartmarx Corporation   *19-1*

20   L.A. Gear, Inc.   *20-1*

21   Kentucky Fried Chicken and the Global Fast-Food Industry   *21-1*

22   Matsushita Industrial de Baja California (A)   *22-1*

23   Matsushita Industrial de Baja California (B)   *23-1*

24   Grand Metropolitan PLC   *24-1*

25   Robin Hood   *25-1*

26   Philip Morris: The Warning Labels Issue   *26-1*

27   Nintendo versus SEGA (A): The Videogame Industry   *27-1*

28   Nintendo versus SEGA (B): The Videogame Wars   *28-1*

29   Banco Comercial Português (1993)   *29-1*

30   Guiness Peat Aviation: The Flotation   *30-1*

Section B   Industry Case Sets   *31-1*

31   Note on the Hazardous Waste Management Industry   *31-1*

32   Chemical Waste Management   *32-1*

33   ICF Kaiser International, Inc.   *33-1*

34   Note on the Oil and Gas Exploration and Production Industry   *34-1*

35   Atlantic Richfield Corporation   *35-1*

36   ICF Resources Incorporated   *36-1*

Section C   Individual Industry Notes   *37-1*

37   Note on the Airline Industry   *37-1*

38   Note on the Personal Computer Industry   *38-1*

39   Note on the Biopharmaceutical Industry   *39-1*

40   Note on the Life Insurance Industry   *40-1*

41   Note on the Motion Picture Industry   *41-1*

Case Index   *CI–1*

Subject Index   *SI*

STRATEGIC MANAGEMENT
FORMULATION, IMPLEMENTATION, AND CONTROL

I OVERVIEW OF STRATEGIC MANAGEMENT

The first chapter of this book introduces strategic management, the set of decisions and actions that result in the design and activation of strategies to achieve the objectives of an organization. The chapter provides an overview of the nature, benefits, and terminology of and the need for strategic management. Subsequent chapters provide greater detail.

The first major section of Chapter 1, "The Nature and Value of Strategic Management," emphasizes the practical value and benefits of strategic management for a firm. It also distinguishes between a firm's strategic decisions and its other planning tasks.

The section stresses the key point that strategic management activities are undertaken at three levels: corporate, business, and functional. The distinctive characteristics of strategic decision making at each of these levels affect the impact of activities at these levels on company operations. Other topics dealt with in this section are the value of formality in strategic management and the alignment of strategy makers in strategy formulation and implementation. The section concludes with a review of the planning research on business, which demonstrates that the use of strategic management processes yields financial and behavioral benefits that justify their costs.

The second major section of Chapter 1 presents a model of the strategic management process. The model, which will serve as an outline for the remainder of the text, describes approaches currently used by strategic planners. Its individual components are carefully defined and explained, as is the process for integrating them into the strategic management process. The section ends with a discussion of the model's practical limitations and the advisability of tailoring the recommendations made to actual business situations.

STRATEGIC MANAGEMENT

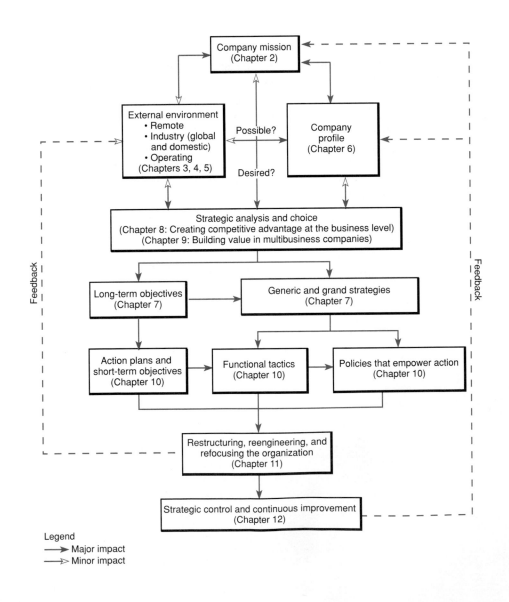

Legend
⟶ Major impact
⟶▷ Minor impact

THE NATURE AND VALUE OF STRATEGIC MANAGEMENT

Managing activities internal to the firm is only part of the modern executive's responsibilities. The modern executive also must respond to the challenges posed by the firm's immediate and remote external environments. The immediate external environment includes competitors, suppliers, increasingly scarce resources, government agencies and their ever more numerous regulations, and customers whose preferences often shift inexplicably. The remote external environment comprises economic and social conditions, political priorities, and technological developments, all of which must be anticipated, monitored, assessed, and incorporated into the executive's decision making. However, the executive often is compelled to subordinate the demands of the firm's internal activities and external environment to the multiple and often inconsistent requirements of its stakeholders: owners, top managers, employees, communities, customers, and country. To deal effectively with everything that affects the growth and profitability of a firm, executives employ management processes that they feel will position it optimally in its competitive environment by maximizing the anticipation of environmental changes and of unexpected internal and competitive demands.

Broad-scope, large-scale management processes became dramatically more sophisticated after World War II. These processes responded to increases in the size and number of competing firms; to the expanded role of government as a buyer, seller, regulator, and competitor in the free enterprise system; and to greater business involvement in international trade. Perhaps the most significant improvement in management processes came in the 1970s, when "long-range planning," "new venture management," "planning, programming, budgeting," and "business policy" were blended. At the same time, increased emphasis was placed on environmental forecasting and external considerations in formulating and implementing plans. This all-encompassing approach is known as strategic management or strategic planning.[1]

Strategic management is defined as the set of decisions and actions that result in the formulation and implementation of plans designed to achieve a company's objectives. It comprises nine critical tasks:

1. Formulate the company's mission, including broad statements about its purpose, philosophy, and goals.
2. Develop a company profile that reflects its internal conditions and capabilities.
3. Assess the company's external environment, including both the competitive and general contextual factors.
4. Analyze the company's options by matching its resources with the external environment.
5. Identify the most desirable options by evaluating each option in light of the company's mission.
6. Select a set of long-term objectives and grand strategies that will achieve the most desirable options.
7. Develop annual objectives and short-term strategies that are compatible with the selected set of long-term objectives and grand strategies.
8. Implement the strategic choices by means of budgeted resource allocations in which the matching of tasks, people, structures, technologies, and reward systems is emphasized.

---

[1] In this text, the term *strategic management* refers to the broad overall process. To some scholars and practitioners, the term connotes only the formulation phase of total management activities.

9. Evaluate the success of the strategic process as an input for future decision making.

As these nine tasks indicate, strategic management involves the planning, directing, organizing, and controlling of a company's strategy-related decisions and actions. By *strategy,* managers mean their large-scale, future-oriented plans for interacting with the competitive environment to achieve company objectives. A strategy is a company's "game plan." Although that plan does not precisely detail all future deployments (of people, finances, and material), it does provide a framework for managerial decisions. A strategy reflects a company's awareness of how, when, and where it should compete; against whom it should compete; and for what purposes it should compete.

DIMENSIONS OF STRATEGIC DECISIONS

What decisions facing a business are strategic and therefore deserve strategic management attention? Typically, strategic issues have the following dimensions.

Strategic Issues Require Top-Management Decisions   Since strategic decisions overarch several areas of a firm's operations, they require top-management involvement. Usually only top management has the perspective needed to understand the broad implications of such decisions and the power to authorize the necessary resource allocations. As top manager of Volvo GM Heavy Truck Corporation, Karl-Erling Trogen, president, wanted to push the company closer to the customer by overarching operations with service and customer relations empowering the work force closest to the customer with greater knowledge and authority. This strategy called for a major commitment to the parts and service end of the business where customer relations was first priority. Trogen's philosophy was to so empower the work force that more operating questions were handled on the line where workers worked directly with customers. He believed that the corporate headquarters should be more focused on strategic issues, such as engineering, production, quality, and marketing.

Strategic Issues Require Large Amounts of the Firm's Resources   Strategic decisions involve substantial allocations of people, physical assets, or moneys that either must be redirected from internal sources or secured from outside the firm. They also commit the firm to actions over an extended period. For these reasons, they require substantial resources. Whirlpool Corporation's "Quality Express" product delivery program exemplified a strategy that required a strong financial and personnel commitment from the company. The plan was to deliver products to customers when, where, and how they wanted them. This proprietary service uses contract logistics strategy to deliver Whirlpool, Kitchen Aid, Roper, and Estate brand appliances to 90 percent of the company's dealer and builder customers within 24 hours and to the other 10 percent within 48 hours. In highly competitive service-oriented businesses, achieving and maintaining customer satisfaction frequently involves a commitment from every facet of the organization.

Strategic Issues Often Affect the Firm's Long-Term Prosperity   Strategic decisions ostensibly commit the firm for a long time, typically five years; however, the impact of such decisions often lasts much longer. Once a firm has committed itself to a particular strategy, its image and competitive advantages usually are tied to that strategy. Firms become known in certain markets, for certain products, with certain technologies. They would jeopardize their previous gains if they shifted from these markets, products, or technologies by adopting a radically different strategy. Thus, strategic decisions have enduring effects on firms—for better or worse.

Strategic Issues Are Future Oriented Strategic decisions are based on what managers forecast, rather than on what they know. In such decisions, emphasis is placed on the development of projections that will enable the firm to select the most promising strategic options. In the turbulent and competitive free enterprise environment, a firm will succeed only if it takes a proactive (anticipatory) stance toward change.

Strategic Issues Usually Have Multifunctional or Multibusiness Consequences Strategic decisions have complex implications for most areas of the firm. Decisions about such matters as customer mix, competitive emphasis, or organizational structure necessarily involve a number of the firm's strategic business units (SBUs), divisions, or program units. All of these areas will be affected by allocations or reallocations of responsibilities and resources that result from these decisions.

Strategic Issues Require Considering the Firm's External Environment All business firms exist in an open system. They affect and are affected by external conditions that are largely beyond their control. Therefore, to successfully position a firm in competitive situations, its strategic managers must look beyond its operations. They must consider what relevant others (e.g., competitors, customers, suppliers, creditors, government, and labor) are likely to do.

Global Strategy in Action 1–1 tells the strategy of a small but rapidly growing restaurant chain. Notice that even such a brief overview of an entrepreneurial firm covers many of the issues that we described above as critical to the strategic management process.

Three Levels of Strategy

The decision-making hierarchy of a firm typically contains three levels. At the top of this hierarchy is the corporate level, composed principally of a board of directors and the chief executive and administrative officers. They are responsible for the firm's financial performance and for the achievement of nonfinancial goals, such as enhancing the firm's image and fulfilling its social responsibilities. To a large extent, attitudes at the corporate level reflect the concerns of stockholders and society at large. In a multibusiness firm, corporate-level executives determine the businesses in which the firm should be involved. They also set objectives and formulate strategies that span the activities and functional areas of these businesses. Corporate-level strategic managers attempt to exploit their firm's distinctive competencies by adopting a portfolio approach to the management of its businesses and by developing long-term plans, typically for a five-year period. A key corporate strategy of Airborne Express's operations involved direct sale to high-volume corporate accounts and developing an expansive network in the international arena. Instead of setting up operations overseas, Airborne's long-term strategy was to form direct associations with national companies within foreign countries to expand and diversify their operations.

Another example of the portfolio approach involved a plan by state-owned Saudi Arabian Oil to spend $1.4 billion to build and operate an oil refinery in Korea with its partner, Ssangyong. To implement their program, the Saudis embarked on a new "cut-out-the-middleman" strategy to reduce the role of international oil companies in the processing and selling of Saudi crude oil.

GLOBAL
STRATEGY IN
ACTION 1–1

WHERE THE MAITRE D' OUTRANKS THE CHEF

Blocking the north side of 54th Street between Fifth and Madison avenues each day at lunchtime is a well-dressed but hungry mob. It's crowding the sidewalk outside Bice, the chic Italian eatery that has made itself the Lourdes of pasta.

The airy dining room seats 160 people and serves some 600 meals a day—average check, about $40 per person at lunch, $60 at dinner. Average daily take: $30,000. But even at these prices, the crowds keep coming. Gianfranco Sorrentino, Bice's unflappable maitre d', dispenses choice front tables to Henry Kissinger and Ronald Perelman, shuffling shoppers and Japanese tourists off behind the massive floral arrangement.

What makes Bice (pronounced beechay) different is owner Roberto Ruggeri's notion that it can be cloned worldwide—doing with a $22.00 black risotto with cuttlefish what McDonald's did with the $1.80 Big Mac.

So Bices are popping up everywhere, 14 so far. Branches in Chicago and Beverly Hills opened in 1989; Paris and Palm Beach in 1990; Washington, Atlanta, Miami, and Scottsdale, Arizona, last year. Bice has since sprouted in San Diego and Tokyo. Coming up are new outposts in Aspen, Montreal, Toronto, Mexico City, Caracas, London, and Sydney. The U.S. operations are all wholly owned. The foreign Bices are joint ventures or are licensed to local owners. "I don't know Caracas," Ruggeri says, explaining why he prefers not to entirely own his deals overseas. "You wake up, they shoot, a new government comes in, and I lose my restaurant."

Potential coups aside, Bice looks enviably solid in a notoriously treacherous industry. The New York flagship had revenues of around $10 million last year, a level that only a handful of New

In the middle of the decision-making hierarchy is the business level, composed principally of business and corporate managers. These managers must translate the statements of direction and intent generated at the corporate level into concrete objectives and strategies for individual business divisions, or SBUs. In essence, business-level strategic managers determine how the firm will compete in the selected product-market arena. They strive to identify and secure the most promising market segment within that arena. This segment is the piece of the total market that the firm can claim and defend because of its competitive advantages.

At the bottom of the decision-making hierarchy is the functional level, composed principally of managers of product, geographic, and functional areas. They develop annual objectives and short-term strategies in such areas as production, operations, research and development, finance and accounting, marketing, and human relations. However, their principal responsibility is to implement or execute the firm's strategic plans. Whereas corporate- and business-level managers center their attention on "doing the right things," managers at the functional level center their attention on "doing things right." Thus, they address such issues as the efficiency and effectiveness of production and marketing systems, the quality of customer service, and the success of particular products and services in increasing the firm's market shares.

Figure 1–1 depicts the three levels of strategic management as structured in practice. In alternative 1, the firm is engaged in only one business and the corporate- and business-level responsibilities are concentrated in a single group of directors, officers, and managers. This is the organizational format of most small businesses.

continued

York restaurants—like Tavern on the Green and Windows on the World—can beat. Pasta ingredients are relatively cheap, so New York profit margins are high: 20 percent. Bice's satellite restaurants have revenues of around $3.0 million to $3.5 million, considered hearty performance by the trade. Only one so far is a dud: Scottsdale. Price cuts loom there.

"This is unique," says Clark Wolf, a New York food and restaurant consultant. "No one before has opened the same restaurant of this caliber all over the world."

To finance his growth, Ruggeri sold a half-interest in his company to a Japanese restaurant chain, WDI, for roughly $2 million in 1989—with the provision that he could buy back his stake. He did so last year for about $6 million. The Japanese got back their $2 million in cash and financed the rest in notes. Now Ruggeri is hoping that investors have noticed his success. He says he's contemplating a public offering to raise $15 million for around 30 percent to 40 percent of the company. With that new money he can expand still further.

Ruggeri, 49, an affable, somewhat rumpled Milanese with unruly brown and gray hair, has a simple marketing strategy: predictability and ambiance, rather than to-die-for food. Explains Ruggeri: "A customer would rather go to a happy place with exceptional food. I'm giving people comfort, not a peak experience." So at Bice the key job is maitre d', not chef. "Italian cuisine is very simple—any good chef can do it. Personality, you can't teach," says Ruggeri.

The trick in the restaurant trade is to survive when the fickle fashion crowd moves on, as they inevitably do. So Ruggeri makes sure he finds locations close to swank stores like Tiffany and Cartier and to commercial hubs to pull in a diverse clientele. "When the trendies stopped coming, the shopping ladies and business people took over," he says.

Alternative 2, the classical corporate structure, comprises three fully operative levels: the corporate level, the business level, and the functional level. The approach taken throughout this text assumes the use of alternative 2. Moreover, whenever appropriate, topics are covered from the perspective of each level of strategic management. In this way, the text presents a comprehensive discussion of the strategic management process.

Characteristics of Strategic Management Decisions

The characteristics of strategic management decisions vary with the level of strategic activity considered. As shown in Figure 1–2, decisions at the corporate level tend to be more value oriented, more conceptual, and less concrete than decisions at the business or functional level. For example, at Alcoa, the world's largest aluminum maker, chairman Paul O'Neill made Alcoa one of the nation's most centralized organizations by imposing a dramatic management reorganization that wiped out two layers of management. He found that this effort not only reduced costs but also enabled him to be closer to the front-line operations managers. Corporate-level decisions are often characterized by greater risk, cost, and profit potential; greater need for flexibility; and longer time horizons. Such decisions include the choice of businesses, dividend policies, sources of long-term financing, and priorities for growth.

Functional-level decisions implement the overall strategy formulated at the corporate and business levels. They involve action-oriented operational issues and are relatively short range and low risk. Functional-level decisions incur only modest costs, because they are

FIGURE 1–1
Alternative Strategic Management Structures

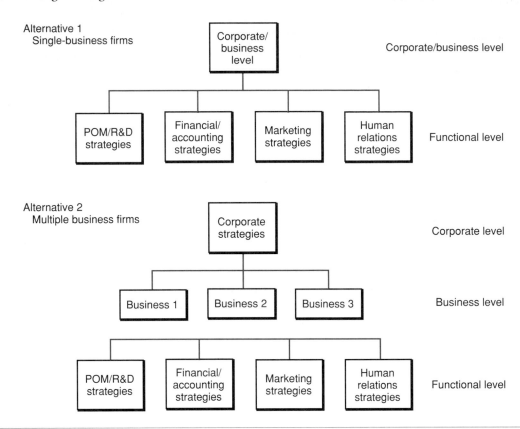

dependent on available resources. They usually are adaptable to ongoing activities and, therefore, can be implemented with minimal cooperation. For example, in 1991, Nordstrom and Dillard Department Stores reported first-quarter profits of $26 million, a 95 percent increase over the previous year. They attributed the increased earnings to tighter inventory and operating controls in the parent company. In a second example, the corporate headquarters of Sears, Roebuck & Company spent $60 million to automate 6,900 clerical jobs by installing 28,000 computerized cash registers at its 868 stores in the United States. Though this move eliminated many functional-level jobs, top management believed that reducing annual operating expenses by at least $50 million was crucial to competitive survival.

Because functional-level decisions are relatively concrete and quantifiable, they receive critical attention and analysis even though their comparative profit potential is low. Common functional-level decisions include decisions on generic versus brand-name labeling, basic versus applied research and development (R&D), high versus low inventory levels, general-purpose versus specific-purpose production equipment, and close versus loose supervision.

Business-level decisions help bridge decisions at the corporate and functional levels. Such decisions are less costly, risky, and potentially profitable than corporate-level decisions, but they are more costly, risky, and potentially profitable than functional-level decisions. Common business-level decisions include decisions on plant location, marketing segmentation and geographic coverage, and distribution channels.

FIGURE 1–2
Hierarchy of Objectives and Strategies

Ends (What is to be achieved?)	Means (How is it to be achieved?)	Strategic Decision Makers			
		Board of Directors	Corporate Managers	Business Managers	Functional Managers
Mission, including goals and philosophy		✓✓	✓✓	✓	
Long-term objectives	Grand strategy	✓	✓✓	✓✓	
Annual objectives	Short-term strategies and policies		✓	✓✓	✓✓

Note: ✓✓ indicates a principal responsibility; ✓ indicates a secondary responsibility.

FORMALITY IN STRATEGIC MANAGEMENT

The formality of strategic management systems varies widely among companies. *Formality* refers to the degree to which participants, responsibilities, authority, and discretion in decision making are specified. It is an important consideration in the study of strategic management, because greater formality is usually positively correlated with the cost, comprehensiveness, accuracy, and success of planning.

A number of forces determine how much formality is needed in strategic management. The size of the organization, its predominant management styles, the complexity of its environment, its production process, its problems, and the purpose of its planning system all play a part in determining the appropriate degree of formality.[2]

In particular, formality is associated with the size of the firm and with its stage of development. Methods of evaluating strategic success also are linked to formality. Some firms, especially smaller ones, follow an *entrepreneurial* mode. They are basically under the control of a single individual, and they produce a limited number of products or services. In such firms, strategic evaluation is informal, intuitive, and limited. Very large firms, on the other hand, make strategic evaluation part of a comprehensive, formal planning system, an approach that Henry Mintzberg called the *planning mode*. Mintzberg also identified a third mode (the *adaptive mode*), which he associated with medium-sized firms in relatively stable environments.[3] For firms that follow the adaptive mode, the identification and evaluation of alternative strategies are closely related to existing strategy. It is not unusual to find different modes within the same organization. For example, Exxon might follow an entrepreneurial mode in developing and evaluating the strategy of its solar subsidiary but follow a planning mode in the rest of the company.

The Strategy Makers

The ideal strategic management team includes decision makers from all three company levels (the corporate, business, and functional)—for example, the chief executive officer (CEO), the product managers, and the heads of functional areas. In addition, the team obtains input from company planning staffs, when they exist, and from lower-level managers and supervisors. The latter provide data for strategic decision making and then implement strategies.

---

[2] M. Goold and A. Campbell, "Managing the Diversified Corporation: The Tensions Facing the Chief Executive," *Long Range Planning,* August 1988, pp. 12–24.

[3] H. Mintzberg, "Strategy Making in Three Modes," *California Management Review* 16, no. 2 (1973), pp. 44–53.

Because strategic decisions have a tremendous impact on a company and require large commitments of company resources, top managers must give final approval for strategic action. Figure 1–2 aligns levels of strategic decision makers with the kinds of objectives and strategies for which they are typically responsible.

Planning departments, often headed by a corporate vice president for planning, are common in large corporations. Medium-sized firms often employ at least one full-time staff member to spearhead strategic data-collection efforts. Even in small firms or less progressive larger firms, strategic planning often is spearheaded by an officer or by a group of officers designated as a planning committee.

Precisely what are managers' responsibilities in the strategic planning process at the corporate and business levels? Top management shoulders broad responsibility for all the major elements of strategic planning and management. It develops the major portions of the strategic plan and reviews, and it evaluates and counsels on all other portions. General managers at the business level typically have principal responsibilities for developing environmental analysis and forecasting, establishing business objectives, and developing business plans prepared by staff groups.

A firm's president or CEO characteristically plays a dominant role in the strategic planning process. In many ways, this situation is desirable. The CEO's principal duty often is defined as giving long-term direction to the firm, and the CEO is ultimately responsible for the firm's success and, therefore, for the success of its strategy. In addition, CEOs are typically strong-willed, company-oriented individuals with high self-esteem. They often resist delegating authority to formulate or approve strategic decisions.

However, when the dominance of the CEO approaches autocracy, the effectiveness of the firm's strategic planning and management processes are likely to be diminished. For this reason, establishing a strategic management system implies that the CEO will allow managers at all levels to participate in the strategic posture of the company.

In implementing a company's strategy, the CEO must have an appreciation for the power and responsibility of the board, while retaining the power to lead the company with the guidance of informed directors. The interaction between the CEO and board is key to any corporation's strategy. Empowerment of the board has been a recent trend across major management teams. Strategy in Action 1–1 presents descriptions of the changes that companies have made in an attempt to monitor the relationships between the role of the board and the role of CEO.

Benefits of Strategic Management

Using the strategic management approach, managers at all levels of the firm interact in planning and implementing. As a result, the behavioral consequences of strategic management are similar to those of participative decision making. Therefore, an accurate assessment of the impact of strategy formulation on organizational performance requires not only financial evaluation criteria but also nonfinancial evaluation criteria—measures of behavior-based effects. In fact, promoting positive behavioral consequences also enables the firm to achieve its financial goals.[4] However, regardless of the profitability of strategic plans, several behavioral effects of strategic management improve the firm's welfare:

1. Strategy formulation activities enhance the firm's ability to prevent problems. Managers who encourage subordinates' attention to planning are aided in their monitoring and forecasting responsibilities by subordinates who are aware of the needs of strategic planning.

---

[4] A. Langely, "The Roles of Formal Strategic Planning," *Long Range Planning*, June 1988, pp. 400–50.

STRATEGY
IN ACTION
1–1

THE PROGRESS OF BOARD EMPOWERMENT

Company	Innovation
Dayton Hudson Corporation	Requires the inside directors to conduct an annual evaluation of the CEO.
Medtronic	Solicits opinions on board procedures by requiring all directors to complete a questionnaire; then the full board reviews the results at an annual meeting and tries to make improvements.
Stanhome	Developed a formal document that specifies the board's purpose, size, proportion of outside directors, annual calendar, and expectations of directors and management.
Mallinckrodt	Separated the roles of chair and CEO.
Lukens	Formed a committee of outside directors to study a major acquisition proposal, hold discussions with management, and recommend action to the full board.
Campbell Soup Company	Designated a lead director with the title of vice chairman.
Monsanto	Increased the proportion of the board's time that would be focused on strategic direction and considered specific capital proposals within that framework.
General Motors	Developed an explicit set of guidelines that outline how the board will function and be structured.

Source: Reprinted by permission of *Harvard Business Review.* An exhibit from "Empowering the Board," by Jay W. Lorsch, January–February 1995. Copyright © 1995 by the President and Fellows of Harvard University, all rights reserved.

2. Group-based strategic decisions are likely to be drawn from the best available alternatives. The strategic management process results in better decisions because group interaction generates a greater variety of strategies and because forecasts based on the specialized perspectives of group members improve the screening of options.

3. The involvement of employees in strategy formulation improves their understanding of the productivity-reward relationship in every strategic plan and, thus, heightens their motivation.

4. Gaps and overlaps in activities among individuals and groups are reduced as participation in strategy formulation clarifies differences in roles.

5. Resistance to change is reduced. Though the participants in strategy formulation may be no more pleased with their own decisions than they would be with authoritarian decisions, their greater awareness of the parameters that limit the available options makes them more likely to accept those decisions.

Risks of Strategic Management

Managers must be trained to guard against three types of unintended negative consequences of involvement in strategy formulation.

First, the time that managers spend on the strategic management process may have a negative impact on operational responsibilities. Managers must be trained to minimize that impact by scheduling their duties to allow the necessary time for strategic activities.

Second, if the formulators of strategy are not intimately involved in its implementation, they may shirk their individual responsibility for the decisions reached. Thus, strategic managers must be trained to limit their promises to performance that the decision makers and their subordinates can deliver.

Third, strategic managers must be trained to anticipate and respond to the disappointment of participating subordinates over unattained expectations. Subordinates may expect their involvement in even minor phases of total strategy formulation to result in both acceptance of their proposals and an increase in their rewards, or they may expect a solicitation of their input on selected issues to extend to other areas of decision making.

Sensitizing managers to these possible negative consequences and preparing them with effective means of minimizing such consequences will greatly enhance the potential of strategic planning.

Executives' Views of Strategic Management

How do managers and corporate executives view the contribution of strategic management to the success of their firms? To answer this question, a survey was conducted that included over 200 executives from the Fortune 500, Fortune 500 Service, and INC 500 companies.[5] Their responses are summarized in Strategy in Action 1–2.

Overall, these responses indicate that corporate America sees strategic management as instrumental to high performance, evolutionary and perhaps revolutionary in its ever-growing sophistication, action oriented, and cost effective. Clearly, the responding executives view strategic management as critical to their individual and organizational success.

THE STRATEGIC MANAGEMENT PROCESS

Businesses vary in the processes they use to formulate and direct their strategic management activities. Sophisticated planners, such as General Electric, Procter & Gamble, and IBM, have developed more detailed processes than less-formal planners of similar size. Small businesses that rely on the strategy formulation skills and limited time of an entrepreneur typically exhibit more basic planning concerns than those of larger firms in their industries. Understandably, firms with multiple products, markets, or technologies tend to use more complex strategic management systems. However, despite differences in detail and the degree of formalization, the basic components of the models used to analyze strategic management operations are very similar.

Because of the similarity among the general models of the strategic management process, it is possible to develop an eclectic model representative of the foremost thought in the strategic management area. This model is shown in Figure 1–3. It serves three major functions. First, it depicts the sequence and the relationships of the major components of the strategic management process. Second, it is the outline for this book. This chapter provides a general overview of the strategic management process, and the major components of the model will be the principal theme of subsequent chapters. Notice that the chapters of the text that discuss each of the strategic management process components are shown in each block. Finally, the model offers one approach

[5] V. Ramanujam, J. C. Camillus, and N. Venkatraman, "Trends in Strategic Planning," in *Strategic Planning and Management Handbook,* ed. W. R. King and D. I. Cleland (New York: Van Nostrand Reinhold, 1987), pp. 611–28.

STRATEGY
IN ACTION
1–2

EXECUTIVES' GENERAL OPINIONS AND ATTITUDES

Item	Percent of Respondents Indicating		
	Agreement	Neutral	Disagreement
1. Reducing emphasis on strategic planning will be detrimental to our long-term performance.	88.7%	4.9%	6.4%
2. Our plans today reflect implementation concerns.	73.6	16.9	9.5
3. We have improved the sophistication of our strategic planning systems.	70.6	18.6	10.8
4. Our previous approaches to strategic planning are not appropriate today.	64.2	16.2	19.6
5. Today's systems emphasize creativity among managers more than our previous systems did.	62.6	20.2	17.2
6. Our strategic planning systems today are more consistent with our organization's culture.	55.6	30.7	13.7
7. We are more concerned about the evaluation of our strategic planning systems today.	54.0	29.7	16.3
8. There is more participation from lower-level managers in our strategic planning.	56.6	18.0	25.4
9. Our tendency to rely on outside consultants for strategic planning has been on the decrease.	50.8	23.0	26.2
10. Our systems emphasize control more than before.	41.3	33.0	25.7
11. Planning in our company or unit is generally viewed as a luxury today.	15.0	13.0	72.0

Source: Adapted from V. Ramanujam, J. C. Camillus, and N. Venkatraman, "Trends in Strategic Planning," in *Strategic Planning and Management Handbook,* ed. W. R. King and D. I. Cleland (New York: Van Nostrand Reinhold, 1987), p. 619.

for analyzing the case studies in this text and thus helps the analyst develop strategy formulation skills.

COMPONENTS OF THE STRATEGIC MANAGEMENT MODEL

This section will define and briefly describe the key components of the strategic management model. Each of these components will receive much greater attention in a later chapter. The intention here is simply to introduce them.

Company Mission

The mission of a company is the unique purpose that sets it apart from other companies of its type and identifies the scope of its operations. In short, the mission describes the company's product, market, and technological areas of emphasis in a way that reflects the values and priorities of the strategic decision makers. For example, Lee Hun-Hee, the new chairman of the Samsung Group, revamped the company mission by stamping his own brand of management on Samsung. Immediately, Samsung separated Chonju

FIGURE 1–3
Strategic Management Model

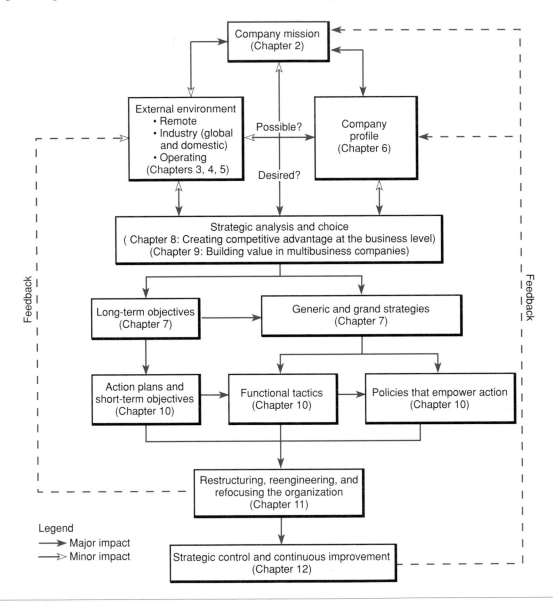

Paper Manufacturing and Shinsegae Department Store from other operations. This corporate act of downscaling reflected a revised management philosophy that favored specialization, thereby changing the direction and scope of the organization.

Company Profile

The company profile depicts the quantity and quality of the company's financial, human, and physical resources. It also assesses the strengths and weaknesses of the company's management and organizational structure. Finally, it contrasts the company's past successes and traditional concerns with the company's current capabilities in an attempt to identify the company's future capabilities.

External Environment

A firm's external environment consists of all the conditions and forces that affect its strategic options and define its competitive situation. The strategic management model shows the external environment as three interactive segments: the operating, industry, and remote environments.

Strategic Analysis and Choice

Simultaneous assessment of the external environment and the company profile enables a firm to identify a range of possibly attractive interactive opportunities. These opportunities are *possible* avenues for investment. However, they must be screened through the criterion of the company mission to generate a set of possible and *desired* opportunities. This screening process results in the selection of options from which a *strategic choice* is made. The process is meant to provide the combination of long-term objectives and generic and grand strategies that optimally position the firm in its external environment to achieve the company mission.

Strategic analysis and choice in single or dominant product/service businesses centers around identifying strategies that are most effective at building sustainable competitive advantage based on key value chain activities and capabilities—core competencies of the firm. Multibusiness companies find their managers focused on the question of which combination of businesses maximizes shareholder value as the guiding theme during their strategic analysis and choice.

Long-Term Objectives

The results that an organization seeks over a multiyear period are its *long-term objectives*. Such objectives typically involve some or all of the following areas: profitability, return on investment, competitive position, technological leadership, productivity, employee relations, public responsibility, and employee development.

Generic and Grand Strategies

Many businesses explicitly and all implicitly adopt one or more *generic strategies* characterizing their competitive orientation in the marketplace. Low cost, differentiation, or focus strategies define the three fundamental options. Enlightened managers seek to create ways their firm possesses both low cost and differentiation competitive advantages as part of their overall generic strategy. They usually combine these capabilities with a comprehensive, general plan of major actions through which their firm intends to achieve its long-term objectives in a dynamic environment. Called the *grand strategy,* this *statement of means* indicates how the objectives are to be achieved. Although every grand strategy is, in fact, a unique package of long-term strategies, 14 basic approaches can be identified: concentration, market development, product development, innovation, horizontal integration, vertical integration, joint venture, strategic alliances, consortia, concentric diversification, conglomerate diversification, turnaround, divestiture, and liquidation.

Each of these grand strategies will be covered in detail in Chapter 7.

Action Plans and Short-Term Objectives

Action plans translate generic and grand strategies into "action" by incorporating four elements. First, they identify *specific* functional *tactics and actions* to be undertaken in the next week, month or quarter as part of the business's effort to build competitive advantage. The second element is a clear *time frame for completion*. Third, action plans *create accountability* by identifying who is responsible for each "action" in the plan. Fourth, each "action" in an action plan has one or more specific, immediate objectives that are identified as *outcomes* that action should generate.

Functional Tactics

Within the general framework created by the business's generic and grand strategies, each business function needs to identify and undertake activities unique to the function that help build a sustainable competitive advantage. Managers in each business function develop tactics which delineate the functional activities undertaken in their part of the business and usually include them as a core part of their action plan. Functional tactics are detailed statements of the "means" or activities that will be used to achieve short-term objectives and establish competitive advantage.

Policies that Empower Action

Speed is a critical necessity for success in today's competitive, global marketplace. One way to enhance speed and responsiveness is to force/allow decisions to be made whenever possible at the lowest level in organizations. *Policies* are broad, precedent-setting decisions that guide or substitute for repetitive or time-sensitive managerial decision making. Creating policies that guide and "preauthorize" the thinking, decisions, and actions of operating managers and their subordinates in implementing the business's strategy is essential for establishing and controlling the ongoing operating process of the firm in a manner consistent with the firm's strategic objectives. Policies often increase managerial effectiveness by standardizing routine decisions and empowering or expanding the discretion of managers and subordinates in implementing business strategies.

The following are examples of the nature and diversity of company policies:

A requirement that managers have purchase requests for items costing more than $5,000 cosigned by the controller.

The minimum equity position required for all new McDonald's franchises.

The standard formula used to calculate return on investment for the 43 strategic business units of General Electric.

A decision that Sears service and repair employees have the right to waive repair charges to appliance customers they feel have been poorly served by their Sears appliance.

Restructuring, Reengineering, and Refocusing the Organization

Until this point in the strategic management process, managers have maintained a decidedly market-oriented focus as they formulate strategies and begin implementation through action plans functional tactics. Now the process takes and internal focus—getting the work of the business done efficiently and effectively so as to make the srategy work. What is the best way to organize ourselves to accomplish the mission? Where should leadership come from? What values should guide our daily activities—what should the organization and its people "be like?" How can we shape rewards to encourage appropriate action? The intense competition in the global marketplace has made this tradition "internally focused" set of questions—how the activities within their business are conducted—recast themselves with unprecedented attentiveness to the marketplace. Downsizing, restructuring, reengineering, outsourcing, and empowerment are all terms that reflect the critical stage in strategy implementation wherein managers attempt to rationalize and recast their organizational structure, leadership, culture, and reward systems to ensure a basic level of cost competitiveness, capacity for responsive quality, and the need to shape each one to accommodate unique requirements of their strategies.

Strategic Control and Continuous Improvement

Strategic control is concerned with tracking a strategy as it is being implemented, detecting problems or changes in its underlying premises, and making necessary adjustments. In contrast to postaction control, strategic control seeks to guide action on behalf of the generic and grand strategies as they are taking place and when the end results are still several years away. The rapid, accelerating change of the global marketplace of the last 10 years has made continuous improvement another aspect of strategic control in many organizations. Continuous improvement provides a way for managers to provide a form of strategic control that allows their organization to respond more proactively and timely to rapid developments in hundreds of areas that influence a business's success.

STRATEGIC MANAGEMENT AS A PROCESS

A *process* is the flow of information through interrelated stages of analysis toward the achievement of an aim. Thus, the strategic management model in Figure 1–3 depicts a process. In the strategic management process, the flow of information involves historical, current, and forecast data on the operations and environment of the business. Managers evaluate these data in light of the values and priorities of influential individuals and groups—often called *stakeholders*—that are vitally interested in the actions of the business. The interrelated stages of the process are the 12 components discussed in the last section. Finally, the aim of the process is the formulation and implementation of strategies that work, achieving the company's long-term mission and near-term objectives.

Viewing strategic management as a process has several important implications. First, a change in any component will affect several or all of the other components. Most of the arrows in the model point two ways, suggesting that the flow of information usually is reciprocal. For example, forces in the external environment may influence the nature of a company's mission, and the company may in turn affect the external environment and heighten competition in its realm of operation. A specific example is a power company that is persuaded, in part by governmental incentives, to include a commitment to the development of energy alternatives in its mission statement. The company then might promise to extend its R&D efforts in the area of coal liquefaction. The external environment has affected the company's mission, and the revised mission signals a competitive condition in the environment.

A second implication of viewing strategic management as a process is that strategy formulation and implementation are sequential. The process begins with development or reevaluation of the company mission. This step is associated with, but essentially followed by, development of a company profile and assessment of the external environment. Then follow, in order, strategic choice, definition of long-term objectives, design of the grand strategy, definition of short-term objectives, design of operating strategies, institutionalization of the strategy, and review and evaluation.

The apparent rigidity of the process, however, must be qualified.

First, a firm's strategic posture may have to be reevaluated in response to changes in any of the principal factors that determine or affect its performance. Entry by a major new competitor, the death of a prominent board member, replacement of the chief executive officer, and a downturn in market responsiveness are among the thousands of changes that can prompt reassessment of a firm's strategic plan. However, no matter where the need for a reassessment originates, the strategic management process begins with the mission statement.

Second, not every component of the strategic management process deserves equal attention each time planning activity takes place. Firms in an extremely stable environment may find that an in-depth assessment is not required every five years. Companies often are satisfied with their original mission statements even after a decade of operation and spend only a minimal amount of time addressing this subject. In addition, while formal strategic planning may be undertaken only every five years, objectives and strategies usually are updated each year, and rigorous reassessment of the initial stages of strategic planning rarely is undertaken at these times.

A third implication of viewing strategic management as a process is the necessity of feedback from institutionalization, review, and evaluation to the early stages of the process. *Feedback* can be defined as the collection of postimplementation results to enhance future decision making. Therefore, as indicated in Figure 1–3, strategic managers should assess the impact of implemented strategies on external environments. Thus, future planning can reflect any changes precipitated by strategic actions. Strategic managers also should analyze the impact of strategies on the possible need for modifications in the company mission.

A fourth implication of viewing strategic management as a process is the need to regard it as a dynamic system. The term *dynamic* characterizes the constantly changing conditions that affect interrelated and interdependent strategic activities. Managers should recognize that the components of the strategic process are constantly evolving but that formal planning artificially freezes those components, much as an action photograph freezes the movement of a swimmer. Since change is continuous, the dynamic strategic planning process must be monitored constantly for significant shifts in any of its components as a precaution against implementing an obsolete strategy.

Changes in the Process

The strategic management process undergoes continual assessment and subtle updating. Although the elements of the basic strategic management model rarely change, the relative emphasis that each element receives will vary with the decision makers who use the model and with the environments of their companies.

Strategy in Action 1–3 is an update on general trends in strategic management, summarizing the responses of over 200 corporate executives. This update shows there has been an increasing companywide emphasis on and appreciation for the value of strategic management activities. It also provides evidence that practicing managers have given increasing attention to the need for frequent and widespread involvement in the formulation and implementation phases of the strategic management process. Finally, it indicates that, as managers and their firms gain knowledge, experience, skill, and understanding in how to design and manage their planning activities, they become better able to avoid the potential negative consequences of instituting a vigorous strategic management process.

STRATEGY
IN ACTION
1–3

GENERAL TRENDS IN STRATEGIC MANAGEMENT

Item	Percent of Respondents Indicating		
	Increase	No Change	Decrease
1. Overall emphasis on strategic planning systems.	81.2%	7.7%	11.1%
2. Perceived usefulness of strategic planning.	82.0	10.2	7.8
3. Involvement of line managers in strategic planning activities.	75.2	21.4	3.4
4. Time spent by the chief executive in strategic planning.	78.7	17.8	3.5
5. Acceptance of the outputs of the strategic planning exercise by top management.	74.0	20.6	5.4
6. Perceived usefulness of annual planning.	53.9	38.7	7.4
7. Involvement of staff managers in the annual planning exercise.	52.9	39.3	7.8
8. Involvement of the board of directors in strategic planning.	51.4	47.0	1.6
9. Resources provided for strategic planning.	62.9	23.9	13.2
10. Consistency between strategic plans and budgets.	53.4	38.2	8.3
11. Use of annual plans in monthly performance review.	42.3	55.6	2.1
12. Overall satisfaction with the strategic planning system.	57.4	24.5	18.1
13. Number of planners (i.e., those management personnel whose primary task is planning).	52.9	24.8	22.3
14. Attention to stakeholders other than stockholders.	32.8	63.0	4.2
15. Use of planning committees.	40.9	46.1	13.1
16. Attention to societal issues in planning.	33.2	59.8	7.0
17. The planning horizon (i.e., the number of years considered in the strategic plan).	28.8	56.6	14.6
18. The distance between the CEO and the chief of planning.	13.3	45.1	41.5
19. Threats to the continuation of strategic planning.	12.0	47.0	41.0
20. Resistance to planning in general.	10.2	31.7	58.0

Source: Adapted from V. Ramanujam, J. C. Camillus, and N. Venkatraman, "Trends in Strategic Planning," in *Strategic Planning and Management Handbook,* ed. W. R. King and D. I. Cleland (New York: Van Nostrand Reinhold, 1987), p. 614.

SUMMARY

Strategic management is the set of decisions and actions that result in the formulation and implementation of plans designed to achieve a company's objectives. Because it involves long-term, future-oriented, complex decision making and requires considerable resources, top-management participation is essential.

Strategic management is a three-tier process involving corporate, business, and functional-level planners, and support personnel. At each progressively lower level, strategic activities were shown to be more specific, narrow, short term, and action oriented, with lower risks but fewer opportunities for dramatic impact.

The strategic management model presented in this chapter will serve as the structure for understanding and integrating all the major phases of strategy formulation and implementation. The chapter provided a summary account of these phases, each of which is given extensive individual attention in subsequent chapters.

The chapter stressed that the strategic management process centers on the belief that a firm's mission can be best achieved through a systematic and comprehensive assessment of both its internal capabilities and its external environment. Subsequent evaluation of the firm's opportunities leads, in turn, to the choice of long-term objectives and grand strategies and, ultimately, to annual objectives and operating strategies, which must be implemented, monitored, and controlled.

QUESTIONS FOR DISCUSSION

1. Find a recent copy of *Business Week* and read the "Corporate Strategies" section. Was the main decision discussed strategic? At what level in the organization was the key decision made?

2. In what ways do you think the subject matter in this strategic management-business policy course will differ from that of previous courses you have taken?

3. After graduation, you are not likely to move directly to a top-level management position. In fact, few members of your class will ever reach the top-management level. Why, then, is it important for all business majors to study the field of strategic management?

4. Do you expect outstanding performance in this course to require a great deal of memorization? Why or why not?

5. You undoubtedly have read about individuals who seemingly have given singled-handed direction to their corporations. Is a participative strategic management approach likely to stifle or suppress the contributions of such individuals?

6. Think about the courses you have taken in functional areas, such as marketing, finance, production, personnel, and accounting. What is the importance of each of these areas to the strategic planning process?

7. Discuss with practicing business managers the strategic management models used in their firms. What are the similarities and differences between these models and the one in the text?

8. In what ways do you believe the strategic planning approach of not-for-profit organizations would differ from that of profit-oriented organizations?

9. How do you explain the success of firms that do not use a formal strategic planning process?

10. Think about your postgraduation job search as a strategic decision. How would the strategic management model be helpful to you in identifying and securing the most promising position?

BIBLIOGRAPHY

Adler, P. S.; D. W. McDonald; and F. MacDonald. "Strategic Management of Technical Functions." *Sloan Management Review* (Winter 1992), pp. 19–38.

Allen, M. G. "Strategic Management Hits Its Stride." *Planning Review* (September 1985), pp. 6–9.

Arkam, J. D., and S. S. Cowen. "Strategic Planning for Increased Profit in the Small Business." *Long Range Planning* (December 1990), pp. 63–70.

Baron, David P. "Integrated Strategy: Market and Nonmarket Components." *California Management Review* 37, no. 2 (Winter 1995), p. 47.

Blair, J. D., and K. B. Boal. "Strategy Formation Processes in Health Care Organizations: A Context-Specific Examination of Context-Free Strategy Issues." *Journal of Management* (June 1991), pp. 305–44.

Borch, Odd Jarl, and Michael B. Arthur. "Strategy Networks among Small Firms: Implications for Strategy Research Methodology." *Journal of Management Studies* 32, no. 4 (July 1995), p. 419.

Brandenburger, Adam M., and Barry J. Nalebuff. "The Right Game: Use Game Theory to Shape Strategy." *Harvard Business Review* 73, no. 4 (July–August 1995), p. 57.

Brooker, R. E., Jr. "Orchestrating the Planning Process." *The Journal of Business Strategy* (July–August 1991), pp. 4–9.

Carlson, F. P. "The Long and Short of Strategic Planning." *The Journal of Business Strategy* (May–June 1990), pp. 15–21.

Collins, James C., and Jerry I. Porras. "Building a Visionary Company." *California Management Review* 37, no. 2 (Winter 1995).

Collis, David J., and Cynthia A. Montgomery. "Competing on Resources: Strategy in the 1990s." *Harvard Business Review* 73, no. 4 (July–August 1995), p. 118.

Goold, M., and A. Campbell. "Many Best Ways to Make Strategy." *Harvard Business Review* (November–December 1987), pp. 70–76.

Gopinath, C., and Richard C. Hoffman. "The Relevance of Strategy Research: Practitioner and Academic Viewpoints." *Journal of Management Studies* 32, no. 5 (September 1995), p. 575.

Hahn, D. "Strategic Management—Tasks and Challenges in the 1990s." *Long Range Planning* (February 1991), pp. 26–39.

Hax, A. C. "Redefining the Concept of Strategy and the Strategy Formation Process." *Planning Review* (May–June 1990), pp. 34–41.

Hinterhuber, H. H., and W. Popp. "Are You a Strategist or Just a Manager." *Harvard Business Review* (January–February 1992), pp. 105–14.

Hitt, M. A.; R. E. Hoskisson; and J. S. Harrison. "Strategic Competitiveness in the 1990s: Challenges and Opportunities for U.S. Executives." *Academy of Management Executive* (May 1991), pp. 7–22.

Larwood, Laurie; Cecilia M. Falbe; Mark P. Krieger; and Paul Miesing. "Structure and Meaning of Organizational Vision." *The Academy of Management Journal* 38, no. 3 (June 1995), p. 740.

Meyer, A. D. "What Is Strategy's Distinctive Competence?" *Journal of Management* (December 1991), pp. 821–34.

Miles, Raymond E.; Henry J. Coleman, Jr.; and W. E. Dougles Creed. "Keys to Success in Corporate Redesign." *California Management Review* 37, no. 3 (Spring 1995), p. 128.

Mintzberg, H. "Strategy Making in Three Modes." *California Management Review* (Spring 1973), pp. 44–53.

Pearce, J. A., II. "An Executive-Level Perspective on the Strategic Management Process." *California Management Review* (Spring 1982), pp. 39–48.

Peker, Peter, Jr., and Stan Abraham. "Is Strategic Management Living Up to Its Promise?" *Long Range Planning* 28, no. 5 (October 1995), p. 32.

Rappaport, A. "CFOs and Strategists: Forging a Common Framework." *Harvard Business Review* (May–June 1992), pp. 84–93.

Rouleau, Linda, and Francine Ségun. "Strategy and Organizational Theories: Common Forms of Discourse." *Journal of Management Studies* 32, no. 1 (January 1995), p. 101.

Schonberger, R. J. "Is Strategy Strategic? Impact of Total Quality Management on Strategy." *Academy of Management Executive* (August 1992), pp. 80–97.

Stalk, G.; P. Evans; and L. E. Shulman. "Competing on Capabilities: The New Rules of Corporate Strategy." *Harvard Business Review* (March–April 1992), pp. 57–69.

Stonich, P. J. "Time: The Next Strategic Frontier." *Planning Review* (November–December 1990), pp. 4–7.

Taylor, Bernard. "The New Strategic Leadership—Driving Charge, Getting Results." *Long Range Planning* 28, no. 5 (October 1995), p. 71.

Veliyath, R. "Strategic Planning: Balancing Short-Run Performance and Longer Term Prospects." *Long Range Planning* (June 1992), pp. 86–97.

Yon, E. T. "Corporate Strategy and the New Europe." *Academy of Management Executive* (August 1990), pp. 61–65.

CHAPTER 1 COHESION CASE ILLUSTRATION

THE COCA-COLA COMPANY

Celebrating its 110th birthday in 1996, The Coca-Cola Company has become perhaps the world's most well-known company. Behind the world's most ubiquitous trademark is an international corporation—or as Coke's management likes to say: "a truly global business system"—that has many lessons to share with strategic management students. As you prepare for a successful business career in the 21st century, you must be fine-tuning your understanding of how to help your company achieve and sustain global competitiveness while building stockholder value in a social and environmentally responsible manner. This book and this Cohesion Case about Coca-Cola will help you do that.

The Cohesion Case is a set of 12 comprehensive illustrations, one accompanying each chapter in the book, that uses The Coca-Cola Company to illustrate and apply key concepts presented in the chapter. Taken together, they provide a "cohesive" journey through experiences, strategies, and decisions at The Coca-Cola Company that will enhance your understanding of strategic management in today's global marketplace.

The remainder of this introductory section will give you a brief history and overview of The Coca-Cola Company. More complete information about The Coca-Cola Company will be provided in the Cohesion Case illustrations following each chapter. And there is a wealth of information about The Coca-Cola Company in various company and trade publications, as well as the popular business press, that we encourage you to seek out as a way to enhance your strategic management skills.

HISTORY OF THE COCA-COLA COMPANY

Coca-Cola's origin dates to 1886 when an Atlanta, Georgia, pharmacist, Dr. John S. Pemberton, cooked up the first medicinal syrup extract of "Coca" in a three-legged brass pot in his backyard. Derived as a potential patent medicine, the first glass of the new soda fountain drink went on sale for 5 cents a glass on May 8, 1886, in an Atlanta pharmacy where, by design or accident, carbonated water was blended with the new syrup to produce the drink. Dr. Pemberton sold 25 gallons of the syrup that year, generating approximately $50 in total sales.

Two years later, Atlanta businessman Asa G. Candler bought all rights to Coca-Cola for $2,300. Candler placed major emphasis on promotional activities and quickly expanded distribution of the syrup and registered the Coca-Cola trademark. The bottling of Coca-Cola started in 1894 in Vicksburg, Mississippi, and continued until 1899, when the company granted rights to bottle and sell Coca-Cola in practically the entire continental United States. By 1904, the annual sales for Coca-Cola syrup reached 1 million gallons, and there were 123 plants authorized or licensed to bottle the finished drink.

Ernest Woodruff, an Atlanta banker, led an investor group that bought The Coca-Cola Company from Candler for $25 million in 1919. Robert Woodruff was made president, and the company moved aggressively to expand sales, establishing a foreign sales office and developing a concentrate for the syrup to reduce transportation costs. Shortly after the Woodruff group purchased the company, Coca-Cola stock was sold to the public at $40 per share, helping to lay the capital foundation for its rapid domestic and international expansion. By 1995, consumers in almost 200 countries purchased over 845 million servings daily of soft drinks provided by The Coca-Cola Company.

COCA-COLA'S RECENT HISTORY

The 1960s saw The Coca-Cola Company expand its business focus beyond soft drinks. In rapid succession, Coca-Cola acquired more than 15 different businesses, ranging from food, wine, and soft drinks to film and water treatment. By 1977, The Coca-Cola Company looked something like this:

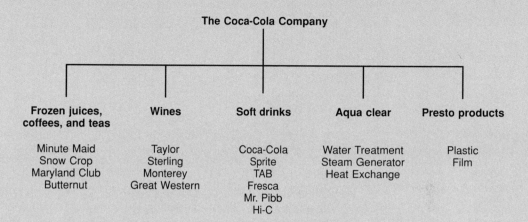

The company reported that, in 1977, 76 percent of total sales ($3.5 billion) and 89 percent of operating profit ($0.6 billion) came from soft drinks. It also reported that 60 percent of worldwide soft-drink volume came from non-U.S. markets. On a companywide basis, sales and profitability looked as follows during that year:

1977 (in millions)

	United States	Latin America	Europe and Africa	Canada and Pacific	Total
Net sales	$2,008	$270	$669	$613	$3,556
Operating profit	264	67	189	114	634
Identifiable assets	1,060	196	414	273	1,943

By 1983, The Coca-Cola Company had become a major player in movie entertainment, acquiring Columbia Pictures. Along the way it sold its wine, water treatment, and plastics businesses. It adopted an aggressive product development effort in soft drinks, with diet, caffeine-free, and citrus soft-drink additions. Introduced one year earlier, Diet Coke became the No. 1 low-calorie beverage in the United States and No. 4 soft drink overall. On a companywide basis, sales and profitability looked as follows during that year:

1983 (in millions)

	United States	Latin America	Europe and Africa	Canada and Pacific	Total
Net sales	$4,071	$401	$1,226	$1,131	$6,829
Operating profit	499	69	295	207	993
Identifiable assets	2,997	421	607	473	4,496

The 12 years that followed saw The Coca-Cola Company make several fundamental changes in its strategic posture, while also accelerating its globalization and achieving some extraordinary results. Having completed the divestiture of Columbia Pictures (to Sony), The Coca-Cola Company of 1994 returned to its roots, operating in only two lines of business:

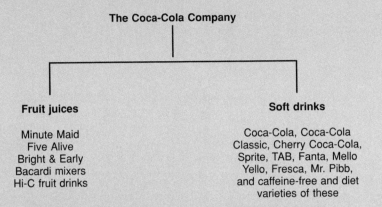

The Coca-Cola Company

Fruit juices

Minute Maid
Five Alive
Bright & Early
Bacardi mixers
Hi-C fruit drinks

Soft drinks

Coca-Cola, Coca-Cola
Classic, Cherry Coca-Cola,
Sprite, TAB, Fanta, Mello
Yello, Fresca, Mr. Pibb,
and caffeine-free and diet
varieties of these

In addition, the company has reversed its traditional approach and started aggressively making major equity investments in bottling facilities. These facilities are owned by bottling franchisees or joint ventures, or are company-owned. Another action was to create and sell 51 percent—the largest IPO in U.S. history—of a new publicly traded company (Coca-Cola Enterprises), which buys and invests in Coca-Cola bottling companies worldwide.

As Coca-Cola generously helped Atlanta host the 1996 Olympics, Coca-Cola's emphasis on globalization is unmistakable. Indeed, Coca-Cola's board chairman and chief executive officer, Robert C. Goizueta, had the following recent remarks about Coca-Cola's global perspective:

The global marketplace is something people have been writing about for years, and, while it may not be completely here yet, it is a fact that most U.S.–based companies of any size today think and act in international terms. At The Coca-Cola Company, we view ourselves today as an international corporation headquartered in the United States, as opposed to a U.S. company with a sizable international business. Coca-Cola's globalization is unquestioned and long a part of our company. Our attention, therefore, has moved beyond, to what we call "the Coca-Cola system," arguably the only truly global business system in existence today.

The trend toward globalization by U.S.–based companies will continue. Not only do 95 percent of the world's 5+ billion people live outside the United States, but the global climate today is generally favorable for companies disposed to expansion:

First, disposable income is rising around the world and, with it, people's ability to purchase more consumer products.

Second, outside the United States and Europe, the world is getting younger, and young people are the most enthusiastic purchasers of many consumer products.

Third, the world's markets are becoming easier to reach. Events in eastern Europe and the former Soviet Union are good examples.

Finally, in many important ways, the world's markets are also becoming more alike. Every corner of the free world is increasingly subjected to intense and similar communications: commercial, cultural, social, and hard news. Thus, people around the world are today connected to each other by brand name consumer products as much as by anything else. Tokyo, London, New York, and Los Angeles resemble each other today far more than they did 25 years ago, in large part because their residents' tastes in consumer products have converged.

Through our advertising and marketing we have encouraged consumers to associate Coca-Cola with their best feelings and memories . . . friends and family . . . joy and laughter . . . sports and music. Through our insistence on product integrity, we have made sure that wherever and whenever they drink a Coke, the product will live up to their expectations.

Through our worldwide business system we have made sure that Coca-Cola is there, so that wherever consumers travel they can always find a point of reference, a friendly reminder of home, regardless of where home may be. And through our efforts to serve our customers and consumers with a passion, they have come to feel passionate about Coca-Cola . . . It is this deep, heartfelt bond shared by Coca-Cola consumers and the members of the Coca-Cola system around the world that The Coca-Cola Company and its management cherish and value above all else. We cherish it because it is, more than anything else, the true measure of success in the global marketplace.

Goizueta, a Cuban refugee who as a young man worked for a Coke bottler in Cuba until fleeing the country with his family after Castro's rise to power, brings a unique perspective to his insistence on a global perspective. And The Coca-Cola Company has prospered under his leadership. Since becoming CEO in 1980, Goizueta has led Coca-Cola to a virtually unsurpassed level of performance. Compounded annual growth rates for several key indicators through 1995 are shown below:

Compound Annual Growth through 1995

	3 Year (%)	5 Year (%)	10 Year (%)
Operating revenues	11%	13%	12%
Operating income	16	17	16
Pretax income	17	16	15
Net income, continuing operations	24	16	17
EPS	23	17	18
EPS, continuing operations	15	17	21
Dividends	18	18	13
Average return on equity	50	47	38
Share appreciation	11	25	27

At January 1, 1982, Coca-Cola's market value stood at $4.3 billion. Fifteen years later, it exceeded $80 billion—an 18-fold growth. By any standard, these results were (and still are) truly extraordinary. It is certainly an indication of sound strategic decision making.

The remainder of this book will provide a Cohesion Case discussion at the end of each chapter. Each segment will examine aspects of strategic management at Coca-Cola that should help you understand Coca-Cola's success, while also serving to illustrate the ideas, concepts, and techniques we will present in each chapter of this book. We are excited about being able to "team up" with Coca-Cola to provide you with this unique perspective. And we strongly encourage you to supplement our coverage by obtaining and reviewing past Coca-Cola annual reports and recent business periodicals about the company to broaden your understanding of the company and its willingness to embrace sensible risk-taking and to welcome global change.

II   STRATEGY FORMULATION

Strategy formulation guides executives in defining the business their firm is in, the ends it seeks, and the means it will use to accomplish those ends. The approach of strategy formulation is an improvement over that of traditional long-range planning. As discussed in the next seven chapters—about developing a firm's competitive plan of action—strategy formulation combines a future-oriented perspective with concern for the firm's internal and external environments.

The strategy formulation process begins with definition of the company mission, as discussed in Chapter 2. In that chapter, the purpose of business is defined to reflect the values of a wide variety of interested parties.

Chapter 3 deals with the principal factors in a firm's external environment that strategic managers must assess so they can anticipate and take advantage of future business conditions. It emphasizes the importance to a firm's planning activities of factors in the firm's remote, industry, and operating environments. A key theme of the chapter is the problem of deciding whether to accept environmental constraints or to maneuver around them.

Chapter 4 describes the key differences in strategic planning and implementation among domestic, multinational, and global firms. It gives special attention to the new vision that a firm must communicate in a revised company mission when it multinationalizes.

Chapter 5 focuses on the environmental forecasting approaches currently used by strategic managers in assessing and anticipating changes in the external environment.

Chapter 6 shows how firms evaluate their internal strengths and weaknesses to produce a company profile. Strategic managers use such profiles to target competitive advantages they can emphasize and competitive disadvantages they should correct or minimize.

Chapter 7 examines the types of long-range objectives strategic managers set and specifies the qualities these objectives must have to provide a basis for direction and evaluation. The chapter also examines the generic and grand strategies that firms use to achieve long-range objectives.

Comprehensive approaches to the evaluation of strategic opportunities and to the final strategic decision are the focus of Chapter 8. The chapter shows how a firm's strategic options can be compared in a way that allows selection of the best available option.

2

DEFINING THE COMPANY MISSION

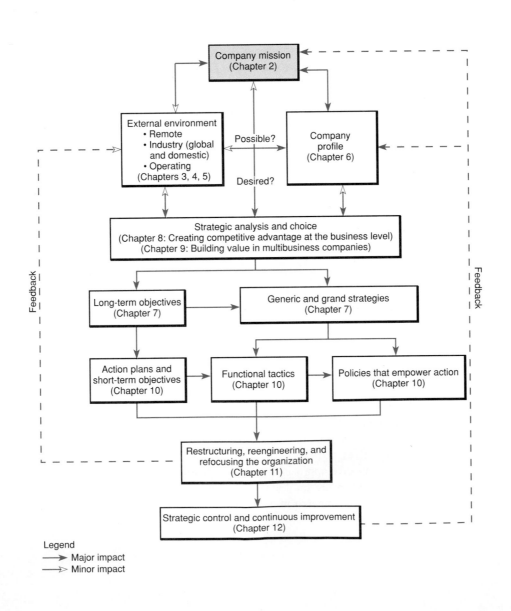

Legend
→ Major impact
⟶▷ Minor impact

WHAT IS A COMPANY MISSION?

Whether a firm is developing a new business or reformulating direction for an ongoing business, it must determine the basic goals and philosophies that will shape its strategic posture. This fundamental purpose that sets a firm apart from other firms of its type and identifies the scope of its operations in product and market terms is defined as the company mission. As discussed in Chapter 1, the company mission is a broadly framed but enduring statement of a firm's intent. It embodies the business philosophy of the firm's strategic decision makers, implies the image the firm seeks to project, reflects the firm's self-concept, and indicates the firm's principal product or service areas and the primary customer needs the firm will attempt to satisfy. In short, it describes the firm's product, market, and technological areas of emphasis, and it does so in a way that reflects the values and priorities of the firm's strategic decision makers. An excellent example is the company mission statement of Nicor, Inc., shown in Strategy in Action 2–1.

The Need for an Explicit Mission

No external body requires that the company mission be defined, and the process of defining it is time-consuming and tedious. Moreover, it contains broadly outlined or implied objectives and strategies rather than specific directives. Characteristically, it is a statement, not of measurable targets but of attitude, outlook, and orientation.

A company mission is designed to accomplish seven outcomes:

1. To ensure unanimity of purpose within the organization.
2. To provide a basis for motivating the use of the organization's resources.
3. To develop a basis, or standard, for allocating organizational resources.
4. To establish a general tone or organizational climate; for example, to suggest a businesslike operation.
5. To serve as a focal point for those who can identify with the organization's purpose and direction and to deter those who cannot do so from participating further in its activities.
6. To facilitate the translation of objectives and goals into a work structure involving the assignment of tasks to responsible elements within the organization.
7. To specify organizational purposes and the translation of these purposes into goals in such a way that cost, time, and performance parameters can be assessed and controlled.[1]

FORMULATING A MISSION

The process of defining the company mission for a specific business can perhaps be best understood by thinking about the business at its inception. The typical business begins with the beliefs, desires, and aspirations of a single entrepreneur. Such an owner-manager's sense of mission usually is based on the following fundamental beliefs:

1. The product or service of the business can provide benefits at least equal to its price.
2. The product or service can satisfy a customer need of specific market segments that is currently not being met adequately.

Note: Portions of this chapter are adopted from John A. Pearce II, "The Company Mission as a Strategic Tool," *Sloan Management Review,* Spring 1992, pp. 15–24.

[1] William R. King and David I. Cleland, *Strategic Planning and Policy* (New York: Van Nostrand Reinhold, 1978), p. 124.

STRATEGY
IN ACTION
2–1

MISSION STATEMENT OF NICOR, INC.

PREAMBLE

We, the management of Nicor, Inc., here set forth our belief as to the purpose for which the company is established and the principles under which it should operate. We pledge our effort to the accomplishment of these purposes within these principles.

BASIC PURPOSE

The basic purpose of Nicor, Inc., is to perpetuate an investor-owned company engaging in various phases of the energy business, striving for balance among those phases so as to render needed satisfactory products and services and earn optimum, long-range profits.

WHAT WE DO

The principal business of the company, through its utility subsidiary, is the provision of energy through a pipe system to meet the needs of ultimate consumers. To accomplish its basic purpose, and to ensure its strength, the company will engage in other energy-related activities, directly or through subsidiaries or in participation with other persons, corporations, firms, or entities.

All activities of the company shall be consistent with its responsibilities to investors, customers, employees, and the public and its concern for the optimum development and utilization of natural resources and for environmental needs.

WHERE WE DO IT

The company's operations shall be primarily in the United States, but no self-imposed or regulatory geographical limitations are placed upon the acquisition, development, processing, transportation, or storage of energy resources, or upon other energy-related ventures in which the company may engage. The company will engage in such activities in any location where, after careful review, it has determined that such activity is in the best interest of its stockholders.

Utility service will be offered in the territory of the company's utility subsidiary to the best of its ability, in accordance with the requirements of regulatory agencies and pursuant to the subsidiary's purposes and principles.

---

3. The technology that is to be used in production will provide a cost- and quality-competitive product or service.

4. With hard work and the support of others, the business can not only survive but also grow and be profitable.

5. The management philosophy of the business will result in a favorable public image and will provide financial and psychological rewards for those who are willing to invest their labor and money in helping the business to succeed.

6. The entrepreneur's self-concept of the business can be communicated to and adopted by employees and stockholders.

As the business grows or is forced by competitive pressures to alter its product–market–technology, redefining the company mission may be necessary. If so, the revised mission statement will contain the same components as the original. It will state the

STRATEGY
IN ACTION
2–2

**IDENTIFYING MISSION STATEMENT COMPONENTS:
A COMPILATION OF EXCERPTS FROM ACTUAL
CORPORATE MISSION STATEMENTS**

1. Customer-market

We believe our first responsibility is to the doctors, nurses, and patients, to mothers and all others who use our products and services. (Johnson & Johnson)

To anticipate and meet market needs of farmers, ranchers, and rural communities within North America. (CENEX)

2. Product-service

AMAX's principal products are molybdenum, coal, iron ore, copper, lead, zinc, petroleum and natural gas, potash, phosphates, nickel, tungsten, silver, gold, and magnesium. (AMAX)

3. Geographic domain

We are dedicated to the total success of Corning Glass Works as a worldwide competitor. (Corning Glass)

4. Technology

Control Data is the business of applying microelectronics and computer technology in two general areas: computer-related hardware and computing-enhancing services, which include computation, information, education, and finance. (Control Data)

The common technology in these areas relates to discrete particle coatings. (NASHUA)

5. Concern for survival

In this respect, the company will conduct its operation prudently, and will provide the profits and growth which will assure Hoover's ultimate success. (Hoover Universal)

6. Philosophy

We are committed to improve health care throughout the world. (Baxter Travenol)

We believe human development to be the worthiest of the goals of civilization and independence to be the superior condition for nurturing growth in the capabilities of people. (Sun Company)

7. Self-concept

Hoover Universal is a diversified, multi-industry corporation with strong manufacturing capabilities, entrepreneurial policies, and individual business unit autonomy. (Hoover Universal)

8. Concern for public image

We are responsible to the communities in which we live and work and to the world community as well. (Johnson & Johnson)

Also, we must be responsive to the broader concerns of the public, including especially the general desire for improvement in the quality of life, equal opportunity for all, and the constructive use of natural resources. (Sun Company)

Source: John A Pearce II and F. R. David, "Corporate Mission Statements: The Bottom Line," *Academy of Management Executive*, May 1987, pp. 109–16.

basic type of product or service to be offered, the primary markets or customer groups to be served, and the technology to be used in production or delivery; the firm's fundamental concern for survival through growth and profitability; the firm's managerial philosophy; the public image the firm seeks; and the self-concept those affiliated with the firm should have of it. This chapter will discuss in detail these components. The examples shown in Strategy in Action 2–2 provide insights into how some major corporations handle them.

Basic Product or Service; Primary Market; Principal Technology

Three indispensable components of the mission statement are specification of the basic product or service, specification of the primary market, and specification of the principal technology for production or delivery. These components are discussed under one heading because only in combination do they describe the company's business activity. A good example of the three components is to be found in the business plan of ITT Barton, a division of ITT. Under the heading of business mission and area served, the following information is presented:

The unit's mission is to serve industry and government with quality instruments used for the primary measurement, analysis, and local control of fluid flow, level, pressure, temperature, and fluid properties. This instrumentation includes flow meters, electronic readouts, indicators, recorders, switches, liquid level system, analytical instruments such as titrators, integrators, controllers, transmitters, and various instruments for the measurement of fluid properties (density, viscosity, gravity) used for processing variable sensing, data collecting, control, and transmission. The unit's mission includes fundamental loop- closing control and display devices, when economically justified, but excludes broadline central control room instrumentation, systems design, and turnkey responsibility.

Markets served include instrumentation for oil and gas production, gas transportation, chemical and petrochemical processing, cryogenics, power generation, aerospace, government, and marine, as well as other instrument and equipment manufacturers.

In only 129 words, this segment of the mission statement clearly indicates to all readers—from company employees to casual observers—the basic products, primary markets, and principal technologies of ITT Barton.

Often the most referenced public statement of a company's selected products and markets appears in "silver bullet" form in the mission statement; for example, "Dayton-Hudson Corporation is a diversified retailing company whose business is to serve the American consumer through the retailing of fashion-oriented quality merchandise."[2] Such an abstract of company direction is particularly helpful to outsiders who value condensed overviews.

Company Goals: Survival, Growth, Profitability

Three economic goals guide the strategic direction of almost every business organization. Whether or not the mission statement explicitly states these goals, it reflects the firm's intention to secure *survival* through *growth* and *profitability.*

A firm that is unable to survive will be incapable of satisfying the aims of any of its stakeholders. Unfortunately, the goal of survival, like the goals of growth and profitability, often is taken for granted to such an extent that it is neglected as a principal criterion in strategic decision making. When this happens, the firm may focus on short-term aims at the expense of the long run. Concerns for expediency, a quick fix, or a bargain may displace the assessment of long-term impact. Too often, the result is near-term economic failure owing to a lack of resource synergy and sound business practice. For example, Consolidated Foods, maker of Shasta soft drinks and L ' eggs hosiery, sought growth through the acquisition of bargain businesses. However, the erratic sales patterns of its diverse holdings forced it to divest itself of more than four dozen companies. This process cost Consolidated Foods millions of dollars and hampered its growth.

Profitability is the mainstay goal of a business organization. No matter how profit is measured or defined, profit over the long term is the clearest indication of a firm's ability to satisfy the principal claims and desires of employees and stockholders. The key phrase here is "over the long term." Obviously, basing decisions on a short-term concern for profitability would lead to a strategic myopia. Overlooking the enduring concerns of customers, suppliers, creditors, ecologists, and regulatory agents may produce profit in the short term, but, over time, the financial consequences are likely to be detrimental.

---

[2] See W. Ouchi, *Theory Z* (Reading, Mass.: Addison-Wesley Publishing, 1981). Ouchi presents more complete mission statements of three of the companies discussed in this chapter: Dayton-Hudson, Hewlett-Packard, and Intel.

The following excerpt from the Hewlett-Packard statement of mission ably expresses the importance of an orientation toward long-term profit:

To achieve sufficient profit to finance our company growth and to provide the resources we need to achieve our other corporate objectives.

In our economic system, the profit we generate from our operation is the ultimate source of the funds we need to prosper and grow. It is the one absolutely essential measure of our corporate performance over the long term. Only if we continue to meet our profit objective can we achieve our other corporate objectives.

A firm's growth is tied inextricably to its survival and profitability. In this context, the meaning of growth must be broadly defined. Although the product impact market studies (PIMS) have shown that growth in market share is correlated with profitability, other important forms of growth do exist. Growth in the number of markets served, in the variety of products offered, and in the technologies that are used to provide goods or services frequently lead to improvements in a firm's competitive ability. Growth means change, and proactive change is essential in a dynamic business environment.

Hewlett-Packard's mission statement provides an excellent example of corporate regard for growth:

Objective: To let our growth be limited only by our profits and our ability to develop and produce technical products that satisfy real customer needs.

We do not believe that large size is important for its own sake; however, for at least two basic reasons, continuous growth is essential for us to achieve our other objectives.

In the first place, we serve a rapidly growing and expanding segment of our technological society. To remain static would be to lose ground. We cannot maintain a position of strength and leadership in our field without growth.

In the second place, growth is important in order to attract and hold high-caliber people. These individuals will align their future only with a company that offers them considerable opportunity for personal progress. Opportunities are greater and more challenging in a growing company.

The issue of growth raises a concern about the definition of the company mission. How can a firm's product, market, and technology be specified sufficiently to provide direction without precluding the exercise of unanticipated strategic options? How can a firm so define its mission that it can consider opportunistic diversification while maintaining the parameters that guide its growth decision? Perhaps such questions are best addressed when a firm's mission statement outlines the conditions under which the firm might depart from ongoing operations. General Electric Company's extensive global mission provided the foundation for its GE Appliances (GEA) in Louisville, Kentucky, to grow in spite of the 1990–91 recession. GEA did not see consumer preferences in the world market becoming Americanized. Instead, its expansion goals allowed for flexibility in examining the unique characteristics of individual foreign markets and tailoring strategies to fit them.

The growth philosophy of Dayton-Hudson also embodies this approach:

The stability and quality of the corporation's financial performance will be developed through the profitable execution of our existing businesses, as well as through the acquisition or development of new businesses. Our growth priorities, in order, are as follows:

1. Development of the profitable market preeminence of existing companies in existing markets through new store development or new strategies within existing stores.

   2. Expansion of our companies to feasible new markets.
   3. Acquisition of other retailing companies that are strategically and financially
      compatible with Dayton-Hudson.
   4. Internal development of new retailing strategies.

Capital allocations to fund the expansion of existing Dayton-Hudson operating companies will be based on each company's return on investment (ROI), in relationship to its ROI objective and its consistency in earnings growth and on the ability of its management to perform up to the forecasts contained in its capital requests. Expansion via acquisition or new venture will occur when the opportunity promises an acceptable rate of long-term growth and profitability, an acceptable degree of risk, and compatibility with Dayton-Hudson's long-term strategy.

Company Philosophy

The statement of a company's philosophy, often called the *company creed,* usually accompanies or appears within the mission statement. It reflects or specifies the basic beliefs, values, aspirations, and philosophical priorities to which strategic decision makers are committed in managing the company. Fortunately, the philosophies vary little from one firm to another. Owners and managers implicitly accept a general, unwritten, yet pervasive code of behavior that governs business actions and permits them to be largely self-regulated. Unfortunately, statements of company philosophy are often so similar and so platitudinous that they read more like public relations handouts than the commitment to values they are meant to be.

Saturn's statement of philosophy, presented in Strategy in Action 2–3, indicates the company's clearly defined initiatives for satisfying the needs of its customers, employees, suppliers, and dealers.

Despite the similarity of these statements, the intentions of the strategic managers in developing them do not warrant cynicism. Company executives attempt to provide a distinctive and accurate picture of the firm's managerial outlook. One such statement of company philosophy is that of Dayton-Hudson Corporation. As Strategy in Action 2–4 shows, Dayton-Hudson's board of directors and executives have established especially clear directions for company decision making and action.

Perhaps most noteworthy in the Dayton-Hudson statement is its delineation of responsibility at both the corporate and business levels. In many ways, the statement could serve as a prototype for the three-tier approach to strategic management. This approach implies that the mission statement must address strategic concerns at the corporate, business, and functional levels of the organization. Dayton-Hudson's management philosophy does this by balancing operating autonomy and flexibility on the one hand with corporate input and direction on the other.

As seen in Global Strategy in Action 2–1, the philosophy of Nissan Motor Manufacturing is expressed by the company's People Principles and Key Corporate Principles. These principles form the basis of the way the company operates on a daily basis. They address the principal concepts used in meeting the company's established goals. Nissan focuses on the distinction between the role of the individual and the corporation. In this way, employees can link their productivity and success to the productivity and success of the company. Given these principles, the company is able to concentrate on the issues most important to its survival, growth, and profitability.

Strategy in Action 2–5 provides an example of how General Motors uses a statement of company philosophy to clarify its environmental principles. Strategy in Action 2–6

STRATEGY
IN ACTION
2–3

SATURN'S STATEMENT OF PHILOSOPHY

We, the Saturn Team, in concert with the UAW and General Motors, believe that meeting the needs of customers, Saturn members, suppliers, dealers, and neighbors is fundamental to fulfilling our mission.

To meet our customers' needs . . .
· our products and services must be world leaders in value and satisfaction.

To meet our members' needs, we . . .
· will create a sense of belonging in an environment of mutual trust, respect, and dignity;
· believe that all people want to be involved in decisions that affect them, care about their jobs and each other, take pride in themselves and in their contributions, and want to share in the success of their efforts;
· will develop the tools, training, and education for each member, recognizing individual skills and knowledge;
· believe that creative, motivated, responsible team members who understand that change is critical to success are Saturn's most important asset.

To meet our suppliers' and dealers' needs, we . . .
· will strive to create real partnerships with them;
· will be open and fair in our dealings, reflecting trust, respect, and their importance to Saturn;
· want dealers and suppliers to feel ownership in Saturn's mission and philosophy as their own.

To meet the needs of our neighbors, the communities in which we live and operate, we . . .
· will be good citizens, protect the environment, and conserve natural resources;
· will seek to cooperate with government at all levels and strive to be sensitive, open, and candid in all our public statements.

Source: Excerpted from Robert R. Rehder, "Is Saturn Competitive?" p. 9. Reprinted from *Business Horizons*, March–April 1994. Copyright 1994 by the Foundation for the School of Business at Indiana University. Used with permission.

describes the changes in corporate philosophy that enabled a subsidiary of Johnson & Johnson to achieve an organizational turnaround.

Public Image

Both present and potential customers attribute certain qualities to particular businesses. Gerber and Johnson & Johnson make safe products; Cross Pen makes high-quality writing instruments; Étienne Aigner makes stylish but affordable leather products; Corvettes are power machines; and Izod Lacoste stands for the preppy look. Thus, mission statements should reflect the public's expectations, since this makes achievement of the firm's goals more likely. Gerber's mission statement should not open the possibility for diversification into pesticides, and Cross Pen's should not open the possibility for diversification into $0.59 brand-name disposables.

On the other hand, a negative public image often prompts firms to reemphasize the beneficial aspects of their mission. For example, in response to what it saw as a disturbing

MANAGEMENT PHILOSOPHY OF
DAYTON-HUDSON CORPORATION

The corporation will:

Set standards for return on investment (ROI) and earnings growth.

Approve strategic plans.

Allocate capital.

Approve goals.

Monitor, measure, and audit results.

Reward performance.

Allocate management resources.

The operating companies will be accorded the freedom and responsibility:

To manage their own business.

To develop strategic plans and goals that will optimize their growth.

To develop an organization that can ensure consistency of results and optimum growth.

To operate their businesses consistent with the corporation's statement of philosophy.

The corporate staff will provide only those services that are:

Essential to the protection of the corporation.

Needed for the growth of the corporation.

Wanted by operating companies and that provide a significant advantage in quality or cost.

The corporation will insist on:

Uniform accounting practices by type of business.

Prompt disclosure of operating results.

A systematic approach to training and developing people.

Adherence to appropriately high standards of business conduct and civic responsibility in accordance with the corporation's statement of philosophy.

---

trend in public opinion, Dow Chemical undertook an aggressive promotional campaign to fortify its credibility, particularly among "employees and those who live and work in [their] plant communities." Dow described its approach in its annual report:

All around the world today, Dow people are speaking up. People who care deeply about their company, what it stands for, and how it is viewed by others. People who are immensely proud of their company's performance, yet realistic enough to realize it is the public's perception of that performance that counts in the long run.

Firms seldom address the question of their public image in an intermittent fashion. Although public agitation often stimulates greater attention to this question, firms are concerned about their public image even in the absence of such agitation. The following excerpt from the mission statement of Intel Corporation is an example of this attitude:

We are sensitive to our *image with our customers and the business community*. Commitments to customers are considered sacred, and we are upset with ourselves when we do not meet our

PRINCIPLES OF NISSAN MOTOR MANUFACTURING (UK) LTD.

People Principles
(All Other Objectives Can Only Be Achieved by People)

Selection	Hire the highest caliber people; look for technical capabilities and emphasize attitude.
Responsibility	Maximize the responsibility; staff by devolving decision making.
Teamwork	Recognize and encourage individual contributions, with everyone working toward the same objectives.
Flexibility	Expand the role of the individual: multiskilled, no job description, generic job titles.
Kaizen	Continuously seek 100.1 percent improvements; give "ownership of change."
Communications	"Every day, face to face."
Training	Establish individual "continuous development programs."
Supervisors	Regard as "the professionals at managing the production process"; give them much responsibility normally assumed by individual departments; make them the genuine leaders of their teams.
Single status	Treat everyone as a "first class" citizen; eliminate all illogical differences.
Trade unionism	Establish single union agreement with AEU emphasizing the common objective for a successful enterprise.

Key Corporate Principles

Quality	Building profitably the highest quality car sold in Europe.
Customers	Achieve target of no. 1 customer satisfaction in Europe.
Volume	Always achieve required volume.
New products	Deliver on time, at required quality, within cost.
Suppliers	Establish long-term relationships with single-source suppliers; aim for zero defects and just-in-time delivery; apply Nissan principles to suppliers.
Production	Use "most appropriate" technology; develop predictable "best method" of doing job; build in quality.
Engineering	Design "quality" and "ease of working" into the product and facilities; establish "simultaneous engineering" to reduce development time.

commitments. We strive to demonstrate to the business world on a continuing basis that we are credible in describing the state of the corporation, and that we are well organized and in complete control of all things that determine the numbers.

Company Self-Concept

A major determinant of a firm's success is the extent to which the firm can relate functionally to its external environment. To achieve its proper place in a competitive situation, the firm realistically must evaluate its competitive strengths and weaknesses. This idea—that

GENERAL MOTORS ENVIRONMENTAL PRINCIPLES

As a responsible corporate citizen, General Motors is dedicated to protecting human health, natural resources, and the global environment. This dedication reaches further than compliance with the law to encompass the integration of sound environmental practices into our business decisions.

The following environmental principles provide guidance to General Motors personnel worldwide in the conduct of their daily business practices:

1. We are committed to actions to restore and preserve the environment.
2. We are committed to reducing waste and pollutants, conserving resources, and recycling materials at every stage of the product life cycle.
3. We will continue to participate actively in educating the public regarding environmental conservation.
4. We will continue to pursue vigorously the development and implementation of technologies for minimizing pollutant emissions.
5. We will continue to work with all governmental entities for the development of technically sound and financially responsible environmental laws and regulations.
6. We will continually assess the impact of our plants and products on the environment and the communities in which we live and operate with a goal of continuous improvement.

Source: 1991 General Motors Public Interest Report, p. 23.

the firm must know itself—is the essence of the company self-concept. The idea is not commonly integrated into theories of strategic management; its importance for individuals has been recognized since ancient times. As one scholar writes, "Man has struggled to understand himself, for how he thinks of himself will influence both what he chooses to do and what he expects from life. Knowing his identity connects him both with his past and with the potentiality of his future."[3]

Both individuals and firms have a crucial need to know themselves. The ability of either to survive in a dynamic and highly competitive environment would be severely limited if they did not understand their impact on others or of others on them.

In some senses, then, firms take on personalities of their own. Much behavior in firms is organizationally based; that is, a firm acts on its members in other ways than their individual interactions. Thus, firms are entities whose personality transcends the personalities of their members. As such, they can set decision-making parameters based on aims different and distinct from the aims of their members. These organizational considerations have pervasive effects.

> Organizations do have policies, do and do not condone violence, and may or may not greet you with a smile. They also manufacture goods, administer policies, and protect the citizenry. These are organizational actions and involve properties of organizations, not individuals. They are carried out by individuals, even in the case of computer-produced letters, which are programmed by individuals—but the genesis of the actions remains in the organization.[4]

[3] J. Kelly, *Organizational Behavior* (Burr Ridge, IL: Irwin, 1974), p. 258.

[4] R. H. Hall, *Organizational Structure and Process* (Englewood Cliffs, NJ: Prentice-Hall, 1972), p. 13.

The characteristics of the corporate self-concept have been summarized as follows:

1. It is based on management's perception of the way in which others (society) will respond to the company.
2. It directs the behavior of people employed by the company.
3. It is determined in part by the responses of others to the company.
4. It is incorporated into mission statements that are communicated to individuals inside and outside the company.[5]

Ordinarily, descriptions of the company self-concept per se do not appear in mission statements. Yet such statements often provide strong impressions of the company self-concept. For example, ARCO's environment, health, and safety (EHS) managers were adamant about emphasizing the company's position on safety and environmental performance as a part of the mission statement. The challenges facing the ARCO EHS managers in the early 1990s included dealing with concerned environmental groups and a public that has become environmentally aware. They hoped to motivate employees toward safer behavior while reducing emissions and waste. They saw this as a reflection of the company's positive self-image.

The following excerpts from the Intel Corporation mission statement describe the corporate persona that its top management seeks to foster:

> Management is self-critical. The leaders must be capable of recognizing and accepting their mistakes and learning from them.
>
> Open (constructive) confrontation is encouraged at all levels of the corporation and is viewed as a method of problem solving and conflict resolution.
>
> Decision by consensus is the rule. Decisions once made are supported. Position in the organization is not the basis for quality of ideas.
>
> A highly communicative, open management is part of the style.
>
> Management must be ethical. Managing by telling the truth and treating all employees equitably has established credibility that is ethical.
>
> We strive to provide an opportunity for rapid development.
>
> Intel is a results-oriented company. The focus is on substance versus form, quality versus quantity.
>
> We believe in the principle that hard work, high productivity is something to be proud of.
>
> The concept of assumed responsibility is accepted. (If a task needs to be done, assume you have the responsibility to get it done.)
>
> Commitments are long term. If career problems occur at some point, reassignment is a better alternative than termination.
>
> We desire to have all employees involved and participative in their relationship with Intel.

Newest Trends in Mission Components

Recently, two new issues have become so prominent in the strategic planning for organizations that they are increasingly becoming integral parts in the development and revisions of mission statements: sensitivity to consumer wants and concern for quality.

Customers

"The customer is our top priority" is a slogan that would be claimed by the majority of businesses in the United States and abroad. For companies including Caterpillar Tractor, General Electric, and Johnson & Johnson, this means analyzing consumer needs before as

---

[5] E. J. Kelley, *Marketing Planning and Competitive Strategy* (Englewood Cliffs, NJ: Prentice Hall, 1972), p. 5.

ORGANIZATIONAL RENEWAL CENTERS ON STRATEGIC COLLABORATION

When William Crouse took over as president of Ortho Diagnostic Systems, Inc. (ODSI), he knew this Johnson & Johnson subsidiary was in danger of becoming yet another victim of growth. In its effort to serve its customers and maintain market share, ODSI hit its markets with a dizzying array of products. Its customer base was deep but too wide. Its sales force devoted as much attention to small hospitals as it did to those with greater potential. All of this pointed to a lack of strategic focus, which usually translates into higher operating costs and profit margin deterioration. Clearly, the company needed to change in order to maintain its leadership position in the competitive diagnostic segment of the global healthcare marketplace.

So change it did. The strategy now is more focused, and there's a greater responsiveness to customers and less product-market clutter. Since the transformation began, turnover has been arrested, volume has more than doubled, profits have skyrocketed, and morale has improved.

The turnaround was achieved through a multistep approach to organizational transformation, which began with setting vision and strategy and included diagnosing an organization's structure, systems, culture, and capabilities for strategic fit. The process also included developing action plans and designing a tracking system for monitoring and updating.

When Crouse assumed the presidency, the first thing he did was nothing—except wander down the hallways of the organization, making stops at all levels and functions, soliciting ideas, asking questions, and listening. "I learned about the company and got to know the people by speaking with them about problems and opportunities," he recalls. "By the end of the first three months, I knew exactly what had to be done."

But Crouse felt that was not enough, so he spent another three months talking with virtually every employee. "I then reported back to them saying, 'This is what you've told me about the company, and here are my conclusions based on what you've told me. This is what I think we should do; now, what do you think?' "

Source: W. A. Schiemann, "Organizational Change: Lessons from a Turnaround," *Management Review,* April 1992, pp. 34–37.

well as after a sale. The bonus plan at Xerox allows for a 40 percent annual bonus, based on high customer reviews of the service that they receive, and a 20 percent penalty if the feedback is especially bad. For these firms and many others, the overriding concern for the company has become consumer satisfaction.

In addition many U.S. firms maintain extensive product safety programs to help assure consumer satisfaction. RCA, Sears, and 3M boast of such programs. Other firms including Calgon Corporation, Amoco, Mobil Oil, Whirlpool, and Zenith provide toll-free telephone lines to answer customer concerns and complaints.

The focus on customer satisfaction is demonstrated by retailer J. C. Penney in this excerpt from its statement of philosophy: "The Penney Idea is (1) To serve the public as nearly as we can to its complete satisfaction; (2) To expect for the service we render a fair remuneration, and not all the profit the traffic will bear; (3) To do all in our power to pack the customer's dollar full of value, quality, and satisfaction."

A focus on customer satisfaction causes managers to realize the importance of providing quality customer service. Strong customer service initiatives have led some firms to gain competitive advantages in the marketplace. Hence, many corporations have made the customer service initiative a key component of their corporate mission. Some key elements of customer service–driven organizations are listed in Figure 2–1.

Strategy then evolved from this broadly based, back-and-forth process of questioning and testing conclusions. "Strategy is not only about what you are going to do, it's also about getting people to buy in and commit to what's going to happen and having them understand their role in implementation."

The evolutionary approach paid off in terms of the quality of thinking that went into the strategy and the commitment to it down through the ranks. It worked because Crouse was personally involved, and he substituted the top-down textbook approach with a more collaboratively strategy-setting model.

At ODSI, an effort was made to channel people's anxiety over change by focusing their energies on a basic strategic mission. That mission had to meet three criteria: uniqueness (it had to set ODSI apart from competitors); altruism (it had to capture employees' spirit and get them to look beyond themselves); and simplicity (it had to be easily understood, remembered, and enacted). As the business mission states: "ODSI provides customers with fast, simple, accurate means of diagnosing patients and protects the safety of the world's blood supply."

This mission could be accomplished only if everyone remained focused. Crouse's six-month journey through the organization taught him that employees were caught in an activity trap. They were bouncing from one crisis to the next and doing too many things. There were too many customers, too many marginal products, and too many small orders. There was a sense that everyone was looking for silver bullets to solve problems, instead of striving to maintain ODSI's leadership position. To move forward, the company had to go back to the basics.

Although the mission provided a good framework, it needed greater specification. The top-management team developed a business protocol that spelled out how ODSI would conduct business; how it would manage and motivate the work force; new decision-making patterns that pushed responsibility downward; and new structures that promoted teamwork and focus. Developing a clear, specific sense of strategic direction and thinking throughout the organization was key to the ODSI turnaround.

Quality

"Quality is job one!" is a rallying point not only for Ford Motor Corporation but for many resurging U.S. businesses as well. Since the 1950s, two U.S. management experts have fostered a worldwide emphasis on quality in manufacturing. W. Edwards Deming and J. M. Juran's messages were first embraced by Japanese managers, whose quality consciousness led to global dominance in several industries including automobile, TV, audio equipment, and electronic components manufacturing. Deming summarizes his approach in 14 now well-known points:

1. Create constancy of purpose.
2. Adopt the new philosophy.
3. Cease dependence on mass inspection to achieve quality.
4. End the practice of awarding business on price tag alone. Instead, minimize total cost, often accomplished by working with a single supplier.
5. Improve constantly the system of production and service.
6. Institute training on the job.
7. Institute leadership.
8. Drive out fear.
9. Break down barriers between departments.

FIGURE 2–1
Key Elements of Customer Service–Driven Organizations

1. A mission statement or sense of mission makes customer service a priority.
2. Customer service goals are clearly defined.
3. Customer service standards are clearly defined.
4. Customer satisfaction with existing products and services is continuously measured.
5. Ongoing efforts are made to understand customers to determine where the organization should be headed.
6. Corrective action procedures are in place to remove barriers to servicing customers in a timely and effective fashion.
7. Customer service goals have an impact on organizational action.

Source: An excerpt from "Peters, 1987," p. 78. Reprinted from *Business Horizons,* July–August 1995. Copyright 1995 by the Foundation for the School of Business at Indiana University. Used with permission.

10. Eliminate slogans, exhortations, and numerical targets.
11. Eliminate work standards (quotas) and management by objective.
12. Remove barriers that rob workers, engineers, and managers of their right to pride of workmanship.
13. Institute a vigorous program of education and self-improvement.
14. Put everyone in the company to work to accomplish the transformation.

Beginning in the late 1980s, firms in the United States responded aggressively. The new philosophy is that quality should be the norm. For example, Motorola's 1993 production goal was 60 or fewer defects per every billion components that it manufactures. Managers who emphasize quality have even created their own jargon, as reviewed in Figure 2–2.

Strategy in Action 2–7 presents the integration of the quality initiative into the mission statements of three corporations. The emphasis on quality has received added emphasis in many corporate philosophies since the Congress created the Malcolm Baldrige Quality Award in 1987. Each year up to two Baldrige Awards can been given in three categories of a company's operations: manufacturing, services, and small businesses.

OVERSEEING THE STRATEGY MAKERS

Who is responsible for determining the firm's mission? Who is responsible for acquiring and allocating resources so the firm can thoughtfully develop and implement a strategic plan? Who is responsible for monitoring the firm's success in the competitive marketplace to determine whether that plan was well designed and activated? The answer to all of these questions is "strategic decision makers." As you saw in Figure 1–3, most organizations have multiple levels of strategic decision makers; typically, the larger the firm, the more levels it will have. The strategic managers at the highest level are responsible for decisions that affect the entire firm, commit the firm and its resources for the longest periods, and declare the firm's sense of values. In other words, this group of strategic managers is responsible for overseeing the creation and accomplishment of the company mission. The term that describes the group is *board of directors.*

In overseeing the management of a firm, the board of directors operates as the representatives of the firm's stockholders. Elected by the stockholders, the board has these major responsibilities:

FIGURE 2–2
A Glossary of Quality-Speak

Acceptable Quality Level (AQL)

Minimum number of parts that must comply with quality standards, usually stated as a percentage.

Competitive Benchmarking

Rating a company's practices, processes, and products against the world's best, including those in other industries.

Continuous-Improvement Process (CIP)

Searching unceasingly for ever-higher levels of quality by isolating sources of defects. The goal: zero defects. The Japanese call it Kaizen.

Control Charts

Statistical plots derived from measuring factory processes, they help detect "process drift," or deviation, before it generates defects. Charts also help spot inherent variations in manufacturing processes that designers must account for to achieve "robust design" (below).

Just-in-Time (JIT)

When suppliers deliver materials and parts at the moment a factory needs them, thus eliminating costly inventories. Quality is paramount: A faulty part delivered at the last minute won't be detected.

Pareto Chart

A bar graph that ranks causes of process variation by the degree of impact on quality.

Poka-Yoke

Making the workplace mistake-proof. A machine fitted with guide rails permits a part to be worked on in just one way.

Quality Function Deployment (QFD)

A system that pays special attention to customer wants. Activities that don't contribute are considered wasteful.

Robust Design

A discipline for making designs "production-proof" by building in tolerances for manufacturing variables that are known to be unavoidable.

Six-Sigma Quality

A statistical measure expressing how close a product comes to its quality goal. One-sigma means 68% of products are acceptable; three-sigma means 99.7%. Six-sigma is 99.999997% perfect: 3.4 defects per million parts.

Statistical Process Control (SPC)

A method of analyzing deviations in production processes during manufacturing.

Statistical Quality Control (SQC)

A method of analyzing measured deviations in manufactured materials, parts, and products.

Taguchi Methods

Statistical techniques developed by Genichi Taguchi, a Japanese consultant, for optimizing design and production. These are used often on "robust design" projects.

Total Quality Control (TQC)

The application of quality principles to all company endeavors, including satisfying internal "customers." Manufacturing engineers, for instance, are customers of the design staff. Also known as total quality management (TQM).

Source: Reprinted from October 25, 1991, issue of *Business Week,* by special permission, copyright © 1991 by McGraw-Hill, Inc.

1. To establish and update the company mission.
2. To elect the company's top officers, the foremost of whom is the CEO.
3. To establish the compensation levels of the top officers, including their salaries and bonuses.
4. To determine the amount and timing of the dividends paid to stockholders.

STRATEGY
IN ACTION
2–7

VISIONS OF QUALITY

CADILLAC

The Mission of the Cadillac Motor Company is to engineer, produce, and market the world's finest automobiles known for uncompromised levels of distinctiveness, comfort, convenience, and refined performance. Through its people, who are its strength, Cadillac will continuously improve the quality of its products and services to meet or exceed customer expectations and succeed as a profitable business.

MOTOROLA

Dedication to quality is a way of life at our company, so much so that it goes far beyond rhetorical slogans. Our ongoing program of continued improvement reaches out for change, refinement, and even revolution in our pursuit of quality excellence.

It is the objective of Motorola, Inc., to produce and provide products and services of the highest quality. In its activities, Motorola will pursue goals aimed at the achievement of quality excellence. These results will be derived from the dedicated efforts of each employee in conjunction with supportive participation from management at all levels of the corporation.

ZYTEC

Zytec is a company that competes on value; is market driven; provides superior quality and service; builds strong relationships with its customers; and provides technical excellence in its products.

Source: Excerpted from Richard M. Hodgets, "Quality Lessons from America's Baldrige Winners," p. 75. Reprinted from *Business Horizons,* July–August 1995. Copyright 1995 by the Foundation for the School of Business at Indiana University. Used with permission.

5. To set broad company policy on such matters as labor-management relations, product or service lines of business, and employee benefit packages.
6. To set company objectives and to authorize managers to implement the long-term strategies that the top officers and the board have found agreeable.
7. To mandate company compliance with legal and ethical dictates.

This chapter considers the board of directors because the board's greatest impact on the behavior of a firm results from its determination of the company mission. The philosophy espoused in the mission statement sets the tone by which the firm and all of its employees will be judged. As logical extensions of the mission statement, the firm's objectives and strategies embody the board's view of proper business demeanor. Through its appointment of top executives and its decisions about their compensation, the board reveals its priorities for organizational achievement.

Board Success Factors

A review of writings and research on the behavior of boards discloses that they are judged to be most successful when:[6]

[6] S. A. Zahra and J. A. Pearce II, "Boards of Directors and Corporate Financial Performance: A Review and Integrative Model," *Journal of Management* 15 (1989), pp. 291–334.

1. They represent the interests of stockholders and carefully monitor the actions of senior executives to promote and protect those interests.[7]

2. They link the firm to influential stakeholders in its external environment, thereby promoting the company mission while ensuring attention to important societal concerns.[8]

3. They are composed of 8 to 12 highly qualified members.

4. They exercise independent and objective thinking in appraising the actions of senior executives and in introducing strategic changes.[9]

5. They pay special attention to their own composition to ensure an appropriate mix of inside and outside directors and the inclusion of minority representatives.[10]

6. They have a well-developed structure; that is, they are organized into appropriate committees to perform specialized tasks (e.g., to review executive compensation and to audit the company's financial transactions).[11]

7. They meet frequently to discuss progress in achieving organizational goals and to provide counsel to executives.[12]

8. They evaluate the CEO's performance at least annually to provide guidance on issues of leadership style.[13]

9. They conduct strategy reviews to determine the fit between the firm's strategy and the requirements of its competitive environment.[14]

10. They formulate the ethical codes that are to govern the behavior of the firm's executives and employees.[15]

11. They promote a future-oriented outlook on the company mission by challenging executives to articulate their visions for the firm and for its interface with society.

These criteria can enable board members, CEOs, and stockholders to judge board behavior. The question "What should boards do?" can be answered largely by studying the criteria.

THE STAKEHOLDER APPROACH TO COMPANY RESPONSIBILITY

In defining or redefining the company mission, strategic managers must recognize the legitimate rights of the firm's claimant. These include not only stockholders and employees but also outsiders affected by the firm's actions. Such outsiders commonly include customers,

---

[7] P. L. Rechner and D. R. Dalton, "The Impact of CEO as Board Chairperson on Corporate Performance: Evidence vs. Rhetoric," *Academy of Management Executive* 3, no. 2 (1989), pp. 141–43.

[8] M. S. Mizruchi, "Who Controls Whom?: An Examination of the Relation between Management and Board of Directors in Large American Corporations," *Academy of Management Review,* August 1983, pp. 426–35.

[9] T. M. Jones and L. D. Goldberg, "Governing the Large Corporation: More Arguments for Public Directors," *Academy of Management Review* 7 (1982), pp. 603–11.

[10] I. F. Kesner, "Directors' Characteristics and Committee Membership: An Investigation of Type, Occupation, Tenure, and Gender," *Academy of Management Journal* 31 (1988), pp. 66–84; and J. A. Pearce II, "The Relationship of Internal versus External Orientations to Financial Measures of Strategic Performance," *Strategic Management Journal* 4 (1983), pp. 297–306.

[11] R. Molz, "Managerial Domination of Boards of Directors and Financial Performance," *Journal of Business Research* 16 (1988), pp. 235–50.

[12] A. Tashakori and W. Boulton, "A Look at the Board's Role Planning," *Journal of Business Strategy* 3, no. 3 (1985), pp. 64–70.

[13] R. Nader, "Reforming Corporate Governance," *California Management Review,* Winter 1984, pp. 126–32.

[14] J. R. Harrison, "The Strategic Use of Corporate Board Committees," *California Management Review* 30 (1987), pp. 109–25; and J. W. Henke, Jr., "Involving the Board of Directors in Strategic Planning," *Journal of Business Strategy* 7, no. 2 (1986), pp. 87–95.

[15] K. R. Andrews, *The Concept of Corporate Strategy* (Burr Ridge, IL: Irwin, 1987).

suppliers, governments, unions, competitors, local communities, and the general public. Each of these interest groups has justifiable reasons for expecting (and often for demanding) that the firm satisfy their claims in a responsible manner. In general, stockholders claim appropriate returns on their investment; employees seek broadly defined job satisfactions; customers want what they pay for; suppliers seek dependable buyers; governments want adherence to legislation; unions seek benefits for their members; competitors want fair competition; local communities want the firm to be a responsible citizen; and the general public expects the firm's existence to improve the quality of life.

According to a recent survey of 2,361 directors in 291 of the largest southeastern U.S. companies:

1. Directors perceived the existence of distinct stakeholder groups.
2. Directors have high stakeholder orientations.
3. Directors view some stakeholders differently, depending on their occupation (CEO directors versus non-CEO directors) and type (inside versus outside directors).

The study also found that the perceived stakeholders were, in the order of their importance, customers and government, stockholders, employees, and society. The results clearly indicated that boards of directors no longer believe that the stockholder is the only constituency to whom they are responsible.

However, when a firm attempts to incorporate the interests of these groups into its mission statement, broad generalizations are insufficient. These steps need to be taken:

1. Identification of the stakeholders.
2. Understanding the stakeholders' specific claims vis-à-vis the firm.
3. Reconciliation of these claims and assignment of priorities to them.
4. Coordination of the claims with other elements of the company mission.

Identification   The left-hand column of Figure 2–3 lists the commonly encountered stakeholder groups, to which the executive officer group often is added. Obviously, though, every business faces a slightly different set of stakeholder groups, which vary in number, size, influence, and importance. In defining the company, strategic managers must identify all of the stakeholder groups and weigh their relative rights and their relative ability to affect the firm's success.

Understanding   The concerns of the principal stakeholder groups tend to center on the general claims listed in the right-hand column of Figure 2–3. However, strategic decision makers should understand the specific demands of each group. They then will be better able to initiate actions that satisfy these demands.

Reconciliation and Priorities   Unfortunately, the claims of various stakeholder groups often conflict. For example, the claims of governments and the general public tend to limit profitability, which is the central claim of most creditors and stockholders. Thus, claims must be reconciled in a mission statement that resolves the competing, conflicting, and contradicting claims of stakeholders. For objectives and strategies to be internally consistent and precisely focused, the statement must display a single-minded, though multidimensional, approach to the firm's aims.

There are hundreds, if not thousands, of claims on any firm–high wages, pure air, job security, product quality, community service, taxes, occupational health and safety regulations, equal employment opportunity regulations, product variety, wide markets, career

FIGURE 2–3
A Stakeholder View of Company Responsibility

Stakeholder	Nature of the Claim
Stockholders	Participation in distribution of profits, additional stock offerings, assets on liquidation; vote of stock; inspection of company books; transfer of stock; election of board of directors; and such additional rights as have been established in the contract with the corporation.
Creditors	Legal proportion of interest payments due and return of principal from the investment. Security of pledged assets; relative priority in event of liquidation. Management and owner prerogatives if certain conditions exist with the company (such as default of interest payments).
Employees	Economic, social, and psychological satisfaction in the place of employment. Freedom from arbitrary and capricious behavior on the part of company officials. Share in fringe benefits, freedom to join union and participate in collective bargaining, individual freedom in offering up their services through an employment contract. Adequate working conditions.
Customers	Service provided with the product; technical data to use the product; suitable warranties; spare parts to support the product during use; R&D leading to product improvement; facilitation of credit.
Suppliers	Continuing source of business; timely consummation of trade credit obligations; professional relationship in contracting for, purchasing, and receiving goods and services.
Governments	Taxes (income, property, and so on); adherence to the letter and intent of public policy dealing with the requirements of fair and free competition; discharge of legal obligations of businesspeople (and business organizations); adherence to antitrust laws.
Unions	Recognition as the negotiating agent for employees. Opportunity to perpetuate the union as a participant in the business organization.
Competitors	Observation of the norms for competitive conduct established by society and the industry. Business statesmanship on the part of peers.
Local communities	Place of productive and healthful employment in the community. Participation of company officials in community affairs, provision of regular employment, fair play, reasonable portion of purchases made in the local community, interest in and support of local government, support of cultural and charitable projects.
The general public	Participation in and contribution to society as a whole; creative communications between governmental and business units designed for reciprocal understanding; assumption of fair proportion of the burden of government and society. Fair price for products and advancement of the state-of-the-art technology that the product line involves.

Source : William R. King and David I. Cleland, *Strategic Planning and Policy.* ©1978 by Litton Educational Publishing, Inc., p. 153. Reprinted by permission of Van Nostrand Reinhold Company.

opportunities, company growth, investment security, high ROI, and many, many more. Although most, perhaps all, of these claims may be desirable ends, they cannot be pursued with equal emphasis. They must be assigned priorities in accordance with the relative emphasis that the firm will give them. That emphasis is reflected in the criteria that the firm uses in its strategic decision making; in the firm's allocation of its human, financial, and physical resources; and in the firm's long-term objectives and strategies.

Coordination with Other Elements   The demands of stakeholder groups constitute only one principal set of inputs to the company mission. The other principal sets are the managerial operating philosophy and the determinants of the product-market offering. Those determinants constitute a reality test that the accepted claims must pass. The key question is: How can the firm satisfy its claimants and at the same time optimize its economic success in the marketplace?

Social Responsibility

As indicated in Figure 2–4, the various stakeholders of a firm can be divided into inside stakeholders and outside stakeholders. The insiders are the individuals or groups that are stockholders or employees of the firm. The outsiders are all the other individuals or groups

FIGURE 2–4
Inputs to the Development of the Company Mission

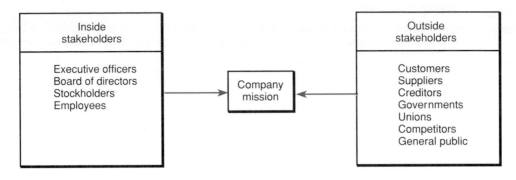

that the firm's actions affect. The extremely large and often amorphous set of outsiders makes the general claim that the firm be socially responsible.[16]

Perhaps the thorniest issues faced in defining a company mission are those that pertain to responsibility. The stakeholder approach offers the clearest perspective on such issues. Broadly stated, outsiders often demand that insiders' claims be subordinated to the greater good of the society; that is, to the greater good of outsiders. They believe that such issues as pollution, the disposal of solid and liquid wastes, and the conservation of natural resources should be principal considerations in strategic decision making. Also broadly stated, insiders tend to believe that the competing claims of outsiders should be balanced against one another in a way that protects the company mission. For example, they tend to believe that the need of consumers for a product should be balanced against the water pollution resulting from its production if the firm cannot eliminate that pollution entirely and still remain profitable. Some insiders also argue that the claims of society, as expressed in government regulation, provide tax money that can be used to eliminate water pollution and the like if the general public wants this to be done.

The issues are numerous, complex, and contingent on specific situations. Thus, rigid rules of business conduct cannot deal with them. Each firm *regardless of size* must decide how to meet its perceived social responsibility. While large, well-capitalized companies may have easy access to environmental consultants, this is not an affordable strategy for smaller companies. However, the experience of many small businesses demonstrates that it is feasible to accomplish significant pollution prevention and waste reduction without big expenditures and without hiring consultants. Once a problem area has been identified, a company's line employees frequently can develop a solution. Other important pollution prevention strategies include changing the materials used or redesigning how operations are bid out. Making pollution prevention a social responsibility can be beneficial to smaller companies. Publicly traded firms also can benefit directly from socially responsible strategies, as indicated in Global Strategy in Action 2–2.

Different approaches adopted by different firms reflect differences in competitive position, industry, country, environmental and ecological pressures, and a host of other factors. In other words, they will reflect both situational factors and differing priorities in the acknowledgment of claims. Obviously, winning the loyalty of the growing legions of

---

[16] J. S. Bracker and A. J. Kinicki, "Strategic Management, Plant Closings and Social Responsibility: An Integrative Process Model," *Employee Responsibilities and Rights Journal* 1, no. 3 (1988), pp. 201–13.

GLOBAL
STRATEGY IN
ACTION 2–2

SOCIAL INDEX LISTS RESPONSIBLE FIRMS

At one time, socially conscious investing was as simple as Just Say No—no investing in companies that produce alcohol, tobacco, or weapons, or are involved in gambling, nuclear energy, or South Africa.

But social investing has matured since arriving in the early 1970s, and it's no longer a cut-and-dried process. "In the past, it has primarily been a boycott movement with social change as a goal," says Amy Domini. "Newer criteria are more about corporate responsibility, and they're more difficult to apply."

Domini, with her husband, Peter Kinder, created the Domini Social Index of 400 socially responsible companies in May 1990. Their Cambridge, Massachusetts, firm screens more than 800 companies for product quality and consumer relations, environmental performance, corporate citizenship, and employee relations.

Companies on the Domini Social Index are not 1960s holdouts making tie-dye T-shirts or macramé plant hangers. The list includes Wal-Mart, Merck, Coca-Cola, PepsiCo, McDonald's, the Federal National Mortgage, and Sears.

The index should perform on a par with the Standard & Poor's 500 index over the long term, says Domini. But it can be more volatile short term, because it has more small companies than the S&P 500.

Source: Excerpted from Chris Wloszczyna, "Social Index Lists Responsible Firms," *USA Today,* March 30, 1992, Section 3B. Copyright 1992, USA TODAY. Reprinted with permission.

consumers will require new marketing strategies and new alliances in the year 2000. Many marketers already have discovered these new marketing facts of life by adopting strategies that can be called the "4 e's": (1) make it easy for the consumer to be green, (2) empower consumers with solutions, (3) enlist the support of the consumer, and (4) establish credibility with all publics and help to avoid a backlash.

Despite differences in their approaches, most American firms now try to assure outsiders that they attempt to conduct business in a socially responsible manner. Many firms, including Abt Associates, Dow Chemical, Eastern Gas and Fuel Associates, Exxon, and the Bank of America, conduct and publish annual social audits. The Equal Employment Opportunity element of an Exxon social audit and the philanthropy element of an audit published in General Motors Public Interest Report are shown in Strategy in Action 2–8 and Strategy in Action 2–9. Such audits attempt to evaluate a firm from the perspective of social responsibility. Private consultants often conduct them for the firm and offer minimally biased evaluations on what are inherently highly subjective issues.

Guidelines for a Socially Responsible Firm

After decades of public debate on the social responsibility of business, the individual firm must still struggle to determine its own orientation. However, public debate and business concern have led to a jelling of perspectives. Sawyer has provided an excellent summary of guidelines for a socially responsible firm that is consistent with the stakeholder approach:

1. The purpose of the business is to make a profit; its managers should strive for the optimal profit that can be achieved over the long run.

STRATEGY
IN ACTION
2–8

EQUAL EMPLOYMENT OPPORTUNITY/
CONTRIBUTION AT EXXON

STEADY PROGRESS FOR WOMEN AND MINORITIES

The percentage of women in Exxon's U.S. work force grew from 25.3 to 25.9 percent, while minority groups increased from 22.5 to 22.9 percent.

At year-end, minorities held 11.4 percent of managerial assignments, compared with 10.3 percent, while minority groups increased from 11.5 to 11.7 percent.

Women employees held 10 percent of managerial posts, compared with 8.9 percent last year, while the women's share of professional jobs rose from 18.9 to 19.5 percent.

The focus on recruitment of minorities and women was expanded through summer jobs, co-op assignments, and scholarships.

EXXON GRANTED $49 MILLION TO NONPROFIT ORGANIZATIONS, INCLUDING $35 MILLION IN THE UNITED STATES

Educational institutions and programs accounted for 59 percent of total U.S. grants. To encourage support for higher education for minority students, the Exxon Education Foundation amended its matching gift program. Employees and annuitants may now make gifts to three organizations with which the donors or their families may have had no prior affiliation. Those educational fits will be matched three-to-one by the Foundation. The three organizations are the United Negro College Fund, the American Indian College Fund, and the Hispanic Association of Colleges and Universities.

A solid grounding in mathematics is a critical asset in many careers in industry. The Exxon Education Foundation began a program in 1988 with these main goals: To foster use of college-level math teaching resources and to address major national math education policy issues.

In its elementary school program, the Foundation's initial 1988 K–3 (kindergarten through third grade) math specialist Planning Grants went to some 50 school districts across America, representing a cross-section of rural, suburban, and inner-city schools. Grantees are now seeking more effective approaches for improving math teaching and learning in these early, formative years.

Of the 24 percent of Exxon's U.S. contributions that were directed to health, welfare, and community service programs, a number addressed problems common to the nation's inner cities. A $50,000 grant was made to the Institute on Black Chemical Abuse in St. Paul, Minnesota, to help develop a national technical assistance, training, and information center.

A $200,000 grant was made to the Environmental and Occupational Health Sciences Institute, a joint program of Rutgers University and the University of Medicine and Dentistry of New Jersey. This grant will contribute to a better understanding of how the environment affects human health.

Source: Exxon 1988 annual report to stockholders.

2. No true profits can be claimed until business costs are paid. This includes all social costs, as determined by detailed analysis of the social balance between the firm and society.

3. If there are social costs in areas where no objective standards for correction yet exist, managers should generate corrective standards. These standards should be based on the managers' judgment of what ought to exist and should simultaneously encourage individual involvement of firm members in developing necessary social standards.

4. Where competitive pressure or economic necessity precludes socially responsible action, the business should recognize that its operation is depleting social capital and, therefore, represents a loss. It should attempt to restore profitable operation through either better management, if the problem is internal, or by advocating corrective legislation, if

PHILANTHROPIC ACTIVITIES

General Motors is committed to being a socially aware and responsible corporate citizen. It believes that it has an obligation to make reasonable and appropriate contributions to charitable and community organizations and educational institutions.

The Corporation has consistently ranked among the top companies in the United States in terms of dollars contributed. While GM seeks to contribute to worthy local activities in the cities and states in which GM facilities are located, it also works to benefit the nation as a whole.

An important tool in managing GM's contributions is the General Motors Foundation, established in 1976 and funded by the Corporation. As a means to offset fluctuations in charitable and educational contributions which result from economic downturns—times when nonprofit organizations most need support—the Foundation helps GM maintain a consistent response to the needs and challenges of these organizations.

In 1990, combined educational and other charitable contributions from the General Motors Corporation and the General Motors Foundation totaled over $65 million.

With a variety of philanthropic activities being supported at both the plant and corporate levels, it is not possible to list all of them.

Source: 1991 General Motors Public Interest Report, p. 55.

society is suffering as a result of the way that the rules for business competition have been made.[17]

Corporate philanthropy dates back to the 17th century when it was common for prominent business leaders to make significant donations. However, these contributions were made solely from wealthy individuals without ties to specific corporations. In the past, legal restrictions made it difficult for firms to become involved in social and philanthropic affairs. However, a Supreme Court ruling in the 1950s put an end to regulations and as a result, corporations began creating their own internal organizations. It became common for larger corporations to give up to 5 percent of their pretax income to charities as a means of improving public image.

Today, as philanthropic strategies become more and more of a key success factor, companies are assuming larger roles on social issues. Strategy in Action 2–10 outlines some of the more prominent national movements in corporate America.

SUMMARY

Defining the company mission is one of the most often slighted tasks in strategic management. Emphasizing the operational aspects of long-range management activities comes much more easily for most executives. But the critical role of the mission statement repeatedly is demonstrated by failing firms whose short-run actions have been at odds with their long-run purposes.

The principal value of the mission statement is its specification of the firm's ultimate aims. A firm gains a heightened sense of purpose when its board of directors and its top

[17] G. E. Sawyer, *Business and Society: Managing Corporate Social Impact* (Boston: Houghton Mifflin, 1979), p. 401.

STRATEGY
IN ACTION
2–10

HOW CORPORATE PHILANTHROPY PROMOTES CAUSES

Now that U.S. companies are adopting strategic philanthropy, they are assuming an activist stance on social issues. As a result, many fringe causes, including the following, have become national movements.

HUNGER

Before the new approach to corporate philanthropy, the foundations of food companies gave cash donations to antihunger organizations. But when the ranks of the hungry increased tenfold in the 1980s, contributions managers in companies such as General Mills, Grand Metropolitan, Kraft General Foods, and Sara Lee decided to play a larger role *and* establish a rallying point around which disparate units of their companies could come together. Marketers arranged for a portion of product sales to be donated to antihunger programs, human resources staffs deployed volunteers, operating units provided free food, and CEOs joined the board of Chicago-based Second Harvest, the food industry's antihunger voice. As a result of those efforts, a complex infrastructure of food banks and soup kitchens was developed.

Now the trend is toward deeper political involvement. In 1993, Kraft General Foods became the first company to use its political capital to press for more funding for food stamps and other federal initiatives.

COMMUNITY AND ECONOMIC DEVELOPMENT

In the late 1980s, major banks such as Bank of America, Chase Manhattan, Citicorp, Morgan Guaranty, and Wells Fargo explored how philanthropy could be tied to marketing, human resources, government affairs, investment, and even trust management. Those banks had given mostly to the arts, but their business managers were concerned about the Community Reinvestment Act, which requires lenders to be responsive to low-income communities. Philanthropy managers used the act to gain internal support for positioning their companies as leaders in the antipoverty struggle. They pointed out that by going beyond the CRA requirements, they could develop positive relationships with regulators while scoring public relations points.

At least 60 banks in the United States have created community development corporations to assist run-down neighborhoods. An executive at Wells Fargo organized a national network of bankers who make low-interest loans to nonprofits working to bring enterprise to inner cities. About 20 percent of those banks' donations now go to those developers.

LITERACY

The effort to increase literacy in the United States is the favorite cause of the communications industry. Print media companies such as McGraw-Hill, Prentice Hall, the *Los Angeles Times,* the

executives address these issues: "What business are we in?" "What customers do we serve?" "Why does this organization exist?" However, the potential contribution of the company mission can be undermined if platitudes or ambiguous generalizations are accepted in response to these questions. It is not enough to say that Lever Brothers is in the business of "making anything that cleans anything" or that Polaroid is committed to

continued

Washington Post, and the *New York Times* are trying to halt the drop in readership, and broadcasters and cable companies are compensating for their role in the decline of literacy. Those companies have mobilized their marketing, human resources, and lobbying power to establish workplace literacy programs. While human resources budgets fund such programs, philanthropy dollars go mostly to volunteer organizations.

SCHOOL REFORM

Under the old corporate philanthropy paradigm, elementary and secondary education received no more than 5 percent of the typical corporate philanthropy budget, and most of the institutions that received aid were private. Now about 15 percent of the country's cash gifts go to school reform, and a recent study estimated that at least one-third of U.S. school districts have partnership programs with business.

Even so, as a recent Conference Board report argues, those programs have not halted the decline of the public school system. The next step toward reform, promoted by the Business Roundtable, is for companies to mobilize their lobbying power at the state level to press for the overhaul of state educational agencies.

AIDS

AIDS is a top cause for insurance companies, who want to reduce claims; pharmaceutical companies, who want public support for the commercialization of AIDS drugs; and design-related companies, who want to support the large number of gays in their work force. Those industries put the first big money into AIDS prevention measures, and they've helped turn the American Foundation for AIDS Research into an advocate for more and better research by the National Institutes of Health.

ENVIRONMENTALISM

Until recently, corporate America feared environmentalism. But the new corporate philanthropy professionals consult their companies' environmental officers to find ways to link donations and volunteer programs to internal efforts at environmental stewardship. Environmental support varies across industries. In high-tech companies, environmentalism is largely a human resources issue because it's the favorite cause of many employees. Contribution managers in such companies typically conduct activities that elicit employee support for conservation. Among the makers of outdoor apparel, environmentalism is largely a marketing issue, so companies donate a portion of the purchase price to environmental nonprofits. In industries that pollute or extract natural resources, environmentalism is often a government affairs matter. Companies in those industries forge alliances with nonprofit adversaries in the hope of circumventing regulations.

---

businesses that deal with "the interaction of light and matter." Only if a firm clearly articulates its long-term intentions can its goals serve as a basis for shared expectations, planning, and performance evaluation.

A mission statement that is developed from this perspective provides managers with a unity of direction transcending individual, parochial, and temporary needs. It promotes a sense of shared expectations among all levels and generations of employees. It consolidates values over time and across individuals and interest groups. It projects a sense of worth and intent that can be identified and assimilated by outside stakeholders; that is, customers, suppliers, competitors, local committees, and the general public. Finally, it asserts the firm's commitment to responsible action in symbiosis with the preservation and protection of the essential claims of insider stakeholders' survival, growth, and profitability.

QUESTIONS FOR DISCUSSION

1. Reread Nicor, Inc.'s mission statement in Strategy in Action 2–1. List five insights into Nicor that you feel you gained from knowing its mission.

2. Locate the mission statement of a company not mentioned in the chapter. Where did you find it? Was it presented as a consolidated statement, or were you forced to assemble it yourself from various publications of the firm? How many of the mission statement elements outlined in this chapter were discussed or revealed in the statement you found?

3. Prepare a two-page typewritten mission statement for your school of business or for a firm selected by your instructor.

4. List five potentially vulnerable areas of a firm without a stated company mission.

5. The partial social audits shown in Strategy in Action 2–8 and 2–9 included only a few of the possible indicators of a firm's social responsibility performance. Name five other potentially valuable indicators and describe how company performance in each could be measured.

6. Define the term *social responsibility*. Find an example of a company action that was legal but not socially responsible. Defend your example on the basis of your definition.

BIBLIOGRAPHY

Board of Directors

Bartlett, Christopher A., and Sumantha Ghoshal. "Changing the Role of Top Management: Beyond Systems to People." *Harvard Business Review* 73, no. 3 (May–June 1995), p. 132.

Donaldson, Gordon. "The New Task for Boards: The Strategic Audit." *Harvard Business Review* 73, no. 4 (July–August 1995), p. 99.

Hambrick, Donald C. "Fragmentation and the Other Problems CEOs Have with Their Top Management Teams." *California Management Review* 37, no. 3 (Spring 1995), p. 110.

Harrison, J. R. "The Strategic Use of Corporate Board Committees." *California Management Review* 30 (1987), pp. 109–25.

Henke, J. W., Jr. "Involving the Board of Directors in Strategic Planning." *Journal of Business Strategy* 7, no. 2 (1986), pp. 87–95.

Hout, Thomas M., and John C. Carter. "Getting It Done: New Roles for Senior Executives." *Harvard Business Review* 73, no. 6 (November–December 1995), p. 133.

Kerr, J., and R. A. Bettis. "Boards of Directors, Top Management Compensation, and Shareholder Returns." *Academy of Management Journal* 30 (1987), pp. 645–64.

Kesner, I. F. "Directors' Characteristics and Committee Membership: An Investigation of Type, Occupation Tenure, and Gender." *Academy of Management Journal* 31 (1988), pp. 66–84.

Lorsch, Jay W. "Empowering the Board." *Harvard Business Review* 73, no. 1 (January–February 1995), p. 107.

Molz, R. "Managerial Domination of Boards of Directors and Financial Performance." *Journal of Business Research* 16 (1988), pp. 235–50.

Park, Jae C. "Reengineering Boards of Directors." *Business Horizons* 38, no. 2 (March–April 1995), p. 63.

Pearce, J. A., II. "The Relationship of Internal versus External Orientations to Financial Measures of Strategic Performance." *Strategic Management Journal* 4 (1983), pp. 297–306.

Pound, John. "The Promise of the Governed Corporation." *Harvard Business Review* 73, no. 2 (March–April 1995), p. 89

Rosenstein, J. "Why Don't U.S. Boards Get More Involved in Strategy?" *Long Range Planning* (June 1987), pp. 20–34.

Savage, G. T.; T. W. Nix; C. J. Whitehead; and J. D. Blair. "Strategies for Assessing and Managing Organizational Stakeholders." *Academy of Management Executive* (May 1991), pp. 61–75.

Smale, John G.; Alan J. Patricot; Denys Henderson; Bernard Marcus; and David N. Johnson. "Redraw the Line Between the Board and the CEO." *Harvard Business Review* 73, no. 2 (March–April 1995), p. 153.

Tichy, Noel M., and Ram Charan. "The CEO as Coach: An Interview with Allied Signal's Lawrence A. Bussidy." *Harvard Business Review* 73, no. 2 (March–April 1995), p. 68.

Zahra, S. A., and J. A. Pearce II. "Boards of Directors and Corporate Financial Performance: A Review and Integrative Model." *Journal of Management* 15 (1989), pp. 291–334.

Mission Statements

Bertodo, R. "Implementing a Strategic Vision." *Long Range Planning* (October 1990), pp. 22–30.

Campbell, A.; M. Gorld; and M. Alexander. "Corporate Strategy—The Quest for Parenting Advantage." *Harvard Business Review* 73, no. 2 (March–April 1995), p. 120.

Ireland, R. D., and M. A. Hitt. "Mission Statements; Importance, Challenge, and Recommendation for Development." *Business Horizons* (May–June 1992), pp. 34–42.

Klemm, M.; S. Sanderson; and G. Luffman. "Mission Statements: Selling Corporate Values to Employees." *Long Range Planning* (June 1991), pp. 73–78.

Osborne, R. L. "Core Value Statements: The Corporate Compass." *Business Horizons* (September–October 1991), pp. 28–34.

Pearce, J. A. II. "The Company Mission as a Strategic Tool." *Sloan Management Review* (Spring 1982), pp. 15–24.

Pearce, J. A. II, and F. R. David. "Corporate Mission Statements: The Bottom Line." *Academy of Management Executive* (May 1987), pp. 109–16.

Pearce, J. A. II; R. B. Robinson, Jr.; and Kendall Roth. "The Company Mission as a Guide to Strategic Action." In *Strategic Planning and Management Handbook,* ed. William R. King and David I. Cleland. New York: Van Nostrand Reinhold, 1987.

Rogers, J. E., Jr. "Adopting and Implementing a Corporate Environmental Charter." *Business Horizons* (March–April 1992), pp. 29–33.

Rothstein, Lawrence R. "The Empowerment Effort that Came Undone." *Harvard Business Review* 73, no. 1 (January–February 1995), p. 20.

Schmitt, Bernd H.; Alex Simonson; and Joshua Marcus. "Managing Corporate Image and Identity." *Long Range Planning* 28, no. 5 (October 1995), p. 82.

Tregoe, B. B.; J. W. Zimmerman; R. A. Smith; and P. M. Tobia. "The Driving Force." *Planning Review* (March–April 1990), pp. 4–17.

Social Responsibility and Business Ethics

Aupperle, K.; A. Carroll; and J. Hatfield. "An Empirical Examination of the Relationship between Corporate Social Responsibility and Profitability." *Academy of Management Journal* 28 (1985), pp. 446–63.

Badaracco, J. L., Jr. "Business Ethics: Four Spheres of Executive Responsibility." *California Management Review* (Spring 1992), pp. 64–79.

Bavaria, S. "Corporate Ethics Should Start in the Boardroom." *Business Horizons* (January–February 1991), pp. 9–12.

Bowie, N. "New Directions in Corporate Social Responsibility." *Business Horizons* (July–August 1991), pp. 56–65.

Cadbury, A. "Ethical Managers Make Their Own Rules." *Harvard Business Review* (September–October 1987), pp. 69–73.

Carroll, A. B. "The Pyramid of Corporate Social Responsibility: Toward the Moral Management of Organizational Stakeholders." *Business Horizons* (July–August 1991), pp. 39–48.

Dalton, D. R., and C. M. Daily. "The Constituents of Corporate Responsibility: Separate, But Not Separable, Interests?" *Business Horizons* (July–August 1991), pp. 74–78.

Day, G. S., and L. Fahey. "Putting Strategy into Shareholder Value Analysis." *Harvard Business Review* (March–April 1990), pp. 156–62.

Freeman, R. E., and J. Liedtka. "Corporate Social Responsibility: A Critical Approach." *Business Horizons* (July–August 1991), pp. 92–98.

Harrington, S. J. "What Corporate America Is Teaching about Ethics." *Academy of Management Executive* (February 1991), pp. 21–30.

Litzinger, W. D., and T. E. Schaefer. "Business Ethics Bogeyman: The Perpetual Paradox." *Business Horizons* (March–April 1987), pp. 16–21.

Waddock, Sandra A., and Mary-Ellen Boyle. "The Dynamics of Change in Corporate Community Relations." *Management Review* 37, no. 4 (Summer 1995), p. 125.

Wood, D. J. "Social Issues in Management: Theory and Research in Corporate Social Performance." *Journal of Management* (June 1991), pp. 383–406.

———. "Toward Improving Corporate Social Performance." *Business Horizons* (July–August 1991), pp. 66–73.

CHAPTER 2 COHESION CASE ILLUSTRATION

COMPANY MISSION AT THE COCA-COLA COMPANY

At the heart of Coca-Cola, especially in its first 100 years, there has been a commitment to intense marketing and to the preservation of its patented formulas and processes to make its special syrup. The intense secrecy that always has surrounded Coke's formula has long fostered an organizational obsession with secrecy pertaining to other information about Coke and its operations. While reaching almost 40,000 employees working in 135 countries and almost 80,000 stockholders by 1978, Coke's statements of mission and long-term goals or values remained very abbreviated and direct. Excerpts from 1978 company documents show its mission to be a brief description of the business and, later in the document, a reference to very general and typical goals or priorities:

> The Coca-Cola Company is the largest manufacturer and distributor of soft-drink concentrates and syrups in the world. Its product, "Coca-Cola," has been sold in the United States since 1886, is now sold in over 135 countries as well, and is the leading soft-drink product in most of these countries . . . Through the Foods Division, the Company manufactures and markets Minute Maid and Snow Crop frozen concentrated citrus juices . . . The Company manufactures and markets still and sparkling wines under the "Taylor" trademark . . . a subsidiary designs and manufactures water treatment systems . . . and a subsidiary is engaged in the manufacture and distribution of plastic film products . . . Our goal is to continue the strong financial growth trends into the future.

By the mid-1980s, Coke had diversified into movie entertainment, yet its commitment to brevity and secrecy remained, as can be seen in these excerpts from its 1986 mission statements:

> The Coca-Cola Company is the worldwide soft-drink leader, as well as one of the world's leading producers and distributors of filmed entertainment and the leading U.S. marketer of orange juice and juice products . . . Management's primary objective is to increase shareholder value. To accomplish this objective, The Coca-Cola Company and subsidiaries have developed a comprehensive business strategy that emphasizes improving volume and margins, maximizing long-term cash flow by increasing investments in areas offering attractive returns, divesting low-return assets, and maintaining appropriate financial policies. The Company operates in three markets: soft drinks, entertainment, and food, each of which is consumer oriented and offers attractive rates of returns. In each market, the Company focuses on maximizing unit volume growth, exercising effective asset management, and increasing utilization of its distribution systems . . . A principal goal for the Soft Drink Business Sector is to increase unit volume at rates in excess of the respective industry rates . . . Key goals of the Entertainment Business Sector are to leverage its motion picture and television distribution systems and to increase its library of filmed entertainment products . . . Following a strategy of product and package segmentation, the Foods Business Sector increases unit volume by adding new products into its existing distribution systems.

By the end of the 1980s, Roberto Goizueta had weathered a few storms and enjoyed several successes in Coca-Cola's last 10 years. "New Coke" had caused an unprecedented consumer revolt. The entertainment business was sold to Sony for an impressive gain. An increasing hallmark of Goizueta's leadership was greater openness about the mission and intention of Coca-Cola. In the early 1990s, Goizueta shared the following mission statement in a booklet entitled *Coca-Cola, a Business System toward 2000: Our Mission in the 1990s:*

OUR OPPORTUNITY

Bringing refreshment to a thirsty world is a unique opportunity for our Company . . . and for all of our Coca-Cola associates . . . to create shareholder value. Ours is the only production and distribution business system capable of realizing that opportunity on a global scale. And we are committed to realizing it.

OUR GOAL

With Coca-Cola as the centerpiece, ours is a worldwide system of superior brands and services through which we, our franchisees, and other business partners deliver satisfaction and value to customers and consumers. By doing so, we enhance brand equity on a global basis. As a result, we increase shareholder wealth over time.

Our goal for the 1990s sounds deceptively simple. *It is to expand our global business system, reaching increasing numbers of consumers who will enjoy our brands and products more and more often.*

OUR CHALLENGE

The 1990s promise to be a paradoxical time for our business. Distribution channels will continue to consolidate, while new ones will emerge . . . yet, *customers* will demand more choices, as well as customized service and marketing programs at the lowest possible cost. *Consumers* in developed countries will grow in age and affluence but not in numbers . . . while strong population growth in lesser developed countries means the vitality of these young consumer markets will depend on job creation and expanding economies.

To succeed in this environment we will make *effective use* of our fundamental resources:

- Brands,
- Systems,
- Capital, and, most important,
- People.

Because these resources are already available, one might assume we need only to draw on them for achieving our goal. Nothing could be more wrong. *The challenge of the 1990s will be not only to use these resources but to expand them . . . to adapt them . . . to reconfigure them in constantly changing ways in order to bring about an ever renewed relationship between the Coca-Cola system and the consumers of the world . . . to make the best even better.*

OUR RESOURCES

Brands Increasing globalization of the communications industry means we can more effectively expose our advertising and other image-building programs through a worldwide brand framework. This places a premium on maintaining our traditional excellence as a premier brand advertiser. Yet, we must remember that it is our franchisee network around the world which will distribute and locally market our brands. To appropriately leverage these brands, we must recognize that we and our franchisees are fundamentally in the business of servicing our customers and meeting the needs, real or perceived, of our consumers.

Tactical decisions regarding the marketing of our products must stay as close to the customer and consumer as possible, within a clear, but flexible, global brand strategy. This is another way of saying that we must think globally but act locally. Thus, intimate knowledge of an account, a channel, or a consumer segment will be required to design specific programs which generate satisfaction and value to that customer or consumer. The Coca-Cola Company does not sell commodities—we will not sell commodities—and we will not cheapen our relationships with customers and consumers.

Coca-Cola, in every form . . . classic, diet, caffeine free, cherry, light . . . is the most widely recognized and esteemed brand in the world. Coca-Cola was, is, and always will be . . . it! It is the centerpiece of our entire refreshment system.

Sprite and Fanta are worldwide brands. They must play a role in our brand strategy. We will continually strive to develop new brands where the opportunity presents itself.

Systems   Moving closer to the consumer both in our own organizational structure and in timely decision-making will be mandated by the global, yet diverse, marketplace of the 1990s.

Structurally, a flatter organization of our Company will be required. Functional groups must be reorganized around business units which focus on market opportunities. And as a company, we must be players, not just cheerleaders or critics.

It will be essential that our franchisees understand this new role we see for ourselves. Our increased equity participation in the Coca-Cola production and distribution network, which may include complete franchise consolidations in some areas of the world, will be carried out only whenever it becomes necessary for achieving our goal. A greater involvement in our franchise system will likely necessitate our making investments to help bring about production and distribution capabilities which meet the service demands of customers at the lowest possible cost. This is to ensure a competitive advantage for the entire system.

Entirely new distribution systems may be needed to realize new opportunities in vending and in new and emerging post-mix markets, particularly outside the United States. Joint ventures, in many forms, with our franchisees and suppliers will put our capital directly into building new avenues to reach consumers.

Success in managing these flatter, market-driven structures will depend largely on our information systems. To reach our goal, our information systems—the processes, reports, procedures, and communication linkages that hold the organization together—must lead, rather than trail, developments in the marketplace. Effective and timely information is vital to effective and timely allocation of resources.

Ours is a multilocal business. Its relative state of development varies dramatically from the soft drink frontiers of Asia to the sophisticated markets of North America. Throughout our 103-year history there has been an evolutionary process or cycle of development continuously at work. That cycle, which often evolved over decades in the past, will quicken in astonishing dimensions in the future. By the year 2000, our business system in developing countries must function at levels nearly equal to those seen in today's sophisticated markets. Where lack of hard currency or difficult political realities are constraints to reaching consumers, we must build new strategic alliances and enhance our trading capabilities to overcome constraints.

Capital   Shaping business systems which are close to consumers will require not only the investment of our capital for new assets but more sophisticated management of existing ones. Existing assets will be evaluated as potential resources for meeting our goal. Those assets include not only physical assets but also equity ownership positions, financial capacity, and information systems, as well as creative management of key business relationships.

Capital management is no longer just the process of earning a rate of return above our cost of capital. It is the innovative endeavor of finding more productive uses and new purposes for assets, of trading or leveraging existing assets to meet our goal and to create new strategic alliances.

Our organization has a rich history of effectively allocating resources and of utilizing our financial strength to build value. That will continue. And given our growing experience at managing greater financial leverage, we will periodically evaluate higher leverage ceilings, primarily for investments in our business system or in strategic alliances and, secondarily, in our own shares.

People   Through the years, The Coca-Cola Company has always had an international cadre of individuals. To capture the global soft-drink opportunity in the 1990s, we need more than the right brands, systems, and infrastructure. We need the right people for the 21st century.

We must have people who use facts and knowledge to add something . . . to add value to our customers' businesses. In an age where everyone has basically the same information at the same time, the advantage goes to people who can take information and quickly put it to effective and profitable use. It means having people with what can be called the "mind of the strategist" . . . people who can create a competitive advantage . . . out of common knowledge.

Few are born with such skill. This skill can be developed, however, and should be rewarded. We must recruit and nurture the growth of associates to match the needs of the business. In the 1990s, "internationalists" with multilingual, multicultural capabilities will be the norm. And we must continue to refine our compensation systems to reflect our operating culture and reward value-adding performance.

The responsibility for developing people cannot be delegated to training courses, academic exercises, or professionals in the area of human resources. Those have a role to play but do not constitute an adequate process. *The development of our best people is the personal responsibility of Management.* It requires each manager to see his or her most important responsibility as teaching and developing people. Our charge is that simple—recruiting and training the best talent by the best managers. As that talent grows and develops, they become the next managers capable of and responsible for developing new talent, thus perpetuating a strength.

This process is the link to maintaining the sense of dissatisfaction that has resulted in much of the success we enjoy today. We must continue to cultivate intelligent risk taking and flexible decision making, realizing that, while not every risk taken or decision made brings success, the alternative is complacency and stagnation . . . a stance totally unacceptable to our Company.

OUR REWARDS

The rewards of meeting these challenges and flourishing in a state of rapid change are enormous:

- Satisfied consumers who return again and again to our brands for refreshment.
- Profitable customers who rely on our worldwide brands and services.
- Communities around the world where we are an economic contributor and welcomed guest.
- Successful business partners.
- Shareholders who are building value through the power of the Coca-Cola system.

OUR SHARED VISION

The Coca-Cola system is indeed a special business. One hundred and three years of dedicated effort by literally millions of individuals have combined to create in Coca-Cola a remarkable trademark presence and economic value unchallenged since the dawn of commercial history.

However, any edge we have is fragile. Our journey to the year 2000 requires that our brands, systems, capital, and people grow and change to meet our goal and thus realize our opportunity. To borrow a recent popular phrase, we see 6 billion points of light in a thirsty world—6 billion consumers in the world of the year 2000—all being refreshed as never before by the Coca-Cola system.

That is a wonderful goal we all can share and strive for as we move together—toward 2000.

The evolution of Coca-Cola's use of mission statements from the 1970s to the 1990s displays a consistent commitment to specific, direct statements defining the business of Coca-Cola, while evidencing a move from brevity and secrecy toward greater clarification of values, priorities, and the "Coca-Cola system." Goizueta's elaborate statement of Coke's mission for the 1990s is rather lengthy by comparison to several mission statements excerpted in Chapter 2. But while sensitive to the virtues of brevity, Mr. Goizueta felt a detailed, complete elaboration upon Coke's mission and related components was essential to focusing a diverse, worldwide group of employees and "partners" on the key ingredients for global success in the next century. He felt that providing order and clarity to a detailed "vision" of what the Coca-Cola system is and what it intends to become would provide a framework for future decisions and actions throughout the Coke system to enhance its opportunity for success.

3 THE EXTERNAL ENVIRONMENT

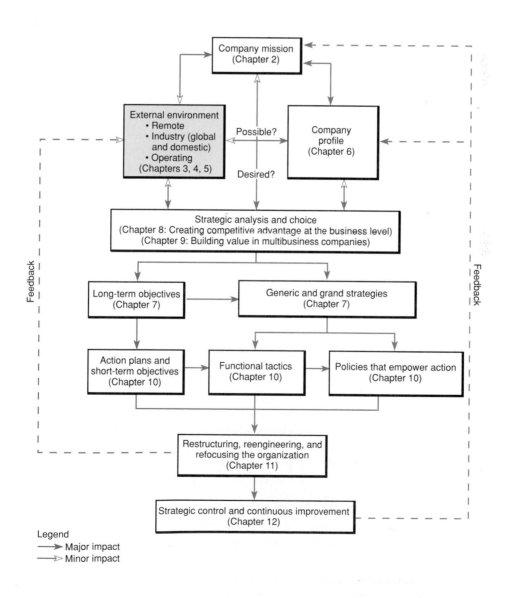

Legend
→ Major impact
⇢ Minor impact

A host of external factors influence a firm's choice of direction and action and, ultimately, its organizational structure and internal processes. These factors, which constitute the *external environment,* can be divided into three interrelated subcategories: factors in the *remote* environment, factors in the *industry* environment, and factors in the *operating* environment.[1] This chapter describes the complex necessities involved in formulating strategies that optimize a firm's market opportunities. Figure 3–1 suggests the interrelationship between the firm and its remote, its industry, and its operating environments. In combination, these factors form the basis of the opportunities and threats that a firm faces in its competitive environment.

REMOTE ENVIRONMENT

The remote environment comprises factors that originate beyond, and usually irrespective of, any single firm's operating situation: (1) economic, (2) social, (3) political, (4) technological, and (5) ecological factors. That environment presents firms with opportunities, threats, and constraints, but rarely does a single firm exert any meaningful reciprocal influence. For example, when the economy slows and construction starts to decrease, an individual contractor is likely to suffer a decline in business, but that contractor's success in stimulating local construction activities would be unable to reverse the overall decrease in construction starts. The trade agreements that resulted from improved relations between the United States and China and the United States and Russia are examples of the effects of political factors on individual firms. The agreements provided individual U.S. manufacturers with opportunities to broaden their international operations.

1. Economic Factors

Economic factors concern the nature and direction of the economy in which a firm operates. Because consumption patterns are affected by the relative affluence of various market segments, in its strategic planning each firm must consider economic trends in the segments that affect its industry. On both the national and international level, it must consider the general availability of credit, the level of disposable income, and the propensity of people to spend. Prime interest rates, inflation rates, and trends in the growth of the gross national product are other economic factors it must consider.

Until recently, the potential impact of international economic forces appeared to be severely restricted and was largely discounted. However, the emergence of new international power brokers has changed the focus of economic environmental forecasting. Among the most prominent of these power brokers are the European Economic Community (EEC, or Common Market), the Organization of Petroleum Exporting Countries (OPEC), and coalitions of developing countries.

The EEC, whose members include most of the West European countries, was established by the Treaty of Rome in 1957. It has eliminated quotas and established a tariff-free trade area for industrial products among its members. By fostering intra-European economic cooperation, it has helped its member countries compete more effectively in non-European international markets.

Vying with the opening of Eastern European borders to commerce as the most significant marketplace occurrence of the 1990s has been the opening of protected markets by the European Community. Commonly referred to as *EC 92,* the stated goal of this cooperative

---

[1] Many authors refer to the operating environment as the *task* or *competitive* environment.

FIGURE 3–1
The Firm's External Environment

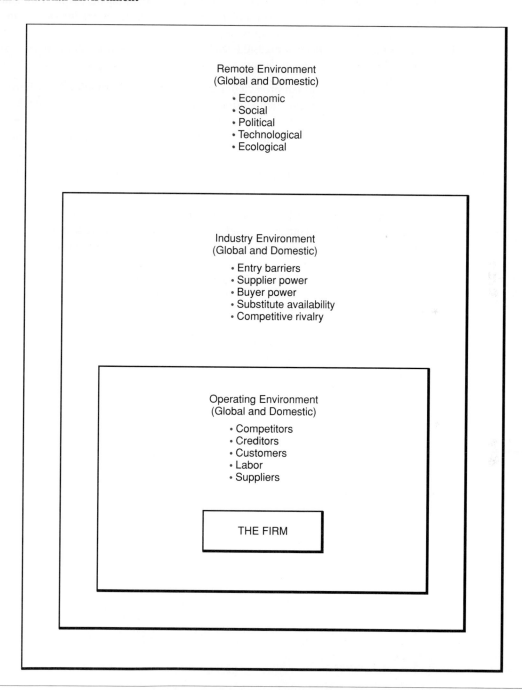

effort is the elimination of all technical, physical, and fiscal barriers to the conduct of international trade in Europe by 1992. While pragmatists see the EC 92 as a concept and not a deadline, significant progress is being made each year toward the attainment of aims of the collaboration. As of early 1990, 125 of the 265 directives related to 1992 had become EC law.

Much of the excitement over EC 92 stems from the size of the market in Europe, which exceeds 320 million consumers. As Europeans' incomes rise and their tastes become less geocentric, a booming market is expected for consumer goods, from appliances to soft drinks. As evidence of their enthusiasm for the EC 92 marketplace, U.S. companies spent $20.9 billion in 1987 alone to build plants and buy companies in Europe, an amount 28 times greater than their expenditures in 1982.

Among the U.S. firms that invested heavily and early in Europe in the hope of profiting from the EC 92 developments were:

American Express, which projected a 20 percent annual growth rate in Europe in the 1990s owing to weak competition from "mom-and-pop" travel agencies.

AT&T, which completed a five-year, $27 billion deal with Italy's state-owned telephone equipment maker to overhaul the country's aging telephone system.

Federal Express, which was among the early organizers of warehousing and distribution services for European companies. Its $200 million-a-year business in Europe is forecasted to grow 80 percent annually during this decade.

Following the original EEC initiative of economic cooperation, the United States, Canada, Japan, the EEC, and other countries conducted multilateral trade negotiations in 1979 to establish rules for international trade and conduct. Those negotiations had a profound effect on almost every aspect of U.S. business activity.

In terms of impact on the United States, OPEC is at present among the most powerful international economic forces. This cartel includes most of the world's major oil and gas suppliers. Its drastic price increases impeded U.S. recovery from the recession of the early 1970s and fueled inflationary fires throughout the world. Those price increases in particular affected the U.S. automobile industry by raising the fuel costs of automobile users and by giving rise to legislation on engine design and performance standards.

Historically underdeveloped countries recently have assumed a greater role in international commerce as a source of both threats and opportunities. Following OPEC's success, these countries found it economically beneficial to directly confront the established powers. Since 1974, producers of primary commodities in the developing countries have formed or greatly strengthened trade organizations to enforce higher prices and achieve larger real incomes for their members. Even developing countries not desiring or unable to form cartels now exhibit an aggressive attitude in their international economic relations. On the other hand, developing countries offer U.S. firms huge new markets for foodstuffs and capital equipment.

The intense nationalism of the developing countries, with nearly three fourths of the world's population, represents perhaps the greatest challenge our industrialized society and multinational corporations will face. As one Third World expert puts it, "the vastly unequal relationship between the rich and poor nations is fast becoming the central issue of our time."[2]

All of these international forces can affect—for better or worse—the economic well being of the U.S. business community. Consequently, firms must try to forecast the repercussions of major actions taken in both the domestic and international economic arenas.

2. Social Factors

The social factors that affect a firm involve the beliefs, values, attitudes, opinions, and lifestyles of persons in the firm's external environment, as developed from cultural, ecological, demographic, religious, educational, and ethnic conditioning. As social attitudes

---

[2] R. Steade, "Multinational Corporations and the Changing World Economic Order," *California Management Review,* Winter 1978, p. 5.

change, so too does the demand for various types of clothing, books, leisure activities, and so on. Like other forces in the remote external environment, social forces are dynamic, with constant change resulting from the efforts of individuals to satisfy their desires and needs by controlling and adapting to environmental factors. Teresa Iglesias-Soloman hoped to benefit from social changes with *Ninos,* a children's catalog written in both English and Spanish. The catalog featured books, videos, and Spanish cultural offerings for English-speaking children who wanted to learn Spanish and for Spanish-speaking children who wanted to learn English. *Ninos'* target market included middle-to-upper income Hispanic parents and a greater number of consumers, educators, bilingual schools, libraries, and purchasing agents. Iglesias-Solomon had reason to be optimistic about the future of *Ninos,* because the Hispanic population was growing five times faster than the general U.S. population.

One of the most profound social changes in recent years has been the entry of large numbers of women into the labor market. This has not only affected the hiring and compensation policies and the resource capabilities of their employers; it also has created or greatly expanded the demand for a wide range of products and services necessitated by their absence from the home. Firms that anticipated or reacted quickly to this social change offered such products and services as convenience foods, microwave ovens, and day-care centers.

A second profound social change has been the accelerating interest of consumers and employees in quality-of-life issues. Evidence of this change is seen in recent contract negotiations. In addition to the traditional demand for increased salaries have been worker demands for such benefits as sabbaticals, flexible hours or four-day workweeks, lump-sum vacation plans, and opportunities for advanced training.

A third profound social change has been the shift in the age distribution of the population. Changing social values and a growing acceptance of improved birth control methods are expected to raise the mean age of the U.S. population, which was 27.9 in 1970, to 34.9 by the year 2000. This trend will have an increasingly unfavorable impact on most producers of predominantly youth-oriented goods and will necessitate a shift in their long-range marketing strategies. Producers of hair- and skin-care preparations already have begun to adjust their research and development to reflect anticipated changes in demand.

A consequence of the changing age distribution of the population has been a sharp increase in the demands made by a growing number of senior citizens. Constrained by fixed incomes, these citizens have demanded that arbitrary and rigid policies on retirement age be modified and have successfully lobbied for tax exemptions and increases in Social Security benefits. Such changes have significantly altered the opportunity-risk equations of many firms—often to the benefit of firms that anticipated the changes.

Translating social change into forecasts of business effects is a difficult process, at best. Nevertheless, informed estimates of the impact of such alterations as geographic shifts in populations and changing work values, ethical standards, and religious orientation can only help a strategizing firm in its attempts to prosper.

3. Political Factors

The direction and stability of political factors is a major consideration for managers on formulating company strategy. Political factors define the legal and regulatory parameters within which firms must operate. Political constraints are placed on firms through fair-trade decisions, antitrust laws, tax programs, minimum wage legislation, pollution and pricing policies, administrative jawboning, and many other actions aimed at protecting employees, consumers, the general public, and the environment. Since such laws and regulations are most commonly restrictive, they tend to reduce the potential profits of firms. However, some political actions are designed to benefit and protect firms. Such actions include patent laws, government subsidies, and product research grants. Thus, political factors either may limit or benefit the firms they influence. For example, when Ethiopian Airlines organized in 1945, it received assistance from TWA and various Ethiopian governments. This support made Ethiopian Airlines one of the most successful members of the African air transport industry. The airline pioneered the hub concept in Africa and arranged its schedules to provide easy connections between many of the continent's countries, as well as between Africa and points in Europe and the Middle East and Asia. Without the political support of the Ethiopian governments, it would have been impossible for the airline to operate.[3]

Political activity also has a significant impact on two governmental functions that influence the remote environment of firms:

Supplier Function

Government decisions regarding the accessibility of private businesses to government-owned natural resources and national stockpiles of agricultural products will affect profoundly the viability of the strategies of some firms.

Customer Function

Government demand for products and services can create, sustain, enhance, or eliminate many market opportunities. For example, in the same way that the Kennedy administration's emphasis on landing a man on the moon spawned a demand for thousands of new products, the Carter administration's emphasis on developing synthetic fuels created a demand for new skills, technologies, and products; and the Reagan administration's strategic defense initiative (the "Star Wars" defense) sharply accelerated the development of laser technologies.

Entrepreneurial firms often feel such influences especially strongly. For example, in the six months following the August invasion of Kuwait, D. M. Offray & Son, a Chester, New Jersey, bow and ribbon manufacturer, sold about 28,409 miles of yellow ribbon in support of the armed forces. In order to keep up with the demand, the plant manager had to go to a triple-shift, six-day work week.[4]

4. Technological Factors

The fourth set of factors in the remote environment involves technological change. To avoid obsolescence and promote innovation, a firm must be aware of technological changes that might influence its industry. Creative technological adaptations can suggest possibilities for new products, for improvements in existing products, or in manufacturing and marketing techniques.

A technological breakthrough can have a sudden and dramatic effect on a firm's environment. It may spawn sophisticated new markets and products or significantly shorten the anticipated life of a manufacturing facility. Thus, all firms, and most particularly those in turbulent growth industries, must strive for an understanding both of the existing technological advances and the probable future advances that can affect their products and services. This quasi-science of attempting to foresee advancements and estimate their impact on an organization's operations is known as technological forecasting.

---

[3] *Air Transport World*, February 1992, pp. 110–12.

[4] *Fortune*, March 11, 1991, p. 14.

Technological forecasting can help protect and improve the profitability of firms in growing industries. It alerts strategic managers to both impending challenges and promising opportunities. As examples: (1) advances in xerography were a key to Xerox's success but caused major difficulties for carbon paper manufacturers, and (2) the perfection of transistors changed the nature of competition in the radio and television industry, helping such giants as RCA while seriously weakening smaller firms whose resource commitments required that they continue to base their products on vacuum tubes.

The key to beneficial forecasting of technological advancement lies in accurately predicting future technological capabilities and their probable impacts. A comprehensive analysis of the effect of technological change involves study of the expected impact of new technologies on the remote environment, on the competitive business situation, and on the business-society interface. In recent years, forecasting in the last area has warranted particular attention. For example, as a consequence of increased concern over the environment, firms must carefully investigate the probable effect of technological advances on quality-of-life factors, such as ecology and public safety.

5. Ecological Factors

As strategic managers forecast past the year 2000, the most prominent factor in the remote environment is often the reciprocal relationship between business and the ecology. The term ecology refers to the relationships among human beings and other living things and the air, soil, and water that support them. Threats to our life-supporting ecology caused principally by human activities in an industrial society are commonly referred to as *pollution*. Specific concerns include global warming, loss of habitat and biodiversity, as well as air, water, and land pollution.

The global climate has been changing for ages; however, it is now evident that humanity's activities are accelerating this tremendously. A change in atmospheric radiation, due in part to ozone depletion, causes global warming. Solar radiation that is normally absorbed into the atmosphere reaches the earth's surface, heating the soil, water, and air.

Another area of great importance is the loss of habitat and biodiversity. Ecologists agree that the extinction of important flora and fauna is occurring at a rapid rate, and if this pace is continued, could constitute a global extinction on the scale of those found in fossil records. The earth's life forms are dependent on a well-functioning ecosystem. In addition, immeasurable advances in disease treatment can be attributed to research involving substances found in plants. As species become extinct, the life-support system is irreparably harmed. The primary cause of extinction on this scale is a disturbance of natural habitat. For example, current data suggest that the earth's primary tropical forests, a prime source of oxygen and potential plant "cure," could be destroyed in only five decades.

Air pollution is created by dust particles and gaseous discharges that contaminate the air. Acid rain, or rain contaminated by sulfur dioxide, which can destroy aquatic and plant life, is believed to result from coal-burning factories in 70 percent of all cases. A health-threatening "thermal blanket" is created when the atmosphere traps carbon dioxide emitted from smokestacks in factories burning fossil fuels. This "greenhouse effect" can have disastrous consequences, making the climate unpredictable and raising temperatures. An interesting example of a way in which the free market system can help to reduce air pollution problems is discussed in Strategy in Action 3–1.

Water pollution occurs principally when industrial toxic wastes are dumped or leak into the nation's waterways. Since fewer than 50 percent of all municipal sewer systems are in compliance with Environmental Protection Agency requirements for water safety, contaminated waters represent a substantial present threat to public welfare.

STRATEGY
IN ACTION
3–1

COLD CASH FOR OLD CLUNKERS

Waddya bid me for this 1971 Ford? Forget the Blue Book. The value of this beauty depends on how much choking black smoke blasts out of its rusted tailpipe—and the more the better. Thanks to the Bush Administration, there is a thriving free market in dirty old cars: companies that pollute the air buy them, junk them, and earn a "pollution credit" for saving however much smog- and ozone-forming exhaust the cars would have belched out before they died. The company—anything from a utility to a paint factory—subtracts the amount of the credit from the quantity of air pollution they're required to cut under the 1990 Clean Air Act. The idea of this and other market-based approaches to environmental cleanup is to get the most clean for the least green. "Lots of little smokestacks on the highway are equivalent to one big smokestack," says energy-policy analyst Will Schroeer of the U.S. Environmental Protection Agency. "But it will be cheaper to scrap cars than to put emission controls on smokestacks."

Adam Smith would love it. Say a factory must reduce its nitrogen oxide (NO_x) emissions by 130,000 pounds a year. And say it will cost $1 million to do that by installing scrubbers on its smokestacks. If the factory buys 1,000 old cars for an average $700 each, and if each car spews out 130 pounds of NO_x a year, the company will have met its clean-air mandate and saved $300,000 in the bargain. People who sold their old clunkers could buy a cleaner, later-model car. That's how it worked in 1990 in California, when Unocal bought 8,376 pre-1971 cars for $700 apiece. The junked cars accounted for nearly 13 million pounds of emissions per year—as much as the hydrocarbons from 250,000 new cars, one large oil refinery, or all the barbecue lighter fluid used in the Los Angeles basin.

Such "green economics" has become as trendy as recycling newspaper. In 1993, southern California allowed factories to meet clean-air standards by buying pollution credits from companies that had exceeded their mandated emissions cuts. Still, although using market forces to clean up the planet has found support in Congress, the administration, and even among environmental groups, cash-for-clunkers has its detractors. Dan Becker of the Sierra Club calls it "the Cheshire Cat approach. Pollution from the car will continue after the [car] has disappeared"—because the car's "quota" is now coming from the smokestack of the buyer, who can avoid cleaning up his own act. But there is no debate that old cars make a tempting target. The 37.6 million cars that predate 1980 are responsible for 86 percent of the smog-making gases from autos but represent only 38 percent of the fleet; the 5.9 million dirtiest cars cause a whopping 50 percent of all hydrocarbons. Next up for the green marketers: giving companies pollution credits if they switch to alternative-fuel fleets. Capitalism may turn out to be an environmentalist's friend after all.

Land pollution is caused by the need to dispose of ever-increasing amounts of waste. Routine, everyday packaging is a major contributor to this problem, as described in Global Strategy in Action 3–1. Land pollution is more dauntingly caused by the disposal of industrial toxic wastes in underground sites. With approximately 90 percent of the annual U.S. output of 500 million metric tons of hazardous industrial wastes being placed in underground dumps, it is evident that land pollution and its resulting endangerment of the ecology have become a major item on the political agenda.

As a major contributor to ecological pollution, business now is being held responsible for eliminating the toxic by-products of its current manufacturing processes and for cleaning up the environmental damage that it did previously. Increasingly, managers are being

PACKAGING FOR THE ENVIRONMENT

Packaging is the ultimate symbol of the 20th century's consumer culture. It protects what we buy and raises our standard of living. In developing countries, 30 percent to 50 percent of food shipments are spoiled because of inadequate packaging and distribution systems. In developed countries with more sophisticated packaging, storage, and distribution, only 2 percent to 3 percent is wasted.

Packaging not only protects goods but also conveys information about their contents and preparation or administration, and—in some cases—foils would-be tamperers. It plays a vital and growing role in the global economy.

At the same time, packaging is on the environmental frontline. It is the largest and fastest growing contributor to one of the most troubling environmental problems: garbage.

In the United States, packaging accounted for more than 30 percent of the municipal solid waste stream in 1990. Where is all this packaging going? In this country, most packaging and other waste is buried in landfills. But even with its abundance of open land, America is running out of room for its garbage.

One quarter of the country's municipalities are expected to exhaust their landfill capacity before 1995, and more than half the population lives in regions with less than 10 years of landfill capacity.

Meanwhile, the environmentally sound alternatives to burying garbage—recycling, reuse, and energy recovery—are only just beginning. For the throwaway society, the 1990s are the decade of reckoning.

While packaging is not the only culprit in the solid waste crisis, it is a highly visible component, and one that directly involves consumers. And its short lifetime exacerbates the problem. Although the useful lives of some packages—such as paint cans and reusable canisters—may be as long as several years, the useful lives of others—such as fast-food hamburger wrappers—can be as fleeting as a few minutes.

Fortunately, because of the sheer volume of packaging in the solid waste stream, even relatively small improvements in packaging can make a real difference in the magnitude of the garbage crisis. Packaging, thus, offers a unique opportunity for companies to assume a leadership role in environmental responsibility.

In terms of packaging choices, industry's response to the environmental challenge has so far focused on recycling and source reduction. But the complexity of the issues involved demands a more systemic, integrated approach based on comprehensive analysis and long-term vision as well as innovative solutions.

Among the analytical tools now being deployed is life-cycle analysis. This is a fairly new technique for exploring the environmental implications of a given product decision—in this case, a packaging choice from raw material acquisition through manufacturing, energy consumption, design, and transportation to final use and disposal of the package. Life-cycle thinking is an important step toward understanding the full environmental implications of packaging choices.

required by the government or are being expected by the public to incorporate ecological concerns into their decision making. For example, between 1975 and 1992, 3M cut its pollution in half by reformulating products, modifying processes, redesigning production equipment, and recycling by-products. Similarly, steel companies and public utilities have invested billions of dollars in costlier but cleaner-burning fuels and pollution control equipment. The automobile industry has been required to install expensive emission controls in

FIGURE 3–2
Environmental Costs and Competitiveness

Several recent efforts to quantify environmental spending have suggested that enormous costs are being incurred. A 1990 study by the U.S. EPA concluded that environmental spending was approaching 2 percent of GNP. Manufacturers then used this information to support their claim that regulation was harming industrial growth and putting the nation at a competitive disadvantage vis-á-vis foreign suppliers. The claims, however, simply did not hold up to closer inspection. First, only a small share of pollution abatement and control spending was incurred by industrial facilities. By one estimate (one used as a source for the EPA study), manufacturers incurred a total of $31.1 billion in environmental costs in 1990. This amounted to only 1.1 percent of product shipments. The costs identified by the EPA resulted from such areas as the requirement for catalytic converters on all automobiles ($14 billion in 1990), the construction and operation of public sewer systems ($20 billion), and the disposal of household wastes ($10 billion).

Even if environmental spending made up only 1 percent of costs, it would not be unreasonable for manufacturers to claim that these costs had a significant influence on competitiveness if international competitors were not required to meet similar requirements. Comparisons of international spending suggest, however, that manufacturers in important production areas around the world are experiencing costs similar to those faced by U.S. producers. Pollution control's share of capital expenditures in Germany was 12 percent in 1990, matching the costs incurred by American manufacturers. Similarly, recent environmental spending by U.S. pulp and paper manufacturers is closely matched by key competitors in Canada and Sweden.

These comparisons suggest that although pollution abatement expenditures are clearly a material part of total costs, the impact of these costs on competitiveness is mild. In fact, no clear link can be made between environmental regulation and measurably adverse effects on net exports, overall trade flows, or plant location decisions. It appear that little advantage has been gained by foreign firms based on the environmental requirements in the areas of their production.

Source: Excerpted from Benjamin C. Bonifant, Matthew R. Arnold, and Frederick J. Long, "Gaining Competitive Advantage through Environmental Investments," p. 39. Reprinted from *Business Horizons,* July–August 1995. Copyright 1995 by the Foundation for the School of Business at Indiana University. Used with permission.

cars. The gasoline industry has been forced to formulate new low-lead and no-lead products. And thousands of companies have found it necessary to direct their R&D resources into the search for ecologically superior products, such as Sears's phosphate-free laundry detergent and Pepsi-Cola's biodegradable plastic soft-drink bottle.

Environmental legislation impacts corporate strategies worldwide. Many companies fear the consequences of highly restrictive and costly environmental regulations. However, some manufacturers view these new controls as an opportunity, capturing markets with products that help customers satisfy their own regulatory standards. Other manufacturers contend that the costs of environmental spending inhibit the growth and productivity of their operations. Figure 3–2 takes a deeper look into the costs of environmental regulations.

The increasing attention by companies to protect the environment is evidenced in the attempts by firms to establish proecology policies. One such approach to environmental activism is described in Global Strategy in Action 3–2.

Despite cleanup efforts to date, the job of protecting the ecology will continue to be a top strategic priority—usually because corporate stockholders and executives choose it, increasingly because the public and the government require it. As evidenced by Figure 3–3, the government has made numerous interventions into the conduct of business for the purpose of bettering the ecology.

Benefits of Eco-Efficiency

Many of the world's largest corporations are realizing that business activities must no longer ignore environmental concerns. Every activity is linked to thousands of other transactions and their environmental impact; therefore, corporate environmental responsibility must be taken seriously and environmental policy must be implemented to ensure a

GLOBAL
STRATEGY IN
ACTION 3–2

TAKING A STEP IN THE RIGHT DIRECTION

"The ongoing occurrence of environmental incidents has become unacceptable in the public's mind," says George Pilko, president of Houston-based Pilko & Associates, an environmental consulting firm. That's why companies today are taking a proactive stance when it comes to managing environmental issues. The public just won't tolerate any more Love Canals, Bhopals, or major oil spills. "You've got strong public sentiment, increasingly stringent environmental regulations at the local, state, and federal level, stricter enforcement of existing regulations, and an exponential rise in environmentally oriented lawsuits. It clearly doesn't make sense for companies to continue to operate as they had been up until the late 1980s where they focused in on just remaining in compliance with existing regulations," Pilko adds.

Instead, according to Pilko, companies need to make sure they've got an environmental policy that clearly explains their commitment to being proactive and is communicated clearly to all employees. Companies also should be aware of the effectiveness of their current programs and where they stand relative to their competitors, because "there is a tremendous discrepancy between executives' perception of how they are doing and what is reality." In fact, a recent Pilko & Associates survey of 200 senior executives representing large industrial firms found that 40 percent of the respondents believed their company was doing an excellent job of managing their environmental problems, while only 8 percent thought their competitors were doing an excellent job.

Regardless of perception, however, management of environmental issues must be supported from the top. "Corporate environmental policy is most effectively communicated by the president or CEO," Pilko says. For those CEOs or senior executives interested in getting out the message that they are serious about dealing with the environment, Pilko advises them to ask themselves the following 10 questions:

1. Do you have a clearly articulated environmental policy that has been communicated throughout the company?
2. Have you had an objective, third-party assessment of the effectiveness of your environmental programs?
3. Have you analyzed how your company's environmental performance compares with that of the leading firms in your industry?
4. Does your company view environmental performance not just as a staff function but as the responsibility of all employees?
5. Have you analyzed the potential impact of environmental issues on the future demand for your products and the competitive economics in your industry?
6. Are environmental issues and activities discussed frequently at your board meetings?
7. Do you have a formal system for monitoring proposed regulatory changes and for handling compliance with changing regulations?
8. Do you routinely conduct environmental due-diligence studies on potential acquisitions?
9. Have you successfully budgeted for environmental expenditures, without incurring surprise expenses that materially affected your profitability?
10. Have you identified and quantified environmental liabilities from past operations, and do you have a plan for minimizing those liabilities?

FIGURE 3–3
Federal Ecological Legislation

Centerpiece Legislation

National Environmental Policy Act, 1969   Established Environmental Protection Agency; consolidated federal environmental activities under it. Established Council on Environmental Quality to advise president on environmental policy and to review environmental impact statements.

Air Pollution

Clean Air Act, 1963   Authorized assistance to state and local governments in formulating control programs. Authorized limited federal action in correcting specific pollution problems.
Clean Air Act, Amendments (Motor Vehicle Air Pollution Control Act), 1965   Authorized federal standards for auto exhaust emission. Standards first set for 1968 models.
Air Quality Act, 1967   Authorized federal government to establish air quality control regions and to set maximum permissible pollution levels. Required states and localities to carry out approved control programs or else give way to federal controls.
Clean Air Act Amendments, 1970   Authorized EPA to establish nationwide air pollution standards and to limit the discharge of six principal pollutants into the lower atmosphere. Authorized citizens to take legal action to require EPA to implement its standards against undiscovered offenders.
Clean Air Act Amendments, 1977   Postponed auto emission requirements. Required use of scrubbers in new coal-fired power plants. Directed EPA to establish a system to prevent deterioration of air quality in clean areas.

Solid Waste Pollution

Solid Waste Disposal Act, 1965   Authorized research and assistance to state and local control programs.
Resource Recovery Act, 1970   Subsidized construction of pilot recycling plants; authorized development of nationwide control programs.
Resource Conservation and Recovery Act, 1976   Directed EPA to regulate hazardous waste management, from generation through disposal.
Surface Mining and Reclamation Act, 1976   Controlled strip mining and restoration of reclaimed land.

Water Pollution

Refuse Act, 1899   Prohibited dumping of debris into navigable waters without a permit. Extended by court decision to industrial discharges.

comprehensive organizational strategy. Because of increases in government regulations and consumer environmental concerns, the implementation of environmental policy has become a point of competitive advantage. Therefore, the rational goal of business should be to limit its impact on the environment, thus ensuring long-run benefits to both the firm and society. To neglect this responsibility is to ensure the demise of both the firm and our ecosystem.

Stephen Schmidheiny, chairman of the Business Council for Sustainable Development, has coined the term *eco-efficiency* to describe corporations that produce more-useful goods and services while continuously reducing resource consumption and pollution. He cites a number of reasons for corporations to implement environmental policy: customers demand cleaner products, environmental regulations are increasingly more stringent, employees prefer to work for environmentally conscious firms, and financing is more readily available for eco-efficient firms. In addition, the government provides incentives for environmentally responsible companies.

Setting priorities, developing corporate standards, controlling property acquisition and use to preserve habitats, implementing energy-conserving activities, and redesigning products (e.g., minimizing packaging) are a number of measures the firm can implement to enhance an eco-efficient strategy. One of the most important steps a firm can take in achieving a competitive position with regard to the eco-efficient strategy is to fully capitalize on technological developments as a method of gaining efficiency.

**FIGURE 3–3
(concluded)**

Federal Water Pollution Control Act, 1956 Authorized grants to states for water pollution control. Gave federal government limited authority to correct specific pollution problems.
Water Quality Act, 1965 Provided for adoption of water quality standards by states, subject to federal approval.
Water Quality Improvement Act, 1970 Provided for federal cleanup of oil spills. Strengthened federal authority over water pollution control.
Federal Water Pollution Control Act Amendments, 1972 Authorized EPA to set water quality and effluent standards; provided for enforcement and research.
Safe Drinking Water Act, 1974 Set standards for drinking water quality.
Clean Water Act, 1977 Ordered control of toxic pollutants by 1984 with best available technology economically feasible.

Other Points

Federal Insecticide, Fungicide and Rodenticide Act, 1947 To protect farmers, prohibited fraudulent claims by salespersons. Required registration of poisonous products.
Federal Insecticide, Fungicide, and Rodenticide Amendments, 1967, 1972 Provided new authority to license users of pesticides.
Pesticide Control Act, 1972 Required all pesticides shipped in interstate commerce to be certified as effective for their stated purposes and harmless to crops, animal feed, animal life, and humans.
Noise Control Act, 1972 Required EPA to set noise standards for major sources of noise and to advise Federal Aviation Administration on standards for airplane noise.
Federal Environmental Pesticide Control Act Amendments, 1975 Set 1977 deadline (not met) for registration, classification, and licensing of many pesticides.
Toxic Substances Control Act, 1976 Required testing of chemicals; authorized EPA to restrict the use of harmful substances.
Comprehensive Environmental Response, Compensation, and Liability Act, 1980 Commonly called "Superfund Act"; created a trust fund (paid for in part by toxic-chemical manufacturers) to clean up hazardous waste sites.

Four key characteristics of eco-efficient corporations are:

· Eco-efficient firms are proactive, not reactive. Policy is initiated and promoted by business because it is in their own interests and the interest of their customers, not because it is imposed by one or more external forces.

· Eco-efficiency is designed in, not added on. This characteristic implies that the optimization of eco-efficiency requires that every business effort regarding the product and process must internalize the strategy.

· Flexibility is imperative for eco-efficient strategy implementation. Continuous attention must be paid to technological innovation and market evolution.

· Eco-efficiency is encompassing, not insular. In the modern global business environment, efforts must not only cross industrial sectors but national and cultural boundaries as well.

INDUSTRY ENVIRONMENT

Harvard professor Michael E. Porter's book *Competitive Strategy* propelled the concept of industry environment into the foreground of strategic thought and business planning. The cornerstone of the book is an article from the *Harvard Business Review,* in which Porter explains the five forces that shape competition in an industry. His well-defined analytic framework helps strategic managers to link remote factors to their effects on a firm's operating environment.

With the special permission of Professor Porter and the *Harvard Business Review,* we present in this section of the chapter the major portion of his seminal article on the industry environment and its impact on strategic management.[5]

OVERVIEW

The nature and degree of competition in an industry hinge on five forces: the threat of new entrants, the bargaining power of customers, the bargaining power of suppliers, the threat of substitute products or services (where applicable), and the jockeying among current contestants. To establish a strategic agenda for dealing with these contending currents and to grow despite them, a company must understand how they work in its industry and how they affect the company in its particular situation. This chapter will detail how these forces operate and suggest ways of adjusting to them, and, where possible, of taking advantage of them.

HOW COMPETITIVE FORCES SHAPE STRATEGY

The essence of strategy formulation is coping with competition. Yet it is easy to view competition too narrowly and too pessimistically. While one sometimes hears executives complaining to the contrary, intense competition in an industry is neither coincidence nor bad luck.

Moreover, in the fight for market share, competition is not manifested only in the other players. Rather, competition in an industry is rooted in its underlying economics, and competitive forces exist that go well beyond the established combatants in a particular industry. Customers, suppliers, potential entrants, and substitute products are all competitors that may be more or less prominent or active depending on the industry.

The state of competition in an industry depends on five basic forces, which are diagrammed in Figure 3–4. The collective strength of these forces determines the ultimate profit potential of an industry. It ranges from intense in industries like tires, metal cans, and steel, where no company earns spectacular returns on investment, to mild in industries like oil-field services and equipment, soft drinks, and toiletries, where there is room for quite high returns.

In the economists' "perfectly competitive" industry, jockeying for position is unbridled and entry to the industry very easy. This kind of industry structure, of course, offers the worst prospect for long-run profitability. The weaker the forces collectively, however, the greater the opportunity for superior performance.

Whatever their collective strength, the corporate strategist's goal is to find a position in the industry where his or her company can best defend itself against these forces or can influence them in its favor. The collective strength of the forces may be painfully apparent to all the antagonists; but to cope with them, the strategist must delve below the surface and analyze the sources of competition. For example, what makes the industry vulnerable to entry? What determines the bargaining power of suppliers?

Knowledge of these underlying sources of competitive pressure provides the groundwork for a strategic agenda of action. They highlight the critical strengths and weaknesses

---

[5] M. E. Porter, "How Competitive Forces Shape Strategy," *Harvard Business Review,* March–April 1979, pp. 137–45.

FIGURE 3–4
Forces Driving Industry Competition

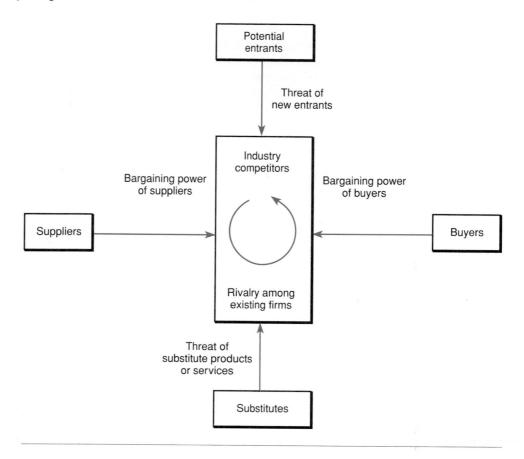

of the company, animate the positioning of the company in its industry, clarify the areas where strategic changes may yield the greatest payoff, and highlight the places where industry trends promise to hold the greatest significance as either opportunities or threats.

Understanding these sources also proves to be of help in considering areas for diversification.

CONTENDING FORCES

The strongest competitive force or forces determine the profitability of an industry and so are of greatest importance in strategy formulation. For example, even a company with a strong position in an industry unthreatened by potential entrants will earn low returns if it faces a superior or a lower-cost substitute product—as the leading manufacturers of vacuum tubes and coffee percolators have learned to their sorrow. In such a situation, coping with the substitute product becomes the number one strategic priority.

Different forces take on prominence, of course, in shaping competition in each industry. In the oceangoing tanker industry, the key force is probably the buyers (the major oil companies), while in tires it is powerful OEM buyers coupled with tough competitors. In the steel industry the key forces are foreign competitors and substitute materials.

Every industry has an underlying structure, or a set of fundamental economic and technical characteristics, that gives rise to these competitive forces. The strategist, wanting to position his or her company to cope best with its industry environment or to influence that environment in the company's favor, must learn what makes the environment tick.

This view of competition pertains equally to industries dealing in services and to those selling products. To avoid monotony, I refer to both products and services as *products*. The same general principles apply to all types of business.

A few characteristics are critical to the strength of each competitive force. They will be discussed in this section.

A. Threat of Entry

New entrants to an industry bring new capacity, the desire to gain market share, and often substantial resources. Companies diversifying through acquisition into the industry from other markets often leverage their resources to cause a shake-up, as Philip Morris did with Miller beer.

The seriousness of the threat of entry depends on the barriers present and on the reaction from existing competitors that the entrant can expect. If barriers to entry are high and a newcomer can expect sharp retaliation from the entrenched competitors, he or she obviously will not pose a serious threat of entering.

There are six major sources of barriers to entry:

1. Economies of Scale

These economies deter entry by forcing the aspirant either to come in on a large scale or to accept a cost disadvantage. Scale economies in production, research, marketing, and service are probably the key barriers to entry in the mainframe computer industry, as Xerox and GE sadly discovered. Economies of scale also can act as hurdles in distribution, utilization of the sales force, financing, and nearly any other part of a business.

2. Product Differentiation

Brand identification creates a barrier by forcing entrants to spend heavily to overcome customer loyalty. Advertising, customer service, being first in the industry, and product differences are among the factors fostering brand identification. It is perhaps the most important entry barrier in soft drinks, over-the-counter drugs, cosmetics, investment banking, and public accounting. To create high fences around their business, brewers couple brand identification with economies of scale in production, distribution, and marketing.

3. Capital Requirements

The need to invest large financial resources in order to compete creates a barrier to entry, particularly if the capital is required for unrecoverable expenditures in up-front advertising or R&D. Capital is necessary not only for fixed facilities but also for customer credit, inventories, and absorbing start-up losses. While major corporations have the financial resources to invade almost any industry, the huge capital requirements in certain fields, such as computer manufacturing and mineral extraction, limit the pool of likely entrants.

4. Cost Disadvantages Independent of Size

Entrenched companies may have cost advantages not available to potential rivals, no matter what their size and attainable economies of scale. These advantages can stem from the effects of the learning curve (and of its first cousin, the experience curve), proprietary technology, access to the best raw materials sources, assets purchased at preinflation prices, government subsidies, or favorable locations. Sometimes cost advantages are enforceable legally, as they are through patents. (For analysis of the much-discussed experience curve as a barrier to entry, see Strategy in Action 3–2.)

5. Access to Distribution Channels

The new boy or girl on the block must, of course, secure distribution of his or her product or service. A new food product, for example, must displace others from the supermarket shelf via price breaks, promotions, intense selling efforts, or some other means. The more limited the wholesale or retail channels are and the more that existing competitors have these tied up, obviously the tougher that entry into the industry will be. Sometimes this barrier is so high that, to surmount it, a new contestant must create its own distribution channels, as Timex did in the watch industry in the 1950s.

6. Government Policy

The government can limit or even foreclose entry to industries, with such controls as license requirements and limits on access to raw materials. Regulated industries like trucking, liquor retailing, and freight forwarding are noticeable examples; more subtle government restrictions operate in fields like ski-area development and coal mining. The government also can play a major indirect role by affecting entry barriers through such controls as air and water pollution standards and safety regulations.

The potential rival's expectations about the reaction of existing competitors also will influence its decision on whether to enter. The company is likely to have second thoughts if incumbents have previously lashed out at new entrants, or if:

The incumbents possess substantial resources to fight back, including excess cash and unused borrowing power, productive capacity, or clout with distribution channels and customers.

The incumbents seem likely to cut prices because of a desire to keep market shares or because of industrywide excess capacity.

Industry growth is slow, affecting its ability to absorb the new arrival and probably causing the financial performance of all the parties involved to decline.

B. Powerful Suppliers

Suppliers can exert bargaining power on participants in an industry by raising prices or reducing the quality of purchased goods and services. Powerful suppliers, thereby, can squeeze profitability out of an industry unable to recover cost increases in its own prices. By raising their prices, soft-drink concentrate producers have contributed to the erosion of profitability of bottling companies because the bottlers—facing intense competition from powdered mixes, fruit drinks, and other beverages—have limited freedom to raise their prices accordingly.

The power of each important supplier (or buyer) group depends on a number of characteristics of its market situation and on the relative importance of its sales or purchases to the industry compared with its overall business.

A *supplier* group is powerful if:

1. It is dominated by a few companies and is more concentrated than the industry it sells.

2. Its product is unique or at least differentiated, or if it has built-up switching costs. Switching costs are fixed costs that buyers face in changing suppliers. These arise because, among other things, a buyer's product specifications tie it to particular suppliers, it has

THE EXPERIENCE CURVE AS AN ENTRY BARRIER

In recent years, the experience curve has become widely discussed as a key element of industry structure. According to this concept, unit costs in many manufacturing industries (some dogmatic adherents say in all manufacturing industries) as well as in some service industries decline with "experience," or a particular company's cumulative volume of production. (The experience curve, which encompasses many factors, is a broader concept than the better-known learning curve, which refers to the efficiency achieved over time by workers through much repetition.)

The causes of the decline in unit costs are a combination of elements, including economies of scale, the learning curve for labor, and capital-labor substitution. The cost decline creates a barrier to entry because new competitors with no "experience" face higher costs than established ones, particularly the producer with the largest market share, and have difficulty catching up with the entrenched competitors.

Adherents of the experience curve concept stress the importance of achieving market leadership to maximize this barrier to entry, and they recommend aggressive action to achieve it, such as price cutting in anticipation of falling costs in order to build volume. For the combatant that cannot achieve a healthy market share, the prescription is usually, "Get out."

Is the experience curve an entry barrier on which strategies should be built? The answer is: not in every industry. In fact, in some industries, building a strategy on the experience curve can be potentially disastrous. That costs decline with experience in some industries is not news to corporate executives. The significance of the experience curve for strategy depends on what factors are causing the decline.

A new entrant may well be more efficient than the more experienced competitors; if it has built the newest plant, it will face no disadvantage in having to catch up. The strategic prescription, "You must have the largest, most efficient plant," is a lot different from "You must produce the greatest cumulative output of the item to get your costs down."

Whether a drop in costs with cumulative (not absolute) volume erects an entry barrier also depends on the sources of the decline. If costs go down because of technical advances known generally in the industry or because of the development of improved equipment that can be copied or purchased from equipment suppliers, the experience curve is not an entry barrier at all—in fact, new or less- experienced competitors may actually enjoy a cost advantage over the leaders. Free of the legacy of heavy past investments, the newcomer or less-experienced competitor can purchase or copy the newest and lowest-cost equipment and technology.

If, however, experience can be kept proprietary, the leaders will maintain a cost advantage. But new entrants may require less experience to reduce their costs than the leaders needed. All this suggests that the experience curve can be a shaky entry barrier on which to build a strategy.

While space does not permit a complete treatment here, I want to mention a few other crucial elements in determining the appropriateness of a strategy built on the entry barrier provided by the experience curve:

> The height of the barrier depends on how important costs are to competition compared with other areas like marketing, selling, and innovation.
>
> The barrier can be nullified by product or process innovations leading to a substantially new technology and, thereby, creating an entirely new experience curve. New entrants can leapfrog the industry leaders and alight on the new experience curve, to which those leaders may be poorly positioned to jump.
>
> If more than one strong company is building its strategy on the experience curve, the consequences can be nearly fatal. By the time only one rival is left pursuing such a strategy, industry growth may have stopped and the prospects of reaping the spoils of victory may long since have evaporated.

invested heavily in specialized ancillary equipment or in learning how to operate a supplier's equipment (as in computer software), or its production lines are connected to the supplier's manufacturing facilities (as in some manufacturing of beverage containers).

3. It is not obliged to contend with other products for sale to the industry. For instance, the competition between the steel companies and the aluminum companies to sell to the can industry checks the power of each supplier.

4. It poses a credible threat of integrating forward into the industry's business. This provides a check against the industry's ability to improve the terms on which it purchases.

5. The industry is not an important customer of the supplier group. If the industry is an important customer, suppliers' fortunes will be tied closely to the industry, and they will want to protect the industry through reasonable pricing and assistance in activities like R&D and lobbying.

C. Powerful Buyers

Customers likewise can force down prices, demand higher quality or more service, and play competitors off against each other—all at the expense of industry profits.

A *buyer* group is powerful if:

1. It is concentrated or purchases in large volumes. Large-volume buyers are particularly potent forces if heavy fixed costs characterize the industry—as they do in metal containers, corn refining, and bulk chemicals, for example—which raise the stakes to keep capacity filled.

2. The products it purchases from the industry are standard or undifferentiated. The buyers, sure that they always can find alternative suppliers, may play one company against another, as they do in aluminum extrusion.

3. The products it purchases from the industry form a component of its product and represent a significant fraction of its cost. The buyers are likely to shop for a favorable price and purchase selectively. Where the product sold by the industry in question is a small fraction of buyers' costs, buyers are usually much less price sensitive.

4. It earns low profits, which create great incentive to lower its purchasing costs. Highly profitable buyers, however, are generally less price sensitive (i.e., of course, if the item does not represent a large fraction of their costs).

5. The industry's product is unimportant to the quality of the buyers' products or services. Where the quality of the buyers' products is very much affected by the industry's product, buyers are generally less price sensitive. Industries in which this situation exists include oil-field equipment, where a malfunction can lead to large losses and enclosures for electronic medical and test instruments, where the quality of the enclosure can influence the user's impression about the quality of the equipment inside.

6. The industry's product does not save the buyer money. Where the industry's product or service can pay for itself many times over, the buyer is rarely price sensitive; rather, he or she is interested in quality. This is true in services like investment banking and public accounting, where errors in judgment can be costly and embarrassing, and in businesses like the mapping of oil wells, where an accurate survey can save thousands of dollars in drilling costs.

7. The buyers pose a credible threat of integrating backward to make the industry's product. The Big Three auto producers and major buyers of cars often have used the threat of self-manufacture as a bargaining lever. But sometimes an industry so engenders a threat to buyers that its members may integrate forward.

Most of these sources of buyer power can be attributed to consumers as a group as well as to industrial and commercial buyers; only a modification of the frame of reference is necessary. Consumers tend to be more price sensitive if they are purchasing products that are undifferentiated, expensive relative to their incomes, and of a sort where quality is not particularly important.

The buying power of retailers is determined by the same rules, with one important addition. Retailers can gain significant bargaining power over manufacturers when they can influence consumers' purchasing decisions, as they do in audio components, jewelry, appliances, sporting goods, and other goods.

D. Substitute Products

By placing a ceiling on the prices it can charge, substitute products or services limit the potential of an industry. Unless it can upgrade the quality of the product or differentiate it somehow (as via marketing), the industry will suffer in earnings and possibly in growth.

Manifestly, the more attractive the price-performance trade-off offered by substitute products, the firmer the lid placed on the industry's profit potential. Sugar producers confronted with the large-scale commercialization of high-fructose corn syrup, a sugar substitute, are learning this lesson today.

Substitutes not only limit profits in normal times but also reduce the bonanza an industry can reap in boom times. In 1978, the producers of fiberglass insulation enjoyed unprecedented demand as a result of high energy costs and severe winter weather. But the industry's ability to raise prices was tempered by the plethora of insulation substitutes, including cellulose, rock wool, and Styrofoam. These substitutes are bound to become an even stronger force once the current round of plant additions by fiberglass insulation producers has boosted capacity enough to meet demand (and then some).

Substitute products that deserve the most attention strategically are those that *(a)* are subject to trends improving their price-performance trade-off with the industry's product or *(b)* are produced by industries earning high profits. Substitutes often come rapidly into play if some development increases competition in their industries and causes price reduction or performance improvement.

E. Jockeying for Position

Rivalry among existing competitors takes the familiar form of jockeying for position—using tactics like price competition, product introduction, and advertising slugfests. This type of intense rivalry is related to the presence of a number of factors:

1. Competitors are numerous or are roughly equal in size and power. In many U.S. industries in recent years, foreign contenders, of course, have become part of the competitive picture.

2. Industry growth is slow, precipitating fights for market share that involve expansion-minded members.

3. The product or service lacks differentiation or switching costs, which lock in buyers and protect one combatant from raids on its customers by another.

4. Fixed costs are high or the product is perishable, creating strong temptation to cut prices. Many basic materials businesses, like paper and aluminum, suffer from this problem when demand slackens.

5. Capacity normally is augmented in large increments. Such additions, as in the chlorine and vinyl chloride businesses, disrupt the industry's supply-demand balance and often lead to periods of overcapacity and price cutting.

6. Exit barriers are high. Exit barriers, like very specialized assets or management's loyalty to a particular business, keep companies competing even though they may be

earning low or even negative returns on investment. Excess capacity remains functioning, and the profitability of the healthy competitors suffers as the sick ones hang on. If the entire industry suffers from overcapacity, it may seek government help—particularly if foreign competition is present.

7. The rivals are diverse in strategies, origins, and "personalities." They have different ideas about how to compete and continually run head-on into each other in the process.

As an industry matures, its growth rate changes, resulting in declining profits and (often) a shakeout. In the booming recreational vehicle industry of the early 1970s, nearly every producer did well; but slow growth since then has eliminated the high returns, except for the strongest members, not to mention many of the weaker companies. The same profit story has been played out in industry after industry—snowmobiles, aerosol packaging, and sports equipment are just a few examples.

An acquisition can introduce a very different personality to an industry, as has been the case with Black & Decker's takeover of McCullough, the producer of chain saws. Technological innovation can boost the level of fixed costs in the production process, as it did in the shift from batch to continuous-line photo finishing in the 1960s.

While a company must live with many of these factors—because they are built into the industry economics—it may have some latitude for improving matters through strategic shifts. For example, it may try to raise buyers' switching costs or increase product differentiation. A focus on selling efforts in the fastest-growing segments of the industry or on market areas with the lowest fixed costs can reduce the impact of industry rivalry. If it is feasible, a company can try to avoid confrontation with competitors having high exit barriers and, thus, can sidestep involvement in bitter price cutting.

INDUSTRY ANALYSIS AND COMPETITIVE ANALYSIS

Designing viable strategies for a firm requires a thorough understanding of the firm's industry and competition. The firm's executives need to address four questions: (1) What are the boundaries of the industry? (2) What is the structure of the industry? (3) Which firms are our competitors? (4) What are the major determinants of competition? The answers to these questions provide a basis for thinking about the appropriate strategies that are open to the firm.

INDUSTRY BOUNDARIES

An industry is a collection of firms that offer similar products or services. By "similar products," we mean products that customers perceive to be substitutable for one another. Consider, for example, the brands of personal computers (PCs) that are now being marketed. The firms that produce these PCs, such as AT&T, IBM, Apple, and Compaq, form the nucleus of the microcomputer industry.

Suppose a firm competes in the microcomputer industry. Where do the boundaries of this industry begin and end? Does the industry include desktops? Laptops? These are the kinds of questions that executives face in defining industry boundaries.

Why is a definition of industry boundaries important? First, it helps executives determine the arena in which their firm is competing. A firm competing in the microcomputer industry participates in an environment very different from that of the broader electronics business. The microcomputer industry comprises several related product families, including personal computers, inexpensive computers for home use, and workstations. The unifying characteristic of these product families is the use of a central processing unit (CPU) in a microchip. On the other hand, the electronics industry is far more extensive; it includes computers, radios, supercomputers, superconductors, and many other products.

The microcomputer and electronics industries differ in their volume of sales, their scope (some would consider microcomputers a segment of the electronics industry), their rate of growth, and their competitive makeup. The dominant issues faced by the two industries also are different. Witness, for example, the raging public debate being waged on the future of the "high-definition TV." U.S. policymakers are attempting to ensure domestic control of that segment of the electronics industry. They also are considering ways to stimulate "cutting-edge" research in superconductivity. These efforts are likely to spur innovation and stimulate progress in the electronics industry. In contrast, the same policymakers are attempting to ensure that microcomputer technology does not reach Eastern Bloc countries. These efforts will restrict the scope of international markets for microcomputer producers.

Second, a definition of industry boundaries focuses attention on the firm's competitors. Defining industry boundaries enables the firm to identify its competitors and producers of substitute products. This is critically important to the firm's design of its competitive strategy.

Third, a definition of industry boundaries helps executives determine key factors for success. Survival in the premier segment of the microcomputer industry requires skills that are considerably different from those required in the lower end of the industry. Firms that compete in the premier segment need to be on the cutting edge of technological development and to provide extensive customer support and education. On the other hand, firms that compete in the lower end need to excel in imitating the products introduced by the premier segment, to focus on customer convenience, and to maintain operational efficiency that permits them to charge the lowest market price. Defining industry boundaries enables executives to ask these questions: Do we have the skills it takes to succeed here? If not, what must we do to develop these skills?

Finally, a definition of industry boundaries gives executives another basis on which to evaluate their firm's goals. Executives use that definition to forecast demand for their firm's products and services. Armed with that forecast, they can determine whether those goals are realistic.

Problems in Defining Industry Boundaries

Defining industry boundaries requires both caution and imagination. Caution is necessary because there are no precise rules for this task and because a poor definition will lead to poor planning. Imagination is necessary because industries are dynamic—in every industry, important changes are under way in such key factors as competition, technology, and consumer demand.

Defining industry boundaries is a very difficult task. The difficulty stems from three sources:

1. The evolution of industries over time creates new opportunities and threats. Compare the financial services industry as we know it today with that of the 1970s and 1980s, and then try to imagine how different the industry will be in the year 2000.

2. Industrial evolution creates industries within industries. The electronics industry of the 1960s has been transformed into many "industries"—TV sets, transistor radios, micro- and macrocomputers, supercomputers, superconductors, and so on. Such transformation allows some firms to specialize and others to compete in different, related industries.

3. Industries are becoming global in scope. Consider the civilian aircraft manufacturing industry. For nearly three decades, U.S. firms dominated world production in that

FIGURE 3–5
Computer Industry Product Segments

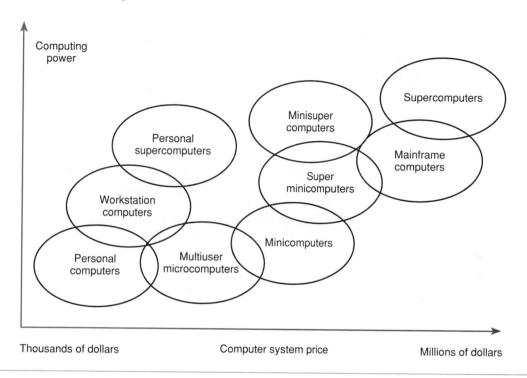

Source: Egil Juliussen and Karen Juliussen, *The Computer Industry Almanac* (New York: Simon & Schuster, 1988), p. 1.11.

industry. But small and large competitors were challenging their dominance by 1990. At that time, Airbus Industries (a consortium of European firms) and Brazilian, Korean, and Japanese firms were actively competing in the industry.

Developing a Realistic Industry Definition

Given the difficulties outlined above, how do executives draw accurate boundaries for an industry? The starting point is a definition of the industry in global terms; that is, in terms that consider the industry's international components as well as its domestic components.

Having developed a preliminary concept of the industry (e.g., computers), executives flesh out its current components. This can be done by defining its product segments, as illustrated in Figure 3–5. Executives need to select the scope of their firm's potential market from among these related but distinct areas.

To understand the makeup of the industry, executives adopt a longitudinal perspective. They examine the emergence and evolution of product families. Why did these product families arise? How and why did they change? The answers to such questions provide executives with clues about the factors that drive competition in the industry.

Executives also examine the companies that offer different product families, the overlapping or distinctiveness of customer segments, and the rate of substitutability among product families.

To realistically define their industry, executives need to examine five issues:

1. Which part of the industry corresponds to our firm's goals?
2. What are the key ingredients of success in that part of the industry?
3. Does our firm have the skills needed to compete in that part of the industry? If not, can we build those skills?
4. Will the skills enable us to seize emerging opportunities and deal with future threats?
5. Is our definition of the industry flexible enough to allow necessary adjustments to our business concept as the industry grows?

INDUSTRY STRUCTURE

Defining an industry's boundaries is incomplete without an understanding of its structural attributes. *Structural attributes* are the enduring characteristics that give an industry its distinctive character. Consider the cable television and financial services industries. Both industries are competitive, and both are important for our quality of life. But these industries have very different requirements for success. To succeed in the cable television industry, firms require vertical integration, which helps them lower their operating costs and ensures their access to quality programs; technological innovation, to enlarge the scope of their services and deliver them in new ways; and extensive marketing, using appropriate segmentation techniques to locate potentially viable niches. To succeed in the financial services industry, firms need to meet very different requirements, among which are extensive orientation of customers and an extensive capital base.

How can we explain such variations among industries? The answer lies in examining the four variables that industry comprises: (1) concentration, (2) economies of scale, (3) product differentiation, and (4) barriers to entry.

Concentration

This variable refers to the extent to which industry sales are dominated by only a few firms. In a highly concentrated industry (i.e., an industry whose sales are dominated by a handful of companies), the intensity of competition declines over time. High concentration serves as a barrier to entry into an industry, because it enables the firms that hold large market shares to achieve significant economies of scale (e.g., savings in production costs due to increased production quantities) and, thus, to lower their prices to stymie attempts of new firms to enter the market.

The U.S. aircraft manufacturing industry is highly concentrated. In 1988, its concentration ratio—the percent of market share held by the top four firms in the industry—was 67 percent. Competition in the industry has not been vigorous. Firms in the industry have been able to deter entry through proprietary technologies and the formation of strategic alliances (e.g., joint ventures).

Economies of Scale

This variable refers to the savings that companies within an industry achieve due to increased volume. Simply put, when the volume of production increases, the long-range average cost of a unit produced will decline.

Economies of scale result from technological and nontechnological sources. The technological sources are a higher level of mechanization or automation and a greater up-to-dateness of plant and facilities. The nontechnological sources include better managerial coordination of production functions and processes, long-term contractual agreements with suppliers, and enhanced employee performance arising from specialization.

Economies of scale are an important determinant of the intensity of competition in an industry. Firms that enjoy such economies can charge lower prices than their competitors. They also can create barriers to entry by reducing their prices temporarily or permanently to deter new firms from entering the industry.

Product Differentiation

This variable refers to the extent to which customers perceive products or services offered by firms in the industry as different.

The differentiation of products can be real or perceived. The differentiation between Apple's Macintosh and IBM's PS/2 Personal Computer is a prime example of real differentiation. These products differ significantly in their technology and performance. Similarly, the civilian aircraft models produced by Boeing differ markedly from those produced by Airbus. The differences result from the use of different design principles and different construction technologies. For example, the newer Airbus planes follow the principle of "fly by wire," whereas Boeing planes utilize the laws of hydraulics. Thus, in Boeing planes, wings are activated by mechanical handling of different parts of the plane, whereas in the Airbus planes, this is done almost automatically.

Perceived differentiation results from the way in which firms position their products and from their success in persuading customers that their products differ significantly from competing products. Marketing strategies provide the vehicles through which this is done. Witness, for example, the extensive advertising campaigns of the automakers, each of which attempts to convey an image of distinctiveness. BMW ads highlight the excellent engineering of the BMW and its symbolic value as a sign of achievement. Some automakers focus on roominess and durability, which are desirable attributes for the family segment of the automobile market.

Real and perceived differentiations often intensify competition among existing firms. On the other hand, successful differentiation poses a competitive disadvantage for firms that attempt to enter an industry.

Barriers to Entry

As Porter noted earlier in this chapter, barriers to entry are the obstacles that a firm must overcome to enter an industry. The barriers can be tangible or intangible. The tangible barriers include capital requirements, technological know-how, resources, and the laws regulating entry into an industry. The intangible barriers include the reputation of existing firms, the loyalty of consumers to existing brands, and access to the managerial skills required for successful operation in an industry.

Entry barriers both increase and reflect the level of concentration, economies of scale, and product differentiation in an industry, and such increases make it more difficult for new firms to enter the industry. Therefore, when high barriers exist in an industry, competition in that industry declines over time.

In summary, analysis of concentration, economies of scale, product differentiation, and barriers to entry in an industry enables a firm's executives to understand the forces that determine competition in an industry and sets the stage for identifying the firm's competitors and how they position themselves in the marketplace.

Industry regulations are a key element of industry structure and can constitute a significant barrier to entry for corporations. Escalating regulatory standards costs have been a

FIGURE 3–6
Innovation-Friendly Regulation

Regulation, properly conceived, need not drive up costs. The following principles of regulatory design will promote innovation, resource productivity, and competitiveness.

Focus on Outcomes, Not Technologies.

Past regulations have often prescribed particular remediation technologies, such as catalysts or scrubbers for air pollution. The phrases "best available technology" (BAT) and "best available control technology" (BACT) are deeply rooted in U.S. practice and imply that one technology is best, thus discouraging innovation.

Enact Strict Rather Than Lax Regulation.

Companies can handle lax regulation incrementally, often with end-of-pipe or secondary treatment solutions. Regulation, therefore, needs to be stringent enough to promote real innovation.

Regulate as Close to the End User as Practical, While Encouraging Upstream Solutions.

This will normally allow more flexibility for innovation in the end product and in all the production and distribution stages. Avoiding pollution entirely or, second best, mitigating it early in the value chain is almost always less costly than late-stage remediation or cleanup.

Employ Phase-In Periods.

Ample but well-defined phase-in periods tied to industry-capital-investment cycles will allow companies to develop innovative resource-saving technologies rather than force them to implement expensive solutions hastily, merely patching over problems.

Use Market Incentives.

Market incentives such as pollution charges and deposit-refund schemes draw attention to resource inefficiencies. In addition, tradable permits provide continuing incentives for innovation and encourage creative use of technologies that exceed current standards.

Harmonize or Converge Regulations in Associated Fields.

Liability exposure in the United States leads companies to stick to safe, BAT approaches, and inconsistent regulation on alternative technologies deters beneficial innovation. For example, one way to eliminate refrigerator cooling agents suspected of damaging the ozone layer involves replacing them with small amounts of propane and butane. But narrowly conceived safety regulations covering these gases seem to have impeded development of the new technology in the United States, while several leading European companies are already marketing the new products.

---

serious concern for corporations for years. As legislative bodies continue their stronghold on corporate activities, businesses feel the impact on their bottom line. In-house counsel departments have been perhaps the most significant additions to corporate structure in the past decade. Legal fees have skyrocketed and managers have learned the hard way about the importance of adhering to regulatory standards. Figure 3–6 presents some key principles that enable corporations to abide by the ever-increasing regulations while keeping costs down, maintaining competitiveness, and enhancing creativity.

COMPETITIVE ANALYSIS

Competitive analysis usually has these objectives: (1) to identify current and potential competitors, (2) to identify potential moves by competitors, and (3) to help the firm devise effective competitive strategies.

How to Identify Competitors

In identifying their firm's current and potential competitors, executives consider several important variables:

FIGURE 3–6
(concluded)

Develop Regulations in Sync with Other Countries or Slightly Ahead of Them.

It is important to minimize possible competitive disadvantages relative to foreign companies that are not yet subject to the same standard. Developing regulations slightly ahead of other countries will also maximize export potential in the pollution-control sector by raising incentives for innovation.

Make the Regulatory Process More Stable and Predictable.

The regulatory process is as important as the standards. If standards and phase-in periods are set and accepted early enough and if regulators commit to keeping standards in place for, say, five years, industry can lock in and tackle root-cause solutions instead of government philosophy.

Require Industry Participation in Setting Standards from the Beginning.

U.S. regulation differs sharply from European regulation in its adversarial approach. Industry should help in designing phase-in periods, the content of regulations, and the most effective regulatory process.

Develop Strong Technical Capabilities among Regulators.

Regulators must understand an industry's economics and what drives its competitiveness. Better information exchange will help avoid costly gaming in which ill-informed companies use an array of lawyers and consultants to try to stall the poorly designed regulations of ill-informed regulators.

Minimize the Time and Resources Consumed in the Regulatory Process Itself.

Time delays in granting permits are usually costly for companies. Self-regulation with periodic inspections would be more efficient than requiring formal approvals. Potential and actual litigation creates uncertainty and consumes resources. Mandatory arbitration procedures or rigid arbitration steps before litigation would lower costs and encourage innovation.

Source: Reprinted by permission of *Harvard Business Review*. An excerpt from "Green and Competitive," by Michael E. Porter and Claas van der Linde, September–October 1995. Copyright © 1995 by the President and Fellows of Harvard University, all rights reserved.

1. How do other firms define the scope of their market? The more similar the definitions of firms, the more likely the firms will view each other as competitors.

2. How similar are the benefits the customers derive from the products and services that other firms offer? The more similar the benefits of products or services, the higher the level of substitutability between them. High substitutability levels force firms to compete fiercely for customers.

3. How committed are other firms to the industry? Although this question may appear to be far removed from the identification of competitors, it is in fact one of the most important questions that competitive analysis must address, because it sheds light on the long-term intentions and goals. To size up the commitment of potential competitors to the industry, reliable intelligence data are needed. Such data may relate to potential resource commitments (e.g., planned facility expansions).

Common Mistakes in Identifying Competitors

Identifying competitors is a milestone in the development of strategy. But it is a process laden with uncertainty and risk, a process in which executives sometimes make costly mistakes. Examples of these mistakes are:

1. Overemphasizing current and known competitors while giving inadequate attention to potential entrants.

2. Overemphasizing large competitors while ignoring small competitors.

3. Overlooking potential international competitors.

4. Assuming that competitors will continue to behave in the same way they have behaved in the past.

5. Misreading signals that may indicate a shift in the focus of competitors or a refinement of their present strategies or tactics.

6. Overemphasizing competitors' financial resources, market position, and strategies while ignoring their intangible assets, such as a top-management team.

7. Assuming that all of the firms in the industry are subject to the same constraints or are open to the same opportunities.

8. Believing that the purpose of strategy is to outsmart the competition, rather than to satisfy customer needs and expectations.

OPERATING ENVIRONMENT

The operating environment, also called the *competitive* or *task environment,* comprises factors in the competitive situation that affect a firm's success in acquiring needed resources or in profitably marketing its goods and services. Among the most important of these factors are the firm's competitive position, the composition of its customers, its reputation among suppliers and creditors, and its ability to attract capable employees. The operating environment is typically much more subject to the firm's influence or control than the remote environment. Thus, firms can be much more proactive (as opposed to reactive) in dealing with the operating environment than in dealing with the remote environment.

1. Competitive Position

Assessing its competitive position improves a firm's chances of designing strategies that optimize its environmental opportunities. Development of competitor profiles enables a firm to more accurately forecast both its short- and long-term growth and its profit potentials. Although the exact criteria used in constructing a competitor's profile are largely determined by situational factors, the following criteria are often included:

1. Market share
2. Breadth of product line.
3. Effectiveness of sales distribution.
4. Proprietary and key-account advantages.
5. Price competitiveness.
6. Advertising and promotion effectiveness.
7. Location and age of facility.
8. Capacity and productivity.
9. Experience.
10. Raw materials costs.
11. Financial position.
12. Relative product quality.
13. R&D advantages position.
14. Caliber of personnel.
15. General images.[6]

Once appropriate criteria have been selected, they are weighted to reflect their importance to a firm's success. Then the competitor being evaluated is rated on the criteria, the ratings are multiplied by the weight, and the weighted scores are summed to yield a numerical profile of the competitor, as shown in Figure 3–7.

---

[6] These items were selected from a matrix for assessing competitive position proposed by C. W. Hofer and D. Schendel, *Strategy Formulation: Analytical Concepts* (St. Paul, MN: West Publishing, 1978), p. 76.

FIGURE 3–7
Competitor Profile

Key Success Factors	Weight	Rating[†]	Weighted Score
Market share	0.30	4	1.20
Price competitiveness	0.20	3	0.60
Facilities location	0.20	5	1.00
Raw materials costs	0.10	3	0.30
Caliber of personnel	0.20	1	0.20
	1.00*		3.30

* The total of the weights must always equal 1.00.

† The rating scale suggested is as follows: very strong competitive position (5 points), strong (4), average (3), weak (2), very weak (1).

   This type of competitor profile is limited by the subjectivity of its criteria selection, weighting, and evaluation approaches. Nevertheless, the process of developing such profiles is of considerable help to a firm in defining its perception of its competitive position. Moreover, comparing the firm's profile with those of its competitors can aid its managers in identifying factors that might make the competitors vulnerable to the strategies the firm might choose to implement.

2. Customer Profiles

Perhaps the most vulnerable result of analyzing the operating environment is the understanding of a firm's customers that this provides. Developing a profile of a firm's present and prospective customers improves the ability of its managers to plan strategic operations, to anticipate changes in the size of markets, and to reallocate resources so as to support forecast shifts in demand patterns. The traditional approach to segmenting customers is based on customer profiles constructed from geographic, demographic, psychographic, and buyer behavior information, as illustrated in Figure 3–8.

   Enterprising companies have quickly learned the importance of identifying target segments. In recent years, market research has increased tremendously as companies realize the benefits of demographic and psychographic segmentation. Research by American Express showed that competitors were stealing a prime segment of the company's business, affluent business travelers. AMEX's competing companies, including Visa and Mastercard, began offering high-spending business travelers frequent flier programs and other rewards including discounts on new cars. In turn, AMEX began to invest heavily in rewards programs, while also focusing on its strongest capabilities, assets, and competitive advantage. Unlike most credit card companies, AMEX cannot rely on charging interest to make money because its customers pay in full each month. Therefore, the company charges higher transaction fees to its merchants. In this way, increases in spending by AMEX customers who pay off their balances each month are more profitable to AMEX than to competing credit card companies. As Strategy in Action 3–3 shows, successful segmentation has paid off.

   Assessing consumer behavior is a key element in the process of satisfying your target market needs. Many firms lose market share as a result of assumptions made about target segments. Market research and industry surveys can help to reduce a firm's chances of relying on illusive assumptions. Firms most vulnerable are those that have had success with one or more products in the marketplace and as a result try to base consumer behavior on past data and trends. Some dangerous implicit assumptions are listed in Figure 3–9.

FIGURE 3–8
Major Segmentation Variables for Consumer Markets

Variable	Typical Breakdowns
Geographic	
Region	Pacific, Mountain, West North Central, West South Central, East North Central, East South Central, South Atlantic, Middle Atlantic, New England.
County size	A, B, C, D.
City or SMSA size	Under 5,000; 5,000–20,000; 20,000–50,000; 50,000–100,000; 100,000–250,000; 250,000–500,000; 500,000–1,000,000; 1,000,000–4,000,000; 4,000,000 or over.
Density	Urban, suburban, rural.
Climate	Northern, southern.
Demographic	
Age	Under 6, 6–11, 12–19, 20–34, 35–49, 50–64, 65+.
Sex	Male, female.
Family size	1–2, 3–4, 5+.
Family life cycle	Young, single; young, married, no children; young, married, youngest child under 6; young, married, youngest child 6 or over; older, married, with children; older, married, no children under 18; older, single; other.
Income	Under $10,000; $10,000–$15,000; $15,000–$20,000; $20,000–$25,000; $25,000–$30,000; $30,000–$50,000; $50,000 and over.
Occupation	Professional and technical; managers, officials, and proprietors; clerical, sales; craftspeople, foremen; operatives; farmers; retired; students; housewives; unemployed.
Education	Grade school or less; some high school; high school graduate; some college; college graduate.
Religion	Catholic, Protestant, Jewish, other.
Race	White, Black, Oriental.
Nationality	American, British, French, German, Scandinavian, Italian, Latin American, Middle Eastern, Japanese.
Psychographic	
Social class	Lower lowers, upper lowers, working class, middle class, upper middles, lower uppers, upper uppers.
Lifestyle	Straights, swingers, longhairs.
Personality	Compulsive, gregarious, authoritarian, ambitious.
Behavioral	
Occasions	Regular occasion, special occasion.
Benefits	Quality, service, economy.
User status	Nonuser, ex-user, potential user, first-time user, regular user.
Usage rate	Light user, medium user, heavy user.
Loyalty status	None, medium, strong, absolute.
Readiness stage	Unaware, aware, informed, interested, desirous, intending to buy.
Attitude toward product	Enthusiastic, positive, indifferent, negative, hostile.

SMSA stands for standard metropolitan statistical area.

Source: *Marketing Management,* 7/e by Kotler, © 1991. Adapted by permission of Prentice Hall, Inc., Upper Saddle River, NJ.

Geographic

It is important to define the geographic area from which customers do or could come. Almost every product or service has some quality that makes it variably attractive to buyers from different locations. Obviously, a Wisconsin manufacturer of snow skis should think twice about investing in a wholesale distribution center in South Carolina. On the other

STRATEGY
IN ACTION
3–3

CUSTOMER SEGMENTATION AT AMEX

Self-selecting, individually correcting offers are new in customer segmentation. American Express is using the approach to reduce cost and shorten time-to-market when it tests new value propositions. One example is its recent *zero spender stimulation test.*

Zero spenders are customers who hold the American Express Card and pay the annual fee but rarely or never use the card. Since those customers not only generate lower profits but also are more likely to defect than an average AMEX customer, they are an obvious target for a loyalty program. However, not all customers in this segment are of equal potential value to American Express. Some are not using the card simply because they can't afford much discretionary spending, but others are using cash or a competitor's card instead. It is the zero spender in the second category that American Express wants to target. Easier said than done.

Although zero spenders consist of two different groups, the behavior of one is indistinguishable from that of the other. To identify the subsegments, AMEX has begun testing a series of self-selecting offers designed to attract the customers who have the highest potential value.

One such offer, high in value and likely to appeal only to those with significant discretionary spending ability, is two airline tickets for heavy card use during a six-month period. The cost of the offer is high, but the cost of losing potentially valuable customers and acquiring new ones would be higher. And trying to identify valuable customers through market research could be expensive and time consuming, given the size of the company's worldwide base of customers.

Customer rewards at AMEX are, in effect, a means of delivering mass-customized value. Most companies think of mass customization as it applies to packaging and delivery, but American Express is using reward to mass-customize the value proposition itself. The approach allows the company to test an unprecedented variety of offers and products while lowering costs and speeding time-to-market. All products and offers are designed not only to appeal to desired target segments but also to allow the customers to select the relevant propositions, thereby identifying themselves and making targeted marketing easier in the future. As a global company, AMEX can correlate lessons learned from one market with other markets—lessons showing which products and offers customers prefer and which behavior and profits each proposition generates.

hand, advertising in the *Milwaukee Sun-Times* could significantly expand the geographically defined customer market of a major Myrtle Beach hotel in South Carolina.

Demographic

Demographic variables most commonly are used to differentiate groups of present or potential customers. Demographic information (e.g., information on sex, age, marital status, income, and occupation) is comparatively easy to collect, quantify, and use in strategic forecasting, and such information is the minimum basis for a customer profile.

Psychographic

Personality and lifestyle variables often are better predictors of customer purchasing behavior than geographic or demographic variables. In such situations, a psychographic study is an important component of the customer profile. Recent advertising campaigns by soft-drink producers—Pepsi-Cola ("the Pepsi generation"), Coca-Cola ("catch the

FIGURE 3–9
Some Dangerous Implicit Assumptions

1. Customers will buy our product because we think it's a good product.

2. Customers will buy our product because it's technically superior.

3. Customers will agree with our perception that the product is "great."

4. Customers run no risk in buying from us instead of continuing to buy from their past suppliers.

5. The product will sell itself.

6. Distributors are desperate to stock and service the product.

7. We can develop the product on time and on budget.

8. We will have no trouble attracting the right staff.

9. Competitors will respond rationally.

10. We can insulate our product from competition.

11. We will be able to hold down prices while gaining share rapidly.

12. The rest of our company will gladly support our strategy and provide help as needed.

Source: Reprinted by permission of *Harvard Business Review*. An excerpt from "Discovery-Driven Planning," by Rita Gunther McGrath and Ian C. MacMillan, July–August 1995. Copyright © by the President and Fellows of Harvard University, all rights reserved.

wave"), and 7UP ("America's turning 7UP")—reflect strategic management's attention to the psychographic characteristics of their largest customer segment—physically active, group-oriented nonprofessionals.

Buyer Behavior

Buyer behavior data also can be a component of the customer profile. Such data are used to explain or predict some aspect of customer behavior with regard to a product or service. As Figure 3–8 indicates, information on buyer behavior (e.g., usage rate, benefits sought, and brand loyalty) can provide significant aid in the design of more accurate and profitable strategies.

A second approach to identifying customer groups is by segmenting industrial markets. As shown in Figure 3–10, there is considerable overlap between the variables used to segment individual and industrial consumers, but the definition of the customer differs.

3. Suppliers

Dependable relationships between a firm and its suppliers are essential to the firm's long-term survival and growth. A firm regularly relies on its suppliers for financial support, services, materials, and equipment. In addition, it occasionally is forced to make special requests for such favors as quick delivery, liberal credit terms, or broken-lot orders. Particularly at such times, it is essential for a firm to have had an ongoing relationship with its suppliers.

In assessing a firm's relationships with its suppliers, several factors, other than the strength of that relationship, should be considered. With regard to its competitive position with its suppliers, the firm should address the following questions:

Are the suppliers' prices competitive? Do the suppliers offer attractive quantity discounts?

How costly are their shipping charges? Are the suppliers competitive in terms of production standards?

In terms of deficiency rates, are the suppliers' abilities, reputations, and services competitive?

Are the suppliers reciprocally dependent on the firm?

FIGURE 3–10
Major Segmentation Variables for Industrial Markets

Demographic

Industry: Which industries that buy this product should we focus on?
Company size: What size companies should we focus on?
Location: What geographical areas should we focus on?

Operating Variables

Technology: What customer technologies should we focus on?
User-nonuser status: Should we focus on heavy, medium, light users or nonusers?
Customer capabilities: Should we focus on customers needing many services or few services?

Purchasing Approaches

Purchasing-function organization: Should we focus on companies with highly centralized or decentralized purchasing organizations?
Power structure: Should we focus on companies that are engineering dominated? financially dominated? other ways dominated?
Nature of existing relationships: Should we focus on companies with which we have strong existing relationships or simply go after the most desirable companies?
General purchase policies: Should we focus on companies that prefer leasing? service contracts? systems purchases? sealed bidding?
Purchasing criteria: Should we focus on companies that are seeking quality? service? price?

Situational Factors

Urgency: Should we focus on companies that need quick and sudden delivery or service?
Specific application: Should we focus on certain applications of our product, rather than all applications?
Size of order: Should we focus on large or small orders?

Perfect Characteristics

Buyer-seller similarity: Should we focus on companies whose people and values are similar to ours?
Attitudes toward risk: Should we focus on risk-taking or risk-avoiding customers?
Loyalty: Should we focus on companies that show high loyalty to their suppliers?

Source: Adapted from Thomas V. Bonoma and Benson P. Shapiro, *Segmenting the Industrial Market* (Lexington, MA: Lexington Books, 1983).

4. Creditors

Because the quantity, quality, price, and accessibility of financial, human, and material resources are rarely ideal, assessment of suppliers and creditors is critical to an accurate evaluation of a firm's operating environment. With regard to its competitive position with its creditors, among the most important questions that the firm should address are the following:

Do the creditors fairly value and willingly accept the firm's stock as collateral?

Do the creditors perceive the firm as having an acceptable record of past payment?

A strong working capital position? Little or no leverage?

Are the creditors' loan terms compatible with the firm's profitability objectives?

Are the creditors able to extend the necessary lines of credit?

The answers to these and related questions help a firm forecast the availability of the resources it will need to implement and sustain its competitive strategies.

5. Human Resources: Nature of the Labor Market

A firm's ability to attract and hold capable employees is essential to its success. However, a firm's personnel recruitment and selection alternatives often are influenced by the nature of its operating environment. A firm's access to needed personnel is affected primarily by three factors: the firm's reputation as an employer, local employment rates, and the ready availability of people with the needed skills.

Reputation

A firm's reputation within its operating environment is a major element of its ability to satisfy its personnel needs. A firm is more likely to attract and retain valuable employees if it is seen as permanent in the community, competitive in its compensation package, and concerned with the welfare of its employees, and if it is respected for its product or service and appreciated for its overall contribution to the general welfare.

Employment Rates

The readily available supply of skilled and experienced personnel may vary considerably with the stage of a community's growth. A new manufacturing firm would find it far more difficult to obtain skilled employees in a vigorous industrialized community than in an economically depressed community in which similar firms had recently cut back operations.

Availability

The skills of some people are so specialized that relocation may be necessary to secure the jobs and the compensation that those skills commonly command. People with such skills include oil drillers, chefs, technical specialists, and industry executives. A firm that seeks to hire such a person is said to have broad labor market boundaries; that is, the geographic area within which the firm might reasonably expect to attract qualified candidates is quite large. On the other hand, people with more common skills are less likely to relocate from a considerable distance to achieve modest economic or career advancements. Thus, the labor market boundaries are fairly limited for such occupational groups as unskilled laborers, clerical personnel, and retail clerks.

EMPHASIS ON ENVIRONMENTAL FACTORS

This chapter has described the remote, industry, and operating environments as encompassing five components each. While that description is generally accurate, it may give the false impression that the components are easily identified, mutually exclusive, and equally applicable in all situations. In fact, the forces in the external environment are so dynamic and interactive that the impact of any single element cannot be wholly disassociated from the impact of other elements. For example, are increases in OPEC oil prices the result of economic, political, social, or technological changes? Or are a manufacturer's surprisingly good relations with suppliers a result of competitors', customers', or creditors' activities or of the supplier's own activities? The answer to both questions is probably that a number of forces in the external environment have combined to create the situation. Such is the case in most studies of the environment.

In a recent study involving more than 200 company executives, the respondents were asked to identify key planning issues in terms of their increasing importance to strategic success. As shown in Figure 3–11, domestic competitive trends, customer or end-user preferences, and technological trends were the issues they selected most often.

Strategic managers are frequently frustrated in their attempts to anticipate the environment's changing influences. Different external elements affect different strategies at different times and with varying strengths. The only certainty is that the impact of the remote and operating environments will be uncertain until a strategy is implemented. This leads many

FIGURE 3–11
Key Planning Issues

Issue	Percent of Respondents Indicating		
	Increase	No Change	Decrease
1. Competitive (domestic) trends	83.6%	13.5%	2.9%
2. Customer or end-user preferences	69.0	29.1	2.0
3. Technological trends	71.4	25.6	3.0
4. Diversification opportunities	61.7	30.3	8.0
5. Worldwide or global competition	59.4	34.4	6.3
6. Internal capabilities	55.4	40.2	4.4
7. Joint venture opportunities	56.6	36.7	6.6
8. Qualitative data	55.9	38.1	5.9
9. General economic and business conditions	46.4	47.3	6.3
10. Regulatory issues	42.8	51.2	6.0
11. Supplier trends	26.0	69.1	5.0
12. Reasons for past failures	27.6	62.3	10.1
13. Quantitative data	36.8	40.7	22.5
14. Past performance	27.3	51.2	21.5

Source: Adapted from V. Ramanujam, J. C. Camillus, and N. Venkatraman, "Trends in Strategic Planning," in *Strategic Planning and Management Handbook,* ed. W. R. King and D. I. Cleland (New York: Van Nostrand Reinhold, 1987), p. 615.

managers, particularly in less-powerful or smaller firms to minimize long-term planning, which requires a commitment of resources. Instead, they favor allowing managers to adapt to new pressures from the environment. While such a decision has considerable merit for many firms, there is an associated trade-off, namely that absence of a strong resource and psychological commitment to a proactive strategy effectively bars a firm from assuming a leadership role in its competitive environment.

There is yet another difficulty in assessing the probable impact of remote, industry, and operating environments on the effectiveness of alternative strategies. Assessment of this kind involves collecting information that can be analyzed to disclose predictable effects. Except in rare instances, however, it is virtually impossible for any single firm to anticipate the consequences of a change in the environment; for example, the precise effect on alternative strategies of a 2 percent increase in the national inflation rate, a 1 percent decrease in statewide unemployment, or the entry of a new competitor in a regional market.

Still, assessing the potential impact of changes in the external environment offers a real advantage. It enables decision makers to narrow the range of the available options and to eliminate options that are clearly inconsistent with the forecast opportunities. Environmental assessment seldom identifies the best strategy, but it generally leads to the elimination of all but the most promising options.

SUMMARY

A firm's external environment consists of three interrelated sets of factors that play a principal role in determining the opportunities, threats, and constraints that the firm faces. The remote environment comprises factors originating beyond, and usually irrespective of, any single firm's operating situation—economic, social, political, technological, and ecological factors. Factors that more directly influence a firm's prospects originate in the environment of its industry, including entry barriers, competitor rivalry, the availability of substitutes, and the bargaining power of buyers and suppliers. The operating environment comprises factors that influence a firm's immediate competitive situation—competitive position, customer profiles, suppliers, creditors, and the labor market. These three sets of factors provide many of the challenges that a particular firm faces in its attempts to attract or acquire needed resources and to profitably market its goods and services. Environmental assessment is more complicated for multinational corporations (MNCs) than for domestic firms because multinationals must evaluate several environments simultaneously.

Thus, the design of business strategies is based on the conviction that a firm able to anticipate future business conditions will improve its performance and profitability. Despite the uncertainty and dynamic nature of the business environment, an assessment process that narrows, even if it does not precisely define, future expectations is of substantial value to strategic managers.

QUESTIONS FOR DISCUSSION

1. Briefly describe two important recent changes in the remote environment of U.S. business in each of the following areas:
   a. Economic.
   b. Social.
   c. Political.
   d. Technological.
   e. Ecological.

2. Describe two major environmental changes that you expect to have a major impact on the wholesale food industry in the next 10 years.

3. Develop a competitor profile for your college and of the one geographically closest to it. Next, prepare a brief strategic plan to improve the competitive position of the weaker of the two colleges.

4. Assume the invention of a competitively priced synthetic fuel that could supply 25 percent of U.S. energy needs within 20 years. In what major ways might this change the external environment of U.S. business?

5. With your instructor's help, identify a local firm that has enjoyed great growth in recent years. To what degree and in what ways do you think this firm's success resulted from taking advantage of favorable conditions in its remote, industry, and operating environments?

6. Choose a specific industry and, relying solely on your impressions, evaluate the impact of the five forces that drive competition in that industry.

7. Choose an industry in which you would like to compete. Use the five-forces method of analysis to explain why you find that industry attractive.

8. Many firms neglect industry analysis. When does this hurt them? When does it not?

9. The model below depicts industry analysis as a funnel that focuses on remote-factor analysis to better understand the impact of factors in the operating environment. Do you find this model satisfactory? If not, how would you improve it?

10. Who in a firm should be responsible for industry analysis? Assume that the firm does not have a strategic planning department.

BIBLIOGRAPHY

Aaker, D. A. "Managing Assets and Skills: The Key to a Sustainable Competitive Advantage." *California Management Review* (Winter 1989), pp. 91–106.

Allen, M. G. "Competitive Confrontation in Consumer Services." *Planning Review* (January–February 1989), pp. 4–9.

Bleeke, J. A. "Strategic Choices for Newly Opened Markets." *Harvard Business Review* (September–October 1990), pp. 158–66.

Bonifant, Benjamin C., Matthew B. Arnold, and Frederick J. Long. "Gaining Competitive Advantage through Environmental Investments." *Business Horizons* 38, no. 1 (July–August 1995), p. 37.

Bylinsky, G. "Manufacturing for Reuse." *Fortune* (February 6, 1995), p. 102.

Covin, J. G., and D. P. Slevin. "Strategic Management of Small Firms in Hostile and Benign Environments." *Strategic Management Journal* (January–February 1989), pp. 75–87.

Cowley, R. R. "Market Structure and Business Performance: An Evaluation of Buyer/Seller Power in the PIMS Database." *Strategic Management Journal* (May–June 1988), pp. 271–78.

Fiesinger, E. G. "Dealing with Environmental Regulations and Agencies: An Industry Perspective." *Business Horizons* (March–April 1992), pp. 41–45.

Filho, P. V. "Environmental Analysis for Strategic Planning." *Managerial Planning* (January–February 1985), pp. 23–30.

Ginter, P. M., and W. J. Duncan. "Macroenvironmental Analysis for Strategic Management." *Long Range Planning* (December 1990), pp. 63–70.

Hooper, T. L., and B. T. Rocca. "Environmental Affairs: Now on the Strategic Agenda." *The Journal of Business Strategy* (May–June 1991), pp. 26–31.

Ilinitch, Anne Y., and Stefan C. Schaltegger. "Developing a Green Business Portfolio." *Long Range Planning* 28, no. 2 (April 1995), p. 79.

Ketelhöhn, Werner. "Re-engineering Strategic Management." *Long Range Planning* 28, no. 3 (June 1995), p. 68.

Lieberman, M. B. "The Learning Curve, Technology Barriers to Entry, and Competitive Survival in the Chemical Processing Industries." (Strategic Management Journal) (September–October 1989), pp. 431–47.

MacMillan, I. C. "Controlling Competitive Dynamics by Taking Strategic Initiative." *Academy of Management Executive* (May 1988), pp. 111–18.

Mascarenhas, B., and D. A. Aaker. "Mobility Barriers and Strategic Groups." *Strategic Management Journal* (September–October 1989), pp. 475–85.

May, Douglas R., and Brenda L. Flannery. "Cutting Waste with Employee Involvement Teams." *Business Horizons* 38, no. 5 (September–October 1995), p. 28.

Mayer, R. "Winning Strategies for Manufacturers in Mature Industries." *Journal of Business Strategy* (Fall 1987), pp. 23–31.

Miles, R. E. "Adapting to Technology and Competition: A New Industrial Relations System for the 21st Century." *California Management Review* (Winter 1989), pp. 9–28.

Miller, D. "Relating Porter's Business Strategies to Environment and Structure: Analysis and Performance Implications." *Academy of Management Journal* (June 1988), pp. 280–308.

Ottman, J. A. "Industry's Response to Green Consumerism." *Journal of Business Strategy* (July–August 1992), pp. 3–7.

Porter, Michael E., and Claas van der Linde. "Toward a New Conception of the Environment-Competitiveness Relationship." *Journal of Economic Perspectives* (Fall 1995).

———. "Green and Competitive: Ending the Stalemate." *Harvard Business Review* 73, no. 5 (September–October 1995), p. 120.

Prescott, J. E., and J. H. Grant. "A Manager's Guide for Evaluating Competitive Analysis Techniques." *Interfaces* (May–June 1988), pp. 10–22.

Rafferty, J. "Exit Barriers and Strategic Position in Declining Markets." *Long Range Planning* (April 1987), pp. 86–91.

Reilly, W. K. "Environment, Inc." *Business Horizons* (March–April 1992), pp. 9–11.

Reimann, B. C. "Sustaining the Competitive Advantage." *Planning Review* (March–April 1989), pp. 30–39.

Robertson, T. S., and H. Gatignon. "How Innovators Thwart New Entrants into Their Market." *Planning Review* (September–October 1991), pp. 4–11.

Sarkis, Joseph, and Abdul Rasheed. "Greening the Manufacturing Function." *Business Horizons* 38, no. 5 (September–October 1995), p. 17.

Schoemaker, Paul J. H., and Joyce A. Shoemaker. "Estimating Environmental Liability." *California Management Review* 37, no. 3 (Spring 1995), p. 29.

———. "Ecocentric Management in Industrial Ecosystems: Management Paradigm for a Risk Society." *Academy of Management Review* 20, no. 1 (1995), p. 118.

Thomas, L. M. "The Business Community and the Environment: An Important Partnership." *Business Horizons* (March–April 1992), pp. 21–24.

Ulrich, D., and F. Wiersema. "Gaining Strategic and Organizational Capability in a Turbulent Business Environment." *Academy of Management Executive* (May 1988), pp. 115–22.

Vesey, J. T. "The New Competitors: They Think in Terms of 'Speed to Market.' " *Academy of Management Executive* (May 1991), pp. 23–33.

Winsemius, P., and U. Guntram. "Responding to the Environmental Challenge." *Business Horizons* (March–April 1992), pp. 12–20.

Yoffie, D. B. "How an Industry Builds Political Advantage." *Harvard Business Review* (May–June 1988), pp. 82–89.

CHAPTER 3 COHESION CASE ILLUSTRATION

ASSESSING THE EXTERNAL ENVIRONMENT AT THE COCA-COLA COMPANY

Coca-Cola managers place a great deal of emphasis on constant renewal and preparedness of their "worldwide business system." Part of their reasoning emanates from the reality of trying to predict future circumstances of different environmental factors across the thousands of essentially local markets in which they compete throughout the world. Roberto Goizueta addressed this when he said:

> Although we cannot foretell the future, we approach it with the premise that in the coming years organizations will be successful to the extent of their effectiveness in managing and coping with change . . . It is our belief that, in the future, fast change, even chaotic change at times, will pose an equal, if not a greater, challenge. If our premise is correct, then organizations must be sharply focused, flexible, and capable of fast reaction to external forces to succeed in this environment that we foresee.

And a year later, he offered:

> We don't view the future as preordained, but as an infinite series of openings, of possibilities. What is required to succeed in the middle of this uncertainty is what the Greeks called "practical intelligence." Above all else, this "practical intelligence" forces adaptability and teaches constant preparedness. It acknowledges that nothing succeeds quite as planned, and that the model is not the reality. But it also teaches that choice and preparedness can influence the future.

While *preparedness* appears the watchword of Coke management, attention to key environmental factors is evident in Coca-Cola's strategic management perspective. Let's look at a few ways this seems evident.

ECONOMIC

Coca-Cola's products are consumer products, and as such are somewhat sensitive to consumers' disposable income. Coca-Cola's management reports two trends that serve to shape its planning related to this factor. First, Coca-Cola consumers view soft drinks as inexpensive pleasure. As such, even in a temporary environment of steady or slightly declining disposable income, Coca-Cola's research suggests that consumers are unlikely to forgo soft drinks. Second, Coca-Cola monitors disposable income in over 200 countries where it sells soft drinks. In 1993, this information suggests that disposable income is generally rising around the world. Coca-Cola interprets this to mean more purchases of consumer products, particularly in countries where consumer product purchasing has been minimal.

Inflation is another economic factor that influences Coca-Cola's success. Asked about this recently, Coca-Cola's CFO offered this comment:

> Inflation is a factor in many markets around the world and consequently impacts the way the company operates. In general, our management believes that we are able to adjust prices to counteract the effects of increasing costs and generate sufficient cash flow to maintain our productive capacity. In highly inflationary countries, Coca-Cola has benefited from its net monetary liability position in recent years. This position is viewed as a hedge against the effects of country-specific inflation, since net liabilities would ultimately be paid with devalued currency.

DEMOGRAPHIC/SOCIAL

Consumption of soft drinks has long been inversely correlated with a person's age. In other words, as you age you drink fewer soft drinks, while younger people drink most soft drinks. Coca-Cola subscribes to this basic phenomenon.

The average age of the populations in the United States and most European countries is increasing. Outside the United States and Europe, Coke management observes, *"The world is getting younger and young people are the most enthusiastic purchasers of consumer products."*

TECHNOLOGICAL

Many of us have heard the phrase, "The world is getting smaller and smaller." Ease of travel and increasingly sophisticated, instantaneous worldwide communication capabilities drive this phenomenon. Coca-Cola's management views this phenomenon as favorable:

> As the world has gotten smaller, a "global teenager" has emerged. In Germany and around the world, these teenagers share similar tastes in music, clothing, and consumer brands. With its global scope and the power of the world's most ubiquitous trademark, the Coca-Cola system is uniquely equipped to market to this group.

These are a few of the remote environmental factors that influence Coca-Cola's future and how Coke management views them. Let's now look at some factors within their more immediate "industry environment" and see how Coca-Cola's management views these, too.

RIVALRY

The Coca-Cola Company is rather vague on how it assesses rivals. Recent comments are both brief and generic, such as:

> The commercial beverages industry, of which the soft-drink business is a part, is competitive. The soft-drink business itself is highly competitive. In any parts of the world in which Coca-Cola does business, demand for soft drinks is growing at the expense of other commercial beverages. Advertising and sales promotional programs, product innovation, increased efficiency in production techniques, the introduction of new packaging, new vending and dispensing equipment, and brand and trademark developments and protection are important competitive factors.

Translated, this statement acknowledges that Coke's intense rivalry with Pepsi results in a "rivalry ante" that virtually eliminates other, lesser rivals. That intense rivalry (known as the "cola wars"), unceasing for 20 years, has resulted in an ever-increasing share of a growing market for both Pepsi and Coke at the expense of other players.

A "third front," *private labels,* has opened up to challenge Coke and Pepsi. Pioneered by Toronto-based Cott Corp., private labels like Wal-Mart's Sam's Choice have begun to impact on cola sales. Cott bottles most of these beverages, and has seen a five-year growth rate exceeding 200 percent, bringing it $1 billion in revenue. Wal-Mart sold over 1 billion 12-ounce servings of Cott-produced cola beverages last year. Cott has over a 23 percent market share of all soda sold in Canadian supermarkets. Douglas Ivester, Roberto Goizueta's heir apparent, said of Cott and other private labelers: "Parasites! On our turf, the parasite is nothing but a tiny bug, waiting to be crushed." Private label beverages typically sell for half Coke or Pepsi's retail price. Cott's profit has slid as its sales increased, leading Goizueta to comment: "Those who continue to rely on pricing as their only point of distinctiveness are meeting with difficult times, on Main Street and Wall Street. In a highly competitive market for every consumer dollar and investment dollar, we believe the failure to differentiate brands in every aspect of marketing eventually erodes the value of the brand and the investment."

The "front line troops" in the cola wars are Coke and Pepsi bottlers, half of whom are independent bottling franchises. Both companies work incessantly to keep these troops at a fever pitch, because of the critical role these local distributors play—soda moves fast in stores and machines; and, if supplies aren't restocked daily, that firm loses sales. At one recent bottlers' convention, Coke bottlers watched a giant screen where a "Coke" battle tank clanked over a valley, swung its turret while zeroing in on a target, and blew a Pepsi vending machine into a million pieces. The attendees went wild! Similarly, a recent Pepsi bottlers' convention featured, along with its regular speakers, a muscle-bound Pepsi bottler who took a sledgehammer and dismantled a Coke machine on stage.

And now, while Coke and Pepsi pummel each other, they must consider retailer comments about Cott-provided products such as "having a store brand improved the way Coke and Pepsi deal with us" and "we can give consumers value and still earn better margins than on national brands." Analysts project Cott to hold 8 percent of U.S. supermarket soda sales by 2000. Cott's beverages already make up over half of the canned soda sold by its first Japanese customer, the 5,000-store Ito Yokado chain, where retail soda prices are sky high.

SUPPLIERS

The principal raw material used by the soft-drink industry in the United States is high fructose corn syrup, a form of sugar, which is available from numerous domestic sources. The principal raw material used by the soft-drink industry outside the United States is sucrose. It likewise is available from numerous sources.

Another raw material increasingly used by the soft-drink industry is aspartame, a sweetening agent used in low-calorie soft-drink products. Until January 1993, in the United States aspartame was available from just one source—the NutraSweet Company, a subsidiary of the Monsanto Company—due to its patent, which expired at the end of 1992.

Coke managers have long held "power" over sugar suppliers. They view the recently expired aspartame patent as only enhancing their power relative to suppliers.

BUYERS

Individual consumers are the ultimate buyers of soft drinks. However, Coke and Pepsi's real "buyers" have been local bottlers who are franchised to bottle the companies' products and to whom each company sells its patented syrups or concentrates. While Coke and Pepsi issue their franchises, these bottlers are in effect the "conduit" through which these international cola brands get to local consumers.

Through the early 1980s, Coke's domestic bottlers were typically independent family businesses deriving from franchises issued early in the century. Pepsi had a collection of similar franchises, plus a few large franchisees that owned many locations. Until 1980, Coke and Pepsi were somewhat restricted in owning bottling facilities, which was viewed as a restraint of free trade. Then President Jimmy Carter, a Coke fan, changed that by signing legislation to allow soft-drink companies to own bottling companies or territories, plus upholding the territorial integrity of soft-drink franchises, shortly before he left office.

Prior to this development, Coke "power" relative to its key buyers was weak when compared with Pepsi, which had fewer, larger, better capitalized franchisees. This advantage helped Pepsi grow aggressively until Coca-Cola was legally allowed to "integrate forward," creating similarly large, modern Coke bottlers.

The other critical buyer is the retailer, particularly grocery chains, which provide the shelf space to products from Coke and other beverage companies. There are numerous chains and stores large and small in virtually every town worldwide. Chain stores have shown increasing interest in private labels or store brands for many national branded products including soft drinks. For example, Wal-Mart now sells over 1 billion 12-ounce bottles or cans of their brand, Sam's Choice, annually. While Coke's power relative to its bottlers' retail outlets has traditionally been imposing, the continued acceptance of private-label brands may begin to change this.

THREAT OF SUBSTITUTES AND POTENTIAL ENTRANTS

Numerous beverages are available as substitutes for soft drinks. Citrus beverages and fruit juices are the more popular substitutes, along with plain ol' water. Availability of shelf space in retail stores, as well as advertising and promotion, has a significant effect on beverage purchasing behavior. Total liquid consumption in the United States has been approximately the following in the 1990s:

Drink	Percent of Liquid Consumed in the United States
Coca-Cola beverages	10%
Other carbonated soft drinks	15
Fruit juices	6
Milk	15
Coffee	11
Beer	12
Tap water	19
Other	12
	100%

For the first half of the 1990s, Coca-Cola USA sales grew at an annualized rate of 4 percent, twice the industry average. Coca-Cola sold almost half of all soft drinks sold in the United States in 1995, finishing off a five-year annualized growth in market share of 18 percent per annum.

"New Age" beverages, the 1,000 to 2,000 new brands or varieties of fruit-flavored drinks, teas, and bottled waters, have been catching some attention in the early 1990s. With rising demand for alternative drinks, small beverage companies have begun to make inroads into places that have long been the strongholds of major cola brands. Snapple, Clearly Canadian, and Tropicana Twisters are among the more well known vanguards in this substitute beverage class. Kroger is one large grocery chain that has allotted considerable space to New Age beverages. Says a key Kroger buyer, "From a retailer's standpoint, it would not bother us at all to see consumers move from the major brands to the New Age beverages."

The New Age beverage category is estimated at 6 percent of 1995 soft-drink sales. But the category seems to be steadily growing at between 10 and 20 percent annually. Observed one Pepsi executive, "The whole New Age, better-for-you phenomenon is out there and it's affecting the soft drink business, especially on the diet side."

4 THE GLOBAL ENVIRONMENT: STRATEGIC CONSIDERATIONS FOR MULTINATIONAL FIRMS

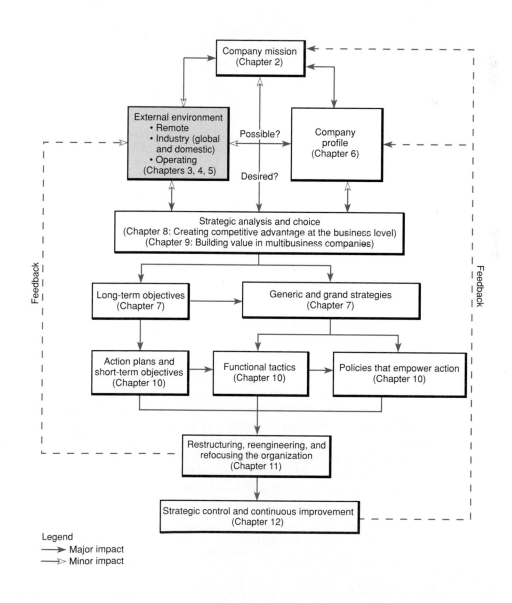

Company mission
(Chapter 2)

External environment
• Remote
• Industry (global
  and domestic)
• Operating
(Chapters 3, 4, 5)

Possible?

Desired?

Company
profile
(Chapter 6)

Strategic analysis and choice
(Chapter 8: Creating competitive advantage at the business level)
(Chapter 9: Building value in multibusiness companies)

Long-term objectives
(Chapter 7)

Generic and grand strategies
(Chapter 7)

Action plans and
short-term objectives
(Chapter 10)

Functional tactics
(Chapter 10)

Policies that empower action
(Chapter 10)

Restructuring, reengineering, and
refocusing the organization
(Chapter 11)

Strategic control and continuous improvement
(Chapter 12)

Feedback

Feedback

Legend
⟶ Major impact
⟶▷ Minor impact

YAMANOUCHI PHARMACEUTICAL READIES ITSELF FOR GLOBALIZATION

The basic policy of the top management of Yamanouchi Pharmaceutical Co., Ltd., represented by Chairman Shigeo Morioka and President Masayoshi Onoda, is summarized by the concepts of big dual enterprise, three-pole tactics, and GBS (global big seven) 005. Big dual enterprise means the dual management diversification into pharmaceuticals and health foods. Three-pole tactics means concentrating activities in Asia (including Japan), America, and Europe, starting from Japan. The GSB 005 envisages the development of seven original new drugs acceptable to the world market until the year 2005, according to Managing Director Junichiro Matsumoto.

The company is actively engaged in project evolution aimed at the establishment of an integrated system covering research and development, and production and sales, as well as a strategy serving local communities. These steps are aimed at converting Yamanouchi into a global enterprise during the first decade of the 21st century.

Yamanouchi achieved excellent business results during fiscal 1994 (March 1995 term). Sales totaled ¥273,048 million, of which exports accounted for ¥12,770 million. Ordinary profit totaled ¥57,990 million. Sales and profit grew by 5.1 percent and 6.6 percent, respectively, from the previous year. The combined group including 54 subsidiaries (for example, Shaklee Corp. of the United States) showed sales of ¥384,323 million and ¥77,390 million, up 4.2 percent and 10.5 percent, respectively. The ordinary profit of the Yamanouchi Group thus achieved even higher growth than the parent company, reflecting the good performance of overseas subsidiaries.

In particular, Yamanouchi Ireland is playing a vital role as the production base of bulk famotidine (Gaster), an anti-ulcer drug agent, which is sold in over 100 countries and recorded annual sales surpassing $1,200 million worldwide. The globalization of Yamanouchi has thus entered a new stage.

Intensified activities related to Yamanouchi's globalization have been seen in the past decade. The firm established Yamanouchi Ireland and started the construction of a manufacturing plant in 1986. The construction was completed in 1988 and the plant moved into full-scale bulk production of

Source: Excerpted from *Japan*, August 21, 1995, p. 30.

Special complications confront a firm involved in the globalization of its operations. *Globalization* refers to the strategy of approaching worldwide markets with standardized products. Such markets are most commonly created by end consumers that prefer lower-priced, standardized products over higher-priced, customized products and by global corporations that use their worldwide operations to compete in local markets.[1] Global corporations headquartered in one country with subsidiaries in other countries experience difficulties that are understandably associated with operating in several distinctly different competitive arenas.

Awareness of the strategic opportunities faced by global corporations and of the threats posed to them is important to planners in almost every domestic U.S. industry. Among corporations headquartered in the United States that receive more than 50 percent of their annual profits from foreign operations are Citicorp, Coca-Cola, Exxon, Gillette, IBM, Otis Elevator, and Texas Instruments. In fact, the 100 largest U.S. globals earn an average of 37 percent of their operating profits abroad. Equally impressive is the impact of foreign-based globals that operate in the United States. Their "direct foreign investment" in the United

[1] T. Levitt, "The Globalization of Markets," *Harvard Business Review*, September-October 1982, p. 91; and T. Hout, M. E. Porter, and E. Rudden, "How Global Companies Win Out," *Harvard Business Review*, September-October 1982, pp. 98–108.

GLOBAL
STRATEGY IN   **continued**
ACTION 4–1

Gaster. Yamanouchi Research Institute (United Kingdom) was inaugurated at Oxford in 1990 as the firm's British research center mainly engaged in basic research centered on cell biology.

In 1991 Yamanouchi bought the pharmaceutical division of Royal Gist–Brocades (the Netherlands) and reorganized it as Brocades Pharma, a base for research and development, and production and sales of pharmaceuticals in Europe. The firm's name was again changed, to Yamanouchi Europe and Yamanouchi Pharma, in 1994 with the establishment of the head office in the Netherlands and sales branches in 12 countries including France, Germany, and Russia. A research center and two plants have been established to bolster development and production.

In the United States, Yamanouchi USA is engaged in clinical development and study. In addition, the firm carried out capital participation (29%) in Roberts, Inc., a middle-level pharmaceutical maker in the United States in 1992.

In the health food sector, in 1989 Yamanouchi bought San Francisco–based Shaklee Corp., a major producer of preparation-enriched foods, with a significant market share and Shaklee Japan, its Japanese subsidiary.

To consolidate its presence in Asia, Yamanouchi established Korea Yamanouchi Pharmaceutical in Seoul, ROK, and Shenyang Yamanouchi Pharmaceutical in Shenyang, China, in 1994. A new plant is slated to start operation in Shenyang in March 1997. The consolidation of the company's foundation in fast-growing Asia is thus making steady progress.

Matsumoto explains: "Our present state is compared to the Step in the Hop, Step, Jump. Jump, the last stage, is crucial." In fact, the next coming few years would be critically important. The structuring of the company's own sales network must be expedited." Overseas production is assisted by the plants of Shacklee and Yamanouchi Europe, but the sales network cannot be established so speedily. "The preparation of a more powerful sales system is essential in order to survive competition with European and American pharmaceutical firms," Matsumoto said. The company's strategy on this point is highly significant.

States now exceeds $90 billion, with Japanese, German, and French firms leading the way. As Global Strategy in Action 4–1 describes, Yamanouchi Pharmaceutical is a fast growth company in the process of globalizing.

Understanding the myriad and sometimes subtle nuances of competing in global markets or against global corporations is rapidly becoming a required competence of strategic managers. For example, experts in the advertising community contend that Korean companies only recently recognized the importance of making their names known abroad. In the 1980s, there was very little advertising of Korean brands, and the country had very few recognizable brands abroad. Korean companies tended to emphasize sales and production more than marketing. The opening of the Korean advertising market in 1991 indicated that Korean firms had acquired a new appreciation for the strategic competencies that are needed to compete globally and created an influx of global firms like Saatchi and Saatchi, J. W. Thompson, Ogilvy and Mather, and Bozell. Many of them established joint ventures or partnerships with Korean agencies. An excellent example of such a strategic approach to globalization by Philip Morris's KGFI is described in Global Strategy in Action 4–2.

Because the growth in the number of global firms continues to overshadow other changes in the competitive environment, this section will focus on the nature, outlook, and operations of global corporations.

THE GLOBALIZATION OF PHILIP MORRIS'S KGFI

Outside of its core Western markets, Kraft General Foods International's (KGFI) food products have a growing presence in one of the most dynamic business environments in the world—the Asia-Pacific region. Its operations there are expanding rapidly, often aided by links with local manufacturers and distributors.

Japan and Korea, two of the world's fastest-growing economies in the last decade, are important examples. In both countries, local alliances can be crucial to market entry and success. Realizing this fact in the early 1970s, General Foods established joint ventures in both Japan and Korea. In 1993, these joint ventures, combined with Kraft General Foods International's (KGFI) stand-alone operations, generated more than $1 billion in revenues. In the aggregate, their combined food operations in Japan and Korea are larger than many Fortune 500 companies.

Whereas soluble coffee accounts for just over 25 percent of the coffee consumed in U.S. homes, it fills over 70 percent of the cups consumed in the homes of convenience-minded Japan. Additionally, Japan is the origin of a unique form of packaged coffee—liquid—and a unique channel of distribution—vending machines. Japanese consumers have purchased packaged liquid coffee for years, and in 1993 it amounted to a $5 billion category. Some 2 million vending machines dispense 9 billion cans of liquid coffee annually—an average of 75 cans per person.

Japan offers a culturally unique distribution channel for coffee products—the gift-set market. Many Japanese exchange specially packaged food or beverage assortments at least twice a year to commemorate holidays as well as special personal or business occasions. The gift-set business has helped Maxim products reinforce their quality image; it also will be a launching pad and support vehicle for Carte Noire coffees.

Outside the Ajinomoto General Foods joint venture, KGFI is developing a freestanding food business under the name Kraft Japan. It is building a cheese business with imported Philadelphia

DEVELOPMENT OF A GLOBAL CORPORATION

The evolution of a global corporation often entails progressively involved strategy levels. The first level, which often entails export-import activity, has minimal effect on the existing management orientation or on existing product lines. The second level, which can involve foreign licensing and technology transfer, requires little change in management or operation. The third level typically is characterized by direct investment in overseas operations, including manufacturing plants. This level requires large capital outlays and the development of global management skills. Although the domestic operations of a firm at this level continue to dominate its policy, such a firm is commonly categorized as a true multinational corporation (MNC). The most involved strategy level is characterized by a substantial increase in foreign investment, with foreign assets comprising a significant portion of total assets. At this level, the firm begins to emerge as a global enterprise with global approaches to production, sales, finance, and control.

Some firms downplay their global nature (to never appear distracted from their domestic operations), whereas others highlight it. For example, General Electric's formal statement of mission and business philosophy includes the following commitment:

> To carry out a diversified, growing, and profitable worldwide manufacturing business in electrical apparatus, appliances, and supplies, and in related materials, products, systems, and services for industry, commerce, agriculture, government, the community, and the home.

Brand cream cheese, the leading cream cheese in the Tokyo metropolitan market, as well as locally manufactured and licensed Kraft Milk Farm cheese slices. The cheese market is expected to grow approximately 5 percent per year. This is a rapid growth rate for a large food category. In addition to cheese, KGFI also imports Oscar Mayer prepared meats and Jocobs Suchard chocolates.

KGFI's joint venture in Korea, Doug Suh Foods Corporation, is one of the top 10 food companies in the country. Doug Suh manufactures coffees and cereals and has its own distribution network. One of Doug Suh's other businesses in Korea, Post Cereals, is also a strong number two, with a 42 percent category share.

Korea's $400 million coffee market is the fastest-growing major coffee market in the world, expanding at an average annual rate of 14 percent in 1990–91. Growing with the market, Maxim and Maxwell soluble coffees, in both traditional "agglomerate" and freeze-dried forms, account for more than 70 percent of the country's soluble coffee sales. The strength of these brands also brings the company a strong number one position in coffee mix, a mixture of soluble coffee, creamer, and sugar. In addition, its Frima brand leads the market in the nondairy creamer segment.

Beyond Australia, where it has a long-established, wholly owned business, and operations in Japan and Korea, KGFI is targeting many other countries for geographic expansion. In Indonesia, for instance, KGFI has established a rapidly growing cheese business through a licensee and introduced other KGFI products in 1993. In Taiwan, the joint venture company, PremierFoods Corporation, holds a 34 percent share of the soluble coffee market and is aggressively developing a Kraft cheese and Jocobs Suchard import business. KGF Philippines, a wholly owned subsidiary, has a leading position in the cheese and powdered soft-drink markets in its country. In the People's Republic of China, the company produces and markets Maxwell House coffees and Tang powdered soft drinks through two successful and rapidly growing joint ventures.

A similar global orientation is evident at IBM, which operates in 125 countries, conducts business in 30 languages and more than 100 currencies, and has 23 major manufacturing facilities in 14 countries.

The question for many firms is not *whether* to globalize, but rather how, how fast, and how to measure progress over time. Six factors that drive global companies are listed in Figure 4–1. They address key aspects of globalizing a business's operations and provide a framework within which companies can effectively pursue the global marketplace.

WHY FIRMS GLOBALIZE

The technological advantage once enjoyed by the United States has declined dramatically during the past 30 years. In the late 1950s, over 80 percent of the world's major technological innovations were first introduced in the United States. By 1990, the figure had declined to less than 50 percent. In contrast, France is making impressive advances in electric traction, nuclear power, and aviation. Germany leads in chemicals and pharmaceuticals, precision and heavy machinery, heavy electrical goods, metallurgy, and surface transport equipment. Japan leads in optics, solid-state physics, engineering, chemistry, and process metallurgy. Eastern Europe and the former Soviet Union, the so-called COMECON (Council for Mutual Economic Assistance) countries, generate 30

FIGURE 4–1
Factors That Drive Global Companies

1. **Global Management Team**
   Possesses global vision and culture.
   Includes foreign nationals.
   Leaves management of subsidiaries to foreign nationals.
   Frequently travels internationally.
   Has cross-cultural training.

2. **Global Strategy**
   Implement strategy as opposed to independent country strategies.
   Develop significant cross-country alliances.
   Select country targets strategically rather than opportunistically.
   Perform business functions where most efficient—no home-country bias.
   Emphasize participation in the triad—North America, Europe, and Japan.

3. **Global Operations and Products**
   Use common core operating processes worldwide to ensure quantity and uniformity.
   Product globally to obtain best cost and market advantage.

4. **Global Technology and R&D**
   Design global products but take regional differences into account.
   Manage development work centrally but carry out globally.
   Do not duplicate R&D and product development; gain economies of scale.

5. **Global Financing**
   Finance globally to obtain lowest cost.
   Hedge when necessary to protect currency risk.
   Price in local currencies.
   List shares on foreign exchanges.

6. **Global Marketing**
   Market global products but provide regional discretion if economies of scale are not affected.
   Develop global brands.
   Use core global marketing practices and themes.
   Simultaneously introduce new global products worldwide.

Source: Robert N. Lussier, Robert W. Baeder, and Joel Corman, "Measuring Global Practices: Global Strategic Planning through Company Situational Analysis," p. 57. Reprinted from *Business Horizons*, September–October 1994. Copyright 1994 by the Foundation for the School of Business at Indiana University. Used with permission.

percent of annual worldwide patent applications. However, the United States can regain some of its lost technological advantage. Through globalization, U.S. firms often can reap benefits from industries and technologies developed abroad. Even a relatively small service firm that possesses a distinct competitive advantage can capitalize on large overseas operations. One such firm that has done this is Domino's Pizza, described in Global Strategy in Action 4–3.

In many situations, global development makes sense as a competitive weapon. Direct penetration of foreign markets can drain vital cash flows from a foreign competitor's domestic operations. The resulting lost opportunities, reduced income, and limited production can impair the competitor's ability to invade U.S. markets. This fact is well understood by the Japanese. As evidence, in 1993 there were 1,500 Japanese-owned or -operated factories in the United States (up 40 percent since 1989) that employed about 300,000 American workers. More than 75 percent of these plants were in six industries, including electronics, food, and cars. Another case in point is IBM's move to establish a position of strength in the Japanese mainframe computer industry before two key competitors, Fiyitsue and Hitachi, could dominate it. Once IBM had achieved a substantial share of the Japanese market, it worked to deny its Japanese competitors the vital cash and production experience they needed to invade the U.S. market.

GLOBAL
STRATEGY IN
ACTION 4–3

THE MULTINATIONALIZATION OF DOMINO'S

Domino's Pizza International, adding stores in Japan at an astounding rate of 1 every four weeks, had 10 in operation by mid-October 1987. By the end of 1988, another 16 stores were to be added. A good reason exists for this expansion. Sales in Japan average $25,000 per store each week, compared with an average of $8,000–$8,500 in the United States.

Domino's works through the Y. Higa Corporation under a licensing agreement to set up pizza franchises. Donald K. Cooper, controller of Domino's Pizza International, said:

> The key to success is spending a lot of time training the workers. It takes a year and a half for a driver to move up to manager-in-training and eventually become a store manager. Early on, managers-in-training learn how to complete a profit and loss statement every four weeks, and, after six months, they know their inventories and how to run a business.

Another reason for Domino's success is the attention it gives to standards. The International stores of Domino's Pizza are kept as close to the U.S. version as possible. Employee uniforms, outdoor signs, and logos are the same as those in the United States. Delivery in 30 minutes or $3 off the price is guaranteed no matter where in the world a Domino's is located, and the menu is always kept simple. Each store must limit the number of toppings it offers, and only two pizza sizes are available.

Domino's operates 200 stores worldwide. It hopes to double that number of stores each year. Cooper said, "Everyone realizes that International is going to be the force in the future."

Source: Adapted from Andrea Chancellor, "Domino's Finds Japanese Sales as Easy as Pie," *Journal of Commerce*, October 13, 1987, p. 1A; and M. R. Czinkota, P. Rivoli, and I. A. Ronkainen, *International Business* (Hinsdale, IL: Dryden Press, 1989).

CONSIDERATIONS PRIOR TO GLOBALIZATION

To begin globalization, firms are advised to take four steps.[2]

Scan the Global Situation   Scanning includes reading journals and patent reports and checking other printed sources—as well as meeting people at scientific-technical conferences and in-house seminars.

Make Connections with Academia and Research Organizations   Firms active in overseas R&D often pursue work-related projects with foreign academics and sometimes enter into consulting agreements with them.

Increase the Firm's Global Visibility   Common methods that firms use to attract global attention include participating in trade fairs, circulating brochures on their products and inventions, and hiring technology acquisition consultants.

Undertake Cooperative Research Projects   Some firms engage in joint research projects with foreign firms to broaden their contacts, reduce expenses, diminish the risk for each partner, or forestall the entry of competitors into their markets.

In a similar vein, external and internal assessments may be conducted before a firm enters global markets. For example, Japanese investors conduct extensive assessments and

---

[2] R. Rondstadt and R. Kramer, "Getting the Most out of Innovation Abroad," *Harvard Business Review*, March–April 1982, pp. 94–99.

GLOBAL
STRATEGY IN
ACTION 4–4

CHECKLIST OF FACTORS TO CONSIDER IN CHOOSING A FOREIGN MANUFACTURING SITE

The following considerations were drawn from an 88-point checklist developed by Business International Corporation.

Economic factors:

1. Size of GNP and projected rate of growth.
2. Foreign exchange position.
3. Size of market for the firm's products; rate of growth.
4. Current or prospective membership in a customs union.

Political factors:

5. Form and stability of government.
6. Attitude toward private and foreign investment by government, customers, and competition.
7. Practice of favored versus neutral treatment for state industries.
8. Degree of antiforeign discrimination.

Geographic factors:

9. Efficiency of transport (railways, waterways, highways).
10. Proximity of site to export markets.
11. Availability of local raw materials.
12. Availability of power, water, gas.

Labor factors:

13. Availability of managerial, technical, and office personnel able to speak the language of the parent company.

---

analyses before selecting a U.S. site for a Japanese-owned firm. They prefer states with strong markets, low unionization rates, and low taxes. In addition, Japanese manufacturing plants prefer counties characterized by manufacturing conglomeration; low unemployment and poverty rates; and concentrations of educated, productive workers.[3]

External assessment involves careful examination of critical features of the global environment, particular attention being paid to the status of the host nations in such areas as economic progress, political control, and nationalism. Expansion of industrial facilities, favorable balances of payments, and improvements in technological capabilities over the past decade are gauges of the host nation's economic progress. Political status can be gauged by the host nation's power in and impact on global affairs.

Internal assessment involves identification of the basic strengths of a firm's operations. These strengths are particularly important in global operations, because they are often the characteristics of a firm that the host nation values most and, thus, offer significant bargaining leverage. The firm's resource strengths and global capabilities must be analyzed. The resources that should be analyzed include, in particular, technical and managerial skills, capital, labor, and raw materials. The global capabilities that should be analyzed include the firm's product delivery and financial management systems.

---

[3] D. Woodward, "Locational Determinants of Japanese Manufacturing Start-Ups in the United States," *Southern Economic Journal*, January 1992, pp. 690–708.

GLOBAL
STRATEGY IN   **continued**
ACTION 4–4

14. Degree of skill and discipline at all levels.
15. Presence or absence of militant or Communist-dominated unions.
16. Degree and nature of labor voice in management.

Tax factors:

17. Tax-rate trends (corporate and personal income, capital, withholding, turnover, excise, payroll, capital gains, customs, and other indirect and local taxes).
18. Joint tax treaties with home country and others.
19. Duty and tax drawbacks when imported goods are exported.
20. Availability of tariff protection.

Capital source factors:

21. Cost of local borrowing.
22. Local availability of convertible currencies.
23. Modern banking systems.
24. Government credit aids to new businesses.

Business factors:

25. State of marketing and distribution system.
26. Normal profit margins in the firm's industry.
27. Competitive situation in the firm's industry: do cartels exist?
28. Availability of amenities for expatriate executives and their families.

A firm that gives serious consideration to internal and external assessment is Business International Corporation, which recommends that seven broad categories of factors be considered. As shown in Global Strategy in Action 4–4, these categories include economic, political, geographic, labor, tax, capital source, and business factors.

COMPEXITY OF THE GLOBAL ENVIRONMENT

Global strategic planning is more complex than purely domestic planning. There are at least five factors that contribute to this increase in complexity:

1. Globals face multiple political, economic, legal, social, and cultural environments as well as various rates of changes within each of them.

2. Interactions between the national and foreign environments are complex, because of national sovereignty issues and widely differing economic and social conditions.

3. Geographic separation, cultural and national differences, and variations in business practices all tend to make communication and control efforts between headquarters and the overseas affiliates difficult.

4. Globals face extreme competition, because of differences in industry structures.

5. Globals are restricted in their selection of competitive strategies by various regional blocs and economic integrations, such as the European Economic Community, the European Free Trade Area, and the Latin American Free Trade Area. Indications of how these

FIGURE 4–2
Differences between Factors That Affect Strategic Management in the United States and Internationally

Factor	U.S. Operations	International Operations
Language	English used almost universally.	Use of local language required in many situations.
Culture	Relatively homogenous.	Quite diverse, both between countries and within countries.
Politics	Stable and relatively unimportant.	Often volatile and of decisive importance.
Economy	Relatively uniform.	Wide variations among countries and among regions within countries.
Government interference	Minimal and reasonably predictable.	Extensive and subject to rapid change.
Labor	Skilled labor available.	Skilled labor often scarce, requiring training or redesign of production methods.
Financing	Well-developed financial markets.	Poorly developed financial markets; capital flows subject to government control.
Media research	Data easy to collect.	Data difficult and expensive to collect.
Advertising	Many media available; few restrictions.	Media limited; many restrictions; low literacy rates rule out print media in some countries.
Money	U.S. dollar used universally.	Must change from one currency to another; problems created by changing exchange rates and government restrictions.
Transportation/ communication	Among the best in the world.	Often inadequate.
Control	Always a problem, but centralized control will work.	A worse problem—centralized control won't work; must walk a tightrope between overcentralizing and losing control through too much decentralizing.
Contracts	Once signed, are binding on both parties even if one party makes a bad deal.	Can be avoided and renegotiated if one party becomes dissatisfied.
Labor relations	Collective bargaining; layoff of workers easy.	Layoff of workers often not possible; may have mandatory worker participation in management; workers may seek change through political process rather than collective bargaining.

Source: Adapted from R. G. Murdick, R. C. Moor, R. H. Eckhouse, and T. W. Zimmerer, *Business Policy: A Framework for Analysis*, 4th ed. (Columbus, OH: Grid, 1984), p. 275.

factors contribute to the increased complexity of global strategic management are provided in Figure 4–2.

CONTROL PROBLEMS OF THE GLOBAL FIRM

An inherent complicating factor for many global firms is that their financial policies typically are designed to further the goals of the parent company and pay minimal attention to the goals of the host countries. This built-in bias creates conflict between the different parts of the global firm, between the whole firm and its home and host countries, and between the home and host countries themselves. The conflict is accentuated by the use of various schemes to shift earnings from one country to another in order to avoid taxes, minimize risk, or achieve other objectives.

Moreover, different financial environments make normal standards of company behavior concerning the disposition of earnings, sources of finance, and the structure of capital more problematic. Thus, it becomes increasingly difficult to measure the performance of international divisions.

In addition, important differences in measurement and control systems often exist. Fundamental to the concept of planning is a well-conceived, future-oriented approach to decision making that is based on accepted procedures and methods of analysis. Consistent approaches to planning throughout a firm are needed for effective review and evaluation by corporate headquarters. In the global firm, planning is complicated by differences in national attitudes toward work measurement, and by differences in government requirements about disclosure of information.

Although such problems are an aspect of the global environment, rather than a consequence of poor management, they are often most effectively reduced through increased attention to strategic planning. Such planning will aid in coordinating and integrating the firm's direction, objectives, and policies around the world. It enables the firm to anticipate and prepare for change. It facilitates the creation of programs to deal with worldwide development. Finally, it helps the management of overseas affiliates become more actively involved in setting goals and in developing means to more effectively utilize the firm's total resources.

As an example of the need for coordination in global ventures and as evidence that firms can successfully plan for global collaboration (e.g., through rationalized production), consider Figure 4–3. Ford Escort (Europe), the best-selling automobile in the world, has a component manufacturing network that consists of plants in 15 countries.

GLOBAL STRATEGIC PLANNING

It should be evident from the previous sections that the strategic decisions of a firm competing in the global marketplace become increasingly complex. In such a firm, managers cannot view global operations as a set of independent decisions. These managers are faced with trade-off decisions in which multiple products, country environments, resource sourcing options, corporate and subsidiary capabilities, and strategic options must be considered.

A recent trend toward increased activism of stakeholders has added to the complexity of strategic planning for the global firm. *Stakeholder activism* refers to demands placed on the global firm by the foreign environments in which it operates, principally by foreign governments. This section provides a basic framework for the analysis of strategic decisions in this complex setting.

Multidomestic Industries and Global Industries

Michael E. Porter has developed a framework for analyzing the basic strategic alternatives of a firm that competes globally.[4] The starting point of the analysis is an understanding of the industry or industries in which the firm competes. International industries can be ranked along a continuum that ranges from multidomestic to global.

Multidomestic Industries

A multidomestic industry is one in which competition is essentially segmented from country to country. Thus, even if global corporations are in the industry, competition in one country is independent of competition in other countries. Examples of such industries include retailing, insurance, and consumer finance.

---

[4] Michael E. Porter, "Changing Patterns of International Competition," *California Management Review*, Winter 1986, pp. 9–40.

FIGURE 4-3
The Global Manufacturing Network for the Ford Escort (Europe)

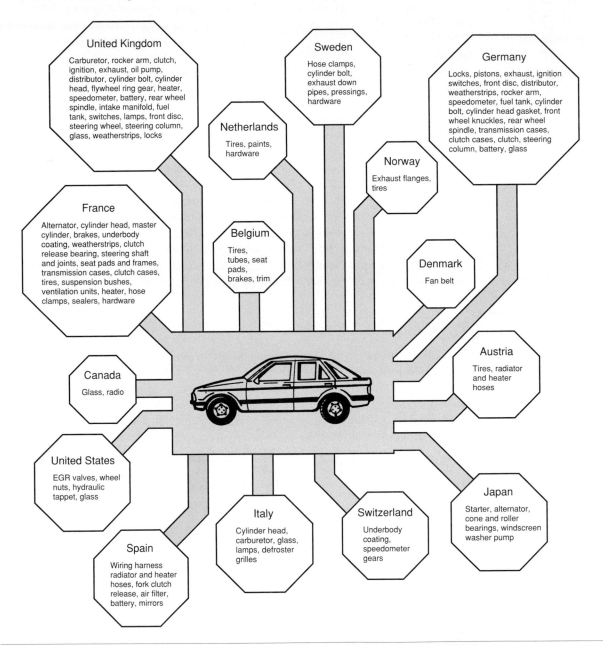

Note: Final assembly takes place in Halewood (United Kingdom) and Saarlouis (Germany).

Source: Peter Dicken, *Global Shift: Industrial Change in a Turbulent World* (London: Harper & Row, 1986), p. 304.

In a multidomestic industry, a global corporation's subsidiaries should be managed as distinct entities; that is, each subsidiary should be rather autonomous, having the authority to make independent decisions in response to local market conditions. Thus, the global strategy of such an industry is the sum of the strategies developed by subsidiaries operating in different countries. The primary difference between a domestic firm and a global firm competing in a multidomestic industry is that the latter makes decisions related to the countries in which it competes and to how it conducts business abroad.

Factors that increase the degree to which an industry is multidomestic include:[5]

The need for customized products to meet the tastes or preferences of local customers.

Fragmentation of the industry, with many competitors in each national market.

A lack of economies of scale in the functional activities of firms in the industry.

Distribution channels unique to each country.

A low technological dependence of subsidiaries on R&D provided by the global firm.

Global Industries

A global industry is one in which competition crosses national borders. In fact, it occurs on a worldwide basis. In such an industry, a firm's strategic moves in one country can be significantly affected by its competitive position in another country. The very rapidly expanding list of global industries includes commercial aircraft, automobiles, mainframe computers, and electronic consumer equipment. Many authorities are convinced that almost all product-oriented industries soon will be global. As a result, strategic management planning must be global for at least six reasons:

1. *The increased scope of the global management task.* Growth in the size and complexity of global firms made management virtually impossible without a coordinated plan of action detailing what is expected of whom during a given period. The common practice of management by exception is impossible without such a plan.

2. *The increased globalization of firms.* Three aspects of global business make global planning necessary: (1) differences among the environmental forces in different countries, (2) greater distances, and (3) the interrelationships of global operations.

3. *The information explosion.* It has been estimated that the world's stock of knowledge is doubling every 10 years. Without the aid of a formal plan, executives can no longer know all that they must know to solve the complex problems they face. A global planning process provides an ordered means for assembling, analyzing, and distilling the information required for sound decisions.

4. *The increase in global competition.* Because of the rapid increase in global competition, firms must constantly adjust to changing conditions or lose markets to competitors. The increase in global competition also spurs managements to search for methods of increasing efficiency and economy.

5. *The rapid development of technology.* Rapid technological development has shortened product life cycles. Strategic management planning is necessary to ensure the replacement of products that are moving into the maturity stage, with fewer sales and declining profits. Planning gives management greater control of all aspects of new product introduction.

6. *Strategic management planning breeds managerial confidence.* Like the motorist with a road map, managers with a plan for reaching their objectives know where they are going. Such a plan breeds confidence, because it spells out every step along the way and assigns responsibility for every task. The plan simplifies the managerial job.

A firm in a global industry must maximize its capabilities through a worldwide strategy. Such a strategy necessitates a high degree of centralized decision making in corporate headquarters so as to permit trade-off decisions across subsidiaries.

---

[5] Y. Doz and C. K. Prahalad, "Patterns of Strategic Control within Multinational Corporations," *Journal of International Business Studies*, Fall 1984, pp. 55–72.

Among the factors that make for the creation of a global industry are:

Economies of scale in the functional activities of firms in the industry.

A high level of R&D expenditures on products that require more than one market to recover development costs.

The presence in the industry of predominantly global firms that expect consistency of products and services across markets.

The presence of homogeneous product needs across markets, which reduces the requirement of customizing the product for each market. The presence of a small group of global competitors.

A low level of trade regulation and of regulation regarding foreign direction investment.[6]

The Multinational Challenge

Although industries can be characterized as global or multidomestic, few "pure" cases of either type exist. A global firm competing in a global industry must be responsive, to some degree, to local market conditions. Similarly, a global firm competing in a multidomestic industry cannot totally ignore opportunities to utilize intracorporate resources in competitive positioning. Thus, each global firm must decide which of its corporate functional activities should be performed where and what degree of coordination should exist among them.

Location and Coordination of Functional Activities

Typical functional activities of a firm include purchases of input resources, operations, research and development, marketing and sales, and after-sales service. A multinational corporation has a wide range of possible location options for each of these activities and must decide which sets of activities will be performed in how many and which locations. A multinational corporation may have each location perform each activity, or it may center an activity in one location to serve the organization worldwide. For example, research and development centered in one facility may serve the entire organization.

A multinational corporation also must determine the degree to which functional activities are to be coordinated across locations. Such coordination can be extremely low, allowing each location to perform each activity autonomously, or extremely high, tightly linking the functional activities of different locations. Coca-Cola tightly links its R&D and marketing functions worldwide to offer a standardized brand name, concentrate formula, market positioning, and advertising theme. However, its operations function is more autonomous, with the artificial sweetener and packaging differing across locations.

Location and Coordination Issues

Figure 4–4 presents some of the issues related to the critical dimensions of location and coordination in multinational strategic planning. It also shows the functional activities that the firm performs with regard to each of these dimensions. For example, in connection with the service function, a firm must decide where to perform after-sale service and whether to standardize such service.

How a particular firm should address location and coordination issues depends on the nature of its industry and on the type of international strategy that the firm is pursuing. As

---

[6] G. Harvel and C. K. Prahalad, "Managing Strategic Responsibility in the MNC," *Strategic Management Journal*, October–December 1983, pp. 341–51.

FIGURE 4–4

Location and Coordination Issues of Functional Activities

Functional Activity	Location Issues	Coordination Issues
Operations	Location of production facilities for components.	Networking of international plants.
Marketing	Product line selection. Country (market) selection.	Commonality of brand name worldwide. Coordination of sales to multinational accounts. Similarity of channels and product positioning worldwide. Coordination of pricing in different countries.
Service	Location of service organization.	Similarity of service standards and procedures worldwide.
Research and development	Number and location of R&D centers.	Interchange among dispersed R&D centers. Developing products responsive to market needs in many countries. Sequence of product introductions around the world.
Purchasing	Location of the purchasing function.	Managing suppliers located in different countries. Transferring market knowledge. Coordinating purchases of common items.

Source: Adapted from Michael E. Porter, "Changing Patterns of International Competition," *California Management Review*, Winter 1986, p. 18.

discussed earlier, an industry can be ranked along a continuum that ranges between multidomestic at one extreme and global at the other. Little coordination of functional activities across countries may be necessary in a multidomestic industry, since competition occurs within each country in such an industry. However, as its industry becomes increasingly global, a firm must begin to coordinate an increasing number of functional activities to effectively compete across countries.

Going global impacts every aspect of a company's operations and structure. As firms redefine themselves as global competitors, work forces are becoming increasingly diversified. The most significant challenge for firms, therefore, is the ability to adjust to a work force of varied cultures and lifestyles and the capacity to incorporate cultural differences to the benefit of the company's mission. Global Strategy in Action 4–5 illustrates Colgate-Palmolive's effort to become a truly global consumer products company, a vision that has impacted virtually every company function, including human resources.

International Strategy Options

Figure 4–5 presents the basic multinational strategy options that have been derived from a consideration of the location and coordination dimensions. Low coordination and geographic dispersion of functional activities are implied if a firm is operating in a multidomestic industry and has chosen a country-centered strategy. This allows each subsidiary to closely monitor the local market conditions it faces and to respond freely to these conditions.

High coordination and geographic concentration of functional activities result from the choice of a pure global strategy. Although some functional activities, such as after-sale

GLOBAL
STRATEGY IN
ACTION 4–5

COLGATE ALIGNS HR WITH ITS GLOBAL VISION

New York City–based Colgate-Palmolive Co. has a clear vision for its future: To become the best truly global consumer products company. This statement is telling. The few carefully chosen words demonstrate the commitment of this $7 billion firm to being more than a U.S.–based company that does business overseas. In the words of CEO Reuben Mark, taken from the company's 1992 annual report: "virtually every aspect of Colgate's business—from how we organize our operations to how we view new product development to how and where we manufacture—reflects our global orientation."

This global mindedness isn't a reaction to recent trends either. The company, which manages such internationally recognized brand-name products as Ajax, Fab, and Soft Soap, has been in 20 countries for more than 50 years, and in more than 50 countries for at least a decade. As far back as 30 years ago, Colgate created a global marketing training program to generate an international cadre of management.

Today, with operations in 75 countries and product distribution in at least 100 more, the company generates 64 percent of sales and 59 percent of operating profits overseas (Canada is included with the United States). As a consequence, two-thirds of the firm's employees now work outside of North America, providing strategic challenges for Colgate's human resources (HR) staff. More than ever before, they must ensure that the company attracts and retains *globalites*—those with the skills and interest to pursue international careers. And they must create systems for the fluid movement of workers across borders.

service, may need to be located in each market, tight control of those activities is necessary to ensure standardized performance worldwide. For example, IBM expects the same high level of marketing support and service for all of its customers, regardless of their location.

Two other strategy options are shown in Figure 4–5. High foreign investment with extensive coordination among subsidiaries would describe the choice of remaining at a particular growth stage, such as that of an exporter. Export-based strategy with decentralized marketing would describe the choice of moving toward globalization, which a multinational firm might make.

GLOBALIZATION OF THE COMPANY MISSION

Few strategic decisions bring about a more radical departure from the existing direction and operations of a firm than the decision to expand globally. Globalization subjects a firm to a radically different set of environmentally determined opportunities, constraints, and risks. To prevent these external factors from dictating the firm's direction, top management must reassess the firm's fundamental purpose, philosophy, and strategic intentions before globalization to ensure their continuation as decision criteria in proactive planning.

Expanding across national borders to secure new market or production opportunities initially may be viewed as consistent with the growth objectives outlined in a firm's existing mission statement. However, a firm's direction inherently is altered as globalization occurs.

continued

In 1991, HR met these challenges head on. Following an initiative by Mark to refocus the company's energies into five key business areas, the company formed a global human resources strategy team to better align HR with the business needs. The team was composed of senior line managers and senior HR leaders. "The objective of our global human resources strategy team was to work in partnership with management to build organizational excellence," says Brian Smith, director of global staffing and strategy. "We define organizational excellence here as the continuous alignment of Colgate people and business processes with vision, values, and strategies to become the best."

The year-long development process yielded: a set of international values that emphasize care for Colgate people, consumers, shareholders, and business partners; an order for all employees to work as part of a global team; and a commitment to continuous improvement. The team also developed strategic initiatives for generating, reinforcing, and sustaining organizational excellence. These initiatives' central feature was the development of recruitment, training, compensation, and recognition systems that reinforce the technical, managerial, and leadership competencies needed to support the global business.

The global human resources strategic team's work was unveiled at a week-long global HR conference in 1992. The conference was attended by the chairman, the president, the chief operating officer, each division's president, and more than 200 of Colgate's HR leaders representing 35 countries. Smith says that the senior leadership's commitment to this project was extraordinary, demonstrating HR's role as a key player in the company's global outlook.

For example, as a firm expands overseas, its operations are physically relocated in foreign operating environments. Since strategic decisions are made in the context of some understanding of the environment, management will absorb information from new sources into its planning processes as the environment becomes pluralistic, with a revised corporate direction as a probable and desirable result. Thus, before reconsidering the firm's strategic choices, management must reassess its mission and institute the required changes as the appropriate environmental information is defined, collected, analyzed, and integrated into existing databases.

Management also must provide a mission that continues to serve as a basis for evaluating strategic alternatives as this information is incorporated into the firm's decision-making processes. Consider the financial component of Zale Corporation's mission statement from this standpoint:

> Our ultimate responsibility is to our shareholders. Our goal is to earn an optimum return on invested capital through steady profit growth and prudent, aggressive asset management. The attainment of this financial goal, coupled with a record of sound management, represents our approach toward influencing the value placed on our common stock in the market.

From a U.S. perspective, this component seems quite reasonable. In a global context, however, it could be unacceptable. Corporate financial goals vary in different countries. The clear preference of French, Japanese, and Dutch executives has been to maximize growth in after-tax earnings, and that of Norwegian executives has been to maximize earnings before interest and taxes. In contrast, these executives have assigned a low priority to the maximization of stockholder wealth. Thus, from a global perspective, a mission

FIGURE 4–5
International Strategy Options

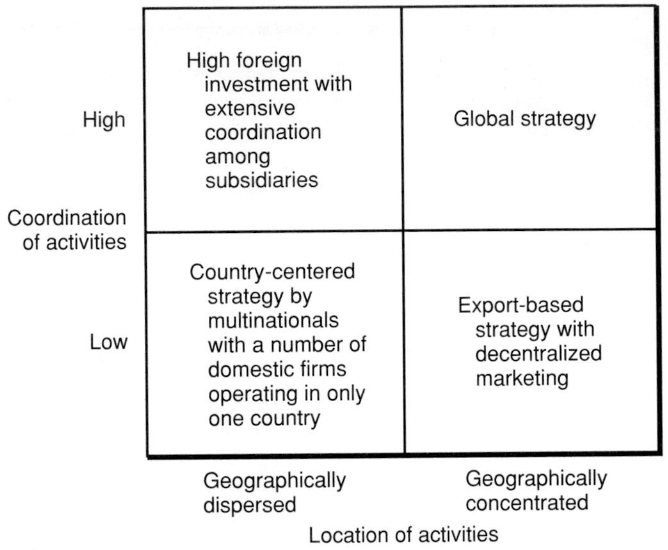

Source: Adapted from Michael E. Porter, "Changing Patterns of International Competition," *California Management Review*, Winter 1986, p. 19.

statement specifying that a firm's ultimate responsibility is to its stockholders may be an inappropriate basis for its financial operating philosophy. This example illustrates the critical need to review and revise the mission statement prior to global expansion so it will maintain its relevance in the new situations confronting the firm.

Components of the Company Mission Revisited

The mission statement must be revised to accommodate the changes in strategic decision making, corporate direction, and strategic alternatives mandated by globalization and must encompass the additional strategic capabilities that will result from globalizing operations. Therefore, each of its basic components needs to be analyzed in light of specific considerations that accompany globalization.

Product or Service, Market, and Technology

The mission statement defines the basic market need that the firm aims to satisfy. This definition is likely to remain essentially intact in the global corporation context, since competencies acquired in the firm's home country can be exploited as competitive advantages when they are transferred to other countries. However, confronted with a multiplicity of contexts, the firm must redefine its primary market to some extent.

The firm could define its market as global, which would necessitate standardization in product and company responses, or it could pursue a "market concept" orientation by focusing on the particular demands of each national market. The mission statement must provide a basis for strategic decision making in this trade-off situation. For example, the directive in Hewlett-Packard's mission statement, "HP customers must feel that they are dealing with one company with common policies and services," implies a standardized approach designed to provide comparable service to all customers. In contrast, Holiday Inn's mission statement reflects the marketing concept: "Basic to almost everything Holiday Inn, Inc., does is its interaction with its market, the consumer, and its consistent capacity to provide what the consumer wants, when, and where it is needed."

Company Goals: Survival, Growth, and Profitability

The mission statement specifies the firm's intention of securing its future through growth and profitability. In the United States, growth and profitability are considered essential to corporate survival. These goals also are acceptable in other countries supportive of the free enterprise system. Following global expansion, however, the firm may operate in countries that are not unequivocally committed to the profit motive. Many countries are committed to state ownership of industries that they view as critical to domestic prosperity. Austria, France, India, Italy, and Mexico are all good examples. A host country may view social welfare and development goals as taking precedence over the goals of free market capitalism. In developing countries, for example, employment and income distribution goals often take precedence over rapid economic growth.

Moreover, even countries that accept the profit motive may oppose the profit goals of global corporations. In such countries, the flow of global corporation profits often is viewed as unidirectional. At the extreme, the global is seen as a tool for exploiting the host country for the exclusive benefit of the parent company's home country, and its profits are regarded as evidence of corporate atrocities. This means that in a global context, a corporate commitment to profits may increase the risk of failure, rather than help secure survival.

Therefore, the mission statement of a global corporation must reflect the firm's intention of securing its survival through dimensions that extend beyond growth and profitability. A global corporation must develop a corporate philosophy that embodies its belief in a bidirectional flow of benefits among the firm and its multiple environments. The mission statement of Gulf & Western Americas Corporation expresses this view deftly: "We believe that in a developing country, revenue is inseparable from mandatory social responsibility and that a company is an integral part of the local and national community in which its activities are based." This statement maintains a commitment to profitability yet acknowledges the firm's responsibility to the host country.

The growth dimension of the mission statement remains closely tied to survival and profitability even in the global corporation context. Globalization disperses corporate resources and operations. This implies that strategic decision makers are no longer located exclusively at corporate headquarters, and that they are less accessible for participation in collective decision-making processes. To maintain the firm's cohesiveness in these circumstances, some mechanism is required to record its commitment to a unifying purpose. The mission statement can provide such a mechanism. It can provide the global corporation's decision makers with a common guiding thread of understanding and purpose.

Company Philosophy

Within the domestic setting, implicit understandings result in a general uniformity of corporate values and behavior even if a firm's philosophy goes unstated. Few domestic events challenge a firm to properly formulate and implement its implied or expressed philosophy. Globalization, however, is clearly such an event. A corporate philosophy developed from a singular perspective is inadequate for a firm that functions in variant cultures. A firm's values and beliefs are primarily culturally defined, reflecting the general philosophical perspective of the society in which the firm operates. Thus, when a firm extends its operations into another society, it encounters a new set of accepted corporate values and beliefs, which it must assimilate and incorporate into its own.

For example, numerous U.S. global corporations have been subjected to considerable criticism about the policies of their South African, Namibian, and Dominican Republic subsidiaries. In general, violations of corporate social responsibility pertaining to working standards have been alleged, not by coalitions within host countries but by coalitions within the United States, such as the Interfaith Center on Corporate Responsibility. Thus, if a global corporation tailors its values and beliefs to those of interest groups in various host countries, it will generate domestic opposition to which it must respond. Consequently, in adopting a company philosophy, a global corporation must recognize its accountability to such opposition.

Self-Concept

The globalized self-concept of a firm is dependent on management's understanding of the firm's strengths and weaknesses as a competitor in each of its operating arenas. The firm's ability to survive in multiple dynamic and highly competitive environments is severely limited if its management does not understand the impact it has or can have on those environments, and vice versa.

Public Image

Domestically, a firm's public image often is shaped from a marketing viewpoint. That image is managed as a marketing tool whose objective is customer acceptance of the firm's product. Although this consideration remains critical in the global environment, in that environment it must be balanced with consideration of other organizational claimants than the customer. In many countries, the global corporation is a major user of national resources and a major force in socialization processes. Thus, it must broaden its image so as to clearly convey its recognition of the additional internal and external claimants resulting from globalization. The following excerpt from Hewlett-Packard's mission statement exemplifies such an image: "As a corporation operating in many different communities throughout the world, we must assure ourselves that each of these communities is better for our presence . . . Each community has its particular set of social problems. Our company must help to solve these problems." These words convey an image of Hewlett-Packard's responsiveness to claimants throughout the world.

COMPETITIVE STRATEGIES FOR U.S. FIRMS IN FOREIGN MARKETS

Strategies for firms that are attempting to move toward globalization can be categorized by the degree of complexity of each foreign market being considered and by the diversity in a company's product line (see Figure 4–6).[7] Complexity refers to the number of critical success factors that are required to prosper in a given competitive arena. When a firm must consider many such factors, the requirements of success increase in complexity. Diversity, the second variable, refers to the breadth of a firm's business lines. When a company offers many product lines, diversity is high.

---

[7] Material in this section was developed in collaboration with Professors J. Kim DeDee, University of Wisconsin–Oskosh, and Shaker A. Zahra, Georgia State University.

FIGURE 4–6
International Strategy Options

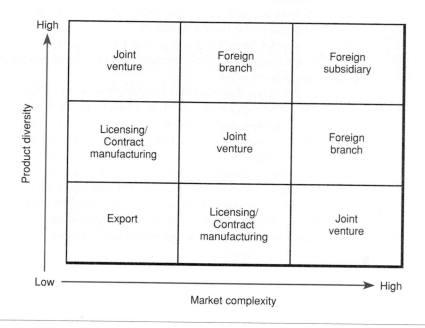

Together, the complexity and diversity dimensions form a continuum of possible strategic choices. Combining these two dimensions highlights many possible actions.

Niche Market Exporting

The primary niche market approach for the company that wants to export is to modify select product performance or measurement characteristics to meet special foreign demands. Combining product criteria from both the U.S. and the foreign markets can be slow and tedious. There are, however, a number of expansion techniques that provide the U.S. firm with the know-how to exploit opportunities in the new environment. For example, copying product innovations in countries where patent protection is not emphasized and utilizing nonequity contractual arrangements with a foreign partner can assist in rapid product innovation. N. V. Philips and various Japanese competitors, such as Sony and Matsushita, now are working together for common global product standards within their markets. Siemens, with a centralized R&D in electronics, also has been very successful with this approach.

Exporting usually requires minimal capital investment. The organization maintains its quality control standards over production processes and finished goods inventory, and risk to the survival of the firm is typically minimal. Additionally, the U.S. Commerce Department through its Export Now Program and related government agencies lowers the risks to smaller companies by providing export information and marketing advice.

Licensing/Contract Manufacturing

Establishing a contractual arrangement is the next step for U.S. companies that want to venture beyond exporting but are not ready for an equity position on foreign soil. Licensing involves the transfer of some industrial property right from the U.S. licensor to a motivated licensee. Most tend to be patents, trademarks, or technical know-how that are granted to the licensee for a specified time in return for a royalty and for avoiding tariffs or import quotas. Bell South and U.S. West, with various marketing and service competitive advantages valuable to Europe, have extended a number of licenses to create personal computer networks in the United Kingdom.

Another licensing strategy open to U.S. firms is to contract the manufacturing of its product line to a foreign company to exploit local comparative advantages in technology, materials, or labor.

U.S. firms that use either licensing option will benefit from lowering the risk of entry into the foreign markets. Clearly, alliances of this type are not for everyone. They are used best in companies large enough to have a combination of international strategic activities and for firms with standardized products in narrow margin industries.

Two major problems exist with licensing. One is the possibility that the foreign partner will gain the experience and evolve into a major competitor after the contract expires. The experience of some U.S. electronics firms with Japanese companies shows that licensees gain the potential to become powerful rivals. The other potential problem stems from the control that the licensor forfeits on production, marketing, and general distribution of its products. This loss of control minimizes a company's degrees of freedom as it reevaluates its future options.

Joint Ventures

As the multinational strategies of U.S. firms mature, most will include some form of joint venture (JV) with a target nation firm. AT&T followed this option in its strategy to produce its own personal computer by entering into several joint ventures with European producers to acquire the required technology and position itself for European expansion. Because JVs begin with a mutually agreeable pooling of capital, production or marketing equipment, patents, trademarks, or management expertise, they offer more permanent cooperative relationships than export or contract manufacturing.

Compared to full ownership of the foreign entity, JVs provide a variety of benefits to each partner. U.S. firms without the managerial or financial assets to make a profitable independent impact on the integrated foreign markets can share management tasks and cash requirements often at exchange rates that favor the dollar. The coordination of manufacturing and marketing allows ready access to new markets, intelligence data, and reciprocal flows of technical information.

For example, Siemens, the German electronics firm, has a wide range of strategic alliances throughout Europe to share technology and research developments. For years, Siemens grew by acquisitions, but now, to support its horizontal expansion objectives, it is engaged in joint ventures with companies like Groupe Bull of France, International Computers of Britain, General Electric Company of Britain, IBM, Intel, Philips, and Rolm. Another example is Airbus Industries, which produces wide-body passenger planes for the world market as a direct result of JVs among many companies in Britain, France, Spain, and Germany.

JVs speed up the efforts of U.S. firms to integrate into the political, corporate, and cultural infrastructure of the foreign environment, often with a lower financial commitment than acquiring a foreign subsidiary. General Electric's (GE) 3 percent share in the European lighting market was very weak and below expectations. Significant increases in competition throughout many of their American markets by the European giant, Philips Lighting, forced GE to retaliate by expanding in Europe. GE's first strategy was an attempted joint venture with the Siemens lighting subsidiary, Osram, and with the British electronics firm, Thorn EMI. Negotiations failed over control issues. When recent events in

Eastern Europe opened the opportunity for a JV with the Hungarian lighting manufacturer, Tungsram, which was receiving 70 percent of revenues from the West, GE capitalized on it.

Although joint ventures can address many of the requirements of complex markets and diverse product lines, U.S. firms considering either equity- or nonequity-based JVs face many challenges. For example, making full use of the native firm's comparative advantage may involve managerial relationships where no single authority exists to make strategic decisions or solve conflicts. Additionally, dealing with host-company management requires the disclosure of proprietary information and the potential loss of control over production and marketing quality standards. Addressing such challenges with well-defined covenants agreeable to all parties is difficult. Equally important is the compatibility of partners and their enduring commitments to mutually supportive goals. Without this compatibility and commitment, a joint venture is critically endangered.

Foreign Branching

A foreign branch is an extension of the company in its foreign market—a separately located strategic business unit directly responsible for fulfilling the operational duties assigned to it by corporate management, including sales, customer service, and physical distribution. Host countries may require that the branch be "domesticated"; that is, have some local managers in middle and upper-level positions. The branch most likely will be outside any U.S. legal jurisdiction, liabilities may not be restricted to the assets of the given branch, and business licenses for operations may be of short duration, requiring the company to renew them during changing business regulations.

Foreign Subsidiaries

Foreign subsidiaries are considered by companies that are willing and able to make the highest investment commitment to the foreign market. These companies insist on full ownership for reasons of control and managerial efficiency. Policy decisions about local product lines, expansion, profits, and dividends typically remain with the U.S. senior managers.

Fully owned subsidiaries can be started either from scratch or by acquiring established firms in the host country. U.S. firms can benefit significantly if the acquired company has complementary product lines or an established distribution or service network.

U.S. firms seeking to improve their competitive postures through a foreign subsidiary face a number of risks to their normal mode of operations. First, if the high capital investment is to be rewarded, managers must attain extensive knowledge of the market, the host nation's language, and its business culture. Second, the host country expects both a long-term commitment from the U.S. enterprise and a portion of their nationals to be employed in positions of management or operations. Fortunately, hiring or training foreign managers for leadership positions is commonly a good policy, since they are close to both the market and contacts. This is especially important for smaller firms when markets are regional. Third, changing standards mandated by foreign regulations may eliminate a company's protected market niche. Product design and worker protection liabilities also may extend back to the home office.

The strategies shown in Figure 4–6 are not mutually exclusive. For example, a firm may engage in any number of joint ventures while maintaining an export business. Additionally, there are a number of other strategies that a firm should consider before deciding on its long-term approach to foreign markets. These will be discussed in detail in Chapter 7 under the topic of grand strategies. However, the strategies discussed in this chapter provide the most popular starting points for planning the globalization of a firm.

SUMMARY

To understand the strategic planning options available to a corporation, its managers need to recognize that different types of industry-based competition exist. Specifically, they must identify the position of their industry along the global versus multidomestic continuum and then consider the implications of that position for their firm.

The differences between global and multidomestic industries about the location and coordination of functional corporate activities necessitate differences in strategic emphasis. As an industry becomes global, managers of firms within that industry must increase the coordination and concentration of functional activities.

The appendix at the end of this chapter lists many components of the environment with which global corporations must contend. This list is useful in understanding the issues that confront global corporations and in evaluating the thoroughness of global corporation strategies.

As a starting point for global expansion, the firm's mission statement needs to be reviewed and revised. As global operations fundamentally alter the direction and strategic capabilities of a firm, its mission statement, if originally developed from a domestic perspective, must be globalized.

The globalized mission statement provides the firm with a unity of direction that transcends the divergent perspectives of geographically dispersed managers. It provides a basis for strategic decisions in situations where strategic alternatives may appear to conflict. It promotes corporate values and commitments that extend beyond single cultures and satisfies the demands of the firm's internal and external claimants in different countries. Finally, it ensures the survival of the global corporation by asserting the global corporation's legitimacy with respect to support coalitions in a variety of operating environments.

Movement of a firm toward globalization often follows a systematic pattern of development. Commonly, businesses begin their foreign nation involvements progressively through niche market exporting, license-contract manufacturing, joint ventures, foreign branching, and foreign subsidiaries.

QUESTIONS FOR DISCUSSION

1. How does environmental analysis at the domestic level differ from global analysis?
2. Which factors complicate environmental analysis at the global level? Which factors are making such analysis easier?
3. Do you agree with the suggestion that soon all industries will need to evaluate global environments?
4. Which industries operate almost devoid of global competition? Which inherent immunities do they enjoy?

BIBLIOGRAPHY

Adler, N. J., and S. Bartholomew. "Managing Globally Competent People." *Academy of Management Executive* (August 1992), pp. 52–65.

Allio, R. J. "Formulating Global Strategy." *Planning Review* (March–April 1989), pp. 22–29.

Banks, Philip, and Ganesh Natarajan. "India: The New Asian Tiger." *Business Horizons* 38, no. 3 (May–June 1995), p. 47.

Beaver, William. "Levi's Is Leaving China." *Business Horizons* 38, no. 2 (March–April 1995), p. 35.

Bolt, J. F. "Global Competitors: Some Criteria for Success." *Business Horizons* (May–June 1988), pp. 62–72.

Calantone, R. J., and C. A. di Benedetto. "Defensive Marketing in Globally Competitive Industrial Markets." *Columbia Journal of World Business* (Fall 1988), pp. 3–14.

Chankin, W., and R. A. Mauborgne. "Becoming an Effective Global Competitor." *Journal of Business Strategy* (January–February 1988), pp. 33–37.

Chaponniere, J. R., and M. Lautier. "Breaking into the Korean Market—Invest or License?" *Long-Range Planning* 28, no. 1 (February 1995), p. 104.

Chilton, Kenneth. "How American Manufacturers Are Facing the Global Marketplace." *Business Horizons* 38, no. 4 (July–August 1995), p. 10.

Copeland, T.; T. Koller; and J. Murrin. "How to Value a Multinational Business." *Planning Review* (May–June 1990), pp. 16–25.

Cox, T., Jr. "The Multicultural Organization." *Academy of Management Executive* (May 1991), pp. 34–47.

Edmunds, John C. "The Multinational as an Engine of Value." *Business Horizons* 38, no. 4 (July–August 1995), p. 5.

Fagan, M. L. "A Guide to Global Sourcing." *The Journal of Business Strategy* (March–April 1991), pp. 21–25.

Franko, L. G. "Global Corporate Competition: Who's Winning, Who's Losing, and the R&D Factor as One Reason Why." *Strategic Management Journal* (September–October 1989), pp. 449–74.

Friedmann, R., and J. Kim. "Political Risk and International Marketing." *Columbia Journal of World Business* (Fall 1988), pp. 63–74.

Gomes-Casseres, B. "Joint Ventures in the Face of Global Competition." *Sloan Management Review* (Spring 1989), pp. 17–26.

Heenan, D. A. "Global Strategy: Why the U.S. Government Should Go to Bat for Business." *The Journal of Business Strategy* (March–April 1990), pp. 46–49.

———. "Global Strategy: The End of Centralized Power." *The Journal of Business Strategy* (March–April 1991), pp. 46–49.

Hitt, Michael A.; Beverly B. Tyler; Camilla Hardel; and Daewoo Park. "Understanding Strategic Intent in the Global Marketplace." *The Academy of Management Executive* 9, no. 2 (May 1995), p. 12.

Hordes, Mark W.; J. Anthony Clancy; and Julie Baddaley. "A Primer for Global Start-Ups." *The Academy of Management Executive* 9, no. 2 (May 1995), p. 7.

Hu, Y. S. "Global or Stateless Corporations Are National Firms with International Operations." *California Management Review* (Winter 1992), pp. 107–26.

Hu, Yao-Su. "The International Transferability of Competitive Advantage." *California Management Review* 37, no. 4 (Summer 1995), p. 73.

James, B. "Reducing the Risks of Globalization." *Long-Range Planning* (February 1990), pp. 80–88.

Johnston, W. B. "Global Work Force 2000: The New World Labor Market." *Harvard Business Review* (March–April 1991), pp. 115–29.

Kanter, Rosabeth Moss. "Thriving Locally in the Global Economy." *Harvard Business Review* 73, no. 5 (September–October 1995), p. 151.

Kester, W. C. "Global Players, Western Tactics, Japanese Outcomes: The New Japanese Market for Corporate Control." *California Management Review* (Winter 1991), pp. 58–70.

Koepfler, E. R. "Strategic Options for Global Market Players." *Journal of Business Strategy* (July–August 1989), pp. 46–50.

Kuhn, R. L. "Japanese-American Strategic Alliances." *Journal of Business Strategy* (March–April 1989), pp. 51–53.

Lasserre, Philippe. "Corporate Strategies for the Asia Pacific." *Long-Range Planning* 28, no. 1 (February 1995), p. 13.

Levy, B. "Korean and Taiwanese Firms as International Competitors." *Columbia Journal of World Business* (Spring 1988), pp. 43–51.

Luthans, Fred; Richard R. Patrick; and Brett C. Luthans. "Doing Business in Central and Eastern Europe: Political, Economic, and Cultural Diversity." *Business Horizons* 38, no. 5 (September–October 1995), p. 9.

Maruyama, M. "Changing Dimensions in International Business." *Academy of Management Executive* (August 1992), pp. 88–96.

Metzger, R. O., and A. Ginsburg. "Lessons from Japanese Global Acquisitions." *Journal of Business Strategy* (May–June 1989), pp. 32–36.

Ohmal, Kenschi. "Putting Global Logic First." *Harvard Business Review* 73, no. 1 (January–February 1995), p. 119.

O'Reilly, A. J. F. "Leading a Global Strategic Charge." *The Journal of Business Strategy* (July–August 1991), pp. 10–13.

Reich, R. B. "Who Is Them?" *Harvard Business Review*, (March–April 1991), pp. 77–89.

Reilly, Tom. "The Harmonization of Standards in the European Union and the Impact on U.S. Business." *Business Horizons* 38, no. 2 (March–April 1995), p. 28.

Reynolds, A. "Competitiveness and the 'Global Capital Shortage.' " Business Horizons (November–December 1991), pp. 23–26.

Sera, K. "Corporate Globalization: A New Trend." *Academy of Management Executive* (February 1992), pp. 89–96.

Shama, Avraham. "Entry Strategies of U.S. Firms to the Former Soviet Bloc and Eastern Europe." *California Management Review* 37, no. 3 (Spring 1995), p. 90.

Shetty, Y. K. "Strategies for U.S. Competitiveness: A Survey of Business Leaders." *Business Horizons* (November–December 1991), pp. 43–48.

Sugiura, H. "How Honda Localizes Its Global Strategy." *Sloan Management Review* (Fall 1990), pp. 77–82.

Von Glinow, Mary Ann, and Linda Clarke. "Vietnam: Tiger or Kitten?" *Academy of Management Executive* 9, no. 4 (November 1995), p. 35.

Williamson, P. "Successful Strategies for Export." *Long Range Planning* (February 1991), pp. 57–63.

Yip, G. S., and G. A. Coundouriotis. "Diagnosing Global Strategy Potential: The World Chocolate Confectionery Industry." *Planning Review* (January–February 1991), pp. 4–15.

COMPONENTS OF THE MULTINATIONAL ENVIRONMENT

Multinational firms must operate within an environment that has numerous components. These components include:

I. Government, laws, regulations, and policies of home country (United States, for example).
   A. Monetary and fiscal policies and their effect on price trends, interest rates, economic growth, and stability.
   B. Balance-of-payments policies.
      1. Mandatory controls on direct investment.
      2. Interest equalization tax and other policies.
   C. Commercial policies, especially tariffs, quantitative import restrictions, and voluntary import controls.
   D. Export controls and other restrictions on trade.
   E. Tax policies and their impact on overseas business.
   F. Antitrust regulations, their administration, and their impact on international business.
   G. Investment guarantees, investment surveys, and other programs to encourage private investments in less-developed countries.
   H. Export-import and government export expansion programs.
   I. Other changes in government policy that affect international business.
II. Key political and legal parameters in foreign countries and their projection.
   A. Type of political and economic system, political philosophy, national ideology.
   B. Major political parties, their philosophies, and their policies.
   C. Stability of the government.
      1. Changes in political parties.
      2. Changes in governments.
   D. Assessment of nationalism and its possible impact on political environment and legislation.
   E. Assessment of political vulnerability.
      1. Possibilities of expropriation.
      2. Unfavorable and discriminatory national legislation and tax laws.
      3. Labor laws and problems.
   F. Favorable political aspects.
      1. Tax and other concessions to encourage foreign investments.
      2. Credit and other guarantees.
   G. Differences in legal system and commercial law.
   H. Jurisdiction in legal disputes.
   I. Antitrust laws and rules of competition.
   J. Arbitration clauses and their enforcement.
   K. Protection of patents, trademarks, brand names, and other industrial property rights.
III. Key economic parameters and their projection.
   A. Population and its distribution by age groups, density, annual percentage increase, percentage of working age, percentage of total in agriculture, and percentage in urban centers.

B. Level of economic development and industrialization.

C. Gross national product, gross domestic product, or national income in real terms and also on a per capita basis in recent years and projections over future planning period.

D. Distribution of personal income.

E. Measures of price stability and inflation, wholesale price index, consumer price index, other price indexes.

F. Supply of labor, wage rates.

G. Balance-of-payments equilibrium or disequilibrium, level of international monetary reserves, and balance-of-payments policies.

H. Trends in exchange rates, currency stability, evaluation of possibility of depreciation of currency.

I. Tariffs, quantitative restrictions, export controls, border taxes, exchange controls, state trading, and other entry barriers to foreign trade.

J. Monetary, fiscal, and tax policies.

K. Exchange controls and other restrictions on capital movements, repatriation of capital, and remission of earnings.

IV. Business system and structure.

A. Prevailing business philosophy: mixed capitalism, planned economy, state socialism.

B. Major types of industry and economic activities.

C. Numbers, size, and types of firms, including legal forms of business.

D. Organization: proprietorship, partnerships, limited companies, corporations, cooperatives, state enterprises.

E. Local ownership patterns: public and privately held corporations, family-owned enterprises.

F. Domestic and foreign patterns of ownership in major industries.

G. Business managers available: their education, training, experience, career patterns, attitudes, and reputations.

H. Business associations and chambers of commerce and their influence.

I. Business codes, both formal and informal.

J. Marketing institutions: distributors, agents, wholesalers, retailers, advertising agencies, advertising media, marketing research, and other consultants.

K. Financial and other business institutions: commercial and investment banks, other financial institutions, capital markets, money markets, foreign exchange dealers, insurance firms, engineering companies.

L. Managerial processes and practices with respect to planning, administration, operations, accounting, budgeting, and control.

V. Social and cultural parameters and their projections.

A. Literacy and educational levels.

B. Business, economic, technical, and other specialized education available.

C. Language and cultural characteristics.

D. Class structure and mobility.

E. Religious, racial, and national characteristics.

F. Degree of urbanization and rural-urban shifts.

G. Strength of nationalistic sentiment.

H. Rate of social change.

I. Impact of nationalism on social and institutional change.

CHAPTER 4 COHESION CASE ILLUSTRATION

THE GLOBAL ENVIRONMENT AND THE COCA-COLA COMPANY

Roberto Goizueta has made it clear that, while Coca-Cola may have its corporate headquarters in the United States, Coca-Cola is an international corporation, rather than a U.S. company with a sizable international business. Table 1 provides per capita consumption of Coca-Cola's soft-drink products in selected countries in 1994. Domestic per capita consumption is way ahead, while also suggesting the future opportunities in other countries where Coke is already strong. By 1995, over 80 percent of Coca-Cola's net revenues from soft drinks were generated outside the United States, as was a whopping 85 percent of its operating profits from soft drinks. Yes, Coca-Cola is certainly a global company. And as Mr. Goizueta claims, it may well be "the only truly global business system" in the 1990s. Recent comments by Mr. Goizueta further explain how Coca-Cola views the global environment:

> Geographic diversity not only helps insulate us from the sputters every economy inevitably endures, it also makes it impossible for us to miss out on the growth spurts—wherever those growth spurts may be.
>
> When an isolated downturn occurs in one of our markets, literally dozens more help take up the slack. When opportunities arise, we stand poised to seize them.
>
> Mexico serves as a timely example. When the sharp devaluation of the peso occurred, most companies ran for cover. Not us, because we view adversity as an opportunity for disciplined companies to shine. And through our long-term investment program in Mexico, we're doing just that. Even now, as the impact of the peso's devaluation continues, our volume and share of industry case sales in Mexico continue to climb.
>
> Our muscle, of course, comes from leading-edge markets such as the United States, Germany, and Japan, all of which generate substantial cash to help fuel our growth.
>
> Our growth potential comes not only from new and rapidly emerging markets such as China, India, East Central Europe, and Russia, but also from our established markets, which offer abundant opportunities for growth.

Fundamental to global growth of the sales of Coca-Cola's products is the need for local and regional bottlers within each country (almost 200 countries by 1996) that will bottle and distribute soft-drink products. Consistent with Figure 4–6 in this chapter, Coca-Cola (low product diversity and high market diversity) has used joint venturing with bottling partners as its major strategy for entering and dominating global markets. The percentage of Coca-Cola's investment in any country's bottler(s) depends on regulations in that country regarding foreign ownership, as well as the capital requirements of prospective bottling partners and the extent to which peculiarities exist within the country's retail distribution practices. Their resulting ownership of key, worldwide bottling operations are shown in the figure, "Worldwide Bottling Investments," on page 133. In just 10 years, Coca-Cola had invested over $2.5 billion in about 41 bottling and canning operations around the world. They ranged from joint ventures to minority positions in public companies to company-owned bottlers. Perhaps more important, this reversed a historical "hands off" approach, allowing Coca-Cola to help capitalize the direct efforts to build retail sales. We will examine this posture more in the Chapter 10 Cohesion Case.

Strategic bottling investments and aggressive marketing have made the Coca-Cola Company's global presence change drastically, as conveyed in Table 2. Since 1984, Coke has solidified a presence in all but 20 countries around the globe.

TABLE 1

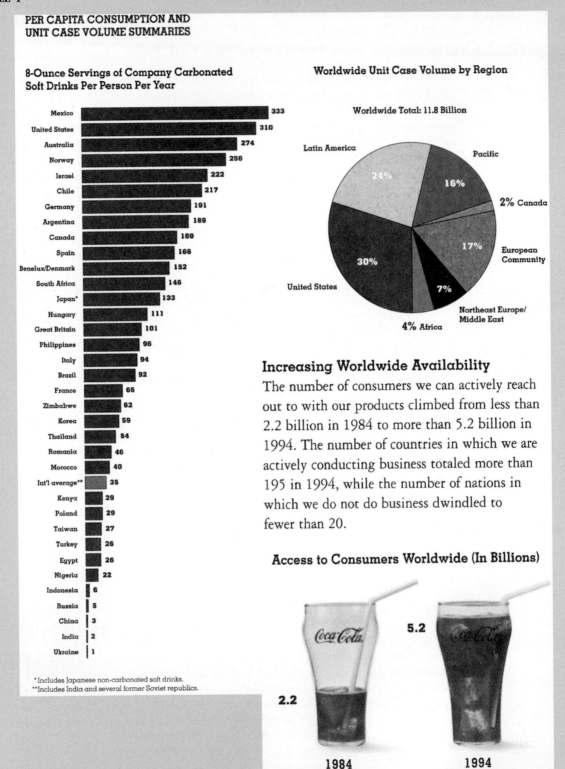

PER CAPITA CONSUMPTION AND UNIT CASE VOLUME SUMMARIES

8-Ounce Servings of Company Carbonated Soft Drinks Per Person Per Year

Mexico	333
United States	310
Australia	274
Norway	256
Israel	222
Chile	217
Germany	191
Argentina	189
Canada	169
Spain	166
Benelux/Denmark	152
South Africa	146
Japan*	133
Hungary	111
Great Britain	101
Philippines	96
Italy	94
Brazil	92
France	65
Zimbabwe	62
Korea	59
Thailand	54
Romania	46
Morocco	40
Int'l average**	35
Kenya	29
Poland	29
Taiwan	27
Turkey	26
Egypt	26
Nigeria	22
Indonesia	6
Russia	5
China	3
India	2
Ukraine	1

* Includes Japanese non-carbonated soft drinks.
**Includes India and several former Soviet republics.

Worldwide Unit Case Volume by Region

Worldwide Total: 11.8 Billion

- Latin America 24%
- Pacific 16%
- 2% Canada
- European Community 17%
- Northeast Europe/Middle East 7%
- 4% Africa
- United States 30%

Increasing Worldwide Availability

The number of consumers we can actively reach out to with our products climbed from less than 2.2 billion in 1984 to more than 5.2 billion in 1994. The number of countries in which we are actively conducting business totaled more than 195 in 1994, while the number of nations in which we do not do business dwindled to fewer than 20.

Access to Consumers Worldwide (In Billions)

2.2 — 1984

5.2 — 1994

Worldwide

Bottling Investments

NCCB 30%
(Netherlands)

Essen CBO 100%
Göttingen CBO 100%
Frankfurt Bottler 44%
Eastern Germany CBO 100%
Cologne CBO 80%
West Berlin CBO 100%
Düsseldorf Bottler 30%

Brussels Bottler 28%
Belgium CBO 100%
(Brugge/Hasselt/Aalst)

Coca-Cola
New York 53%

France CBO 100%

Brucephil 29%

Coca-Cola Beverages 49%
(Canada)

Coca-Cola &
Schweppes
Beverages 49%

Refresca AG 33%
(Switzerland)

Hainan 25%
Tianjin Bottler 50%
(China)

Coca-Cola
Consolidated
30%

Taiwan Bottling
Company 34%

Coca-Cola
Enterprises 44%

Swire Bottlers
(Hong Kong)
14%

Coca-Cola
Philippines 30%

Grupo Continental 11%
(Mexico)

Industria de Cafe 37%
(Guatemala)

BONAGUI
(Guinea)
44%

ANSAN 88%
MAKSAN 100%
(Turkey)

Industrias Roman 20%
(Colombia)

IAWC
(Egypt) 100%

Jakarta
Bottler 29%

Refrescos
do Brasil 13%
(Brazil)

Nairobi CBO 77%

Coca-Cola
Amatil 51%

Coca-Cola S.A. 100%
Inti S.A. 57%
(Argentina)

Montevideo
Refrescos 55%
(Uruguay)

Zambia Bottlers Ltd.
100%

Thai Pure
Drinks Ltd.
44%

Bucharest
CBO 51%

Milan CBO 100%
Rome CBO 100%
Turin CBO 100%
Piacenza CBO 100%

TABLE 2
The Coca-Cola Company's Expanding Global Presence

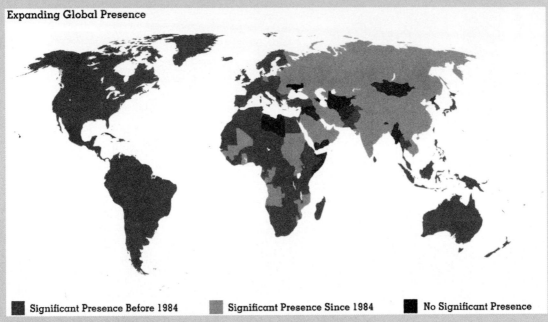

Expanding Global Presence

■ Significant Presence Before 1984   ■ Significant Presence Since 1984   ■ No Significant Presence

Trends in global markets, while impressive, are beginning to present Coca-Cola with some challenges. Consider the following two examples, one from Eastern Europe and another from Japan:

TOKYO—Tomiichi Murayama, Japan's Socialist prime minister, has been saying all the right things about deregulation. But of course everybody in Japan now favors deregulation—some just want it slower than others. That's why foreign marketers are better off putting their faith in Isao Nakauchi.

Mr. Nakauchi's Daiei department-store chain is groaning under a heavy load of debt, and that has helped motivate the maverick retailer to take on his country's brand-name cartels. In the process, he's offering Japan's consumers a better deal.

Specifically, Mr. Nakauchi has been driving pins into the Coca-Cola folks, who've had their markets locked up for decades and have gouged the Japanese mercilessly. Coke shows that Japan isn't closed to Western companies, just as long as they're willing to front the money to play by the same rules as Japanese firms. That means investing heavily in the capacity and troops to make and distribute your product locally—and to freeze out potential competitors.

Coke runs 17 bottling plants in Japan, including the world's biggest in Tokyo. Like any good Japanese giant—Coke controls 90% of Japan's cola market—it uses its clout to punish mom-and-pop retailers who dare to place a rival on the shelves.

It dawned on Mr. Nakauchi that Japanese consumers probably weren't thrilled to pay the equivalent of $1.10, even for "the real thing." He's begun importing a no-name Canadian cola, pasting on the Daiei label and selling pop for the equivalent of 39 cents a pop. That he has a big success on his hands is clear from Coke's response last week. The company announced plans to import Coca-Cola Classic from North America to compete with its own high-cost Japanese bottlers. The imported brew will sell for about 40% less.

Coke isn't happy about this, as indeed other entrenched U.S. companies in Japan aren't happy about the coming of a freer market. You won't notice Procter & Gamble, NCR and other such companies cheering deregulation from the rooftops. They've invested millions in doing things the Japanese way, and now the Japanese way is becoming obsolete.

BUDAPEST—Sitting at an outdoor cafe overlooking the Danube in the Hungarian capital, Istvan Fischer breaks into a smile as he picks up a glass of Coca-Cola.

"I drank my first Coke in 1963, in Vienna, and my hands trembled," says Mr. Fischer, a 69-year-old pensioner. "I was afraid because the Communists told us that Coca-Cola was an intoxicating potion that left people in a stupor."

Today, Eastern Europeans are guzzling soda after decades of a Western soft-drink drought. That's because a battle raging between those icons of American consumer culture, Coca-Cola and Pepsi, has filled shop shelves to overflowing. Since the collapse of communism in 1989, the two companies have been bent on capturing the markets of Eastern Europe, pouring a total of $2 billion into the region to modernize production and distribution facilities.

After just a few years, Coke, Pepsi and a slew of other cola brands can be found not only in Budapest and Warsaw, but also along the back roads to remote Transylvanian towns and secluded villages from Bohemia to central Bulgaria.

Yet the skirmish for this largely untapped market is just now reaching a fever pitch. After years of clashes in which Coca-Cola Co. emerged as the clear winner, PepsiCo Inc. is striking back.

The payoff could be huge, officials from both companies predict. Like China and India, Eastern Europe is a premier emerging market, they note, with more than 300 million consumers. Analysts forecast as many as two decades of dramatic growth in Eastern Europe before it levels off.

5

ENVIRONMENTAL FORECASTING

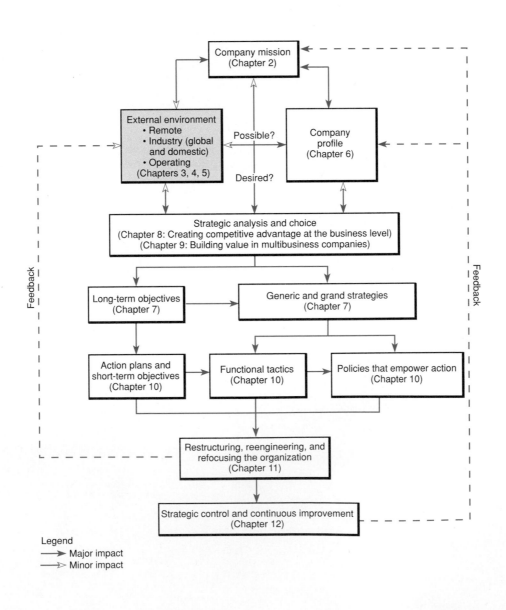

Legend
→ Major impact
⟶▷ Minor impact

IMPORTANCE OF FORECASTING

Change is occurring rapidly, and even greater changes and challenges are forecast for the year 2000. The crucial responsibility for managers will be ensuring their firm's capacity for survival. This will be done by anticipating and adapting to environmental changes in ways that provide new opportunities for growth and profitability. The impact of changes in the remote industry and task environments must be understood and predicted.

Even large firms in established industries will be actively involved in transitions. The $5.5 billion loss in the U.S. auto industry in the early 1980s is a classic example of what can happen when firms fail to place a priority on environmental forecasting. The preceding decade saw a 20 percent penetration of the U.S. new car market by foreign competition, a nation-crippling oil embargo, rapidly climbing fuel prices, and uncertain future supplies of crude oil. Yet the long-range implications of these predictable factors on future auto sales were largely ignored by U.S. automakers. Because it was not open to changes in technology, Detroit was left without viable, fuel-efficient, quality alternatives for the American market. On the other hand, Japanese automakers anticipated the future need for fuel efficiency, quality, and service through careful market research and environmental forecasting. As a result, they gained additional market share at Detroit's expense.

In retaliation, American automakers spent $80 billion over a three-year period on product and capital-investment strategies that were meant to recapture their lost market share. They realized that success in strategic decisions rests not solely on dollar amounts but also on anticipation of and preparation for the future.

Accurate forecasting of changing elements in the environment is an essential part of strategic management. Forecasting the business environment for the 1990s led many firms to diversify. For example, USX Corporation (formerly U.S. Steel) purchased Marathon Oil so as to have a profit generator whose proceeds could be used to turn USX into a low-cost steel producer. Similarly, predicting future demand for new products is an arduous process. As Strategy in Action 5–1 suggests, the accuracy of new product forecasts can be critically important.

Other firms have forecast a need for massive retrenchment. One such firm is IBM, which laid off 40,000 employees in 1991–92 and another 25,000 employees in 1993 to streamline its cost of doing business. Still other firms have cut back in one area of operations to underwrite growth in another. For example, CBS sold its records division to Sony for $2 billion to raise the capital it needed for its planned expansion in television stations in the 1990s.

These and many other examples indicate that strategic managers need to develop skills in predicting significant environmental changes. To aid in the search for future opportunities and constraints, they should take the following steps:

1. Select the environmental variables that are critical to the firm.
2. Select the sources of significant environmental information.
3. Evaluate forecasting techniques.
4. Integrate forecast results into the strategic management process.
5. Monitor the critical aspects of managing forecasts.

SELECT CRITICAL ENVIRONMENTAL VARIABLES

Management experts have argued that an important cause of the turbulent business environment is the change in population structure and dynamics. This change, in turn, produced other major changes in the economic, social, and political environments.

FORECASTING DEMAND FOR NEW PRODUCTS ALWAYS DIFFICULT

The major new project of the 90s, the so-called information superhighway, is developing rapidly. One sure sign is the increasing frequency of reported misuse for stock swindles, assorted sexual solicitations, slanderous communications, and other undesirable traffic.

When the Haloid company developed the dry-process copier in the later 1950s, it retained Stewart, Dougall & Associates, a now-defunct research and consulting firm, to estimate market potential and assist in developing market strategy. A common initial reaction to the product concept was that it seemed like a good idea that could replace some then-current methods like thermography because of the better appearance and durability of its plain-paper copies. The forecast seemed unbelievably high and turned out to be a serious underestimate.

It is difficult to project uses that go beyond replacements of current use and beyond the needs currently anticipated by potential users, even assuming that all potential users have been correctly identified. A little earlier, the same firm had forecast demand for another new product, polyethylene film; this forecast also turned out to be far short of reality.

The main obstacle to the prediction of demand is our limited vision. It is hard for us to realize how severely we are hemmed in by assumptions of the persistence of current patterns. Because early xerography equipment turned out relatively expensive copies compared to the mimeograph and multigraph, few analysts foresaw that it would virtually eliminate their use, and even affect traditional printing.

We tend to resist the notion of great supply-driven demand growth. It smacks of hucksterism that runs counter to the traditionally desirable posture of conservatism in forecasting and in research generally. This conservative posture has a severe downside, a risk of underestimation resulting in opportunity loss.

A closely related risk is failure to recognize problems that may arise, such as undesirable uses. In the last century, the great advantages offered by dynamite in mining and construction obscured realization of its destructive potential. Similarly, the information superhighway's potential for misuse, while realized by some, could not compete with the enthusiastic media hype of its benefits.

Anyone trying to forecast new-product demand should be well aware of the trade-off between the optimistic and the conservative views. That trade-off should be carefully modulated in accordance with the relative risks involved, an assessment that requires close cooperation of top management. After all, the company's future may depend on it.

There is no such thing as objectivity when we try to look into the future, except in data collection. The decision as to what data to collect, how to collect them, and how to interpret them cannot be objective, no matter how hard we try and it shouldn't be.

Source: "Forecasting Demand for New Products Always Difficult," by Thomas T. Semon, *Marketing News*, March 27, 1995, p. 10. Reprinted by permission of the American Marketing Association.

Historically, population shifts tended to occur over 40–50 year periods and, therefore, had little relevance to business decisions. During the second half of the 20th century, however, population changes have become radical, erratic, contradictory, and, therefore, of great importance.

For example, the U.S. baby boom between 1945 and the mid-1960s has had and will have a dramatic impact on all parts of society—from maternity wards and schools to the labor force and the marketplace. This population bulge is facing heavy competition for jobs, promotions, and housing, despite a highest-ever educational level. Compounding the problem are the heightened expectations of women and of racial minorities. The lack of high-status jobs to fit these expectations poses a potential impetus for major social and

FIGURE 5–1
The New Work Force

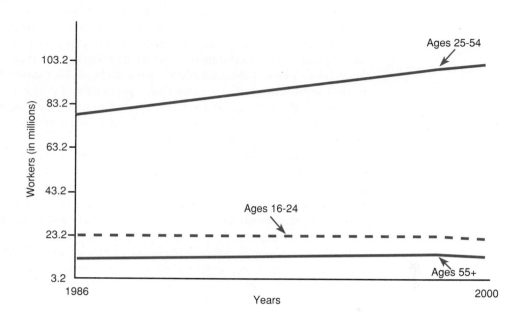

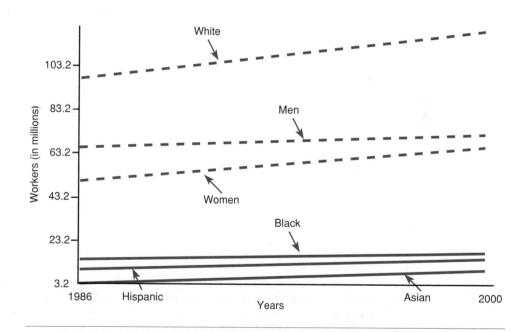

Source: *American Demographics*

economic changes. In addition, an increasingly aging labor force finds it difficult to give up status, power, and employment when retirement programs are either not financially attractive or not available at the traditional age of 65. (See Figure 5–1 for work force projections through the year 2000.)

Obviously, the demands of these groups will have important effects on social and political changes in terms of lifestyle, consumption patterns, and political decisions. In economic terms, the size and potential affluence of these groups suggest increasing markets for housing, consumer products, and leisure goods and services.

Interestingly, the same shifts in population, life expectancy, and education have occurred in many developed nations. However, developing nations face the opposite population configurations. Although birthrates have declined, high survival rates resulting from medical improvements have created a large population of people who are reaching adulthood in the 1990s. Jobs and food are expected to be in short supply. Therefore, many developing countries will face severe social and political instability unless they can find appropriate work for their surplus labor.

The rates of population increase obviously can be of great importance, as indicated by the contrasting effects forecast above. If a growing population has sufficient purchasing power, new markets will be developed to satisfy its needs. However, too much growth in a country with a limited amount of resources or a drastic inequity in their distribution may result in major social and political upheavals that pose substantial risks for businesses.

If forecasting were as simple as predicting population trends, strategic managers would only need to examine census data to predict future markets. But economic interpretations are more complex. Population statistics are complicated by migration rates; mobility trends; birth, marriage, and death rates; and racial, ethnic, and religious structures. In addition, resource development and its political use in this interdependent world further confuse the problem—as evidenced by the actions of some of the oil states (e.g., Saudi Arabia, Iraq, Libya, and Kuwait). Changes in political situations, technology, or culture add further complications.

Domestically, the turbulence is no less severe. Continually changing products and services, changing competitors, uncertain government priorities, rapid social change, and major technological innovations all add to the complexity of planning for the future. To grow, to be profitable, and at times even to survive in this turbulent world, a firm needs sensitivity, commitment, and skill in recognizing and predicting these variables that will most profoundly affect its future.

Who Selects the Key Variables?

Although executives or committees in charge of planning may assist in obtaining the forecast data, the responsibility for environmental forecasting usually lies with top management. This is the case at the Sun (Oil) Company, where responsibility for the firm's long-range future is assigned to the chairman and vice chairman of the board of directors. A key duty of the vice chairman is environmental assessment. In this context, environment refers not to air, water, and land but rather to the general business setting created by the economic, technological, political, social, and ecological forces in which Sun plans to operate.

The environmental assessment group consists of Sun's chief economist, a specialist in technological assessment, and a public issues consultant—who all report to the vice president of environmental assessment. The chief economist evaluates and forecasts the state of the economy; the technological assessment specialist covers technology and science; and the public issues consultant concentrates on politics and society.

However, headquarters may lack the capability and proficiency needed to analyze political, economic, and social variables around the world. Therefore, on-the-spot personnel, outside consultants, or company task forces may be assigned to assist in forecasting.

What Variables Should Be Selected?

A list of the key variables that will have make-or-break consequences for the firm must be developed. Some of these variables may have been crucial in the past, and others may be expected to have future importance. This list can be kept manageable by limiting it in the following ways:[1]

1. Include all variables that would have a significant impact although their probability of occurrence is low (e.g., trucking deregulation). Also include highly probable variables regardless of their impact (e.g., a minimal price increase by a major supplier). Delete others with little impact and low probabilities.

2. Disregard major disasters, such as nuclear war.

3. When possible, aggregate variables into gross variables (e.g., a bank loan is based more on the dependability of a firm's cash flow than on the flow's component sources).

4. If the value of one variable is based on the value of another, separate the dependent variable for future planning.

Limits of money, time, and forecasting skill prevent a firm from predicting many variables. The task of predicting even a dozen is substantial. Firms often try to select a set of key variables by analyzing the environmental factors in the industry that are most likely to foster sharp growth or decline in the marketplace. For the furniture, appliance, and textiles industries, housing starts are a key variable. Housing starts, in turn, are greatly affected by interest rates. Figure 5–2 identifies some issues that may have critical impacts on a firm's future success.

Another key consideration in attempting to forecast future performance is the amount of data needed. Data requirements are situation specific, but, as Figure 5–3 shows, depend on how quickly the data patterns change, the type of industry, the type of product, the analytical model selected, the forecast horizon, and ex-post forecast results.

SELECT SOURCES OF SIGNIFICANT ENVIRONMENTAL INFORMATION

Before formal forecasting can begin, appropriate sources of environmental information should be identified. Casual gathering of strategic information—through reading, interactions, and meetings—is part of the normal course of executive behavior but is subject to bias and must be balanced with alternative viewpoints. Although *The Wall Street Journal, Business Week, Fortune, Harvard Business Review, Forbes*, and other popular trade and scholarly journals are important sources of forecasting information, formal, deliberate, and structured searches are desirable. Appendix 5–A lists published sources that strategic managers can use to meet their specific forecasting needs. If the firm can afford the time and expense, it should also gather primary data in such areas as market factors, technological changes, and competitive and supplier strategies.

EVALUATE FORECASTING TECHNIQUES

Debate exists over the accuracy of quantitative versus qualitative approaches to forecasting (see Figure 5–4), with most research supporting quantitative models. However, the differences in the predictions derived from these approaches are often minimal. Moreover, subjective or judgmental approaches are often the only practical method of forecasting political, legal, social, and technological trends in the remote external environment. The same is true of several factors in the task environment, especially customer and competitive considerations.

---

[1] R. E. Linneman and J. D. Kennell, "Shirt-Sleeve Approach to Long-Range Plans," *Harvard Business Review*, March–April 1977, p. 145.

FIGURE 5–2
Strategic Forecasting Issues

Key Issues in the Remote Environment

Economy

What are the probable future directions of the economies in the firm's regional, national, and international markets? What changes in economic growth, inflation, interest rates, capital availability, credit availability, and consumer purchasing power can be expected? What income differences can be expected between the wealthy upper-middle class, the working class, and the underclass in various regions? What shifts in relative demand for different categories of goods and services can be expected?

Society and demographics

What effects will changes in social values and attitudes regarding childbearing, marriage, lifestyle, work, ethics, sex roles, racial equality, education, retirement, pollution, and energy have on the firm's development? What effects will population changes have on major social and political expectations—at home and abroad? What constraints or opportunities will develop? What pressure groups will increase in power?

Ecology

What natural or pollution-caused disasters threaten the firm's employees, customers, or facilities? How rigorously will existing environmental legislature be enforced? What new federal, state, and local laws will affect the firm, and in what ways?

Politics

What changes in government policy can be expected with regard to industry cooperation, antitrust activities, foreign trade, taxation, depreciation, environmental protection, deregulation, defense, foreign trade barriers, and other important parameters? What success will a new administration have in achieving its stated goals? What effect will that success have on the firm? Will specific international climates be hostile or favorable? Is there a tendency toward instability, corruption, or violence? What is the level of political risk in each foreign market? What other political or legal constraints or supports can be expected in international business (e.g., trade barriers, equity requirements, nationalism, patent protection)?

Technology

What is the current state of the art? How will it change? What pertinent new products or services are likely to become technically feasible in the foreseeable future? What future impact can be expected from technological breakthroughs in related product areas? How will those breakthroughs interface with the other remote considerations, such as economic issues, social values, public safety, regulations, and court interpretations?

Key Issues in the Industry Environment

New entrants

Will new technologies or market demands enable competitors to minimize the impact of traditional economies of scale in the industry? Will consumers accept our claims of product or service differentiation? Will potential new entrants be able to match the capital requirements that currently exist? How permanent are the cost disadvantages (independent of size) in our industry? Will conditions change so that all competitors have equal access to marketing channels? Is government policy toward competition in our industry likely to change?

Bargaining power of suppliers

How stable are the size and composition of our supplier group? Are any suppliers likely to attempt forward integration into our business level? How dependent will our suppliers be in the future? Are substitute suppliers likely to become available? Could we become our own supplier?

Ultimately, the choice of technique depends not on the environmental factor under review but on such considerations as the nature of the forecast decision, the amount and accuracy of available information, the accuracy required, the time available, the importance of the forecast, the cost, and the competence and interpersonal relationships of the managers and forecasters involved. Frequently, assessment of such considerations leads to the selection of a combination of quantitative and qualitative techniques, thereby strengthening the accuracy of the ultimate forecast.

FIGURE 5–2
concluded

Substitute products or services

Are new substitutes likely? Will they be price competitive? Could we fight off substitutes by price competition? By advertising to sharpen product differentiation? What actions could we take to reduce the potential for having alternative products seen as legitimate substitutes?

Bargaining power of buyers

Can we break free of overcommitment to a few large buyers? How would our buyers react to attempts by us to differentiate our products? What possibilities exist that our buyers might vertically integrate backward? Should we consider forward integration? How can we make the value of our components greater in the products of our buyers?

Rivalry among existing firms

Are major competitors likely to undo the established balance of power in our industry? Is growth in our industry slowing such that competition will become fiercer? What excess capacity exists in our industry? How capable are our major competitors of withstanding intensified price competition? How unique are the objectives and strategies of our major competitors?

Key Issues in the Operating Environment

Competitive position

What strategic moves are expected by existing rivals—inside and outside the United States? What competitive advantage is necessary in selected foreign markets? What will be our competitors' priorities and ability to change? Is the behavior of our competitors predictable?

Customer profiles and market changes

What will our customer regard as needed value? Is marketing research done, or do managers talk to each other to discover what the customer wants? Which customer needs are not being met by existing products? Why? Are R&D activities under way to develop means for fulfilling these needs? What is the status of these activities? What marketing and distribution channels should we use? What do demographic and population changes portend for the size and sales potential of our market? What new market segments or products might develop as a result of these changes? What will be the buying power of our customer groups?

Supplier relationships

What is the likelihood of major cost increases because of dwindling supplies of a needed natural resource? Will sources of supply, especially of energy, be reliable? Are there reasons to expect major changes in the cost or availability of inputs as a result of money, people, or subassembly problems? Which suppliers can be expected to respond to emergency requests?

Creditors

What lines of credit are available to help finance our growth? What changes may occur in our creditworthiness? Are creditors likely to feel comfortable with our strategic plan and performance? What is the stock market likely to feel about our firm? What flexibility would our creditors show toward us during a downturn? Do we have sufficient cash reserves to protect our creditors and our credit rating?

Labor market

Are potential employees with desired skills and abilities available in the geographic areas in which our facilities are located? Are colleges and vocational-technical schools that can aid in meeting our training needs located near our plant or store sites? Are labor relations in our industry conducive to meeting our expanding needs for employees? Are workers whose skills we need shifting toward or away from the geographic location of our facilities?

Techniques Available

Economic Forecasts

At one time, only forecasts of economic variables were used in strategic management. The forecasts were primarily concerned with remote factors, such as general economic conditions, disposable personal income, the consumer price index, wage rates, and productivity. Derived from government and private sources, these economic forecasts served as the framework for industry and company forecasts, which dealt with task-environment concerns, such as sales, market share, and other pertinent economic trends.

FIGURE 5–3
How Much Data Should You Use to Prepare Forecasts?

Sooner or later a decision has to be made as to how much data should be used to prepare the next period's forecast. Should you use all the data you have or a part of it? If you use part of the data, which part should be used? There is no simple answer to these questions; it depends on: (1) how quickly the data pattern changes, (2) the type of industry, (3) the type of product, (4) the model selected, (5) the forecast horizon, and (6) ex-post forecast results.

Data Pattern

As we know: Actual value = Pattern + Error. The best forecasting model is the one that most accurately captures the underlying pattern in a data set. The more a given model captures the pattern, the less will be the error. In a given company, the data pattern can change from one time to another because of a change in legislation, product mix, socio-demographic makeup, and the competitive environment. Technological developments and acquisitions and mergers can also change the data pattern. In that case, you need data from where the most recent data pattern starts. For example, if the most recent pattern starts in 1991, you should be using data starting 1991.

Type of Industry

The change in the data pattern is not the same in each and every industry. Some industries experience changes more rapidly than others. This may be because some industries are more prone to technological developments and/or mergers and acquisitions than others. In industries where the data pattern changes rapidly, forecasters often use data of a shorter period. In consumer product industries, for example, forecasters use data of the previous three years in preparing operations forecasts—forecasts of less than one year.

Type of Product

The type of product also makes a difference. Some products have a longer life than others. The life of essential products is generally much longer than that of fashion products. Other things being constant, the longer the life of a product the more data will be required and vice versa.

Forecast Horizon

How much data is needed also depends on whether we wish to prepare a short- or long-term forecast. Generally speaking, less data are needed for short-term forecasts and more data for long-term forecasts. If you wish to make a forecast for the next week or month, by and large, projecting the current trend adjusted for seasonal elements will be sufficient. This means a couple of years of data will be enough. However, if you wish to make a forecast for four or five years into the future, you will need much more data.

Model Selected

The data required also depends on the selected model because each model has its own requirement. For example, the "three-period moving average change model" needs at least four periods of data, and at the same time the "three-period double moving average change model" requires at least six periods of data. For a Box Jenkins model, some feel at least six years of data are needed if weekly or monthly forecasts are to be prepared and the data contain seasonality. In a regression-based model, the minimum observations required depend, among other things, on the number of independent variables. The more independent variables you incorporate in a model, the more observations will be needed.

Ex-Post Forecasts

Above all, the data required depend on how many observations, on the average, give the best forecasts. Using the best model, one can prepare ex-post forecasts on the basis of, say, one year of data, two years of data, and three years of data. (Ex-post forecasts are forecasts of those periods for which actuals are known.) If, on the average, three years of data give the lowest error, you need three years of data; if two years of data give the lowest error, you need two years of data; and so on.

Source: Chaman L. Jain, "How Much Data Should You Use to Prepare Forecasts?" *The Journal of Business Forecasting*, Winter 1994–1995, p. 2.

Econometric Models

With the advent of sophisticated computers, the government and some wealthy firms contracted with private consulting firms to develop "casual models," especially models involving econometrics. These econometric models utilize complex simultaneous regression equations to relate economic occurrences to areas of corporate activity. They are especially useful when

FIGURE 5–4
Popular Approaches to Forecasting

Technique	Short Description	Cost	Popularity	Complexity	Association with Life-Cycle Stage
Quantitative–Causal Models					
Econometric models	Simultaneous systems of multiple regression equations.	High	High	High	Steady state
Single and multiple regression	Variations in dependent variables are explained by variations in one or more independent variables.	High/ medium	High	Medium	Steady state
Time series models	Linear, exponential, S-curve, or other types of projections.	Medium	High	Medium	Steady state
Trend extrapolation	Forecasts obtained by linear or exponential smoothing or averaging of past actual values.	Medium	High	Medium	Steady state
Qualitative or Judgmental Models					
Sales force estimate	A bottom-up approach aggregating salespersons' forecasts.	Low	High	Low	All stages
Juries of executive opinion	Forecasts jointly prepared by marketing, production, finance, and purchasing executives.	Low	High	Low	Product development
Customer surveys; market research	Learning about intentions of potential customers or plans of businesses.	Medium	Medium	Medium	Market testing and early introduction
Scenario development	Impacts of anticipated conditions imagined by forecasters.	Low	Medium	Low	All stages
Delphi method	Experts guided toward a consensus.	Low	Medium	Medium	Product development
Brainstorming	Idea generation in a noncritical group situation.	Low	Medium	Medium	Product development

information on casual relationships is available and large changes are anticipated. During the relatively stable decade of the 1970s, econometrics was one of the nation's fastest-growing industries. In the 1980s, however, the three biggest econometric firms—Data Resources (McGraw-Hill), Chase Econometric (Chase Manhattan Bank), and Wharton Econometric Forecasting Associates (Ziff-Davis Publishing)—fell on hard times. The explosion of oil prices, inflation, and the growing interdependence in the world economy created problems that fell beyond the inherent limits of econometric models. And despite enormous technological resources, such models still depend on the often undependable judgment of the model builders.

Two more widely used and less expensive forecasting techniques are *time series models* and *judgmental models*. Time series models attempt to identify patterns based on combinations of historical trends and seasonal and cyclical factors. This technique assumes that the past is a prologue to the future. Time series techniques, such as exponential smoothing and linear projections, are relatively simple, well known, inexpensive, and accurate.

Of the time series models, *trend analysis* models are the most frequently used. Such models assume that the future will be a continuation of the past, following some long-range trend. If sufficient historical data are available, such as annual sales, a trend analysis can be done quickly at a modest cost.

In the trend analysis depicted in Figure 5–5, concern should focus on long-term trends, such as Trend C, which is based on 11 years of fluctuating sales. Trend A, which is based

FIGURE 5–5
Interpretations in Trend Analysis

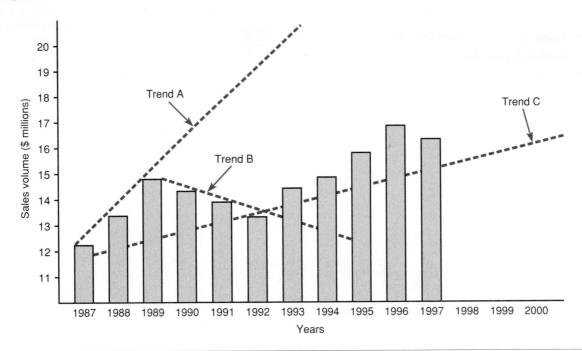

on three excellent years, is much too optimistic. Similarly, Trend B, which is based on four bad years, is much too pessimistic.

The major limitation of trend analysis is the assumption that all of the relevant conditions will remain relatively constant. Sudden changes in these conditions falsify trend predictions.

Judgmental models are useful when historical data are unavailable or hard to use. *Sales force estimates* and *juries of executive opinion* are examples of such models. Sales force estimates consolidate salespeople's opinions of customer intentions regarding specific products. These estimates can be relevant if customers respond honestly and their intentions remain consistent. Juries of executive opinion average the estimates made by executives from marketing, production, finance, and purchasing. No elaborate math or statistics are required.

Customer surveys are conducted by means of personal interviews or telephone questionnaires. The questions must be well stated and easily understood. The respondents are a random sample of the relevant population. Customer surveys can provide valuable in-depth information. Although they are often difficult to construct and time-consuming to administer, many marketing research firms use them.

Social Forecasts

If strategic forecasting relies only on economic indicators, social trends that can have a profound impact may be neglected. Some firms have recognized this and identify social trends and underlying attitudes as part of their environmental scanning. Recent social forecasting efforts have involved analysis of such areas as population, housing, Social Security and welfare, health and nutrition, education and training, income, and wealth and expenditures.

A variety of approaches are used in social forecasting, including time series analysis and the judgmental techniques described earlier. However, *scenario development* is probably the most popular approach. Scenarios, the imagined stories that integrate objective and subjective parts of other forecasts, are designed to help prepare strategic managers for alternative possibilities, thus enabling them to develop contingency plans. Because scenarios can be presented in easily understood forms, they often are used in social forecasting. They can be developed by the following process:

1. Prepare the background by assessing the overall social environment under investigation (such as social legislation).
2. Select critical indicators, and search for future events that may affect them (e.g., growing distrust of business).
3. Analyze the reasons for the past behavior of each indicator (e.g., perceived disregard for air and water quality).
4. Forecast each indicator in three scenarios—showing the least favorable environment, the likely environment, and the most favorable environment.
5. Write the scenarios from the viewpoint of someone at a given future time.
6. Condense each scenario to a few paragraphs.

Strategy in Action 5–2 presents the "most likely" scenario of the ecology in the 21st century as judged by a panel of experts. It shows how social, political, and technological concerns can be blended to produce a useful forecast.

Strategy in Action 5–3 presents a scenario that was developed in 1987 for Georgia Power Company. Its purpose was to determine how the future environment might influence the firm's load and energy growth to the year 1995. With the help of Battelle Columbus Division, a consulting firm, Georgia Power identified five broad areas of influence—the same areas you studied in Chapter 3 as the constituents of the remote external environment. From these areas, 15 key factors were isolated for investigation, of which 5 were judged to be critical to Georgia Power's planning. The scenario in Strategy in Action 5–3 was built on forecasts regarding these five factors. Several scenarios were developed, of which the one presented in Strategy in Action 5–3 showed the greatest economic growth.

Political Forecasts

Some strategic planners want to give political forecasts the same serious consideration that is given to economic forecasts. They believe that business success can be profoundly affected by shifts in a broad range of political factors, such as the size of government budgets, tariffs, tax rates, defense spending, the growth of regulatory bodies, and the extent of business leaders' participation in government planning.

Political forecasts for foreign countries also are important. Political risks in those countries affect firms that are in any way dependent on international subsidiaries, on suppliers for customers, or on critical resources. Increasing worldwide interdependence makes it imperative for firms of all sizes to consider the international political implications of their strategies.

Because of the billions of U.S. dollars lost in the last two decades as a result of revolutions, nationalization, and other manifestations of political instability, multinational firms and consultants have developed a variety of approaches to international forecasting. Some of the better known are:

Haner's Business Environmental Risk Index, which monitors 15 economic and political variables in 42 countries.

STRATEGY
IN ACTION
5–2

SCENARIO ON THE ECOLOGY IN THE 21ST CENTURY

Imagine how the world will look from a technological standpoint in the year 2050. It seems likely that the combination of environmental constraints and consumer desires for functionality rather than ownership will have had profound impacts on the global economy, government policies, private corporations, and individuals. As a result of environmental constraints, for example, energy and resource conservation will have become increasingly critical. Energy- and resource-efficient corporations will have gained substantial competitive advantages. This trend in particular may favor Japanese companies, because as an island nation, the Japanese have already internalized a parsimonious attitude toward energy and resources. This attitude, which at least initially was quite independent of the environment, will serve them well in an environmentally constrained world. Americans, on the other hand, with their "cowboy economy" and propensity for resource depletion, may have a considerably rougher time.

Price structures, a serious impediment to industrial ecology during the 1990s, will undergo considerable evolution in the next few decades, as more and more externalities become captured either through market mechanisms or fees and taxes. The adjustment of the pricing structure will be sporadic and will make business planning quite difficult. Those corporations that fail to internalize environmental considerations into their product and process planning in the late twentieth or early twenty-first centuries will find their costs escalating wildly and unpredictably, and will have few options when changes have to be made rapidly.

A concomitant development will be the ascendancy of materials science in many corporations. The ability to predict environmental impacts of materials across their life cycles and to implement alternatives in response to regulatory bans and rapidly changing costs will prove to be an important competency for any extractive or manufacturing corporation. Much of the progress in achieving sustainable manufacturing practices will rely on new materials—superconductors, buckyball derivatives, and enzymes used in bioprocessing factories, for example—and those corporations that stay abreast of the "learning curve" on new materials will do well.

The crucial role of new materials will be reinforced by an explicit policy on the part of many governments to allocate the transfer of functionality to the consumer marketplace and to place the responsibility for the underlying product on manufacturing corporations. The trend, initiated by postconsumer product take-back legislation in Germany and Japan in the 1990s, will be extended to most product categories. Governments will increasingly realize that environmental impacts arise predominantly from the nature of the material stocks and flows underlying the economy rather than

Source: *Industrial Ecology* by Graedel/Allenby, © 1995. Adapted by permission of Prentice Hall, Inc., Upper Saddle River, NJ.

Frost and Sullivan's World Political Risks Forecasts, which predict the likelihood of various catastrophes befalling an individual firm.

Probe International's custom reports for specific firms, which examine broad social trends.

The developmental forecasts of Arthur D. Little (ADL), which examine a country's progress.

Of all the approaches in use, those of ADL may be the most ambitious and sophisticated. With computer assistance, ADL follows the progress of each country by looking at five criteria: social development, technological advancement, abundance of natural resources, level of domestic tranquility, and type of political system. When a country's

from the quality of life the economy provides to consumers. They will react more and more by imposing on business the responsibility for materials, from extraction to rebirth to safe disposal.

On a broader front, as more and more operations of corporations become subject to public approval processes, either formally through regulatory mechanisms or informally through public activism, manufacturing will become a true partnership among the corporation, the community in which it exists, and the society in which it is embedded. The idea of a corporation as responsible to only its shareholders and perhaps to its employees or management is rapidly becoming obsolescent, although the details of balancing desirable competitive incentives against a broader social role are difficult and still evolving. Nonetheless, in the future corporations will not quickly put profit ahead of social responsibility; so deeply will environmental concerns redefine our society.

What of various industrial sectors? Electronics manufacturing and software development will boom as the creation of intelligent resource- and energy-conserving systems permeates the economy. Some power utilities will suffer, but many will prosper by increasing their energy networking capabilities and becoming turnkey energy-efficiency consultants, an extension of the demand management efforts that began in the early 1990s. The transportation sector will see enormous change, best characterized by saying that customers will be offered "transparent transportation" for goods and services, where conditions and timing are specified but modes and interconnections are chosen by the service vendor. "Transparent commuting" will operate much the same way, except that many people will remain where they are and commute electronically. An economy based on intellectual capital requires an infrastructure emphasizing electronic networks, not civil engineering.

A Summary of The Vision

The future for purposes of the practitioner of industrial ecology is essentially captured in two propositions: that it is an increasingly environmentally constrained world, and that customers will soon be buying functionality, not material. Thus, the long-term vision of industrial ecology centers both on a technological development and on changes in the structure of societal demand. Industrial ecology recognizes that technology is the source of our environmental problems and that it may be the only feasible way to solve them. Technology alone cannot achieve the transformation we envision; it must work within the societal system to move closer to that goal.

development in any one of these areas gets too far ahead of its development in the other areas, tension builds and violence often follows. Using this system, ADL forecast political turbulence in Iran eight years before the U.S. hostage crisis. ADL foresees that uneven development probably will produce similar turmoil in 20 other countries, such as Peru, Chile, Malaysia, and the Philippines. It believes the world is highly predictable if the right questions are asked. Unfortunately, too many executives fail to use the same logic in analyzing political affairs that they use in other strategic areas. Political analysis should be routinely incorporated into economic analyses. Ford, General Motors, PepsiCo, Singer, Du Pont, and United Technologies are among the many firms that follow ADL's advice.

Global Strategy in Action 5–1 provides a guide to political evaluation that is popular among executives who are responsible for international operations. Global Strategy in Action 5–2 presents an actual scenario that was developed to assess political and economic conditions in the Americas.

GEORGIA POWER PLANNING SCENARIOS FOR 1995

HIGH ECONOMIC GROWTH SCENARIO

The average annual growth rate of the real U.S. gross national product (GNP) will exceed 3.2 percent between now and the year 2010. This growth rate is about the same as the growth rate of 3.4 percent experienced during the post–World War II era but is greater than the average growth rate for the 1980s. Economic growth in Georgia will exceed that of the nation as a whole by as much as one percentage point. This growth pattern is expected to result from a continuation of the Sunbelt phenomenon that drove Georgia's strong growth over the past two decades. With higher economic growth elsewhere, net migration to Georgia will slow down.

Higher productivity growth and lower real interest rates will be associated with higher U.S. economic growth. Higher productivity growth will occur as the baby boom generation matures and the work experience of its members increases. Interest rates will remain lower as long as inflationary pressures do not reemerge.

The average price of oil in 1985 dollars will remain under $18 per barrel as a result of the transformation of the OPEC-dominated world oil market into a commodity-based market. The surplus of natural gas will diminish, but not until the middle 1990s. Industrial demand for natural gas will dampen, as lower oil prices encourage substitution to oil. Coal prices will increase more slowly. Real electricity prices will decline if the free market energy policy pursued by the Reagan Administration continues. Emissions will remain essentially stable through 1995.

Real U.S. GNP will grow at an annual rate of less than 2.7 percent, a rate lower than the average growth rate experienced so far in the 1980s. This decline will result from a worsening trade imbalance and from large deficit spending that exerts an upward pressure on interest rates. Georgia's personal income growth will exceed that of the United States as a whole by over one percentage point. Higher levels of net migration into Georgia will occur as economic circumstances worsen elsewhere. This will accelerate growth in the state.

The annual increase in U.S. productivity will be less than 1.5 percent, an increase consistent with the slow growth of the 1970s. The low growth rate will result from a decline in demand for most goods and services as the population ages. Taxes will increase to support the aged population. Both higher taxes and higher interest rates will accelerate the shift from a manufacturing to a service economy.

By 1995, oil prices will average over $30 per barrel in 1985 dollars. The current world surplus will erode quickly in the early years as the current strong economic growth increases oil demand. This will cause a return to OPEC price controls. Deregulation will free natural gas prices to adjust rapidly to supply and demand imbalances. Exploration and development will be dampened by the initial lower prices and by inconsistent and unpredictable government energy policy. Real electricity prices will decline. Some acid rain legislation will be passed, but not enough to significantly discourage growth in the utility industry.

Source: D. L. Goldfarb and W. R. Huss, "Building Scenarios for an Electric Utility," *Long Range Planning*, June 1988, pp. 78–85.

Technological Forecasts

Such rapidly developed and revolutionary technological innovations as lasers, nuclear energy, satellites and other communication devices, desalination of water, electric cars, and miracle drugs have prompted many firms to invest in technological forecasts. Knowledge of probable technological development helps strategic managers prepare their firms to benefit from change. Except for econometrics, all of the previously described techniques can be used to make technological forecasts. However, uncertainty of information favors the use of scenarios and two additional forecasting approaches: brainstorming and the Delphi technique.

Brainstorming helps a group generate new ideas and forecasts. With this technique, analysis or criticisms of participants' contributions are postponed so creative thinking is not stifled or restricted. Because there are no interruptions, group members are encouraged to offer original ideas and to build on one another's innovative thoughts. The most promising ideas generated in this way are thoroughly evaluated at a later time.

The *Delphi method* is a systematic procedure for obtaining consensus among a group of experts. This method includes:

1. A detailed survey of opinions of experts, usually obtained through a mail questionnaire.
2. Anonymous evaluation of the responses by the experts involved.
3. One or more revisions of the experts' answers until convergence has been achieved.

Relatively inexpensive, the Delphi method can be successful in social and political forecasting.

A firm's use of a particular forecasting technique is often highly dependent on the industry in which it is involved. For product necessities such as electric power, food, and pharmaceuticals, corporations are often able to perform forecasts several months in advance. However, for newly introduced products or products with volatile demand, forecasting efforts become daily challenges in satisfying fluctuating demand patterns. A means to alleviate the pressures of dealing with such patterns can be the recognition of early warning signals. Proactive steps such as customer surveys or early tests of response can help to promote early warning signs. Figure 5–6 provides a comparison of where early warning systems have greater or less value in predicting demand.

At the end of this chapter, Appendix 5–B briefly describes the 20 most frequently used forecasting approaches.

INTEGRATE FORECAST RESULTS INTO THE STRATEGIC MANAGEMENT PROCESS

Once the forecasting techniques have been selected and the forecasts made, the results must be integrated into the strategic management process. For example, the economic forecast must be related to analyses of the industry, suppliers, competition, and key resources. Figure 5–7 presents a format for displaying interrelationships between forecast remote environment variables and the influential task environment variables. The resulting predictions become a part of the assumed environment in formulating strategy.

It is critical that strategic decision makers understand the assumptions on which environmental forecasts are based. The experience of Itel, a computer-leasing firm, illustrates the consequences of a failure to understand these assumptions. Itel had been able to lease 200 plug-in computers made by Advance Systems and by Hitachi largely because IBM could not deliver its newest AT systems. Consequently, Itel bullishly forecast that it would place 430 of its systems in the following year—despite the rumor that IBM would announce a new line of aggressively priced systems in the first quarter of that year. Even Itel's competitors felt that customers would hold off their purchasing decisions until IBM made the announcement. However, Itel signed long-term purchase contracts with its suppliers and increased its marketing staff by 80 percent. Itel's forecasting mistake and its failure to examine its sales forecasts in relationship to the actions of competitors and suppliers were nearly disastrous. It slipped close to bankruptcy within less than a year.

A GUIDE TO POLITICAL EVALUATION

The following is an abridged version of the popular Political Agenda Worksheet developed by Probe, a consulting firm that specializes in political analysis, which may serve as a guide for corporate executives initiating their own political evaluations.

EXTERNAL FACTORS AFFECTING SUBJECT COUNTRY

Prospects for foreign conflict.

Relations with border countries.

Regional instabilities.

Alliances with major and regional powers.

Sources of key raw materials.

Major foreign markets.

Policy toward United States.

U.S. policy toward country.

INTERNAL GROUPINGS (POINTS OF POWER)

Government in Power

Key agencies and officials.

Legislative entrenched bureaucracies.

Policies—economic, financial, social, labor, and so on.

Pending legislation.

Attitude toward private sector.

Power networks.

Political Parties (in and out of power)

Policies.

Leading and emerging personalities.

Source: Benjamin Weiner, "What Executives Should Know about Political Risk," *Management Review,* January 1992, p. 21.

Forecasting external events enables a firm to identify its probable requirements for future success, to formulate or reformulate its basic mission, and to design strategies for achieving its goals and objectives. If the forecast identifies any gaps or inconsistencies between the firm's desired position and its present position, strategic managers can respond with plans and actions. When Apple successfully introduced its new low-priced personal computers, sales climbed 85 percent for the quarter. However, because the firm failed to forecast that sales of the low-price computers would cannibalize the sales of its more expensive models, profits slipped, forcing Apple to lay off 10 percent of its work force, or 1,500 employees.

Dealing with the uncertainty of the future is a major function of strategic managers. The forecasting task requires systematic information gathering coupled with the utilization of a

Internal power struggles.

Sector and area strengths.

Future prospects for retaining or gaining power.

Other Important Groups

Unions and labor movements.

Military, special groups within military.

Families.

Business and financial communities.

Intelligentsia.

Students.

Religious groups.

Media.

Regional and local governments.

Social and environmental activists.

Cultural, linguistic, and ethnic groups.

Separatist movements.

Foreign communities.

Potential competitors and customers.

INTERNAL FACTORS

Power struggles among elites.

Ethnic confrontations.

Regional struggles.

Economic factors affecting stability (consumer inflation, price and wage controls, unemployment, supply shortages, taxation, and so on).

Anti-establishment movements.

variety of forecasting approaches. A high level of insight also is needed to integrate risks and opportunities in formulating strategy. However, intentional or unintentional delays or the inability to understand certain issues may prevent a firm from using the insights gained in assessing the impact of broad environmental trends. Sensitivity and openness to new and better approaches and opportunities, therefore, are essential.

MONITOR THE CRITICAL ASPECTS OF MANAGING FORECASTS

Although almost all aspects of forecast management may be critical in specific situations, three aspects are critical over the lifetime of a firm.

THE AMERICAS

In general, political and economic conditions are likely to be more stable in Central and South America in 1992 than they have been for several years. The debt crisis has receded as a prime concern; and while political violence may increase, most regimes are not likely to change during 1992. The biggest headlines will be devoted to the free-trade movements in the region, especially the North American Free Trade Area (NAFTA).

Some type of free-trade agreement between Mexico and the United States is likely in 1992, but its economic impact will not be nearly as important as its symbolic significance. Rather than stimulating new trade in Mexico, it will open up new opportunities for joint venture investments. The most important consequence of such an agreement may well be to sustain political support for President Salinas of Mexico. Other free-trade agreements among South American countries will also evolve during 1992, but they will have only limited impact on the local economies.

Since Brazil and Argentina together account for 50 percent of all economic activity in South America, these are the countries to watch closely. Brazil continues to make little headway against inflation or toward meaningful economic reform. Prospects for improvement are not good while President Collor battles a recalcitrant congress and the stubbornly independent state governments.

Argentina, on the other hand, has shown significant signs of economic improvement under a new minister of the economy and President Menem, who has regained much of his earlier popularity. As more privatization has occurred, the international financial community appears to have talked itself back into believing in Argentina. Nevertheless, prospects for comprehensive privatization remain limited, and labor is becoming increasingly opposed to Menem's policies. A new acceleration of inflation could destroy Menem's chances of implementing the nascent program of far-reaching economic reform now in process.

Source: *Planning Review* 20, no. 2 (March–April 1992), p. 27. Published with permission of The Planning Forum, P.O. Box 70, Oxford, OH 45056.

The first is the identification of the environmental factors that deserve forecasting. Hundreds of factors may affect a firm, but often the most important of these factors are a few of immediate concern, such as sales forecasts and competitive trends. The time and resources needed to completely understand all the environmental factors that might be critical to the success of a strategy are seldom available. Therefore, executives must depend on their collective experience and perception to determine which factors are worth the expense of forecasting.

The second aspect is the selection of reputable, cost-efficient forecasting sources outside the firm that can expand its forecasting database. Strategic managers should identify federal and state government agencies, trade and industry associations, and individuals or other groups that can provide data forecasts at reasonable costs.

The third aspect is the selection of forecasting tasks that are to be done in-house. Given the great credence that often is accorded to formally developed forecasts—despite the inherent uncertainty of the database—the selection of forecasting techniques is indeed critical. A firm beginning its forecasting efforts is well advised to start with less technical methods, such as sales force estimates and the jury of executive opinion, rather than highly sophisticated forecasting techniques, such as econometrics, and to add approaches requiring greater analytic sophistication as its experience and understanding increase. In this way, its managers can learn how to deal with the varied weaknesses and strengths of forecasting techniques.

FIGURE 5–6
Where an Early Warning System Has Greater or Less Value in Business

Greater Value	Less Value
Long or lengthening supply lead times.	Easy resupply "off the shelf."
Lean inventories.	Ample inventories.
High fraction of new products; apparel, book publishing.	Well-established products such as aspirin and corn flakes.
Customers can easily go elsewhere if item is unavailable: department stores, airlines.	Unique items with limited competition: high-performance car accessories.
Perishable or rapid-obsolescence items: theater seats, cut flowers.	Products can be easily carried over for future sale: blue jeans, office supplies.
Short, intense selling season: Christmas decorations, skiwear.	Selling seasons that permit enough time to expand or contract supplies.
Suppliers to JIT or Quick Response customers, for example, to auto companies, Wal-Mart.	Suppliers of capital equipment and systems that are made to order: mainframe computers, aircraft.

Source: Paul V. Teplitz, "Do You Need an Early Warning System?" *The Journal of Forecasting*, 1995, p. 9.

SUMMARY

Environmental forecasting starts with the identification of critical factors external to the firm that might provide opportunities or pose threats in the future. Both quantitative and qualitative strategic forecasting techniques are used to project the long-range direction and impact of these factors in the remote and task environments. To select the forecasting techniques that are most appropriate for the firm, the strengths and weaknesses of the various techniques must be understood. To offset the potential biases or errors individual techniques involve, employment of more than one technique usually is advisable.

Critical aspects in forecast management include the identification of the environmental factors that deserve forecasting, the selection of forecasting sources outside the firm, and the selection of forecasting tasks that are to be done in-house.

QUESTIONS FOR DISCUSSION

1. Identify five changes in the remote environment that you believe will affect major U.S. industries over the next decade. What forecasting techniques could be used to assess the probable impact of these changes?

2. Construct a matrix with forecasting techniques on the horizontal axis and at least five qualities of forecasting techniques across the vertical axis. Indicate the relative strengths and weaknesses of each technique.

3. Develop three rules of thumb for guiding strategic managers in their use of forecasting.

4. Develop a typewritten two-page forecast of a variable that you believe will affect the prosperity of your business school over the next 10 years.

5. Using prominent business journals, find two examples of firms that either benefited or suffered from environmental forecasts.

6. Describe the background, skills, and abilities of the individual you would hire as the environmental forecaster for a firm with $500 million in annual sales. How would the qualifications of such an individual differ for a much smaller firm? For a much larger firm?

FIGURE 5–7
Task and Remote Environment Impact Matrix

Remote Environments	Task Environments			
	Key Customer Trends	**Key Competitor Trends**	**Key Supplier Trends**	**Key Labor Market Trends**
Economic	*Example:* Trends in inflation and unemployment rates.		*Example:* Annual domestic oil demand and worldwide sulfur demand through the year 2020.	
Social	*Example:* Increasing numbers of single-parent homes.			*Example:* Rising education level of U.S. population.
Political	*Example:* Increasing numbers of punitive damage awards in product liability cases.		*Example:* Possibility of oil boycotts	
Technological		*Example:* Increasing use of superchips and computer-based instrumentation for synthesizing genes.	*Example:* Use of cobalt 60 gamma irradiation to extend shelf life of perishables.	
Ecological		*Example:* Increased use of biodegradable fast-food packaging.		*Example:* Increasing availability of mature workers with experience in "smokestack" industries.

BIBLIOGRAPHY

Alerthal, Lester M., Jr. "Keeping the Lead in an Ever-Changing Global Landscape." *Planning Review* 23, no. 8 (September–October 1995), p. 13.

Alexander, Marcus; Andrew Campbell; and Michael Gorld. "A New Model for Reforming the Planning Review Process." *Planning-Review* 23, no. 1 (January–February 1995), p. 12.

Allaire, Y., and M. E. Firsirotu. "Coping with Strategic Uncertainty." *Sloan Management Review*, Spring 1989, pp. 7–16.

Barndt, W. D., Jr. "Profiling Rival Decision Makers." *The Journal of Business Strategy*, January–February 1991, pp. 8–11.

Barrett, F. D. "Strategies for the Use of Artificial and Human Intelligence." *Business Quarterly*, Summer 1986, pp. 18–27.

Coplin, W. D., and M. K. O'Leary. "1991 World Political Risk Forecast." *Planning Review*, January–February 1991, pp. 16–23.

Czinkota, M. R. "International Information Needs for U.S. Competitiveness." *Business Horizons*, November–December 1991, pp. 86–91.

Fuld, L. "A Recipe for Business Intelligence Success." *The Journal of Business Strategy*, January–February 1991, pp. 12–17.

———. "Achieving Total Quality through Intelligence." *Long Range Planning*, February 1992, pp. 109–15.

Fulmer, W., and R. Fulmer. "Strategic Group Technique: Involving Managers in Strategic Planning." *Long Range Planning*, April 1990, pp. 79–84.

Gelb, B. D.; M. J. Saxton; G. M. Zinkhan; and N. D. Albers. "Competitive Intelligence: Insights from Executives." *Business Horizons*, January–February 1991, pp. 43–47.

Gilad, B. "U.S. Intelligence System: Model for Corporate Chiefs?" *The Journal of Business Strategy*, May–June 1991, pp. 20–25.

Herring, J. P. "The Role of Intelligence in Formulating Strategy." *The Journal of Business Strategy*, September–October 1992, pp. 54–60.

Kahane, A. "Scenarios for Energy: Sustainable World vs. Global Mercantilism." *Long Range Planning*, August 1992, pp. 38–46.

Keiser, B. "Practical Competitor Intelligence." *Planning Review*, September 1987, pp. 14–19.

Lederer, A. L., and V. Sethi. "Guidelines for Strategic Information Planning." *The Journal of Business Strategy*, November–December 1991, pp. 38–43.

Pant, P. N., and W. H. Starbuck. "Innocents in the Forest: Forecasting and Research Methods." *Yearly Review of Management*, June 1990, pp. 433–60.

Pine, B. Joseph, II. "Peter Schwartz Offers Two Scenarios for the Future." *Planning Review* 23, no. 5 (September–October 1995), p. 30.

Premkumar, G., and W. R. King. "Assessing Strategic Information Systems Planning." *Long Range Planning*, October 1991, pp. 41–58.

Rousch, G. B. "A Program for Sharing Corporate Intelligence." *The Journal of Business Strategy*, January–February 1991, pp. 4–7.

Schoemaker, Paul J. H. "Scenario Planning: A Tool for Strategic Thinking." *Sloan Management Review* 36, no. 2 (Winter 1995), p. 25.

———. "Getting the Most Out of Scenarios: Some Questions and Answers." *Planning Review* 23, no. 6 (November–December 1995), p. 37.

Schriefer, Audrey E. "Getting the Most Out of Scenarios: Advice from the Experts." *Planning Review* 23, no. 5 (September–October 1995), p. 33.

Simpson, Daniel. "The Planning Process and the Role of the Planner." *Planning Review* 23, no. 1 (January–February 1995), p. 20.

———. "Planning in a Global Business." *Planning Review* 23, no. 2 (March–April 1995), p. 25.

Stokke, P. R.; W. K. Ralston; T. A. Boyce; and I. H. Wilson. "Scenario Planning for Norwegian Oil and Gas." *Long Range Planning*, April 1990, pp. 17–26.

Thurow, Lester C. "Surviving in a Turbulent Environment." *Planning Review* 23, no. 5 (September–October 1995), p. 24.

Wilson, Ian; Oliver W. Markley; Joseph F. Coates; and Clement Bezold. "A Forum of Futurists." *Planning Review* 23, no. 6 (November–December 1995), p. 10.

APPENDIX 5–A

SOURCES FOR ENVIRONMENTAL FORECASTS

REMOTE AND INDUSTRY ENVIRONMENTS

A. Economic considerations:
  1. *Predicasts* (most complete and up-to-date review of forecasts).
  2. National Bureau of Economic Research.
  3. *Handbook of Basic Economic Statistics.*
  4. *Statistical Abstract of the United States* (also includes industrial, social, and political statistics).
  5. Publications by Department of Commerce agencies:
     a. Office of Business Economics (e.g., *Survey of Business*).
     b. Bureau of Economic Analysis (e.g., *Business Conditions Digest*).
     c. Bureau of the Census (e.g., *Survey of Manufacturers* and various reports on population, housing, and industries).
     d. Business and Defense Services Administration (e.g., *United States Industrial Outlook*).
  6. Securities and Exchange Commission (various quarterly reports on plant and equipment, financial reports, working capital of corporations).
  7. The Conference Board.
  8. *Survey of Buying Power.*
  9. *Marketing Economic Guide.*
  10. *Industrial Arts Index.*
  11. U.S. and national chambers of commerce.
  12. American Manufacturers Association.
  13. *Federal Reserve Bulletin.*
  14. *Economic Indicators*, annual report.
  15. *Kiplinger Newsletter.*
  16. International economic sources:
     a. *Worldcasts.*
     b. Master key index for business international publications.
     c. Department of Commerce.
        (1) Overseas business reports.
        (2) Industry and Trade Administration.
        (3) Bureau of the Census—*Guide to Foreign Trade Statistics.*
  17. *Business Periodicals Index.*
B. Social considerations:
  1. Public opinion polls.

Sources: Adapted with numerous additions from C. R. Goeldner and L. M. Kirks, "Business Facts: Where to Find Them," *MSU Business Topics*, Summer 1976, pp. 23–76, reprinted by permission of the publisher, Division of Research, Graduate School of Business Administration, MSU; F. E. deCarbonnel and R. G. Donance, "Information Source for Planning Decisions," *California Management Review*, Summer 1973, pp. 42–53; and A. B. Nun, R. C. Lenz, Jr., H. W. Landford, and M. J. Cleary, "Data Source for Trend Extrapolation in Technological Forecasting," *Long Range Planning*, February 1972, pp. 72–76.

2. Surveys such as *Social Indicators and Social Reporting,* the annals of the American Academy of Political and Social Sciences.
3. Current controls: Social and behavioral sciences.
4. Abstract services and indexes for articles in sociological, psychological, and political journals.
5. Indexes for *The Wall Street Journal, New York Times,* and other newspapers.
6. Bureau of the Census reports on population, housing, manufacturers, selected services, construction, retail trade, wholesale trade, and enterprise statistics.
7. Various reports from such groups as the Brookings Institution and the Ford Foundation.
8. World Bank Atlas (population growth and GNP data).
9. World Bank–World Development Report.

C. Political considerations:
1. *Public Affairs Information Services Bulletin.*
2. CIS Index (Congressional Information Index).
3. Business periodicals.
4. Funk & Scott (regulations by product breakdown).
5. Weekly compilation of presidential documents.
6. *Monthly Catalog of Government Publications.*
7. *Federal Register* (daily announcements of pending regulations).
8. *Code of Federal Regulations* (final listing of regulations).
9. Business International Master Key Index (regulations, tariffs).
10. Various state publications.
11. Various information services (Bureau of National Affairs, Commerce Clearing House, Prentice Hall).

D. Technological considerations:
1. *Applied Science and Technology Index.*
2. *Statistical Abstract of the United States.*
3. Scientific and Technical Information Service.
4. University reports, congressional reports.
5. Department of Defense and military purchasing publishers.
6. Trade journals and industrial reports.
7. Industry contacts, professional meetings.
8. Computer-assisted information searches.
9. National Science Foundation annual report.
10. *Research and Development Directory* patent records.

E. Industry considerations:
1. *Concentration Ratios in Manufacturing* (Bureau of the Census).
2. *Input-Output Survey* (productivity ratios).
3. *Monthly Labor Review* (productivity ratios).
4. *Quarterly Failure Report* (Dun & Bradstreet).
5. *Federal Reserve Bulletin* (capacity utilization).
6. *Report on Industrial Concentration and Product Diversification in the 1,000 Largest Manufacturing Companies* (Federal Trade Commission).
7. Industry trade publications.
8. Bureau of Economic Analysis, Department of Commerce (specialization ratios).

INDUSTRY AND OPERATING ENVIRONMENTS

A. Competition and supplier considerations:
1. Target Group Index.
2. U.S. Industrial Outlook.
3. Robert Morris annual statement studies.
4. Troy, Leo Almanac of Business & Industrial Financial Ratios.
5. Census of Enterprise Statistics.
6. Securities and Exchange Commission (10-K reports).
7. Annual reports of specific companies.
8. *Fortune 500 Directory, The Wall Street Journal, Barron's, Forbes, Dun's Review.*
9. Investment services and directories: Moody's, Dun & Bradstreet, Standard & Poor's, Starch Marketing, Funk & Scott Index.
10. Trade association surveys.
11. Industry surveys.
12. Market research surveys.
13. *Country Business Patterns.*
14. *Country and City Data Book.*
15. Industry contacts, professional meetings, salespeople.
16. *NFIB Quarterly Economic Report for Small Business.*

B. Customer profile:
1. *Statistical Abstract of the United States*, first source of statistics.
2. *Statistical Sources* by Paul Wasserman (a subject guide to data—both domestic and international).
3. *American Statistics Index* (Congressional Information Service Guide to statistical publications of U.S. government—monthly).
4. Office to the Department of Commerce:
   a. Bureau of the Census reports on population, housing, and industries.
   b. *U.S. Census of Manufacturers* (statistics by industry, area, and products).
   c. *Survey of Current Business* (analysis of business trends, especially February and July issues).
5. Market research studies (*A Basic Bibliography on Market Review*, compiled by Robert Ferber et al., American Marketing Association).
6. *Current Sources of Marketing Information: A Bibliography of Primary Marketing Data* by Gunther & Goldstein, AMA.
7. *Guide to Consumer Markets*, The Conference Board (provides statistical information with demographic, social, and economic data—annual).
8. *Survey of Buying Power.*
9. *Predicasts* (abstracts of publishing forecasts of all industries, detailed products, and end-use data).
10. *Predicasts Basebook* (historical data from 1960 to present, covering subjects ranging from population and GNP to specific products and services; series are coded by Standard Industrial Classifications).
11. *Market Guide* (individual market surveys of over 1,500 U.S. and Canadian cities; includes population, location, trade areas, banks, principal industries, colleges and universities, department and chain stores, newspapers, retail outlets, and sales).
12. *Country and City Data Book* (includes bank deposits, birth and death rates, business firms, education, employment, income of families, manufacturers, population, savings, and wholesale and retail trade).

13. *Yearbook of International Trade Statistics* (UN).
14. *Yearbook of National Accounts Statistics* (UN).
15. *Statistical Yearbook* (UN—covers population, national income, agricultural and industrial production, energy, external trade, and transport).
16. *Statistics of (Continents): Sources for Market Research* (includes separate books on Africa, America, Europe).

C. Key natural resources:
1. *Minerals Yearbook, Geological Survey* (Bureau of Mines, Department of the Interior).
2. *Agricultural Abstract* (Department of Agriculture).
3. Statistics of electric utilities and gas pipeline companies (Federal Power Commission).
4. Publications of various institutions: American Petroleum Institute, Atomic Energy Commission, Coal Mining Institute of America, American Steel Institute, and Brookings Institution.

APPENDIX 5–B

STRATEGIC PLANNING FORECASTING TOOLS AND TECHNIQUES

1. **Dialectical Inquiry.**
   Development, evaluation, and synthesis of conflicting points of view by (1) having separate assigned groups use debate format to formulate and refine each point of view and (2) then bringing two groups together for presentation of debate between and synthesis of their points of view.

2. **Nominal Group Technique.**
   Development, evaluation, and synthesis of individual points of view through an interactive process in a group setting.

3. **Delphi Method.**
   Development, evaluation, and synthesis of individual points of view by systematically soliciting and collating judgments on a particular topic through a set of carefully designed sequential questionnaires interspersed with summarized information and feedback of opinions derived from earlier responses.

4. **Focus Groups.**
   Bringing together recognized experts and qualified individuals in an organized setting to develop, evaluate, and synthesize their individual points of view on a particular topic.

5. **Simulation Technique.**
   Computer-based technique for simulating future situations and then predicting the outcome of various courses of action against each of these situations.

6. **PIMS Analysis.**
   Application of the experiences of a diverse sample of successful and unsuccessful firms.

7. **Market Opportunity Analysis.**
   Identification of markets and market factors in the economy and the industry that will affect the demand for and marketing of a product or service.

8. **Benchmarking.**
   Comparative analysis of competitor programs and strategic positions for use as reference points in the formulation of organization objectives.

9. **Situational Analysis** (SWOT or TOWS).
   Systematic development and evaluation of past, present, and future data to identify internal strengths and weaknesses and external threats and opportunities.

10. **Critical Success Factors/Strategic Issues Analysis.**
    Identification and analysis of a limited number of areas in which high performance will ensure a successful competitive position.

11. **Product Life Cycle Analysis.**
    Analysis of market dynamics in which a product is viewed according to its position within distinct stages of its sales history.

12. **Future Studies.**
    Development of future situations and factors based on agreement of a group of "experts," often from a variety of functional areas within a firm.

Source: Excerpted with updates from J. Webster, W. Reif, and J. Bracker, "The Manager's Guide to Strategic Planning Tools and Techniques," *Planning Review*, November–December 1989, pp. 4–13, 48.

13. **Multiple Scenarios.**

Smoothly unfolding narratives that describe an assumed future expressed through a sequence of time frames and snapshots.

14. **SPIRE** (Systematic Procedure for Identification of Relevant Environments).

A computer-assisted, matrix-generating tool for forecasting environmental changes that can have a dramatic impact on operations.

15. **Environmental Scanning, Forecasting, and Trend Analysis.**

Continuous process, usually computer based, of monitoring external factors, events, situations, and projections of forecasts of trends.

16. **Experience Curves.**

An organizing framework for dynamic analyses of cost and price for a product, a company, or an industry over an extended period.

17. **Portfolio Classification Analysis.**

Classification and visual display of the present and prospective positions of firms and products according to the attractiveness of the market and the ability of the firms and products to compete within that market.

18. **Metagame Analysis.**

Arriving at a strategic direction by thinking through a series of viewpoints on a contemplated strategy in terms of every competitor and every combination of competitive responses.

19. **Strategic Gap Analysis.**

Examination of the difference between the extrapolation of current performance levels (e.g., current sales) and the projection of desired performance objectives (e.g., a desired sales level).

20. **Sustainable Growth Model.**

Financial analysis of the sales growth rate that is required to meet market share objectives and the degree to which capacity must be expanded to achieve that growth rate.

CHAPTER 5 COHESION CASE ILLUSTRATION

FORECASTING AND THE COCA-COLA COMPANY

Coca-Cola's chief executive officer, Roberto Goizueta, communicating with Coke share-holders, appeared to suggest that Coke's strategic management process avoids significant emphasis on forecasting when he said:

> As an organization we are not wasting our energy forecasting what the soft-drink industry will be like in the many countries around the world in which we operate. And neither are we spending our time forecasting what the future holds for this company. We will use our resources to construct today the foundation on which OUR future . . . THE FUTURE WE ARE CREATING FOR OURSELVES . . . will be built.

* * * * *

> We do not want to leave our shareowners with the false impression that this wonderful soft-drink business of The Coca-Cola Company is totally impervious to any and all setbacks. How-ever, we are running this business today at a high efficiency, and we have the attitude and the financial resources, as well as the management team, needed to take care of any negative eventu-ality which may come our way. So . . . when it does, if we don't completely neutralize it, at the very least, we will minimize its impact.
>
> On the other hand, and as with everything in life, there will also surely be unexpected positive events in the future of this Company. When they happen, we will quickly put them to work to our advantage. In the past we have demonstrated our system has such capabilities, and we will continue to take advantage of every opportunity in the future.

On the surface, it would appear that Mr. Goizueta places little faith in efforts to forecast future events. A closer reading and review of Coke's management actions suggest other-wise. In other words, Mr. Goizueta is at least in part saying that Coca-Cola is a very focused company. While it serves a myriad of markets worldwide, it has learned some very simple and powerful lessons about the fundamentals of success in the soft-drink business. And it is his belief that Coke's ability to do those things and to adjust those things to changing conditions will perhaps more profoundly influence its success in an unknown future than will reactions generated by any single forecast. According to Mr. Goizueta, successful global marketing of soft-drink products requires certain conditions be in place that require a long time to develop: (1) a company must have, build, or buy a powerful trademark to be a globally successful soft-drink company, and (2) that company must have a global business system through which to reach consumers. (3) Such a business system must be able to appeal to cultures as diverse as Switzerland and Swaziland—to tailor products and messages to local markets. And finally, (4) there must be an intangible yet powerful ingredient—a central theme, idea, or symbol—that binds together the business system, the brands, and the consumers into an association with their best feelings and memories each time they drink a Coke. And it is sensitivity to ways that these key condi-tions can be applied, refined, and expanded that shapes future success at Coke.

While Goizueta eschews forecasts, he recently told *Financial World*:

> In the United States, we will be growing 6 percent in volume with double-digit earnings growth. But outside the United States, where we have 9–10 percent volume growth, we will have higher double-digit earnings increases.

Apparently there is keen management interest in charting and projecting soft-drink consumption patterns. An internal company trend analysis of soft-drink consumption during 1991 and the preceding 10 years is shown in the table, "Selected Country Results," from The Coca-Cola Company 1994 Annual Report.

Another area where Coca-Cola management appears sensitive to monitoring are changes in key countries, which have large populations, that support introduction or re-introduction of the "Coca-Cola Business System." Coke management calls this "seeding for the future," as is illustrated regarding India, China, and Indonesia in the excerpt on page 167.

Finally, several soft-drink-related facts or trends have appeared in various industry forums that provide Coke management with confirmation of its inclinations or possible "forecasts." Some of these include:

1. While annual per capita soft-drink consumption in the United States is about 770 servings, in markets abroad per capita rates average only 62 servings. In less developed markets, such as India, consumers drink less than three servings a year.

2. In international markets, most soft drinks are sold in single-serve bottles, one at a time. Getting consumers to take home bigger packages means they'll drink more.

3. In the United States, vending machines account for 12 percent of soft-drink sales; but they're still a rarity in many countries.

4. Soft drinks represent about one quarter of all beverages consumed in the United States. That means replacing other beverages or expanding into them represents growth for soft-drink companies.

5. Eastern Europe is developing rapidly as a soft-drink market from a negligible base in 1992. The breakup of the Soviet Union has opened new markets that represent sustained volume growth opportunities.

SELECTED COUNTRY RESULTS

Estimated Unit Case[1] Volume

	Average Annual Growth				1994 Results			
	10 Years		5 Years		Unit Case Growth		Company	
	Company[3]	Industry[4]	Company[3]	Industry[4]	Company[3]	Industry[4]	Share[4]	Per Capita[4] Consumption
Worldwide[6]	7%	5%	6%	3%	10%	6%	46%	49
North America Business Sector[2]	4	3	4	3	7	4	41	296
United States	4	3	4	3	7	4	41	310
International Business Sector[6]	8	5	7	3	11	7	49	35
European Community	9	5	6	3	7	5	49	130
Benelux/Denmark	8	4	8	4	9	4	46	152
France	13	7	11	5	9	(1)	47	65
Germany	7	5	8	1	4	3	55	191
Great Britain	12	6	2	3	7	10	31	101
Italy	8	6	4	3	5	2	55	94
Spain	8	4	5	2	9	8	54	166
Pacific[5]	8	8	7	6	12	12	39	20
Australia	9	7	8	3	10	9	65	274
Japan[5]	6	1	6	2	8	8	30	133
Korea	5	5	4	1	11	5	52	59
Philippines	6	3	3	3	14	14	75	96
Thailand	12	14	9	9	14	11	48	54
Northeast Europe/Middle East (NEME)[6]	14	4	17	1	35	17	32	11
Egypt	5	2	4	0	47	4	55	26
Hungary	20	2	37	6	4	12	42	111
Norway	11	7	8	5	9	15	59	256
Poland	33	2	69	8	44	47	24	29
Africa	5	2	5	(1)	1	(7)	84	23
Nigeria	2	0	6	0	(14)	(25)	82	22
South Africa	5	3	5	1	4	0	88	146
Zimbabwe	8	6	5	(1)	9	4	87	62
Latin America	8	6	6	4	10	4	55	148
Argentina	7	6	14	11	12	12	57	189
Brazil	8	7	0	1	10	14	56	92
Chile	15	14	12	8	8	6	64	217
Mexico	8	6	6	4	11	7	57	333

[1]Unit case equals 24 8-ounce drinks.
[2]Consists of United States and Canada.
[3]Includes non-carbonated soft drinks.
[4]Includes only flavored, carbonated soft drinks.
[5]Company share and per capita include Japanese non-carbonated soft drinks; revised to conform with
    Japanese industry standards (equivalent Company share for Japan in 1993 was 31).
[6]The calculation of per capita consumption includes India and several former Soviet republics.

the Future

Seeding for

Over the past five years, the Company's international unit case sales have increased at an average annual rate of 8 percent. No countries better exemplify the Company's long-term opportunity to maintain or exceed that sort of growth than the three profiled on this page. **Nearly 45 percent of the more than 5 billion people on earth live in China, India or Indonesia, but the per capita soft drink consumption rates for the countries are only 8, 3 and 6, respectively.** *While explosive short-term growth is unlikely, the potential for tremendous, sustained growth over time is extraordinary, and the Company is taking aggressive actions now to prepare the ground. Set forth below are some of the ways in which we are seeding for the future.*

INDIA

With 860 million people, India is, by far, the largest market in which Company products are not currently produced. That should change in 1993, thanks to the Indian government's approval of a joint venture formed in late 1991.

The Company will not, however, be starting from scratch. During the 1970s, the Coca-Cola system in India comprised 21 bottlers selling more than 32 million unit cases annually and accounting for 60 percent of the country's carbonated soft drink sales. The Company left India in 1977, but the Coca-Cola trademark continues to enjoy strong, positive recognition and recall among consumers.

The immediate task is to re-establish bottling and distribution networks in and around large metropolitan areas. Once up and running, we will be addressing several marketing opportunities, including packaging, where we see tremendous potential for large, multiserve containers.

Last year, the entire Indian carbonated soft drink industry sold only 113 million unit cases, less than the Company sold in Korea, a country with only 5 percent as many people. To say that the opportunity is enormous is an understatement. No market in the world shows greater promise for rapid, sustained growth for years to come.

CHINA

The Company resumed operations in China in 1981 after an absence of 41 years. Since our re-entry, we have invested $75 million in 13 bottling plants and a concentrate plant in Shanghai, which makes it possible for bottlers to purchase concentrate with local currency, a distinct advantage.

Company products have long been acceptable in China — in 1933 the country became the first market outside the United States to post annual sales of more than a million unit cases — and we are continuing to invest as necessary to make them available and affordable to every one of China's 1.2 billion people.

INDONESIA

If there is such a thing as an ideal soft drink market, it probably looks like Indonesia. Fifty-five percent of its 180 million people are under age 25; the average year-round temperature is a humid 80°F; gross national product is growing 6 to 7 percent a year; and the government welcomes foreign investment.

Last year, the Coca-Cola system sold 34 million unit cases of Company products, accounting for 71 percent of all carbonated soft drinks sold in the country. Because we see the potential for a vastly larger market, we have, over the past few years, rationalized our bottling system and entered, directly and indirectly, into three joint ventures that last year posted 87 percent of our system's unit case sales. Since we began making these investments in 1987, unit case sales have grown at a compound annual rate of 15 percent, and the business is well positioned for continued rapid growth in the years to come.

35

6

INTERNAL ANALYSIS

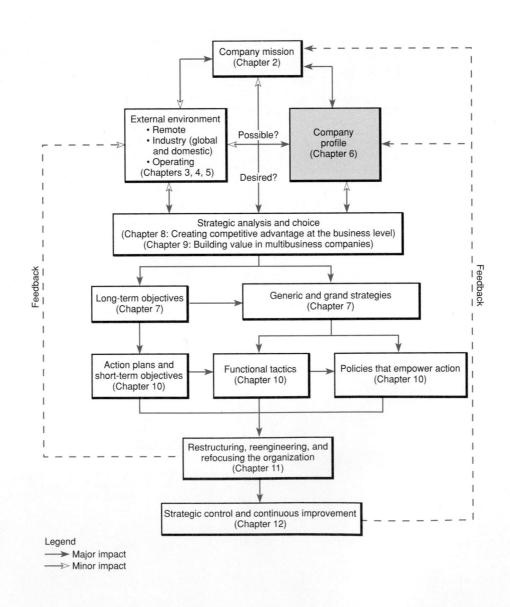

Company mission
(Chapter 2)

External environment
• Remote
• Industry (global and domestic)
• Operating
(Chapters 3, 4, 5)

Possible?

Desired?

Company profile
(Chapter 6)

Strategic analysis and choice
(Chapter 8: Creating competitive advantage at the business level)
(Chapter 9: Building value in multibusiness companies)

Long-term objectives
(Chapter 7)

Generic and grand strategies
(Chapter 7)

Action plans and short-term objectives
(Chapter 10)

Functional tactics
(Chapter 10)

Policies that empower action
(Chapter 10)

Restructuring, reengineering, and refocusing the organization
(Chapter 11)

Strategic control and continuous improvement
(Chapter 12)

Feedback

Feedback

Legend
⟶ Major impact
⟶ Minor impact

Three ingredients are critical to the success of a strategy. First, the strategy must be *consistent* with conditions in the competitive environment. Specifically, it must take advantage of existing or projected opportunities and minimize the impact of major threats. Second, the strategy must place *realistic* requirements on the firm's internal capabilities. In other words, the firm's pursuit of market opportunities must be based not only on the existence of such opportunities but also on the firm's key internal strengths. Finally, the strategy must be *carefully executed*. The focus of this chapter is on the second ingredient: *realistic analysis of the firm's internal capabilities.*

Managers often do this subjectively, based on intuition and "gut feel." Years of seasoned industry experience positions managers to make sound subjective judgments. But just as often, or more often, this may not be the case. In fast-changing environments, reliance on past experiences can cause management myopia or a tendency to accept the status quo and disregard signals that change is needed. And with managers new to strategic decision making, subjective decisions are particularly suspect. A lack of experience is easily replaced by emotion, narrow functional expertise, and the opinions of others creating the foundation on which newer managers build strategic recommendations. So it is that new managers' subjective assessments often come back to haunt them.

This chapter looks at several ways managers achieve greater objectivity and rigor as they analyze their company's internal capabilities. Managers often start their internal analysis with questions like: "How well is the current strategy working? What is our current situation? Or what are our strengths and weaknesses?" *SWOT analysis* and *functional analysis* are two approaches discussed in this chapter that managers frequently use to introduce realism and greater objectivity into their attempts to answer these questions. More recently, insightful managers have begun to look at their business as a chain of activities that add value by creating the products or services they sell. Associated with this perspective is a powerful concept for introducing rigor and objectivity into internal analysis, the *value chain*, which this chapter will examine in great detail. Finally, objectivity and realism are enhanced when managers use meaningful standards for comparison regardless of the particular analytical framework they employ in internal analysis. We conclude this chapter examining how managers do this using *past performance*, stages of industry evolution, *comparison with competitors* or other *"benchmarks," industry norms*, and traditional *financial analysis.*

Laura Ashley Holdings PLC, the famous United Kingdom-based retail chain, recently convinced American Ann Iverson to leave her position as President and CEO of Kay Bee Toys to move to London and become Laura Ashley's new President and CEO. She is the first female CEO since the late Laura Ashley founded the company 42 years ago. Iverson spent the first four months traveling to stores in the United Kingdom, Europe, and the United States conducting a realistic analysis of Laura Ashley's internal capabilities and situation. You should read Global Strategy in Action 6–1 to see what she found and you should use this example to help you understand the focus of this chapter.

TRADITIONAL APPROACHES TO INTERNAL ANALYSIS

Managers have historically relied on two approaches to structure their analysis of internal capabilities so that they introduce greater objectivity into their firm's strategic decision-making process: SWOT analysis and functional analysis.

ENGLAND'S FAMOUS RETAILER LAURA ASHLEY HOLDINGS PLC NEEDED A WOMAN AT THE HELM TO CONDUCT A REALISTIC INTERNAL ANALYSIS

When Ann Iverson became CEO of Laura Ashley, she found the Laura Ashley name meant different things to different people. Unfortunately, most of those people worked at Laura Ashley stores. Stores in the United States and Europe offered vastly different items. Buyers and designers around the globe created hundreds of styles, and many clashed with Laura Ashley's English country fashions.

The chain's mail-order catalog showed the problem. Fall 1995 found three different versions for the United States, United Kingdom, and European markets. Iverson traveled throughout the various stores and quickly concluded that Laura Ashley had lost its focus. "We didn't have a single point of view or great conviction . . . people didn't understand what we stood for or even who they reported to." Iverson went to work.

First, she was the fourth CEO in five years. She was the first woman since the founder 40 years earlier, and she was the first with retail experience among the last five. Heading into 1996 she offered the following assessment of Laura Ashley's current internal capabilities.

"One of our main problems is a vast range of product lines, many filled with weak sellers and duplicate styles." When she joined the firm, 83 percent of its sales came from 22 percent of the merchandise. She quickly eliminated 30 percent of the clothing styles and 20 percent of the home furnishings.

"Our U.S. stores are too small and cramped for our large range. Most U.S. stores are only 600 square feet while newer shops in the United Kingdom average 4,700 square feet. And many U.S. stores are second rate. Of the 500 best U.S. shopping malls, Laura Ashley has stores in only 150."

Although the famous Laura Ashley "green box" store front is likely to remain intact, Iverson says she hopes to create a common store front design and format. "Of the famous brands in more than one market—Estee Lauder, Ralph Lauren, the Gap—they all have a common theme. They have a common way they talk to the customer. We don't.

"Many of our costs are too high. Distribution costs rose 1.6 million pounds in six months due to a contract with a shipper that costs the company far too much money. And shipping is chaotic at times—products shipped from the Far East go to a facility in Wales where they were then packaged and reshipped to the United States—and then repackaged and sent to Japan."

Iverson is also reviewing the company's heavy vertical integration with significant manufacturing capacity. She says retailers should not be manufacturers and distributors as well as retailers.

British analysts are encouraged for 1997 based on her initial efforts. They are optimistic about her predictions that Laura Ashley can move from operating margins around 2 percent to double-digit levels in 1998. Her concluding comment after completing her internal analysis and charting her direction: "There's no question that it's a brilliant brand, but we're finally behaving like a retailer."

It appears Iverson conducted a realistic internal analysis.

SWOT Analysis

SWOT is an acronym for the internal Strengths and Weaknesses of a firm and the environmental Opportunities and Threats facing that firm. SWOT analysis is an easy technique through which managers create a quick overview of a company's strategic situation. It is based on the assumption that an effective strategy derives from a sound "fit" between a firm's internal capabilities (strengths and weaknesses) and its external situation (opportunities and threats). A good fit maximizes a firm's strengths and opportunities and minimizes its weaknesses and threats. Accurately applied, this simple assumption has powerful implications for the design of a successful strategy.

Environmental industry analysis (Chapters 3 through 5) provides the information needed to identify opportunities and threats in a firm's environment, the first fundamental focus in SWOT analysis. We define opportunities and threats first.

Opportunities

An *opportunity* is a major favorable situation in a firm's environment. Key trends are one source of opportunities. Identification of a previously overlooked market segment, changes in competitive or regulatory circumstances, technological changes, and improved buyer or supplier relationships could represent opportunities for the firm.

Threats

A *threat* is a major unfavorable situation in a firm's environment. Threats are key impediments to the firm's current or desired position. The entrance of new competitors, slow market growth, increased bargaining power of key buyers or suppliers, technological changes, and new or revised regulations could represent threats to a firm's success.

Japanese acceptance of superior U.S. technology in personal computers is proving a major opportunity for Apple and IBM. Deregulation of the airline industry was a major opportunity for regional carriers (such as Southwest Airlines) to serve routes previously closed to them. Some traditional carriers (such as United) saw deregulation as a threat to the profitability of their high-traffic routes. So an opportunity for one firm can be a threat to another. Moreover, the same factor can be seen as both an opportunity and a threat. For example, the baby boom generation moving into its prime earning years presents a major opportunity for financial service firms like Merrill Lynch. However, this generation wants convenient inexpensive financial services, which is a major threat to Merrill Lynch's established broker network—historically a Merrill Lynch strength.

Understanding the key opportunities and threats facing a firm helps its managers identify realistic options from which to choose an appropriate strategy and clarifies the most effective niche for the firm.

The second fundamental focus in SWOT analysis is the identification of internal strengths and weaknesses.

Strengths

A *strength* is a resource, skill, or other advantage relative to competitors and the needs of the markets a firm serves or expects to serve. It is a *distinctive competence* when it gives the firm a comparative advantage in the marketplace. Strengths may exist with regard to financial resources, image, market leadership, buyer-supplier relations, and other factors.

Weaknesses

A *weakness* is a limitation or deficiency in resource, skills, or capabilities that seriously impedes a firm's effective performance. Facilities, financial resources, management capabilities, marketing skills, and brand image can be sources of weaknesses.

The sheer size and level of Microsoft's user base have proven to be a key strength on which it built its initially successful strategy in applications software like word processing, financial services, and operating systems. Limited financial capacity was a weakness recognized by Southwest Airlines, which charted a selective route expansion strategy to build the best profit record in a deregulated airline industry.

FIGURE 6–1
SWOT Analysis Diagram

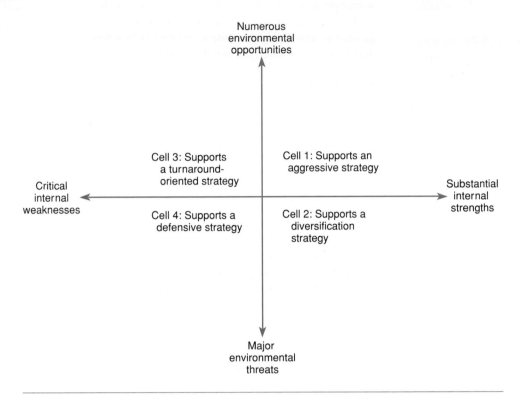

SWOT analysis can be used in many ways to aid strategy analysis. The most common way is to use it as a logical framework guiding systematic discussion of a firm's situation and the basic alternatives that the firm might consider. What one manager sees as an opportunity, another may see as a potential threat. Likewise, a strength to one manager may be a weakness to another. Different assessments may reflect underlying power considerations within the firm or differing factual perspectives. Systematic analysis of these issues facilitates objective internal analysis.

A second way in which SWOT analysis can be used to aid strategic analysis is illustrated in Figure 6–1. Key external opportunities and threats are systematically compared with internal strengths and weaknesses in a structured approach. The objective is identification of one of four distinct patterns in the match between a firm's internal and external situations. These patterns are represented by the four cells in Figure 6–1. Cell 1 is the most favorable situation; the firm faces several environmental opportunities and has numerous strengths that encourage pursuit of those opportunities. This situation suggests growth-oriented strategies to exploit the favorable match. America OnLine's intensive market development strategy in the online services market is the result of a favorable match of its strengths of technical expertise, early entry, and reputation with an opportunity for impressive market growth as millions of people joined the "information highway" in the latter 1990s. Cell 4 is the least favorable situation, with the firm facing major environmental threats from a position of relative weakness. This situation clearly calls for strategies that reduce or redirect involvement in the products or markets examined by means of SWOT analysis. Citicorp's successful turnaround from the verge of insolvency due to massive defaults on many international loans is an example of such a strategy in the early 1990s.

In cell 2, a firm with key strengths faces an unfavorable environment. In this situation, strategies would use current strengths to build long-term opportunities in more opportunistic product markets. Greyhound, possessing many strengths in intercity bus transportation, still faced an environment dominated by fundamental, long-term threats, such as airline competition and high costs. The result was product development into nonpassenger (freight) services, followed by diversification into other businesses (e.g., financial services).

A firm in cell 3 faces impressive market opportunity but is constrained by internal weaknesses. The focus of strategy for such a firm is eliminating the internal weaknesses so as to more effectively pursue the market opportunity. Disney's late 1995 acquisition of ABC/Capital Cities was in part an attempt to overcome key weaknesses in Disney's control of distribution outlets for its varied, excellent programming so that it could more easily pursue global opportunities in the entertainment industry of the 21st century.

Overall, SWOT analysis highlights the central role that the identification of internal strengths and weaknesses plays in a manager's search for effective strategies. The careful matching of a firm's opportunities and threats with its strengths and weaknesses is the essence of sound strategy formulation. Global Strategy in Action 6–2 shows three key players in the global PC industry attempting to do just this in 1996.

Although SWOT analysis provides an excellent framework through which managers can view their firm's strategic situation, it does not explain how managers identify internal strengths and weaknesses. The functional approach is one way managers have traditionally sought to isolate and evaluate internal strengths and weaknesses.

The Functional Approach

Key internal factors are a firm's basic capabilities, limitations, and characteristics. Figure 6–2 lists typical internal factors, some of which would be the focus of internal analysis in most firms. The list is broken along functional lines for one logical reason. Most firms organize their operations at some level along functional lines to get their products or services sold, produced, delivered, financed, and accounted. It stands to reason that close scrutiny of each of these functions serves as a compelling, strategically relevant focus for internal analysis.

Firms are not likely to evaluate all of the factors listed in Figure 6–2 (pp. 176–77) as potential strengths or weaknesses. To develop or revise a strategy, managers would prefer to identify the few factors on which its success is most likely to depend. Equally important, a firm's reliance on particular internal factors will vary by industry, market segment, product life cycle, and the firm's current position. Managers are looking for what Chester Barnard calls the "strategic factors," those internal capabilities that are most critical for success in a particular competitive area. The strategic factors of firms in the oil industry, for example, will be quite different from those of firms in the construction industry or the hospitality industry. Strategic factors also can vary among firms within the same industry. In the mechanical writing industry, for example, the strategies of BIC and Cross, both successful firms, are based on different internal strengths: BIC's on its strength in mass production, extensive advertising, and mass distribution channels; Cross's on high quality, image, and selective distribution channels.

Strategists examine a firm's past performance to isolate key internal contributors to favorable (or unfavorable) results. What did we do well, or poorly, in marketing, operations, and financial management that had a major influence on our past results? Was our sales force effectively organized? Were we in the right channels of distribution? Did we have the financial resources needed to support our past strategy? The same examination can be applied to a firm's current situation, with particular emphasis on changes in the

THREE GLOBAL PC MAKERS TAKE A "SWOT" AT THE U.S. HOME PC MARKET

The PC industry is becoming very competitive. Forrester Research, which predicted a "golden age" for home PCs in the late 1990s, now says the market will slow significantly by 1998. They say that "PC makers will need new strategies to endure, such as really cheap, specialized models. Dell Computer's wizard founder Mr. Dell says: "There's no way all these companies are going to survive." Here's what other "experts" are saying:

Profit margins are very thin, the products are obsolete in six months, and buyers are fickle with endless options. More and more companies are jumping into the home PC market. But 1996 sees too many players and cut-throat competition.

Packard Bell leads the home PC market with a 32 percent share, but doesn't make much money and recently sold 20 percent of itself to NEC–Japan. Hewlett Packard operates at a loss; IBM lost $1 billion in 1995. "We don't know if anyone is making money,"says an IBM spokesman, "yet you need a lot of inventory on which prices come down all the time!"

New players keep coming. NEC and ACER–Taiwan re-entered the home PC market. And solid players like Dell, Gateway, Apple, AST, and Compaq already have serious positions. AT&T and Radio Shack have cut their losses and exited.

PC makers argue that the business segment is 90 percent penetrated; the home market is growing and only 30 percent of U.S. homes (smaller overseas) have PCs, leaving 68 million homes without them. "We have the opportunity to become a market leader in the major growth opportunities—home PCs—over the next 20 years" say HP's home PC general manager.

But recent surveys suggest only 5 percent of homes without PCs are likely to purchase within one year. Replacement sales are less likely with easily upgraded Pentium models. The price tag of $2,000 + is way above mass merchandising standards. Some outsiders like Oracle's Larry Ellison are pushing a $500 stripped-down model that will "surf" the Internet. It's hotly rejected by major PC makers, maybe because it could redefine the whole industry.

Gross profit margins for PC makers range from 8 percent to 14 percent—well below the 20 percent to 30 percent in traditional consumer electronics. Microsoft generates an 80 percent margin on its Windows operating system; Intel gets a 50 percent gross margin on its Pentium chips.

Source: Bart Ziegler, "PC Makers' Big Push into the Home Market Comes at Risky Time," *The Wall Street Journal* 226, no. 86; Jeff Trachtenberg and Bart Ziegler, "Sony Expected in U.S. Market for Home PCs,"*The Wall Street Journal*, November 13, 1995; "Making Over the IBM PC Co.," *Information Week*, November 13, 1995, p. 97; Peter Burrows, "Is Spindler A Survivor?" *Business Week*, October 2, 1995, p. 62.

importance of key dimensions over time. For example, heavy advertising, mass production, and mass distribution were strategic internal factors in BIC's initial strategy for ballpoint pens and disposable lighters. With the product life cycle fast reaching maturity, BIC later determined that cost-conscious mass production was a strategic factor, whereas heavy advertising was not.

Analysis of past trends in a firm's sales, costs, and profitability is of major importance in identifying its strategic internal factors. And that identification should be based on a clear picture of the nature of the firm's sales. An anatomy of past sales trends broken down by product lines, channels of distribution, key customers or types of customers, geographic region, and sales approach should be developed in detail. A similar anatomy should be developed on costs and profitability. Detailed investigation of the firm's performance history helps isolate the internal factors that influence its sales, costs, and profitability or their interrelationships. For example, one firm may find that 83 percent of its sales result from 25 percent of its products, and another firm may find that 30 percent of its products (or

Let's look at three industry players.

SONY—Japanese electronic giant Sony chose 1996 to enter the U.S. home PC market. It has concluded that it can use its powerful brand name and reservoir of electronics expertise to elbow its way into this "growth market." It also believes synergies with its semiconductor and computer peripheral businesses, which are its fastest growing U.S. businesses, represent key strengths. Unknown to many is the fact that Sony has long manufactured portable computers and workstations for Dell and Apple. It also sells monitors to virtually all U.S. computer manufacturers.

IBM—The new head of the IBM PC Co., Robert Stephenson, taking over a group that lost $1 billion in 1995, said this: "I'm spending my time reengineering the whole process of becoming a reliable supplier. We have good strategies. We just are not executing well. If we can get the reengineering of our manufacturing, procurement, and distribution right, marketing and sales will follow. To put it bluntly, if we can't correct our reliability as a supplier, we won't be in business. . . . In home PCs, we have a good product but its $2,000–$3,000 price is too high . . . And we have got to change the way we develop products and make brand managers and marketing people think in tune."

Apple—Demand for Macintosh has been booming with a $1 billion backlog in 1996. But Apple's stock price has plunged. Apple can't cash in on the surge because it lacks critical parts, especially modems and custom chips. That's because many of its components are custom-designed and sourced to only one supplier. That makes accurate forecasts critical . . . and that's where Apple screwed up. 1995 sales surged 25 percent, Apple predicted 15 percent growth based on "sandbagged" estimates Apple salespeople gave Apple executives that they knew they could easily surpass in order to enhance their bonuses. And analysts predict consumers unable to buy Macintosh will opt for computers running Windows 95 and will not return to the Apple fold. Michael Spindler, Apple's CEO, says "I resent the idea that we have systemic problems" as he argues their problems are fixable.

When you apply a SWOT analysis to the home PC market and these three players, what do you see and what do you think will happen?

services) contribute 78 percent of its profitability. On the basis of such results, a firm may determine that certain key internal factors (e.g., experience in particular distribution channels, pricing policies, warehouse location, technology) deserve major attention in the formulation of future strategy.

The identification of strategic internal factors requires an external focus. A strategist's efforts to isolate key internal factors are assisted by analysis of industry conditions and trends and by comparisons with competitors. BIC's identification of mass production and advertising as key internal factors was based as much on analysis of industry and competitive characteristics as on analysis of its own past performance. Changing conditions in an industry can lead to the need to reexamine a firm's internal strengths and weaknesses in light of newly emerging determinants of success in that industry.

It is important for you to see that a functional approach, regardless of situational differences, focuses managers on basic business functions leading to a more objective, relevant internal analysis that enhances strategic decision making. Whether looking at attributes of marketing, production, financing, information systems, or human resource management, the functional approach structures managers' thinking in a focused, potentially objective manner.

FIGURE 6–2
Key Internal Factors: Potential Strengths or Weaknesses

Marketing

Firm's products-services: breadth of product line.
Concentration of sales in a few products or to a few customers.
Ability to gather needed information about markets.
Market share or submarket shares.
Product-service mix and expansion potential: life cycle of key products; profit-sales balance in
    product-service.
Channels of distribution: number, coverage, and control.
Effective sales organization; knowledge of customer needs.
Product-service image, reputation, and quality.
Imaginativeness, efficiency, and effectiveness of sales promotion and advertising.
Pricing strategy and pricing flexibility.
Procedures for digesting market feedback and developing new products, services, or markets.
After-sale service and follow-up.
Goodwill—brand loyalty.

Financial and Accounting

Ability to raise short-term capital.
Ability to raise long-term capital; debt-equity.
Corporate-level resources (multibusiness firm).
Cost of capital relative to that of industry and competitors.
Tax considerations.
Relations with owners, investors, and stockholders.
Leverage position; capacity to utilize alternative financial strategies, such as lease or sale and
    leaseback.
Cost of entry and barriers to entry.
Price-earnings ratio.
Working capital; flexibility of capital structure.
Effective cost control; ability to reduce cost.
Financial size.
Efficiency and effectiveness of accounting system for cost, budget, and profit planning.

Production, Operations, Technical

Raw materials cost and availability, supplier relationships.
Inventory control systems; inventory turnover.
Location of facilities; layout and utilization of facilities.
Economies of scale.
Technical efficiency of facilities and utilization of capacity.
Effectiveness of subcontracting use.
Degree of vertical integration; value added and profit margin.
Efficiency and cost-benefit of equipment.

While the functional approach offers logical advantages focusing internal analysis, managers that endured the downsizing and reengineering 1990s found the need for an approach that focused them even more narrowly on how work actually took place within their companies as they sought to meet customer needs. What these managers were responding to was the reality that producing goods or services and handling customers often necessitated the simultaneous involvement of multiple functions to be effective. They needed a way to look at their business as a series of activities that took place to create value for a customer—and to use this view as the framework to guide internal analysis. The value chain concept became their framework.

Value Chain Analysis

Value chain analysis is based on the assumption that a business's basic purpose is to create value for users of its products or services. In value chain analysis, managers divide the activities of their firm into sets of separate activities that add value. Their firm is viewed as

FIGURE 6-2
(concluded)

Production, Operations, Technical (cont.)

Effectiveness of operation control procedures: design, scheduling, purchasing, quality control, and efficiency.

Costs and technological competencies relative to those of industry and competitors.

Research and development–technology–innovation.

Patents, trademarks, and similar legal protection.

Personnel

Management personnel.

Employees' skill and morale.

Labor relations costs compared to those of industry and competitors.

Efficiency and effectiveness of personnel policies.

Effectiveness of incentives used to motivate performance.

Ability to level peaks and valleys of employment.

Employee turnover and absenteeism.

Specialized skills.

Experience.

Quality Management

Relationship with suppliers, customers.

Internal practices to enhance quality of products and services.

Procedures for monitoring quality.

Information Systems

Timeliness and accuracy of information about sales, operations, cash, and suppliers.

Relevance of information for tactical decisions.

Information to manage quality issues; customer service.

Ability of people to use the information that is provided.

Organization and General Management

Organizational structure.

Firm's image and prestige.

Firm's record in achieving objectives.

Organization of communication system.

Overall organizational control system (effectiveness and utilization).

Organizational climate; organizational culture.

Use of systematic procedures and techniques in decision making.

Top-management skill, capabilities, and interest.

Strategic planning system.

Intraorganizational synergy (multibusiness firms).

a chain of value-creating activities starting with procuring raw materials or inputs and continuing through design, component production, manufacturing and assembly, distribution, sales, delivery, and support of the ultimate user of its products or services. Each of these activities can add value and each can be a source of competitive advantage. By identifying and examining these activities, managers often acquire an in-depth understanding of their firm's capabilities, its cost structure, and how these create competitive advantage or disadvantage.

Value chain analysis divides a firm's activities into two major categories, primary activities and support activities, as shown in Figure 6–3. *Primary activities* are those involved in the physical creation of the product, marketing and transfer to the buyer, and after-sale support. *Support activities* assist the primary activities by providing infrastructure or inputs that allow them to take place on an ongoing basis. The value chain includes a *profit margin* since a markup above the cost of providing a firm's value-adding activities is normally part of the price paid by the buyer—creating value that exceeds cost so as to generate a return for the effort.

FIGURE 6–3
The Value Chain

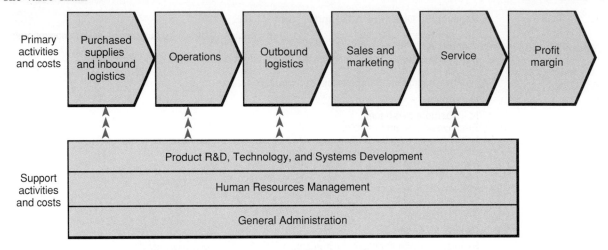

Primary Activities

· **Purchased Supplies and Inbound Logistics**—Activities, costs, and assets associated with purchasing fuel, energy, raw materials, parts components, merchandise, and consumable items from vendors; receiving, storing, and disseminating inputs from suppliers; inspection; and inventory management.

· **Operations**—Activities, costs, and assets associated with converting inputs into final product form (production, assembly, packaging, equipment maintenance, facilities, operations, quality assurance, environmental protection).

· **Outbound Logistics**—Activities, costs, and assets dealing with physically distributing the product to buyers (finished goods warehousing, order processing, order picking and packing, shipping, delivery vehicle operations).

· **Sales and Marketing**—Activities, costs, and assets related to sales force efforts, advertising and promotion, market research and planning, and dealer/distributor support.

· **Service**—Activities, costs, and assets associated with providing assistance to buyers, such as installation, spare parts delivery, maintenance and repair, technical assistance, buyer inquiries, and complaints.

Support Activities

· **Research, Technology, and Systems Development**—Activities, costs, and assets relating to product R&D, process R&D, process design improvement, equipment design, computer software development, telecommunications systems, computer-assisted design and engineering, new database capabilities, and development of computerized support systems.

· **Human Resources Management**—Activities, costs, and assets associated with the recruitment, hiring, training, development, and compensation of all types of personnel; labor relations activities; development of knowledge-based skills.

· **General Administration**—Activities, costs, and assets relating to general management, accounting and finance, legal and regulatory affairs, safety and security, management information systems, and other "overhead" functions.

Note: Purchasing, also called *procurement*, was listed as a support activity in the original value chain model. We have chosen to list it as part of the inbound primary activities because of the prominent role it plays at this stage for most value-sensitive companies today. At the same time, keep in mind that many companies retain a procurement function that provides purchasing support to all the organization's primary activities. For example, office supplies or other routine supplies, from safety gear in operations to recurring ads in newspapers sought by marketing, may all be handled through one suport activity or procurement department.

Source: Adapted from Michael E. Porter, *Competitive Advantage* (New York: The Free Press, 1985), pp 37–43; and A. A. Thompson and A. Strickland, *Strategic Management* (Burr Ridge, IL: Richard D. Irwin, 1995), p. 98.

FIGURE 6–4

The Difference between Traditional Cost Accounting and Activity-Based Cost Accounting

Traditional Cost Accounting in a Purchasing Department		Activity-Based Cost Accounting in the Same Purchasing Department	
Wages and Salaries	$350,000	Evaluate supplier capabilities	$135,750
Employee benefits	115,000	Process purchase orders	82,100
Supplies	6,500	Expedite supplier deliveries	23,500
Travel	2,400	Expedite internal processing	15,840
Depreciation	17,000	Check quality of items purchased	94,300
Other fixed charges	124,000	Check incoming deliveries against purchase orders	48,450
Miscellaneous operating expenses	25,250	Resolve problems	110,000
		Internal administration	130,210
	$640,150		$640,150

Source: Terence P. Pare, "A New Tool for Managing Costs," *Fortune*, June 14, 1993, pp. 124–29. © 1993, Time, Inc. All rights reserved.

Conducting a Value Chain Analysis

The initial step in value chain analysis is to divide a company's operations into specific activities or business processes, usually grouping them similarly to the primary and support activity categories provided in Figure 6–3. Within each category, a firm typically performs a number of discrete activities that may represent key strengths or weaknesses. Service activities, for example, may include such discrete activities as installation, repair, parts distribution, and upgrading—any of which could be a major source of competitive advantage or disadvantage. The manager's challenge at this point is to be very detailed attempting to "disaggregate" what actually goes on into numerous distinct, analyzable activities rather than settling for a broad, general categorization.

The next step is to attempt to attach costs to each discrete activity. Each activity in the value chain incurs costs and ties up time and assets. Value chain analysis requires managers to assign costs and assets to each activity, thereby providing the basis to estimate costs of each activity. The result provides managers with a very different way of viewing costs than traditional cost accounting procedures would produce, as seen in Figure 6–4. Many managers find the value activity costs more useful in drawing conclusions about and managing internal strengths and weaknesses.

The data necessary to support value chain analysis can be formidable, particularly given its nontraditional format. Traditional accounting identifies costs in broad expense categories—wages, benefits, travel, supplies, depreciation, and so on. Activity-based costing requires managers to "disaggregate" these broad numbers across specific tasks and activities. Figure 6–5 gives a good illustration of the challenge, and the benefit, in doing this in a purchasing department.

Once the company's value chain has been documented and costs determined, managers need to identify the activities that are critical to buyer satisfaction and market success. It is those that are deserving major scrutiny in an internal analysis. Three considerations are essential at this stage in the value chain analysis. First, the company's basic mission needs to influence managers' choice of activities they examine in detail. If the company is focused on being a low-cost provider, then management attention to lower costs should be very visible; and missions built around commitment to differentiation should find managers spending more on activities that are differentiation cornerstones. Retailer Wal-Mart focuses intensely on costs related to inbound logistics and purchasing to build its competitive advantage while

FIGURE 6–5
The Value Chain System

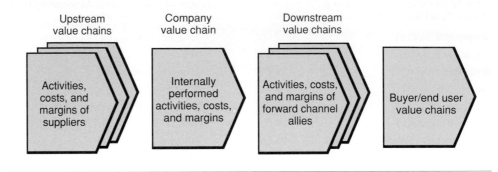

Source: Adapted from Michael E. Porter, *Competitive Advantage* (New York: The Free Press, 1985), p. 35.

Nordstrom builds its distinct position in retailing emphasizing sales and support activities on which they spend twice the retail industry average. The Gap's use of value chain analysis to guide its spectacular retail success is described in Strategy in Action 6–1.

Second, the nature of value chains and the relative importance of the activities within them vary by industry. Lodging firms like Holiday Inn's major costs and concerns involve operational activities—it provides its service instantaneously at each location—and marketing activities, while having minimal concern for outbound logistics. Yet for a distributor, such as the food distributor PYA, inbound and outbound logistics are the most critical area. Major retailers like Wal-Mart have built value advantages focusing on purchasing and inbound logistics while the most successful personal computer companies have built via sales, outbound logistics, and service through the mail order process.

Third, the relative importance of value activities can vary by a company's position in a broader value system that includes the value chains of its upstream suppliers and downstream customers or partners involved in providing products or services to end users (see Figure 6–5). A producer of roofing shingles depends heavily on the activities of wholesale distributors and building supply retailers to reach roofing contractors and do-it-yourselfers. Paint manufacturers typically have a similar situation, although some strong regional independent paint producers (Kelly-Moore in California; Rose Talbert in the Carolinas) have built their own wholesale/retail outlets creating a whole different position in the value system that exists to provide paint products to home and business paint users. They created value-building activities that meet customer needs more cost effectively than the downstream retail partners of typical paint producers. Kelly-Moore has also worked closely with pigment suppliers and equipment suppliers to ensure coordinated shipment of paint supplies and state-of-the-art mixing capabilities—thereby building a value-creating inbound logistics and operation advantage via upstream suppliers'/partners' service activities in the California paint industry.

As these examples suggest, it is important that managers take into account their level of vertical integration when comparing their cost structure for activities on their value chain to the value chain of key competitors. Comparing a fully integrated rival with a partially integrated one requires adjusting for the scope of activities performed to achieve meaningful comparison. It also suggests the need for examining costs associated with activities provided by upstream or downstream companies the activities of which ultimately determine comparable, final costs to end users. Said another way, one company's comparative cost disadvantage (or advantage) may emanate more from activities undertaken by upstream or downstream "partners" than from activities under the direct control of that company—therefore suggesting less of a relative advantage or disadvantage within the company's direct value chain.

The final basic consideration when applying value chain analysis is the need to have a meaningful comparison to use when evaluating a value activity as a strength or weakness. Whether using the value chain approach or an examination of functional areas, or both approaches, the strategist's next step in a systematic internal analysis is to compare the firm's status with meaningful standards to determine which of its value activities are strengths or weaknesses. Four sources of meaningful standards for evaluating internal factors and value activities are discussed in the next section.

INTERNAL ANALYSIS: MAKING MEANINGFUL COMPARISONS

Managers need an objective standard to use when examining internal capabilities or value-building activities. Whether using SWOT analysis, the functional approach, or the value chain, strategists rely on four basic perspectives to evaluate where their firm stacks up on its internal capabilities. These four perspectives are discussed in this section.

Comparison with Past Performance

Strategists use the firm's historical experience as a basis for evaluating internal factors. Managers are most familiar with the internal capabilities and problems of their firm because they have been immersed in its financial, marketing, production, and R&D activities. Not surprisingly, a manager's assessment of whether a certain internal factor—such as production facilities, sales organization, financial capacity, control systems, or key personnel—is a strength or a weakness will be strongly influenced by his or her experience in connection with that factor. In the capital-intensive airline industry, for example, debt capacity is a strategic internal factor. Delta Airlines managers view Delta's debt-equity ratio of less than 1.5 brought on by its acquisition of PanAm's international operations as a real weakness limiting its flexibility to invest in facilities because it maintained a ratio less than 0.6 for over 20 years. American Airlines managers, on the other hand, view American's much higher 1.8 debt-equity ratio as a growing strength, because it is down 50 percent from its 3.5 level five years earlier.

Although historical experience can provide a relevant evaluation framework, strategists must avoid tunnel vision in making use of it. NEC, Japan's IBM, has dominated Japan's PC market with a 70 percent market share using a proprietary hardware system, much higher screen resolution, powerful distribution channels, and a large software library from third-party vendors. Far from worried, Hajime Ikeda, manager of NEC's planning division, said recently: "We don't hear complaints from our users." But the 1990s has seen IBM and Macintosh filling shelves in Japan's famous consumer electronics district, Akihabara. Hiroki Kamata, president of a Japanese computer research firm, reports that Japan's PC market is worth over $15 billion in 1996, with Apple and IBM compatibles each having more market share than NEC because of better technology, software, and the restrictions created by NEC's proprietary technology. Clearly, using only historical experience as a basis for identifying strengths and weaknesses can prove dangerously inaccurate.

Stage of Industry Evolution

The requirements for success in industry segments change over time. Strategists can use these changing requirements, which are associated with different stages of industry evolution, as a framework for identifying and evaluating the firm's strengths and weaknesses.

THE GAP'S SPECTACULAR RETAILING SUCCESS WAS BASED ON VALUE CHAIN ANALYSIS

Melvin Jacobs, chairman of the New York–based Saks Fifth Avenue, observed: "The Gap is a huge success, while retailers around the world are struggling like crazy." Dean Witter analyst Donald Trott says The Gap hit 2,000 stores and $5 billion in sales in 1995—an impressive accomplishment for its 25th birthday after a one-store start in San Francisco. While The Gap has been a Wall Street darling for some time, president Mickey Drexler says, "We've been doing the same thing for seven or eight years. This company is no overnight success."

What Drexler and founder Donald Fisher did was apply a type of value chain look at specialty retail clothing to identify key value activities around which they could build a long-term competitive advantage. They identified four components of the value chain within which they saw the opportunity to create new, value-added approaches that could become sustained competitive advantages.

1. PROCUREMENT

Drexler's concept for The Gap was and is: simple, quality, and comfort. Gap's designers are told to design clothes they themselves would wear, to guide their search for merchandise. At an early 1992 meeting in San Francisco, about 30 merchandisers were showing their proposed fall collection for GapKids to Drexler and his staff. The woman in charge of jackets held up a hooded coat. After viewing it, Drexler's reaction: "I hate it." A loud cheer among the staff goes up—the New York designers were pushing the item, but The Gap staff found it ugly.

The Gap staff members feel their strong involvement in clothing design choices, rather than the usual reliance on New York or Dallas merchandisers, is a distinct advantage. The Gap designs its own clothes, chooses its own material, and monitors manufacturing so closely that it can keep quality high and costs low.

2. INBOUND LOGISTICS

The Gap has over 200 quality-control inspectors working inside factories in 40 countries to make sure specifications are met right from the start. Like Wal-Mart, The Gap has computerized, highly automated, carefully located distribution centers serving as hubs directly linked to store groupings. For example, a $75 million automated distribution center recently opened outside Baltimore,

Source: The Gap annual reports, 1991–1995; The Gap, *Business Week*, March 9, 1992, p. 58.

Figure 6–6 depicts four stages of industry evolution and the typical changes in functional capabilities that are often associated with business success at each of these stages. The early development of a product market, for example, entails minimal growth in sales, major R&D emphasis, rapid technological change in the product, operating losses, and a need for sufficient resources or slack to support a temporarily unprofitable operation. Success at this introduction stage may be associated with technical skill, with being first in new markets, or with having a marketing advantage that creates widespread awareness. Radio Shack's initial success with its TRS–80 home computer was based in part on its ability to gain widespread exposure and acceptance in the ill-defined home computer market via the large number of existing Radio Shack outlets throughout the country.

The strengths necessary for success change in the growth stage. Rapid growth brings new competitors into the product market. At this stage, such factors as brand recognition, product differentiation, and the financial resources to support both heavy marketing expenses and the

allowing The Gap to supply New York City stores daily instead of three times a week. Few in specialty retailing can match this logistical capability.

3. OPERATIONS

Every Gap store is the same—a clean, well-lit place where harried consumers can shop easily and quickly. Every detail is fussed over, from cleaning the store's floors to rounding the counter corners at GapKids for safety's sake to the detailed instructions on where to display clothes and touching up white walls weekly and polishing wood floors every three days. Already in 800 of the U.S.'s 1,500 largest malls, it lowered operating costs long term by taking advantage of the 1992 recession's impact, locking up sweet lease deals, moving into downtowns and urban neighborhoods, and opening new stores on the declining main streets of midsized cities. Each of these operational activities ensured higher quality and ease of management, and sustained lower costs.

4. HUMAN RESOURCE MANAGEMENT

In an industry that is low base pay and commission based, The Gap salespeople receive no commission. But compensation exceeds the industry average. The Gap's COO motivates salespeople with constant contests. The most multiple purchases to the register in one day wins a Gap-logo watch. The Thanksgiving weekend rush saw COO O'Donnell have Pizza Hut and Domino's deliver 15,000 pizzas and 72,000 Pepsis to store personnel on the job. And The Gap's training program is detailed and rigorous before you are free to "work the floor." Again, The Gap pursues policies that differentiate it from current industry practices in a way that adds incremental value—well trained, fairly compensated, highly motivated store personnel, resulting in lower turnover costs and a favorable image for service-leery retail shoppers.

Drexler and Fisher have driven The Gap's success in these and many other ways. But disaggregating specialty clothing retailing into distinct activities in order to better understand their costs and sources of differentiation has led them to design unique approaches (described above) in four strategically important activities that created sustained competitive advantages through lower costs, higher quality, and clear differentiation from all other clothing retailers.

effect of price competition on cash flow can be key strengths. IBM entered the personal computer market in the growth stage and was able to rapidly become the market leader with a strategy based on its key strengths in brand awareness and possession of the financial resources needed to support consumer advertising. But IBM lost that lead in the next stage as speed in distribution and cost structures became the key success factors—strengths for Compaq and several mail order–oriented computer assemblers.

As the industry moves through a shakeout phase and into the maturity stage, industry growth continues, but at a decreasing rate. The number of industry segments expands, but technological change in product design slows considerably. As a result, competition usually becomes more intense, and promotional or pricing advantages and differentiation become key internal strengths. Technological change in process design becomes intense as the many competitors seek to provide the product in the most efficient manner. Where R&D was critical in the introduction stage, efficient production is now crucial to continued success in the broader industry segments. Ford's emphasis on quality control and modern,

FIGURE 6–6
Sources of Distinctive Competence at Different Stages of Industry Evolution

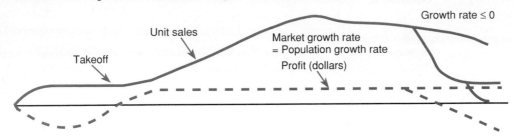

Functional Area	Introduction	Growth	Maturity	Decline
Marketing	Resources/skills to create widespread awareness and find acceptance from customers; advantageous access to distribution	Ability to establish brand recognition, find niche, reduce price, solidify, strong distribution relations, and develop new channels	Skills in aggressively promoting products to new markets and holding existing markets; pricing flexibility; skills in differentiating products and holding customer loyalty	Cost-effective means of efficient access to selected channels and markets; strong customer loyalty or dependence; strong company image
Production operations	Ability to expand capacity effectively, limit number of designs, develop standards	Ability to add product variants, centralize production, or otherwise lower costs; ability to improve product quality; seasonal subcontracting capacity	Ability to improve product and reduce costs; ability to share or reduce capacity; advantageous supplier relationships; subcontracting	Ability to prune product line; cost advantage in production, location or distribution; simplified inventory control; subcontracting or long production runs
Finance	Resources to support high net cash overflow and initial losses; ability to use leverage effectively	Ability to finance rapid expansion, to have net cash outflows but increasing profits; resources to support product improvements	Ability to generate and redistribute increasing net cash inflows; effective cost control systems	Ability to reuse or liquidate unneeded equipment; advantage in cost of facilities; control system accuracy; streamlined management control
Personnel	Flexibility in staffing and training new management; existence of employees with key skills in new products or markets	Existence of an ability to add skilled personnel; motivated and loyal work force	Ability to cost effectively, reduce work force, increase efficiency	Capacity to reduce and reallocate personnel; cost advantage
Engineering and research and development	Ability to make engineering changes, have technical bugs in product and process resolved	Skill in quality and new feature development; ability to start developing successor product	Ability to reduce costs, develop variants, differentiate products	Ability to support other grown areas or to apply product to unique customer needs
Key functional area and strategy focus	Engineering: market penetration	Sales: consumer loyalty; market share	Production efficiency; successor products	Finance; maximum investment recovery

Source: Adapted from Peter Doyle, "The Realities of the Product Life Cycle," *Quarterly Review of Marketing*, Summer 1976, pp. 1–6; Harold Fox, "A Framework for Functional Coordination," *Atlantic Economic Review* November–December 1973; Charles W. Hofer, *Conceptual Conflicts for Formulating Corporate and Business Strategy* (Boston: Intercollegiate Case Clearing House 1977), p. 7; Philip Kotler, *Marketing Management* (Englewood Cliffs, NJ: Prentice Hall, 1988); and Charles Wasson, *Dynamic Competitive Strategy and Product Cycles* (Austin, TX: Austin Press, 1978).

AVERY DENNISON USES BENCHMARKING AND STAGE OF INDUSTRY EVALUATION TO TURN WEAKNESS INTO STRENGTH

Avery Dennison has long made adhesives and what it calls "sticky papers" for business customers. Ten years ago, AD decided to take on 3M with its own version of 3M's highly successful Post-It notes and Scotch transparent tape.

How frequently did you buy Avery Notes and Avery Tape? You probably have never heard of them, right? That is because Avery was beat up in that market by 3M and AD exited the business after just a few years. Key strengths, distribution and brand name, that 3M used to build those products were major weaknesses at AD. Plus, in President Charles Miller's way of viewing it, 3M remained aggressive and true to an innovative culture to back its products while AD had grown rusty and "me too" rather than being the innovator it had traditionally been with pressure-sensitive papers. So faced with considerable weakness competing against a major threat (see Figure 6–2), Miller refocused AD on getting innovative in areas of traditional technical strength.

Today, AD has 30 percent of its sales from products introduced in the past five years. It has half the market for adhesive paper stock and 40 percent of the market for coated paper films for package labels. Says Miller, "We believe in market evolution. The best way to control a market is to invent it. With innovative products, superstores aren't able to squeeze margins, as they can in commodity products." New products now pour out of AD labs to position AD strengths against early life cycle stage opportunities.

Source: Damon Darlin, "Thank You, 3M," *Forbes*, September 25, 1995, p. 86. Reprinted by permission of *Forbes* Magazine © Forbes, Inc., 1995.

efficient production has helped it prosper in the maturing U.S. auto industry, while General Motors, which pays almost 50 percent more than Ford to produce a comparable car, continues to decline.

When the industry moves into the decline stage, strengths and weaknesses center on cost advantages, superior supplier or customer relationships, and financial control. Competitive advantage can exist at this stage, at least temporarily, if a firm serves gradually shrinking markets that competitors are choosing to leave.

Figure 6–6 is a rather simple model of the stages of industry evolution. These stages can and do vary from the model. What should be borne in mind is that the relative importance of various determinants of success differs across the stages of industry evolution. Thus, the state of that evolution must be considered in internal analysis. Figure 6–6 suggests dimensions that are particularly deserving of in-depth consideration when a company profile is being developed.

Benchmarking—Comparison with Competitors

A major focus in determining a firm's strengths and weaknesses is comparison with existing (and potential) competitors. Firms in the same industry often have different marketing skills, financial resources, operating facilities and locations, technical know-how, brand images, levels of integration, managerial talent, and so on. These different internal capabilities can become relative strengths (or weaknesses) depending on the strategy a firm chooses. In choosing a strategy, managers should compare the firm's key internal capabilities with those of its rivals, thereby isolating its key strengths and weaknesses.

SAS AIRLINES BENCHMARKS
USING DELTA AIRLINES

For many years, Scandinavian Airline System (SAS) was a premier European airline. Benefiting from International Airline Transportation Association (IATA), a protective European airline industry trade organization, SAS was profitable for 17 straight years. But changes in the global

We've got some tough competition. Like the "street fighters" from the rough-and-tumble American domestic

market. Efficient. In shape. Like Delta. . .

Or European companies which have pursued more consistent and purposeful policies than we have.

And who keep making money, hard times or not.

In the home appliance industry, for example, Sears and General Electric are major rivals. Sears's principal strength is its retail network. For GE, distribution—through independent franchised dealers—has traditionally been a relative weakness. GE's possession of the financial resources needed to support modernized mass production has enabled it to maintain both cost and technological advantages over its rivals, particularly Sears. This major strength for GE is a relative weakness for Sears, which depends solely on subcontracting to produce its Kenmore appliances. On the other hand, maintenance and repair service are important in the appliance industry. Historically, Sears has had strength in this area because it maintains fully staffed service components and spreads the costs of components over numerous departments at each retail location. GE, on the other hand, has had to depend on regional service centers and on local contracting with independent service firms by its independent local dealers. Among the internal factors that Sears and GE must

continued

airline industry caused its earnings to plummet in the last few years. When SAS was on the verge of folding, its new CEO undertook an extensive competitor comparison as a basis for finding a strategy to turn it around. The CEO shared the following assessment in an employee pamphlet communicating the firm's new strategy and rationale behind it.

Look at the Differences:

	Swissair International	SAS International
Cabin Factor	63.60	59.30
Load Factor	59.20	47.60
Passenger revenue USD/RPK*	0.09	0.08
Cargo revenue USD/RFTK	0.37	0.31
Total revenue USD/RTK	0.79	0.73
Operating cost USD/ATK	0.45	0.42
Revenue-cost relationship (Over 100% profit)	103.50	99.70
Average flight leg/km	1051.00	967.00

Delta Has:

40% more revenue tonne kms per employee

120% more passengers per employee

14% more available tonne kms per pilot

40% more passenger kms per cabin attendant

35% more passenger kms per passenger sales employee

It is difficult to make similar comparisons in the technical and maintenance fields, but even in these areas Delta has a substantially higher productivity than SAS.

* USD = U.S. Dollars; RPK = Revenue passenger-kilometers; RFTK = Revenue freight tonne-kilometers; RTK = Revenue tonne-kilometers; ATK = Available tonne-kilometers. Exchange rate: one USD = 4.65 Swedish kronor.

consider in developing a strategy are distribution networks, technological capabilities, operating costs, and service facilities. Managers in both organizations have built successful strategies yet those strategies are quite different. Benchmarking each other, they have identified ways to build on relative strengths while avoiding dependence on capabilities at which the other firm excels.

Benchmarking, comparing the way "our" company performs a specific activity with a competitor or other company doing the same thing, has become a central concern of managers in quality commitment companies worldwide. Particularly as the value chain framework has taken hold in structuring internal analysis, managers seek to systematically benchmark the costs and results of the smallest value activities against relevant competitors or other useful standards because it has proven to be an effective way to continuously improve that activity. The ultimate objective in benchmarking is to identify the "best

KMART GETS SOME BAD NEWS BY BENCHMARKING INDUSTRY SUCCESS FACTORS AGAINST A KEY RIVAL

Kmart's new management team has a problem. Kmart is in serious trouble, perhaps more so than they originally thought when they took over the firm in 1995.

Key success factors in discount retailing include the obvious—good locations, solid supplier relations, selection, and efficient inbound logistics. But recent focus among investment analysts charting the industry has centered around four key indicators: Core customers, sales/square foot, shopper visits/year, and loyalty to the chain.

Their 1996 benchmarking of Kmart compared to Wal-Mart revealed the following on these key success factors:

Key Success Factor to Benchmark	Kmart	Wal-Mart
Core customer	Over 55; more than $20k income and no kids at home	Under 44, $40k income and kids at home
Sales/square foot	$185	$379
Shopper visits/year	15 times per year	32 times per year
Loyal to the chain	19 percent of Kmart customers	46 percent of Wal-Mart customers
Location	36 percent of Americans find their newest Kmart inconvenient compared to other stores	49 percent of Wal-Mart customers drive past a Kmart to go to Wal-Mart

Sources: Wal-Mart 1995 Annual Report; Kmart 1995 Annual Report; "Can This Chain Be Saved?" *Chain Store Age Executive,* May 1995, pp. 31–44; "Kmart Is Down for the Count," *Fortune,* January 15, 1996, pp. 102–3; "As Kmart Teeters, an Industry Holds Its Breath," *Chain Store Age Executive,* January 1996, p. 70.

practices" in performing an activity, to learn how lower costs, fewer defects, or other outcomes linked to excellence are achieved. Companies committed to benchmarking attempt to isolate and identify where their costs or outcomes are out of line with what the best practicers of a particular activity experience (competitors and noncompetitors) and then attempt to change their activities to achieve the new best practices standard.

Comparison with key competitors can prove useful in ascertaining whether their internal capabilities on these and other factors are strengths or weaknesses. Significant favorable differences (existing or expected) from competitors are potential cornerstones of a firm's strategy. Moreover, through comparison with major competitors, a firm may avoid strategic commitments that it cannot competitively support. Global Strategy in Action 6–4 shows how the Scandinavian Airline System (SAS) used competitor comparison to assess its strengths and weaknesses in the global airline industry.

Comparison with Success Factors in the Industry

Industry analysis (see Chapter 3) involves identifying the factors associated with successful participation in a given industry. As was true for the evaluation methods discussed above, the key determinants of success in an industry may be used to identify a firm's internal strengths and weaknesses. By scrutinizing industry competitors, as well as customer needs, vertical industry structure, channels of distribution, costs, barriers to entry, availability of substitutes, and suppliers, a strategist seeks to determine whether a firm's current internal capabilities represent strengths or weaknesses in new competitive arenas. The discussion in Chapter 3 provides a useful framework—five industry forces—against which to examine a firm's potential strengths and weaknesses. General Cinema Corporation, the largest U.S. movie theater operator, determined that its internal skills in marketing, site analysis, creative financing, and management of geographically dispersed operations were key strengths relative to major success factors in the soft-drink bottling industry. This assessment proved accurate. Within 10 years after it entered the soft-drink bottling industry, General Cinema became the largest franchised bottler of soft drinks in the United States, handling Pepsi, 7UP, Dr Pepper, and Sunkist. Strategy in Action 6–2 provides a very current example where Kmart has used industry factors to benchmark itself against industry leader Wal-Mart to find out just how weak Kmart is on some key factors. Global Strategy in Action 6–3 describes how Avery Dennison used similar industry evolution benchmarking versus 3M to create a new, successful strategy.

SUMMARY

This chapter looked at several ways managers achieve greater objectivity and rigor as they analyze their company's internal capabilities. Managers often start their internal analysis with questions like: "How well is the current strategy working? What is our current situation? Or what are our strengths and weaknesses?" *SWOT analysis* and *functional analysis* are two traditional approaches discussed in this chapter. Managers frequently use them to introduce realism and greater objectivity into their attempts to answer these questions. This chapter then described how insightful managers have begun to look at their business as a chain of activities that add value creating the products or services they sell. Associated with this perspective is a powerful concept for introducing rigor and objectivity into internal analysis, *value chain analysis*, which this chapter examined in great detail. Managers who use value chain to understand the value structure within their firm's activities and look at the value system, which also includes upstream suppliers and downstream partners and buyers, often gain very meaningful insights into their company's strategic capabilities and options. Finally, this chapter covered four ways objectivity and realism are enhanced when managers use meaningful standards for comparison regardless of the particular analytical framework they employ in internal analysis. This chapter is followed by an appendix covering traditional financial analysis to serve as a refresher and reminder about this basic internal analysis tool.

When matched with management's environmental analyses and mission priorities, the process of internal analysis provides the critical foundation for strategy formulation. Armed with an accurate, thorough, and timely internal analysis, managers are in a better position to formulate effective strategies. The next chapter describes basic strategy alternatives that any firm may consider.

QUESTIONS FOR DISCUSSION

1. Describe SWOT analysis as a way to guide internal analysis. How does this approach reflect the basic strategic management process?
2. Why would the functional approach be considered a "traditional" approach to internal analysis? Would you expect managers to prefer this approach or shy away from it? Why? What do you think are the strengths and weaknesses of this approach?

3. Apply SWOT analysis to yourself and your career aspirations. What are your major strengths and weaknesses? How might you use your knowledge of these strengths and weaknesses to develop your future career plans?

4. Why do you think value chain analysis has become a preferred approach to guide internal analysis? What are its strengths? Weaknesses?

5. In what ways do the approaches to internal analysis at The Gap (see Strategy in Action 6–1) and Scandinavian Airline Systems (see Global Strategy in Action 6–4) appear to be similar and different?

BIBLIOGRAPHY

Aaker, David A. "Managing Assets and Skills: The Key to a Sustainable Competitive Advantage." *California Management Review*, Winter 1989, pp. 91–106.

Barney, J. B. "Firm Resources and Sustained Competitive Advantage." *Journal of Management* 17 (1991), pp. 99–120.

Berman, S. J., and R. F. Kautz. "A Sophisticated Tool That Facilitates Strategic Analysis." *Planning Review* 18, no. 4 (1990), pp. 35–39.

Bukszar, Ed, and Terry Connolly. "Hindsight Bias and Strategy Choice." *Academy of Management Journal*, September 1988, p. 828.

Cvitkovic, Emillo. "Profiling Your Competitors." *Planning Review*, May–June 1989, pp. 28–31.

De Geus, A. P. "Planning as Learning." *Harvard Business Review*, March 1988. pp. 70–74.

Fann, G. L., and L. R. Smittzer. "The Use of Information from and about Competitors in Small Business Management." *Entrepreneurship: Theory and Practice*, Summer 1989, pp. 35–46.

Feinman, B. C. "Sustaining the Competitive Market Advantage." *Planning Review*, May 1989, pp. 30–39.

Fifer, R. M. "Cost Bench Marketing Approach: Functions in Value Chain." *Planning Review*, May 1989, pp. 18–27.

Gale, B. T., and R. D. Buzzel. "Market Perceived Quality: Key Strategic Concept." *Planning Review*, March 1989, pp. 6–15.

Hergert, M., and D. Morris. "Accounting Data for Value Chain Analysis." *Strategic Management Journal*, March 1989, pp. 175–88.

Hinterhuber, H. H., and W. Popp. "Are You a Strategist or Just a Manager?" *Harvard Business Review* 70, no. 1 (1992), pp. 105–13.

Kazanjian, Robert K. "Relation of Dominant Problems to Stages of Growth in Technology-Based New Ventures." *Academy of Management Journal*, September 1988, p. 628.

Lado, A.; N. Boyd; and P. Wright. "A Competency-Based Model of Sustainable Competitive Advantage: Toward a Conceptual Integration." *Journal of Management* 18 (1992), pp. 77–91.

Langley, A. "The Roles of Formal Strategic Planning." *Long Range Planning*, June 1988, pp. 40–50.

Leigh, T. W. "Competitive Assessment in Service Industries." *Planning Review*, January 1989, pp. 10–19.

Morrisey, George L. "Executive Guide to Strategic Thinking." *Executive Excellence* 7, no. 6 (1990), pp. 5–6.

Porter, Michel E. "From Competitive Advantage to Corporate Strategy." *Harvard Business Review*, May–June 1987, p. 43.

Potts, G. W. "Exploit Your Product's Service Life Cycle." *Harvard Business Review*, September 1988, pp. 32–39.

Prahalad, C. K., and G. Hamel. "The Core Competence of the Corporation." *Harvard Business Review* 68, no. 3 (1990), pp. 79–91.

Quinn, J. B. "Strategic Change: Logical Incrementalism." *Sloan Management Review*, Summer 1989, pp. 45–60.

Schmidt, J. A. "The Strategic Review," *Planning Review*, July 1988, pp. 14–19.

Stalk, G.; P. Evans; and L. E. Shulman. "Competing on Capabilities: The New Rules for Corporate Strategy." *Harvard Business Review* 70 (1992), pp. 57–69.

Steiner, M. P., and O. Solem. "Factors for Success in Small Manufacturing Firms." *Journal of Small Business Management*, January 1988, pp. 51–56.

Stoner, Charles R. "Distinctive Competence and Competitive Advantage." *Journal of Small Business Management*, April 1987, p. 33.

APPENDIX

USING FINANCIAL ANALYSIS

One of the most important tools for assessing the strength of an organization within its industry is financial analysis. Managers, investors, and creditors all employ some form of this analysis as the beginning point for their financial decision making. Investors use financial analyses in making decisions about whether to buy or sell stock, and creditors use them in deciding whether or not to lend. They provide managers with a measurement of how the company is doing in comparison with its performance in past years and with the performance of competitors in the industry.

Although financial analysis is useful for decision making, some weaknesses should be noted. Any picture that it provides of the company is based on past data. Although trends may be noteworthy, this picture should not automatically be assumed to be applicable to the future. In addition, the analysis is only as good as the accounting procedures that have provided the information. When making comparisons between companies, one should keep in mind the variability of accounting procedures from firm to firm.

There are four basic groups of financial ratios: liquidity, leverage, activity, and profitability.

Depicted in Exhibit 6–1 are the specific ratios calculated for each of the basic groups. Liquidity and leverage ratios represent an assessment of the risk of the firm. Activity and profitability ratios are measures of the return generated by the assets of the firm. The interaction between certain groups of ratios is indicated by arrows.

Typically, two common financial statements are used in financial analyses: the balance sheet and the income statement. Exhibit 6–2 is a balance sheet and Exhibit 6–3 an income statement for the ABC Company. These statements will be used to illustrate the financial analyses.

LIQUIDITY RATIOS

Liquidity ratios are used as indicators of a firm's ability to meet its short-term obligations. These obligations include any current liabilities, including currently maturing long-term debt. Current assets move through a normal cash cycle of inventories–sales—accounts receivable—cash. The firm then uses cash to pay off or reduce its current liabilities. The best-known liquidity ratio is the current ratio: current assets divided by current liabilities. For the ABC Company, the current ratio is calculated as follows:

$$\frac{\text{Current assets}}{\text{Current liabilities}} = \frac{\$4,125,000}{\$2,512,500} = 1.64 \ (1999)$$

$$= \frac{\$3,618,000}{\$2,242.250} = 1.161 \ (1998)$$

Most analysts suggest a current ratio of 2 to 3. A large current ratio is not necessarily a good sign; it may mean that an organization is not making the most efficient use of its assets. The optimum current ratio will vary from industry to industry, with the more volatile industries requiring higher ratios.

EXHIBIT 6–1
Financial Ratios

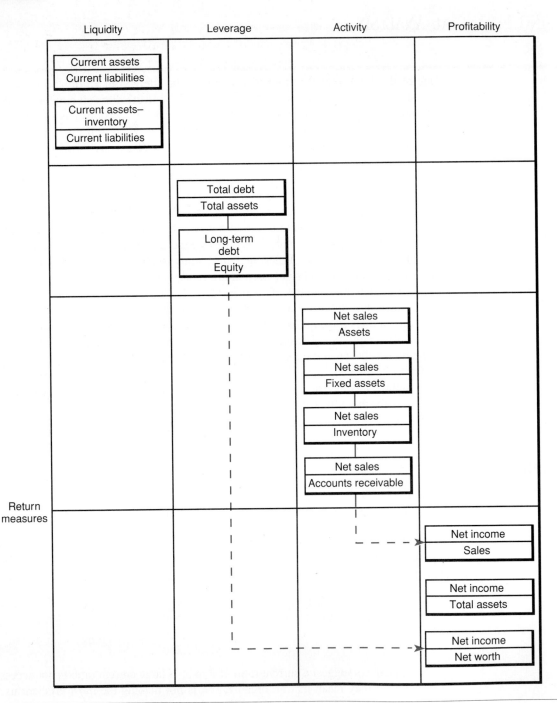

EXHIBIT 6–2

ABC COMPANY
Balance Sheet
As of December 31, 1998, and 1999

		1999		1998
Assets				
Current assets:				
Cash		$ 140,000		$ 115,000
Accounts receivable		1,760,000		1,440,000
Inventory		2,175,000		2,000,000
Prepaid expenses		50,000		63,000
Total current assets		4,125,000		3,618,000
Fixed assets:				
Long-term receivable		1,255,000		1,090,000
Property and plant	$2,037,000		$2,015,000	
Less: Accumulated depreciation	862,000		860,000	
Net property and plant		1,175,000		1,155,000
Other fixed assets		550,000		530,000
Total fixed assets		2,980,000		2,775,000
Total assets		$7,105,000		$6,393,000
Liabilities and Stockholders' Equity				
Current liabilities:				
Accounts payable		$1,325,000		$1,225,000
Bank loans payable		475,000		550,000
Accrued federal taxes		675,000		425,000
Current maturities (long-term debt)		17,500		26,000
Dividends payable		20,000		16,250
Total current liabilities		2,512,500		2,242,250
Long-term liabilities		1,350,000		1,425,000
Total liabilities		3,862,000		3,667,250
Stockholders' equity:				
Common stock (104,046 shares outstanding in 1995; 101,204 shares outstanding in 1994)		44,500		43,300
Additional paid-in capital		568,000		372,450
Retained earnings		2,630,000		2,310,000
Total stockholders' equity		3,242,500		2,725,750
Total liabilities and stockholders' equity		$7,105,000		$6,393,000

Since slow-moving or obsolescent inventories could overstate a firm's ability to meet short-term demands, the quick ratio is sometimes preferred to assess a firm's liquidity. The quick ratio is current assets minus inventories, divided by current liabilities. The quick ratio for the ABC Company is calculated as follows:

$$\frac{\text{Current assets} - \text{Inventories}}{\text{Current liabilities}} = \frac{\$1,950,000}{\$2,512,500} = 0.78 \ (1999)$$

$$= \frac{\$1,618,000}{\$2,242,250} = 0.72 \ (1998)$$

EXHIBIT 6–3

ABC COMPANY
Income Statement
For the Years Ending December 31, 1998, and 1999

	1999		1998
Net sales		$8,250,000	$8,000,000
Cost of goods sold	$5,100,000		$5,000,000
Administrative expenses	1,750,000		1,680,000
Other expenses	420,000		390,000
Total		7,270,000	7,070,000
Earnings before interest and taxes		980,000	930,000
Less: Interest expense		210,000	210,000
Earnings before taxes		770,000	720,000
Less: Federal income taxes		360,000	325,000
Earnings after taxes (net income)		$ 410,000	$ 395,000
Common stock cash dividends		$ 90,000	$ 84,000
Addition to retained earnings		$ 320,000	$ 311,000
Earnings per common share		$ 3.940	$ 3.90
Dividends per common share		$ 0.865	$ 0.83

A quick ratio of approximately 1 would be typical for American industries. Although there is less variability in the quick ratio than in the current ratio, stable industries would be able to operate safely with a lower ratio.

LEVERAGE RATIOS

Leverage ratios identify the source of a firm's capital—owners or outside creditors. The term *leverage* refers to the fact that using capital with a fixed interest charge will "amplify" either profits or losses in relation to the equity of holders of common stock. The most commonly used ratio is total debt divided by total assets. Total debt includes current liabilities and long-term liabilities. This ratio is a measure of the percentage of total funds provided by debt. A total debt–total assets ratio higher than 0.5 is usually considered safe only for firms in stable industries.

$$\frac{\text{Total debt}}{\text{Total assets}} = \frac{\$3,862,500}{\$7,105,000} = 0.54 \ (1999)$$

$$= \frac{\$3,667,250}{\$6,393,000} = 0.57 \ (1998)$$

The ratio of long-term debt to equity is a measure of the extent to which sources of long-term financing are provided by creditors. It is computed by dividing long-term debt by the stockholders' equity.

$$\frac{\text{Long-term debt}}{\text{Equity}} = \frac{\$1,350,000}{\$3,242,500} = 0.42 \ (1999)$$

$$= \frac{\$1,425,000}{\$2,725,750} = 0.52 \ (1998)$$

ACTIVITY RATIOS

Activity ratios indicate how effectively a firm is using its resources. By comparing revenues with the resources used to generate them, it is possible to establish an efficiency of operation. The asset turnover ratio indicates how efficiently management is employing total assets. Asset turnover is calculated by dividing sales by total assets. For the ABC Company, asset turnover is calculated as follows:

$$\text{Asset turnover} = \frac{\text{Sales}}{\text{Total assets}} = \frac{\$8,250,000}{\$7,105,000} = 1.16 \ (1999)$$

$$= \frac{\$8,000,000}{\$6,393,000} = 1.25 \ (1998)$$

The ratio of sales to fixed assets is a measure of the turnover on plant and equipment. It is calculated by dividing sales by net fixed assets.

$$\text{Fixed asset turnover} = \frac{\text{Sales}}{\text{Net fixed assets}} = \frac{\$8,250,000}{\$2,980,000} = 2.77 \ (1999)$$

$$= \frac{\$8,000,000}{\$2,775,000} = 2.88 \ (1998)$$

Industry figures for asset turnover will vary with capital-intensive industries, and those requiring large inventories will have much smaller ratios.

Another activity ratio is inventory turnover, estimated by dividing sales by average inventory. The norm for American industries is 9, but whether the ratio for a particular firm is higher or lower normally depends on the product sold. Small, inexpensive items usually turn over at a much higher rate than larger, expensive ones. Since inventories normally are carried at cost, it would be more accurate to use the cost of goods sold in place of sales in the numerator of this ratio. Established compilers of industry ratios, such as Dun & Bradstreet, however, use the ratio of sales to inventory.

$$\text{Inventory turnover} = \frac{\text{Sales}}{\text{Inventory}} = \frac{\$8,250,000}{\$2,175,000} = 3.79 \ (1999)$$

$$= \frac{\$8,000,000}{\$2,000,000} = 4 \ (1998)$$

The accounts receivable turnover is a measure of the average collection period on sales. If the average number of days varies widely from the industry norm, it may be an indication of poor management. A too-low ratio could indicate the loss of sales because of a too restrictive credit policy. If the ratio is too high, too much capital is being tied up in accounts receivable, and management may be increasing the chance of bad debts. Because of varying industry credit policies, a comparison for the firm over time or within an industry is the only useful analysis. Because information on credit sales for other firms generally is unavailable, total sales must be used. Since not all firms have the same percentage of credit sales, there is only approximate comparability among firms.

$$\text{Accounts receivable turnover} = \frac{\text{Sales}}{\text{Accounts receivable}} = \frac{\$8,250,000}{\$1,760,000} = 4.69 \ (1999)$$

$$= \frac{\$8,000,000}{\$1,440,000} = 5.56 \ (1998)$$

$$\text{Average collection period} = \frac{360}{\text{Accounts receivable turnover}}$$

$$= \frac{360}{4.69} = 77 \text{ days (1999)}$$

$$= \frac{360}{5.56} = 65 \text{ days (1998)}$$

PROFITABILITY RATIOS

Profitability is the net result of a large number of policies and decisions chosen by an organization's management. Profitability ratios indicate how effectively the total firm is being managed. The profit margin for a firm is calculated by dividing net earnings by sales. This ratio is often called *return on sales* (ROS). There is wide variation among industries, but the average for American firms is approximately 5 percent.

$$\frac{\text{Net earnings}}{\text{Sales}} = \frac{\$410,000}{\$8,250,000} = 0.0497 \text{ (1999)}$$

$$= \frac{\$395,000}{\$8,000,000} = 0.0494 \text{ (1998)}$$

A second useful ratio for evaluating profitability is the return on investment—or *ROI*, as it is frequently called—found by dividing net earnings by total assets. The ABC Company's ROI is calculated as follows:

$$\frac{\text{Net earnings}}{\text{Total assets}} = \frac{\$410,000}{\$7,105,000} = 0.0577 \text{ (1999)}$$

$$= \frac{\$395,000}{\$6,393,000} = 0.0618 \text{ (1998)}$$

The ratio of net earnings to net worth is a measure of the rate of return or profitability of the stockholders' investment. It is calculated by dividing net earnings by net worth, the common stock equity and retained earnings account. ABC Company's return on net worth, also called ROE, is calculated as follows:

$$\frac{\text{Net earnings}}{\text{Net worth}} = \frac{\$410,000}{\$3,242,500} = 0.1264 \text{ (1999)}$$

$$= \frac{\$395,000}{\$2,725,750} = 0.1449 \text{ (1998)}$$

It is often difficult to determine causes for lack of profitability. The Du Pont system of financial analysis provides management with clues to the lack of success of a firm. This financial tool brings together activity, profitability, and leverage measures and shows how these ratios interact to determine the overall profitability of the firm. A depiction of the system is set forth in Exhibit 6–4.

The right side of the exhibit develops the turnover ratio. This section breaks down total assets into current assets (cash, marketable securities, accounts receivable, and inventories) and fixed assets. Sales divided by these total assets gives the turnover on assets.

The left side of the exhibit develops the profit margin on sales. The individual expense items plus income taxes are subtracted from sales to produce net profits after taxes. Net profits divided by sales gives the profit margin on sales. When the asset turnover ratio on the right side of Exhibit 6–4 is multiplied by the profit margin on sales developed on the left side of the exhibit, the product is the return on assets (ROI) for the firm. This can be shown by the following formula:

EXHIBIT 6–4
Du Pont's Financial Analysis

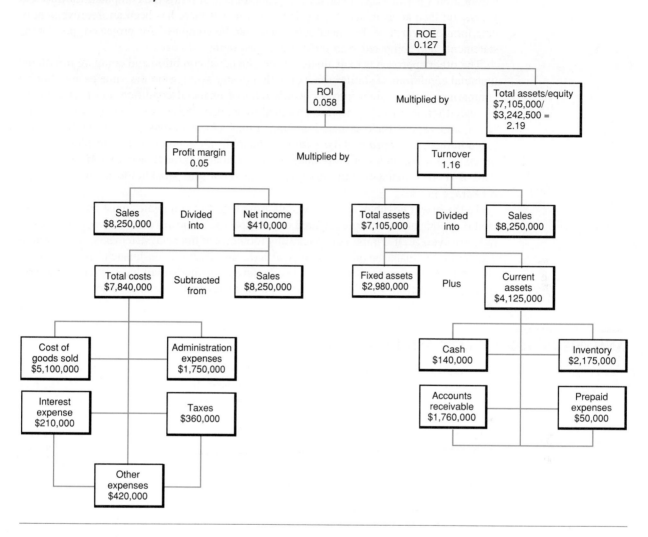

$$\frac{\text{Sales}}{\text{Total assets}} \times \frac{\text{Net earnings}}{\text{Sales}} = \frac{\text{Net earnings}}{\text{Total assets}} = \text{ROI}$$

The last step in the Du Pont analysis is to multiply the rate of return on assets (ROI) by the equity multiplier, which is the ratio of assets to common equity, to obtain the rate of return on equity (ROE). This percentage rate of return, of course, could be calculated directly by dividing net income by common equity. However, the Du Pont analysis demonstrates how the return on assets and the use of debt interact to determine the return on equity.

The Du Pont system can be used to analyze and improve the performance of a firm. On the left, or profit, side of the exhibit, attempts to increase profits and sales could be investigated. The possibilities of raising prices to improve profits (or lowering prices to improve volume) or seeking new products or markets, for example, could be studied. Cost accountants and production engineers could investigate ways to reduce costs. On the right, or turnover, side, financial officers could analyze the effect of reducing investment in various assets as well as the effect of using alternative financial structures.

There are two basic approaches to using financial ratios. One approach is to evaluate the corporation's performance over several years. Financial ratios are computed for different years, and then an assessment is made about whether there has been an improvement or deterioration over time. Financial ratios also can be computed for projected, pro forma, statements and compared with present and past ratios.

The other approach is to evaluate a firm's financial condition and compare it with the financial conditions of similar firms or with industry averages in the same period. Such a comparison gives insight into the firm's relative financial condition and performance. Financial ratios for industries are provided by Robert Morris Associates, Dun & Bradstreet, and various trade association publications. (Associations and their addresses are listed in the *Encyclopedia of Associations* and in the *Directory of National Trade Associations*.) Information about individual firms is available through *Moody's Manual*, Standard & Poor's manuals and surveys, annual reports to stockholders, and the major brokerage houses.

To the extent possible, accounting data from different companies must be so standardized that companies can be compared or so a specific company can be compared with an industry average. It is important to read any footnotes of financial statements, since various accounting or management practices can have an effect on the financial picture of the company. For example, firms using sale-leaseback methods may have leverage pictures quite different from what is shown as debts or assets on the balance sheet.

ANALYSIS OF THE SOURCES AND USES OF FUNDS

The purpose of this analysis is to determine how the company is using its financial resources from year to year. By comparing balance sheets from one year to the next, one may determine how funds were obtained and how these funds were employed during the year.

To prepare a statement of the sources and uses of funds, it is necessary to (1) classify balance sheet changes that increase and decrease cash, (2) classify from the income statement those factors that increase or decrease cash, and (3) consolidate this information on a sources and uses of funds statement form.

Sources of funds that increase cash are:

1. A net decrease in any other asset than a depreciable fixed asset.
2. A gross decrease in a depreciable fixed asset.
3. A net increase in any liability.
4. Proceeds from the sale of stock.
5. The operation of the company (net income, and depreciation if the company is profitable).

Uses of funds include:

1. A net increase in any other asset than a depreciable fixed asset.
2. A gross increase in depreciable fixed assets.
3. A net decrease in any liability.
4. A retirement or purchase of stock.
5. Payment of cash dividends.

We compute gross changes to depreciable fixed assets by adding depreciation from the income statement for the period to net fixed assets at the end of the period and then subtracting from the total net fixed assets at the beginning of the period. The residual represents the change in depreciable fixed assets for the period.

For the ABC Company, the following change would be calculated:

Net property and plant (1999)	$1,175,000
Depreciation for 1999	+ 80,000
	$1,255,000
Net property and plant (1998)	−1,155,000
	$ 100,000

To avoid double counting, the change in retained earnings is not shown directly in the funds statement. When the funds statement is prepared, this account is replaced by the earnings after taxes, or net income, as a source of funds, and dividends paid during the year as a use of funds. The difference between net income and the change in the retained earnings account will equal the amount of dividends paid during the year. The accompanying sources and uses of funds statement was prepared for the ABC Company.

A funds analysis is useful for determining trends in working-capital positions and for demonstrating how the firm has acquired and employed its funds during some period.

ABC COMPANY
Sources and Uses of Funds Statement
For 1999

Sources:

Prepaid expenses	$ 13,000
Accounts payable	100,000
Accrued federal taxes	250,000
Dividends payable	3,750
Common stock	1,200
Additional paid-in capital	195,000
Earnings after taxes (net income)	410,000
Depreciation	80,000
Total sources	$1,053,500

ABC COMPANY
Sources and Uses of Fund Statement
For 1999

Uses:

Cash	$ 25,000
Accounts receivable	320,000
Inventory	175,000
Long-term receivables	165,000
Property and plant	100,000
Other fixed assets	20,000
Bank loans payable	75,000
Current maturities of long-term debt	8,500
Long-term liabilities	75,000
Dividends paid	90,000
Total uses	1,053,500

CONCLUSION

It is recommended that you prepare a chart, such as that shown in Exhibit 6–5, so you can develop a useful portrayal of these financial analyses. The chart allows a display of the ratios over time. The "Trend" column could be used to indicate your evaluation of the ratios over time (e.g., "favorable," "neutral," or "unfavorable"). The "Industry Average" column could include recent industry averages on these ratios or those of key competitors. These would provide information to aid interpretation of the analyses. The "Interpretation" column could be used to describe your interpretation of the ratios for this firm. Overall, this chart gives a basic display of the ratios that provides a convenient format for examining the firm's financial condition.

Finally, Exhibit 6–6 is included to provide the quick reference summarizing the calculation and meaning of the ratios discussed earlier.

EXHIBIT 6–5
A Summary of the Financial Position of a Firm

Ratios and Working Capital	1995	1996	1997	1998	1999	Trend	Industry Average	Interpretation
Liquidity: Current								
Quick								
Leverage: Debt-assets								
Debt-equity								
Activity: Asset turnover								
Fixed asset ratio								
Inventory turnover								
Accounts receivable turnover								
Average collection period								
Profitability: ROS								
ROI								
ROE								
Working-capital position								

EXHIBIT 6–6
A Summary of Key Financial Ratios

Ratio	Calculation	Meaning
Liquidity Ratios:		
Current ratio	$\dfrac{\text{Current assets}}{\text{Current liabilities}}$	The extent to which a firm can meet its short-term obligations.
Quick ratio	$\dfrac{\text{Current assets} - \text{Inventory}}{\text{Current liabilities}}$	The extent to which a firm can meet its short-term obligations without relying on the sale of inventories.
Leverage Ratios:		
Debt-to-total-assets ratio	$\dfrac{\text{Total debt}}{\text{Total assets}}$	The percentage of total funds that are provided by creditors.
Debt-to-equity ratio	$\dfrac{\text{Total debt}}{\text{Total stockholders' equity}}$	The percentage of total funds provided by creditors versus the percentage provided by owners.
Long-term-debt-to-equity ratio	$\dfrac{\text{Long-term debt}}{\text{Total stockholders' equity}}$	The balance between debt and equity in a firm's long-term capital structure.
Times-interest-earned ratio	$\dfrac{\text{Profits before interest and taxes}}{\text{Total interest charges}}$	The extent to which earnings can decline without the firm becoming unable to meet its annual interest costs.
Activity Ratios:		
Inventory turnover	$\dfrac{\text{Sales}}{\text{Inventory of finished goods}}$	Whether a firm holds excessive stocks of inventories and whether a firm is selling its inventories slowly compared to the industry average.
Fixed assets turnover	$\dfrac{\text{Sales}}{\text{Fixed assets}}$	Sales productivity and plant equipment utilization.
Total assets turnover	$\dfrac{\text{Sales}}{\text{Total assets}}$	Whether a firm is generating a sufficient volume of business for the size of its assets investment.
Accounts receivable turnover	$\dfrac{\text{Annual credit sales}}{\text{Accounts receivable}}$	In percentage terms, the average length of time it takes a firm to collect on credit sales.
Average collection period	$\dfrac{\text{Accounts receivable}}{\text{Total sales/365 days}}$	In days, the average length of time it takes a firm to collect on credit sales.
Profitability Ratios:		
Gross profit margin	$\dfrac{\text{Sales} - \text{Cost of goods sold}}{\text{Sales}}$	The total margin available to cover operating expenses and yield a profit.
Operating profit margin	$\dfrac{\text{Earnings before interest and taxes (EBIT)}}{\text{Sales}}$	Profitability without concern for taxes and interest.
Net profit margin	$\dfrac{\text{Net income}}{\text{Sales}}$	After-tax profits per dollar of sales.
Return on total assets (ROA)	$\dfrac{\text{Net income}}{\text{Total assets}}$	After-tax profits per dollar of assets; this ratio is also called *return on investment* (ROI).
Return on stockholders' equity (ROE)	$\dfrac{\text{Net income}}{\text{Total stockholders' equity}}$	After-tax profits per dollar of stockholders' investment in the firm.

EXHIBIT 6–6
(concluded)

Ratio	Calculation	Meaning
Earnings per share (EPS)	$$\frac{\text{Net income}}{\text{Number of shares of common stock outstanding}}$$	Earnings available to the owners of common stock.
Growth Ratio:		
Sales	Annual percentage growth in total sales	Firm's growth rate in sales.
Income	Annual percentage growth in profits	Firm's growth rate in profits.
Earnings per share	Annual percentage growth in EPS Firm's growth rate in EPS.	
Dividends per share	Annual percentage growth in dividends per share	Firm's growth rate in dividends per share.
Price-earnings ratio	$$\frac{\text{Market price per share}}{\text{Earnings per share}}$$	Faster-growing and less risky firms tend to have higher price-earnings ratios.

CHAPTER 6 COHESION CASE ILLUSTRATION

INTERNAL ANALYSIS AT THE COCA-COLA COMPANY

One way to gauge the strengths and weaknesses at Coca-Cola is to compare it to competitors on key indicators. Perhaps the best starting point for comparison is to look at recent data on sales and market share. Listed below are the sales results in the U.S. market for the first half of the 1990s.

CORPORATE COLA LEADERS
Top 10 Parent Companies in 1995

Rank	Brand	Gallonage (millions)	Market Share	1994 Growth	Industry Growth Index Factor*	Five-Year Growth
1	Coca-Cola	*5,580.8*	*42.0%*	+5.1%	*+49.0%*	+18.1%
2	Pepsi-Cola	4,070.6	30.7	+4.4	+31.1	+12.1
3	Dr Pepper/Seven-Up*	1,520.8	11.5	+6.3	+16.4	+33.9
4	Cadbury Beverages†	632.3	4.8	+1.1	+1.2	+10.3
5	Cott‡	300.7	2.3	*+37.7*	+14.9	NA
6	Royal Crown	267.3	2.0	−3.2	−1.6	−12.8
7	National Beverage	227.8	1.7	+5.5	+2.2	+13.6
8	Monarch	208.0	1.6	−0.4	−0.1	+8.4
9	Barq's	82.5	0.6	+6.5	+0.9	*+66.7*
10	Double-Cola	53.2	0.4	+2.9	+0.3	−2.7
	Top 10 Soft-Drink Companies	12,944.0	97.6	+5.1	+114.3	+21.4
	All Others	331.0	2.4	−19.2	−14.3	−68.8
	Total Soft-Drink Industry	13,275.0	100.0	+4.3	+100.0	+13.5

Bold italics indicate best among top 10.
*GIF = Brand gallonage growth ÷ Industry gallonage growth.
†Acquired by Cadbury Schweppes in 1995.
‡Includes A&W Brands, acquired in 1993.
§Cott tracked since 1992.
Source: Beverage Marketing Corporation.

Coca-Cola has sustained a dominant domestic market share lead over Pepsi throughout the decade. Internationally, Coca-Cola is even more dominant as the following exhibit indicates:

THE WORLD'S FAVORITE SOFT DRINK?

	Market Leader	Leadership Margin	Second Place
Australia	Coca-Cola	3.9–1	Diet Coke
Belgium	Coca-Cola	9.0–1	Fanta
Brazil	Coca-Cola	3.7–1	Brazilian brand
Chile	Coca-Cola	4.5–1	Fanta
France	Coca-Cola	4.2–1	French brand
Germany	Coca-Cola	3.5–1	Fanta
Great Britain	Coca-Cola	1.8–1	Diet Coke
Greece	Coca-Cola	3.7–1	Fanta
Italy	Coca-Cola	2.8–1	Fanta
Japan	Coca-Cola	2.2–1	Fanta
Korea	Coca-Cola	1.6–1	Korean brand
Norway	Coca-Cola	2.7–1	Coca-Cola light
South Africa	Coca-Cola	3.8–1	Sparletta
Spain	Coca-Cola	2.4–1	Spanish brand
Sweden	Coca-Cola	3.6–1	Fanta

Share of flavored, carbonated soft drink sales.
Source: Company data/store audit data.

Further comparison of Coca-Cola, Pepsi-Cola, and upstart Cott Corporation gives a sense that Coke has major strength in traditional brands and is experiencing the best growth in the diet and "new age" categories among these major players. Cott's success with retailers is impressive, representing a potential challenge to Coke's traditional dominance.

Soft Drink	Gallonage (millions)	Market Share	Corporate Share	1994 Growth	Industry Growth Index Factor*	Five-Year Growth
Coca-Cola	**5,580.8**	**42.0%**	**100.0%**	**+5.1%**	**+49.0%***	**+18.1%**
Coca-Cola Classic	2,621.1	19.7	47.0	+5.7	+25.6	+16.4
Diet Coke	1,267.5	9.5	22.7	+3.6	+8.0	+16.8
Sprite	580.6	4.4	10.4	+10.8	+10.2	+37.6
Caffeine-Free Diet Coke	264.8	2.0	4.7	−1.7	−0.8	+10.0
Diet Sprite	97.1	0.7	1.7	−3.2	−0.6	+3.1
Cherry Coke	94.6	0.7	1.7	+4.9	+0.8	−20.8
Mello Yello	89.0	0.7	1.7	+1.0	+0.2	+65.7
Fanta	73.9	0.6	1.4	−0.1	(−)0.0	−11.4
Minute Maid	69.4	0.5	1.2	+16.1	+1.7	+37.4
Caffeine-Free Coca-Cola Classic	69.3	0.5	1.1	+11.1	−1.2	+179.4
Mr. PIBB	54.2	0.4	1.0	+10.4	+0.9	+160.6
Diet Minute Maid	49.6	0.4	0.9	+11.5	+0.9	+49.8
Coke II	37.6	0.3	0.8	−29.5	−2.8	−77.2
Fresca	17.9	0.1	0.3	+13.3	+0.4	+588.5
Tab	15.8	0.1	0.3	−5.4	−0.2	−54.2
Diet Cherry Coke	10.8	0.1	0.2	−15.6	−0.4	−55.6
All other Coke products	167.6	1.3	2.9	+14.6	+3.9	+805.9

Soft Drink	Gallonage (millions)	Market Share	Corporate Share	1994 Growth	Industry Growth Index Factor*	Five-Year Growth
Pepsi-Cola	**4,070.6**	**30.7**	**100.0**	**+4.4**	**+31.1**	**+12.1**
Pepsi-Cola	2,066.3	15.6	50.7	+5.4	+19.2	+1.3
Diet Pepsi	760.3	5.7	18.7	+4.0	+5.3	+15.8
Mountain Dew	682.6	5.1	16.8	+17.4	+18.3	+61.5
Caffeine-Free Diet Pepsi	152.7	1.2	3.8	+1.7	+0.5	+10.2
Slice	126.8	1.0	3.1	+6.8	+1.5	+23.6
Caffeine-Free Pepsi	105.8	0.8	2.6	−6.4	+0.6	+3.1
Diet Mountain Dew	85.0	0.6	2.1	+3.4	+1.3	+66.0
Mug	38.2	0.3	0.9	+9.5	+0.2	+32.6
Diet Slice	22.5	0.2	0.6	+1.1	−0.7	−63.2
Caffeine-Free Mountain Dew	12.1	0.1	0.3	NA	+2.2[†]	NA
Caffeine-Free Diet Mountain Dew	7.8	0.1	0.2	NA	+1.4[†]	NA
Crystal Pepsi	5.6	0.0	0.1	−90.4	−9.5	NA
Diet Crystal Pepsi	1.9	0.0	0.0	−94.0	−5.4	NA
All other Pepsi products	3.0	0.0	0.0	−91.1	−3.7	−87.3
Cott Total‡	**300.7**	**2.3**	**100.0**	**+37.7**	**+14.9**	**218.5**
Sam's Choice	104.0	0.8	34.6	+31.5	+4.5	+54.3
Safeway Select	50.8	0.4	16.9	+11.6	+1.0	NA
President's Choice	38.0	0.3	12.6	+33.3	+1.7	+544.1
World Classics	13.2	0.1	4.4	+37.5	+0.7	NA
Marquee	9.6	0.1	3.2	NA	NA	NA
Q&V	7.5	0.1	2.5	NA	NA	NA
Bi-Lo	6.6	NS	2.2	NA	NA	NA
Smith's	5.4	NS	1.8	NA	NA	NA
Wegman's	4.5	NS	1.5	NA	NA	NA
Ralph's	4.5	NS	1.5	NA	NA	NA
Top's	4.2	NS	1.4	NA	NA	NA
Master Choice	3.0	NS	1.0	NA	NA	NA
Randall's	2.5	NS	0.8	NA	NA	NA
Schnuck's	2.4	NS	0.8	NA	NA	NA
All other Cott products	44.5	0.3	14.8	−20.0	−1.8	+110.9

‡Cott tracked since 1992.

NA = Not available. NS = not significant.

*IGIF = Brand gallonage growth ÷ Industry gallonage growth.

†Represents first-year gallonage.

Source: Beverage Marketing Corporation.

Pepsi's main strength is in the supermarket area, but Coca-Cola maintains a virtually equal portion of this market. Pepsi has strong sales through the restaurant chains it owns (Pizza Hut, Kentucky Fried Chicken, Taco Bell), although a recent decision by Burger King to leave Pepsi for Coke, plus McDonald's continued relationship with Coca-Cola, seem to confirm Goizueta's long-held policy that Coca-Cola will not compete with its customers, such as restaurant chains, by entering their industry.

Coca-Cola was a weak relative to Pepsi in the early 1980s in terms of the strength of franchisee bottlers. Coke's bottlers, as mentioned in an earlier case, were second- and third-generation family businesses that had been with Coke from its very early days. Pepsi's franchises, led by what was then the world's largest soft-drink bottler, General Cinema Corporation, had better capitalized and more sophisticated bottlers in many key urban areas in the United States. But Coca-Cola recognized this and, over the 1980s, became more aggressively involved with its bottlers, including over $2 billion in investment, which makes its bottling network, particularly abroad, a relative advantage in the 1990s.

Cott Corporation's efforts to reach Japanese consumers through large Japanese retailers by selling cola beverages for less than half Coke's price has begun to cause Coca-Cola management to question its relative weakness in this geographic region and channel. Coca-Cola's conclusion appears to be that a relative weakness could potentially develop unless Coca-Cola responds to minimize the threat and reestablish its competitive advantage.

Coca-Cola likes to assess its strengths and weaknesses against an internal sense of what is required for success in the global soft-drink industry. Based on quotes of Roberto Goizueta, Coca-Cola's chief executive officer, provided in the Chapter 5 Cohesion Case, it appears Coke is exceptionally strong on dimensions it deems key determinants of success. An outside evaluation of Coke's strengths vis-à-vis international markets appears to confirm Coke's perception:

> International volume growth [at Coke] has outpaced domestic growth for several years, reflecting the relative immaturity of those markets in terms of soft-drink consumption and, more importantly, The Coca-Cola Company's aggressive efforts to expand distribution and emphasize marketing. While The Coca-Cola Company participates in U.S. bottling activities primarily as an equity investor (albeit a highly involved investor), the international involvement has been varied. In most countries, the preferred avenue has been to establish a joint venture with a strong local business entity, with Coke contributing equity and management expertise. In some markets, notably France and the former East Germany, Coca-Cola has stepped in with direct ownership and investment.

Overall the company's increasing emphasis on bottling investment and support represent a major strength for the company in virtually every market.

Brand loyalty is another major strength for Coca-Cola. In the United States, Coke's mid-1980s debacle—withdrawing regular Coke in favor of New Coke only to have consumers react so negatively that regular Coke, "Coke Classic," was brought back to head off consumer lawsuits and other demands—showed Coke the depth of brand loyalty it had engendered. The net result was greater market share and profitability for Coke as it realized the depth of its brand loyalty. The selected financial data provided on the following two pages portray the strong position of the Coke brand abroad, and suggest a similar brand loyalty in those markets.

1995 saw Coca-Cola using the billboard below to communicate the strength of its brand identity. A recent global analysis ranked Coca-Cola as the world's most valuable brand, assigning it a value of $39 billion.

SELECTED FINANCIAL DATA

(In millions except per share data, ratios and growth rates)	Compound Growth Rates		Year Ended December 31,	
	5 Years	10 Years	1994[2]	1993[3]
Summary of Operations				
Net operating revenues	13.4%	11.5%	$ 16,172	$ 13,957
Cost of goods sold	11.7%	8.5%	6,167	5,160
Gross profit	14.5%	14.0%	10,005	8,797
Selling, administrative and general expenses	13.5%	13.0%	6,297	5,695
Operating income	16.5%	15.9%	3,708	3,102
Interest income			181	144
Interest expense			199	168
Equity income			134	91
Other income (deductions)-net			(96)	4
Gain on issuance of stock by equity investees			—	12
Income from continuing operations before income taxes and changes in accounting principles	16.1%	15.2%	3,728	3,185
Income taxes	16.2%	12.5%	1,174	997
Income from continuing operations before changes in accounting principles	16.1%	16.6%	$ 2,554	$ 2,188
Net income	10.7%[5]	15.0%	$ 2,554	$ 2,176
Preferred stock dividends			—	—
Net income available to common share owners	11.0%[5]	15.0%	$ 2,554	$ 2,176
Average common shares outstanding			1,290	1,302
Per Common Share Data				
Income from continuing operations before changes in accounting principles	18.1%	18.9%	$ 1.98	$ 1.68
Net income	12.5%	17.3%	1.98	1.67
Cash dividends	18.1%	13.0%	.78	.68
Market price at December 31	21.7%	25.8%	51.50	44.63
Balance Sheet Data				
Cash, cash equivalents and current marketable securities			$ 1,531	$ 1,078
Property, plant and equipment–net			4,080	3,729
Depreciation			382	333
Capital expenditures			878	800
Total assets			13,873	12,021
Long-term debt			1,426	1,428
Total debt			3,509	3,100
Share-owners' equity			5,235	4,584
Total capital[1]			8,744	7,684
Other Key Financial Measures[1]				
Total-debt-to-total-capital			40.1%	40.3%
Net-debt-to-net-capital			22.6%	26.2%
Return on common equity			52.0%	51.7%
Return on capital			32.7%	31.2%
Dividend payout ratio			39.4%	40.6%
Economic profit			$ 2,012	$ 1,495

[1]See Glossary on page 70.
[2]In 1994, the Company adopted SFAS No. 115, "Accounting for Certain Investments in Debt and Equity Securities."
[3]In 1993, the Company adopted SFAS No. 112, "Employers' Accounting for Postemployment Benefits."
[4]In 1992, the Company adopted SFAS No. 106, "Employers' Accounting for Postretirement Benefits Other Than Pensions."
[5]The Company adopted SFAS No. 109, "Accounting for Income Taxes," in 1992 by restating financial statements beginning in 1989.

THE COCA-COLA COMPANY AND SUBSIDIARIES

1992[4,5]	1991[5]	1990[5]	1989[5]	1988	1987	1986	1985	1984
$ 13,074	$ 11,572	$ 10,236	$ 8,622	$ 8,065	$ 7,658	$ 6,977	$ 5,879	$ 5,442
5,055	4,649	4,208	3,548	3,429	3,633	3,454	2,909	2,738
8,019	6,923	6,028	5,074	4,636	4,025	3,523	2,970	2,704
5,249	4,604	4,076	3,348	3,038	2,701	2,626	2,163	1,855
2,770	2,319	1,952	1,726	1,598	1,324	897	807	849
164	175	170	205	199	232	154	151	133
171	192	231	308	230	297	208	196	128
65	40	110	75	92	64	45	52	42
(82)	41	13	66	(33)	—	35	69	13
—	—	—	—	—	40	375	—	—
2,746	2,383	2,014	1,764	1,626	1,363	1,298	883	909
863	765	632	553	537	496	471	314	360
$ 1,883	$ 1,618	$ 1,382	$ 1,211	$ 1,089	$ 867	$ 827	$ 569	$ 549
$ 1,664	$ 1,618	$ 1,382	$ 1,537	$ 1,045	$ 916	$ 934	$ 722	$ 629
—	1	18	21	7	—	—	—	—
$ 1,664	$ 1,617	$ 1,364	$ 1,516[6]	$ 1,038	$ 916	$ 934	$ 722	$ 629
1,317	1,333	1,337	1,384	1,458	1,509	1,547	1,573	1,587
$ 1.43	$ 1.21	$ 1.02	$ .86	$ .74	$ .57	$ .53	$ .36	$ .35
1.26	1.21	1.02	1.10[6]	.71	.61	.60	.46	.40
.56	.48	.40	.34	.30	.28	.26	.25	.23
41.88	40.13	23.25	19.31	11.16	9.53	9.44	7.04	5.20
$ 1,063	$ 1,117	$ 1,492	$ 1,182	$ 1,231	$ 1,489	$ 895	$ 843	$ 768
3,526	2,890	2,386	2,021	1,759	1,602	1,538	1,483	1,284
310	254	236	181	167	152	151	130	119
1,083	792	593	462	387	304	346	412	300
11,052	10,189	9,245	8,249	7,451	8,606	7,675	6,341	5,241
1,120	985	536	549	761	909	996	801	631
3,207	2,288	2,537	1,980	2,124	2,995	1,848	1,280	1,310
3,888	4,239	3,662	3,299	3,345	3,187	3,479	2,948	2,751
7,095	6,527	6,199	5,279	5,469	6,182	5,327	4,228	4,061
45.2%	35.1%	40.9%	37.5%	38.8%	48.4%	34.7%	30.3%	32.3%
31.9%	19.2%	23.7%	14.7%	18.9%	15.4%	10.9%	15.6%	19.7%
46.4%	41.3%	41.4%	39.4%	34.7%	26.0%	25.7%	20.0%	19.4%
29.4%	27.5%	26.8%	26.5%	21.3%	18.3%	20.1%	16.8%	16.7%
44.3%	39.5%	39.2%	31.0%[6]	42.1%	46.0%	43.1%	53.8%	57.9%
$ 1,293	$ 1,029	$ 878	$ 821	$ 748	$ 417	$ 311	$ 269	$ 268

[6]Net income available to common share owners in 1989 includes after-tax gains of $604 million ($.44 per common share) from the sales of the Company's equity interest in Columbia Pictures Entertainment, Inc. and the Company's bottled water business and the transition effect of $265 million related to the change in accounting for income taxes. Excluding these nonrecurring items, the dividend payout ratio in 1989 was 39.9 percent.

7 FORMULATING LONG-TERM OBJECTIVES AND GRAND STRATEGIES

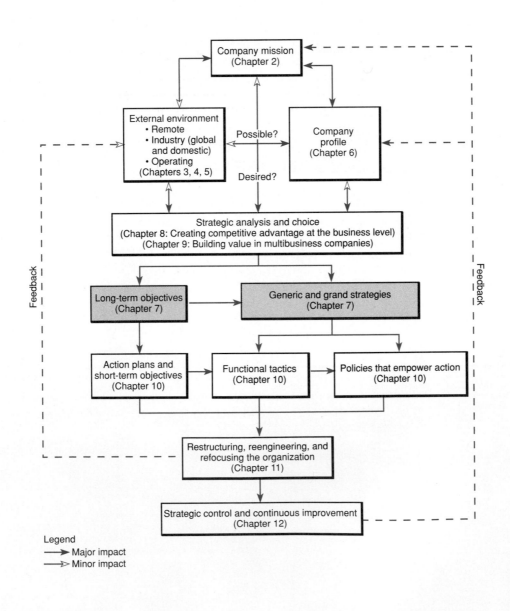

Legend
———▶ Major impact
———▷ Minor impact

The company mission was described in Chapter 2 as encompassing the broad aims of the firm. The most specific statement of aims presented in that chapter appeared as the goals of the firm. However, these goals, which commonly dealt with profitability, growth, and survival, were stated without specific targets or time frames. They were always to be pursued but could never be fully attained. They gave a general sense of direction but were not intended to provide specific benchmarks for evaluating the firm's progress in achieving its aims. Providing such benchmarks is the function of objectives.[1]

The first part of this chapter will focus on long-term objectives. These are statements of the results a firm seeks to achieve over a specified period, typically five years. The second part will focus on the formulation of grand strategies. These provide a comprehensive general approach in guiding major actions designed to accomplish the firm's long-term objectives.

The chapter has two major aims: (1) to discuss in detail the concept of long-term objectives, the topics they cover, and the qualities they should exhibit; and (2) to discuss the concept of grand strategies and to describe the 14 principal grand strategy options that are available to firms singly or in combination, including three newly popularized options that are being used to provide the basis for global competitiveness.

LONG-TERM OBJECTIVES

Strategic managers recognize that short-run profit maximization is rarely the best approach to achieving sustained corporate growth and profitability. An often repeated adage states that if impoverished people are given food, they will eat it and remain impoverished; however, if they are given seeds and tools and shown how to grow crops, they will be able to improve their condition permanently. A parallel choice confronts strategic decision makers:

1. Should they eat the seeds to improve the near-term profit picture and make large dividend payments through cost saving measures such as laying off workers during periods of slack demand, selling off inventories, or cutting back on research and development?
2. Or should they sow the seeds in the effort to reap long-term rewards by reinvesting profits in growth opportunities, committing resources to employee training, or increasing advertising expenditures?

For most strategic managers, the solution is clear—distribute a small amount of profit now but sow most of it to increase the likelihood of a long-term supply. This is the most frequently used rationale in selecting objectives.

To achieve long-term prosperity, strategic planners commonly establish long-term objectives in seven areas:

Profitability   The ability of any firm to operate in the long run depends on attaining an acceptable level of profits. Strategically managed firms characteristically have a profit objective, usually expressed in earnings per share or return on equity.

---

[1] Throughout this text, the terms *goals* and *objectives* are each used to convey a special meaning, with goals being the less specific and more encompassing concept. Most authors follow this usage; however, some use the two words interchangeably, while others reverse the usage.

GLOBAL
STRATEGY IN
ACTION 7–1

From Strategic Intent to Corporate Purpose: The Remaking of Komatsu

When he succeeded his father as Komatsu's president in 1964, Ryoichi Kawai articulated an objective that the company would pursue for more than 20 years. Komatsu's strategic intent, Kawai announced, was to "catch up with and surpass Caterpillar."

The management approach Kawai adopted to pursue this goal became a well-studied and widely emulated model in the West. Each year, Kawai would define a clear and specific operating priority—for example, improving quality, reducing costs, or expanding exports—that used Catepillar's performance as a standard and sited Caterpillar itself as the competitive target. Then each year's priority would be translated into detailed action plans through PDCA (plan, do, check, act), Komatsu's tightly controlled management system.

Kawai's strategy worked well, and by 1982, when he was choosing his successor, Komatsu had grown from a tiny local competitor with poor product quality to Caterpillar's most serious global challenger in the construction equipment market. But the market was about to change. By 1989, when Tetsuya Katada became the third president to follow Kawai, worldwide demand for construction equipment was down, competition was up, and Komatsu's profits were in steady decline.

As Katada saw the situation, Komatsu's management had become so obsessed with catching Caterpillar that it had stopped thinking about strategic choices. For instance, its product development efforts were biased toward Caterpillar's high-end bulldozers rather than toward smaller, lower-priced products like hydraulic excavators, for which market demand was growing. Katada worried that Komatsu's top management had stopped questioning the business the company was in. Further, he was concerned that the inflexible, top-down style that had become embedded at Komatsu had crushed "the spirit of enterprise" among middle and frontline managers.

Source: Reprinted by permission of *Harvard Business Review*. An excerpt from "Changing the Role of Top Management: Beyond Strategy to Purpose," by Christopher A. Bartlett and Sumantra Ghoshal, November–December 1994. Copyright © 1995 by the President and Fellows of Harvard University, all rights reserved.

Productivity   Strategic managers constantly try to improve the productivity of their systems. Firms that can improve the input-output relationship normally increase profitability. Thus, firms almost always state an objective for productivity. Commonly used productivity objectives are the number of items produced or the number of services rendered per unit of input. However, productivity objectives sometimes are stated in terms of desired cost decreases. For example, objectives may be set for reducing defective items, for customer complaints leading to litigation, or for overtime. Achieving such objectives increases profitability if unit output is maintained.

Competitive Position   One measure of corporate success is relative dominance in the marketplace. Larger firms commonly establish an objective in terms of competitive position, often using total sales or market share as measures of their competitive position. An objective with regard to competitive position may indicate a firm's long-term priorities. For example, Gulf Oil set a five-year objective of moving from third to second place as a producer of high-density polypropylene. Total sales were the measure.

Competitive positioning, however, may sometimes result in a firm subordinating its main objective. As was the case with Komatsu, management became so concerned with the company's performance relative to its competitor, Caterpillar, that the company found itself forgoing opportunities for growth, which led to the company's decline in profits. As Global Strategy in Action 7–1 demonstrates, the company's strategy was successfully restructured before any further damage was caused.

Managers, Katada decided, "can no longer operate within the confines of a defined objective. They need to go out and see the needs and opportunities and operate in a creative and innovative way, always encouraging initiative from below." In other words, he told the company, "I want everyone to stop concentrating simply on catching up with Caterpillar."

At meetings and discussions, Katada challenged managers at several levels to find ways for the company to double its sales by the mid-1990s. What emerged from these and subsequent discussions was a new definition of the company. Rather than thinking of Komatsu as a construction equipment company trying to catch Caterpillar, management began to describe it as a "total technology enterprise" with an opportunity to leverage its existing resources and expertise in electronics, robotics, and plastics.

Under a new banner of "Growth, Global, Groupwide" (the Three Gs), Katada encouraged management at all levels to find new growth opportunities through expanding geographically and leveraging competences. He appointed a Committee for the 1990s to determine how Komatsu could enrich its corporate philosophy, broaden its social contributions, and revitalize its human resources. His objective was to create an organization that could attract and stimulate the best people. "Compared with our old objective," Katada acknowledged, "the Three Gs slogan may seem abstract, but it was this abstract nature that stimulated people to ask what they could do and respond creatively."

More than a strategy, Komatsu now had a corporate purpose, to which its managers could commit and in which they had a voice. In the first three years after Katada articulated the Three Gs, Komatsu's sales, which had been declining since 1982, perked up. That surge was driven almost entirely by a 40 percent growth in Komatsu's nonconstruction equipment business.

Employee Development   Employees value growth and career opportunities. Providing such opportunities often increases productivity and decreases turnover. Therefore, strategic decision makers frequently include an employee development objective in their long-range plans. For example, PPG has declared an objective of developing highly skilled and flexible employees and, thus, providing steady employment for a reduced number of workers.

Employee Relations   Whether or not they are bound by union contracts, firms actively seek good employee relations. In fact, proactive steps in anticipation of employee needs and expectations are a characteristic concern of strategic managers. Strategic managers believe that productivity is linked to employee loyalty and to perceived management interest in workers' welfare. They, therefore, set objectives to improve employee relations. Among the outgrowths of such objectives are safety programs, worker representation on management committees, and employee stock option plans.

Technological Leadership   Firms must decide whether to lead or follow in the marketplace. Either approach can be successful, but each requires a different strategic posture. Therefore, many firms state an objective with regard to technological leadership. For example, Caterpillar Tractor Company established its early reputation and dominant position in its industry by being in the forefront of technological innovation in the manufacture of large earthmovers. Because of an advanced technological design, Daihatsu Mira became the most popular car in Japan in 1991. The four-seat minicar held a 660cc engine that provided the customer with 30 percent more miles per gallon than any competitor, and it had a 25 percent smaller sales tax.

Public Responsibility   Firms recognize their responsibilities to their customers and to society at large. In fact, many firms seek to exceed the demands made by government. They work not only to develop reputations for fairly priced products and services but also to establish themselves as responsible corporate citizens. For example, they may establish objectives for charitable and educational contributions, minority training, public or political activity, community welfare, or urban revitalization. In an attempt to exhibit their sense of public responsibility in the United States, Japanese companies, such as Toyota, Hitachi, and Matsushita, contributed more than $500 million to American educational projects, charities, and nonprofit organizations, a 67 percent increase over the previous year.

Qualities of Long-Term Objectives

What distinguishes a good objective from a bad one? What qualities of an objective improve its chances of being attained? Perhaps these questions are best answered in relation to seven criteria that should be used in preparing long-term objectives: acceptable, flexible, measurable over time, motivating, suitable, understandable, and achievable.

Acceptable   Managers are most likely to pursue objectives that are consistent with their preferences. They may ignore or even obstruct the achievement of objectives that offend them (e.g., promoting a non-nutritional food product) or that they believe to be inappropriate or unfair (e.g., reducing spoilage to offset a disproportionate allocation of fixed overhead). In addition, long-term corporate objectives frequently are designed to be acceptable to groups external to the firm. An example is efforts to abate air pollution that are undertaken at the insistence of the Environmental Protection Agency.

Flexible   Objectives should be adaptable to unforeseen or extraordinary changes in the firm's competitive or environmental forecasts. However, such flexibility usually is increased at the expense of specificity. Moreover, employee confidence may be tempered because adjustment of flexible objectives may affect their jobs. One way of providing flexibility while minimizing its negative effects is to allow for adjustments in the level, rather than in the nature, of objectives. For example, the personnel department objective of providing managerial development training for 15 supervisors per year over the next five-year period might be adjusted by changing the number of people to be trained. In contrast, changing the personnel department's objective of "assisting production supervisors in reducing job-related injuries by 10 percent per year" after three months had gone by would understandably create dissatisfaction.

Measurable   Objectives must clearly and concretely state what will be achieved and when it will be achieved. Thus, objectives should be measurable over time. For example, the objective of "substantially improving our return on investment" would be better stated as "increasing the return on investment on our line of paper products by a minimum of 1 percent a year and a total of 5 percent over the next three years."

Motivating   Studies have shown that people are most productive when objectives are set at a motivating level—one high enough to challenge but not so high as to frustrate or so low as to be easily attained. The problem is that individuals and groups differ in their perceptions of what is high enough. A broad objective that challenges one group frustrates another and minimally interests a third. One valuable recommendation is that objectives be tailored to specific groups. Developing such objectives requires time and effort, but objectives of this kind are more likely to motivate.

CACI'S LONG-TERM OBJECTIVES, 1990–1997

REVENUE

Increase revenue range to $167–$176M or better in FY 90 (FY 90 bookings at $170M).

FY 91: Revenue in the $193–$202M range; bookings at $195–$205M range.

Increase company revenue 15–20 percent per year steadily over next decade.

Consistently increase revenues to $500 M per annum by 1997 or earlier. Steady manageable and consistent profitable growth.

PROFITABILITY

Achieve 4 percent NAT or better as an annual corporate target for return on revenues, moving to 5 percent CAT by mid-90s.

Individual departments and divisions must target NAT percentage profits at 50–100 percent above company levels (i.e., 6–8 percent moving to 7.5–10 percent).

SHAREHOLDERS' VALUE

Increase stock price (market value) to $20 per share or better by 1997 (current share basis).

Suitable   Objectives must be suited to the broad aims of the firm, which are expressed in its mission statement. Each objective should be a step toward the attainment of overall goals. In fact, objectives that do not coincide with the company mission can subvert the firm's aims. For example, if the mission is growth oriented, the objective of reducing the debt-to-equity ratio to 1.00 would probably be unsuitable and counterproductive.

Understandable   Strategic managers at all levels must understand what is to be achieved. They also must understand the major criteria by which their performance will be evaluated. Thus, objectives must be so stated that they are as understandable to the recipient as they are to the giver. Consider the misunderstandings that might arise over the objective of "increasing the productivity of the credit card department by 20 percent within five years." What does this objective mean? Increase the number of outstanding cards? Increase the use of outstanding cards? Increase the employee workload? Make productivity gains each year? Or hope that the new computer-assisted system, which should improve productivity, is approved by year 5? As this simple example illustrates, objectives must be clear, meaningful, and unambiguous.

Achievable   Finally, objectives must be possible to achieve. This is easier said than done. Turbulence in the remote and operating environments affects a firm's internal operations, creating uncertainty, and limiting the accuracy of the objectives set by strategic management. To illustrate, the wildly fluctuating prime interest rates in 1980 made objective setting extremely difficult for the years 1981 to 1985, particularly in such areas as sales projections for producers of consumer durable goods like General Motors and General Electric.

An especially fine example of long-term objectives is provided in CACI, Inc.'s strategic plan. Shown in Strategy in Action 7–1 are CACI's major financial objectives for the period. The firm's approach is wholly consistent with the list of desired qualities for long-term objectives. In particular, CACI's objectives are flexible, measurable over time, understandable, and suitable for a high-technology and professional services organization.

GENERIC STRATEGIES

Many planning experts believe that the general philosophy of doing business declared by the firm in the mission statement must be translated into a holistic statement of the firm's strategic orientation before it can be further defined in terms of a specific long-term strategy. In other words, a long-term or grand strategy must be based on a core idea about how the firm can best compete in the marketplace.

The popular term for this core idea is *generic strategy*. From a scheme developed by Michael Porter, many planners believe that any long-term strategy should derive from a firm's attempt to seek a competitive advantage based on one of three generic strategies:

1. Striving for overall low-cost leadership in the industry.
2. Striving to create and market unique products for varied customer groups through *differentiation*.
3. Striving to have special appeal to one or more groups of consumer or industrial buyers, *focusing* on their cost or differentiation concerns.

Advocates of generic strategies believe that each of these options can produce above-average returns for a firm in an industry. However, they are successful for very different reasons.

Low-cost leaders depend on some fairly unique capabilities to achieve and sustain their low-cost position. Examples of such capabilities are: having secured suppliers of scarce raw materials, being in a dominant market share position, or having a high degree of capitalization. Low-cost producers usually excel at cost reductions and efficiencies. They maximize economies of scale, implement cost-cutting technologies, stress reductions in overhead and in administrative expenses, and use volume sales techniques to propel themselves up the earning curve. The commonly accepted requirements for successful implementation of the low-cost and other two generic strategies are overviewed in Figure 7–1.

A low-cost leader is able to use its cost advantage to charge lower prices or to enjoy higher profit margins. By so doing, the firm effectively can defend itself in price wars, attack competitors on price to gain market share, or, if already dominant in the industry, simply benefit from exceptional returns. As an extreme case, it has been argued that National Can Company, a corporation in an essentially stagnant industry, is able to generate attractive and improving profits by being the low-cost producer.

Strategies dependent on differentiation are designed to appeal to customers with a special sensitivity for a particular product attribute. By stressing the attribute above other product qualities, the firm attempts to build customer loyalty. Often such loyalty translates into a firm's ability to charge a premium price for its product. Cross-brand pens, Brooks Brothers suits, Porsche automobiles, and Chivas Regal Scotch whiskey are all examples.

The product attribute also can be the marketing channels through which it is delivered, its image for excellence, the features it includes, and the service network that supports it. As a result of the importance of these attributes, competitors often face "perceptual" barriers to entry when customers of a successfully differentiated firm fail to see largely identical products as being interchangeable. For example, General Motors hopes that customers will accept "only genuine GM replacement parts."

A focus strategy, whether anchored in a low-cost base or a differentiation base, attempts to attend to the needs of a particular market segment. Likely segments are those that are ignored by marketing appeals to easily accessible markets, to the "typical" customer, or to

FIGURE 7–1
Requirements for Generic Competitive Strategies

Generic Strategy	Commonly Required Skills and Resources	Common Organizational Requirements
Overall cost leadership	Sustained capital investment and access to capital. Process engineering skills. Intense supervision of labor. Products designed for ease in manufacture. Low-cost distribution system.	Tight cost control. Frequent, detailed control reports. Structured organization and responsibilities. Incentives based on meeting strict quantitative targets.
Differentiation	Strong marketing abilities. Product engineering. Creative flare. Strong capability in basic research. Corporate reputation for quality or technological leadership. Long tradition in the industry or unique combination of skills drawn from other businesses. Strong cooperation from channels.	Strong coordination among functions in R&D, product development, and marketing. Subjective measurement and incentives instead of quantitative measures. Amenities to attract highly skilled labor, scientists, or creative people.
Focus	Combination of the above policies directed at the particular strategic target.	Combination of the above policies directed at the regular strategic target.

Source: Free Press *COMPETITIVE STRATEGY: Techniques for Analyzing Industries and Competitors*, pp. 40–41. Reprinted with permission of the Free Press, a division of Simon & Schuster, from *Competitive Strategy: Techniques for Analyzing Industries and Competitors*, by Michael E. Porter. Copyright © 1980 by Michael E. Porter.

customers with common applications for the product. A firm pursuing a focus strategy is willing to service isolated geographic areas; to satisfy the needs of customers with special financing, inventory, or servicing problems; or to tailor the product to the somewhat unique demands of the small-to-medium-sized customer. The focusing firms profit from their willingness to serve otherwise ignored or under-appreciated customer segments. The classic example is cable television. An entire industry was born because of a willingness of cable firms to serve isolated rural locations that were ignored by traditional television services. Brick producers that typically service a radius of less than 100 miles and commuter airlines that serve regional geographic areas are other examples of industries where a focus strategy frequently yields above-average industry profits.

While each of the generic strategies enables a firm to maximize certain competitive advantages, each one also exposes the firm to a number of competitive risks. For example, a low-cost leader fears a new low-cost technology that is being developed by a competitor; a differentiating firm fears imitators; and a focused firm fears invasion by a firm that largely targets customers. As Figure 7–2 suggests, each generic strategy presents the firm with a number of risks.

GRAND STRATEGIES

While the need for firms to develop generic strategies remains an unresolved debate, designers of planning systems agree about the critical role of grand strategies. Grand strategies, often called *master* or *business strategies*, provide basic direction for strategic

FIGURE 7–2
Risks of the Generic Strategies

Risks of Cost Leadership	Risks of Differentiation	Risk of Focus
Cost of leadership is not sustained: • Competitors imitate. • Technology changes. • Other bases for cost leadership erode.	Differentiation is not sustained: • Competitors imitate. • Bases for differentiation becomes less important to buyers.	The focus strategy is imitated. The target segment becomes structurally unattractive: • Structure erodes. • Demand disappears.
Proximity in differentiation is lost.	Cost proximity is lost.	Broadly targeted competitors overwhelm the segment: • The segment's differences from other segments narrow • The advantages of a broad line increase.
Cost focusers achieve even lower cost in segments.	Differentiation focusers achieve even greater differentiation in segments.	New focusers subsegment the industry.

Source: Free Press *Competitive Advantage: Creating and Sustaining Superior Performance*, p. 21. Adapted with the permission of the Free Press, a division of Simon & Schuster, from *Competitive Strategy: Creating and Sustaining Superior Performance*, by Michael E. Porter. Copyright © 1985 by Michael E. Porter.

actions. They are the basis of coordinated and sustained efforts directed toward achieving long-term business objectives.

The purpose of this section is twofold: (1) to list, describe, and discuss 14 grand strategies that strategic managers should consider and (2) to present approaches to the selection of an optimal grand strategy from the available alternatives.

Grand strategies indicate the time period over which long-range objectives are to be achieved. Thus, a grand strategy can be defined as a comprehensive general approach that guides a firm's major actions.

The 14 principal grand strategies are: concentrated growth, market development, product development, innovation, horizontal integration, vertical integration, concentric diversification, conglomerate diversification, turnaround, divestiture, liquidation, joint ventures, strategic alliances, and consortia. Any one of these strategies could serve as the basis for achieving the major long-term objectives of a single firm. But a firm involved with multiple industries, businesses, product lines, or customer groups—as many firms are—usually combines several grand strategies. For clarity, however, each of the principal grand strategies is described independently in this section, with examples to indicate some of its relative strengths and weaknesses.

Concentrated Growth

Many of the firms that fell victim to merger mania were once mistakenly convinced that the best way to achieve their objectives was to pursue unrelated diversification in the search for financial opportunity and synergy.[2] By rejecting that "conventional wisdom," such firms as **Martin-Marietta**, Kentucky Fried Chicken, Compaq, Avon, Hyatt Legal Services, and **Tenant** have demonstrated the advantages of what is increasingly proving to be sound business strategy. A firm that has enjoyed special success through a strategic emphasis

---

[2] Portions of this section were adapted from John A. Pearce II and J. Harvey, "Risks and Rewards of a Concentrated Growth Strategy," *Academy of Management Executive*, February 1990, pp. 62–69.

on increasing market share through concentration is Chemlawn. With headquarters in Columbus, Ohio, Chemlawn is the North American leader in professional lawn care. Like others in the lawn-care industry, Chemlawn is experiencing a steadily declining customer base. Market analysis shows that the decline is fueled by negative environmental publicity, perceptions of poor customer service, and concern about the price versus the value of the company's services, given the wide array of do-it-yourself alternatives. Chemlawn's approach to increasing market share hinges on addressing quality, price, and value issues; discontinuing products that the public or environmental authorities perceive as unsafe; and improving the quality of its work force.

These firms are just a few of the majority of American firms that pursue a concentrated growth strategy by focusing on a specific product and market combination. Concentrated growth is the strategy of the firm that directs its resources to the profitable growth of a single product, in a single market, with a single dominant technology. The main rationale for this approach, sometimes called a *market penetration* or *concentration strategy*, is that the firm thoroughly develops and exploits its expertise in a delimited competitive arena.

Rationale for Superior Performance

Concentrated growth strategies lead to enhanced performance. The ability to assess market needs, knowledge of buyer behavior, customer price sensitivity, and effectiveness of promotion are characteristics of a concentrated growth strategy. Such core capabilities are a more important determinant of competitive market success than are the environmental forces faced by the firm. The high success rates of new products also are tied to avoiding situations that require undeveloped skills, such as serving new customers and markets, acquiring new technology, building new channels, developing new promotional abilities, and facing new competition.

A major misconception about the concentrated growth strategy is that the firm practicing it will settle for little or no growth. This is certainly not true for a firm that correctly utilizes the strategy. A firm employing concentrated growth grows by building on its competences, and it achieves a competitive edge by concentrating in the product-market segment it knows best. A firm employing this strategy is aiming for the growth that results from increased productivity, better coverage of its actual product-market segment, and more efficient use of its technology. Strategy in Action 7–2 provides an excellent example of how Hechinger, the home supply chain, is attempting to improve its competitiveness by refocusing its concentration strategy.

Conditions That Favor Concentrated Growth

Specific conditions in the firm's environment are favorable to the concentrated growth strategy. The first is a condition in which the firm's industry is resistant to major technological advancements. This is usually the case in the late growth and maturity stages of the product life cycle and in product markets where product demand is stable and industry barriers, such as capitalization, are high. Machinery for the paper manufacturing industry, in which the basic technology has not changed for more than a century, is a good example.

An especially favorable condition is one in which the firm's targeted markets are not product saturated. Markets with competitive gaps leave the firm with alternatives for growth, other than taking market share away from competitors. The successful introduction of traveler services by Allstate and Amoco demonstrates that even an organization as entrenched and powerful as the AAA could not build a defensible presence in all segments of the automobile club market. Similarly, General Motors attempted to increase its share of the Japanese car market in 1992 with the introduction of its Pontiac Grand AM and Buick

HECHINGER REBUILDS STORE CONCEPT

Hechinger—the company that's helped thousands of weekend do-it-yourselfers with everything from fixing a leaky faucet to building a deck—is kicking up a little dust of its own with the remodeling of its Washington area stores to a new "Home Project Center" format.

In addition to new warehouse-style shelving, the stores cluster products around "project areas" and displays and have more workers on hand to answer questions.

"The most important thing we must do as a retailer . . . is to focus on what the customer wants and give it to them better than anyone else," said John W. Hechinger, Jr., the company's president since 1986. "That's really what's driving us."

"The wave of the present, if not the future, is the warehouse concept," said Neal Kaplan, an analyst at Scott & Stringfellow, a Richmond-based brokerage. "It seems some Hechinger stores aren't really as competitive as they'd like them to be."

Analysts also see Hechinger's rapid move as a "preemptive strike" against expansion by Atlanta-based The Home Depot, Inc., and other specialty hardware retailers, such as Lowes, a North Carolina-based chain that is opening larger "superstores."

The Home Depot, rapidly becoming the dominant company in the nation's $25 billion home improvement products industry, has 200 stores in 18 states and is looking to open its first Washington store in Alexandria next year.

Hechinger expects to convert its two dozen Washington area stores to Home Project Centers by the middle of the decade. In early 1992, the Landover, Maryland-based, company set aside $83 million for the work, which also involves closing or consolidating some stores.

It costs about $6 million to open a new store and about $2 million to convert an older Hechinger to the Home Project Center format. Most of the Washington area stores—in prime locations—will be remodeled.

Hechinger's new centers sell more goods, but operating costs are higher, meaning lower gross margins, according to the company's financial records. In response to competition, the company also cut prices in several markets and started a lowest-price guarantee, which has pared profits.

Analysts say it's important for Hechinger to pick its battles in key markets, in part because of the evolution of the home improvement supplies business. For example, they point to the fact that it's possible to buy a tub of spackle or a hacksaw at a drug store or mulch at the neighborhood grocery.

"We need to be the most flexible, leanest operator in the business," Hechinger said.

Source: Excerpted from "Hechinger Rebuilds Store Concept," by Lloyd Batzler, *The Fairfax Journal Weekly*, December 2, 1992, p. A3.

Park Avenue. The move was based on GM's knowledge that import auto sales in Japan rose 5.2 percent in 1990, with large cars accounting for most of those sales.

A third condition that favors concentrated growth exists when the firm's product markets are sufficiently distinctive to dissuade competitors in adjacent product markets from trying to invade the firm's segment. John Deere scrapped its plans for growth in the construction machinery business when mighty Caterpillar threatened to enter Deere's mainstay, the farm machinery business, in retaliation. Rather than risk a costly price war on its own turf, Deere scrapped these plans.

A fourth favorable condition exists when the firm's inputs are stable in price and quantity and are available in the amounts and at the times needed. Maryland-based Giant Foods is able to concentrate in the grocery business largely due to its stable long-term arrangements with suppliers of its private-label products. Most of these suppliers are makers of the national brands that compete against the Giant labels. With a high market share and aggressive retail distribution, Giant controls the access of these brands to the consumer. Consequently, its suppliers have considerable incentive to honor verbal agreements, called *bookings*, in which they commit themselves for a one-year period with regard to the price, quality, and timing of their shipments to Giant.

The pursuit of concentrated growth also is favored by a stable market—a market without the seasonal or cyclical swings that would encourage a firm to diversify. Night Owl Security, the District of Columbia market leader in home security services, commits its customers to initial four-year contracts. In a city where affluent consumers tend to be quite transient, the length of this relationship is remarkable. Night Owl's concentrated growth strategy has been reinforced by its success in getting subsequent owners of its customers' homes to extend and renew the security service contracts. In a similar way, Lands' End reinforced its growth strategy by asking customers for names and addresses of friends and relatives living overseas who would like to receive Lands' End catalogs.

A firm also can grow while concentrating, if it enjoys competitive advantages based on efficient production or distribution channels. These advantages enable the firm to formulate advantageous pricing policies. More efficient production methods and better handling of distribution also enable the firm to achieve greater economies of scale or, in conjunction with marketing, result in a product that is differentiated in the mind of the consumer. Graniteville Company, a large South Carolina textile manufacturer, enjoyed decades of growth and profitability by adopting a "follower" tactic as part of its concentrated growth strategy. By producing fabrics only after market demand had been well established, and by featuring products that reflected its expertise in adopting manufacturing innovations and in maintaining highly efficient long production runs, Graniteville prospered through concentrated growth.

Finally, the success of market generalists creates conditions favorable to concentrated growth. When generalists succeed by using universal appeals, they avoid making special appeals to particular groups of customers. The net result is that many small pockets are left open in the markets dominated by generalists, and that specialists emerge and thrive in these pockets. For example, hardware store chains, such as Stanbaugh-Thompsons and Hechinger, focus primarily on routine household repair problems and offer solutions that can be easily sold on a self-service, do-it-yourself basis. This approach leaves gaps at both the "semiprofessional" and "neophyte" ends of the market—in terms of the purchaser's skill at household repairs and the extent to which available merchandise matches the requirements of individual homeowners.

Risk and Rewards of Concentrated Growth

Under stable conditions, concentrated growth poses lower risk than any other grand strategy; but, in a changing environment, a firm committed to concentrated growth faces high risks. The greatest risk is that concentrating in a single product market makes a firm particularly vulnerable to changes in that segment. Slowed growth in the segment would jeopardize the firm because its investment, competitive edge, and technology are deeply entrenched in a specific offering. It is difficult for the firm to attempt sudden changes if its product is threatened by near-term obsolescence, a faltering market, new substitutes, or changes in technology or customer needs. For example, the manufacturers of IBM clones faced such a problem when IBM adopted the OS/2 operating system for its personal computer line. That change made existing clones out of date.

The concentrating firm's entrenchment in a specific industry makes it particularly susceptible to changes in the economic environment of that industry. For example, Mack Truck, the second-largest truck maker in America, lost $20 million as a result of an 18-month slump in the truck industry.

Entrenchment in a specific product market tends to make a concentrating firm more adept than competitors at detecting new trends. However, any failure of such a firm to properly forecast major changes in its industry can result in extraordinary losses. Numerous makers of inexpensive digital watches were forced to declare bankruptcy because they failed to anticipate the competition posed by Swatch, Guess, and other trendy watches that emerged from the fashion industry.

A firm pursuing a concentrated growth strategy is vulnerable also to the high opportunity costs that result from remaining in a specific product market and ignoring other options that could employ the firm's resources more profitably. Overcommitment to a specific technology and product market can hinder a firm's ability to enter a new or growing product market that offers more attractive cost-benefit trade-offs. Had Apple Computers maintained its policy of making equipment that did not interface with IBM equipment, it would have missed out on what have proved to be its most profitable strategic opinions.

Concentrated Growth Is Often the Most Viable Option

Examples abound of firms that have enjoyed exceptional returns on the concentrated growth strategy. Such firms as McDonald's, Goodyear, and Apple Computers have used firsthand knowledge and deep involvement with specific product segments to become powerful competitors in their markets. The strategy is associated even more often with successful smaller firms that have steadily and doggedly improved their market position.

The limited additional resources necessary to implement concentrated growth, coupled with the limited risk involved, also make this strategy desirable for a firm with limited funds. For example, through a carefully devised concentrated growth strategy, medium-sized John Deere & Company was able to become a major force in the agricultural machinery business even when competing with such firms as Ford Motor Company. While other firms were trying to exit or diversify from the farm machinery business, Deere spent $2 billion in upgrading its machinery, boosting its efficiency, and engaging in a program to strengthen its dealership system. This concentrated growth strategy enabled it to become the leader in the farm machinery business despite the fact that Ford was more than 10 times its size.

The firm that chooses a concentrated growth strategy directs its resources to the profitable growth of a narrowly defined product and market, focusing on a dominant technology. Firms that remain within their chosen product market are able to extract the most from their technology and market knowledge and, thus, are able to minimize the risk associated with unrelated diversification. The success of a concentration strategy is founded on the firm's use of superior insights into its technology, product, and customer to obtain a sustainable competitive advantage. Superior performance on these aspects of corporate strategy has been shown to have a substantial positive effect on market success.

A grand strategy of concentrated growth allows for a considerable range of action. Broadly speaking, the firm can attempt to capture a larger market share by increasing the usage rates of present customers, by attracting competitors' customers, or by selling to nonusers. In turn, each of these options suggests more specific options, some of which are listed in the top section of Figure 7–3.

When strategic managers forecast that their current products and their markets will not provide the basis for achieving the company mission, they have two options that involve moderate costs and risk: market development and product development.

Market Development

Market development commonly ranks second only to concentration as the least costly and least risky of the 14 grand strategies. It consists of marketing present products, often with only cosmetic modifications, to customers in related market areas by adding

FIGURE 7–3
Specific Options under the Grand Strategies of Concentration, Market Development, and Product Development

Concentration (increasing use of present products in present markets):
1. Increasing present customers' rate of use:
   a. Increasing the size of purchase.
   b. Increasing the rate of product obsolescence.
   c. Advertising other uses.
   d. Giving price incentives for increased use.
2. Attracting competitors' customers:
   a. Establishing sharper brand differentiation.
   b. Increasing promotional effort.
   c. Initiating price cuts.
3. Attracting nonusers to buy the product:
   a. Inducing trial use through sampling, price incentives, and so on.
   b. Pricing up or down.
   c. Advertising new uses.

Market development (selling present products in new markets):
1. Opening additional geographic markets:
   a. Regional expansion.
   b. National expansion.
   c. International expansion.
2. Attracting other market segments:
   a. Developing product versions to appeal to other segments.
   b. Entering other channels of distribution.
   c. Advertising in other media.

Product development (developing new products for present markets):
1. Developing new product features:
   a. Adapt (to other ideas, developments).
   b. Modify (change color, motion, sound, odor, form, shape).
   c. Magnify (stronger, longer, thicker, extra value).
   d. Minify (smaller, shorter, lighter).
   e. Substitute (other ingredients, process, power).
   f. Rearrange (other patterns, layout, sequence, components).
   g. Reverse (inside out).
   h. Combine (blend, alloy, assortment, ensemble; combine units, purposes, appeals, ideas).
2. Developing quality variations.
3. Developing additional models and sizes (product proliferation).

Source: Adapted from Philip Kotler, *Marketing Management Analysis, Planning, and Control*, 6th ed., 1987. Reprinted by permission of Prentice Hall, Inc., Englewood Cliffs, NJ.

channels of distribution or by changing the content of advertising or promotion. Several specific approaches are listed under this heading in Figure 7–3. Thus, as suggested by the figure, firms that open branch offices in new cities, states, or countries are practicing market development. Likewise, firms are practicing market development if they switch from advertising in trade publications to advertising in newspapers or if they add jobbers to supplement their mail-order sales efforts. One company that has mastered the strategy of market development is Tandy Corporation, as explained in Strategy in Action 7–3.

Market development allows firms to practice a form of concentrated growth by identifying new uses for existing products and new demographically, psychographically, or geographically defined markets. Frequently, changes in media selection, promotional appeals, and distribution are used to initiate this approach. Du Pont used market development when it found a new application for Kevlar, an organic material that police, security, and military personnel had used primarily for bulletproofing. Kevlar now is being used to refit and maintain wooden-hulled boats, since it is lighter and stronger than glass fibers and has 11 times the strength of steel.

STRATEGY
IN ACTION
7–3

TANDY REMAKES ITSELF AGAIN AND AGAIN AND AGAIN

Only months after heralding its Incredible Universe megastore as the shop of the future, the venerable merchant Tandy Corp. announced that it would open mini electronics and computer stores in several big cities. In another surprising flip-flop, the $3.8 billion retailer scrapped plans to spin off its computer-manufacturing subsidiary, TE Electronics. Instead, it agreed to sell its money-losing plants to computer maker AST Research for an estimated $175 million.

If the reshuffling seems to defy logic, there may be some method in the madness. Central to Tandy's hope for redemption is Incredible Universe, which some analysts have called the most exciting retailing concept in years. The 160,000-square-foot stores, which are about 70 times larger than a Radio Shack, seem to offer 70 times more products than anyone else. They peddle, for instance, 315 kinds of televisions, 181 varieties of refrigerators, and 45,000 music and movie titles. As Tandy CEO John Roach puts it, "If it's not in the Universe, it doesn't exist."

If the stores' guaranteed low prices don't draw the crowds, the Disney-like atmosphere may. Customers are greeted by karaoke singers and salespeople dubbed "cast members" who offer product information and door-prize entry blanks. The stores have their own child-care center stocked with—what else?—electronic toys sold elsewhere in the store. The hope, of course, is that the kid will beg Mom and Dad to take some home. Said one father in Dallas: "One hour of babysitting cost me $400."

If Incredible Universe wants to be everything to everybody, Tandy's latest concepts promise specialized merchandise to a few. A sampling: Energy Express Plus stores will be free-standing kiosks in high-traffic malls that sell mostly impulse purchases like batteries and electronic date books. And Computer City Express will stock the top-selling products carried by the chain's larger computer superstores. Tandy is also out to capitalize on the outlet mall craze. Its new Famous Brand Electronics will carry factory overstocks and clearance merchandise.

Tandy executives report that the first of 16 planned Incredible Universe stores is expected to ring up sales of $60 million in its first year.

The medical industry provides other examples of new markets for existing products. The National Institutes of Health's report of a study showing that the use of aspirin may lower the incidence of heart attacks was expected to boost sales in the $2.2 billion analgesic market. It was predicted that the expansion of this market would lower the market share of nonaspirin brands, such as industry leaders Tylenol and Advil. Product extensions currently planned include Bayer Calendar Pack, 28-day packaging to fit the once-a-day prescription for the prevention of a second heart attack.

Another example is Chesebrough-Ponds, a major producer of health and beauty aids, which decided several years ago to expand its market by repacking its Vaseline Petroleum Jelly in pocket-size squeeze tubes as Vaseline "Lip Therapy." The corporation decided to place a strategic emphasis on market development, because it knew from market studies that its petroleum-jelly customers already were using the product to prevent chapped lips. Company leaders reasoned that their market could be expanded significantly if the product were repackaged to fit conveniently in consumers' pockets and purses.

As shown in Global Strategy in Action 7–2, a British joint venture called "Mercury One 2 One" was able to successfully market its cellular service to a new target segment. The company changed the promotion of its existing product to appeal to more than the

IN ENGLAND THEY GIVE IT AWAY

As U.S. companies try to figure out how to sell consumers on national cellular service, they should ponder the Pythonesque misadventures of a British operator called Mercury One 2 One that dared to cut prices too much.

A joint venture of US West and Britain's Cable 7 Wireless, Mercury was determined to make cellular more than a plaything for rich businessmen. So it launched a marketing campaign in which it offered customers across England free calling services 7 PM to 7 AM when call volume had been low.

The two-year campaign, which ended in September, was successful beyond hope. Mercury signed up over 300,000 new customers, two-thirds of whom had never used a cellular phone. In Britain, even local calls are metered, costing you more the longer you speak. Besides adapting their behavior in obvious ways, like never using the regular phone to make a call in the evening, the happy multitude showed typical British pluck in making the best of a good thing. Some customers took to keeping a line open all night and using their cell phones as crib monitors. The night hours became the time of peak traffic, and circuits soon overloaded. To avoid a PR disaster, Mercury had to install additional transmitters—for calls that brought in zero revenue.

Mercury points out that each customer pays a monthly fee, and that the volume of calls during the daylight hours has also soared. Still, the company now has 300,000 customers who will get free nighttime phone service for as long as they keep their contracts up, which can mean the rest of their lives. Says Mercury spokesman Andrew Donovan: "They can't, however, pass these rights on to their heirs."

traditional wealthy businessman, offering free calling services during downtime hours. The company's strategy proved disastrously successful as the company has gained over 300,000 new customers.

Product Development

Product development involves the substantial modification of existing products or the creation of new but related products that can be marketed to current customers through established channels. The product development strategy often is adopted either to prolong the life cycle of current products or to take advantage of a favorite reputation or brand name. The idea is to attract satisfied customers to new products as a result of their positive experience with the firm's initial offering. The bottom section in Figure 7–3 lists some of the options available to firms undertaking product development. A revised edition of a college textbook, a new car style, and a second formula of shampoo for oily hair are examples of the product development strategy.

The product development strategy is based on the penetration of existing markets by incorporating product modifications into existing items or by developing new products with a clear connection to the existing product line. The telecommunications industry provides an example of product extension based on product modification. To increase its estimated 8–10 percent share of the $5–$6 billion corporate user market, MCI Communication Corporation extended its direct-dial service to 146 countries, the same as those serviced by AT&T, at lower average rates than those of AT&T. MCI's recent addition of 79 countries to its network underscores its belief in this market, which it expects to grow 15–20 percent annually. Another example of expansions linked to existing lines is Gerber's decision to engage in general merchandise marketing. Gerber's recent introduction included 52 items that ranged from feeding accessories to toys and children's wear. Likewise, Nabisco Brands seeks competitive advantage by placing its strategic emphasis on product development. With headquarters in Parsippany, New Jersey, the company is one of three operating units of RJR Nabisco. It is the leading producer of biscuits, confections, snacks, shredded cereals, and processed fruits and vegetables. To maintain its position as leader, Nabisco pursues a strategy of developing and introducing new products and expanding its existing product line. Spoon Size Shredded Wheat and Ritz Bits crackers are two examples of new products that are variations on existing products.

Innovation

In many industries, it has become increasingly risky not to innovate. Both consumer and industrial markets have come to expect periodic changes and improvements in the products offered. As a result, some firms find it profitable to make innovation their grand strategy. They seek to reap the initially high profits associated with customer acceptance of a new or greatly improved product. Then, rather than face stiffening competition as the basis of profitability shifts from innovation to production or marketing competence, they search for other original or novel ideas. The underlying rationale of the grand strategy of innovation is to create a new product life cycle and thereby make similar existing products obsolete. Thus, this strategy differs from the product development strategy of extending an existing product's life cycle. For example, Intel, a leader in the semiconductor industry, pursues expansion through a strategic emphasis on innovation. With headquarters in California, the company is a designer and manufacturer of semiconductor components and related computers, of microcomputer systems, and of software. Its Pentium microprocessor gives a desktop computer the capability of a mainframe. The innovation strategy pursued at Nippondenso has led to a creative research approach of micronization as described in Global Strategy in Action 7–3.

While most growth-oriented firms appreciate the need to be innovative occasionally, a few firms use it as their fundamental way of relating to their markets. An outstanding example is Polaroid, which heavily promotes each of its new cameras until competitors are able to match its technological innovation; by this time, Polaroid normally is prepared to introduce a dramatically new or improved product. For example, it introduced consumers in quick succession to the Swinger, the SX-70, the One Step, and the Sun Camera 660.

Few innovative ideas prove profitable because the research, development, and premarketing costs of converting a promising idea into a profitable product are extremely high. A study by the Booz Allen & Hamilton management research department provides some understanding of the risks. As shown in Figure 7–4, Booz Allen & Hamilton found that less than 2 percent of the innovative projects initially considered by 51 companies eventually reached the marketplace. Specifically, out of every 58 new product ideas, only 12 pass an initial screening test that finds them compatible with the firm's mission and long-term objectives, only 7 remain after an evaluation of their potential, and only 3 survive development attempts. Of the three survivors, two appear to have profit potential after test marketing and only one is commercially successful.

GLOBAL
STRATEGY IN
ACTION 7–3

THE TINIEST TOYOTA

The technological edge in the car industry is shifting away from vehicle assemblers to the components makers. They are the ones responsible for such wonders as engine-management chips and antilock braking systems. Now, one of the world's biggest car-components companies, Japan's Nippondenso, has taken the process even further, and built its own car. Although it has yet to make some bits work—such as the engine—the car is still pretty impressive. That is because it is just 4.8mm long.

Nippondenso's microcar is a classic: a replica of the Toyota Model AA, which was developed in 1936 when the Toyota Automatic Loom Works decided to open an automobile division. That division became the third-biggest carmaker in the world. Toyota is Nippondenso's largest shareholder.

It took staff at Nippondenso's basic-research laboratory (one of the first to be opened by a carparts firm) 2½ months to build the little car. It was assembled from components produced by a number of processes.

Nippondenso now is trying to make the microcar go under its own steam, so to speak. An internal combustion engine is out of the question: too complex to make small enough to fit under the bonnet. Instead, the laboratory has decided to use an environmentally friendly miniaturized electric engine. There is still a problem, though, in supplying the energy. Shrinking the batteries and the necessary electrical connections to fit inside such a small vehicle appear impossible with current technology. So the company plans to supply the engine's energy externally.

The plan is to make what Nippondenso calls an *electromagnetic wave engine*—a tiny device capable of converting the energy contained in microwaves (which would be beamed at the car) into some kind of driving force. The laboratory is coy about the details, but it hopes to put together the components of such an engine within the next two years.

The purpose of all this, of course, is not to build cars for amoebae but to develop micromachining techniques that may be useful in making future products—and not just cars. Nippondenso talks of a self-propelled microcamera that can be driven through human blood vessels, or a microrobot that can repair, from the inside, the small cooling tubes surrounding the core of a nuclear reactor. Toyotas soon could be everywhere.

Source: Excerpted from "The Tiniest Toyota," *The Economist*, July 20, 1991, p. 103. © The Economist Newspaper Group, Inc. Reprinted with permission. Further reproduction prohibited.

Horizontal Integration

When a firm's long-term strategy is based on growth through the acquisition of one or more similar firms operating at the same stage of the production-marketing chain, its grand strategy is called *horizontal integration*. Such acquisitions eliminate competitors and provide the acquiring firm with access to new markets. One example is Warner-Lambert's acquisition of Parke Davis, which reduced competition in the ethical drugs field for Chilcott Laboratories, a firm that Warner-Lambert previously had acquired. Another example is the long-range acquisition pattern of White Consolidated Industries, which expanded in the refrigerator and freezer market through a grand strategy of horizontal integration, by acquiring Kelvinator Appliance, the Refrigerator Products Division of Bendix Westinghouse Automotive Air Brake, and Frigidaire Appliance from General Motors. Nike's acquisition in the dress shoes business and N. V. Homes's purchase of Ryan Homes have vividly exemplified the success that horizontal integration strategies can bring.

FIGURE 7–4
Decay of New Product Ideas (51 Companies)

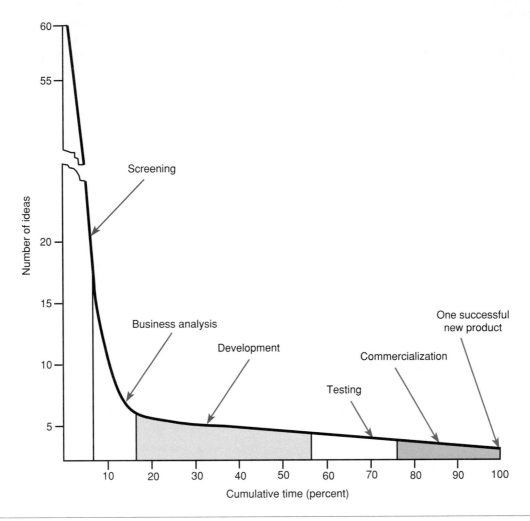

Vertical Integration

When a firm's grand strategy is to acquire firms that supply it with inputs (such as raw materials) or are customers for its outputs (such as warehousers for finished products), *vertical integration* is involved. To illustrate, if a shirt manufacturer acquires a textile producer—by purchasing its common stock, buying its assets, or exchanging ownership interests—the strategy is vertical integration. In this case, it is *backward* vertical integration, since the firm acquired operates at an earlier stage of the production-marketing process. If the shirt manufacturer had merged with a clothing store, it would have been *forward* vertical integration—the acquisition of a firm nearer to the ultimate consumer.

Amoco emerged as North America's leader in natural gas reserves and products in 1988 as a result of its acquisition of Dome Petroleum. This backward integration by Amoco was made in support of its downstream businesses in refining and in gas stations, whose profits made the acquisition possible.

FIGURE 7–5
Vertical and Horizontal Integrations

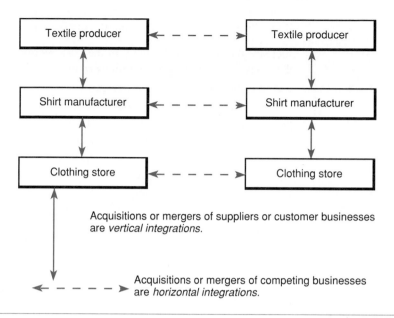

Acquisitions or mergers of suppliers or customer businesses are *vertical integrations*.

Acquisitions or mergers of competing businesses are *horizontal integrations*.

Figure 7–5 depicts both horizontal and vertical integration. The principal attractions of a horizontal integration grand strategy are readily apparent. The acquiring firm is able to greatly expand its operations, thereby achieving greater market share, improving economies of scale, and increasing the efficiency of capital use. In addition, these benefits are achieved with only moderately increased risk, since the success of the expansion is principally dependent on proven abilities.

The reasons for choosing a vertical integration grand strategy are more varied and sometimes less obvious. The main reason for backward integration is the desire to increase the dependability of the supply or quality of the raw materials used as production inputs. That desire is particularly great when the number of suppliers is small and the number of competitors is large. In this situation, the vertically integrating firm can better control its costs and, thereby, improve the profit margin of the expanded production-marketing system. Forward integration is a preferred grand strategy if great advantages accrue to stable production. A firm can increase the predictability of demand for its output through forward integration; that is, through ownership of the next stage of its production-marketing chain.

Some increased risks are associated with both types of integration. For horizontally integrated firms, the risks stem from increased commitment to one type of business. For vertically integrated firms, the risks result from the firm's expansion into areas requiring strategic managers to broaden the base of their competences and to assume additional responsibilities.

Concentric Diversification

Grand strategies involving diversification represent distinctive departures from a firm's existing base of operations, typically the acquisition or internal generation (spin-off) of a separate business with synergistic possibilities counterbalancing the strengths and weaknesses of the two businesses. For example, Head Ski initially sought to diversify into summer sporting goods and clothing to offset the seasonality of its "snow" business. However, diversifications occasionally are undertaken as unrelated investments, because of their high profit potential and their otherwise minimal resource demands.

Regardless of the approach taken, the motivations of the acquiring firms are the same:

Increase the firm's stock value. In the past, mergers often have led to increases in the stock price or the price-earnings ratio.

Increase the growth rate of the firm.

Make an investment that represents better use of funds than plowing them into internal growth.

Improve the stability of earnings and sales by acquiring firms whose earnings and sales complement the firm's peaks and valleys.

Balance or fill out the product line.

Diversify the product line when the life cycle of current products has peaked.

Acquire a needed resource quickly (e.g., high-quality technology or highly innovative management).

Achieve tax savings by purchasing a firm whose tax losses will offset current or future earnings.

Increase efficiency and profitability, especially if there is synergy between the acquiring firm and the acquired firm.[3]

Concentric diversification involves the acquisition of businesses that are related to the acquiring firm in terms of technology, markets, or products. With this grand strategy, the selected new businesses possess a high degree of compatibility with the firm's current businesses. The ideal concentric diversification occurs when the combined company profits increase the strengths and opportunities and decrease the weaknesses and exposure to risk. Thus, the acquiring firm searches for new businesses whose products, markets, distribution channels, technologies, and resource requirements are similar to but not identical with its own, whose acquisition results in synergies but not complete interdependence.

Conglomerate Diversification

Occasionally a firm, particularly a very large one, plans to acquire a business because it represents the most promising investment opportunity available. This grand strategy is commonly known as conglomerate diversification. The principal concern, and often the sole concern, of the acquiring firm is the profit pattern of the venture. Unlike concentric diversification, *conglomerate diversification* gives little concern to creating product-market synergy with existing businesses. What such conglomerate diversifiers as ITT, Textron, American Brands, Litton, U.S. Industries, Fuqua, and I.C. Industries seek is financial synergy. For example, they may seek a balance in their portfolios between current businesses with cyclical sales and acquired businesses with countercyclical sales, between high-cash/low-opportunity and low-cash/high-opportunity businesses, or between debt-free and highly leveraged businesses.

The principal difference between the two types of diversification is that concentric diversification emphasizes some commonality in markets, products, or technology, whereas conglomerate diversification is based principally on profit considerations.

---

[3] Godfrey Devlin and Mark Bleackley, "Strategic Alliances—Guidelines for Success," *Long Range Planning*, October 1988, pp. 18–23.

Several of the grand strategies discussed above, including concentric and conglomerate diversification and horizontal and vertical integration, often involve the purchase or acquisition of one firm by another. It is important to know that the majority of such acquisitions fail to produce the desired results for the companies involved. Strategy in Action 7–4 provides seven guidelines that can improve a company's chances of a successful acquisition.

Turnaround

For any one of a large number of reasons, a firm can find itself with declining profits. Among these reasons are economic recessions, production inefficiencies, and innovative breakthroughs by competitors. In many cases, strategic managers believe that such a firm can survive and eventually recover if a concerted effort is made over a period of a few years to fortify its distinctive competences. This grand strategy is known as *turnaround*. It typically is begun through one of two forms of retrenchment, employed singly or in combination:

1. *Cost reduction.* Examples include decreasing the work force through employee attrition, leasing rather than purchasing equipment, extending the life of machinery, eliminating elaborate promotional activities, laying off employees, dropping items from a production line, and discontinuing low-margin customers.

2. *Asset reduction.* Examples include the sale of land, buildings, and equipment not essential to the basic activity of the firm and the elimination of "perks," such as the company airplane and executives' cars.

Interestingly, the turnaround most commonly associated with this approach is in management positions. In a study of 58 large firms, researchers Shendel, Patton, and Riggs found that turnaround almost always was associated with changes in top management.[4] Bringing in new managers was believed to introduce needed new perspectives on the firm's situation, to raise employee morale, and to facilitate drastic actions, such as deep budgetary cuts in established programs.

Strategic management research provides evidence the firms that have used a *turnaround strategy* have successfully confronted decline. The research findings have been assimilated and used as the building blocks for a model of the turnaround process shown in Figure 7–6 on page 234.[5]

The model begins with a depiction of external and internal factors as causes of a firm's performance downturn. When these factors continue to detrimentally impact the firm, its financial health is threatened. Unchecked decline places the firm in a turnaround situation.

A *turnaround situation* represents absolute and relative-to-industry declining performance of a sufficient magnitude to warrant explicit turnaround actions. Turnaround situations may be the result of years of gradual slowdown or months of sharp decline. In either case, the recovery phase of the turnaround process is likely to be more successful in accomplishing turnaround when it is preceded by planned retrenchment that results in the achievement of near-term financial stabilization. For a declining firm, stabilizing operations and restoring profitability almost always entail strict cost reduction followed by a shrinking back to those segments of the business that have the best prospects of attractive profit margins. The need for retrenchment was shown during the 1990–92 recession when

---

[4] Other forms of joint ventures (such as leasing, contract manufacturing, and management contracting) offer valuable support strategies. They are not included in the categorization, however, because they seldom are employed as grand strategies.

[5] J. A. Pearce II and D. K. Robbins, "Toward Improved Theory and Research on Business Turnaround," *Journal of Management*, 1993; D. K. Robbins and J. A. Pearce II, "Turnaround: Recovery and Retrenchment," *Strategic Management Journal* 13, no. 4 (1992), pp. 287–309.

SEVEN DEADLY SINS OF STRATEGY ACQUISITION

1. *The wrong target.* This error becomes increasingly visible as time passes after the acquisition, when the acquiror may realize that anticipated synergies just don't exist, that the expanded market just isn't there, or that the acquiror's and target's technologies simply were not complementary.

   The first step to avoid such a mistake is for the acquiror and its financial advisors to determine the strategic goals and identify the mission. The product of this strategic review will be specifically identified criteria for the target.

   The second step required to identify the right target is to design and carry out an effective due diligence process to ascertain whether the target indeed has the identified set of qualities selected in the strategic review.

2. *The wrong price.* Even in a strategic acquisition, paying too much will lead to failure. For a patient strategic acquiror with long-term objectives, overpaying may be less of a problem than for a financial acquiror looking for a quick profit. Nevertheless, overpaying may divert needed acquiror resources and adversely affect the firm's borrowing capacity. In the extreme case, it can lead to continued operating losses and business failure.

   The key to avoiding this problem lies in the acquiror's valuation model. The model will incorporate assumptions concerning industry trends and growth patterns developed in the strategic review.

3. *The wrong structure.* Both financial and strategic acquisitions benefit by the structure chosen. This may include the legal structure chosen for the entities, the geographic jurisdiction chosen for newly created entities, and the capitalization structure selected for the business after the acquisition. The wrong structure may lead to an inability to repatriate earnings (or an ability to do so only at a prohibitive tax cost), regulatory problems that delay or prevent realization of the anticipated benefits, and inefficient pricing of debt and equity securities or a bar to chosen exit strategies due to inflexibility in the chosen legal structure.

   The two principal aspects of the acquisition process that can prevent this problem are a comprehensive regulatory compliance review and tax and legal analysis.

half of all U.S. companies reduced their work forces by an average of 11 percent (especially hard hit were real estate, transportation, and electronic company middle managers).

The immediacy of the resulting threat to company survival posed by the turnaround situation is known as *situation severity.* Severity is the governing factor in estimating the speed with which the retrenchment response will be formulated and activated. When severity is low, a firm has some financial cushion. Stability may be achieved through cost retrenchment alone. When turnaround situation severity is high, a firm must immediately stabilize the decline or bankruptcy is imminent. Cost reductions must be supplemented

continued

4. *The lost deal.* Lost deals often can be traced to poor communication. A successful strategic acquisition requires agreement upon the strategic vision, both with the acquiring company and between the acquiror and the continuing elements of the target. This should be established in the preliminary negotiations that lead to the letter of intent.

The letter must spell out not only the price to be paid but also many of the relational aspects that will make the strategic acquisition successful. Although an acquiror may justifiably focus on expenses, indemnification, and other logical concerns in the letter of intent, relationship and operational concerns are also important.

5. *Management difficulties.* Lack of attention to management issues may lead to a lost deal. These problems can range from a failure to provide management continuity or clear lines of authority after a merger to incentives that cause management to steer the company in the wrong direction.

The remedy for this problem must be extracted from the initial strategic review. The management compensation structure must be designed with legal and business advisors to help achieve those goals. The financial rewards to management must depend upon the financial and strategic success of the combined entity.

6. *The closing crisis.* Closing crises may stem from unavoidable changed conditions, but most often they result from poor communication. Negotiators sometimes believe that problems swept under the table maintain a deal's momentum and ultimately allow for its consummation. They are sometimes right—and often wrong. Charting a course through an acquisition requires carefully developed skills for every kind of professional—business, accounting, and legal.

7. *The operating transition crisis.* Even the best conceived and executed acquisition will prevent significant transition and postclosing operation issues. Strategic goals cannot be achieved by quick asset sales or other accelerated exit strategies. Management time and energy must be spent to assure that the benefits identified in the strategic review are achieved.

The principal constraints on smooth implementation are usually human: poor interaction of personnel between the two preexisting management structures and resistance to new systems. Problems also may arise from too much attention to the by now well-communicated strategic vision and too little attention to the nuts and bolts of continuing business operations.

---

with more drastic asset reduction measures. Assets targeted for divestiture are those determined to be underproductive. In contrast, more productive resources are protected from cuts and represent critical elements of the future core business plan of the company (i.e., the intended recovery response).

Turnaround responses among successful firms typically include two stages of strategic activities: retrenchment and the recovery response. *Retrenchment* consists of cost-cutting and asset-reducing activities. The primary objective of the retrenchment phase is to stabilize the firm's financial condition. Situation severity has been associated with retrenchment responses among successful turnaround firms. Firms in danger of bankruptcy or failure (i.e., severe situations) attempt to halt decline through cost and asset reductions. Firms in

FIGURE 7–6
A Model of the Turnaround Process

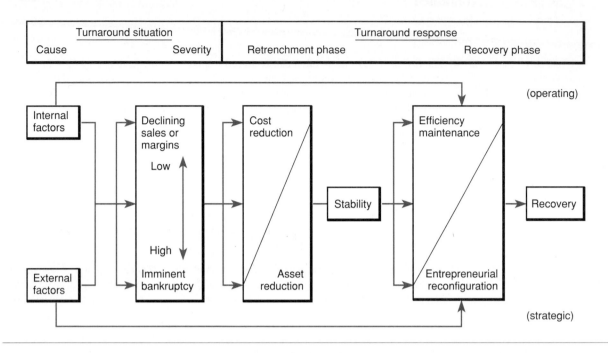

Source: J. A. Pearce II and D. K. Robbins, "Toward Improved Theory and Research on Business Turnaround," *Journal of Management*, 1993.

less severe situations have achieved stability merely through cost retrenchment. However, in either case, for firms facing declining financial performance, the key to successful turnaround rests in the effective and efficient management of the retrenchment process.

The primary causes of the turnaround situation have been associated with the second phase of the turnaround process, the *recovery response*. For firms that declined primarily as a result of external problems, turnaround most often has been achieved through creative new entrepreneurial strategies. For firms that declined primarily as a result of internal problems, turnaround has been most frequently achieved through efficiency strategies. *Recovery* is achieved when economic measures indicate that the firm has regained its predownturn levels of performance.

Divestiture

A *divestiture strategy* involves the sale of a firm or a major component of a firm. For example, in March 1992, Goodyear Tire and Rubber announced its decision to sell its polyester business to Shell Chemical to cut its $2.6 billion debt. The sale was part of Goodyear's strategy to bring its debt below $2 billion within 18 months.

When retrenchment fails to accomplish the desired turnaround, as was the Goodyear situation, or when a nonintegrated business activity achieves an unusually high market value, strategic managers often decide to sell the firm. However, because the intent is to find a buyer willing to pay a premium above the value of a going concern's fixed assets, the term *marketing for sale* is often more appropriate. Prospective buyers must be convinced that, because of their skills and resources or because of the firm's synergy with their existing businesses, they will be able to profit from the acquisition.

The reasons for divestiture vary. They often arise because of partial mismatches between the acquired firm and the parent corporation. Some of the mismatched parts cannot be integrated into the corporation's mainstream activities and, thus, must be spun off. A second reason is corporate financial needs. Sometimes the cash flow or financial stability of the corporation as a whole can be greatly improved if businesses with high market value can be sacrificed. The result can be a balancing of equity with long-term risks or of long-term debt payments to optimize the cost of capital. A third, less frequent reason for divestiture is government antitrust action when a firm is believed to monopolize or unfairly dominate a particular market.

Although examples of the divestiture grand strategy are numerous, CBS, Inc., recently provided an outstanding example. In a two-year period, the once diverse entertainment and publishing giant sold its Records Division to Sony, its magazine publishing business to Diamandis Communications, its book publishing operations to Harcourt Brace Jovanovich, and its music publishing operations to SBK Entertainment World. Other firms that recently have pursued this type of grand strategy include Esmark, which divested Swift & Company, and White Motors, which divested White Farm.

The unfortunate but frequent consequence of a firm's failure to achieve turnaround—through a combination of retrenchment, divestiture, and new strategies—is financial bankruptcy. Firms filing for Chapter 11 bankruptcy protection are allowed by federal law to undertake a comprehensive reorganization while being protected from creditor actions. Believed to be in trouble because of serious mismanagement, such firms are allowed to reorganize with "proper management" in the hope they may be able to repay their debts over time and to become profitable operations. One of the hundreds of thousands of troubled businesses that have sought protection under Chapter 11 is Wang, as described in Strategy in Action 7–5.

Liquidation

When liquidation is the grand strategy, the firm typically is sold in parts, only occasionally as a whole—but for its tangible asset value and not as a going concern. In selecting liquidation, the owners and strategic managers of a firm are admitting failure and recognize that this action is likely to result in great hardships to themselves and their employees. For these reasons, liquidation usually is seen as the least attractive of the grand strategies. As a long-term strategy, however, it minimizes the losses of all the firm's stockholders. Faced with bankruptcy, the liquidating firm usually tries to develop a planned and orderly system that will result in the greatest possible return and cash conversion as the firm slowly relinquishes its market share.

Planned liquidation can be worthwhile. For example, Columbia Corporation, a $130 million diversified firm, liquidated its assets for more cash per share than the market value of its stock.

CORPORATE COMBINATIONS

The 11 grand strategies discussed above, used singly and much more often in combinations, represent the traditional alternatives used by firms in the United States. Recently, three new grand types have gained in popularity; all fit under the broad category of corporate combinations. Although they do not fit the criterion by which executives retain a high degree of control over their operations, these grand strategies deserve special attention and consideration especially by companies that operate in global, dynamic, and technologically

STRATEGY
IN ACTION
7–5

BLINDSIDED BY THE FUTURE

On the streets of Boston, they're calling it Black Tuesday. The same day that basketball legend Larry Bird said he would end his career with the Boston Celtics, computer giant Wang Laboratories announced it would file for Chapter 11 bankruptcy protection and lay off 5,000 of its 13,000 workers. In many ways, it seemed fitting that Wang, based in Lowell, Massachusetts, and once a heroic player in the computer industry, bowed out during the same 24-hour period as did Boston's beloved hoopster. Like Bird, the 41-year-old industry icon was an old-timer crippled by past injuries that had failed to heal; a pain-racked veteran, it could no longer compete in a world filled with fastmoving rookies. Calling the bankruptcy "a drastic step that I deeply regret," chairman Richard W. Miller said the company, which will continue to operate, had simply "run out of resources."

The announcement was the end of a long, slow slide for the computer maker. Founded by Dr. An Wang, a Harvard-educated Chinese immigrant, Wang Laboratories revolutionized offices around the world with its minicomputers. But as the industry began to shift to personal computers in the mid-1980s, Wang was left behind. Its meteoric growth rates slowed, and earnings fell dramatically. Before the elder Wang's death from esophageal cancer in 1990, he already was preparing bankruptcy papers—but just in case the company rose from the ashes, he named Miller, an experienced turn-around artist, to succeed him.

Since then, Miller has been fighting to stave off the inevitable: The company has talked with more than 40 investors and has bargained with lenders for 56 amendments to its borrowing plan over the last three years. But analysts say Miller wasn't listening to customers—and last week Wang reported an operating loss of $45.4 million for the last fiscal year. "[The company] fell prey to the enormous success of the PC," says Thomas Willmont, a Boston-based computer consultant. "They simply did not react fast enough to compete in the workplace."

Wang could undergo transformation. In any case, the company will emerge from Chapter 11 much changed—if it emerges at all. Miller says, "We're in business today just as we were yester-day." Some analysts are doubtful. Like a wornout basketball player, they say, Wang may finally have benched itself for good.

driven industries. These three newly popularized grand strategies are joint ventures, strategic alliances, and consortia.

Joint Ventures

Occasionally two or more capable firms lack a necessary component for success in a particular competitive environment. For example, no single petroleum firm controlled sufficient resources to construct the Alaskan pipeline. Nor was any single firm capable of processing and marketing all of the oil that would flow through the pipeline. The solution was a set of *joint ventures*, which are third commercial companies (children) created and operated for the benefit of the co-owners (parents). These cooperative arrangements provided both the funds needed to build the pipeline and the processing and marketing capacities needed to profitably handle the oil flow.

The particular form of joint ventures discussed above is *joint ownership*. In recent years, it has become increasingly appealing for domestic firms to join foreign firms by means of this form. For example, Diamond-Star Motors is the result of a joint venture between a U.S. company, Chrysler Corporation, and Japan's Mitsubishi Motors corporation. Located in Normal, Illinois, Diamond-Star was launched because it offered Chrysler and Mitsubishi a chance to expand on their long-standing relationship in which subcompact cars (as well as Mitsubishi engines and other automotive parts) are imported to the United States and sold under the Dodge and Plymouth names.

The joint venture extends the supplier-consumer relationship and has strategic advantages for both partners. For Chrysler, it presents an opportunity to produce a high-quality car using expertise brought to the venture by Mitsubishi. It also gives Chrysler the chance to try new production techniques and to realize efficiencies by using the work force that was not included under Chrysler's collective bargaining agreement with the United Auto Workers. The agreement offers Mitsubishi the opportunity to produce cars for sale in the United States, without being subjected to the tariffs and restrictions placed on Japanese imports.

As a second example, Bethlehem Steel acquired an interest in a Brazilian mining venture to secure a raw material source. The stimulus for this joint ownership venture was grand strategy, but such is not always the case. Certain countries virtually mandate that foreign firms entering their markets do so on a joint ownership basis. India and Mexico are good examples. The rationale of these countries is that joint ventures minimize the threat of foreign domination and enhance the skills, employment, growth, and profits of local firms.

It should be noted that strategic managers understandably are wary of joint ventures. Admittedly, joint ventures present new opportunities with risks that can be shared. On the other hand, joint ventures often limit the discretion, control, and profit potential of partners, while demanding managerial attention and other resources that might be directed toward the firm's mainstream activities. Nevertheless, increasing globalization in many industries may require greater consideration of the joint venture approach, if historically national firms are to remain viable. Advantages and disadvantages of an international joint venture are highlighted in Global Strategy in Action 7–4.

Strategic Alliances

Strategic alliances are distinguished from joint ventures because the companies involved do not take an equity position in one another. In many instances, strategic alliances are synonymous with licensing agreements. Licensing involves the transfer of some industrial property right from the U.S. licensor to a motivated licensee in a foreign country. Most tend to be patents, trademarks, or technical know-how that are granted to the licensee for a specified time in return for a royalty and for avoiding tariffs or import quotas. Bell South and U.S. West, with various marketing and service competitive advantages valuable to Europe, have extended a number of licenses to create personal computer networks in the United Kingdom (U.K.).

Another licensing strategy open to U.S. firms is to contract the manufacturing of its product line to a foreign company to exploit local comparative advantages in technology, materials, or labor. For example, MIPS Computer Systems has licensed Digital Equipment Corporation, Texas Instruments, Cypress Semiconductor, and Bipolar Integrated Technology in the United States, and Fujitsu, NEC, and Kubota in Japan to market computers based on its designs in the partner's country.

Service and franchise-based firms—including Anheuser-Busch, Avis, Coca-Cola, Hilton, Hyatt, Holiday Inns, Kentucky Fried Chicken, McDonald's, and Pepsi—have long engaged in licensing arrangements with foreign distributors as a way to enter new markets with standardized products that can benefit from marketing economies.

JOINT VENTURE BOOSTS SIBERIAN OIL FLOW

The name White Nights Joint Enterprise plays off the Siberian summer and off the reason U.S. oil companies are here. And while the mission of the first working Russian–U.S. oil venture is simple, the details aren't.

"This is the first arrangement of its kind in all of the oil industry," says Gerald Walston, the Denver oil man who is White Nights' director.

The arrangement he refers to is incremental sharing, which entitles White Nights to all the oil recovered from three fields, above what the Russians had expected to get out, for 25 years.

Varyegan Oil and Gas, the state-owned company that controls the oil, is the Russian partner in White Nights. In exchange for turning its oil fields over to the joint venture, Varyegan gets all the oil up to its production estimates, plus half the oil that comes in addition to that. It also gets 10 percent in royalties.

The U.S. partners, Anglo-Suisse and Philbro Energy Production, split what's left, which is 40 percent of the extra production. They can make their money by shipping their oil out of the country to sell for hard currency.

The venture is pumping ahead of the Russians' estimated production. "Production in all of Russia was down 9.5 percent in 1991. Our fields were up about 40 percent," says Walston.

Anatoly Sivak, director general of Varyegan Oil and Gas, says, "This joint venture will serve as an example. It is the wave of the future."

The reason Sivak turned to the West for help was simple: "The question was how to stop the production decline. For that, we needed money and equipment and technology not available here." Completed wells were sitting idle for lack of parts.

Although the venture has succeeded in boosting production, "We've had some problems," Sivak says.

Anglo-Suisse was designated operator of the venture, and Russian oil people, who have been drilling here since the 1960s, couldn't understand why a U.S. company is running the show.

On top of that resentment were more obvious obstacles: different languages, clashing cultures, huge gaps in economic circumstances among the workers, different drilling techniques, and radically different organizational mindsets.

The Russians, with their five-year plans and strict instructions, "tended to organize and plan down to the last jot and tiddle," says Walston, a graying, unflappable gentleman who appears to keep the joint venture on an even keel via strings of Post-It notes splayed over the top of his desk. "The watchword for us is flexibility," he says.

Outsourcing is another approach to strategic alliances that enables firms to gain a competitive advantage. Corporate use of outsourcing has increased dramatically in recent years as corporations realize its tremendous benefits. Significant changes within many segments of American business have encouraged the use of outsourcing practices. Within the healthcare arena, an industry survey recorded 67 percent of hospitals using provider outsourcing for at least one department within their organization. Services such as information systems, reimbursement, and risk and physician practice management are outsourced by 51 percent of the hospitals that use outsourcing.

Another successful application of outsourcing is found in human resources. A survey of human resource executives revealed 85 percent having personal experience with leading an

FIGURE 7–7
The Top Five Strategic Reasons for Outsourcing

1. **Improve Business Focus.**
   For many companies, the single most compelling reason for outsourcing is that several "how" issues are siphoning off huge amounts of management's resources and attention.

2. **Access to World-Class Capabilities.**
   By the very nature of their specialization, outsourcing providers bring extensive worldwide, world-class resources to meeting the needs of their customers. According to Norris Overton, vice president of reengineering, AMTRAK, partnering with an organization with world-class capabilities, can offer access to new technology, tools, and techniques that the organization may not currently possess; better career opportunities for personnel who transition to the outsourcing provider; more structured methodologies, procedures, and documentation; and competitive advantage through expanded skills.

3. **Accelerated Reengineering Benefits.**
   Outsourcing is often a byproduct of another powerful management tool—business process reengineering. It allows an organization to immediately realize the anticipated benefits of reengineering by having an outside organization—one that is already reengineered to world-class standards—take over the process.

4. **Shared Risks.**
   There are tremendous risks associated with the investments an organization makes. When companies outsource they become more flexible, more dynamic, and better able to adapt to changing opportunities.

5. **Free Resources for Other Purposes.**
   Every organization has limits on the resources available to it. Outsourcing permits an organization to redirect its resources from noncore activities toward activities that have the greater return in serving the customer.

Source: Material prepared for a paid advertising section which appeared in the October 16, 1995, issue of *Fortune* © 1995, Time, Inc. All rights reserved.

outsourcing effort within their organization. In addition, it was found that two-thirds of pension departments have outsourced at least one human resource function.

Within customer service and sales departments, outsourcing increased productivity in such areas as product information, sales and order taking, sample fulfillment, and complaint handling. Figure 7–7 presents the top five strategic and five tactical reasons for exploiting the benefits of outsourcing.

Consortia, Keiretsus, and Chaebols

Consortia are defined as large interlocking relationships between businesses of an industry. In Japan such consortia are known as *keiretsus*, in South Korea as *chaebols*.

In Europe, consortia projects are increasing in number and in success rates. Examples include the Junior Engineers' and Scientists' Summer Institute, which underwrites cooperative learning and research; the European Strategic Program for Research and Development in Information Technologies, which seeks to enhance European competitiveness in fields related to computer electronics and component manufacturing; and EUREKA, which is a joint program involving scientists and engineers from several European countries to coordinate joint research projects.

A Japanese *keiretsu* is an undertaking involving up to 50 different firms that are joined around a large trading company or bank and are coordinated through interlocking directories and stock exchanges. It is designed to use industry coordination to minimize risks of competition, in part through cost sharing and increased economies of scale. Examples include Sumitomo, Mitsubishi, Mitsui, and Sanwa.

FIGURE 7–8
A Profile of Strategic Choice Options

	Six Strategic Choice Options					
	1	**2**	**3**	**4**	**5**	**6**
Interactive opportunities	West Coast markets present little competition		Current markets sensitive to price competition		Current industry product lines offer too narrow a range of markets	
Appropriate long-range objectives (limited sample): Average 5-year ROI. Company sales by year 5. Risk of negative profits.	15% +50% .30	19% +40% .25	13% +20% .10	17% +0% .15	23% +35% .20	15% +25% .05
Grand strategies	Horizontal integration	Market development	Concentration	Selective retrenchment	Product development	Concentration

A South Korean chaebol resembles a consortium or keiretsu except that they are typically financed through government banking groups and largely are run by professional managers trained by participating firms expressly for the job.

SELECTION OF LONG-TERM OBJECTIVES AND GRAND STRATEGY SETS

At first glance, the Strategic Management Model, which provides the framework for study throughout this book, seems to suggest that strategic choice decision making leads to the sequential selection of long-term objectives and grand strategies. In fact, however, strategic choice is the simultaneous selection of long-range objectives and grand strategies. When strategic planners study their opportunities, they try to determine which are most likely to result in achieving various long-range objectives. Almost simultaneously, they try to forecast whether an available grand strategy can take advantage of preferred opportunities so the tentative objectives can be met. In essence, then, three distinct but highly interdependent choices are being made at one time. Several triads, or sets, of possible decisions are usually considered.

A simplified example of this process is shown in Figure 7–8. In this example, the firm has determined that six strategic choice options are available. These options stem from three interactive opportunities (e.g., West Coast markets) that present little competition. Because each of these interactive opportunities can be approached through different grand strategies—for options 1 and 2, the grand strategies are horizontal integration and market development—each offers the potential for achieving long-range objectives to varying degrees. Thus, a firm rarely can make a strategic choice only on the basis of its preferred opportunities, long-range objectives, or grand strategy. Instead, these three elements must be considered simultaneously, because only in combination do they constitute a strategic choice.

In an actual decision situation, the strategic choice would be complicated by a wider variety of interactive opportunities, feasible company objectives, promising grand strategy options, and evaluative criteria. Nevertheless, Figure 7–8 does partially reflect the nature and complexity of the process by which long-term objectives and grand strategies are selected.

In the next chapter, the strategic choice process will be fully explained. However, knowledge of long-term objectives and grand strategies is essential to understanding that process.

Sequence of Objectives and Strategy Selection

The selection of long-range objectives and grand strategies involves simultaneous, rather than sequential, decisions. While it is true that objectives are needed to prevent the firm's direction and progress from being determined by random forces, it is equally true that objectives can be achieved only if strategies are implemented. In fact, long-term objectives and grand strategies are so interdependent that some business consultants do not distinguish between them. Long-term objectives and grand strategies are still combined under the heading of company strategy in most of the popular business literature and in the thinking of most practicing executives.

However, the distinction has merit. Objectives indicate what strategic managers want but provide few insights about how they will be achieved. Conversely, strategies indicate what types of actions will be taken but do not define what ends will be pursued or what criteria will serve as constraints in refining the strategic plan.

Does it matter whether strategic decisions are made to achieve objectives or to satisfy constraints? No, because constraints are themselves objectives. The constraint of increased inventory capacity is a desire (an objective), not a certainty. Likewise, the constraint of an increase in the sales force does not assure that the increase will be achieved, given such factors as other company priorities, labor market conditions, and the firm's profit performance.

Summary

Before learning how strategic decisions are made, it is important to understand the two principal components of any strategic choice; namely, long-term objectives and the grand strategy. The purpose of this chapter was to convey that understanding.

Long-term objectives were defined as the results a firm seeks to achieve over a specified period, typically five years. Seven common long-term objectives were discussed: profitability, productivity, competitive position, employee development, employee relations, technological leadership, and public responsibility. These, or any other long-term objectives, should be acceptable, flexible, measurable over time, motivating, suitable, understandable, and achievable.

Grand strategies were defined as comprehensive approaches guiding the major actions designed to achieve long-term objectives. Fourteen grand strategy options were discussed: concentrated growth, market development, product development, innovation, horizontal integration, vertical integration, concentric diversification, conglomerate diversification, turnaround, divestiture, liquidation, joint ventures, strategic alliances, and consortia.

Questions for Discussion

1. Identify firms in the business community nearest to your college or university that you believe are using each of the 14 grand strategies discussed in this chapter.
2. Identify firms in your business community that appear to rely principally on 1 of the 14 grand strategies. What kind of information did you use to classify the firms?
3. Write a long-term objective for your school of business that exhibits the seven qualities of long-term objectives described in this chapter.
4. Distinguish between the following pairs of grand strategies:
   a. Horizontal and vertical integration.
   b. Conglomerate and concentric diversification.

     c. Product development and innovation.

     d. Joint venture and strategic alliance.

5. Rank each of the 14 grand strategy options discussed in this chapter on the following three scales:

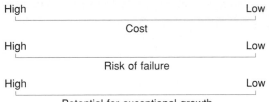

6. Identify firms that use one of the eight specific options shown in Figure 7–1 under the grand strategies of concentration, market development, and product development.

BIBLIOGRAPHY

Anderson, E. "Two Firms, One Frontier: On Assessing Joint Venture Performance." *Sloan Management Review*, Winter 1990, pp. 19–30.

Badaracco, J. L. "Alliances Speed Knowledge Transfer." *Planning Review*, March–April 1991, pp. 10–17.

Beamish, Paul W., and Andrew C. Inkpen. "Keeping International Joint Ventures Stable and Profitable." *Long Range Planning* 28, no. 3 (June 1995), p. 26.

Bleeke, J., and D. Ernst. "The Way to Win in Cross-Border Alliances." *Harvard Business Review*, November–December 1991, pp. 127–35.

Brannen, M. Y. "Culture as the Critical Factor in Implementing Innovation." *Business Horizons*, November–December 1991, pp. 59–67.

Bronthers, Keith D.; Lane Eliot Bronthers; and Timothy J. Wilkinson. "Strategic Alliances: Choose Your Partners." *Long Range Planning* 28, no. 3 (June 1995), p. 68.

Clarke, C. J., and K. Brennan. "Defensive Strategies against Takeovers: Creating Shareholder Value." *Long Range Planning*, February 1990, pp. 95–101.

Erickson, T. J.; J. F. Magee; P. A. Roussel; and K. N. Saad. "Managing Technology as a Business Strategy." *Sloan Management Review*, Spring 1990, pp. 73–78.

Ettlie, J. E. "What Makes a Manufacturing Firm Innovative?" *Academy of Management Executive*, November 1990, pp. 7–20.

Evan, W. M., and P. Olk. "R&D Consortia: A New U.S. Organizational Form." *Sloan Management Review*, Spring 1990, pp. 37–46.

Gopinath, C. "Turnaround: Recognizing Decline and Initiating Intervention." *Long Range Planning*, December 1991, pp. 96–101.

Grossi, G. "Promoting Innovation in a Big Business." *Long Range Planning*, February 1990, pp. 41–52.

Haspeslagh, P. C., and D. B. Jemison. "The Challenge of Renewal through Acquisitions." *Planning Review*, March–April 1991, pp. 27–33.

Houlden, Brian T. "How Corporate Planning Adopts and Survives." *Long Range Planning* 28, no. 4 (August 1995), p. 99.

Hughes, G. D. "Managing High-Tech Product Cycles." *Academy of Management Executive*, May 1990, pp. 44–55.

Kanter, R. M. "When Giants Learn Cooperative Strategies." *Planning Review*, January–February 1990, pp. 15–25.

Keller, R., and R. Chinta. "International Technology Transfer: Strategies for Success." *Academy of Management Executive*, May 1990, pp. 33–43.

Kukolis, Sal, and Mark Jungemann. "Strategic Planning for a Joint Venture." *Long Range Planning* 28, no. 3 (June 1995), p. 46.

Lengnick-Hall, C. A. "Innovation and Competitive Advantage: What We Know and What We Need to Learn." *Journal of Management*, June 1992, p. 399.

Leontiades, M. "The Case for Nonspecialized Diversification." *Planning Review*, January–February 1990, pp. 26–33.

Lewis, J. "Using Alliances to Build Market Power." *Planning Review*, September–October 1990, pp. 4–9.

Littler, Dole, and Fiona Leverick. "Joint Ventures for Product Development: Learning from Experience." *Long Range Planning* 28, no. 3 (June 1995), p. 58.

Lowry, James R. "A Partnering Approach to Mass Merchandising in Russia." *Business Horizons* 38, no. 4 (July–August 1995), p. 28.

McLeod, Raymond, Jr.; Jack William Jones; and Carol Saunders. "The Difficulty in Solving Strategic Problems: The Experiences of Three CIO's." *Business Horizons* 38, no. 1 (January–February 1995), p. 28.

Miller, D. "The Generic Strategy Trap." *The Journal of Business Strategy*, January–February 1992, pp. 37–41.

Newman, W. H. "Focused Joint Ventures in Transforming Economies." *Academy of Management Executive*, February 1992, pp. 67–75.

Paap, J. E. "A Venture Capitalist's Advice for Successful Strategic Alliances." *Planning Review*, September–October 1990, pp. 20–26.

Pearce, J. A., II, and J. W. Harvey. "Concentrated Growth Strategies." *Academy of Management Executive*, February 1990, pp. 61–68.

Pearce, J. A., II, and D. K. Robbins. "Toward Improved Theory and Research on Business Turnaround." *Journal of Management*, 1993.

———. "Entrepreneurial Recovery Strategies among Small Market Share Manufacturers." *Journal of Business Venturing*, 1994.

Peters, T. "Get Innovative or Get Dead." *California Management Review*, Winter 1991, pp. 9–23.

Randall, R. M. "The Coyote and the Bear Form a Strategic Alliance." *Planning Review*, September–October 1990, p. 27.

Reimann, B. C. "Corporate Strategies That Work." *Planning Review*, January–February 1992, pp. 41–46.

Robbins, D. K., and Pearce, J. A., II. "Entrepreneurial Retrenchment among Small Manufacturing Firms." *Journal of Business Venturing*, July 1993, pp. 301–18.

Sankar, Chetan S.; William R. Boulton; Nancy W. Davidson; Charles A. Snyder; and Richard W. Ussery. "Building a World-Class Alliance: The Universal Card—TSYS Case." *The Academy of Management Executive* 9, no. 2 (May 1995), p. 20.

Shanklin, William L. "Offensive Strategies for Defense Companies." *Business Horizons* 38, no. 4 (July–August 1995), p. 53.

Stiles, Jan. "Collaboration for Competitive Advantage: The Changing World of Alliances and Partnerships." *Long Range Planning* 28, no. 5 (October 1995), p. 109.

CHAPTER 7 COHESION CASE ILLUSTRATION

FORMULATING LONG-TERM OBJECTIVES AND GRAND STRATEGIES AT THE COCA-COLA COMPANY

Coca-Cola management sets forth several long-term objectives toward which the company is focused for the year 2000. First, they offer a statement about what they call "rewards." In the booklet entitled *Coca-Cola, a Business System toward 2000: Our Mission in the 1990s*, Coke management sets forth the four key "rewards" it seeks:

- Satisfied consumers who return again and again to our brands for refreshment.
- Profitable customers who rely on our worldwide brands and services.
- Communities around the world where we are an economic contributor and welcomed guest.
- Successful business partners.
- Shareholders who are building value through the power of the Coca-Cola system.

LONG-TERM OBJECTIVES

The company identifies several long-term objectives that support these reward intentions. The first objective most often mentioned is:

Management's primary objective is to maximize shareowner value over time.

The company then indicates that the following objectives help accomplish this over-arching objective:

Maximize long-term cash flow by increasing gallon sales, optimizing profit margins, expanding global business systems through investment in areas offering attractive returns.

The principal objective of bottling investments is to ensure the strongest and most efficient production, distribution, and marketing systems possible, in order to maximize long-term growth in volume, cash flow, and shareowner value of the bottler and the Company.

The Coca-Cola Company pursues several inherent objectives as follows:

Profitability. Double-digit levels annually equal to or exceeding historical levels.
Productivity. Each Coca-Cola facility has as its objective maintenance or improvement of its operating profit margin.
Competitive Position. Coca-Cola seeks to be the market leader in markets in which it competes.
Technological Leadership. Coca-Cola seeks to be the leader in the production and marketing technologies used in the markets in which it competes.

What are the qualities of Coca-Cola's long-term objectives? It would appear Coca-Cola's objectives meet several criteria that this chapter has suggested characterize effective objectives. Specifically, each of these publicly stated Coke objectives appears to be acceptable, flexible, motivating, suitable, reasonable, and achievable.

These objectives all appear deficient in terms of being measurable. None of these publicly stated objectives identifies a quantifiable result to be achieved or a specific time period within which to accomplish those results. Coke officials indicate a preference for stating objectives publicly in broad terms. They prefer to retain key results and timetables for internal consumption only. While this may be quite appropriate, you should nonetheless be able to recognize that objectives without measurable results or measurable timetables within which to accomplish them lose a lot of their value in focusing and directing strategic activities. A recent interview with Coca Cola USA president Jack Stahl and vice president Charlie Frenette about their Year 2000 goals for the U.S. market shows that Coca Cola's use of measurable objectives is very much a way they work internally. It also suggests a willingness to be more open publicly. Finally, some people question whether the market share objectives are too ambitious. What do you think?

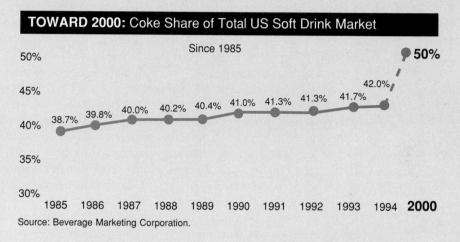

TOWARD 2000: Coke Share of Total US Soft Drink Market

Source: Beverage Marketing Corporation.

Frenette: Right now we estimate that the average person consumes 64 ounces of liquid daily. We have about 11 percent of that intake in the U.S., which translates into per capita consumption of 333 eight-ounce servings of our beverage products annually. We want to position our product portfolio to satisfy this physiological need for refreshment. As we set an aspiration for 400 per capita consumption and a 50 percent share—which is what our international business enjoys today—we're going to source everything, including tap water.

Beverage World [BW]: What makes 50 percent the right share target? Why not more?

Stahl: We had 42 percent entering 1995. We have to look at the power of our system today, look at the capabilities that we believe we can put in place over the next several years, and then say, "How much better can we do all of that vis-à-vis our competitors." We believe we can really distance ourselves in terms of our ability to service customers and meet the needs of consumers. We believe we can grow at a dramatically higher rate than the 3 percent industry average.

BW: Your recent history of share growth makes 50 a pretty ambitious number, doesn't it?

Stahl: That's right. It's somewhat ambitious. Although, if you look at where we've been and look at our capturing most of the growth [90 percent of the U.S. cola growth in 1995], that kind of performance over time can get you there.

BW: But 50 by 2000? Having procured 4 corporate share points since 1985, Coke entered 1995 with 42 percent of the whole U.S. soft drink market. That means it must snare 8 percentage points in six years.

Salmon Brothers [analyst Andrew Conway]: It's extremely aggressive. Coke will have to grow two to three times faster than the total industry to pull it off.

COCA-COLA STRATEGIES

Coca-Cola is in the enviable position of being able to pursue numerous strategies. Among generic strategies, Coke is able to pursue low-cost strategies and still enjoy higher profit margins. Its unparalleled trademarks and syrup patent protection offer strong support for differentiation strategies. And the global reality that its success is determined in one local market at a time puts it in the unique posture of needing focus strategies by local geographic markets.

Among grand strategies, Coke has several options available to it. Concentrated growth appears a viable strategy, at least in key major markets like the U.S. market. But given its sizable financial resources, concentrated growth alone may not achieve long-term objectives. Rather, its extraordinary global "system" makes market development a related and potentially advantageous strategy. The many underdeveloped global markets available to Coca-Cola represent attractive targets for Coke's excess resources.

Coke long has been committed to a product development strategy, which creates new but related products that can be marketed to current customers through established channels. Not only does this allow Coke to penetrate existing markets and channels but it preempts new product efforts of weaker competitors.

The diversification strategies, concentric and conglomerate, are available to Coca-Cola given its financial resources and market clout. Since 1975, Coke has included both diversification strategies in the options it has chosen. Coke's move into movie entertainment, water treatment, plastic films, and certain foods were clear diversifications.

Finally, the latter part of the 1980s has seen Coca-Cola seriously consider a forward vertical integration strategy, allowing greater involvement in and control over bottling activity, given the removal of regulatory restrictions on doing so, and combined with the critical role local bottlers play in distributing national brands and the relative strength in this regard of PepsiCo's bottling network.

The global commitments and aspirations of Coca-Cola are another reason forward vertical integration in some form must be considered by the company. Whether this takes the form of joint ventures, strategic alliances, or consortia appears dependent on market and regulatory conditions within each country that Coke targets.

Coke has little need for retrenchment, turnaround, and liquidation strategies. It has a strong position in most of its businesses. Divestiture has been used by Coke when it has chosen to exit a variety of related and unrelated businesses. This strategy was continually considered by Coke's management as it increasingly emphasized the need to focus on soft-drink and clearly related business sectors.

8

STRATEGIC ANALYSIS AND CHOICE IN SINGLE- OR DOMINANT-PRODUCT BUSINESSES: BUILDING SUSTAINABLE COMPETITIVE ADVANTAGES

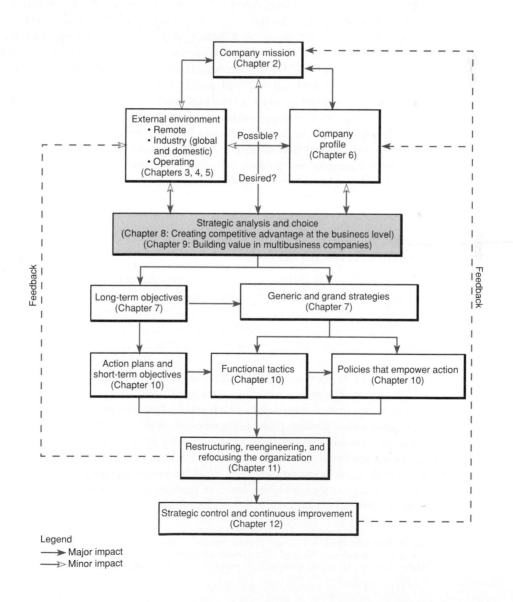

Strategic analysis and choice is the phase of the strategic management process when business managers examine and choose a business strategy that allows their business to sustain or create a sustainable competitive advantage. Their starting point is to evaluate and determine which value chain activities provide the basis for distinguishing itself in the customer's mind from other reasonable alternatives. Businesses with a dominant product or service line must also choose among alternate grand strategies to guide the firm's activities, particularly when they are trying to decide about broadening the scope of the firm's activities beyond its core business.

This chapter examines strategic analysis and choice in single- or dominant-product/ service businesses by addressing two basic issues:

1. **What strategies are most effective at building sustainable competitive advantages for single business units?** What competitive strategy positions a business most effectively in its industry? For example, Scania, the most productive truck manufacturer in the world, joins its major rival Volvo as two anchors of Sweden's economy. Scania's return on sales of 9.9 percent far exceeds Mercedes (2.6 percent) and Volvo (2.5 percent), which it has done most of the last 60 years. Scania has built a sustainable competitive advantage with a strategy of focusing solely on heavy trucks, in a limited geographic area—Europe—and by providing customized trucks with standardized components (20,000 components per truck versus 25,000 for Volvo and 40,000 for Mercedes). Scania is a low-cost producer of a differentiated truck that can be custom manufactured quickly and sold to a regionally focused market.

2. **Should dominant-product/service businesses diversify** to build value and competitive advantage? What grand strategies are most appropriate? For example, Compaq Computers and Coca-Cola managers have examined the question of diversification and apparently concluded that continued concentration on their core products and services and development of new markets for those same core products and services are best. IBM and Pepsi examined the same question and concluded that related diversification and vertical integration were best. Why?

EVALUATING AND CHOOSING BUSINESS STRATEGIES: SEEKING SUSTAINED COMPETITIVE ADVANTAGE

Business managers evaluate and choose strategies that they think will make their business successful. Businesses become successful because they possess some advantage relative to their competitors. The two most prominent sources of competitive advantage can be found in the business's cost structure and its ability to differentiate the business from competitors. Disney World in Orlando offers theme park patrons several unique, distinct features that differentiate it from other entertainment options. Wal-Mart offers retail customers the lowest prices on popular consumer items because they have created a low-cost structure resulting in a competitive advantage over most competitors.

Businesses that create competitive advantages from one or both of these sources usually experience above-average profitability within their industry. Businesses that lack a cost or differentiation advantage usually experience average or below-average profitability. Two recent studies found that businesses that do not have either form of competitive advantage perform the poorest among their peers while businesses that possess both forms of competitive advantage enjoy the highest levels of profitability within their industry.[1] The average return on investment for over 2,500 businesses across seven industries looked as follows:

---

[1] R. B. Robinson and J. A. Pearce, "Planned Patterns of Strategic Behavior and Their Relationship to Business Unit Performance," *Strategic Management Journal* 9, no. 1 (1988), pp. 43–60; G. G. Dess and A. Miller, *Strategic Management* (New York: McGraw Hill, 1993), pp. 110–11.

Differentiation Advantage	Cost Advantage	Overall Average ROI across Seven Industries
High	High	35.0%
Low	High	26.0
High	Low	22.0
Low	Low	9.5

Initially, managers were advised to evaluate and choose strategies that emphasized one type of competitive advantage. Often referred to as *generic strategies*, firms were encouraged to become either a differentiation-oriented or low-cost-oriented company. In so doing, it was logical that organizational members would develop a clear understanding of company priorities and, as these studies suggest, likely experience profitability superior to competitors without either a differentiation or low-cost orientation.

The studies mentioned above, and the experience of many other businesses, indicate that the highest profitability levels are found in businesses that possess both types of competitive advantage at the same time. In other words, businesses that have one or more value chain activities that truly differentiate them from key competitors and also have value chain activities that let them operate at a lower cost will consistently outperform their rivals that don't. So the challenge for today's business managers is to evaluate and choose business strategies based on core competencies and value chain activities that sustain both types of competitive advantage simultaneously.

Evaluating Cost Leadership Opportunities

Business success built on cost leadership requires the business to be able to provide its product or service at a cost below what its competitors can achieve. And it must be a sustainable cost advantage. Through the skills and resources identified in Figure 8–1, a business must be able to accomplish one or more activities in its value chain activities— procuring materials, processing them into products, marketing the products, and distributing the products or support activities—in a more cost-effective manner than that of its competitors or it must be able to reconfigure its value chain so as to achieve a cost advantage. Figure 8–1 provides examples of ways this might be done.

Strategists examining their business's value chain for low-cost leadership advantages evaluate the sustainability of those advantages by *benchmarking* (refer to Chapter 6 for a discussion of this comparison technique) their business against key competitors and by considering the impact of any cost advantage on the five forces in their business's competitive environment. Low-cost activities that are sustainable and that provide one or more of these advantages relative to key industry forces should become the basis for the business's competitive strategy.[2]

Low-Cost Advantages That Reduce the Likelihood of Pricing Pressure from Buyers   When key competitors cannot match prices from the low-cost leader, customers pressuring the leader risk establishing a price level that drives alternate sources out of business.

Truly Sustained Low-Cost Advantages May Push Rivals into Other Areas, Lessening Price Competition   Intense, continued price competition may be ruinous for all rivals, as seen occasionally in the airline industry.

---

[2] G. G. Dess and A. Miller, *Strategic Management* (New York: McGraw Hill, 1993), pp. 116.

FIGURE 8–1
Evaluating a Business's Cost Leadership Opportunities

A. Skills and Resources That Foster Cost Leadership

Sustained capital investment and access to capital.
Process engineering skills.
Intense supervision of labor or core technical operations.
Products or services designed for ease of manufacturer or delivery.
Low-cost distribution system.

B. Organizational Requirements to Support and Sustain Cost Leadership Activities

Tight cost control.
Frequent, detailed control reports.
Continuous improvement and benchmarking orientation.
Structured organization and responsibilities.
Incentives based on meeting strict, usually quantitative targets.

C. Examples of Ways Businesses Achieve Competitive Advantage via Cost Leadership

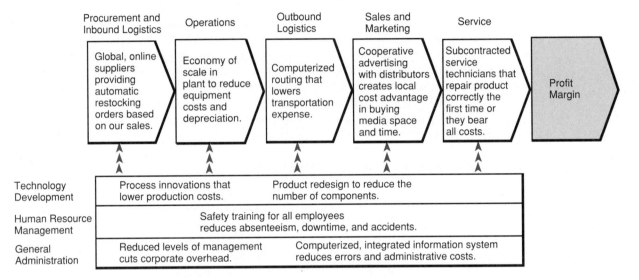

Source: Adapted with permission of The Free Press, a Division of Simon and Schuster, from *Competitive Advantage: Creating and Sustaining Superior Performance*, by Michael E. Porter. Copyright © 1985 by Michael E. Porter.

New Entrants Competing on Price Must Face an Entrenched Cost Leader without the Experience to Replicate Every Cost Advantage   Delite entered the fast food market with great fanfare in the 1980s as the first low-fat fast food chain emphasizing salads and lean hamburgers. Wendy's simply expanded its inexpensive salad bar and, already serving fresh lean meat, quickly saw Delite disappear from NASDAQ. Delite could not begin to match Wendy's cost structure, built on inbound logistics and lower location costs, and still charge a price close to what Wendy's charged for lean, fresh fast food.

Low-Cost Advantages Should Lessen the Attractiveness of Substitute Products   A serious concern of any business is the threat of a substitute product in which buyers can meet their original need. Low-cost advantages allow the holder to resist this happening because it allows them to remain competitive even against desirable substitutes and it allows them to lessen concerns about price facing an inferior, lower priced substitute.

Higher Margins Allow Low-Cost Producers to Withstand Supplier Cost Increases and Often Gain Supplier Loyalty over Time   Sudden, particularly uncontrollable increases in the costs suppliers face can be more easily absorbed by low-cost, higher margin producers. Severe droughts in California quadrupled the price of lettuce—a key restaurant demand. Some chains absorbed the cost; others had to confuse customers with a "lettuce tax." Furthermore, chains that worked well with produce suppliers gained a loyal, cooperative "partner" for possible assistance in a future, competitive situation.

Once managers identify opportunities to create cost advantage–based strategies, they must consider whether key risks inherent in cost leadership are present in a way that may mediate sustained success. The key risks with which they must be concerned are discussed next.

Many Cost-Saving Activities Are Easily Duplicated   Computerizing certain order entry functions among hazardous waste companies gave early adopters lower sales costs and better customer service for a brief time. Rivals quickly adapted, adding similar capabilities with similar impacts on their costs.

Exclusive Cost Leadership Can Become a Trap   Firms that emphasize lowest price and can offer it via cost advantages where product differentiation is increasingly not considered must truly be convinced of the sustainability of those advantages. Particularly with commodity-type products, the low-cost leader seeking to sustain a margin superior to lesser rivals may encounter increasing customer pressure for lower prices with great damage to both leader and lesser players.

Obsessive Cost Cutting Can Shrink Other Competitive Advantages Involving Key Product Attributes   Intense cost scrutiny can build margin, but it can reduce opportunities for or investment in innovation—processes and products. Similarly, such scrutiny can lead to the use of inferior raw materials, processes, or activities that were previously viewed by customers as a key attribute of the original products. Some mail order computer companies that sought to maintain or enhance cost advantages found reductions in telephone service personnel and automation of that function backfiring with a drop in demand for their products even though their low prices were maintained.

Cost Differences Often Decline over Time   As products age, competitors learn how to match cost advantages. Absolute volumes sold often decline. Market channels and suppliers mature. Buyers become more knowledgeable. All of these factors present opportunities to lessen the value or presence of earlier cost advantages. Said another way, cost advantages that are not sustainable over a period of time are risky.

Once business managers have evaluated the cost structure of their value chain, determined activities that provide competitive cost advantages, and considered their inherent risks, they start choosing the business's strategy. Those managers concerned with differentiation-based strategies, or those seeking optimum performance incorporating both sources of competitive advantage, move to evaluating their business's sources of differentiation.

Evaluating Differentiation Opportunities

Differentiation requires that the business have sustainable advantages that allow it to provide buyers with something uniquely valuable to them. A successful differentiation strategy allows the business to provide a product or service of perceived higher value to buyers at a "differentiation cost" below the "value premium" to the buyers. In other words, the buyer feels the additional cost to buy the product or service is well below what the product or service is worth compared to other available alternatives.

Differentiation usually arises from one or more activities in the value chain that create a unique value important to buyers. Perrier's control of a carbonated water spring in France,

FIGURE 8–2
Evaluating a Business's Differentiation Opportunities

A. Skills and Resources That Foster Differentiation

Strong marketing abilities.
Product engineering.
Creative talent and flair.
Strong capabilities in basic research.
Corporate reputation for quality or technical leadership.
Long tradition in an industry or unique combination of skills drawn from other businesses.
Strong cooperation from channels.
Strong cooperation from suppliers of major components of the product or service.

B. Organizational Requirements to Support and Sustain Differentiation Activities

Strong coordination among functions in R&D, product development, and marketing.
Subjective measurement and incentives instead of quantitative measures.
Amenities to attract highly skilled labor, scientists, and creative people.
Tradition of closeness to key customers.
Some personnel skilled in sales and operations—technical and marketing.

C. Examples of Ways Businesses Achieve Competitive Advantage via Differentiation

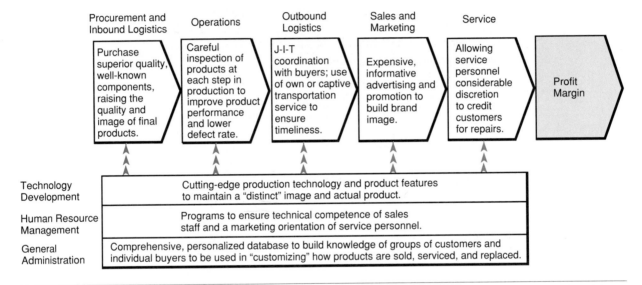

Source: Adapted with permission of The Free Press, a division of Simon and Schuster, from *Competitive Advantage: Creating and Sustaining Superior Performance*, by Michael E. Porter. Copyright © 1985 by Michael E. Porter.

Stouffer's frozen food packaging and sauce technology, Apple's highly integrated chip designs in its Macintosh computers, American Greeting Card's automated inventory system for retailers, and Federal Express's customer service capabilities are all examples of sustainable advantages around which successful differentiation strategies have been built. A business can achieve differentiation by performing its existing value activities or reconfiguring in some unique way. And the sustainability of that differentiation will depend on two things—a continuation of its high perceived value to buyers and a lack of imitation by competitors.

Figure 8–2 suggests key skills that managers should ensure are present to support an emphasis on differentiation. Examples of value chain activities that provide a differentiation advantage are also provided.

Strategists examining their business's value chain for differentiation advantages evaluate the sustainability of those advantages by *benchmarking* (refer to Chapter 6 for a discussion of this comparison technique) their business against key competitors and by considering the impact of any differentiation advantage on the five forces in their business's competitive environment. Sustainable activities that provide one or more of the following opportunities relative to key industry forces should become the basis for differentiation aspects of the business's competitive strategy:

Rivalry Is Reduced When a Business Successfully Differentiates Itself BMW's new Z23 made up the road in Greer, South Carolina, does not compete with Saturns made in central Tennessee. A Harvard education does not compete with a local technical school. Both situations involve the same basic needs, transportation or education. However, one rival has clearly differentiated itself from others in the minds of certain buyers. In so doing, they do not have to respond competitively to that competitor.

Buyers Are Less Sensitive to Prices for Effectively Differentiated Products The Highlands Inn in Carmel, California, and the Ventana Inn along the Big Sur charge a minimum of $400 per night for a room with a kitchen, fireplace, hot tub, and view. Other places are available along this beautiful stretch of California's spectacular coastline, but occupancy rates at these two locations remain over 90 percent. Why? You can't get a better view and a more relaxed, spectacular setting to spend a few days on the Pacific Coast. Similarly, buyers of differentiated products tolerate price increases low-cost–oriented buyers would not accept. The former become very loyal to certain brands.

Brand Loyalty Is Hard for New Entrants to Overcome Many new beers are brought to market in the United States, but Budweiser continues to gain market share. Why? Brand loyalty is hard to overcome! And Anheuser Busch has been clever to extend its brand loyalty from its core brand into newer niches, like nonalcohol brews, that other potential entrants have pioneered.

Managers examining differentation-based advantages must take potential risks into account as they commit their business to these advantages. Some of the more common ways risks arise are discussed next.

Imitation Narrows Perceived Differentiation, Rendering Differentiation Meaningless AMC pioneered the Jeep passenger version of a truck 40 years ago. Ford created the Explorer, or luxury utility vehicle, in 1990. It took luxury car features and put them inside a jeep. Ford's payoff was substantial. The Explorer has become Ford's most popular domestic vehicle. However, virtually every vehicle manufacturer offered a luxury utility in 1997, with customers beginning to be hard pressed to identify clear distinctions between lead models. Ford's Explorer managers were looking for a new business strategy for the next decade that relied on new sources of differentiation and placed greater emphasis on low-cost components in their value chain.

Technological Changes That Nullify Past Investments or Learning The Swiss controlled over 95 percent of the world's watch market into the 1970s. The bulk of the craftspeople, technology, and infrastructure resided in Switzerland. U.S.-based Texas Instruments decided to experiment with the use of its digital technology in watches. Swiss producers were not interested. Strategy in Action 8–1 shows how the Internet may be doing this to *Penthouse* magazine.

The Cost Difference between Low-Cost Competitors and the Differentiated Business Becomes Too Great for Differentiation to Hold Brand Loyalty Buyers may begin to choose to sacrifice some of the features, services, or image possessed by the differentiated business for large cost savings. The rising cost of a college education, particularly at several "premier" institutions, has caused many students to opt for lower-cost destinations that offer very similar courses without image, frills, and professors that seldom teach undergraduate students anyway.

THE INTERNET ERASES *PENTHOUSE* MAGAZINE'S FUNDAMENTAL DIFFERENTIATION COMPETITIVE ADVANTAGE

WHY *PENTHOUSE* IS IN THE DOG HOUSE

The Pet of the Year may bear a come-hither look on the cover of the latest *Penthouse*, but there's much to be modest about at the skin mag these days.

Circulation continues to sag—off 61% over the past ten years—and for the nine months ended in September, the magazine's parent, General Media, lost $7.6 million, vs. a $2.2 million profit last year. Cash is tighter than a corset, and at least one analyst wonders whether the company can cover interest on $85 million of newly downgraded junk bonds.

Penthouse's woes are similar to those bedeviling such staid publishers as Times Mirror and Knight-Ridder. Competing electronic media—in *Penthouse*'s case, vavavoom videos and XXX Internet Web-sites—have readers browsing elsewhere. (Guess they weren't buying it for the articles after all.) Rising paper prices, up 50% last year, sent costs spiraling, as have postal rate hikes.

Skinzines also have distribution problems, stemming from the lingering effects of a 1990 boycott by religious groups against stores that displayed adult publications. *Penthouse* often gets bad exposure in the aisles, a fact that General Media President Richard Cohen admits cuts into sales. Says he: "For many people, we're an impulse buy." No kidding.

All of this has prompted retrenchment. The magazine, says Cohen, has cut costs by laying off employees, rejiggering production, and switching to cheaper paper stock. There are fewer pages too. General Media is also moving briskly into electronic distribution overseas: It recently rolled out a joint venture pay-per-view outlet in the U.K.

That may be too little too late, says analyst Brian Oak of Moody's Investors Service. He recently downgraded General Media debt from B2, just below investment grade, all the way to Caa, a scant two steps up from rock bottom. In particular, Oak is worried the company won't be able to make an interest payment of $4.2 million that's due on its junk bonds next June. Cohen insists the company has more than enough dough to meet current interest charges, but a closer look between General Media's balance sheets is revealing. Analyst Oak asserts the company's cash balance of some $9 million consists mostly of unearned revenue—upfront money paid by distributors that is supposed to pay for operating costs.

Penthouse founder and General Media CEO Bob Guccione need not fear for his tasteful art collection—Renoir to Van Gogh to Holbein. That isn't collateral. His two other publications, a health magazine called *Longevity* and science-fiction monthly *Omni*, operate separately.

Evaluating Speed as a Competitive Advantage

While most telecommunication companies used 1995 to leap aboard the information super-highway, GTE continued its impressive turnaround (income up 7% to $5 billion; revenues up 4%) focusing on its core business—providing local telephone services. Long lagging behind the Baby Bells in profitability and efficiency, GTE has emphasized improving its poor customer service that dates back to the 1980s. The service was so bad in Santa Monica, California, that officials once tried to remove GTE as the local phone company. Candidly saying "we were the pits," new CEO Chuck Lee largely did away with its old system of taking customer service requests by writing them down and passing them along for resolution. Now, using personal communication services and specially designed software, service reps can solve 70 percent of all problems on the initial call—triple the

FIGURE 8–3
Evaluating a Business's Rapid Response (Speed) Opportunities

A. Skills and Resources That Foster Speed

Process engineering skills.
Excellent inbound and outbound logistics.
Technical people in sales and customer service.
High levels of automation.
Corporate reputation for quality or technical leadership.
Flexible manufacturing capabilities.
Strong downstream partners.
Strong cooperation from suppliers of major components of the product or service.

B. Organizational Requirements to Support and Sustain Rapid Response Activities

Strong coordination among functions in R&D, product development, and marketing.
Major emphasis on customer satisfaction in incentive programs.
Strong delegation to operating personnel.
Tradition of closeness to key customers.
Some personnel skilled in sales and operations—technical and marketing.
Empowered customer service personnel.

C. Examples of Ways Businesses Achieve Competitive Advantage via Speed

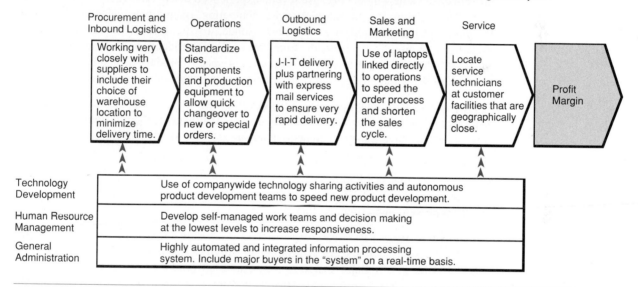

Procurement and Inbound Logistics	Operations	Outbound Logistics	Sales and Marketing	Service	
Working very closely with suppliers to include their choice of warehouse location to minimize delivery time.	Standardize dies, components and production equipment to allow quick changeover to new or special orders.	J-I-T delivery plus partnering with express mail services to ensure very rapid delivery.	Use of laptops linked directly to operations to speed the order process and shorten the sales cycle.	Locate service technicians at customer facilities that are geographically close.	Profit Margin

Technology Development: Use of companywide technology sharing activities and autonomous product development teams to speed new product development.

Human Resource Management: Develop self-managed work teams and decision making at the lowest levels to increase responsiveness.

General Administration: Highly automated and integrated information processing system. Include major buyers in the "system" on a real-time basis.

Source: Adapted with permission of The Free Press, a Division of Simon and Schuster, from *Competitive Advantage: Creating and Sustaining Superior Performance*, by Michael E. Porter. Copyright © 1985 by Michael E. Porter.

success rate at the beginning of the last decade. Repair workers meanwhile plan their schedules on laptops, cutting down time and speeding responses. CEO Lee has spent $1.5 billion on reengineering that slashed 17,000 jobs, replaced people with technology, and prioritized *speed* as the defining feature of GTE's business practices.

Speed, or rapid response to customer requests or market and technological changes, has become a major source of competitive advantage for numerous firms in today's intensely competitive global economy. Speed is certainly a form of differentiation, but it is more than that. Speed involves the *availability of a rapid response* to a customer by providing current products quicker, accelerating new product development or improvement, quickly adjusting production processes, and making decisions quickly. While low cost and differentiation may provide important competitive advantages, managers in tomorrow's successful companies will base their strategies on creating speed-based competitive advantages. Figure 8–3 describes and illustrates key skills and organizational requirements that are associated with speed-based competitive advantage. Jack Welch, the CEO who transformed General Electric from a fading company into one of Wall Street's best performers over the last 10 years, had this to say about speed:

> Speed is really the driving force that everyone is after. Faster products, faster product cycles to market. Better response time to customers. . . . Satisfying customers, getting faster communications, moving with more agility, all these things are easier when one is small. And these are all characteristics one needs in a fast-moving global environment.[3]

Speed-based competitive advantages can be created around several activities.

Customer Responsiveness   All consumers have encountered hassles, delays, and frustration dealing with various businesses from time to time. The same holds true when dealing business to business. Quick response with answers, information, and solutions to mistakes can become the basis for competitive advantage . . . one that builds customer loyalty quickly.

Product Development Cycles   Japanese car makers have focused intensely on the time it takes to create a new model because several experienced disappointing sales growth in the mid-1990s in Europe and North America competing against new vehicles like Ford's Explorer and Renault's Megane. By 1997, Honda, Toyota, and Nissan had lowered the cycle from 24 months to 11 months from conception to production. This capability is old hat to 3M Corporation, which is so successful at speedy product development that one-fourth of its sales and profits each year are from products that didn't exist five years earlier.

Product or Service Improvements   Like development time, companies that can rapidly adapt their products or services and do so in a way that benefits their customers or creates new customers have a major competitive advantage over rivals that cannot do this.

Speed in Delivery or Distribution   Firms that can get you what you need when you need it, even when that is tomorrow, realize that buyers have come to expect that level of responsiveness. Federal Express's success reflects the importance customers place on speed in inbound and outbound logistics.

Information Sharing and Technology   Speed in sharing information that becomes the basis for decisions, actions, or other important activities taken by a customer, supplier, or partner has become a major source of competitive advantage for many businesses. Telecommunications, the Internet, and networks are but a part of a vast infrastructure that is being used by knowledgeable managers to rebuild or create value in their businesses via information sharing.

These rapid response capabilities create competitive advantages in several ways. They create a way to lessen rivalry because they have *availability* of something that a rival may not have. It can allow the business to charge buyers more, engender loyalty, or otherwise enhance the business's position relative to its buyers. Particularly where impressive customer response is involved, businesses can generate supplier cooperation and concessions since their business ultimately benefits from increased revenue. Finally, substitute products and new entrants find themselves trying to keep up with the rapid changes rather than introducing them.

While the notion of speed-based competitive advantage is exciting, it has risks managers must consider. First, speeding up activities that haven't been conducted in a fashion that prioritizes rapid response should only be done after considerable attention to training,

---

[3] "Jack Welch on the Art of Thinking Small," *Business Week*, Enterprise 1993 issue, p. 212.

reorganization, and/or reengineering. Second, some industries—stable, mature ones that have very minimal levels of change—may not offer much advantage to the firm that introduces some forms of rapid response. Customers in such settings may prefer the slower pace or the lower costs currently available or they may have long time frames in purchasing such that speed is not that important to them.

Evaluating Market Focus as a Way to Competitive Advantage

Small companies, at least the better ones, usually thrive because they serve narrow market niches. This is usually called *focus*, the extent to which a business concentrates on a narrowly defined market. Take the example of Soho Beverages, a business former Pepsi manager Tom Cox bought from Seagram after Seagram had acquired it and was unable to make it thrive. The tiny brand, once a healthy niche product in New York and a few other east coast locations, muddled within Seagrams because its sales force was unused to selling in delis. Cox was able to double sales in one year. He did this on a lean marketing budget that didn't include advertising or database marketing. He hired Korean- and Arabic-speaking college students and had his people walk into practically every deli in Manhattan in order to reacquaint owners with the brand, spot consumption trends, and take orders. He provided rapid stocking services to all Manhattan-area delis, regardless of size. The business has continued sales growth at over 50 percent per year. Why? Cox says "It is attributable to focusing on a niche market, delis; differentiating the product and its sales force; achieving low costs in promotion and delivery; and making rapid, immediate response to any deli owner request its normal practice."

Two things are important in this example. First, this business focused on a narrow niche market in which to build a strong competitive advantage. But focus alone was not enough to build competitive advantage. Rather, Cox created several value chain activities that achieved differentiation, low cost, and rapid response competitive advantages within this niche market that would be hard for other firms, particularly mass market–oriented firms, to replicate.

Focus allows some businesses to compete on the basis of low cost, differentiation, and rapid response against much larger businesses with greater resources. Focus lets a business "learn" its target customers—their needs, special considerations they want accommodated—and establish personal relationships in ways that "differentiate" the smaller firm or make it more valuable to the target customer. Low costs can also be achieved filling niche needs in a buyer's operations that larger rivals either do not want to bother with or cannot do as cost effectively. Cost advantage often centers around the high level of customized service the focused, smaller business can provide. And perhaps the greatest competitive weapon that can arise is rapid response. With enhanced knowledge of its customers and intricacies of their operations, the small, focused company builds up organizational knowledge about timing sensitive ways to work with a customer. Often the needs of that narrow set of customers represent a large part of the small, focused business's revenues. Global Strategy In Action 8–1 illustrates how Sweden's Scania has become the global leader in heavy trucks via the focused application of low cost, differentiation, and speed.

The risk of focus is that you attract major competitors that have waited for your business to "prove" the market. Dominoes proved that a huge market for pizza delivery existed and now faces serious challenges. Likewise, publicly traded focused companies become takeover targets for large firms seeking to fill out a product portfolio. And perhaps the greatest risk of all is slipping into the illusion that it is focus itself, and not some special form of low cost, differentiation, or rapid response, that is creating the business's success.

GLOBAL
STRATEGY IN
ACTION 8–1

SCANIA LEAVES VOLVO AND OTHER GLOBAL TRUCK MANUFACTURERS IN ITS DUST

The preeminent consulting firm McKinsey and Company recently studied the global truck industry to understand which producers had the strongest competitive advantages and why they did. It quickly became a study of the Swedish firm, Scania, and its long time rival, Volvo. On an index that measured value added per hour worked, Scania scored 100 with Volvo close behind. The best Japanese, U.S., and German truck makers trailed by more than 25 points.

Leif Ostling, Scania's burly CEO, attributes the business's success to a determination to stick to its strategy of concentrating on heavy trucks, and rely on its own resources to deliver quality products commanding market leading prices. McKinsey's analysis broadens the explanation as it sought an answer to how Scania had arrived at its enviable position and what its prospects were for remaining a world leader. McKinsey concluded:

1. Intense competition between Scania and Volvo in tiny Sweden prepared them both to compete better than other rivals in the global market because the truck industry is much less international than the car industry, leaving newer rivals less competitive even on their home turf. Scania and Volvo have been benchmarking each other for years.

2. Scania uses a building principle of maximization of standardization of parts across many brands while also leading the industry in responding to the demand for customization of each vehicle that is sold. How? While every truck is a unique order, Scania uses less than 20,000 components to build their truck compared to 25,000 for Volvo and 40,000 for Mercedes. Fewer parts mean lower development costs, lower manufacturing costs, and lower distribution costs.

3. Scania produces all main components in house, which allows them to maximize integration of design, development, and production, thus saving time, allowing for greater customization, and fewer parts.

4. There is strong emphasis on customization of each vehicle: "We have to supply a specific truck to a customer's specific needs," said Kaj Holmelius, head of chassis development, pointing to a production line, "Each of these is for a specific order and almost every one will be different in some way when they come off the end of the line. At the same time we want to get as large volumes as possible for individual components."

5. Scania will not expand into lighter trucks because it would dilute the efficiencies it has wrung out of its modular system. It has no plans to enter the North American market because of very different truck specifications and lower margins. The intention is to grow chiefly in Central and Eastern Europe and in the Pacific region. "We will stick to what we know how to do in limited, margin favorable markets," said Ostling.

The bottom line is, Scania has built a variety of sustainable competitive advantages that promise to keep it on top the world heavy truck market for a long time.

Source: "Scania Pulls Ahead of the Crowd," *Financial Times*, October 16, 1995, p. 10.

Managers evaluating opportunities to build competitive advantage should link strategies to value chain activities that exploit low cost, differentiation, and rapid response competitive advantages. When advantageous, they should consider ways to use focus to leverage these advantages. One way business managers can enhance their likelihood of identifying these opportunities is to consider several different "generic" industry environments from the perspective of the typical value chain activities most often linked to sustained competitive advantages in those unique industry situations. The next section discusses five key generic industry environments and the value chain activities most associated with success.

SELECTED INDUSTRY ENVIRONMENTS AND BUSINESS STRATEGY CHOICES

The analysis and choice of the ways a business will seek to build competitive advantage can be enhanced when managers take industry conditions into account. Chapters 3 and 5 discussed ways to examine industry conditions, so we do not seek to repeat that here. Likewise, Chapter 6 shows how the market life cycle concept can be used to examine business strengths. What is important to recognize as managers evaluate opportunities to emphasize a narrow set of core competencies and potential competitive advantages is that different sets appear to be more useful in different, unique industry environments. We examine five "typical" industry settings and opportunities for generating competitive advantages that strategists should look for in their deliberations. Three of these five settings relate to industry life cycle. Managers use these as ways to evaluate their value chain activities and then select the ones around which it is most critical to build competitive advantage.[4]

Competitive Advantage in Emerging Industries

Emerging industries are newly formed or re-formed industries that typically are created by technological innovation, newly emerging customer needs, or other economic or sociological changes. Emerging industries of the last decade have been the Internet browser, fiber optic, solar heating, cellular telephone, and on-line services industries.

From the standpoint of strategy formulation, the essential characteristic of an emerging industry is that there are no "rules of the game." The absence of rules presents both a risk and an opportunity—a wise strategy positions the firm to favorably shape the emerging industry's rules.

Business strategies must be shaped to accommodate the following characteristics of markets in emerging industries.

Technologies that are mostly proprietary to the pioneering firms and technological uncertainty about how product standardization will unfold.

Competitor uncertainty because of inadequate information about competitors, buyers, and the timing of demand.

High initial costs but steep cost declines as the experience curve takes effect.

Few entry barriers, which often spurs the formation of many new firms.

First-time buyers requiring initial inducement to purchase and customers confused by the availability of a number of nonstandard products.

Inability to obtain raw materials and components until suppliers gear up to meet the industry's needs.

Need for high-risk capital because of the industry's uncertainty prospects.

For success in this industry setting, business strategies require one or more of these features:

1. The ability to *shape the industry's structure* based on the timing of entry, reputation, success in related industries or technologies, and role in industry associations.
2. The ability to *rapidly improve product quality* and performance features.
3. *Advantageous relationships* with key suppliers and promising distribution channels.

---

[4]These industry characterizations draw heavily on the work of Michael E. Porter, *Competitive Advantage: Creating and Sustaining Superior Performance*. (New York: Free Press, 1985).

STRATEGY
IN ACTION
8–2

DOES NETSCAPE HAVE A REAL, SUSTAINABLE COMPETITIVE ADVANTAGE IN THE EMERGING "INTERNET INDUSTRY?"

AS THE BIG GUYS AWAKE, CAN NETSCAPE PREVAIL?

Netscape, the tiny software company that the stock market values at nearly $6 billion, has come to symbolize the Internet the way Microsoft does PC computing. Investors treat this pup as a bellwether for the Internet phenomenon, the presumed Next Big Thing. Now, rapid-fire changes in the market are posing a threat to Netscape's ability to dominate Internet computing. Absent that, Netscape's hypervaluation is impossible to justify.

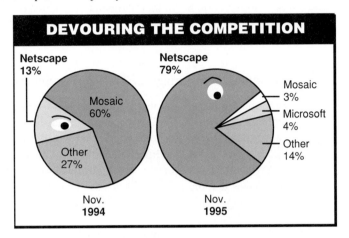

Source: "As the Big Guys Awake, Can Netscape Prevail?" January 15, 1996, p. 16. By David Kirkpatrick, *Fortune*, © 1996, Time, Inc. All rights reserved.

4. The ability to *establish the firm's technology as the dominant one* before technological uncertainty decreases.
5. The early acquisition of *a core group of loyal customers* and then the expansion of that customer base through model changes, alternative pricing, and advertising.
6. The ability to *forecast future competitors* and the strategies they are likely to employ.

A firm that has had repeated successes with business in emerging industries is 3M Corporation. In each of the last 20 years, over 25 percent of 3M's annual sales have come from products that did not exist 5 years earlier. Start-up companies enhance their success by having experienced entrepreneurs at the helm, a knowledgeable management team and board of directors, and patient sources of venture capital. Netscape's dramatic debut on Wall Street symbolically ushering in the emerging "Internet Industry" era for investors will certainly lead to questions about the lasting competitive advantage at Netscape. Strategy in Action 8–2 examines whether Netscape has the capacity to prevail in this emerging industry.

Competitive Advantage in the Transition to Industry Maturity

As an industry evolves, its rate of growth eventually declines. This "transition to maturity" is accompanied by several changes in its competitive environment:

Netscape's business consists primarily of two sectors—Internet "browsers" and software for the servers to which the browsers go for data. But new products announced by Microsoft and IBM's Lotus Development will be "Internet-enabled." That means such software as Microsoft Word or Excel, or Lotus Notes, can transport the user to the Internet directly, without help from Netscape's browser.

The company's biggest business right now—70% of this year's $60 million in revenues—is providing browsers and server software for so-called intranets. In these setups, businesses use Internet tools to build internal information-sharing systems. But if Microsoft inserts a browser in its operating systems, as it intends to in Windows 95, why should a customer buy another one? And Lotus Notes' primary function is for creating intranet-like systems but with vastly greater information control and security. In mid-December, Lotus raised the stakes by slashing Notes prices.

To fend off competitors like Lotus, Netscape has to add features to its software without raising prices. It also has to provide the kind of expensive support corporate customers demand. Given that its rivals are expert at just that, says David Marshak, a communications software expert at Boston's Patricia Seybold Group, "Netscape is vulnerable."

Jonathan Cohen, an analyst at Smith Barney, thinks naive investors assume Netscape can eventually rule the Internet and vanquish the challengers. "But it really will be difficult," he explains, "for any company to gain a proprietary competitive advantage by controlling the operating system of the Internet." At Netscape's recent price of $140, Cohen says sell.

Netscape co-founder Marc Andreessen takes a feisty view toward the more established competition. "Microsoft should have been all over this three years ago," he says. "It's premature to say a bunch of moribund companies are going to catch up and kill us."

Competition for market share becomes more intense as firms in the industry are forced to achieve sales growth at one another's expense.

Firms in the industry sell increasingly to experienced, repeat buyers that are now making choices among known alternatives.

Competition becomes more oriented to cost and service as knowledgeable buyers expect similar price and product features.

Industry capacity "tops out" as sales growth ceases to cover up poorly planned expansions.

New products and new applications are harder to come by.

International competition increases as cost pressures lead to overseas production advantages.

Profitability falls, often permanently, as a result of pressure to lower prices and the increased costs of holding or building market share.

These changes necessitate a fundamental strategic reassessment. Strategy elements of successful firms in maturing industries often include:

1. *Pruning the product line* by dropping unprofitable product models, sizes, and options from the firm's product mix.
2. *Emphasis on process innovation* that permits low-cost product design, manufacturing methods, and distribution synergy.

3. *Emphasis on cost reduction* through exerting pressure on suppliers for lower prices, switching to cheaper components, introducing operational efficiencies, and lowering administrative and sales overhead.
4. *Careful buyer selection* to focus on buyers that are less aggressive, more closely tied to the firm, and able to buy more from the firm.
5. *Horizontal integration* to acquire rival firms whose weaknesses can be used to gain a bargain price and are correctable by the acquiring firms.
6. *International expansion* to markets where attractive growth and limited competition still exist and the opportunity for lower-cost manufacturing can influence both domestic and international costs.

Business strategists in maturing industries must avoid several pitfalls. First, they must make a clear choice among the three generic strategies and avoid a middle-ground approach, which would confuse both knowledgeable buyers and the firm's personnel. Second, they must avoid sacrificing market share too quickly for short-term profit. Finally, they must avoid waiting too long to respond to price reductions, retaining unneeded excess capacity, engaging in sporadic or irrational efforts to boost sales, and placing their hopes on "new" products, rather than aggressively selling existing products.

Competitive Advantage in Mature and Declining Industries

Declining industries are those that make products or services for which demand is growing slower than demand in the economy as a whole or is actually declining. This slow growth or decline in demand is caused by technological substitution (such as the substitution of electronic calculators for slide rules), demographic shifts (such as the increase in the number of older people and the decrease in the number of children), and shifts in needs (such as the decreased need for red meat).

Firms in a declining industry should choose strategies that emphasize one or more of the following themes:

1. *Focus* on segments within the industry that offer a chance for higher growth or a higher return.
2. *Emphasize product innovation and quality improvement,* where this can be done cost effectively, to differentiate the firm from rivals and to spur growth.
3. *Emphasize production and distribution efficiency* by streamlining production, closing marginal productions facilities and costly distribution outlets, and adding effective new facilities and outlets.
4. *Gradually harvest the business*—generate cash by cutting down on maintenance, reducing models, and shrinking channels and make no new investment.

Strategists who incorporate one or more of these themes into the strategy of their business can anticipate relative success, particularly where the industry's decline is slow and smooth and some profitable niches remain. At the same time, three pitfalls must be avoided: (1) being overly optimistic about the prospects for a revival of the industry, (2) getting trapped in a profitless war of attrition, and (3) harvesting from a weak position.

Competitive Advantage in Fragmented Industries

A fragmented industry is one in which no firm has a significant market share and can strongly influence industry outcomes. Fragmented industries are found in many areas of the economy and are common in such areas as professional services, retailing, distribution, wood and metal fabrication, and agricultural products. Business strategists in fragmented industries pursue low-cost, differentiation, or focus competitive advantages in one of five ways.

Tightly Managed Decentralization

Fragmented industries are characterized by a need for intense local coordination, a local management orientation, high personal service, and local autonomy. Recently, however, successful firms in such industries have introduced a high degree of professionalism into the operations of local managers.

"Formula" Facilities

This alternative, related to the previous one, introduces standardized, efficient, low-cost facilities at multiple locations. Thus, the firm gradually builds a low-cost advantage over localized competitors. Fast food and motel chains have applied this approach with considerable success.

Increased Value Added

The products or services of some fragmented industries are difficult to differentiate. In this case, an effective strategy may be to add value by providing more service with the sale or by engaging in some product assembly that is of additional value to the customer.

Specialization

Focus strategies that creatively segment the market can enable firms to cope with fragmentation. Specialization can be pursued by:

1. *Product type.* The firm builds expertise focusing on a narrow range of products or services.
2. *Customer type.* The firm becomes intimately familiar with and serves the needs of a narrow customer segment.
3. *Type of order.* The firm handles only certain kinds of orders, such as small orders, custom orders, or quick turnaround orders.
4. *Geographic area.* The firm blankets or concentrates on a single area.

Although specialization in one or more of these ways can be the basis for a sound focus strategy in a fragmented industry, each of these types of specialization risks limiting the firm's potential sales volume.

Bare Bones/No Frills

Given the intense competition and low margins in fragmented industries, a "bare bones" posture—low overhead, minimum wage employees, tight cost control—may build a sustainable cost advantage in such industries.

Competitive Advantage in Global Industries

A global industry is one that comprises firms whose competitive positions in major geographic or national markets are fundamentally affected by their overall global competitive positions. To avoid strategic disadvantages, firms in global industries are virtually required to compete on a worldwide basis. Oil, steel, automobiles, apparel, motorcycles, televisions, and computers are examples of global industries.

Global industries have four unique strategy-shaping features:

Differences in prices and costs from country to country due to currency exchange fluctuations, differences in wage and inflation rates, and other economic factors.

Differences in buyer needs across different countries.

Differences in competitors and ways of competing from country to country.

Differences in trade rules and governmental regulations across different countries.

These unique features and the global competition of global industries require that two fundamental components be addressed in the business strategy: (1) the approach used to gain global market coverage and (2) the generic competitive strategy.

Three basic options can be used to pursue global market coverage:

1. *License* foreign firms to produce and distribute the firm's products.
2. *Maintain a domestic production base* and export products to foreign countries.
3. *Establish foreign-based plants and distribution* to compete directly in the markets of one or more foreign countries.

Along with the market coverage decision, strategists must scrutinize the condition of the global industry features identified earlier to choose among four generic global competitive strategies:

1. *Broad-line global competition*—directed at competing worldwide in the full product line of the industry, often with plants in many countries, to achieve differentiation or an overall low-cost position.
2. *Global focus* strategy—targeting a particular segment of the industry for competition on a worldwide basis.
3. *National focus* strategy—taking advantage of differences in national markets that give the firm an edge over global competitors on a nation-by-nation basis.
4. *Protected niche* strategy—seeking out countries in which governmental restraints exclude or inhibit global competitors or allow concessions, or both, that are advantageous to localized firms.

Competing in global industries is an increasing reality for many U.S. firms. Strategists must carefully match their skills and resources with global industry structure and conditions in selecting the most appropriate strategy option.

In conclusion, the analysis and choice of business strategy involves three basic considerations. First, strategists must recognize that their overall choice revolves around three sources of competitive advantage that require total, consistent commitment. Second, strategists must carefully weigh the skills, resources, organizational requirements, and risks associated with each source of competitive advantage. Finally, strategists must consider the unique influence that the generic industry environment most similar to the firm's situation will have on the set of value chain activities they choose to build competitive advantage.

DOMINANT-PRODUCT/SERVICE BUSINESSES: EVALUATING AND CHOOSING TO DIVERSIFY TO BUILD VALUE

McDonald's has frequently looked at numerous opportunities to diversify into related businesses or to acquire key suppliers. Its decision has consistently been to focus on its core business using the grand strategies of concentration, market development, and product development. Rival Pepsi, on the other hand, has chosen to diversify into related businesses and vertical integration as the best grand strategies for it to build long-term value. Both firms experienced unprecedented success during the last 20 years.

FIGURE 8–4
Grand Strategy Selection Matrix

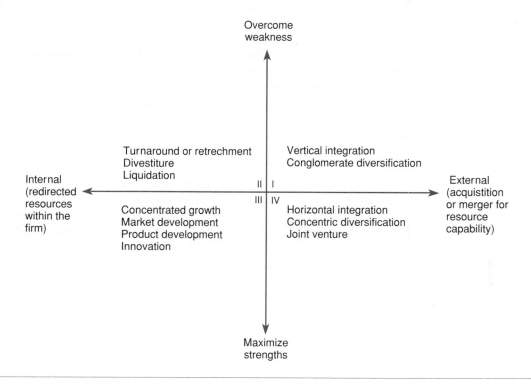

Many dominant product businesses face this question as their core business proves successful: What grand strategies are best suited to continue to build value? Under what circumstances should they choose an expanded focus (diversification, vertical integration); steady continued focus (concentration, market or product development); or a narrowed focus (turnaround or divestiture)? This section examines two ways you can analyze a dominant product company's situation and choose among the 12 grand strategies identified in Chapter 7.

Grand Strategy Selection Matrix

One valuable guide to the selection of a promising grand strategy is the matrix shown in Figure 8–4. The basic idea underlying the matrix is that two variables are of central concern in the selection process: (1) the principal purpose of the grand strategy and (2) the choice of an internal or external emphasis for growth or profitability, or both.

In the past, planners were advised to follow certain rules or prescriptions in their choice of strategies. Now, most experts agree that strategy selection is better guided by the conditions of the planning period and by the company strengths and weaknesses. It should be noted, however, that even the early approaches to strategy selection sought to match a concern over internal versus external growth with a desire to overcome weaknesses or maximize strengths.

The same considerations led to the development of the grand strategy selection matrix. A firm in quadrant I, with "all its eggs in one basket," often views itself as overcommitted to a particular business with limited growth opportunities or high risks. One reasonable solution is *vertical integration*, which enables the firm to reduce risk by reducing uncertainty about inputs or access to customers. Another is *conglomerate diversification*, which provides a profitable investment alternative with diverting management attention from the original business. However, the external approaches to overcoming weaknesses usually result in the most costly grand strategies. Acquiring a second business demands large investments of time and sizable financial resources. Thus, strategic managers considering these approaches must guard against exchanging one set of weaknesses for another.

More-conservative approaches to overcoming weaknesses are found in quadrant II. Firms often choose to redirect resources from one internal business activity to another. This approach maintains the firm's commitment to its basic mission, rewards success, and enables further development of proven competitive advantages. The least disruptive of the quadrant II strategies is *retrenchment*, pruning the current activities of a business. If the weaknesses of the business arose from inefficiencies, retrenchment can actually serve as a *turnaround* strategy—that is, the business gains new strength from the streamlining of its operations and the elimination of waste. However, if those weaknesses are a major obstruction to success in the industry and the costs of overcoming them are unaffordable or are not justified by a cost-benefit analysis, then eliminating the business must be considered. *Divestiture* offers the best possibility for recouping the firm's investment, but even *liquidation* can be an attractive option if the alternatives are bankruptcy or an unwarranted drain on the firm's resources.

A common business adage states that a firm should build from strength. The premise of this adage is that growth and survival depend on an ability to capture a market share that is large enough for essential economies of scale. If a firm believes that this approach will be profitable and prefers an internal emphasis for maximizing strengths, four grand strategies hold considerable promise. As shown in quadrant III, the most common approach is *concentrated growth*, that is, market penetration. The firm that selects this strategy is strongly committed to its current products and markets. It strives to solidify its position by reinvesting resources to fortify its strengths.

Two alternative approaches are *market development* and *product development*. With these strategies, the firm attempts to broaden its operations. Market development is chosen if the firm's strategic managers feel that its existing products would be well received by new customer groups. Product development is chosen if they feel that the firm's existing customers would be interested in products related to its current lines. Product development also may be based on technological or other competitive advantages. The final alternative for quadrant III firms is *innovation*. When the firm's strengths are in creative product design or unique production technologies, sales can be stimulated by accelerating perceived obsolescence. This is the principle underlying the innovative grand strategy.

Maximizing a firm's strengths by aggressively expanding its base of operations usually requires an external emphasis. The preferred options in such cases are shown in quadrant IV. *Horizontal integration* is attractive because it makes possible a quick increase in output capability. Moreover, in horizontal integration, the skills of the managers of the original business often are critical in converting newly acquired facilities into profitable contributors to the parent firm; this expands a fundamental competitive advantage of the firm—its management.

Concentric diversification is a good second choice for similar reasons. Because the original and newly acquired businesses are related, the distinctive competencies of the diversifying firm are likely to facilitate a smooth, synergistic, and profitable expansion.

The final alternative for increasing resource capability through external emphasis is a *joint venture* or *strategic alliance*. This alternative allows a firm to extend its strengths into competitive arenas that it would be hesitant to enter alone. A partner's production, technological, financial, or marketing capabilities can reduce the firm's financial investment significantly and increase its probability of success.

FIGURE 8–5
Model of Grand Strategy Clusters

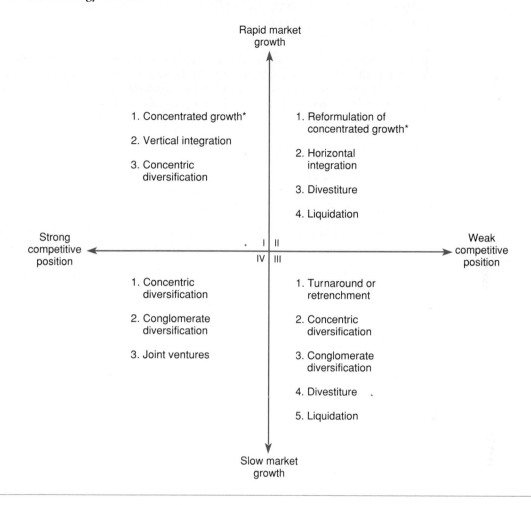

*This is usually via market development, product development, or a combination of both.

Model of Grand Strategy Clusters

A second guide to selecting a promising grand strategy is shown in Figure 8–5. The figure is based on the idea that the situation of a business is defined in terms of the growth rate of the general market and the firm's competitive position in that market. When these factors are considered simultaneously, a business can be broadly categorized in one of four quadrants: (I) strong competitive position in a rapidly growing market, (II) weak position in a rapidly growing market, (III) weak position in a slow-growth market, or (IV) strong position in a slow-growth market. Each of these quadrants suggests a set of promising possibilities for the selection of a grand strategy.

Firms in quadrant I are in an excellent strategic position. One obvious grand strategy for such firms is continued concentration on their current business as it is currently defined. Because consumers seem satisfied with the firm's current strategy, shifting notably from it would endanger the firm's established competitive advantages. McDonald's Corporation has followed this approach for 25 years. However, if the firm has resources that exceed the

CHOOSING AMONG GRAND STRATEGY ALTERNATIVES AT PEPSICO

Twenty-five years ago, PepsiCo was a sleepy and distant second to Coca-Cola in the U.S. soft-drink industry. Soda consumption by the baby boom generation made it easy for PepsiCo to double its sales to almost $1 billion while maintaining a steady ROE in the high teens and a 5 percent return on sales. This profitability allowed the company to generate an additional $40 million in working capital over that needed to operate the company's existing business.

PepsiCo's management team led by Donald Kendall and Andrall Pearson sought to heat up the company's growth, given the predictability of its soft-drink income stream. As they examined alternative grand strategies, they viewed PepsiCo as possessing proven strengths in selling an inexpensive consumable product (Pepsi) to a young, energetic consumer. Their first choice of strategy was one that sought to redirect internal resources (excess cash generated) toward maximizing these strengths. Their conclusion in this regard was a four-part program:

1. Continue to build sales of their Pepsi product in existing outlets. (Concentrated growth)
2. Expand distribution (and sales) of Pepsi by aggressively pursuing new and different outlets, especially grocery stores and international. (Market development)
3. Create related but new products like diet drinks to appeal to baby boomers reaching adulthood. (Product development)
4. Design revolutionary new packaging to reinforce the sales efforts emanating from above. (Innovation—plastics and 32 oz.)

Wisely anticipating that these strategies would continue to generate a growing stream of excess cash, these managers also realized that PepsiCo did not possess other resources (people, experience, and products) necessary to take advantage of related growth opportunities. So PepsiCo had to look externally for the management, experience, and product opportunities that could blend well with and maximize its proven strengths in cola marketing and sales. Their add-on grand strategies to pursue these conclusions were:

5. Acquire 7UP, Mountain Dew, and Mug Rootbeer to expand their product offerings. (Horizontal integration)
6. Diversify via acquisition into related products including Frito Lay. (Concentric diversification)

PepsiCo also rationalized the acquisition of Wilson Sporting Goods and United Van Lines as a part of this strategy. Wilson was seen as selling products to the same market—active young people. United complemented PepsiCo's growing transportation network by bringing the expertise to run it efficiently.

Source: PepsiCo, Inc., 1971 and 1994 annual reports.

demands of a concentrated growth strategy, it should consider vertical integration. Either forward or backward integration helps a firm protect its profit margins and market share by ensuring better access to consumers or material inputs. Finally, to diminish the risks associated with a narrow product or service line, a quadrant I firm might be wise to consider concentric diversification; with this strategy, the firm continues to invest heavily in its basic area of proven ability. Strategy in Action 8–3 describes how PepsiCo, a clear quadrant I firm, has followed these guidelines.

Firms in quadrant II must seriously evaluate their present approach to the marketplace. If a firm has competed long enough to accurately assess the merits of its current grand

continued

PepsiCo's choice of grand strategies generally proved successful. In 10 years net sales had increased sixfold to over $6 billion. Profitability and cash generation ratios remained consistent, meaning even greater excess financial resources to work with. Along the way, Wilson and United were divested, because management saw both businesses to contain several weaknesses not worth (from PepsiCo's perspective) investment to correct. With this overall growth in financial resources, PepsiCo managers concluded the same grand strategies applied that led to the acquisition of Pizza Hut, Kentucky Fried Chicken, and Taco Bell as a logical concentric diversification.

PepsiCo, now in soft drinks, snack foods, and restaurants, saw its net sales, net income, and cash flow grow at compounded annual rates of 17 percent, 19 percent, and 15 percent, respectively, into the first half of the 1990s. Over this period, operations generated over $15 billion for reinvestment, dividends, or acquisition.

Contributing to and reaping the bounty of this legacy, PepsiCo's colorful chairman and CEO, Wayne Calloway, observed:

At PepsiCo, we've increased sales and net income at an exhilarating rate of nearly 15 percent for 26 years. That means we've doubled our business about every five years. But now that we're about $30 billion big, you might well ask, How long can this keep going on? Forever, as far as we're concerned. At least that's our intention.

Mr. Calloway views PepsiCo as being in the fortunate position of maximizing strengths via redirection of internally generated resources in each of its three business sections. Some of the specific strategies he outlines to back up his above assertion are:

1. In many international markets, consumers drink fewer soft drinks in a year than most Americans consume in a week. We're going to change that. (Concentrated growth)
2. Our (snack food) products are still unavailable to about 60 percent of the world's population. We're changing that. (Market development)
3. Soft drinks represent about one quarter of all beverages consumed in the United States. That means that three quarters of the beverage market provides opportunity. (Product development)
4. More than 40 percent of all adults in the United States have a meal delivered from a restaurant at least once a month. We're becoming a front runner in this market segment. (Concentrated growth)
5. International consumers eat about one sixth the amount of snack chips consumed by their U.S. counterparts, but snacking is becoming more popular every day. (Market and product development)

strategy, it must determine (1) why that strategy is ineffectual and (2) whether it is capable of competing effectively. Depending on the answers to these questions, the firm should choose one of four grand strategy options: formulation or reformulation of a concentrated growth strategy, horizontal integration, divestiture, or liquidation.

In a rapidly growing market, even a small or relatively weak business often is able to find a profitable niche. Thus, formulation or reformulation of a concentrated growth strategy is usually the first option that should be considered. However, if the firm lacks either a critical competitive element or sufficient economies of scale to achieve competitive cost efficiencies, then a grand strategy that directs its efforts toward horizontal integration is often a desirable alternative. A final pair of options involve deciding to stop competing in the market or product area of the business. A multiproduct firm may conclude that it is most likely to achieve the goals of its mission if the business is dropped through divestiture. This grand strategy not only eliminates a drain on resources but also may provide funds to promote other business activities. As an option of last resort, a firm may decide to liquidate the business. This means that the business cannot be sold as a going concern and is at best worth only the value of its tangible assets. The decision to liquidate is an undeniable admission of failure by a firm's strategic management and, thus, often is delayed—to the further detriment of the firm.

Strategic managers tend to resist divestiture because it is likely to jeopardize their control of the firm and perhaps even their jobs. Thus, by the time the desirability of divestiture is acknowledged, businesses often deteriorate to the point of failing to attract potential buyers. The consequences of such delays are financially disastrous for firm owners because the value of a going concern is many times greater than the value of its assets.

Strategic managers who have a business in quadrant III and expect a continuation of slow market growth and a relatively weak competitive position will usually attempt to decrease their resource commitment to that business. Minimal withdrawal is accomplished through retrenchment; this strategy has the side benefits of making resources available for other investments and of motivating employees to increase their operating efficiency. An alternative approach is to divert resources for expansion through investment in other businesses. This approach typically involves either concentric or conglomerate diversification because the firm usually wants to enter more promising arenas of competition than integration or concentrated growth strategies would allow. The final options for quadrant III businesses are divestiture, if an optimistic buyer can be found, and liquidation.

Quadrant IV businesses (strong competitive position in a slow-growth market) have a basis of strength from which to diversify into more promising growth areas. These businesses have characteristically high cash flow levels and limited internal growth needs. Thus, they are in an excellent position for concentric diversification into ventures that utilize their proven acumen. A second option is conglomerate diversification, which spreads investment risk and does not divert managerial attention from the present business. The final option is joint ventures, which are especially attractive to multinational firms. Through joint ventures, a domestic business can gain competitive advantages in promising new fields while exposing itself to limited risks.

Opportunities for Building Value as a Basis for Choosing Diversification or Integration

The grand strategy selection matrix or the model of grand strategy clusters are useful tools to help dominant product company managers evaluate and narrow their choices among alternative grand strategies. When considering grand strategies that would broaden the scope of their company's business activities through integration, diversification, or joint venture strategies, managers must examine whether opportunities to build value are present. Opportunities to build value via diversification, integration, or joint venture strategies are usually found in market-related, operating-related, and management activities. Such opportunities center around reducing costs, improving margins, or providing access to new revenue sources more cost effectively than traditional internal growth options via concentration, market development, or product development. Major opportunities for sharing and value building as well as ways to capitalize on core competencies are outlined in the next section about strategic analysis and choice in diversified companies.

Dominant product company managers who choose diversification or integration eventually create another management challenge. That challenge is charting the future of a company that becomes a collection of several distinct businesses. These distinct businesses often encounter different competitive environments, challenges, and opportunities. The next chapter examines ways managers of such diversified companies attempt to evaluate and choose corporate strategy. Central to their challenge is the continued desire to build value, particularly shareholder value.

SUMMARY

This chapter examined how managers in businesses that have a single or dominant product or service evaluate and choose their company's strategy. Two critical areas deserve their attention: first, their business's value chain; second, the appropriateness of 12 different grand strategies based on matching environmental factors with internal capabilities.

Managers in single-product-line business units examine their business's value chain to identify existing or potential activities around which they can create sustainable competitive advantages. As managers scrutinize their value chain activities, they are looking for three sources of competitive advantage: low cost, differentiation, and rapid response capabilities. They also examine whether focusing on a narrow market niche provides a more effective, sustainable way to build or leverage these three sources of competitive advantage.

Managers in single or dominant product/service businesses face two interrelated issues. First, they must choose which grand strategies make best use of their competitive advantages. Second, they must ultimately decide whether to diversify their business activity. Twelve grand strategies were identified in this chapter along with three frameworks that aid managers to choose which grand strategies should work best and when diversification or integration should be the best strategy for the business. The next chapter expands the coverage of diversification to look at how multibusiness companies evaluate continued diversification and how they construct corporate strategy.

QUESTIONS FOR DISCUSSION

1. Explain/illustrate how a business can build low-cost competitive advantages? Differentiation? Speed?
2. Is it better to concentrate on one type of competitive advantage or to nurture all three?
3. How does market focus help a business create any competitive advantage?
4. Select three grand strategies. Under what circumstances would you recommend one and not the other two for a business to pursue?

BIBLIOGRAPHY

Allaire, Yvon, and Michaela E. Firsirotu. "Coping with Strategic Uncertainty." *Sloan Management Review*, Spring 1987, p. 7.

Barwise, Patrick; Paul R. Marsh; and Robin Wensley. "Must Finance and Strategy Clash?" *Harvard Business Review*, September–October 1989, p. 85.

Berman, S. J., and R. F. Kautz. "Complete! A Sophisticated Tool That Facilitates Strategic Analysis." *Planning Review* 18 no. 4 (1990) pp. 35–39.

Bitner, Larry N., and Judith D. Powell. "Expansion Planning for Small Retail Firms." *Journal of Small Business Management*, April 1987, p. 47.

Chaganti, Rajeswararao, and Vijay Mahajan. "Portfolio Small Business Strategies under Different Types of Competition." *Entrepreneurship: Theory and Practice*, Spring 1989, p. 21.

Cravens, David W. "Gaining Strategic Marketing Advantage." *Business Horizons*, September–October 1988, p. 44.

Dess, Gregory G., and Nancy K. Orizer. "Environment, Structure, and Consensus in Strategy Formulation." *Academy of Management Review*, April 1987, p. 313.

Dodge, H. R.; S. Fullerton; and J. E. Robbins. "Stage of the Organizational Life Cycle and Competition as Mediators of Problem Perceptions for Small Businesses." *Strategic Management Journal* 15 (1994), pp. 121–34.

Eisenhardt, K. M. "Speed and Strategic Choice: How Managers Accelerate Decision Making." *California Management Review* 32, no. 3 (1990), pp. 39-54.

Eynn, P. J. "Avoid the Seven Deadly Sins of Strategic Risk Analysis." *Journal of Business Strategy*, September 1988, pp. 18–23.

Farnham, A. "America's Most Admired Companies." *Fortune*, February 7, 1994, pp. 50–62.

Fulmer, William E., and Jack Goodwin. "Differentiation: Begin with the Consumer." *Business Horizons*, September–October 1988, p. 55.

Govindarajan, Vijay. "A Contingency Approach to Strategy Selection at the Business Unit Level." *Academy of Management Journal*, December 1988, p. 828.

Hamilton, W. F.; J. Vila; and M. D. Dibner. "Patterns of Strategic Choice in Emerging Firms." *California Management Review* 32, no. 3 (1990), pp. 73–86.

Jones, T., and G. Seiler. "The Rapidly Growing Pump Company: Marketing for Competitive Advantage." *Planning Review*, May–June 1988, pp. 30–35.

Kelly, K. "Suddenly, Big Airlines Are Saying: 'Small Is Beautiful.' " *Business Week*, January 1994, p. 37.

Kennedy, C. "Planning Global Strategies for 3M." *Long Range Planning*, February 1988, pp. 9–17.

Krubasik, E. G. "Customize Your Product Development." *Harvard Business Review*, September–October 1988, pp. 46–53.

Lado, A. A.; N. G. Boyd; and P. Wright. "A Competency-Based Model of Sustainable Competitive Advantage: Toward a Conceptual Integration." *Journal of Management* 18, no. 1 (1992), pp. 77–91.

Mason, David H., and Robert G. Wilson. "Future-Mapping: A New Approach to Managing Strategic Uncertainty." *Planning Review*, May–June 1987, p. 20.

McConkey, Dale D. "Planning in a Changing Environment." *Business Horizons*, September–October 1988, p. 64.

Pelham, A. M., and D. E. Clayson. "Receptivity to Strategic Planning Tools." *Journal of Small Business Management*, January 1988, pp. 43–50.

Rudnitsky, H. "The King of Off-Price." *Forbes*, January 31, 1994, pp. 54–55.

Schofield, M., and D. Arnold. "Strategies for Mature Businesses." *Long Range Planning*, October 1988, p. 69–76.

Schrage, Michael. "A Japanese Firm Rethinks Globalization: Interview with Yoshihisa Tabuchi." *Harvard Business Review*, July–August 1989, p. 70.

Sfiligh, E. "Ice Beers Give Stroh Another Excuse to Keep Coming Out With New Brews." *Beverage World*, January 31, 1994, p. 3.

Stalk, G. "Time—The Next Source of Competitive Advantage." *Harvard Business Review*, July–August 1988, pp. 41–53.

———.; P. Evans; and L. E. Shulman. "Competing on Capabilities: The New Rules of Corporate Strategy." *Harvard Business Review* 70, no. 2 (1992), pp. 57–69.

Ulrich David. "Tie the Corporate Knot: Gaining Complete Customer Commitment." *Sloan Management Review*, Summer 1987, p. 139.

Varadarajan, P. R. "Product Portfolio Analysis and Market Share Objectives: An Exposition of Certain Underlying Relationships." *Journal of the Academy of Marketing Science* 18, no. 1 (1990), pp. 17–29.

———.; T. Clark; and W. M. Pride. "Controlling the Uncontrollable: Managing Your Market Environment." *Sloan Management Review* 33, no. 2 (1992), pp. 39–47.

Watts, L. R. "Degrees of Entrepreneurship and Small Firm Planning." *Journal of Business and Entrepreneurship* 2, no. 2 (1992), pp. 59–67.

CHAPTER 8 COHESION CASE ILLUSTRATION

BUILDING SUSTAINABLE COMPETITIVE ADVANTAGES AT COCA-COLA

Strategic analysis and choice at Coca-Cola in the 1990s has centered around how to build sustainable competitive advantages that create long-term shareholder value. Coca-Cola managers have emphasized differentiation, rapid response, and market focus competitive advantages during this time. Chief Executive Officer Roberto Goizueta likes to talk about these three sources of competitive advantage in terms of four key themes that define Coca-Cola's business strategy for the 1990s:

> Since 1984, we have changed ourselves dramatically, a fact made obvious as our market value has climbed from $8 billion to nearly $66 billion. With a clear eye on the long run, we have deliberately assembled and fine-tuned a global machine capable of sustaining strong, profitable growth well into the next century. That assembly process continues today, but thus far, it can be characterized by these major initiatives: 1. Geographic expansion, 2. Financial reformation, 3. Infrastructure fortification, and 4. Consumer marketing.

Geographic Expansion

Refusing to neglect any territory anywhere in the world, we have long pursued geographic expansion as a fundamental means of growth. Through our own persistence, the end of the Cold War and the fundamental transformations of many important local economies, we have more than doubled since 1980 the number of potential consumers truly within our reach.

This has not been rocket science, just good, common business sense. After all, we market a brand with a uniquely universal appeal, and we have not entered a single new market where we did not benefit from a substantial existing demand for Coca-Cola.

Financial Reformation

We also began to capitalize on another significant resource: the naturally strong cash flow of our business. By the early 1980s, the financial prudence that protected our Company so well earlier in the century had ossified, effectively trapping a live organism within the hard constrictions of its own fossil shell.

One by one, we began taking important steps to reform our financial policies. We also shifted our focus to new, clearly superior measurements of our performance. We now evaluate our business units and opportunities based primarily on their ability to generate attractive economic profit, not just growth in revenues or earnings. We define economic profit as net operating profit after taxes, less a charge for the average cost of the capital employed to produce that profit.

Infrastructure Fortification

As we were moving ahead with geographic expansion and financial reformation, we began a third, complementary thrust. We began using our financial resources to fortify our global bottling network, taking a global distribution system that was already the world's most widespread and making it also the world's strongest and most efficient.

The methods we used varied. Some were as simple as encouraging the sale of bottling companies to owners who shared our prejudice for action and heavy reinvestment. Others involved injecting equity capital and management expertise in bottlers eager to have our participation. And still others were as complex as helping create the largest soft drink bottling company in the world, Coca-Cola Enterprises Inc.

Consumer Marketing

To drive that demand, we are taking the decisive actions that will effectively make us the world's premier consumer marketing company.

Some people tell us we're already there. After all, they would argue, wouldn't the company that has built the world's best-known and most admired brand also have to be the world's premier marketing organization?

Others would debate it, because there are a number of truly great marketing companies around the world.

To be perfectly honest, we don't care one way or the other what people say today. We simply intend to keep taking all the actions that will make our consumer marketing leadership undeniable tomorrow.

That's a bold proposition, and we know it. But we also know our success in generating value for you is largely tied to our ability to turn that proposition into reality.

When you think about it, any company can grow by expanding geographically and entering new markets. Only the best companies—the companies most worthy of your investment—can grow by building their businesses in their most developed markets.

For us, that means being able to generate solid growth in markets such as the United States, Japan, Western Europe, Mexico and Brazil. In 1994, we clearly showed that we can do just that.

We were able to do it because, while we continued to expand our brands *horizontally* across new geography in the Chinas and Indias of the world, we were also building our brands *vertically* in our established markets.

Building brands vertically means continually building new value into those brands, giving the people who buy your products more reasons to buy them than ever before. That task is particularly daunting when the brand you are building is already the world's most powerful.

How do we find new ways to make the world's most powerful brand even more powerful? How do we make that brand generate increased sales volume in a market like the United States, where, on average, every person is coming increasingly closer to consuming one of our products *every day*?

Through differentiation.

Differentiation

If the three keys to selling real estate are location, location, location, then the three keys to selling consumer products are differentiation, differentiation, differentiation. In recent years, whether it's product quality, packaging, advertising or any other element of the brand, our aim is to enhance the uniqueness of Coca-Cola by continuously making it different, better and special, relative to every possible competitor.

By further differentiating ourselves with consumers, we also further differentiated ourselves with our highly valued customers, adding value to their businesses with reliable sales growth, effective service and superior profitability.

And ultimately, by differentiating ourselves in the consumer marketplace, we were also able to differentiate ourselves in the investment marketplace, outperforming most other comparable investments while significantly enhancing the value of our Company.

In contrast, those who continued to rely on pricing as their *only* point of distinctiveness met with difficult times, on both Main Street and Wall Street. In a highly competitive environment for the consumer dollar and the investment dollar, we believe the failure to differentiate brands in *every* aspect of marketing eventually erodes the value of both the brand and the investment.

We will not allow ourselves to fall into that trap.

Market Focus

In sports, coaches can only be as good as their players. In business, the same holds true, as managers can only be as good as their businesses. Eager to be worthy managers of your investment, we purposefully narrowed our lines of business to those that would inherently make us shine. Today, we operate as an enterprise focused almost entirely on a soft drink concentrate business that consistently generates returns nearly three times greater than our average cost of capital. That core business is augmented by our selective holdings in key bottling operations around the world, and nicely complemented by Coca-Cola Foods, a solid long-term performer.

If you refer back to Figures 8–2, 8–3, and 8–4, the skills and resources required to support differentiation, rapid response, and market focus appear to be consistent with the resources available to Coke. Its decision to employ differentiation is easily apparent to any consumer. Its choice of market focus—beverages worldwide—leverages its increasing global presence and power. Rapid response through unmatched inbound and outbound logistics is supported and reinforced through its continued investment in infrastructure.

Another way to visualize strategic analysis and choice at Coke centers around the basic notion that strategists seek strategy alternatives offering a strong "fit" with a firm's overall situation. Two approaches—the grand strategy selection matrix and the model of grand strategy clusters—suggest sets of strategic alternatives associated with different strategic situations. Applying the first approach, Coca-Cola has long been in the situation of maximizing several strengths, while also preferring to emphasize "internally" generated growth. The grand strategy selection matrix would suggest concentrated growth, market development, product development, and innovation. These strategies are just what Coca-Cola has emphasized in its core soft-drink business, which it has returned to even more in the 1990s. Coke seeks first to hold and expand current market positions; then expand into new, particularly international as well as previously underemphasized outlets (e.g., restaurants, airlines); and also gradually add new product versions or those preferred in key local markets.

At the same time, Coca-Cola's management watched with some apprehension during the late 1970s as Pepsi's increasingly concentrated bottling network was out-distributing and out-marketing Coke's independent (franchised) bottlers in many local domestic markets. Pepsi's fewer, newer, and larger franchise bottlers were able to bring extra resources and professional management of marketing activities to bear in markets where they competed with smaller and usually older family-business franchises of Coca-Cola in the United States and in selected European countries. Applying the grand strategy selection matrix to overcome this relative "weakness," Coca-Cola had to look outside the company (externally) toward its existing bottling franchise network and seek to overcome a critical weakness—a situation wherein the matrix suggests a vertical integration strategy. Coca-Cola's analysis and choice reached the same conclusion—integrate forward into soft-drink bottling. To pursue this capital-intensive strategy, Coke decided to sell Columbia Pictures (net $1.3 billion) as well as create and take Coca-Cola Enterprises (CCE—a bottling franchise company) public to raise another source of funds. Coke remained a 49 percent owner and used CCE to buy old Coke bottling franchises in the United States and abroad so it could create bigger, more modern, and aggressive distributors-marketers of Coca-Cola's soft drinks in each local market. This allowed Coke to neutralize Pepsi's previous advantage in key markets.

The model of grand strategy clusters would focus on the market growth and strength of Coke's competitive position. The conclusion suggested by that model as portrayed in Figure 8–5 would have Coca-Cola's management following concentrated growth (includes market and product development), vertical integration, and, perhaps, concentric diversification when the success of the other strategies starts to fade. Indeed, this set of grand strategies is very similar to those suggested by the model of grand strategy clusters and appears to be the basic grand strategies Coca-Cola's management has charted toward the 21st century.

9 STRATEGIC ANALYSIS AND CHOICE IN THE MULTIBUSINESS COMPANY: RATIONALIZING DIVERSIFICATION AND BUILDING SHAREHOLDER VALUE

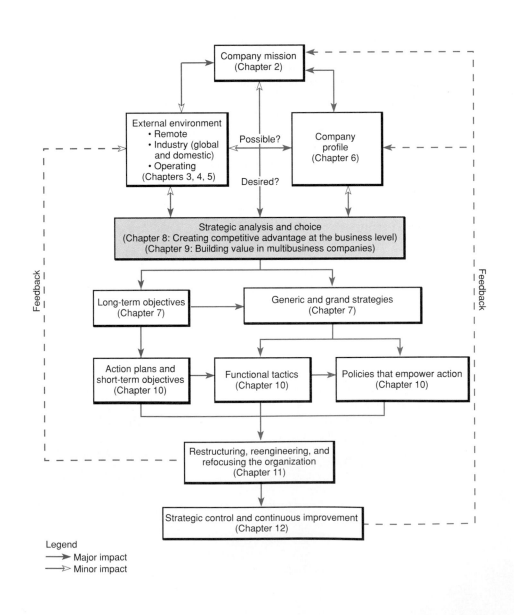

Legend
⟶ Major impact
⟶▷ Minor impact

Strategic analysis and choice is more complicated for corporate-level managers because they must create a strategy to guide a company that contains numerous businesses. They must examine and choose which businesses to own and which ones to forgo or divest. They must consider business managers' plans to capture competitive advantage, and then decide how to allocate resources among businesses as part of this phase. This chapter will first examine diversified, multibusiness companies. Specifically, how should the diversified business build shareholder value? For example, MCI has decided to pursue an aggressive diversification program to expand its presence in a variety of different industries; AT&T has recently decided to split into three separate companies while divesting itself of other businesses. Why?

A final topic that is important to an understanding of strategic analysis and choice in business organization is the "nonbusiness," behavioral factors that often exert a major influence on strategic decisions. This is true in the single-product business as well as the multibusiness company. What behavioral considerations often influence how managers analyze strategic options and make strategic choices? For example, J. E. Schrempp became CEO of Germany's Daimler Benz in mid-1995 as planned, having taken over from his mentor, Edzard Reuter, with whom he had charted a steady 10-year diversification to build a $74 billion company. Three months later, Schrempp reversed the strategy to break up the company, focus on core businesses, and reconstruct a new management team. How could such a dramatic, sudden shift take place? Answering that question requires you to consider behavioral factors as well as strategic issues at Daimler Benz.

RATIONALIZING DIVERSIFICATION AND INTEGRATION

When a single- or dominant-business company is transformed into a collection of numerous businesses across several industries, strategic analysis becomes more complex. Managers must deal not only with each business's strategic situation, they must set forth a corporate strategy that rationalizes the collection of businesses they have amassed. Two key audiences are listening. First, managers within the organization want to understand their role and access to resources relative to other businesses within the company. Second, and of greatest importance, stockholders deserve to understand how this collection of businesses is expected to build shareholder value over the long term more effectively than simply investing in separate businesses. In a sense the question is: "Are there compelling reasons why corporate management is better able to invest shareholder value in a variety of other businesses versus allowing shareholders to make that decision themselves?"

Stockholder value in a diversified company is ultimately determined by how well its various businesses perform and/or how compelling potential synergies and opportunities appear to be. Business-level performance is enhanced by sustained competitive advantages. Wise diversification has at its core the search for ways to build value and sustained competitive advantage across multiple business units. We saw several ways opportunities for sharing and building value may be present across different businesses. The bottom line is that diversification that shares skills and core competencies across multiple businesses to strengthen value chains and build competitive advantage enhances shareholder value. And so it is that strategic analysis and choice for corporate managers overseeing multibusiness companies involves determining whether their portfolio of business units is capturing the synergies they intended, how to respond accordingly, and choosing among future diversification or divestiture options. Managers address the following four basic questions to do this.

FIGURE 9–1
Value Building in Multibusiness Companies

Opportunities to Build Value or Sharing	Potential Competitive Advantage	Impediments to Achieving Enhanced Value
Market-Related Opportunities:		
Shared sales force activities or shared sales office, or both.	Lower selling costs. Better market coverage. Stronger technical advice to buyers. Enhanced convenience for buyers (can buy from single source). Improved access to buyers (have more products to sell).	• Buyers have different purchasing habits toward the products. • Different salespersons are more effective in representing the product. • Some products get more attention than others. • Buyers prefer to multiple-source rather than single-source their purchases.
Shared after-sale service and repair work.	Lower servicing costs. Better utilization of service personnel (less idle time). Faster servicing of customer calls.	• Different equipment or different labor skills, or both, are needed to handle repairs. • Buyers may do some in-house repairs.
Shared brand name.	Stronger brand image and company reputation. Increased buyer confidence in the brand.	• Company reputation is hurt if quality of one product is lower.
Shared advertising and promotional activities.	Lower costs. Greater clout in purchasing ads.	• Appropriate forms of messages are different. • Appropriate timing of promotions is different.
Common distribution channels.	Lower distribution costs. Enhanced bargaining power with distributors and retailers to gain shelf space, shelf positioning, stronger push and more dealer attention, and better profit margins.	• Dealers resist being dominated by a single supplier and turn to multiple sources and lines. • Heavy use of the shared channel erodes willingness of other channels to carry or push the firm's products.
Shared order processing.	Lower order processing costs. One-stop shopping for buyer enhances service and, thus, differentiation.	• Differences in ordering cycles disrupt order processing economies.

Are Opportunities for Sharing Infrastructure and Capabilities Forthcoming?

Opportunities to build value via diversification, integration, or joint venture strategies are usually found in market-related, operating-related, and management activities. Each business's basic value chain activities or infrastructure become a source of potential synergy and competitive advantage for another business in the corporate portfolio. Morrison's Cafeteria, long a mainstay in U.S. food services markets, rapidly accelerated its diversification into other restaurant concepts like Ruby Tuesdays. Numerous opportunities for shared operating capabilities and management capabilities drove this decision and, upon repeated strategic analysis, has accelerated corporate managers to move Morrison's totally out of the cafeteria segment by 1999. Some of the more common opportunities to share value chain activities and build value are identified in Figure 9–1.

Strategic analysis is concerned with whether or not the potential competitive advantages expected to arise from each value opportunity have materialized. Where advantage has not materialized, corporate strategists must take care to scrutinize possible impediments to achieving the synergy or competitive advantage. We have identified in Figure 9–1 several impediments associated with each opportunity, which strategists are well advised to examine. Good strategists assure themselves that their organization has ways to avoid or

FIGURE 9–1
concluded

Opportunities to Build Value or Sharing	Potential Competitive Advantage	Impediments to Achieving Enhanced Value
Operating Opportunities:		
Joint procurement of purchased inputs.	Lower input costs. Improved input quality. Improved service from suppliers.	• Input needs are different in terms of quality or other specifications. • Inputs are needed at different plant locations, and centralized purchasing is not responsive to separate needs of each plant.
Shared manufacturing and assembly facilities.	Lower manufacturing/assembly costs. Better capacity utilization, because peak demand for one product correlates with valley demand for other. Bigger scale of operation improves access to better technology and results in better quality.	• Higher changeover costs in shifting from one product to another. • High-cost special tooling or equipment is required to accommodate quality differences or design differences.
Shared inbound or outbound shipping and materials handling.	Lower freight and handling costs. Better delivery reliability. More frequent deliveries, such that inventory costs are reduced.	• Input sources or plant locations, or both, are in different geographic areas. • Needs for frequency and reliability of inbound/outbound delivery differ among the business units.
Shared product and process technologies or technology development or both.	Lower product or process design costs, or both, because of shorter design times and transfers of knowledge from area to area. More innovative ability, owing to scale of effort and attraction of better R&D personnel.	• Technologies are the same, but the applications in different business units are different enough to prevent much sharing of real value.
Shared administrative support activities.	Lower administrative and operating overhead costs.	• Support activities are not a large proportion of cost, and sharing has little cost impact (and virtually no differentiation impact).
Management Opportunities:		
Shared management know-how, operating skills, and proprietary information.	Efficient transfer of a distinctive competence—can create cost savings or enhance differentiation. More effective management as concerns strategy formulation, strategy implementation, and understanding of key success factors.	• Actual transfer of know-how is costly or stretches the key skill personnel too thinly, or both. • Increased risks that proprietary information will leak out.

Source: Adapted with the permission of The Free Press, a Division of Simon and Schuster, from *Competitive Advantage: Creating and Sustaining Superior Performance,* by Michael E. Porter. Copyright © 1985 by Michael E. Porter.

minimize the impact of any impediments or they recommend against further integration or diversification and consider divestiture options.

Two elements are critical in meaningful shared opportunities. First, the shared opportunities must be a significant portion of the value chain of the businesses involved. Returning to Morrison's Cafeteria, its purchasing and inbound logistics infrastructure give Ruby Tuesday's operators an immediate cost-effective purchasing and inventory management capability that lowered its cost in a significant cost activity. Second, the businesses involved must truly have shared needs—need for the same activity—or there is no basis for synergy in the first place. Novell, the U.S.-based networking software giant, paid $900 million for WordPerfect in late 1994, envisioning numerous synergies serving offices

GLOBAL
STRATEGY IN
ACTION 9–1

DAIMLER'S DIVERSIFICATION DILEMMA

Inspired by the success of General Electric in the United States, where a dull electrical firm was turned into a successful diversified group by the drive and deal-making of Jack Welch, Edzard Reuter at Daimler Benz thought he could do the same by accelerating from luxury cars into aerospace and transport equipment. The early 1990s saw Germany's biggest company handing out a glossy document called *The New Age* in which Reuter boasted that he had transformed the firm from a luxury car maker into an "integrated technology group" involved in aerospace, microelectronics, and many kinds of transportation.

With a sense of conquest and closure, Reuter boasted of returning the company to profitability in 1994 ($DM 750 million on $DM 74 billion in diversified sales) as he predicted higher profits for 1995 and turned over the reins of the company to his heir-apparent of 10 years, Jurgen Schrempp. Three months into 1995, Daimler Benz was in disarray.

The soaring German mark, management disputes, and losses from Reuter's diversification strategy were causing analysts to turn negative on the company as Schrempp reversed Reuter's parting forecast and warned of severe 1995 losses by year-end ($DM 1.6 billion by mid-year).

By late 1995 analysts were saying that Schrempp had to act quickly and dismantle and reverse the diversification strategy his mentor, with Schrempp's help, had spent the previous 10 years implementing. Here were some of the recommendations analysts were making:

1. Make a decisive break with the failed diversification strategy.
2. Focus on the core automotive and truck business, which provides most of the profit anyway.
3. Close the money-losing Daimler Benz Industrie unit; sell off or transfer profitable operations.
4. Downsize Daimler Benz Aerospace by cutting its work force of 40,000 to 20,000 and accelerate outsourcing of parts from weak-currency areas. Consider divesting.
5. Accelerate globalization of manufacturing by locating big-ticket plants outside Germany.

Bottom line, analysts do not think the synergies originally expected in Reuter's diversification have occurred. Daimler's stock price, down 30 percent during Reuter's reign, doesn't compare with BMW's 50 percent increase.

Schrempp's remarks to the financial press during this uncertain time in late 1995 continued to publicly defend Reuter's strategy; however, he has begun to distance himself a bit by talking about strengthening Daimler as an "integrated transportation company" rather than the "integrated high-tech concern" as Reuter did.

Now it is your turn. What do you think he should have done? What do you suspect he has done since late 1995? Did diversification make sense or were the analysts right? Look up Daimler's stock price on the German DAX or the NYSE and read an article about Daimler Benz to see what Schrempp has done.

Sources: "A Tale of Two Conglomerates," *The Economist*, November 18, 1995, p. 20; "Dismantling Daimler Benz," *The Economist*, November 18, 1995, pp. 67–68, 77–78; "Failed Diversification," *German Brief*, April 8, 1994, pp. 4–5; and "There's Virtue in Diversification," *Euromoney*, November 1994, pp. 70–71.

globally not to mention 15 million WordPerfect users. By late 1995 Novell would sell WordPerfect for less than $300 million, because, as new CEO Bob Frankenberg said, "It is not because WordPerfect is not a business without a future, but for Novell it represented a distraction from our strategy." Corporate strategies have repeatedly rushed into diversification only to find perceived opportunities for sharing were nonexistent because the businesses did not really have shared needs. Global Strategy in Action 9–1 examines just this dilemma at Germany's Daimler Benz.

Are We Capitalizing on Our Core Competencies?

Perhaps the most compelling reason companies should diversify can be found in situations where core competencies—key value-building skills—can be leveraged with other products or into markets that are not a part of where they were created. Where this works well, extraordinary value can be built. Managers undertaking diversification strategies should dedicate a significant portion of their strategic analysis to this question.

General Cinema was a company that grew from drive-in theaters to eventually dominate the multicinema, movie exhibition industry. Next, they entered soft-drink bottling and became the largest bottler of soft drinks (Pepsi) in North America. Their stock value rose 2,000 percent in 10 years. They found that core competencies in movie exhibition—managing many small, localized businesses; dealing with a few large suppliers; applying central marketing skills locally; and acquiring or crafting a "franchise"—were virtually the same in soft-drink bottling. Disney and ABC see shared core competencies as central in the entertainment industry of the 21st century (see Strategy in Action 9–1). AT&T and McCall Cellular see shared core competencies as central to telecommunications success. These and many more companies look to three basic considerations to evaluate whether they are capitalizing on core competencies.[1]

Is Each Core Competency Providing a Relevant Competitive Advantage to the Intended Businesses?

The core competency must assist the intended business in creating strength relative to key competition. This could occur at any step in the business's value chain. But it must represent a major source of value to be a basis for competitive advantage—and the core competence must be transferrable. Honda of Japan viewed itself as having a core competence in manufacturing small, internal combustion engines. It diversified into small garden tools, perceiving that traditional electric tools would be much more attractive if powered by a lightweight, mobile, gas combustion motor. Their core competency created a major competitive advantage in a market void of gas-driven hand tools. When Coca-Cola added bottled water to its portfolio of products, it expected its extraordinary core competencies in marketing and distribution to rapidly build value in this business. Ten years later, Coke sold its water assets concluding that the product did not have enough margin to interest its franchised bottlers and that marketing was not a significant value-building activity among many small suppliers competing primarily on the cost of "producing" and shipping water.

Are Businesses in the Portfolio Related in Ways That Make the Company's Core Competence(s) Beneficial?

Earlier, we described General Cinema's spectacular success in both movie exhibition and soft-drink bottling. Seemingly unrelated, their management found that core competencies in various aspects of managing diverse business locations were key value chain components in both industries. So the products of various businesses do not necessarily have to be similar to leverage core competencies. While their products may not be related, it is essential that some activities in their value chains require similar skills to create competitive advantage if the company is going to leverage its core competence(s) in a value-creating way.

---

[1] C. K. Prahalad and G. Hamel, "The Core Competence of the Corporation," *Harvard Business Review*, May–June 1990, pp. 79–91; and M. Porter, "From Competitive Advantage to Corporate Strategy," *Harvard Business Review*, May–June 1987, pp. 43–59.

DISNEY DEMONSTRATES THE ABC'S
OF DIVERSIFICATION

The recent acquisition of ABC/Capital Cities by Disney was the most visible merger among the many that took place in 1995 as the rapidly changing media industry continued its dramatic upheavals. It was the second largest corporate takeover ever done. Walt Disney and ABC/Capital Cities have joined their businesses, including the following.

	Walt Disney	ABC/Capital Cities
Production	Walt Disney Pictures Touchstone Pictures	ABC Productions
Distribution		11 company-owned TV stations 228 TV affiliates 21 radio stations
Cable	Disney Channel	ESPN, Lifetime, A&E
Publishing		Newspapers in 13 states Fairchild Publications Chilton Publications

Most analysts viewed the Disney-ABC merger favorably. Here is what they said shortly after the deal was done:

1. The combination of the two companies creates a sizable player that transforms the balance of power in the entertainment industry by becoming the industry's most influential player.
2. Recent rule changes will permit networks (like ABC) to own more of their own programming, enhancing their value and challenging outside suppliers (like Disney), leaving the suppliers fearful of less "shelf space" for their products.

Are Our Combination of Competencies Unique or Difficult to Recreate?

Skills that corporate strategists expect to transfer from one business to another, or from corporate to various businesses, may be transferrable. They may also be easily replicated by competitors. When this is the case, no sustainable competitive advantage is created. Sometimes strategists look for a combination of competencies, a package of various inter-related skills, as another way to create a situation where seemingly easily replicated competencies become unique, sustainable competitive advantages. 3M Corporation has the enviable record of having 25 percent of its earnings always coming from products introduced within the last five years. 3M has been able to "bundle" the skills necessary to accelerate the introduction of new products so that it consistently extracts early life cycle value from adhesive-related products that hundreds of competitors with similar technical or marketing competencies cannot touch.

Does the Company's Business Portfolio Balance Financial Resources?

Multibusiness companies usually find that their various businesses generate and consume very different levels of cash. Some generate more cash than they can use to maintain or expand their business while others consume more than they generate. Corporate managers

STRATEGY
IN ACTION   **continued**
9–1

3. The more forms of information delivery a company owns, the greater their power. Brands such as ABC and ESPN get people's attention.

4. "Content is king" was the traditional view attributing power to a studio like Disney; More recently distribution outlets have become key as demonstrated by Rupert Murdoch's Fox Network—many stations and satellite and cable channels to deliver product to viewers.

5. Eisner previously thought distribution was distasteful. Rupert Murdoch changed all of that. Cap Cities thrusts Disney into the distribution business in a big way. Eisner says it does more, since ABC produces and delivers programming over air and cable. And it provides a guaranteed platform for its first-run syndicated programs—shows that might otherwise die on the vine.

6. Financially, Disney takes on $10 billion in debt; however, it expects $5 billion annually in cash flow to quickly pay down the debt. Now Disney's growth can continue strongly like it has the last five years.

7. Disney has been weak internationally, but ABC has been strong. ESPN is well known. Disney can learn from ABC about developing foreign contacts and building distribution. In foreign markets, entertainment has become a leading U.S. export.

8. ABC is among the industry's best run. Disney reaps profits from all the shows the network airs, whether it produces them or not.

9. Disney has creative capabilities and a production track record second to none, which ABC can leverage.

face the very important challenge of determining the best way to generate and use financial resources among the businesses within their company. Faced with this challenge, managers historically looked to balance cash generators and cash users so that, along with outside capital sources, they can efficiently manage the cash flows across their business portfolio.

Responding to this challenge during the diversification explosion of the 1970s, the Boston Consulting Group pioneered an approach called *portfolio techniques* that attempted to help managers "balance" the flow of cash resources among their various businesses while also identifying their basic strategic purpose within the overall portfolio. Three of these techniques are reviewed here. Once reviewed, we will identify some of the problems with the portfolio approach that you should keep in mind when considering its use.

The BCG Growth-Share Matrix

Managers using the BCG matrix plotted each of the company's businesses according to market growth rate and relative competitive position. Market growth rate is the projected rate of sales growth for the market being served by a particular business. Usually measured as the percentage increase in a market's sales or unit volume over the two most recent years, this rate serves as an indicator of the relative attractiveness of the markets served by each business in the firm's portfolio of businesses. Relative competitive position usually is

FIGURE 9–2
The BCG Growth-Share Matrix

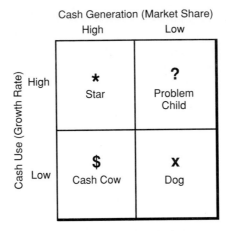

Cash Generation (Market Share)

High   Low

Cash Use (Growth Rate)

High

*
Star

?
Problem
Child

Low

$
Cash Cow

X
Dog

Description of Dimensions

Market Share: Sales relative to those of other competitors in the market
(dividing point is usually selected to have only the two–three largest
competitors in any market fall into the high market share region)

Growth Rate: Industry growth rate in constant dollars
(dividing point is typically the GNP's growth rate)

Source: The growth-share matrix was originally developed by the Boston Consulting Group.

expressed as the market share of a business divided by the market share of its largest competitor. Thus, relative competitive position provides a basis for comparing the relative strengths of the businesses in the firm's portfolio in terms of their positions in their respective markets. Figure 9–2 illustrates the growth-share matrix.

The *stars* are businesses in rapidly growing markets with large market shares. These businesses represent the best long-run opportunities (growth and profitability) in the firm's portfolio. They require substantial investment to maintain (and expand) their dominant position in a growing market. This investment requirement is often in excess of the funds that they can generate internally. Therefore, these businesses are often short-term, priority consumers of corporate resources.

Cash cows are businesses with a high market share in low-growth markets or industries. Because of their strong positions and their minimal reinvestment requirements, these businesses often generate cash in excess of their needs. Therefore, they are selectively "milked" as a source of corporate resources for deployment elsewhere (to stars and question marks). Cash cows are yesterday's stars and the current foundation of corporate portfolios. They provide the cash needed to pay corporate overhead and dividends and provide debt capacity. They are managed to maintain their strong market share while generating excess resources for corporatewide use.

Low market share and low market growth businesses are the *dogs* in the firm's portfolio. Facing mature markets with intense competition and low profit margins, they are managed for short-term cash flow (through ruthless cost cutting, for example) to supplement corporate-level resource needs. According to the original BCG prescription, they are divested or liquidated once this short-term harvesting has been maximized.

Question marks are businesses whose high growth rate gives them considerable appeal but whose low market share makes their profit potential uncertain. Question marks are cash guzzlers because their rapid growth results in high cash needs, while their small market share results in low cash generation. At the corporate level, the concern is to identify the question marks that would increase their market share and move into the star group if extra corporate resources were devoted to them. Where this long-run shift from question mark to star is unlikely, the BCG matrix suggests divesting the question mark and repositioning its resources more effectively in the remainder of the corporate portfolio.

The Industry Attractiveness–Business Strength Matrix

Corporate strategists found the growth-share matrix's singular axes limiting in their ability to reflect the complexity of a business's situation. Therefore, some companies adopted a matrix with a much broader focus. This matrix, developed by McKinsey & Company at General Electric, is called the Industry Attractiveness–Business Strength Matrix. This matrix, shown in Figure 9–4, uses multiple factors to assess industry attractiveness and business strength rather than the single measures (market share and market growth, respectively) employed in the BCG matrix. It also has nine cells as opposed to four—replacing the high/low axes with high/medium/low axes to make finer distinctions among business portfolio positions.

The company's businesses are rated on multiple strategic factors within each axis, such as the factors described in Figure 9–3.[2] The position of a business is then calculated by "subjectively" quantifying its rating along the two dimensions of the matrix. Depending on the location of a business within the matrix, one of the following strategic approaches is suggested: (1) invest to grow, (2) invest selectively and manage for earnings, or (3) harvest or divest for resources. The resource allocation decisions remain quite similar to those of the BCG approach.

Although the strategic recommendations generated by the Industry Attractiveness–Business Strength Matrix are similar to those generated by the BCG matrix, the Industry Attractiveness–Business Strength Matrix improves on the BCG matrix in three fundamental ways. First, the terminology associated with the Industry Attractiveness–Business Strength Matrix is preferable because it is less offensive and more understandable. Second, the multiple measures associated with each dimension of the business strength matrix tap many factors relevant to business strength and market attractiveness besides market share and market growth. And this, in turn, makes for broader assessment during the planning process, bringing to light considerations of importance in both strategy formulation and strategy implementation. Strategy in Action 9–2 illustrates the matrix approach as applied at Holiday Inns over the last 20 years.

The Life Cycle–Competitive Strength Matrix

One criticism of the first two portfolio methods was their static quality—their portrayal of businesses as they exist at one point in time, rather than as they evolve over time. A third portfolio approach was introduced that attempted to overcome these deficiencies and better identify "developing winners" or potential "losers."[3] This approach used the multiple-factor approach to assess competitive strength as one dimension and stage of the market life cycle as the other dimension.

---

[2] G. G. Dess and A. Miller, *Strategic Management* (New York: McGraw-Hill, 1993), pp. 110–11.

[3] Attributed to Arthur D. Little, a consulting firm, and to Charles W. Hofer in "Conceptual Constructs for Formulating Corporate and Business Strategies" (Boston: Harvard Case Services, #9-378-754, 1977).

FIGURE 9–3
Factors Considered in Constructing an Industry Attractiveness–Business Strength Matrix

Industry Attractiveness	Business Strength
Nature of Competitive Rivalry	**Cost Position**
Number of competitors	Economies of scale
Size of competitors	Manufacturing costs
Strength of competitors' corporate parents	Overhead
Price wars	Scrap/waste/rework
Competition on multiple dimensions	Experience effects
	Labor rates
Bargaining Power of Suppliers/Customers	Proprietary processes
Relative size of typical players	**Level of Differentiation**
Numbers of each	Promotion effectiveness
Importance of purchases from or sales to	Product quality
Ability to vertically integrate	Company image
	Patented products
Threat of Substitute Products/New Entrants	Brand awareness
Technological maturity/stability	**Response Time**
Diversity of the market	Manufacturing flexibility
Barriers to entry	Time needed to introduce new products
Flexibility of distribution system	Delivery times
	Organizational flexibility
Economic Factors	
Sales volatility	**Financial Strength**
Cyclicality of demand	Solvency
Market growth	Liquidity
Capital intensity	Break-even point
	Cash flows
Financial Norms	Profitability
Average profitability	Growth in revenues
Typical leverage	
Credit practices	**Human Assets**
	Turnover
Sociopolitical Considerations	Skill level
Government regulation	Relative wage/salary
Community support	Morale
Ethical standards	Managerial commitment
	Unionization
	Public Approval
	Goodwill
	Reputation
	Image

The life cycle dimension allowed users to consider multiple strategic issues associated with each life cycle stage (refer to the discussion in Chapter 6), thereby enriching the discussion of strategic options. It also gave a "moving indication" of both issues—those strategy needs to address currently and those that could arise next. Figure 9–5 on page 291 provides an illustration of this matrix. It includes basic strategic investment parameters recommended for different positions in the matrix. While this approach seems valuable, its recommendations are virtually identical to the previous two portfolio matrices.

Limitations of Portfolio Approaches

Portfolio approaches made several contributions to strategic analysis by corporate managers convinced of their ability to transfer the competitive advantage of professional management across a broad array of businesses. They helped convey large amounts of information about diverse business units and corporate plans in a greatly simplified format. They

FIGURE 9–4
The Industry Attractiveness–Business Strength Matrix

Industry Attractiveness

	High	Medium	Low
High	Invest	Selective Growth	Grow or Let Go
Medium	Selective Growth	Grow or Let Go	Harvest
Low	Grow or Let Go	Harvest	Divest

(Row labels on left axis: Business Strength)

Description of Dimensions

Industry Attractiveness: Subjective assessment based on broadest possible range of external opportunities and threats beyond the strict control of management

Business Strength: Subjective assessment of how strong a competitive advantage is created by a broad range of the firm's internal strengths and weaknesses.

Source: McKinsey & Company and General Electric.

illuminated similarities and differences between business units and helped convey the logic behind corporate strategies for each business with a common vocabulary. They simplified priorities for sharing corporate resources across diverse business units that generated and used those resources. They provided a simple prescription that gave corporate managers a sense of what they should accomplish—a balanced portfolio of businesses—and a way to control and allocate resources among them. While these approaches offered meaningful contributions, they had several critical limitations and shortcomings:

· A key problem with the portfolio matrix was that it did not address how value was being created across business units—the only relationship between them was cash. Because of this, its valued simplicity encouraged a tendency to trivialize strategic thinking among users that did not take proper time for thorough underlying analysis.

· Truly accurate measurement for matrix classification was not as easy as the matrices portrayed. Identifying individual businesses, or distinct markets, was not often as precise as underlying assumptions required.

· The underlying assumption about the relationship between market share and profitability—the experience curve effect—varied across different industries and

FROM HOLIDAY INNS TO HOLIDAY CORPORATION TO THE PROMUS COMPANIES: A STORY OF CORPORATE PORTFOLIO MANAGEMENT

In 1952, Kemmons Wilson started Holiday Inns to meet what he perceived to be a glaring need for affordable, consistent lodging throughout the United States and ultimately the world. Extraordinarily successful, Holiday Inns became and still is the largest lodging chain in the world, with three times the number of rooms as its nearest competitor. While this story generally is known to most of us, the fact Holiday Inns became a portfolio of businesses that has changed dramatically over the last 20 years is not. Following this latter story is an interesting journey in the application of corporate portfolio analysis.

By 1977, its 25th year, Holiday Inns Corporation was seen as a travel-related company, with several businesses Kemmons Wilson viewed as strategically related. The corporate portfolio looked as follows:

1977: Holiday Inn Corporation

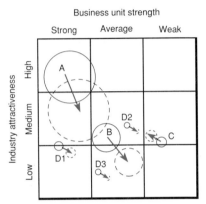

	Revenue	Operating Income
A. Holiday Inns	$590 mm	$90 mm
B. Trailways Bus Lines	244 mm	16 mm
C. Delta Steamships	80 mm	17 mm
D. Products Group: 1. InnKeepers Supply 2. Dohrmann 3. Innkare	144 mm	6 mm

Over the next five years, Kemmons Wilson would step down to be replaced by his long-time vice chairman and COO, Roy Winegardner. Holiday Inns' board, spurred by their young president, Mike Rose, began to view Holiday Inns as a portfolio of businesses needing significant change. Acting consistently with the strategic suggestions arising from the above portfolio analysis, Trailways, Delta, and the Products Group were divested, raising approximately $280 million. That money, along with new stock and debt, was used to reposition Holiday Inns as a "hospitality company" by acquiring Harrah's and Perkins Restaurants and by seeding two new hospitality ventures.

Source: Holiday Inns Corporation 1977 annual report; Holiday Corporation 1983 annual report; The Promus Companies 1995 annual report.

market segments. Some have no such link. Some find that firms with low market share can generate superior profitability with differentiation advantages.

· The limited strategic options, intended to describe the flow of resources in a company, came to be seen more as basic strategic missions. Doing this creates a false sense of what strategies were when none really existed. This becomes more acute when attempting to use the matrices to conceive strategies for average businesses in average growth markets.

· The portfolio approach portrayed the notion that firms needed to be self-sufficient in capital. This ignored capital raised in capital markets.

STRATEGY
IN ACTION   **continued**
9–2

1983: Holiday Corporation

	Revenue	Operating Income

A. Hotel Group:
  1. Holiday Inns
  2. Holiday Inn Crowne Plaza
	$882 mm	$168 mm

B. Gaming Group:
  1. Harrah's Nevada
  2. Harrah's Atlantic City
	592 mm	116 mm

C. Perkins Restaurants	106 mm	5 mm

D. New Ventures:
  1. Hampton Inns
  2. Embassy Suites
	0	–8 mm

Mike Rose soon became chairman and CEO of what in 1983 was renamed Holiday Corporation. He offered these observations at the time:

> We have completed the divestiture of our nonhospitality businesses. The major story for 1983 and the remainder of the decade is execution of our segmentation strategy in the hotel industry and in the casino gaming markets.

What Mr. Rose had done was to restructure Holiday's business portfolio, diverting resources from weak or inconsistent businesses into those with greater future promise. The real question beginning to arise via portfolio analysis was the long-term status of the Holiday Inns chain with its segment, midpriced hotel accommodations, facing increased competition and less demand. By 1992, dramatic change had occurred again.

· The portfolio approach typically failed to compare the competitive advantage a business received from being owned by a particular company with the costs of owning it. The 1980s saw many companies build enormous corporate infrastructures that created only small gains at the business level. The deconstruction in the 1990s of some "model" portfolio companies reflects this important omission.

Constructing business portfolio matrices must be undertaken with these limitations in mind. Perhaps it is best to say that they provide one form of input to corporate managers seeking to balance financial resources. They should be used merely to provide a basis for further discussion of corporate strategy and the allocation of corporate resources, and to

STRATEGY IN ACTION 9–2   **continued**

1994: The Promus Companies

	Revenue	Operating Income
A. Gaming Group:	$1.1 billion	$210 mm
1. Harrah's Atlantic City		
2. Harrah's Lake Tahoe		
3. Harrah's Las Vegas		
4. Harrah's Laughlin		
5. Harrah's Reno		
B. Hotel Group:	225 mm	75 mm
1. Hampton Inns		
2. Embassy Suites		
3. Homewood Suites		

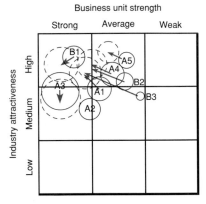

Consistent with the trend predicted and strategic recommendations emanating from the 1983 portfolio analysis, Holiday Corporation's board eventually would sell the Holiday Inns chain to the Bass group for approximately $2.5 billion. Also during this time, the Perkins Restaurant chain was sold at a net loss and Holiday Inn Crowne Suites was sold in a separate transaction. The newly created portfolio of businesses has what was originally the Holiday Inns, now Promus, positioned with two groups of businesses focused in the faster growing segments of gaming and lodging industries with what Mike Rose called "the leading brands" in each respective segment.

The evolution of Holiday Inns over the last 20 years to include getting out of the Holiday Inns business reflects a corporate portfolio management perspective very consistent with the suggestions of the BCG matrix or Industry Attractive–Business Strength matrix approaches. Indeed, so seriously were those suggestions taken to heart that Promus's largest business and the one from which it was founded was "harvested" to raise resources to support more promising business opportunities and building shareholder value.

A portfolio approach at Promus continued into 1995. On January 30, 1995, Promus announced plans to split the company into two separate, publicly traded companies. Said Mr. Rose:

> There are many good reasons for this decision. The most basic is we feel the two companies will achieve greater success as separate businesses than joined together. Like many other important decisions of the past two decades, this split narrows our focus. There are certainly similarities in our businesses and many lessons have been shared over the years. As the businesses have grown, however, the different attributes and needs of each have become more pronounced. Differences in such critical areas as sources of growth, regulatory and political issues, market visibility and capital needs all support the concept of a spin-off.

provide a picture of the "balance" of resource generators and users to test underlying assumptions about these issues in more involved corporate planning efforts to leverage core competencies to build sustained competitive advantages. For while the portfolio approaches have serious limitations, the challenge for corporate managers overseeing the allocation of resources among a variety of business units is still to maintain a balanced use of the company's financial resources.

FIGURE 9–5
The Market Life Cycle–Competitive Strength Matrix

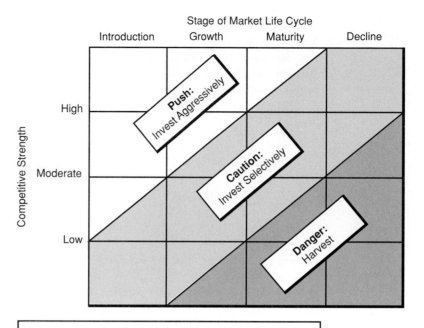

Description of Dimensions

Stage of Market Life Cycle: See page 184.

Competitive Strength: Overall subjective rating, based on a wide range of factors regarding the likelihood of gaining and maintaining a competitive advantage

Does Our Business Portfolio Achieve Appropriate Levels of Risk and Growth?

Diversification has traditionally been recommended as a way to manage, or diversify, risk. Said another way, "not having all your eggs in one basket" allows corporate managers to potentially reduce risk to company stockholders. Balancing cyclical revenue streams to reduce earnings volatility is one way diversification may reduce risk. So managers need to ask this question as a part of their strategic analysis and subsequent choice. Likewise, revenue growth can be enhanced by diversification. Many companies in the hazardous waste industry maintained the steady growth investors had come to expect by continuously making acquisitions of other businesses to gain immediate sales growth.

Both risk and growth are assumptions or priorities corporate managers should carefully examine as they undertake strategic analysis and choice. Is growth always desirable? Can risks truly be managed most effectively by corporate management? Many companies have pursued growth to gain market share without accompanying attention to profitability. Similarly, companies have built diverse business portfolios in part to manage overall risk. In both instances, the outcome is often a later time when subsequent management must "look in the bag" of businesses and aggressively divest and downsize the company until true value-adding activities and synergies linked to sustained competitive advantages are uncovered. Global Strategy-in-Action 9–1 describes just such a situation at Germany's largest company, Daimler Benz.

BEHAVORIAL CONSIDERATIONS AFFECTING STRATEGIC CHOICE

After alternative strategies have been analyzed, managers choose one of those strategies. If the analysis identified a clearly superior strategy or if the current strategy will clearly meet future company objectives, then the decision is relatively simple. Such clarity is the exception, however, and strategic decision makers often are confronted with several viable alternatives rather than the luxury of a clear-cut choice. Under these circumstances, several factors influence the strategic choice. Some of the more important are:

1. Role of the current strategy.
2. Degree of the firm's external dependence.
3. Attitudes toward risk.
4. Internal political considerations.
5. Timing.
6. Competitive reaction.

Role of the Current Strategy

Current strategists are often the architects of past strategies. If they have invested substantial time, resources, and interest in those strategies, they logically would be more comfortable with a choice that closely parallels or involves only incremental alterations to the current strategy.

Such familiarity with and commitment to past strategy permeates the entire firm. Thus, lower-level managers reinforce the top managers' inclination toward continuity with past strategy during the choice process. Research in several companies found lower-level managers suggested strategic choices that were consistent with current strategy and likely to be accepted while withholding suggestions with less probability of approval. Research by Henry Mintzberg suggests that past strategy strongly influences current strategic choice. The older and more successful a strategy has been, the harder it is to replace. Similarly, once a strategy has been initiated, it is very difficult to change because organizational momentum keeps it going. Even as a strategy begins to fail due to changing conditions, strategists often increase their commitment to it. Thus, firms may replace top executives when performance has been inadequate for an extended period because replacing these executives lessens the influence of unsuccessful past strategy on future strategic choice.

Degree of the Firm's External Dependence

If a firm is highly dependent on one or more environmental elements, its strategic alternatives and its ultimate strategic choice must accommodate that dependence. The greater a firm's external dependence, the lower its range and flexibility in strategic choice.

Bama Pies is a great family business success story. It makes excellent pies—apple turnovers. For many years, Bama Pies sold most of its pie output to one customer—McDonald's. With its massive retail coverage and its access to alternative suppliers. McDonald's was a major external dependence for Bama Pies. Bama Pies' strategic alternatives and ultimate choice of strategy were limited and strongly influenced by McDonald's demands. Bama Pies carefully narrowed its grand strategy and important related decisions in areas such as research and development, pricing, distribution, and product design with its critical dependence on McDonald's in mind.

Progressive firms accept external dependencies as a more positive reality—perhaps a source of competitive advantage. In the push for higher, more consistent quality, these firms seek to view key suppliers and customers as "partners" in strategic and operating decisions. More on this in Chapter 11.

Attitudes toward Risk

Attitudes toward risk exert considerable influence on strategic choice. Where attitudes favor risk, the range of the strategic choices expands and high-risk strategies are acceptable and desirable. Where management is risk averse, the range of strategic choices is limited and risky alternatives are eliminated before strategic choices are made. Past strategy exerts far more influence on the strategic choices of risk-averse managers.

Industry volatility influences the propensity of managers toward risk. Top managers in highly volatile industries absorb and operate with greater amounts of risk than do their counterparts in stable industries. Therefore, top managers in volatile industries consider a broader, more diverse range of strategies in the strategic choice process.

Industry evolution is another determinant of managerial propensity toward risk. A firm in the early stages of the product-market cycle must operate with considerably greater risk and uncertainty than a firm in the later stages of that cycle.

In making a strategic choice, risk-oriented managers lean toward opportunistic strategies with higher payoffs. They are drawn to offensive strategies based on innovation, company strengths, and operating potential. Risk-averse managers lean toward safe, conservative strategies with reasonable, highly probable returns. They are drawn to defensive strategies that minimize a firm's weaknesses, external threats, and the uncertainty associated with innovation-based strategies.

Internal Political Considerations

Power/political factors influence strategic choice. The use of power to further individual or group interest is common in organizational life. A major source of power in most firms is the chief executive officer (CEO). In smaller firms, the CEO is consistently the dominant force in strategic choice. Regardless of firm size, when the CEO begins to favor a particular choice, it is often selected unanimously.

Coalitions are power sources that influence strategic choice. In large firms, subunits and individuals (particularly key managers) have reason to support some alternatives and oppose others. Mutual interest draws certain groups together in coalitions to enhance their position on major strategic issues. These coalitions, particularly the more powerful ones (often called *dominant coalitions*), exert considerable influence on the strategic choice process. Numerous studies confirm the frequent use of power and coalitions in strategic decision making.

Figure 9–6 shows that the *content* of strategic decisions and the *processes* of arriving at such decisions are politically charged. Each phase in the process of strategic choice presents an opportunity for political action intended to influence the outcome. The challenge for strategists lies in recognizing and managing this political influence. For example, selecting the criteria used to compare alternative strategies or collecting and appraising information regarding those criteria may be particularly susceptible to political influence. This possibility must be recognized and, where necessary, "managed" to avoid dysfunctional political bias. Relying on different sources to collect and appraise information might serve this purpose.

Organizational politics must be viewed as an inevitable dimension of organizational decision making that strategic management must accommodate. Some authors argue that politics is a key ingredient in the "glue" that holds an organization together. Formal and

FIGURE 9–6
Political Activities in Phases of Strategic Decision Making

Phases of Strategic Decision Making	Focus of Political Action	Examples of Political Activity
Identification and diagnosis of strategic issues.	Control of: Issues to be discussed. Cause-and-effect relationships to be examined.	Control agenda. Interpretation of past events and future trends.
Narrowing the alternative strategies for serious consideration.	Control of alternatives.	Mobilization: Coalition formation. Resource commitment for information search.
Examining and choosing the strategy.	Control of choice.	Selective advocacy of criteria. Search and representation of information to justify choice.
Initiating implementation of the strategy.	Interaction between winners and losers.	Winners attempt to "sell" or co-opt losers. Losers attempt to thwart decisions and trigger fresh strategic issues.
Designing procedures for the evaluation of results.	Representing oneself as successful.	Selective advocacy of criteria.

Source: Adapted from Liam Fahey and V. K. Naroyanan, "The Politics of Strategic Decision Making," in *The Strategic Management Handbook*, ed. Kenneth J. Albert (New York: McGraw-Hill, 1983), pp. 21–20.

informal negotiating and bargaining between individuals, subunits, and coalitions are indispensable mechanisms for organizational coordination. Accommodating these mechanisms in the choice of strategy will result in greater commitment and more realistic strategy. The costs of doing so, however, are likely to be increased time spent on decision making and incremental (as opposed to drastic) change.

Timing

The time issue can have considerable influence on strategic choice. The most obvious way is when a time limit constrains strategic choice. A company has a six-month option to acquire another company or a key location is an example.

Another aspect of the time issue is the timing of a strategic decision. A good strategy may be disastrous if it is undertaken at the wrong time. The sudden outbreak of the Gulf War in 1991 proved disastrous for many small U.S. retailers who had expanded inventories for Spring 1991. And the sudden end of the war proved equally problematic for small military suppliers of products like Patriot missiles and body bags who had geared up for considerably increased demand.

Competitive Reaction

In weighing strategic choices, top management frequently incorporates perceptions of likely competitor reactions to those choices. For example, if it chooses an aggressive strategy directly challenging a key competitor, that competitor can be expected to mount an aggressive counterstrategy. In weighing strategic choices, top management must consider the probable impact of such reactions on the success of the chosen strategy.

The beer industry provides a good illustration. In the early 1970s, Anheuser-Busch dominated the industry, and Miller Brewing Company, recently acquired by Philip Morris, was a weak and declining competitor. Miller's management decided to adopt an expensive advertising-oriented strategy that challenged the big three (Anheuser-Busch, Pabst, and Schlitz) head-on because it assumed that their reaction would be delayed due to Miller's current declining status in the industry. This assumption proved correct, and Miller was able to reverse its trend in market share before Anheuser-Busch countered with an equally intense advertising strategy.

Miller's management took another approach in its next major strategic decision. In the mid-1970s, it introduced (and heavily advertised) a low-calorie beer—Miller Lite. Other industry members had introduced such products without much success. Miller chose a strategy that did not directly challenge its key competitors and was not expected to elicit immediate counterattacks from them. This choice proved highly successful, because Miller was able to establish a dominant share of the low-calorie beer market before those competitors decided to react. In this case, as in the preceding case, expectations regarding the reactions of competitors were a key determinant in the strategic choice made by Miller's management.

SUMMARY

This chapter examined how managers evaluate and choose their company's strategy in multibusiness settings. They look to rationalize their efforts to diversify and their current or anticipated collection of businesses. Doing this means identifying opportunities to share skills and core competencies across businesses or from corporate capabilities to business operational needs. Such opportunities usually arise in marketing, operations, management, or a combination of these activities when a capability in one area contributes to a competitive advantage in another.

Diversified, multibusiness companies face yet another, more complicated process of strategy analysis and choice. This chapter looked at the evolution of this challenge from portfolio approaches to value-based ways to decide which set of businesses maximizes opportunities to build sharcholder value.

Critical, often overlooked in the process of strategic analysis and choice, are behavioral considerations that may well determine a company's choice of strategy as much or more so than solely rational analysis. Commitment to the current strategy, external dependence, political considerations, timing, and competitive considerations combine to exercise a major influence on how managers eventually evaluate and choose strategies.

QUESTIONS FOR DISCUSSION

1. How does strategic analysis at the corporate level differ from strategic analysis at the business unit level? How are they related?

2. When would multi-industry companies find the portfolio approach to strategic analysis and choice useful?

3. What are three types of opportunities for sharing that form a sound basis for diversification or vertical integration? Give an example of each from companies you have read about.

4. What role might power and politics play in strategic analysis within a multibusiness company? Strategic choice within that same company? Would you expect these issues to be more prominent in a diversified company or in a single–product line company? Why or why not?

5. Read Global Strategy in Action 9–1 about the German manufacturer Daimler Benz. Which behavioral considerations discussed in this chapter appear to have influenced strategic analysis and choice within that company over the last 10 years? Explain.

BIBLIOGRAPHY

Bart, K. Christopher. "Implementing 'Growth' and 'Harvest' Product Strategies." *California Management Review*, Summer 1987, p. 139.

Barwise, Patrick; Paul R. Marsh; and Robin Wensley. "Must Finance and Strategy Clash?" *Harvard Business Review*, September–October 1989, p. 85.

Bettis, Richard A., and William K. Hall. "Strategic Portfolio Management in the Multibusiness Firm." *California Management Review* 24 (Fall 1981), pp. 23–38.

———. "The Business Portfolio Approach—Where It Falls Down in Practice." *Long Range Planning* 16, no. 2 (April 1983), pp. 95–104.

Buzzell, R. D. "Is Vertical Integration Profitable?" *Harvard Business Review* 61 (January–February 1994), pp. 92–102.

Christensen, H. Kurt; Arnold C. Cooper; and Cornelius A. Dekluyuer. "The Dog Business: A Reexamination." *Business Horizons* 25, no. 6 (November–December 1982), pp. 12–18.

Davis, R., and L. G. Thomas "Direct Estimation of Synergy: A New Approach to the Diversity-Performance Debate." *Management Science* 39 (1993), pp. 1334–46.

Dess, Gregory G., and Nancy K. Orizer. "Environment, Structure, and Consensus in Strategy Formulation." *Academy of Management Review*, April 1987, p. 313.

Fry, J. N., and P. J. Killing. "Vision-Check." *Business Quarterly* [Canada] 54, no. 2 (1989), pp. 64–69.

Ginter, P. M.; W. J. Duncan; L. E. Swayne; and A. G. Shelfer. "When Merger Means Death: Organizational Euthanasia and Strategic Choice." *Organizational Dynamics* 20, no. 3 (1992), pp. 21–33.

Haspeslagh, Phillippe. "Portfolio Planning: Uses and Limits." *Harvard Business Review* 60, no. 1 (January–February 1982), pp. 58–73.

Haspeslagh, Phillippe C., and David B. Jamison. *Managing Acquisitions: Creating Value through Corporate Renewal*. New York: Free Press, 1991.

Hax, Arnoldo, and Nicolas S. Majluf. *Strategic Management: An Integrative Perspective*. Englewood Cliffs, NJ: Prentice Hall, 1984, chaps. 7–9.

———. *The Strategy Concept and Process*. Englewood Cliffs, NJ: Prentice Hall, 1991, chaps. 8–11 and 15.

Henderson, Bruce D. "The Application and Misapplication of the Experience Curve." *Journal of Business Strategy* 4, no. 3 (Winter 1984), pp. 3–9.

———. "The Origin of Strategy." *Harvard Business Review*, November–December 1989, p. 139.

Hill, Charles W. L., and Robert E. Hoskisson. "Strategy and Structure in the Multi-Product Firm." *Academy of Management Review*, April 1987, p. 331.

Hoskisson, Robert E. "Multidivisional Structure and Performance: The Contingency of Diversification Strategy." *Academy of Management Journal*, December 1987, p. 621.

Kelly, K. "Learning from Japan." *Business Week*, January 27, 1992, p. 53.

Lubatkin, M., and S. Chatterjee. "Extending Modern Portfolio Theory into the Domain of Corporate Diversification: Does It Apply?" *Academy of Management Journal* 37 (1994), pp. 109–136.

Mason, David H., and Robert G. Wilson. "Future-Mapping: A New Approach to Managing Strategic Uncertainty." *Planning Review*, May–June 1987, p. 20.

McConkey, Dale D. "Planning in a Changing Environment." *Business Horizons*, September–October 1988, p. 64.

Naugle, David G., and Garret A. Davies. "Strategic-Skill Pools and Competitive Advantage." *Business Horizons* 30, no. 6 (November–December 1987), pp. 35–42.

Porter, Michael E. *Competitive Advantage*. New York: Free Press, 1984, chaps. 9–11.

———. "From Competitive Advantage to Corporate Strategy." *Harvard Business Review* 65, no. 3 (May–June 1987), pp. 43–59.

Zweig, L. "Who Says the Conglomerate is Dead?" *Business Week*, January 23, 1995, p. 92.

CHAPTER 9 COHESION CASE ILLUSTRATION

BUILDING SHAREHOLDER VALUE AS A MULTIBUSINESS COMPANY AT COCA-COLA

A historical synopsis is useful to illustrate the "evolutionary perspective" on strategic choice at Coca-Cola. Coca-Cola focused its initial efforts on single-business concentration for an extended time. Through the 1960s, The Coca-Cola Company focused on market development and product development in its core business—soft drinks. This focus on a single-business concentration built Coke a domestic dominance and a growing dominance in the selected overseas markets it gradually entered. Facing some regulatory restrictions from vertically integrating into bottling—as well as hesitance to aggressively commit to such a capital-intensive arena when it "controlled" these businesses through franchising the rights to bottle Coke and other soft drinks—Coke found itself with a "cash cow" in the early 1970s.

Similar to other large U.S. companies, The Coca-Cola Company chose to pursue diversification as a way to spread its risks and opportunities. It principally chose the acquisition approach, entering over 15 diverse businesses already described in the cohesion case at the end of Chapter 1. By the early 1980s, Coke's management found itself facing increased losses to a rejuvenated PepsiCo, with weaknesses in its bottling franchise network relative to Pepsi's, and gradual maturation of the domestic market while facing rapidly expanding market opportunities abroad. While Coke remained financially strong, it found itself needing resources to respond to challenges and opportunities facing its core business at home and abroad. So Coke gradually divested itself of most of its nonbeverage businesses, culminating in the divestiture of Columbia Pictures, which alone generated $1.3 billion for investment in Coca-Cola's beverage-related businesses. Each of these shifts in strategy at Coke including its mid-1990s refocus on its core business, soft drinks (along with its citrus beverage business), and soft-drink bottling (vertical integration forward) is consistent with the evolutionary pattern discussed in Chapter 9.

As we described at the end of Chapter 1, Coca-Cola was a multibusiness company in the 1970s and early 1980s. Strategic analysis and choice during this period could be aided by a matrix approach similar to the industry attractive–business strength matrix. A selective assessment of some of Coke's businesses at the time would look something like this:

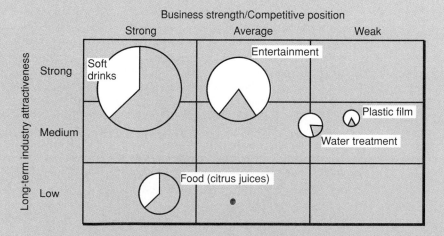

This assessment would suggest increased investment in soft drinks, harvesting water treatment and plastic films, selective investment and managing the juice business for cash generation, and investment to grow entertainment or harvesting the attractive opportunity if the company couldn't financially support the opportunity represented by both this business and soft drinks.

Strategic analysis and choice of Coca-Cola's generic strategy toward the 21st century is an important element we must consider to appreciate this perspective on strategic management and to understand fundamentals behind Coke's key strategic decisions. Coca-Cola's management under the new leadership of Roberto Goizueta set a new tone within The Coca-Cola Company of the 1980s. Some analysts have likened it to waking a sleeping giant. Regardless of the analogy you choose, it is abundantly clear that Coca-Cola reinvigorated the "Cola Wars" with aggressive behavior toward competitors and toward proving its uniqueness in every market it served throughout the world. If you refer back to Figures 9–2 to 9–4 in Chapter 9, you will see the commonly required skills, resources, and organizational requirements of the three basic generic business strategies. Coca-Cola has long possessed most of those required by a differentiation strategy—strong marketing abilities, product engineering, reputation for quality, a long tradition in the industry, and a strong coordination among R&D, product development, and marketing. The decisions made by Goizueta and his management team at that time and followed today seek to build Coke's success on differentiating it from every other source of refreshment in the world.

Finally, Coke's decision to focus on soft drinks, expand control of its primary distribution channel, and aggressively expand internationally is consistent with an industry that is in a transition to maturity in the United States, while the global market is rapidly emerging as a stable (for the sale of soft drinks) modern setting worldwide. And Coca-Cola's industry analysis shows that the main threats to industry profitability come from buyer power (bottlers), rivalry (Pepsi), and, perhaps, substitutes. Suppliers and potential entrants offer little concern. Coke is very strong relative to suppliers, and the capital requirement of serious entry is high. So Coca-Cola's differentiation strategy, combined with its swift, aggressive program of vertical integration acquiring bottlers or major interests in them, is a logical strategy to deal with rivalry and substitutes on the one hand and buyer power on the other. Coca-Cola's strategic decision to sell Columbia Pictures to Sony, whereby Coke netted $1.3 billion, was a clear decision to redirect substantial resources toward an aggressive vertical integration strategy suggested by the industry analysis as well as the other approaches outlined earlier.

Goizueta, speaking in late 1995, described Coca-Cola's "portfolio analysis" this way:

> We decided to evaluate our businesses based on economic value added [EVA], which we define as net operating profit after taxes less a charge for the average cost of debt and equity capital employed to produce that profit. The difference, if positive, is contributing value to shareholders. If negative, it is not. This shift in evaluation methodology prompted us to begin divesting ourselves of businesses with financial characteristics inferior to the remarkable fundamentals of our core soft drink business. Over ten years we divested our entertainment business, water treatment, plastic film, and other investments that did not produce an acceptable EVA. We have purposefully narrowed our businesses to focus almost entirely on a soft drink concentrate business that consistently generates returns 3Xs greater than our cost of capital. That business is augmented by selected bottling investments around the world and Coca Cola Foods.

So Coca-Cola management took an EVA-based look at the value-building capability of its portfolio of businesses and, based on that analysis, chose to divert resources from lesser performers toward the business that added the greatest value and held the best promise to continue to do so.

Focusing on Superior Lines of Business
By selling off businesses not sharing the same attractive financial fundamentals as the soft drink business, we now operate only in high-return businesses.

1994 Operating Income

97% Soft Drinks   3% Other

77% Soft Drinks   23% Other

1984 Operating Income

III STRATEGY IMPLEMENTATION

The last section of this book examines what is often called the *action phase* of the strategic management process: implementation of the chosen strategy. Up to this point, three phases of that process have been covered—strategy formulation, analysis of alternative strategies, and strategic choice. Although important, these phases alone cannot ensure success. To ensure success, the strategy must be translated into carefully implemented action. This means that:

1. The strategy must be translated into guidelines for the daily activities of the firm's members.
2. The strategy and the firm must become one—that is, the strategy must be reflected in the way the firm organizes its activities and in the firm's values, beliefs, and tone.
3. In implementing the strategy, the firm's managers must direct and control actions and outcomes and adjust to change.

Chapter 10 explains how organizational action is successfully initiated in three interrelated steps:

1. Creation of clear *action plans* and *short-term objectives*.
2. Development of specific *functional tactics* that create competitive advantage.
3. Empowerment of operating personnel through *policies* to guide decisions.

Action plans guide implementation by converting long-term objectives into short-term actions and targets. Functional tactics translate the business strategy into activities that build advantage. Policies empower operating personnel by defining guidelines for making decisions.

Today's competitive environment often necessitates restructuring and reengineering the organization to sustain competitive advantage. Chapter 11 examines how restructuring and reengineering are pursued in four organizational elements that provide fundamental, long-term means for institutionalizing the firm's strategy:

1. The firm's *structure*.
2. The *leadership* provided by the firm's CEO and key managers.
3. The fit between the strategy and the firm's *culture*.
4. The firm's *reward systems*.

Since the firm's strategy is implemented in a changing environment, successful implementation requires that execution be controlled and continuously improved. The control and improvement process must include at least these dimensions:

1. *Strategic controls* that "steer" execution of the strategy.
2. *Operations control systems* that monitor performance, evaluate deviations, and initiate corrective action.
3. *Continuous improvement* through total quality initiatives.

Chapter 12 examines the dimensions of the control and improvement process. It explains the essence of change as an ever-present force driving the need for strategic control. The chapter concludes with a look at the global "quality imperative," which is redefining the essence of control into the 21st century.

Implementation is "where the action is." It is the arena that most students enter at the start of their business careers. It is the strategic phase in which staying close to the customer, achieving competitive advantage, and pursuing excellence become realities. The chapters in this part will help you understand how this is done.

10

IMPLEMENTING STRATEGY THROUGH ACTION PLANS, FUNCTIONAL TACTICS AND EMPLOYEE EMPOWERMENT

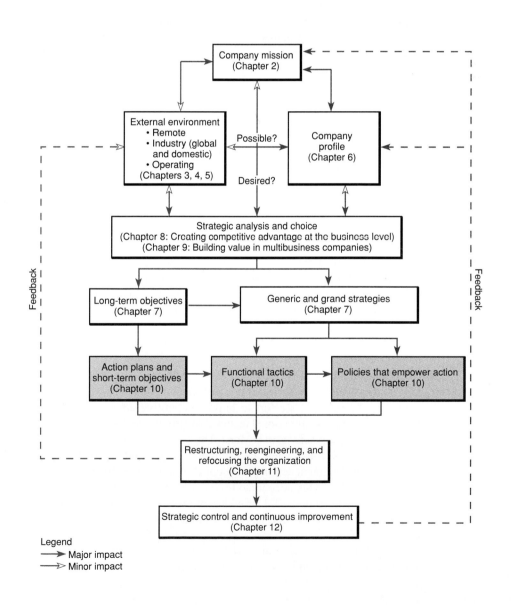

Company mission
(Chapter 2)

External environment
• Remote
• Industry (global and domestic)
• Operating
(Chapters 3, 4, 5)

Possible?

Desired?

Company profile
(Chapter 6)

Strategic analysis and choice
(Chapter 8: Creating competitive advantage at the business level)
(Chapter 9: Building value in multibusiness companies)

Long-term objectives
(Chapter 7)

Generic and grand strategies
(Chapter 7)

Action plans and short-term objectives
(Chapter 10)

Functional tactics
(Chapter 10)

Policies that empower action
(Chapter 10)

Restructuring, reengineering, and refocusing the organization
(Chapter 11)

Strategic control and continuous improvement
(Chapter 12)

Feedback

Feedback

Legend
→ Major impact
⇢ Minor impact

303

Once corporate and business strategies have been agreed upon and long-term objectives set, the strategic management process moves into a critical new phase—translating strategic thought into organizational action. In the words of two well-worn phrases, they move from "planning their work" to "working their plan" as they shift their focus from strategy formulation to strategy implementation. This shift gives rise to four interrelated concerns:

1. Identifying action plans and short-term objectives.
2. Initiating specific functional tactics.
3. Communicating policies that empower people in the organization.
4. Committing to continuous improvement.

Action plans and short-term objectives translate long-range aspirations into this year's actions. If well developed, these objectives provide clarity, a powerful motivator and facilitator of effective strategy implementation.

Functional tactics translate business strategy into daily activities people need to execute. Functional managers participate in the development of these tactics, and their participation, in turn, helps clarify what their units are expected to do in implementing the business's strategy.

Policies are empowerment tools that simplify decision making by empowering operating managers and their subordinates. Policies can empower the "doers" in an organization by reducing the time required to decide and act.

Continuous improvement has become essential to the ability of any business to remain competitive. This quality orientation wherein functional managers seek best practices in each area's activities keeps businesses current, competitive, and value oriented.

ACTION PLANS AND SHORT-TERM OBJECTIVES

Chapter 7 described business strategies, grand strategies, and long-term objectives that are critically important in crafting a successful future. To make them become a reality, however, the people in an organization that actually "do the work" of the business need guidance in exactly what needs to be done today and tomorrow to make those long-term strategies become reality. Action plans and short-term objectives help do this. They provide much more specific guidance for what is to be done, a clear delineation of impending actions needed, which helps translate vision into action.

Action plans are effective when they incorporate four elements. First, they identify specific functional tactics and actions that will be done in the next week, month, or quarter as part of the business's effort to build competitive advantage. The next major section examines some of the functional tactics they usually deal with. The important point here is *specificity*—what exactly is to be done. The second element of an action plan is a clear *time frame for completion*—when the effort will begin and when its results will be accomplished. A third element action plans contain is identification of *who is responsible* for each action in the plan. This accountability is very important to ensure action plans are acted upon. Strategy in Action 10–1 provides excerpts from the action plan of a small oil distribution company in the northeastern United States that was part of its 1996–98 strategic plan.

The fourth element associated with action plans are short-term objectives. Usually, each action in an action plan has one or more specific objectives that are identified as outcomes

FIGURE 10–1
Creating Measurable Objectives

Examples of Deficient Objectives	Examples of Objectives with Measurable Criteria for Performance
To improve morale in the division (plant, department, etc.)	To reduce turnover (absenteeism, number of rejects, etc.) among sales managers by 10 percent by January 1, 1998.
	Assumption: Morale is related to measurable outcomes (i.e., high and low morale are associated with different results).
To improve support of the sales effort	To reduce the time lapse between order data and delivery by 8 percent (two days) by June 1, 1998.
	To reduce the cost of goods produced by 6 percent to support a product price decrease of 2 percent by December 1, 1998.
	To increase the rate of before- or on-schedule delivery by 5 percent by June 1, 1998.
To improve the firm's image	To conduct a public opinion poll using random samples in the five largest U.S. metropolitan markets to determine average scores on 10 dimensions of corporate responsibility by May 15, 1998. To increase our score on those dimensions by an average of 7.5 percent by May 1, 1999.

Source: Adapted from Laurence G. Hrebiniak and William F. Joyce, *Implementing Strategy* (New York: Macmillan, 1984), p. 116.

the action generates. There is also the need for other short-term objectives to be identified that "operationalize" long-term objectives. If we commit to a 20 percent gain in revenue over five years, what is our specific target or objective in revenue during the current year, month, or week to indicate we are making appropriate progress. Finally, short-term objectives are often useful topics to help raise issues that require coordination across functional activities within an organization. Meeting certain revenue objectives for the next month may cause difficulties for production managers or marketing managers also concerned with other objectives as well. Identifying and discussing short-term objectives help raise such issues. Because of the particular importance of short-term objectives in action plans, the following section addresses how to develop meaningful short-term objectives.

Qualities of Effective Short-Term Objectives

Measurable

Short-term objectives are more consistent when they clearly state *what* is to be accomplished, *when* it will be accomplished, and *how* its accomplishment will be *measured*. Such objectives can be used to monitor both the effectiveness of each activity and the collective progress across several interrelated activities. Figure 10–1 illustrates several effective and ineffective short-term objectives. Measurable objectives make misunderstanding less likely among interdependent managers who must implement action plans. It is far easier to quantify the objectives of *line* units (e.g., production) than of certain *staff* areas (e.g., personnel). Difficulties in quantifying objectives often can be overcome by initially focusing on *measurable activity* and then identifying *measurable outcomes*.

Priorities

Although all annual objectives are important, some deserve priority because of a timing consideration or their particular impact on a strategy's success. If such priorities are not established, conflicting assumptions about the relative importance of annual objectives

FROM OBSCURITY TO BEING A LEADER IN FUEL DISTRIBUTION ALONG VIRGINIA'S COAST

EnergyCo is an exciting, closely-held fuel distribution company located in coastal Virginia. Its management team has undertaken regular strategic analysis and planning to guide its growth aspirations. Its most recent planning efforts generated a comprehensive strategic plan to exploit several attractive opportunities. A key part of their ongoing strategic planning effort is the identification of action plans and annual objectives to make their wide-ranging planning discussions and efforts become concrete actions for which each member of the management team accepts some responsibility. They also insist on reducing the action plans into a few pages with minimal wording so that they can easily be reviewed, updated, and discussed at each weekly management meeting. Included below is an excerpt from their most recent action plan.

Objective	Assumption	1996	1998
Sales: Commercial fuels	12.5% annual growth	$16.9 mm	$21.0 mm
Sales: Oil Futures Hedging	Approximately 5% annual growth	$ 6.5 mm	$ 7.0 mm
Sales: Retail/C stores	Approximately 5% annual growth	$ 4.3 mm	$ 5.0 mm
Sales: Branding	4 sites per year 97–98	$ 4.0 mm	$12.0 mm
Sales: Home heat	1 or 2 acquisitions 97–98	$ 1.5 mm	$ 3.0 mm
Sales: Fleet pump	Aggressive growth 97–98	$ 750 k	$ 2.5 mm
Sales: Lubricants	12.5% + growth	$ 2.3 mm	$ 2.6 mm
Sales: Marine	Approximately 5% annual growth	$ 3.7 mm	$ 4.0 mm
Sales: Heating & cooling	Flat with 1998 acquisition?	$ 530 k	$ 800 k
Sales: Trucking	Approximately 5% annual growth	$ 2.7 mm	$ 3.0 mm
Total sales		$43.9 mm	$60.9 mm
Operating income		$ 1.2 mm	$ 1.7 mm
Return on equity		40%	37%
Debt to equity		3.5/1	3/1

may inhibit progress toward strategic effectiveness. Facing the most rapid, dramatic decline in profitability of any major computer manufacturer as it confronted relentless lower pricing by Dell Computer and AST, Compaq Computer formulated a retrenchment strategy with several important annual objectives in pricing, product design, distribution, and financial condition. But its highest priority was to dramatically lower overhead and production costs so as to satisfy the difficult challenge of dramatically lowering prices while also restoring profitability.

Priorities are established in various ways. A simple *ranking* may be based on discussion and negotiation during the planning process. However, this does not necessarily communicate the real difference in the importance of objectives, so such terms as *primary, top,* and

Strategic Assignment	Who's Responsible	Due
Present outline of timing/format for sharing the results of EnergyCo planning retreat and the 1998 Vision with Eees (see 3/1/96 too).	Sam	Xmas Party
Get info on employee leasing from Laser Tech to Sarah	Richard	12/20/96
Sales—Operations Coordination and Integration—Report on initial ideas to increase the level of coordination and to pursue group meetings; after work meetings; coordination and interaction with admin personnel to. . . . Report on initial thoughts & get input	Leigh Jack Kate	Report initial ideas by 1/3/97
Real good assessment & recommendations on HVAC situation	Jack and Ginger	2/3/97
Create drawings and explanation of the adjacent property deal/use	Jack, Sarah, & Sam	3/3/97
Sales—Operations (Administration) Coordination Procedure Plan (the plan that results from the above ideas discussed, refined, etc.)	Leigh and Jack	4/30/97
Assess, do P&L, & implement hiring of Harbor Lube sales rep	Sam & Sarah	5/30/97
Computerization Task Force—assemble team, set agenda, and plan to proceed to examine, get a handle on, get input/involvement of EnergyCo employees doing the real work, and implement a comprehensive, integrated computer automation of the daily management of all of EnergyCo's sales, operations, administrative activities . . . & consideration of hiring someone to help early on	Sarah Kate Leigh Jack	6/30/97
Analysis, evaluation & develop a plan to deal with out of town product acquisition & $0.015 premium on low rack	Sarah & Jack	7/15/97
Retail Joint Venture: Evaluate EnergyCo direct ownership; franchise operations; owner equity lease financing to EnergyCo; and the potential for real estate syndication	Sam Sarah Kate	8/15/97
Partner buyout life insurance and evaluate risk of shared ownership	Leigh & Jack	9/15/97
EnergyCo Proformas on D/E ratios with capital proposed; set up EnergyCo's financial report to reflect investment by revenue stream/division and calculate ROI & SPI for each, etc.	Sarah	10/1/97
Implement series of meetings with employees to explain EnergyCo 1998 strategic plan and to answer questions; get their feedback, etc. One of the key issues to develop and discuss with EnergyCo employees is the new, greater emphasis and commitment to the retail and branding sides of the business.	Sam with management team	11/1/97
Finish Commission Program for Sales organization	Sarah and Leigh	12/30/97

secondary may be used to indicate priority. Some firms assign *weights* (e.g., 0 to 100 percent) to establish and communicate the relative priority of objectives. Whatever the method, recognizing priorities is an important dimension in the implementation value of short-term objectives.

Linked to Long-Term Objectives

Short-term objectives can add breadth and specificity in identifying *what* must be accomplished to achieve long-term objectives. For example, Wal-Mart's top management recently set out "to obtain 45 percent market share in five years" as a long-term objective. Achieving that objective can be greatly enhanced if a series of specific short-term objectives identify what must be accomplished each year in order to do so. If Wal-Mart's market share is now 25 percent, then one likely annual objective might be "to have each regional office achieve a minimum 4 percent increase in market share in the next year." "Open two regional distribution centers in the Southwest in 1998" might be an annual objective that Wal-Mart's marketing and distribution managers consider essential if the firm is to achieve a 45 percent market share in five years. "Conclude arrangements for a $1 billion line of credit at 0.25 percent above prime in 1994" might be an annual objective of Wal-Mart's financial managers to support the operation of new distribution centers and the purchase of increased inventory in reaching the firm's long-term objective.

The link between short-term and long-term objectives should resemble cascades through the firm from basic long-term objectives to specific short-term objectives in key operation areas. The cascading effect has the added advantage of providing a clear reference for communication and negotiation, which may be necessary to integrate and coordinate objectives and activities at the operating level.

The qualities of good objectives discussed in Chapter 7—acceptable, flexible, suitable, motivating, understandable, and achievable—also apply to short-term objectives. They will not be discussed again here, but the reader should review the discussion in Chapter 7 to appreciate these qualities, common to all good objectives.

The Value-Added Benefits of Action Plans and Short-Term Objectives

One benefit of action plans and short-term objectives is that they give operating personnel a better understanding of their role in the firm's mission. "Achieve $2.5 million in 1998 sales in the Chicago territory," "Develop an OSHA-approved safety program for handling acids at all Georgia Pacific plants in 1998," and "Reduce Ryder Truck's average age of accounts receivable to 31 days by the end of 1998" are examples of how short-term objectives clarify the role of particular personnel in their firm's broader mission. Such *clarity of purpose* can be a major force in helping use a firm's "people assets" more effectively, which may add tangible value.

A second benefit of action plans and short-term objectives comes from the process of developing them. If the managers responsible for this accomplishment have participated in their development, action plans and short-term objectives provide valid bases for addressing and accommodating conflicting concerns that might interfere with strategic effectiveness. Meetings to set action plans and short-term objectives become the forum for raising and resolving conflicts between strategic intentions and operating realities.

A third benefit of action plans and short-term objectives is that they provide *a basis for strategic control*. The control of strategy will be examined in detail in Chapter 12. However, it is important to recognize here that action plans and short-term objectives provide a clear, measurable basis for developing budgets, schedules, trigger points, and other mechanisms for controlling the implementation of strategy.

A fourth benefit is often a *motivational payoff*. Action plans and short-term objectives that clarify personal and group roles in a firm's strategies and are also measurable, realistic, and challenging can be powerful motivators of managerial performance—particularly when these objectives are linked to the firm's reward structure.

Strategy in Action 10–1 excerpts selected short-term objectives and action plans from the strategic plan of EnergyCo Fuel Company. Bought out of bankruptcy 10 years ago, founder Sam Rutledge has led an outstanding management team that has made EnergyCo a major player in eastern Virginia. One of the key aspects the firm emphasizes is action plans and annual objectives.

FIGURE 10–2
Role of Functional Tactics at General Cinema Corporation

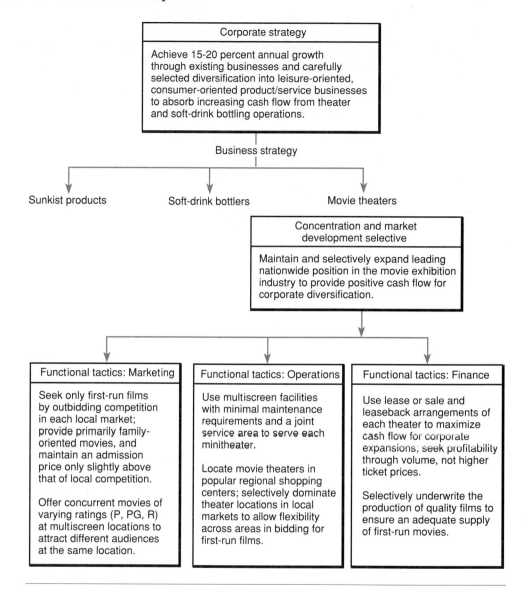

Corporate strategy
Achieve 15-20 percent annual growth through existing businesses and carefully selected diversification into leisure-oriented, consumer-oriented product/service businesses to absorb increasing cash flow from theater and soft-drink bottling operations.

Business strategy

Sunkist products   Soft-drink bottlers   Movie theaters

Concentration and market development selective
Maintain and selectively expand leading nationwide position in the movie exhibition industry to provide positive cash flow for corporate diversification.

Functional tactics: Marketing	Functional tactics: Operations	Functional tactics: Finance
Seek only first-run films by outbidding competition in each local market; provide primarily family-oriented movies, and maintain an admission price only slightly above that of local competition. Offer concurrent movies of varying ratings (P, PG, R) at multiscreen locations to attract different audiences at the same location.	Use multiscreen facilities with minimal maintenance requirements and a joint service area to serve each minitheater. Locate movie theaters in popular regional shopping centers; selectively dominate theater locations in local markets to allow flexibility across areas in bidding for first-run films.	Use lease or sale and leaseback arrangements of each theater to maximize cash flow for corporate expansions; seek profitability through volume, not higher ticket prices. Selectively underwrite the production of quality films to ensure an adequate supply of first-run movies.

FUNCTIONAL TACTICS THAT IMPLEMENT BUSINESS STRATEGIES

Functional tactics are the key, routine activities that must be undertaken in each functional area—marketing, finance, production/operations, R&D, and human resource management—to provide the business's products and services. In a sense, functional tactics translate thought (grand strategy) into action designed to accomplish specific short-term objectives. Every value chain activity in a company executes functional tactics that support the business's strategy and help accomplish strategic objectives.

Figure 10–2 illustrates the difference between functional tactics and corporate and business strategy. It also shows that functional tactics are essential to implement business strategy. The corporate strategy defined General Cinema Corporation's general posture in the broad economy. The business strategy outlined the competitive posture of its operations in the movie theater industry. To increase the likelihood that these strategies would be successful, specific functional tactics were needed for the firm's operating components. These functional tactics clarified the business strategy, giving specific, short-term guidance to operating managers in the areas of marketing, operations, and finance.

Differences between Business Strategies and Functional Tactics

Functional tactics are different from business or corporate strategies in three fundamental ways:

1. Time horizon.
2. Specificity.
3. Participants who develop them.

Time Horizon

Functional tactics identify activities to be undertaken "now" or in the immediate future. Business strategies focus on the firm's posture three to five years out. Delta Air lines is committed to a concentration/market development business strategy that seeks competitive advantage via differentiation in its level of service and focus on the business traveler. Its pricing tactics are often to price above industry averages, but it often lowers fares on selected routes to thwart low-cost competition. Its business strategy is focused 10 years out; its pricing tactics change weekly.

The shorter time horizon of functional tactics is critical to the successful implementation of a business strategy for two reasons. First, it focuses the attention of functional managers on what needs to be done *now* to make the business strategy work. Second, it allows functional managers like those at Delta to adjust to changing current conditions.

Specificity

Functional tactics are more specific than business strategies. Business strategies provide general direction. Functional tactics identify the specific activities that are to be undertaken in each functional area and thus allow operating managers to work out *how* their unit is expected to pursue short-term objectives. General Cinema's business strategy gave its movie theater division broad direction on how to pursue a concentration and selective market development strategy. Two functional tactics in the marketing area gave managers specific direction on what types of movies (first-run, primarily family-oriented, P, PG, R) should be shown and what pricing strategy (competitive in the local area) should be followed.

Specificity in functional tactics contributes to successful implementation by:

· Helping ensure that functional managers know what needs to be done and can focus on accomplishing results.
· Clarifying for top management how functional managers intend to accomplish the business strategy, which increases top management's confidence in and sense of control over the business strategy.
· Facilitating coordination among operating units *within* the firm by clarifying areas of interdependence and potential conflict.

Participants

Different people participate in strategy development at the functional and business levels. Business strategy is the responsibility of the general manager of a business unit. That manager typically delegates the development of functional tactics to subordinates charged with running the operating areas of the business. The manager of a business unit must establish long-term objectives and a strategy that corporate management feels contributes to corporate-level goals. Similarly, key operating managers must establish short-term objectives and operating strategies that contribute to business-level goals. Just as business strategies and objectives are approved through negotiation between corporate managers and business managers, so, too, are short-term objectives and functional tactics approved through negotiation between business managers and operating managers.

Involving operating managers in the development of functional tactics improves their understanding of what must be done to achieve long-term objectives and, thus, contributes to successful implementation. It also helps ensure that functional tactics reflect the reality of the day-to-day operating situation. And perhaps most important, it can increase the commitment of operating managers to the strategies developed.

The next several sections will highlight key tactics around which managers can build competitive advantage and add value in each of the various functional areas.

Functional Tactics in Production/Operations

Basic Issues

Production/operations management (POM) is the core function of any organization. That function converts inputs (raw materials, supplies, machines, and people) into value-enhanced output. The POM function is most easily associated with manufacturing firms, but it also applies to all other types of businesses (service and retail firms, for example). POM tactics must guide decisions regarding (1) the basic nature of the firm's POM system, seeking an optimum balance between investment input and production/operations output and (2) location, facilities design, and process planning on a short-term basis. Figure 10–3 highlights key decision areas in which the POM tactics should provide guidance to functional personnel.

POM facility and equipment tactics involve decisions regarding plant location, size, equipment replacement, and facilities utilization that should be consistent with grand strategy and other operating strategies. In the mobile home industry, for example, the facilities and equipment tactic of Winnebago was to locate one large centralized, highly integrated production center (in Iowa) near its raw materials. On the other extreme, Fleetwood, Inc., a California-based competitor, located dispersed, decentralized production facilities near markets and emphasized maximum equipment life and less-integrated, labor-intensive production processes. Both firms are leaders in the mobile home industry, but have taken very different tactical approaches.

The interplay between computers and rapid technological advancement has made flexible manufacturing systems (FMS) a major consideration for today's POM tacticians. FMS allows managers to automatically and rapidly shift production systems to retool for different products or other steps in a manufacturing process. Changes that previously took hours or days can be done in minutes. The result is decreased labor cost, greater efficiency, and increased quality associated with computer-based precision. Global Strategy in Action 10–1 summarizes the "responsive factory" of tomorrow based on a global study by *Business Week*.

Purchasing has become an increasingly important component in the POM area. Many companies now accord purchasing a separate status like any other functional area. Purchasing tactics provide guidelines about questions like: Are the cost advantages of using only a

FIGURE 10–3
Key Functional Strategies in POM

Functional Strategy	Typical Questions That the Functional Strategy Should Answer
Facilities and equipment	How centralized should the facilities be? (One big facility or several small facilities?)
	How integrated should the separate processes be?
	To what extent should further mechanization or automation be pursued?
	Should size and capacity be oriented toward peak or normal operating levels?
Purchasing	How many sources are needed?
	How should suppliers be selected, and how should relationships with suppliers be managed over time?
	What level of forward buying (hedging) is appropriate?
Operations planning and control	Should work be scheduled to order or to stock?
	What level of inventory is appropriate?
	How should inventory be used (FIFO/LIFO), controlled, and replenished?
	What are the key foci for control efforts (quality, labor cost, downtime, product use, other)?
	Should maintenance efforts be oriented to prevention or to breakdown?
	What emphasis should be placed on job specialization? Plant safety? The use of standards?

few suppliers outweighed by the risk of overdependence? What criteria (e.g., payment requirements) should be used in selecting vendors? Which vendors can provide "just-in-time" inventory and how can the business provide it to our customers? How can operations be supported by the volume and delivery requirements of purchases?

POM planning and control tactics involve approaches to the management of ongoing production operations and are intended to match production/operations resources with longer range, overall demand. These tactical decisions usually determine whether production/operations will be demand oriented, inventory oriented, or outsourcing oriented to seek a balance between the two extremes. Tactics in this component also address how issues like maintenance, safety, and work organization are handled. Quality control procedures are yet another focus of tactical priorities in this area.

Just in time (JIT) delivery, outsourcing, and statistical process control (SPC) have become prominent aspects of the way today's POM managers create tactics that build greater value and quality in their POM system. JIT delivery was initially a way to coordinate with suppliers to reduce inventory carrying costs of items needed to make products. It also became a quality control tactic because smaller inventories made quality checking easier on smaller, frequent deliveries. It has become an important aspect of supplier-customer relationships in today's best businesses.

Outsourcing, or the use of a source other than internal capacity to accomplish some task or process, has become a major operational tactic in today's downsizing-oriented firms. Outsourcing is based on the notion that strategies should be built around core competencies that add the most value in the value chain, and functions or activities that add little value or that cannot be done cost effectively should be done outside the firm—outsourced. When done well, the firm gains a supplier that provides superior quality at lower cost than it could provide itself. JIT and outsourcing have increased the strategic importance of the purchasing function. Outsourcing must include intense quality control by the buyer. ValuJet's

GLOBAL
STRATEGY IN
ACTION 10–1

WHAT DOES THE TRULY "RESPONSIVE" FACTORY OF THE 21ST CENTURY GLOBAL ECONOMY LOOK LIKE?

Manufacturers worldwide are scrambling to create the factories of the future today. Flexible manufacturing systems are an important component. But that's not all. Total quality control, concurrent engineering, process reengineering, computerization, and computer-aided logistical support are just some of today's insisted-upon characteristics. Convened by *Business Week* to probe the vision of the responsive factory more clearly, operations managers around the globe agreed on five key characteristics.

CHARACTERISTICS OF THE TRULY RESPONSIVE FACTORY

Concurrent everything	Enterprisewide computer integration, with electronic links to customers and suppliers, means that transactions occur mostly between computers, which will automatically route information to all the proper departments or operations.
Fast development cycles	A real-time database will unite the distributed-processing computers used by design, engineering, production, logistics, marketing, and customer service—whether the work is done in-house or outsourced. All parties will have instant access to the latest information, eliminating the rework now caused by delays in shuffling paper.
Flexible production	Flexibility will be built into all levels of manufacturing, from the controls on each machine to the computers that coordinate work cells and factorywide systems. Products can thus be turned out in greater variety and customized easily, with no cost penalty for small production runs.
Quick response	Dynamic factory-scheduling systems will put production "on call" and thus pare inventories to the bone. Production will begin only after a customer places an order.
Commitment to lifelong quality	Ongoing quality programs will lead to continuous improvement of both processes and products. A primary focus will be to make products easier to recycle or dispose of in environmentally sound ways.

Source: Reprinted from October 22, 1993, issue of *Business Week* by special permission. Copyright © 1993 by The McGraw-Hill Companies.

tragic 1996 crash in the Everglades was caused by poor quality control over its outsourced maintenance providers.

Statistical process control (SPC) refers to a series of quantitative-oriented management practices designed to improve quality at several phases in the production/operations process. Identifying measurable aspects of every function from inbound logistics through operations and then outbound parts of the value chain—and then subjecting them to systematic scrutiny to ensure that every phase is in control and compliance—is the heart of SPC. At the heart of the total quality management (TQM) movement, SPC has become very important tactically, particularly for businesses selling solely to other businesses that seek to meet international quality certifications.

Functional Tactics in Marketing

The role of the marketing function is to achieve the firm's objectives by bringing about the profitable sale of the business's products/services in target markets. Marketing tactics should guide sales and marketing managers in determining who will sell what, where, to

FIGURE 10–4
Key Functional Tactics in Marketing

Functional Tactic	Typical Questions That the Functional Tactic Should Answer
Product (or service)	Which products do we emphasize? Which products/services contribute most to profitability? What product/service image do we seek to project? What consumer needs does the product/service seek to meet? What changes should be influencing our customer orientation?
Price	Are we competing primarily on price? Can we offer discounts or other pricing modifications? Are our pricing policies standard nationally, or is there regional control? What price segments are we targeting (high, medium, low, and so on)? What is the gross profit margin? Do we emphasize cost/demand or competition-oriented pricing?
Place	What level of market coverage is necessary? Are there priority geographic areas? What are the key channels of distribution? What are the channel objectives, structure, and management? Should the marketing managers change their degree of reliance on distributors, sales reps, and direct selling? What sales organization do we want? Is the sales force organized around territory, market, or product?
Promotion	What are the key promotion priorities and approaches? Which advertising/communication priorities and approaches are linked to different products, markets, and territories? Which media would be most consistent with the total marketing strategy?

whom, in what quantity, and how. Marketing tactics at a minimum should address four fundamental areas: products, price, place, and promotion. Figure 10–4 highlights typical questions marketing tactics should address. Strategy in Action 10–2 shows how the San Luis Sourdough Company, a small California baker, developed pricing tactics to address different levels of service they rendered to different customers with the bread they sold.

In addition to the basic issues raised in Figure 10–4, marketing tactics today must guide managers addressing the impact of *the communication revolution* and the *increased diversity* among market niches worldwide. The Internet and the accelerating blend of computers and telecommunications has facilitated instantaneous access to several places around the world. A producer of plastic kayaks in Easley, South Carolina, receives orders from somewhere in the world about every 30 minutes over the Internet without any traditional distribution structure or global advertising. It fills the order within five days without any transportation capability. Speed linked to the ability to communicate instantaneously is causing marketing tacticians to radically rethink what they need to do to remain competitive and maximize value.

Diversity has accelerated because of communication technology, logistical capability worldwide, and advancements in flexible manufacturing systems. The diversity that has resulted is a virtual explosion of market niches, adaptations of products to serve hundreds of distinct and diverse customer segments that would previously have been served with more mass-market, generic products or services. Where firms used to rely on volume associated with mass markets to lower costs, they now encounter smaller niche players carving out subsegments they can serve more timely *and* more cost effectively. These new, smaller players lack the bureaucracy and committee approach that burdens the larger firms. They make decisions, outsource, incorporate product modifications, and make other agile adjustments to niche market needs before their larger competitors get through the first phase of committee-based decision making. Jack Welch, the CEO of General Electric, commented on this recently with the editors of *Business Week*:

> Size is no longer the trump card it once was in today's brutally competitive world marketplace—a marketplace that is unimpressed with logos and sales numbers but demands, instead, value and performance. At GE we're trying to get that small-company soul—and small-company speed— inside our big-company body. Faster products, faster product cycles to market. Better response time. New niches. Satisfying customers, getting faster communications, moving with more agility, all these are easier when one is small. All these are essential to succeed in the diverse, fast-moving global environment.

Functional Tactics in Accounting and Finance

While most functional tactics guide implementation in the immediate future, the time frame for functional tactics in the area of finance varies, because these tactics direct the use of financial resources in support of the business strategy, long-term goals, and annual objectives. Financial tactics with longer time perspectives guide financial managers in long-term capital investment, debt financing, dividend allocation, and leveraging. Financial tactics designed to manage working capital and short-term assets have a more immediate focus. Figure 10–5 highlights some key questions that financial tactics must answer.

Accounting managers have seen their need to contribute value increasingly scrutinized. Traditional expectations centered around financial accounting—reporting requirements from bank and SEC entities and tax law compliance—remain areas in which actions are dictated by outside governance. Managerial accounting, where managers are responsible for keeping records of costs and the use of funds within their company, has taken on increased strategic significance in the 1990s. This change has involved two tactical areas: (1) how to account for costs of creating and providing their business's products and services, and (2) valuing the business, particularly among publicly traded companies.

Managerial cost accounting has traditionally provided information for managers using cost categories like those shown on the left side below. However, value chain advocates have been increasingly successful getting managers to seek activity-based cost accounting information like that shown on the right side below. In so doing, accounting is becoming a more critical, relevant source of information that truly benefits strategic management.

Traditional Cost Accounting in a Purchasing Department		Activity-Based Cost Accounting in the Same Purchasing Department	
Wages and salaries	$350,000	Evaluate supplier capabilities	$135,750
Employee benefits	115,000	Process purchase orders	82,100
Supplies	6,500	Expedite supplier deliveries	23,500
Travel	2,400	Expedite internal processing	15,840
Depreciation	17,000	Check quality of items purchased	94,300
Other fixed charges	124,000	Check incoming deliveries against purchase orders	48,450
Miscellaneous operating expenses	25,250	Resolve problems	110,000
		Internal administration	130,210
	$640,150		$640,150

Source: Adapted from information in Terence P. Paré, "A New Tool for Managing Costs," *Fortune*, June 14, 1993, pp. 124–29. *Fortune,* © 1993, Time, Inc. All rights reserved.

REAL-WORLD PRICING DILEMMAS:
PRICING SERVICE

Most companies charge their customers the same price for a product—even if it costs more to satisfy some of them. Some customers require no after-sale service; others demand a tremendous amount of hand holding, support, and service. To David and Linda ("Charlie") West, owners of the San Luis Sourdough Company, it didn't make sense to charge *everyone* the same price. So the Wests designed a system that sets prices for their sourdough bread based on how much service their customers—local supermarkets and specialty food shops—require.

Here's how the pricing strategy works: If a customer chooses Level 1 service, having San Luis Sourdough deliver the bread to its back door, the wholesale price is 97 cents per loaf. If the store also wants to be able to return day-old bread for a full credit (Level 2 service) the cost of a loaf is $1.02. If the customer wants the convenience of returns plus the service of having San Luis Sourdough put the bread on the shelf and price it by sticking a bar code label on each bag and another on the shelf (Level 3 service), the price is $1.05 per loaf.

The Wests' prices are not arbitrary; they simply cover the cost of the extra service. The 5-cent premium per loaf for the privilege of returning day-old loaves covers the cost of the bread and handling the returns. Similarly, the 8-cent-per-loaf charge for stocking, pricing, and accepting returns pays for the Level 3 service. Studies show it takes a driver 30 minutes to stock and price a shelf, and drivers earn $8 per hour (salary and benefits). The average customer order is 100 loaves, producing a cost of 8 cents per loaf. "We don't care which pricing option you choose," says Dave. "They're all the same to us." About 60 percent of San Luis Sourdough's customers choose Level 2 service; the remainder are evenly divided between Levels 1 and 3.

In essence, San Luis Sourdough is passing the cost of service on to its customers. Rather than absorb the extra 5 cents or 8 cents per loaf to charge everyone the same price, the Wests let their customers pay for it. How can they get away with it? After all, Sourdough's customers typically require their other bread suppliers to charge one price, whatever the level of service.

Source: Adapted from Paul Brown, "You Get What You Pay For," *Inc.*, October 1990, pp. 155–56; and N. Scarborough and T. Zimmerer, *Effective Small Business Management* (Englewood Cliffs, NJ: Prentice Hall, 1995), p. 395.

Another area of concern is value—whether or not business strategies and management actions are creating real value for stockholders. Perhaps the most prominent technique that has guided tactical decisions for many companies during the last five years is *economic value added* (EVA). EVA is simply a way of measuring an operation's real profitability. It takes into account the "true" cost of capital—after-tax operating profit minus the total annual cost of capital. Incredibly, most corporate groups have looked at the cost of their borrowed capital, but the cost of equity capital that shareholders have contributed appears nowhere in their financial statements. Until managerial accounting takes this into account, so that managers know whether they are covering all their costs and adding value to the company, company managers won't achieve the benefits that have accrued to several companies described in Strategy in Action 10–3 on page 320.

Functional Tactics in Research and Development

With the increasing rate of technological change in most competitive industries, research and development (R&D) has assumed a key strategic role in many firms. In the technology-intensive computer and pharmaceutical industries, for example, firms typically spend

continued

The Wests cite three reasons. First, their big customers recognize that Sourdough is a small business, and they're willing to give the little guy a break. Second, the Wests bake a superior loaf of bread. Their customers recognize Sourdough's higher quality product and are willing to be more flexible in order to stock it. Third, the Wests are honest when dealing with their customers. "What we've told all our customers—and it's true—is that we just don't have the resources of a huge bread company," says Charlie. "We have to compete on the quality of our product, not our level of service."

Very few customers ever complain. Costco Wholesale, Inc., a national supermarket chain touting its reputation for the lowest prices, has no problem paying the 8-cent premium for Level 3 service. "I'm happy," explains the buyer. "We don't have the manpower here to stock the shelves, price, and handle returns. As long as I'm still able to offer the lowest price on their bread, it's a very workable arrangement."

Charlie and David West offer these rules for keeping customers happy while asking them to pay for extra service:

Don't gouge. Charge exactly what the service costs. Don't add a surcharge; it only alienates customers.

Don't play favorites. If customers choose to get extra service, they pay for it. "If we started providing Level 3 service to one company for the price of Level 2 or even Level 1, pretty soon we'd have to do it for everybody," says Dave. "By handling every customer the same way, we don't run the risk of alienating anyone."

Give them a reason to go along. Unless your product is unique, it's difficult to convince customers to pay a premium for service.

Let them establish the level of service they want. Don't force service on customers; let them tell you what service they want. You'll both be better off.

---

between 4 and 6 percent of their sales dollars on R&D. In other industries, such as the hotel/motel and construction industries, R&D spending is less than 1 percent of sales. Thus, functional R&D tactics may be more critical instruments of the business strategy in some industries than in others.

Figure 10–6, on page 322, illustrates the types of questions addressed by R&D tactics. First, R&D tactics should clarify whether basic research or product development research will be emphasized. Several major oil companies now have solar energy subsidiaries in which basic research is emphasized, while the smaller oil companies emphasize product development research.

The choice of emphasis between basic research and product development also involves the time horizon for R&D efforts. Should these efforts be focused on the near term or the long term? The solar energy subsidiaries of the major oil companies have long-term per-spectives, while the smaller oil companies focus on creating products now in order to establish a competitive niche in the growing solar industry.

R&D tactics also involve organization of the R&D function. For example, should R&D work be conducted solely within the firm, or should portions of that work be contracted out? A closely related issue is whether R&D should be centralized or decentralized. What emphasis should be placed on process R&D versus product R&D?

Decisions on all of the above questions are influenced by the firm's R&D posture, which can be offensive or defensive, or both. If that posture is offensive, as is true for small

FIGURE 10–5
Key Functional Tactics in Finance

Functional Tactic	Typical Questions That the Functional Tactics Should Answer
Capital acquisition	What is an acceptable cost of capital?
	What is the desired proportion of short- and long-term debt? Preferred and common equity?
	What balance is desired between internal and external funding?
	What risk and ownership restrictions are appropriate?
	What level and forms of leasing should be used?
Capital allocation	What are the priorities for capital allocation projects?
	On what basis should the final selection of projects be made?
	What level of capital allocation can be made by operating managers without higher approval?
Dividend and working capital management	What portion of earnings should be paid out as dividends?
	How important is dividend stability?
	Are things other than cash appropriate as dividends?
	What are the cash flow requirements? The minimum and maximum cash balances?
	How liberal/conservative should the credit policies be?
	What limits, payment terms, and collection procedures are necessary?
	What payment timing and procedure should be followed?

high-technology firms, the firm will emphasize technological innovation and new product development as the basis for its future success. This orientation entails high risks (and high payoffs) and demands considerable technological skill, forecasting expertise, and the ability to quickly transform innovations into commercial products.

A defensive R&D posture emphasizes product modification and the ability to copy or acquire new technology. Converse Shoes is a good example of a firm with such an R&D posture. Faced with the massive R&D budgets of Nike and Reebok, Converse placed R&D emphasis on bolstering the product life cycle of its prime products (particularly canvas shoes).

Large companies with some degree of technological leadership often use a combination of offensive and defensive R&D strategy. GE in the electrical industry, IBM in the computer industry, and Du Pont in the chemical industry all have a defensive R&D posture for currently available products *and* an offensive R&D posture in basic, long-term research.

Functional Tactics in Human Resource Management (HRM)

The strategic importance of HRM tactics received widespread endorsement in the 1990s. HRM tactics aid long-term success in the development of managerial talent and competent employees; the creation of systems to manage compensation or regulatory concerns; and guiding the effective utilization of human resources to achieve both the firm's short-term objectives and employees' satisfaction and development. HRM tactics are helpful in the areas shown in Figure 10–7, on page 323. The recruitment, selection, and orientation should establish the basic parameters for bringing new people into a firm and adapting them to "the way things are done" in the firm. The career development and training component should guide the action that personnel takes to meet the future human resources needs of the overall business strategy. Merrill Lynch, a major brokerage firm whose long-term corporate strategy is to become a diversified financial service institution, has moved into such areas as investment banking, consumer credit, and venture capital. In support of its long-term objectives, it has incorporated extensive early-career training and ongoing career development programs to meet its expanding need for personnel with multiple competencies. Larger organizations need HRM tactics that guide decisions regarding labor relations; EEOC requirements; and employee compensation, discipline, and control.

Current trends in HRM parallel the reorientation of managerial accounting by looking at their cost structure anew. HRM's "paradigm shift" involves looking at people expense as an investment in human capital. This involves looking at the business's value chain and the "value" of human resource components along the various links in that chain. One of the results of this shift in perspective has been the downsizing phenomenon of the late 1980s and 1990s. While this has been traumatic for millions of employees in companies worldwide, its underlying basis involves an effort to examine the use of "human capital" to create value in ways that maximize the human contribution. This scrutiny continues to challenge the HRM area, as the recent *FORTUNE* article reprinted in Strategy in Action 10–4 details on page 324. The emerging implications for human resource management tactics may be a value-oriented perspective on the role of human resources in a business's value chain as suggested below.

Traditional HRM Ideas	Emerging HRM Ideas
Emphasis solely on physical skills	Emphasis on total contribution to the firm
Expectation of predictable, repetitious behavior	Expectation of innovative and creative behavior
Comfort with stability and conformity	Tolerance of ambiguity and change
Avoidance of responsibility and decision making	Accepting responsibility for making decisions
Training covering only specific tasks	Open-ended commitment; broad continuous development
Emphasis placed on outcomes and results	
High concern for quantity and throughput	Emphasis placed on processes and means
Concern for individual efficiency	High concern for total customer value
Functional and subfunctional specialization	Concern for overall effectiveness
Labor force seen as unnecessary expense	Cross-functional integration
Work force is management's adversary	Labor force seen as critical investment
	Management and work force are partners

Source: G. G. Dess and A. Miller, *Strategic Management*, p. 159. © 1993 by McGraw-Hill, Inc. Reproduced with the permission of The McGraw-Hill Companies.

To summarize, functional tactics reflect how each major activity of a firm contributes to the implementation of the business strategy. The specificity of functional tactics and the involvement of operating managers in their development help ensure understanding of and commitment to the chosen strategy. A related step in implementation is the development of policies that empower operating managers and their subordinates to make decisions and to act autonomously.

**THE HIP MANAGERIAL ACCOUNTANT:
"WHAT'S YOUR EVA?"**

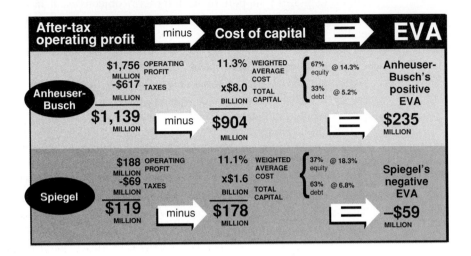

The power of the economic value added (EVA) concept comes from the insight that you can't know if an operation is really creating value until you apply the *true* cost of capital to *all* the capital employed. Most operations within companies—and some companies themselves—have no idea what either amount is. Finding out is fascinating and often startling.

▶Question No. 1: What's the true cost of your capital? You know the cost of your borrowed capital; at least in the short term it's the interest you pay, adjusted to reflect its tax deductibility. (In the longer term it's more complicated, and we'll leave that aside.) But what about equity capital, the money the shareholders provided? Since you aren't required to pay for it, you may think it's free. But it isn't—and its cost is much more than many managers would imagine.

Your true cost of equity is what your shareholders could be getting in price appreciation and dividends if they invested instead in a portfolio of companies about as risky as yours. It's what

EMPOWERING OPERATING PERSONNEL: THE ROLE OF POLICIES

Specific functional tactics provide guidance and initiate action implementing a business's strategy, but more is needed. Supervisors and personnel in the field have been charged in today's competitive environment with being responsible for customer value—for being the "front line" of the company's effort to truly meet customers' needs. Meeting customer needs, becoming obsessed with quality service, was the buzzword that started organizational revolutions in the 1980s. Efforts to do so often failed because employees that were the real contact point between the business and its customers were not *empowered* to make decisions or act to fulfill customer needs. One solution has been to empower operating personnel by pushing down decision making to their level. General Electric allows

STRATEGY
IN ACTION
10–3   **continued**

economists call the opportunity cost. Many managers resist this idea—how can it be a real cost if I don't have to write a check every month?

If that's your reaction, think of it from the point of view of the shareholder who has given his money to you instead of to Coca-Cola or Berkshire Hathaway or the Magellan Fund. If you're not employing his money as successfully as they are—and not showing any promise of doing so—he will take his money back by selling your stock, sending its price down. Other investors will be less inclined to supply any capital. So as long as you're not at least matching the investor's opportunity cost, you're on the road to oblivion. Says Talton Embry, an EVA enthusiast whose New York investment firm owns stakes in a host of big companies: "Capital looks free to a lot of managers. It doesn't look free to investors who hand them the money."

So what is equity's cost today? Over time, shareholders have received on average a return that is six percentage points higher on stocks than on long-term government bonds. With bond rates around 6.3%, that puts the average cost of equity at 12.3%, though it goes much higher for companies with volatile stocks and lower for those with more stable stocks. Assuming you use debt as well as equity capital, the cost is the weighted average of the two.

▶Question No. 2: How much capital is tied up in your operation? Even if you don't know the answer, you know what it consists of: what you paid for real estate, machines, vehicles, and the like, plus working capital. But proponents of EVA say there's more. What about the money your company spends on R&D? On employee training? Those are investments meant to pay off for years, but accounting rules say you can't treat them that way; you have to call them expenses, like the amount you spend on electricity. EVA proponents say forget the accounting rules. For internal purposes, call these things what they are: capital investments. No one can say what their useful life is, so make your best guess—say five years. It's truer than calling them expenses.

When you've answered these questions, you can multiply the capital from Question 2 by the rate from Question 1 and get the dollar cost of the capital in your operation. Now it's a simple matter to figure your EVA. Start with the commonest management yardstick, operating earnings. Subtract taxes. Then subtract the capital cost. What's left is your EVA.

If it's positive, congratulations—your operation is creating wealth. If it's negative, you've just learned your operation is destroying capital. You'd better fix it, fast.

Don't assume that because capital costs a lot, it's a bad thing. Look at the EVAs of Anheuser-Busch and Spiegel (above). It isn't how much capital you've got, but how you manage it.

appliance repair personnel to decide about warranty credits on the spot, a decision that used to take several days and multiple organizational levels. Delta Air Lines allows customer service personnel and their supervisors wide range in resolving customer ticket pricing decisions. Federal Express couriers make decisions and handle package routing information that involves five management levels in the U.S. Postal Service.

Empowerment is being created in many ways. Training, self-managed work groups, eliminating whole levels of management in organizations, and aggressive use of automation are some of the ways and ramifications of this fundamental change in the way business organizations function. At the heart of the effort is the need to ensure that decision making is consistent with the mission, strategy, and tactics of the business while at the same time allowing considerable latitude to operating personnel. One way operating managers do this is through the use of policies.

FIGURE 10–6
Key Functional Tactic in R&D

R&D Decision Area	Typical Questions That the Functional Tactic Should Answer
Basic research versus product and process development	To what extent should innovation and breakthrough research be emphasized? In relation to the emphasis on product development, refinement, and modification?
	What critical operating processes need R&D attention?
	What new projects are necessary to support growth?
Time horizon	Is the emphasis short term or long term?
	Which orientation best supports the business strategy? The marketing and production strategy
Organizational fit	Should R&D be done in-house or contracted out?
	Should R&D be centralized or decentralized?
	What should be the relationship between the R&D units and product managers? Marketing managers? Production managers?
Basic R&D posture	Should the firm maintain an offensive posture, seeking to lead innovation in its industry?
	Should the firm adopt a defensive posture, responding to the innovations of its competitors?

Policies are directives designed to guide the thinking, decisions, and actions of managers and their subordinates in implementing a firm's strategy. Previously referred to as *standard operating procedures*, policies increase managerial effectiveness by standardizing many routine decisions and clarifying the discretion managers and subordinates can exercise in implementing functional tactics. Logically, policies should be derived from functional tactics (and, in some instances, from corporate or business strategies) with the key purpose of aiding strategy execution.[1] Strategy in Action 10–5, on page 326, illustrates selected policies of several well-known firms.

Creating Policies That Empower

Policies communicate guidelines to decisions. They are designed to control decisions while defining allowable discretion within which operational personnel can execute business activities. They do this in several ways:

1. *Policies establish indirect control over independent action* by clearly stating how things are to be done *now*. By defining discretion, policies in effect control decisions yet empower employees to conduct activities without direct intervention by top management.

2. *Policies promote uniform handling of similar activities.* This facilitates the coordination of work tasks and helps reduce friction arising from favoritism, discrimination,

---

[1] The term *policy* has various definitions in management literature. Some authors and practitioners equate policy with strategy. Others do this inadvertently by using "policy" as a synonym for company mission, purpose, or culture. Still other authors and practitioners differentiate policy in terms of "levels" associated respectively with purpose, mission, and strategy. "Our policy is to make a positive contribution to the communities and societies we live in" and "our policy is not to diversify out of the hamburger business" are two examples of the breadth of what some call policies. This book defines *policy* much more narrowly as specific guides to managerial action and decisions in the implementation of strategy. This definition permits a sharper distinction between the formulation and implementation of functional strategies. And, of even greater importance, it focuses the tangible value of the policy concept where it can be most useful—as a key administrative tool to enhance effective implementation and execution of strategy.

FIGURE 10–7
Key Functional Tactics in HRM

Functional Tactic	Typical Questions That HRM Tactics Should Answer
Recruitment, selection, and orientation	What key human resources are needed to support the chosen strategy?
	How do we recruit these human resources?
	How sophisticated should our selection process be?
	How should we introduce new employees to the organization?
Career development and training	What are our future human resource needs?
	How can we prepare our people to meet these needs?
	How can we help our people develop?
Compensation	What levels of pay are appropriate for the tasks we require?
	How can we motivate and retain good people?
	How should we interpret our payment, incentive, benefit, and seniority policies?
Evaluation, discipline, and control	How often should we evaluate our people? Formally or informally?
	What disciplinary steps should we take to deal with poor performance or inappropriate behavior?
	In what ways should we "control" individual and group performance?
Labor relations and equal opportunity requirements	How can we maximize labor-management cooperation?
	How do our personnel practices affect women/minorities?
	Should we have hiring policies?

and the disparate handling of common functions—something that often hampers operating personnel.

3. *Policies ensure quicker decisions* by standardizing answers to previously answered questions that otherwise would recur and be pushed up the management hierarchy again and again—something that required unnecessary levels of management between senior decision makers and field personnel.

4. *Policies institutionalize basic aspects of organization behavior.* This minimizes conflicting practices and establishes consistent patterns of action in attempts to make the strategy work—again, freeing operating personnel to act.

5. *Policies reduce uncertainty in repetitive and day-to-day decision making,* thereby providing a necessary foundation for coordinated, efficient efforts and freeing operating personnel to act.

6. *Policies counteract resistance to or rejection of chosen strategies by organization members.* When major strategic change is undertaken, unambiguous operating policies clarify what is expected and facilitate acceptance, particularly when operating managers participate in policy development.

7. *Policies offer predetermined answers to routine problems.* This greatly expedites dealing with both ordinary and extraordinary problems—with the former, by referring to these answers; with the latter, by giving operating personnel more time to cope with them.

8. *Policies afford managers a mechanism for avoiding hasty and ill-conceived decisions in changing operations.* Prevailing policy can always be used as a reason for not yielding to emotion-based, expedient, or temporarily valid arguments for altering procedures and practices.

STRATEGY
IN ACTION
10–4

WHAT'S NEXT FOR HRM? AN EXPERT SAYS IT'S TIME FOR HRM DEPARTMENTS TO PUT UP OR SHUT UP!

*F*ortune magazine editor Tom Stewart (74774.3555@compuserve.com) made these observations recently:

> Nestling warm and sleepy in your company is a department whose employees spend 80 percent of their time on routine administrative tasks. Nearly every function of this department can be performed more expertly for less by others. It is your human resources department. Consider what HR does and whether it should do it.

Start with payroll. Outside providers now cut an estimated 25 percent of all paychecks issued in the United States. The reason, says payroll services leader ADP's CFO: "As companies move off mainframes, they are taking a look at what applications are strategic to them. When they decide that payroll and HR functions are not strategic, they outsource them."

The same is happening with benefits administration. A 1995 survey of 314 large U.S. companies found 87 percent outsource record keeping and 59 percent administration service. The Corporate Leadership Council conducts research for 500 member companies concluded that there is significant potential and value in outsourcing four HR functions: benefit design and administration; information systems and record keeping; employee services such as retirement counseling, outplacement, and relocation; and health and safety. None, the Council noted, have much potential to produce competitive advantage for a company that does them especially well in-house.

But why stop there? Take recruiting. The rule of thumb among managers is to involve HR as little as possible in the recruiting process. While HR professionals are themselves looking for work, two-thirds of the time they find it by networking or using (outside) search firms. Another candidate is

Policies may be written and formal or unwritten and informal. Informal, unwritten policies are usually associated with a strategic need for competitive secrecy. Some policies of this kind, such as promotion from within, are widely known (or expected) by employees and implicitly sanctioned by management. Managers and employees often like the latitude granted by unwritten and informal policies. However, such policies may detract from the long-term success of a strategy. Formal, written policies have at least seven advantages:

1. They require managers to think through the policy's meaning, content, and intended use.
2. They reduce misunderstanding.
3. They make equitable and consistent treatment of problems more likely.
4. They ensure unalterable transmission of policies.
5. They communicate the authorization or sanction of policies more clearly.
6. They supply a convenient and authoritative reference.
7. They systematically enhance indirect control and organizationwide coordination of the key purposes of policies.

The strategic significance of policies can vary. At one extreme are such policies as travel reimbursement procedures, which are really work rules and may not be linked to the implementation of a strategy. At the other extreme are organizationwide policies that are virtually functional strategies, such as Wendy's requirement that every location invest 1 percent of its gross revenue in local advertising.

**STRATEGY
IN ACTION
10–4**   **continued**

designing and running compensation and reward systems—ironically, especially when state-of-the-art reward mechanisms are of paramount importance to competing. Many managers have decided that it is much better to buy the state of the art from outside, customize it, and instill responsibility for running it as far down in the organization as possible. And as for training: Will every reader who has taken a training course sponsored by their HR department and found it very valuable raise his hand? There's lot of evidence that training is a good thing . . . if it's just-in-time, close-to-the-work training—training that should be lodged in the line function, not off the shelf.

Says Vikesh Mahendroo, Executive VP of HR consultants W.M. Mercer says "HR is often out of sync with the needs of the business." He thinks reengineering HR can fix that. But how far should they go? Steel giant Nucor, with 6,000 employees, runs HR with a headquarters staff of three people—a secretary and two HR professionals, one HR agent at each plant reporting to the plant manager, and a set of company HR principles. Says Corporate Leadership Council executive director Matt Olsen: "This is a make-or-break moment for the HR function."

HR people say that they are the trustee of the asset that matters above all others, proactive custodians of our core competence, holders of the keys to competitive advantage in the new economy. Just so much rhetoric say others. There may be a reason that more and more new HR executives come to the post with backgrounds in line management or consulting rather than from HR's own ranks. Says Mahendroo, "There are two messages here. One is that human capital management is important enough that it is an acceptable career path for an up-and-comer. The second is that many people doing the work now can't cut it in the HR of the future."

Policies can be externally imposed or internally derived. Policies regarding equal employment practices are often developed in compliance with external (government) requirements, and policies regarding leasing or depreciation may be strongly influenced by current tax regulations.

Regardless of the origin, formality, and nature of policies, the key point to bear in mind is the valuable role that they can play in strategy implementation. Existing policies should be reviewed periodically so as to ensure their guidance and control of operating activities in a manner consistent with current business and functional strategies. Lotus Development Corporation (Lotus 1–2–3) recently halted a policy forcing customers to destroy spreadsheet programs from competing software makers. Aimed at preventing unauthorized use of 1–2–3 software, Lotus found it was creating major problems for some customers. Communicating specific policies will help overcome resistance to strategic change and foster commitment to successful strategy implementation.

SUMMARY

The first concern in the implementation of business strategy is to translate that strategy into action throughout the organization. This chapter discussed three important tools for accomplishing this.

Action plans and short-term objectives are derived from long-term objectives, which are then translated into current actions and targets. They differ from long-term objectives in time frame, specificity, and measurement. To be effective in strategy implementation, they must be integrated and coordinated. They also must be consistent, measurable, and prioritized.

SELECTED POLICIES THAT
AID STRATEGY IMPLEMENTATION

3M Corporation has a *personnel policy*, called the *15 percent rule*, that allows virtually any employee to spend up to 15 percent of the workweek on anything that he or she wants to, as long as it's product related.

(This policy supports 3M's corporate strategy of being a highly innovative manufacturer, with each division required to have a quarter of its annual sales come from products introduced within the past five years.)

Wendy's has a *purchasing policy* that gives local store managers the authority to buy fresh meat and produce locally, rather than from regionally designated or company-owned sources.

(This policy supports Wendy's functional strategy of having fresh, unfrozen hamburgers daily.)

General Cinema has a *financial policy* that requires annual capital investment in movie theaters not to exceed annual depreciation.

(By seeing that capital investment is no greater than depreciation, this policy supports General Cinema's financial strategy of maximizing cash flow—in this case, all profit—to its growth areas. The policy also reinforces General Cinema's financial strategy of leasing as much as possible.)

IBM had a *marketing policy* of not giving free IBM personal computers (PCs) to any person or organization.

(This policy attempted to support IBM's image strategy by maintaining its image as professional, high-value, service business as it sought to dominate the PC market.)

Crown, Cork, and Seal Company has an *R&D policy* of not investing any financial or people resources in basic research.

(This policy supports Crown, Cork, and Seal's functional strategy, which emphasizes customer services, not technical leadership.)

NationsBank of South Carolina has an *operating policy* that requires annual renewal of the financial statement of all personal borrowers.

(This policy supports NationsBank's financial strategy, which seeks to maintain a loan-to-loss ratio below the industry norm.)

Functional tactics are derived from the business strategy. They identify the specific, immediate actions that must be taken in key functional areas to implement the business strategy.

Employee empowerment through policies provides another means for guiding behavior, decisions, and actions at the firm's operating levels in a manner consistent with its business and functional strategies. Effective policies channel actions, behavior, decisions, and practices to promote strategic accomplishment.

Action plans, functional tactics, and policies represent only the start of the strategy implementation. The strategy must be institutionalized—must permeate the firm. The next chapter examines this phase of strategy implementation.

QUESTIONS FOR DISCUSSION

1. How does the concept "translate thought into action" bear on the relationship between business strategy and operating strategy? Between long-term and short-term objectives?

2. How do functional tactics differ from corporate and business strategies?

3. What key concerns must functional tactics address in marketing? Finance? POM? Personnel?

4. How do policies aid strategy implementation? Illustrate your answer.

5. Illustrate a policy, an objective, and a functional tactic in your personal career strategy.

6. Why are short-term objectives needed when long-term objectives are already available.

BIBLIOGRAPHY

Allio, R. J. "Formulating Global Strategy." *Planning Review*, March–April 1989, pp. 22–29.

Boag, David A., and Ali Dastmalchian. "Market Vulnerability and the Design and Management of the Marketing Function in Small Firms." *Journal of Small Business Management*, October 1988, p. 37.

Charalambides, L. C. "Designing Communication Support Systems for Strategic Planning." *Long Range Planning*, December 1988, pp. 93–100.

Coates, N. "The Globalization of the Motor Vehicle Manufacturing Industry." *Planning Review*, January–February 1989, pp. 34–39.

Coy, P. "The New Realism in Office Systems." *Business Week*, June 15, 1992, p. 128.

David, F. R. "How Companies Define Their Mission." *Long Range Planning*, February 1989, pp. 90–97.

Freund, Y. P. "Critical Success Factors." *Planning Review*, March–April 1988, pp. 20–23.

Fulmer, William E. "Human Resource Management: The Right Hand of Strategy Implementation." *Human Resource Planning* 13, no. 1 (1990), pp.1–11.

Garavan, Thomas N. "Strategic Human Resource Development." *International Journal of Manpower* 12, no. 6 (1991), pp. 21–34.

Giles, William D. "Making Strategy Work." *Long Range Planning* 24, no. 5 (1991), pp. 75–91.

Lado, A. A., and M. C. Wilson. "Human Resource Systems and Sustained Competitive Advantage: A Competency Based Perspective." *Academy of Management Review* 19 (1994), pp. 699–727.

Marucheck, Ann; Ronald Pamnesi; and Carl Anderson. "An Exploratory Study of the Manufacturing Strategy Process in Practice." *Journal of Operations Management* 9, no. 1 pp. 101–23.

Miller, J. G., and W. Hayslip. "Implementing Manufacturing Strategic Planning." *Planning Review*, July–August 1989, pp. 22–29.

Nielson, Richard P. "Cooperative Strategy in Marketing." *Business Horizons*, July–August 1987, p. 61.

Ohmae, K. "Getting Back to Strategy." *Harvard Business Review*, September–October 1988, pp. 149–56.

Parnell, J. A. "Functional Background and Business Strategy: The Impact of Executive Strategy Fit on Performance." *Journal of Business Strategies* 11, no. 1 (1994), pp. 49–62.

Perkins, A. G. "Manufacturing: Maximizing Service, Minimizing Inventory." *Harvard Business Review* 72, no. 2, pp. 13–14.

Peterson, R. T. "An Analysis of New Product Ideas." *Journal of Small Business Management*, April 1988, pp. 25–31.

Prahalad, C. K., and Gary Hamel. "The Core Competence of the Corporation." *Harvard Business Review* 68 (May–June 1990), pp. 79–93.

Quinn, James Brian. *Intelligent Enterprise.* (New York: Free Press, 1992), chaps. 2 and 3.

Randolph, W. A., and B. Z. Posner. "What Every Manager Needs to Know about Project Management." *Sloan Management Review*, Summer 1988, pp. 64–74.

Roth, Kendall; David M. Schweiger; and Allen J. Morrison. "Global Strategy Implementation at the Business Unit Level: Operational Capabilities and Administrative Mechanisms." *Journal of International Business Studies* 22, no. 3 (1991), pp. 369–402.

Shank, J. K., and V. Govindarajan. "Making Strategy Explicit in Cost Analysis." *Sloan Management Review*, Spring 1988, pp. 19–30.

Stalk, George; Philip Evans; and Lawrence E. Shulman. "Competing on Capabilities: The New Rules of Corporate Strategy." *Harvard Business Review* 70, no. 2 (March–April 1992), pp. 57–69.

Stern, Joel. "Think Cash and Risk—Forget ESP." *Planning Review*, January–February 1988, p. 6.

Stonich, Paul. *Implementing Strategy: Making Strategy Happen.* (New York: Ballinger, 1982).

Wheelwright, S., and N. S. Langowitz. "Plus Development Corporation: Joint Venturing a Breakthrough Product." *Planning Review*, July–August 1989, pp. 6–21.

Wright, Norman B. "The Driving Force: An Action-Oriented Solution to Strategy Implementation." *Canadian Business Quarterly* 54, no. 1 (1989), pp. 51–54, 66.

Yip, George S. *Total Global Strategy: Managing for Worldwide Competitive Advantage.* (Englewood Cliffs, NJ: Prentice Hall, 1992), chap. 8.

CHAPTER 10 COHESION CASE ILLUSTRATION

IMPLEMENTING STRATEGY THROUGH THE BUSINESS FUNCTIONS AT COCA-COLA

The Coca Cola Company is exciting to examine when it comes to the detail with which they craft and execute value chain activities and functional tactics designated to accomplish their business strategy. In this case we show you some of the activities and tactics Coca-Cola has used to implement the four elements of its business strategy.

Before we do that, it is useful to see how Coca-Cola management views their company from a value chain perspective. Their value chain view of themselves is as a "global business system," as they describe below:

> A successful global company must have a global business system through which to reach consumers. In our case, the system comprises not only the Company itself, but a worldwide network of employees, bottling partners, vendors, and customers. This system is made up of dedicated people working long and hard to sell products they believe in. . . . Such a system must do much more than just deliver products. In order to appeal to cultures as diverse as those in Switzerland and Swaziland, it must also tailor products and messages to local markets. . . . Graphically, this system can best be represented as an inverted triangle or pyramid comprising many levels, of which the Company is only the base. The following figure depicts this incomparable global system, which builds from 650,000 employees through more than 8 million customers to satisfy the thirst of the world's more than 5 billion consumers. And most important, the system is growing and expanding every day. As impressive as the numbers in the figure are, by the time, you read them, they will have been surpassed.

Remember that Coca Cola's business strategy had four elements: (1) geographic expansion, (2) infrastructure fortification, (3) financial reformation, and (4) differentiation. Let's look at some specific ways they implement these four elements.

GEOGRAPHIC EXPANSION

Says Roberto Goizueta, "We refuse to neglect any territory anywhere in the world. We have long pursued geographic expansion as a fundamental means of growth. We have divided the world into six regions in which we have major organizations in place to pursue aggressive expansion." A summary of Coca Cola's geographic expansion efforts over the last three years is provided below and on pages 329–32.

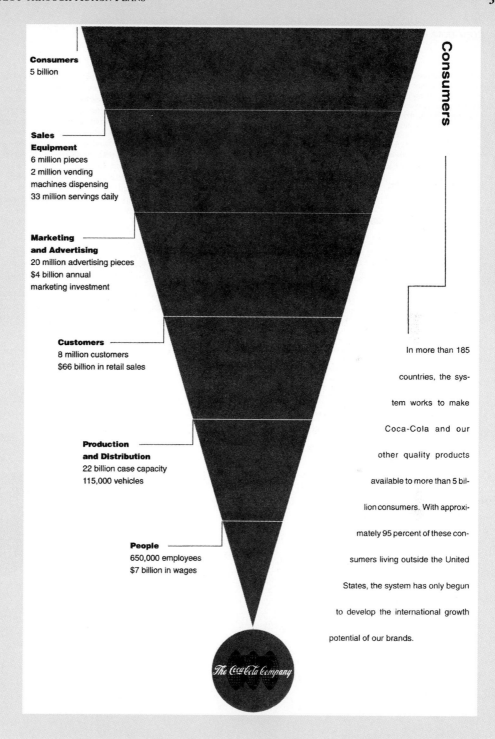

Consumers
5 billion

Sales Equipment
6 million pieces
2 million vending machines dispensing
33 million servings daily

Marketing and Advertising
20 million advertising pieces
$4 billion annual marketing investment

Customers
8 million customers
$66 billion in retail sales

Production and Distribution
22 billion case capacity
115,000 vehicles

People
650,000 employees
$7 billion in wages

Consumers

In more than 185 countries, the system works to make Coca-Cola and our other quality products available to more than 5 billion consumers. With approximately 95 percent of these consumers living outside the United States, the system has only begun to develop the international growth potential of our brands.

The Coca-Cola Company

COCA-COLA USA

Led by solid increases in the Company's core brands, the world's largest market for Coca-Cola achieved solid growth in 1994, again outperforming the industry. Unit case volume grew 7 percent, while gallon sales grew 8 percent. Complementing the strong growth of Coca-Cola and Sprite, supporting brands such as Fruitopia, Powerāde and Minute Maid Juices To Go contributed meaningful volume gains. Continued focus on programs designed to help customers increase their profits through the sale of our products also contributed to the results.

Average Annual Growth
Unit Case Volume*

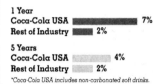

1 Year
Coca-Cola USA   7%
Rest of Industry   2%

5 Years
Coca-Cola USA   4%
Rest of Industry   2%

*Coca-Cola USA includes non-carbonated soft drinks.

Coca-Cola USA Per Capita Consumption**
Even in leading-edge markets such as the United States, enormous opportunities for growth still exist. If we were to elevate territories with below-average per capitas to our national average, our overall per capita would increase 27 drinks, generating 300 million incremental unit cases – roughly the equivalent of our total 1994 unit case volume in Spain, one of our top 10 markets worldwide.

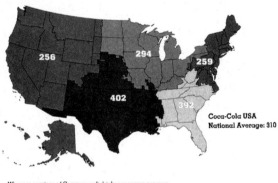

Coca-Cola USA
National Average: 310

**8-ounce servings of Company soft drinks per person per year.

AFRICA GROUP

Difficult economic and political conditions in key markets continued to affect industry performance in Africa. Declines in economically troubled Nigeria offset unit case increases throughout most of the Group. Gallon sales declined slightly, affected primarily by a decrease in Nigeria. Nonetheless, the Africa Group continues to improve and expand the foundations for strong long-term growth. Those foundations include restructured bottling operations, increasingly efficient business systems, aggressive marketing programs and improved customer service. While Company products account for 84 percent of industry sales, overall per capita consumption of Company products remains a relatively low 23 servings per year, representing significant potential for growth.

Growth Rate
(1994 vs. 1993)

Africa	Gallon Sales	Unit Case Sales
Central Africa Region	7%	11%
Nigeria	(19)%	(14)%
Southern Africa Division	(5)%	3%
Other	12%	9%
Total	**(4)%**	**1%**

Africa Group
1994 Unit Case Sales

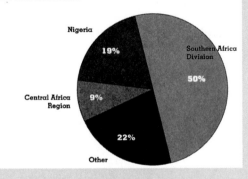

PACIFIC GROUP

Aggressive marketing and expanded production and distribution capacity fueled strong across-the-board volume increases in the Pacific Group in 1994. Unit case volume grew 12 percent and gallon sales increased 13 percent, as an unusually warm summer over most of Asia offset continued weakness in the Japanese economy. In 1995, the Group assumed responsibility for India and the Middle East, markets with opportunities that mirror those of many of our developed markets in Asia. Accordingly, the Group was renamed the Middle and Far East Group.

Growth Rate
(1994 vs. 1993)

Pacific	Gallon Sales	Unit Case Sales
Australia	13%	10%
China	50%	36%
Japan	9%	8%
Korea	19%	11%
Philippines	12%	14%
Thailand	14%	14%
Other	10%	10%
Total	**13%**	**12%**

Pacific Group
1994 Unit Case Sales

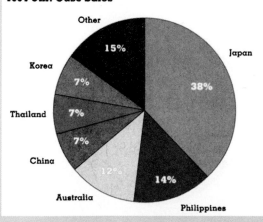

EUROPEAN COMMUNITY GROUP

Focused marketplace activity, complemented by favorable summer weather and a recovering economy, yielded strong results in 1994. Momentum accelerated in the second half of the year as unit case volume grew 13 percent. For the full year, unit case volume grew 7 percent and gallon sales rose 5 percent. These gains were fueled by a number of initiatives, including a new push behind contour packaging and strong World Cup and Olympic Winter Games marketing efforts. In early 1995, Eastern Europe, Scandinavia and the former Soviet Union were added to the Group's responsibilities, providing a single leadership point for greater Europe. The combined group was renamed the Greater Europe Group.

Growth Rate
(1994 vs. 1993)

European Community	Gallon Sales	Unit Case Sales
Benelux/Denmark	4%	9%
France	7%	9%
Germany	3%	4%
Great Britain	6%	7%
Italy	3%	5%
Spain	7%	9%
Other	11%	11%
Total	**5%**	**7%**

European Community Group
1994 Unit Case Sales

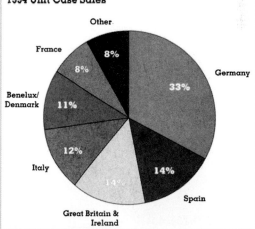

NORTHEAST EUROPE/MIDDLE EAST GROUP

The diverse markets of the Northeast Europe/Middle East (NEME) Group recorded another year of exceptionally strong growth. Unit case volume grew 35 percent and gallon shipments increased 32 percent, continuing the strong momentum of 1993. The NEME Group also picked up significant volume in India, where Coca-Cola returned in late 1993 after a 16-year absence.

Growth Rate
(1994 vs. 1993)

Northeast Europe/ Middle East (NEME)	Gallon Sales	Unit Case Sales
East Central European Division	17%	23%
Middle East Division	34%	33%
Nordic and N. Eurasia Division	13%	16%
India	*	*
Total	**32%**	**35%**

*Sales began in late 1993.

LATIN AMERICA GROUP

The Latin America Group continued to capitalize on the liberalization of economies throughout the region with aggressive infrastructure investments and new product and package introductions. These measures, coupled with focused brand-building initiatives, contributed to a solid performance in 1994. Driven by strong growth from Mexico and Argentina and a second-half surge in demand in Brazil, unit case volume grew 10 percent and gallon sales increased 9 percent, while profitability increased significantly.

Growth Rate
(1994 vs. 1993)

Latin America	Gallon Sales	Unit Case Sales
Argentina	11%	12%
Brazil	8%	10%
Chile	8%	8%
Colombia	4%	4%
Mexico	11%	11%
Other	7%	9%
Total	**9%**	**10%**

**Northeast Europe/Middle East Group
1994 Unit Case Sales**

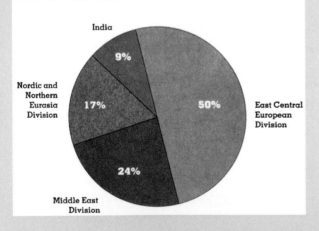

**Latin America Group
1994 Unit Case Sales**

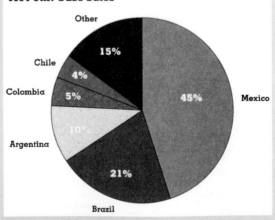

INFRASTRUCTURE FORTIFICATION

Coca-Cola has sought to improve and expand its inbound logistics, operating capabilities, and outbound logistics throughout its global bottling system. Management had this to say about infrastructure tactics:

> As our customers grow and expand, we continue to stimulate positive changes in our global bottling system, equipping it to meet their needs more effectively and efficiently. Depending on the situation, we have used three approaches: 1. Taking noncontrolling ownership positions, infusing capital and management. 2. Facilitating the creation of large, efficient anchor bottlers who share our commitment to growth. 3. Investing in consolidated operations, compensating for limited local resources. Bottling companies in which we hold an ownership position sold over 5 billion unit cases for 42 percent of our worldwide volume. Unit case volume grew at approximately the same rate in both those bottling companies in which we have ownership positions and those in which we have no holdings, reaffirming the effectiveness of the strategy of infrastructure fortification.

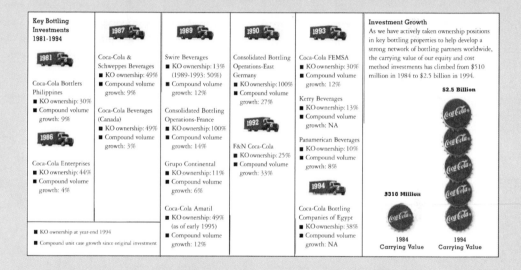

Another way to see this more graphically is to look at what Coca-Cola has invested in nonbottling infrastructure to consolidate production and distribution networks and to adapt the latest operating technology and information systems:

	Year Ended December 31		
	1994	**1993**	**1992**
Capital expenditures	**$878**	$800	$1,083
United States	**32%**	23%	22%
Africa	**3%**	1%	1%
European Community	**26%**	33%	41%
Latin America	**16%**	19%	20%
Northeast Europe/Middle East	**19%**	18%	13%
Pacific & Canada	**4%**	6%	3%

FINANCIAL REFORMATION

Coca-Cola management has used four financial/accounting tactics to implement its business strategy and to generate the capacity to support the other parts of its strategy to build competitive advantage. Those four tactics are:

1. Increase the use of debt.
2. Lower the dividend payout rate to increase reinvestment.
3. Repurchase Coca-Cola shares.
4. Adopt the economic value-added approach to evaluate results.

These tactics are described below and on the next page.

Using Debt Effectively

Capitalizing on our ability to generate returns well above our borrowing rates, we began taking on prudent amounts of debt in the early 1980s. With a return on capital roughly three times our cost of capital, this strategy makes even more sense now than before.

Reinvestment Rate

1983
35%

1994
60%

Lowering Dividend Payout Ratio

With our dividend payout ratio cresting as high as 65 percent in 1983, we began increasing our dividends at a slower rate than our earnings growth, eventually lowering that ratio to 40 percent. Reducing our payout ratio allowed us to reinvest over $660 million into our business in 1994 alone, bringing the total amount freed up for reinvestment since 1983 to $3.4 billion.

Repurchasing of Shares

Acting on the conviction that our shares represent one of the best uses of our excess cash, we repurchased 25 million of our own shares in 1994, bringing our total repurchases since 1984 to approximately 454 million, at an average cost of $15.45 per share.

$15.45

$51.50

Average Purchase Price

1994 Market Value

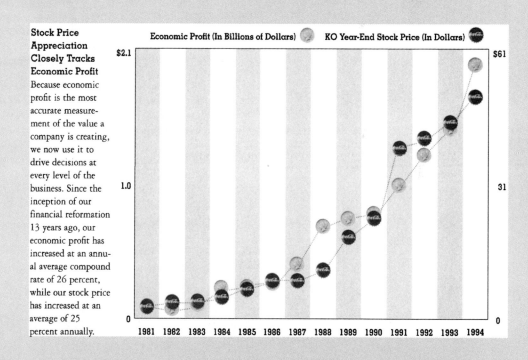

Stock Price Appreciation Closely Tracks Economic Profit

Because economic profit is the most accurate measurement of the value a company is creating, we now use it to drive decisions at every level of the business. Since the inception of our financial reformation 13 years ago, our economic profit has increased at an annual average compound rate of 26 percent, while our stock price has increased at an average of 25 percent annually.

Economic Profit (In Billions of Dollars)   KO Year-End Stock Price (In Dollars)

$2.1

1.0

0

$61

31

0

1981 1982 1983 1984 1985 1986 1987 1988 1989 1990 1991 1992 1993 1994

DIFFERENTIATION

Focusing on the Consumer

4 If our ongoing geographic expansion, financial reformation and infrastructure fortification initiatives are designed to gear up the machine, then our fourth initiative is designed to put that machine to work. Where we once might have been tempted to rely on the sheer strength of our global availability, our substantial financial resources and our powerful distribution network, we now are driving growth by aggressively expanding demand for our brands. **1994** To increase that demand to levels that will meet our own ambitious expectations, we have set out to become undeniably the world's premier consumer marketing company, taking decisive actions to differentiate our brands wherever we do business.

Differentiation With Customers

Further differentiating our brands with consumers also helps us further differentiate ourselves with our customers, the people who make our products available at the retail level. The logic is simple: the greater the consumer demand for our brands, the greater our ability to add value to our customers' businesses by attracting more consumers into their outlets.

This important point of differentiation is complemented by our ability to provide superior delivery, promotional services and sales support that clearly differentiate us as the beverage supplier most capable of driving sustained, profitable growth in their businesses.

Disappearing at stores daily.

Differentiation in Size and Scope Already the world's largest beverage company, we continued to increase in size and scope in 1994, further enhancing another key point of differentiation we bring to any marketplace.

- In 1994, the *increase* in our market value exceeded the *total* 1994 market value of all but 106 of the publicly traded companies based in the United States.
- In 1994, unit case sales for Fanta and Sprite, our third and fourth largest-selling brands, respectively, each crossed the **1,**   mark for the first time. If the two brands existed as independent companies, Fanta would rank as the third largest soft drink marketer in the world, while Sprite would be the fourth.
- In 1994, our unit case sales in Latin America alone exceeded our nearest international competitor's total international unit case sales.
- In 1994, sales of Coca-Cola *increased* by 500 million unit cases – more than we sold in our first 34 years *combined*.
- In 1995, Coca-Cola made its third trip into space – aboard the *Discovery*.

Differentiation with Consumers

Through the decades, we have quite effectively built brand Coca-Cola on a horizontal basis, extending its appeal across national boundaries

Time magazine
May 15, 1950

until there is virtually no place on earth where the people do not both know and like Coca-Cola. That horizontal expansion continues to serve us well in driving growth. But now, as the number of nations where Coca-Cola is not sold dwindles to fewer than 20, we are intensifying our efforts to build our brands vertically.

Building a brand vertically means simply creating deeper consumer desire for that brand than existed the day before. It's simply making sure we continue to give people additional reasons to

Tokyo's Ginza
1994

buy our brands instead of somebody else's. That's the essence of *differentiation*, and we are determined to make sure every consumer understands that our brands are different, better and special.

In building brand Coca-Cola vertically, our challenge is daunting. Increasing the strength of a new brand is relatively easy; making the world's most powerful brand even more powerful is not. After all, most of the world's 5.6 billion people already have a well-established understanding of what Coca-Cola means to them.

But if our challenge is daunting, our tools are uniquely suited to the task. First, the Coca-Cola trademark itself is a remarkably resilient and multi-dimensional piece of cultural iconography. Second, we are continually building on our unique marketing expertise, consumer understanding, financial firepower and access to creative resources. And third, we are developing an increasingly strong penchant for action.

Differentiation in Action

Differentiation is not created by mere philosophy. Differentiation is created by action.

In other words, the world will judge us as its premier consumer marketing company based not on how much we know or how clever our ideas are, but on how well we translate those ideas into actions that produce results in the marketplace.

Consequently, if our marketing efforts are guided by our bias for differentiation, then they are propelled by our prejudice for action. This means that we must be willing to take risks. And, yes, it means we must be willing to

MIND

BODY

Fruitopia

PLANET

Fruitopia: taking action to meet changing consumer needs

fail occasionally.

In 1994, all of our major consumer marketing actions

generated significant value for The Coca-Cola Company, either by directly driving volume increases or by helping us gain a deeper understanding of our consumers, on which we will build with future actions.

11

IMPLEMENTING STRATEGY THROUGH RESTRUCTURING AND REENGINEERING THE COMPANY'S STRUCTURE, LEADERSHIP, CULTURE, AND REWARDS

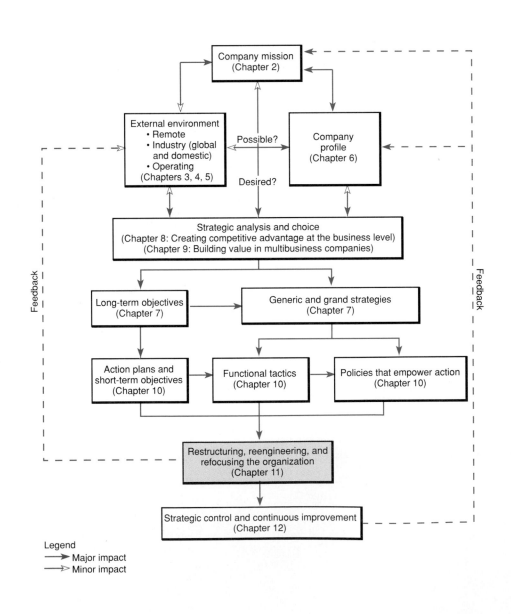

Legend
→ Major impact
⇒ Minor impact

Until this point in the strategic management process, managers have maintained a decidedly market-oriented focus as they formulate strategies and begin implementation through action plans detailing the tactics and actions that will be taken in each functional activity. Now the process takes a decidedly operations focus—getting the work of the business done efficiently and effectively so as to make the strategy work. What is the best way to organize ourselves to accomplish the mission? Where should leadership come from? What values should guide our activities each day? What should this organization and its people be like? How can we shape rewards that encourage appropriate action? These are some of the fundamental issues managers face as they turn to the heart of strategy implementation.

While the focus is internal, the firm must still consider external factors as well. The intense competition in the global marketplace of the 1990s has led most companies to consider their structure, or how the activities within their business are conducted, with an unprecedented attentiveness to what that marketplace—customers, competitors, suppliers, distribution partners—suggests or needs from the "internal" structure, business processes, leadership, and culture of their company. *Downsizing, restructuring, reengineering, outsourcing*, and *empowerment* are all emblazoned in our minds as a result of the extraordinary speed with which companies worldwide have incorporated them as part of their adjustment to the rigors of competing as a part of the global economic village of the 21st century. You no doubt recognize and have been touched in several ways by the ramification of these concepts over the last five years. This contemporary vocabulary reflects managers' attempts to rationalize their organizational structure, leadership, culture, and reward systems to ensure a basic level of cost competitiveness, capacity for responsive quality, and the need to shape each one of them to accommodate the requirements of their strategies.

These topics received considerable attention from executives, authors, and researchers during the last decade as they sought to understand the reasons behind the superior performance of the world's "best companies." One of the early and widely accepted frameworks that identify the key factors that best explain superior performance was the McKinsey 7-S Framework, provided in Figure 11–1. This framework provides a useful visualization of the key components managers must consider in making sure a strategy permeates the day-to-day life of the firm.

Once the strategy has been designed, the McKinsey Framework suggests that managers focus on six components to ensure effective execution: structure, systems, shared values (culture), skills, style, and staff. This chapter organizes these six components into four basic elements through which managers can implement strategy. The first is structure—the basic way the firm's different activities are organized. Second is leadership, encompassing the need to establish an effective style as well as the necessary staff and skills to execute the strategy. The third element is culture—the shared values that create the norms of individual behavior and the tone of the organization. The final elements are the systems for rewarding performance as well as monitoring and controlling organizational action. Reward systems are examined in this chapter, while a discussion of systems for monitoring and controlling organizational action is reserved for Chapter 12.

STRUCTURING AN EFFECTIVE ORGANIZATION

Successful strategy implementation depends in large part on the firm's primary organizational structure. Structure helps identify the firm's key activities and the manner in which they will be coordinated to achieve the firm's strategic purpose. IBM changed from a highly centralized, functional structure in the early 1990s to a highly decentralized, strategic business unit structure that IBM's top managers viewed as more consistent with the firm's "network-centric" product development strategy for the 21st century.

FIGURE 11–1
McKinsey 7-S Framework

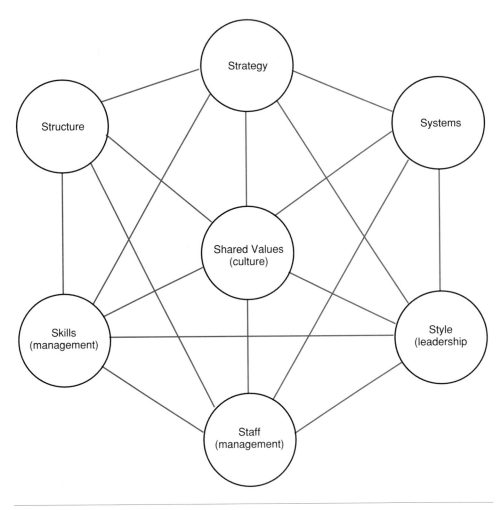

A primary organizational structure comprises the firm's major elements, components, or differentiated units. Such a structure portrays how key tasks and activities have been divided to achieve efficiency and effectiveness.

The primary structure is not the only means for getting "organized" to implement the strategy. Reward systems, coordination terms, planning procedures, alliances, information, and budgetary systems are among the other means that facilitate getting organized. However, it is through the primary structure that strategists attempt to position the firm so as to execute its strategy in a manner that balances internal efficiency and overall effectiveness.

Primary Organizational Structures and Their Strategy-Related Pros and Cons

Matching the structure to the strategy is a fundamental task of company strategists. To understand how that task is handled, we first must review the five basic primary structures. We will then turn to guidelines for matching structure to strategy.

FIGURE 11–2
Functional Organization Structures

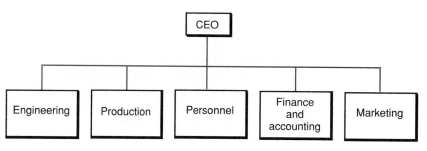

A process-oriented functional structure (an electronics distributor):

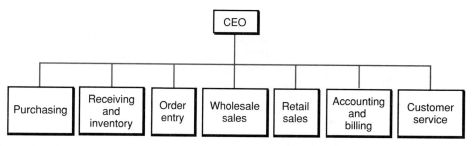

Strategic Advantages	Strategic Disadvantages
1. Achieves efficiency through specialization.	1. Promotes narrow specialization and functional rivalry or conflict.
2. Develops functional expertise.	2. Creates difficulties in functional coordination and interfunctional decision making.
3. Differentiates and delegates day-to-day operating decisions.	3. Limits development of general managers.
4. Retains centralized control of strategic decisions.	4. Has a strong potential for interfunctional conflict—priority placed on functional areas, not the entire business.
5. Tightly links structure to strategy by designating key activities as separate units.	

The five basic primary structures are: (1) functional organization, (2) geographic organization, (3) divisional organization, (4) strategic business units, and (5) matrix organization. Each structure has advantages and disadvantages that strategists must consider when choosing an organization form.

Functional Organizational Structure

Functional structures predominate in firms with a single or narrow product focus. Such firms require well-defined skills and areas of specialization to build competitive advantages in providing their products or services. Dividing tasks into functional specialties enables the personnel of these firms to concentrate on only one aspect of the necessary work. This allows use of the latest technical skills and develops a high level of efficiency.

Product, customer, or technology considerations determine the identity of the parts in a functional structure. A hotel business might be organized around housekeeping (maids), the front desk, maintenance, restaurant operations, reservations and sales, accounting, and personnel. An equipment manufacturer might be organized around production, engineering/quality control, purchasing, marketing, personnel, and finance/accounting. Two examples of functional organizations are illustrated in Figure 11–2.

The strategic challenge presented by the functional structure is effective coordination of the functional units. The narrow technical expertise achieved through specialization can lead to limited perspectives and to differences in the priorities of the functional units. Specialists may see the firm's strategic issues primarily as "marketing" problems or "production" problems. The potential conflict among functional units makes the coordinating role of the chief executive critical. Integrating devices (such as project teams or planning committees) are frequently used in functionally organized firms to enhance coordination and to facilitate understanding across functional areas.

Geographic Organizational Structure

Firms often grow by expanding the sale of their products or services to new geographic areas. In these areas, they frequently encounter differences that necessitate different approaches in producing, providing, or selling their products or services. Structuring by geographic areas is usually required to accommodate these differences. Thus, Holiday Inns is organized by regions of the world because of differences among nations in the laws, customs, and economies affecting the lodging industry. And even within its U.S. organization, Holiday Inns is organized geographically because of regional differences in traveling requirements, lodging regulations, and customer mix.

The key strategic advantage of geographic organizational structures is responsiveness to local market conditions. Figure 11–3 illustrates a typical geographic organizational structure and itemizes the strategic advantages and disadvantages of such structures.

Divisional Organizational Structure

When a firm diversifies its product/service lines, utilizes unrelated market channels, or begins to serve heterogeneous customer groups, a functional structure rapidly becomes inadequate. If a functional structure is retained under these circumstances, production managers may have to oversee the production of numerous and varied products or services, marketing managers may have to create sales programs for vastly different products or sell through vastly different distribution channels, and top management may be confronted with excessive coordination demands. A new organizational structure is often necessary to meet the increased coordination and decision-making requirements that result from increased diversity and size, and the divisional organizational structure is the form often chosen.

For many years, Ford and General Motors have used divisional structures organized by product groups. Manufacturers often organize sales into divisions based on differences in distribution channels.

A divisional structure allows corporate management to delegate authority for the strategic management of distinct business entities—the divisions. This expedites decision making in response to varied competitive environments and enables corporate management to concentrate on corporate-level strategic decisions. The divisions usually are given profit responsibility, which facilitates accurate assessment of profit and loss.

Figure 11–4 illustrates a divisional organizational structure and specifies the strategic advantages and disadvantages of such structures.

Strategic Business Units

Some firms encounter difficulty in evaluating and controlling the operations of their divisions as the diversity, size, and number of these units continue to increase. Under these conditions, a firm may add another layer of management to improve strategy implementation, to promote synergy, and to gain greater control over the firm's diverse business interests. This can be accomplished by creating groups that combine various divisions (or parts of some divisions)

FIGURE 11–3
A Geographic Organizational Structure

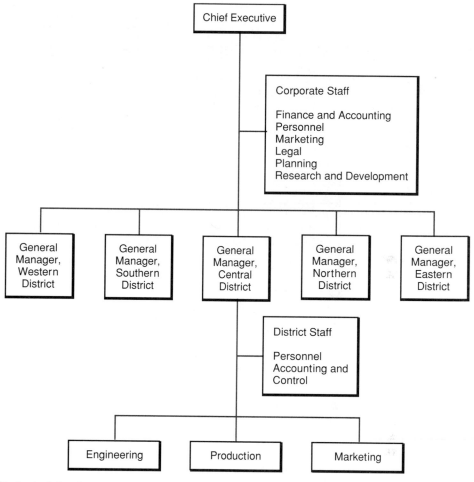

Strategic Advantages

1. Allows tailoring of strategy to needs of each geographic market.
2. Delegates profit/loss responsibility to lowest strategic level.
3. Improves functional coordination within the target market.
4. Takes advantage of economies of local operations.
5. Provides excellent training grounds for higher level general managers.

Strategic Disadvantages

1. Poses problem of deciding whether headquarters should impose geographic uniformity or geographic diversity should be allowed.
2. Makes it more difficult to maintain consistent company image/reputation from area to area.
3. Adds layer of management to run the geographic units.
4. Can result in duplication of staff services at headquarters and district levels.

in terms of common strategic elements. These groups, commonly called *strategic business units* (SBUs), usually are based on the independent product-market segments served by the firm. Figure 11–5 illustrates an SBU organizational structure.

As companies grow, they often adopt a new structure from among the alternatives we have described as a way to help them manage complexity brought on by growth. The SBU structure's main value appears to be that it provides a way for the largest companies to

FIGURE 11–4
Divisional Organization Structure

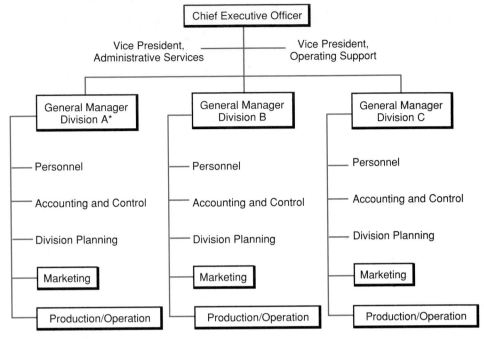

Strategic Advantages

1. Forces coordination and necessary authority down to the appropriate level for rapid response.
2. Places strategy development and implementation in closer proximity to the unique environments of the divisions.
3. Frees chief executive officer for broader strategic decision making.
4. Sharply focuses accountability for performance.
5. Retains functional specialization within each division.
6. Provides good training grounds for strategic managers.

Strategic Disadvantages

1. Fosters potentially dysfunctional competition for corporate-level resources.
2. Presents the problem of determining how much authority should be given to division managers.
3. Creates a potential for policy inconsistencies among divisions.
4. Presents the problem of distributing corporate overhead costs in a way that's acceptable to division managers with profit responsibility.

regain focus in different parts of their business that were central to earlier success yet which became "lost" or dysfunctional in the complexity and size brought on by the company's success. IBM adopted the SBU approach in 1995 by creating 11 distinct SBUs, or "Baby Blues," out of its highly centralized structure. These SBUs are distinct SBUs that provide marketing, services, and support for their customers in five global regions. These SBUs have worldwide responsibility for product development, manufacturing, and delivery of their own distinct product lines.

Matrix Organization

In large companies, increased diversity leads to numerous product and project efforts of major strategic significance. The result is a need for an organizational form that provides skills and resources where and when they are most vital. The matrix organization has been used increas-

FIGURE 11–5
Strategic Business Unit Organizational Structure

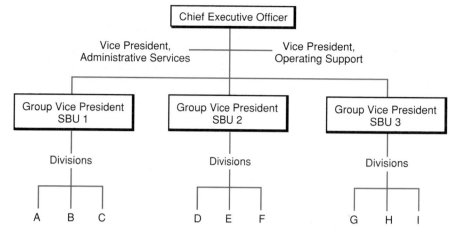

Strategic Advantages	**Strategic Disadvantages**
1. Improves coordination between divisions with similar strategic concerns and product-market environments.	1. Places another layer of management between the divisions and corporate management.
2. Tightens the strategic management and control of large, diverse business enterprises.	2. May increase dysfunctional competition for corporate resources.
3. Facilitates distinct and in-depth business planning at the corporate and business levels.	3. May present difficulties in defining the role of the group vice president.
4. Channels accountability to distinct business units.	4. May present difficulties in defining how much autonomy should be given to the group vice presidents and division managers.

ingly to meet this need. Among the firms that now use some form of matrix organization are Citicorp, Matsushita, Unilever, Shell Oil, Dow Chemical, and Texas Instruments.

The matrix organization provides dual channels of authority, performance responsibility, evaluation, and control, as shown in Figure 11–6. Essentially, subordinates are assigned both to a basic functional area and to a project or product manager. The matrix form is intended to make the best use of talented people within a firm by combining the advantages of functional specialization and product-project specialization.

The matrix structure also increases the number of middle managers who exercise general management responsibilities (through the project manager role) and, thus, broaden their exposure to organizationwide strategic concerns. In this way, the matrix structure overcomes a key deficiency of functional organizations while retaining the advantages of functional specialization.

Although the matrix structure is easy to design, it is difficult to implement. Dual chains of command challenge fundamental organizational orientations. Negotiating shared responsibilities, the use of resources, and priorities can create misunderstanding or confusion among subordinates. These problems are heightened in an international context with the complications introduced by distance, language, time, and culture.

To avoid the deficiencies that might arise from a permanent matrix structure, some firms are accomplishing particular strategic tasks, by means of a "temporary" or "flexible" *overlay structure*. This approach, used recently by such firms as NEC, Matsushita, Phillips, and Unilever, is meant to take *temporary* advantage of a matrix-type team while preserving an

FIGURE 11–6
Matrix Organizational Structure

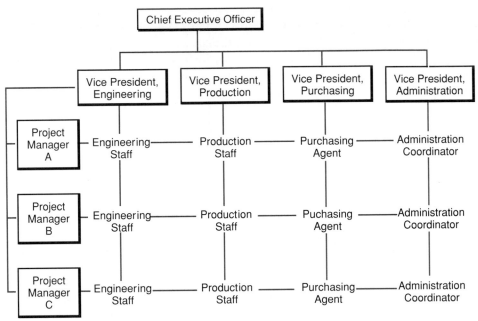

Strategic Advantages

1. Accommodates a wide variety of project-oriented business activity.
2. Provides good training grounds for strategic managers.
3. Maximizes efficient use of functional managers.
4. Fosters creativity and multiple sources of diversity.
5. Gives middle management broader exposure to strategic issues.

Strategic Disadvantages

1. May result in confusion and contradictory policies.
2. Necessitates tremendous horizontal and vertical coordination.
3. Can proliferate information logjams and excess reporting.
4. Can trigger turf battles and loss of accountability.

underlying divisional structure. Thus, the basic idea of the matrix structure—*to simplify and amplify the focus of resources on a narrow but strategically important product, project, or market*—appears to be an important structural alternative for large, diverse organizations.

Guidelines to Match Structure to Strategy

Which organizational structure is the best? Considerable research has addressed this issue, and the consensus is that *it depends on the strategy of the firm.* Since the structural design ties together key activities and resources of the firm, it must be closely aligned with the demands of the firm's strategy. What follows are some guidelines that emerge from this line of research and the restructuring revolution that has altered the corporate landscape at the dawn of the 21st century.

Restructure to Emphasize and Support Strategically Critical Activities

Restructuring has been the buzzword of global enterprise for the last 10 years. Its contemporary meaning is multifaceted. At the heart of the restructuring trend is the notion that some activities within a business's value chain are more critical to the success of the business's strategy than others. Wal-Mart's organizational structure is designed to ensure that its impressive logistics and purchasing competitive advantages operate flawlessly. Coordinating daily logistical and purchasing efficiencies among separate stores lets Wal-Mart lead the industry in profitability yet sell retail for less than many competitors buy the same merchandise at wholesale. Motorola's organizational structure is designed to protect and nurture its legendary R&D and new product development capabilities—spending over twice the industry average in R&D alone each year. Motorola's R&D emphasis continually spawns proprietary technologies that support its technology-based competitive advantage. Coca-Cola emphasizes the importance of distribution activities, advertising, and retail support to its bottlers in its organizational structure. All three of these companies emphasize very different parts of the value chain process, but they are extraordinarily successful in part because they have designed their organizational structures to emphasize and support strategically critical activities. Strategy in Action 11–1 provides some guidelines that should influence how an organization is structured depending on which among five different sources of competitive advantage are emphasized in its strategy.

Two critical considerations arise when restructuring the organization to emphasize and support strategically critical activities. First, managers need to make the strategically critical activities the central building blocks for designing organization structure. Those activities should be identified and separated as much as possible into self-contained parts of the organization. Then the remaining structure must be designed so as to ensure timely integration with other parts of the organization.

While this is easily proposed, managers need to recognize that strategically relevant activities may still reside in different parts of the organization, particularly in functionally organized structures. Support activities like finance, engineering, or information processing are usually self-contained units, often outside the unit around which core competencies are built. This often results in an emphasis on departments obsessed with performing their own tasks more than emphasizing the key results (customer satisfaction, differentiation, low costs, speed) the business as a whole seeks. So the second consideration is to design the organizational structure so that it helps coordinate and integrate these support activities to (1) maximize their support of strategy-critical primary activities in the firm's value chain and (2) does so in a way to minimize the costs for support activities and the time spent on internal coordination. Managerial efforts to do this in the 1990s have placed reengineering, downsizing, and outsourcing as prominent tools for strategists restructuring their organizations.

Reengineer Strategic Business Processes

Business process reengineering (BPR), popularized by consultants Michael Hammer and James Champy,[1] is one of the more popular methods by which organizations worldwide are undergoing restructuring efforts to remain competitive in the 21st century. BPR is intended to reorganize a company so that it can best create value for the customer by eliminating barriers that create distance between employees and customers. It involves fundamental rethinking and radical redesign of a business process. It is characterized as radical because it strives to structure organizational efforts and activities around results and value creation by focusing on the processes that are undertaken to meet customer needs, not specific tasks and functional areas such as marketing and sales.

Business reengineering reduces fragmentation by crossing traditional departmental lines and reducing overhead to compress formerly separate steps and tasks that are

---

[1] Michael Hammer and James Champy, *Reengineering the Corporation* (New York: HarperBusiness, 1993).

STRATEGY
IN ACTION
11–1

GUIDELINES FOR DESIGNING A STRUCTURE TO ACCOMMODATE FIVE DIFFERENT STRATEGIC PRIORITIES

One of the key things business managers should keep in mind when restructuring their organizations is to devise the new structure so that it emphasizes strategically critical activities within the business's value chain. This means that the structure should allow those activities to have considerable autonomy over issues that influence their operating excellence and timeliness; they should be in a position to easily coordinate with other parts of the business—to get decisions made fast.

Below are five different types of critical activities that may be at the heart of a business's effort to build and sustain competitive advantage. Beside each one are typical conditions that will affect and shape the nature of the organization's structure:

Potential Strategic Priority and Critical Activities	Concomitant Conditions That May Affect or Place Demands on the Organizational Structure and Operating Activities to Build Competitive Advantage
1. Compete as low-cost provider of goods or services.	Broadens market. Requires longer production runs and fewer product changes. Requires special-purpose equipment and facilities.
2. Compete as high-quality provider.	Often possible to obtain more profit per unit, and perhaps more total profit from a smaller volume of sales. Requires more quality-assurance effort and higher operating cost. Requires more precise equipment, which is more expensive. Requires highly skilled workers, necessitating higher wages and greater training efforts.
3. Stress customer service.	Requires broader development of servicepeople and service parts and equipment. Requires rapid response to customer needs or changes in customer tastes, rapid and accurate information system, careful coordination. Requires a higher inventory investment.
4. Provide rapid and frequent introduction of new products.	Requires versatile equipment and people. Has higher research and development costs. Has high retraining costs and high tooling and changeover costs. Provides lower volumes for each product and fewer opportunities for improvements due to the learning curve.
5. Seek vertical integration.	Enables firm to control more of the process. May not have economies of scale at some stages of process. May require high capital investment as well as technology and skills beyond those currently available within the firm.

strategically intertwined in the process of meeting customer needs. This "process orientation," rather than a traditional functional orientation, becomes the perspective around which various activities and tasks are then grouped to create the building blocks of the organization's structure. This is usually accomplished by assembling a multifunctional, multilevel team that begins by identifying customer needs and how the customer wants to deal with the firm. Customer focus must permeate all phases. Companies that have successfully reengineered their operations around strategically critical business processes have pursued the following steps:[2]

---

[2] Judy Wade, "How to Make Reengineering Really Work," *Harvard Business Review* 71, no. 6 (November–December 1993), pp. 119–31.

· Develop a flow chart of the total business process, including its interfaces with other value chain activities.

· Try to simplify the process first, eliminating tasks and steps where possible and analyzing how to streamline the performance of what remains.

· Determine which parts of the process can be automated (usually those that are repetitive, time-consuming, and require little thought or decision); consider introducing advanced technologies that can be upgraded to achieve next-generation capability and provide a basis for further productivity gains down the road.

· Evaluate each activity in the process to determine whether it is strategy-critical or not. Strategy-critical activities are candidates for benchmarking to achieve best-in-industry or best-in-world performance status.

· Weigh the pros and cons of outsourcing activities that are noncritical or that contribute little to organizational capabilities and core competencies.

· Design a structure for performing the activities that remain; reorganize the personnel and groups who perform these activities into the new structure.

When asked recently about his new networking-oriented direction for IBM, IBM CEO Gerstner responded: "It's called *reengineering*. It's called *getting competitive*. It's called *reducing cycle time and cost, flattening organizations, increasing customer responsiveness*. All of these require a collaboration with the customer and with suppliers and with vendors."

Downsize, Outsource, and Self-Manage

Reengineering and a value orientation have led managers to scrutinize even further the way their organizational structures are crucial to strategy implementation. That scrutiny has led to downsizing, outsourcing, and self-management as three important themes influencing the organizational structures into the 21st century. *Downsizing* is eliminating the number of employees, particularly middle management, in a company. The arrival of a global marketplace, information technology, and intense competition caused many companies to reevaluate middle management activities to determine just what value was really being added to the company's products and services. The result of this scrutiny, along with continuous improvements in information processing technology, has been widespread downsizing in the number of management personnel in thousands of companies worldwide. These companies often eliminate whole levels of management. General Electric went from 400,000 to 280,000 employees in this decade while its sales have almost tripled and its profit risen fivefold. AT&T has experienced similar numbers of job reductions. The results of a survey of companies worldwide that have been actively downsizing (which attempts to extract guidelines for downsizing) is shown in Global Strategy in Action 11–1.

One of the outcomes of downsizing was increased *self-management* at operating levels of the company. Cutbacks in the number of management people left those that remained with more work to do. The result was that they had to give up a good measure of control to workers, and they had to rely on those workers to help out. Spans-of-control, traditionally thought to maximize under 10 people, have become much larger due to information technology, running "lean and mean," and delegation to lower levels. Ameritech, one of the Baby Bells, has seen its spans-of-control rise to as much as 30 to 1 in some divisions because most of the people that did staff work—financial analysts, assistant managers, and so on—have disappeared. This delegation, also known as empowerment, is accomplished through concepts like self-managed work groups, reengineering, and automation. It is also seen through efforts to create distinct businesses within a business—conceiving a business

HOW LEAN IS YOUR COMPANY?

It's hard to find a major corporation that hasn't downsized in recent years. But simple reductions in staffing don't make for lean management. Here's a checklist, developed from interviews with executives and consultants, that may tell you if your company needs a diet.

Company Characteristic	Analysis
1. Layers of management between CEO and the shop floor.	Some companies, such as Ameritech, now have as few as four or five where as many as 12 had been common. More than six is most likely too many.
2. Number of employees managed by the typical executive.	At lean companies, spans of control range up to one manager to 30 staffers. A ratio of lower than 1:10 is a warning of arterial sclerosis.
3. Amount of work cut out by your downsizing.	Eliminating jobs without cutting out work can bring disaster. A downsizing should be accompanied by at least a 25% reduction in the number of tasks performed. Some lean companies have hit 50%.
4. Skill levels of the surviving management group.	Managers must learn to accept more responsibility and to eliminate unneeded work. Have you taught them how?
5. Size of your largest profit center by number of employees.	Break down large operating units into smaller profit centers—less than 500 employees is a popular cutoff—to gain the economies of entrepreneurship and offset the burdens of scale.
6. Post-downsizing size of staff at corporate headquarters.	The largest layoffs, on a percentage basis, should be at corporate headquarters. It is often the most overstaffed—and the most removed from customers.

as a confederation of many "small" businesses, rather than one large, interconnected business. Whatever the terminology, the idea is to push decision making down in the organization by allowing major management decisions to be made at operating levels. The result is often the elimination of up to half the levels of management previously existing in an organizational structure.

Another driving force behind downsizing has been outsourcing. *Outsourcing* is simply obtaining work previous done by employees inside the companies from sources outside the company. Managers have found that as they attempt to restructure their organizations, particularly if they do so from a business process orientation, numerous activities can often be found in their company that are not "strategically critical activities." This has particularly been the case of numerous staff activities and administrative control processes previously the domain of various middle management levels in an organization. But it can also refer to primary activities that are steps in their business's value chain—purchasing, shipping, making certain parts, and so on. Further scrutiny has led managers to conclude that these activities not only add little or no value to the product or services, but that they are either unnecessary or they can be done much more cost effectively (and competently) by other businesses specializing in these activities. If this is so, then the business can enhance its competitive advantage by outsourcing the activities it can't outright eliminate. Many organizations have outsourced information processing, various personnel activities, and production of parts that can be done better outside the company. Outsourcing, then, can be a source of competitive advantage and result in a leaner, flatter organizational structure.

Recognize That Strategy and Structure Often Evolve in a Predictable Pattern

Predating some of the recent guidelines reviewed above, still-relevant research suggests businesses frequently grow in a rather predictable pattern that has ramifications for which structure would be most effective. Alfred Chandler first observed a common sequence of evolution in strategy and structure among American firms.[3] The sequence reflected their increasing scope. Most firms began as simple functional units operating at a single site (e.g., a plant, a warehouse, or a sales office) and within a single industry. The initial growth strategy of such firms was *volume expansion*, which created a need for an administrative office to manage the increased volume. The next growth strategy was *geographic expansion*, which required multiple field units, still performing the same function but in different locations. Administrative problems with regard to standardization, specialization, and interunit coordination then gave rise to the need for geographic units and for a central administrative unit to oversee them. *Vertical integration* was usually the next growth strategy. Firms remained within the same industry but performed additional functions. Problems associated with the flow of information and materials among the various functions led to the functional organization, in which staff personnel developed forecasts and schedules that facilitated overall coordination.

The final growth strategy was *product diversification*. Firms entered other industries in which they could use their existing resources. Problems in managing diverse product divisions and evaluating their capital investment proposals led to the multidivisional structure in which similar activities were grouped. Separate divisions handled independent products and were responsible for short-run operating decisions. General managers (i.e., group managers) at a central office were responsible for long-term strategic decisions. These managers had to relate divisional decisions and performance to strategic direction and to balance divisional autonomy against central control.

Larry Wrigley and Richard Rumelt built on Chandler's work by examining how a firm's degree of diversification from its core business affected its choice of structure. They identified four growth strategies: (1) *single-product businesses*; (2) *single dominant businesses*, with one business accounting for 70–95 percent of sales; (3) *related diversified businesses* based on a common distribution channel or technology, with more than 30 percent of sales outside the primary business; and (4) *unrelated diversified businesses*, with more than 30 percent of sales outside the primary business.[4] They found that greater diversity led to greater divisionalization: single-product businesses used a functional structure; related and unrelated businesses used a divisionalized structure; and single dominant businesses used a functional structure in the dominant business and a divisional structure in the remaining businesses.

More-recent research has extended our understanding of the strategy-structure fit.[5] This research continues to suggest that, in smaller firms with a single product or product line, the

---

[3] Alfred D. Chandler, *Strategy and Structure* (Cambridge, MA: MIT Press, 1962).

[4] Larry Wrigley, *Divisional Autonomy and Diversification*, doctoral dissertation, Harvard Business School, 1970; Richard Rumelt, *Diversification Strategy and Performance, Strategic Management Journal* 3 (January–February 1982), pp. 359–69; Richard Rumelt, *Strategy, Structure and Economic Performance* (Boston: HBS Press, 1986). Rumelt used a similar, but more detailed classification scheme.

[5] D. A. Nathanson and J. S. Cassano, "Organization, Diversity, and Performance," *Wharton's Magazine* 6 (1982), pp. 19–26; and Christopher A. Bartlett and Sumantra Ghoshal, "Matrix Management: Not a Structure, a Frame of Mind," *Harvard Business Review* 68, no. 4 (1990), pp. 138–45.

functional structure significantly outperforms the multidivisional structure. In larger firms, however, the roles of corporate- and lower-level staffs significantly affect performance. The greater the diversity among a firm's businesses, the more desirable it is to have strong, decentralized staffs within the businesses (or divisions); with less diversity, firms with strong staffs at higher organizational levels are more effective. In other words, the greater the diversity among the businesses in multibusiness firms, the greater is the necessary degree of decentralization and self-containment. This need has only been heightened by the rapid globalization among many countries. On the other hand, where the diversity among a firm's businesses is low and the interdependence of these businesses is high, more integration at the corporate level is needed.

Four significant conclusions can be drawn from this research:[6]

1. *A single-product firm or single dominant business firm should employ a functional structure.* This structure allows for strong task focus through an emphasis on specialization and efficiency, while providing opportunity for adequate controls through centralized review and decision making.

2. *A firm in several lines of business that are somehow related should employ a multidivisional structure.* Closely related divisions should be combined into groups within this structure. When synergies (i.e., shared or linked activities) are possible within such a group, the appropriate location for staff influence and decision making is at the group level, with a lesser role for corporate-level staff. The greater the degree of diversity across the firm's businesses, the greater should be the extent to which the power of staff and decision-making authority is lodged within the divisions.

3. *A firm in several unrelated lines of business should be organized into strategic business units.* Although the strategic business unit structure resembles the multidivisional structure, there are significant differences between the two. With a strategic business unit structure, finance, accounting, planning, legal, and related activities should be centralized at the corporate office. Since there are no synergies across the firm's businesses, the corporate office serves largely as a capital allocation and control mechanism. Otherwise, its major decisions involve acquisitions and divestitures. All operational and business-level strategic plans are delegated to the strategic business units.

4. *Early achievement of a strategy-structure fit can be a competitive advantage.* A competitive advantage is obtained by the first firm among competitors to achieve appropriate strategy-structure fit. That advantage will disappear as the firm's competitors also attain such a fit. Moreover, if the firm alters its strategy, its structure must obviously change as well. Otherwise, a loss of fit will lead to a competitive disadvantage for the firm.

ORGANIZATIONAL LEADERSHIP

The introduction to this chapter showed the McKinsey 7-S framework as a way to understand the implementation challenge. Figure 11–1 shows that framework identifies management and leadership as two separate elements. Management is identified with skills and leadership with style. This distinction is important. John Kotter, a widely recognized leadership expert, helps explain this distinction:[7]

---

[6] V. R. Galbraith and R. K. Kazanjian, *Strategy Implementation: Structure, Systems & Processes* (St. Paul, MN: West Publishing, 1986).

[7] John P. Kotter, "What Leaders Really Do," *Harvard Business Review* 68, no. 3 (May–June 1990), p. 104.

Management is about coping with complexity. Its practices and procedures are largely a response to one of the most significant developments of the 20th century: the emergence of large organizations. Without good management, complex enterprises tend to become chaotic in ways that threaten their very existence. Good management brings a degree of order and consistency to key dimensions like the quality and profitability of products.

Leadership, by contrast, is about coping with change. Part of the reason it has become so important in recent years is that the business world has become more competitive and more volatile. . . . The net result is that doing what was done yesterday, or doing it 5 percent better, is no longer a formula for success. Major changes are more and more necessary to survive and compete effectively in this new environment. More change always demands more leadership.

Organizational leadership, then, involves two considerations. One is strategic leadership, usually coming from the CEO. The other is management skill to cope with complexity.

Strategic Leadership: Embracing Change

The blending of telecommunications, computers, the Internet, and one global marketplace have increased the pace of change exponentially during the last 10 years. All business organizations are affected. Change has become an integral part of what leaders and managers deal with daily.

The leadership challenge is to galvanize commitment among people within an organization as well as stakeholders outside the organization to embrace change and implement strategies intended to position the organization to do so. Leaders galvanize commitment to embrace change through three, interrelated activities: clarifying strategic intent, building an organization, and shaping organizational culture.

Clarifying Strategic Intent

Leaders help stakeholders embrace change by setting forth a clear vision of where the business's strategy needs to take the organization. Traditionally, the concept of vision has been a description or picture of what the company could be that accommodates the needs of all its stakeholders. The intensely competitive, rapidly changing global marketplace has refined this to be targeting a very narrowly defined strategic intent—*an articulation of a simple criterion or characterization of what the company must become to establish and sustain global leadership.* Lou Gerstner is a good example of a leader in the middle of trying to shape strategic intent. "One of the great things about this industry is that every decade or so, you get a chance to redefine the playing field," said Gerstner. "We're in that phase of redefinition right now, and winners or losers are going to emerge from it. We've got to become *the leader in 'network-centric computing.'* " It's an opportunity brought about by telecommunications-based change that will change IBM more than semiconductors did in the 1980s. Says Gerstner, "I sensed there were too many people inside IBM who wanted to fight the war we lost," referring to PCs and PC software, so now he is aggressively trying to shape network-centric computing as the strategic intent for IBM in the next century.

Clarifying strategic intent can come in many different forms. Coca-Cola's CEO and Chairman Roberto Goizueta says that the company he leads is "a global business system for which we raise capital to make concentrate and sell it at an operating profit. Then we pay the cost of that capital. Shareholders pocket the difference." Coke has average 27% annual return on stockholder equity for 18 years under his leadership. Travelers Insurance lost $200 million in 1992. Sanford Weill assumed leadership, focusing on a short term turnaround. Among other things, he says, "We sent letters to all suppliers saying: Dear Supplier, either we rebid your business or you lower your costs 15%." Within two years, nonpersonnel costs were cut 49% in addition to 15,000 jobs. Travelers' made $700 million in 1996. Mr. Weill was effective in setting forth strategic intent for Travelers' turnaround. While Coke and Travelers are very different situations, their leaders were both very effective in shaping and clarifying strategic intent in a way that helped stakeholders understand what needed to be done.

Building an Organization

The previous section examined alternative structures to use in designing the organization necessary to implement strategy. Leaders spend considerable time shaping and refining their organizational structure and making it function effectively to accomplish strategic intent. Since leaders are attempting to embrace change, they are often rebuilding or remaking their organization to align it with the ever changing environment and needs of the strategy. And since embracing change often involves overcoming resistance to change, leaders find themselves addressing problems like the following as they attempt to build or rebuild their organization:

· Ensuring a common understanding about organizational priorities
· Clarifying responsibilities among managers and organizational units
· Empowering newer managers and pushing authority lower in the organization
· Uncovering and remedying problems in coordination and communication across the organization
· Gaining the personal commitment to a shared vision from managers throughout the organization
· Keeping closely connected with "what's going on in the organization and with its customers"

Leaders do this through many ways. Larry Bossidy, the CEO who had quadrupled Allied Signal's stock price in the last four years, spends 50 percent of his time each year flying to Allied Signal's various operations around the world meeting with managers, discussing decisions, results and progress. Bill Gates at Microsoft spends two hours each day reading and sending E-mail to any of Microsoft's 16,000 employees that want to contact him. All managers adapt structures, create teams, implement systems, and otherwise generate ways to coordinate, integrate and share information about what their organization is doing and might do. Others create customer advisory groups, supplier partnerships, R&D joint ventures and other adjustments to build an adaptable, learning organization that embraces the leader's vision, strategic intent and the change driving the future opportunities facing the business. These, in addition to the fundamental structural guidelines described in the previous section for restructuring to support strategically critical activities, are the issues leaders constantly address as they attempt to build a supportive organization.

Shaping Organization Culture

Leaders know well that the values and beliefs shared throughout their organization will shape how the work of the organization is done. And when attempting to embrace accelerated change, reshaping their organization's culture is an activity that occupies considerable time for most leaders. Listen to these observations by and about MCI and CEO Bert Roberts about competing in the rapidly changing telecommunications industry:[8]

---

[8] Alison Sprout, "MCI: Can It Become the Communications Company of the Next Century?" *Fortune*, October 2, 1995, p. 110.

Says Roberts: "We run like mad and then we change directions." Indeed, the ever-changing wireless initiative (reselling wireless services rather than creating its own capacity) illustrates a trait that sets apart MCI from its competitors—a willingness to try new things, and if they don't work, to try something else. "Over at AT&T, people are afraid to make mistakes," says Jeff Kagan, president of Kagan Telecom in Atlanta, Ga. "At MCI, people are afraid not to make mistakes."

It appears that MCI CEO Bert Roberts wants an organizational culture that is risk taking and somewhat free wheeling in order to take advantage of change in the telecommunications industry. He is doing this by example, by expectations felt by his managers, and in the way decision making is approached within MCI.

Leaders use reward systems, symbols, and structure among other means to shape the organization's culture. Travelers' turnaround was accomplished in part by changing its "hidebound" culture through a change in its agent reward system. Employees previously on salary with occasional bonuses were given rewards that involved substantial cash bonuses and stock options. Observed a customer and risk management director at drugmaker Becton Dickinson, "They're hungrier now. They want to make deals. They're different than the old, hidebound Travelers' culture."

As leaders clarify strategic intent, build an organization, and shape their organization's culture, they look to one key element to help—their management team throughout their organization. As Allied Signal's visible CEO Lary Bossidy candidly observed when asked about how after 38 years at General Electric and now at Allied Signal with seemingly drab businesses he could expect exciting growth: "There's no such thing as a mature market. What we need is mature executives who can find ways to grow." Leaders look to managers they need to execute strategy as another source of leadership to accept risk and cope with the complexity that change brings about. So assignment of key managers becomes a leadership tool.

Assignment of Key Managers

A major concern of top management in implementing a strategy, particularly if it involves a major change, is that the right managers be in the right positions to facilitate execution of the new strategy. Of all the means for ensuring successful implementation, this is the one that CEOs mention first. Confidence in the individuals occupying pivotal managerial positions is directly correlated with top-management expectations that a strategy can be executed successfully.

This confidence is based on the answers to two fundamental questions:

1. Which persons hold the leadership positions that are especially critical to execution of the strategy?
2. Do these persons have the characteristics needed to ensure effective implementation of the strategy?

Although it is impossible to specify the characteristics that are most important in this context, they probably include (1) ability and education, (2) previous track record and experience, and (3) personality and temperament. An individual's suitability on these counts, combined with top managers' gut feelings about the individual, provides the basis for top management's confidence in the individual.

One practical consideration in making key managerial assignments when implementing strategy is whether to utilize current (or promotable) executives or bring in new personnel. This is obviously a difficult, sensitive, and strategic issue. Figure 11–7 highlights the key advantages and disadvantages of these alternatives.

FIGURE 11–7
**Using Existing Executives versus Bringing in Outsiders in
Managerial Assignments to Implement a New Strategy**

	Advantages	**Disadvantages**
Using existing executives to implement a new strategy	Existing executives already know key people, practices, and conditions. Personal qualities of existing executives are better known and understood by associates. Existing executives have established relationships with peers, subordinates, suppliers, buyers, and the like. Use of existing executives symbolizes organizational commitment to individual careers.	Existing executives are less adaptable to major strategic changes because of their knowledge, attitudes, and values. Past commitments of existing executives hamper the hard decisions required in executing a new strategy. Existing executives have less ability to become inspired and credibly convey the need for change.
Bringing in outsiders to implement a new strategy	Outsiders may already believe in and have "lived" the new strategy. Outsiders are unencumbered by internal commitments to people. Outsiders come to the new assignment with heightened commitment and enthusiasm. Bringing in outsiders can send powerful signals throughout the organization that change is expected.	Bringing in outsiders often is costly in terms of both compensation and "learning-to-work-together" time. Candidates suitable in all respects (i.e., exact experience) may not be available, leading to compromise choices. Uncertainty exists in selecting the right outsiders to bring in. "Morale costs" are incurred when an outsider takes a job that several insiders want. The "what to do with poor ol' Fred" problem arises when outsiders are brought in.

The other consideration that has become prominent in an environment of restructuring, downsizing, and self-management is managers' ability to delegate and to handle larger spans of control. As companies adapt employee empowerment and self-managed work group practices, managers that remain face greater workloads and different management challenges. The result is the need for skills consistent with this new environment—delegation, coaching, electronic savvy, and a results orientation.

ORGANIZATIONAL CULTURE

Organizational culture is the set of important assumptions (often unstated) that members of an organization share in common. Every organization has its own culture. An organization's culture is similar to an individual's personality—an intangible yet ever-present theme that provides meaning, direction, and the basis for action. In much the same way as personality influences the behavior of an individual, the shared assumptions (beliefs and values) among a firm's members influence opinions and actions within that firm.

A member of an organization can simply be aware of the organization's beliefs and values without sharing them in a personally significant way. Those beliefs and values have more personal meaning if the member views them as a guide to appropriate behavior in the organization and, therefore, complies with them. The member becomes fundamentally committed to the beliefs and values when he or she internalizes them; that is, comes to hold them as personal beliefs and values. In this case, the corresponding behavior is *intrinsically rewarding* for the member—the member derives personal satisfaction from his or her actions in the organization because those actions are congruent with corresponding personal beliefs and values. *Assumptions become shared assumptions through internalization among an organization's individual members.* And those shared, internalized beliefs and values shape the content and account for the strength of an organization's culture.

Leaders typically attempt to manage and create distinct cultures through a variety of ways. Some of the most common ways are as follows:

Emphasize Key Themes or Dominant Values   Businesses build strategies around distinct competitive advantages they possess or seek. Quality, differentiation, cost advantages, or speed are three key sources of competitive advantage. So insightful leaders nurture key themes or dominant values within their organization that reinforce competitive advantages they seek to maintain or build. Key themes or dominant values may center around wording in an advertisement. They are often found in internal company communications. They are most often found as a new vocabulary used by company personnel to explain "who we are." At Xerox, the key themes include respect for the individual and services to the customer. At Procter & Gamble (P&G), the overarching value is product quality; McDonald's uncompromising emphasis on QSCV—quality, service, cleanliness, and value—through meticulous attention to detail is legendary; Delta Airlines is driven by the "family feeling" theme, which builds a team spirit and nurtures each employee's cooperative attitude toward others, cheerful outlook toward life, and pride in a job well done. Du Pont's safety orientation—a report of every accident must be on the chairman's desk within 24 hours—has resulted in a safety record that was 17 times better than the chemical industry average and 68 times better than the all-manufacturing average.

Encourage Dissemination of Stories and Legends about Core Values   Companies with strong cultures are enthusiastic collectors and tellers of stories, anecdotes, and legends in support of basic beliefs. Frito-Lay's zealous emphasis on customer service is reflected in frequent stories about potato chip route salespeople who have slogged through sleet, mud, hail, snow, and rain to uphold the 99.5 percent service level to customers in which the entire company takes great pride. Milliken (a textile leader) holds "sharing" rallies once every quarter at which teams from all over the company swap success stories and ideas. Typically, more than 100 teams make five-minute presentations over a two-day period. Every rally is designed around a major theme, such as quality, cost reduction, or customer service. No criticisms are allowed, and awards are given to reinforce this institutionalized approach to storytelling. L. L. Bean tells customer service stories; 3M tells innovation stories; P&G, Johnson & Johnson, IBM, and Maytag tell quality stories. These stories are very important in developing an organizational culture, because organization members identify strongly with them and come to share the beliefs and values they support.

Institutionalize Practices That Systematically Reinforce Desired Beliefs and Values
Companies with strong cultures are clear on what their beliefs and values need to be and take the process of shaping those beliefs and values very seriously. Most important, the values these companies espouse undergird the strategies they employ. For example, McDonald's has a yearly contest to determine the best hamburger cooker in its chain. First, there is a competition to determine the best hamburger cooker in each store; next, the store winners compete in regional championships; finally, the regional winners compete in the

"All-American" contest. The winners, who are widely publicized throughout the company, get trophies and All-American patches to wear on their McDonald's uniforms.

Adapt Some Very Common Themes in Their Own Unique Ways   The most typical beliefs that shape organizational culture include (1) a belief in being the best (or, as at GE, "better than the best"); (2) a belief in superior quality and service; (3) a belief in the importance of people as individuals and a faith in their ability to make a strong contribution; (4) a belief in the importance of the details of execution, the nuts and bolts of doing the job well; (5) a belief that customers should reign supreme; (6) a belief in inspiring people to do their best, whatever their ability; (7) a belief in the importance of informal communication; and (8) a belief that growth and profits are essential to a company's well-being. Every company implements these beliefs differently (to fit its particular situation), and every company's values are the handiwork of one or two legendary figures in leadership positions. Accordingly, every company has a distinct culture that it believes no other company can copy successfully. And in companies with strong cultures, managers and workers either accept the norms of the culture or opt out from the culture and leave the company.

The stronger a company's culture and the more that culture is directed toward customers and markets, the less the company uses policy manuals, organization charts, and detailed rules and procedures to enforce discipline and norms. The reason is that the guiding values inherent in the culture convey in crystal-clear fashion what everybody is supposed to do in most situations. Poorly performing companies often have strong cultures. However, their cultures are dysfunctional, being focused on internal politics or operating by the numbers as opposed to emphasizing customers and the people who make and sell the product.

Managing Organizational Culture in a Global Organization[9]

The reality of today's global organizations is that organizational culture must recognize cultural diversity. *Social norms* create differences across national boundaries that influence how people interact, read personal cues, and otherwise interrelate socially. *Values* and *attitudes* about similar circumstances also vary from country to country. Where individualism is central to a North American's value structure, the needs of the group dominate the value structure of their Japanese counterparts. *Religion* is yet another source of cultural differences. Holidays, practices, and belief structures differ in very fundamental ways that must be taken into account as one attempts to shape organizational culture in a global setting. Finally, *education*, or ways people are accustomed to learning, differ across national borders. Formal classroom learning in the United States may teach things that are only learned via apprenticeship in other cultures. Since the process of shaping an organizational culture often involves considerable "education," leaders should be sensitive to global differences in approaches to education to make sure their cultural education efforts

---

[9]Differing backgrounds, often referred to as *cultural diversity*, is something that most managers will certainly see more of, both because of the growing cultural diversity domestically and the obvious diversification of cultural backgrounds that result from global acquisitions and mergers. For example, Harold Epps, manager of DEC's computer keyboard plant in Boston, manages 350 employees representing 44 countries of origin and 19 languages. Useful reading on cultural diversity can be found in David Jamieson and Julie O'Mara, *Managing Workforce 2000: Gaining the Diversity Advantage* (San Francisco: Josey-Bass, 1991), and R. R. Thomas, *Beyond Race and Gender: Unleashing the Power of Your Total Workforce by Managing Diversity* (New York: AMACOM Books, 1991). To get an informative appreciation of the global scene, see Rosabeth Moss Kanter, "Transcending Business Boundaries: 12,000 World Managers View Change," *Harvard Business Review* 69, no. 3 (1991), pp. 151–64.

FIGURE 11–8
Managing the Strategy-Culture Relationship

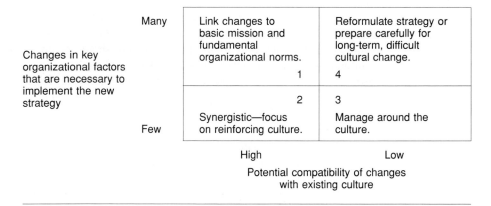

Managing the Strategy-Culture Relationship

Managers find it difficult to think through the relationship between a firm's culture and the critical factors on which strategy depends. They quickly recognize, however, that key components of the firm—structure, staff, systems, people, style—influence the ways in which key managerial tasks are executed and how critical management relationships are formed. And implementation of a new strategy is largely concerned with adjustments in these components to accommodate the perceived needs of the strategy. Consequently, managing the strategy-culture relationship requires sensitivity to the interaction between the changes necessary to implement the new strategy and the compatibility or "fit" between those changes and the firm's culture. Figure 11–8 provides a simple framework for managing the strategy-culture relationship by identifying four basic situations a firm might face.

Link to Mission

A firm in cell 1 is faced with a situation in which implementing a new strategy requires several changes in structure, systems, managerial assignments, operating procedures, or other fundamental aspects of the firm. However, most of the changes are potentially compatible with the existing organizational culture. Firms in this situation usually have a tradition of effective performance and are either seeking to take advantage of a major opportunity or are attempting to redirect major product-market operations consistent with proven core capabilities. Such firms are in a very promising position: they can pursue a strategy requiring major changes but still benefit from the power of cultural reinforcement.

Four basic considerations should be emphasized by firms seeking to manage a strategy-culture relationship in this context. First, *key changes should be visibly linked to the basic company mission*. Since the company mission provides a broad official foundation for the organizational culture, top executives should use all available internal and external forums to reinforce the message that the changes are inextricably linked to it. Second, *emphasis should be placed on the use of existing personnel* where possible to fill positions created to implement the new strategy. Existing personnel embody the shared values and norms that help ensure cultural compatibility as major changes are implemented. Third, *care should be taken if adjustments in the reward system are needed.* These adjustments should be consistent with the current reward system. If, for example, a new product-market thrust requires significant changes in the way sales are made, and, therefore, in incentive compensation, common themes (e.g., incentive oriented) should be emphasized. In this way, current and future reward approaches are related and the changes in the reward system are justified (encourage development of less familiar markets). Fourth, *key attention should be paid to the changes that are least compatible with the current culture,* so current norms are not disrupted. For example, a firm may choose to subcontract an important step in a production process because that step would be incompatible with the current culture.

IBM's strategy in entering the Internet-based market is an illustration. Serving this radically different market required numerous organizational changes. To maintain maximum compatibility with its existing culture while doing so, IBM went to considerable public and internal effort to link its new Internet focus with its long-standing mission. Numerous messages relating the network-centric computing to IBM's tradition of top-quality service appeared on television and in magazines, and every IBM manager was encouraged to go online. Where feasible, IBM personnel were used to fill the new positions created to implement the strategy. But because the software requirements were not compatible with IBM's current operations, virtually all of its initial efforts were linked to newly acquired Lotus Notes.

Maximize Synergy

A firm in cell 2 needs only a few organizational changes to implement its new strategy, and those changes are potentially quite compatible with its current culture. A firm in this situation should emphasize two broad themes: (1) *take advantage of the situation to reinforce and solidify the current culture* and (2) *use this time of relative stability to remove organizational roadblocks to the desired culture.* Holiday Inns' move into casino gambling required a few major organizational changes. Holiday Inns saw casinos as resort locations requiring lodging, dining, and gambling/entertainment services. It only had to incorporate gambling/entertainment expertise into its management team, which was already capable of managing the lodging and dining requirements of casino (or any other) resort locations. It successfully inculcated this single major change by selling the change internally as completely compatible with its mission of providing high-quality accommodations for business and leisure travelers. The resignation of Roy Clymer, its CEO, removed an organizational roadblock, legitimizing a culture that placed its highest priority on quality service to the middle-to-upper-income business traveler, rather than a culture that placed its highest priority on family-oriented service. The latter priority was fast disappearing from Holiday Inns' culture, with the encouragement of most of the firm's top management, but its disappearance had not yet been fully sanctioned because of Clymer's personal beliefs. His voluntary departure helped solidify the new values that top management wanted.

Manage around the Culture

A firm in cell 3 must make a few major organizational changes to implement its new strategy, but these changes are potentially inconsistent with the firm's current organizational culture. The critical question for a firm in this situation is whether it can make the changes with a reasonable chance of success.

A firm can manage around the culture in various ways: create a separate firm or division; use task forces, teams, or program coordinators; subcontract; bring in an outsider; or sell out. These are a few of the available options, but the key idea is to create a method of achieving the change desired that avoids confronting the incompatible cultural norms. As cultural resistance diminishes, the change may be absorbed into the firm.

In the 1970s, Rich's was a highly successful, quality-oriented department store chain that served higher income customers in several southeastern locations. With Wal-Mart and Kmart experiencing rapid growth in the sale of mid- to low-priced merchandise, Rich's decided to serve this market as well. Finding such merchandise inconsistent with the successful values and norms of its traditional business, it created a separate business called *Richway* to tap this growth area in retailing. Through a new store network, it was able to *manage around its culture*. Both Rich's and Richway have since flourished, though their cultures are radically different in some respects.

Reformulate the Strategy or Culture

A firm in cell 4 faces the most difficult challenge in managing the strategy-culture relationship. To implement its new strategy, such a firm must make organizational changes that are incompatible with its current, usually entrenched, values and norms. A firm in this situation faces the complex, expensive, and often long-term challenge of changing its culture; it is a challenge that borders on impossible. Strategy in Action 11–2 describes the challenge faced by Robert Daniell, CEO of United Technologies, as he attempted to change the culture of his firm.

When a strategy requires massive organizational change and engenders cultural resistance, a firm should determine whether reformulation of the strategy is appropriate. Are all of the organizational changes really necessary? Is there any real expectation that the changes will be acceptable and successful? If these answers are yes, then massive changes in management personnel are often necessary. AT&T offered early retirement to over 20,000 managers as part of a massive recreation of its culture to go along with major strategic changes in 1996. If the answer to these questions is no, the firm might reformulate its strategic plan so as to make it more consistent with established organizational norms and practices.

Merrill Lynch faced the challenge of strategy-culture incompatibility in the last decade. Seeking to remain number one in the newly deregulated financial services industry, it chose to pursue a product development strategy in its brokerage business. Under this strategy, Merrill Lynch would sell a broader range of investment products to a more diverse customer base and would integrate other financial services, such as real estate sales, into the Merrill Lynch organization. The new strategy could succeed only if Merrill Lynch's traditionally service-oriented brokerage network became sales and marketing oriented. Initial efforts to implement the strategy generated substantial resistance from Merrill Lynch's highly successful brokerage network. The strategy was fundamentally inconsistent with long-standing cultural norms at Merrill Lynch that emphasized personalized service and very close broker-client relationships. Merrill Lynch ultimately divested its real estate operation, reintroduced specialists that supported broker/retailers, and refocused its brokers more narrowly on basic client investment needs.

REWARD SYSTEMS: MOTIVATING STRATEGY EXECUTION

The execution of strategy ultimately depends on individual organizational members, particularly key managers. So motivating and rewarding good performance by individuals and organizational units are key ingredients in effective strategy implementation. If strategy accomplishment is a top priority, then the reward system must be clearly and tightly linked to strategic performance. Motivating and controlling managerial personnel in the execution

TRANSFORMING ORGANIZATIONAL CULTURE AT UNITED TECHNOLOGIES

It was with some urgency that Robert F. Daniell, the newly appointed CEO of United Technologies Corporation, summoned his top executives. Just weeks after taking the reins from Harry J. Gray, Daniell called a management powwow at the Jupiter Beach Hilton in Florida. The subject? UTC's shaky future. Customers of its Pratt & Whitney jet engines, outraged by lousy service, were defecting in droves to archrival General Electric Company. Market shares at UTC's once dominant Otis elevator unit and Carrier air-conditioning company were evaporating. Profits had hit a 13-year low. "Things had to change," says Daniell.

Unlike the iron-fisted Gray, however, Daniell did not lecture at management meetings. Instead, a Boston consultant moderated a roiling discussion in which managers put forth their remedies: dump divisions wholesale, diversify, pump up research-and-development spending. "Just the fact that we went through all of that yelling and screaming was unusual," says one executive who attended. After two days, Daniell and his team decided to remake UTC—to level its autocratic structure and bring more of its 186,800 employees into the decision-making process. *The ultimate goal: To get UTC's haughty culture to take marching orders from its customers.*

Worker empowerment. Team building. Getting close to your customer. While a lot of companies are just starting to talk about such methods, Bob Daniell is already proving that they can work wonders on the bottom line. The changes are nowhere more apparent than at jet-engine maker Pratt & Whitney, which pulls in more than half of UTC's operating profit. Orders have increased eightfold, to nearly $8 billion, since 1987.

When Daniell finally became CEO, he inherited a divided, argumentative management. Executives were too frightened to admit mistakes, and they directed their staffs like armies. All the way down the line, staffers refused to take responsibility for errors.

At the same time, Daniell was working on a long-term goal: changing Pratt's by-the-book structure. Dictatorial management and a Byzantine approval process made employees feel powerless. Take the case of an airplane builder who wants to mount an engine a fraction of a millimeter closer to the wing than the blueprint specifies. Normally, a good engineer at Pratt could just eyeball the

Source: "Changes at United Technologies," *Forbes*, August 28, 1989, pp. 42–46.

of strategy are accomplished through a firm's reward mechanisms—compensation, raises, bonuses, stock options, incentives, benefits, promotions, demotions, recognition, praise, criticism, more (or less) responsibility, group norms, performance appraisal, tension, and fear. These mechanisms can be positive and negative, short run and long run.

Guidelines for Structuring Effective Reward Systems

Regardless of the short- or long-term strategic considerations, managers face additional challenges in structuring rewards in a manner that energizes every person in their organization. One success story in meeting this challenge has been Nucor Corporation. Described in Strategy in Action 11–3, Nucor's reward system is largely credited with driving the success of its strategy in a U.S. steel industry where experts have said the United States has "lost its comparative advantage, can no longer compete in world markets, and should exit the business altogether." Managers at every level within Nucor, and any other business, can improve the effectiveness of their reward system by following these nine guidelines:

1. **Link rewards tightly to the strategic plan.** As the earlier discussion pointed out, rewards linked to a firm's strategy logically enhance its chance of success. Linking rewards

continued

blueprint and give the customer the nod for such a change. But until Pratt changed the system in February 1988, the request would wind through nine departments, including a committee that met only once a week.

Now, the design engineer makes the decision and only needs to get three signatures. Says Garvey: "It's all part of quality—taking responsibility." As a result, average response time has gone from 82 days to 10, and the request backlog has shrunk from 1,900 cases to fewer than 100.

Daniell went further with this campaign to improve service. He increased the number of service representatives in the field by nearly 70 percent—despite 30 percent staff cuts in the rest of the company.

Overall, Daniell's effort to change the culture is based on four approaches:

Flatten the hierarchy. Daniell leveled a Byzantine corporate structure by cutting many layers of decision making. At Pratt & Whitney, for instance, he cut eight levels of management to as few as four.

Empower your workers. Managers pushed decision making down. For instance, field representatives at Pratt & Whitney now make multimillion-dollar decisions about reimbursing customers on warranty claims. Before, they would have to wait for approvals from numerous layers above.

Get close to your customers. This is Daniell's battle cry. Worker empowerment helps, but the imperative goes even further than that. For instance, Pratt & Whitney lends some of its top engineers to customers for a year—and pays their salaries.

Train, train, train. Daniell uses training to revamp the corporate culture. More than 5,000 senior and middle managers are getting at least 40 hours of classroom work. In some classes, customers are brought in for gripe sessions, and a problem-solving team gathered from many different departments must come up with solutions.

to the accomplishment of key objectives, milestones, completion of key projects, or actions that sustain competitive advantage (like Nucor's high productivity) keeps people energized and focused on the right things and on doing them right.

2. **Use variable incentives and make them a major part of everyone's compensation.** If a significant portion of a person's compensation (usually 25 to 60 percent) varies with successful execution of his or her responsibilities, then a person should be very attentive to do them well. Nucor did this with low base pay and virtually open-ended bonus capability. AT&T has introduced "internal venturing," whereby employees with approved new product ideas can forgo a part of their compensation as a "co-investment" in their own internal venture and receive up to eight times that investment if the venture is successful within five years. This guideline obviously can backfire on any manager if the incentive is not fair, not understood, and not consistent with the next guideline.

3. **Rewards and incentives must be linked to an individual's job and the outcomes the individual can personally effect.** People are more accepting of incentive compensation when they control what needs to be done to accomplish the outcomes that earn them the incentive. While easier for salespeople to visualize than for production or administrative personnel, effective managers strive to introduce this guideline in all areas of the

NUCOR'S SECRET TO SUCCESS: A LOGICAL REWARD SYSTEM

The last 10 years have seen most analysts write off the U.S. steel industry as outdated, inefficient, and no match for Japan, Taiwan, and Europe. But they should come down to Charlotte, North Carolina. In an industry where the giants are hemorrhaging red ink, closing plants, and diversifying, midsized Nucor Corporation is an unprecedented success. Nucor is taking market share *away* from Japan and Taiwan!

Nucor is the low-cost producer, combining outfront technology with innovative incentive systems. The results are globally competitive steel products, highly productive steel mills, and a well-paid work force.

Nucor's reward system is based on four principles: (1) earnings according to productivity, (2) job security for proper performance, (3) fair and consistent treatment, and (4) easy and direct avenues of appeal. Nucor believes that "money is the best motivator." The compensation system is incentive oriented, with those incentives tied directly to productivity. Base salaries are low; but incentives can easily add 50 to 100 percent of base salary to total compensation, with no upper limit. All employees have a significant part of their compensation based around productivity. All incentive systems are designed around groups, not individuals. This applies to everyone, from production workers to clerks and secretaries to senior officers.

In the production incentive program, groups range from 25 to 35 people who are working as a team on some complete task. There are nine production bonus groups in Nucor's typical minimill—three each in melting and casting (M&C), rolling, and finishing and shipping. The M&C group begins with a base goal of 12 tons of good billets per hour; above this, every person in the group gets a 4 percent bonus for every ton per hour produced. If over a week they average 30 tons per hour—which is considered low—they earn a 72 percent bonus $[4 \times (30 - 12)]$ for that week. The multiplier affects all pay—overtime and regular. In the joist production line, bonuses are based on 90 percent of the historical time it takes to make a particular product. If during the week a group makes the product at 40 percent less than standard time, its members receive a 40 percent bonus—with the *next* paycheck.

Source: Nucor Corporation 1994 annual report.

company. Team bonuses are one way this is done. Employee participation in designing the rewards is another.

4. **Reward performance and link value to success, rather than to position in the hierarchy.** While seniority has its place, and positions of responsibility in a management hierarchy often correlate with contribution to results, progressive managers increasingly are recognizing the importance of structuring incentives and compensation to reward the key skills or expertise necessary for a strategy to be successful. In the rapidly growing environmental and bio-engineering industries, several companies have compensation and bonus programs under which technical personnel can earn significantly more than managers of their units or managers at higher levels in the organization. The reason is simple. The skills those people possess are essential to successful strategic outcomes.

5. **Reward everyone and be sensitive to discrepancies between the top and bottom of the organization.** A successful strategy requires energized, cooperative effort from every organization member. Incentive-based reward systems should reflect this by including programs wherein every member participates in some fashion. And while varying skills, levels of responsibility, and roles must be recognized with significantly different incentive amounts, inexplicably high rewards at high executive levels with little or none at the lowest level can erode confidence and commitment. A major controversy has arisen in

continued

Managerial bonuses are based on return on assets. Top managers have no employment contracts, nor do they receive guaranteed or discretionary bonuses, profit sharing, pension plans, or other executive perks (no company cars, planes, country club memberships, executive dining rooms, or reserved parking). Base salaries are set at 75 percent of what executives earn in comparable positions in other companies. If the company produces below par (9 percent return on equity), that's all they get. For every pretax dollar above this base, 5 percent goes into an officers' pool that is divided according to salary. For example, if return on equity goes to 24 percent, which it has, Nucor executives receive up to 270 percent of their base in cash and an additional 180 percent in stock.

All Nucor employees receive the same insurance, holidays, and vacations. Everyone, including the CEO, flies coach. There is a profit-sharing plan for all nonexecutive employees. Nucor provides a scholarship of $2,000 per year for four years of college or vocational training for every child of every employee. (When the children graduate, many come to work for Nucor.) The company has not laid off a single employee for more than 20 years. Ken Iverson, Nucor's president, confessed he was proud to be the lowest compensated Fortune 500 CEO in the recession of the early 1980s. Why? During that period, to avoid layoffs, Nucor had to cut back to four- or even three-and-a-half-day workweeks, which cut employee pay 20 to 25 percent below normal. But few complained: they knew that department heads were cut more (35 to 40 percent) and officers even more (60 to 70 percent). Iverson calls it our "Share the Pain" program. If a company isn't successful, the reasons are irrelevant. Management should take the biggest cut because they are the most responsible.

Can Nucor's incentive compensation be applied to other companies and industries? There are limitations. Two elements are necessary: (1) it must make sense to break out small groups of people who work as a team on a particular function and (2) that particular function must be both self-contained and measurable.

the United States over CEO compensation as a result of extraordinary bonuses accruing to selected executives in the auto industry and others while their companies were losing billions, massive layoffs were commonplace, and their highly successful Japanese and German counterparts were much more modestly compensated.[10] In smaller firms the discrepancy usually arises in perks or special founding-family compensation. But whether the reward involves cash, stock, options, perks, or other benefits, a reward system designed to incentivize everyone in the organization to share in strategic success (or a lack thereof) will be more effective long term.

6. **Be scrupulously fair, accurate, and informative.** Related to the previous guideline, reward systems that are perceived to be fair work better than those that are not. Where

---

[10] The issue of CEO compensation is a complex, highly charged issue. Some people question the high compensation and bonus package accruing to executives like Lee Iacocca (Chrysler), Steve Ross (Time-Warner), Mike Eisner (Disney), and Roberto Goizueta (Coke) to name a few. Others strongly defend their high compensation, pointing to the rise in market value of their respective firm's stock since they took control. For thoughtful analyses of this issue, see Andrew R. Brownstein and Morris J. Panner, "Who Should Set CEO Pay? The Press? Congress? Shareholders?" *Harvard Business Review* 70, no. 3 (1992), pp. 28–39; and "CEO Pay: How Much Is Enough?" *Harvard Business Review* 70, no. 4 (1992), pp. 130–39. For practical guidelines on handling executive pay in an atmosphere of increased public scrutiny, see John D. McMillan, "Executive Pay a New Way," *HRMagazine* 37, no. 6 (1992), pp. 46–48, 194.

incentives are linked to work teams, groups, or units, fairness among individuals' contribution and reward often will be an issue facing operating-level managers. Accurate measurement of the outcomes triggering rewards, timing considerations, and amounts paid play a key role in perceived fairness. Complete openness in sharing information about "how we're doing," so participants can see clearly the reasons behind compensation results, is another important way to reinforce fairness.

7. **Reward generously when successful; minimally when not.** Reward systems that reinforce success do just that. Systems that provide similar rewards (or a lack thereof) whether successful or not can send the message that extra effort doesn't matter. Food Lion has butchers and cashiers, while Wal-Mart has greeters and cashiers that have seen their small stock incentives valued at a few thousand dollars 20 years ago make them worth in excess of $2 million today. Nucor's management took 40 to 70 percent cuts and employees 20 to 25 percent cuts (via shorter work weeks) during the recession-induced reduction in demand for steel. Whether long term or short term, incentive compensation linked to results provides appropriate reinforcement of the need to formulate and implement good strategies effectively, regardless of organizational level.

8. **Don't underestimate the value of a rewarding and motivational environment.** While cash, stock, and perks get people's attention, a motivating environment is a very important part of a sound reward system. Increased responsibility, autonomy, participation in decision making, recognition, and opportunity for growth are long-advocated and proven "rewards" that motivate most people. Significant attention to creating ways to structure these elements into an individual and work team environment can provide any manager with a powerful tool for motivating strategy execution.

9. **Be open to changing the reward systems.** Strategies and tactics change. Situations change. Organization members come and go or encounter different needs. Certain aspects of a reward system prove inappropriate or counterproductive. These and other reasons should keep managers looking at reward systems as evolving, rather than permanent, indefinitely. Tempered with the need to avoid confusion and any sense of unfairness, a thoughtful change in reward systems can be an effective management option.

Following these guidelines in structuring reward systems will not guarantee successful strategy implementation. But a system so designed will make a big difference, particularly at operating levels of the company. For decisions on incentive compensations, salary increases, promotions, and key assignments, as well as perks, praise, and recognition are operational managers' foremost attention-getting and commitment-generating devices.

SUMMARY

This chapter examined the idea that a key aspect of implementing a strategy is the *institutionalization* of the strategy so it permeates daily decisions and actions in a manner consistent with long-term strategic success. Four fundamental elements must be managed to "fit" a strategy if the strategy is to be effectively institutionalized: *organizational structure, leadership, culture*, and *rewards*.

Five fundamental organizational structures were examined, and the advantages and disadvantages of each were identified. Institutionalizing a strategy requires a good strategy-structure fit. This chapter dealt with how this requirement often is overlooked until performance becomes inadequate and then indicated the conditions under which the various structures would be appropriate.

Organizational leadership is essential to effective strategy implementation. The CEO plays a critical role in this regard. Assignment of key managers, particularly within the top-management team, is an important aspect of organizational leadership. Deciding whether to promote insiders or hire outsiders is often a central leadership issue in strategy implementation. This chapter showed how this decision could be made in a manner that would best institutionalize the new strategy.

Organizational culture has been recognized as a pervasive influence on organizational life. Organizational culture, which is the shared beliefs and values of an organization's members, may be a major help or hindrance to strategy implementation. This chapter discussed an approach to managing the strategy-culture fit. It identified four fundamentally different strategy-culture situations and provided recommendations for managing the strategy-culture fit in each of these situations.

The reward system is a key ingredient in motivating managers to execute a firm's strategy. Firms should emphasize incentive systems that ensure adequate attention to strategic thrusts. This usually requires a concerted effort to emphasize long-term strategic performance as well as short-term measures of performance. In addition to timing, nine key guidelines must be accommodated to have an effective reward system.

QUESTIONS FOR DISCUSSION

1. What key structural considerations must be incorporated into strategy implementation? Why does structural change often lag a change in strategy?

2. Which organizational structure is most appropriate for successful strategy implementation? Explain how state of development affects your answer.

3. Why is leadership an important element in strategy implementation? Find an example in a major business periodical of the CEO's key role in strategy implementation.

4. Under what conditions would it be more appropriate to fill a key management position with someone from outside the firm when a qualified insider is available?

5. What is organizational culture? Why is it important? Explain two different situations a firm might face in managing the strategy-culture relationship.

6. How would you vary an incentive system for a growth-oriented versus a harvest-oriented business?

7. What do you anticipate your first management job may be? Outline a reward system for your employees based on the guidelines provided at the end of this chapter.

BIBLIOGRAPHY

Bailey, G., and J. Szerdy. "Is There Life after Downsizing?" *Journal of Business Strategy*, January 1988, pp. 8–11.

Barney, J. B. "Organizational Culture: Can It Be a Source of Sustained Competitive Advantage?" *Academy of Management Review*, July 1986, p. 656.

Bethel, J. E., and J. Liebeskind. "The Effects of Ownership Structure on Corporate Restructuring." *Strategic Management Journal* 14 (1993), pp. 15–31.

Bettinger, Cass. "Use Corporate Culture to Trigger High Performance." *Journal of Business Strategy* 10, no. 2 (March–April 1989), pp. 38–42.

Block, Barbara. "Creating a Culture All Employees Can Accept." *Management Review*, July 1989, p. 41.

Botterill, M. "Changing Corporate Culture." *Management Services* (UK) 34, no. 6 (1990), pp. 14–18.

Bower, Joseph Lyon, and Martha Wagner Weinberg. "Statecraft, Strategy, and Corporate Leadership." *California Management Review*, Winter 1988, p. 107.

Bowman, E. H., and H. Singh. "Corporate Restructuring: Reconfiguring the Firm." *Strategic Management Journal* 14 (1993), pp. 5–14.

Byles, C. M., and R. J. Keating. "Strength of Organizational Culture and Performance: Strategic Implications." *Journal of Business Strategy*, Spring 1989, pp. 45–55.

Chapman, P. "Changing the Corporate Culture of Rank Xerox." *Long Range Planning*, April 1988, pp. 23–28.

Chandler, A. D., *Strategy and Structure*. Cambridge: MIT Press, 1962.

Chingos, P. T., and V. J. Elliott. "Using Incentives to Foster Business Unit Results." *Bottomline* 8, no. 3 (1991), pp. 15–19.

Cowherd, D. M., and R. H. Luchs. "Linking Organization Structures and Processes to Business Strategy." *Long Range Planning*, October 1988, pp. 47–53.

"Cultural Transition at AT&T." *Sloan Management Review*, Fall 1983, pp. 15–26.

Daft, R. L.; J. Sormunen; and D. Parks. "Chief Executive Scanning." *Strategic Management Journal*, March 1988, pp. 123–40.

Donaldson, G. "Voluntary Restructuring: The Case of General Mills." *Journal of Financial Economics* 27 (1990), pp. 117–41.

Drake, Bruce H., and Eileen Drake. "Ethical and Legal Aspects of Managing Corporate Cultures." *California Management Review*, Winter 1988, p. 107.

Eccles, Robert G. "The Performance Measurement Manifesto." *Harvard Business Review* 69 (January–February 1991), pp. 131–37.

Fitzgerald, T. H. "Can Change in Organizational Culture Really Be Managed?" *Organizational Dynamics* 17, no. 2 (1988), pp. 5–15.

Floyd, Steven W., and Bill Wooldridge. "Managing Strategic Consensus: The Foundation of Effective Implementation." *Academy of Management Executive* 6, no. 4 (November 1992), pp. 27–39.

Forman, R. "Strategic Planning and the Chief Executive." *Long Range Planning*, August 1988, pp. 57–64.

Fredrickson, James W.; Donald C. Hambrick; and Sara Bawmrin. "A Model of CEO Dismissal." *Academy of Management Review*, April 1988, p. 255.

Freeman, R. Edward, and Daniel R. Gilbert, Jr. *Corporate Strategy and the Search for Ethics*. Englewood Cliffs, NJ: Prentice Hall, 1988.

Freund, York P. "Critical Success Factors." *Planning Review*, July–August 1988, p. 20.

Gabarro, J. J. "When a New Manager Takes Charge." *Harvard Business Review* 64, no. 3 (May–June 1985), pp. 110–23.

Ginsburg, Lee, and Neil Miller. "Value-Driven Management." *Business Horizons* (May–June 1992), pp. 25–27.

Gomez-Mejia, Luis R.; Henri Tose; and Timothy Hinkin. "Managerial Control, Performance, and Executive Compensation." *Academy of Management Journal*, March 1987, p. 51.

Gomez-Mejia, L. R., and T. Welbourne. "Compensation Strategies in a Global Context." *Human Resource Planning* 14, no. 1 (1991), pp. 29–41.

Green, Sebastian. "Strategy, Organizational Culture, and Symbolism." *Long Range Planning* 21, no. 4 (August 1988), pp. 121–29.

Gupta, Anil K. "SBU Strategies, Corporate-SBU Relations, and SBU Effectiveness in Strategy Implementation." *Academy of Management Journal*, September 1987, p. 477.

Hinterhuber, H. H., and W. Popp. "Are You a Strategist or Just a Manager?" *Harvard Business Review* 70, no. 1 (1992), pp. 105–14.

Hosking, D. M. "Organizing, Leadership and Skillful Process." *Journal of Management Studies*, March 1988, pp. 147–66.

Jensen, M. C., and K. J. Murphy. "Performance Pay and Top-Management Incentives." *Journal of Political Economy* 98 (1990), pp. 225–64.

Johnson, G. "Managing Strategic Change—Strategy, Culture, and Action." *Long Range Planning* 25, no. 1 (1992), pp. 28–36.

Kim, W. C., and R. A. Mauborgne. "Parables of Leadership." *Harvard Business Review* 70, no. 4 (1992), pp. 123–28.

Kirkpatrick, Shelley A., and Edwin A. Locke. "Leadership: Do Traits Matter?" *Academy of Management Executive* 5, no. 2 (May 1991), pp. 48–60.

Koch, D. L., and D. W. Steinhauser. "Changing the Corporate Culture." *Datamotion*, October 1983, pp. 247–52.

Kotter, John P. "What Leaders Really Do." *Harvard Business Review* 68 (May–June 1990), pp. 103–11.

Kotter, John P., and James L. Heskett. *Corporate Culture and Performance*. New York: Free Press, 1992.

Larson, Erik W., and David H. Gobeli. "Matrix Management: Contradictions and Insights." *California Management Review*, Summer 1987, p. 126.

Lei, D.; J. Slocum; and R. Slater. "Global Strategy and Reward Systems: The Key Roles of Management Development and Corporate Culture." *Organizational Dynamics* 19, no. 2 (1990), pp. 27–41.

Lewis, P. "Performance Related Pay: Pretexts and Pitfalls." *Employee Relations* (U.K.) 13, no. 1 (1991), pp. 12–16.

Liden, Robert C., and Terence R. Mitchell. "Ingratiatory Behavior in Organizational Settings." *Academy of Management Review*, October 1988, p. 572.

Main, John G., and John Thackray. "The Logic of Restructuring." *Planning Review*, May–June 1987, p. 5.

Meindl, James R., and Sanford B. Ehrlich. "The Romance of Leadership and Evaluation of Organizational Performance." *Academy of Management Journal*, March 1987, p. 91.

Miller, Danny. "Strategy Making and Structure: Analysis and Implications for Performance." *Academy of Management Journal*, March 1987, p. 7.

Nichols, Don. "Bottom-Up Strategies." *Management Review*, December 1989, p. 44.

O'Toole, James. "Employee Practices at the Best-Managed Companies." *California Management Review* 28, no. 1 (Fall 1985), pp. 35–66.

Paine, Lynn Sharp. "Managing for Organizational Integrity." *Harvard Business Review* 72, no. 2 (March–April 1994), pp. 106–117.

Putz, B. J. "Productivity Improvement: Changing Values, Beliefs, and Assumptions." *SAM Advanced Management Journal* 56, no. 4 (1991), pp. 9–12.

Reed, R., and M. Reed. "CEO Experience and Diversification Strategy Fit." *Journal of Management Studies*, March 1988, pp. 251–70.

Reimann, Bernard C., and Yoash Wiener. "Corporate Culture: Avoiding the Elitist Trap." *Business Horizons*, March–April 1988, p. 36.

Saffold, Guy S., III. "Culture Traits, Strength, and Settings." *Academy of Management Review*, October 1988, p. 546.

Schneier, C. E. "Capitalizing on Performance Management, Recognition, and Rewards Systems." *Compensation and Benefit Review* 21, no. 2 (1989), pp. 20–30.

Spector, Bert A. "From Bogged-Down to Fired-Up: Inspiring Organizational Change." *Sloan Management Review*, Summer 1989, p. 29.

Spohn, A. G. "The Relationship of Reward Systems and Employee Performance." *Compensation and Benefits Management* 6, no. 2 (1990), pp. 128–32.

Stone, N. "Building Corporate Character." *Harvard Business Review* 70, no. 2 (1992), pp. 94–104.

"Strategic Leaders and Leadership." *Strategic Management Journal*, special issue, Summer 1989.

Vancil, Richard F. "A Look at CEO Succession." *Harvard Business Review*, March–April 1987, p. 107.

Vincent, D. R. "Understanding Organization Power." *Journal of Business Strategy*, March 1988, pp. 40–44.

Wagner, John A., III, and Richard Z. Gooding. "Shared Influence and Organizational Behavior: A Meta-Analysis of Situational Variables Expected to Moderate Participation-Outcome Relationships." *Academy of Management Review*, September 1987, p. 524.

Webber, Alvin M. "The CEO Is the Company." *Harvard Business Review*, January–February 1987, p. 114.

———. "Consensus, Continuity, and Common Sense." *Harvard Business Review* 68, no. 4 (1990), pp. 115–23.

Zabriskie, N., and A. Huellmantel. "Implementing Strategies for Human Resources." *Long Range Planning*, April 1989, pp. 70–77.

Zajac, E. J., and M. S. Kraatz. "A Diametric Forces Model of Strategic Change: Assessing the Antecedents and Consequences of Restructuring in the Higher Education Industry." *Strategic Management Journal* 14 (1993), pp. 83–102.

Zaleznik, A. "Managers and Leaders: Are They Different?" *Harvard Business Review* 70, no. 2 (1992), pp. 126–35.

Zemke, R. "Rewards and Recognition: Yes, They Really Work." *Training* 25, no. 1 (1988), pp. 48–53.

CHAPTER 11 COHESION CASE ILLUSTRATION

IMPLEMENTING STRATEGY BY RESTRUCTURING AND REENGINEERING COCA-COLA'S ORGANIZATIONAL STRUCTURE, LEADERSHIP, CULTURE, AND REWARDS

STRUCTURE

The Coca-Cola Company had the following basic structure at the beginning of the 1980s:

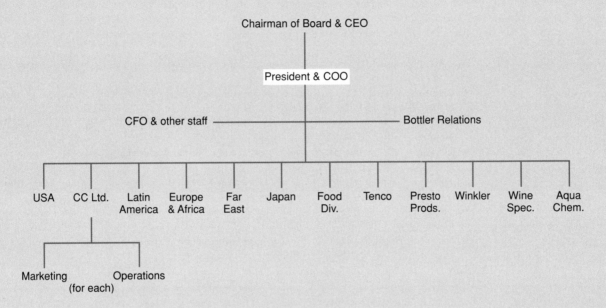

The figure suggests Coke was a rather decentralized company with relatively autonomous operating units based on both the product-service of the business and geographic location. This facilitated local decision making and aided Coke's rapid advance in international markets.

By the mid-1980s, Roberto Goizueta had completed significant restructuring and consolidation of Coca-Cola to allow for decentralized decision making while also retaining more centralized control. The following figure shows Coke's structure by 1984. According to Goizueta:

> To operate more effectively in today's business environment and more sharply focus management's attention on the expansion opportunities within the industries in which they operate, we have regrouped the Company's various units into four business sectors . . . Each of our four business sectors is operating according to a well-defined plan. Each is moving forward in line with a broad strategy to capitalize on its superior positioning and expertise, while drawing from complementary corporate resources that bind the sectors into a single, powerful enterprise.

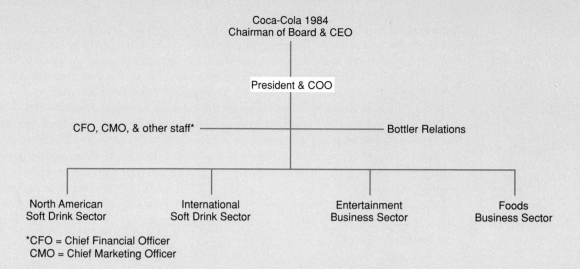

Coca-Cola 1984
Chairman of Board & CEO

President & COO

CFO, CMO, & other staff* ———————————————— Bottler Relations

North American Soft Drink Sector | International Soft Drink Sector | Entertainment Business Sector | Foods Business Sector

*CFO = Chief Financial Officer
CMO = Chief Marketing Officer

By 1993, the structure looked as follows:

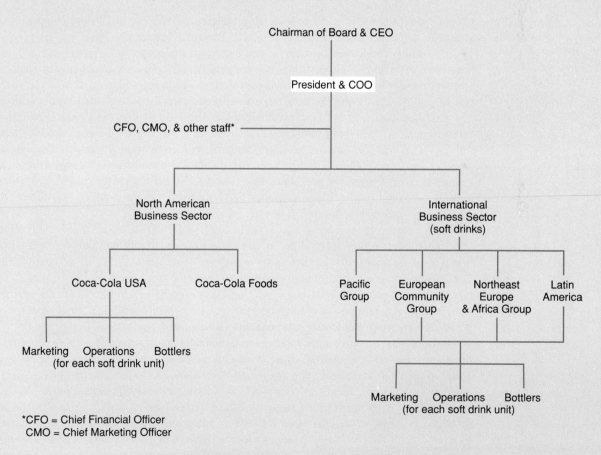

Chairman of Board & CEO

President & COO

CFO, CMO, & other staff*

North American Business Sector

Coca-Cola USA   Coca-Cola Foods

Marketing   Operations   Bottlers
(for each soft drink unit)

International Business Sector (soft drinks)

Pacific Group | European Community Group | Northeast Europe & Africa Group | Latin America

Marketing   Operations   Bottlers
(for each soft drink unit)

*CFO = Chief Financial Officer
CMO = Chief Marketing Officer

The Coke structure of the mid-1990s reflected subtle but key adjustments designed to implement its key strategies more effectively. First, it had essentially two lines of business—soft drinks and foods (citrus juices). Second, it operated in two broad arenas—domestic (United States) and international. Goizueta's management team felt geographic focus was the most logical and fundamental organizing dimension to implement an international emphasized strategy. Then, in the case of the United States, the team's preference was to place the two main U.S. businesses (soft drinks and foods) within the U.S. geographic organization. Perhaps synergies involving deliveries to many retail outlets could be better supported or conflicts overcome by having these two under one roof.

A second dimension of this new organization kept bottling relations and overall marketing support as a corporate function, while giving each unit control of operations and day-to-day marketing and distribution. This allowed corporate control of broad themes, resources, and guidelines, while also allowing significant autonomy within each basic geographic sector. It also allowed for greater coordination of resources across international markets—an essential ingredient if Coke's aggressive international growth posture was to be maintained or indeed accelerated. Overall, the changes reflected in this structure point to Coca-Cola's major emphasis on international development and aggressive marketing adapted to local markets.

LEADERSHIP

Coca-Cola has many incidents of leadership selection that appear well coordinated with its strategies and changing strategic needs. Let's look at a few examples.

First, and perhaps most notable, was the selection of Roberto Goizueta as CEO and soon thereafter chairman in 1980. As we have briefly described earlier, Goizueta is Cuban by birth. His family owned a sugar refinery, which had made them wealthy. After finishing school in Cuba, Roberto chose to start to work for a major Coke bottler in Cuba, rather than join his family's business. Soon thereafter, Fidel Castro's rebellion took control of the island nation and, stripped of their sugar business, the Goizueta family left Cuba for the United States. Roberto Goizueta soon joined his family and went to work for a Florida bottler partially owned by the parent company. His background was in engineering and chemistry, which aided his rise within the organization, quickly turning into a position in Atlanta. From there he became a star in operations and rose quickly to the executive V.P. level.

When Paul Austin decided to step down in 1978, Coke had embarked on a serious effort to grow its international sales. While facing some lingering doubt as a rather conservative group, Coke's board was impressed with Roberto Goizueta's ability to articulate what Coke stood for and certainly was aware of the positive message it would convey to its budding international partners, employees, and investors. His appointment also reinforced Coke's long-standing policy of promotion from within, while sending a clear message to domestic personnel that it was serious about its long-term international commitment.

Goizueta has set a precedence of expecting managers to bring results-oriented commitment and dedication to their assignments at Coke. When results miss expectations, he is quick to move to support his managers and their ideas for improvement—or to change managers where their ideas engender a lack of confidence. In 1989, Coca-Cola USA—the big domestic arm selling Coke syrups and concentrates—was steadily losing modest market share to Pepsi in selected outlets. Goizueta's reaction was to suddenly bring in then 61-year-old Ira Herbert out of headquarters staff obscurity and put him in charge of this subsidiary. Herbert, marketing guru during Coca-Cola's very successful "Coke is it" and "It's the real thing" campaigns, insisted that he had not been called in "to pull the cart out of a ditch." Business writers thought otherwise. By 1992, Herbert had returned to staff duties and pending retirement, with Coca-Cola USA now leading Pepsi in every distribution outlet, including Pepsi's powerful grocery store channel. The lesson we see from this is the decisive decision to adjust leadership to the growth demands and aggressive marketing posture inherent in Coke's strategy for the 1990s. Rather than just talk about what it will take, Goizueta communicated his total commitment and expectation of the same from others by this action.

Goizueta, 65 in 1996, has been the subject of much speculation about the possibility of retirement. This speculation began in 1994. A story about Coke's handling this helps illustrate Coke's leadership orientation. Other illustrations of Coke's leadership priorities, which center around speeding up decision making and taking initiative, can be seen in the next section on culture. First the story:

> ATLANTA, 1994: Coca-Cola Co. was gripped with succession fever. Who would become the next in line to succeed Roberto C. Goizueta, the company's chairman and chief executive officer, who normally would be due to retire in 1996?
>
> Employees gossiped behind closed doors. They totted up the stock options of the company's young turks. They tried to divine the real reasons certain top executives were deciding such minutiae as where to place Olympic billboards or whether Diet Coke needed a new logo.
>
> "People constantly are speculating over who's going to succeed whom in top-level jobs," even on their car phones, one former employee said not long ago.
>
> The guessing game is over. Three weeks ago, the company announced that Mr. Goizueta, who turns 63 later this year, would remain at the helm for "an indefinite period" beyond the normal retirement age of 65. And the chairman seems in no rush to move on. Let's say "that I'm going to stay until 1999," he says cagily. "You mean to tell me you can pick in 1994 who is going to be the chief executive in 1999? Only God can do that. So many things happen in five years."
>
> The move to keep Mr. Goizueta was widely regarded by both insiders and outsiders as smart, coming at a time when Coke's stock has been weak and it faces new challenges both at home and abroad. The Cuban-born aristocrat, who joined Coke as a chemical engineer 40 years ago, has had a wildly successful run at Coke and has been a big hit on Wall Street.
>
> Many of the company's followers simply see no reason to turn him out. He is passionate about his job, regularly working 10-hour days, traveling to Coke's far-flung operations and perusing overseas strategy reports over weekends. He is in good health. And although he has been the CEO for 13 years, few believe that his management has ossified.
>
> Indeed, Coca-Cola may be representative of a new way of thinking enunciated by management experts and echoed by Coke's directors: There really is no reason—in fact, it may be foolish—to let go an experienced, successful chief executive just because he turns 65.
>
> "Talent is so scarce that when you have it, you don't let an arbitrary age retire it," says Warren Buffett, the respected Omaha, Neb., investor and Coke board member. "As long as the board thinks Roberto is the best person in the world to be head of the Coca-Cola company, there is no room for anyone else to head it."

BUILDING A SPEED-ORIENTED CULTURE AND REWARD SYSTEM

The culture Goizueta and other Coca-Cola managers think best reinforces their strategy is one that is synonymous with speed, rapid response, and aggressive decisions and actions. They seek to continually build an organization of people with initiative, commitment, understanding of how to make Coke forever remain the true pause that refreshes; people who take unabashed pleasure in (and are rewarded for) their efforts. Goizueta feels this must be the very foundation of Coke's worldwide business system. An interesting way to illustrate this culture is to look at Coke's reaction to the sudden fall of the Berlin Wall as the decade of the 1990s was about to begin.

The Berlin Wall was daily being destroyed in 1991 as millions watched on worldwide TV. Coke's chairman, Roberto Goizueta, and president, Don Keough, worried that a large, fast push into eastern Germany—with its ill-suited market structure—might become a colossal failure. But Horst Muller and Heinz Weizorek pressed their argument and quickly succeeded in changing the minds of Coke's top brass, especially Goizueta. The two Germans argued that monetary union would come faster than most people expected, which in turn would make doing business in eastern Germany much easier. They also saw economic advantages via tax breaks and investment assistance going to those companies and investors that moved quickly into a decrepit East Germany once it opened to the West. Also, they were aware of pent-up demand among East Germans, who consumed colas as frequently as their West German counterparts but were forced to drink poor-quality sodas provided by state-run factories.

Horst Muller, the new head of Coca-Cola's East German operations, first asked himself how to find sales reps in a country that has never had any. He needed people to handle store merchandising, order taking, and delivery. For Muller the dilemma, or one of many, was that East Germans lived in a culture where "selling" was a completely foreign idea.

Muller's choice was to scrutinize his 2,000+ employees in East Germany, most of whom worked at six old bottling plants Coca-Cola had bought from East Germany just weeks earlier. With the aid of his West German managers, Muller picked out the most friendly and engaging clerks, factory workers, and technicians from the old East German work force and sent them off to West Germany (and the United States) for a special version of Coke's sales personnel training programs. They returned in 30 days as obsessed market ambassadors and hustlers for Coca-Cola.

German personnel used "anything with wheels" to get their product and vending machines and other items into any outlet that would sell it. They jury-rigged the old East German bottling plants to keep up with demand and worked long hours, resulting in a dominant cola position in East Germany by the end of 1993—even before Pepsi had been seriously able to attempt to compete. And at the heart of this success was again a "can-do culture" found throughout the Coca-Cola worldwide business system.

Within one year, Coke had taken East Germany by storm and sold over 75 million cases in a territory where none were sold the previous year. Sales topped 100 million cases in 1992. Since Muller started, Coke has invested $500 million in eastern Germany, and Germany has become Coke's largest market in the European Community, which in turn generated more operating profits than the U.S. market since 1990. Indeed, it appears that Coke will usurp Pepsi's previous advantage in most of Eastern Europe and the old Soviet Union based on its aggressive move into East Germany from its strong position in West Germany. Today, unified Germany is one of Coke's strongest markets.

Another story from late 1995 describes how Coke's actions in Russia and other spots around the world seek to foster its culture and leadership to make *speed* synonymous with Coca-Cola:

> Late one recent night, Neville Isdell, Coca-Cola Co.'s European chief, got a frantic call at home in Atlanta.
>
> It was one of his managers in Russia asking for $340,000 to buy a stake in a bottling plant in the remote town of Nagutsky. The manager hadn't done any of the usual studies or liability checks. He wasn't even sure if local laws would permit Coke to own the property.
>
> Mr. Isdell's response: Go for it. Two hours later, Coke was a part owner of the plant and later gained controlling interest. "The old Coca-Cola would have picked over every detail in the book, and maybe lost the chance to bid," he says. "Now, we know the value of intelligent risks."
>
> In the race to quench the world's thirst, Coca-Cola has always had a reputation as the soft-drink industry's plodding old giant. Though a successful marketer, when it came to speed or innovation, the company faltered. It was swamped by the wave of teas, juices and flavored waters in the U.S. in the early 1990s. It was late entering India when that market began opening in the late

1980s. It shrugged off attacks by private-label soft-drink makers in the United Kingdom until they had siphoned off sizable sales.

But lately, Coca-Cola is charging around faster than a 10-year-old on a soda buzz—and with equal daring.

In the U.S., after nearly a decade without a new product, the company is pushing new drinks out the door at a record pace—everything from Mountain Blast Powerade sports drink to Strawberry Passion Awareness Fruitopia fruit drink. Its new marketing force has unleashed a flood of new packaging and promotions, including its signature curvy bottle, lucratively reborn in plastic. Coca-Cola says the efforts have helped it capture more than 80% of the growth in the U.S. soft-drink market this year—nearly twice last year's rate.

"Nothing energizes an organization like speed," says Roberto Goizueta, the company's chairman and chief executive.

Coca-Cola's hyperactivity has posed special challenges for PepsiCo Inc., which has always banked on its image as the industry's young rebel. It prided itself on coming out with the latest products and the hippest advertising campaigns (even if they flopped, as did Crystal Pepsi), and touted its flexibility overseas.

Now that Coca-Cola is assuming some of those same qualities, Pepsi acknowledges that it is scrambling to keep its edge. "Coke has definitely raised the bar," says Brian Swette, Pepsi's marketing chief.

The most important battles are in developing markets. With growth in soft-drink consumption maturing in markets such as the U.S., Western Europe, Mexico and Japan, most agree that the future of the beverage industry lies in emerging nations such as China and Russia.

Just this year, Coca-Cola has opened plants in Romania, Norway, Fiji and India. At least 10 more are slated, including plants in China, Hungary, Lithuania, Russia and Thailand. Big Red also is the first U.S. company to enter a joint venture in Vietnam since the embargo was lifted this summer. Coca-Cola now derives about 80% of its earnings from overseas, and makes more than half the soft drinks consumed outside the U.S.

In part, Coca-Cola is adapting to a changing industry, where teas, juices, sports drinks, bottled waters and other elixirs have transformed a largely two-cola world. Having recovered from the failure of New Coke, Coca-Cola is more willing to enter the fray and risk its name.

Credit new personalities. Coca-Cola's president, Douglas Ivester, is a fiercely competitive former financial chief who made his debut as president last year with a speech comparing company managers to a pack of "hungry wolves." What's more, as part of a recent marketing shake-up, Sergio Zyman, the creative whiz who left the company after New Coke bombed, has returned as chief marketing officer. He now is prodding his staff to make bolder, swifter moves.

For the most part, though, the changes are an extension of Mr. Goizueta's own career-long campaign to break institutional habits. During his 14-year tenure, he has overhauled the company's financial operations, trimmed the corporate structure, redefined its relationship with bottlers and reined in overseas operations that used to be run as distant fiefs. What is different about the latest moves, he says, is that many of them relate to marketing "and that's what people see."

Indeed, while Mr. Goizueta first started preaching "fast and flexible" in 1990, the effort has accelerated under Mr. Ivester. A champion of technology, Mr. Ivester has imposed a culture of voice and electronic mail and video conferencing, cutting the blizzard of memos by more than a third. He is known to send messages late at night and on weekends, leaving few excuses for delays.

"Neville's in Europe this morning, but I've already left him five voice mails," says Mr. Ivester, rushing through the halls of headquarters in Atlanta early one recent morning. "I've dealt with Spain, Italy, France and a personnel issue in Eastern Europe. And I didn't even need to talk to him once."

The company also has brought in new blood, especially in marketing. When Mr. Zyman took over, he went on a search for the "best marketing minds in the world" to bring in fresh ideas and keep pace with the company's growth. He has since hired between 40 and 50 new officers—some from sports teams and entertainment companies. Coca-Cola also has pushed its system of cross-training managers—shuttling them through different divisions—further down into the ranks, making it more difficult for the bureaucracy to solidify.

Coca-Cola's stuffy culture also is loosening up. Along with the company's collection of 19th-century oil paintings, basketball hoops now are popping up. And during a recent meeting between Coke's Asian manager and the company's Philippine bottler, Mr. Ivester and other top executives frequently dropped in to ask questions and give advice—a big change from the formal, closed-door sessions of old.

"The bottler told me, 'Doug, we used to just sit here and have a boring conversation. Now I'm talking to the president and working out all kinds of things,'" says Douglas Daft, the Asian manager. "He couldn't believe it."

Lower-level staff meetings also have taken on a more freewheeling air. "Now, in the Monday meetings, it's cool to talk about the movie you saw, or rock concert you went to and how it relates to Coke," says John Kao, a Harvard management professor who recently studied the rise in creativity at Coca-Cola.

Clearly, Coca-Cola is still a far cry from becoming the industry's wild child. The company continues to roll over competitors with its heaps of capital and tight control over bottlers, and it remains conservative among scrappier rivals.

What's more, continuing to engineer a faster, more daring Coca-Cola may be a tough task. Obsessed with shareholder value and steady growth, Coca-Cola has gained a reputation as a reliable earnings wonder. Largely on the strength of its international performance, the company's stock is up more than 50% in the past year—it closed yesterday at $63.125—boosting its market value by about $28 billion. A more-adventurous company, some say, might become a riskier investment.

"That's the hard balance," Prof. Kao says. "They have to simultaneously feed the machine that thrives on efficiency, format and market share and at the same time try to be a lab for risk-taking and invention."

Adds Mr. Isdell, the European chief: "Change driven by crisis is easy. Changing the way an organization thinks while it's successful, without being dysfunctional to what's good, that's the interesting challenge."

But it is a challenge the company will have to face as it enters new markets. Whereas the West may have been won with money and marketing muscle, emerging markets also will require quick response, a healthy thirst for risk and the ability to forge ties with a new breed of consumers. In these markets, politics and economies can change daily, demand is uncertain and customers can crave everything from pepper colas to rice punch.

In this new environment, Coke's new personality appears to be paying off.

Consider Japan, Coke's most-profitable market. Consumers there are notorious for constantly demanding fresh products. Companies typically launch between 700 and 800 drinks a year, and few stay in vending machines for more than a month.

While dominant in the market, Coca-Cola had trouble for years keeping pace. Two years ago, the company built a sophisticated product-development center to crank out new beverages faster. The result: Launch time for new drinks has been cut to 30 days from 90 days, and the company now releases as many as 50 new beverages a year. The development center has begun to serve the rest of Asia, and the lessons learned in Japan are being applied to the U.S. and Europe, too.

"We're getting it down to a fine art," says Mr. Daft, the Asian manager.

Japan also has taught the company the art of retreat. Traditionally, Coca-Cola stayed behind its products no matter how disastrous, fearing public defeat. Mr. Goizueta tells the story of a fortified tomato juice launched in the 1960s called ViProMin. The juice stayed on the shelves for several years, even though sales never materialized. "We tried to make it work for too long," he says.

Now, the company pushes products in and out of markets with greater ease, and shrugs off failures. In Japan, it launched a "lactic-based" drink called Ambasa Whitewater that initially sold millions of cases. But the market started to fade after 18 months and Ambasa was pulled.

"We see that as taking advantage of an opportunity," Mr. Daft says, "not failure."

Speed also has become more important in financial decisions. In a meeting with managers in Hanoi last month, Mr. Ivester made a quick decision to double the size of the company's new plant with a $10 million investment—even though the market was untested. To further speed things up, Mr. Ivester ordered a manufacturing line rerouted to Hanoi from a dock in Singapore.

"We had good information from our people on the ground, so we went for it," says Mr. Ivester. The plant will open next month.

In Eastern Europe, and especially in Russia, Coca-Cola's newfound agility has helped it blow past Pepsi. When the Soviet Union collapsed, for instance, the two companies followed opposite strategies. PepsiCo clung to its network of rickety, state-run bottlers, hoping to make use of their ties to old-line management. Coca-Cola quickly severed its links to the government system and built a new business from scratch. The company spent more than $1.5 billion in former East bloc countries to bring in manufacturing, distribution and marketing operations. Coca-Cola is now seen as the "milk of capitalism," especially among the young.

Of course, Coca-Cola's record overseas is far from perfect, and some spills have been costly. In Europe, the company's Tab Clear bombed. In Poland, Coca-Cola got stuck with a giant plant full of returnable bottles in its scramble to capture the expected market. And in Southeast Asia, the company's partnership with a politically well-connected bottler floundered and the company had to find an additional partner with more business acumen.

Still, Coca-Cola seems more willing than ever to swallow its failures in the name of risk and speed.

"You can't stumble if you're not moving," Mr. Goizueta says. "And if you stumble and make a decision that doesn't pan out, then you move quickly to change it. But it's better than standing still."

The Wall Street Journal, August 22, 1995, p. A1.

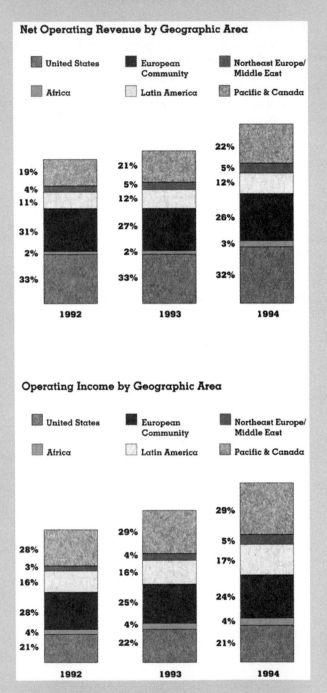

Net Operating Revenue by Geographic Area

United States   European Community   Northeast Europe/ Middle East

Africa   Latin America   Pacific & Canada

1992: 19%, 4%, 11%, 31%, 2%, 33%

1993: 21%, 5%, 12%, 27%, 2%, 33%

1994: 22%, 5%, 12%, 26%, 3%, 32%

Operating Income by Geographic Area

United States   European Community   Northeast Europe/ Middle East

Africa   Latin America   Pacific & Canada

1992: 28%, 3%, 16%, 28%, 4%, 21%

1993: 29%, 4%, 16%, 25%, 4%, 22%

1994: 29%, 5%, 17%, 24%, 4%, 21%

12

STRATEGIC CONTROL AND CONTINUOUS IMPROVEMENT

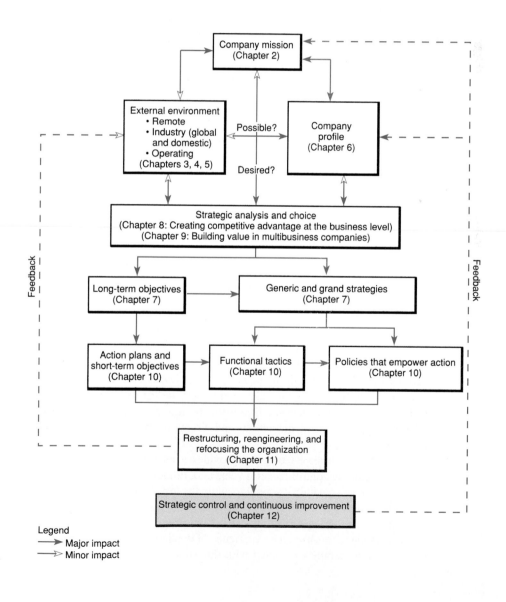

Company mission
(Chapter 2)

External environment
• Remote
• Industry (global and domestic)
• Operating
(Chapters 3, 4, 5)

Possible?

Desired?

Company profile
(Chapter 6)

Strategic analysis and choice
(Chapter 8: Creating competitive advantage at the business level)
(Chapter 9: Building value in multibusiness companies)

Long-term objectives
(Chapter 7)

Generic and grand strategies
(Chapter 7)

Action plans and short-term objectives
(Chapter 10)

Functional tactics
(Chapter 10)

Policies that empower action
(Chapter 10)

Restructuring, reengineering, and refocusing the organization
(Chapter 11)

Strategic control and continuous improvement
(Chapter 12)

Feedback

Feedback

Legend
⟶ Major impact
⟶ Minor impact

Strategies are forward looking, designed to be accomplished several years into the future, and based on management assumptions about numerous events that have not yet occurred. How should managers control a strategy? The traditional approach to control compares actual results against a standard. After work is done, the manager evaluates it and then uses that evaluation as input to control further work. Although this approach has its place, it is inappropriate as a means for controlling a strategy. The full execution of a strategy often takes five or more years, during which time many changes occur that have major ramifications for the strategy's ultimate success. Consequently, the traditional approaches to control must be replaced by an approach that recognizes the unique control needs of long-term strategies.

Strategic control is concerned with tracking a strategy as it is being implemented, detecting problems or changes in its underlying premises, and making necessary adjustments. In contrast to postaction control, strategic control is concerned with guiding action in behalf of the strategy as that action is taking place and when the end result is still several years off. Managers responsible for the success of a strategy typically are concerned with two sets of questions:

1. Are we moving in the proper direction? Are key things falling into place? Are our assumptions about major trends and changes correct? Are we doing the critical things that need to be done? Should we adjust or abort the strategy?
2. How are we performing? Are objectives and schedules being met? Are costs, revenues, and cash flows matching projections? Do we need to make operational changes?

The rapid, accelerating change of the global marketplace of the last 10 years has made *continuous improvement* another aspect of strategic control in many business organizations. Synonymous with the total quality movement, continuous improvement provides a way for organizations to provide strategic control that allows an organization to respond more proactively and timely to rapid developments in hundreds of areas that influence a business's success. This chapter discusses traditional strategic controls and then explains ways that the *continuous improvement quality imperative* can be a vehicle for strategic control.

ESTABLISHING STRATEGIC CONTROLS

The control of strategy can be characterized as a form of "steering control." Ordinarily, a good deal of time elapses between the initial implementation of a strategy and achievement of its intended results. During that time, investments are made and numerous projects and actions are undertaken to implement the strategy. Also, during that time, changes are taking place in both the environmental situation and the firm's internal situation. Strategic controls are necessary to steer the firm through these events. They must provide the basis for adapting the firm's strategic actions and directions in response to these developments and changes.

Prudential Insurance Company provides a useful example of the proactive, steering nature of strategic control. Several years ago, Prudential adopted a long-term market development strategy in which it sought to attain the top position in the life insurance industry by differentiating its level of service from those of its competitors. It decided to achieve a differential service advantage by establishing regional home offices. Exercising strategic control, its managers used the experience of the first regional offices to reproject the overall expenses and income associated with this strategy. The predicted expenses were so high

FIGURE 12–1
Four Types of Strategic Control

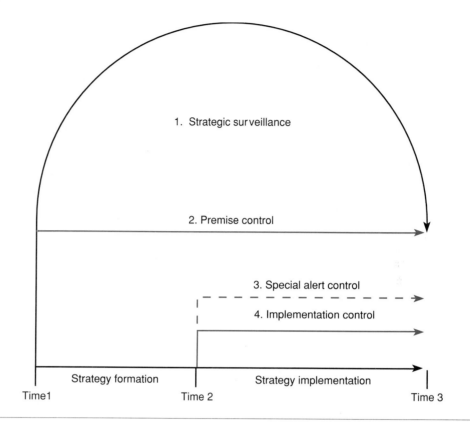

Source: Adapted from G. Schreyogg and H. Steinmann, "Strategic Control: A New Perspective," *Academy of Management Review* 12, no. 1 (1987), p. 96.

that the original schedule for establishing other regional offices had to be modified. And on the basis of other early feedback, the restructuring of the services performed at Prudential's corporate headquarters was sharply revised. Thus, the steering control (or strategic control) exercised by Prudential managers significantly altered the firm's strategy. In this case, the major objectives of the strategy remained in place; in other cases, strategic control has led to changes in the major strategic objectives.

The four basic types of strategic control are:

1. Premise control.
2. Implementation control.
3. Strategic surveillance.
4. Special alert control.

The nature of these four types is summarized in Figure 12–1.

Premise Control

Every strategy is based on certain planning premises—assumptions or predictions. *Premise control is designed to check systematically and continuously whether the premises on which the strategy is based are still valid.* If a vital premise is no longer valid, the strategy may have to be changed. The sooner an invalid premise can be recognized and rejected, the better are the chances that an acceptable shift in the strategy can be devised.

Which Premises Should Be Monitored?

Planning premises are primarily concerned with environmental and industry factors. These are described next.

Environmental Factors   Although a firm has little or no control over environmental factors, these factors exercise considerable influence over the success of its strategy, and strategies usually are based on key premises about them. Inflation, technology, interest rates, regulation, and demographic/social changes are examples of such factors.

EPA regulations and federal laws concerning the handling, use, and disposal of toxic chemicals have a major effect on the strategy of Velsicol Chemical Company, a market leader in pesticide chemicals sold to farmers and exterminators. So Velsicol's management makes and constantly updates premises about future regulatory actions.

Industry Factors   The performance of the firms in a given industry is affected by industry factors. These differ among industries, and a firm should be aware of the factors that influence success in its particular industry. Competitors, suppliers, product substitutes, and barriers to entry are a few of the industry factors about which strategic assumptions are made.

Rubbermaid has long been held up as a model of predictable growth, creative management, and rapid innovation in the plastic housewares and toy industry. Its premise going into the 21st century was that large retail chains would continue to prefer its products over competitors' because of this core competence. This premise included continued receptivity to regular price increases when necessitated by raw materials costs. Late 1995 found retailers, most notably Wal-Mart, balking at Rubbermaid's attempt to raise prices to offset the doubling of resin costs. Furthermore, traditionally overlooked competitors have begun to make inroads with computerized stocking services. Rubbermaid is moving aggressively to adjust its strategy because of the response of Wal-Mart and other key retailers.

Strategies are often based on numerous premises, some major and some minor, about environmental and industry variables. Tracking all of these premises is unnecessarily expensive and time consuming. Managers must select premises whose change (1) is likely and (2) would have a major impact on the firm and its strategy.

How Are Premise Controls Enacted?

A strategy's key premises should be identified and recorded during the planning process. Responsibility for monitoring those premises should be assigned to the persons or departments that are qualified sources of information. To illustrate, members of the sales force might be assigned to monitor the expected price policy of major competitors and the finance department might be assigned to monitor interest rate trends. The required amount of monitoring effort varies for different premises; to avoid information overload, emphasis should be placed on the monitoring of key premises. These premises should be updated (and new predictions should be made) on the basis of updated information. Finally, key areas within the firm, or key aspects of the strategy that would be significantly affected by changes in certain premises, should be preidentified so adjustments necessitated by revisions in those premises can be determined and initiated. For example, senior marketing executives should be alerted to changes in competitors' pricing policies so these executives can determine whether revised pricing, product repositioning, or other strategy adjustments are necessary. Global Strategy in Action 12–1 reports an interview with IBM CEO Lou Gerstner that discusses the premise control changes in IBM's strategy that IBM has made in response to the Internet.

Implementation Control

Strategy implementation takes place as series of steps, programs, investments, and moves that occur over an extended time. Special programs are undertaken. Functional areas initiate strategy-related activities. Key people are added or reassigned. Resources are mobilized. In other words, managers implement strategy by converting broad plans into the concrete, incremental actions and results of specific units and individuals.

Implementation control is the type of strategic control that must be exercised as those events unfold. *Implementation control is designed to assess whether the overall strategy should be changed in light of the results associated with the incremental actions that implement the overall strategy.* Prudential's updating of cost and revenue projections based on early experiences with regional home offices is an example of implementation control. The two basic types of implementation control are (1) monitoring strategic thrusts and (2) milestone reviews.

Monitoring Strategic Thrusts

As a means of implementing broad strategies, narrow strategic projects often are undertaken—projects that represent part of what needs to be done if the overall strategy is to be accomplished. These strategic thrusts provide managers with information that helps them determine whether the overall strategy is progressing as planned or needs to be adjusted.

Although the utility of strategic thrusts seems readily apparent, it is not always easy to use them for control purposes. It may be difficult to interpret early experience or to evaluate the overall strategy in light of such experience. One approach is to agree early in the planning process on which thrusts or which phases of thrusts are critical factors in the success of the strategy. Managers responsible for these implementation controls will single them out from other activities and observe them frequently. Another approach is to use stop/go assessments that are linked to a series of meaningful thresholds (time, costs, research and development, success, and so forth) associated with particular thrusts. A program of regional development via company-owned inns in the Rocky Mountain area was a monitoring thrust that Days Inn used to test its strategy of becoming a nationwide motel chain. Problems in meeting time targets and unexpectedly large capital needs led Days Inn's executives to abandon the overall strategy and eventually sell the firm.

Milestone Reviews

Managers often attempt to identify significant milestones that will be reached during strategy implementation. These milestones may be critical events, major resource allocations, or simply the passage of a certain amount of time. The milestone reviews that then take place usually involve a full-scale reassessment of the strategy and of the advisability of continuing or refocusing the firm's direction.

A useful example of implementation control based on milestone review is offered by Boeing's product development strategy of entering the supersonic transport (SST) airplane market. Boeing had invested millions of dollars and years of scarce engineering talent during the first phase of its SST venture, and competition from the British/French

WHOOSH . . . THE INTERNET, WORLDWIDE WEB, AND IBM: PREMISE CONTROL AT IBM

IBM was supposed to be dying. And it may still die. But it is endeavoring to apply premise control to build its future in "network-centric" directions. Let's see what this involves by looking at IBM's old premise and the effects of the Internet.

1. *Old premise.* Software programs are written for specific types of hardware (IBM or Apple). Programs don't go from one hardware configuration to the other. And even if written for the same operating system, programs don't adapt from one to the other. Even same-supplier programs don't always work together. Solution: bloatware, "suites," with a bunch of applications thrown together to interface better. But this requires greater speed and capacity on your computer so a new chip and new computer is needed. And so begins an "unholy" alliance between software and hardware makers. Not always best for the computer consumer but few alternatives exist.

2. *Enter the Internet.* Since the Web and Mosaic and Netscape programs for viewing pages emerged, the Web has turned into a huge virtual disk drive. Suddenly, barriers that kept information from flowing between brands of computers and software are gone. Next, using the Web not only to make the same information available to all wired machines but to let them share the same programs. If it works, the software industry is destroyed and reconstructed overnite. That's exactly what's beginning to happen—at a pace nobody in the computer industry anticipated.

IBM's CEO Lou Gerstner, speaking with *Business Week* editor Ira Sager in a conference room where Gerstner keeps a couple of computers to check on everything from kids' software to Web browsers, shared IBM's premise control reactions, as reported in the following *Business Week* article:

> *Louis V. Gerstner Jr. caused a stir two summers ago when he declared that the last thing IBM needed was to proclaim a grand vision. Gerstner proceeded to focus on cost-cutting and other management issues and proved the vision-hungry pundits wrong. But having studied IBM, the computer industry, and technology trends, the former McKinsey & Co. consultant has come up with, if not a vision, at least a plan for IBM. Relaxing in a conference room where he keeps a couple of computers to check out everything from kids' software to Web browsers, Gerstner shared his ideas with Information Processing Editor Ira Sager.*
>
> **Q:** *You speak of "network-centric" computing. What is it?*
>
> **A:** The first wave of computing, 30 years ago, was driven by the technologies of host-based processors [mainframes] and storage devices. Twenty years later, we moved into a second wave, which was driven by microprocessors and simplified operating systems. The third wave of computing is being driven by very powerful networked technologies that provide very inexpensive and very wide [communications] bandwidth.
>
> **Q:** *What will happen to existing computers?*
>
> **A:** People have argued that the host-based [mainframe] model is dead. Well, it isn't dead. People are buying more of those units than they ever have. And no one should say that the stand-

Source: "Lou Gerstner on Catching the Third Wave," *Business Week*, October 30, 1995, p. 152.

Concorde effort was intense. Since the next phase represented a billion-dollar decision, Boeing's management established the initiation of the phase as a milestone. The milestone reviews greatly increased the estimates of production costs; predicted relatively few passengers and rising fuel costs, thus raising the estimated operating costs; and noted that the Concorde, unlike Boeing, had the benefit of massive government subsidies. These factors led Boeing's management to scrap its SST strategy in spite of high

alone personal computer is going to go away. But there is no question that the PC-based model is now not the future. The future is a network-centric model. The focus moves to a network that draws out the best of both worlds. That model drives the strategy of this company. When people talk about IBM, it's interesting to hear them say: "Well, I wonder if they'll get their new businesses to grow fast enough while their old businesses die." What they don't understand is, we are reconceptualizing our old businesses. We're bringing them into this new model.

Q: *Will IBM put applications on a network and charge per-transaction or volume-based fees?*

A: Absolutely. We call this business process outsourcing. For example, this Internet or networked world will put extreme pressure on traditional providers of financial services. We have no interest in going into the banking business. But we do have an interest in working with a series of banks in which we will provide networking capability through the IBM Global Network and networking applications that we will build. We'll take part of the transaction revenue. It could very well be on a per-click, per-communication unit. It is a strategy that brings our customers into this world of network services. Yes, we will be compensated in nontraditional ways.

Q: *That provides a recurring source of revenue—as opposed to one-time product sales. Is this where you see network computing leading IBM?*

A: That's the model IBM created with its mainframe software—monthly license revenue. We understand the concept of software paid for on a usage basis as opposed to a shrink-wrap, buy-it-once basis. Now, all of this is going to take time. It's going to evolve differently in different industries, in different companies, depending on their strategies. Large customers are going to take a very long time before they're going to rent mission-critical applications. People will not convert their own legacy systems to this. What will go on a rental model is the new stuff, like electronic commerce.

Q: *In a wired world, must IBM remain a big maker of hardware and software?*

A: People are going to need a lot of very powerful servers. They're going to need a lot of transaction software. They're going to need a lot of database software. They're going to need a lot of communications software. You don't necessarily have to provide all of these things, but we do. And as long as we're successful in each of them, we're going to continue to provide them. [If] we're not successful, we'll get out of the business.

Q: *How does Prodigy fit into IBM's network-computing plans?*

A: We are taking a hard look at our Prodigy strategy right now, along with [Prodigy partner] Sears. Short term, we're making a lot of changes. We brought in new management. They've done some new things with their system. Certainly their merchandising and marketing has gotten better. But the long-term strategy for IBM and Prodigy is not clear. We will sort that out in a relatively short time. The fundamental issue is: In the world of the Internet, is there a place for a packager of services? Does the customer want to go surf the Net and go to every one of 50,000 Web sites? Or will people pay a reasonable amount for somebody to go out and preselect and package what they want? My guess is they will both coexist.

---

sunk costs, pride, and patriotism. Only an objective, full-scale strategy reassessment could have led to such a decision.

In this example, a milestone review occurred at a major resource allocation decision point. Milestone reviews may also occur concurrently when a major step in a strategy's implementation is being taken or when a key uncertainty is resolved. Managers even may set an arbitrary period, say two years, as a milestone review point. Whatever the basis for

EXAMPLES OF STRATEGIC CONTROL

IMPLEMENTATION CONTROL AT DAYS INN

When Days Inn pioneered the budget segment of the lodging industry, its strategy placed primary emphasis on company-owned facilities and it insisted on maintaining a roughly 3-to-1 company-owned/franchise ratio. This ratio ensured the parent company's total control over standards, rates, and so forth.

As other firms moved into the budget segment, Days Inn saw the need to expand rapidly throughout the United States and, therefore, reversed its conservative franchise posture. This reversal would rapidly accelerate its ability to open new locations. Longtime executives, concerned about potential loss of control over local standards, instituted *implementation controls* requiring both franchise evaluation and annual milestone reviews. Two years into the program, Days Inn executives were convinced that a high franchise-to-company ratio was manageable, and so they accelerated the growth of franchising by doubling the franchise sales department.

STRATEGIC SURVEILLANCE AT CITICORP

Citicorp has been pursuing an aggressive product development strategy intended to achieve an annual earnings growth of 15 percent while it becomes an institution capable of supplying clients with any kind of financial service anywhere in the world. A major obstacle to the achievement of this earnings growth is Citicorp's exposure to default because of its extensive earlier loans to troubled Third World countries. Citicorp is sensitive to the wide variety of predictions about impending Third World defaults.

Source: Adapted from conversations with selected Days Inn executives; "Is the Worst over for Citi?" *Forbes,* May 11, 1992; and "How Companies Prepare for the Worst," *Business Week,* December 23 1985, p. 74.

selecting that point, the critical purpose of a milestone review is to thoroughly scrutinize the firm's strategy so as to control the strategy's future.

Strategic Surveillance

By their nature, premise control and implementation control are focused controls; strategic surveillance, however, is unfocused. *Strategic surveillance is designed to monitor a broad range of events inside and outside the firm that are likely to affect the course of its strategy.*[1] The basic idea behind strategic surveillance is that important yet unanticipated information may be uncovered by a general monitoring of multiple information sources.

Strategic surveillance must be kept as unfocused as possible. It should be a loose "environmental scanning" activity. Trade magazines, *The Wall Street Journal,* trade conferences, conversations, and intended and unintended observations are all subjects of strategic surveillance. Despite its looseness, strategic surveillance provides an ongoing, broad-based vigilance in all daily operations that may uncover information relevant to the firm's strategy. Citicorp benefited significantly from a Peruvian manager's strategic surveillance of political speeches by Peru's former president, as discussed in Strategy in Action 12–1.

[1] G. Schreyogg and H. Steinmann, "Strategic Control: A New Perspective," *Academy of Management Review* 12, no. 1 (1987), p. 101.

continued

Citicorp's long-range plan assumes an annual 10 percent default on its Third World loans over any five-year period. Yet it maintains active *strategic surveillance control* by having each of its international branches monitor daily announcements from key governments and from inside contacts for signs of changes in a host country's financial environment. When that surveillance detects a potential problem, management attempts to adjust Citicorp's posture. For example, when Peru's former president, Alan Garcia, stated that his country would not pay interest on its debt as scheduled, Citicorp raised its annual default charge to 20 percent of its $100 million Peruvian exposure.

SPECIAL ALERT CONTROL AT UNITED AIRLINES

The sudden impact of an airline crash can be devastating to a major airline. United Airlines has made elaborate preparations to deal with this contingency. Its executive vice president, James M. Guyette, heads a crisis team that is permanently prepared to respond. Members of the team carry beepers and are always on call. If United's Chicago headquarters receives word that a plane has crashed, for example, they can be in a "war room" within an hour to direct the response. Beds are set up nearby so team members can catch a few winks; while they sleep, alternates take their places.

Members of the team have been carefully screened through simulated crisis drills. "The point is to weed out those who don't hold up well under stress," says Guyette. Although the team was established to handle flight disasters, it has since assumed an expanded role. The crisis team was activated when American Airlines launched a fare war. And according to Guyette, "We're brainstorming about how we would be affected by everything from a competitor who had a serious problem to a crisis involving a hijacking or taking a United employee hostage."

Special Alert Control

Another type of strategic control, really a subset of the other three, is special alert control. *A special alert control is the thorough, and often rapid, reconsideration of the firm's strategy because of a sudden, unexpected event.* A political coup in the Middle East, an outside firm's sudden acquisition of a leading competitor, an unexpected product difficulty, such as the poisoned Tylenol capsules—events of these kinds can drastically alter the firm's strategy.

Such an event should trigger an immediate and intense reassessment of the firm's strategy and its current strategic situation. In many firms, crisis teams handle the firm's initial response to unforeseen events that may have an immediate effect on its strategy. Increasingly, firms have developed contingency plans along with crisis teams to respond to circumstances such as those illustrated in Strategy in Action 12–1.

Figure 12–2 summarizes the major characteristics of the four types of strategic control. Unlike operational controls, which are concerned with the control of action, strategic controls are designed to continuously and proactively question the basic direction and appropriateness of a strategy. Each type of strategic control shares a common purpose: to assess whether the strategic direction should be altered in light of unfolding events. Many of us have heard the axiom, "The only thing that is constant is change itself." Organizations face the constancy of change from endless sources within and without the organization, all occurring at an ever accelerating pace. There is very little that organizations can do to directly control the many sources of change. Yet, with performance and long-term

FIGURE 12–2
Characteristics of the Four Types of Strategic Control

Basic Characteristics	Types of Strategic Control			
	Premise Control	Implementation Control	Strategic Surveillance	Special Alert Control
Objects of control	Planning premises and projections	Key strategic thrusts and milestones	Potential threats and opportunities related to the strategy	Occurrence of recognizable but unlikely events
Degree of focusing	High	High	Low	High
Data acquisition:				
Formalization	Medium	High	Low	High
Centralization	Low	Medium	Low	High
Use with:				
Environmental factors	Yes	Seldom	Yes	Yes
Industry factors	Yes	Seldom	Yes	Yes
Strategy-specific factors	No	Yes	Seldom	Yes
Company-specific factors	No	Yes	Seldom	Seldom

Source: Adapted from G. Schreyogg and H. Steinmann, "Strategic Control: A New Perspective," *Academy of Management Review* 12, no. 1 (1987), pp. 91–103.

survival at stake, better organizations adopt and regularly refine strategic controls as a way to deal with pervasive change.

IBM's CEO Lou Gerstner's explanation of the rationale behind some of the fundamental changes at IBM toward the end of the 20th century illustrates the pervasive, dramatic character of change and the essence of strategic control as a means to deal with it:

> One of the great things about this [computer] industry is that every decade or so, you get a chance to redefine the playing field. We're in that phase of redefinition right now, and winners or losers are going to emerge from it . . . Network centric computing . . . Providing time on computers rather than selling the hardware . . . The Internet . . . There's no question that the speed with which the Internet has emerged has caught all industries related to this technology by surprise . . . But there is no question that the PC-based model is now not the future.

Both operational and strategic controls are needed to guide the strategic management process. The next section examines the key types of operational control systems that are used to aid the strategic management process.

OPERATIONAL CONTROL SYSTEMS

Operational control systems guide, monitor, and evaluate progress in meeting short-term objectives. While strategic controls attempt to steer the company over an extended period (usually five years of more), operational controls provide postaction evaluation and control over short periods—usually from one month to one year. To be effective, operational control systems must take four steps common to all postaction controls:

1. Set standards of performance.
2. Measure actual performance.
3. Identify deviations from standards set.
4. Initiate corrective action.

Three types of operational control system are *budgets, schedules,* and *key success factors.* The nature and use of these three types of systems are described in the next sections.

Budgets

The budgetary process was the forerunner of strategic planning. A budget is a resource allocation plan that helps managers coordinate operations and facilitates managerial control of performance. Budgets themselves do not control anything. They simply set standards against which action can be measured. They also provide a basis for negotiating short-term resource requirements to implement strategy at the operating level. Most firms employ at least three budgets as a part of their planning and control activities. These types of budgets are the following:

1. *Profit and loss (P&L) budgets* are perhaps the most common. These budgets serve as the basis to monitor sales on a monthly or more frequent basis, as well as to monitor expense categories on a comparable time frame against what has actually occurred. Sales and expense numbers often are subdivided by department, location, product lines, and other relevant subunits to more closely project and monitor organizational activities.

2. *Capital budgets* usually are developed to show the timing of specific expenditures for plant, equipment, machinery, inventories, and other capital items needed during the budget period.

3. *Cash flow budgets* forecast receipt and disbursement of cash during the budget period. They tie together P&L expectations, capital expenditures, collection of receivables, expense payments, and borrowing needs to show just where the life blood of any business—cash—will come from and go to each month.

The budgeting system serves as an important and early indicator about the effectiveness of a firm's strategy by serving as a frame of reference against which to examine month-to-month results in the execution of that strategy.

Scheduling

Timing is often a key factor in the success of a strategy. Scheduling considerations in allocating time-constrained resources and sequencing interdependent activities often determine the success of strategy implementation. Scheduling offers a mechanism with which to plan for, monitor, and control these dependencies.[2] For example, a firm committed to a vertical integration strategy must carefully absorb expended operations into its existing core. Such absorption, given either forward or backward integration, will require numerous changes in the operational practices of the firm's organizational units. A good illustration is Coors Brewery's decision to integrate backward by producing its own beer cans. A comprehensive two-year schedule of actions and targets for incorporating the manufacture of beer cans and bottles into the product chain contributed to the success of this strategy. Purchasing, production scheduling, machinery, and production systems were but a few of the critical operating areas that Coors's scheduling efforts were meant to accommodate and coordinate.

---

[2] A useful primer on scheduling considerations in strategic project planning is provided by Steven Wheelwright and Kim Clark in "Creating Project Plans to Focus Project Development," *Harvard Business Review* 70, no. 2 (1992), pp. 70–82; and Steven Wheelwright and Kim Clark, *Revolutionizing Product Development: Quantum Leaps in Speed, Efficiency, and Quality* (New York: The Free Press, 1992).

FIGURE 12–3
Key Success Factors at Lotus Corporation

Key Success Factor	Measurable Performance Indicator
1. Product quality	a. Performance data versus specification. b. Percentage of product returns. c. Number of customer complaints.
2. Customer service	a. Delivery cycle in days. b. Percentage of orders shipped complete. c. Field service delays.
3. Employee morale	a. Trends in employee attitude survey. b. Absenteeism versus plan. c. Employee turnover trends.
4. Competition	a. Number of firms competing directly. b. Number of new products introduced. c. Percentage of bids awarded versus the standard.

Key Success Factors

Another useful way to effect operational control is to focus on "key success factors." These factors identify the performance areas that are of greatest importance in implementing the company's strategies and, therefore, must receive continuous management attention. Each key success factor must have measurable performance indicators. Lotus Corporation management, for example, having identified product quality, customer service, employee morale, and competition as the key determinants of success in the firm's strategy of rapidly expanding its software offerings, then specified three indicators to monitor and control each of these key success factors, as shown in Figure 12–3.

Key success factors succinctly communicate the critical elements for which operational managers are responsible. These factors require the successful performance of several key individuals and, thus, can be a foundation for teamwork among managers in meeting the firm's strategic objectives.

Budgeting, scheduling, and monitoring key success factors are important means of controlling strategy implementation at the operational level. Common to all of these operational control systems is the need to establish measurable standards and to monitor performance against those standards. The next section examines how to accomplish this.

USING OPERATIONAL CONTROL SYSTEMS: MONITORING PERFORMANCE AND EVALUATING DEVIATIONS

Operational control systems require performance standards. *Control* is the process of obtaining timely information on deviations from these standards, determining the causes of the deviations, and taking corrective action.

Figure 12–4 illustrates a simplified report that links the current status of key performance indicators to a firm's strategy. These indicators represent progress after two years of a five-year strategy intended to differentiate the firm as a customer-service-oriented provider of high-quality products. Management's concern is to compare *progress to date* with *expected progress*. The *current deviation* is of particular interest, because it provides a basis for examining *suggested actions* (usually suggested by subordinate managers) and for finalizing decisions on changes or adjustments in the firm's operations.

FIGURE 12-4
Monitoring and Evaluating Performance Deviations

Key Success Factors	Objective, Assumption, or Budget	Forecast Performance at This Time	Current Performance	Current Deviation	Analysis
Cost control: Ratio of indirect overhead costs to direct field and labor costs	10%	15%	12%	+3 (ahead)	Are we moving too fast, or is there more unnecessary overhead than was originally thought?
Gross profit	39%	40%	40%	0%	
Customer service: Installation cycle in days	2.5 days	3.2 days	2.7 days	+0.5 (ahead)	Can this progress be maintained?
Ratio of service to sales personnel	3.2	2.7	2.1	−0.6 (behind)	Why are we behind here? How can we maintain the installation-cycle progress?
Product quality: Percentage of products returned	1.0%	2.0%	2.1%	−0.1% (behind)	Why are we behind here? What are the ramifications for other operations?
Product performance versus specification	100%	92%	80%	−12% (behind)	
Marketing: Monthly sales per employee	$12,500	$11,500	$12,100	+$600 (ahead)	Good progress. Is it creating any problems to support?
Expansion of product line	6	3	5	+2 products (ahead)	Are the products ready? Are the perfect standards met?
Employee morale in service area: Absenteeism rate	2.5%	3.0%	3.0%	(on target)	
Turnover rate	5%	10%	15%	−8% (behind)	Looks like a problem! Why are we so far behind?
Competition: New product introductions (average number)	6	3	6	−3 (behind)	Did we underestimate timing? What are the implications for our basic assumptions?

From Figure 12–4, it appears that the firm is maintaining control of its cost structure. Indeed, it is ahead of schedule on reducing overhead. The firm is well ahead of its delivery cycle target, while slightly below its target service-to-sales personnel ratio. Its product returns look OK, although product performance versus specification is below standard. Sales per employee and expansion of the product line are ahead of schedule. The absenteeism rate in the service area is on target, but the turnover rate is higher than that targeted. Competitors appear to be introducing products more rapidly than expected.

After deviations and their causes have been identified, the implications of the deviations for the ultimate success of the strategy must be considered. For example, the rapid product-line expansion indicated in Figure 12–4 may have been a response to the increased rate of competitors' product expansion. At the same time, product performance is still low; and, while the installation cycle is slightly above standard (improving customer service), the ratio of service to sales personnel is below the targeted ratio. Contributing to this substandard ratio (and perhaps reflecting a lack of organizational commitment to customer service) is the exceptionally high turnover in customer service personnel. The rapid reduction in indirect overhead costs might mean that administration integration of customer service and product development requirements has been cut back too quickly.

This information presents operations managers with several options. They may attribute the deviations primarily to internal discrepancies. In that case, they can scale priorities up or down. For example, they might place more emphasis on retaining customer service personnel and less emphasis on overhead reduction and new product development. On the other hand, they might decide to continue as planned in the face of increasing competition and to accept or gradually improve the customer service situation. Another possibility is reformulating the strategy or a component of the strategy in the face of rapidly increasing competition. For example, the firm might decide to emphasize more standardized or lower-priced products to overcome customer service problems and take advantage of an apparently ambitious sales force.

This is but one of many possible interpretations of Figure 12–4. The important point here is the critical need to monitor progress against standards and to give serious in-depth attention to both the causes of observed deviations and the most appropriate responses to them. After the deviations have been evaluated, slight adjustments may be made to keep progress, expenditure, or other factors in line with the strategy's programmed needs. In the unusual event of extreme deviations—generally because of unforeseen changes—management is alerted to the possible need for revising the budget, reconsidering certain functional plans related to budgeted expenditures, or examining the units concerned and the effectiveness of their managers.

An acceptable level of deviation should be allowed; otherwise, the control process will become an administrative overload. Standards should not be regarded as absolute, because the estimates used to formulate them typically are based on historical data, which, by definition, are after the fact. Absolute standards (keep equipment busy 100 percent of the time or meet 100 percent of quota) make no provision for variability. Standards are also often derived from averages, which, by definition, ignore variability. These difficulties suggest the need to define acceptable *ranges* of deviation in budgetary figures or key indicators of strategic success. This approach helps in avoiding administrative difficulties, in recognizing measurement variability, in delegating more realistic authority for short-term decisions to operating managers, and in improving motivation.

Some firms use trigger points for the clarification of standards, particularly in monitoring key success factors. A *trigger point* is a level of deviation of a key indicator or figure (such as a competitor's actions or a critical cost category) that management identifies in the planning process as representing either a major threat or an unusual opportunity. When that point is reached, management immediately is altered (triggered) to consider necessary adjustments in the firm's strategy. Some firms take this idea a step forward and develop one or more *contingency plans* that are to be implemented when predetermined trigger points are reached. These contingency plans redirect priorities and actions so rapidly that valuable reaction time is not wasted on administrative assessment of the extreme deviation.

Correcting deviations in performance brings the entire management task into focus. Managers can correct such deviations by changing measures or plans. They also can eliminate poor performance by changing how things are done, by hiring or retraining workers, by changing job assignments, and so on. Correcting deviations, therefore, can involve all of the functions, tasks, and responsibilities of operations managers. Managers in other cultures, most notably Japan, have for some time achieved operational control by seeking their unit's continuous improvement. Companies worldwide have adapted this point of view that operational control is best achieved through a pervasive commitment to quality, often called *total quality management* (TQM), which is seen as essential to strategic success into the 21st century.

THE QUALITY IMPERATIVE: CONTINUOUS IMPROVEMENT TO BUILD CUSTOMER VALUE

The initials TQM have become the most popular abbreviation in business management literature since MBO (management by objectives).[3] TQM Stands for *total quality management,* an umbrella term for the quality programs that have been implemented in many businesses worldwide in the last two decades. TQM was first implemented in several large U.S. manufacturers in the face of the overwhelming success of Japanese and German competitors. Japanese manufacturers embraced the quality messages of Americans W. Edward Deming and J. M. Juran following World War II, and by the 1970s Japanese products had acquired unquestioned reputations for superior high quality.

Growing numbers of U.S. manufacturers have attempted to change this imbalance with their own quality programs, and the practice has spread to large retail and service companies as well. Increasingly, smaller companies that supply big TQM companies have adopted quality programs, often because big companies have required small suppliers to adopt quality programs of their own. Strategy in Action 12–2 describes the quality program in one such company, Dallas-based Marlow Industries, a recent winner of the Malcolm Baldrige National Quality Award.

TQM is viewed as virtually a new organizational culture and way of thinking. It is built around an intense focus on customer satisfaction; on accurate measurement of every critical variable in a business's operation; on continuous improvement of products, services, and processes; and on work relationships based on trust and teamwork. One useful explanation of the quality imperative suggests 10 essential elements of implementing total quality management, as follows:[4]

1. **Define *quality* and *customer value.*** Rather than be left to individual interpretation, company personnel should have a clear definition of what *quality* means in the job, department, and throughout the company. It should be developed from your customer's perspective and communicated as a written policy.

Thinking in terms of customer value broadens the definition of *quality* to include efficiency and responsiveness. Said another way, quality to your customer often means that the product performs well; that it is priced competitively (efficiency); and that you provide it quickly and adapt it when needed (responsiveness). Customer value is found in the combination of all three—quality, price, and speed.

2. **Develop a customer orientation.** Customer value is what the customer says it is. Don't rely on secondary information—talk to your customers directly. Also recognize your "internal" customers. Usually less than 20 percent of company employees come into contact with external customers, while the other 80 percent serve internal customers—other units with real performance expectations.

The value chain provides an important way to think about customer orientation, particularly to recognize *internal* as well as external (ultimate) customers. Operating personnel

---

[3] This section draws on total quality management ideas found in the following: G. Stalk, P. Evans, and L. E. Shulman, "Competing on Capabilities: The New Rules of Corporate Strategy," *Harvard Business Review,* March–April 1992, pp. 57–69; M. Barrier, "Small Firms Put Quality First," *Nation's Business,* May 1992, pp. 22–31; Ernst & Young, *Total Quality,* SCORE Retrieval File no. A49003, 1991; and Mary Walton, *The Deming Management Method* (New York: Perigee Books, 1986).

[4] Ideas about these 10 elements are based in part on excellent work by the firm Ernst and Young, in *Total Quality,* SCORE Retrieval File no. A49003, 1991.

STRATEGY IN ACTION 12–2

DO OR DIE: MARLOW INDUSTRIES ADOPTS TOTAL QUALITY MANAGEMENT

Congress created the Baldrige Award in 1987 to recognize U.S. firms with outstanding records of quality improvement and quality management. Marlow Industries, the Dallas-based firm that was the 1992 small-business winner of the Malcolm Baldrige National Quality Award, is one of those companies that adopted TQM under pressure from its customers.

There's a simple reason for such customer pressure: When an appliance maker is trying to produce defect-free products, it cannot tolerate defects in the parts provided by its small suppliers.

Marlow, with 160 employees, is the smallest business yet to win the award. Only three small firms have ever won, out of 125 that have applied. Marlow makes thermoelectric coolers—small solid-state devices used to spot cooling in critical applications for telecommunications, aerospace, and the military. Most of Marlow's products are custom made for customers who impose their own quality requirements on their suppliers. Marlow had to come up with comprehensive quality systems that would meet all of those requirements.

That might sound like an intimidating task for so small a company, but Marlow successfully introduced profound changes in the way it operates. For example, about two years ago Marlow broke up its quality-assurance department, assigning product inspectors to "minifactories"—self-contained units, made up of approximately 15 people each. Today, according to Chris Witzke, Marlow's COO, the inspectors "look after the quality systems, set training standards, do audits—but they're not in the product-inspection business."

In other words, Marlow switched from product inspection to process control—from catching and correcting defects at the end of the process to monitoring the process itself, so defects do not occur. It was not easy to adopt TQM at Marlow. Raymond Marlow, founder and president of Marlow, said "You've got to have patience, because it takes a couple of years" before employees can work together smoothly in problem-solving teams. While the transition is taking place, Marlow says, top management must display "consistency of purpose. You have to keep the quality thing moving."

Measurement was critical at Marlow. "If you measure something," said Chris Witzke, "it improves." Simply posting measurements—putting up a chart showing how well departments

Source: Excerpted from "Small Firms Put Quality First," *Nation's Business,* May 1992, pp. 22–31.

are *internal* customers of the accounting department for useful information and also the purchasing department for quality, timely supplies. When they are "served" with quality, efficiency, and responsiveness, value is added to their efforts, and is passed on to their internal customers and, eventually, external (ultimate) customers.

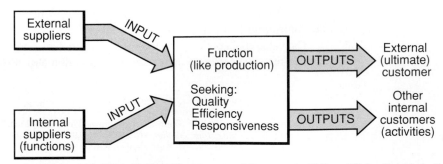

Source: G. G. Dess and A. Miller, *Strategic Management,* p. 143. © 1993 by McGraw-Hill, Inc. Reprinted with the permission of The McGraw-Hill Companies.

continued

are doing at turning in their time cards on schedule, for instance—can sometimes solve a problem. But deciding what to measure is not always easy. Marlow devoted a full year to developing statistical process controls. "We really dedicated ourselves to understanding our processes and finding the key variables," Witzke said. "All this stuff used to be black art. Now it's science." Marlow at one time measured 52 variables in a plating process—but had constant problems anyway. Now it measures only 14 variables (including seven new ones), and the problems have disappeared. Measurements sometimes can reveal things about a business that no one would have suspected if the measurements hadn't been made. When Marlow began subjecting employee turnover to Pareto analysis, it discovered that a 90-day probationary period was contributing to turnover by encouraging supervisors to make marginal hires. Once the supervisors understood the cost of that turnover, they tightened their hiring practices. At Marlow, decisions on what should be measured usually have followed surveys of "internal customers" so what was important could be measured.

As any TQM company would be expected to do, Marlow measures its suppliers' performances—and it also tells them how they're doing. "It's amazing how quick a reaction you can get just from sending out a letter saying, 'Hey, your supplier index has dropped to 1.1,' " said Marlow's Witzke. One of Marlow's minifactories, responding to just such a review, came up with a "service guarantee" for its internal customers. Posted prominently in a hall at the plant, the guarantee promises replacement of any unsatisfactory part within 24 hours. After that guarantee went up, Witzke said, "it wasn't long before they started popping up in other places. That's the ideal situation—where management doesn't have to spend all of its time making things happen."

Marlow does a lot of in-house training, in both work skills and quality techniques—the average employee spent almost 50 hours in training last year—and the training helps managers as well as employees. Said Witzke: "By the time you've taught a course three or four times, you begin to believe it."

When a quality program is working, Witzke says—when customers are happy, products are defect-free, deliveries are on time—"all of a sudden you've got 30 percent more staff than you thought you had," because employees are spending less time correcting problems.

3. **Focus on the company's business processes.** Break down every minute step in the process of providing the company's product or service and look at ways to improve it, rather than focusing simply on the finished product or service. Each process contributes value in some way, which can be improved or adapted to help other processes (internal customers) improve. Examples of ways customer value is enhanced across business processes in several functions are:

	Quality	Efficiency	Responsiveness
Marketing	Provides accurate assessment of customer's product preferences to R&D	Targets advertising campaign at customers, using cost-effective medium	Quickly uncovers and reacts to changing market trends
Operations	Consistently produces goods matching engineering design	Minimizes scrap and rework through high-production yield	Quickly adapts to latest demands with production flexibility
Research and development	Designs products that combine customer demand and production capabilities	Uses computers to test feasibility of idea before going to more expensive full-scale prototype	Carries out parallel product/process designs to speed up overall innovation

(*continued*)

	Quality	Efficiency	Responsiveness
Accounting	Provides the information that managers in other functions need to make decisions	Simplifies and computerizes to decrease the cost of gathering information	Provides information in "real time" (as the events described are still happening)
Purchasing	Selects vendors for their ability to join in an effective "partnership"	Given the required vendor quality, negotiates prices to provide good value	Schedules inbound deliveries efficiently, avoiding both extensive inventories and stock-outs
Personnel	Trains work force to perform required tasks	Minimizes employee turnover reducing hiring and training expenses	In response to strong growth in sales, finds large numbers of employees and quickly teaches needed skills

Source: G. G. Dess and A. Miller, Strategic Management, p. 143 ©1993 by McGraw-Hill, Inc. Reproduced with the permission of The McGraw-Hill Companies.

4. **Develop customer and supplier partnerships.** Organizations have a destructive tendency to view suppliers and even customers adversarily. It is better to understand the horizontal flow of a business—outside suppliers to internal suppliers/customers (a company's various departments) to external customers. This view suggests suppliers are partners in meeting customer needs, and customers are partners by providing input so the company and suppliers can meet and exceed those expectations.

Ford Motor Company's Dearborn, Michigan, plant is linked electronically with supplier Allied Signal's Kansas City, Missouri, plant. A Ford computer recently sent the design for a car's connecting rod to an Allied Signal factory computer, which transformed the design into instructions that it fed to a machine tool on the shop floor. The result: quality, efficiency, and responsiveness.

5. **Take a preventive approach.** Many organizations reward "fire fighters," not "fire preventers," and identify errors after the work is done. Management, instead, should be rewarded for being prevention oriented and seeking to eliminate nonvalue-added work.

Strategy in Action 12–2 describes how Marlow Industries discovered that a traditional 90-day probationary period for new hires was increasing employee turnover, encouraging marginal hires, and lowering all three sources of customer value.

6. **Adopt an error-free attitude.** Instill an attitude that "good enough" is not good enough anymore. "Error free" should become each individual's performance standard, with managers taking every opportunity to demonstrate and communicate the importance of this imperative.

Strategy in Action 12–2 describes how Marlow Industries reoriented its complete organization from a "get the job done no matter what" attitude to a "no job is done until it's done right" way of thinking.

7. **Get the facts first.** Continuous improvement–oriented companies make decisions based on facts, not on opinions. Accurate measurement, often using readily available statistical techniques, of every critical variable in a business's operation—and using those measurements to trace problems to their roots and eliminate their causes—is a better way.

8. **Encourage every manager and employee to participate.** Employee participation, empowerment, participative decision making, and extensive training in quality techniques, in statistical techniques, and in measurement tools are the ingredients continuous improvement companies employ to support and instill a commitment to customer value.

9. **Create an atmosphere of total involvement.** Quality management cannot be the job of a few managers or of one department. Maximum customer value cannot be achieved unless all areas of the organization apply quality concepts simultaneously.

10. **Strive for continuous improvement.** Stephen Yearout, director of Ernst & Young's Quality Management Center, recently observed that, "In the '80s, meeting your customers' expectations would distinguish you from your competitors. The '90s will require you to anticipate customer expectations and deliver quality service faster than the competition." Quality, efficiency, and responsiveness are not one-time programs of competitive response, for they create a new standard to measure up to. Organizations quickly find that continually improving quality, efficiency, and responsiveness in their processes, products, and services is not just good business; it's a necessity for long-term survival.

Continuous improvement and strategic control are two sides of the same "coin"—attention to factors that, in themselves, or because of change impacting them, influence the long-term success and survival of an organization. So it is not surprising, in the face of increasing global competition, that continuous improvement has evolved as a prominent factor that strategic-thinking managers are instilling in the way their organizations do business in the 21st century.

SUMMARY

Three fundamental perspectives—strategic control, operational control, and total quality/continuous improvement—provide the basis for designing strategy control systems. Strategic controls are intended to steer the company toward its long-term strategic goals. Premise controls, implementation controls, strategic surveillance, and special alert controls are types of strategic control. All four types are designed to meet top management's needs to track the strategy as it is being implemented, to detect underlying problems, and to make necessary adjustments. These strategic controls are linked to the environmental assumptions and the key operating requirements necessary for successful strategy implementation. Ever-present forces of change fuel the need for and focus of strategic control.

Operational control systems identify the performance standards associated with allocation and use of the firm's financial, physical, and human resources in pursuit of its strategy. Budgets, schedules, and key success factors are the primary means of operational control.

Operational control systems require systematic evaluation of performance against predetermined standards or targets. A critical concern here is identification and evaluation of performance deviations, with careful attention paid to determining the underlying reasons for and strategic implications of observed deviations before management reacts. Some firms use trigger points and contingency plans in this process.

The "quality imperative" of the last 20 years has redefined global competitiveness to include reshaping the way many businesses approach strategic and operational control. What has emerged is a commitment to continuous improvement in which personnel across all levels in an organization define customer value, identify ways every process within the business influences customer value, and seek continuously to enhance the quality, efficiency, and responsiveness with which the processes, products, and services are created and supplied. This includes attending to internal as well as external customers.

QUESTIONS FOR DISCUSSION

1. Distinguish strategic control from operating control. Give an example of each.
2. Select a business whose strategy is familiar to you. Identify what you think are the key premises of the strategy. Then select the key indicators that you would use to monitor each of these premises.

3. Explain the differences between implementation controls, strategic surveillance, and special alert controls. Give an example of each.

4. Why are budgets, schedules, and key success factors essential to operations control and evaluation?

5. What are key considerations in monitoring deviations from performance standards?

6. What are five key elements of quality management? How are quality imperative and continuous improvement related to strategic and operational control?

7. How might customer value be linked to quality, efficiency, and responsiveness?

8. Is it realistic that a commitment to continuous improvement could actually replace operational controls? Strategic controls?

BIBLIOGRAPHY

Asch, D. "Strategic Control: A Problem Looking for a Solution." *Long Range Planning* 25, no. 2 (1992), pp. 97–104.

Baysinger, B., and R. E Hoskisson. "The Composition of Boards of Directors and Strategic Control: Effects on Corporate Strategy." *Academy of Management Review* 15, no. 1 (1990), pp. 72–87.

Boeker, Warren. "Strategic Change: The Effects of Founding and History." *Academy of Management Journal,* September 1989, p. 489.

Bungay, S., and M. Goold. "Creating a Strategic Control System." *Long Range Planning* 24, no. 3 (1991), pp. 32–39.

Cowen, S. S., and J. K. Middaugh. "Designing an Effective Financial Planning and Control System," *Long Range Planning,* December 1988, pp. 83–92.

Duchessi, P., and J. Hobbs. "Implementing a Manufacturing Planning and Control System." *California Management Review,* Spring 1989, pp. 75–90.

Finkin, E. F. "Expense Control in Sales and Marketing." *Journal of Business Strategy,* May 1988, pp. 52–55.

Goold, M. "Strategic Control in the Decentralized Firm." *Sloan Management Review* 32, no. 2 (1991), pp. 69–81.

Goold, M., and J. J. Quinn. "The Paradox of Strategic Control." *Strategic Management Journal* 11, no. 1 (1990), pp. 43–57.

Grant, Robert M.; Rami Shani; and R. Krishnan. "TQM's Challenge to Management Theory and Practice." *Sloan Management Review,* Winter 1994, pp. 25–35.

Gundy, T., and D. King. "Using Strategic Planning to Drive Strategic Change." *Long Range Planning* 25, no. 1 (1992), pp. 100–09.

Gupta, A. K., and V. Govindarajan. "Knowledge Flows and the Structure of Control within Multinational Corporations." *Academy of Management Review* 16, no. 4 (1991), pp. 768–92.

Harrison, E. F. "Strategic Control at the CEO Level." *Long Range Planning* 24, no. 6 (1991), pp. 78–87.

Herzberg, Frederick. "One More Time: How Do You Motivate Employees?" *Harvard Business Review* 65, no. 4 (September–October 1987), pp. 109–20.

Hill, C. W. L. "Corporate Control Type, Strategy, Size and Financial Performance," *Journal of Management Studies,* September 1988, pp. 403–18.

Johnson, G. N. "Managing Strategic Change: Strategy, Culture and Action," *Long Range Planning* 25, no. 1 (1992), pp. 28–36.

Johnson, H. Thomas. *Relevance Regained.* New York: Free Press, 1992.

Kellinghusen, G., and K. Wiebbenhorst. "Strategic Control for Improved Performance." *Long Range Planning* 25, no. 3 (1992), pp. 30–37.

Kelly, D., and T. L. Amburgey. "Organizational Inertia and Momentum: A Dynamic Model of Strategic Change." *Academy of Management Journal* 34, no. 3 (1991), pp. 591–612.

Kiernan, Matthew J. "The New Strategic Architecture: Learning to Compete in the Twenty-First Century." *Academy of Management Executive* 7, no. 1 (February 1993), pp. 7–21.

King, E. M.; W. Norvell; and D. Deines. "Budgeting: A Strategic Managerial Tool." *Journal of Business Strategy,* Fall 1988, pp. 69–75.

Klein, Howard J. "An Integrated Control Theory Model of Work Motivation." *Academy of Management Review,* April 1989, p. 50.

Kohn, Alfie. "Why Incentive Plans Cannot Work." *Harvard Business Review* 71, no. 5 (September–October 1993), pp. 54–63.

Murphy, T. "Pay for Performance—An Instrument of Strategy." *Long Range Planning,* August 1989, pp. 40–45.

Norburn, D., and S. Birley. "The Top Management Team and Corporate Performance." *Strategic Management Journal,* May 1988, pp. 225–38.

Odiorne, George S. "Measuring the Unmeasurable: Setting Standards for Management Performance." *Business Horizons,* July–August 1987, p. 69.

Olian, Judy D., and Sara L. Rynes, "Making Total Quality Work: Aligning Organizational Processes, Performance Measures, and Stakeholders." *Human Resource Management* 30, no. 3 (Fall 1991), pp. 303–333.

Quinn, James Brian. *Intelligent Enterprise.* New York: Free Press, 1992, chap. 4.

Reichheld, F. F., and W. E. Sasser. "Zero Defects: Quality Comes to Services." *Harvard Business Review* 68, no. 3 (1990), pp. 94–111.

Rogers, T. J. "No Excuses Management." *Harvard Business Review* 68, no. 4 (1990), pp. 105–13.

Ross, Joel, and David Georgoff. "A Survey of Productivity and Quality Issues in Manufacturing: The State of the Industry." *Industrial Management* 33, no. 1 (1991), pp. 3–5, 22–25.

Shetty, Y. K. "Aiming High: Competitive Benchmarking for Superior Performance," *Long Range Planning* 26, no. 1 (February 1993), pp. 39–44.

Taguchi, G., and D. Clausing. "Robust Quality." *Harvard Business Review* 68, no. 1 (1990), pp. 65–75.

Wiley, Carolyn. "Incentive Plan Pushes Production." *Personnel Journal* (August 1993), pp. 86–91.

Zahra, S. "Increasing the Board's Involvement in Strategy." *Long Range Planning* 23, no. 6 (1990), pp. 10–16.

Zent, Charles H. "Using Shareholder Value to Design Business Unit Manager Incentive Plans." *Planning Review,* March–April 1988, p. 40.

CHAPTER 12 COHESION CASE ILLUSTRATION

STRATEGIC CONTROL AND CONTINUOUS IMPROVEMENT AT COCA-COLA

Fundamental to Coca-Cola's strategic control in its soft-drink business is daily monitoring of unit case sales in each of the thousands of markets Coke serves around the world. The following table of selected country results illustrates Coke's unit case volume in selected countries on an annual basis. The same scrutiny is applied to all markets, sales territories, routes, and customers (stores selling or disbursing soft drinks) on a weekly basis throughout the Coca-Cola system.

A second critical strategic variable monitored by Coke management is the sales volume or market share attained by independently owned as well as company-owned (full or partially) bottling franchises worldwide. You will recall that a major element of Coke's strategy for the 1990s has been its decision to vertically integrate forward into bottling as necessary to ensure accelerated access to consumers. And where Coke already has long-time franchisees in place, it is aggressively monitoring and evaluating their sales results, choosing quickly when necessary to buy out underperforming franchises. This has been true even in international markets, where some international business experts consider such a move, usually accompanied with inserting an American manager in charge, as being too aggressive. Yet Coke has pushed forward and done so successfully, most notably in Great Britain and France. Recent comments by Coke management on this activity include:

> Our accelerated growth rate of the past five years would seem to indicate that we are doing business differently than before, and we are. Without question, the biggest difference is our willingness to do whatever is advisable to grow our concentrate and syrup business around the world. In large measure, around the world we are able to maximize profitable growth with the traditional bottler system. Sometimes, however, the practical action is taking significant equity positions in important components of our global bottling network. Taking ownership positions in approximately 60 different bottling, canning, and distribution operations around the world and, often, assuming management responsibility has been a way to ensure ourselves of working with the bottling partners who share our commitment to reinvestment in, and profitable growth of, the business.
>
> The results speak for themselves. The accompanying table illustrates the success we have had in a number of individual markets (and also serves to show the focus of a key aspect of Coke's strategic control system).

Another element of Coca-Cola's strategic control centers around the basic goal the company seeks to accomplish. Speaking to business analysts, Roberto Goizueta put it simply: "Management doesn't get paid to make the shareholders comfortable. We get paid to make the shareholders rich." So fundamental strategic control at Coca-Cola monitors the market valuation of Coke and continuously tries to evaluate strategies, assumptions, and actions in light of their effect on this situation. Coca-Cola's chief financial officer recently explained this approach to strategic control:

> Economic Profit and Economic Value Added provide a direct framework for measuring the impact of value-oriented actions. Economic Profit is defined as net operating profit after taxes in excess of a computed capital charge for average operating capital employed. Economic Value Added represents the growth in Economic Profit from year to year.
>
> Beginning in 1994, the Company expanded the use of Economic Value Added as a performance measurement tool. Measured over a three year time frame, long-term incentive bonuses for

Bottling Investments

Region	Year of Investment	Company Ownership (%)	Share (%)		Annual Unit Case Sales Growth (%)
			Before	1995	
Philippines	1981	30%	31%	78%	14%
Taiwan	1985	35	10	52	48
Great Britain	1986	49	21	36	22
Indonesia	1987	29	58	79	18
Netherlands	1988	30	24	34	16
France	1989	100	32	41	24
Australia	1989	51	52	57	9

certain employees of the Company are now determined, in part, by comparison against Economic Profit target levels. This change in performance measures was made to more closely align management's focus on the key drivers of the business. Management believes that a clear focus on the components of Economic Profit, and the resultant growth in Economic Value Added over time, leads to the creating of share-owner wealth.

Over the last 13 years, the Company has increased its Economic Profit at an average annual compound rate of 26 percent, resulting in Economic Value Added to the Company of $1.9 billion. Over the same period, the Company's stock price has increased at an average annual compound rate of 25 percent. During the past decade, share owners of the Company have received an excellent return on their investment. A $100 investment in the Company's common stock at December 31, 1984, together with reinvested dividends, would be worth approximately $1,237 at December 31, 1994, an average annual compound return of 29 percent.

SELECTED COUNTRY RESULTS

Estimated Unit Case[1] Volume

| | Average Annual Growth | | | | 1994 Results | | | |
| | 10 Years | | 5 Years | | Unit Case Growth | | Company | |
	Company[3]	Industry[4]	Company[3]	Industry[4]	Company[3]	Industry[4]	Share[4]	Per Capita[4] Consumption
Worldwide[6]	7%	5%	6%	3%	10%	6%	46%	49
North America Business Sector[2]	4	3	4	3	7	4	41	296
United States	4	3	4	3	7	4	41	310
International Business Sector[2]	8	5	7	3	11	7	49	35
European Community	9	5	6	3	7	5	49	130
Benelux/Denmark	8	4	8	4	9	4	46	152
France	13	7	11	5	9	(1)	47	65
Germany	7	5	8	1	4	3	55	191
Great Britain	12	6	2	3	7	10	31	101
Italy	8	6	4	3	5	2	55	94
Spain	8	4	5	2	9	8	54	166
Pacific[5]	8	8	7	6	12	12	39	20
Australia	9	7	8	3	10	9	65	274
Japan[5]	6	1	6	2	8	8	30	133
Korea	5	5	4	1	11	5	52	59
Philippines	6	3	3	3	14	14	75	96
Thailand	12	14	9	9	14	11	48	54
Northeast Europe/Middle East (NEME)[6]	14	4	17	1	35	17	32	11
Egypt	5	2	4	0	47	4	55	26
Hungary	20	2	37	6	4	12	42	111
Norway	11	7	8	5	9	15	59	256
Poland	33	2	69	8	44	47	24	29
Africa	5	2	5	(1)	1	(7)	84	23
Nigeria	2	0	6	0	(14)	(25)	82	22
South Africa	5	3	5	1	4	0	88	146
Zimbabwe	8	6	5	(1)	9	4	87	62
Latin America	8	6	6	4	10	4	55	148
Argentina	7	6	14	11	12	12	57	189
Brazil	8	7	0	1	10	14	56	92
Chile	15	14	12	8	8	6	64	217
Mexico	8	6	6	4	11	7	57	333

[1]Unit case equals 24 8-ounce drinks.
[2]Consists of United States and Canada.
[3]Includes non-carbonated soft drinks.
[4]Includes only flavored, carbonated soft drinks.
[5]Company share and per capita include Japanese non-carbonated soft drinks; revised to conform with Japanese industry standards (equivalent Company share for Japan in 1993 was 31).
[6]The calculation of per capita consumption includes India and several former Soviet republics.

Perhaps the best-known example of its willingness to react quickly is Coke's reaction to consumers' reception of New Coke in the mid-1980s. After extensive market tests showed Pepsi's slightly sweeter cola was preferred in blind taste tests to traditional Coke, and after still further ruminations, Goizueta's relatively new management team introduced New Coke in an extraordinarily expensive promotional and distribution blitz while also having it take the place of Coke's traditional beverage. Coke was surprised by the consumer rebellion of loyal Coke drinkers who adamantly refused to let the old Coke die. While Coke management had invested millions in this new move—literally changing distribution practices, promotional material, and the like nationwide in 1985—it quickly readjusted its strategy, apologized for its decision, brought back a new "Coke Classic," and ended up with more shelf space in grocery stores (Pepsi's stronghold) as retailers allowed Coke to keep both New Coke & Coke Classic (as well as other brands) for sale. Even with the huge mistake, Coke management's rapid response (strategic control) resulted in yet another record year, in terms of sales and profitability, as well as a valuable lesson in and reinforcement of consumer loyalty to the Coke brand.

Two key trends in global markets will occupy the attention of Coke executives' strategic control:

· Private-label colas sold by large retailers.
· Rise in demand for noncola, "new age" beverages.

For example, Cott Corporation, still a very small player in the beverage industry, has made some inroads in key markets like Japan, Canada, Great Britain, and the United States with an improved quality beverage that it sells to retailers who relabel it using their own labels and sell it to consumers at prices 50 percent below Coke's retail price. They also receive greater profit margins, even at this drastically lower price, than they receive from handling Coke products. Developments in Japan help illustrate this dilemma.[5]

TOKYO—Coke is no longer "It" in Japan, as big retailers come out with discount colas and force the giant U.S. beverage maker Coca-Cola Co. to trim its prices.

"Coca-Cola's biggest fear right now is price deflation for soft drinks spreading to vending machines," which account for about 55% of Coca-Cola's overall soft-drink sales in Japan, said Nikko's Ms. Sudo. That is already happening: Coca-Cola has recently slashed the price of its soft drinks to 100 yen ($1.19) from 110 yen at some of its vending machines.

The root of Coca-Cola's problem in Japan is the brand's slipping ability to defend its suggested retail prices. The problem stems from tougher competition from other beverage companies and the onslaught of inexpensive, generic soft drinks, which last year began flooding Japanese supermarkets at prices as low as 40 yen a can, hurting the sales and influence of brand-name sodas.

Together, Japan's 17 Coca-Cola bottlers, which produce soft drinks with syrups provided by Coca-Cola (Japan) Co., still sell almost one out of every three soft drinks in the country. But at the retail level, excluding vending-machine sales, their dominance is waning. At some major chain stores, analysts said, Coca-Cola's share now is as little as 10%.

As a result of Coca-Cola's diminishing presence in retail stores, the balance of power has tipped in favor of large retailers, so much so that Coca-Cola is under growing pressure to do something it hasn't done much in the past: hand out discounts for retailers.

---

[5] Norihiko Shirouzu, "World Markets: Stocks of Coca-Cola Bottlers in Japan Pressured by Price-driven Inroads by Retailers, Rivals," *The Wall Street Journal,* May 2, 1995, p. C12.

The clearest indication of Coca-Cola's compromised position, Ms. Sudo said, is recent talk among the Coca-Cola bottlers about unifying their distribution, now segmented into 17 regional blocks—a system that has achieved stable retail prices. While a new operation could boost efficiency, it is being considered only at the strong urging of large retail chains such as Seven-Eleven Japan Co. and Daiei Inc. "It's not something Coca-Cola is volunteering to do," Ms. Sudo said.

Because Coca-Cola products, which include coffees and Chinese and Japanese teas, are distributed exclusively by one Coca-Cola bottler per region, large retailers are prevented from using volume buying as leverage for discounts or other incentives. So for the bottlers, altering this system may be necessary but suicidal, analysts said, because a superstore chain could demand lower Coke prices in return for shelf space.

Coke's strategic control has focused on creating alternate responses as it monitors the developments in this critical Pacific region market. Reactions include selling colas, at least Coke Classic, directly from the U.S. West Coast, bypassing Coca-Cola's 17 Japanese bottlers. But long term, the issue speaks to the need for Coke to reconsider its cost structure to address this price-based competition and the high relative strength of large retailers.

Coke's response to the development of new age beverages has been much more direct. Coke has introduced several new beverages to compete directly with these beverages. It has rapidly and aggressively introduced new beverages to leverage the strength of its existing infrastructure and relationship with retailers to immediately take market share away from new entrants once they prove a viable niche exists. The next page highlights some of Coke's recent successes with this approach, which it calls *capitalizing on supporting brands*.

Action: Capitalize On Supporting Brands

Objective: Strengthen consumer loyalty; tap into shifting consumer preferences; source volume from competitors.

Tactics: Positioned supporting brands to address specific market opportunities.

Point of Differentiation: A portfolio of unparalleled strength and depth.

Results: Strong growth from virtually all major supporting brands.

The Complete Beverage Source

Our Company owns some 100 supporting brands around the world. Some have an appeal that transcends geographic and cultural boundaries. Others fill uniquely local needs, often with modest investment. We're eyeing each one with the same scrutiny we used to refocus our lines of business, energizing those that complement our core brands and justify their costs of capital and shedding the rest.

Powerāde Introduced in 1990. Expanding to 20 countries in 1995.	Advertising campaign featuring new look and attitude launched in 1995.		Compounded unit case volume growth*: **346%**
Aquarius Introduced in 1983. Available in 20 countries.		Two new flavors launched in Japan; new advertising under way in Europe.	Compounded unit case volume growth*: **19%**
Hi-C Acquired in 1960. Available in 21 countries.	New packaging graphics and advertising introduced in 1995.		Compounded unit case volume growth**: **6%**
Georgia Introduced in 1975. Available in Japan.		Japan's canned coffee segment leader.	Compounded unit case volume growth*: **30%**
Thums Up & Limca Acquired in late 1993. Available primarily in India.		Leaders in respective flavor segments in India.	No prior year comparison.
Sparletta Brands Once a bottler brand. Available primarily in South Africa.	Our second largest brand in South Africa behind Coca-Cola.		Compounded unit case volume growth***: **22%**

Teas

Ready-to-drink teas represent a small but growing fraction of the soft drink industry. In 1995, we will enhance our product line with new iced teas under the Fruitopia and Nestea trademarks, complemented by local teas in select markets.

Fruitopia Teas New in 1995.	Initial line to include four all-natural flavors.		No prior year comparison.
Nestea Distributed by the Company since 1992. Now in 41 countries.		Customized flavors and styles with pure iced tea taste launched in 1995.	Compounded unit case volume growth*: **104%**
Seiryusabo Introduced in 1994. Available in Japan.	Nearly 19 million unit cases sold in 1994; one of the fastest growing brands in its category.		No prior year comparison.

*Since first full year after introduction/acquisition.
**Since 1975. ***Since 1970.

SEEKING CONTINUOUS IMPROVEMENT

Coca-Cola has placed much greater emphasis on empowering operating personnel to seek continuous improvement and quality, believing that it is critical to control the strategic priority to keep their global business system better than any other in the world. This often translates into continuously improving local operations, syrup plants, and other parts of Coca-Cola. Below are two internal documents that characterize what Coke seeks to do in empowering plant personnel to act and react quickly—with the speed long utilized by executives.

**Managing in the New System vs.
Managing in the Old System**

Old System (Traditional)	New System (Contemporary)
Individual	Team
Fickleness	Commitment
Generalities	Details
Finance focus	Production focus
Dollars	Things and ideas
Sales focus	Marketing focus
Printed or spoken word	Diagram oriented
Single function	System
Opinion	Data
Why?	How?
Fragmented (single focus)	Holistic (integrated)
Deductive	Inductive
Short range	Long range
Product	Process
Debate/conversation	Planning/action
Correction	Prevention
Blame	Help
Just-in-case	Just-in-time
Management control	Leadership
Technology/machines	Human resources
Bureaucratic	Entrepreneurial
Information is power	Communicative
Compartmentalized	Cooperation
Quality-problem	Quality-solution
Control	Breakthrough
Fire fighting to preserve the status quo	Continuous improvement

Source: Coca-Cola USA

Values Sustain Continuous Improvement

· Belief in the employees' ability to solve problems
· Belief that the people doing the work know the most about it and, therefore, are the best able to improve it
· Belief that innovation requires tapping into the resources, contributions, and growth of all employees
· Belief that CIP, team building, and problem solving can create a culture where everyone is responsible for quality
· Willingness to respond fairly and promptly to team recommendations
· Willingness to allow time for team meetings
· Willingness to develop incentives which reward team performance for quality improvement
· Willingness to change structure, policies, and the system as teams develop skills
· Willingness to place decisions for quality with the individuals who do the work
· Willingness to create the opportunity for personal growth, development, and contributions of all employees.

GUIDE TO STRATEGIC MANAGEMENT CASE ANALYSIS

THE CASE METHOD

Case analysis is a proven educational method that is especially effective in a strategic management course. The case method complements and enhances the text material and your professor's lectures by focusing attention on what a firm has done or should do in an actual business situation. Use of the case method in a strategic management course offers you an opportunity to develop and refine analytical skills. It also can provide exciting experience by allowing you to assume the role of the key decision maker for the organizations you will study.

When assuming the role of the general manager of the organization being studied, you will need to consider all aspects of the business. In addition to drawing on your knowledge of marketing, finance, management, production, and economics, you will be applying the strategic management concepts taught in this course.

The cases in this book are accounts of real business situations involving a variety of firms in a variety of industries. To make these opportunities as realistic as possible, the cases include a variety of quantitative and qualitative information in both the presentation of the situation and the exhibits. As the key decision maker, you will need to determine which information is important, given the circumstances described in the case. Keep in mind that the results of analyzing one firm will not necessarily be appropriate for another since every firm is faced with a different set of circumstances.

PREPARING FOR CASE DISCUSSION

The case method requires an approach to class preparation that differs from the typical lecture course. In the typical lecture course, you can still benefit from each class session even if you did not prepare, by listening carefully to the professor's lecture. This approach will not work in a course using the case method. For a case course, proper preparation is essential.

Suggestions for Effective Preparation

1. *Allow adequate time in preparing a case.* Many of the cases in this text involve complex issues that are often not apparent without careful reading and purposeful reflection on the information in the cases.

2. *Read each case twice.* Because many of these cases involve complex decision making, you should read each case at least twice. Your first reading should give you an overview of the firm's unique circumstances and the issues confronting the firm. Your second reading allows you to concentrate on what you feel are the most critical issues and to understand what information in the case is most important. Make limited notes identifying key points during your first reading. During your second reading, you can add details to your original notes and revise them as necessary.

3. *Focus on the key strategic issue in each case.* Each time you read a case you should concentrate on identifying the key issue. In some cases, the key issue will be identified by the case writer in the introduction. In other cases, you might not grasp the key strategic issue until you have read the case several times. (Remember that not every piece of information in a case is equally important.)

This guide was developed by John A. Pearce II, Richard B. Robinson, Jr., and William R. Bayer.

4. *Do not overlook exhibits.* The exhibits in these cases should be considered an integral part of the information for the case. They are not just "window dressing." In fact, for many cases you will need to analyze financial statements, evaluate organizational charts, and understand the firm's products, all of which are presented in the form of exhibits.

5. *Adopt the appropriate time frame.* It is critical that you assume the appropriate time frame for each case you read. If the case ends in 1994, that year should become the present for you as you work on that case. Making a decision for a case that ends in 1994 by using data you could not have had until 1996 defeats the purpose of the case method. For the same reason, although it is recommended that you do outside reading on each firm and industry, you should not read material written after the case ended unless your professor instructs you to do so.

6. *Draw on all of your knowledge of business.* As the key decision maker for the organization being studied, you will need to consider all aspects of the business and industry. Do not confine yourself to strategic management concepts presented in this course. You will need to determine if the key strategic issue revolves around a theory you have learned in a functional area, such as marketing, production, finance, or economics, or in the strategic management course.

PARTICIPATING IN CLASS

Because the strategic management course uses the case method, the success and value of the course depend on class discussion. The success and value of the class discussion, in turn, rely on the roles both you and your professor perform. Following are aspects of your role and your professor's, which, if kept in mind, will enhance the value and excitement of this course.

The Students as Active Learner

The case method requires your active participation. This means your role is no longer one of sitting and listening.

1. *Attend class regularly.* Not only is your grade likely to depend on your involvement in class discussions, but the benefit you derive from this course is directly related to your involvement in and understanding of the discussions.

2. *Be prepared for class.* The need for adequate preparation already has been discussed. You will benefit more from the discussions, will understand and participate in the exchange of ideas, and will avoid the embarrassment of being called on when not prepared. By all means, bring your book to class. Not only is there a good chance you will need to refer to a specific exhibit or passage from the case, you may need to refresh your memory of the case (particularly if you made notes in the margins while reading).

3. *Participate in the discussion.* Attending class and being prepared are not enough; you need to express your views in class. You can participate in a number of ways: by addressing a question asked by your professor, by disagreeing with your professor or your classmates (by all means, be tactful), by building on an idea expressed by a classmate, or by simply asking a relevant question.

4. *Participate wisely.* Although you do not want to be one of those students who never raises his or her hand, you also should be sensitive to the fact that others in your class will want to express themselves. You have probably already had experience with a student who attempts to dominate each class discussion. A student who invariably tries to dominate the class discussion breeds resentment.

5. *Keep a broad perspective.* By definition, the strategic management course deals with the issues facing general managers or business owners. As already mentioned, you need to consider all aspects of the business, not just one particular functional area.

6. *Pay attention to the topic being discussed.* Focus your attention on the topic being discussed. When a new topic is introduced, do not attempt to immediately introduce another topic for discussion. Do not feel you have to have something to say on every topic covered.

Your Professor as Discussion Leader

Your professor is a discussion leader. As such, he or she will attempt to stimulate the class as a whole to share insights, observations, and thoughts about the case. Your professor will not necessarily respond to every comment you or your classmates make. Part of the value of the case method is to get you and your classmates to assume this role as the course progresses.

The professor in a strategic management case course performs several roles:

1. *Maintaining focus.* Because multiple complex issues need to be explored, your professor may want to maintain the focus of the class discussion on one issue at a time. He or she may ask you to hold your comment on another issue until a previous issue is exhausted. Do not interpret this response to mean your point is unimportant; your professor is simply indicating there will be a more appropriate time to pursue that particular comment.

2. *Getting students involved.* Do not be surprised if your professor asks for input from volunteers and nonvolunteers alike. The value of the class discussion increases as more people share their comments.

3. *Facilitating comprehension of strategic management concepts.* Some professors prefer to lecture on strategic management concepts on a "need-to-know" basis. In this scenario, a lecture on a particular topic will be followed by an assignment to work on a case that deals with that particular topic. Other professors will have the class work through a case or two before lecturing on a topic to give the class a feel for the value of the topic being covered and for the type of information needed to work on cases. Still other professors prefer to cover all of the theory in the beginning of the course, thereby allowing uninterrupted case discussion in the remaining weeks of the term. All three of these approaches are valued.

4. *Playing devil's advocate.* At times your professor may appear to be contradicting many of the comments or observations being made. At other times your professor may adopt a position that does not immediately make sense, given the circumstances of the case. At other times your professor may seem to be equivocating. These are all examples of how your professor might be playing devil's advocate. Sometimes the professor's goal is to expose alternative viewpoints. Sometimes he or she may be testing your resolve on a particular point. Be prepared to support your position with evidence from the case.

ASSIGNMENTS

Written Assignments

Written analyses are a critical part of any strategic management course. In fact, professors typically put more weight on written analyses than on exams or quizzes. Each professor has a preferred format for these written analyses, but a number of general guidelines will prove helpful to you in your written assignments.

1. *Analyze.* Avoid merely repeating the facts presented in the case. Analyze the issues involved in the case and build logically toward your recommendations.

2. *Use headings or labels.* Using headings or labels throughout your written analysis will help your reader follow your analysis and recommendations. For example, when you are analyzing the weaknesses of the firm in the case, include the heading Weaknesses. Note the headings in the cases that follow.

3. *Discuss alternatives.* Follow the proper strategic management sequence by (1) identifying alternatives, (2) evaluating each alternative, and (3) recommending the alternative you think is best.

4. *Use topic sentences.* You can help your reader more easily evaluate your analysis by putting the topic sentence first in each paragraph and following with statements directly supporting the topic sentence.

5. *Be specific in your recommendations.* Develop specific recommendations logically and be sure your recommendations are well defended by your analysis. Avoid using generalizations, clichés and

ambiguous statements. Remember that any number of answers are possible, and so your professor is most concerned about how your reasoning led to your recommendations and how well you develop and support your ideas.

6. *Do not overlook implementation.* Many good analyses receive poor evaluations because they do not include a discussion of implementation. Your analysis will be much stronger when you discuss how your recommendation can be implemented. Include some of the specific actions needed to achieve the objectives you are proposing.

7. *Specifically state your assumptions.* Cases, like all real business situations, involve incomplete information. Therefore, it is important that you clearly state any assumptions you make in your analysis. Do not assume your professor will be able to fill in the missing points.

Oral Presentations

Your professor is also quite likely to ask you and your classmates to make oral presentations on a particular case. Oral presentations usually are done by groups of students. In these groups, each member will typically be responsible for one aspect of the overall case. Keep the following suggestions in mind when you are faced with an oral presentation:

1. *Use your own words.* Avoid memorizing a presentation. The best approach is to prepare an outline of the key points you want to cover. Do not be afraid to have the outline in front of you during your presentation, but do not just read the outline.

2. *Rehearse your presentation.* Do not assume you can simply read the outline you have prepared or that the right words will come to you when you are in front of the class making your presentation. Take the time to practice your speech, and be sure to rehearse the entire presentation with your group.

3. *Use visual aids.* The adage "a picture is worth a thousand words" contains quite a bit of truth. The people in your audience will more quickly and thoroughly understand your key points—and will retain them longer—if you use visual aids. Think of ways you and your team members can use the blackboard in the classroom; a graph, chart, or exhibit on a large posterboard; or, if you will have a number of these visual aids, a flip chart.

4. *Be prepared to handle questions.* You probably will be asked questions by your classmates. If questions are asked during your presentation, try to address those that require clarification. Tactfully postpone more elaborate questions until you have completed the formal phase of your presentation. During your rehearsal, try to anticipate the types of questions that you might be asked.

Working as a Team Member

Many professors assign students to groups or teams for analyzing cases. This adds more realism to the course, since most strategic decisions in business are addressed by a group of key managers. If you are a member of a group assigned to analyze a case, keep in mind that your performance is tied to the performance of the other group members, and vice versa. The following are some suggestions to help you be an effective team member:

1. *Be sure the division of labor is equitable.* It is not always easy to decide how the workload can be divided equitably, since it is not always obvious how much work needs to be done. Try breaking down the case into the distinct parts that need to be analyzed to determine if having a different person assume responsibility for each part is equitable. All team members should read and analyze the entire case, but different team members can be assigned primary responsibility for each major aspect of the analysis. Each team member with primary responsibility for a major aspect of the analysis also will be the logical choice to write that portion of the written analysis or to present it orally in class.

2. *Communicate with other team members.* This is particularly important if you encounter problems with your portion of the analysis. Since, by definition, the team members are dependent on each other, it is critical that you communicate openly and honestly with each other. It, therefore, is essential that your team members discuss problems, such as some members not doing their fair share of work or members insisting that their point of view dominate the team's report.

3. *Work as a team.* Since a group's output should reflect a combined effort, the whole group should be involved in each part of the analysis, even if different individuals assume primary responsibility for different parts of the analysis. Avoid having the marketing major do the marketing portion of the analysis, the production major handle the production issues, and so forth. This will both hamper the group's aggregate analysis and do all of the team members a disservice by not giving each member exposure to decision making involving the other functional areas. The strategic management course provides an opportunity to look at all aspects of the business situation, to develop the ability to see the big picture, and to integrate the various functional areas.

4. *Plan and structure team meetings.* When working with a group on case analysis, it is impossible to achieve the team's goals and objectives without meeting outside of class. As soon as the team is formed, establish mutually convenient times for regular meetings, and be sure to keep this time available each week. Be punctual in going to the meetings, and manage the meetings so they end at a predetermined time. Plan several shorter meetings, as opposed to one longer session right before the case is due. (This, by the way, is another way realism is introduced in the strategic management course. Planning and managing your time is essential in business, and working with others to achieve a common set of goals is a critical part of life in the business world.)

SUMMARY

The strategic management course is your opportunity to assume the role of a key decision maker in a business organization. The case method is an excellent way to add excitement and realism to the course. To get the most out of the course and the case method, you need to be an active participant in the entire process.

The case method offers you the opportunity to develop your analytical skills and to understand the interrelationships of the various functional areas of business; it also enables you to develop valuable skills in time management, group problem solving, creativity, organization of thoughts and ideas, and human interaction. All of these skills will prove immensely valuable when you enter the job market and begin your career.

IV CASES

A COMPANY CASES

CASE 1

NTN COMMUNICATIONS, INC.—INTERACTIVE TELEVISION: THE FUTURE IS NOW

> "In the next five years, interactive television is going to take off.
> The whole industry is going to explode."
> *Daniel Downs, co-founder, NTN Communications, Inc.*

1   On June 28, 1994, Patrick Downs, Daniel Downs, and Don Klosterman met to decide the future strategic direction of NTN Communications. NTN's interactive television programming products, QB1 and Diamond Ball, designed to run on a variety of platforms including television and personal computers, were big hits. But the continual advent of new technologies, such as direct satellite communication, made it hard to stay current. The three principals needed to decide where to focus their efforts and resources in light of the veritable explosion of new technologies in the marketplace.

QB1—INTERACTIVE FOOTBALL

2   QB1 is an interactive television game that allows patrons of hotels, taverns, and restaurants to play the role of quarterback during live television coverage of college and professional football games. Patrons watch a live football game on television and predict the quarterback's calls by punching their play of choice (pass, middle, deep is one option) on a portable playmaker box. Once the real action begins, their choices are locked in and beamed by satellite to NTN's Carlsbad, California, headquarters. Viewers win or lose points based on the accuracy of their predictions. Using sophisticated computers and software, the score of each QB1 competitor is tabulated instantaneously and bounced back via satellite to each game site. As the game progresses, QB1 players can track how they are

This case was prepared by Julie Driscoll, Alan N. Hoffman, Alison Rude, Carol Rugg, and Bonnie Silvieria of Bentley College. Published by permission of Alan N. Hoffman, Bentley College.

doing against every single individual competing across the country as their scores and results are flashed on the television screen. "QB1 is definitely a game of skill; you cannot be successful at it if you approach it as a game of chance," says Dan Klosterman, co-founder of NTN Communications, who, together with NFL coaches Don Shula, Hank Stram, and Bill Walsh (collective winners of six Superbowl games), developed QB1 for NTN.

WHAT IS INTERACTIVE TELEVISION?

3   Interactive communication, a synthesis of television, games, education, and information systems, is potentially the "mega-industry" of the 1990s. Although interactive communication is popular with restaurant/bar owners, educators, business professionals, and home owners, there are many consumers who do not understand the concepts behind it, and some who are not even aware that interactive options exist.

4   Interactive communication is two-way (or more) communication between a viewer and a device, usually a television screen. A viewer may interact with a television program as if a dialogue were taking place between two people. For example, a person can play "Jeopardy" interactively by answering the questions on the show via a remote control device. While one viewer answers the questions, viewers at any number of other locations may also answer; thus all participating viewers compete against each other simultaneously, making for a more active and enjoyable viewing experience through interactive participation.

THE HISTORY OF INTERACTIVE TELEVISION

5   The earliest form of interactive communication was the Morse code machine, which made two-way communication possible via a transmitter and a receiver. Next, the telephone enabled virtually any two people to be linked; and now more than two people can communicate instantly via sophisticated teleconferencing technology. Companies such as AT&T, Picturetel, and Intel have also developed video conferencing, which enables participants from remote locations to see each other via satellite or long-distance telephone lines while they talk. Universities also use video-conferencing to conduct classes for students in inaccessible locations. Now, the development of the "information highway" by companies such as America Online, CompuServe, and Prodigy allows users to communicate with a vast database of information, and with other users, via computer hook-up.

6   Interactive television is a natural development of current technology. The potential for interactive communications is so great that no single firm will be able to dominate all aspects of the industry. Consequently, many alliances are forming among cable, telephone, and computer firms to develop the necessary technology and infrastructure. Time Warner has joined forces with Silicon Graphics to develop computer equipment for an interactive television network, and with US West to develop a full-service interactive system. In addition, the Federal Communications Commission has granted regional telephone companies permission to offer audiovisual services, and, thus, to compete directly with cable companies.

COMPANY HISTORY

7   NTN was founded in 1983 by three sports executives: Donald C. Klosterman, Patrick J. Downs, and Daniel C. Downs. Pat Downs was vice president and business manager of the San Diego Padres baseball team from 1964 to 1969 and director of special projects for Time/Life Broadcast properties in San Diego from 1970 to 1973. Dan Downs began his career in the early 1960s in the Los Angeles Dodgers' management training program. In 1966, he became stadium manager and director of sales for the Houston Oilers football team, and was later promoted to assistant general manager. His

interest in interactivity dates back to those Houston Oilers days when he and his boss, Don Kloster-man, were working on ways to get more fans to the Astrodome to watch the Oilers play.

8 Pat and Dan Downs made ambitious plans, but more than once their interactive ventures teetered on the brink of financial ruin. Nevertheless, they persevered, marketing their first game, QB1, to restaurants and bars. After losing the financial backing of Time Inc.'s Home Box Office, they risked everything to build the interactive network themselves, going without pay for three years, even losing their homes. Still the Downs brothers never considered turning back, though many advised them to quit. "In retrospect, we were ahead of the times. But we hung on long enough to raise enough capital to keep going," said Dan Downs. "At times it felt really lonely out there. But we believed so much in what we were doing, we just kept going." Now people who scoffed at them years ago want to deal. "We've put ourselves in a position to succeed and that's what we intend to do," Pat says. "Deals with the big players (ABC, AT&T, and Sony) are in the works, and when the superhighway comes along, we will be ready to go."

9 NTN Communications, Inc., an international provider of interactive television games and educational programs, and a pioneer in developing interactive television, was formed from the merger of Alroy Industries, Inc., and National Telecommunicator Network, Inc. The company's revenues presently derive from three sources: broadcasting, the sale of interactive equipment, and the licensing of technology. NTN owns and operates the only interactive television network in North America that broadcasts 24 hours a day, every day of the week.

10 A number of games are now available through NTN's interactive network. The company began with sports games because this was the founders' area of expertise, and has since broadened its product base to include Diamond Ball (baseball), Power Play (hockey), Passport (an interactive travel game), Spot Light (an entertainment game), and Playback (a music game). NTN's niche is public venues and special event productions such as the Superbowl, the Grammy Awards, the Academy Awards, all game shows on the ABC television network, and trade shows, sales conferences, and charity events. NTN has the capability to allow many people to participate at the same time through the use of their 200-unit playmaker system, which is perfect for large events. The wide variety of their games is a strength because there is something for everyone.

NTN's Target Markets

11 The NTN network is currently marketed to group viewing locations such as bars and restaurants. There are approximately 700 location subscribers in the United States and 220 in Canada. All NTN network programming is produced at NTN corporate headquarters in Carlsbad, California, and transmitted to subscribers using multiple data transmission techniques including FM radio transmission, direct satellite broadcast, and television transmission via vertical blanking intervals. Using the same technology as that used for pay-per-view movies, NTN can provide simultaneous transmission of up to eight live events for interactive play, allowing the company to broadcast different programs to different geographic locations at the same time. The NTN feed is carried via satellite and each establishment has a decoder that enables it to receive advertisements and games designated specifically for that location.

12 Bars and restaurants are capitalizing on interactive trends by offering games tied to popular sporting events to increase traffic into their establishments and increase sales. However, observers have noted that the success of their interactive offerings is tied directly to the bar's or restaurant's successful promotion of the event. For example, a pub in Chicago gets at least 30 extra people specifically to play NTN's QB1 game, while another bar down the street, although full, may have only a few people using the interactive game.

13 NTN currently services four domestic markets: hospitality, home, education, and video games markets. For the hospitality market, NTN has joined with LodgeNet to provide over 14,000 hotel rooms nationwide with an interactive network of games that allows hotel guests to play along with live sporting events. For the home market, NTN has joined forces with Prodigy, AT&T ImagiNation Network, GEnie, and GTE's Main Street to offer interactive computer games. For the interactive education market, NTN provides surveys, academic competitions, and testing capabilities that can be

EXHIBIT 1
NTN Communications Divisional Overview

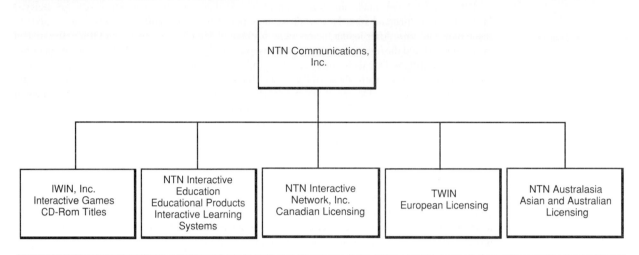

performed within a single classroom at a particular site, or at several different locations, all with instantaneous feedback via satellite networks. And NTN's wholly owned subsidiary, IWIN, Inc., is a full-service provider of interactive applications and transactions services for the interactive games industry. See Exhibit 1 for an overview of NTN's divisions.

14   NTN also operates internationally. In Canada, NTN has an exclusive license with NTN Interactive Network, Inc. NTN also has an agreement with TWIN, its licensee for Europe (owned by Whitebread Breweries, PLC, and BBC Enterprises) to license the rights to all of NTN's products and services throughout Europe. Australasia became an operational company in November 1993 with a broadcast facility in Sydney, Australia. NTN is currently pursuing interactive education opportunities in Mexico, and has received some approval from the Mexican Ministry of Education.

NEW PRODUCTS

15   In 1993, NTN formed a wholly owned subsidiary, IWIN (I Win), to take advantage of the legalization of home betting on horses. IWIN is a full-service provider of interactive applications and transactions services to the worldwide gaming industry, and is currently testing a new pari-mutuel game called Triples, which allows cable TV subscribers in California to wager on the races at the Los Alamitos Race Course. NTN plans further expansion into the gaming industry using a vertical market strategy to break into the lottery and casino gaming markets in the near future.

16   In January 1994, NTN teamed up with Replica Corporation to offer Replica's interactive investment and sports fantasy games through NTN's distribution system. The agreement boosts NTN's offerings, adding to its appeal to new target markets as well as current customers. In March of the same year, NTN cut a deal with Event Entertainment and Kingvision Pay-Per-View to form the NTN Event Network, which will offer interactive boxing for 8 to 12 fights per year.

17   Interactive programming has many potential uses beyond allowing players to participate in games, for instance, enlivening training and education. To expand its capabilities in more markets, NTN formed an Interactive Education Division in 1993. Interactive education can provide rural or disadvantaged students with the same opportunities as those from wealthier school districts by allowing students to actively participate in the learning process and communicate with teachers at remote locations as if they were in the same classroom. At the same time, teachers effectively control the process by quickly monitoring student progress and providing instant feedback. NTN has had

success in developing and licensing its interactive technology to KET, an education network in Kentucky. NTN has also developed the Interactive Learning System, a unique tool for teaching students in a more enjoyable environment. It operates via satellite and has been used for conducting surveys, academic competitions, and testing. The Interactive Learning System has been used in 19 states for more than five years and regional centers are currently being established in California and Arizona.

18   NTN is also working with the Mexican government to provide educational services. Field tests were conducted in which Mexican schools received a satellite broadcast transmitted from Mexico City. These tests were successful, and NTN anticipates making a final agreement with the Mexican government to provide interactive educational services to approximately 3,000 schools in the near future. Under this arrangement, NTN will receive $695 per month, per system, for the next five years in addition to a one-time installation fee of $250 and a monthly maintenance fee of $150 per system. In addition to the 3,000 schools already targeted, there are 5,700 schools that could benefit from NTN's services. However, NTN has not yet received a signed contract, and, if the deal falls through, NTN stands to lose millions of dollars in potential revenue.

19   NTN seeks to expand into the corporate world by using their products for corporate training, product knowledge testing, employee testing, and certification and technical training. They plan to market interactive training as a way to help companies cut their training and development costs by combining training with other branches of the company or by eliminating the need for an on-site trainer.

NTN's COMPETITIVE LANDSCAPE

20   The competition in the field of interactive television is fierce. Many new entrants are adept at using both current technologies such as television and telephone lines, and state-of-the-art technologies such as satellites, cellular networks, and personal computers. NTN's direct competitor in the interactive television home market is the Interactive Network, Inc. (IN). IN distributes their own interactive network whose programming is very similar to that of NTN. IN's subscriber-based service allows television viewers to play along in real time with televised sporting events, game shows, dramas, news, and talk show programming. Currently testing in Sacramento, California, and Chicago, Illinois, IN's system, like that of NTN, is designed to run on many different delivery platforms. The biggest threat IN poses to NTN, however, is that it is backed by Tele-Communications, Inc., Gannett Co., Cablevision, NBC, and A.C. Nielsen, large media investors with "deep pockets," all of whom are significant players in their respective industries.

21   Because NTN's services are designed to utilize various already existing delivery mechanisms, their competitors are diverse. Recent entrants into the interactive television marketplace are local and long-distance telephone companies such as AT&T and Bell Atlantic, which can use their existing telephone infrastructure and a combination of both television and personal computers to deliver interactive programming.

22   Many cable TV companies across the United States are also interested in interactive television both as a future programming alternative and as an opportunity to expand their revenue stream. The cable companies pose a real threat because they have large financial resources, their delivery infrastructure via cable networks is already in place, and they have access to a wide variety of programming possibilities.

23   In addition, online services such as Prodigy, CompuServe, and America Online pose a competitive risk to NTN. They have been in the interactive marketplace for over 10 years; they have the infrastructure in place; and their products already provide high levels of interactivity through interactive chat and gaming capabilities.

24   As is characteristic of most growth industries, many new players will compete directly with NTN. The threat to NTN is real, especially because competition can take so many different forms. And, because there are so many ways a company wishing to compete can proceed, the current climate in the industry is volatile and unpredictable. In addition, since there are no industry standards, a

company developing its own technology runs the risk of being side-tracked by an alternative technology. NTN relies on distribution networks, such as radio stations, and telephone and cable companies, to supply their products to customers. Consequently, they are at the mercy of their distributors to get their products to clients. Mergers and alliances are one way to reduce this threat. Alternatively, a concerted effort to offer the best services (those most desired by consumers) would shift the balance of power in NTN's favor by outdoing the competition.

25   In the home and hospitality segments, NTN relies heavily on information providers (NHL, NFL, Trivia, the Academy Awards) to supply content for their products, which are, in turn, evaluated primarily on the basis of their association with major sporting events or game shows.

THE INFORMATION SUPERHIGHWAY

26   Technological advances have given consumers access to many services without having to leave home, and it is interactive technology (the ability of the consumer to respond and communicate directly and interactively with a television or computer) that makes it all possible. Because it is so responsive to consumer needs, the growth potential for interactive technology is huge. Cable subscriptions currently represent approximately 61 percent of the total television household market, and are on the rise. Many consumers spend a significant portion of their time watching movies, playing video or electronic games, or watching sports programs.

27   Industry experts predict that television and cable services are still in their infancy, and that the near future holds a wider selection of cable channels, the ability to select and watch a movie on demand, and the ability to interact directly with the television. However, television is not the only medium competing for a share of the interactive market. A recent study revealed that the average household spends almost twice as much time using a computer as watching television. Some experts even predict that PCs will replace televisions as the household electronic appliance of choice and that the majority of homes will have a PC by the year 2000, despite the extra expense. Software and cable companies currently offer very similar products such as news services, home shopping, and electronic games, suggesting that computer and video marketing are beginning to converge in a competition for the same consumers. Microsoft plans to capitalize on this trend by developing software that works with both platforms. The company is currently working on a network that will operate not only on phone networks but on cable TV networks as well, which could have a tremendous impact on the interactive television segment. For example, Microsoft Baseball, a CD-ROM program that dials into an electronic service to retrieve daily scores, will eventually become a video update program that will allow consumers to scan for the baseball footage they missed the night before. In addition, Microsoft is forming alliances with Hollywood film studios and other software companies to combine computing and video technologies more effectively. As Microsoft's president, Bill Gates, puts it, "The PC industry has come a long way, but that's nothing compared with what's going to happen."

THE FUTURE

28   The future of the information superhighway is promising, but uncertain. Because technology is constantly changing there are very few industry standards relevant to the development of interactive television. Companies developing a product must take all the risks and may very well end up with an already obsolete new product. A recent FCC ruling granting permission to telephone companies to offer audiovisual services opens even more doors for players to enter the market. However, because it is unclear which avenue or mode of technology will be the wave of the future, cable, telephone, and computer companies are forming alliances that not only combine technologies, but secure markets within the industry. Cable companies, for example, already enjoy concessions such as right of ways and legal easements for cable installations, and monopolies on particular service territories, which prevent other cable companies from competing directly with them.

29   The future of the information superhighway becomes even more uncertain when satellite technology is factored in. As satellite technology advances, satellite dishes are becoming smaller and more inexpensive, and will soon be offering greater opportunities for interactive technology. In fact, satellites may very well supersede cable and telephone technology, which would tremendously benefit all involved. For instance, digging permits or right of way issues, a large source of aggravation and cost for cable companies today, would be eliminated. In fact, many businesses currently opt for satellite television services instead of cable because cable companies cannot provide access, either because of awkward location or building and right of way issues. There are, however, problems with satellite technology, especially with regard to the "line of sight" when satellite signals are obstructed by large buildings or other impediments.

DEMOGRAPHIC TRENDS

30   One potential problem for NTN is the public's lack of product awareness. In a recent survey, 66 percent of the population stated they did not have much interest in or awareness of interactive television, although 22 percent indicated they were interested in subscribing to interactive television in their homes. However, the survey did reveal a rise in interest among consumers between 18 and 34; and as the income levels of those surveyed rose, so did interest in interactive services. Thus consumer education, especially education targeted to particular demographic markets, is crucial to the promotion of interactive products.

31   The elderly currently represent 13 percent of the U.S. population, and population growth statistics predict that the group of those over 65 will grow at a faster rate than any other age group between 1994 and 2000. Although the elderly population often have a great deal of leisure time, historically speaking, they have not been comfortable with high-tech devices. While interactive television could offer useful services to this age group (e.g., at-home bingo, shopping), it is not clear whether there is sufficient interest among this demographic group.

32   The 0 to 15 age segment currently represents 23 percent of the total population. Although this age segment shows slow growth within the next few years, it will continue to be, proportionately, the largest population segment in the United States through the year 2002.

MARKETING

33   Within the interactive industry, NTN has positioned itself in an enviable niche: programming and programming distribution. NTN's ongoing marketing objectives include:

  · Attracting important new sponsors and advertisers.
  · Forming new strategic alliances and securing new contracts.
  · Entering into agreements that expand the distribution of their programs and services.

34   At the same time, the interactive industry is continually changing and NTN's marketing strategies must reflect this. In 1992, NTN repositioned itself as a leader in interactive communications, rebuilding its core product offerings and recasting NTN's marketing operation.

35   NTN's primary market focus is hospitality, especially restaurants, bars, and hotels. NTN's plan is to garner expertise in this segment before moving into the home market, its next growth segment. In North America alone, there are approximately 330,000 bars and restaurants NTN can target: a tremendous growth area. Some of NTN's subscribers include: Bennigan's, Steak and Ale, Hooters, TGI Friday's, Chili's, Ground Round, and Chi Chi's. In 1993, NTN added military bases, college campuses, hospitals, country clubs, fraternal organizations, and bowling centers to its list of subscribers. These subscribers are easy markets for NTN products because they can afford them, and it is not necessary to sell them television-set-top boxes.

36   NTN entered the hotel segment of the hospitality industry through an agreement with LodgeNet Entertainment Corporation, which gave NTN access to 14,000 guest rooms. The full hotel segment

potential is 250,000 guest rooms in major hotel chains such as Marriott, Hilton, ITT Sheraton, Radisson, Ramada, and Holiday Inn. Interactive marketing to the hospitality industry grew significantly during 1993, the subscriber base nearly doubling from 776 to 1,420. By the end of 1993, the number of interactive participants has increased to 55 million, with the largest increase, 112 percent, during the last year. These increases mark significant growth and are considered reliable indicators of future industry growth.

37   Advertisers are also finding creative ways to take advantage of interactive television services. Infomercials are using interactive TV to review feedback about their products, and Oceanspray has teamed up with NTN to create interactive advertisements that sponsor prizes for top-scoring customers. Indeed, the latest challenge for advertisers will be marketing their products effectively using interactive media. Anticipated trends include:

· More sponsor-oriented programs focused on specific interest groups.
· Product channels that allow for comparison shopping.
· Increased use of infomercials.
· Increased availability of commercial spots.

38   Currently, NTN has national advertisers such as Paddington, Seagrams, Miller Brewing (which sponsored NTN's game QB1 for the past three years), and American Express (which advertises on NTN's Passport game). Advertisers view the interactive network as a powerful medium and an effective way to target many different segments of their markets at the same time. In addition, advertising on this medium is more cost effective. The flexibility of interactive programming allows advertisers to tailor their product promotions to different geographical areas and age groups, especially the hard-to-reach 21-to-35-year-olds. Advertisers are thus able to reach more than 5 million players each month, with a year-end 1994 estimate of 10 million per month, a major attraction for many corporate sponsors.

FINANCIAL SITUATION

39   NTN's financial objectives are: increase shareholder value by reaching profitability; fund future growth from revenues generated by the company; and contain costs. The company achieved its first objective of reaching profitability in the fourth quarter of 1993, realizing a profit of $160,000; and continued to show a profit into the first quarter of 1994. (See Exhibits 2 and 3 for financial statement data.) Total consolidated revenues for 1993 increased 61 percent over 1992 to $17.3 million. These figures include revenues from New World Computing, which was acquired in 1993. The profits of the past two quarters make NTN the *only* profitable company in the interactive TV industry.

40   NTN's stock price has fluctuated from a low of ⅛ in 1990 to 11½ in 1993. As of July 15, 1994, the price was 7¼. One of management's objectives is to "have a stock that can properly reflect both the current results, as well as future potential which entails expenses for which no financial benefits may be available for the short term."

41   NTN currently has a sale-leaseback arrangement for its equipment, which allows for an off-balance sheet financing method. Under this arrangement, NTN pays for the equipment, sells the assembled equipment to another company for a higher price, then leases it back, an arrangement NTN found necessary because of insufficient working capital to finance the cost of the equipment itself. In the future, NTN will finance the equipment purchases by exercising the warrants and options.

42   In 1993, sales grew by 61 percent, a rise attributable to increases in sales of equipment, numbers of subscribers, and retail sales of products. NTN's other sources of revenue include license fees and royalties from foreign licensees, and the advertising and sponsorship revenues from companies advertising on its games and shows.

EXHIBIT 2

NTN COMMUNICATIONS, INC., AND SUBSIDIARIES
Consolidated Balance Sheets
December 31, 1994, and 1993

	1994	1993
Assets		(Note 2)
Current assets:		
Cash and cash equivalents	$ 2,429,000	$ 7,208,000
Marketable securities—available for sale	1,000,000	3,554,000
Interest-bearing security deposits	1,225,000	200,000
Accounts receivable—trade, net of allowance for doubtful accounts of $435,000 in 1994 and $180,000 in 1993	5,881,000	2,366,000
Accounts receivable—officers and directors	100,000	180,000
Accounts receivable—other	600,000	1,642,000
Notes receivable—officers and directors (note 3)	3,262,000	2,856,000
Software development costs, net of accumulated amortization of $177,000	1,212,000	—
Inventories	4,628,000	3,756,000
Prepaid expenses and other current assets	1,769,000	1,340,000
Total current assets	22,106,000	23,102,00
Fixed assets, net (note 4)	1,405,000	846,000
Interest-bearing security deposits	1,975,000	900,000
Software development costs, net of accumulated amortization of $408,000 in 1994 and $87,000 in 1993	2,193,000	639,000
Other investments	1,630,000	807,000
Deposits and other assets	1,930,000	946,000
Total assets	$31,239,000	$27,240,000
Liabilities and Shareholders' Equity		(Note 2)
Current liabilities:		
Accounts payable and accrued liabilities	$ 2,744,000	$ 1,668,000
Short-term borrowings and current portion of long-term debt (note 5)	468,000	237,000
Deferred revenue	740,000	378,000
Customer deposits	1,006,000	650,000
Total current liabilities	4,958,000	2,933,000
Deferred revenue	816,000	491,000
Long-term debt, excluding current portion (note 5)	8,000	163,000
Total liabilities	5,782,000	3,587,000
Shareholders' equity (notes 7, 8 and 9):		
10% Cumulative convertible preferred stock, $.005 par value, 10,000,000 shares authorized; issued and outstanding 197,612 in 1994 and 255,000 in 1993	1,000	1,000
Common stock, $.005 par value, 50,000,000 shares authorized; issued and outstanding 19,178,060 in 1994 and 18,855,550 in 1993	96,000	94,000
Additional paid-in capital	44,599,000	43,504,000
Accumulated deficit	(19,239,000)	(19,946,000)
Total shareholder's equity	25,457,000	23,653,000
Commitments and contingencies (notes 12 and 13)		
Total liabilities and shareholders' equity	$31,239,000	$27,240,000

EXHIBIT 3

NTN COMMUNICATIONS, INC., AND SUBSIDIARIES
Consolidated Statements of Operations
For the Years Ended December 31, 1994, 1993, and 1992

	1994	1993	1992
		(Note 2)	(Note 2)
Broadcast and production services	$12,244,000	$ 6,778,000	$ 3,225,000
Product sales	5,263,000	5,468,000	3,652,000
Equipment sales	4,387,000	3,970,000	2,108,000
License fees and royalties	1,934,000	802,000	1,328,000
Other revenue	818,000	240,000	389,000
Total revenues	24,646,000	17,258,000	10,702,000
Cost of services—broadcast and production services	5,198,000	3,261,000	1,378,000
Cost of sales—product sales	1,502,000	1,537,000	1,346,000
Cost of sales—equipment	2,753,000	2,716,000	1,476,000
Total cost of sales	9,453,000	7,514,000	4,200,000
Gross profit	15,193,000	9,744,000	6,502,000
Operating expenses:			
Selling, general, and administrative	12,926,000	10,125,000	7,298,000
Research and development	1,972,000	1,073,000	1,338,000
Total operating expenses	14,898,000	11,198,000	8,636,000
Operating income (loss)	295,000	(1,454,000)	(2,134,000)
Interest income, net of interest expense of $54,000, $71,000, and $129,000 in 1994, 1993, and 1992, respectively	412,000	434,000	—
Earnings (loss) before income taxes	707,000	(1,020,000)	(2,134,000)
Income taxes (note 6)	—	281,000	106,000
Net earnings (loss)	$ −707,000	$ (1,301,000)	$ (2,240,000)
Net earnings (loss) per share	$ 0.03	$ (0.08)	$ (0.20)
Weighted-average number of shares outstanding	21,123,955	17,135,430	11,343,601

LEGAL ISSUES

43   The legal environment for interactive services is uncertain. The major obstacle to NTN's effort to provide an interactive betting service is that in many states home betting is illegal. Senate Bill 1431 legalizes home betting in California, but mandates blackout areas of 15 miles around satellite facilities and 30 miles around racetracks. The process for legalizing home betting in other states has been slower than expected, hindering penetration of the market. However, there are five states where betting is legal: Kentucky, Pennsylvania, Michigan, Ohio, and New York, making them potential candidates for a home betting service. This number will most likely increase as state governments seek additional revenue through gambling profits.

44   Other legal hassles include a patent infringement case with Interactive Network, Inc. (IN). The dispute involves NTN's royalty-free use of IN's patent to lock out responses from viewers during a live sports telecast. Under a partial settlement agreement, IN licensed NTN's QB1 trivia game for a fee, but the license expired on March 31, 1993, and has not yet been renewed. As of now, IN is the only other company developing subscription-based interactive television service, and it has formed powerful alliances that could lock NTN out of certain key markets. For example, Cablevision, an

affiliate of Rainbow Programming, Inc., currently services all of Boston and a great deal of New York's residential and business market. However, NTN does not think that patent technology is key to their success in the interactive industry. Rather, it is NTN's corporate philosophy that they can maintain a competitive edge by differentiating their product and service offerings, and by fostering consumer loyalty.

45   Licensing arrangements, which are similar to patents, also act as barriers to new firms entering the interactive sports entertainment market, and may allow NTN to gain a competitive advantage in the marketplace. NTN currently holds a license to use live NFL football game telecasts for their interactive games such as QB1. The license expires in 1995 but NTN has the option to renew for another five years. Under this arrangement, NTN can also sublicense the use of NFL games for interactive television to other cable service companies and delivery systems.

STRATEGIC DIRECTION?

47   NTN is at a critical point in its life cycle. NTN faces several opportunities and challenges on the technological and competitive fronts. NTN must confront tremendous competitive pressures from other interactive service providers such as America Online, Prodigy, CompuServe, and the Internet, any of which could, from another perspective, provide opportunities for NTN to cultivate strategic alliances. Given NTN's limited resources, Patrick, Dan, and Don know they need to focus on a particular strategic direction for NTN and concentrate NTN's resources on one or two technologies—either cable, telephone, online, satellite, or wireless communication—if NTN is to survive and prosper in the long run.

REFERENCES

Aho, Debra. "Miller Calls an Interactive Play." *Advertising Age*, October 11, 1993, p. 41.

Armstrong, Larry. "I Have Seen the Future and Its—Urp!" *Business Week*, January 24, 1994, p. 41.

Armstrong, Larry; Ira Sager; Kathy Rebello; and Peter Burrows. "Home Computers." *Business Week*, November 28, 1994, p. 88.

Bhattacharya, Sanjoy. "NTN Communications, Inc." *D. Blech and Company*, November 16, 1993, pp. 1–10.

Fawcett, A. W. "Interactive TV's Toughest Question." *Advertising Age*, October 11, 1993, pp. 39–40.

Hartke, James; Tarum Chandra; and Peter Kambourakis. "NTN Communications, Inc." *Laidlaw Equities, Inc.*, June 18, 1993, pp. 1–20.

Hunger, J. David, and Thomas L. Wheelan. *Strategic Management*. Reading, MA: Addison-Wesley Publishing Company, 1993.

Interactive Network. Annual Report. 1993.

Interactive Services Association. "Interactive Television Today and Tomorrow." San Francisco, July 18, 1994.

NTN—At a Glance. Leedom's San Diego Stock Report, San Diego, 1994.

NTN Communications. Annual Report. 1993.

NTN Communications. First Quarter Bulletin. 1994.

NTN Communications. Standard American Stock Exchange Stock Reports. New York: McGraw-Hill, 1994.

"NTN Communications Is Teaming with Event Entertainment and Kingvision Pay-Per-View." *Broadcasting and Cable*, March 14, 1994, p. 12.

Quinn, James Brian. *Intelligent Enterprises*. New York: The Free Press, 1992.

Smith, Virginia. "The Consumer Market For Interactive Television: Today and Tomorrow." *AT&T Consumer Video Services*, July 18, 1994, p. 1–9.

CASE 2

LIZ CLAIBORNE, 1993: TROUBLED TIMES FOR THE WOMAN'S RETAIL GIANT

1   In 1986, Liz Claiborne, Inc., became the first company started by a woman to make the Fortune 500. Described by *Working Woman* magazine as "the wizard of the working woman's wardrobe,"[1] Liz Claiborne, Inc., provides quality career and casual clothing, accessories, and fragrances at prices working women can afford. In fact, the company's philosophy, to produce "simple, straightforward fashion designed for women who have more important things to think about than what to wear,"[2] has made it the largest women's apparel manufacturer in the world. In 1993, Liz Claiborne sold 65 million garments, and more than 20 million accessories.

THE EARLY YEARS

2   The daughter of a banker at Morgan Guaranty Trust Company, Liz Claiborne spent her early childhood in Brussels before moving with her family to New Orleans in 1934. She never finished high school, but after the War, her father sent her to Europe to study at the Art School in Brussels, and then to the Academie in Nice, France, to study fine arts. She returned to the United States only to discover that her family opposed her desire to work in the fashion industry. Nevertheless, Liz entered a sketch of a woman's high-collared coat in a design contest sponsored by *Harper's Bazaar*, and won. At 21, she began her career as a sketcher, model, and, later, designer on "Fashion Avenue," the insiders' name for New York's Seventh Avenue garment district, where much of America's ready-to-wear is designed, and was, at one time, produced. Soon afterward, while working at Rhea Manufacturing Company in Milwaukee, she met Arthur Ortenberg, a design executive, whom she married in 1957.

3   In 1960, Liz Claiborne embarked on a 15-year career as the chief designer for Youth Guild, the junior dress division of Jonathan Logan. It was during these years that the seeds of Liz Claiborne, Inc., were sown: More and more women were entering the work force, and Liz perceived that there was an opening in the market for tasteful, moderately priced career clothes. She could not sell Youth Guild on her vision of a mix-and-match sportswear line to fill that gap, so she decided to set up her own company.

4   Liz Claiborne, Inc., was launched on January 19, 1976. Financed by $50,000 in personal savings and $200,000 from family, friends, and business associates, the company began small; Liz Claiborne was President and head designer, and her husband, Arthur Ortenberg, an expert in textiles and business administration, was Secretary and Treasurer of the corporation, and, later, Chairman. A third partner, Leonard Boxer, contributed production expertise, and, in 1977, Jerome Chazen, a personal friend, was named Vice President of Marketing. Within its first year, the company was operating in the black, with sales of over $2 million. In 1985, sales reached the half billion dollar mark; the next year, retail sales surpassed $1.2 billion, and Liz Claiborne, Inc., made it into the Fortune 500.

5   In February 1989, Liz Claiborne and Arthur Ortenberg announced their retirement from active management of the company to pursue environmental, social, and other interests. Jerome Chazen, one of the company's original partners, was named CEO, and Jay Margolis was hired as Vice Chair and President of Women's Sportswear, Liz Claiborne, Inc.'s, core division. Committed to taking Liz

This case was prepared by Sharon Ungar Lane, Patricia Bilafer, Mary Fandel, Barbara Gottfried, and Professor Alan N. Hoffman of Bentley College. The authors would like to thank Jane Moreno, Jeffrey Shuman, and Sally Strawn for their valuable contributions to this case. Photographic contribution by Scott Lane.

Claiborne into the 1990s debt-free, they and a team of designers have expanded product lines, adding accessories and fragrances to meet customer demand. They also purchased Russ Togs Company to sustain company growth. Today Liz Claiborne can claim a full 2 percent of the women's apparel market—more than any other publicly held company.

THE FASHION INDUSTRY

6   The fashion industry is highly competitive. The maturing market for women's clothing is dominated by Liz Claiborne and its major competitors: Jones New York, Chaus, Evan Picone, JH Collectibles, and VF Corporation. Retailers, the interface between the fashion industry and the consumer, have suffered in recent years from the recession and volatile consumer tastes, necessitating major restructuring, which has had a significant impact on the fashion industry. Mergers, acquisitions, and bankruptcies of major retailers have created powerful retail rivals with the financial resources to create large economies of scale and withstand new entrants, strict governmental regulation, and technological advances. For instance, when Macy's, which had accounted for a significant percentage of Liz Claiborne sales, went bankrupt in 1992, Liz Claiborne's sales figures suffered in the ensuing bankruptcy settlement.

7   The retail clothing industry is also highly vulnerable to shifting tastes. Predicting fashion is risky and expensive because what is considered stylish today may be out tomorrow. Yet significant lead time is required to bring new styles to market. A company may invest a year or more in the design and production stages of a new design concept only to have the line fail upon introduction. In fact, clothing lines are usually either complete successes or complete failures; yet at the same time, inventory levels for successful lines must be adequate to meet consumer demand, which doesn't leave much margin for error. Establishing name recognition is a priority for designers. Consumers consistently shop their favorite designers, and remain loyal to those whose clothes fit best. Indeed, strong designer loyalty dominates the retail industry. Thus fashion industry marketing strategies must take many contingencies into account at all times, while remaining flexible enough to respond to continually shifting consumer tastes.

PRODUCT LINES

8   Liz Claiborne's principal lines are designed to meet the work and leisure clothing needs of working women. Today 57.7 percent of all women in the United States work outside the home; and women with children under the age of six are the fastest growing segment of the work force. The dual-income family has become the norm, and stay-at-home moms the exception rather than the rule. Consequently, many women no longer have the kind of leisure time they once had to shop; rather they prefer to maximize any shopping outing. Liz Claiborne, Inc., has carved out a niche for itself by targeting these women as its primary constituency, designing mix-and-match coordinating outfits rather than separates, that can be variously combined to suit individual needs and tastes—thus, simplifying both shopping and dressing for the busy lifestyles of working women. To market this concept, Liz Claiborne was one of the first companies to merchandise their clothing lines as outfits rather than single items, arranging them on the display floor to demonstrate that they can dress the customer from head to toe, rather than displaying single garments by classification. Furthermore, the clothes are modern and classic rather than trendy, designed with practicality, style, and fashion longevity in mind. Liz Claiborne's goal is to offer clothing and accessories that are not only aesthetically and technically well designed, but which make the customer feel confident, addressing all the needs of her busy life.

9   As of 1993, Liz Claiborne, Inc., had 18 divisions (Exhibit 1) offering various products aimed at specific target markets and covering a wide gamut of career wear, active wear, and accessories for women, as well as for men. Liz Claiborne is continually adding new products to their apparel line, such as the women's suits introduced in 1991, not simply to increase sales, but to garner more

EXHIBIT 1
Liz Claiborne, Inc.'s Product Line Overview

Sportswear

Includes Collection, Lizsport, Lizwear, and Petite Sportswear. Liz Claiborne, Inc., launched into the fashion industry with its sportswear line in 1976. Designed to be modern and classic rather than trendy, so as to ensure fashion longevity, the sportswear division divided into three distinct lines. The first, Collection, is primarily a career-oriented, tailored, and professional line. Lizsport provides sportswear for leisure time as well as for more casual work environments. Lizwear is a highly denim-driven sportswear division. Our Petite sportswear was developed in 1982 to fulfill an unmet need in the market for the 5'4" and under customer. Petite sizes are offered in all three sportswear lifestyles.

Dresses:

Misses and Petite. Misses dresses were launched in 1982, followed by Petite in 1985. Our dresses include a wide range of fabrications and styles, from career to knit to social occasion dresses. Furthermore, the dress division offers a large selection of dresses that can be worn from day to dinner, encompassing the ease and professionalism necessary for a work environment with the style and fun for an evening on the town.

Suits:

In 1991 Liz Claiborne, Inc., ventured into the Suits market. The division differentiates itself by offering a wide variety of skirt and jacket lengths, seasonless fabrics, pant suits, and day-to-dinner designs.

Liz & Co.:

Liz & Co., launched in 1989, consists primarily of comfortable and coordinated knitwear separates with a relaxed fit and a youthful attitude.

Dana Buchman:

Sportswear, Petite Sportswear, and Dresses. Founded in 1987, Dana Buchman is our bridge sportswear division with prices that range from better sportswear to designer merchandise. It offers sophisticated styles of the highest quality fabrics with an exceptional attention to detail. Dana Buchman's distribution is selective.

Elisabeth:

Sportswear, Petite Sportswear, and Dresses. In response to a previously neglected market, Liz Claiborne, Inc., developed its large-size division called Elisabeth in 1989. The line includes a wide range of products from active wear to career clothing to evening dressing in sizes 14 to 24 and 14P to 22P. Through Elisabeth's high attention to design, quality, and fit, it has become a market leader.

Claiborne:

Men's Sportswear and Men's Furnishings. Liz Claiborne, Inc., launched into the men's market in 1985 with our Claiborne sportswear division and in 1987 with men's furnishings. Furnishings include men's dress shirts and ties, while our men's sportswear incorporates the same high level of fashion and quality as offered in our women's sportswear areas.

Crazy Horse:

Acquired in 1992, Crazy Horse is a casual line with a young and modern attitude that is merchandised in department and specialty stores. Its fashion-forward appearance appeals to a younger customer.

Russ:

Also acquired in 1992, Russ offers career as well as casual dressing and is displayed in the moderate areas of department stores.

The Villager:

The Villager, acquired in 1992 along with Crazy Horse and Russ, focuses on career clothing but offers some casual wear as well. It will be distributed to national and regional chain department stores. Thus, with these three new labels, Liz Claiborne, Inc., has expanded both its product offerings and its distribution to include moderate career and casual dressing.

EXHIBIT 1
concluded

Accessories:

Includes Handbags/Small Leather Goods and Fashion Accessories.
Our fashion accessories, organized in 1980, include scarves, belts, hats, tights, socks, and hair accessories. Also introduced in 1980 were Liz Claiborne handbags and small leather goods. Many of the Liz Claiborne accessories are designed and developed to coordinate with our sportswear and can be used for anything from work to play. Recently, the Accessories division launched our bodywear, offering the same fit, fashion, and quality of all Liz Claiborne products.

Shoes:

Shoes and Sport Shoes. Also designed to coordinate and complement our sportswear, Liz Claiborne, Inc., moved into the shoe market in 1981. This division includes casual shoes, dress shoes, and, as of 1991, fashionable and athletic sport shoes. Of course, like all our apparel divisions, all styles are comfortable and of the highest fashion sense.

Jewelry:

Liz Claiborne, Inc., also offers a wide range of fashion jewelry designed for both casual and work. Many of the designs coordinate with the seasonal apparel trends and colors. Introduced in 1990, this division offers a full range of jewelry including earrings, necklaces, bracelets, and pins.

Cosmetics

Our Cosmetics division was launched in 1987 and consists of a collection of fragrances that captures and completes the whole Liz Claiborne attitude. The first, our signature fragrance, is entitled Liz Claiborne and is bottled in Liz Claiborne's trademark triangle. Claiborne for men was developed in 1989, followed by Realities in 1990. In the Fall of 1993, Liz Claiborne, Inc., will be launching its new fragrance, Vivid. Various complimentary fragrance items are also carried in the lines, including shampoo, conditioners, and body lotion, to name a few.

---

department store space. Their perfume, "Liz Claiborne," has been particularly successful. The versatile scent was conceived to be worn around the clock, at work or out on the town; it was based on Liz Claiborne's instinctive preferences rather than on market research, as was the triangle-shaped logo and the red, yellow, and blue color scheme for the packaging.

10   The company also carved out a niche for itself marketing to the "forgotten" woman. Over 30 percent of adult women are overweight. Liz Claiborne, Inc., entered the large-sized women's clothing market with its Elisabeth line, which successfully serves a long-neglected group of consumers by offering large-sized sportswear that provides the excellent fit, fashion, and quality of its regular sportswear lines. The gambit has paid off, and Liz Claiborne, Inc., has plans to continue extending the Elisabeth line. In yet another ploy to extend its markets and increase its sales, Liz Claiborne, Inc., has ignored the industry standard of four seasons and has opted for six seasonal lines to offer women clothes they can wear right away and to allow for a constant flow of new merchandise to generate consumer interest. The net result of the company's versatility and market savvy: Liz Claiborne outfits more women than any other designer.

11   To stay on top of its huge volume of business, Liz Claiborne uses both direct customer feedback, and a unique computerized system, SURF (System Updated Retail Feedback), which provides weekly sales trends reports on what is and isn't selling nationwide. At the end of each week, data on sales, styles, sizes, and colors are reviewed by division heads to determine both short- and long-term planning needs. Most importantly, SURF allows the company to respond quickly to mistakes. For example, for the Spring 1988 season, Liz Claiborne had decided to fall in line with current trends—and market miniskirts. When it became obvious through SURF that the company's regular customers had no intention of baring their thighs, Liz Claiborne was able to adjust their Fall 1988 designs quickly and order longer skirts for the fall fashion season to avoid losing loyal customers.

12   Nevertheless, Liz Claiborne, Inc., has had a few disappointments, such as its girls' line for 5-to-12-year-olds begun in 1984, but phased out in 1987. Also, 1992 sales of the men's sportswear and furnishings

lines were a big disappointment, falling 24.6 percent; as a result, the Claiborne collection of men's sportswear, originally styled for young customers, has shifted to a more upscale, conservative look.

13   While saturation is always a possibility, especially as the core sportswear line matures, Liz Claiborne works hard to stay one step ahead of the game. Recently the company saw in the moderate market, which targets working women with more sophisticated, yet reasonably priced clothes than those at The Gap or The Limited stores, the potential for new business and a broadened customer base. In 1992, Liz Claiborne entered the moderate women's sportswear market by acquiring Russ Togs (Russ, Crazy Horse, and The Villager labels), which broadened their distribution by expanding Liz Claiborne's position in both national and regional chain department stores, in addition to the moderate areas of traditional department stores.

LIZ CLAIBORNE: 1993

14   Liz Claiborne, Inc., markets its various lines primarily through 3,500 leading department stores such as Bloomingdale's, Filene's, Lord & Taylor, Macy's, and Jordan Marsh, delivering a consistent product at a fair price. Within these stores, the company usually sets up "Liz Claiborne boutiques," which carry the full line of Liz merchandise to allow for one-stop shopping for women who don't have time to shop (the store within a store concept pioneered by Ralph Lauren).

15   However, because many of its best retailers were in financial trouble, Liz Claiborne made an ambitious move into retailing. By 1993, the company had opened 16 Liz Claiborne company-owned retail stores, 39 First Issue stores, and 55 outlet stores nationwide. The 16 company-owned retail stores help give Liz Claiborne fashions a unique identity, and play an important role in testing new products and new merchandising ideas, functioning as laboratories to observe consumer taste and measure reactions to such elements as fit, selling, size, group, and fabric. The company also owns three Elisabeth retail stores.

16   The 39 First Issue stores, opened in 1993, are designed to compete with retailers like The Limited and The Gap. The stores exclusively market First Issue merchandise, related separates and basics similar to Liz Claiborne sportswear but less career oriented, designed by a separate team and priced approximately 15 percent lower than the Liz Claiborne label lines.

17   Liz Claiborne also has 55 outlet stores where they sell unsold merchandise from previous seasons, providing the company with control over the disposition of unsold inventories. The outlets are deliberately located at some distance from the department and specialty stores where Liz products are regularly sold in order to preserve brand image.

18   Since many segments of the U.S. fashion industry are maturing, overseas markets represent new and substantial sources of growth for U.S. designers. An internationally recognized brand name and world-wide advertising campaign are critical to competing successfully in European and Asian markets. To effectively market its products outside the United States, Liz Claiborne, Inc., is tailoring its sales strategies specifically for each country. To date, Liz Claiborne has met with some success in Canada and England, where women tend to shop and dress like Americans, but less success in other parts of the world. One problem lies in the fact that Liz Claiborne is essentially a department store line in the United States, while in Europe most business is done in small boutiques. In some British stores, Liz Claiborne is leasing space and selling their goods themselves. In Japan the company is selling through a mail order catalog in addition to two Liz Claiborne stores that were opened in Tokyo during Fall 1993. International expansion has, however, suffered the adverse impact of recessions in both Europe and Japan.

INTERNATIONAL MANUFACTURING

19   Currently, 100 percent of Liz Claiborne's product lines are manufactured overseas. Global outsourcing is widespread in the textile industry, capitalizing on lower labor and production costs at overseas manufacturing sites. Outsourcing creates the flexibility to shift production to various sites depending on wage differentials. Yet many of these sites have high risk due to the political and economic instability of

developing and Third World countries. Nevertheless, very few firms have manufacturing facilities in the United States, so they vary their sources by using a combination of domestic, Caribbean, and foreign sources to ensure minimal instability. However, scattered production sites can jeopardize quality control. In addition, reliance on foreign suppliers is not without its disadvantages, since those suppliers are not always consistent, and cannot be easily relied upon to operate on the tight schedules necessitated by the time pressures of an industry that turns around four to six seasonal lines a year.

20   U.S. import regulations are currently favorable for retailers, which further contributes to the marketing of goods made overseas; however, these conditions are subject to change. As imports rise, quota restrictions are more strictly enforced; and recently, the government has shifted to a more protectionist policy. The garment industry has been criticized both for exporting U.S. manufacturing jobs and for exploiting foreign labor. Indeed, the shift of clothing production to overseas sites has been economically significant for the United States because "apparel production alone employs more people than the entire printing and publishing field and more than the automobile manufacturing industry."[3]

WOMEN'S WORK

21   Liz Claiborne, Inc., has a long-standing commitment to the welfare of others, especially women. In the past, the Liz Claiborne Foundation, funded by company profits, actively assisted organizations involved in social welfare programs, for example, helping the homeless, serving people with AIDS and their families, and enhancing opportunities for underprivileged children. The company also strongly encourages its employees to volunteer and support local nonprofit organizations.

22   Over the years Liz Claiborne has learned a great deal about the lives of the women who buy their products—about their careers, their dreams, and their struggles outside of work. The company wanted both to give something back to the millions of women who had contributed to the company's success, and to contribute to social change by making a difference in peoples lives. To do so, Liz Claiborne, Inc., recently developed "Women's Work." "Women's Work" develops and funds multi-year, nationwide programs designed to heighten awareness of social problems and encourage positive social change with regard to issues of particular concern to women and their families, such as domestic violence and work-family conflicts.

23   The specific "Women's Work" project supported in each target community is based on issues of particular concern to that community, for example, domestic violence in San Francisco, Boston, and Miami; the needs and concerns of working mothers in Chicago. In San Francisco, Boston, and Miami, Liz Claiborne builds innovative, collaborative partnerships with organizations active in confronting domestic violence. In Chicago, a local artist and children from a local elementary school published a book that addresses the impact of working mothers on their families, especially their children. All proceeds resulting from the sale of the book are donated to literacy programs nationwide.

24   In 1993, to coincide with National Domestic Violence Awareness Month, Liz Claiborne launched domestic violence awareness programs in Boston and Miami, and formed a partnership with the Jane Doe Safety Fund sponsored by the Massachusetts Coalition of Battered Women. To raise money for the fund, Claiborne solicited the help of Barbara Kruger, a contemporary artist whose work advocates social change. The Fund's public awareness campaign on domestic violence includes billboards, city bus signs, transit stop posters, and educational brochures (Exhibits 2A and 2B), as well as broadcast and print public service announcements. Additionally, Liz Claiborne launched a collection of special commemorative products (Exhibit 3), which can be purchased at local Liz Claiborne stores, participating department stores, or through a special toll-free number, whose proceeds will be donated to domestic violence programs such as the Jane Doe Safety Fund in Boston. Liz Claiborne has also donated money to establish the first centralized 24-hour domestic violence hot line, which the company hopes will become permanent with the support of local foundations and organizations.

25   "Women's Work" is a way for Liz Claiborne, Inc., to give something back to the communities and the American women who have contributed to Liz Claiborne's success by funding programs for the future welfare of women. In addition, Liz Claiborne, Inc., is exploring the possibility of sponsoring educational programs about the detection and treatment of breast cancer, and already offers free

EXHIBIT 2A

mammograms to all its women employees. While the company acknowledges that they do not expect sales to increase as a result of the Liz Claiborne Foundation or "Women's Work," they hope that by responding to concerns important to women and their families, "Women's Work" will reinforce Liz Claiborne, Inc.'s reputation as a company that cares.

1993: THE WRONG PRODUCT—AND TOO MUCH OF IT

26   By the late 1980s, Liz Claiborne had branched beyond clothes for working women into petites, large sizes, accessories, fragrances, men's clothing, and other lines. With so much to watch over, managers began to lose their focus on the core merchandise. Customers yawned at many outfits, which too often repeated past styles. Retailers, who had allowed Liz Claiborne's presence in their stores to reach King Kong–like proportions, say top managers were slow to admit the problem. According to a former senior Claiborne executive: "If the product didn't sell, it was always someone else's fault. The buyers didn't show it right, or it wasn't delivered in the right way. They didn't allow themselves to think that maybe they just weren't listening to the customer."[4]

27   1993 was a difficult year for Liz Claiborne. A weak retail environment, conservative buying by customers, the start-up costs associated with the Russ Division, and the surprise resignation of Jay Margolis in July 1993 led industry analysts to question the strength of Liz Claiborne, Inc. Sales were flat for the first nine months of 1993 and earnings dropped by 40 percent in the third quarter after double-digit declines in the first and second quarters. The consensus opinion on the problem: the wrong product and too much of it.

28   The following excerpt appeared in the January 1994 edition of *SmartMoney* magazine:

EXHIBIT 2B

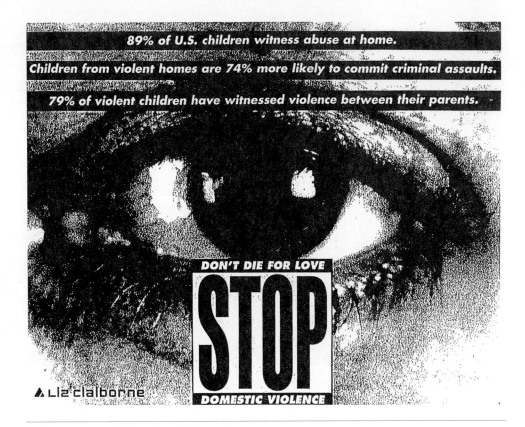

In late 1992, Louis Lowenstein, a Claiborne director, bragged that the apparel maker's balance sheet was so solid it would bring tears to [his] mother's eyes. Save the hanky. Investors watched Liz's earnings slide all year. The company overestimated shopper's appetites after a strong 1992 Christmas season and made too many clothes. Then its uninspired 1993 fashion collections failed to entice thrift shoppers. The inventory overload prevented Liz from being able to react quickly to the slow retail environment, causing profits to slide an estimated 40% for the year. Liz Claiborne's stock traded at $42.38 on January 7, 1993 and was $18.13 on October 21, 1993.

Clearly, 1993 was a disappointing year for Liz Claiborne, Inc.

THE OUTLOOK FOR THE FUTURE

29   Consumers today are demanding more and are adamant about paying less. A global economy has given them a "sultan's power to command exactly what they want, the way they want it, when they want it, and at a price that will make [companies] weep."[5] Companies will have to either meet these expectations or be forced out of business by those competitors that do.

30   The prolonged recession, low consumer confidence, a four-year national decline in per capita clothing spending, and numerous bankruptcies among several of the nation's largest department stores have wreaked havoc in the apparel industry. Many companies are cutting costs through sophisticated inventory control systems and computer-aided design and manufacturing, as well as enhanced fabric production systems. But the industry must also comply with federal legislation that regulates

EXHIBIT 3A

WOMEN'S WORK
Liz claiborne, inc.

Contact: Maria Kalligeros/Lisa Schmidt
Patrice Tanaka & Company, Inc.
(212) 505-9332

LIZ CLAIBORNE, INC. TO LAUNCH COMMEMORATIVE COLLECTION; PROCEEDS WILL BENEFIT DOMESTIC VIOLENCE ORGANIZATIONS

Items Feature Special Images by Artist Barbara Kruger

COMMEMORATIVE COLLECTION

To increase awareness of domestic violence, Liz Claiborne, Inc. will be launching a special collection of products, proceeds from which will raise funds for domestic violence organizations. Each piece in the collection features contemporary artist **Barbara Kruger's** striking red, black and white images and the message, "DON'T DIE FOR LOVE – STOP DOMESTIC VIOLENCE," specially commissioned by Liz Claiborne, Inc. for this program. Startling statistics, running across the top and bottom of the image, read – "Every 12 seconds a woman is beaten in the U.S." and "52% of female murder victims are killed by their partners."

ITEMS AVAILABLE VIA PHONE ORDER

<u>T-Shirt</u> ($12) in white 100% cotton. Available in X-large with the image silk screened on the front.

<u>Tote Bag</u> ($20) in natural color canvas (15" x 13" x 5") silk screened with the image on the front. Natural color twill straps, a zippered center section and two zippered interior compartments.

Over...

THE WOMEN'S WORK PROGRAM IS SUPPORTED AND FUNDED BY **LIZ** CLAIBORNE, INC.

WOMEN'S WORK, c/o PT&Co.,141 Fifth Avenue, New York, NY 10010 212·505·9332 Fax 212·505·9928

EXHIBIT 3B

LIZ CLAIBORNE, INC. COMMEMORATIVE COLLECTION/FACT SHEET   page 2

	<u>Baseball Cap</u> ($10) in black twill with the Kruger message silk screened in red and white above the brim. Available in adjustable one-size-fits-all.
PHONE ORDERING INFORMATION	The collection can be ordered by calling 1-800-449-STOP (1-800-449-7867). American Express, VISA, Mastercard, checks or money orders will be accepted; New York/New Jersey residents must add sales tax. Shipping is <u>not</u> included. Consumers should allow four to six weeks for delivery.
ITEMS AVAILABLE AT RETAIL	The **T-shirt, tote bag, baseball cap** *and:* <u>Mug</u> ($6) in white featuring the Kruger image in red and black. <u>Sunglasses</u> ($15) are a classic black frame with the Kruger message displayed on the outside of each lens. View is unobstructed for the wearer.

RETAIL LOCATIONS	• several Boston-area Filene's
	
	 • Burdines stores in Miami's Dade and Broward Counties
	
	 • Museum shops nationwide
	
	 • Liz Claiborne Stores:
	  -Copley Place, Boston, MA
	  -Town Center, Boca Raton, FL
	
	 • Selected campus stores

WHO DO PROCEEDS BENEFIT?	• <u>Through 800 #</u>: The Family Violence Prevention Fund, a national, non-profit organization devoted to public policy, education and advocacy. • <u>In Miami</u>: The Women's Fund of Dade County which will administer grants to local domestic violence programs. • <u>In Boston</u>: The Jane Doe Safety Fund, a statewide fundraising and public education campaign of the Massachusetts Coalition of Battered Women Service Groups.

# # #

competition and requires product labeling with content and care instructions designed to protect consumers, both of which contribute to higher costs.

31   At the same time, Americans are changing the way they shop. Many designers, including Liz Claiborne, rely on large department stores located in shopping malls for a large percentage of their

sales. However, the appeal of shopping malls is diminishing and the trend is toward specialty stores. Consumers, especially women, have less time to shop, so convenience is becoming even more important than it already was.

32   Clearly, for 1994 and beyond, questions abound. Liz Claiborne, Inc., must rethink both its product lines and its entire marketing strategy, considering whether it has grown too fast, spread itself too thin, and/or set itself up to compete with itself by branching out into retailing lines under other labels that are too similar to its own name-brand lines. The company must also consider how best to fill the void left by the departure of Liz Claiborne herself, clearly a visionary who carved out a fashion empire that may now be on the brink of decline.

CONSOLIDATED STATEMENTS OF INCOME
Liz Claiborne, Inc. and Subsidiaries

	Fiscal Years Ended		
All dollar amounts in thousands except per common share data	December 25, 1993	December 26, 1992	December 28, 1991
Net Sales	$2,204,297	$2,194,330	$2,007,177
Cost of goods sold	1,453,381	1,364,214	1,207,502
Gross Profit	750,916	830,116	799,675
Selling, general and administrative expenses	568,286	507,541	471,060
Operating Income	182,630	322,575	328,615
Investment and other income—net	16,151	19,349	22,133
Income Before Provision for Income Taxes and Cumulative Effect of a Change in Accounting Principle	198,781	341,924	350,748
Provision for income taxes	73,500	123,100	128,000
Income Before Cumulative Effect of a Change in Accounting Principle	125,281	218,824	222,748
Cumulative effect of a change in the method of accounting for income taxes	1,643	—	—
Net Income	$ 126,924	$ 218,824	$ 222,748
Earnings per Common Share:			
Income Before Cumulative Effect of a Change in Accounting Principle	$ 1.54	$ 2.61	$ 2.61
Cumulative effect of a change in the method of accounting for income taxes	.02	—	—
Net Income per Common Share	$ 1.56	$ 2.61	$ 2.61
Dividends Paid per Common Share	$ .44	$ .39	$ .33

The accompanying notes to consolidated financial statements are an integral part of these statements.

CONSOLIDATED BALANCE SHEETS
Liz Claiborne, Inc. and Subsidiaries

All amounts in thousands except share data	December 25, 1993	December 26, 1992
ASSETS		
Current Assets:		
Cash and cash equivalents	$ 104,720	$ 130,721
Marketable securities	204,571	294,892
Accounts receivable—trade	174,435	200,183
Inventories	436,593	385,879
Deferred income tax benefits	15,065	13,907
Other current assets	69,055	55,384
Total current assets	1,004,439	1,080,966
Property and Equipment—net	202,068	145,695
Other Assets	29,831	29,647
	$1,236,338	$1,256,308
LIABILITIES AND STOCKHOLDERS' EQUITY		
Current Liabilities:		
Accounts payable	$ 141,126	$ 138,738
Accrued expenses	97,765	87,330
Income taxes payable	15,547	22,109
Total current liabilities	254,438	248,177
Long-Term Debt	1,334	1,434
Deferred Income Taxes	2,275	8,922
Commitments and Contingencies		
Stockholders' Equity:		
Preferred stock, $.01 par value, authorized shares—50,000,000, issued shares—none	—	—
Common stock, $1 par value, authorized shares—250,000,000, issued shares—88,218,617	88,219	88,219
Capital in excess of par value	56,699	55,528
Retained earnings	1,123,413	1,034,280
Cumulative translation adjustment	(1,279)	(1,410)
	1,267,052	1,176,617
Common stock in treasury, at cost—9,371,217 shares in 1993 and 5,436,864 shares in 1992	(288,761)	(178,842)
Total stockholders' equity	978,291	997,775
	$1,236,338	$1,256,308

The accompanying notes to consolidated financial statements are an integral part of these statements.

LIZ CLAIBORNE
Five-Year Sales, Net Income, and EPS
Summary
(in thousands)

Year	Sales	Net Income	EPS
1993	$2,204,297	$126,924	$1.56
1992	2,194,330	218,824	2.61
1991	2,007,177	222,748	2.61
1990	1,728,868	205,800	2.37
1989	1,410,677	164,591	1.87

5-year growth rate: Sales: 11.8; net income: −6.2;
and EPS: −4.4.

ENDNOTES

1. Morris, Michele, "The Wizard of Working Women's Wardrobe," *Working Woman*, June 1988, p. 74.
2. Better, Nancy Marx, "The Secret of Liz Claiborne's Success," *Working Woman*, April 1992, p. 68.
3. Guenciro, Miriam, and Jeannette Jarnow, *Inside the Fashion Industry*, 5th ed. (New York: MacMillian Publishing Company, 1991), p. 5.
4. Caminiti, Susan, " Liz Claiborne: How to Get Focused Again," *Fortune*, January 24, 1994, p. 85
5. Jacob, Rahul, "Beyond Quality and Value," *Fortune*, Autumn/Winter 1993, p. 8.

CASE 3

PERDUE FARMS, INC.—1994

BACKGROUND/COMPANY HISTORY

> I have a theory that you can tell the difference between those who have inherited a fortune and those who have made a fortune. Those who have made their own fortune forget not where they came from and are less likely to lose touch with the common man. (Bill Sterling, "Just Browsin' " column in *Eastern Shore News*, March 2, 1988)

1 In 1917, Arthur W. Perdue, a Railway Express agent and descendent of a French Huguenot family named Perdeaux, bought 50 leghorn chickens for a total of $5 and began selling table eggs near the small town of Salisbury, Maryland. A region immortalized in James Michener's *Chesapeake*, it is alternately known as the "Eastern Shore" or the "Delmarva Peninsula" and includes parts of Delaware, Maryland and Virginia.

2 Initially, the business amounted to little more than a farm wife's chore for "pin money," raising a few "biddies" in a cardboard box behind the wood stove in the kitchen until they were old enough to fend for themselves in the barnyard. But, in 1920, when Railway Express asked "Mr. Arthur" to move to a station away from the Eastern Shore, at age 36 he quit his job as Salisbury's Railway Express agent and entered the egg business full-time. His only child, Franklin Parsons Perdue, was born that same year.

3 Mr. Arthur soon expanded his egg market and began shipments to New York. Practicing small economies such as mixing his own chicken feed and using leather from his old shoes to make hinges for his chicken coops, he stayed out of debt and prospered. He tried to add a new chicken coop every year. By the time young Frank was 10, he had 50 chickens or so of his own to look after, earning money from their eggs. He worked along with his parents, not always enthusiastically, to feed the chickens, clean the coops, dig the cesspools, and gather and grade eggs. A shy introverted country boy, he went for five years to a one-room school, eventually graduated from Wicomico High School, and attended the State Teachers College in Salisbury for two years before returning to the farm in 1939 to work full-time with his father.

4 By 1940, it was obvious to father and son that the future lay in selling chickens, not eggs. But, the Perdues made the shift to selling broilers only after careful attention to every detail—a standard Perdue procedure in the years to come. In 1944, Mr. Arthur made his son Frank a full partner in what was then A. W. Perdue and Son, Inc., a firm already known for quality products and fair dealing in a toughly competitive business. In 1950, Frank took over leadership of Perdue Farms, a company with 40 employees. By 1952, revenues were $6,000,000 from the sale of 2,600,000 broilers.

5 By 1967, annual sales had increased to about $35,000,000 but it was becoming increasingly clear that additional profits lay in processing chickens. Frank recalled in an interview for *Business Week* (September 15, 1972) "processors were paying us 10 cents a live pound for what cost us 14 cents to produce. Suddenly, processors were making as much as 7 cents a pound."

This case was prepared by George C. Rubenson and Frank Shipper of Salisbury State University and Jean M. Hanebury of Texas A&M University, Corpus Christi.

Acknowledgments: The authors are indebted to Frank Perdue, Jim Perdue, and the numerous associates at Perdue Farms, Inc., who generously shared their time and information about the company. In addition, the authors would like to thank the anonymous librarians who routinely review area newspapers and file articles about the poultry industry—the most important industry on the Delmarva peninsula. Without their assistance, this case would not be possible.

6   A cautious, conservative planner, Arthur Perdue had not been eager for expansion and Frank Perdue himself was reluctant to enter poultry processing. But, economic forces dictated the move and, in 1968, Perdue Farms became a vertically integrated operation, hatching eggs, delivering the chicks to contract growers, buying grain, supplying the feed and litter, and, finally, processing the broilers and shipping them to market.

7   The company bought its first plant in 1968, a Swift and Company operation in Salisbury, renovated it, and equipped it with machines capable of processing 14,000 broilers per hour. Computers were soon employed to devise feeding formulas for each stage of growth so birds reached their growth potential sooner. Geneticists were hired to breed larger-breasted chickens and veterinarians were put on staff to keep the flocks healthy, while nutritionists handled the feed formulations to achieve the best feed conversion.

8   From the beginning, Frank Perdue refused to permit his broilers to be frozen for shipping, a process that resulted in unappetizing black bones and loss of flavor and moistness when cooked. Instead, Perdue chickens were (and some still are) shipped to market packed in ice, justifying the company's advertisements at that time that it sold only "fresh, young broilers." However, this policy also limited the company's market to those locations that could be serviced overnight from the Eastern Shore of Maryland. Thus, Perdue chose for its primary markets the densely populated towns and cities of the East Coast, particularly New York City, which consumes more Perdue chicken than all other brands combined.

9   During the 1970s, the firm entered the Baltimore, Philadelphia, Boston, and Providence markets. Facilities were expanded rapidly to include a new broiler processing plant and protein conversion plant in Accomac, Virginia; a processing plant in Lewiston, North Carolina; a hatchery in Murfreesboro, North Carolina; and several Swift and Company facilities including a processing plant in Georgetown, Delaware; a feedmill in Bridgeville, Delaware; and a feedmill in Elkin, North Carolina.

10 In 1977, Mr. Arthur died at the age of 91, leaving behind a company with annual sales of nearly $200 million, an average annual growth rate of 17 percent compared to an industry average of 1 percent a year, the potential for processing 78,000 broilers per hour, and annual production of nearly 350 million pounds of poultry per year. Frank Perdue, who says without a hint of self-deprecation that "I am a B-minus student. I know how smart I am. I know a B-minus is not as good as an A," said of his father simply, "I learned everything from him."

11 Stew Leonard, owner of a huge supermarket in Norwalk, Connecticut, and one of Perdue's top customers, describes Frank Perdue as "What you see is what you get. If you ask him a question you will get an answer." Perdue disapproves the presence of a union between himself and his associates and adds, "The absence of unions makes for a better relationship with our associates. If we treat our associates right, I don't think we will have a union." On conglomerates, he states, "Diversification is the most dangerous word in the English language." His business philosophy is, "I'm interested in being the best rather than the biggest. Expansion is OK if it has a positive effect on product quality. I'll do nothing that detracts from product quality."

12 Frank Perdue is known for having a temper. He is as hard on himself, however, as he is on others, readily admitting his shortcomings and even his mistakes. For example, in the 70s, he apparently briefly discussed using the influence of some unsavory characters to help alleviate union pressure. When an investigative reporter in the late 1980s asked him about this instance, he admitted that it was a mistake, saying "it was probably the dumbest thing I ever did."

13 In 1981, Frank Perdue was in Massachusetts for his induction into the Babson College Academy of Distinguished Entrepreneurs, an award established in 1978 to recognize the spirit of free enterprise and business leadership. Babson College President Ralph Z. Sorenson inducted Perdue into the academy, which, at that time, numbered 18 men and women from four continents. Perdue had the following to say to the college students:

> There are none, nor will there ever be, easy steps for the entrepreneur. Nothing, absolutely nothing, replaces the willingness to work earnestly, intelligently towards a goal. You have to be willing to pay the price. You have to have an insatiable appetite for detail, have to be willing to accept constructive criticism, to ask questions, to be fiscally responsible, to surround yourself with good people and most of all, to listen. (Frank Perdue, speech at Babson College, April 28, 1981).

14   The early 1980s proved to be a period of further growth as Perdue diversified and broadened its market. New marketing areas included Washington, D.C.; Richmond, Virginia; and Norfolk, Virginia. Additional facilities were opened in Cofield, Kenly, Halifax, Robbins, and Robersonville, North Carolina. The firm broadened its line to include value added products such as "Oven Stuffer" roasters and "Perdue Done It!," a new brand of fresh, prepared chicken products featuring cooked chicken breast nuggets, cutlets, and tenders. James A. (Jim) Perdue, Frank's only son, joined the company as a management trainee in 1983.

15   But, the latter 1980s also tested the mettle of the firm. Following a period of considerable expansion and concentric diversification, a consulting firm was brought in to recommend ways to cope with the new complexity. Believing that the span of control was too broad, the consulting firm recommended that strategic business units, responsible for their own operations, be formed. In other words, the firm should decentralize.

16   Soon after, the chicken market leveled off and eventually began to decline. At one point the firm was losing as much as $1 million a week and, in 1988, Perdue Farms experienced its first year in the red. Unfortunately, the decentralization had created duplication of duties and enormous administrative costs. Management information systems costs, for example, had tripled. The firm's rapid plunge into turkeys and other food processing, where it had little experience, contributed to the losses. Waste and inefficiency had permeated the company. Characteristically, Frank Perdue took the firm back to basics, concentrating on efficiency of operations, improving communications throughout the company, and paying close attention to detail.

17   On June 2, 1989, Frank celebrated 50 years with Perdue Farms, Inc. At a morning reception in downtown Salisbury, the Governor of Maryland proclaimed it "Frank Perdue Day." The Governors of Delaware and Virginia did the same.

18   The 1990s have been dominated by market expansion to North Carolina; Atlanta, Georgia; Pittsburgh, Pennsylvania; Cleveland, Ohio; Chicago, Illinois; and Florida. New product lines have included fresh ground chicken, fresh ground turkey, sweet Italian turkey sausage, turkey breakfast sausage, fun-shaped chicken breast nuggets in star and drumstick shapes, and BBQ and oven roasted chicken parts in the "Perdue Done It!" line. A new "Fit 'n Easy" label was introduced as part of a nutrition campaign using skinless, boneless chicken and turkey products.

Jim, Frank, and Mr. Arthur Perdue—three generations of Perdue Farms leadership.

19   In 1991, 12,500 associates and 3,000 producers generated an estimated $1.2 billion in revenue. Frank was named Chairman of the Executive Committee and Jim Perdue became Chairman of the Board. Sitting in the small unpretentious office that had been his dad's for 40 years, Jim looked out the window at the house where he had grown up, the broiler houses Frank built in the 1940s, his grandfather's homestead across the road where Frank was born, and a modern hatchery. "Dad would come home for dinner, then come back here and work into the early hours of the morning. There's a fold-out cot behind that credenza. He got by on three or hour hours of sleep a night."

MISSION STATEMENT AND STATEMENT OF VALUES

20   From the beginning, Mr. Arthur's motto had been to "create a quality product, be aware of your customers, deal fairly with people, and work hard, work hard, work hard." In a speech in September 1991 to the firm's leaders, accountants, and Perdue associates, Frank reiterated these values, saying:

> If you were to ask me what was the biggest factor in whatever success we have enjoyed, I would answer that it was not technology, or economic resources, or organizational structure. It . . . has been our conscious decision that, in order to be successful, we must have a sound set of beliefs on which we premise all our policies and actions . . . Central to these beliefs is our emphasis on quality . . . Quality is no accident. It is the one absolutely necessary ingredient of all the most successful companies in the world.

21   The centrality of quality to the firm is featured in its mission statement and its statement of values. To ensure that all associates know what the company's mission, quality policy, values, and annual goals are, managers receive a fold-up, wallet size card with them on it (see Exhibit 1).

SOCIAL RESPONSIBILITY

22   To realize its corporate statement of values, Perdue Farms works hard to be a good corporate citizen. Two areas in which this is especially clear are its code of ethics and its efforts to minimize the environmental damage it causes.

Code of Ethics

23   Perdue Farms has taken the somewhat unusual step of setting forth explicitly the ethical standards it expects all associates to follow. Specifically, the code of ethics calls upon associates to conduct every aspect of business in the full spirit of honest and lawful behavior. Further, all salaried associates and certain hourly associates are required to sign a statement acknowledging that they understand the code and are prepared to comply with it. Associates are expected to report to their supervisor dishonest or illegal activities as well as possible violations of the code. If the supervisor does not provide a satisfactory response, the employee is expected to contact either the Vice President for Human Resources or the Vice President of their division. The code notes that any Perdue manager who initiates or encourages reprisal against any person who reports a violation commits a serious violation of the code.

Minimizing Environmental Damage

24   Historically, chicken processing has been the focus of special interest groups whose interests range from animal rights to repetitive-motion disorders to environmental causes. Perdue Farms has accepted the challenge of striving to maintain an environmentally friendly workplace as a goal that requires the commitment of all of its associates, from Frank Perdue down. Frank Perdue states it best: "We know that we must be good neighbors environmentally. We have an obligation not to pollute, to police ourselves, and to be better than EPA requires us to be."

EXHIBIT 1
PERDUE Farms Mission Statement, Quality Policy, Statement of Values, and Company Goals, 1995

Mission Statement

Our mission is to provide the highest quality poultry and poultry-related products to retail and food service customers.

We want to be the recognized industry leader in quality and service, providing more than expected for our customers, associates, and owners.

We will accomplish this by maintaining a tradition of pride in our products, growth through innovation, integrity in the management of our business, and commitment to Team Management and the Quality Improvement Process.

Quality Policy

We shall produce products and provide services at all times which meet or exceed the expectations of our customers.

We shall not be content to be of equal quality to our competitors.

Our commitment is to be increasingly superior.

Contribution to quality is a responsibility shared by everyone in the Perdue organization

Statement of Values

Our success as a company, and as individuals working at Perdue, depend upon:

· Meeting customer needs with the best quality, innovative food and food-related products and services.

· Associates being team members in the business and having opportunities to influence, make contributions, and reach their full potential.

· Working together as business partners by implementing the principles of the QIP so that mutual respect, trust, and a commitment to being the best are shared among associates, customers, producers, and suppliers.

· Achieving the long-term goals of the company and providing economic stability and a rewarding future for all associates through well-planned, market-driving growth.

· Being the best in our industry in profitability as a low-cost producer, realizing that our customers won't pay for our inefficiencies.

· Staying ahead of the competition by investing our profits to provide a safe work environment; to pay competitive wages; to maintain up-to-date facilities, equipment, and processes; and to create challenging opportunities for associates.

· Serving the communities in which we do business with resources, time, and the creative energies of our associates.

FY 1995 Company Goals

People—provide a safe, secure, and productive work environment.

· Improve workplace safety. Measurements include reduction in lost-time accidents and per-capita workers compensation cost.

· Improve associate satisfaction. Goal is completion of associate survey throughout the company.

Products—Provide the highest quality products and services at competitive costs.

· Improve consumer satisfaction. Measured by consumer rating of the brand.

· Improve the "Customer Service Satisfaction Index" (CSI). Each division has an individual improvement goal.

· Improve Perdue quality spread over competition. Measurements include plant-weighted ranking scores and quality consistency scores.

Profitability—grow profitably.

· Achieve planned ROE target.

· Improve competitiveness. Measurement is Agrimetrics IOE deviation in Fresh Poultry, Perdue Foods, and Turkey.

25   For example, over the years, the industry had explored many alternative ways of disposing of dead birds. Perdue research provided the solution—small composters on each farm. Using this approach, dead birds are reduced to an end product that resembles soil in a matter of a few days. This has become a major environmental activity. Another environmental challenge is the disposal of hatchery wastes. Historically, manure and unhatched eggs that make up these wastes were shipped to a landfill. Perdue produces about 10 tons of this waste per day! However, Perdue has reduced the waste by 50 percent by selling the liquid fraction to a pet food processor who cooks it for protein. The other 50 percent is recycled through a rendering process. In 1990, Perdue spent $4.2 million to construct a state-of-the-art waste water treatment facility at its Accomac, Virginia, plant. This facility used forced hot air heated to 120 degrees to cause the microbes to digest all traces of ammonia, even during the cold winter months. In April 1993, the company took a major step with the creation of the Environmental Steering Committee. Its mission is "to provide all Perdue Farms work sites with vision, direction, and leadership so that they can be good corporate citizens from an environmental perspective today and in the future." The committee oversees how the company is doing in such environmentally sensitive areas as waste water, storm water, hazardous waste, solid waste, recycling, biosolids, and human health and safety.

26   Jim Perdue sums it up as follows: "we must not only comply with environmental laws as they exist today, but look to the future to make sure we don't have any surprises. We must make sure our policy statement is real, and that there's something behind it, and that we do what we say we're going to do."

MARKETING

27   In the early days, chicken was sold to groceries as a commodity, that is, producers sold it in bulk and butchers cut and wrapped it. The consumer had no idea what company grew the chicken. Frank Perdue was convinced that higher profits could be made if Perdue's products were premium quality so they could be sold at a premium price. But the only way the premium quality concept would work was if consumers asked for it by name—and that meant the product must be differentiated and "branded" to identify what the premium qualities are. Hence, the emphasis over the years on superior quality, a higher meat-to-bone ratio, and a yellow skin (the result of mixing marigold petals in the feed), which is an indicator of bird health.

28   In 1968, Perdue spent $40,000 on radio advertising. In 1969, the company spent $80,000 on radio, and in 1970 spent $160,000 split 50-50 between radio and television. The advertising agency had recommended against television advertising, but the combination worked. TV ads increased sales and Frank Perdue decided the old agency he was dealing with did not match one of the basic Perdue tenets: "The people you deal with should be as good at what they do as you are at what you do."

29   That decision set off a storm of activity on Frank's part. In order to select a new ad agency, Frank studied intensively and personally learned more about advertising than any poultry man before him. He began a 10-week immersion on the theory and practice of advertising. He read books and papers on advertising. He talked to sales managers of every newspaper and radio and television station in the New York City area, consulted experts, and interviewed 48 ad agencies. On April 2, 1971, Perdue Farms selected Scali, McCabe, Sloves as their new advertising agency. As the agency tried to figure out how to successfully "brand" a chicken—something that had never been done—they realized that Frank Perdue was their greatest ally. "He looked a little like chicken himself, and he sounded a little like one, and he squawked a lot!" Ed McCabe, partner and chief copywriter of the firm, decided that Frank Perdue should be the firm's spokesperson. Initially Frank resisted. But, in the end, he accepted the role and the campaign based on "It takes a tough man to make a tender chicken" was born. Frank set Perdue Farms apart by educating consumers about chicken quality. The process catapulted Perdue Farms into the ranks of the top poultry producers in the country.

30   The firm's very first television commercial showed Frank on a picnic in the Salisbury City Park saying:

A chicken is what it eats . . . And my chickens eat better than people do . . . I store my own grain and mix my own feed . . . And give my Perdue chickens nothing but pure well water to drink . . . That's why my chickens always have that healthy golden yellow color . . . If you want to eat as good as my chickens, you'll just have to eat my chickens . . . Mmmm, that's really good!

31   Additional ads, touting superior quality and more breast meat read as follows:

Government standards would allow me to call this a grade A chicken . . . but my standards wouldn't. This chicken is skinny . . . It has scrapes and hairs . . . The fact is, my graders reject 30% of the chickens government inspectors accept as grade A . . . That's why it pays to insist on a chicken with my name on it . . . If you're not completely satisfied, write me and I'll give you your money back . . . Who do you write in Washington? . . . What do they know about chickens?

Never go into a store and just ask for a pound of chicken breasts . . . Because you could be cheating yourself out of some meat . . . Here's an ordinary one-pound chicken breast, and here's a one-pound breast of mine . . . They weigh the same. But as you can see, mine has more meat, and theirs have more bone. I breed the broadest breasted, meatiest chicken you can buy . . . So don't buy a chicken breast by the pound . . . Buy them by the name . . . and get an extra bite in every breast.

32   The ads paid off. In 1968, Perdue Farms held about three percent of the New York market. By 1972, one out of every six chickens eaten in New York was a Perdue chicken. Fifty-one percent of New Yorkers recognized the label. Scali, McCabe, Sloves credited Frank Perdue's "believability" for the success of the program. "This was advertising in which Perdue had a personality that lent credibility to the product." Today, 50 percent of the chickens consumed in New York are Perdue.

33   Frank had his own view. As he told a Rotary audience in Charlotte, North Carolina, in March 1989, "the product met the promise of the advertising and was far superior to the competition. Two great sayings tell it all: 'nothing will destroy a poor product as quickly as good advertising' and 'a gifted product is mightier than a gifted pen!' "

34   Today, the Perdue marketing function is unusually sophisticated. Its responsibilities include deciding (1) how many chickens and turkeys to grow; (2) what the advertising and promotion pieces should look like, where they should run, and how much the company can afford; and (3) which new products the company will pursue. The marketing plan is derived from the company's five-year

EXHIBIT 2
Milestones in the Quality Improvement Process at Perdue Farms

1924	Arthur Perdue buys leghorn roosters for $25.
1950s	Adopts the company logo of a chick under a magnifying glass.
1984	Frank Perdue attends Philip Crosby's Quality College.
1985	Perdue recognized for its pursuit of quality in "A Passion for Excellence."
	200 Perdue managers attend Quality College.
	Adopted the Quality Improvement Process (QIP).
1986	Established Corrective Action Teams (CATs).
1987	Established Quality Training for all associates.
	Implemented Error Cause Removal Process (ECR).
1988	Steering Committee formed.
1989	First Annual Quality Conference held.
	Implemented Team Management.
1990	Second Annual Quality Conference held.
	Codified Values and Corporate Mission.
1991	Third Annual Quality Conference held.
	Customer Satisfaction defined.
1992	Fourth Annual Quality Conference held.
	How to implement Customer Satisfaction explained for team leaders and QITs.

business plan and includes goals concerning volume, return on sales, market share, and profitability. The internal Marketing Department is helped by various service agencies including:

· Lowe & Partners/SMS: advertising campaigns, media buys.
· R. E. Auletta & Co.: public relations, company image.
· Gertsman & Meyers: packaging design.
· Group Williams: consumer promotional programs.
· Various research companies for focus groups, telephone surveys, and in-home-use tests.

OPERATIONS

35   Two words sum up the Perdue approach to operations—quality and efficiency—with emphasis on the first over the latter. Perdue more than most companies represents the Total Quality Management (TQM) slogan, "Quality, a journey without end." Some of the key events are listed in Exhibit 2. The pursuit of quality began with Arthur Perdue in 1924 when he purchased breeding roosters from Texas for the princely sum of $25 each. For comparison, typical wages in 1925 were $1.00 for a 10-hour workday. Frank Perdue's own pursuit of quality is legendary. One story about his pursuit of quality was told in 1968 by Ellis Wainwright, the state of Maryland grading inspector, during start-up operations at Perdue's first processing plant. Frank had told Ellis that the standards that he wanted were higher than the Government Grade A standard. The first two days had been pretty much disastrous. On the third day, as Wainwright recalls,

> We graded all morning, and I found only five boxes that passed what I took to be Frank's standards. The rest had the yellow skin color knocked off by the picking machines. I was afraid Frank was going to raise cain that I had accepted so few. Then Frank came through and rejected half of those.

36   To ensure that Perdue continues to lead the industry in quality, it buys about 2,000 pounds of competitors' products a week. Inspection associates grade these products and the information is

EXHIBIT 3
Perdue Farms Cultural Transformation

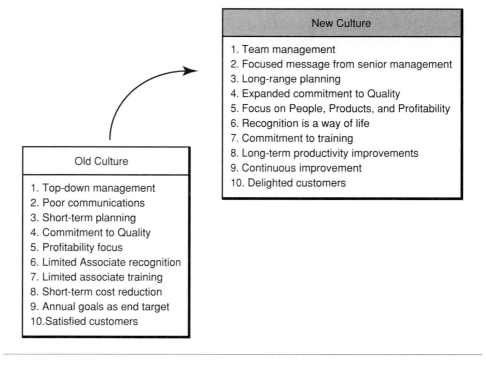

New Culture

1. Team management
2. Focused message from senior management
3. Long-range planning
4. Expanded commitment to Quality
5. Focus on People, Products, and Profitability
6. Recognition is a way of life
7. Commitment to training
8. Long-term productivity improvements
9. Continuous improvement
10. Delighted customers

Old Culture

1. Top-down management
2. Poor communications
3. Short-term planning
4. Commitment to Quality
5. Profitability focus
6. Limited Associate recognition
7. Limited associate training
8. Short-term cost reduction
9. Annual goals as end target
10. Satisfied customers

shared with the highest levels of management. In addition, the company's Quality Policy is displayed at all locations and taught to all associates in quality training (see Exhibit 1).

37 Perdue insists that nothing artificial be fed or injected into its birds. The company will not take any shortcuts in pursuit of the perfect chicken. A chemical- and steroid-free diet is fed to the chickens. Young chickens are vaccinated against disease. Selective breeding is used to improve the quality of the chickens sold. Chickens are bred to yield more breast meat because that is what the consumer wants.

38 Efficiency is improved through management of details. As a vertically integrated producer of chickens, Perdue manages every detail including breeding and hatching its own eggs, selecting growers, building Perdue-engineered chicken houses, formulating and manufacturing its own feed, overseeing care and feeding, operating its own processing plants, distributing via its own trucking fleet, and marketing. Improvements are measured in fractional cents per pound. Nothing goes to waste. The feet that used to be thrown away are now processed and sold in the Orient as a barroom delicacy.

39 Frank's knowledge of details is also legendary. He not only impresses people in the poultry industry, but those in others as well. At the end of one day the managers and engineers of a new Grumman plant in Salisbury, Maryland, were reviewing their progress. Through the door unannounced came Frank Perdue. The Grumman managers proceeded to give Frank a tour of the plant. One machine was an ink-jet printer that labeled parts as they passed. Frank said he believed he had some of those in his plants. He paused for a minute and then he asked them if it clogged often. They responded yes. Frank exclaimed excitedly, "I am sure that I got some of those!" To ensure that this attention to detail pays off, eight measurable items—hatachability, turnover, feed conversion, livability, yield, birds per man-hour, utilization, and grade—are tracked.

40 Frank Perdue credits much of his success to listening to others. He agrees with Tom Peters that "Nobody knows a person's 20 square feet better than the person who works there." To facilitate the transmission of ideas through the organization, it is undergoing a cultural transformation beginning with Frank (see Exhibit 3). He describes the transition from the old to the new culture and himself as follows:

We also learned that *loud and noisy* were worth a lot more than mugs and pens. What I mean by this is, we used to spend a lot of time calling companies to get trinkets as gifts. Gradually, we learned that money and trinkets weren't what really motivated people. We learned that when a man or woman on the line is going all out to do a good job, that he or she doesn't care that much about a trinket of some sort; what they really want is for the manager to get up from behind his desk, walk over to them and, in front of their peers, give them a hearty and sincere "thank you."

When we give recognition now, we do it when there's an audience and lots of peers can see. This is, I can tell you, a lot more motivating than the "kick in the butt," that was part of the old culture—*and I was the most guilty!"*

41   Changing the behavioral pattern from writing up people who have done something wrong to recognizing people for doing their job well has not been without some setbacks. For example, the company started what it calls the "Good Egg Award," which is good for a free lunch. Managers in the Salisbury plant were all trained and asked to distribute the awards by "catching" someone doing a good job. When the program manager checked with the cafeteria the following week to see how many had been claimed, the answer was none. A meeting of the managers was called to see how many had been handed out. The answer was none. When the managers were asked what they had done with their award certificates, the majority replied they were in their shirt pocket. A goal was set for all managers to hand out five a week.

42   The following week, the program manager still found that very few were being turned in for a free lunch. When employees were asked what they had done with their awards, they replied that they had framed them and hung them on walls at home or put them in trophy cases. The program was changed again. Now the "Good Egg Award" consists of both a certificate and a ticket for a free lunch.

43   Perdue also has a beneficial suggestion program that it calls "Error Cause Removal." It averages better than one submission per year per three employees. Although that is much less than the 22 per employee per year in Japan, it is significantly better than the national average in the United States of one per year per 5 employees. As Frank has said, "We're 'one up' . . . because with the help of the Quality Improvement Process and the help of our associates, we have *thousands* of 'better minds' helping us."

MANAGEMENT INFORMATION SYSTEMS (MIS)

44   In 1989, Perdue Farms employed 118 information systems (IS) people who spent 146 hours per week on IS maintenance—"fix it" jobs. Today, the entire department has been reduced to 50 associates who spend only 52 hours per week on "fix it," and 94 percent of their time building new systems or reengineering old ones. Even better, a six-year backlog of projects has been eliminated and the average "build-it" cost for a project has dropped from $1,950 to $568—an overall 300 percent increase in efficiency.

45   According to Don Taylor, Director of MIS, this is the payoff from a significant management reorientation. A key philosophy is that a "fix-it" mentality is counterproductive. The goal is to determine the root cause of the problem and reengineer the program to eliminate future problems.

46   Developer-user partnerships—including a monthly payback system—were developed with five functional groups: sales and marketing, finance and human resources, logistics, quality assurance, and fresh-poultry and plant systems. Each has an assigned number of IS hours per month and defines its own priorities, permitting it to function as a customer.

47   In addition, a set of critical success factors (CSFs) were developed. These include (1) automation is never the first step in a project; it occurs only after superfluous business processes are eliminated and necessary ones simplified; (2) senior management sponsorship—the vice president for the business unit—must sponsor major projects in their area; (3) limited size, duration, and scope—IS has found that small projects have more success and a cumulative bigger payoff than big ones (all major projects are broken into three- to six-month segments with separate deliverables and benefits; (4) precise definition of requirements—the team must determine up front

EXHIBIT 4
Perdue Farms, Inc., Technological Accomplishments

· Bred chickens with 15 percent more breast meat.
· First to use digital scales to guarantee weights to customers.
· First to package fully cooked chicken products on microwaveable trays.
· First to have a box lab to define quality of boxes from different suppliers.
· First to test both its chickens and competitors' chickens on 52 quality factors every week.
· Improved on-time deliveries 20 percent between 1987 and 1993.

exactly what the project will accomplish; and (5) commitment of both the IS staff and the customer to work as a team.

48   Perdue considers IS key to the operation of its business. For example, IS developed a customer ordering system for the centralized sales office (CSO). This system automated key business processes that link Perdue with its customers. The CSO includes 13 applications including order entry, product transfers, sales allocations, production scheduling, and credit management.

49   When ordering, the Perdue salesperson negotiates the specifics of the sale directly with the buyer in the grocery chain. Next, the salesperson sends the request to a dispatcher who determines where the various products are located and designates a specific truck to make the required pickups and delivery, all within the designated one-hour delivery window that has been granted by the grocery chain. Each truck is even equipped with a small satellite dish that is connected to the LAN so that a trucker on the New Jersey Turnpike headed for New York can call for a replacement tractor if his rig breaks down.

50   Obviously, a computer malfunction is a possible disaster. Four hours of downtime is equivalent to $6.2 million in lost sales. Thus, Perdue has separate systems and processes in place to avoid such problems. In addition to maximizing on-time delivery, this system gives the salespeople more time to discuss wants and needs with customers, handle customer relations, and observe key marketing issues such as Perdue shelf space and location.

51   On the other hand, Perdue does not believe that automation solves all problems. For example, it was decided that electronic monitoring in the poultry houses is counterproductive and not cost effective. While it would be possible to develop systems to monitor and control almost every facet of the chicken house environment, Perdue is concerned that doing so would weaken the invaluable link between the farmer and the livestock; Perdue believes that poultry producers need to be personally involved with conditions in the chicken house in order to maximize quality and spot problems or health challenges as soon as possible.

RESEARCH AND DEVELOPMENT

52   Perdue is an acknowledged industry leader in the use of technology to provide quality products and service to its customers. A list of some of its technological accomplishments is given in Exhibit 4. As with everything else he does, Frank Perdue tries to leave nothing to chance. Perdue employs 25 people full-time in the industry's largest research and development effort, including five with graduate degrees. It has specialists in avian science, microbiology, genetics, nutrition, and veterinary science. Because of its research and development capabilities, Perdue is often involved in U.S.D.A. field tests with pharmaceutical suppliers. Knowledge and experience gained from these tests can lead to a competitive advantage. For example, Perdue has the most extensive and expensive vaccination program among its breeders in the industry. As a result, Perdue growers have more disease-resistant chickens and one of the lowest mortality rates in the industry.

53   Perdue is not complacent. According to Dr. Mac Terzich, Doctor of Veterinary Medicine and Laboratory manager, Perdue really pushes for creativity and innovation. Currently, they are working with and studying some European producers who use a completely different process.

EXHIBIT 5
Human Resource Corporate Strategic Goals

· Provide leadership to the corporation in all aspects of human resources including safety, recruitment and retention of associates, training and development, employee relations, compensation, benefits, communication, security, medical, housekeeping, and food services.

· Provide leadership and assistance to management at all levels in communicating and implementing company policy to ensure consistency and compliance with federal, state, and local regulations.

· Provide leadership and assistance to management in maintaining a socially responsible community image in all our Perdue communities by maintaining positive community relations and encouraging Perdue associates to be active in their community.

· Provide leadership and assistance to management in creating an environment wherein all associates can contribute to the overall success of the company.

· Be innovative and cost efficient in developing, implementing, and providing to all associates systems which will reward performance, encourage individual growth, and recognize contribution to the corporation.

HUMAN RESOURCE MANAGEMENT

54   When entering the Human Resource Department at Perdue Farms, the first thing one sees is a prominently displayed set of human resource corporate strategic goals (see Exhibit 5). Besides these strategic goals, Perdue sets annual company goals that deal with "people." FY 1995's strategic "people" goals center on providing a safe, secure, and productive work environment. The specific goals are included on the wallet-size, fold-up card mentioned earlier (see Exhibit 1).

55   Strategic Human Resource planning is still developing at Perdue Farms. According to Tom Moyers, Vice President for Human Resource Management, "Every department in the company has a mission statement or policy which has been developed within the past 18 months . . . Department heads are free to update their goals as they see fit . . . Initial strategic human resource plans are developed by teams of three or four associates . . . These teams meet once or twice a year company-wide to review where we stand in terms of meeting our objectives."

56   To keep associates informed about company plans, Perdue Farms holds "state of the business" meetings for all interested associates twice a year. For example, during May 1994, five separate meetings were held near various plants in Delmarva, the Carolinas, Virginia, and Indiana. Typically, a local auditorium is rented, overhead slides are prepared, and the company's progress toward its goals and its financial status is shared with its associates. Discussion revolves around what is wrong and what is right about the company. New product lines are introduced to those attending and opportunities for improvement are discussed.

57   Upon joining Perdue Farms, each new associate attends an extensive orientation that begins with a thorough review of the "Perdue Associate Handbook." The handbook details Perdue's philosophy on quality, employee relations, and drugs and alcohol, and its code of ethics. The orientation also includes a thorough discussion of the Perdue benefit plans. Fully paid benefits for all associates include (1) paid vacation, (2) eight official paid holidays, (3) health, accident, disability, and life insurance, (4) savings and pension plans, (5) funeral leave, and (6) jury duty leave. The company also offers a scholarship program for children of Perdue associates.

58   Special arrangements can be made with the individual's immediate supervisor for a leave of absence of up to 12 months in case of extended nonjob-related illness or injury, birth or adoption of a child, care of a spouse or other close relative, or other personal situations. Regarding the Family and Medical Leave Act of 1993, although opposed by many companies because its requirements are far more than their current policies, the act will have little impact on Perdue Farms since existing leave of absence policies are already broader than the new federal law.

59   Perdue Farms is a nonunion employer. The firm has had a long-standing open door policy and managers are expected to be easily accessible to other associates, whatever the person's concern. The open door has been supplemented by a formal peer review process. While associates are expected to discuss problems with their supervisors first, they are urged to use peer review if they are still dissatisfied.

EXHIBIT 6
Annual Compound Growth Rate—Revenues and Associates

	Revenue Growth	Associate Growth
Past 20 years	13%	10%
Past 15 years	11	8
Past 10 years	9	5
Past 5 years	5	2

60　　Wages and salaries, which are reviewed at least once a year, are determined by patterns in the poultry industry and the particular geographic location of the plant. Changes in the general economy and the state of the business are also considered.

61　　Informal comparisons of turnover statistics with others in the poultry industry suggest that Perdue's turnover numbers are among the lowest in the industry. Perdue also shares workers' compensation claims data with their competitors and incidence rates (for accidents) are also among the lowest in the industry. Supervisors initially train and coach all new associates about the proper way to do their jobs. Once trained, the philosophy is that all associates are professionals and, as such, should make suggestions about how to make their jobs even more efficient and effective. After a 60-day introductory period, the associate has seniority based on the starting date of employment. Seniority is the determining factor in promotions where qualifications (skill, proficiency, dependability, work record) are equal. Also, should the work force need to be reduced, this date is used as the determining factor in layoffs.

62　　A form of Management by Objectives (MBO) is used for annual performance appraisal and planning review. The format includes a four-step process:

1. Establish accountability, goals, standards of performance, and their relative weights for the review period.
2. Conduct coaching sessions throughout the review period and document these discussions.
3. Evaluate performance at the end of the review period and conduct appraisal interview.
4. Undertake next review period planning.

63　　The foundation of human resources development includes extensive training and management development plus intensive succession planning and career pathing. The essence of the company's approach to human resource management is captured in Frank Perdue's statement:

> We have gotten where we are because we have believed in hiring our own people and training them in our own way. We believe in promotion from within, going outside only when we feel it is absolutely necessary—for expertise and sometimes because our company was simply growing faster than our people development program. The number one item in our success has been the quality of our people.

FINANCE

64　Perdue Farms, Inc., is a privately held firm and considers financial information to be proprietary. Hence, available data is limited. Stock is primarily held by the family and a limited amount by Perdue management. Common numbers used by the media and the poultry industry peg Perdue Farms' revenues for 1994 at about $1.5 billion and the number of associates at 13,800.

65　　The firm's compound sales growth rate has been slowly decreasing during the past 20 years, mirroring the industry, which has been experiencing market saturation and overproduction. However, Perdue has compensated by wringing more efficiency from its associates, for example, 20 years ago, a 1 percent increase in associates resulted in a 1.3 percent increase in revenue; today, a 1 percent increase in associates results in a 2.5 percent increase in revenues (see Exhibit 6).

66　　Perdue Farms has three operating divisions: Retail Chicken (62% of sales, growth rate 5%), Foodservice Chicken and Turkey (20% sales, growth rate 12%), and Grain and Oilseed (18% of

EXHIBIT 7
Nation's Top Four Broiler Companies, 1993*

	Million Head	Million Pounds
1. Tyson Foods, Inc.	26.50	84.15
2. ConAgra, Inc.	11.25	40.53
3. Gold Kist, Inc.	12.60	39.70
4. Perdue Farms, Inc.	7.51	28.28

*Based on average weekly slaughter.
Source: Broiler Industry Survey, 1993.

sales, growth rate 10%). Thus, the bulk of sales comes from the sector—retail chicken—with the slowest growth rate. Part of the reason for the slow sales growth in retail chicken may stem from Perdue Farm's policy of selling only fresh—never frozen—chicken. This has limited their traditional markets to cities that can be serviced overnight by truck from production facility locations (New York, Boston, Philadelphia, Baltimore, and Washington), which are pretty well saturated. (Developing markets include Chicago, Cleveland, Atlanta, Pittsburgh, and Miami.) On the other hand, food-service and grain and oilseed customers are nationwide and include export customers in eastern Europe, China, Japan, and South America.

67   Perdue Farms has been profitable every year since its founding with the exception of 1988. Company officials believe the loss in 1988 was caused by a decentralization effort begun during the early 80s. At that time, there was a concerted effort to push decisions down through the corporate ranks to provide more autonomy. When the new strategy resulted in higher costs, Frank Perdue responded quickly by returning to the basics, reconsolidating, and downsizing. Now the goal is to constantly streamline in order to provide cost-effective business solutions.

68   Perdue Farms uses a conservative approach to financial management, using retained earnings and cash flow to finance asset replacement projects and normal growth. When planning expansion projects or acquisitions, long-term debt is used. The target debt limit is 55 percent of equity. Such debt is normally provided by domestic and international bank and insurance companies. The debt strategy is to match asset lives with liability maturities, and have a mix of fixed rate and variable rate debt. Growth plans require about two dollars in projected incremental sales growth for each one dollar in invested capital.

THE U.S. POULTRY INDUSTRY

69   U.S. annual per capita consumption of poultry has risen dramatically during the past 40 years—from 26.3 pounds in 1950 to almost 80 pounds in 1990. Consumption continued to grow through 1993, according to a broiler industry survey of the largest integrated broiler companies. Output of ready-to-cook product increased 5.8 percent in 1991, 5.3 percent in 1992, and 6.0 percent in 1993 to 476 million pounds per week.

70   Recent growth is largely the result of consumers moving away from red meat due to health concerns and the industry's continued development of increased value products such as precooked or roasted chicken and chicken parts. Unfortunately, this growth has not been very profitable due to chronic overcapacity throughout the industry, which has pushed down wholesale prices. The industry has experienced cyclical troughs before and experts expect future improvement in both sales and profits. Still, razor-thin margins demand absolute efficiency.

71   Fifty-four integrated broiler companies account for approximately 99 percent of ready-to-cook production in the United States. While slow consolidation of the industry appears to be taking place, it is still necessary to include 22 companies to get to 80 percent of production. Concentration has been fastest among the top four producers. For example, since 1986 market share of the top four has grown from 35 percent to 40.5 percent (see Exhibit 7).

EXHIBIT 8
Integrated Broiler Producers Operating on Delmarva Peninsula

	National Rank
Tyson Foods, Inc.	1
ConAgra, Inc.	2
Perdue Farms, Inc. (headquartered in Salisbury, MD)	4
Hudson Foods, Inc.	7
Townsend, Inc. (headquartered in Millsboro, DE)	9
Showell Farms, Inc. (headquartered in Showell, MD)	10
Allen Family Foods, Inc. (headquartered in Seaford, DE)	17
Mountaire Farms of Delmarva, Inc. (headquartered in Selbyville, DE)	28

Source: Delmarva Poultry Industry, Inc., 1993 fact sheets.

72   Although the Delmarva Peninsula (home to Perdue Farms, Inc.) has long been considered the birthplace of the commercial broiler industry, recent production gains have been most rapid in the Southeast. Arkansas, Georgia, and Alabama are now the largest poultry producing states—a result of abundant space and inexpensive labor. The Southeast accounts for approximately 50 percent of the $20 billion U.S. chicken industry, employing 125,000 across the region. Still, Delmarva chicken producers provide about 10 percent of all broilers grown in the United States. This is due largely to the region's proximity to Washington, Baltimore, Philadelphia, New York, and Boston. Each weekday, more than 200 tractor-trailers loaded with fresh-dressed poultry leave Delmarva headed for these metropolitan markets.

73   Eight integrated companies operate 10 feed mills, 15 hatcheries, and 13 processing plants on Delmarva, employing approximately 22,000 people and producing approximately 10 million broilers each week (see Exhibit 8).

THE FUTURE

74   Considering Americans' average annual consumption of chicken (almost 80 pounds per person in 1990), many in the industry wonder how much growth is left. For example, after wholesale prices climbed from 14 cents per pound in 1960 to about 34 cents per pound in 1990, the recession and a general glut in the market have caused prices to fall back (see Exhibit 9). In real terms, the price of chicken is at an all-time low. A pound of chicken is down from 30 minutes of an average workers' 1940 wage to only 4.5 minutes of a worker's 1990 wage.

75   While much of this reduction can be justified by improved production efficiencies, prices are clearly depressed due to what some consider overcapacity in the industry. For example, in 1992, ConAgra, Inc., temporarily stopped sending chicks to 30 Delmarva growers to prevent an oversupply of chickens and several chicken companies have started to experiment with producing other kinds of meats—from pork to striped bass—to soften the impact. (Kim Clark, *The Sun*, July 4, 1993).

76   The trend is away from whole chickens to skinless, boneless parts. Perdue has responded with its line of "Fit 'n Easy" products with detailed nutrition labeling. It is also developing exports of dark meat to Puerto Rico and chicken feet to China. Fresh young turkey and turkey parts have become an important product and the "Perdue Done It!" line has been expanded to include fully cooked or roasted broilers, Cornish hens, and parts. Recently the company has expanded its lines to include ground chicken and turkey sausage.

77   Frank Perdue reflected recently that "we have a very high share of the available supermarket business in the Middle Atlantic and Northeastern United States, and if we were to follow that course which we know best—selling to the consumer through the retailer—we'd have to consider the Upper Midwest—Pittsburgh, Chicago, Detroit, with 25 to 30 million people."

EXHIBIT 9
Price/Pound of Live Broilers as Received by Farmers

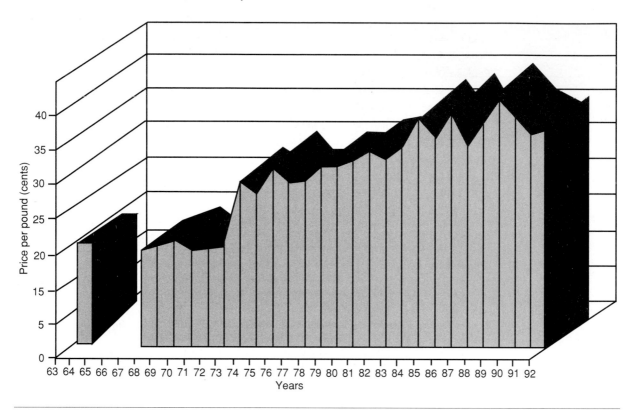

PUBLIC SOURCES OF INFORMATION

Barmash, Isadore. "Handing Off to the Next Generation." *The New York Times*, July 26, 1992, Business, p. 1.

Bates, Eric, and Bob Hall. "Ruling the Roost." *Southern Exposure*, Summer 1989, p. 11.

Clark, Kim. "Tender Times: Is Sky Falling on the Chicken Boom?" *The Sun*, July 4, 1993, p. 4F/Business.

DelMarVa Poultry Industry, Inc. "Facts About the DelMarVa Poultry Industry." July 28, 1994.

"Facts About the DelMarVa Broiler Industry—1973." Industry Bulletin, February 25, 1974.

Fahy, Joe. "All Pain, No Gain." *Southern Exposure*, Summer 1989, pp. 35–39.

Flynn, Ramsey. "Strange Bird." *The Washingtonian*, December 1989, p. 165.

Gale, Bradley T. "Quality Comes First When Hatching Power Brands." *Planning Review*, July/August, 1992, pp. 4–48.

"Golden Jubilee! Company Honors Frank Perdue for His 50 Years of Service." *Perdue Courier*, Special Edition, July 1989.

Goldoftas, Barbara. "Inside the Slaughterhouse." *Southern Exposure*, Summer 1989, pp. 25–29.

Hall, Bob. "Chicken Empires." *Southern Exposure*, Summer 1989, pp. 12–19.

"In the Money: Downhome Retailer Is Nation's Richest, Forbes Says." *The Washington Post*, October 14, 1986.

MacPherson, Myra. "Chicken Big." *The Washington Post, Potomac Magazine*, May 11, 1975, p. 15.

"Perdue Chicken Spreads Its Wings." *Business Week*, September 16, 1972, p. 113.

Perdue Farms. *Perdue Farms Incorporated—Historical Highlights*. September 1992.

Perdue Farms, Inc. "The Perdue Story. And the Five Reasons Why Our Consumers Tell It Best." October, 1991.

Perdue, Frank. Speech at Babson College. April 28, 1981.

Perdue, Frank. Speech to firm's leaders, accountants, and Perdue associates. September 1991.

Poultry industry file—miscellaneous newspaper clippings from 1950 to 1994. The Maryland Room, Blackwell Library, Salisbury State University.

Santosus, Megan. "Perdue's New Pecking Orders." *CIO*, March 1993, pp. 60–68.

Scarupa, Henry. "When Is a Chicken Not a Football?" *The (Baltimore) Sun Magazine*, March 4, 1973, pp. 5–12.

"Silent Millionaires in America." *Economist* 270, no. 7072 (March 17, 1979).

Sterling, Bill. "Just Browsin' ." *Eastern Shore News*, March 2, 1988.

Thornton, Gary. "Data from BROILER INDUSTRY." Elanco Poultry Team, Partner with the Poultry Industry, December 1993.

Yeoman, Barry. "Don't Count Your Chickens." *Southern Exposure*, Summer 1989, pp. 21–24.

CASE 4

FRIENDS PROVIDENT: REENGINEERING CUSTOMER SERVICES

INTRODUCTION

1   Our products differ from almost everything else the consumer buys. The purchaser's premiums are spread over many years and the monetary benefit is not received until the end of the contract. So our customers are with us for a long time, often quite literally for life. This makes us very conscious of the vital importance of ensuring our customers are given the best possible service.

Friends Provident Annual Report, 1992

2   In 1993 Friends Provident (FP), a major UK insurance company, was in the midst of a complete reorganization of its administrative structures to support its strategy of providing the highest level of customer service. In 1989, the administrative activities within FP were organized by product and function and split between the branches and Head Office. Such an organization was causing several problems in the provision of a high level of customer service. Starting in 1990, FP embarked on a quick-paced reorganization that redefined the relationship between Branch and Head Office activities and focused on the gradual reorganization of administrative processes to support the company's customer focus. Functional demarcations within Head Office were blurred with the creation of Service Centers to handle all needs of a particular set of customers. Increased emphases were laid on cross-functional teams and multi-skilled individuals. FP was also actively investigating whether further improvements in important processes were possible with the use of work-flow and image technologies.

3   While most of the changes associated with the reorganization had been fairly successful, several questions on the scope and depth of the change effort remained to be answered. Had the reorganization gone far enough? Was the reorganization too focused on Head Office? Were the current structures and processes best suited for ensuring the highest levels of customer service? Should FP consider a more radical redesign of its customer facing processes? What were the organizational implications of any such future changes?

COMPANY AND INDUSTRY BACKGROUND

4   The UK insurance market is large, sophisticated, and profitable. It ranks only behind the United States, Japan, and West Germany in terms of total gross premiums. The market is very fragmented with nearly 200 authorized insurance companies (the largest company, Prudential, has under 10 percent of the market share). Mutuals[1] control about 50 percent of the UK market. The market is witnessing a gradual consolidation with new entrants such as large non-UK insurance companies, banks, building societies, and even retailers (such as Marks and Spencer) from outside the financial services. Exhibit 1 provides some general information about the UK insurance market.

This case was written by Professors Soumitra Dutta and James Téboul from the Technology Management Area at INSEAD. Copyright © 1994 INSEAD, Fontainebleau, France. Financial support from the INSEAD Alumni Fund European Case Programme is gratefully acknowledged.

[1] A mutual is wholly owned by its policy owners (similar to a cooperative).

EXHIBIT 1
Major UK Insurance Companies (1993)

Company	Assets (£M)
AXA Equity & Law	5,847
Clerical Medical and General	5,329
Cooperative Insurance Society	7,871
Eagle Star	6,211
Equitable Life	9,565
Friends Provident	8,800
Legal & General	14,821
London Life	12,312
National Provident Institution	5,439
Norwich Union	20,822
Pearl Assurance	9,184
Prudential	29,233
Royal Life	5,243
Scottish Amicable	7,141
Scottish Widows	9,884
Standard Life	24,461
Sun Alliance	5,458
Sun Life	6,857

Source: *Money Management*, November 1993, pp. 8–10;
and Friends Provident 1992 Report and Accounts.

5   Friends Provident is one of the United Kingdom's leading mutual life insurance and investment companies with a little less than 4 percent of the market share. It has major business activities in the areas of Life Insurance, Personal Pensions, Company Pensions, and Health Insurance. In the United Kingdom, FP has almost 2 million individual policyholders and also writes substantial volumes of group business. In 1992, total assets under management at FP Group exceeded £8 billion and Group premium income was £1.2 billion.

6   Established by the Society of Friends in 1832, FP has a network of branches in major towns and cities throughout the United Kingdom. Friends Provident was one of the first insurance companies in the United Kingdom to adopt a multi-distribution strategy comprising independent financial advisers, appointed representatives,[2] direct (field) sales, and direct (telephone and mail) marketing. Friends Provident expects its new business for individual policies in 1994 to be distributed among these four distribution channels in the following proportion: independent financial advisers (50%), appointed representatives (14%), direct sales (25%), and direct marketing (11%).

7   Exhibit 2 gives the position of FP relative to other major insurance companies along different product lines. Exhibit 2 also provides a summary of the image of FP relative to its competitors as perceived by independent financial advisers. A senior FP manager commented on the perception of FP among the brokers: "We are among the top four or five choices of the brokers, but quite often not their first or second choice."

8   Faced with the opening of the European financial services market and increasing demands from sophisticated customers for international services, FP entered in 1992 into a new pan-European alliance, Eureko, in partnership with three major continental insurance companies: Wasa (Sweden),

---

[2] While independent financial advisers (or brokers) are free to sell the products of any insurance company, appointed representatives are agents who are independent but have a special agreement to sell only FP products.

EXHIBIT 1
Value Index Ratings: Performance of Low-Cost Endowment Policies
(continued)

Company	Value Index
Equitable Life	253
Friends Provident	235
Eagle Star	231
NatWest	*231*
Standard Life	229
Gen Accident Life	225
TSB	*222*
Clerical Medical	220
Midland	*215*
Lloyds (Black Horse)	211
Barclays Life	*210*

Note: (1) Banks are italicized in the above table. This highlights the threat of new entrants in the traditional insurance market. (2) The Value Index is obtained by dividing the maturity value by the total outlay.

Source: Savings market as quoted in *The Sunday Times*, April 3, 1994.

AVCB (Holland), and Topdanmark (Denmark). While each alliance partner retained autonomy in its home country, Eureko promised to give FP increased representation in the continent.

CUSTOMER SERVICES ADMINISTRATION

9   The Customer Services Division (CSD), or alternatively known as the Head Office, provides the back office administrative support function for FP. Headed by Roger Hallett (since 1989), the CSD is organized in two areas: Individual Business and Group Business distributed over three different locations: Dorking, Salisbury and Manchester. Exhibit 3 describes the overall organization of FP and provides details about the structure of CSD (in 1993).

10   There are three broad categories of "customers" served by CSD: FP branches, independent financial advisers and appointed representatives, and individual policyholders and groups (e.g., companies). FP branches are distributed all over the UK and report to the Sales Division of FP. Individual and group customers contact PF branches directly or more commonly through independent financial advisers to purchase FP products. Both individual and group customers usually contact CSD directly for servicing and claims processing on existing policies. To maintain a high level of customer service, FP encourages independent financial advisers to allow their customers to contact CSD directly for servicing and claims. Exhibit 4 lists the most important aspects of "service" to the independent financial advisers.

11   Each FP branch has an administration manager and a sales manager reporting to the branch manager. The sales support staff under the administration manager is responsible for functions such as new business quotes, the processing of new business proposals, and selective "one-touch"[3] servicing of policies. The new business inspectors under the branch sales manager focus on obtaining new sales by visiting brokers and agents. The Head Office provides help on complex underwriting

---

[3] New business policies that can be underwritten and processed to completion at the branches without the necessity of referral to the Customer Services Division (Head Office).

EXHIBIT 1
Friends Provident Portfolio: Individual Policies, November 1993
(concluded)

	Distribution Channels			
Products	Appointed Representatives (000s)	Independent Financial Advisers (000s)	Direct Sales and Marketing (000s)	Total (000s)
Unit-linked life*	70	230	140	440
With-profit life†	120	610	430	1,160
Unit-linked pensions*	30	120	130	280
With-profit pensions†	10	80	20	110
Permanent health insurance	10	50	10	70
			Total	2,060

*The payouts on unit-linked policies are linked to the particular investments associated with the investments. Insurance companies tend to prefer unit-linked policies as it helps to reduce their risk exposure.
†The payouts on with-profit policies are linked to the overall profitability of the insurance company.
Source: Internal Friends Provident documents.

cases, completes the processing of new business proposals, and services policies. Exhibit 5 illustrates how a proposal for a new policy is currently processed at both branch and Head Office.

12   There were considerable differences in view and culture between the branches and Head Office. Joanne Hamblet, an Assistant General Manager in CSD explained:

> The knowledge profile of branches was horizontal—wide but thinly spread. In contrast, the Head Office had vertical knowledge—narrow but deep. Also, the branch staff felt that the Head Office people were remote and did not appreciate sales. In return the Head Office staff felt that the branches were inefficient and could do a better job with administration. Under such conditions, one did not really trust the other. Staff in both branches and Head Office would check and recheck each other's work leading to inefficiencies in the entire system.

13   Roger Hallett, General Manager of CSD elaborated on the origins of the rivalry between branches and Head Office: "In the 1970s Friends Provident had a sophisticated real-time computer system which helped to propagate the mentality of a 'Head Office in every Branch.' Also, brokers tended to have the view that it was done better if it was done locally."

STIMULI FOR CHANGE

14   Until the end of 1989, the functions performed by CSD were distributed over two separate divisions, Marketing and Administration as illustrated in Exhibit 6A. Pensions reported to the Marketing General Manager for primarily historical reasons. A reorganization in January 1990 aggregated all departments responsible for servicing customers (shown shaded in Exhibit 6A) into a new division called the Customer Services Division. The name "Customer Services Division" was deliberately chosen to emphasize a customer orientation in the activities of the concerned departments. Exhibit 6B illustrates the partial structure of the CSD after the reorganization of 1990.

15   After the reorganization, CSD retained its organization around product and functional lines such as new business, claims, premium administration, and servicing (see Exhibit 6B). Such a structure often caused problems and inefficiencies within CSD. A senior CSD manager described some of these problems:

> The functional demarcation lines within CSD were quite dysfunctional. No one had a clear responsibility for the customer and this led to a degradation in the level of customer service we could provide. For example, assume that a customer sent us a claims letter with a request for premium adjustments. This letter would first be processed by the claims group, and then passed to the premium administration group where it would wait to

EXHIBIT 2
Business Placed with Independent Financial Advisers (1993)

The following table gives the companies with whom the surveyed independent financial advisers (IFAs) have placed the most business during the past six months. The data comes from face-to-face interviews of more than 500 IFAs in the period March 8th to April 2nd, 1993. The survey was conducted by an industry market research association consisting of Friends Provident and 18 other major UK insurance companies. The names of other companies participating in the survey have been disguised due to the confidentiality of the data.

Product	Company	Percent IFAs Using Company Most	Position of Company in Overall Ranking (out of 19)
Mortgages	Company 1	28	1
	Company 2	21	2
	Friends Provident	10	5
Savings and investments	Company 1	25	1
	Company 3	24	2
	Friends Provident	12	7
Personal protection	Company 4	30	1
	Company 5	26	2
	Friends Provident	8	7
Corporate protection	Company 4	17	1
	Company 6	11	2
	Friends Provident	4	7
Individual pensions	Company 1	29	1
	Company 7	26	2
	Friends Provident	18	8
Group pensions	Company 7	15	1
	Company 1	13	2
	Friends Provident	4	12

be processed. The delays added up within CSD—leading to a degradation of the overall level of customer service we could provide.

16   Several customers were also visibly dissatisfied with the level of service they were receiving from FP. For example, Endsleigh[4] had communicated the need for better customer service to FP management. Roger Hallett summarized the service offered by FP in 1989: "Our speed was variable, quality was indifferent and cost was worrying!" In 1987, when Abbey National (a major building society) joined FP on a five-year contract, Roger Hallett was given a free hand in quickly setting up a servicing facility for Abbey National. He decided to pilot a new customer service model for servicing Abbey National in Manchester. Roger elaborated:

Starting afresh in a place 200 miles away from Dorking and Salisbury gave us an opportunity to try out something new. We had sensed for some time that our functional demarcations were not helpful for providing high quality customer service, but that was the first time we actually grouped several different functions together to service a particular customer. That was the origin of the concept of Service Centers within CSD.

17   The Manchester site was operational in 1988 and by mid-1990 it was clear that the Manchester site was incurring lower expenses and generating fewer complaints from its customer (Abbey National). In December 1990, a four-member group consisting of managers from CSD and Sales (branch) Administration was formed to determine ways to improve the level of customer service

---

[4] Endsleigh is an independent sales company associated with Friends Provident as an appointed representative.

EXHIBIT 2
Image Ratings of Friends Provident (1993)
(concluded)

The following table gives the percent of independent financial advisers (IFAs) stating that Friends Provident was excellent/good along different dimensions of the company's image. As before, the data come from face-to-face interviews of more than 500 IFAs in the period March 8th to April 2nd, 1993. The survey was conducted by an industry market research association consisting of Friends Provident and 18 other major UK insurance companies.

Image Dimension	Percent IFAs Rating FP as Excellent/Good Along Dimension	Rank of FP in Ranking Along Dimension (out of 19 Companies)	Percent of IFAs Rating Company Ranked No. 1 as Excellent/Good
Financial strength	73	5	87
Past performance	79	3	90
Price of products	68	5	68
Technical literature	56	9	72
Overall service	72	1	72
Past performance (with profit)	82	2	91
Past performance (unit linked)	59	9	82
Quotation service	80	1	80
Product range	66	3	71
Consultant support	67	2	71
Client literature	61	6	69

Source: Internal Friends Provident documents.

provided to Endsleigh. The group looked at the Manchester site in detail and recommended the creation of a new Service Center at Manchester to service all Endsleigh needs (which were previously serviced from the departments at Salisbury).

18   The Endsleigh Service Center was operational in Manchester by 1st April 1991. The notion of a Service Center was relatively new for CSD. A Service Center implied a reorganization across functional lines to focus the responsibility for customers at one point and allow a single center to satisfy all customer needs. However, the need for change was not perceived by many managers within Head Office. Jane Stevens, Manager for Individual Customer Services in CSD, commented on this:

> The pressure to change was not really recognized—except by the likes of Roger (Hallett). There was a lot of complacency—people did not really see the need to change. If something had happened in a particular way, people tended to believe that it would always be done in that way. In fact, many of the senior managers within Friends Provident were actually in favor of reinforcing functional specialization.

ORGANIZING FOR CHANGE

19   We have tremendous strengths within Customer Services Division and the aim of the reorganization is to build on these qualities to put Friends Provident in an even better position in the market place.

Roger Hallett (August 1991)

In May 1991, a Branch/Head office project was started with the aim to "improve administration of office insurance products at branch and Head Office locations." The project team consisted of four managers—two from Head Office and two administration managers from branches—and was given the charter to focus on improving the quality of service and determine ways to deliver that service cost-effectively. The team visited several branches, Head Office departments, brokers, appointed representatives, and Endsleigh Insurance offices and conducted interviews over a period of five

EXHIBIT 3
Structure of Friends Provident and Customer Services Division (1993)

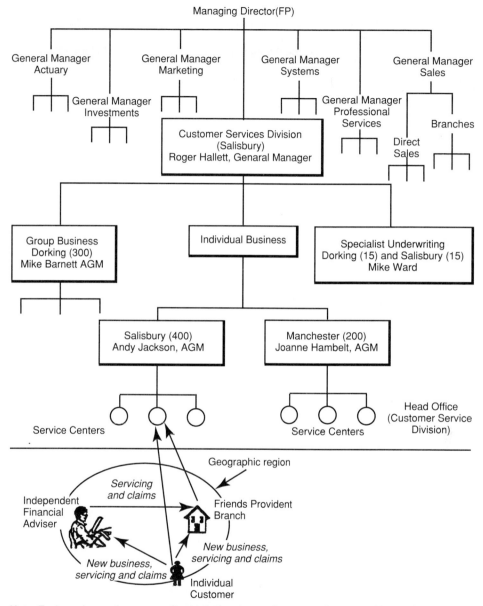

Note: Each service center serves a fixed set of customers from a certain geographical region. Customers include FP branches, independent financial advisers, and individual customers.

Source: Internal Friends Provident documents.

weeks. Their study led to a better understanding of the needs of branches and agreed service levels between Head Office and branches. The team arrived at the following conclusions:

· Branches should concentrate on the acquisition of new business.
· CSD should be reorganized into Service Centers.

EXHIBIT 4
Important Aspects of Service

The following table gives the most important aspects of "service" as perceived by independent financial advisers (IFAs).
Similar to the tables of Exhibit 2, the data comes from face-to-face interviews of more than 500 IFAs in the period March 8th to
April 2nd, 1993. The survey was conducted by an industry market research association consisting of Friends Provident and 18
other major UK insurance companies.

Aspect of Service	Percent IFAs Saying Very Important	Relative Rank of Friends Provident
Fast rectification of errors	79	1
Efficient premium collection	71	1
Well trained branch staff	63	1
Inform of failure to collect direct debit mandate (DDM)	67	2
Fast, flexible underwriting	48	3
Inform of delays	61	1
Staff on top of administration	60	2
Speed of response	65	1

Source: Internal Friends Provident documents.

· Policy servicing work should be transferred from branches to Head Office.

· Staff should be transferred from branches to Head Office to increase their customer awareness.

· The number and roles of branches should be reviewed.

20   In response to the conclusions of the Branch/Head office project an external consultant was brought in on 20th June 1991 to organize a one-day "Change Day" for 16 CSD managers. At the end of the Change Day, the 16 managers were asked about what should be done next. All of them said there was need to spread awareness about the need for change. Fifteen of them recommended that a dedicated task force should be formed to devise a new coordinated Customer Service approach. Interestingly, no one said do nothing. Jane Stevens commented on the results of the Change Day vote: "If you had asked the managers two days earlier about change, most of them would not have even though about change, let alone agree that change was necessary."

21   In response to the recommendations of the Change Day, a group of seven managers from Head Office was set up on 1st July 1991 and given the task of coming up with the practical details for reorganizing CSD. Any proposed solution had to address the following needs:

· To clearly identify the customer and thus gain a greater understanding of their requirements.

· To provide flexibility for changing needs in the future.

· To gain the commitment of the CSD management and staff.

· To maintain technical knowledge/skills.

· To ensure service provision did not deteriorate during any change.

22   Roger Hallett was not a member of the group, but interacted periodically with them. Jane Stevens, a member of the group, elaborated on the influence of Roger on the group:

The group was meeting in the Boardroom which was across from Roger's office. Roger would often walk in and drop a few gems. After he walked away, we would think about his comments and add them to our plans. The end result of this was that the group ended up presenting ideas which were very much in agreement with Roger's vision, but the group felt at the time that they had come up with a forward thinking but practical plan.

EXHIBIT 5
Processing of a Proposal for a New Insurance Policy (1993)

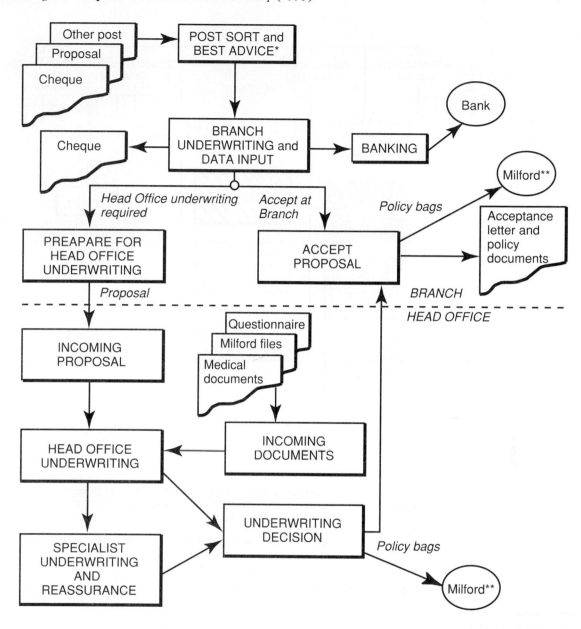

Note:
* Best advice refers to checking compliance with the U.K. Financial Services Act requiring all financial services institutions to offer the right product for the customers' needs.
** Originals of all documents are stored in Milford.

Source: Internal Friends Provident documents.

EXHIBIT 6A
Structure of Friends Provident and the Administration and Marketing Divisions (1989)

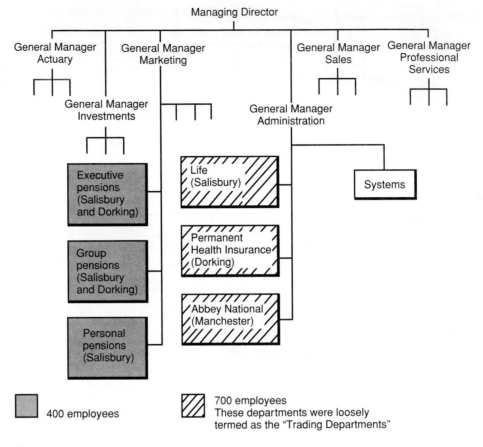

Note:

1. The shaded departments were consolidated into the Customer Services Division. The "Systems" department under the Administration Division was moved to the Information Systems Division during the reorganization of January 1990.

2. The total number of employees in the shaded departments is as mentioned above.

Source: Internal Friends Provident documents.

PLAN FOR CHANGE

23   The group of seven managers presented their view of the change process to Roger Hallett on 11th July 1991. The recommendations of the group outlined how CSD should be reorganized (see Exhibit 7) into nine Service Centers, each focused on a known customer, that is, a group of geographically co-located FP branches or a particular distribution agent (such as Endsleigh). Each Service Center would contain the expertise necessary to provide complete service for all products for its assigned customers. Each team within a Service Center would remain focused on one particular function but would have to work alongside other functional teams. Staff were not expected to become "multi-functional" overnight but it was envisaged that the proximity to other functional teams would make them more aware of the customer service process as a whole.

EXHIBIT 6B
Traditional (Partial) Structure of Customer Services Division (1990)

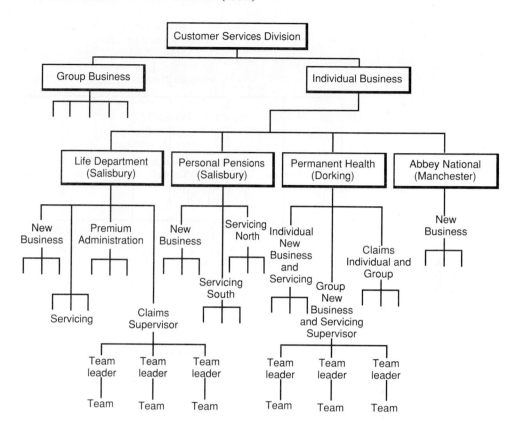

Note: Within each function, there were several teams. Members of the team worked largely individually on projects, but helped each other out on specific tasks when required. The team leader was responsible for allocating work among the team members.

Source: Internal Friends Provident documents.

24   To ensure the maintenance of high technical standards, the group also recommended the formation of a few specialist units to support the Service Centers. The distinction between the Service Center and Specialist Units would be invisible to the customer, and the Service Center would always be responsible for all customer needs. Agreed service levels would be measured from the date of receipt of post to date of despatch to the customer inclusive of all referrals to Specialist Units.

25   Of special importance was a new specialist group under the heading Operating Standards that would be set up at each site and led by a small number of senior people. This group was to be responsible for systems, processes, and training and for ensuring consistency of approach and standards over all sites and for building on "Best Practice."

26   Another important initiative in the reorganization was the creation of a Customer Information Center at each site staffed by experts in each function to provide an interface between Head Office and its customers and give a "one-stop" answering service for simple queries. The Customer

EXHIBIT 7
New (Partial) Structure of Customer Services Division (1991)

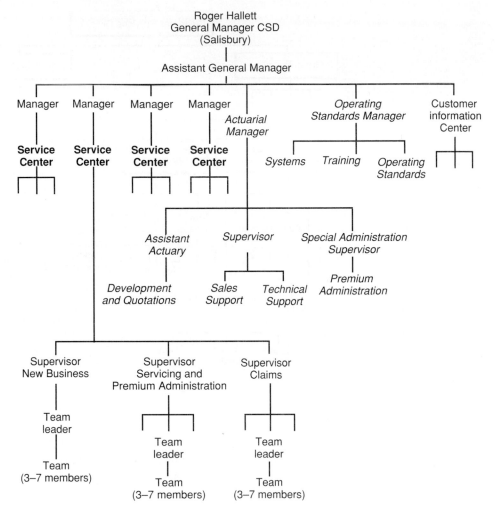

Note:

1. The partial structure of Salisbury shown above is after the reorganization of the CSD into service centers in August 1991.

2. Service centers are shown in bold and specialist units are italicized.

Source: Internal Friends Provident documents.

Information Center would forward a customer call to the relevant Service Center only if it needed specialized assistance.[5] Jane Stevens explained the importance of the Customer Information Center:

> Previously when a policyholder called Friends Provident, the receptionist decided the functional division to which the call would be forwarded. Receptionists frequently made errors and as a result, customers were

---

[5] In 1993, the Customer Information Center had a staff of 16 employees. It received an average of 3,000 calls each week. Less than 10 percent of incoming calls needed to be forwarded to a service center.

passed around from one function to the other. Answering customer queries quickly and efficiently is important as 80% of our policyholders contact us directly for service.

27   The group also considered some key implementation issues related to work transfers (across locations), personnel requirements, training, technology changes, and communication. Technology changes were kept to the minimal (such as entering new function codes, changing addresses, and modifying sign-on authorities) and no new systems were planned. A detailed implementation plan was drawn up and the group concluded that the earliest possible date for implementation was October 1st, 1991.

IMPLEMENTING CHANGE

28   On 19th July 1991, a "Customer Day" was organized for all managers (about 50 in number) from within CSD. To develop awareness about customer needs, the managers first went through exercises pretending to be customers and trying to ascertain problems faced by customers while dealing with CSD. Next, the group of seven managers presented their view of change and asked the managers to brainstorm about issues related to the proposed changes. Jane Stevens elaborated on the process:

> The Customer Day was critical for getting the entire management group involved in the change process. With only a couple of exceptions, all managers realized the importance of what was being attempted and were generally happy with what we were doing. We also found their feedback very useful. Besides filling in details in some parts of our proposals, it indicated areas where we had to be very careful with what we communicated to the rest of the organization.

29   Having obtained the backing of CSD managers, a presentation of the proposed changes was made to the General Management of FP on 2nd August. Roger added:

> General management was very supportive as they could see the potential for reducing costs, improving service, and increasing the sales focus of branches. While they were convinced of the utility of the ideas, they were not equally sure whether we could make it work—at least within the time frame specified. We however very much believed in what we had come up with and would do everything to make it work.

30   With the support of FP General Management behind them, Roger and the group started matching new job descriptions with manager competencies. It was clearly understood at the start of the process that there would be no redundancies. Jane explained:

> We did not want to change the culture by introducing redundancies. Clearly, no job in the new world was the same as before. So everyone was going to have a new job. This gave us an opportunity to ensure that the right people were there in the right jobs. With hindsight, we probably should have faced up to a few more problems than we did. There were a few people who really did not fit, but we made them fit.

31   Two days later, the management team communicated the changes to all supervisors (the next level down from managers). Specially prepared documents were given to them to aid the presentation and emphasize the fact that the customer was the focus of the changes. The fact that there would be no redundancies in the new organization was also stressed. The supervisors were assigned the task of distributing their staff within the Service Centers and ensuring that the skills were correctly distributed within each center. Whenever possible, entire (functional) teams were relocated together.

32   A day later, all lower level staff were informed about their new positions. Jane commented on the reactions of the staff:

> The staff knew that change was coming. They were on the front line and were living through the kind of problems which were now being voiced by the managers group. There was little resistance to the new assignments. We also tried to be as flexible as possible in accommodating requests for changes.

33   The staff were not expected to become multi-functional from day one, but it was clear that there would be increased amounts of cross-training in the future with the aim of breaking boundaries between teams within a Service Center. However, some training was necessary prior to implementation as there were only a few experts in some areas and it was not possible to split these people evenly among the Service Centers. All necessary pre-implementation changes were done within the next five weeks and the Service Centers were up and running as scheduled on 1st October 1991.

34   Roger Hallett commented on the change process:

> Process changes are essentially about people. I spent a lot of time talking to small groups of my staff at all levels about the challenges facing Friends Provident in the future and what we should be doing about them. This helped to create an awareness of the need for change.
>
> I also believe that people will make change happen. You give them a vision, create an environment conducive for change, and empower them to make the change happen. This is what we did.

CHANGE IN WORK PROCESSES

35   Prior to the creation of Service Centers, product and functional divisions were organized into teams. Team members worked individually on cases, but often interacted with others while handling a complex assignment. Team leaders were responsible for allocating work among team members according to the complexity of tasks and skills of team members. Customer queries requiring processing by multiple functional departments flowed from one functional team to another with arbitrary hand-off delays across functions. As no one function was responsible for servicing a customer, the level of service provided was often inadequate. There was poor continuity in customer relationships as service requests were allocated to different teams on an ad hoc basis.

36   The creation of Service Centers changed the work flow dramatically. Each Service Center contained different functional teams and handled all aspects of service related to a particular set of customers. The overall work flow changed from an ad hoc hand-off across teams to a "focused" flow across co-located teams. Responsibility for servicing customers was localized in the managers of the concerned Service Centers. There was increased continuity in customer relationships as the same Service Center satisfied all requests from a particular customer. These differences in the overall work flows are represented in Exhibit 8.

37   A more concrete (but simplified) example of the change in work flows induced by the Service Centers is shown in Exhibit 9. In the pre-Service Center period, every aspect of processing a new business proposal was a "multi-touch" process in which clerks would pass on a file using a pend/post tray only to receive it back later. It was quite common to have work transferred back and forth between geographically distant locations midway through processes. Service Centers co-located different clerks and reorganized work to eliminate internal hand-off delays. Note that in Exhibit 9, work has been moved from the branch office to Head Office and the nature of the tasks of the new business clerk and underwriter have changed. For example, the underwriter directly contacts the medical doctor in the post-Service Center work flows. The physical co-location of the new business clerk and the underwriter within the same Service Center has eliminated "double touch" and minimized the use of the post/pend tray to the time while awaiting external action.

CONSEQUENCES OF THE REORGANIZATION

38   After the reorganization, an overall customer service plan was formed and each individual Service Center was asked to make its own plan in accordance with the overall plan. Due to the mutually agreed service level objectives, each Service Center had incentives to follow up on different aspects of service to a customer. A manager commented on the Service Center plans: "It all seems simple, but it was the first time we had ever done it. Why had we not done it before? I think that it was the fact that now people had a clear customer they were trying to achieve for." Staff within Service Centers also seemed to be more motivated by knowing "who they were working for" and by "seeing the whole picture." Pay for performance was introduced and salaries could vary by as much as 60 percent of the base salary. A number of non-monetary rewards and incentive plans were also introduced to reward excellent ideas and/or performance.

EXHIBIT 8
Work Flows before and after Creation of Service Centers

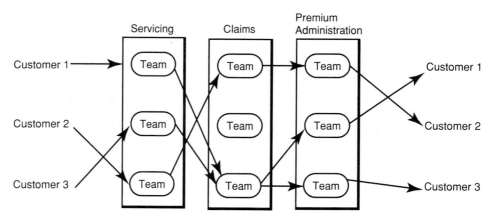

Work flow prior to Service Centers

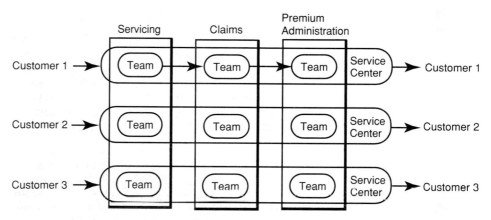

Work flow after creation of Service Centers

Note: Before the creation of service centers, work was handed off across functional departments in an "ad-hoc" manner. No one was responsible for the customer. After the creation of service centers, work flowed through different teams within a service center serving the same customer.

Source: Internal Friends Provident documents.

39   The Service Centers changed the relations between CSD and branches. Joanne Hamblet explained the nature of these changes:

> Prior to the Service Centers the branches did not know who within CSD was responsible for providing them with service. We had very little interaction with our branches. The introduction of Service Centers changed that completely. Now each Service Center is responsible for a fixed set of branches. There is continuity in our relation with branches.

40   The branches were also pleased with the changes. A branch administration manager explained: "Prior to the changes, the branches frequently complained about the lack of customer awareness within CSD. Today, the CSD is in increased direct contact with customers and more aware of customer needs."

41   A branch sales manager noted the following:

EXHIBIT 9
Processing New Policy Proposal: Request for Medical Information Process
(Pre-Service Centers)

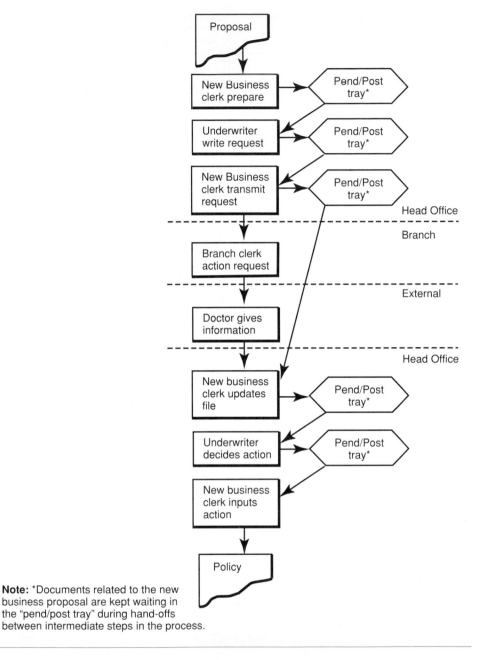

Note: *Documents related to the new business proposal are kept waiting in the "pend/post tray" during hand-offs between intermediate steps in the process.

Source: Internal Friends Provident documents.

If I went a long way to visit a broker and spent the first ten minutes listening to him complain about our service, then there is little use in me discussing our products any further with him. The provision of a higher quality customer service from CSD has helped to alleviate such concerns.

Also, the branches had for a certain period lost their focus on sales. These changes (within CSD) have helped to increase awareness about the importance of sales to the company's future.

EXHIBIT 9
Processing New Policy Proposal: Request for Medical Information Process
(Post-Service Centers)
(concluded)

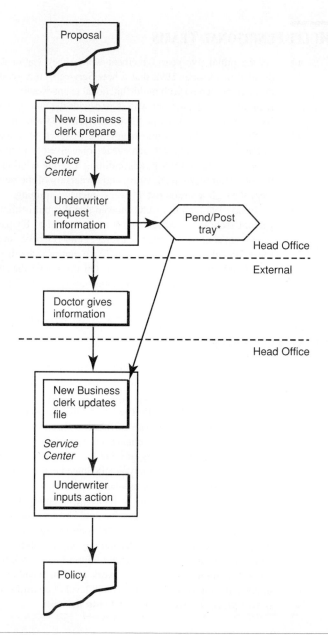

Source: Internal Friends Provident documents.

42   The role of a "minder" was created within CSD. The minder was responsible for managing the relation with the branches and was expected to be in frequent (weekly) contact with them. Branches also started inviting CSD managers to their sales meetings. This became feasible because now one manager (the corresponding Service Center manager) was responsible for servicing a fixed set of branches.

43   Cost savings were also realized from the reorganization. Administrative work (such as group business processing) was moved from the branches to CSD with no increase in staff. Further cost savings were obtained with a reduction in branch administrative staff by 12 percent to 400.

MOVE TO MULTI-FUNCTIONAL TEAMS

44   As the initial five-year agreement with Abbey National was terminating in January 1993, it was decided in October 1992 that a new Service Center (called the Northern Service Center to service northern branches) with multi-functional teams would be formed at Manchester. A dedicated and job-focused training program was started with the aim of making the first multi-functional team of the Northern Service Center go "live" in April 1993 with the entire Center being "live" by October 1993.

45   Staff were divided into teams and assigned to a specific Northern region branch office. This "branch focus" helped to achieve the objective of "reinforcing a positive customer services attitude, offering a personal touch, and building a strong relation." This team-based training also helped to develop teamwork, team spirit, and ownership of the new Service Center goals. Each staff member went through a structured 14-week intensive training.

46   In late 1993, audit results showed that the multi-functional teams showed an overall result of 91 percent technically correct work as compared to 83 percent for a similar period in the previous functional team structure. The average trained worker showed an improvement of at least two levels (on a 5-level scale) in more than 70 percent of tasks. Eighty-eight percent of work was being dealt with inside new tighter schedules. On the whole the teams were achieving similar service level results but on a turn-around time improvement of 25 percent.

TECHNOLOGICAL INITIATIVES

47   In late 1993, FP was in the midst of two major technology initiatives: rebuilding Gladis, its central mainframe system, and piloting work-flow and image technologies. The former initiative was necessary because Gladis was appearing increasingly obsolete in its ability to keep up with the changes in work practices within CSD. The latter initiative was motivated by internal studies within FP that had shown that the average team member spent approximately 40 percent of his time handling paper. Besides, it was felt that reliance on paper-based processes was generating excessive paper and hampering the productivity of CSD. For example, a customer file could be stored in more than six different locations. As work typically flowed in paper form from one team to another, delays accumulated in work processes even when several teams could possibly work on the file simultaneously.

48   With the help of imaging technology, incoming documents were to be scanned in the mailroom and stored as electronic images that could be accessed simultaneously by employees in branches and Head Office. This could enable employees to work simultaneously on the same document and reduce delays significantly. Imaging technology was also expected to increase the accessibility of documents and customer files to all employees within FP. A work flow capability in the imaging system would allow the automatic routing of work to team members and provide more accurate and complete management information. The overall level of control and quality assurance in Head Office administrative processes was also expected to increase.

QUALITY INITIATIVES

The reorganization created a motivation for change and improvement. This created a conducive atmosphere for introducing formal quality initiatives—things which we had not done actively and on a systematic basis before.

                                                           Jane Stevens, Manager, Individual Customer Services

49   In December 1992, two Service Centers (one each in Dorking and Salisbury) started on a special quality program termed the "Pursuit of Excellence" (POE). Specific objectives were set for the program:

· To reduce start to finish processing time by 25 percent for six key functions.
· To achieve 5 percent productivity gain.
· To maintain 100 percent agreed service levels.
· To reduce "rework"[6] by 50 percent.
· To create an environment of continuous improvement.

50   The initiative started with a brainstorming session with all Service Center staff on 125 different issues. The brainstorming revealed the 10 most important issues for becoming centers of excellence. The top two issues were:

· Need to improve knowledge/learning.
· Too much emphasis on agreed service levels, not enough on quality.

51   Next, teams were set up to produce solutions. One team, the "Quick Fix" team looked at minor problems that could be fixed easily for quick gains. The other team, the "Top 10" team focused on the top 10 issues identified in the brainstorming session. Process groups were created to redesign three key processes: maturities, new business, and personal pension quotations. A project group was also set up to coordinate all POE activities and to communicate all plans, actions, and achievements.

52   In September 1993, the POE initiative had made some tangible progress. The "Quick Fix" team was finished and the "Top 10" team was still engaged in tackling larger issues. Unit costs had come down by 5 to 10 percent and changes to procedures had produced yearly savings of 2,750 hours. Reworks had dropped by 40 percent and agreed service levels had been maintained between 94 percent and 100 percent since the start of the POE initiative. Of the three process groups, one group (maturities) had almost finished its task. The POE Review Group was holding regular meetings and communicating its results via a dedicated POE notice board. Jane commented on the results:

The most important benefit of the quality initiatives is the change it has produced in the attitude of staff. Now they always question: "is this the best way to do it?" Before, they would not do so. The bigger challenge for us is to decide how to spread best practices to other centers.

FUTURE CHALLENGES

The more that we do, the more we see we have to do. Most of our changes thus far have been primarily structural. We have to work very hard now to better understand our customer needs, to train our staff, and shape our organizational culture.

Roger Hallett, General Manager, CSD

53   When Roger Hallett took charge of the CSD in late 1989, he set himself two short-term (two-year) and two long-term (five-year) goals. The two short-term objectives were: (a) standardizing business results and (b) restructuring CSD. The two five-year objectives were (a) winning a major UK Service Award and (b) reducing servicing costs to 1985 levels in absolute terms (without accounting for inflation).

54   In late 1993, Roger Hallett could take some pride in having achieved his initial objectives to a fair degree. Business results for most aspects of CSD has been standardized and important aspects of the restructuring of CSD had been completed successfully. More important was the fact that FP won a major service award for the first time in October 1993 from the National Federation of Independent Financial Advisers, who rated FP as No. 1 in overall service. Unit servicing costs were also headed

---

[6] *Rework* is defined as work returned by customer due to error or incompleteness.

EXHIBIT 10

The following graph depicts the changes in the perception of Friends Provident along key dimensions during the period September 1991 through March 1993. The base comprises all independent financial advisers using Friends Provident.

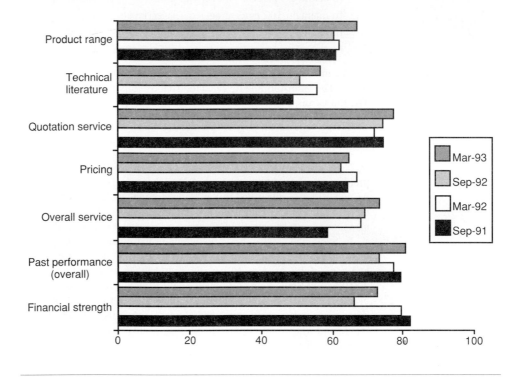

Source: Internal Friends Provident documents.

downwards. Taking the unit servicing cost in 1990 as 100, unit servicing costs in 1992 had fallen to 77 (in absolute terms). The goal was to achieve the unit servicing cost of 1985 (equal to 66). Exhibit 10 summarizes the changes in the perception of FP by independent financial advisers during the period September 1991 through March 1993.

55   FP had gone through major changes in its administrative processes over the last couple of years. The benefits of the reorganization were becoming evident. Customer satisfaction had increased significantly and costs were down. A clustering of branches had reduced the number of branches from 40 in 1991 to 28 in late 1993. This had enabled the administrative staff in branches to be reduced further by 26 percent to about 320.[7] Roger Hallett commented on the changes:

> The top few insurance companies now have very similar products with comparable prices. Systems and investment returns are not that different either. So the quality of service provided becomes a key differentiator from a competitive perspective.

56   However some important concerns remained related to the management of relationships with customers. While the degree of satisfaction among the brokers and branches had increased, could CSD do more to understand its end customers (individual policyholders)? Most individual policyholders contacted CSD directly for service. Could FP exploit these interactions with the end customer

---

[7] The headcount reduction was occurring largely through "managed attrition." With only a few exceptions, there were no forced layoffs.

further? Were the current systems and procedures adequately focused on the individual customer? Roger Hallett elaborated on these concerns:

> We don't have a good system in place for measuring (end) customer satisfaction. Often the customer doesn't actually know what he wants. What they often appreciate the most is not the technical details of our response, but its presentation, its accessibility, and the speed of response.
>
> The culture of a significant part of our organization is very technical and "expert" driven. I worry about how far we have succeeded in changing this to a more customer-oriented culture. When I read the literature on process management, I also wonder if we have gone far enough with our process changes. There are also several risks to be managed, such as the risk of loss of expertise.

CASE 5

MOBIL CHEMICAL AND THE VPP

INTRODUCTION

1   In 1982, the Occupational Safety and Health Administration (OSHA) undertook to elicit cooperation between government and industry. Specifically, OSHA set up a Voluntary Protection Program (VPP) that would recognize and encourage positive voluntary improvements in workplace safety and health practices. As with most private corporations, Mobil Chemical was initially hesitant to involve themselves with this governmental regulatory agency. The 1982 issue was: could such a voluntary involvement with an agency known for enforcing regulations and imposing punitive fines possibly lead to anything good? Mobil Chemical wanted to know the answer. By 1993, new issues in occupational safety and health had been raised. Now, the question was: how should Mobil Chemical stay abreast with all the new federal, state, local regulations, and voluntary initiatives that appear to be in conflict with each other?

2   Mobil Chemical also recognizes that new experiments in "employee empowerment" are occurring throughout the country. Plant management at a Washington, New Jersey, plant has introduced such a program at their facility. Specifically, this group developed and implemented a 5-Star Quality program that plant and company personnel find successful. Mobil Chemical wonders: what useful lesson can be transferred from this plant to other facilities within Mobil's domain? Exactly how is the attention to safety and health programs paying off, and is there a logical way such benefits can be quantified? How does safety relate to the concepts of "quality" and "productivity"?

ISSUES ASSOCIATED WITH THE CHEMICAL INDUSTRY AND OSHA

3   The federal agency charged with investigating workplace safety and health is the Occupational Safety and Health Administration (OSHA), established with the passage of the Occupational Safety and Health Act of 1970. This Act states that management has a legal obligation to provide employees with a workplace that is free from all recognized hazards and dangers. The Act also specifies that risks must be minimized and employees trained in the safety aspects of their jobs. This enables the employee to perform his or her work without worry of injury or illness.

4   The Act specifies that management must be willing to deliver the best possible protection for workers' well-being. This means furnishing proper protective equipment, tools, machinery, safeguards, and training as well as taking all necessary precautions to reduce injury and illness. It is OSHA's job to make sure that management fulfills its obligations. This means OSHA has to watch over 92 million workers in more than 6 million U.S. establishments.

5   In the recent past, due to a series of unfortunate incidents, the public's perception of the chemical industry has been quite negative. For example, in 1984, deadly industrial gases from a Union Carbide plant in Bhopal, India, killed 10,000 people and injured 5 to 10 times that many. In 1990, a series of

This case was prepared by Sue Greenfeld, D.B.A., and Harold Dyck, Ph.D., of California State University. Special thanks to Delbert L. Flowers, Director, Office of Academic and Professional Affairs of the Occupational Safety and Health Administration, who facilitated and helped to make this case possible, and to Bob Brant, Chairman of the Voluntary Protection Programs Participants' Association, and Manager of Safety, Health, and Loss Prevention, Mobil Chemical.

chemical explosions occurred in a Phillips 66 Pasadena, Texas, facility, leaving 23 dead and 314 employees injured. In 1992, Lockheed Corporation settled with 624 plaintiffs who accused the company of concealing 35 deaths and failing to warn workers of the risks. Such dramatic occurrences as these alarm the public who call upon governmental officials to do something.

6   Thus, one controversy has emerged. How should OSHA carry out this role in relationship to business? Should OSHA be merely an enforcer of regulations, or should OSHA help business meet the standards? On one side, critics contend that OSHA should be tougher on business, that OSHA should have more enforcement clout, that standards need to be tougher, and that firms should be mandated to have safety committees composed of management and workers. Some feel that OSHA fines are not high enough, and that many firms just receive a "slap on the hand." To illustrate one such case in the chemical industry, in 1992 OSHA inspectors discovered 47 "willful," 156 "serious," and 22 other incidents of violations against a Formosa Plastics Company facility in Texas. Yet, the total assessed penalty was only $330,300 (about $1,467 per violation). Many thought this penalty was far too low given the belief that some violations had the potential for catastrophic effects (i.e., either fire and/or explosions).

7   On the other hand, others maintain that a more conciliatory and cooperative approach with business would result in more effective safety and health procedures. They maintain that, if OSHA works with businesses and settles cases, it would result in more timely hazard abatement than if OSHA has to litigate the cases. Secretary of Labor Robert B. Reich says that one of his goals is "to encourage employers and employees to join together in order to achieve mutual gains. Few workplace issues offer as obvious a common ground for meaningful collaboration as safety and health." With respect to OSHA's regulatory efforts, he is "especially eager to find ways to create a nonadversarial climate of rulemaking in which all parties—employers, employees, government, and others with knowledge—work together to identify and resolve safety and health problems." The progress made with OSHA's Voluntary Protection Programs (VPP) may be considered a better approach than a "rigid judicial interpretation of current statutory language which impose heavy evidentiary burdens on OSHA."

8   The difficulty of dealing with 50 different states and many more county and city governments, each setting up their own regulations, is also a major concern, according to John Morton, Manager, Mobil Chemical's Hazardous Materials Program. The growing trend seems to be for communities "to regulate something new which may be in many cases the opposite of what the federal regulations told us to do." Mobil Chemical feels hampered by such a diverse set of local regulations, and questions whether the international trend toward standardization (e.g., codes in the European Community) should be encouraged in the United States.

9   Another critical problem is the public's negative perceptions of chemicals in general. According to a 1991 *New York Times* article, oil spills, hazardous waste, underground storage tanks, and releases of radioactive materials top the list of public concerns. To recognize and respond to these community sensitivities, the Chemical Manufacturers Association (CMA) developed a Responsible Care® program in 1988, borrowed from the Canadian Chemical Association. This program is designed to set standards for development, production, and transportation of chemicals; to set emergency response procedures; and to participate with government in creating "responsible laws, regulations and standards to safeguard the community, workplace and environment." Mobil Chemical belongs to the CMA, but asks: how can Mobil Chemical best demonstrate their commitment to make this Responsible Care program work?

THE VOLUNTARY PROTECTION PROGRAMS (VPP)

10   In 1982, OSHA initiated the Voluntary Protection Programs in which management, labor, and government establish a cooperation relationship at the workplace in order to recognize and promote effective safety and health management. Approved VPP participants must meet all relevant criteria and have an on-going safety program. OSHA has very rigorous requirements, including site inspections. They look for inadequate training in hazard recognition, repeated incidents with the same type

of hazards, and the ability to achieve hazard correction. Companies must apply to participate in the VPP at one of the three levels of accomplishment: Star, Merit, and Demonstration.

11   Star worksites are those with comprehensive, successful safety and health programs. They are evaluated on-site every three years and undergo annual injury rate reviews. Merit facilities work toward Star qualifications and are evaluated annually, while Demonstration worksites are still exploring the use of VPP. OSHA-approved VPP participants meeting all relevant OSHA standards are exempted from regularly scheduled OSHA inspections.

12   By October 1992, 77 U.S. facilities had achieved Star, and an additional 22 had reached Merit in 50 different companies. Of these sites, 75 were non-union and 24 were unionized. This means about 78,356 U.S. workers are in a VPP site.

13   In 1991, OSHA established the Office of Academic and Professional Affairs under the Directorate of Policy to help integrate occupational safety and health material into the curricula of medicine, engineering, and business. Through this Office, visitors were invited to observe a Mobil Chemical Star plant.

COMPANY BACKGROUND

14   Mobil Chemical is a wholly-owned subsidiary of Mobil Corporation and is an integrated manufacturer of petrochemicals, polypropylene packaging films, additives and synthetics, and fabricated plastics products for institutional and consumer markets. Figures for 1992 show that Mobil Chemical employs over 14,000 employees with a total sales revenue of more than $4 billion. It operates 27 domestic facilities and six international sites. If Mobil Chemical were an independent company, separate from Mobil Corporation, it would be a Fortune 200 company in its own right. See Exhibit 1 for a breakdown of the Mobil Chemical divisions. The Safety, Health and Loss Prevention Department falls under the Vice President, Environmental Affairs, who reports directly to the President of Mobil Chemical. Exhibit 2 gives financial highlights of Mobil Chemical for the years 1989 to 1992.

MOBIL CHEMICAL ENTERS THE VPP

15   Mobil Chemical became one of the first companies to take an active part in OSHA's Voluntary Protection Programs. According to insiders, the emphasis on safety and health has always been a leading priority at Mobil Chemical. However, as Dick Fricke, Manager, Evaluation and Regulatory Affairs at Mobil Chemical, stated, there was some hesitation about the VPP when OSHA first started the program in 1982. Mobil Chemical, like many other companies, was not interested in volunteering anything to OSHA, and believed there was no need to have OSHA help them to be safe because "we knew how to be safe, and we were better off keeping them out of our plants because they couldn't help us anyway. If there was an incident that would justify OSHA coming in, they would usually not find anything wrong, and our [safety] rates were well below the industry average and we weren't on any target lists . . . We felt we were managing our program quite well."

16   In early 1982, the Corporate Safety Manager of Mobil Corporation attended an Organizational Resource Councilors (ORC) meeting in Washington, D.C. At that meeting, OSHA made a pitch to get the councilors involved in the VPP. The Corporate Safety Manager asked which division of Mobil Corporation should enter the program first, just as an experiment. Mobil Chemical decided it would lead off Mobil Corporation's entry into the VPP. Each of the five divisions of Mobil Chemical were given the green light to volunteer at least one site. Seven sites were finally chosen to be part of the VPP–OSHA experiment, and so began Mobil Chemical's involvement with VPP.

17   Being part of the OSHA VPP is not easy. OSHA first gives a company a four-page application guideline sheet. The company then has to document what it does for occupational safety and health. The company's completed application can run 200–400 pages, and will include such items as the following:

EXHIBIT 1
Mobil Chemical Company

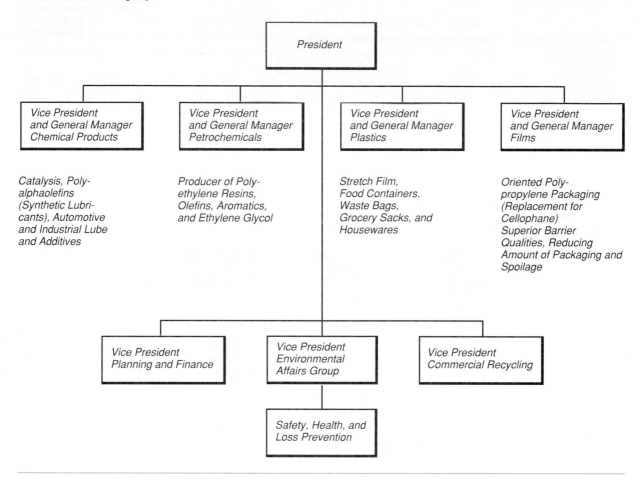

1. General information (company and corporate name, collective bargaining agent(s), number of employees, type of work performed, products, SIC code, injury incidence rate, lost workday injury case rate).
2. Management Commitment and Planning (documentation of safety and health policies, how safety fits into the overall management organization, responsibility, accountability, resources, planning, contract workers, employee notification, site plan).
3. Worksite analysis (surveys, self-inspections, job hazard analysis, employee notification of hazards, accident investigations, medical program).
4. Hazard Prevention and Control (professional expertise, safety and health rules, personal protective equipment, emergency preparedness, preventive maintenance).
5. Safety and Health Training (description of programs).
6. Employee Involvement (List the ways employees are involved; safety committees, etc.).
7. Program Evaluation (self-evaluation, rate reduction, etc.).
8. Statement of Commitment and Assurances (union and management; signature of the plant manager).

18   After the application has been reviewed and accepted by OSHA, an OSHA site visitation team then examines the facility firsthand. In 1983, the opening and closing OSHA Star review meetings at the seven Mobil Chemical plants included only senior staff, plant managers, the division safety manager and supervisors who made their presentations to OSHA. Hourly employees were excluded.

EXHIBIT 2
Financial Highlights of Mobil Chemical: 1989–1992 (in millions)

Chemical Financial Indicators	1989	1990	1991	1992
Petrochemical earnings	$ 424	$ 225	$ 142	$ 120
Plastics and other earnings	134	97	75	16
Total	558	322	217	136
Segment revenues	4,205	4,277	4,149	3,878
Capital expenditures	199	402	317	371
Segment assets	2,702	3,265	3,294	3,397

Sources: 1992 & 1991 Mobil Annual Reports.

19   Some at Mobil Chemical though the successful completion of the seven sites into the Star program would be enough, but this was not the case. Management then decided that all Mobil Chemical plants would become Star certified workplaces. By 1987, after five years of hard work, all Mobil Chemical sites had achieved Star certification. Mobil Chemical's new acquisitions, such as Tucker Housewares purchased in 1991, are all required to become Star certified as well.

20   Implementing the Star program at Mobil Chemical has also changed the tenor of the plant meetings with OSHA. For example, there is much more employee involvement now as compared to the early Star reviews. The opening Star meetings with OSHA are now attended by plant employees, including hourly personnel. They are the ones making the opening presentation to OSHA, informing OSHA about the workplace. They also participate in the final presentations by OSHA.

Costs and Benefits of Involvement in the VPP

21   The cornerstone of VPP is employee involvement integrated with management commitment. Employee involvement meshes with the total quality management (TQM) concept of "employee empowerment." Thus, management becomes the catalyst and/or facilitator in the Star certified sites. *A dramatic change in culture may be necessary if plants are run by managers of the "old school" who believe in "control and command" management (Theory X), whereby managers make all the decisions while employees are expected to follow orders without question.*

22   Mobil Chemical's injury incident rate over time has fallen from 4.1 in 1980 before the VPP to around 2.4 since entering the program. The Standard Industrial Classification Code (SIC) rate for the industry is around 15.0. Refer to Exhibit 3, which also shows the drop in lost workday case rate, and decreases in worker compensation and accident costs. The workday severity rate initially dropped for Mobil Chemical, but then rose to 1980 levels. Exhibit 3 also shows how incident rates are calculated for OSHA. Though the frequency of accidents has been much reduced, being in the Star program has not guaranteed a perfect record for Mobil Chemical. Two fatalities have occurred since starting the program: one in Covington, Georgia, another in Bakersfield, California.

23   For Bob Brant, Manager, Safety, Health and Loss prevention at Mobil Chemical, one key issue is how to better quantify the benefits of VPP. He knows there has been an improvement in morale and attitude. There is a great deal of anecdotal evidence from plant personnel who feel VPP is working, but Bob would like to see more meaningful numbers. His concern is how to go about getting more data that substantiate these gut feelings about the importance of VPP.

THE WASHINGTON, NEW JERSEY, FACILITY

24   Built in 1972, the Washington facility is 1 of 11 plants in Mobil Chemical's Plastics Division. The plant, located on 75 acres in Washington, New Jersey, has 225,000 sq. ft. with 80,000 sq. ft. for production and the balance for warehousing and storage. There are 9,000 skids located on-site and 32,000 skids at an off-site location. The primary products are plastic trash bags of the Hefty® line,

EXHIBIT 3
Mobil Chemical Company Injury and Workers Compensation Summary: 1980–1992

	80	81	82	83	84	85	86	87	88	89	90	91	92†
Injury incident rate*	4.1*	4.0*	3.5*	3.3*	3.2*	2.7*	2.2*	1.8	1.8	1.9	1.9	2.0	2.4
Lost workday case rate (people)	2.0	1.8	1.2	.8	.6	.5	.5	.8	.9	1.1	1.2	1.2	1.4
Workday lost—severity rate (in days)	36.1	28.4	26.3	22.8	18.4	11.2	17.3	24.2	23.8	32.4	32.9	32.6	36.5
Workers compensation costs (Millions $)†	n.a.	n.a.	3.0	2.3	2.1	1.2	1.5	1.7	2.1	2.2	2.1	2.6	3.8
Total accident costs (Millions $)† (includes workers compensation costs)	n.a.	n.a.	18.0	8.1	7.5	6.7	6.2	5.8	6.6	7.1	6.4	5.4	3.9

*Adjusted after records review. Injury incidence rates are calculated (N/EH) x 200,000 where

    N = Number of recordable injuries in one year

    EH =Total number of hours worked by all employees in one year

    200,000 = Equivalent of 100 full-time workers working 40-hour weeks for 50 weeks per year

†Not adjusted for inflation.

Source: Mobil Chemical's Safety, Health, & Loss Prevention Manager.

including "Twist-Tie,"® and "Cinch-Sak."® The "Twist-Tie"® can run six lines capable of producing 46 million lbs. per year. The "Cinch-Sak,"® started in 1988, can run four lines with a yearly capacity of 27 million lbs. The reclaim department has two lines capable of 18 million lbs. per year, for internally generated scrap and outside purchased scrap. The plant, with 143 people, has three shifts and runs seven days a week, 24 hours per day (8A.M.–4 P.M., 4 P.M.–midnight, midnight–8 A.M.). The plant manager, Win Clemmons, indicated that the Washington facility became OSHA Star certified for the first time in 1986 and recertified in 1989 and 1992. The plant layout is presented in Exhibit 4.

THE PRODUCTION PROCESS

25 The production process begins when polyethylene resin is unloaded from railcars located behind the plant facilities. It is then stored in silos that hold up to 190,000 lbs. (equivalent to one railcar). The resin is piped into blending systems by the use of blowers. Controls and power are designed to minimize noise, dust, and employee exposure to fire or explosion risks. A dust collector keeps dust from entering the atmosphere. Refer to Exhibit 5 for a picture of the extrusion flow diagram.

26 The resin pellets are fed into the extruders through a hopper. There are six extruders for "Twist-Tie"® and two extruders for "Cinch-Sak."® The extruders heat (300°F) the resin pellets to a liquid form. Coloring takes place with a dye which has been shipped by large trucks and unloaded at the loading docks. An operator monitors the extrusion process through a system of controls, alarms, and warning devices.

27 Once melted, the resin is forced out through a circular device called a die. Almost like a large cyclone, a bubble of continuous plastic is pulled upward, inflated and cooled as it extends to four stories in height. Some of the cooled extruded material will go directly into bag making machines in the "Twist-Tie"® lines while other material will be placed on large rolls for "Cinch-Sak"® lines. "Twist-Tie"® is a continuous process while "Cinch-Sak"® is a two-step process. One advantage of the latter process is the flexibility that rolls provide. They can be moved around to different lines, or placed in storage. However, the just-in-time manufacturing philosophy may not see this as an advantage. Throughout the process, statistical quality control charts are used to insure uniformity of the product.

28 The collapsed bubble of plastic forms one long double-layered sheet that is cut and sealed into bags (e.g., "Hefty"® kitchen and trash bags) The bags are folded, counted, and packed into predetermined box sizes (e.g., 18, 24, or 30 counts). After the product is boxed, finished product is placed on wooden

EXHIBIT 4

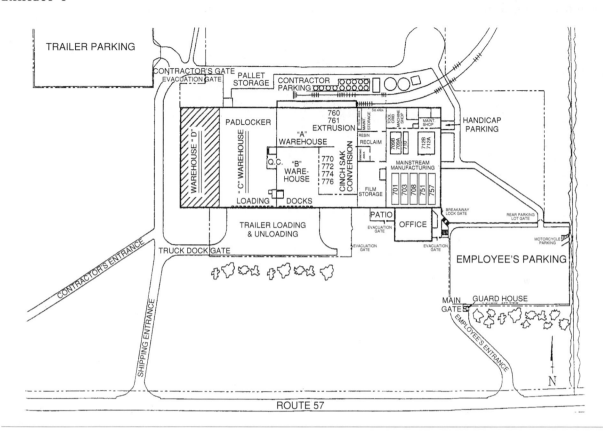

pallets where it is wrapped with stretch material before being stored or shipped. Scrap material is returned to the two reclaim lines to be turned eventually into new bags.

29   Until 1987, the packaging was labor intensive, but "now, no one touches the bags anymore, except for quality checking," says Donna Murling, Safety/Training Facilitator at the Washington, New Jersey, facility. Previously, people worked eight hours a day slapping coupons on a stack of bags going by on a conveyer belt. Back injuries, carpal tunnel syndrome, and other ergonomic problems have been greatly reduced through automation.

30   Safety and quality are two distinct aspects related to the automation of a manufacturing system. All machinery in the Washington, New Jersey, plant has protective Plexiglas guards to prevent unauthorized access. Conveyer belts over walkways and aisles have yellow safety netting underneath them. Throughout the plant, railings and other guarded areas are painted bright yellow. When maintenance is performed on any machine, the machine is completely turned off and secured with a safety lock, preventing it from being turned on accidentally during the maintenance procedure. Quality is also affected by automation through standardization. Variation in process time and other variables are minimized.

MANAGEMENT STYLE AND EMPLOYEE EMPOWERMENT

31   Win Clemmons, a 38-year-old college graduate from the University of North Carolina, and a former U.S. military officer, is indicative of the new breed of plant manager that Mobil Chemical wants to develop. He joined Mobil Chemical in 1983 as a first-line supervisor in Bakersfield, California, and after five and a half years, he moved to general supervisor at a plant in Illinois. Win was then transferred to the Washington facility in 1991 as production superintendent in charge of all the plant's

EXHIBIT 5
Extrusion Flow Diagram

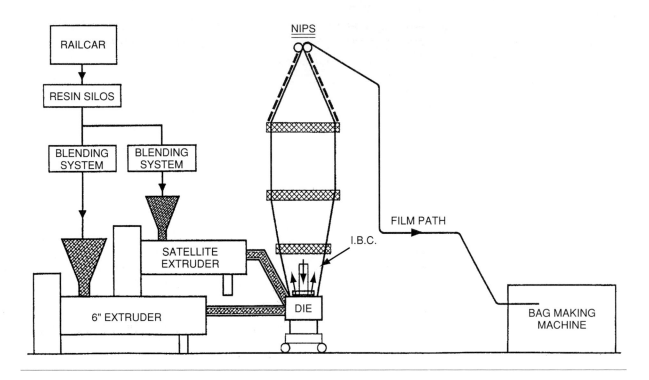

production. During a reorganization in which his predecessor was promoted, Clemmons moved into the plant manager's position.

32   Clemmons says his major challenge is to help the plant personnel understand what is going on. In the old management style, only a few people knew the "big picture" in the plant. Today, with high employee involvement and empowerment, the emphasis is on communication, sharing information with all employees, and also to "get them to make decisions on their own without having to call six people first." This is especially true now that the number of salaried employees has decreased from about 32 to 15. With fewer salaried employees, it is more important than ever to involve the 128 hourly employees in the decision-making process.

33   The employees are making more decisions on their own, but some are hesitant. Clemmons wonders how he should proceed to encourage this independent employee decision making.

TQM AND CONTINUOUS PRODUCT IMPROVEMENT EFFORTS

34   Total quality management (TQM) is a management philosophy that strives to involve the entire organization in efforts to satisfy customers. This can take the form of customer surveys, products and/or processes designed for quality, statistical process control, preventive maintenance, greater involvement with suppliers and distributors, and extensive employee training programs. TQM involves employee empowerment and the use of team problem solving. An important component of TQM is continuous quality improvement (CQI), which seeks gradual, continuous improvements of products and processes as opposed to dramatic steps in improvement. One way for companies to do this is through competitive benchmarking. This entails identifying firms known for "excellence in manufacturing" (world-class leaders), and by visiting these plants in order to analyze the disparities between world-class plants and one's own firm. At the Washington, New Jersey, plant, efforts toward TQM and benchmarking began in 1991.

EXHIBIT 6
The Star Model

Why:	To improve the way we operate the Washington plant	
Purpose:	Produce higher quality products by maximizing individual contributions	
How:	A five-point organization structure (STAR) focusing personal involvement on the most important activity areas in the plant	
What:	The STAR model will:	

- Enhance competitiveness through maximizing teamwork.
- Increase individual involvement and contributions (more as a stakeholder).
- Provide the framework for the plant's CQI efforts.
- Enable more pride, satisfaction, and motivation.
- Increase leadership and team skills at all levels.

Vision: Our goal is total commitment to the Continuous Quality Improvement process. Our standard of performance will be to constantly strive to safely provide cost competitive products and services that fully satisfy the requirements of our customers.

We will develop responsibility and accountability at all levels of the organization so that everyone's efforts will make a difference.

35   Prior to 1991, there was a Quality Leadership Team (QLT) composed of the plant manager and staff who met monthly to discuss strategic issues. The QLT did not include hourly workers close to the process. Following a consultant's recommendation, the QLT was expanded to 20 individuals (including 10 hourly and 10 salaried workers) who participated in a "High Involvement Seminar." The focus of the QLT meetings changed from informative to participative, and the team was challenged to look at where the plant needed the most help. One issue was how could they translate information from these monthly meetings into meaningful implementation. Some questions resulting from those early meetings included: Should they create an organizational design team? Should they call in another consultant? Should they visit other facilities? Which management practices could they adopt? Also, it became apparent that there was some frustration for hourly personnel who did not have a means to channel their suggestions. The QLT wanted to address this frustration.

36   In 1991, as a means for resolving some of these issues, the plant created its own internal 5-point Star Quality Program (no relation to OSHA's Star level certification). This 5-point Star Quality Program is divided along five functional areas: Safety; Planning; Learning and Development; Personnel; and Quality and Productivity. A quality and productivity facilitator was also hired to help launch the new program. These plant initiatives complemented divisional activities, such as the implementation of Juran's philosophy, and statistical process control. Exhibit 6 shows the purpose and the vision of the Star model.

37   To help them address some of their concerns, the QLT wanted to see how other organizations used teams. Specifically, in April of 1991, Mark Geuss, Manager of Employee Relations, and production superintendent, Jeff Phillips, visited a Du Pont plant in Pennsylvania. This visit was prompted by a *Fortune* magazine article in which Du Pont's team-based organizations were referenced. A second visit with the entire QLT group to Du Pont's plant followed in May 1991. The group also visited Stanley Vidmar, part of Stanley Works of Connecticut. These visits proved invaluable, giving them working examples of how to organize their natural work teams.

The Safety Point of the Five-Point Star

38   Safety is one point on the 5-point star. A structured weekly meeting occurs that includes about 34 people (or 26% of the total plant); of these 34 people about 28 are hourly employees. A typical meeting involves introducing guests, reviewing first aid/near miss/recordable injuries, reviewing the incident rate, giving reports, discussing OSHA 1910 regulations, VPP business, and other agenda items. Currently, a "Cinch-Sak"® operator, Bob Keating, is the Chair (or Strategic Leader) of the Safety Leadership Committee.

39   As an example of the preventive role it plays, the committee reviewed a Safety Improvement Opportunity Form (IOF) which noted a potential problem close to a doorway inside the plant where 3–4 foot heavy metal bins had been stacked three high. The danger existed of a fork-lift knocking these bins over, possibly injuring a worker. As a result of an investigation, foot traffic was re-routed and a guardrail erected, creating a buffer zone. Bins were required to be stacked no more than two high along the buffer zone, thus averting an unsafe incident. A potentially dangerous situation had been corrected before an accident had occurred.

40   To heighten safety awareness in the plant, past committee projects have included a "safety passport" and a yearly calendar. The "safety passport" is an incentive plan that awards $50 gift certificates for those who perform 12 safety actions (3 per quarter) over a year. Safety actions include becoming CPR certified, submitting a safety suggestion, attending safety circle meetings, and nine other types of activities. The design of the yearly plant calendar is also used to promote safety. A safety contest is conducted where employees' children and grandchildren submit illustrated safety posters, with slogans such as "Stay away from buzzing bees. If you bother them, they will sting," or "Don't jump on the bed, you might fall and hit your head." An outside panel of judges selects the 12 or so pictures to be included. Although the calendar is expensive to produce, it has been very popular with the employees.

41   The implementation of the internal Star program has caused a number of issues to surface. These include peer appraisal, employee assistance programs, policy and procedures, and recreation. For example, should doctors come and give annual hearing tests or blood tests, or prescribe smoking cessation patches? What would be the benefits? How well would these be received? Could there be possible problems of privacy?

42   In terms of safety, the net result has been impressive. One measure of the plant's success has included a 1991 President's Cup award to the facility as the plant with lowest incident rate among the 11 plants in the Plastics Division. Washington achieved an incident rate of 1.35 in 1991.

ROTATING SHIFTS

43   One recurring issue at the Washington, New Jersey, plant is the policy regarding rotating shifts. The current system divides the hourly shift workers into A,B,C, and D groups, and rotates their eight-hour system counterclockwise. For example, members of group A work the midnight to 8 a.m. shift for six days, then, two days off; return for six days on 4 p.m. to midnight. Again, off two days, and then work six days on the 8 a.m.–4 p.m. shift. This counterclockwise sleep rotation is contrary to the advice of most sleep experts who recommend a clockwise sleep rotation as better for one's body.

44   In 1990, the Washington facility developed a committee to investigate this issue. The committee came up with a number of alternatives, including 12-hour shifts. One proposal suggested an alternating weekly rotation. The first week, an hourly person would work daytime on Monday, Tuesday; have Wednesday, Thursday off, and work daytime on Friday, Saturday, and Sunday (or 48 hours). The following week he or she would have Monday and Tuesday off and would work Wednesday and Thursday nights (or 36 hours). One limitation placed on the plant was cost; the new plan could not exceed current spending. According to Bob Keating, "they didn't want to raise their labor costs . . . Even the twelve hour system would cost money." The problem was the overtime charges associated with the 48-hour week. The next week one would only work 36 hours, but the two weeks could not be averaged due to government regulations.

45   Of the 70% of the 130 hourly shift workers needed to make this dramatic change, only 56% approved. Even though this change in rotation was voted down, the concern about rotating shifts still lingers.

CONCLUSION

46   As visitors toured the Washington, New Jersey, plant, they were impressed with the plant's commitment toward safety and quality. However, they also saw Mobil Chemical as a company in transition with a number of challenges to overcome. For example, most customers prefer plastic bags. Yet as reported in *Chemical and Engineering News*, the Environmental Defense Fund believes the plastics

industry has a poor record with respect to recycling. Mobil Chemical's response has been its commercial recycling group formed in 1991 to implement large-scale recycling. It currently has plastic bag recycling programs in more than 4,000 supermarkets and other retail outlets nationwide.

47   Another challenge for the Washington facility is to be competitive with their sister Mobil Chemical plants located in Texas and Illinois where costs are lower. Utilities, labor, and taxes are just some of the factors that make business more expensive in New Jersey.

48   In addition, the entire bag making industry has become extremely competitive. At one time, there were only two major players: Mobil Chemical's "Hefty"® and Dow Chemical's "Glad"® bags. Today, there are more than 10 competitors successfully marketing to customers who are increasingly price sensitive.

49   Finally, for Mobil Chemical in general, the visitors considered the direction Mobil Chemical should take towards improving the government-industry relationship. Is there excessive government regulation? Is the industry burdened by overlapping regulatory jurisdictions? Are government procedures too complex and lengthy? Are they excessively detailed and too prescriptive? Or perhaps, through cooperative efforts with government, such as the VPP, Mobil Chemical can gain a competitive edge for their products, and a safe and healthy environment for their workers and their workers' communities.

CASE 6

TQM AND MOBIL CHEMICAL'S WASHINGTON, NEW JERSEY, FACILITY

INTRODUCTION

1   Total quality management (TQM) is a management philosophy that strives to involve the entire organization in efforts to satisfy customers. This can take the form of customer surveys, products/processes designed for quality, statistical process control, preventive maintenance, and greater involvement with suppliers and distributors, and extensive employee training programs. TQM involves employee empowerment and the use of team problem solving. An important component of TQM is continuous improvement (CI), which seeks gradual, continuous improvements of products and processes as opposed to dramatic steps in improvement. One way for companies to do this is through competitive benchmarking. This entails identifying firms known for "excellence in manufacturing" (world-class leaders), and by visiting their plants in order to analyze the disparities between world-class plants and one's own firm.

2   Many organizations including Mobil Chemical are looking to TQM as one mechanism for becoming more competitive in a global marketplace. At Mobil Chemical's Washington, New Jersey, plant, efforts in this direction began in 1991.

MOBIL CHEMICAL AND ITS WASHINGTON, NEW JERSEY, FACILITY

3   Mobil Chemical is a wholly-owned subsidiary of the Mobil Corporation and is an integrated manufacturer of petrochemicals, polypropylene packaging films, additives and synthetics, and fabricated plastics products for institutional and consumer markets. Figures for 1992 show that Mobil Chemical employs over 14,000 employees with a total sales revenue of more than $4 billion. It operates 27 domestic facilities and six international sites. If Mobil Chemical were an independent company separate from Mobil Corporation, it would be a Fortune 200 company in its own right. Mobil Chemical's four major divisions are Chemical Products, Petrochemicals, Plastics, and Films.

4   Built in 1972, Mobil Chemical's Washington facility is one of 11 plants in Mobil Chemical's Plastics division. The plant, located on 75 acres in Washington, New Jersey, has 225,000 sq. ft. with 80,000 sq. ft. for production and the balance for warehousing and storage. There are 9,000 skids located on-site and 32,000 skids at an off-site location. The primary products are plastic trash bags of the Hefty line including "Twist-Tie®," and "Cinch-Sak®." The "Twist-Tie" can run six lines capable of producing 46 million lbs. per year. The "Cinch-Sak," started in 1988, can run four lines with a yearly capacity of 27 million lbs. The reclaim department has two lines capable of 18 million lbs. per year, for internally generated scrap and outside purchased scrap. The plant, with 143 people, has three shifts and runs seven days a week, 24 hours per day (8 a.m.–4 p.m., 4 p.m.–midnight, midnight–8 a.m.). The plant layout is presented in Exhibit 1.

This case was prepared by Harold Dyck, PhD., and Sue Greenfeld, D.B.A., of California State University. Special thanks to Delbert L. Flowers, Director, Office of Academic and Professional Affairs of the Occupational Safety and Health Administration who facilitated and helped to make this case possible, and to Bob Brant, Chairman of the Voluntary Protection Programs Participants' Association, and Manager of Safety, Health, and Loss Prevention, Mobil Chemical.

EXHIBIT 1

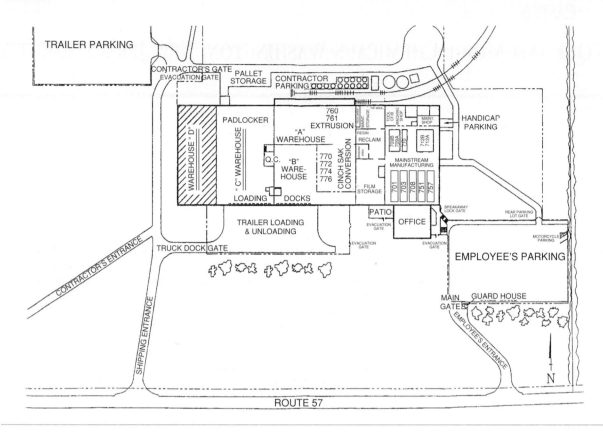

5   Plant manager, Win Clemmons, indicated that the Washington facility became OSHA Star certified for the first time in 1986 and recertified in 1989 and 1992. This certification is part of OSHA's Voluntary Protection Program (VPP). This program was initiated in 1982 to establish a cooperative relationship in the workplace between management, labor, and government, and to recognize and promote effective safety and health management.

THE PRODUCTION PROCESS

6   The production process begins when polyethylene resin is unloaded from railcars located behind the plant facilities. It is then stored in silos that hold up to 120,000 lbs. (equivalent to one railcar). The resin is piped into blending systems by the use of blowers. Controls and power are designed to minimize noise, dust, and employee exposure to risk of fire or explosion. A dust collector keeps dust from entering the atmosphere. Refer to Exhibit 2 for the extrusion flow diagram.

7   The resin pellets are fed into the extruders through a hopper. There are six extruders for "Twist-Tie" and two extruders for "Cinch-Sak." The extruders heat (300°F) the resin pellets to a liquid form. Coloring takes place with a dye, which has been shipped by large trucks and unloaded at the loading docks. An operator monitors the extrusion process through a system of controls, alarms, and warning devices.

8   Once melted, the resin is forced out through a circular device called a die. Almost like a large cyclone, a bubble of continuous plastic is pulled upward, inflated, and cooled as it extends to four stories in height. Some of the cooled extruded material will go directly into bag making machines in the "Twist-Tie" lines while other material will be placed on large rolls for "Cinch-Sak" lines.

EXHIBIT 2
Extrusion Flow Diagram

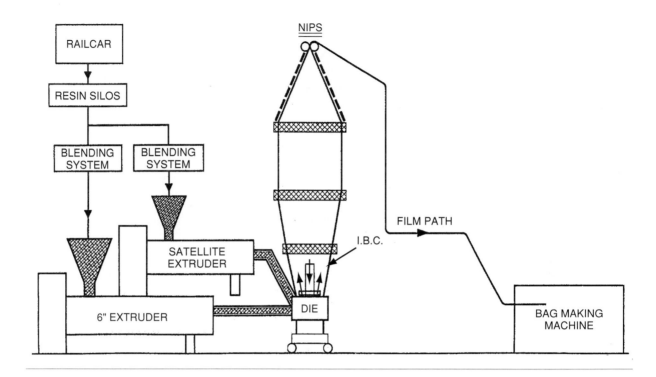

"Twist-Tie" is a continuous process while "Cinch-Sak" is a two-step process. One advantage of the latter process is the flexibility that rolls provide. They can be moved around to different lines, or placed in storage. However, the just-in-time manufacturing philosophy may not see this as an advantage. Throughout the process, statistical quality control charts are used to insure uniformity of the product.

9   The collapsed bubble of plastic forms one long double-layered sheet that is cut and sealed into bags (e.g., "Hefty" kitchen and trash bags). The bags are folded, counted, and packed into predetermined box sizes (e.g. 18, 24, 30 counts). After the product is boxed, the finished product is placed on wooden pallets where they are wrapped with stretch material before being either stored or shipped. Scrap material is returned to the two reclaim lines to be eventually turned into new bags.

10   Until 1992, the packaging was labor intensive, but "now, no one touches the bags anymore, except for quality checking," says Donna Murling, Safety/Training Facilitator at the Washington, New Jersey, facility. Previously, people worked eight hours a day slapping coupons on a stack of bags going by on a conveyor belt. Back injuries, carpal tunnel syndrome, and other ergonomic problems were eliminated through automation. Equipment is now run by programmable logic controllers (PLCs).

11   Safety and quality are two distinct aspects related to the automation of a manufacturing system. All machinery in the Washington, New Jersey, plant has protective Plexiglas guards to prevent unauthorized access. Conveyor belts over walkways and aisles have yellow safety netting underneath them. Throughout the plant, railings and other guarded areas are painted bright yellow. When maintenance is performed on any machine, the machine is completely turned off and secured with a safety lock, preventing it from being turned on accidentally during the maintenance procedure. Quality is also affected by automation through standardization. Variation in process time and other variables are minimized.

EXHIBIT 3
The Star Model

Why:	To improve the way we operate the Washington plant
Purpose:	Produce higher quality products by maximizing individual contributions
How:	A five-point organization structure (STAR) focusing personal involvement on the most important activity areas in the plant
What:	The STAR model will:

· Enhance competitiveness through maximizing teamwork.
· Increase individual involvement and contributions (more as a stakeholder).
· Provide the framework for the plant's Continuous Quality Improvement efforts.
· Enable more pride, satisfaction, and motivation.
· Increase leadership and team skills at all levels.

Vision:	Our goal is total commitment to our CQI process. Our standard of performance will be to constantly strive to safely provide cost competitive products and services that fully satisfy the requirements of our customers.
	We will develop responsibility and accountability at all levels of the organization so that everyone's efforts will make a difference.

TQM AND CONTINUOUS PRODUCT IMPROVEMENT EFFORTS

12   Prior to 1991, there was a Quality Leadership Team (QLT) composed of the plant manager and staff who met monthly to discuss strategic issues. The QLT did not include hourly workers close to the process. Following a consultant's recommendation, the QLT was expanded to 20 individuals (including 10 hourly and 10 salaried workers) who participated in a "High Involvement Seminar." The focus of the QLT meetings changed from informative to participative, and the team was challenged to look at where the plant needed to most help. One issue was: how could they translate information from these monthly meetings into meaningful implementation? Some questions from those early meetings included: should they create an organizational design team? Should they call in another consultant? Should they visit other facilities? Which management practices could they adopt? Also it became apparent that there was some frustration from hourly personnel who did not have a means to channel their suggestions. The QLT wanted to address this frustration.

13   In 1991, as a means for resolving some of these issues, the plant created its own internal 5-point Star Quality Program. This 5-point Star Quality Program is divided along five functional areas: Quality and Productivity; Safety; Planning; Learning and Development; and Personnel. A quality and productivity facilitator was also hired to help launch the new program. These plant initiatives complemented divisional activities, such as the implementation of Juran's philosophy, and statistical process control. Exhibit 3 shows the purpose of the vision of the Star model.

14   To help them address some of their concerns, the QLT wanted to see how other organizations used teams. Specifically, in April of 1991, Mark Geuss, Manager of Employee Relations, and Production Manager, Jeff Phillips, visited a Du Pont plant in Pennsylvania. This visit was prompted by a *Fortune* magazine article in which Du Pont's team-based organizations were referenced. A second visit by the entire QLT group to Du Pont's plant followed in May 1991. Du Pont has been engaged in implementing ISO 9000, which is a certification process for those companies desiring to trade with the European Community (EC). International Organization for Standardizations (ISO) Quality Management and Quality Assurance Committees created the ISO 9000 standards to "force the establishment of quality management procedures on firms doing business in the EC. . . . The standards may achieve worldwide acceptance."[1]

15   They also visited Stanley Vidmar, part of Stanley Works of Connecticut. These visits proved invaluable, giving them working examples of how to organize natural work teams. According to Mark Geuss, "It really does pay to get the people closest to the process involved in the decision making. You can't pay lip service. If anything will shoot you in the foot faster, it is trying to

EXHIBIT 4
Quality and Productivity Subcommittee Mission Statements

"Cinch-Sak" PIT	Work toward developing a manufacturing environment that is dedicated to meeting our customers' needs, expectations, and desires, improving quality and reducing costs.
"Twist-Tie" PIT	Improve "Twist-Tie" operations in all areas. We will do this by getting ideas from suggestion forms, people on the floor, fellow team members, and any other available source.
Recycle PIT	Strive to safely produce and distribute cost effective reprocessed materials that consistently meet our customers' expectations. We will establish a solid base of operations involving every member of the department in the process of continual improvement of both existing processes and in the implementation of new technology.
Warehouse PIT	Continually improve the distribution function. This will be accomplished through teamwork and the implementation of warehouse improvement projects.
Maintenance PIT	Strive to be a cohesive, well informed, knowledgeable maintenance department, capable of performing quality workmanship to the satisfaction of all with a commitment to continually improve through progressive concepts.
Q.C. PIT	Work together as a team to educate and guide the plant in the manufacturing of quality products.
Downgauging	Implement the division request for reduced caliper production in the "Twist-Tie" area without any incremental increase in reclaim or downtime.

implement high involvement, but retaining control. They see through that like you wouldn't believe. It is difficult for some of our managers to grasp."

THE QUALITY AND PRODUCTIVITY POINT OF THE FIVE-POINT STAR

16   Quality and productivity is one point of the 5-point Star with a leadership committee of 14 employees including management and hourly employees. The overall mission statement for this point is to "develop and facilitate the process of improvement in the plant by providing guidance for the [Process Improvement Teams] PITs." Individual mission statements have been developed for "Cinch-Sak," "Twist-Tie," Recycle, Warehouse, Maintenance, Q.C., and Downgauging. Exhibit 4 presents the Quality and Productivity Subcommittee mission statements.

17   To improve the quality of the "Hefty" bags, statistical process improvement (SPI) charts track variables at various points of the production process. Exhibit 5 shows an example of an SPI $\overline{X}$ and R chart for the variable "width" on line 776A. Notice that on the 14th subsample action was taken to increase the width when the range became large. Also notice the out-of-control point on the 37th subsample.

18   In terms of improving the scheduling process, scheduler Sam Rafalko receives a monthly rough cut of the production requirements for each line from Mobil Chemical Plastics headquarters in Rochester, New York, where 2–3 month forecasts for product demand takes place. Headquarters gives case quantities for each line. After the weekly production meeting with the plant manager and personnel from production, engineering, and maintenance, Sam puts a 10-day schedule for the operating lines onto a magnetic wall board. For example, there may be 1,600 cases of "Twist-Ties" that will run on line 703 from the 11th and until the 20th of the month. The schedule assumes 100% line utilization, but he modifies the schedule as the plant runs ahead or behind its production goals. He updates the schedule as changes come in.

19   The schedule shows the item number, the case quantity, the day Rochester wants the line to start, and specifics about the item itself (e.g. count, gauge, nonpoly part numbers, ship dimension, corrugate dimension, and the approximate number of cases to be produced daily). From that, Sam orders

EXHIBIT 5

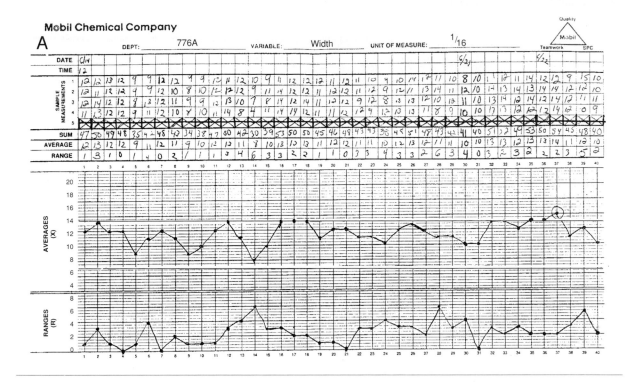

the "nonpoly" corrugated cardboard, glue, tape, drawstrings, coupons, and any other items in the right quantities so that delivery will be in time for each production run. Warehousing time is minimal. For example, nonpoly and other items used to arrive two weeks prior to their scheduled use, but now, warehousing runs around three days. This has decreased warehousing costs and has minimized problems associated with the nonpoly becoming damaged or dirty.

20   Purchase orders for some items are sent to Rochester, New York, where they are bought in large quantities. The Washington, New Jersey, plant has its own suppliers for such items as corrugate, drawstrings, and glue. Currently, there are two corrugate suppliers, but Mobil Chemical may be moving to one supplier in the near future.

21   Inventories of finished goods (e.g., "Cinch-Saks" and "Twist-Ties") have also decreased over time as these goods are shipped as they are made on a regular basis. This has helped to reduce obsolescence of finished goods, and minimize the need for repackaging. A distribution information system keeps track of the locations and status of all items in transit.

22   Planned preventive maintenance occurs continually, but a complete plant shutdown for a total maintenance servicing occurs twice a year. These times are two weeks in the summer and the period between Christmas and New Year's Day.

THE SAFETY POINT OF THE FIVE-POINT STAR

23   Safety is another point on the five-point star. A structured weekly meeting occurs that includes about 34 people (or 26% of the total plant); of these 34 people about 28 are hourly employees. A typical meeting involves introducing guests, reviewing first aid/near miss/recordable injuries, reviewing the injury incident rates,[2] giving reports, discussing OSHA regulations, VPP business, and other agenda items. Currently, a "Cinch-Sak" operator, Bob Keating, is the Chair (or Strategic Leader) of the Safety Leadership Committee.

24   As an example of the preventive role it plays, the committee reviewed a Safety Improvement Opportunity Form (IOF) which noted a potential problem close to a doorway inside the plant where 3–4 foot heavy metal bins had been stacked three high. The danger existed of a fork-lift knocking these bins over, possibly injuring a worker. As a result of an investigation, foot traffic was re-routed, and a guardrail was erected, creating a buffer zone. Bins were required to be stacked no more than two high along the buffer zone, thus, averting an unsafe incident. A potentially dangerous situation had been corrected before an accident had occurred.

25   To heighten safety awareness in the plant, past committee projects have included a "safety passport" and a yearly calendar. The "safety passport" is an incentive plan that awards $50 gift certificates for those who perform 12 safety actions (3 per quarter) over a year. Safety actions include becoming CPR certified, submitting a safety suggestion, attending safety circle meetings, and nine other types of activities. The design of the yearly plant calendar is also used to promote safety. A safety contest is conducted where employees' children and grandchildren submit illustrated safety posters, with slogans such as "Stay away from buzzing bees. If you bother them, they will sting." or "Don't jump on the bed, you might fall and hit your head." An outside panel of judges selects the 12 or so pictures to be included. Although the calendar is expensive to produce, it has been very popular with the employees.

26   The implementation of the internal Star program has caused a number of issues to surface. These include peer appraisal, employee assistance programs, policy and procedures, and recreation. For example, should doctors come and give annual hearing tests or blood tests, or prescribe smoking cessation patches? What would be the benefits? How well would these be received? Could there be possible problems of privacy?

27   In terms of safety, the net result has been impressive. One measure of the plant's success has included a 1991 President's Cup award to the facility as the plant with the lowest incidence rate among 11 plants in the Plastics Division. Their incidence rate in 1991 was 1.35.

The Debate over Worker-Management Teams

28   Worker-management teams, such as the QLT, have not been without controversy. According to a *Wall Street Journal* article, a major ruling by the National Labor Relations Board (NLRB) in June of 1993 ordered Du Pont to "disband seven such panels and to deal instead with the company's chemical workers union."[3] The Board maintained that Du Pont circumvented the union because decisions made by these management-labor teams were actually subject to management approval. Unions assert that the company cannot bypass the union as the bargaining agent.

29   However, U.S. Department of Labor Secretary Robert B. Reich is a supporter of worker-management teams, and views them as a mechanism to solve problems in the workplace. At the state level, some states are already *requiring* worker-management teams for workplace safety issues. In Connecticut, "companies must begin establishing worker management teams to investigate accidents, evaluate prevention programs, and determine possible safety fixes."[4] Other states following suit include Alaska, Minnesota, Nebraska, North Carolina, Oregon, Tennessee, Washington, and West Virginia. As a nonunionized plant, the Washington, New Jersey, facility is somewhat removed from the legal debate surrounding worker-management teams.

Conclusion

30   As Mobil Chemical's Washington, New Jersey, facility looks towards meeting its customers' needs, plant personnel wonder: Will they be able to establish a solid base of operation whereby every member is involved in continual improvement? Will they be able to build a cohesive, informed work force capable of performing quality workmanship with cost reduction and technology improvement? Will they be able to work together as a team, and how does teamwork lead to individual promotion and compensation? Will direct employee involvement in safety improve plant safety performance, and long-run cost savings?

FOOTNOTES

1. Barry Render and Jay Heizer, *Principles of Operations Management: Building and Managing World-Class Operations* (Boston, MA: Allyn and Bacon, 1994), p. 93.

2. Injury incidence rates are calculated as $(N/EH) \times 200{,}000$ where

$$N = \text{Number of recordable injuries in one year}$$
$$EH = \text{Total number of hours worked by all employees in one year}$$
$$200{,}000 = \text{Equivalent of 100 full-time workers working 40-hour}$$
$$\text{weeks for 50 weeks per year}$$

3. Kevin Salwen, "Du Pont Is Told It Must Disband Nonunion Panels," *The Wall Street Journal*, June 7, 1993, p. A2.

4. Jyoti Thottman and Kevin G. Salwen, "As U.S. Mulls Worker-Safety Mandate, Some States Require Company Action," *The Wall Street Journal*, June 22, 1993, pp. A2, A4.

CASE 7

PERRIGO COMPANY

1   Mike Jandernoa, the Chief Executive Officer and Chairman of the Board of Perrigo Company, was driving along Michigan State Highway 222 toward the city of Allegan, the site of the company's corporate headquarters. It was the first week of March 1993. As he passed snow-covered farmlands, Mike thought about the upcoming week-long strategic planning meeting. This was the meeting where critical long-term plans were made for the company. He smiled at the recollection of an executive who described these meetings as "5 or 6 days of pure hell." Yet, argued Mike to himself, these meetings were vital for Perrigo. The store brand industry was in a boom period with tremendous opportunities for a company that was well positioned.

2   Pulling into the employee (the company had no executive parking spaces) parking lot, Mike parked his car and walked briskly to his office. After greeting his executive secretary he told her that he was not to be disturbed for the next 3–4 hours. He wanted to spend the time reviewing the company's present position so that he was well prepared for the strategic planning meeting.

COMPANY HISTORY

3   Headquartered in Allegan, Michigan, the Perrigo Company was founded in 1887 by Luther Perrigo, who sold curative elixirs from a horse-drawn cart. In the late 1940s, William L. Tripp, grandson of Luther Perrigo, and Dr. Lem Curlin, an investor, helped guide the conversion of the company from a repacker of generic home remedies to a quality manufacturer of branded health and beauty aids.

4   In 1981, the founding family sold the company to a management group. The acquisition, which was a leveraged buyout, also marked the transition from a family-owned branded products company to a professionally managed maker of products for the store brand market. In 1986, the company was sold to Grow Group, Inc., (for $45 million) a New York–based publicly held company that owned (at that time) 23 diverse manufacturing firms. Perrigo became the largest unit of Grow Group, Inc., contributing almost one-third of total sales. In April 1988, a management group bought Perrigo from Grow Group, Inc., for $61 million through a leveraged buyout. Key management personnel, however, stayed with the company throughout these transitions.

5   In December 1991, the company made an initial public offering of 9.2 million shares of common stock for a purchase price of $16 per share. Of the more than $122 million (net of commissions) that was raised by the offering, approximately $35 million was used to acquire Cumberland-Swan, a major manufacturer of personal care products located in Smyrna, Tennessee. The rest of the proceeds was used to reduce the debt that resulted from the series of leveraged buyouts.

6   In September 1992, 5 million shares of common stock were sold at $32 per share by some of the existing shareholders. The company's common stock was traded in the over-the-counter market and was included in the NASDAQ National Market System under the symbol "PRGO." In March 1993, approximately 40% of the shares were owned by institutions and the general public, while 60% of the shares were owned by the management group together with the Hillman Company and its affiliates.

7   Citing a cooperative relationship with the workforce and a strong commitment to low-cost production and customer service as causes, Perrigo Company reported fiscal 1992 sales of $409.8

This case was prepared by Ram Subramanian of Grand Valley State University.

EXHIBIT 1
Price Comparison of Selected National Brands and Their Store Brand Equivalents

Product	National Brand		Store Brand		Consumer Savings
	Retail Price	Retail Profit	Retail Price	Retail Profit	
Advil (OTC)	$7.88	$1.55	$4.49	$2.76	43%
Head & Shoulders (Personal care)	3.49	0.74	2.69	1.44	23%
Centrum (Vitamins)	8.99	0.99	5.75	2.25	36%

Note: Advil, Head & Shoulders, and Centrum are registered trademarks.
Source: Perrigo Company.

million and a net income of $28.6 million. It was the nation's largest manufacturer of over-the-counter (non-prescription) pharmaceuticals and personal care products for the store brand market as well as a leading player in the private label vitamin market.

8   The vast majority (about 98% in 1992) of Perrigo's products were sold under the retailer's brand name and competed with nationally advertised brand names. In addition, the company also marketed its own brand of vitamins, personal care products, and over-the-counter pharmaceutical products under the "Nature's Glo," "Perrigo," "Swan," and "Good Sense" labels.

THE STORE BRAND PRODUCTS INDUSTRY

9   In 1991, the $26 billion store brand (or private label) industry accounted for 18.2% unit share and 13.7% dollar share of the total supermarket revenue. This was an increase from 15.3% in units and 11.6% in dollars from 1988.[1] Brian Sharoff, the President of the Private Label Manufacturers Association (PLMA) identified the factors responsible for the explosive growth of the store brand industry as: good packaging, high quality, aggressive promotion, and increased corporate commitment by retailers.[2]

10   Store brand products encompassed all merchandise sold under a retailer's private label. These products, which were usually identical to branded products, were found in categories such as food, snacks, soft drinks, health and beauty aids, and over-the-counter (OTC) drugs.

11   Store brand products had long been a staple of most supermarket chains. They offered customers savings of around 30 to 40 percent over national brands (Exhibit 1). However, despite offering significant price savings for consumers, sales of store brand products were low until the late 1980s. This was because store brands, like the low cost generic products that mushroomed during the 1980s, had a reputation for uneven quality, cheap packaging, and poor store display. The store brand industry came into the limelight in 1985 with the success of Loblaw's, the Toronto-based grocery chain's, private-label President's Choice line.[3] The popularity of this line along with the significantly high profit margins for the retailer (approximately 10–15% for national brands versus 30% for store brands) because of lower marketing and promotional costs, enabled the industry to register strong sales growth in the next few years. National brands ignored the growth in popularity of store brands, arguing that the switch was due to the recession and that customers would come back to branded products once good times returned. This was not to be as store brand industry sales increased each year from 1988 to 1991.

12   The PLMA attributed four reasons for the renaissance of store brand products. First, retailers saw themselves as more directly in touch with their customers than most manufacturers and therefore believed they were the ones who had the most to lose from customer dissatisfaction. They wanted to control their own destiny. Second, there was a decline in brand loyalty. Marcia Smith, the publisher of *Private Label Products News*, an industry trade magazine, talked about this decline:

> Brand loyalty is mostly dead. Consumers want quality products, they want value for their money, but they've discovered extremely good value in private labels. They've gotten smarter.[4]

EXHIBIT 2
Overall Market Size, Store Brand's Share, and Perrigo's Market Share in 1992

Perrigo's Product Categories	Total Market Size (in billions)	Store Brand Share	Perrigo's Market Share
OTC	$ 7.2	12%	65%
Personal care	8.7	7	44
Vitamins	1.7	31	13
Total	$17.6	11%	45%

Note: Total market size includes sales of branded plus store brand product (retail value).
Source: Perrigo Company.

13   Aggressive couponing by national brands helped in dissipating brand loyalty. As a result, consumers placed several brands (including store brands) on par with each other and made their shopping decisions according to price and promotion. The third reason was the major shift in consumer attitudes toward private label. A 1991 Gallup poll indicated greater acceptance of store brands, primarily because retailers improved the quality and merchandizing of these products. Finally, the fourth reason was the internationalization of retailing. Many major U.S. supermarket chains were owned by European companies, where store brands had been accepted for a long time.[5] 1991 market share for private label in Great Britain was around 29%, 24% in France, and 20% in Holland and Belgium.[6]

14   Exhibit 2 gives the overall market size, store brand's share of total market, and Perrigo's market share in 1992. Exhibit 3 indicates store brands' share of total market in each of the three segments (mentioned above) for the period 1990–1992.

15   The store brand industry was highly fragmented along product and geographic lines. Nearly 200 manufacturers vied with one another to supply retailers. Competition was driven primarily by cost and quality, though Perrigo executives constantly emphasized customer service as a key success factor. Since most players in the store brand industry were small, closely-held companies, individual data about competitors was impossible to obtain. Exhibit 4 profiles the competition in the OTC, personal care, and vitamin segments of the store brand industry. Perrigo considered itself to be the leader in the OTC and personal care segments and the third big player (both P-Leiner and Pharmavite had broader vitamin product lines and larger sales volume than Perrigo) in the vitamin segment of the store brand industry.

COMPANY PROFILE

A. Company Organization and Management

16   Perrigo Company operated through three wholly-owned subsidiaries. L. Perrigo Company (located in Allegan, Michigan) manufactured over-the-counter pharmaceuticals and certain lines of personal care products. Perrigo Company of South Carolina (located in Greenville, South Carolina) produced vitamins, and Cumberland-Swan (in Smyrna, Tennessee) primarily produced personal care products and "wets" or traditional liquid "home remedy" products such as rubbing alcohol, hydrogen peroxide, castor oil, and witch hazel.

17   Michael J. Jandernoa was the Chief Executive Officer and Chairman of the Board of Perrigo Company. Elected a Director of the company in 1981, he became the CEO in 1986, 7 years after joining the company. The other principal officers were: Richard Hansen, the Chief Operating Officer and President of L. Perrigo Company, Lonnie Smith, President of Cumberland-Swan, and M. James Gunberg, Treasurer and Chief Financial Officer.

EXHIBIT 3
Store Brands' Share of Total Market, 1990–1992

Category	1990	1991	1992
Over-the-counter (OTC)	9%	11%	12%
Personal care	5	6	7
Vitamins	29	30	31

Source: Information provided by Perrigo Company.

18   Exhibit 5 gives a condensed organizational chart for the company. Within the L. Perrigo and Cumberland-Swan subsidiaries, a functional structure was observed. The South Carolina subsidiary was operated from Allegan, Michigan. The finance department and the Executive Vice President's office provided support functions in the areas of finance and operations, respectively.

B. Marketing and Sales

19   In contrast to national brand manufacturers who focused on the consumer (i.e., the end user), Perrigo sought to establish close relationships with its customers, the retailers. Its marketing efforts were directed at developing customized marketing plans and programs for its customers' store brands. One important aspect of this store brand management approach was that it enabled retailers to promote their own brand name products at the point of purchase. In addition, because the cost to the retailer of a store brand product was generally significantly lower than that of a national brand product, the retailer was able to commit funds to promote its store brand products through coupons, rebates, and other individualized promotions, while still realizing a higher profit margin on its store brand products than on comparable national brand products. Jeff Needham, L. Perrigo Company's Vice President of Marketing, talked about the company's marketing focus:

> Our customer universe is very well-defined. We are doing business today in some way, shape, or form with just about every retailer in the country. There are some retailers we aren't doing business with that we'd like to, but that's a pretty short list. That is not to say we're doing all the business we want to with all of our customers, obviously, but our customer universe is pretty well-defined and we're talking to those people on a regular basis. So we kind of pride ourselves on understanding what's going on with all of our customers, and certainly our major customers. We have to be very well attuned to them, seeing them on a regular basis. As our customers' store brand program becomes increasingly important to them, it is necessary that they execute a well thought-out marketing plan to support it. Perrigo's marketing role is to support our customers in helping to direct this brand management planning process and to provide the necessary programs and tools to them so that they can execute successful in-store programs. Aside from a couple of vitamin companies, Perrigo was the first company (in the store brand industry) to have invested tremendous resources in its marketing function. It clearly gives us an edge over our competitors.

20   The marketing department was responsible for managing product introductions and conversions, promotional planning support, and market research. It used both primary and secondary market research (Perrigo had performed or authorized some of the largest primary and secondary market studies ever completed on store brand customer buying habits), monitored data and trends for products and categories, and provided market information and educational training aids to its customers.

21   The company's products were sold by its own sales force primarily to major retail drug, supermarket, and mass merchandise chains, and major wholesalers and to industry brokers for sales to smaller retailers.

22   In fiscal 1992, Perrigo had approximately 2,250 customers, one of which, Wal-Mart, accounted for approximately 12% of total sales. According to Perrigo Company officials, most, though not all, customers sole source their private label products.

23   In the late 1980s, the company introduced a program to reduce retailer inventory costs while maintaining the optimum level of product on store shelves. This program, called the Minimum Inventory–Maximum Service (MIMS) program, used Electronic Data Interchange (EDI) to allow

EXHIBIT 4
Store Brand Competition*

Company	1992 Sales† (Millions)	Segment Company Competes In		
		OTC	Personal Care	Vitamins
Perrigo	$409	Yes	Yes	Yes
P. Leiner	225	Yes	Yes	Yes
Pharmarite	150	No	No	Yes
Rexall/Pennex	70	Yes	Yes	Yes
ViJon	50	No	Yes	No
Granutec	35	Yes	No	No
PFI	35	Yes	No	No
Hall Labs	35	Yes	No	Yes
American Vitamins	30	No	No	Yes

*Selected companies.
†Except for Perrigo, sales of other companies are estimates by Perrigo executives.
Source: Perrigo Company.

Perrigo to monitor and manage customer inventory levels. As of fiscal 1992, about 10% of their customers were involved in the MIMS program.

24　　Exhibit 6 shows the company's product sales by class. In fiscal 1992, Perrigo offered an increased number of vitamin products to its customers. Sales of the personal care segment increased significantly over the previous year because of the Cumberland-Swan acquisition, while the increase in OTC segment sales was attributed to the introduction of several new products through the Abbreviated New Drug Application process. Exhibit 7 gives examples of products marketed by the company and their national brand equivalents. In 1993, Perrigo marketed approximately 857 store brand products to their customers.

25　　In 1984, the company introduced the "Good Sense" brand of products. Jeff Needham, the Vice President of Marketing, explained the purpose and rationale of the program:

> About nine years ago we identified the need for a brand program, what we call the "control label" program. That was as much as anything designed to provide us a program that we could sell to customers who weren't large enough or for whatever reason didn't want to have their own store brand program. So the Good Sense program was developed to fill that need. That business has been growing quite significantly in the last several years.

26　　Apart from the Good Sense line, the company also manufactured and marketed Nature's Glo and Perrigo lines of natural vitamins and Swan brand "wets." In addition, the company used the Equate brand name, for which it gave Wal-Mart an exclusive license.

C. Operations

27　　The company had six manufacturing facilities located throughout the country (Exhibit 8). These facilities occupied approximately 1,467,000 square feet. New facilities were added when needed, and in 1993, to support their anticipated growth, the company embarked on a $60 million capital investment plan to increase its production and distribution capacities. A $25 million tablet manufacturing facility at Allegan, Michigan, an $8 million mouthwash (personal care) manufacturing plant at Smyrna, Tennessee, and a $3 million vitamin plant at Greenville, South Carolina, were in the planning stages as part of the $60 million investment. In fiscal 1992, the company operated at an average of 86% of capacity.

28　　Each manufacturing plant was characterized by flexible manufacturing capabilities which were designed to allow low cost production of a wide variety of products of different quantities, sizes, and packaging. The focus of the manufacturing function was on flexibility to respond to customer needs.

EXHIBIT 5
Perrigo Company's Organization Chart (Condensed)

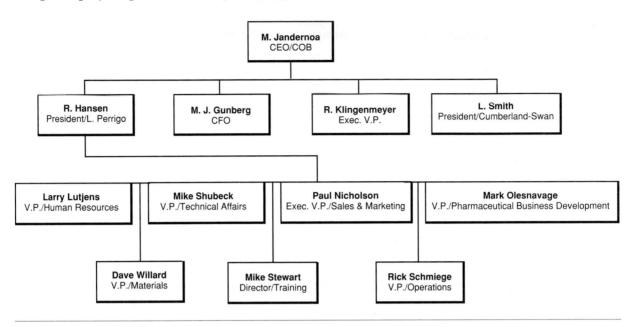

Note: Cumberland-Swan followed a functional structure similar to that of the L. Perrigo subsidiary shown above.

Source: Perrigo Company.

Flexible production line change-over capabilities and reduced cycle times enabled the company to respond quickly to changes in manufacturing schedules.

29　　　Richard Schmiege, Vice President of Operations for the L. Perrigo subsidiary, talked about the company's production function:

> Something that we constantly talk about in our regular meetings is customer service. Our goal is, as you would expect, continuous improvement. We have many programs in place to help support that objective. We meet every Monday morning in a production meeting which involves operation departmental managers, and we invite other people from scheduling, inventory control, purchasing, customer service—basically, anyone who wants to attend our meeting. Sometimes, we have as many as 35 people in these meetings. We report the production numbers from the previous week, we talk about the problems that we've had for the week, and assign responsibility if there's a problem that needs to be fixed. We have a very open session and talk about things that need to be done on a weekly basis. We also have many formal programs to support our objective of continuous improvement. We have installed a state-of-the-art manufacturing resource planning (MRP II) system which enables the company to develop realistic and attainable production schedules and related material and capacity requirements. We have also introduced a JIT/TQC system, which we call the "Advantage" program. Our interpretation of the JIT/TQC concept led to the formation of work teams. In the past we had line workers whose job was to watch the lines to make sure they were running smoothly and to shut them down if they weren't running smoothly. We also had another set of people who would come in when machines needed to be fixed or set up. Today, we have all of the employees, including set-up people, unit leaders and line workers, doing the same thing—fixing, setting up and running the machines as a team.

30　　　The company had a supplier certification program whose objective was to improve quality, save time, and eliminate duplication of efforts between Perrigo and its suppliers, thus reducing costs. Dave Kiddy, Director of Purchasing for the Allegan subsidiary, talked about the certification process.

> Our supplier certification program was developed by a crossfunctional team from within the company. We developed various measurements and supplier evaluation criteria which we use when auditing suppliers and their facilities. We measure quality and service for all items purchased from suppliers being considered for

EXHIBIT 6
Perrigo Product Sales Breakdown

	1988	1989	1990	1991	1992
Sales in Millions of Dollars					
OTC	$100.5	$144.1	$165.4	$187.7	$259.4
Personal Care	40.3	46.0	53.9	65.2	114.3
Vitamins	23.5	24.7	26.2	27.9	35.2
	$164.3*	$214.8	$245.5	$280.8	$408.9
Sales as Percent of Total Sales					
OTC	61.2%	67.1%	67.4%	66.8%	63.4%
Personal Care	24.5	21.4	22.0	23.2	28.0
Vitamins	14.3	11.5	10.6	10.0	8.6
	100.00%	100.00%	100.00%	100.00%	100.00%

*The total of the three segments' sales differs from Perrigo's total reported sales because of revenues from contract work that Perrigo performs for certain national brand manufacturers. These contract sales amount to less than 1 percent of total sales. In 1992, for example, contract sales were $885,000 or 0.22% of total sales.
Source: Perrigo Company, 1992 Annual Report.

certification as well as those already certified. Our intent is to improve the quality and reduce our total cost of the materials we purchase by working closely with our suppliers. We attempt to clearly communicate our needs and expectations, evaluate suppliers' capabilities to meet a high standard, and take redundancy out of the system if we are confident the suppliers' processes are under control. We have been able to improve our total cost by reducing or eliminating the amount of incoming inspection, rerouting the flow of certified materials through the production departments, and by reducing leadtimes and inventory levels. Another benefit of our certification program has been in the improvement of communication and strengthened relationships with our suppliers. I feel we are better customers to them and they are better suppliers to us because we have improved our understanding of each other's needs and capabilities. Also, multi-level relationships have been developed or enhanced during the certification process.

31   The certification process had been in place since 1992. Only a few of the company's suppliers had been certified by March 1993, but they represented a significant number of the items and dollars spent. All of the company's certified suppliers were considered strategic suppliers.

32   The company did not make any of the chemicals required for production. The company was vertically integrated to the extent that it processed all the raw materials in-house before being used in the production process. The acquisition of Cumberland-Swan gave the company a bottle blow molding facility. In addition, the company made 75 percent of its labels and printed 35 percent of its cartons in-house.

33   Perrigo's Graphic Arts and Printing Department was a 66,000 square foot facility that employed 239 graphic arts experts including 43 artists. The objective of this department was to provide excellent customer service. Extensive consumer research was used to design and produce packaging that invited comparison with national brands. In addition, the department also created point-of-sale materials custom-designed to help the retailer attract customers. Jack Godfrey, the Printing Manager, talked about the Graphics Department:

About six years ago (in 1987) we invested in a proprietary design software that we use to design on a terminal. It is similar to designing on a Macintosh, only much larger. Our department currently runs 1,500 to 1,700 jobs per month. In designing the labels our Regulatory Affairs Department provides us with guidelines to follow.

34   Products were shipped from six geographically dispersed distribution facilities (Exhibit 9). Several large customers picked up their products directly from these distribution facilities. In most cases, contract or common carriers were used to deliver products.

D. Research and Development

35   The company did not do primary or basic research in which it would develop new products which had not been previously sold to consumers. Instead, the company's research efforts were focused on

EXHIBIT 7
Examples of Company Products and National Brand Equivalents

Company Products	Competing National Brands
OTC Pharmaceuticals	
Ibuprofen Tablets	Advil Tablets
Acetaminophen Tablets	Tylenol Tablets
Aspirin	Bayer
Nite Time Cough Syrup	Nyquil
Stress Liquid	Pepto-Bismol
Flavored Antacid Tablets	Tums
Personal Care Products	
Green Mouthwash	Scope
Anti-Plaque Rinse	Plax
Smoker's Toothpaste	Topol
Shampoo Plus Conditioner	Pert
Antiperspirant Stick	Sure
Vitamins	
Therapeutic M	Theragran M
A-Shapes Chewables	Flintstones
Century IV Vitamins	Centrum

Source: Perrigo Company, 1992 Annual Report.

developing store brand equivalents of national brands, and in reformulating existing products in response to changes in national brand formulas. Thirty-two employees made up this department which spent approximately $3.4 million in fiscal 1992.

E. Human Resources

36 Larry Lutjens, Vice President of Human Resources for the L. Perrigo subsidiary, traced the company's labor-management situation:

> Perrigo, when I joined them in 1980, was about a $40 million company and we employed about 800 people. It was an interesting situation. The company's employees had just gone through an organizing campaign and management had won by a very small margin. Bill Swaney, the CEO of the company after the first management-led leveraged buyout, felt that we needed to take a different approach with people here, to try to get away from an adversarial type relationship. I wanted to start with the basics. The first thing I did was to establish some practices here so that we knew what people we had on the third shift, what people we had on the second shift, etc. We wanted to know something about the history of each employee's work experience so that when we had to make promotion decisions, we had a basis for that. The big problem we had, let's say in 1979, was favoritism. That was the biggest issue on the table at that time. Without good personnel practices, that's how it was going to be perceived. If they didn't get the job and there's no system in place, they're going to feel, "well, it's because he knew the boss."

37   Lutjens and his group spent almost two years working on personnel practices. A committee of employees was formed to put together an employee handbook. Training sessions were conducted for supervisors on using a non-adversarial approach in the workplace. Lutjens decided that compensation was a critical area that needed to be addressed and began looking around for a plan that would motivate employees by allowing them to share the rewards of their productivity. He explained his approach:

> In looking at compensation, we tried to get away from the idea that no matter what you did, no matter what your performance, no matter how the company was doing, everybody got the same thing. At that time employees received cost of living or wage increases, maybe 3 percent or 4 percent each year. In 1982, we just eliminated that. We eliminated cost of living increases, and we eliminated general increases. We came across something called Improshare (a trademarked product). It is a productivity-based bonus plan where employees

EXHIBIT 8
Perrigo's Manufacturing Facilities

Location	Approximate Square Feet	Leased or Owned
Allegan, Michigan	791,000	Owned
Greenville, South Carolina	75,000	Owned
Montague, Michigan	37,000	Owned
Smyrna, Tennessee	580,000	Leased*
San Bernardino, California	68,000	Leased*
Holland, Michigan	101,000	Owned

Note: The Allegan, Michigan, and Smyrna, Tennessee, facilities also housed corporate offices. Total manufacturing area was 1,467,000 square feet.
*As part of the acquisition of Cumberland-Swan, Perrigo contracted to purchase these facilities in December 1994.
Source: Perrigo Company, 1992 Annual Report.

EXHIBIT 9
Perrigo's Distribution Facilities

Location	Approximate Square Feet	Leased or Owned
Holland, Michigan	381,000	Leased*
Greenville, South Carolina	104,000	Leased*
Sacramento, California	79,000	Leased
Lavergne, Tennessee	311,000	Leased
San Bernardino, California	68,000	Leased†
Cranbury, New Jersey	114,000	Leased

Note: This location houses both manufacturing and distribution facilities.
*With an option to purchase all or part of the facility.
†As part of the acquisition of Cumberland-Swan, Perrigo contracted to purchase this facility in December 1994.
Source: Perrigo Company, 1992 Annual Report.

receive a weekly bonus based on their productivity in that particular period. The amount of the bonus is based on performance for a particular period as compared to performance during a base period. If employees improve their productivity over a formula that is established during the base period, we pay a bonus on that and that bonus is paid weekly. Today, we are averaging about a 17 percent bonus per week. The plan is also marked by employee involvement with its implementation, active participation by employees and their supervisors in increasing productivity, and constant communication that tells employees what their bonus is for a particular period as well as why it is that particular amount.

38   According to Lutjens, Improshare not only improved productivity, but, more importantly, it introduced a change in the company's culture. Employees began to be more concerned about hours worked and absenteeism, not only their own but also of others, since Improshare was a group, not an individual plan.

39   The number of job classifications were reduced from 68 (in the mid-1980s) to 8 and all employees were put on salary. Employees did not have to punch in or out on production. They maintained their own time cards. Also, barriers between management and labor were non-existent. There were no designated parking lots and all employees shared a common lunchroom.

40   Pay rates were competitive and the company offered good benefits. More than 50 percent of the job openings were filled from within. A tuition reimbursement program encouraged employees to further their formal education.

41   A bi-monthly newsletter acted as the forum for formal communication. In addition, Michael Jandernoa, the CEO, met with employee groups on a quarterly basis to discuss the company's performance. In 1993 the company employed a total of around 3,500 people in all its subsidiaries.

EXHIBIT 10

Balance Sheets at June 30, 1991, and 1992 (in thousands)

	1992	1991
Assets		
Current assets		
Cash	$ 538	$ 64
Accounts receivables (net)	50,460	31,261
Inventories	106,504	58,604
Prepaid expenses and other current assets	6,092	3,950
Total current assets	163,594	93,879
Property and equipment (at cost)		
Land	7,419	4,292
Buildings	70,515	45,975
Machinery and equipment	67,951	38,704
	145,885	88,971
Less accumulated depreciation	28,737	19,324
	117,148	69,647
Cost in excess of net assets of acquired businesses	33,177	16,412
Other	3,027	2,785
	$316,946	$182,723
Liabilities & Shareholders' Equity		
Current liabilities:		
Accounts payable	$ 41,896	$ 25,989
Payrolls and related taxes	8,411	5,929
Accrued expenses	16,929	9,928
Income taxes	4,358	1,718
Current installments on long-term debt	871	11,557
Total current liabilities	72,465	55,121
Deferred income taxes	14,744	12,600
Long-term debt (less current installments)	45,999	82,100
Shareholders' equity:		
Common stock	132,285	10,000
Retained earnings	51,453	22,902
Total shareholders' equity	183,738	32,902
	$316,946	$182,723

Source: Perrigo Company, 1992 Annual Report.

F. Finances

42   Perrigo was a high growth company. Between fiscal 1989 (the first full year after the final management-led buyout) and fiscal 1992, the company's sales and net income grew at compounded annual rates of approximately 24% and 107%, respectively. However, the two leveraged buyouts resulted in a high long-term debt-to-equity ratio of 13.3:1 in June 1990 (before the initial public issue of its stock). Primarily as a result of the initial stock offering, this ratio decreased to 0.25:1 by June 1992. Perrigo did not break down the sales and profits of its Cumberland-Swan and South Carolina subsidiaries. Perrigo's sales and net income had historically peaked in the second and third quarters of the fiscal year while the first quarter had been its least profitable. Sales of cough and cold remedies traditionally peaked during the second and third fiscal quarters as customers stocked inventories for the winter months. Sales of suntan products peaked in the third and fourth quarters as customers stocked up for the summer months. To fund its high growth, the company noted in its 1992 Annual Report that it does not currently pay cash dividends. Exhibit 10 gives the company's financial data.

G. New Product Development

43   Perrigo's new product development efforts had contributed to its growth and had enabled it to be among the first companies to manufacture and market certain store brand products. From the

EXHIBIT 10
(continued)

Income Statements June 30, 1990, 1991, and 1992 (in thousands)

	1992	1991	1990
Net sales	$409,785	$281,265	$247,026
Cost of sales	290,626	204,614	181,699
Gross profit	119,159	76,651	65,327
Operating expenses:			
Distribution	11,369	5,305	4,375
Research & development	3,373	1,565	1,518
Selling & administrative	50,585	38,057	31,646
Operating income	53,832	31,724	27,788
Interest expense	8,781	12,420	15,356
Income before income taxes	45,051	19,304	12,432
Income taxes	16,500	7,100	4,800
Net income	$ 28,551	$ 12,204	$ 7,632

Source: Perrigo Company, 1992 Annual Report.

company's standpoint, new products included not only new store brand products which were comparable to newly introduced national brand products, but also variations of existing products such as new sizes, flavors, and product forms. During fiscal 1992, more than $17 million of the company's net sales (approximately 4.25%) were attributable to new products introduced after fiscal 1990.

44   Most new products introduced by Perrigo do not require prior approval of the Food and Drug Administration (FDA) for their manufacture or marketing. The company, however, sought significant opportunities for growth through the introduction of products requiring prior FDA approval using the Abbreviated New Drug Application (ANDA) process. Such products were typically those for which patent protection was expiring and/or "prescription only" status was being changed to over-the-counter status. Mark Olesnavage, Vice President of Pharmaceutical Business Development for Perrigo, talked about the FDA's ANDA process:

> If Merck or Sandoz or Glaxo wanted to introduce a new drug, a new chemical entity, or an old drug with a new claim, then the manufacturer has to show that the drug is effective in meeting the claim. If you want to say that you have a brand new cure for acne, then you've got to show that it is effective in clinical studies. There are different phases in this testing process. First is usually animal testing. This is followed by a series of clinicals on humans. All such tests can take 3–4 years. Tests should also show that the product is safe. So the two things the manufacturer has to show are that the product is effective and that it is safe. In 1984, the Waxman-Hatch Act was passed. Prior to this Act, the generic manufacturer had to conduct tests to indicate that the efficacy and safety of the generic drug matches the prescription drug. The Act allowed generic drug companies (once a drug was off patent) to market a drug after getting an ANDA approval. What this meant was that the generic manufacturer did not have to prove the effectiveness and safety of the drug. They just had to show that the generic drug was bio-equivalent to the original drug. A typical ANDA approval takes about 18 months. We can file an ANDA application before patent expiration and the FDA can conditionally approve it, but we cannot market the product until it is off patent. Perrigo likes to introduce new products through the ANDA process because these products have typically higher margins.

45   The New Product Group made the decision to file an ANDA application. Once the approval was obtained, then the top management of the company made the decision to manufacture the product. Once the decision to manufacture was made, then a matrix organizational structure (made up of production, marketing and research and development people) developed specific plans for manufacturing and product introduction. The mission of the matrix structure was to take the product through introduction. Several months after launch the product was turned over to the regular marketing department.

46   By 1993, three years after the company began applying for approval of drugs through the ANDA process, Perrigo had obtained approval to market 7 formulas constituting 30 products. For example, in January 1992, the company received approval to manufacture and market Loperamide Hydrochloride liquid—a drug used for treating acute diarrhea and comparable to the national brand Imodium

EXHIBIT 10
(continued)

Statement of Cash Flows June 30, 1990, 1991, and 1992 (in thousands)

	1992	1991	1990
Cash Flows from (for) Operating Activities			
Net income	$ 28,551	$ 12,204	$ 7,632
Depreciation	9,432	7,131	6,330
Amortization of intangible assets	2,610	2,382	1,762
Deferred income taxes	(930)	10	990
Provision for losses on accounts receivable	947	533	480
Changes in:			
Accounts receivable	(7,080)	(1,687)	(2,716)
Inventories	(27,762)	(4,957)	11,761
Prepaid expenses and other current assets	148	(681)	(316)
Accounts payable	8,901	6,208	(9,254)
Payrolls and related taxes	1,926	2,432	(223)
Accrued expenses	(260)	(439)	882
Income taxes	2,668	895	(475)
Net cash from operating activities	19,151	24,031	16,853
Cash Flows for Investing Activities			
Additions to property and equipment	(19,692)	(7,525)	(13,964)
Acquisition of Cumberland-Swan	(35,000)	—	—
Purchase of certain assets of J.B. Laboratories	(4,900)	—	—
Other	(559)	(56)	(667)
Net cash for investing activities	(60,151)	(7,581)	(14,631)
Cash Flows from (for) Financing Activities			
Borrowings of long-term debt	—	—	5,075
Repayments of long-term debt	(80,811)	(16,442)	(7,337)
Proceeds from issuance of common stock	122,285	—	—
Net cash from (for) financing activities	41,474	(16,442)	(2,262)
Net increase (decrease) in cash	474	8	(40)
Cash, at beginning of period	64	56	96
Cash, at end of period	538	64	56

Note: Long-term debt matures as follows: 1993—$871,000; 1994—$773,000; 1995—$12.786 million; 1996—$30.3 million; 1997—$300,000; and 1998—$1.84 million (total long-term debt is $46.87 million).

Source: Perrigo Company, 1992 Annual Report.

AD. Olesnavage talked about the success of the company's Pharmaceutical Business Development group:

> We've [i.e., the group] only been around for a short period of time. The industry has never had an unsuccessful switch [from prescription to over-the-counter] yet. But, I'm sure it is going to happen. Let me give you a scenario. For new products, we monitor the success of the introduction of the original product. Let's say Johnson and Johnson tested its Tylenol PM in certain markets and we think it is a great new product because the retailer said it was selling well in test. We develop it and it's ready to go, and all of a sudden Johnson and Johnson says "we're not going to go national." Maybe it wasn't good enough, or maybe it took too much money to support. What we've got is a formula that we've spent money on but is a skeleton in our closet. And that could happen. But that's a small risk. We stress the importance of working in partnership with our customers in developing new products.

47   In an effort to be among the first companies to offer comparable store brand products, in addition to selling its own ANDA products, Perrigo also entered into exclusive arrangements with various generic pharmaceutical manufacturers (some of whom were their direct competitors) to market their ANDA products. For example, prior to obtaining approval for its own ibuprofen tablets (the active ingredient in national brands such as Advil and Nuprin), the company marketed such tablets produced by another manufacturer and was the first company to market a store brand equivalent.

EXHIBIT 10
(concluded)

PERRIGO COMPANY
Investor Information

NASDAQ Ticker Symbol: PRGO
Shares outstanding at June 30, 1992: 36,568,471
Fiscal 1992 share price range: Low 20
                                                    High 35¾
Market Capitalization:
    at low price range: $731.36 million
    at high price range: $1.307 billion
Value Line Beta: 1.65
                Timeliness: 3 (average)
                Safety: 3 (average)
                Financial strength: B++
Price/Earnings ratio:
    Fiscal 1990: 36.1
    Fiscal 1991: 63.5

Sources: Perrigo Company 1992 Annual Report; and
Value Line Investment Survey.

H. Subsidiaries

48   Until the early 1980s, Cumberland-Swan (CS) primarily manufactured and sold products under the Swan brand. Thereafter, it pursued a strategy of expansion into the store brand market. In 1991, approximately 30 percent of CS's sales came from the Swan brand and the remaining from store brands. The Swan brand enabled CS to sell products to smaller retail chains that did not have the volume for their own store brands. The acquisition of CS provided Perrigo access to such smaller retail chains (their own "Good Sense" brand had only limited penetration into such chains) as well as increased manufacturing capacity for store brand products. In addition, the acquisition helped Perrigo vertically integrate into producing bottles for its needs. However, the rate of sales growth of CS historically was lower than that of Perrigo. CS had its own group of managers (all of its top managers were long-term employees) whose president, Lonnie Smith, reported to Mike Jandernoa.

49   Perrigo Company of South Carolina produced and sold vitamins for the store brand market. This subsidiary was managed (except for the production function, which was local) by the L. Perrigo subsidiary from Allegan.

THE FUTURE

50   As Mike Jandernoa reviewed Perrigo's performance, he realized that the upcoming strategic planning meeting was important for the company. While the company did not publicly announce specific goals in terms of percentage of annual sales growth, he and his management team had set the following broad objective for the company: to be the leader in the store brand industry through internal product development including those that are switched from prescription to OTC status, as well as through strategic acquisitions. The meetings were important to position Perrigo to take advantage of the booming store brand market. While buying Cumberland-Swan made strategic sense to Perrigo, the historical growth rate of CS was slower than that of Perrigo. In the future, should the company focus more on expanding internally rather than through acquisitions? If they expanded through acquisitions, how should they finance them?

51   In addition, a number of branded, prescription drugs were coming off patents in the next few years (Exhibit 11). Many of them were likely to be converted to branded OTC products by their manufacturers. Should the company allocate additional resources (production facilities, funds for product development, etc.) to expand its OTC segment to take advantage of the opportunity? Would giving the OTC segment additional funds weaken the company's personal care and vitamin segments?

EXHIBIT 11
Major Drugs Losing Patent Protection: 1993–1995

Brand Name	Manufacturer	Patent Expires	1989 Sales (millions)
Naprosyn	Syntex	1993	$ 410
Xanax	Upjohn	1993	358
Tagamet	SmithKline	1994	570
Capoten	Squibb	1995	500
Zantac	Glaxo	1995	1,200

Source: Michael F. Conlan, "Future Is Sunny for Generics as Popular Rxs Come Off Patent," *Drug Topics*, October 22, 1990, pp. 14–16.

ENDNOTES

1. "Latest Market Statistics Show Private Label Renaissance," a PLMA Press Release, May 4, 1992.
2. Ibid.
3. Gary Strauss, "Shoppers Find Value Beyond Big Names," *USA Today*, January 7, 1993, pp. D1, D2.
4. Ibid.
5. "A Strategic Guide to Private Label," *Discount Store News*, October 1992.
6. "Store Brands: The Next Generation," *Progressive Grocer*, May 1992.

CASE 8

BEN & JERRY'S HOMEMADE, INC.: "YO! I'M YOUR CEO!"

"Ben & Jerry's Grows Up"
Boston Globe

"Ben, Jerry Losing Their Values?"
Washington Times

"Ben & Jerry's Melting Social Charter"
The Washington Post

"Life Won't Be Just a Bowl of Cherry Garcia"
Business Week

"Say It Ain't So, Ben & Jerry"
Business Week

1 The headlines said it all. Ben & Jerry's, the company that had built its success as much on its down-home image and folksy idealism as on its super-rich ice cream, was at a crossroads. Having been started in 1978 in a renovated Vermont gas station by childhood friends Ben Cohen and Jerry Greenfield, the unconventional company soon grew into a $140 million powerhouse that was rivaled only by Haagen-Dazs in the superpremium category of the ice cream market. With its many donations and policies promoting corporate responsibility, Ben & Jerry's took great pride in its success combining social activism with financial viability. But in mid-1994, the outlook was not so rosy. Sales were flat, profits were down, and the company's stock price had fallen to half what it was at the end of 1992. In its 1993 annual report, Ben & Jerry's admitted that some flavors of its "all natural" ice cream included ingredients that were not, in fact, all natural. And staffers within the company reportedly criticized it for lack of leadership.

2 On June 13, Ben & Jerry's announced that Ben was stepping down as CEO, and that it would abandon its longtime cap on executive salaries in order to help it find a new one. The message was clear: Ben & Jerry's was no longer the company it once was. For many, the question then was, what would it become?

THE CONTEST

3 With a marketing flair befitting its tradition of wacky promotional tactics, Ben & Jerry's set out to find its new leader by announcing the "Yo! I'm Your CEO!" contest. Customers were asked to send in a lid from a container of their favorite Ben & Jerry's ice-cream flavor along with a 100-word essay explaining "Why I Would Be a Great CEO for Ben & Jerry's." The winner would get to run the company, the runner-up would get a lifetime supply of ice cream, and the losers would get a rejection letter "suitable for framing."

4 "We have never had an experienced CEO and we have reached the point in our life when we need one," said Ben, adding that he planned to continue with the company as chairman and concentrate on "fun stuff" like product development.

This case was prepared by Katherine A. Auer of Indiana University and Alan N. Hoffman of Bentley College. Published by permission of Alan N. Hoffman, Bentley College.

5   But the search wasn't all fun and games. Ben & Jerry's also announced that it would abandon its long-time policy that no executive be paid more than seven times the salary of the lowest-paid employee, and hired an executive recruiting firm to help find the right person. Under the old policy, Ben was paid $133,212 in 1993 and no bonuses; the going rate for executives at companies of like size was $300,000 to $500,000.

6   "I think we are looking for a rare bird," said Ben. "I guess there are about five or 10 executives who will be interested and have the skills." The key, he added, is experience in keeping "everyone aligned and moving the same direction" as the company grows—something he admitted he was learning but not good at. "I haven't found the happy medium between autocratic and laissez-faire," he explained.

7   Some 22,500 aspiring leaders around the world flooded the company with their responses, which were as varied as the flavors in its ice-cream line. Entries came from places as far away as Australia, Thailand, East Africa, and Saudi Arabia. An entire fifth-grade class sent in letters, with offers from some of the students to develop new flavors. One woman sent in a near-nude photo of herself, while an advertising executive attached his resumé to a Superman costume.

8   An Indiana schoolteacher scrawled her essay on a painting of a woman reading a book, while Allen Stillman, head of New York restaurant chain Smith & Wollensky, put a full-page ad in *The New York Times*. "I propose a whole new line of flavors," he wrote. "Red Meat Swirl, Potato Gravy Chunk, Starchie Bunker." Stillman also proposed a merger and a new name: Ben Smith & Jerry Wollensky Steaks and Shakes.

9   Other response tactics included a resumé written entirely on a giant sheet cake, another engraved on a brass plaque and mounted on marble, and one written in crayon by a hopeful couple's 2 1/2-year-old son. A Milwaukee car salesman sent in a mock two-foot-wide lid of a New York Super Fudge Chunk carton, folded in half. When the lid was unfolded, an electronic device made a sound like a telephone ring; the opener then read "Please call me—I'm the one you want to be your CEO."

10   "Some of them may not be right for the CEO's job, but they sure would be right for marketing jobs," Ben said. "We may not have to advertise for people for the next several years."

THE WINNER

11   On February 2, 1995, Ben & Jerry's announced that they had at last found the leader they wanted: Robert Holland, Jr., a former partner at management consultancy McKinsey & Co. By taking the helm of Ben & Jerry's, the 55-year-old MBA became one of the most visible African-American chief executives among the nation's publicly traded corporations.

12   Holland was found not through the essay contest, but through New York executive recruiter Russell Reynolds. Some 500 candidates were initially considered by that firm, and Ben & Jerry's board members ultimately reviewed about 15 applicants. The race eventually narrowed down to six competitors (one of which did come from the essay contest), and from there, it came down to two finalists, both of whom spent considerable time over dinner and ice cream with Ben, Jerry, and board members. Rumor had it that Holland's competitor preferred frozen yogurt, while he himself was a passionate ice-cream fan.

13   Having grown up in Michigan, Holland spent 13 years as an associate and partner at McKinsey, where he worked with consumer and industrial clients including the soft-drink division of Heineken. He left McKinsey in 1981, going on to become an independent consultant and businessman. Among his subsequent roles were chairman of Gilreath Manufacturing, Inc., a plastic injection-molding company, and chairman and CEO for Rokher-J Inc., a White Plains, New York, consulting and takeover firm. Holland earned his MBA at Baruch College in New York.

14   But at least as important as his experience in turning troubled companies around were Holland's social values. He was chairman of the board of trustees at Spelman College in Atlanta, a school traditionally attended by black women, as well as the founder of a dropout-prevention program for Detroit high-school students and a board member of the Harlem Junior Tennis program for inner-city youth.

EXHIBIT 1
Time, Values and Ice Cream*
By Robert Holland

Born before the baby boom
as war drums raged cross distant waters—way
beyond my family's lore since our 1600s coming to this far off land called
America.

'Twas a simple time, as I grew tall.
Shucks! Uncle Sam really wanted you (so the poster said)—pride
in work, parades and proms, company picnics 'tween eve'ns spent with "Suspense,"
"The Shadow," and everybody's "Our Miss Brooks."
Good ole days in the summertime, indeed! . . . in
America.

Yet, some nostalgia stayed 'yond one's grasp,
like Sullivans,
the ice cream place on Main—swivel stools, cozy booths, and sweet,
sweet smells with no sitting place for all of some of us.
Could only dream such humble pleasure. Sometimes, dear 'Merica,
of thee I simply hum.

Much, so much has changed in twenty springs. Sputnik
no longer beeps so loud;
Bay of Pigs, Vietnam and contentions in Chicago . . .
come and gone . . .
All that noise almost drowning out "One small step for man . . . "
and " . . . Willie, time to say goodbye to baseball."
Confusing place, this melodious mix,
called America.

Now I sit by eyeing distant twilight,
Engineer and MBA,
smiling wide on M.L.K.'s day,
CEO of Cherry Garcia and Peace Pops' fountain
having not forgotten the forbidden seats of Sullivans',
with miles to go before we sleep . . .
and time left yet to get there.
Only in America!

*Only 100 words before translation from the language of Chunky Mandarin Orange With Natural Wild Brazil Nuts

15   "We were very impressed not only with Bob's operational expertise, but with his social commitment, as expressed in both his business experience and his active involvement with the nonprofit sector," said Ben.

16   Holland's salary was to be $250,000 plus options on 180,000 shares of stock and a bonus of up to $125,000 if he met certain financial goals. Though significantly higher than what Ben had been earning, that was still at the low end of the pay scale for CEOs at midsized manufacturers, and reportedly less than what Holland had been earning as a management consultant.

17   Though he didn't submit an essay as part of the contest, Holland did submit something—a poem—upon request after he was chosen. The poem, entitled "Time, Values and Ice Cream" (see Exhibit 1), reflected his background in poor, working-class, south-central Michigan.

18   Though his appointment at Ben & Jerry's made Holland one of just a few African-American CEOs at public companies, Holland declined to be called a role model for other blacks, calling the term "too presumptuous." Nevertheless, he said, "I'm looking forward to dispelling whatever concerns people have."

19   In any case, Holland faced a formidable challenge at Ben & Jerry's. The company was expected to post its first quarterly loss ever for the fourth quarter of fiscal 1994, and when Holland's appointment was announced, Chuck Lacy, the company's longtime president, resigned.

20   While Holland won the executive slot, what some may say was the better prize—a lifetime supply of ice cream—went to three runners-up. Among them was Taylor James Caldwell, the toddler, by then three years old, who had submitted an entry for his parents. In addition, about 100 honorable mentions received limited-edition T-shirts.

EXHIBIT 2
Five-Year Financial Highlights
(In thousands except per share data)

	Year Ended				
	12/31/94	12/25/93	12/26/92	12/28/91	12/29/90
Summary of Operations:					
Net sales	$148,802	$140,328	$131,969	$96,997	$77,024
Cost of sales	109,760	100,210	94,389	68,500	54,203
Gross profit	39,042	40,118	37,580	28,497	22,821
Selling, general, and administrative expenses	36,253	28,270	26,243	21,264	17,639
Asset write-down	6,779				
Other income (expense)—net	229	197	(23)	(729)	(709)
Income (loss) before income taxes	(3,761)	12,045	11,314	6,504	4,473
Income taxes	(1,893)	4,845	4,639	2,765	1,864
Net income (loss)	(1,868)	7,200	6,675	3,739	2,609
Net income (loss) per common share[1]	$ (0.26)	$ 1.01	$ 1.07	$ 0.67	$ 0.50
Weighted average common shares outstanding[1]	7,148	7,138	6,254	5,572	5,225
Balance Sheet Data:					
Working capital	$ 37,456	$ 29,292	$ 18,053	$11,035	$ 8,202
Total assets	120,295	106,361	88,207	43,056	34,299
Long-term debt	32,419	18,002	2,641	2,787	8,948
Stockholders' equity[2]	72,502	74,262	66,760	26,269	16,101

[1]The per share amounts and average shares outstanding have been adjusted for the effects of all stock splits, including stock splits in the form of stock dividends.

[2]No cash dividends have been declared or paid by the Company on its capital stock since the Company's organization. The Company intends to reinvest earnings for use in its business and to finance future growth. Accordingly, the Board of Directors does not anticipate declaring any cash dividends in the foreseeable future.

THE "GOOD OLD" DAYS

21   The birth of Ben & Jerry's can be traced to a $5 correspondence course in ice cream making taken by Ben Cohen and Jerry Greenfield. The duo, who had been friends since growing up together in Merrick, New York, then gathered $12,000 ($4,000 of which was borrowed), and in May 1978 opened an ice cream shop in a renovated Burlington, Vermont, gas station. Featuring an antique rock-salt ice cream freezer and a Volkswagen squareback for its delivery man, the shop soon became popular for its innovative flavors made from fresh Vermont milk and cream.

22   At the heart of Ben & Jerry's was the very distinct business philosophy shared by its founders. In essence, they believed that companies have a responsibility to do good for society, not just for themselves. This philosophy is best explained by the company's three-part mission statement, formally stated in 1988 and reproduced here in its entirety:

Ben & Jerry's is dedicated to the creation and demonstration of a new corporate concept of linked prosperity. Our mission consists of three interrelated parts:

Product Mission: To make, distribute, and sell the finest quality, all-natural ice cream and related products in a wide variety of innovative flavors made from Vermont dairy products.

Social Mission: To operate the company in a way that actively recognizes the central role that business plays in the structure of society by initiating innovative ways to improve the quality of life of a broad community—local, national, and international.

Economic Mission: To operate the company on a sound financial basis of profitable growth, increasing value for our shareholders, and creating career opportunities and financial rewards for our employees.

Underlying the mission of Ben & Jerry's is the determination to seek new and creative ways of addressing all three parts, while holding a deep respect for the individuals, inside and outside the company, and for the communities of which they are a part.

EXHIBIT 3
Consolidated Balance Sheets

	12/31/94	12/25/93
Assets		
Current assets:		
Cash and cash equivalents	$ 20,777,746	$ 14,704,795
Accounts receivable, less allowance for doubtful accounts: $504,000 in 1994 and $229,000 in 1993	11,904,844	11,679,222
Inventories	13,462,572	13,452,863
Deferred income taxes	3,146,000	1,689,000
Income taxes receivable	2,097,743	
Prepaid expenses	534,166	847,851
Total current assets	51,923,071	42,373,731
Property, plant, and equipment, net	57,980,567	40,261,538
Investments	8,000,000	22,000,000
Other assets	2,391,465	1,725,316
	$120,295,103	$106,360,585
Liabilities & Stockholders' Equity		
Current liabilities:		
Accounts payable and accrued expenses	$ 13,914,972	$ 12,068,424
Income taxes payable		344,519
Current portion of long-term debt and capital lease obligations	552,547	669,151
Total current liabilities	14,467,519	13,082,094
Long-term debt and capital lease obligations	32,418,565	18,002,076
Deferred income taxes	907,000	1,014,000
Commitments and contingencies		
Stockholders' equity:		
$1.20 noncumulative Class A preferred stock—$1.00 par value, redeemable at the Company's option at $12.00 per share; 900 shares authorized, issued, and outstanding, aggregate preference on voluntary or involuntary liquidation: $9,000	900	900
Class A common stock—$.033 par value; authorized 20,000 shares; issued: 6,290,580 shares at December 31, 1994, and 6,266,772 shares at December 25, 1993	208,010	207,224
Class B common stock—$.033 par value; authorized 3,000,000 shares; issued: 932,448 shares at December 31, 1994, and 947,637 shares at December 25, 1993	30,770	31,271
Additional paid-in capital	48,366,185	48,222,445
Retained earnings	25,316,309	27,185,003
Unearned compensation		(19,815)
Treasury stock, at cost: 69,032 Class A and 1,092 Class B shares at December 31, 1994, and 66,353 Class A and 1,092 Class B shares at December 25, 1993	(1,420,155)	(1,364,613)
Total stockholders' equity	72,502,019	74,262,415
	$120,295,103	$106,360,585

See accompanying notes.

23   This unconventional philosophy touched everything the company did, from the way it treated its employees to the way it dealt with its suppliers.

24   The company enjoyed a strong team and family oriented atmosphere, for example, supported by progressive family-leave, health-insurance, and other benefit plans. Reasoning that happy employees would reduce stress and improve the workplace in general, Ben and Jerry kept the culture extremely casual and relaxed, and had even formed a "Joy Committee" to spread joy among their employees. Some of the spontaneous events coordinated by the Joy Committee included an Elvis Presley recognition day, with an Elvis look-alike contest, a Barry Manilow appreciation day, and a car race derby in which employees raced their own toy cars. Pranks abounded at all gatherings, including the annual shareholders' meetings, and most were followed by entertainment such as 1960s musicians Richie

EXHIBIT 4
CEO's Letter

Dear Shareholders,

As I said at the press conference announcing my appointment as CEO of Ben & Jerry's, it is difficult to say what you are going to do for a company when you are speaking to people who know more about that company than you do.

I came to Ben & Jerry's because I like what I see in this Company. Ben & Jerry's enjoys a tremendous consumer franchise. It has consistently delivered pleasant surprises to its followers in the form of great products and a unique commitment to innovation both in the marketplace and in its vision of the critical role business must play in improving our society. This is a consumer franchise fairly brimming with goodwill between customers and the Company.

I have run businesses of my own and have consulted with many others. What I intend to offer to Ben & Jerry's is the business management and strategic planning skills that it has been my good fortune to learn throughout my career. Despite the difficulties Ben & Jerry's has noted in its most recent results—which are a combination of internal issues and marketplace conditions—I see a host of opportunities in front of this unique Company. As this Annual Report is being prepared, I am brand-new on the job. As such, it is more my task to begin the process of assessing and prioritizing these opportunities than to describe them in detail here.

What impresses me most is what is already here. The people resources of this Company are a tremendous asset; these are skilled, dedicated people whose talents and experience I can complement but not supplant. High on my list of priorities is to analyze the strengths and the deployment of our people and to fill what missing pieces may exist. I stress, though, that much of what we need is already well rooted in the functions and the traditions of this Company.

It is true that I did not write an essay for the "Yo! I'm Your CEO!" contest until I had been selected for the position. There were, as I hear it, some strong entrants from the contest though. The contest itself was a perfect snapshot of what is unique and wonderful about Ben & Jerry's, for two reasons. First, the Company had the imagination to see that it made sense to cast a wide net in its search; that the regular route—a standard executive search—might not be the only place to find what it was looking for. (As the founders note in their letter in this Annual Report, if they had taken the regular route, they would not have gotten to where the Company is today.) Second, the contest created an explosion of creativity and fascination on the part of customers and friends. Precious few companies have the kind of rapport with their customers that can engender such excitement. I have seen it clearly in the many letters sent to me since my arrival here, without return addresses, that simply say, "Good luck!" or "Welcome to our family."

In the poem I wrote to celebrate the spirit of the contest and the Company, I closed with the words, "With miles to go before we sleep, and time left to get there . . . only in America." I ask you for a bit of that time to make real what I know that Ben & Jerry's can do. I want my actions to speak best, not my words on this page. It is my belief and commitment that next year at this time, you will be close to as glad to have me here as I am today to be here.

With thanks & best wishes,

Bob Holland

Havens, Livingston Taylor, and dozens of other bands. In essence, Ben and Jerry truly seemed to live by their motto, "If it's not fun, why do it?"

25   Yet in their desire to create a healthy and equitable workplace, Ben and Jerry's did more than just promote fun and games: Their longtime cap on executive salaries required that no executive be paid more than seven times the salary of the lowest-paid employee. Typical staff meetings included all employees, not just executives, and issues affecting women, minorities, and gays in their workforce were always discussed openly.

26   In choosing suppliers for the ingredients of their products, Ben & Jerry's tried to be equally responsible. For example, the brownies used in its Chocolate Fudge Brownie ice cream were bought from a bakery in Yonkers, New York, that hired undertrained and underskilled workers and used its

EXHIBIT 5
What We Make

1994 was a banner year for packaging changes for most consumer goods companies including Ben & Jerry's. With the advent of the FDA regulated nutritional labeling requirements, we took the opportunity to modify and enhance every one of our 39 packages in '94.

Original

The 14 chunky, Original ice cream flavors now have colorful flavor icons on the pints and the standard nutritional label. Our newest indulgent flavor, Chubby Hubby®, was released to market on March 1, 1995. It's a customer-suggested concoction of chocolate-covered peanut-butter-filled pretzel nuggets in a vanilla malt ice cream with a fudge and peanut butter ripple. Wow!

· Butter Pecan
· Cherry Garcia®
· Chocolate Fudge Brownie
· Chocolate Chip Cookie Dough
· Chubby Hubby®
· Chunky Monkey®
· Coconut Almond Fudge Chip
· Coffee Toffee Crunch
· English Toffee Crunch
· Mint Chocolate Cookie
· New York Super Fudge Chunk
· Peanut Butter Cup
· Rainforest Crunch™
· Wavy Gravy

Smooth, No Chunks!

After a successful Spring '94 line launch, we attained over a 6% national market share with our 8 new Smooth, No Chunks! flavors.

· Aztec Harvests® Coffee
· Deep Dark Chocolate
· Double Chocolate Fudge Swirl
· Mocha Fudge
· Vanilla Caramel Fudge
· Vanilla Bean
· Vanilla
· White Russian™

Frozen Yogurt

In 1995, we'll be rounding out (or rather slimming down) our regular & lowfat frozen yogurt pint offerings with three, all natural, NO FAT flavors: Strawberry, Cappuccino, and Vanilla Fudge. They're everything you'd expect from Ben & Jerry's, without the fat.

· Coffee Almond Fudge
· English Toffee Crunch
· Low Fat Apple Pie
· Low Fat Cherry Garcia®
· Low Fat Chocolate Fudge Brownie
· No Fat Cappuccino
· No Fat Strawberry
· No Fat Vanilla Fudge

Peace Pops

True to the Company's objective of source reduction in packaging, our Peace Pops are packaged in colorful, flavor-specific wraps, not in individual boxes. The case of 24 pops doubles as a display box and shipper.

· Cherry Garcia® Frozen Yogurt
· Cookie Dough
· English Toffee Crunch
· New York Super Fudge Chunk
· Vanilla

Quarts

You may have noticed the larger size Quart container of Ben & Jerry's in some freezer cases.

· Cherry Garcia®
· Chocolate Fudge Brownie
· Chocolate Chip Cookie Dough
· Vanilla

Scoop Shop Flavors
ICE CREAM

· Apple Pie
· Aztec Harvests® Coffee
· Butter Pecan
· Cappuccino Chocolate Chunk
· Cherry Garcia®
· Chocolate Chip Cookie Dough
· Chocolate Fudge Brownie
· Chubby Hubby®

· Chunky Monkey®
· Coconut Almond Fudge Chip
· Coffee Toffee Crunch
· Deep Dark Chocolate
· Double Chocolate Fudge Swirl
· English Toffee Crunch
· Maple Walnut
· Mint Chocolate Chunk
· Mint Chocolate Cookie
· Mocha Fudge
· New York Super Fudge Chunk
· Peach
· Peanut Butter Cup
· Pistachio Pistachio
· Praline Pecan
· Rainforest Crunch™
· Strawberry
· Sweet Cream & Cookie
· Vanilla Caramel Fudge
· Vanilla Chocolate Chunk
· Vanilla
· Vanilla Bean
· Wavy Gravy
· White Russian™

FROZEN YOGURT

· Coffee Almond Fudge
· English Toffee Crunch
· Low Fat Cherry Garcia®
· Low Fat Chocolate Fudge Brownie
· No Fat Cappuccino
· No Fat Chocolate
· No Fat Strawberry
· No Fat Vanilla
· No Fat Vanilla Fudge

FRUIT ICES

· Lemon Daiquiri
· Mandarin
· Raspberry

profits to house the homeless and teach them trades. Ben & Jerry's Rainforest Crunch ice cream featured nuts grown in South American rain forests; the firm paid the harvesters directly, and donated a portion of the proceeds from sales of the ice cream to environmental preservation causes. Wild Maine Blueberry ice cream was made with blueberries grown and harvested by the Passamaquoddy Indians of Maine. Fresh Georgia Peach ice cream was made from Georgia-grown peaches as part of the company's policy of supporting family farms.

27   Similarly, for the milk and cream that forms the bulk of its products, Ben & Jerry's was committed to buying from Vermont dairy farms, to whom it paid above-market prices. When rBGH, a genetically engineered drug to increase cows' milk production, was approved by the FDA, Ben & Jerry's declared it would buy only from farms not using the drug, citing health concerns and a desire to protect smaller farms. To ensure that its products stayed wholesome and pure, the company paid the premium to suppliers in exchange for their written assurance that they would not use rBGH.

28   Finally, the company also established the Ben & Jerry's Foundation, which donated 7.5 percent of its pretax profits to nonprofit organizations. These causes included, among others, the American Wildlands in Montana; Burch House in New Hampshire (a safe house); the Burlington Peace and Justice Coalition in Vermont; the Citizens Committee for Children in New York (aid for drug-addicted pregnant women); Natural Guard (an environmental group for school-age children and teens); the Brattleboro Area AIDS Project (providing free services to HIV-positive individuals and their families); and the Massachusetts Coalition for the Homeless.

29   Such efforts won the hearts of scores of like-minded consumers, many of whom had grown up in the same socially conscious generation as Ben and Jerry. Indeed, because of its values and its unconventional nature, the company had to do very little marketing: Media coverage of its various antics was virtually guaranteed on a regular basis, providing free publicity for the company, its products, and its values. Thanks in part to the size of the "baby boom" generation of which its leaders were a part, Ben & Jerry's flourished in the 1980s, growing to more than 100 franchises. In 1984 the company went public in Vermont, and by 1986 it had achieved 100 percent growth.

RECENT TROUBLES

30   While Ben & Jerry's thrived during the 1980s, the 1990s presented a very different picture. One of the primary reasons was that the baby boom generation—Ben & Jerry's primary target market—was entering middle age and becoming more health-conscious. Whereas during the 80s these consumers enjoyed the socially conscious self-indulgence of Ben & Jerry's ice cream, they had since become averse to high-fat foods such as superpremium ice cream. At the same time, new labeling requirements imposed by the FDA meant that customers could see with painful clarity the amount of fat each scoop of Ben & Jerry's ice creams contained, thus bringing home the reality about their less-than-healthful nature.

31   One step Ben & Jerry's took to respond was to introduce a reduced-fat, reduced-calorie ice milk, called Ben & Jerry's Lite. That line failed, reportedly due to poor quality, but the subsequent introduction of a low-fat, low-cholesterol frozen yogurt line met with much better success. In addition, the company was expected to begin rolling out the first flavors in its non-fat yogurt line by the summer of 1995. Nevertheless, the fact remained that ice-cream sales were slowing.

32   Ben & Jerry's was also facing increased competition from the deep-pocketed Haagen-Dazs, which had expanded its selection of flavors to better rival Ben & Jerry's (including its chunky "Extraas," a low-fat ultrapremium ice cream as well as frozen yogurt) and had brought on a price war by reducing its prices and offering a variety of promotions and discounts. During the weakened economy of the 1990s, competing on price became the name of the game.

33   Indeed, the superpremium category as a whole was witnessing increased competition from lower-cost, lower-fat premium ice creams. Among those were Edy's, manufactured by Dreyer's, which produced roughly half of Ben & Jerry's output. Not only that, but Dreyer's had recently received a huge cash infusion from Nestlé, giving the firm increased competitive muscle.

34   Despite the fact that U.S. ice-cream exports had tripled in recent years, and the fact that Haagen-Dazs had already begun exporting (even opening a factory in France), Ben & Jerry's so far had paid little attention to markets outside the United States. Said Chuck Lacy, the company's president, "It's something that we're starting to think about, but we've got a lot of work to do here in the U.S." Sales to restaurants was another option for growth outside of the heated grocery-store market, but again, Lacy said, while "there's huge potential, it's a completely different business. It requires completely different distributors and sales staff, a completely different head."

35   Software glitches, meanwhile, had repeatedly delayed the opening of Ben & Jerry's new $40 million ice-cream plant in St. Albans, which had been planned to dramatically increase production. But with sales down, it was not even clear that the company would be able to use even half the plant's capacity when it did finally open, making it a roughly break-even proposition.

36   Management problems were also plaguing the firm, reducing morale and drawing criticism from employees, who said there was a lack of direction. By the end of 1994, the mood had reportedly

become so dark that the company asked author Milton Moskowitz to remove them from the most recent edition of "The 100 Best Companies to Work for in America."

37   Finally, on December 19, 1994, Ben & Jerry's had announced that it expected to report a loss of $700,000 to $900,000 for the fourth quarter of 1994—its first since going public in 1984.

THE INDUSTRY LANDSCAPE

38   The packaged ice-cream industry included ordinary, premium, and superpremium products. These types were distinguished primarily by their butterfat content and density, as well as the freshness of their ingredients and the way they were blended and treated.

39   Ordinary ice creams typically contained the minimum of 10 to 12 percent butterfat and the maximum proportion of air; one four-ounce scoop contained 150 calories or less. Premium ice creams contained 12 to 16 percent butterfat and less air than regular types; a four-ounce scoop usually contained 180 calories. Superpremium ice creams, which included Ben & Jerry's, generally contained about 16 to 20 percent fat (excluding add-ins) and less than 20 percent air. The caloric value of a four-ounce scoop was generally about 260 calories. This type of ice cream was characterized by a greater richness than the other types, and was sold in packaged pints priced between $2.29 and $2.89 each.

40   The total annual sales in U.S. supermarkets for the ice-cream and frozen yogurt market as a whole were more than $3.6 billion in 1994. The superpremium market (ice cream, frozen yogurt, ice milk, and sorbet) accounted for about $415 million. Ninety-three percent of American households consumed ice cream, but demand was seasonal, with summer levels as much as 30 percent higher than those in the winter. Sales for frozen yogurt (superpremium and regular) were $550 million in supermarkets in 1994; Ben & Jerry's was clearly ahead of Haagen-Dazs in the superpremium frozen yogurt market.

41   Gross margins in the ice-cream industry as a whole were about 30.6 percent, compared with only 20 percent for the frozen-food department as a whole. Premium and superpremium varieties outperformed other ice-cream types, accounting for 45.8 percent of sales and 45.9 percent of profits of the ice-cream category as a whole, and earning a gross margin of 31.5 percent.

42   The superpremium ice cream and frozen yogurt business was highly competitive. Ben & Jerry's principal competitor was the Haagen-Dazs Company, Inc., which roughly matched Ben & Jerry's 42 percent share of the market; others, including Columbo, Dannon, Healthy Choice, Simple Pleasures, Elan, Frusen Gladje, Yoplait, Honey Hill Farms, and Steve's, constituted less than 10 percent of the market.

43   Haagen-Dazs was owned by the Pillsbury Company, which in turn was owned by Grand Metropolitan PLC, a British food and liquor conglomerate with resources significantly greater than those of Ben & Jerry's. Haagen-Dazs entered the market well before Ben & Jerry's, and also became well-established in certain markets in Europe and the Pacific Rim. And to compete with Ben & Jerry's, it introduced in 1992 its Extraas line of products that included a variety of add-ins like cookies, candies, and nuts.

44   Ben & Jerry's also competed with several well-known brands in the ice-cream novelty segment, including Haagen-Dazs and Dove Bars, which are manufactured by a division of Mars, Inc. Both Haagen-Dazs and Dove Bars achieved significant market share before Ben & Jerry's entered their markets.

MARKET SHARE

45   The total U.S. sales for superpremium ice cream, frozen yogurt, ice milk, and sorbet were more than $415 million in 1994. The market was dominated by Haagen-Dazs and Ben & Jerry's: In 1993, the former held 62 percent of the market while Ben & Jerry's held 36 percent, but by early 1995, both held roughly 42 percent.

46   Haagen-Dazs had entered the superpremium market back in 1961. Though success was not achieved overnight, the brand remained on the market and became the industry leader. Early success was linked to word-of-mouth advertising, but by 1983 Haagen-Dazs spent $14 million on advertising, while average ice-cream manufacturers spent less than 1 percent of sales on advertising.

47   When new competitors began entering the market in the early 1980s, namely Ben & Jerry's, Haagen-Dazs attempted to keep them out by threatening distributors. Ben & Jerry's fought back with

a lawsuit and a campaign including bumper stickers and T-shirts displaying the statement, "What's the Pillsbury Doughboy Afraid of?" The litigation was settled and the campaign brought to an end within about a year.

48   Between 1989 and 1993, overall growth in the market had been sluggish, rising by only 14 percent. During that same period, however, Ben & Jerry's market share rose by 120 percent, while Haagen-Dazs' share decreased by 10 percent. In 1992, Ben & Jerry's increased its U.S. market share by 10 percent; Haagen-Dazs, on the other hand, lost 8 percent. Thus, while Ben & Jerry's entered late into the mature, low-growth ice-cream market, it gained substantial market share, primarily at the expense of Haagen-Dazs.

49   Ben & Jerry's products were distributed primarily by independent regional ice-cream distributors. With certain exceptions, only one distributor was appointed to each territory. In some areas, sub-distributors were used. Ben & Jerry's trucks also distributed some of the ice cream and frozen yogurt sold in Vermont and upstate New York. Ben & Jerry's had a distribution agreement with Dreyer's whereby Dreyer's had exclusivity, in general, for sales to supermarkets and similar accounts of Ben & Jerry's products in most of its markets outside New England, upstate New York, Pennsylvania, and Texas. Net sales to Dreyer's accounted for about 54 percent and 52 percent of Ben & Jerry's net sales for 1993 and 1994, respectively.

50   While Dreyer's marketed its own premium ice cream, as well as frozen dessert products made by other companies, it did not produce or market any other superpremium ice cream or frozen yogurt. Were it to begin doing so, Dreyer's would lose its exclusivity as a Ben & Jerry's distributor.

51   Because of instances of legal action over distribution agreements, manufacturers and distributors generally opted for verbal rather than written contracts.

52   In recent years, two independent distributors claimed that Ben & Jerry's and Dreyer's had squeezed them out of the business, and at least three others claimed they had lost access to the brand after building it for years. Furthermore, Amy Miller, founder of Amy's Ice Creams in Austin, Texas, claimed that Ben & Jerry's pressured the best distributor in that area to not carry Amy's pints or risk losing the immensely popular Ben & Jerry's. But Ben and Jerry categorically denied any such involvement, and was backed up by the distributor. There were also a few other instances in which distributors claimed that they had been pressured to not carry brands competing with Ben & Jerry's. Said one retailer, who sued Ben & Jerry's after it cut him off, "corporately, they are absolutely vicious."

53   Ben & Jerry's admitted that while its relationships with Dreyer's and other distributors have been generally satisfactory, they were not always easy to maintain. But alternatives were few: According to the company, the loss of one or more of the related distribution agreements could have a material adverse effect on the company's business.

54   When it came to choosing suppliers, Ben & Jerry's insistence on social responsibility earned it much acclaim, but developing such relationships was not always easy. Its search for the perfect coffee bean, for example, took more than five years and led to one of its most complex, yet successful, supplier relationships. The company's goal was to give much of the profits back to the grower, rather than to a middleman broker; accomplishing this required a significant commitment of time and resources to learn each party's needs and expectations.

55   Because working directly with suppliers required so much energy, Ben & Jerry's planned to establish only one or two new relationships each year. R&D, Quality Assurance, finance, and manufacturing all had to be involved in the evaluation and education of each new supplier. Although the work involved was much more than would have been required if it simply made calls to existing suppliers, Ben & Jerry's felt the result made it worthwhile.

FINANCE

56   Ben & Jerry's sales had been steadily increasing from 1988 through 1992, but then slowed dramatically in 1993. Sales increased by about 30 percent annually from 1990 to 1992, but that dropped to 6 percent in 1993. Furthermore, the company indicated that virtually all of its growth in 1993 came from its frozen-yogurt line, which grew by 35 percent during that year. Sales for fiscal 1993 were $140 million and $149 million for fiscal 1994.

57   Net income had grown steadily along with sales growth, and exceeded that pace during 1991 and 1992. While sales grew at 26 percent and 36 percent during 1991 and 1992, respectively, net income grew at 42 percent and 81 percent. During 1993, sales grew 6 percent while net income grew at 7 percent. For 1994, however, the company reported a net loss of $1.87 million.

58   The company's net profit margin was 5.1 percent, compared with the industry average of 3.4 percent. The net loss per share for 1994 was ($0.26); during previous years, earnings per share had risen steadily, from $0.32 in 1988 to a high of $1.07 in 1992, then falling to $1.01 in 1993. Consequently, its stock price had since been driven down nearly 50 percent from its 1993 high of $32 by investors impatient with the company's lack of momentum. On February 1, 1995, the company's stock price was $12.125.

MARKETING

Product

59   Ben & Jerry's "product" was a carefully orchestrated combination of premium ice-cream products and social consciousness—"Caring Capitalism"—created through bottom-up management and cause-generated marketing and public-relations efforts. The physical products included superpremium ice cream, in both chunky and smooth flavors, low-fat frozen yogurt, and ice-cream novelties. The company operated in the focused niche of superpremium ice-cream products, with the driving competitive factor traditionally being diversity and uniqueness of flavor.

60   As such, the primary marketing goal at Ben & Jerry's was to develop and deliver great new products and flavors. It maintained a full-time research and development team dedicated to the development of unconventional, cutting-edge flavors. It is this strength that had placed Ben & Jerry's at the forefront of the superpremium ice-cream market, with 6 of the top 10 and 13 of the top 20 best selling flavors.

61   In its traditional line, Ben & Jerry's distinguished its flavors and products through "chunkiness," maintaining specifications not only for chunk size, but for number per spoonful and quality of the fruits and nuts they contain. Although such requirements added a great deal more to the cost of the finished product, the enhancement in taste differentiated Ben & Jerry's product from the competition.

62   The company also distinguished its product by its use of pure, natural and socially conscious milk from Vermont dairy farmers who agreed not to use rBGH. The FDA allowed the voluntary labeling of dairy products made from non-rBGH treated cows, so Ben & Jerry's aggressively promoted its products' purity on its packaging.

63   Ben & Jerry's products were sold by the pint in recycled paper board cups, a practice that was standard in the superpremium market. Ben & Jerry's arrived at that strategy based on the demographics of its target market–25- to 40-year-old consumers in the upper middle class sector who had no children. People in this segment did not need to purchase larger quantities of ice cream at one time.

64   Ice-cream pints accounted for only about 13 percent of supermarket ice-cream sales. Nonetheless, Ben & Jerry's strategy had been to obtain an increasingly large piece of a shrinking pie, but that was becoming more difficult as the competitive landscape changed.

65   It soon became apparent that the company would have to work harder to continue success based on its "new flavor" strategy because competitors began imitating its flavors with rapidly increasing speed. While originally it could count on about six months before imitations arrived, Ben & Jerry's now "owned" a flavor for only about 60 days. As a result, the company revised its marketing goal to establish a standard of product quality that cannot be imitated, to introduce more "euphoric" new flavors, and to improve the selection of the company's flavors in grocery stores.

66   In March 1994, Ben & Jerry's had introduced its line of Smooth, No Chunks flavors in response to market research indicating that a large portion of the superpremium market did not like chunks. The company targeted the segment that was " just too tired to chew" at the end of a busy day and who would rather "experience their ice cream without having to exert too much energy." That move placed Ben & Jerry's in a fortified position in its battle with Haagen-Dazs.

67   Other product innovations included novelty items such as Brownie Bars, which failed, and Peace Pops, which were marginally successful. Peace Pops were wrapped in a message to redirect one percent of the military budget to social programs; they did well only at convenience stores, suggesting to the company that they were primarily impulse buys. Recently, 70 percent of the Pops were sold in convenience stores.

Place

68   Ben & Jerry's marketed its superpremium ice-cream products to supermarkets, grocery stores, convenience stores, and restaurants that had demonstrated corporate consciousness in the way they did business. Roughly 105 Ben & Jerry's franchises or licensed "scoop shops" existed across the United States, in addition to some in Canada and Israel and a 50-50 joint venture in Russia. In addition, in March 1994 the company began shipping a small amount of its products to small specialty stores in the United Kingdom.

69   The company had also attempted to increase its distribution channels by offering gifts by mail. This concept featured a brochure advertising earthy, tie-dyed gifts, as well as ice cream, coffee, and candy, and offered consumers the ability to have the ice cream dry-ice packed and delivered overnight anywhere in the country. So far, the concept had met with limited success, due in part to limited promotion.

70   Restaurants were another venue the company was exploring in order to maintain growth, but to date, Ben & Jerry's had not placed this opportunity as a primary goal. Same went for global expansion. The company had been successful abroad, but efforts had been haphazard and cause-generated, and outcomes had been based solely on luck. The company admitted that it did not have an international strategy and that true commitment to global exporting would require that it learn much more about the market—something it had not made a current priority.

Price

71   Ben & Jerry's ice-cream products were premium-priced at the high end of the ice-cream market. A pint of its ice cream retailed for approximately $2.69. Although this pricing strategy worked extremely well within the exploding market of the late 1980s and early 1990s, it had been experiencing some difficulty in recent years, as demand shifted toward lower-priced and/or private-label products in grocery stores. Price elasticity had declined, and whereas before Ben & Jerry's could impose significant price increases (8 percent in 1991, 4 percent in early 1993), price became the pivotal issue.

72   Pricing pressure also resulted from the apparent consolidation of sales in a few players' hands and the stagnation of the market, with new forms of pricing competition coming into play. Until recently, all superpremium ice-cream and frozen-yogurt makers priced their products roughly equivalently. But Haagen-Dazs, the "sleeping giant" that had allowed Ben & Jerry's to gain market share at its expense during the late 1980s, had recently "woken up" and soon started "throwing dollars and incentives at the marketplace."

73   Haagen-Dazs was much bigger than Ben & Jerry's and so capable of waging a significant price war without fear of any lasting harm. The result was two-for-one sales and discounts in certain parts of the country. Ben & Jerry's guardedly followed suit with price discounts and store coupons for $1.49 pints, recognizing that the battle had become solely financial.

Promotion

74   Ben & Jerry's product promotion relied primarily on cause-generated marketing. It was the company's belief that marketing should not be performed simply to sell the product, but to have an effect on society. This marketing theory was called "Edible Activism."

75   The company's cause-related events included such things as traveling vaudeville shows in buses with solar-powered freezers—the more unconventional and politically correct, the better. The largest part of Ben & Jerry's budget went to major music festivals around the country, including the Newport Folk Festival in Rhode Island. In addition, the company's own plant was the largest tourist attraction in Vermont, hosting 275,000 visitors annually; thus, just by opening its own doors, Ben & Jerry's was promoting its products.

76   The company's socially conscious practices also earned it regular publicity, thereby saving it millions in public expenditures annually. As Ben once said, "the media can supply the ink and Ben & Jerry's will supply the wackiness."

77   Responsibility for marketing had not been farmed out to outside design and advertising firms. Rather, the company chose to maintain control for this function in-house. In March 1994, for example, Ben & Jerry's had created its first 30-second commercial to sell its new Smooth, No Chunks flavors; directed by Spike Lee, the ad featured socially minded stars who received nothing but a lifetime supply of ice cream for their efforts. The $6 million campaign to launch the line also included print ads featuring high-profile activists such as Carlos Santana, Bobby Seal, and Pete Seeger.

78   As competitive pressures increased and market growth slowed, Ben & Jerry's was forced to reexamine its exclusive use of socially oriented promotion. Many publicity events were abandoned so that funds could be diverted instead to promotional priorities such as store coupons and price discounts. While apparently rational, such a shift also garnered criticism that the company had been simply using the "world's ills and social needs to sell a product."

OPERATIONS

79   In February 1995, Ben & Jerry's had two manufacturing plants located in Waterbury and Springfield, Vermont; its St. Albans plant, whose opening had been delayed several times, was currently scheduled to come online in the second half of 1995. The company's main factory, in Waterbury, was located just over the hill from company headquarters, and generally operated two shifts a day, six days a week. Production averaged about 4.7 million gallons a year. The Springfield plant was used for the production of ice-cream novelties, bulk ice cream and frozen yogurt, and packaged pints; its production averaged about 1.2 million dozen novelties, and 2.3 million gallons of bulk ice cream and frozen yogurt, and packaged pints and quarts per year. It, too, operated six days a week. Overall, the company had a maximum manufacturing capacity at its own facilities of about 10.2 million gallons per year of packaged pints.

80   During 1992 and 1993, Ben & Jerry's had increased its manufacturing capacity to support its phenomenal sales growth. After seeing a surge in sales in the winter of 1991, the company added pint production lines at its Springfield plant and at the St. Albans Cooperative Creamery, in space loaned to the company by the site's family farmer owners.

81   The new St. Albans plant would have a maximum ice-cream and yogurt production capacity of about 17 million gallons per year when operated six days a week. It was being built with energy-efficient lighting, motors, and compressors to reduce the total amount of energy required for production. At the same time, Ben & Jerry's was inventing $2 million in the Waterbury plant to improve efficiency there. In the early 1990s the company was fined for dumping too much waste into the Waterbury system; since then, it launched a pilot cleanup product using a solar greenhouse to treat sewage.

82   The production equipment used at Ben & Jerry's was not the most efficient available; in fact, the only new machine added in recent years had been a wrapping machine, which replaced an antiquated predecessor. The company felt that increased automation might eliminate jobs, which would undermine its philosophy of social responsibility. In discussing the labor-intensive nature of the packaging line, the company has said that it would choose versatility over speed, should the choice be necessary. They admitted that there were several new machines available that were faster than what they currently used: It took the company about two hours to change from one size packaging capability to another.

83   Until the new plant was ready, Ben & Jerry's had a manufacturing and warehouse agreement with Edy's Grand Ice Cream, a subsidiary of Dreyer's Grand Ice Cream, Inc., to manufacture certain pint

ice-cream flavors at its plant in Fort Wayne, Indiana. The agreement was set in accordance with Ben & Jerry's quality-control specifications, and used dairy products shipped from Vermont. About 5 million gallons, or 40 percent of the packaged pints, were manufactured under this agreement in 1994, compared with about 37 percent in 1993. For 1995, the company expected that to be 2 million gallons.

HUMAN RESOURCES

84   Since its inception, Ben & Jerry's had been run entrepreneurially by Ben and Jerry and "built on the cult of these two counter-cultural personalities." As the company grew to almost 600 employees, the challenge became to maintain the original spirit while managing an increasingly large organization.

85   The key to Ben & Jerry's human resources success lay in keeping employees at all levels involved in bottom-up decision making. The company attempted to create ownership at all levels and followed the new-age management model of worker empowerment. Because they had the power to make decisions and influence how things were done, employees were energized and committed.

86   Of course, as the company grew, it became difficult to preserve the feel of a small company in which people matter amid the firm's transformation into an immense corporate entity. Both Ben and Jerry drew considerable praise from those inside as well as outside the company for their efforts to achieve this, and were viewed by many as the company's two biggest assets.

87   At the same time, however, there were those who criticized the company for "not walking its talk" in terms of employee treatment. Despite the firm's much hailed and publicized politically correct culture, for instance, employees nonetheless held less than half of 1 percent of company stock. And while Ben and Jerry frequently drew attention to the fact that their own salaries were a relatively paltry $130,000 per year, they failed to note that their combined stock was worth in excess of $50 million.

88   Finally, known for occasionally getting bored with the daily grind and going off on some sabbatical, Ben and Jerry did not enjoy an untarnished reputation on Wall Street. The company's stock consistently underperformed the market and irritated many investors, largely as a result of the firm's insistence on putting its principles—the promotion of charity, peace, and environmental preservation—ahead of its public shareholders.

89   The benefits offered to employees at the company were widely regarded as being on the cutting edge. Tuition reimbursement, flexible spending accounts, opinion surveys, evaluate-your-boss polls, paid health-club fees, 12 unpaid weeks of maternity, paternity and adoption leave, child-care centers, free body and foot massages, sabbatical leave, profit sharing, paid adoption expenses, wellness plans, an insurance plan that covered unmarried heterosexual and homosexual domestic partners, and free ice cream were all among the offerings employees could take advantage of. Ben & Jerry's management also reflected a commitment to minorities and women: Of the five senior positions filled in 1990, four were women or minorities.

90   Minimum wage at Ben & Jerry's was $8 per hour. While top salaries had been capped at roughly $150,000 (the sum earned in 1993 by Charles Lacy, president and COO), that policy was abandoned with the hiring of Holland. Nevertheless, while the average per capita income of Vermont residents was $17,436, the lowest-paid employee at Ben & Jerry's earned salary and benefits worth roughly $22,000.

91   Not surprisingly, the result of all its attention to employees earned Ben & Jerry's a generally happy workforce; its turnover rate was only 12 percent.

THE CHALLENGE

92   When Robert Holland took the helm as CEO, Ben & Jerry's future direction was far from clear. While the company had built its success by selling high-fat ice creams to consumers who were willing to pay more for the unique flavors and for Ben & Jerry's social causes, those days were gone. Health concerns, increased competition, pressure on prices, and its own massive size meant that Ben & Jerry's had to change. For Holland, the question was not "if" but "how."

CASE 9

SNAPPLE BEVERAGE CORPORATION

1   In 1972, Arnold Greenberg, the owner of a Manhattan health food store, Hyman Golden, and Leonard Marsh came up with the idea to sell all-natural drinks to health food distributors in the New York area. Over the next 20 years, the small grassroots company, Unadulterated Food Products became a $520 million dollar business and, now known as Snapple Beverage Company, one of the hottest stocks on Wall Street.

2   Greenberg, Golden, and Marsh have built Snapple into a major competitor in the natural beverage market at a time when diet-, health-, and environment-conscious consumers are shifting from carbonated, artificially flavored sodas to natural beverages. In developing, producing, and marketing their beverages, Snapple focuses on product excellence, targeting consumers who seek great-tasting natural products. Snapple's growth in this target market is evidenced by its rapid distribution growth: 26 states in 1990, 35 states by 1991, and all 50 states by 1992. To continue growing, Snapple plans to expand to new domestic and international markets and further penetrate existing markets through brand loyalty.

3   Although Snapple is the current market leader in the ready-to-drink (RTD) tea market, the company did not create that market. Rather, it merely capitalized on an opportunity to fulfill an unsatisfied need among health-conscious iced tea drinkers. The RTD tea market has existed since 1904. Lipton invented a tea with preservatives in it, which gave it a tin-like taste. Other companies packaged their iced teas in half-gallon milk cartons with minimal success. The Snapple Beverage Company found a way to produce the first hot-brewed, no preservative, all-natural, glass bottled iced tea, using Tetley, Inc., as their predominant supplier of nondecaffeinated tea. Snapple's consumer appeal lies in its authentic taste, and it has now become the standard to beat for good tasting ready-to-drink tea.

4   Part of Snapple's success derives from the company's concern for the well being of its customers. Health-conscious consumers choose Snapple's 64 flavors of all-natural iced teas, sports drinks, and fruit drinks because they are "made from the best stuff on earth." To fulfill this claim, Snapple incorporates a water purification technique into its manufacturing process, then packages its single-serving beverages in generous 16-ounce recyclable glass containers. For weight-conscious consumers, Snapple provides beverages sweetened with NutraSweet. Consumers have responded to Snapple's commitment to healthful products and environmental sensitivity with terrific consumer acceptance and word-of-mouth sponsorship.

5   Despite Snapple's attention to social concerns, the company has not been exempt from negative publicity. In the 1990s the Department of Health and Human Services began developing labeling standards for the food and beverage industry. The Food and Drug Administration (FDA) conducted inquiries into Snapple's use of the terminology "real brewed iced tea" and "all-natural" on their iced tea and fruit drink labels. Although the FDA concluded its investigation without finding fault with Snapple, its stock nevertheless fell two points.

6   The negative impact of the FDA inquiry on Snapple stock was compounded by several boycott threats from groups supporting social causes. In 1992 the company was threatened with a boycott based on rumors that it supports the anti-abortion group Operation Rescue. In the summer of 1993, an unknown source spread a rumor that Snapple iced tea labels actually depict slave ships rather than the intended Boston Tea Party ship. In addition, students at the University of Oregon challenged Premier, one of Snapple's distributors, to support the "Keep America Beautiful" campaign by providing

This case was prepared by Karen Hare, Alan N. Hoffman, Roland Larose, Linda Merrill, and Karen Mullen of Bentley College. The authors would like to thank Barbara Gottfried and Sally Strawn for their valuable comments and suggestions.

recycling bins to collect bottles not yet covered by deposit laws and bottle bills. The Snapple Beverage Company quickly reacted to these social pressures by declaring its neutral stance on the issue of abortion, launching a costly campaign to squelch false rumors about its labels, and providing recycling bins for the university.

7   Despite recessionary times and social challenges, consumer demand for Snapple products continues to grow. In 1993 sales volume doubled over the previous year. In fact consumer demand became so high, the company had to temporarily cut production of some of its flavors to meet the demand for its 15 most popular flavors. The company realizes its greatest sales and profitability during the summer season (April through September, the second and third quarters). During those months of peak demand, Snapple arranges for co-packing capacity in excess of anticipated demand to avoid shortages and ensure its ability to satisfy customer demand.

8   Snapple Beverage Company takes great pride in the high quality and great taste of its beverages, and has taken steps to secure its continued success by protecting the proprietary nature of its products. The company owns the Snapple trademark, which is registered with the United States Patent and Trademark Office, and has entered into confidentiality agreements with its co-packers and flavor houses. The future of Snapple Beverage Company depends on its ability to keep its beverage formulas a trade secret and on its ability to continue to develop innovative products that appeal to a diverse group of consumers.

9   Snapple is committed to product excellence and to a future of continued growth in market share, sales, and earnings. Much of Snapple's success may be attributed to the efforts of a team of employees, contract packers, and distributors who produce Snapple products and distribute the beverages nationally. Snapple's commitment to high quality and good taste, as well as its ongoing concern for the well-being of consumers, has been the key to its success with its customers.

THE SOFT DRINK INDUSTRY

Overview

10   Soft drinks are the largest segment of the beverage industry, responsible for 54 percent of overall beverage sales for an estimated $48.9 billion dollars in revenue in 1993 (Exhibit 1). With their large marketing budgets and extensive distribution systems, the industry's two main competitors, PepsiCo and Coca-Cola, dominate both the overall industry and many of the segments within the industry.

11   In such an intensely competitive industry, where the products are essentially similar, successful marketing is the key to increasing both revenue and market share. The stakes are high and the tactics ruthless, as war games rhetoric of "The Cola Wars" and the "Pepsi Challenge" makes clear. The marketing campaign must appeal to consumers, playing on their perception of the product. The "Pepsi Challenge" was superb marketing because it positively shaped consumers' perception of Pepsi at Coke's expense (see below for details).

Background

12   In the 1970s, the soft drink industry was dominated by the six largest concentrate producers: Coca-Cola, PepsiCo, Seven-Up, Dr. Pepper, Royal Crown, and Canada Dry, who together held over 75 percent of the market share. Each firm had achieved its position by creating extensive promotional, advertising, and marketing programs to differentiate its products from those of its competitors. The rest of the market was made up of small national and regional companies (e.g., Hires, Orange Crush, Squirt, Schweppes, A&W Root Beer), supermarket private labels, and small local firms.

13   The Coca-Cola Company was the largest of these six firms in terms of marketing, sales, profit, market share, and financial strength, and the first U.S. company to begin international soft drink operations. In fact, in 1975 analysts estimated that Coke's international sales were growing more rapidly than its domestic sales. While Coke's sales were largely from cola products, in the 1960s and

EXHIBIT 1
Beverage Industry

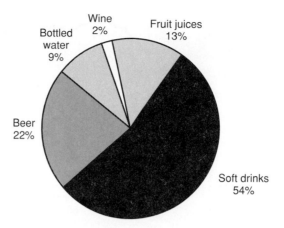

1970s Coke began introducing many flavored soft drinks, for example, Fanta, Sprite, Mr. PiBB, Tab, and Fresca.

14   PepsiCo was the industry's second largest company. The company competed with the six top soft drink producers in four product areas, and internationally. Its main soft drinks were regular and diet Pepsi-Cola, Mountain Dew (a lemon-lime soft drink), and Pepsi Light (a semidiet cola). PepsiCo also had a food division that was the leading U.S. producer of snack foods (e.g., potato and corn chip products), with its own delivery system. By 1975 PepsiCo's sales were eighty percent of Coca-Cola's, while its net profit was 44 percent of Coke's.

15   In the early 1970s, competition began to increase among the major national soft drink producers, particularly between the industry leaders, Coca-Cola and PepsiCo. Many industry analysts began to call this intense rivalry the "Cola Wars," because of the war games mentality exhibited by each of the competitors. The battles were fought with innovative new advertising and promotional campaigns to increase market share. In April 1974 PepsiCo launched what will always be remembered as one of the great advertising campaigns, the "Pepsi Challenge." In Dallas, Texas, consumers were "challenged" in a blind taste test to choose between Pepsi and Coke. The taste tests took place in local supermarkets to ensure a large number of participants. Pepsi "won," but Coke did not take the challenge lightly, increasing its advertising budget and offering price promotions. Pepsi responded in kind. The net result was a small market share increase for Coke, to about 30 percent, while PepsiCo almost doubled its market share, from 7 percent to 14 percent. Ironically, the challenge benefited not only Pepsi, but its rival, Coke, as well. Together the two companies increased their combined market share from 36 percent to over 44 percent, at the expense of smaller brands, especially Dr Pepper. Consumers were also winners as retail soft drink prices fell to almost half their prechallenge levels, and the stage was set for the Cola Wars to continue into the 1980s and 1990s.

Bottling and Distribution Entities

16   Bottling and distribution companies also play a key role in the soft drink industry, especially in local markets. Some are family owned, but many are now owned by conglomerates or by the concentrate companies themselves. Since the late 1970s, the number of small bottlers has steadily decreased, as they have been pushed out of the market by increased operating costs and higher capital requirements, while larger volume bottlers have achieved greater economies of scale.

17   Smaller bottling and distribution companies do not produce their own flavors, they purchase syrup directly from the concentrate manufacturers. Their market advantage lies in their sales forces, which are right on the spot to negotiate for shelf space, rotate the stock, and run in-store promotions.

EXHIBIT 2
Cola Sales

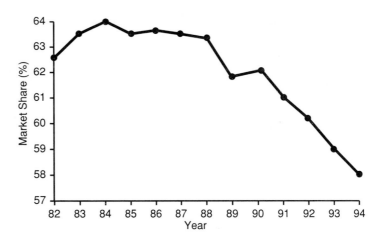

The two largest concentrate companies, Coca-Cola and PepsiCo, own many of their own bottling and distribution companies, thereby controlling a sprawling distribution network, which, combined with their marketing strength, makes them the two global giants of the soft drink industry.

Recent Trends

18   In the last decade, many niches have developed within the soft drink industry, which has led to greater levels of competition. A company's direct competitors are determined by the niche or market segment in which it competes. For example, in the cola segment of the market, Coke and Pepsi clearly dominate, so any potential new entrant must compete head to head with these large and powerful firms. However, Cola sales have declined over the past eight years (Exhibit 2), and current growth in the soft drink industry is most rapid in the segments other than the cola market, especially in the new niches that have developed in the past few years. From 1991–1992 the overall soft drink industry grew only very slowly, about 1–2 percent per year, although in 1993 growth increased to about 3 percent in the domestic United States, and 6–9 percent internationally. Nevertheless, while the industry as a whole is growing at a relatively slow rate, many of the niche segments within the industry are growing rapidly.

19   One of the fastest growing niches in the soft drink industry is the ready-to-drink (RTD) iced tea segment, with 122 different RTD tea labels currently on the market. This segment has experienced double-digit growth over the past few years (Exhibit 3), from $300 million in 1991 to $1 billion in 1993, and growth was expected to continue for at least the next two years. Snapple is the industry leader in the RTD iced tea market with a 43.7 percent market share, a niche Snapple itself created in 1988 when Unadulterated Food Products, Inc., introduced Snapple iced tea. As of 1992 Snapple distributes its products nationally, in all 50 states, whereas its competitors in the RTD tea market are primarily regional, private label, and global companies, for example, Island Natural Beverage, Empire Beverage Group, Celestial Seasonings (owned by Perrier), and Tropicana Fruit Teas. While 50 percent of Snapple's sales are in the RTD tea market, Snapple also competes in other soft drink market segments including the fruit drink, sports drink, and New Age beverage niches. New Age beverages, which are less sweet and less carbonated than most soft drinks, were developed in response to consumer demand for more natural carbonated drinks. Many of these products are clear, with fructose and fruit juice typically used for sweetening, rather than corn syrup or refined sugar. The New Age beverage market is growing at more than 10 percent annually. Some of Snapple's competitors in this market are Clearly Canadian, Crystal Pepsi, and other flavored sparking waters.

EXHIBIT 3
RTD Tea Market Growth

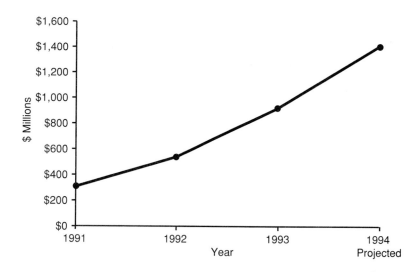

20   Exhibit 4 shows a strategic group mapping of the soft drink industry for the cola segment and the market segments in which Snapple competes. The chart helps illustrate how the industry is structured, and who some of the competitors are in each of the areas. The map's two axes indicate market segment growth rate and market segment size.

MARKETING

21   The Snapple Beverage Corporation's marketing objectives include increased penetration of existing markets, development of new markets, building product awareness and loyalty, and focused differentiation, all of which it hopes to achieve by emphasizing the excellence of its product.

The Product

22   Snapple Beverages are separated into five product categories: real brewed iced teas, fruit-based drinks, natural sodas and seltzers, fruit juices, and isotonic sports drinks, all marketed under the Snapple brand name. The beverages are available in 10-ounce, 16-ounce, and 32-ounce glass bottles and 11.5-ounce cans. Snapple is made from costly, high quality natural ingredients without adding artificial colors or preservatives, although the Diet products contain NutraSweet, a low-calorie sweetener, and the Sport Drinks contain synthetic vitamins and minerals. The company pioneered the "hot-fill" bottling technique whereby the tea is brewed at such high temperatures that preservatives are not required during the bottling process. Snapple is diligent in ensuring that all products satisfy corporate quality standards, and monitors its co-packers (bottlers) to ensure adherence to its production procedures, analyzing samples from each production run to ensure quality control.

23   To increase its appeal, and, thereby, its market share, Snapple has developed and introduced new products on a regular basis, adding four to five new products per year. Snapple products attract people who want something more natural than ordinary soft drinks and more substantial than water.

24   Snapple's 64 flavors and 105 sku's offer something for everyone to maximize its public exposure. The company works with independent flavor houses that cover much of the expense of new product

EXHIBIT 4
Strategic Group Mapping

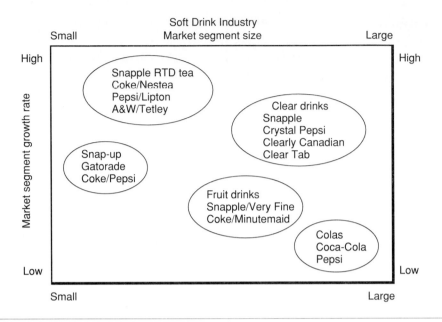

Soft Drink Industry
Market segment size
Small   Large

development, enabling Snapple to develop new products at a relatively low cost. Snapple currently plans to expand its product lines of both fruit-based drinks and diet drinks to attract new customers.

Price

25   Snapple currently sells at full retail markup, offering retailers 35 percent to 43 percent margins, which gives them high profit margins in the traditionally unprofitable loss-leader beverage aisle. Pricing varies widely depending on the channel of distribution:

	Supermarkets	Convenience Stores	Other Food Services
16 oz.	.79	.99	$1.29
32 oz.	$1.39	n/a	n/a

26   To date, Snapple has resisted all forms of price cutting and discounting. Outlets in the convenience store and food service categories, where Snapple does much of its business, do not require price cutting, and Snapple has been highly successful as a result. The supermarket class of trade (which Snapple entered in 1993) traditionally requires that manufacturers offer co-op advertising dollars to support advertising programs and price reductions, but Snapple has not yet offered supermarkets anything other than full list pricing.

Distribution: Increased Penetration of Existing Markets

27   Most soft drink companies manufacture a syrup that is then sold to independent bottlers who add water, carbonation, and so on; bottle the final product; and distribute it in their regions. Snapple's distribution system is unlike that of any other soft drink company. The Snapple Beverage Company is involved in the whole process of manufacturing a finished product even though they use co-packers.

What Snapple does is buy the ingredients, develop the products and preparation processes, and retain ownership of the product until it is shipped from the 16 independent co-packers with whom it has contracts to various independent distributors. The independent contract packers purchase the natural ingredients, including flavors and water, from Snapple, and produce, bottle, and warehouse the product themselves. Each packer has its own quality control standards supplemented by corporate standards. Thus, although Snapple's transportation costs are much higher because they are shipping finished products in bottles, rather than just syrup that will be bottled locally, its capital expenditure is nominal because production needs are met by existing and new co-packers, rather than by the company itself.

28   Independent trucking companies then transport the product to one of 300 distributors, who in turn sell Snapple to delis, mom-and-pop markets, convenience stores, supermarkets, office buildings, and school cafeterias. This distribution strategy enables the company to maintain influence over shelf space allocation and merchandising while reducing Snapple's reliance on any one distributor. When a distributor requires the product, an order is placed at corporate headquarters. The company selects a co-packer with available inventory closest to the distributor and contracts with outside trucking companies to deliver Snapple products from the co-packer to the distributor. The distributor then resells and delivers products directly to the retail outlet, and stocks the retailers' shelves with Snapple.

29   Distributors are given exclusive rights to their territories and share the cost of advertising and promotion with the corporation. A distributor has the exclusive rights to distribute Snapple beverages but may also sell competing beverage brands. Nevertheless, Snapple products often account for 85 to 100 percent of a distributor's business.

30   Distribution in supermarket chains is one of the keys to growth for Snapple. As the cola market matures, consumers are looking for alternative beverages. Snapple has now achieved 100 percent distribution in U.S. supermarkets and is selling extremely well without in-store advertising, displays, or promotion. Even so, Snapple and its distributors are currently attempting to increase shelf and display space within the supermarket class of trade by racking up enough product sku's to occupy a "billboard" of shelf space in retail outlets. To promote billboard display, Snapple and its distributors share the cost of purchasing cold coolers for retail stores and place them in retail outlets in exchange for primary product display within those coolers.

31   The Snapple Beverage Corporation sees the vending market as its next distributional frontier and has begun a program to assist vending machine operators in their purchase of Snapple vending machines. The company has ordered 10,000 vending machines, which hold 52 varieties of Snapple, for office buildings, schools, and public areas. Distributors are working with Snapple to expand into the vending machine market because they find the high profit margins that vending machines offer very attractive.

32   Snapple currently has no clear international strategy and is simply responding to foreign distributors' requests for its products. In 1993 Snapple was available in Canada, the United Kingdom, the Caribbean, and 11 other countries. The company plans to expand into Ireland, Japan, and Australia during 1994 by appointing regional distributors. Snapple has increased the size of its international management group at its corporate headquarters and will continue to prospect for new markets.

Advertising and Promotion: Building Awareness and Loyalty

33   Snapple is working to build customer loyalty and market share through down-to-earth advertising and promotions focusing on ordinary people. Their commercials are spontaneous, not scripted, and feature Snapple-worshipping consumers who have written unsolicited letters of appreciation to the company. Since the quirky commercials began airing on TV and radio in the spring of 1993, consumer correspondence has jumped from 100 to over 3,500 letters per week. The testimonials (or "love letters," as the company likes to call them) validate the company's overall marketing strategy: unpretentious word-of-mouth growth. Nevertheless, Snapple's advertising budget increased threefold, from $10 million in 1992 to $30 million in 1993.

34   Snapple's advertising agency, Kirshenbaum & Bond in New York has identified its primary target market as adults aged 18 to 49, and its secondary market as teens aged 12 to 17. The company has positioned its products as a healthy, good-for-you, natural alternative to soda, and used a mixture of

consumer and trade promotion to market its products. The majority of its promotional budget is invested in radio and television spots, but by and large, the company has benefited from high consumer demand at the point of purchase, which has thus far made it unnecessary for it to pursue aggressive advertising and promotion.

Sales Force

35 Snapple's 56-person sales force is organized by region. Salespeople are responsible for the large retail accounts located in their regions, for managing existing distributor relationships, and for selection of new distributors as needed. The sales force concentrates on opening new accounts and increasing shelf space. Area managers work with distributors to identify local marketing opportunities and share advertising and promotional costs. Sales reps also install Snapple refrigerated coolers in retail outlets with "billboard" displays of Snapple products in centralized high-traffic locations. Snapple sales managers receive only minimal training and support, as the company is scrambling to grow as quickly as possible. For instance, the company does not supply personal computers for managers to track sales as well as manage their businesses, a practice that may prove to be penny-wise, but pound-foolish.

In-Store Display

36 Snapple sales managers work with regional distributors to increase shelf space and display of the product in all classes of trade, particularly supermarkets. Snapple has set the following Display Objectives for supermarkets and convenience stores:

- four-foot vertical sets in all chains.
- Distribution of cans in chains stores (6 packs).
- Full cold box doors in convenience stores.

Snapple's most effective sales gimmick has been to give supermarkets their own Snapple refrigerators, making it possible for grocers to take a chance on the brand without having to discontinue better known soft drinks and juices to make space on the shelves for Snapple.

FINANCE

37 In March of 1992, Snapple Beverage Corporation was formed through a leveraged buyout of Unadulterated Food Products, Inc., by its three original owners, Greenberg, Marsh, and Golden, and the Thomas H. Lee Company. The purchase price of the assets of Unadulterated Food Products was $144 million, of which $89 million was for the Snapple name, trademarks, patents, and contract. On December 14, 1992, the company went public using the net proceeds to significantly reduce the indebtedness incurred at the time of the original acquisition. In 1993 the company's stock split twice, in June and September.

38   1993 earnings per share were 49 cents and its price to earnings (P/E) ratio was 66 based on a stock price of 32 1/4 as of February 15, 1994. This P/E ratio is much higher than the Value Line industry average of 27.

39   The company's financial performance shows significant growth over the last five years (Exhibit 5). In 1991 the company had revenues of $95 million. In the next two years since then revenues have grown 5.5 times to the 1993 level of $516 million, a growth of 250 percent over 1992 levels. This growth has been driven by the company's desire to expand into new markets and gain a stronger foothold in the markets in which it already competes. Throughout this period of exponential growth, the company's net profit margin has increased to 13.1 percent, while its gross profit margins continue to be in the 38 percent range.

40   As stated earlier, the company took on significant debt during its acquisition. Although this debt was substantially paid off through the issuing of common stock, there was still a very large increase

EXHIBIT 5

SELECTED HISTORICAL FINANCIAL DATA

Set forth below are the historical financial data of Snapple Beverage Corp. (the "Company") and its predecessor, Unadulterated Food Products, Inc. (the "Predecessor Company").

(000's except per share amounts)	Predecessor Company Year ended December 31, 1899	1990	1991	Three months ended March 31, 1992	Combined Year ended Dec. 31, 1992	The Company Nine months ended Dec. 31, 1992	Year ended Dec. 31, 1993
STATEMENT OF OPERATIONS DATA:							
Net revenues	$23,594	$44,183	$95,017	$26,468	$231,934	$205,446	**$516,005**
Cost of sales	16,330	29,376	58,875	16,129	143,227[1]	127,098[1]	**298,724**
Gross profit	7,264	14,807	36,142	10,339	88,707	78,368	**217,281**
Selling, general and administrative expenses	5,566	10,232	20,208	5,526	50,982[2]	45,456[2]	**105,694**
Incentive bonus expense.[3]	—	—	—	—	5,700	5,700	**—**
Distributor termination expense, net	—	125	160	833	2,978	2,145	**93**
Amortization of intangible assets	—	—	—	—	6,657	6,657	**9,387**
Operating income	1,698	4,450	15,774	3,980	22,390	18,410	**102,107**
Interest expense	108	103	98	22	19,108[4]	19,086[4]	**2,459**
Interest income	(1)	(6)	(17)	(14)	(3,889)	(3,875)	**(459)**
Asset sale expense	—	—	324	514	514	—	**—**
Minority interest	—	—	—	—	—	—	**96**
Other income	(91)	(149)	(188)	—	—	—	
Income before income taxes and extraordinary item	1,682	4,502	15,557	3,458	6,657	3,199	**100,011**
Income taxes.[5]	137	348	832	135	1,398	1,263	**32,388[6]**
Extraordinary item	—	—	—	—	(2,633)	(2,633)	
Net income (loss)	$ 1,545	4,154	$14,725	$ 3,323	$ 2,626	(697)	**$ 67,623**
Income (loss) per share						$ (0.01)	**$ 0.56**
PRO FORMA STATEMENT OF OPERATIONS DATA:							
Income before pro forma income tax	$ 1,682	$ 4,502	$15,557	$ 3,458	$ 6,657	—	—
Pro forma income tax	725	1,890	6,403	1,423	2,686	—	—
Extraordinary item	—	—	—	—	(2,633)	—	—
Pro forma net income	$ 957	$ 2,612	$ 9,154	$ 2,035	$ 1,338	—	—
OPERATING DATA:							
Total case sales, in units	2,783	5,124	10,743	2,925	25,327	22,402	**55,578**
Capital expenditures	$ 25	$ 212	$ 148	$ 3	$ 487	$ 484	**$ 9,029**
BALANCE SHEET DATA (AT PERIOD END):							
Working capital	$ 1,549	$ 4,021	$ 9,997	$ 8,837	$ 24,173	$ 24,173	**$ 67,778**
Total assets	4,533	7,912	18,894	26,336	226,737	226,737	**238,952**
Long-term debt	532	110	189	181	18,226	18,226	**26,219**
Total shareholders' equity	1,415	4,515	11,555	10,318	90,814	90,814	**162,477**

[1] Includes non-cash expense of approximately $3.7 million for a write-up of inventory to recorded value related to the Acquisition, which represented the entire amount of such inventory write-up.

[2] Includes approximately $1.0 million for certain one-time non-cash compensation expenses relating to stock issuances and the granting of non-qualified stock options related to the Acquisition.

[3] Represents certain one-time incentive bonus payments.

[4] Includes $8.0 million of incremental interest expense.

[5] The Predecessor Company was an S Corporation and accordingly not subject to federal and certain state income taxes during the periods indicated.

[6] Includes $8.1 million or $0.07 per share of one-time tax benefit related to the Company's election of certain new provisions of 1993 tax legislation.

[7] Reflects approximate federal and state income tax expense the Predecessor Company would have incurred had it been treated as a C Corporation, based on the tax rates which would have been in effect during the respective periods shown.

EXHIBIT 5

SNAPPLE BEVERAGE CORP. AND SUBSIDIARIES
CONSOLIDATED BALANCE SHEETS

	December 31 1992	December 31 1993
ASSETS (Note 9):		
Current assets:		
Cash and cash equivalents (Note 12)	$ 7,486,632	$ 9,396,949
Restricted cash (Notes1, 8, and 12)	90,000,000	4,000,000
Accounts receivable, less allowance for doubtful accounts of		
$308,796 and $1,030,548, respectively (Note 12)	17,428,379	53,010,325
Inventory (Note 3)	16,166,183	40,922,888
Income tax receivable	2,738,236	1,109,550
Deferred tax asset (Note 5)	2,135,798	789,787
Other current assets	1,914,551	2,293,422
Total current assets	137,869,779	111,522,921
Fixed assets, net (Notes 4 and 7)	1,053,399	10,751,597
Intangible assets, net (Notes 1a and 6)	82,770,827	97,819,997
Deferred tax asset, net (Notes 1b and 5)	2,953,950	17,668,675
Deferred financing costs, net of accumulated amortization of zero and		
$420,448, respectively (note 2)	751,051	883,950
Other non-current assets	1,338,166	304,745
Total assets	$226,737,172	$238,951,885
LIABILITIES AND SHAREHOLDERS' EQUITY:		
Current liabilities:		
Notes payable to Predecessor Company (Notes 1a and 8)	90,000,000	$ —
Payable to seller of Mr. Natural, Inc. (Note 1b)	—	3,860,844
Accounts payable	6,100,345	7,326,411
Accrued expenses and other current liabilities (Notes 1, 10 and 14)	16,999,258	17,573,454
Income taxes payable	446,892	6,034,860
Current portion of long-term debt, including obligations under capital leases (Notes 7 and 9)	150,469	8,949,665
Total current liabilities	113,696,964	43,745,234
Long-term debt, including obligations under capital leases (Notes 7 and 9)	18,226,138	26,218,911
Other non-current liabilities (Notes 1 and 14)	4,000,000	5,011,000
Minority interest in subsidiary (Note 1b)	—	1,499,717
Total liabilities	135,923,102	76,474,862
Commitments and contingencies (Notes 7, 11, and 18)		
Shareholders' equity (Notes 1, 9, 14 and 16):		
Preferred stock $.01 par value per share; 1,000,000 shares authorized;		
no shares issued or outstanding	—	—
Common stock, $.01 par value per share; 140,000,000 shares authorized;		
121,376,560 and 121,609,568 issued and outstanding	1,213,766	1,216,096
Additional paid-in capital, net	90,297,391	94,334,533
(Accumulated deficit) retained earnings	(697,087)	66,926,394
Total shareholders' equity	90,814,070	162,477,023
Total liabilities and shareholders' equity	$226,737,172	$238,951,885

The accompanying notes are an integral part of these consolidated financial statements.

EXHIBIT 6
Boston Consulting Group Matrix

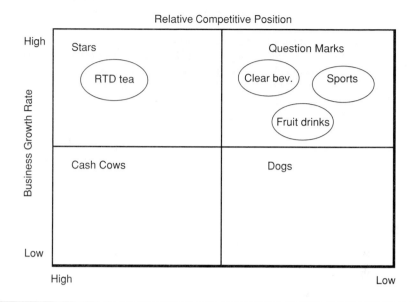

in the level of debt in 1992 (Exhibit 5). At the end of 1993, this long-term debt was 16 percent of total assets, or $26.2 million. Snapple's objective is to finance its operations through profits and not debt. Due to the cyclical nature of the beverage industry, Snapple sometimes needs to increase working capital at peak times of the year. In order to accomplish this, the company has a working capital credit line agreement with the Banque Nationale de Paris for $20 million. Its current outstanding debt on that credit line is $18.1 million at an interest rate of 5.25 percent, which will be reduced on a quarterly basis beginning in 1994.

41   Net income for the company has also grown steadily in the last five years. In 1991 Unadulterated Food Products had net income of $14.2 million, restated to $9.2 million on a pro-forma basis after the effects of the change in income tax rates were taken into account. In 1992 company income dropped significantly, to $1.3 million, for reasons related to the acquisition. In 1992 the company made interest payments of $19.1 million, which completely cleared its acquisition debt. In 1993 net income returned to a respectable $67.6 million dollars.

42   The company currently has what amounts to a four-year contract with Greenberg, Golden, and Marsh. According to this agreement, the company pays each of them an annual salary of $300,000 and a bonus based on operating income each year. An additional bonus of $5.7 million was paid to the three in 1992 since the company went public before April 1, 1993. Thomas Lee also has a consulting agreement with the company that pays him $120,000 per year through 1997, at which time the agreement can be renewed on an annual basis. While these figures are low compared to company sales, they represented a substantial hit to the bottom line in 1992, and are seen as management's way of taking operating profits out of the company.

OPERATIONS

43   Snapple's major strength has been its ability to grow without incurring large amounts of debt, a process facilitated by the company's use of co-packers. Snapple beverages are produced in 16 plants strategically located across the United States, which are owned and operated by independent contract packers. Snapple selects only modern, high-quality facilities and is involved in every step of the

production process, from managing product development, purchasing, and inventory to overseeing shipping from their New York headquarters. Snapple buys the ingredients, develops the recipes and preparation processes, and retains ownership of the product until it is shipped to the distributor. Snapple's production and quality assurance representatives then work directly with the contract packers at the packers' facilities to guarantee that every bottle of Snapple measures up to the company's exacting standards of quality.

44   In 1993 Snapple acquired its largest distributor, Mr. Natural, located in its largest market, the metropolitan New York area. Mr. Natural purchased 10 percent of Snapple's sales in both 1992 and the first quarter of 1993. By acquiring its largest distributor, Snapple reduces the power that their largest distributor would have had over them.

45   Snapple currently has a contract through 1995 to purchase virtually all its tea from Tetley, with semi-annual price adjustments. After contracting with Snapple, Tetley entered into a joint venture with A&W Root Beer to produce and market its own RTD tea under the Tetley name. A&W is currently being pursued by Cadbury Schweppes, another big-league player, which could add to the RTD iced tea competition that Snapple already faces from Coca Cola and PepsiCo.

FALL 1994: TROUBLE AHEAD

46   The RTD tea segment continues to change and grow. While the primary arena for survival was once convenience stores and delicatessens, it has now shifted to the supermarket segment. Currently, there are three major competitors joining the fray. Snapple continues to be the market leader, followed by Pepsi, with its Lipton product, and Coke, with its Nestea product. However, InfoScan data for a 12-week period in 1994 shows Snapple losing 17 market share points, primarily to the Lipton line of teas, even though the market for this segment continues to grow at a rapid rate. Over the same 12-week period, Snapple sales grew by 82 percent, but its competitors' sales grew at an even greater rate, Lipton showing 352 percent growth, and Nestea nearly doubling its sales.

47   To offset threats from the competition, Snapple has decided to double its advertising budget to $65 million in 1994. To counter this bold move by Snapple, Nestea has developed its own media blitz. In a $30 million promotional campaign, Nestea (Coca Cola) will sponsor the Association of Volleyball Professionals beach volleyball tour, and offer samples of their products in their "Cool Out Caravan" at tour stops. Lipton (PepsiCo), on the other hand, is reverting to Cola War tactics, attacking Snapple's claim that it is made from real brewed iced tea, and alleging that it is made from powdered iced tea. Pepsi has introduced its Lipton RTD tea product into markets by coupling it with two other new drinks, Ocean Spray Lemonade and All Sport, in a discounted trial pack, all three of which compete in the same markets as Snapple beverages, although they cannot make the same claim of "naturalness."

48   The latest competitive threat to Snapple comes from the niche player Arizona Iced Tea. An unknown in 1992, Arizona finished fourth in the RTD tea market in 1993 with a 12.6 percent market share. In 1994 Arizona projects their sales will exceed $300 million, triple their 1993 sales.

49   Another trend threatening Snapple's bottom line is a shift in consumer preference. People who once consumed Snapple's RTD tea are now purchasing lower margin fruit juices. While overall case sales of Snapple are increasing, this shift in product mix is proving to be detrimental to profits.

50   Recognizing that its domestic dominance is now in question, Snapple has implemented two strategies aimed at defending its market share. The first is an agreement to sell Snapple in vending machines. The second is to expand internationally. Vending machine sales should make Snapple products more visible to consumers and allow them to be sold in a larger variety of venues: office buildings, schools, and public areas. The second line of defense, international distribution, although it is currently hurting company profits, may help Snapple to remain ahead of Lipton and Nestea in the long run. In the second quarter of 1994, Snapple's sales, general, and administrative expenses rose 110 percent as a result of the cost of implementing aggressive advertising campaigns and international launches. The increased expenses, combined with the change in product mix, resulted in Snapple's stock dropping to a 52-week low of 13 3/4 in November 1994 after hitting a peak of 32 1/4 just 10 months earlier.

51   Ironically, while Snapple is currently at the height of its popularity with consumers, increased competition from Coca-Cola and PepsiCo, in the form of lower prices, may force Snapple to cuts its prices to retain market share. Falling prices for Snapple products will directly impact the company's bottom line. It appears that Snapple's best days may be behind them and they may have a tough road ahead, going head-to-head with the soft drink industry giants.

CASE 10

EASTMAN KODAK COMPANY

> An organization cannot be sound unless its spirit is. That is the lesson the man on top must learn. He must be a man of vision and progress who can understand that. One can muddle along a basis in which the human factor takes no part, but eventually there comes a fall. He must be willing to adopt the very best there is in industrial reform and, in addition, must find the "something else" that will engender the respect and loyalty of his employees.
>
> George Eastman, 1923[1]

INTRODUCTION

1   As of 1993, Eastman Kodak Company processed one of the world's most valuable brand names, due to excellent product quality and reliability. However, the Kodak organization was often depicted as bloated, slow-moving, myopic, and incapable of coping with the loss of its once invincible market power in the photographic film business. Product obsolescence and technological substitution were serious challenges in most of Kodak's largest market segments. Over the 1983–93 decade, profits repeatedly came in below security analysts' expectations, and the company incurred billions of dollars in so-called "one-time" charges, as it undertook incremental efforts to streamline and improve its performance.

2   Kodak was a major participant in the $20 billion U.S. photographic industry, a mature industry facing competition from other leisure time products. Industry shipments were expected to grow at a sluggish annual rate of 1 to 2 percent during the 1990s. While Kodak's core businesses were photographic imaging equipment and supplies, the company had ventured into a broad array of related product lines, as illustrated in Exhibit 1.

3   In October 1993, the Board of Directors of Eastman Kodak Company selected George M. C. Fisher to be its new Chairman, President, and Chief Executive Officer (CEO). He was the first outsider in Kodak's 113-year history to occupy the top management position. His background also diverged from Kodak's traditional realm, since he was well versed in the fields of electronics and communications rather than chemistry.

4   Fisher faced the pressing challenge of increasing shareholder returns and adapting Kodak's mission, capabilities, resources, and product-market orientation. During the first six months on the job, Fisher's principal challenge was to develop an appreciation of Kodak's recent history as well as its major competencies and deficiencies, as a prelude to the formulation and implementation of successful long-term strategic changes.

RECENT SYMPTOMS OF DECLINE

5   Measured by *Fortune* magazine's annual survey of "America's Most Admired Corporations," Eastman Kodak's reputation among top executives, directors, and financial analysts had declined from the top 5 percent to the bottom 18 percent of surveyed companies over a 10-year period. Rankings were based upon eight key attributes of reputation, namely: quality of management; quality of products or services; innovativeness; long-term investment value; financial soundness; ability to

This case was prepared by James A. Kidney of Southern Connecticut State University.

[1]Interview, *New York Times,* February 4, 1923.

EXHIBIT 1
Eastman Kodak Company Business Segments as of 1993

Imaging Segment (SIC 3069, 3827, 3861, 7384)

Products were used for capturing, recording, or displaying an image. Examples were black and white films, color films, cameras, projectors, photographic paper, photographic plates, processing chemicals, processing services, Photo CD systems, videotapes, batteries, albums, and frames.

Major customers included amateur and professional photographers, motion picture and television producers, cinematographers, motion picture laboratories, special effects houses, schools, services, managerial and professional offices, photojournalists, newspapers, printers, advertising agencies.

Major competitors included 3DO, Bayer (Agfa brand), Fuji Photo, Konica, International Paper (Anitec, Horsell, Ilford brands), Minnesota Mining and Mfg. (3M brand), and Polaroid.

Information Segment (SIC 1038, 1046, 3861, 7372)

Products were used to capture, store, process, and display images in a variety of forms. Examples were copier-duplicators, graphics imaging systems, microfilm and related equipment, mass memory discs, diconix printers, sensors, scanners, and audio-visual equipment.

Major customers were in commercial printing, publishing, office automation, and government markets.

Major competitors included Alco Standard, Canon, Harris (Lanier brand), IBM, Minolta, Pitney Bowes, and Xerox.

Health Segment (SIC 2830, 2842, 2844)

Products were used to advance the well-being of consumers by providing solutions to health and home-care needs. Examples were life science chemicals, x-ray films and equipment, *in vitro* diagnostics, aspirin, milk of magnesia, pharmaceuticals, household cleaners, disinfectants, deodorants, baby care products, hair care products, floor-maintenance products, pesticides, rodenticides, wood stains, and wood protectors.

Major customers were hospitals, doctors, pharmacists, household consumers, and maintenance services.

Major competitors included American Home Products, Amway, Bristol-Myers Squibb, Carter Wallace, Colgate-Palmolive, Dial, Johnson & Johnson, S.C. Johnson, Pfizer, Procter & Gamble, Schering-Plough, and Upjohn.

Most of this segment, including L & F Products, was targeted for divestiture during 1994.

Chemicals Segment (SIC 2820, 2860)

Products were ingredients or applications for photography, packaging, fabrics, cigarette filters, health care, and nutrition. Examples were film, Kodel polyester, alcohols, acids, coatings, solvents, glycols, waxes, plasticizers.

Major customers included other Kodak divisions and industrial firms.

Major competitors included Bayer, Clorox, Dow Chemical, DuPont, General Electric.

This segment disappeared at the end of 1993 as the result of a tax-free spin-off to shareholders.

Sources: Developed from Annual Reports from 1987 through 1993 and Hoover's Handbook, 1993.

attract, develop, and keep talented people; responsibility to the community and the environment; and wise use of corporate assets.

6   In 1988, the company held 80 percent of the U.S. conventional film market and remained first in global sales (Exhibit 2). However, during the following five years, Fuji, 3M, Agfa, and other competitors took 10 percent of the U.S. market away from Kodak, thus narrowing the company's global leadership.

7   Over the 10-year period from 1984 through 1993, total returns to shareholders averaged 10 percent per annum. Because of investor discontent with such returns, enhancement of economic value for shareholders became an increasingly important goal of the outside members of Kodak's Board of Directors (Exhibit 3).

THE 1960S AND 1970S: INCREASING TECHNOLOGICAL AND COMPETITIVE CHALLENGES

8   The seeds of Kodak's problems were planted several decades ago. While its Japanese and European competitors recovered from the devastation of World War II, Kodak was able to offer the best technology, quality, and value in the field of silver-halide photography. However, during the 60s and 70s, Kodak began to face increasing competition from firms such as Polaroid, Berkey Photo, 3M, Agfa, and Fuji. The growth rate of Kodak's highly profitable photography business dwindled down to

EXHIBIT 2
Eastman Kodak Company Market Share Data for Conventional Film, 1988 ($4.8 billion)

Global Film Sales by Region		Global Film Sales by Manufacturer	
U.S.	35%	Kodak	51%
Japan	30	Fuji	28
Europe	26	3M	6
Rest of World (ROW)	9	Others	12

U.S. Film Sales by Manufacturer		Japan Film Sales by Manufacturer	
Kodak	80%	Fuji	60%
Fuji	12	Konica	20
3M	4	Kodak	14
Agfa	2	Others	6
Others	2		

Europe Film Sales by Manufacturer		ROW Film Sales by Manufacturer	
Kodak	45%	Kodak	70%
Agfa	20	Fuji	15
Fuji	17	Others	15
3M	15		
Others	4		

Market Share Data for Global Photocopy Equipment Market, 1991

	By Manufacturer and Size of Unit		
	Large	**Medium**	**Small**
Canon	ins.	24	29
Kodak	12	26	ins.
Xerox	85	5	17
Other	3	45	54

ins. = insignificant

Source: *Market Share Reporter,* 1991 and 1994.

2 percent to 4 percent per year, and management began to search for new ways to increase the rate of growth. As a result, the Instamatic line of "foolproof" cameras was launched and became a major marketing success. Around the same time, Kodak became one of the first companies to develop a camcorder, but management decided not to launch it, because it would be very costly and might detract from sales of amateur movie products.

9 Kodak started to take an interest in related product markets it had previously neglected. In 1975, Kodak introduced the Ektaprint Copier-Duplicator, putting itself in direct competition with two firmly entrenched rivals, Xerox and IBM. Having committed to a line of high-volume machines, Kodak found itself in the wrong niche as more users turned to low-volume photocopiers. Despite appealing innovative features and high-quality image production, this line lost $150 million during its first five years. In 1976, believing it had developed a product that did not infringe upon Polaroid's patents, Kodak entered the instant camera market. Polaroid launched, and eventually won, a lengthy patent infringement suit against Kodak.[2]

CHANDLER NAMED PRESIDENT

10 Colby H. Chandler, a soft-spoken engineer who had been heavily involved in managing both of the foregoing ill-fated projects, was named President in 1977. Chandler had joined Kodak as an engineer

---

[2] The Court required Kodak to withdraw from the instant camera market in 1986 and to pay Polaroid an award of $873 million in 1991.

EXHIBIT 3
Eastman Kodak Company Board of Directors, as of December 1993

Richard S. Braddock, 52, CEO of Medco Containment Services, Inc.

Martha Layne Collins, 57, President of St. Catharine College in Springfield, KY, former governor of Kentucky.

Charles T. Duncan, 69, Senior counsel in the law firm of Reid & Priest.

Alice F. Emerson, 62, Fellow of the Andrew W. Mellon Foundation, and former President of Wheaton College in Massachusetts.

George M. C. Fisher, 53, Chairman, President, and Chief Executive Officer of Eastman Kodak Company, effective December 1, 1993.

Roberto C. Goizueta, 62, Chairman and CEO of The Coca-Cola Company.

Paul E. Gray, 62, Chairman of the Corporation of Massachusetts Institute of Technology.

Karlheinz Kaske, 64, retired. Former President and CEO of Siemens AG.

John J. Phelan, Jr., 62, retired. Former Chairman and CEO of the New York Stock Exchange.

Wilber J. Prezzano, 53, Group Vice President of Eastman Kodak Company and President of Kodak's Health Group.

Leo J. Thomas, 57, Group Vice President of Eastman Kodak Company and President of Kodak's Imaging Group.

Richard A. Zimmerman, 62, Chairman and CEO of Hershey Foods.

Source: 1993 Annual Report and 10-K.

in 1950. Facing one of his first external challenges, Chandler responded to increasing competition from 3M Company, Fuji Photo, and private label brands by announcing film price reductions designed to protect market share. The result was lower earnings and a decreasing level of investor confidence. While sales revenues for the company's consumer photographic products were deteriorating, high sales in other areas helped to offset the bad news.

11   Attributing Kodak's earnings stagnation to a lack of strategic planning, Chandler promptly hired the company's first director of corporate planning. Chandler encouraged new measures to improve performance. These included a stronger emphasis on non-photographic products with high profit potential such as electronic publishing, videocassettes, floppy discs, batteries, office equipment, and health care products; a more aggressive approach to protecting core capabilities in chemical imaging; an acceleration of the company's slow-moving product introduction process; a broader international marketing strategy; and a concerted effort to find new businesses with appropriate technologies, particularly in video and electronics.

12   In the post–World War II era, Kodak had neglected to establish manufacturing or research facilities in Japan and had no direct control over its sales in the Japanese market. Japanese companies such as Canon, Nikon, Minolta, and Olympus developed 35mm autofocus cameras that were superior to Kodak's Instamatic cameras. In response, Kodak launched a unique new line of small cameras employing film discs in 1983. After a brief initial period of success, sales were below expectations. Although 25 million disc cameras were sold, the product line was eventually discontinued due to an inferior, grainy picture quality.

RESTRUCTURING: THE END OF TRADITIONAL JOB SECURITY

13   Chandler was promoted to Chairman and CEO in mid-1983. Kay R. Whitmore, another long-term Kodak engineer, moved into the President's position. Since revenues had not been increasing as rapidly as payroll and overhead expenses, cost control immediately became management's top priority issue.

14   In 1983, management was obliged to reduce the work force by 5 percent and delay pay increases to cut costs and fortify profits. Employing generous incentives, the reduction was achieved magnanimously through buyouts and voluntary departures; but Kodak's long-standing tradition of lifetime employment was shattered.

EXHIBIT 4
Workforce Reductions: Published Announcements, 1983–1993

January 5, 1983—Voluntary early retirement and separation incentives at age 55.

January 11, 1983—Layoff of 1,100 workers in apparatus division.

May 7, 1983—Layoff of another 1,600 workers in apparatus division.

October 18, 1983—Eliminate 800 jobs at Rochester, NY, and Windsor, CO, plants through voluntary retirements, separation incentives, and layoffs.

March 20, 1984—Eliminate 820 employees in Rochester area, through separation incentives.

May 1, 1984—Eliminate 80 jobs in Rochester communications and publications groups.

September 10, 1985—Eliminate 300 jobs in Clinical Products division.

January 18, 1986—Dismiss 800 employees for financial reasons.

February 14, 1986—Eliminate 10 percent of global work force, equivalent to 12,900 employees (about 6,000 in the U.S.).

March 13, 1986—Trim work force by 5 percent in chemical division.

October 1, 1986—Close photo-finishing laboratory in Rochester, idling 650 workers.

June 17, 1989—Cut hundreds of jobs, by consolidating consumer photography products and photofinishing operations.

December 1, 1989—Eliminate 4,500 to 5,000 jobs, or about 3 percent of global work force, through voluntary severance incentives.

August 13, 1991—Reduce U.S. work force by 3,000 through early retirement and separation incentives.

October 3, 1992—Eliminate 8,320 employees through voluntary early retirement.

January 19, 1993—Eliminate 2,000 to 4,000 research and development jobs, through layoffs mainly in the copy products division.

March 18, 1993—Break promise to hire students in Japan, paying them compensation.

August 19, 1993—Cut 10,000 jobs globally over the next two years.

Sources: *The Wall Street Journal* and *New York Times*.

15   From this point onward, goodwill between managers and employees began to dissolve. As downsizing, corporate restructuring, and use of temporary employees (called supplementals) became recurring gambits, anxiety, fatigue, and resentment began to permeate the organization. Union organizers began to take an interest in enlisting Kodak's blue collar workforce, while "headhunters" began to recruit its professional managers for positions in other companies.

16   Announcements of staff cuts totaling more than 45,000 positions over a 10-year period are listed in Exhibit 4. Since staff reductions were linked to retirement incentives, Kodak was able to replace older workers with younger ones. Younger replacements tended to earn less, were easier to train, and possessed more up-to-date skills.

FUJI PHOTO AND EXCESS GLOBAL CAPACITY

16   Global capacity for producing photographic supplies grew faster than demand during the 1980s. The industry experienced an erosion in consumer interest due to growing popular acceptance of home video cameras and VCR/TV viewing. While Hollywood continued to use Kodak movie film, the amateur home movie business had faded away by the late 1980s.

17   As often happens when there is excess capacity in an industry, Kodak faced intensifying price competition from Fuji, 3M, and private label brands of film and paper. The Japanese competitive challenge first began to be taken seriously when Fuji won the title of official film for the 1984 Summer Olympics in Los Angeles, California.

18   Fuji was generally perceived to be bottom-line, rather than market-share, oriented. However, as competition intensified, Kodak eventually accused Fuji of subsidizing its photographic paper sales in the United States by charging as low as one-fourth of what Fuji charged in Japan and the Netherlands, where its paper production facilities were located. Suspecting that the United States might impose punitive tariffs for illegal "dumping," Fuji started to set up its own production facilities in the United States (i.e., South Carolina), thereby threatening to exacerbate overcapacity problems.

19   Since three out of four households throughout the world still did not have a camera to take snapshots, it was debatable whether photography had become a mature global industry. Large, untapped markets existing in Latin America (e.g., Mexico, Brazil), Eastern Europe (e.g., Poland, Russia), and Asia (e.g., China, India, Indonesia). Unlike Director Roberto Goizueta's company, Kodak had not aggressively pursued such markets. Nevertheless, during the strategic planning process, management arrived at the conclusion that the core photographic business was at a mature stage.

20   To break away from the emphasis on conventional photography, Chandler began to emphasize that Kodak was in the "imaging" business. He felt that it was crucial to introduce video product lines into the company as rapidly as possible, to keep up with the pace of technological change.

DIVERSIFICATION THROUGH ACQUISITIONS

21   In 1988, IBM's copier service business was acquired and melded into the information systems sector. Diversifying into a related line of chemistry, Kodak also purchased Sterling Drug, Inc., a manufacturer of products such as over-the-counter and prescription drugs. As a result, Kodak's health segment encompassed not only Sterling's medicinal brand names such as Bayer, Phillips, Andrews, Midol, Campho-Phenique, Neo-Synephrine, Valda, and Panadol, but also L&F Products' household and do-it-yourself consumer brand names such as Lysol, Love My Carpet, Cling, Resolve, Formby, Thompson's Water Seal, Minwax, Red Devil, Rid-X, and d-Con. Sterling had 22,000 employees and annual sales of $2 billion. This $5.1 billion acquisition was financed through a steep rise in long-term debt.

22   From the outset, this was a controversial strategic decision. It denoted a strengthened commitment to chemistry rather than electronics. Critics believed it was unwise to saddle the company with debt, particularly while Polaroid Corporation's lawsuit for patent infringements remained unsettled. Sterling was a laggard in its industry and might not have enough critical mass to be competitive with very large pharmaceutical companies like Merck, SmithKline Beechman, and Bristol-Myers Squibb.

23   Skeptics complained that Kodak management faced enough problems in familiar businesses and should not have plunged into problems that they barely understood. Optimists felt that Sterling had some potential blockbuster products in the product development pipeline that would make the acquisition a highly successful sector of the company by the year 1995.

24   To forge the elements of a coherent corporate strategy for the 1990s, Chandler began to promote his idea of the "Spheres of Success," which appeared in the 1989 Annual Report (Exhibit 5). Emphasizing that imaging was the core business, this exhibit not only depicted the four related sectors but also linked them to critical elements: people, technology/manufacturing, and marketing.

WHITMORE PROMOTED TO CHAIRMAN

25   Retiring in May of 1990, upon attaining the age of 65, Chandler handed over his recently enunciated strategic vision to Kay Whitmore, his successor has Chairman and CEO. An engineer with a degree in chemistry, Whitmore had joined Kodak in 1957. Most of his early experience was in film manufacturing in Rochester, New York, and Mexico. He subsequently held general management positions in the Photographic Division in Latin America, Canada, and the United States.

26   While holding the number two position on Chandler's management team, Whitmore had served as the main planner of the Sterling Drug acquisition; directed efforts to increase Kodak's marketing,

EXHIBIT 5
Kodak Business Sectors Share Vital Links

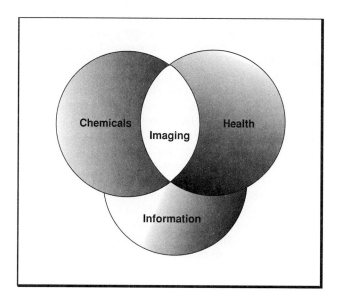

Spheres of Success

Kodak's involvement in four sectors—Imaging, Chemicals, Health, and Information—is as natural as 19th century physicist James Clerk Maxwell's discovery of additive color.

Passing light through red, blue, and green filters, Maxwell found that the combination of light produced white at the center and secondary colors of magenta, cyan, and yellow. This understanding proved to be the key to modern-day color photography.

At Kodak's center, Imaging, Chemicals, Health, and Information form natural growth lines. From the very start, the manufacture of film, as well as its processing, required chemicals.

Kodak's entry into Health and Information markets started with film products; in Health there were x-ray films and in Information there were graphics films and microfilms.

Extensive knowledge of controlled chemical reactions in the photographic process led to Kodak's development of dry chemistry slides for clinical testing. And for more than 70 years Kodak has supplied chemical intermediates to the pharmaceutical industry.

Depth in Imaging science has further led the company to more electronically linked developments in copiers and optical storage.

As you can see, Kodak today, like photography itself, is the result of a natural additive process—each business interrelated and strengthened by the other.

What supports our four sectors is not simply their bond but the strengths of three critical elements: people, technology, and marketing.

People— Employee pride is a strong taproot of Kodak success. It nourishes policies and traditions of dealing fairly with each other and the ability to see the future with optimism. No company embarks on the adventure of the 1990s with more depth and skill, nor with more reason to believe in its own vision. All four sectors abound with qualified personnel, well equipped and prepared for the demands ahead.

Technology/Manufacturing— Scientists and support teams in research and development create unique opportunities, linking longstanding Kodak strengths in chemistry and optics with new directions in electronics and magnetics, as well as hybrid technologies. Kodak engineers and technicians have literally pushed themselves to new levels of process technology, promoting an atmosphere of continuous improvement that enhances manufacturing performance.

Marketing— Quality is the cornerstone of the company's marketing efforts. Products of quality and value, presented with integrity in 150 countries, give all Kodak business groups a clear identity. The common drive is to know customer wants, then to respond in creative ways to help customers succeed.

Source: 1989 Annual Report.

distribution, film finishing, and research activities within Japan; and promoted a strong business presence in the Pacific Rim.

27   As Whitmore took over the chairmanship, Kodak faced huge debts, tough price and quality competition in its core photographic film business, threats from new electronic technologies, and incoherent diversification. According to critics, R&D objectives had become confused; Kodak's management culture had become stifling, dispirited, and intensely hierarchical; and division executives frequently operated with vague budgetary targets and infrequent progress reviews.

28   Whitmore continued Chandler's efforts to focus the direction of the company and interrelate its four basic business segments: Imaging, Information, Chemicals, and Health. To a greater extent than Chandler, Whitmore preached that the traditional photographic business had entered an era of slow growth and heavy competition. He favored development of new electronic products to record, store, transmit, and deliver image outputs. Initially, these were envisioned to be hybrid products linking both film and electronic imaging, since chemistry remained Kodak's forte.

29   Wall Street seemed dissatisfied with return on equity (ROE) under Whitmore. During 1989 through 1992, overhead expenditures on research, development, marketing, and administrative activities escalated from 33 to 37 percent of revenues. These expenditures seemed excessive to many analysts. Over the years Kodak had developed leading-edge electronic imaging technologies but had not marketed many of them. Procrastination occurred not only because of lack of marketing and commercial skills in electronic products but also because of an implicit fear of cutting into existing photographic film and paper markets. Consequently, the first all-electronic camera was launched by Sony, a consumer electronics company.

30   Kodak's reputation also suffered from a series of recent performance disappointments in endeavors undertaken with considerable enthusiasm, such as the acquisition of Verbatim, a maker of computer floppy discs, and the acquisition of Atex, a computer text and image software maker. Sales from new products such as Bayer's Select brand of non-aspirins and digital Photo CDs (magnetic disks) were also floundering.

31   Despite management's contention that the Photo CD had tremendous untapped potential for business and consumer applications, it remained a widely misunderstood product. Akin to an audio compact disc, the Photo CD was capable of storing up to 100 pictures that could be retrieved and displayed on a television or computer screen. It was also suitable for emerging telephone transmission and multimedia applications. While the product had potential to become an industry standard, sluggish sales forced Kodak to lower the price by 15 percent.

HIRING OF AN OUTSIDER AS CFO

32   One of the most traumatic episodes of Whitmore's tenure was the turmoil that followed the appointment of Christopher J. Steffan, an outsider, as Chief Financial Officer (CFO). Having been trained as an accountant, Steffan had earned a reputation as a tough asset manager at Honeywell, Inc., and Chrysler Corporation. At both of those companies he had been involved in extensive restructuring and disposition of assets. He reportedly left Honeywell because he felt that they would never promote him to the top job, due to his nontechnical background.

33   Looked upon favorably by the Board and major investors, Steffan's appointment appeared to signal that Kodak would stop trying to grow its way to greater profitability and would accept slow growth and downsizing as ways to enhance profitability. It also signaled a new willingness to hire outsiders. The price of Kodak's stock immediately rose, due to expectations tied to Steffan's tough reputation.

34   Steffan and Whitmore clashed over how quickly the company should sell assets and cut research, development, and marketing costs in slow-growing lines of business. Whitmore perceived the exercise in "right sizing" as a strategic question, rather than a tactical response to current events. He observed that Steffan was interested in financial issues but seemed uninterested in learning about the business.

35   Unable to generate a sense of crisis and instigate an aggressive restructuring program, Steffan abruptly resigned at the end of April 1993, just three months after starting his new position. The price

of Kodak's stock immediately dropped nearly 10 percent, seemingly out of fear that the culture was inhospitable to outsiders and that its cautious, home-grown management was unlikely to increase shareholder value soon.

SPINOFF OF EASTMAN CHEMICAL COMPANY

36   Following Steffan's departure, a new sense of urgency was forced upon Whitmore by the Board. Thus, in June 1993, he announced that a tax-free spinoff of Eastman Chemical Co. to Kodak shareholders would occur at year end.

37   Although Kodak retained ownership of patents for its photochemicals, the decision to exit from the chemical manufacturing industry was heavily symbolic, because it signaled a decreasing commitment to chemical imaging. It also unleashed the chemical company's management, allowing them to determine the destiny of over 400 products.

38   Eastman Chemical had become a leading manufacturer of fibers, packaging plastics, cigarette filters, and specialty chemicals. While Kodak's film business had long ago been the major customer of the chemical division, it currently accounted for only about 8 percent of its sales. During 1993, this division had roughly 18,500 employees (96% in the U.S.), $4.3 billion in assets, $3.9 billion in sales, and $270 million in earnings. The spinoff had little impact on shareholder value, since it chiefly redistributed Kodak's earnings and debt.

SHAREHOLDER AND BOARD SENTIMENTS

39   Two-thirds of Kodak's shares were held by institutional investors, such as colleges, banks, mutual funds, insurance companies, and pension funds. Beginning in 1991, the California Public Employees Retirement System (CalPERS) included Kodak on a list of firms that it considered the worst performers in its investment portfolio. In addition, other institutional investors such as the College Retirement Equities Fund (CREF), Fidelity Investments Group, and several activist "relationship investment funds" began to push for strategic and managerial changes at Kodak. Critics tended to want the company to maximize cash flow, downplay growth, reduce debt, raise dividends, and/or repurchase outstanding common shares.

40   Although Whitmore came up with a new proposal to trim 10,000 jobs by year end, major investors were hoping for twice that number of layoffs. They also favored spinoffs of the photocopier business, the pharmaceutical product lines of Sterling Winthrop, Inc., and L&F's household and do-it-yourself products. Spinoffs would bring an infusion of cash and permit debt reduction. However, these were not opportune maneuvers. The copier business was related to Kodak's core competencies in imaging, and the valuation of the pharmaceutical business was diminished by U.S. government pressures to reduce health care costs.

41   On August 6, 1993, a group of restive outside directors—including John J. Phelan, Jr., Roberto C. Goizueta, Richard S. Braddock, and Charles T. Duncan—ousted Whitmore, indicating that, despite ample warnings from them, he was not doing enough to cut costs and improve the company's financial performance. Financial performance for 1987–93 is reported in Exhibits 6 and 7. Additional performance data are supplied in Exhibits 8, 9, and 10.

FISHER ACCEPTED LUCRATIVE OFFER

42   It took two months for the Board to find Whitmore's successor, because they were determined to find the right kind of outsider. During the search, the Board indicated that marketing and cost cutting, rather than technical, skills would have top priority. When the selection of George M. D. Fisher was announced, the price of Kodak's stock surged well above its $40 to $50 trading range. Investors were

EXHIBIT 6

EASTMAN KODAK COMPANY
Income Statement
(in millions)

	1993	1992	1991	1990	1989	1988	1987
Statement of Earnings							
Sales to customers in the U.S.	8,287	10,610	10,312	10,118	10,302	9,554	7,611
Sales to customers outside the U.S.	8,077	9.573	9,107	8,790	8,096	7,480	5,694
Total Sales	16,364	20,183	19,419	18,908	18,398	17,034	13,305
Cost of goods sold	8,063	10,392	9,985	9,637	9,822	8,580	7,045
Marketing and administrative expenses	4,989	5,869	5,565	5,098	4,857	4,495	3,190
Research and development costs	1,301	1,587	1,494	1,329	1,253	1,147	992
Interest expense	635	813	844	855	895	697	181
Restructuring/litigation/unusual charges	538	220	1,605	888	875		
Other charges	259	95	170	133		11	
Total costs	15,785	18,976	19,663	17,940	17,702	14,930	11,408
Investment income, including equity interests	277	394	255	289	148	132	83
Other extraordinary income (expense)	178				81		4
Earnings before income taxes	1,034	1,601	11	1,257	925	2,236	1,984
Provision (benefit) for income taxes	381	607	–6	554	396	839	806
Effect of accounting changes	–2,168	152					
Net earnings	–1,515	1,146	17	703	529	1,397	1,178
Cash dividends declared	657	650	649	649	649	616	572
Depreciation and amortization (in above)	1,111	1,539	1,477	1,309	1,326	1,183	995

Note: Eastman Chemical Company was treated as a discontinued operation in 1993. Cumulative effects of changes in accounting principles for continuing and discontinued operations are reported on the accounting changes line.

Net income of the discontinued Chemical business is reported as 1993 Other Income ($178 mil.).

Kodak shareholders received one share of Eastman Chemical stock for every four shares of Kodak common stock held after the close of business on Dec. 31, 1993.

Sources: Adapted by casewriter from Kodak's annual reports, 10-K's, *Moody's Industrials.*

impressed by the Board's pronouncement that the new chairman would be expected to deliver fast and deep cost cuts.

43   Kodak's Board offered Fisher a generous performance-based compensation package to entice him away from his $1.5 million per year position as Chairman and CEO of Motorola, Inc., a semiconductor and mobile communications equipment manufacturer, known as a technology leader and a producer of quality products.

44   Motorola had long been regarded as a well-managed company. It was known for its dedication to hard work and quality, as exemplified by the Six Sigma defect reduction program, which made it the first large company to win a Malcolm Baldrige National Quality Award. Motorola was also esteemed as a learning and teaching organization, deeply dedicated to maintaining a competent, committed work force known for its responsiveness, adaptability, and creativity. With the average employee receiving more than 40 hours of training per year, Motorola's culture was reputed to be "regimented, efficient, and more than a little driven."[3]

45   Fisher's compensation package was one of the most lucrative "golden hellos" ever awarded. It included a sign-on bonus of $5 million, an annual base salary of $2 million, a minimum incentive bonus of $1 million for each of the first two years, an $8.3 million loan to be forgiven if he remained with Kodak for five years, a $1.3 million restricted stock grant, and long-term options to buy 1,323,000 shares of Kodak stock at a fixed price of $50.47. The options could eventually net him capital gains of over $100 million, if Kodak's stock price were to average a 10 percent annual increase over the next 10 years. In addition he was provided with relocation assistance, term life insurance of $7 million, a car and driver, a plane available for personal use,

---

[3] "Motorola: Training for the Millennium," *Business Week*, March 28, 1994.

EXHIBIT 7

EASTMAN KODAK COMPANY
Balance Sheet
(in millions)

	DEC 93	DEC 92	DEC 91	DEC 90	DEC 89	DEC 88	DEC 87
Assets							
Cash & marketable securities	$ 1,966	$ 560	$ 924	$ 916	$ 1,279	$ 1,075	$ 992
Receivables, inventories, and other c/a	6,055	6,845	7,334	7,692	7,312	7,609	5,799
Total current assets	8,021	7,405	8,258	8,608	8,591	8,684	6,791
Net properties	6,366	9,835	9,602	8,978	8,628	8,013	6,663
Unamortized goodwill, net	4,186	4,273	4,349	4,448	4,579	4,610	424
Other non-current assets	1,752	1,625	1,961	2,102	1,854	1,657	820
Total assets	$20,325	$23,138	$24,170	$24,136	$23,652	$22,964	$14,698
Liabilities							
Payables, including taxes and dividends	$ 4,255	$ 4,262	$ 4,289	$ 4,207	$ 6,573	$ 5,850	$
Short-term borrowings	655	1,736	2,610	2,956			
Total current liabilities	4,910	5,998	6,899	7,163	6,573	5,850	4,140
Long-term borrowings	6,853	7,202	7,597	6,989	7,376	7,779	2,382
Other long-term liabilities	5,127	2,312	2,080	1,406	1,371	990	743
Deferred income tax credits	79	1,069	1,490	1,830	1,690	1,565	1,420
Total liabilities	16,969	16,581	18,066	17,388	17,010	16,184	8,685
Total shareholders' equity	3,356	6,557	6,104	6,748	6,642	6,780	6,013
Total liabilities and shareholders' equity	$20,325	$23,138	$24,170	$24,136	$23,652	$22,964	$14,698

Sources: Adapted by casewriter from Kodak's annual reports, 10-Ks, and *Moody's Industrials*.

luncheon and country club memberships, a residential security system, financial/tax counseling, and six weeks vacation.

FISHER'S BACKGROUND AND EXPERIENCE

46   Fisher received a bachelor's degree in engineering from the University of Illinois followed by a master's degree in engineering and a doctorate in applied mathematics from Brown University. He began working as a researcher at AT&T's Bell Laboratories before joining Motorola as a manufacturing director in 1976. In his five years as Motorola's CEO, Fisher displayed an instinct for marketable innovative technologies. He helped double sales from $8 billion to $16 billion and earned a reputation for technological foresight and patience in nurturing new products such as cellular telephones, two-way radios, pagers, modems, and computer chips. He also successfully employed political pressure to protect Motorola's position in the Jananese market. During this period, he was widely perceived to be an accessible, hands-off manager who preferred to set high expectations and leave implementations to others, subject to rigorous accountability measures.

47   His speedy decision to accept the offer from Kodak's Board caught Motorola's Board members by surprise. It was rumored that the founding family's grip on Motorola might have impeded his future prospects with that company. Furthermore, Fisher revealed that he perceived Kodak's strengths to be its huge market franchise, brand name, and technology. Those strengths could give Kodak potential to become a leader in the upcoming era of electronic images. information networks, and wireless communications. Fisher envisioned a corporate strategy that would relay upon the conventional photographic business to serve as a cash cow to finance Kodak's transformation into a high-growth, high-technology company. Considering the coming "information revolution," potential endeavors that could bring success included filmless cameras, photo compact discs for digital images, digital photo-finishing systems for home use, electronic store catalogs, image archives, and image distribution systems employing communications networks.

EXHIBIT 8
Eastman Kodak Annual Business Segment Data

	1993	1992	1991	1990	1989	1988	1987
Sales ($ millions)							
Imaging	7,253	7,401	7,066	7,122	6,985	6,638	6,200
Information	3,862	4,063	3,968	4,140	4,200	3,937	3,494
Health	5,249	5,081	4,917	4,349	4,009	3,597	1,206
Chemicals	none	3,638	3,468	3,297	3,204	2,862	2,405
Earnings from operations ($ millions)							
Imaging	1,109	1,216	489	1,611	821	1,280	1,231
Information	−137	−151	−688	5	−360	311	225
Health	560	588	433	626	487	591	244
Chemicals	none	494	538	602	643	630	378
Assets ($ millions)							
Imaging	6,482	6,391	6,586	6,611	7,039	7,186	6,836
Information	3,669	3,808	3,844	3,939	4,331	4,319	3,814
Health	8,402	8,227	8,353	8,142	7,793	7,278	1,100
Chemicals	none	4,255	4,035	3,952	3,238	2,967	2,548
Corporate and intersegment	1,772	457	1,352	1,492	1,251	1,214	400
Margin on sales (percent)							
Imaging	15	16	7	23	12	19	20
Information	−4	−4	−17	0	−9	8	6
Health	11	12	9	14	12	16	20
Chemicals	none	14	16	18	20	22	16

Sources: Adapted by casewriter from Kodak's annual reports, 10-K's *Moody's Industrials.*

FISHER'S INITIAL ASSESSMENT OF SITUATION

48   Shortly after his installation as Chairman of Eastman Kodak Company, Fisher issued his first public assessment of the situation he encountered, and his remarks differed from Board and investor expectations. Looking toward the company's fiscal year-end, he announced that 1993 earnings per share would be nearly the same as for the prior year. In addition, he warned shareholders that security analysts' consensus estimates of Kodak's 1994 earnings were well above what he would be able to deliver.

49   The bleakness of Fisher's near-term assessment caught Wall Street by surprise. Within hours of his December 1993 announcement, stockbrokers received a heavy volume of "sell" orders, as analysts trimmed their 1994 earnings projections and downgraded their investment recommendations.

50   Later, when actual 1993 results were released, they were worse than expected. Kodak reported a $1.5 billion loss, which reflected major one-time adjustments not only for the divestiture of the chemical company but also for the initial accrual of long-term obligations for postretirement and postemployment benefits. The latter adjustment meant that benefit expenses would thereafter be recognized at the time they were being earned rather than when they were ultimately paid.

51   The investment community had been anticipating that the new chairman would promptly lay off up to 20,000 of the company's 132,000 employees; but Fisher's outlook was that of a builder, not a blood-letter. He seemed unwilling to promise more than 10,000 layoffs, spread over the next two years, as previously announced by his predecessor.

52   During the interview, Fisher asserted that "cost-cutting alone is not the long-term answer . . . growth is critical, and we will create that profitable growth through cost-cutting, better marketing , selective asset sales, prudent investment leading to new products, a rigorous portfolio review, and better balance sheet management."[4]

---

4 "At Kodak, Lower Expectations Begin with Stock," *New York Times,* December 16, 1993.

EXHIBIT 9
Eastman Kodak Other Periodic Data as of Year End

	1993	1992	1991	1990	1989	1988	1987
Employees, worldwide (thousands)	110.4	132.6	133.2	134.5	137.8	145.3	124.4
Employees, U.S. alone (thousands)	57.2	77.1	76.9	80.4	82.9	87.9	81.8
Return on sales (percent)	−9	6	0	4	3	8	9
Return on equity (percent)	−45	17	0	10	8	21	20
Equity/assets (percent)	16	28	25	28	28	30	41
Number of shareholders (thousands)	157.8	166.5	169.1	168.9	172.0	174.1	168.5
Average shares outstanding (millions)	330.6	325.1	324.7	324.5	324.3	324.2	334.7
Cash flow per share ($)	−1.26	7.96	4.60	7.94	5.72	7.96	6.49
Net earnings per share, primary ($)	−4.62	3.53	0.05	2.17	1.63	4.31	3.52
Dividends per share ($)	2.00	2.00	2.00	2.00	2.00	1.90	1.71
Book value per share ($)	10.15	20.12	18.79	20.75	20.48	20.91	18.55
Stock price high ($)	65.00	50.75	49.75	43.88	52.38	53.25	70.67
Stock price low ($)	40.25	37.75	37.63	33.75	40.00	39.13	41.92
Stock price year-end close ($)	56.25	40.50	48.25	41.63	41.13	45.13	49.00
Total yearly return to stockholders (percent)	44.5	−12.2	9.2	6.3	−4.9	−4.1	10.4
S&P index year-end close (500 stocks)	466.5	435.7	376.2	334.6	323.1	265.9	268.8
U.S. consumer price index (1982–84 = 100)	144.1	140.3	136.2	130.7	124.0	118.3	113.6

Note: Stock prices and return to shareholders for 1993 do not reflect any adjustment for Eastman Chemical Company spin-off. Other 1993 data do exclude Eastman Chemical Company.

Sources: Adapted by casewriter from Kodak's annual reports, 10-Ks, *Value Line, Hoover's Handbook, Fortune, S&P Stock Reports,* and *World Almanac.*

CUTTING BACK TO THE IMAGING CORE

53   During a follow-up press conference five months later, Fisher again repeated his reluctance to wage a war on costs: "Rather than simply take an ax to budgets and manpower, we are trying to change, in significant ways, how this company operates."[5] He noted that "to achieve maximum success, we have concluded that we must commit our entire resource base to imaging opportunities and divest noncore businesses."[6] He revealed that the company from now on would "focus on profitable participation in the five links of the imaging chain: image capture, processing, storage, output, and delivery of images for people and machines anywhere in Kodak's worldwide market."[7]

54   Fisher also announced that Health segment businesses with 1993 net sales of $3.7 billion were for sale. Medical and dental imaging and x-ray businesses with 1993 sales of $1.5 billion would be retained. Proceeds would be used to pay down roughly $7 billion in long-term debt, thereby reducing interest expense.

55   He also described the formation of 10 special team projects to improve profitability and lower costs, with the objective of doubling return on net assets (RONA) by 1999. Those programs included: growth of market, asset management, span-of-control, cost of quality, research and development productivity, marketing opportunities, business portfolio review, process reengineering, cycle time improvement, and policy opportunities.

56   A securities analyst reacted to Fisher's pronouncements in a skeptical manner: "The big question beyond the disposition of assets is what is going to happen to the core business? How are they going

---

[5] "Kodak's New Strategy: Just Pictures," *New York Times,* May 5, 1994.

[6] Ibid.

[7] Ibid.

EXHIBIT 10
1993 Comparisons of Employee and Capital Productivity for Global Competitors in
Imaging and Information Sectors

Company (Country)	Number of Employees thousands (Rank)	Financial Productivity Per Person			
		Sales (Rank)	Assets ($000 per employee) (Rank)	Equity (Rank)	Profits (Rank)
Bayer (Agfa) (Germany)	156.4 (1)	$170.2 (8)	$151.3 (9)	$66.9 (5)	$6.2 (4)
Eastman Kodak (U.S.)	110.4 (2)	181.7 (6)	184.1 (7)	30.4 (10)	−13.7 (10)
Xerox (U.S.)	97.0 (3)	183.4 (5)	399.5 (2)	54.0 (8)	−1.3 (7)
Minn. Mining (3 M) (U.S.)	86.2 (4)	162.7 (9)	141.5 (10)	75.6 (4)	14.7 (2)
Canon (Japan)	64.5 (5)	255.8 (2)	300.4 (3)	100.1 (2)	2.9 (5)
Pitney Bowes (U.S.)	32.5 (6)	108.9 (10)	208.9 (5)	57.5 (7)	10.9 (3)
Fuji Photo (Japan)	25.1 (7)	381.1 (1)	605.2 (1)	402.3 (1)	21.3 (1)
Konica (Japan)	18.0 (8)	253.8 (3)	288.4 (4)	93.6 (3)	2.2 (6)
Minolta (Japan)	16.8 (9)	177.6 (7)	198.6 (6)	31.9 (9)	−2.7 (8)
Polaroid (U.S.)	12.0 (10)	186.3 (4)	183.6 (8)	63.7 (6)	−4.3 (9)

Source: Derived from *Fortune's* "500" and "Global 500."

to offset tremendous negative factors in film and paper and demonstrate they can make money in electronic imaging?"[8]

57   A movement from traditional photographic products to electronic imaging products and services would put photographic films in competition with some electronic and computer companies and in alliances with others. Although computer manufacturers were beginning to incorporate improved CD-ROM drives with photo CD capability into personal computers, industry watchers noted that the highest growth would probably occur within a complex array of niche markets with well-established, nimble, and low-cost players paving the way[9] They predicted that the appeal of digital photography for the consumer market would remain weak, until prices fell significantly and applications became easier to appreciate. Over the near term, digital cameras and copiers were likely to serve primarily commercial and medical applications.

THE LONG-TERM ANSWER?

58   Since vertical integration into chemicals no longer existed, and Chandler's four sector "Spheres of Success" were no longer relevant, a new corporate vision was needed. As Fisher launched his quest for long-term solutions to Kodak's problems, he was seeking ways to strengthen the core businesses

---

[8] Ibid.

[9] Among the foremost companies are Agfa, Alias, Apple, Avid, Canon, Cognex, Colorbus, Cornerstone, Electronics for Imaging, FileNet, IBM, Indigo, International Imaging Materials, MacroMedia, Optika, Perception, Ricoh, Scitex, Sonic Solutions, Tektronix, ViewStar, Visioneer, Xeikon, Xerox, Wang, Watermark, WaveFront, and Westbrooke.

and to raise the proportion of sales attributed to electronics. Human and technical reforms would be needed, since Kodak's digital electronic imaging business accounted for less than 1 percent of 1993 sales, and fierce price wars were hurting the traditional film business.

59   Drawing upon his experience at Motorola, Fisher's future strategic themes might include: a search for overlooked ideas in Kodak's labs;[10] research on products with high-growth and high-profit potentials; mergers or new strategic alliances with high-tech, market-oriented computer, cable, telephone, photocopier, and archiving businesses; reorganizing of business segments to give digital technology a separate identity; and requirement of key managers from outside the company.

60   Six months into his new job, key considerations for Fisher were: Would he be able to retain the confidence of internal and external stakeholders? Would he also be able to reorient Kodak's technology and reshape organizational culture? If so, how?

---

[10] With its long-established research tradition, Kodak ranked among the top five firms in the number of patents awarded annually by the U.S. Patent and Trademark Office.

CASE 11

DIESEL TECHNOLOGY COMPANY

1   Derek Kaufman, the president of Diesel Technology Company (DTC), a Michigan-based manufacturer of fuel injectors for diesel engines, put down the telephone and walked over to Bob Joseph's office. He told Joseph (vice president of finance) that he had just been on the telephone with Roger Penske (the company's Chairman) and that Penske wanted to hold a Business Review meeting in Detroit in four weeks' time. Penske had indicated to Kaufman that, in addition to discussing the current performance of the company, he wanted to spend time talking about the company's future. Penske had specifically reiterated his desire to have DTC go beyond selling merely to sister company Detroit Diesel in the U.S. market and explore the possibility of entering the world market. In the last two months, Mercedes-Benz (a division of Daimler-Benz AG) and Robert Bosch GmbH of Germany had each separately indicated an interest in a collaboration with DTC. Should DTC go in for a collaboration to enter the European market? Should the company look for other collaborations such as the one offered by Benz and Bosch to enter other markets? Kaufman indicated to Joseph that they better have answers to these questions before the December meeting.

COMPANY HISTORY

2   Roger Penske, the race car owner and industrialist, agreed in 1988 to buy the diesel fuel injection component (for an undisclosed amount) of General Motors' (GM) 1.9 million square foot AC Rochester Products plant in Wyoming, Michigan. Effective October 31, 1988, the new company, called Diesel Technology Corporation,* was owned jointly by Penske Corporation's Transportation Group (80%) and Detroit Diesel Corporation (20%). Exhibit 1 shows the composition of Penske Corporation. In addition, in February 1989, DTC purchased the assets of Injector Corporation and established a business to remanufacture fuel injectors in Kentwood, Michigan.

3   To determine the reasons for Roger Penske's acquisition of DTC, one had to look back to his decision to purchase Detroit Diesel Corporation from GM. Penske Corporation was a closely held company that reported annual sales of $2.6 billion in 1991. Major units included Penske Leasing, which serviced a fleet of 56,000 trucks in a joint venture with General Electric, and car dealerships including Longo Toyota of California, the largest Toyota dealership in the U.S. When GM wanted to sell Detroit Diesel, its troubled diesel engine division, an investment banker sounded Penske out on this opportunity. At that time, Penske owned a Detroit Diesel dealership. He saw the strategic advantages that his truck leasing unit would have by acquiring a diesel engine producer and acquired 60% of Detroit Diesel and later increased his stake to 80%. The AC Rochester Products Division of GM was a supplier to Detroit Diesel, and with his purchase of Detroit Diesel Penske acquired an option to buy the fuel injection unit. Derek Kaufman, the President of DTC, described Penske's rationale for acquiring the fuel injection unit:

> Penske exercised the option for three strategic reasons. First, he wanted to safeguard his supply of injectors for engines today. Second, he wanted to assure the proper level of research and development for Detroit Diesel tomorrow. And third, he saw the potential of selling fuel injectors on the world market.[1]

This case was prepared by Ram Subramanian, Jaideep Motwani, and Earl Harper of Grand Valley State University.

* The company's name was changed from Diesel Technology Corporation to Diesel Technology Company in February 1992.

EXHIBIT 1

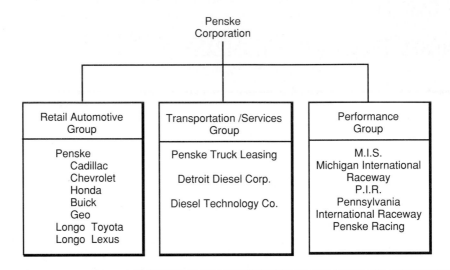

Penske
Corporation

Retail Automotive Group	Transportation /Services Group	Performance Group
Penske Cadillac Chevrolet Honda Buick Geo Longo Toyota Longo Lexus	Penske Truck Leasing Detroit Diesel Corp. Diesel Technology Co.	M.I.S. Michigan International Raceway P.I.R. Pennsylvania International Raceway Penske Racing

4   Penske made an offer to all employees of GM's fuel injection unit to join DTC. About 450 employees (both hourly and salaried) joined the new company. Penske appointed Derek Kaufman as President of the new company and charged him with the task of turning it around (DTC, as part of GM's Detroit Diesel unit, was losing money and market share, though GM would not reveal actual details). Kaufman came with a long track record of experience in the American trucking industry having worked in various positions at Freightliner, Inc. (a subsidiary of Daimler-Benz), a manufacturer of custom-built trucks.

The Turnaround Process

5   Kaufman started the process of turning around the new company by first eliciting cooperation from the United Auto Workers, the union that represented the hourly workers of DTC. He described the process in these words:

> Penske stresses a working relationship with the unions. We came in the door realizing that the UAW is an asset, not a liability. The UAW has been great to work with. They are very progressive. They are strong in their stances for UAW people, yet flexible when working with Penske people.

6   Kaufman held several meetings with employee groups. In each of these meetings, he asked them four questions: did they like working here, where did they see themselves three years from now, what was the single most important success factor for DTC, and what three things would make the company better. Kaufman noted all the answers and began to get a better idea as to where the company was and how to turn it around.

7   Kaufman felt that the most important finding that emerged from his meetings with employee groups was that employees had no idea what the cost of products were and the relationship of what they did to overall company profitability. He described his findings as follows:

> I realized that I had a very compartmentalized group of people. One was running a machine that made plungers, one of the 30–40 parts to an injector. But this person for fifteen years made only that one part. He said at the meeting, "I've been making this part for 15 years and I don't even know where it goes." The other thing that came out strongly in the meetings was that this was a plant within GM that transferred its products to sister divisions of GM. To say there was no customer focus is one of the greater understatements. It was antagonistic. The feeling here was that "the idiots over at Detroit Diesel don't know how to forecast," and the feeling at Detroit Diesel was that "the idiots over at Diesel Technology can't make a quality part." To

emphasize our situation, I drew a circle on the screen and sliced a small pie out of it. I said, "Here are our two customers. Detroit Diesel is 95 percent and EMD (a division of GM) is 5 percent. If Detroit Diesel gets sick, we're going to get pneumonia real quick. We are a stand-alone company. We're going to live or die with our P&L and balance sheet." I felt from these meetings that this was an intelligent group of people with an extremely good work ethic. People on the manufacturing floor really cared about quality. It was evident to me that a lot of people came over to DTC from "across the wall" [DTC's plant in Wyoming, Michigan, shares a common wall with GM's AC Rochester plant, which makes precision auto parts, hence the expression] to escape a system that they perceived as strangling them.

8   To elicit cooperation, the company began holding monthly financial meetings with employees where profits and losses were discussed. Also, hourly workers were included in product design committees so that they could contribute practical experience of machining problems. In 1991 the company reported that more than 600 employee suggestions were implemented in the last three years. The managers tried to inculcate in all employees the philosophy of flexibility, team spirit, and customer focus.

9   The company also benefited from the turnaround at Detroit Diesel, its major customer. Detroit Diesel increased its North American diesel-engine market share from 3% in 1987 to 25.6% in 1991 (versus 53% in 1987 and 37% in 1991 for industry leader Cummins) primarily by becoming more customer oriented and focusing on product development.

10   DTC's turnaround was also helped by new exhaust emission and fuel economy standards set for truck companies by the Environmental Protection Agency for the 1990s. Fleet owners perceived fuel injectors as extremely important components in meeting the new standards.

11   In 1992, DTC was a leading manufacturer of fuel injectors for diesel engines. Its sales increased from $48 million in 1988 (when it was part of GM) to around $60[†] million in 1992. More importantly, the company reported profits for both 1991 and 1992. The company's operations consisted of its fuel injection equipment manufacturing plant at Wyoming, Michigan, a remanufacturing unit at Kentwood, Michigan, and a licensed operation in Mexico to rebuild fuel injectors for the Mexican market.

COMPANY PROFILE

Organization Structure

12   The company was structured along functional lines (see Exhibit 2) with five vice presidents reporting directly to the president. Ken Oberholtzer, the Controller, reported to Bob Joseph, the Vice President of Finance. Exhibit 3 provides brief profiles of the company's top managers.

Manufacturing

13   DTC produced a wide range of unit fuel injectors for diesel engine applications ranging from 200 to 3,200 horsepower. These injectors were used in large marine crafts, off-highway equipment, and on-highway trucks, buses, and locomotives. Fuel injectors came in two different types: the mechanical unit injector (MUI), which was first produced in 1947, and the electronic unit injector (EUI), which was pioneered by DTC in 1985 (when the company was part of GM). EUIs cost twice as much as MUIs, but were more accurate in controlling fuel flow. The U.S. military was the major market for diesel engines with MUIS, while large fleet owners preferred diesel engines with EUIs because they saved fuel.

14   85 percent of the components that went into both types of injectors were manufactured internally. In the manufacture of MUIs (Exhibit 4 shows a diagram of the MUI), steel was purchased in bars and tubes and sent to an outside vendor for heat treatment after different turning operations were

---

[†] Figures are disguised as per company's request.

EXHIBIT 2
DTC Organization Chart (Condensed)

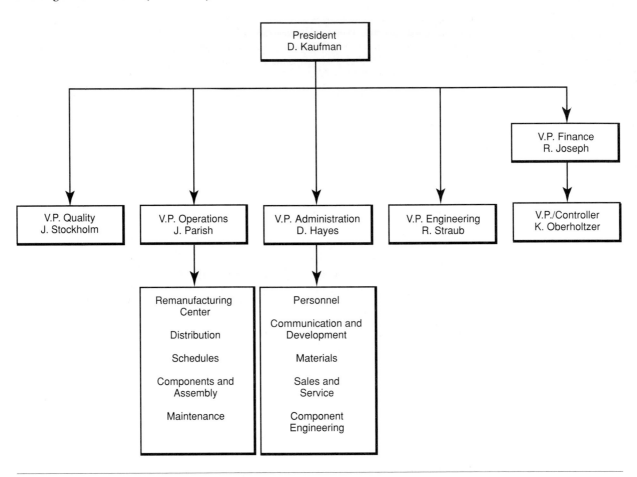

completed. The turning operations cut the steel into the different parts (31 for the MUI) that went into
the assembly of an injector. The manufacturing process used tool steel, cold roll steel, and alloy steel,
each of which required a different heat treatment process. The heat treatment hardened the injector
parts. Once the steel was heat treated it came back to the plant where it underwent different types of
grinding. Many of these grinding operations were of close tolerances which required the use of
computer numerical controlled machines. Each operator in the grinding process was responsible for
product quality. Operators did quality checks as part of the grinding process. Depending on the
capability of the machines, some operators checked more frequently than others. In-process quality
auditors also verified or validated the quality of the parts. After the parts were ground to specific
tolerances, they were calibrated to specifications and assembled to form injectors. The assembled
injectors were then tested for functionality. For example, the injector was checked to ensure that its
calibrations met specifications, and also that it was leakproof.

15   The production process for EUIs (Exhibit 4 shows a diagram of an EUI and Exhibit 5 a photograph of a complete EUI) was very similar to that of the MUIs. The process started with cutting steel
bars and tubes into different shapes and sizes to conform to individual parts (47 for the EUI) which
formed the injector. As in the case of the mechanical injector, the cut steel pieces were sent to an
outside vendor for heat treatment. The individual components then went through grinding, calibra-
tion, and testing as in the case of the MUI. However, the tolerances were stricter for the EUI, as were
also the processes used to test individual components and the assembled injector.

EXHIBIT 3
Profiles of DTC's Management Team

Derek Kaufman: President. Previously vice president of marketing at Freightliner, Inc., a leading manufacturer of truck chassis currently owned by Mercedes-Benz.

Robert Joseph: Vice President of Finance. Previously at Penske Corporation's automotive retail unit.

Jack Stockholm: Vice President of Quality. Previously superintendent of manufacturing at the fuel injector unit of GM's AC Rochester plant.

Jim Parish: Vice President of Operations. Previously plant manager of the fuel injector unit at GM's AC Rochester plant.

Doyle Hayes: Vice President of Administration. Previously superintendent of manufacturing at the fuel injector unit at GM's AC Rochester plant.

Ken Oberholtzer: Controller. Previously cost accountant in the fuel injector unit at GM's AC Rochester plant.

16   The main manufacturing plant at Wyoming, Michigan, had around 780 machining centers and a 33,000 square meter process area. Based on tolerances, the plant manufactured 149 different injector models. Production was around 60,000 injectors a month, roughly divided into 70 percent EUIs and 30 percent MUIs. Reject rates for MUIs were around 5 to 10 percent, while they were between 20 and 30 percent for EUIs. Jack Addington, Group Manager of Engineering, talked about reject rates:

> We would like to have zero defect. But, because of the way technology is and the way our system is set up, the capability isn't quite there to get to zero defects. One of the things we try to do is a Pareto‡ (analysis) of each defect. Which defect is the big one that we need to concentrate on and try to reduce? Then we go on to the next one. At one point, the reject rate for one particular model of MUIs was around 22 percent. By looking at the Pareto and doing some changes in the system, we were able to reduce that to less than 5 percent.

17   A customer contact person provided feedback to the manufacturing department. Complaints ranged from 1–2 to occasionally 10 a week. Jack Addington described the way complaints were handled:

> We have an audit crib that takes all the returned material and thoroughly checks for cause of defect. The audit crib then brings the material back into the plant and talks to the specific department and/or operator that ran it to see if the defect can be rectified. By signing off on a tag that accompanies each unit on the assembly line, defects can be traced to an individual operator or a department. Returns for each week are posted prominently on a bulletin board. Also, the weekly publication "Update" informs production employees of the past week's returns. Finally, a quality report that comes out periodically describes a historical Pareto analysis of the defects that are found in the field.

18   The company moved from a large batch, process centered operating system to one that used a lean production concept, manufacturing cells, and visual just-in-time pull systems. By changing the production system, the company reported reduced inventory, accelerated product flow, optimized material handling, improved product quality, and increased operator awareness of the entire product. Two robots were used in the manufacturing process. Also, an Automated Guided Vehicle ran four machines.

19   The company's EUI production amounted to 110 percent of capacity, while it used only 50 percent capacity for MUIs. As need arose, the company planned to switch more production lines to EUIs from MUIs. No capacity problems were foreseen in the near future.

20   The Remanufacturing Center rebuilt injectors to factory standards using a duplicate of the original equipment manufacturing process. The remanufacturing process provided the company with real life information about the product. Injectors that arrived for rebuilding (injectors were typically good for

‡ Pareto analysis applies the 80/20 rule to identify the significant few causes that account for most of the problems. It separates the "vital few" from the "trivial many." All potential causes of problems or variations are ranked according to their contribution to cost, variation, or other measures. See Richard Chase and Nicholas Aquilano, *Production and Operations Management*, 6th ed. (Burr Ridge, IL: Richard D. Irwin, 1992).

EXHIBIT 4
Diagrams of Electronic Unit Injector and Mechanical Unit Injector

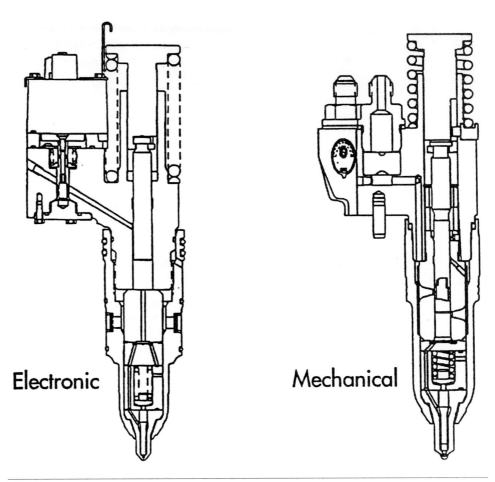

Electronic   Mechanical

around 100,000 miles) were analyzed to gain insight that was used to increase the life of OEM injectors. Typical problems that were "corrected" at the Remanufacturing Center included replacing spray tips that wear out and checking the injector for proper fuel flow.

Quality Control

21 A quality control department headed by a vice president reported directly to the company president. Quality auditors covered individual departments. Also, a quality group oversaw the quality of the entire plant. Jack Addington, Group Manager of Engineering, talked about the relationship between the Quality Control Department and Manufacturing:

> I think historically in a lot of plants it's probably adversarial. We have progressed to a point where we're working together. At one point, people felt that a quality group creates or causes a problem and then they go back and turn it over to manufacturing. Here, in our plant, quality actually takes the next step when they help us investigate the cause of the problem. We're trying to get past the adversarial part. We try to get more into problem solving and focusing on getting it right the first time.

22 The company's emphasis on quality was articulated in its "Quality Statement" (Exhibit 6).

EXHIBIT 5
Electronic Fuel Injector

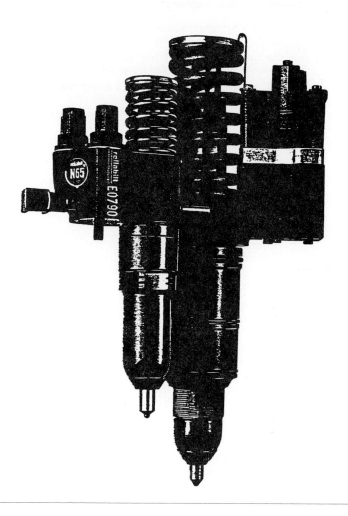

Marketing

23 DTC's biggest customer was Detroit Diesel, which accounted for around 95 percent of sales. The other 5 percent was sold to a division of GM.

24 Detroit Diesel was also a Penske company that had 1991 sales of $1.154 billion. When Roger Penske bought Detroit Diesel from GM in 1988, the company's share of the heavy duty diesel engine market had dropped from a high of 30% in the early 1980s to 3% by 1987. The main reason for the drop in market share was GM's failure to spend money on this division. When Penske bought what critics dubbed as "Destroyed Diesel," the conventional wisdom was that the acquisition would provide engines and spare parts for his Penske Truck Leasing operation. But Penske had gone on record as saying that the acquisition of Detroit Diesel was a vital cog in making the closely held Penske Corp. a major global transportation company.

25 Immediately on making the acquisition, Penske laid off several hundred workers, eliminated redundant computer costs, and consolidated manufacturing operations. More importantly, he supported aggressive new product development. Detroit Diesel's Series 60 electronically controlled diesel engines were introduced in late 1988 to enthusiastic reception. The new engine offered better fuel efficiency and had the capacity to monitor engine use through a built-in computer. Detroit Diesel's market share rose to 22% in 1991 and to 25.6% by 1992. In 1992, 73% of Detroit Diesel's

EXHIBIT 6
Diesel Technology Company's Quality Statement

This is a customer focused company. As such, it is our goal to provide a quality product that satisfies our customers' needs and expectations the first time, every time.

Our customers deserve timely delivery, efficient and courteous service, superior design quality, reliability, and durability. Our value is established by committing ourselves to the following:

1. Listening. Each customer has unique needs and challenges. We need to listen first, then provide solutions.
2. Providing "Proven Designs," monitored by full statistical process control with complete historical documentation.
3. Developing a highly trained and positively motivated workforce.
4. Establishing excellent relationships with our suppliers.
5. Constantly improving our manufacturing process.
6. Providing an atmosphere where our people enjoy the challenge of working.

Diesel Technology Company understands that consistent quality is the foundation of our success.

Roger S. Penske   Derek Kaufman
Chairman   President

---

sales were from U.S.-based customers with the balance from international customers located in over 88 countries.

26   DTC's sales were handled by the sales and service department, consisting of two employees who reported to the Vice President of Administration. The company did no advertising.

Personnel

27   Currently, DTC employed 720 people, of which 120 were salaried and 600 were hourly employees represented by the United Auto Workers (UAW). When Roger Penske took control of the A.C. Rochester facility of GM, an offer was made to all employees working in that division to either join the fledgling company or remain with GM. Bill Krystiniak, DTC's Director of Personnel, headed the transition program at GM. He described the changeover process:

> First of all it was my responsibility when I was at GM to head up the program relative to the transition of the people end of it. I had to take all the people that had made application to go to the Penske organization and see to it that we had a proper transition. Some people came to DTC, while others who didn't stayed back at GM. I'd say about 20% of those people that worked on the fuel injector product line stayed back at GM. You have to keep in mind, a lot of people that came with us are people that if the product line was pulled and moved would have been out of a job. And then you have a percentage of people that came with us because they really wanted a challenge. By the way, for the hourly employees there is not really the risk there is with salaried employees, because with the hourly employees there is a clause in the contract where they can apply to go back to GM. We have had around 15 people go back. They went back primarily because they didn't like our absenteeism policy, some of them thought it was more stringent than what they wanted to deal with, and some felt they had to be much more accountable with us than what they were used to at GM.

28   When the company was formed, 391 hourly and 60 salaried employees came over from GM. DTC hired around 200 people across the board (skilled tradespeople, general factory workers, tool makers, machine repairmen, and engineers) to bring their workforce to their current strength.

29   At GM the employees had narrow job descriptions, and one of the first things that DTC did was to broaden these rigid descriptions. As Bill Krystiniak put it:

> At GM we had very stringent lines of demarcation, especially in the areas of skilled trades. We still have problems of lines of demarcation, primarily between tool makers and machine repairmen. We like to think that we moved quite a ways away from the GM system when it comes to that. To give you an example, at GM they have a lot of janitors, and the janitors do a lot of work out in the plant. One of the things that we did when we

became a company was that we tried to instill in the people the philosophy, "hey, let's clean up after ourselves at the end of the day." Therefore we reduced the number of janitors. At the GM side of the house, it would be much more difficult to do that. They feel over there, you have janitors and janitors should do the cleaning up, there again your strict lines of demarcation.

30   General factory workers were paid $15.54 an hour plus a $0.94 per hour cost of living adjustment, while skilled tradespeople such as tool and die makers got $18.16 plus $0.94. Salaried employees were paid at market rate or better. When the company opened a remanufacturing center in 1989, they negotiated with the union to have a $7.00 an hour starting wage in that unit. The company asked each hourly employee at the fuel injection unit to turn in one referral and this formed the employee pool for the new unit. These referrals were also used to fill vacancies that arose from time to time in the remanufacturing unit. Senior people at the remanufacturing unit were hired to fill vacancies at the fuel injection unit. Hiring for skilled trade and salaried positions was done through newspaper advertisements and employment agencies. Job openings were posted on the shop floor and both hourly and salaried employees could apply for these openings.

31   Bill Krystiniak described the company's safety record:

GM had an excellent safety record on this product line, and we likewise have a very, very good record. We have had a couple of incidents . . . we had a millwright who cut the top of his finger off when the spring door in the loading area accidently came down. We've had a couple of other slip-and-fall type things, but fortunately as far as lost time is concerned, we have been very, very fortunate. Right now the big thing for us is out at the Remanufacturing Center and some of the coolant solutions that we use in there, we are finding out that some of our employees are rather sensitive to it. We don't know why and we are having our chemist work on it as well as our doctor. We are trying to get to the bottom of it to see why we have had certain people break out in rashes. But by and large we are pretty fortunate.

32   Both formal and informal internal communication were constantly encouraged. A weekly newsletter called the *Update* was distributed to all employees Monday mornings. It gave employees information about the previous week's production, scrap, and customer feedback. In addition, the newsletter also cited employees who had been involved in community service or had turned in suggestions that benefited the company.

33   Employees were encouraged to supplement their skills by undergoing training. The company had a tuition assistance program to help employees take courses at city colleges. Also, a number of training programs (e.g., CAD/CAM training) were provided in-house to increase employee skills. According to Bill Krystiniak, the union was responsible for many of the training programs encouraged by the company:

The UAW was very instrumental in this. They suggested, during negotiations, that we have a special fund set up for training. We can't touch that fund unless we get the union's concurrence. Right now, we have around $200,000 in the fund that we use for a variety of training programs.

34   The personnel department, consisting of Bill Krystiniak and five assistants, reported to the Vice President of Administration.

Financial Controls and Reporting System

35   Bob Joseph, the Vice President of Finance, was responsible for introducing periodic reporting procedures as well as introducing systems to produce regular information for decision making. He talked about his early days on the job trying to change people's minds about the financial manager:

The carryover from GM was that the finance manager was the guy that always told you that you were off budget and "no, this expense can't be approved because you don't have the right signature." I learned a long time ago that economic activity drives accounting and not vice versa. So when you talk to operations people you are talking about the economics of what is going on. What Ken [Oberholtzer, the Controller] and I tried to do was to educate everybody in the organization on the balance sheet and the income statement. We constantly tell people that the financial guy is not just a watchdog or a policeman or just somebody complaining about something constantly, but somebody who wants to help people make better decisions. I think we've made a lot of progress in that area.

36   As part of this education, manufacturing people were taught traditional investment analysis tools such as Return on Investment and Internal Rate of Return and encouraged to do preliminary evaluations of the projects before sending them to the finance department for approval.

37   Hourly workers were allowed to make purchases up to $1,000 worth of materials, while expenses of $1,000 or above had to be authorized by the controller. Bob Joseph approved expenditures between $25,000 and $2 million. Expenses beyond $2 million required board approval.

38   Monthly meetings were held with Roger Penske and members of his holding company. These, called Business Review meetings, were attended by Bob Joseph and Derek Kaufman, the President of DTC. Bob Joseph described typical activities at these meetings:

> The principal thing at these meetings is the review, where we look at three months at a time, always looking at performance versus plan versus last year. We also spend a lot of time on non-financial topics. Quality issues are always actively discussed, as well as the relationship between us and Detroit Diesel [major customer], whether they be supply type things such as what back orders have not been filled, or product issues. Also, strategy issues, such as what direction DTC should take in the future, are also discussed.

39   When DTC was formed in 1988, it continued to have its accounting done by Detroit Diesel. Ken Oberholtzer, the Controller of the company, and a staff of 5 people were primarily charged with providing cost figures to Detroit Diesel. When DTC bought the assets of Injector Corporation to set up a remanufacturing unit, the company decided to insource accounting in order to reduce costs. Computer software for various accounting functions was purchased and staff were trained in their use. Since GM's accounting was done by Electronic Data Systems (a subsidiary of GM), the computer programs were proprietary and DTC was not allowed to use them. The new accounting software that the company now used required a lot of training time for the accounting department. In installing the computerized accounting system, Oberholtzer's objective was to have a fully integrated system instead of islands of automation. Currently, all accounting except payroll (handled by Detroit Diesel) was done by DTC and a contract with EDS provided technical support for computers.

Finances

40   Exhibit 7 gives the financial statements from 1989 to 1992 for the company. Though the company reduced its long-term debt and increased its equity between 1989 and 1992, according to Bob Joseph, the VP of Finance, Roger Penske wanted DTC to finance its growth through debt rather than equity. The company had recently leased capital equipment worth about $15 million. The loss reported in 1990 was due largely to changes in certain accounting policies.

Culture

41   The company's culture stressed employee involvement, team spirit, and customer focus. Also, racing metaphors (because of Roger Penske's involvement in the company) such as "running at high speed" and "staying light" were frequently used in everyday communication.

42   To allow employees to become familiar with the total production process and experience first hand where the many different components fit into the finished product, a campaign called "I Got It Together" was started. To participate in this campaign, an employee had to assemble the injector, identify each component part, and give a brief explanation of its functions to a Quality Team. Upon successful completion, the employee received an "I Got It Together" T-shirt. Within a few months of the campaign's inception, over 75 percent of the employees had participated.

43   The company's customer focus was best illustrated by an incident that Derek Kaufman, the President of DTC, described in a magazine interview:

> Once, when I was visiting Detroit Diesel, I saw a shipment of fuel injectors arrive from DTC. The receiving department tore open the box and threw it away. The injectors were pulled out haphazardly, with no way of matching sets of injectors. I came back to DTC and had returnable plastic crates made up, each one able to hold a matched and calibrated set of injectors. The savings in cardboard alone are incredible, but the idea also made it easier for customers to do their jobs.[2]

EXHIBIT 7
DIESEL TECHNOLOGY COMPANY* Income Statement
(in $ 000s)

	1989	1990	1991	1992
Revenues	38,500	43,600	53,700	60,700
Cost of goods sold	34,400	39,700	45,700	51,900
Engineering expenses	700	1,800	2,000	2,100
Depreciation/amortization	1,300	1,900	2,100	2,200
Administrative expenses	1,400	1,300	2,100	1,900
Earnings before interest and taxes	700	(1,100)	1,800	2,600
Interest	1,700	1,900	1,400	1,100
Earnings before taxes	(1,000)	(3,000)	400	1,600

Balance Sheet
(in $ 000s)

Assets	1989	1990	1991	1992
Accounts receivable	4,600	10,700	5,400	5,800
Inventories	13,400	11,700	11,300	10,400
Prepaid expenses	300	400	900	100
Capital assets	15,200	15,400	15,300	14,400
Miscellaneous assets	2,300	2,000	2,200	1,700
	35,800	40,200	35,100	32,400

Liabilities/Equity				
Notes payable	7,600	13,500	4,000	1,400
Accounts payable	3,200	3,500	4,100	2,900
Accrued expenses	3,400	3,300	4,000	4,700
Long-term debt	15,600	7,900	5,600	4,400
Paid-in capital	7,000	16,000	21,000	21,000
Retained earnings	(1,000)	(4,000)	(3,600)	(2,000)
	35,800	40,200	35,100	32,400

*Disguised, per company's request.

44   Kaufman described another incident that emphasized the turnaround he and his management group had accomplished at the company:

> I think I heard in the barbershop the other day the key point in our turnaround process. I was having my hair cut and I had one of my company T-shirts on. The barber said to me, "Oh, Roger Penske is doing a fantastic job with the company." I said, "How do you know that?" He replied, "I have a number of DTC employees as my customers. These days I can tell a Diesel Tech person even when he comes into the barbershop without the company T-shirt on. If he is sitting in my chair and sees a Diesel Tech truck go by, he would say 'There goes our truck.' They never used 'our' and 'we' before in talking about the company."

THE FUEL INJECTION EQUIPMENT INDUSTRY

45   The fuel injection equipment industry (part of Standard Industrial Classification code 3714—motor vehicle parts and accessories) consisted primarily of diesel engine manufacturers who had integrated into the production of injectors and pumps. Apart from DTC, the other manufacturers were CAV Lucas (a U.K.-based company), who supplied Caterpillar (which also made injectors on its own), and Cummins, the U.S. market leader in heavy-duty diesel engines. Three Japanese companies—Nippondenso, Mitsubishi, and Zexel—had unit injectors in the development stage but not in production. The other major competition for unit injectors were manufacturers of fuel pumps such as Robert Bosch GmbH and Nippondenso. Bosch's fuel pumps were currently used in some Cummins' diesel engines. While fuel pumps and fuel injectors performed the same function in an engine, fuel injectors were better at controlling fuel flow (resulting in fuel savings) and also at meeting emission standards. In addition, fuel injectors were cheaper than fuel pumps. Exhibit 8 gives the worldwide market share

EXHIBIT 8
Fuel Injection Industry: Worldwide Market Share

Company	Market Share
Bosch	50%
Nippondenso	15
Zexel	10
Stanadyne	10
Lucas	9
DTC	2
Cummins	2
Caterpillar	2
Total	100%

Note: This list includes companies that make fuel pumps as well as companies that make unit injectors.

of companies in the fuel injection equipment industry. Exhibit 9 profiles fuel pumps and points out the differences between fuel pumps and unit injectors.

46   Derek Kaufman, the President of DTC, described the key success factor in the industry as follows:

> What companies are really reacting to are total business solutions. By this I mean that apart from performance, quality, and price of the product, the customer is interested in how the product is shipped, how the manufacturer supports the product in the field, and ways by which the injector manufacturer can help the engine makers' customer. Injector manufacturers are trying to bring a much bigger sphere of thinking into the situation.

47   In assessing DTC and its competitors on the industry's key success factors, Derek Kaufman had this to say:

> I think we [DTC] might be leading in the area of total business solutions a little bit. I see CAV Lucas as being more traditional in price. But in recent times, they have also shown the capacity to meet customers' needs. So our advantage does not last very long. One thing you have to understand is that in the diesel engine industry, primarily due to capital constraints, some form of partnership is taking place worldwide. For example, our biggest customer Detroit Diesel has a marketing agreement with U.K. based Perkins (which makes engines of a different capacity from Detroit Diesel). Perkins has an agreement to sell its engines to Navistar. Navistar's biggest customer for its engines is Ford. Now, Ford in turn owns 10 percent of Cummins which competes with Detroit Diesel in the North American heavy-duty diesel engine market. I think the key for DTC is to understand how we can take advantage of the trend in the industry toward partnerships.

48   The U.S. diesel engine industry experienced steady growth following World War II as engine designs improved in the areas of fuel economy, power density, reliability, and durability. In the post-war economic expansion and the related development of the on-highway transportation and urban transit infrastructures, the demand for heavy-duty diesel engines in on-highway trucks, transit buses, and in construction and industrial equipment increased significantly. However, by the early 1980s, the heavy-duty engine market was becoming more sophisticated. Demands for improved fuel economy and reduced engine emissions during this period had a major impact on the diesel engine business and became the focus of product development. As emissions standards for heavy-duty engines became more prevalent around the world, the ability of a manufacturer to meet the regulatory requirements and at the same time to deliver an efficient and durable engine product for the intended application had become critical aspects of the market.

49   In the U.S., the principal heavy-duty engine manufacturers were Cummins Engine Company, Caterpillar, and Detroit Diesel. Exhibit 10 shows the market share breakdown in the U.S. heavy-duty diesel engine industry. Industry analysts forecasted modest growth in heavy-duty truck sales after a slump in 1990 and 1991. The economic slump, the nationwide credit crunch, and uncertainty over the impact of new federal air-quality standards had reduced the demand for truck orders, directly affecting diesel engine makers. From a high of 165,000 engines in 1988, diesel engine sales slumped to

EXHIBIT 9
Fuel Pumps versus Unit Injectors: A Profile

Pros	Cons
Fuel Pumps	
High product volume—competitive price	Increased trapped volume of fuel in lines—makes control more difficult
High level of installed base—good for service education, exchange parts, etc.	Electronic control expensive
Options available	Increased pressures require larger pump size
	Single pump failure stops engine
	Large production volume discourages flexible change
Unit Injectors	
Improved control	Requires engine redesign
Less trapped volume	Removal/replacement time
Failure of one injector does not stop engine	
More flexible manufacturing process	

90,000 in 1991. However, industry observers forecasted an upturn in the demand for heavy-duty trucks (because the economy was expected to improve) starting toward the end of 1992 and continuing into 1993. Engine sales were expected to be around 115,000 to 120,000 units in 1992, and between 130,000 and 165,000 units in 1993 and 1994.[3]

50   New environmental regulations affected the diesel engine industry. Under the Clean Air Act, the Environmental Protection Agency had stipulated that by 1994 exhaust particles must be cut by 60 percent, and by 1998 levels of nitrogen oxides (NOx) must be cut to 4.0 compared with 5.0 in 1992. While all the major diesel engine manufacturers had invested heavily in new products to meet emission standards, Detroit Diesel's Series 60 diesel engines currently met the 1994 standard by increasing injection pressure. Emission standards for heavy-duty engines were becoming more prevalent around the world. Current European emission standards were not as stringent as those of the U.S. but a set of standards (called Euro I) which were similar to the 1994 U.S. standards were scheduled to go into effect in 1996 and a tighter set of standards (called Euro II) were expected by 1999.[4]

51   In 1992 the European trucking industry was predicted to be on the verge of a shakeout following unification. Experts forecast that the opening of the markets by countries in the European Community would ultimately result in consolidation among truck companies and their component suppliers. In 1991, 190,000 trucks were produced in Europe (the U.S. produced around 98,000 trucks in 1991) for sales within the continent and another 57,000 were produced for export.

52   Of the six primary truck manufacturers in Europe, the big three were Daimler-Benz AG, AB Volvo, and Renault SA. In response to the anticipated consolidation and the consequent margin reductions, it was expected that these major truck manufacturers would "go in for less vertical integration and more technological cooperation with component suppliers to spread their fixed costs across a broader base."[5] The big three manufacturers produced their own diesel engines and bought fuel pumps from Bosch. The market for diesel engine manufacturers (Perkins and U.S.-based suppliers such as Detroit Diesel, Cummins, and Caterpillar) centered around the after-market as well as in supplying the three smaller truck manufacturers (Iveco, Scania, and British Leyland) who did not have the capabilities to produce diesel engines for their trucks. Exhibit 11 gives the world sales forecast for commercial vehicles (medium and heavy-duty diesel trucks).

Profiles of Potential Partners

53   Daimler-Benz AG, based in Stuttgart was Germany's largest company and the world's leading heavy truck maker. It also owned Freightliner, the U.S.-based truck manufacturer. In 1990, 65 percent of the company's sales were from the European Community countries, 15% from North America, and the

EXHIBIT 10
U.S. Heavy-Duty Engine
Market Share

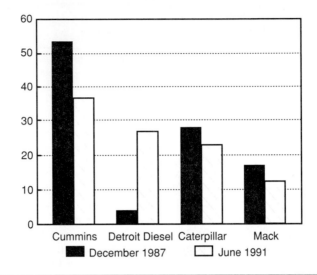

rest from Asia, Latin America, and non-EC countries. Sixty-eight percent of the company's total sales for 1990 were accounted for by the passenger car and truck divisions. The diversified company also operated in the electrical equipment, aerospace, and financial services industries. The diversification was achieved principally through acquisitions made since 1987. Employing over 376,000 people, the company's 1990 sales were $57.382 billion and net income was $1.13 billion.

54   In 1990, the Stuttgart, Germany–based Robert Bosch GmBH was the world's number one electronic automobile equipment manufacturer and also owned 6% of Nippondenso, the number two player in the industry. The company is owned 90% by the Robert Bosch Foundation, a charitable organization. Long known for pioneering work in the antilock braking system (ABS) and fuel injection areas, the company employed 13,483 (7.50% of total work force) R&D personnel in 1990. A diversified company with 1990 sales of $21.358 billion and net income of $375.83[||] million, Bosch was in automotive equipment (50% of sales), communications technology (23% of sales), consumer (20%), and capital goods (7%) industries. However, Europe accounted for 83% of sales in 1990. The Robert Bosch Corporation was the company's wholly owned subsidiary in the U.S.

THE FUTURE

55   As Derek Kaufman thought about the upcoming Business Review meeting, he realized that Penske's concerns about the company's future were indeed understandable. After all, he thought, while two of the three strategic reasons for which Penske acquired DTC from GM were achieved, the third, selling fuel injectors on the world market, still needed to be addressed. Should the company try to tap the world market on its own or look for potential joint ventures such as the one discussed with Benz and Bosch? If the company did decide on a partnership, should it be with a customer (Benz) or a supplier of fuel pumps (Bosch)? Would it lose its entrepreneurial spirit if it grew at a fast pace? Kaufman and his management team also realized that they had to make their decision with very limited knowledge of the European fuel injection market and its major players.

[||] § At December 31, 1990, exchange rate of 1 U.S. = 1.49 DM.

EXHIBIT 11
Global Commercial Vehicle Sales Forecast by Region
Class 8 Heavy-Duty Diesel Trucks (sales in 000s of units)

Region	1990	1995	2000	2005	2010
United States	4,847	5,177	5,441	5,648	5,790
Europe	2,628	2,913	3,303	3,743	4,259
Asia	1,841	2,434	3,170	4,017	5,078
Africa	338	401	488	606	754

Source: Adapted from Stephen E. Plumb, "Competition Will Be Cut-Throat in the 90s," *Ward's Auto World,* August 1992, p. 46.

56   Kaufman mentally prepared himself to put in long hours of thought and discussions with top managers prior to the Business Review meeting with Roger Penske.

ENDNOTES

1. Robin Luymes, "Diesel Gears Up to Pursue Growth," *Grand Rapids Business Journal,* October 28, 1991, pp. B7–B8.
2. Robin Luymes, "Diesel Gears Up to Pursue Growth," *Grand Rapids Business Journal,* October 28, 1991, pp. B7–B8.
3. Based on Ellen Benoit, "Jump Start," *Financial World,* October 18, 1988, pp. 42–44; Kevin Kelly, "Does Cummins Have the Oomph to Climb This Hill?" *Business Week,* November 4, 1991, pp. 66–68; and Stephen E. Plumb, "Competition Will be Cut-Throat in the 90s," *Ward's Auto World,* August 1992, pp. 45–46.
4. Stephen E. Plumb, "Alternate Fuels a Puzzlement for Big Rigs," *Ward's Auto World,* June 1992, pp. 47–50.
5. Stephen E. Plumb, "EC '92 Creates Opportunity and Consolidation," *Ward's Auto World,* July 1992, pp. 83, 87.

CASE 12

MERRILL ELECTRONICS CORPORATION (A)

1　In early July 1991, Patricia Merrill, the President and largest shareholder of Merrill Electronics, was preparing to evaluate her company's operating results for the first half of 1991. She was particularly interested in these results for two reasons: first, she wanted to determine the effectiveness of the policies and efforts of the company's new general manager, Charles Brown; and, second, she was to meet with Brown later in the day to discuss the company's cash position and the renegotiation of the lines of credit with its banks.

2　Since its founding in 1950 by Thomas Merrill, Merrill Electronics had been a distributor for GEC,[1] a large manufacturer of electrical and electronics products for consumer and institutional markets. Over the years, in addition to the GEC products, the company had added noncompeting lines of electrical appliances, records, compact disks, and cassettes. In 1980, it began to broaden its product lines by importing Japanese consumer electronics. Four years later, it entered into an exclusive import agreement with the Goldstone Corporation of Taiwan, a major producer of television and other electronic equipment. These products were distributed to retail firms and dealers throughout a broad geographical area.

3　By the mid-1980s, Merrill had entered into the personal computer (PC) market distributing both hardware and software products. It became the national distributor for Fuji Electronics, a major Japanese manufacturer of PCs and related products, in March 1989. This had proven to be a fast growing market, accounting for close to half of total sales and even more of the profits during the latest six-month period; but at the same time, it was becoming more and more competitive. By 1991, price-cutting had become rampant as mail order and discount houses entered the business.

4　Patricia Merrill had been working in the company for two years when her father, Thomas Merrill, died in January 1989. As the only family member with experience in the company, she succeeded him as President. Together with her mother, she controlled 75 percent of the share capital of the firm. The remaining shares were held by her father's brother and sister and their families. Although she herself received a salary from the company, Patricia Merrill's mother and the other shareholders in the family relied on dividends from the company for a portion of their income.

5　Twenty-nine at the time of her father's death, Patricia Merrill had been working the company as his personal assistant and heir apparent. During that period, he had delegated relatively little responsibility to her. Anxious to prove herself in her newly assumed capacity, she set ambitious growth targets for the company, and then began to try to recruit a seasoned operating manager to help achieve those objectives. When she reviewed the operating statements for the first half of 1990, generally regarded as a good year in the industry, she was convinced she needed help. That October, she was able to attract Charles Brown into the company as general manager by offering him a share of the profits in addition to salary. Brown had been the general sales manager of a distributor handling the products of a major GEC competitor. It was agreed by them that as general manager, Brown would have full authority to execute any changes he desired.

6　At the time of her father's death, Merrill had been troubled by the question of whether the family should retain its interest in the company or sell out. She had been aware of her father's concern over the steadily declining margins in the electrical distribution business in recent years, and, while the

This case was written by H. Lee Remmers, Professor at INSEAD. It is intended to be used as a basis for class discussion rather than to illustrate either effective or ineffective handling of an administrative situation. Reprinted with the permission of INSEAD. Copyright © 1992 INSEAD, Fontainebleau, France.

[1] Formerly the Global Electrical Company. In 1982, the company's name and logo had been changed to create a new image.

family enjoyed considerable wealth, she wondered whether they should not sell all or part of their shareholdings and invest the proceeds elsewhere. In fact, her uncle had been putting pressure on her to put the company up for sale ever since the death of her father.

7   At the end of 1990, her first year at the head of the company, Patricia Merrill had almost decided that they should sell out. In fact, she had told Brown at their first meeting that she might be interested in finding a buyer for the company because margins had fallen so drastically in recent years. "My father worked on an average gross margin of about 20 percent not many years ago," she said. "Nowadays, aside from the computer line and records, we don't average 14 percent any more. Television, which used to yield 15 percent, is now below 12 percent. The market for computers and software has become cutthroat and margins have fallen drastically during the past year and a half. So how can we make money? My feeling is that, if this keeps up, the distribution business will soon disappear. That's why I feel we should get out of this business now."

8   Brown replied that he was certainly familiar with the declining margins problem and that he had given it a great deal of thought. He was convinced, he said, that the answer lay in doing a high-volume business. "I don't think we'll ever see average gross margins of 20 percent in the traditional lines of our business again, but I do think we can maintain the return on investment by building volume, adding new product lines and rationalizing or possibly dropping old ones, and controlling costs. It won't be easy, but I think it can be done." Brown's confidence had been an important element in Merrill's decision to leave the family's money in the company, at least for the time being.

9   During his first few weeks with the company, Brown reviewed in detail the records of the operating and sales departments. He was particularly concerned with the market penetration achieved by the company's sales force in 1990 in relation to the estimated market potential as supplied by GEC, Fuji, and certain other suppliers. He was also interested in the gross margin trends and in the earnings shown by product lines.

10   As a result of his review, and with the aid of the operations manager, Julian McNeil, and the sales manager, Michael Teresi, Brown developed a forecast of sales, gross margins, operating expenses, and earnings for the first six months of 1991 (see Exhibit 1). The forecast was submitted to Merrill in late December of 1990, along with the following memorandum:

To: Patricia Merrill

From: Charles Brown

Summary of sales, gross margin and operating earnings objectives, January 1 to June 30, 1991.

1. The budgeted sales increase of $4,565,000 over the first six months of this past year is based primarily on the distribution of Fuji personal computers and accessories, and further growth in GEC's Vortex line of white goods,[2] which the company took on in late Spring 1990. Sales of all other lines are also expected to increase. The primary emphasis in 1991 will be on adding volume to the PC Division while maintaining margins, and bringing white goods into a position where they will be a profitable addition to the company's existing lines of products.

2. The budgeted gross margins are in accordance with 1990 experience, except for television and VCRs where a slight increase is predicted. PC margins have been under pressure, but we believe that our figures are realistic. The gross margin percentages on new products are based on factory representatives' estimates.

3. The budgeted operating earnings percentages are expected to be above 1990 figures since fixed costs will be spread over the greater volume that we expect to sell. In making these projections, we have included the cost of additional sales, office, service, and warehouse personnel to handle the planned increase in sales. We will continue to spend heavily on promotion and other investments to maintain a quality after-sales service.

4. Every effort will be made to speed up collection of accounts receivable and to obtain an overall inventory turnover of eight times in order to obtain the greatest use of the company's financial resources.

---

[2] Clothes washers and dryers, dishwashers, refrigerators, and freezers.

EXHIBIT 1
Budgeted versus Actual Performance: January 1 to June 30, 1991

	Budget ($)	Percent of Sales	Actual ($)	Percent of Sales	Variance (in $)	Actual as Percent of Budget	Difference (in percent)
Net Sales							
PC products and services	$ 6,500,000	100.0	$ 7,261,500	100.0	+$778,020	112	
Records, CDs, cassettes	736,125	100.0	986,730	100.0	+250,605	134	
Television and VCR	3,289,425	100.0	3,153,765	100.0	−135,660	96	
HiFi and electronics	1,311,840	100.0	1,397,160	100.0	+85,320	107	
Vortex	2,520,000	100.0	2,546,670	100.0	+26,670	101	
Small appliances	863,560	10.0	956,535	100.0	+92,970	111	
Total sales	$15,220,950		$16,302,360		$1,097,925	1.07	
Gross Margin							
PC products and services	$ 1,718,120	26.5	$ 1,724,600	23.7	+$6,480		−2.8
Records, CDs, cassettes	147,220	20.0	202,280	20.5	+55,060		+0.5
Television and VCR	332,240	10.1	352,365	11.1	+20,125		+1.0
HiFi and electronics	204,650	15.6	205,095	14.7	+445		−0.9
Vortex	348,090	13.8	312,225	12.3	−35,865		−1.5
Small appliances	99,730	11.5	107,130	11.2	+7,400		−0.3
Total gross margin	$ 2,850,050	18.7	$ 2,903,695	17.8	$53,645		−0.9
Operating Expenses							
PC products and services	$ 1,170,000	18.0	$ 1,430,520	19.7	+$260,520		+1.7
Records, CDs, cassettes	113,700	15.4	115,170	11.7	+1,470		−3.7
Television and VCR	250,000	7.6	253,380	8.0	+3,380		+0.4
HiFi and electronics	177,110	13.5	168,285	12.0	−8,825		−1.5
Vortex	317,850	12.6	285,290	11.2	−32,560		−1.4
Small appliances	91,550	10.6	105,720	11.1	+14,170		+0.5
Total expenses	$ 2,120,210	13.9	$ 2,358,365	14.5	$238,155		
Earnings before Interest and Tax (EBIT)							
PC products and services	$ 548,120	8.5	$ 294,080	4.1	−$254,040		−4.4
Records, CDs, cassettes	33,520	4.0	87,110	8.8	+53,590		+4.2
Television and VCR	82,230	2.5	98,985	3.1	+16,755		+0.6
HiFi and electronics	27,540	2.1	36,810	2.6	+9,270		+0.5
Vortex	30,240	1.2	26,935	1.1	−3,305		−0.1
Small appliances	8,180	0.9	1,410	0.1	−6,770		−0.8
Total earnings before tax	$ 729,830	4.8	$ 545,330	3.4	−$184,500		

11   During the first six months of 1991, Brown began to put his plans into effect. Additional personnel were added to the staff and, as the monthly sales reports were received, Merrill observed a substantial overall increase in sales in comparison with the same period in 1990.

12   With the increased volume, however, the company began to have difficulty meeting payments to suppliers while holding borrowing within the credit lines agreed with its banks.

13   During the last three months of 1990, the company had found it necessary to increase the overall bank credit line limit to $2,500,000 to finance larger inventories and receivables. It was planned that the credit line should be partially, if not wholly, paid off during the first three months of 1991. However, sales in the first quarter of 1991 ran higher than had been anticipated, thus prolonging the

company's need for borrowed funds. The problem was compounded by the arrival in February and March of large computer and software inventories; it worsened in May and June as white goods and small appliances moved more slowly than expected.

14   Accordingly, Merrill and Brown approached the company's banks in March and arranged for an increase in their credit lines to $3 million and for them to be extended to September 30, 1991. During the next three months, sales continued to expand so that in late June they made a further request to the banks for an extension of the $3 million limit to March 31, 1992. The request was turned down. However, the bankers told Merrill and Brown they would consider continuing the current line until December 31, 1991. But they would have to be presented with a realistic operating plan including a cash flow forecast to show that the company could stay within the $3 million credit limit during the second half of the year, *and* reduce the amount of credit lines used to no more than $500,000 by December 31.

15   The chairman of the loan committee of the company's principal bank told Merrill and Brown that he believed part of the company's financial needs were long term in nature and, therefore, should be supplied by an increase in equity or long-term capital. He insisted that without an increase of capital from the shareholders, his bank would find it very difficult to extend its present credit line of $1.5 million beyond the end of December if the conditions outlined above (preceding paragraph) were not met.

16   At the beginning of the second week in July, Merrill received from McNeil, the operations manager, copies of the company's income statement and balance sheet for the six months ended June 30, 1991, together with his comments on sales, gross margins, and earnings. (See Exhibits 1, 2, 3 and 4). For comparative purposes, McNeil also gave Merrill a set of selected financial and operating statistics drawn from a sample of other companies in the consumer electronics distribution industry (see Exhibit 5). On receipt of these reports, Merrill began to analyze the effectiveness of Brown's plans and operations during the first half of 1991.

17   She next turned her attention to the company's financial position, giving consideration to a number of alternative ways of meeting its cash needs during the second half of 1991. In assessing these needs, she bore in mind that both Fuji and GEC recently had sent reminders that the credit terms *net 30 days* meant just that, that is, that they were going to be enforced. This could take a number of forms: interest could be charged on past due payables, perhaps at considerably above market rates; much worse, the suppliers could stop shipping or ship only upon receipt of cash payment. Merrill also discussed with Brown, McNeil, and Teresi the expected sales targets for the company until the end of June 1991. Between them they agreed upon a sales forecast for the next 12 months (Exhibit 6).

18   Second, Merrill wondered to what extent the funds required for their ambitious sales program could be met internally—specifically, through a combination of reduced operating expenses, reduced inventory levels, improved collection of receivables, and possibly, the dropping of one or more product lines.

19   Finally, she wondered whether—on the basis of Brown's performance to date and the long-term prospects of the business —the Merrill family might be justified in investing additional funds of their own in the company or, instead, begin to look for someone to buy them out sooner rather than later. Even if the family were to hold onto the company for now, investing additional capital if needed, she believed that within the next three to five years they should try to realize part of their investment by placing some of their shares on the over-the-counter market. To keep peace in the family, one way or another she would have to give the other shareholders a way to realize part of their investment. And she was well aware that to go public would require a solid track record —strong, stable growth of sales revenues and earnings, and a sound financial position.

EXHIBIT 2
Report of Operations: January 1 to June 30, 1991

To: Patricia Merrill, President

From: Julian McNeil, Operations Manager

Re: Report of operations for 6 months ending 30 June 1991

1. Summary results are shown for the first half of 1991 on the previous page (Exhibit 1).

2. Division Analysis

PC Products Division

Sales volume during the past 6 months exceeded forecasts by over three quarters of a million dollars. The new Fuji 2500XEC laptop has been especially popular and accounted for close to 20 percent of the total—in spite of some teething problems discussed below. However, gross margins have been under considerable pressure from discounters, especially for software products. We are concerned that this will continue and very likely become even more severe during the next few months. Margins overall may fall to as low as 20 percent before stabilizing. In addition, since well over half of this division's products are purchased from Japanese suppliers, margins may also be affected by currency fluctuations. Finally, we are beginning to explore the possibility of starting a mail order operation with our own brand label—similar to Dell Computers.

Operating expenses are also running above those forecast. Part of this is due to problems with the color screens on the new F2500XEC laptop, but a number of other products have needed more service than planned. As our service and repair personnel become more experienced, expenses should be easier to control in this area. Inventories are still more than $500,000 over our target level, and competition will make it difficult to improve this situation much in the short term. There is some $200,000 in obsolete merchandise; we may be able to return some of this to our suppliers, but most will have to be sold off below cost.

Records Division

1991 should make history. Sales were especially strong in compact disks. Our most recent analysis of obsolete inventories indicates that we have approximately $30,000 to dispose of. We will probably have to sell this stock at below cost.

We are negotiating with another major producer and hope to add their label to our existing lines. This should have a favorable effect on revenues. On the other hand, margins continue to be under pressure from discounters.

Television and VCR Division

TV sales for the first six months are slightly below last year, although gross margin and operating earnings are ahead. On the negative side, ending June inventory is well above target and includes roughly $250,000 worth of older models. We will try to move these as fast as possible, but will probably mean discounting below cost.

According to GEC factory reports on television distributor sales to dealers, our market share in this area for the year to date is 14.7 percent. This compares to GEC's overall market share of 17.8 percent for this same period. In 1990, our market share was 15.2 percent compared to the GEC national average of 16.9 percent. In 1989, we had 17.0 percent of the market in our area compared to the GEC national average of 16.5 percent. Fortunately, our market share for Fuji TVs is up from the same period a year ago.

VCR sales of the new Fuji and Goldstone lines as well as earnings are better than forecast, somewhat offsetting the currently weak TV market. We have had some servicing problems with the Goldstone VCRs, and although the factory has promised help, repair expenses may rise.

HiFi and Electronics Division

Sales for the first half of 1991 have exceeded 1990 by $225,000. Although gross margins have decreased slightly in percentage terms, our operating earnings have increased.

Factory reports of distributor sales of HiFi equipment to dealers show our market share for the first months of 1991 to be 19.4 percent. This compares to the GEC national average of 12.0 percent for the same period. In 1990, our market share was 18.2 percent compared to the GEC national average of 11.8 percent. In 1989, the figures were 15.6 percent and 12.0 percent, respectively. Likewise, our market share for Fuji products is better than their overall national average.

Our order backlog amounts to more than $125,000. If business remains at or near the present level, this will be a banner year for this department. However, there are some orders in jeopardy because of slow delivery of merchandise from suppliers. Given this situation, our inventory target of 45 days may prove to be unrealistic.

Vortex Division

Because we took on the Vortex line in the middle of 1990, there are no comparable figures for the first half of the year. We realize that this division has not done much more than break even for the first six months of 1991; however, in view of the promotional costs we had (approximately $85,000) and some discounting, it may be considered satisfactory. Since most of these costs have been incurred, the balance of the year should be profitable.

Small Appliance Division

Sales in this division include portable air conditioners, small kitchen appliances, and lamps. Sales and gross margins are running ahead of last year, but increased expenses from repairs on defective merchandise have virtually wiped out operating earnings.

The principal challenge we are facing is excessively high inventories. With interest rates at current levels, carrying costs exceed operating earnings.

We need to follow closely this division's performance during the next months. If results cannot be improved substantially, we might be advised to phase it out and focus our attention on the more promising lines.

EXHIBIT 2
(concluded)

3. Accounts receivable
   Our receivables are in good condition with 91.25 percent current. Bad debt expense for the latest six months was $81,500, 0.5 percent of total sales. This amount is based on past experience, but may be conservative. Our bad debt reserve is $191,410 of which about $120,000 will probably be written off when the final accounts for the year are prepared. The condition of our accounts receivable is shown by the following aging schedule:

	June 18, 1991	May 17, 1991
Current	91.25%	93.05%
Past due:		
1 to 30 days	4.15	3.85
31 to 60 days	1.85	1.55
61 to 90 days	1.10	0.81
91 days and over	1.65	0.74

4. Inventories
   Our inventories as at June 30, 1991, amounted to $5,591,470. They are up considerably from a year ago, primarily as a result of the addition of a new line of personal computers, obsolete merchandise in the PC and TV divisions, problems with TVs that were mentioned earlier, and the need to carry a relatively broader range of Vortex washers and dryers than was previously the case. Our inventory position by product line is as follows:

Product Line	Actual Inventory Level Amount	Actual Inventory Level In days*	Target Inventory Level Amount	Target Inventory Level In days†
PC products and services	$2,092,400	68	$1,526,000	50
Records, CDs, etc.	255,365	58	183,560	45
Television, VCRs	1,319,945	75	739,600	50
HiFi, electronics	450,300	65	285,750	45
Vortex	723,110	60	530,580	45
Small appliances	750,350	110	266,000	60
Total	$5,591,470	67	$3,541,490	49

*Based on anticipated sales volume (valued at cost) for period July–October 1991.

†Based on our best estimates of optimum inventory levels taking into account expected cost of products, delivery lead-time from suppliers, diversity of products, sales forecasting uncertainties.

EXHIBIT 3
Income Statements

	6 Months to 30 June 1990		6 Months to 31 December 1990		6 Months to 30 June 1991	
Net sales	$10,654,900	100.0	$18,096,400	100.0	$16,203,360	100.0
Cost of sales	8,939,610	83.9	15,020,010	83.0	13,398,665	82.2
Gross margin	1,715,290	16.1	3,076,390	17.0	2,903,695	17.8
Operating expenses:						
Direct selling	460,280	4.3	742,780	4.1	665,400	4.1
Advertising & promotion	119,680	1.1	231,300	1.3	205,200	1.3
After sales service	253,250	2.4	522,650	2.9	566,800	3.5
Warehouse & Shipping	178,150	1.7	262,400	1.5	236,400	1.5
General administration	542,550	5.1	575,005	3.1	608,115	3.7
Depreciation	44,175	0.4	54,590	0.3	76,450	0.5
Total expenses	1,598,085	15.0	2,388,725	13.2	2,358,365	14.5
Operating earnings (EBIT)	117,205	1.1	687,665	3.8	545,330	3.4
Interest expense	62,650	0.6	143,225	0.8	178,800	1.1
Earnings before taxes	54,555	0.5	544,440	3.0	366,530	2.3
Corporate taxes	22,900	0.2	206,890	1.2	146,850	0.9
Earnings after taxes	31,655	0.3	337,550	1.9	219,680	1.4
Dividends paid	20,000		50,000		50,000	

EXHIBIT 4
Balance Sheets (amounts in dollars)

	30 June 1990	31 December 1990	30 June 1991
Assets			
Current assets:			
Cash and bank	58,900	38,850	35,220
Accounts receivable (net)	2,841,100	4,826,600	4,166,180
Inventories	2,895,200	3,534,120	5,591,470
Other current assets	29,700	41,450	65,980
Total current assets	5,824,900	8,441,020	9,858,850
Fixed assets:			
Buildings and equipment (net)	632,900	718,200	789,750
Goodwill	100,000	100,000	100,000
Total	732,900	818,200	889,750
Total assets	6,557,800	9,259,220	10,748,600
Capital and Liabilities			
Current liabilities:			
Short-term bank loans	455,000	2,050,000	2,985,000
Long-term debt due in one year	80,000	80,000	80,000
Accounts payable *domestic*	1,155,700	1,819,130	1,705,110
Accounts payable *foreign**	241,200	391,250	895,620
Accrued expenses	171,980	217,370	251,720
Total current liabilities	2,103,880	4,557,750	5,917,450
Long-term debt	560,000	520,000	480,000
Capital stock	1,000,000	1,000,000	1,000,000
Retained earnings	2,893,920	3,181,470	3,351,150
Owners' equity	3,893,920	4,181,470	4,351,150
Total capital and liabilities	6,557,800	9,259,220	10,748,600

*Primarily Yen-denominated invoices.

EXHIBIT 5
Selected Financial and Operating Data Electronics Equipment Distributors[a]

	Average Lower Quartile	Median	Average Upper Quartile
Current ratio	1.5	2.0	2.7
Acid test ratio	0.6	1.0	1.3
Debt ratio[b]	41.2%	48.6%	55.1%
Asset turnover[c]	3.0	3.5	3.9
Collection period[d]	28 days	33 days	39 days
Payment period[e]	29 days	31 days	35 days
Inventory turnover[f]	7.5 times	8.6 times	9.2 times
Gross margin	12.7%	15.4%	18.0%
Operating expenses/sales	9.8%	12.2%	14.4%
Operating earnings (EBIT)/sales	2.9%	3.2%	3.6%
Earnings after tax (EAT)/sales	1.1%	1.3%	1.5%
Return on equity (ROE)[g]	4.7%	6.9%	9.5%

[a]Based on latest six-month results (January–June 1990).
[b]Total liabilities divided by total assets.
[c]Sales revenue for January–June 1991 divided by total assets for June 30, 1991 (annualized by multiplying by 2).
[d]Receivables on 30 June 1991 divided by sales revenue for January–June 1991 multiplied by 180 days.
[e]Payables on 30 June 1991 divided by purchases for January–June 1991 multiplied by 180 days.
[f]Inventories on 30 June 1991 divided by cost of sales for January–June 1991 (annualized by multiplying by 2).
[g]Earnings after tax for January–June 1991 divided by owners' equity for 30 June 1991 (annualized by multiplying by 2).

EXHIBIT 6
Sales Forecasts: July 1991–June 1992
(thousands of dollars)

Product line	Jul	Aug	Sept	Oct	Nov	Dec	Jan	Feb	Mar	Apr	May	Jun
PC products	1,200	1,200	1,350	1,450	1,600	1,500	1,300	1,450	1,750	1,900	1,850	1,800
Records, etc.	150	175	290	450	570	240	170	230	250	280	300	270
TVs and VCRs	470	550	930	1,400	1,850	1,260	650	750	820	850	900	800
HiFI	210	250	400	630	800	640	225	325	345	360	350	320
Vortex	380	450	750	1,120	1,470	1,150	500	600	650	700	720	680
Appliances	135	170	275	420	550	450	180	240	250	270	280	250
Total	2,545	2,795	3,995	5,470	6,840	5,240	3,025	3,595	4,065	4,360	4,400	4,120

CASE 13

MERRILL ELECTRONICS CORPORATION (B)

1   Patricia Merrill, President and majority shareholder of Merrill Electronics, was pleased with her company's results over the past year (see Exhibits 2 and 3). Sales had increased by over 40 percent and profits by more than 50 percent compared to the previous year, in line with her ambitious growth objectives for the company. A number of operational improvements had been implemented with considerable success in reducing the working capital and cash needs of the firm. Also, she had secured additional long-term financing and an increase in the company's credit line. Although continued growth would require some additional investment in new computer and office equipment, and other fixed assets, she expected this could be largely financed out of cash flow—if margins held up and working capital could be kept under control.

2   Since its founding in 1950 by Thomas Merrill, Merrill Electronics had been a distributor for GEC,[1] a large manufacturer of electrical and electronics products for consumer and institutional markets. Over the years, in addition to the GEC products, the company had added noncompeting lines of electrical appliances, records, compact disks, and cassettes. In 1980, it began to broaden its product lines by importing Japanese consumer electronics. Four years later, it entered into an exclusive import agreement with the Goldstone Corporation of Taiwan, a major producer of television and other electronic equipment. These products were distributed to retail firms and dealers throughout a broad geographical area.

3   By the mid-1980s, Merrill had entered into the personal computer (PC) market distributing both hardware and software products. It became the national distributor for Fuji Electronics, a major Japanese manufacturer of PCs and related products, in March 1989. This had proven to be a fast growing market, accounting for close to half of total sales and even more of the profits during the latest six-month period; but at the same time, it was becoming more and more competitive. By 1991, price-cutting had become rampant as mail order and discount houses entered the business.

4   Patricia Merrill had been working in the company for two years when her father, Thomas Merrill, died in the Spring of 1989. As the only family member with experience in the company, she succeeded him as President. Together with her mother, she controlled 75 percent of the share capital of the firm. The remaining shares were held by her father's brother and sister and their families.

5   During that first week of July 1992, she had been taking advantage of the relative calm that usually marked that time of the year. This was when they took the semi-annual inventory, tended to various small problems that had been pushed aside during the past two or three months, and thought about the future.

6   One of the things that had been bothering her for some time was the volatility of the yen. About half of the equipment sold in the PC, TV and VCR, and Hifi product lines were imported from Japanese suppliers. From a volume of about $12 million in the year ending in June 1991, yen-denominated purchases had exceeded $20 million during the past 12 months. With the growing volume expected in the PC product line, Merrill foresaw yen purchases from Fuji Electronics, Merrill's principal supplier, and other Japanese manufacturers to increase substantially in the future.

7   Typical of most Japanese exporters, Merrill's suppliers insisted on invoicing in yen. On average, once an order was placed the Japanese suppliers shipped by airfreight within 60 days. Payment terms

This case was written by H. Lee Remmers, Professor at INSEAD. It is intended to be used as a basis for class discussion rather than to illustrate either effective or ineffective handling of an administrative situation. Reprinted with the permission of INSEAD. Copyright © 1992 INSEAD, Fontainebleau, France.

[1] Formerly the Global Electrical Company. In 1982, the company's name and logo had been changed to create a new image.

EXHIBIT 1
Currency and Other Financial Market Data
July 8, 1992

> Spot Yen: 124.60–124.70 ($0.008019–$0.008026)
> 90-Day Forward Yen: 124.95–125.10 ($0.007994–$0.008003)
>
> 90-Day EuroYen interest rates: 4.3125%–4.4375% p.a.
> 90-Day EuroDollar interest rates: 3.3750%–3.5000% p.a.
> Merrill short-term borrowing rate: Prime (6.00%) + 25 basis points
>
> September yen futures (IMM): $0.8046; December yen futures (IMM): $0.8036
>
> October yen call options (IMM): $0.8000 strike–$0.0170 per 100 yen

---

were 30 days from the end of the delivery month; hence the ¥225 million value of goods delivered in June 1992 would be paid at the end of July. With few exceptions, the yen spot price on the last day of the month in which the order was placed was used for the invoice. This meant that Merrill had on average a 90-day yen currency exposure for each order. Concerned about the potential impact from a varying exchange rate on the dollar cost of these purchases, Merrill had asked her general manager, Charles Brown, to gather some data on the monthly volume of purchases from Japanese suppliers as well as the yen/dollar exchange rates and interest rates over the past year. These appear on Exhibits 4 and 5.

8   The data gathered by Brown stunned Patricia Merrill. The effect of the yen's continual appreciation against the dollar between July and December 1991 meant that purchases during that period had cost Merrill over $370,000 more than if the exchange rate had been stable. Put another way, pre-tax profits were over 30 percent lower. Although Brown explained that a similar analysis performed on the January–June period in both 1991 and 1992 showed "gains" due to a weakening yen, Merrill decided that they could no longer leave a major element of cost hostage to uncertain market conditions. She immediately got on the phone to her banker and arranged a meeting for that same afternoon.

9   Listening to Merrill and Brown's story, their banker agreed that Merrill did face significant currency risk, observing that the cost impact of a strong yen was amounting to more than the interest it was paying on loans. Further, he reminded them that since Merrill Electronics imported a higher portion of its products from Japan than other distributors competing in the market, its profit margins were much more sensitive to the value of the yen than theirs were. He explained there were several ways of dealing with their problem.

10   First, Merrill could continue as before, buying yen on the spot market each time payments to the Japanese suppliers were made. If the ¥580 [2] million worth of goods on order or already invoiced at the end of June were to be settled at the current spot rate of ¥124.60,[3] Merrill would suffer higher purchase costs of about $225,000, compared to the dollar costs that would have been incurred at the spot rates when the orders were placed. On the other hand, if the yen weakened in the future, Merrill would benefit from lower dollar costs for the goods imported. The banker cautioned that neither he, nor anyone else for that matter, could guess what the yen would do during the next few months. He showed Merrill and Brown some news commentary on the currency markets (Exhibit 6), and other evidence that the dollar was undervalued in terms of its relative purchasing power (see Exhibit 7), but stressed that the various market uncertainties were such as to make predictions highly risky.

11   Second, there were other alternatives: (1) "lock-in" today an exchange rate that would be close to the current spot rate, or (2) enter into an option contract that would set the upper limit on the cost of yen, but allow Merrill to take advantage of a cheaper yen if that should occur over the next few months. Since foreign currency was something that Merrill and Brown had never given much thought to before, the banker decided to go over the basic issues with them. To help them follow, he handed them a copy of the currency markets quotations page from the *Wall Street Journal* (Exhibit 8).

---

[2] The goods were worth $4.43 million at the spot rates prevailing when the orders were placed.

[3] ¥124.60 per dollar ($0.8026 per 100 yen) was the spot rate on 8 July 1992 for transactions of at least $1 million equivalent. Merrill Electronics usually bought yen from its bankers at from 1% to 2% less favorable rates since most transactions were under $250,000.

EXHIBIT 2
Comparative Income Statements
(thousands of dollars)

	Actual Year Ending 30 June 1991	Proforma Year Ending 30 June 1992
Sales revenue	34,398	50,118
Cost of goods sold	28,419	41,866
Gross margin	5,979	8,252
Variable expenses	2,100	3,060
Fixed expenses	2,516	3,245
Depreciation	131	180
Operating earnings (EBIT)	1,232	1,767
Interest expense	322	340
Earnings before taxes	910	1,427
Income taxes	354	562
Earnings after taxes	556	865

12   To lock in an exchange rate, the banker explained, meant that the future price of a foreign currency—*the future spot rate*—would in effect be set today. This type of hedge insured that whatever the future spot rate might turn out to be, the *effective* price paid for yen would still be that which was agreed today. There were three ways to lock in an exchange rate: a forward contract, a money market transaction, and a currency futures contract. Each of these carried precisely defined terms with regard to price, maturity, and certain other performance measures. Any changes in the terms of the contract, such as lengthening its maturity, would have to be negotiated and agreed with the counterparty, possibly resulting in additional cost.

13   The **forward contract hedge** would be an arrangement in which Merrill would buy from the bank a specified quantity of yen to be delivered at a specified date in the future. The exchange rate would be fixed at the outset. At ¥124.95, a 90 day forward contract was at present slightly cheaper than the spot rate. If this hedge was used, Merrill would receive yen from the bank on the agreed date, pay the bank the amount of dollars at the forward exchange rate set earlier, and then use the yen to pay the Japanese suppliers.

14   The **money market hedge** was also an arrangement with the bank. Merrill would buy yen today on the spot market and place it in a yen time deposit or some other yen asset until needed to pay the suppliers. The purchase of yen would be financed in dollars by a short term loan or by using cash reserves if they were available. The cost of this hedge would be the difference between the interest paid on the dollar loan and that received from the yen deposit. The banker reminded them that Merrill could borrow dollars at 25 *basis points*[4] over the current *prime* rate [6.00 percent], and earn 4.3125 percent on a 3-month Euroyen time deposit.

15   The **yen futures hedge** was provided by an instrument traded on the *International Monetary Market* (IMM) exchange in Chicago.[5] As protection against loss from currency fluctuations, this hedge was very similar to the forward contract provided by the bank. Merrill would *buy* a sufficient number of futures to create the hedge. It could then wait until the futures contracts came to maturity and take delivery of the yen. Alternatively, if Merrill decided the hedge was no longer needed, but the futures contracts had not yet come to maturity, they could be *sold*. If a rise in the value of the yen

[4] A basis point is 1/100 of a percent, i.e., 0.0001. Basis points are generally used in pricing loans and certain other financial instruments.

[5] Currency futures are also traded on exchanges in London [LIFFE], Singapore [SIMEX], Sidney, and elsewhere in the world.

EXHIBIT 3
Comparative Balance Sheets
(thousands of dollars)

	30 June 1991	30 June 1992
Assets		
Current assets:		
Cash and deposits	35	45
Prepaid expenses	66	75
Accounts receivable	4,166	5,312
Inventories	5,591	4,530
	9,858	9,962
Fixed assets (Net)	790	1,031
Goodwill	100	100
Total assets	10,748	11,093
Capital and Liabilities		
Current liabilities:		
Bank credit	2,985	853
Mortgage—current	80	80
Accrued expenses	252	561
Accounts payable:		
Domestic	1,705	1,452
Foreign (yen)*	896	1,784
	5,918	4,650
Mortgage loan	480	400
Subordinated loan	—	250
Capital stock	1,000	1,500
Retained earnings	3,351	4,213
Owners' equity	4,351	5,713
Total capital and liabilities	10,749	11,093

*Dollar value of ¥224.8 million order at spot rate on 30 June
(¥126 = $).

meant it cost more dollars to settle the purchase account with the Japanese suppliers, it also meant that the futures would be sold at a profit, thereby providing an offset. However, the mechanics of futures contracts differ considerably from forwards. The contracts are made through a member of the futures exchange, usually a broker. Currency futures come in standard sizes (¥12.5 million), and standard maturity dates (the third Wednesday of March, June, September, December). They are revalued daily (*marked-to-market*) with any profit or loss immediately settled between broker and client. To trade on the futures market, the client must open and maintain a margin account with the broker. At present, this is a minimum of $1,500 per contract. In addition, the broker will charge a small commission.

16 The **currency option contract** was available from either banks or exchanges. Option contracts give the *right but not the obligation* to buy (**a call**) or to sell (**a put**) currency or some other asset within a specified period and at a predetermined price.

17 Bank or OTC[6] options can be tailored to meet the clients precise needs for maturity, amount, or currency. They are usually "European" type options, i.e., they may only be exercised at expiration. Most bank options are on spot currency. Merrill's banker pointed out that besides dealing in call and put options, he could also offer them *synthetic* instruments. These were combinations of calls, puts, and sometimes forward contracts which were designed to meet particular risk/return objectives of a client.

18 Like futures, exchange-traded options have standardized maturities and amounts. The expiration dates are similar to those for futures: March, June, September, and December. In addition, the American exchanges offer some "near-by" expiration dates. For example, at the beginning of July,

[6] OTC = Over the counter.

EXHIBIT 4
Actual Purchases from Japanese Suppliers
July 1991–June 1992

Purchase Amount ¥ Million	Order Date	¥/$ Spot	Delivery and Invoice Date	Payment Date	¥/$ Spot	Gain/Loss (in $000s)
210.2	Jul 91	138	Sept 91	Oct 91	131	−81.4
244.1	Aug 91	137	Oct 91	Nov 91	130	−95.9
327.8	Sept 91	133	Nov 91	Dec 91	125	−157.7
274.3	Oct 91	131	Dec 91	Jan 92	125	−100.5
156.0	Nov 91	130	Jan 92	Feb 92	127	−28.3
192.5	Dec 91	125	Feb 92	Mar 92	133	+92.6
186.3	Jan 92	125	Mar 92	Apr 92	133	+89.6
216.5	Feb 92	127	Apr 92	May 92	130	+39.3
229.4	Mar 92	133	May 92	Jun 92	128	−67.4
224.8	Apr 92	133	Jun 92	Jul 92	?	?
195.0	May 92	130	Jul 92	Aug 92	?	?
159.4	Jun 92	128	Aug 92	Sept 92	?	?

Forecasted Purchases from Japanese Suppliers

July–October 1992

225.3	Jul 92	?	Sept 92	Oct 92	?	?
325.0	Aug 92	?	Oct 92	Nov 92	?	?
395.0	Sept 92	?	Nov 92	Dec 92	?	?
385.0	Oct 92	?	Dec 92	Jan 93	?	?

contracts were offered for July and August expiration as well as for the September standard month. Only a few major currencies are available. Most are priced in U.S. dollars including those traded on European or Asian exchanges. They are typically so-called "American" type options, i.e., they may be exercised at any time before expiration. Those traded on the Philadelphia exchange are on spot currency. Chicago's IMM and London's LIFFE contracts are on currency futures. To buy an option on an exchange, the full premium[7] must be paid in advance. To sell (or write) an option requires a specified margin to be maintained with the broker.

19   There was yet another aspect to Merrill Electronics' currency management problem. The company imported goods from its Japanese suppliers on a continuous basis throughout the year. If they did decide to hedge these purchases, should it be done when the orders were placed, when the purchase invoice was actually received, or periodically for a longer period of 6 to 12 months based on operating plans and budgets?

20   The banker concluded his exposé by stressing there was no "correct" hedging approach. It depended on the particular needs and financial position of the company, and the attitudes of its management and shareholders towards risk. The efficiency of the hedge would only be known *ex post*—after the supplier was paid. In the case of Merrill's currency problem, if yen strengthened, "locking in" the rate would have been the correct decision. If yen weakened, either no hedge or an option hedge would have produced the best results.

---

[7] The LIFFE exchange uses a margin system similar to that for futures trading. Hence, a specified minimum margin is maintained with the broker rather than paying a cash premium up front.

EXHIBIT 5A
Yen-Dollar Spot Rates
January 1990–July 1992

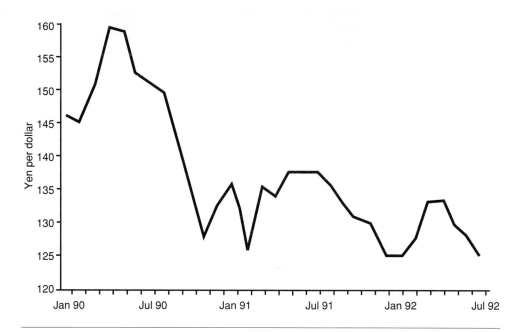

Source: *International Herald Tribune,* various issues.

21   The banker's explanation of the various hedging methods left Merrill and Brown somewhat bewildered. As they were leaving, they told their banker that they would need a few days to decide what they wanted to do. On their way back to the office, Merrill told Brown that she was convinced that they should begin to manage actively their currency position. There was simply too much money at risk to allow things to continue as they had during the past several months. The problem was how should they go about it?

22   Not wanting to let the matter drag on any longer, Patricia Merrill asked Brown to prepare a brief report on how their company's currency risk should be managed. In particular, she asked him to set out the relative advantages in terms of cost and risk for each of the alternatives that had been described to them by the banker. To provide a practical example, he could use the ¥225 million (rounded off) exposure arising from the goods that were being ordered during July and which would be due for payment in October, 90 days from then. She suggested he use the July 8 market rates which they had picked up at the bank (Exhibit 1), and assume that the suppliers would be paid and the hedges lifted on the 8th of October. She also asked if he would give some thought to *when and under what circumstances* any currency hedging should be done.

EXHIBIT 5B
EuroYen Interest Rates
January 1990–July 1992

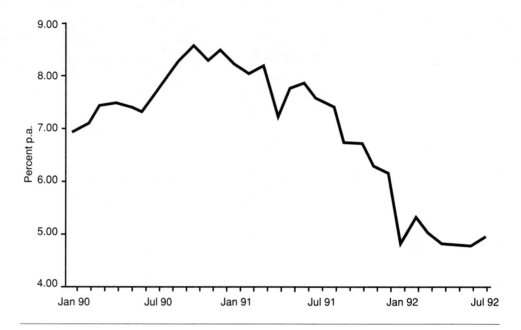

Sources: DRI; *International Herald Tribune,* various issues.

Dollar Falls on Mark; Sell-Off Is Stemmed

CURRENCY MARKETS

By CHARLENE LEE
AP-Dow Jones News Service

NEW YORK - The dollar declined against the mark on Wednesday, but rose from its lows on frantic short-covering after Treasury Secretary Nicholas Brady said the U.S. isn't actively "seeking to depreciate the dollar."

Mr. Brady, speaking in Munich after the conclusion of the annual economic summit of the Group of Seven most industrialized nations, backed away from remarks made in a television interview aired in the U.S. late on Tuesday.

In that interview, Mr. Brady said he wasn't bothered by the dollar's fall below 1.5000 marks or its proximity to the historical low of 1.4425 marks. Those comments opened the floodgates to a dollar sell-off, sending the currency to a new 1992 low of 1.4770 marks early on Wednesday.

In late New York trading, the dollar was quoted at 1.4885 marks, down from 1.4900 marks late Tuesday in New York. The U.S. currency also was changing hands at 124.70 yen, up from 124.10 yen. Sterling fell to $1.9300 from $1.9340.

During the session, the U.S. unit also set new lows for the year at 1.3291 Swiss francs and $1.9430 to the pound.

"I think what happened was Mr. Brady didn't realize what effect he would have on the market," said Joseph Cambria, foreign exchange manager in New York for Banque Paribas. "It was some sort of damage control," he added, referring to Mr. Brady's statements on Wednesday clarifying his remarks in the interview.

The Treasury secretary's back-pedaling triggered a flurry of short-covering and helped the currency rally to a session high of 1.5010 marks. Nevertheless, the U.S. unit's rally was greeted by heavy selling interest as dealers took the opportunity to establish fresh short positions at the higher levels and forced the dollar back down.

Traders noted that Mr. Brady's comments and the G-7's final communique did little to change bearish sentiment toward the U.S. currency. And they likely won't deter the market from testing the dollar's all-time low in the coming weeks.

"I think this trend is still intact for the dollar to go down. It's been around for several weeks, and there's nothing to change that," Mr. Cambria said.

Observers said this year's G-7 communique was more significant for what it didn't say, rather than its actual contents. The statement, issued around midday in Europe, indicated to the currency market that "all around, things are pretty much status quo" in the U.S., Germany, Japan, Britain, France, Canada, and Italy, said Peter Iversen, a trader for Shawmut Bank of Boston NA. Those seven countries make up the G-7.

Unlike G-7 statements issued in January and April, the latest contained no specific reference to the yen. In its previous statements, the G-7 frowned upon the yen's weakness, calling it an undesirable factor in the global economy.

Traders and analysts said the lack of a strongly unified call by the G-7 for a stronger yen was somewhat surprising, especially after Japan on Wednesday released figures that continued to show a ballooning trade surplus. A stronger yen would, in theory, help shrink that surplus by making Japanese goods more expensive abroad while making imports more attractive to Japanese consumers.

The absence of a reference to the yen in the communique weakened the yen against the dollar and mark, and left many observers wondering whether the Bank of Japan has any room to ease monetary policy.

Late in New York, the mark changed hands at 83.78 yen, well above 83.29 yen on Tuesday. During the session the mark set a new 1992 peak of 83.91 yen.

With the economic summit now concluded, traders said the market's attention will return to the U.S. economy and today's release of the weekly jobless claims and money supply reports. Market watchers said participants will be paying close attention to jobless claims data in the next several weeks in the wake of the surprisingly bleak June employment report.

According to an average of estimates from economists surveyed by Dow Jones Capital Markets Report, initial claims for state unemployment benefits are seen falling 4,000 to 416,000 in the week ended June 27. The market isn't expected to regard the jobless claims figure favorably until the total drops below 400,000.

The closely watched M2 aggregate of money supply is expected to contract by $4 billion in the week ended June 29 after failing by $10.6 billion the previous week. The M2 growth rate is currently running at 1.3% from the fourth quarter 1991 base, well below the Fed's targeted range of 2.5% to 6.5%. M2 consists of cash and all private deposits except very large ones left for a specified period of time. It also includes certain short-term assets such as the amounts held in money-market mutual funds.

Also on Wednesday, the Canadian dollar firmed after a breakthrough. in constitutional reform talks late Tuesday. The Canadian government and nine of the country's 10 provinces agreed on major constitutional changes aimed at keeping Quebec in Canada.

The agreement would constitutionally recognize French-speaking Quebec as a distinct society. It also would provide for a Senate with equal representation for all provinces.

"I think this agreement more than anything, just limits the weakness rather than providing strength" to the Canadian currency, said Dave Glowacki, a senior trader for National Bank of Detroit.

Late in New York, the U.S. dollar was quoted at C$1.1916, down from C$1.1948 a day earlier.

European Trading

The dollar was bolstered in European trading earlier Wednesday after U.S. Treasury Secretary Nicholas Brady said the G-7 and U.S. aren't encouraging a weaker currency. But it slipped again in late trading.

The currency fetched 1.4965 marks late Wednesday, off from 1.4985 marks late Tuesday. The dollar also was trading at 124.80 yen, up from 124.45 yen a day earlier.

Source: *The Wall Street Journal,* Thursday, July 9, 1992.

EXHIBIT 6B

Future Of Dollar Darkens

Further Falls Seen As Unit Tumbles

By Erik Ipsen

International Herald Tribune

LONDON - The dollar suffered another bruising day against the Deutschemark on Wednesday, as hopes for a pickup in the U.S. economy continued to recede.

"The latest figures all suggest yet another false dawn for the American recovery," said Jane Edwards, senior international economist at Lehman Brothers International.

With no growth spurt in America to boost or even to stabilize interest rates, and with no sign from Germany that it will cut its interest rates, the huge gap between the two is proving irresistible. "If interest rates are 3 percent in the U.S. and 10 percent in Europe, it is easy to see where I'd like to have my money," said Steven Bell. chief economist with Morgan Grenfell.

In late London trading, the dollar declined to 1.4950 Deutsche marks from Tuesday's close of 1.4990, after meeting a 17-month low during the day of 1.4760 DM. But it edged up to 124.675 yen, from 124.305 yen.

In New York, the currency was also weaker against the mark, closing at 1.4897 DM, down from 1.4903 DM. But it was slightly higher against other major currencies, gaining to 124.78 yen from 124.05, to 5.0165 French francs from 5.0160, and to 1.3425 Swiss francs from 1.3406. The British pound stood at $1.9277, down from the previous day's $1.9332.

Most foreign exchange traders think that the dollar will soon test its all-time low of 1.4460 DM, set in February 1991. With the interest rate gap widely expected to persist well into next year, the dollar looks like its in for a long, hard slog. In fact, some economists argue that the only reason that the American currency has not fallen even further and faster is that it has already fallen too far. "The dollar is greatly undervalued if you look at purchasing power parity," said David Twynam, a currency trader with Swiss Bank Corp.

Many economists calculate that on the basis of purchasing power parity, the dollar ought to be worth around 2 DM. American tourists stepping off planes from Manchester to Madrid will note almost instantly that their currency has seen far better days.

Nonetheless, most economists argue that a further drop in the currency is desirable.

Calling it fairly "benign," Mr. Bell said "it helps the two key countries - the U.S. and Germany - with their No. 1 problems."

For the Americans, a lower dollar should give the economy a boost, he said. By making its exports less expensive it will boost U.S. competitiveness and sales in international markets. For the Germans the fact that basic commodities such as oil are priced in dollars means that the cheaper dollar will help to keep inflation under control.

Political uncertainties in the United States will test the benevolent decline theories in coming weeks.

Many currency traders fear that the Federal Reserve Board will cut interest rates in the early autumn in one last stab at setting the economy on its feet again before the November election. "Politicians will be concerned with letting the economy moving not the fate of the dollar." said Ms. Edwards.

Against the yen, the outlook for the dollar is a bit cloudier. With Japanese overnight interest rates currently around 4.75 percent versus 3.3 percent in the U.S., the gap is not overpowering.

Not all observers said they felt the Japanese were keen to do whatever they could to maintain a strong yen and thus reduce their politically embarrassing current-account surplus. "By cutting interest rates and stimulating domestic demand the Japanese will be able to tackle their current-account problem," said Ifty Islam, a currency strategist with Barclays de Zoete Wedd.

Source: *International Herald Tribune,* July 8, 1992.

EXHIBIT 7
Real Effective Exchange Rate: Value of the U.S. Dollar versus 40 Currencies

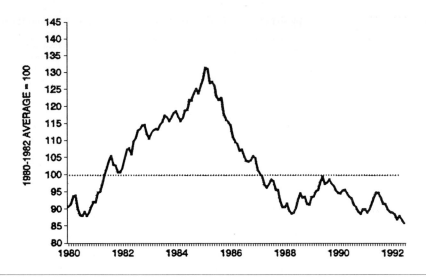

Source: World Financial Markets, Morgan Guaranty Trust Company.

The index number 100 represents the average value of the dollar in 1980–1982 as measured against the currencies of the 40 principal U.S. trading partners, each weighted by its relative importance.

"The *Economist's* Big Mac index was first launched in 1986 as a ready reckoner to whether currencies are at their "correct" exchange rate. It is time for our annual update.

The case for munching our way around the globe on Big Macs is based on the theory of purchasing-power parity. This argues that the exchange rate between two currencies is in equilibrium when it equalizes the prices of an identical basket of goods and services in both countries. Advocates of PPP argue that in the long run currencies tend to move towards their PPP".

"The Big Mac PPP is the exchange rate that leaves hamburgers costing the same in each country. Comparing the current exchange rate with its PPP gives a measure of whether a currency is under- or over-valued.

For example, the average price of a Big Mac in four American cities is $2.19. In Japan our Big Mac watcher had to fork out ¥380 ($2.86) for the same gastronomic delight. Dividing the yen price by the dollar price gives a Big Mac PPP of $1=¥174. On April 10th the actual dollar exchange rate was ¥133, which implies that on PPP grounds the dollar is 24% undervalued against the yen".

"Some readers find the Big Mac index hard to digest. To be sure, hamburgers are primitive predictors of exchange rates. Local price differences may be distorted by taxes, property costs or trade barriers. Nevertheless, the Big Mac can provide a rough and ready guide to how currencies might move over the long term. Experts who calculate PPPs by more sophisticated means come up with results that are not radically different. Indeed, many of them suggest that the dollar is even more under-valued than the hamburger standard indicates".

- Excerpts from *The Economist*, April 18th, 1992

The hamburger standard

Big Mac prices Country	Prices* in local currency	Implied PPP** of the dollar	Actual exchange rate 10/4/92	% over(+) or under(-) valuation of dollar
Argentina	Peso3.30	1.51	0.99	–34
Australia	A$2.54	1.16	1.31	+13
Belgium	BFr108	49.32	33.55	–32
Brazil	Cr3,800	1,735	2,153	+24
Britain	£1.74	0.79	0.57	–28
Canada	C$2.76	1.26	1.19	–6
China	Yuan6.30	2.88	5.44	+89
Denmark	DKr27.25	12.44	6.32	–49
France	FFr18.10	8.26	5.55	–33
Germany	DM4.50	2.05	1.64	–20
Holland	Fl5.35	2.44	1.84	–24
Hong Kong	HK$8.90	4.06	7.73	+91
Hungary	Forint133	60.73	79.70	+31
Ireland	I£1.45	0.66	0.61	–8
Italy	Lire4,100	1872	1,233	–34
Japan	¥380	174	133	–24
Russia	Rouble58	26.48	98.95†	+273
Singapore	S$4.75	2.17	1.65	–24
S.Korea	Won2,300	1,050	778	–26
Spain	Ptas315	144	102	–29
Sweden	SKr25.50	11.64	5.93	–49
United States††	$2.19	—	—	—
Venezuela	Bs 170	77.63	60.63	–22

Source: McDonald's. * prices may vary locally. ** Purchasing-power parity; local price divided by dollar price. † Market rate. †† New York, Chicago, San Francisco and Atlanta

EXHIBIT 8A
Currency and Options Markets

CURRENCY TRADING

Tuesday, July 7, 1992

EXCHANGE RATES

The New York foreign exchange selling rates below apply to trading among banks in amounts of $1 million and more, as quoted at 3 p.m. Eastern time by Bankers Trust Co., Telerate and other sources. Retail transactions provide fewer units of foreign currency per dollar.

Country	U.S. $ equiv. Tues.	U.S. $ equiv. Mon.	Currency per U.S. $ Tues.	Currency per U.S. $ Mon.
Argentina (Peso)	1.01	1.01	.99	.99
Australia (Dollar)	.7422	.7443	1.3473	1.3435
Austria (Schilling)	.09521	.09398	10.49	10.64
Bahrain (Dinar)	2.6522	2.6522	.3771	.3771
Belgium (Franc)	.03258	.03214	30.69	31.11
Brazil (Cruzeiro)	.00029	.00029	3460.21	3430.00
Britain (Pound)	1.9325	1.9115	.5175	.5231
30-Day Forward	1.9213	1.9001	.5205	.5263
90-Day Forward	1.9016	1.8815	.5259	.5315
180-Day Forward	1.8734	1.8543	.5338	.5393
Canada (Dollar)	.8361	.8331	1.1960	1.2004
30-Day Forward	.8345	.8316	1.1983	1.2025
90-Day Forward	.8321	.8291	1.2018	1.2061
180-Day Forward	.8294	.8262	1.2057	1.2104
Czechoslovakia (Koruna)				
Commercial rate	.0368732	.0368732	27.1200	27.1200
Chile (Peso)	.002895	.002895	345.40	345.47
China (Renminbi)	.182815	.182815	5.4700	5.4700
Colombia (Peso)	.001722	.001722	580.64	580.64
Denmark (Krone)	.1745	.1721	5.7315	5.8100
Ecuador (Sucre)				
Floating rate	.000717	.000717	1394.00	1394.00
Finland (Markka)	.24606	.24284	4.0640	4.1180
France (Franc)	.19928	.19641	5.0180	5.0915
30-Day Forward	.19811	.19523	5.0478	5.1222
90-Day Forward	.19598	.19319	5.1026	5.1762
180-Day Forward	.19292	.19026	5.1835	5.2560
Germany (Mark)	.6709	.6616	1.4905	1.5115
30-Day Forward	.6672	.6579	1.4987	1.5200
90-Day Forward	.6605	.6514	1.5140	1.5351
180-Day Forward	.6508	.6422	1.5365	1.5572
Greece (Drachma)	.005488	.005423	182.20	184.40
Hong Kong (Dollar)	.12932	.12932	7.7325	7.7330
Hungary (Forint)	.0130293	.0130582	76.7500	76.5800
India (Rupee)	.03550	.03550	28.17	28.17
Indonesia (Rupiah)	.0004921	.0004921	2032.02	2032.02
Ireland (Punt)	1.7892	1.7641	.5589	.5669
Israel (Shekel)	.4164	.4194	2.4013	2.3846
Italy (Lira)	.0008877	.0008741	1126.53	1143.98
Japan (Yen)	.008058	.008045	124.10	124.30
30-Day Forward	.008050	.008037	124.22	124.42
90-Day Forward	.008040	.008027	124.38	124.58
180-Day Forward	.008035	.008022	124.45	124.65
Jordan (Dinar)	1.5207	1.5207	.6576	.6576
Kuwait (Dinar)	3.4614	3.4614	.2889	.2889
Lebanon (Pound)	.000587	.000587	1705.00	1705.00
Malaysia (Ringgit)	.4002	.3998	2.4987	2.5010
Malta (Lira)	3.3058	3.3058	.3025	.3025
Mexico (Peso)				
Floating rate	.0003210	.0003210	3115.75	3115.75
Netherland (Guilder)	.5951	.5870	1.6803	1.7037
New Zealand (Dollar)	.5437	.5445	1.8392	1.8365
Norway (Krone)	.1711	.1688	5.8430	5.9255
Pakistan (Rupee)	.0400	.0400	25.00	25.00
Peru (New Sol)	.8752	.8752	1.14	1.14
Philippines (Peso)	.04008	.04008	24.95	24.95
Poland (Zloty)	.00007741	.00007741	12918.01	12918.00
Portugal (Escudo)	.007997	.007909	125.05	126.44
Saudi Arabia (Riyal)	.26738	.26738	3.7400	3.7400
Singapore (Dollar)	.6198	.6203	1.6135	1.6120
South Africa (Rand)				
Commercial rate	.3637	.3625	2.7493	2.7583
Financial rate	.2558	.2525	3.9100	3.9600
South Korea (Won)	.0012721	.0012721	786.10	786.10
Spain (Peseta)	.010614	.010468	94.21	95.53
Sweden (Krona)	.1856	.1830	5.3885	5.4635
Switzerland (Franc)	.7460	.7386	1.3405	1.3540
30-Day Forward	.7423	.7349	1.3472	1.3608
90-Day Forward	.7357	.7285	1.3592	1.3727
180-Day Forward	.7262	.7192	1.3771	1.3904
Taiwan (Dollar)	.041186	.041152	24.28	24.30
Thailand (Baht)	.03954	.03954	25.29	25.29
Turkey (Lira)	.0001464	.0001461	6830.03	6843.00
United Arab (Dirham)	.2723	.2723	3.6725	3.6725
Uruguay (New Peso)				
Financial	.000316	.000316	3160.01	3160.01
Venezuela (Bolivar)				
Floating rate	.01522	.01523	65.70	65.65
SDR	1.44632	1.43898	.69494	.69494
ECU	1.37280	1.35490	....	....

Special Drawing Rights (SDR) are based on exchange rates for the U.S., German, British, French and Japanese currencies. Source: International Monetary Fund.

European Currency Unit (ECU) is based on a basket of community currencies.

ECU VALUES

The value of one ECU in terms of other currencies as reported by the European Community Commission.

Currency	Tue.	Prev.	Currency	Tue.	Prev.
Belg Fr.	42.153	42.148	D-Mark	2.0475	2.0476
Guilder	2.3082	2.3080	Pound Stg.	0.7097	0.7080
Dan Kr.	7.8740	7.8706	French Fr.	6.8909	6.8972
It Lira (100)	1547.0	1549.7	Irish Pound	0.7680	0.7678
Gr Drachma	250.37	249.86	Sp Peseta	129.38	129.39
Por Escudo	171.57	171.10	U.S. Dollar	1.3692	1.3520
Swiss Franc	1.8362	1.8353	Swed Kr.	7.4030	7.4032
Nor Kr.	8.0240	8.0268	Can Dollar	1.6386	1.6217
Aus Sch.	14.410	14.412	Fin-Mark	5.5839	5.5810
Aust Dollar	1.8404	1.8160	Nz Dollar	2.5138	2.4853
Malt Pound	0.4140	0.4125	Tur Lira	9471.4	9339.7
Yen	169.52	168.26			

TRADE-WEIGHTED VALUES

Morgan Guaranty Trust Co.'s trade-weighted currency statistics show a currency's percentage change against average market rates in the period 1980-82. The statistics show the devaluation or upvaluation of each currency against 15 other major currencies, weighted by each country's 1980 bilateral trade patterns.

Currency	Tue	Prev	Currency	Tue	Prev
Dollar	− 18.2	− 17.9	Sterling	− 18.9	− 19.1
D Mark	+ 26.3	+ 26.1	Fr Franc	− 10.8	− 11.1
Sw Franc	+ 16.5	+ 16.9	Lire	− 19.6	− 19.8
Yen	+ 77.9	+ 78.3	Nor Krone	− 15.5	− 15.7
Can Dlr	− 3.2	− 3.4			

OPTIONS

PHILADELPHIA EXCHANGE

Option & Underlying	Strike Price	Calls—Last Jul	Calls—Last Aug	Calls—Last Sep	Puts—Last Jul	Puts—Last Aug	Puts—Last Sep
50,000 Australian Dollars-cents per unit.							
ADollr	73	r	r	r	r	r	0.43
74.43	74	r	r	0.93	r	r	0.77
74.43	76	r	r	0.22	r	r	r
31,250 British Pounds-European Style.							
BPound	180	r	r	r	r	r	0.60
191.13	182½	9.40	r	8.35	r	r	r
191.13	187½	r	4.98	r	r	r	r
191.13	190	r	3.40	r	r	r	r
191.13	192½	r	r	r	r	3.60	r
191.13	195	r	r	r	r	3.18	r
191.13	197½	r	0.82	r	r	r	r
31,250 British Pounds-cents per unit.							
BPound	177½	r	r	r	r	r	0.34
191.13	185	r	r	6.98	r	0.76	1.61
191.13	187½	r	5.30	r	r	1.38	2.60
191.13	190	2.78	3.60	r	0.30	2.22	r
191.13	192½	1.16	r	3.05	0.90	r	4.85
191.13	195	0.28	r	r	2.65	r	r
191.13	197½	r	r	1.30	r	6.75	r
50,000 Canadian Dollars-cents per unit.							
CDollr	81	2.59	r	r	r	r	r
83.29	83½	0.15	0.27	r	r	r	r
83.29	84	r	0.13	0.26	r	r	r
83.29	85	0.02	r	r	r	r	r
250,000 French Francs-10ths of a cent per unit.							
FFranc	19¾	r	r	r	r	r	4.90
250,000 French Francs-European Style.							
FFranc	19¾	1.50	r	r	r	r	r
1,000,000 GermanMark-JapaneseYen cross.							
GMk-JYn	82	r	r	r	0.10	r	r
82.22	83	0.25	r	r	0.36	r	r
62,500 German Marks-European Style.							
DMark	61	r	r	5.05	r	r	r
66.14	62½	r	3.55	3.39	r	r	r
66.14	63	r	3.12	2.99	r	r	r
66.14	63½	r	2.68	2.50	r	r	r
66.14	64½	r	2.16	r	r	r	r
66.14	65	r	r	r	r	1.12	r
66.14	66	r	1.16	r	0.20	r	r
66.14	67	0.30	r	r	r	r	r
66.14	67½	r	r	r	r	1.75	r
66.14	68	r	r	r	r	2.03	r
66.14	69	r	0.24	r	r	2.81	r
66.14	70	r	0.13	r	r	r	r
62,500 German Marks-cents per unit.							
DMark	62	4.40	r	4.72	r	r	0.21
66.14	62½	r	r	r	r	r	0.25
66.14	63	3.73	3.31	3.30	r	0.14	r
66.14	63½	r	2.83	2.84	0.01	0.20	r
66.14	64	2.75	r	2.93	0.02	0.31	r
66.14	64½	2.26	3.00	r	r	0.37	r
66.14	65	r	r	0.96	0.34	0.51	r
66.14	65½	r	r	r	0.12	r	1.07
66.14	66	0.81	1.23	1.51	0.15	0.87	1.27
66.14	67	0.22	0.76	1.00	0.60	r	r
66.14	67½	0.15	0.57	0.54	0.86	r	r
66.14	68	0.10	0.44	0.65	r	1.96	r
66.14	68½	r	0.27	r	r	r	r
66.14	69	r	r	r	r	r	3.35
6,250,000 Japanese Yen-100ths of a cent per unit.							
JYen	78	r	r	r	r	0.21	r
80.45	78½	r	r	r	r	0.33	r
80.45	79	r	r	r	0.04	r	r
80.45	80	0.60	r	r	0.18	r	1.03
80.45	80½	0.30	0.96	1.19	0.45	1.86	1.40
80.45	81	0.16	0.73	r	r	r	r
80.45	82	r	r	0.75	r	r	r
6,250,000 Japanese Yen-European Style.							
JYen	79½	r	1.56	s	r	0.54	s
80.45	81	r	0.78	r	r	r	r
62,500 Swiss Francs-European Style.							
SFranc	66	r	r	r	r	r	0.06
73.85	71	r	r	r	r	0.28	r
73.85	72½	1.65	r	s	r	r	s
73.85	75	r	0.70	r	r	r	r
62,500 Swiss Francs-cents per unit.							
SFranc	69	r	5.50	r	r	r	r
73.85	71	r	3.30	3.27	r	0.32	r
73.85	71½	r	r	r	r	r	0.69
73.85	72	r	2.54	r	r	0.50	0.87
73.85	72½	r	r	s	r	0.63	s
73.85	73	r	r	r	r	r	1.24
73.85	74	0.65	r	r	0.47	r	r
73.85	74½	0.39	r	1.25	r	r	r
73.85	75	0.32	0.56	0.94	r	r	r
73.85	75½	r	r	r	1.14	r	r
73.85	76	r	0.56	r	r	r	r

Total Call Vol 29,658   Call Open Int 247,571
Total Put Vol 39,477   Put Open Int 539,131

Source: *The Wall Street Journal Europe,* July 8, 1992.

EXHIBIT 8B

CURRENCY

Currency Futures Contracts

	Open	High	Low	Settle	Change	Lifetime High	Lifetime Low	Open Interest
JAPAN YEN (IMM)—12.5 million yen; $ per yen (.00)								
Sept	.8030	.8067	.8000	.8046	+ .0017	.8090	.7265	52,191
Dec	.8057	.8057	.7987	.8036	+ .0017	.8070	.7410	3,065
Mr93	...	...	...	.8036	+ .0016	.8050	.7445	2,140

Est vol 21,071; vol Mon 15,533; open int 57,396, +1,938.

	Open	High	Low	Settle	Change	Lifetime High	Lifetime Low	Open Interest
DEUTSCHEMARK (IMM)—125,000 marks; $ per mark								
Sept	.6528	.6641	.6503	.6639	+ .0102	.6641	.5685	65,868
Dec	.6513	.6549	.6490	.6543	+ .0101	.6549	.5645	6,110
Mr93	.6440	.6465	.6425	.6459	+ .0100	.6465	.5724	760

Est vol 52,713; vol Mon 36,981; open int 72,740, +7,996.

	Open	High	Low	Settle	Change	Lifetime High	Lifetime Low	Open Interest
CANADIAN DOLLAR (IMM)—100,000 dlrs.; $ per Can $								
Sept	.8325	.8338	.8322	.8337	+ .0038	.8774	.8191	21,240
Dec	.8291	.8300	.8291	.8303	+ .0038	.8740	.8130	992
Mr93	...	...	...	.8274	+ .0038	.8712	.8115	237

Est vol 2,869; vol Mon 2,261; open int 22,506, −125.

	Open	High	Low	Settle	Change	Lifetime High	Lifetime Low	Open Interest
BRITISH POUND (IMM)—62,500 pds.; $ per pound								
Sept	1.9072	1.9110	1.8986	1.9104	+ .0222	1.9110	1.6490	27,347
Dec	1.8770	1.8830	1.8704	1.8820	+ .0218	1.8830	1.6280	832
Mr93	1.8550	1.8570	1.8550	1.8570	+ .0212	1.8570	1.7620	138

Est vol 12,856; vol Mon 9,751; open int 28,317, −532.

	Open	High	Low	Settle	Change	Lifetime High	Lifetime Low	Open Interest
SWISS FRANC (IMM)—125,000 francs; $ per franc								
Sept	.7377	.7394	.7327	.7391	+ .0081	.7394	.6335	29,871
Dec	.7280	.7300	.7230	.7295	+ .0078	.7300	.6280	685

Est vol 21,460; vol Mon 14,092; open int 30,619, −946.

	Open	High	Low	Settle	Change	Lifetime High	Lifetime Low	Open Interest
AUSTRALIAN DOLLAR (IMM)—100,000 dlrs.; $ per A.$								
Sept	.7401	.7415	.7392	.7394	− .0015	.7610	.7388	1,814

Est vol 132; vol Mon 675; open int 1,928, +272.

	Open	High	Low	Settle	Change	Lifetime High	Lifetime Low	Open Interest
U.S. DOLLAR INDEX (FINEX)—1,000 times USDX								
Sept	84.24	84.33	83.13	83.14	− 1.07	94.20	83.13	4,410
Dec	85.50	84.86	84.75	84.44	− 1.02	94.93	84.75	416

Est vol 3,750; vol Mon 1,734; open int 4,827, +162.
The index: High 83.24; Low 82.15; Close 82.15 −.98

Futures and Options Markets

CURRENCY

Currency Futures Options Contracts

JAPANESE YEN (IMM)
12,500,000 yen; cents per 100 yen

Strike Price	Calls—Settle Aug	Sep	Oct	Puts—Settle Aug	Sep	Oct
7900	1.54	1.85	....	0.40	0.71	....
7950	1.21	1.54	....	0.57	0.90	....
8000	0.94	1.27	1.52	0.80	1.13	1.49
8050	0.70	1.04	....	1.06	1.40	....
8100	0.52	0.84	....	1.38	1.70	....
8150	0.38	0.68	....	....	....	....

Est. vol. 3,903;
Tues vol. 1,500 calls; 4,026 puts
Op. int. Tues 21,013 calls; 27,607 puts

DEUTSCHEMARK (IMM)
125,000 marks; cents per mark

Strike Price	Calls—Settle Aug	Sep	Oct	Puts—Settle Aug	Sep	Oct
6550	1.56	1.86	....	0.59	0.89	....
6600	1.26	1.58	1.18	0.79	1.11	....
6650	0.99	1.30	....	1.02	1.33	....
6700	0.77	1.09	....	1.30	1.62	....
6750	0.58	0.89	....	....	....	....
6800	0.43	0.73	....	....	2.26	....

Est. vol. 38,873;
Tues vol. 11,288 calls; 15,250 puts
Op. int. Tues 124,636 calls; 153,736 puts

CANADIAN DOLLAR (IMM)
100,000 Can.$, cents per Can.$

Strike Price	Calls—Settle Aug	Sep	Oct	Puts—Settle Aug	Sep	Oct
8250	....	1.32	....	0.07	0.19	....
8300	0.78	0.94	....	0.15	0.31	....
8350	0.45	0.63	....	0.32	0.50	....
8400	0.23	0.40	....	0.60	0.77	....
8450	0.10	0.24	....	0.97	....	....
8500	0.03	0.12	....	....	1.48	....

Est. vol. 833;
Tues vol. 422 calls; 516 puts
Op. int. Tues 7,635 calls; 7,884 puts

BRITISH POUND (IMM)
62,500 pounds; cents per pound

Strike Price	Calls—Settle Aug	Sep	Oct	Puts—Settle Aug	Sep	Oct
1850	6.50	7.16	....	0.78	1.50	....
1875	4.64	5.46	4.72	1.40	2.28	....
1900	3.12	4.04	....	2.38	3.32	....
1925	1.96	2.88	....	3.70	4.64	....
1950	1.16	1.98	....	5.40	....	....
1975	0.66	1.30	....	7.36	....	....

Est. vol. 2,236;
Tues vol. 540 calls; 797 puts
Op. int. Tues 12,107 calls; 10,292 puts

SWISS FRANC (IMM)
125,000 francs; cents per franc

Strike Price	Calls—Settle Aug	Sep	Oct	Puts—Settle Aug	Sep	Oct
7300	1.66	2.01	....	0.75	1.10	....
7350	1.36	1.72	....	0.95	1.31	....
7400	1.11	1.47	....	1.20	1.56	....
7450	0.89	1.25	....	1.48	....	....
7500	0.70	1.05	....	....	....	....
7550	0.55	....	....	....	....	....

Est. vol. 2,668;
Tues vol. 4,667 calls; 1,774 puts
Op. int. Tues 15,615 calls; 19,724 puts

MARK/YEN CROSS RATE (CME)
125,000 marks; yen per mark

Strike Price	Calls—Settle Aug	Sep	Oct	Puts—Settle Aug	Sep	Oct
8200	1.40	1.69	....	....	0.78	....
8250	....	....	....	....	....	....
8300	0.83	1.15	....	....	....	....
8350	0.63	....	....	....	....	....
8400	0.47	0.76	....	....	....	....
8450	....	....	....	....	....	....

Est. vol. 32;
Tues vol. 60 calls; 0 puts
Op. int. Tues 1,602 calls; 1,373 puts

Source: *The Wall Street Journal Europe*, July 8, 1992.

CASE 14

VIDEOTON (A)

1   Videoton began as a shotgun cartridge manufacturer in 1938 and was nationalized by the Communists a few years later. Mass production of radios began in 1955, and television sets in 1959. The assembly of computers started in the following decade, and the manufacture of computer peripherals was added in the 1970s. In the economic liberalization introduced by the New Economic Mechanism (discussed below), Videoton was granted the right to trade with the West on its own account through a captive foreign trade company (FTO). The bulk of its sales remained, however, within the socialist bloc.

2   By the late 1980s, Videoton was a diversified group employing 20,000 with sales totaling HuF 21.5 billion (about US$ 300 million). A rationalization program implemented in late 1989 and early 1990, combined with natural attrition and an early-retirement program, reduced the workforce to about 14,000.

3   Most of Videoton's business fell into one of three core areas: consumer electronics, including television, audio, and compact disc production; defense electronics, essentially communication and control equipment for the Warsaw Pact armed forces; and computer hardware and software, with specialization in process control equipment for Soviet natural-resource industries (mining, petroleum exploitation, distribution of electricity), and the mass production of line and dot-matrix printers. The five-year plan for the first half of the 1990s/projected a large and profitable quota for sales of television sets to the USSR, and an ambitious investment program was well underway to meet it.

THE HUNGARIAN ECONOMIC SYSTEM: FROM PLAN TO MARKET

4   The Stalinist command system that dominated Hungary's economy for its first 20 years under Communism gradually gave way to a more liberal system with the introduction of the New Economic Mechanism (NEM) in 1968. There had been earlier efforts at reform, but they were severely limited both in scale and in scope; little more was done than to encourage private handicraft and retail trade. In 1968, however, the emphasis was on unfettering enterprises in the state sector.

5   Although the economy remained largely controlled and directed by the "plan," the NEM introduced important elements of autonomy to enterprise managers. Horizontal links between state-owned firms, in contrast to vertical linkages between firms and the state bureaucracy, strengthened. Bureaucratic and party interference was common, but the beginnings of genuine market contracting between firms regarding prices, quality standards, and delivery dates were visible. Firms also received increased autonomy, although not freedom from bureaucratic interference, regarding their choices of technology.

6   As administrative controls were relaxed, pricing policy changed—not to a system of "free market pricing," certainly, but to a system of relative pricing that was closer to world markets than in other socialist bloc countries. For many goods, a "cost-plus" pricing formula was required, with strict rules on how costs should be calculated and what profit margins would be permitted. Nevertheless,

This case was written by S. David Young, Associate Professor at INSEAD, with the assistance of Thomas Howell, Research Associate. It is intended to be used as a basis for class discussion rather than to illustrate either effective or ineffective handling of an administrative situation. Financial support from the INSEAD Alumni Fund European Case Programme is gratefully acknowledged.
Reprinted with the permission of INSEAD.

even when prices were decided within the firm, they were still subject to influence, and sometimes even veto, by bureaucratic authorities.

7   The NEM also increased the firm's discretion over investment decisions. Although the bulk of investment capital continued to be centrally, and thus politically, allocated, a substantial fraction of profits could be retained for investment purposes. It has been estimated that, as of the mid-1980s, about one-fifth of capital investments were decided at the firm level and financed exclusively from retained profits. The central bureaucracy's control over capital investment, therefore, remained decisive.

8   To summarize, the NEM granted managers of state-owned enterprises (SOEs) a degree of autonomy substantially greater than was possible in Hungary prior to 1968 and greater than their counterparts enjoyed elsewhere in the Soviet bloc at the time. The position of large-company managements grew stronger still throughout the 1970s and into the 1980s. The Hungarian Socialist Workers' (i.e., Communist) Party (hereafter, the Party), accepted that while central planning might work passably well for simple commodities such as coal or wheat, the same could not be said for complex industrial products requiring numerous inputs. Therefore, the Party encouraged, or at the very least did not resist, the trend toward less central control. The Party could see that the coordination effort required for even a modest product range stretched the bureaucracy to breaking point. Moreover, decentralization was acceptable because power was largely transferred to people who were themselves senior members of the Party.

9   Under this system, all important aspects of managerial decision making—e.g., entry, exit, output, input, wages, investment—were subject to a seemingly endless series of negotiations and lobbying efforts with bureaucratic and Party authorities. The Hungarian economist, Janos Kornai, sums up the situation nicely: "The firm's manager watched the customer and the supplier with one eye and his superiors in the bureaucracy with the other." When Kornai speaks of "bureaucracy," of course, he means "the Party."

10   Through all of these changes, the CMEA (Council for Mutual Economic Assistance, or COMECON) continued to exert a profound influence on economic activity in its member states. Based in Moscow, the CMEA functioned as the planning apparatus for the entire Soviet bloc. For Hungary, the planning apparatus had three tiers—the CMEA in Moscow, the National Planning Office in Budapest, and the corporate planning departments at the enterprise level. In the case of televisions, for example, Moscow dictated the number of sets Hungary was to make and specified how many sets were to be black and white and how many color. The planning office in Budapest allocated this quota between Hungary's two domestic producers, one of which was Videoton. Huge administrative and planning departments in each company then worked out their own plans to ensure that the target was met.

11   In addition to planning the final level of products, the CMEA and National Planning Office clearly had to provide for inter-enterprise trade in the various raw materials, components, and subassemblies needed to complete production. The nature of the various relationships that existed between enterprises in this supply chain influenced the forms the organizations assumed. Generally speaking, if the relationship was between a Hungarian enterprise such as Videoton and an enterprise within the CMEA but in a different country, the supplier and purchaser had no contractual relationship; both merely obeyed the plan. Even payment was effected centrally and cleared in "soft" roubles. This clearing system acted as a form of trade finance with suppliers paid (in local currency) by the trading agency on delivery, which allowed the enterprise to avoid credit risk. Because no direct contractual relationship existed, neither did any legal recourse to enforce the terms of delivery, such as timing or quality, nor could a different specification to that envisaged in the plan be ordered. The only possible remedy for defects was via political channels (if the unsuitability of input was particularly obvious) or through personal connections and exchange of favors among the mangers of the transacting companies. Such control was generally weak, however. Companies lessened the risks of dependence on outside supply by establishing departments to rectify faulty inputs and by holding large buffer inventories.

12   For defense electronics parts, the planning process required the placement of orders at least two years in advance. Civil protection was slightly more flexible, but lead times were still at least several months. A buyer might have to wait several weeks for a required product even if it had already been manufactured and was waiting in stock at the supplier's premises.

13　　If both the supplier and purchaser were Hungarian, an enforceable contract did exist, at least in theory. Because manufacturers were generally dependent on designated suppliers, however, the cumbersome legal apparatus was rarely used to enforce contracts. Accusations and litigation could threaten a breakdown of the ongoing business relationship, and the supplier's power to withhold supplies long enough to prevent the manufacturer achieving plan targets was too great to risk a breach. Orders could be placed directly with suppliers for above-quota (surplus) production and would be delivered in a reasonably quick manner. On the other hand, if current production was already allocated, the lead time was about one year.

14　　As for trade with Western companies, all transactions had to take place through licensed FTOs, also known as Impexes (because they handled imports and exports). The system was created to regulate access to foreign exchange, always in scarce supply because of Hungary's artificially high exchange rates. One of the many distorting effects of this system was to insulate manufacturers from contact with sophisticated Western markets, adding technological obsolescence to the cost-management problems that arise whenever achieving production targets takes precedence over profits. The government used the FTOs to sell to, then collect the hard currency from, Western customers. The FTOs also arranged imports of components and materials available only in the West. An enterprise was eligible for hard-currency imports up to 70–75 percent of its hard-currency sales. Components were imported from the West usually for technological rather than cost reasons, particularly after the microchip revolution gained momentum and the socialist bloc slipped farther and farther behind technologically.

15　　To complicate matters for Hungarian enterprises, the key Soviet market was lost almost completely beginning in 1989. The Hungarians became increasingly wary of their escalating soft-rouble trade surplus with the USSR. In effect, the surplus was a free loan to the Soviets, because the CMEA envisaged rough parity of trade flows and had no mechanism for the settlement of imbalances. From the beginning of 1991, as part of the dismantling of the CMEA, the governments of the region decided that trade had to be denominated and settled in American dollars. The Soviets may have been earning dollar prices for their oil, but their internal problems left almost no hard currency for finished-goods imports from their former socialist allies.

VIDEOTON: GENERAL BACKGROUND

16　　The NEM allowed companies such as Videoton greater say in the planning process than previously, but until the 1980s, any input from Videoton in terms of what it required and what it was to supply still had to be approved by the National Planning Office. In addition, freedom from the planning process was largely (though not entirely) illusory because of Videoton's dependence on other (still planned) CMEA markets for most of its sales. As one of its managers said, "We had the freedom to sell them more but they did not have the freedom to buy."

17　　Before the introduction of the NEM, all Videoton prices were centrally (i.e., bureaucratically) determined. Data covering materials and labor cost had to be submitted to the Ministry of Industry, which set the prices without further discussion. In the 1970s, the system was modified to free domestic prices within limits. Indeed, after an agonizing public debate, even a small "profit" was permitted in pricing. Later reforms allowed Videoton and other large companies to submit their own plans without the need for approval. This policy change was made possible by economic reforms that partially decentralized the planning function. In Videoton's case, the company's requirements and sales were sometimes negotiated directly with representatives from CMEA member states. Thus, Videoton was able to coordinate much of its nonmilitary buying and selling activities without intervention from the national planning authorities. The company plan presented to the Hungarian National Planning Office was a "done deal"; any further planning effort, at least for the activities prearranged by Videoton, would have been superfluous. Of course, military contracts (an important part of Videoton's business) continued to be negotiated at the governmental level.

18　　While these changes reflected growing economic liberalism on the part of the government, they also demonstrated the increasing power, relative to the government's planning bureaucracy, of large hard-currency generating enterprises such as Videoton. In the 1970s and early 1980s, the Hungarian government borrowed heavily from the West, mainly to stock the shops and mollify the population. The growing influence of large companies resulted from this indebtedness.

19   By the late 1980s, a market was growing for trading above plan, or surplus, production, which introduced an additional element of flexibility for the company. Nevertheless, this system was still a long way from a "free" market in the sense that Videoton could simply buy whatever it wanted or modify output to accommodate shifts in costs or consumer preferences. The plan continued to represent the enterprise's main channel for ordering outside supplies, and for disposing of most of its output.

20   In addition, all of Videoton's senior managers and all decision makers in Hungary's planning apparatus were Party members and, therefore, subject to a variety of constraining influences. Boundaries between Party, bureaucracy, and enterprise were, as always, difficult to distinguish. Because of its strategic (i.e., military) importance, Videoton was directly controlled by the Ministry of Industry; all the top managers were employed and directly remunerated by the Ministry, which was effectively controlled by the Party. Although the Industry Minister had, in theory, the power to appoint senior management, no appointment would be made until after discussion with the "personnel department" at Party headquarters. Videoton's long-time chief executive (until late 1990, when he was fired by the democratically-elected government) was a member of the Party's Central Committee, one of Hungary's ruling organs under Communism.

21   Videoton enjoyed strong Party support (as, for example, in the allocation of funds for capital investment) chiefly because its performance was viewed, within the framework of Hungary's planning system, as highly successful. It was big (in itself a virtue), generated hard currency, and was of great strategic importance because it supplied electronics to the Warsaw Pact armed forces.

22   As political reform accelerated in the socialist bloc, Videoton came under severe pressure. It had borrowed heavily to invest in television production for the Soviet market, but this market was fast disappearing. Demand for defense electronics vanished almost overnight. In response, management, increasingly free from political control, started to reorganize the company in order to (1) create entities suitable as targets for Western investment and thus take advantage of the new law that allowed tax breaks for joint ventures formed with foreign investors, (2) create some sort of structural logic for its wide-ranging activities, and (3) find other activities for the defense electronics divisions. The resulting structure is shown in Exhibit 1; Exhibit 2 provides employment numbers and a brief description of each entity's activities.

23   These measures proved wholly insufficient in addressing the company's most fundamental problems. It was, for example, unable to service interest charges of 40 percent on its huge debt (compared with the 7 percent rate at which it had originally borrowed). Although the main bank creditor had granted the company a moratorium on interest and capital payments to give it time to complete negotiations on an offer for the whole group, this offer proved to be more illusory than real. Compounding Videoton's difficulties was the collapse of the CMEA trading system. Efforts to direct exports to the West were frustrated by high costs and EC restrictions on imports from Eastern Europe. Thus by the end of 1990, Videoton, allegedly one of the gems of Hungarian industry, found itself in grave difficulties.

HOW DID VIDEOTON GET THAT WAY?

24   Until the 1970s, the principal objective of Videoton's managers was to satisfy the plan, on which basis they were largely compensated, rewarded, and even promoted. Under the central planning system, the rewards came largely after the performance period in the form of lump-sum bonuses for the company to distribute among its employees. To link the reward more closely to the plan, this system was modified to include bonus advances for performance against monthly, quarterly, and six-month plans. These mini-bonuses could total up to 15 percent of annual salary for the half-dozen top executives who were directly remunerated by the state. By the late 1970s, the state began tying bonuses to achievement of other specified objectives such as inventory control and, later, a measure of "profit."

EXHIBIT 1
Videoton's Organizational Chart as of December 1990

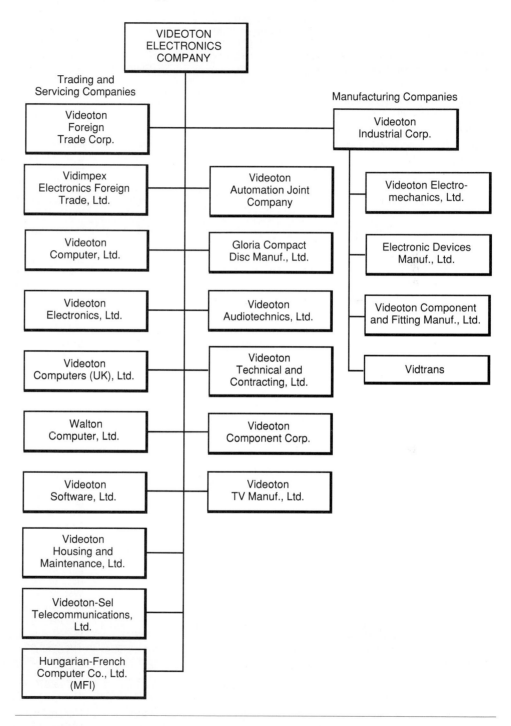

Source: KPMG, Videoton company literature.

EXHIBIT 2
The Videoton Group's Structure as of December 1990

Company Name	Number of employees at End of 1990	Majority Shareholder	Brief Description of Activities
Holding Company/Head Office			
Videoton Electronics Vallalat (VEV)	70	State	
Videoton Industrial Rt (VIRT)— Head Office Division	1,140	VEV	
Information Technology Group			
Videoton Bull Hungarian-French Computer Co., Ltd.	8	VEV	49% owned by Bull of France; planned to distribute Bull products in Eastern Europe and to mass-produce peripherals and PCs
Videoton Computer, Ltd.	150	VEV	The service and sales network for Videoton's former IT operations
Videoton Computers (UK), Ltd.	2	VEV	Inactive joint venture with a British company
Walton Computer, Ltd.	10	VEV	Joint venture with a British company since 1985 for the manufacture and sale of matrix printers
Videoton Software, Ltd.	30	VEV	Joint venture with a West German company; specializing in application program packages
Videoton Industrial Rt (VIRT)— Computer Division	1,650	VEV	Started with a contract to build French CII (now Bull) computers under license in 1969; manufactures "super-mini" computers, particularly for production management, printers (line and matrix), terminals and monitors, all under license; also, software production for specialist (process-control) applications
Consumer Electronics Group			
Videoton Audiotechnics, Ltd.	1,400	VEV	Loudspeaker and TV cabinets in wood and plastic; computer-technology casings; manufacture of loudspeakers (2 million per annum) and of completed loudspeaker/cabinet units (400,000 per annum) for own-label sales or for Akai and Fisher
Gloria Compact Disc Manufacturing, Ltd.	90	VEV	Relatively new-tech (1988) facility for the production of 6.5 million CDs per year; 95% of capacity contracted to four Western editing/publishing companies; largely independent of other group companies
Videoton Industrial Rt (VIRT)— TV Division & Videoton TV Manufacturing, Ltd.	1,190	VEV	Highly automated production line for TVs; 160,000 produced in 1989, although capacity 2 to 3 times this number; main products for screens, from 14″ to 37″, made under a license with Thomson of France
Videoton Electronics, Ltd.	490	VEV	National service network for TVs, with 28 service units and 19 shops countrywide; contracts for guarantee repairs for some Western goods sold in Hungary

EXHIBIT 2
(concluded)

Company Name	Number of employees at End of 1990	Majority Shareholder	Brief Description of Activities
Other Businesses*			
Videoton Industrial Rt (VIRT)— Radio Division	1,300	VEV	Military electronics
Videoton Industrial Rt (VIRT)— Chemical Division	650	VEV	Plastic injection, metal plating
Videoton-SEL Telecommunications, Ltd.	8	VEV	Joint venture with a German subsidiary of the French Alcatel Group, formed to build SYSTEM 12 digital telephone exchanges and other telecommunications equipment
Electronic Devices Manufacturing, Ltd.	1,610	VIRT	Manufacture of radio and electronic equipment capable of operating in "extreme conditions"
Videoton Automation Joint Company	970	VEV	Various licenses to build electronic and mechanical parts of electronically controlled machine tools
Videoton Electromechanics, Ltd.	280	VIRT	Radio telecommunication equipment, slot machines, and small agricultural machinery
Videoton Component and Fitting Manufacturing, Ltd.	1,370	VIRT	Sophisticated printed circuit boards (PCBs) and chemicals transportation
Videoton Technical and Contracting, Ltd.	460	VEV	Manufacture of single-purpose machines, maintenance and repair of machine tools and air-conditioning equipment; manufacture of iron structures; masonry, painting, joinery, and carpentry
Vidtrans	250	VEV	Providing transport services to the group
Videoton Components Corporation	340	VEV	Design and manufacture of multilayer PCBs
Videoton Housing and Maintenance, Ltd.	5	VEV	Maintenance of company housing
Trading Companies			
Videoton Foreign Trade Corporation	770	VEV	Foreign sales and imports
Vidimpex Electronics Foreign Trade, Ltd.	60	VEV	Foreign sales and imports

*These businesses represent largely an attempt to redeploy the 45% of the work force that was employed in "radio" operations, i.e., military electronics, before 1990.
Source: KMPG, Videoton company literature.

25   Through all of these changes, because achieving the plan in East bloc markets was vitally important to Videoton's bureaucratic sponsors, and because the enterprise could not sell its products in the West if components were of poor quality, the reliability of supply in terms of timing and quality remained critical. Cost efficiency was relatively unimportant, because costs could be passed on to CMEA consumers as part of what was, effectively, cost-plus pricing, and whether the price Western customers paid was profitable or not was secondary to the fact that the price was paid in hard currency. (Indeed, the very fact that the product could be sold for hard currency was considered adequate proof of its "profitability.")

26   In deciding whether to make something in-house for the next plan, Videoton managers made calculations on the basis of what was called "base cost" (materials and direct labor plus an overhead element related to direct labor). Thus, the cost of a company's administrative bureaucracy—a cost far higher in a socialist enterprise than in Western firms because of the layers of planners and Party officials—was implicitly assumed to be zero. Similarly, capital resources were assumed to be costless. In the extreme short term, the first of these assumptions may have been valid given the excess capacity inherent in a "full" employment economy, but once the capacity had been established, the company had no way to reduce it. Job reductions were rarely an option, nor was there much of a market for used plant and machinery; it was usually too dated to be of interest to the West, and there were no domestic competitors to sell to. In effect, the decision to make or buy was a one-way buy: "First we invested to establish capacity, then we had to find ways to fill it," as one Videoton financial executive admits. Moreover, no accounting rules for evaluating make-or-buy decisions were apparent, presumably because direct quantifiable factors were not really the key drivers of the decision. For example, a company accountant described what happened when he was asked to evaluate a decision to install productive capacity to build some television parts under license. His calculations showed that the investment would not be profitable: "I got into a lot of trouble. The decision had already been made by engineers and technical people, and accountants were only required after the event to justify it."

27   Given its captive markets, Videoton did not need to be at the leading edge of technology; the choice-starved socialist bloc customer was quite happy with last decade's model. Thus, Videoton did not have the research-and-development potential to innovate in product design. Instead, the 2,000 employees in the company's various R&D departments devised processes for manufacturing other companies' products and also served as a "fire-fighting force" to find solutions to problems which threatened the meeting of deadlines. The great diversity of R&D effort, covering all of Videoton's wide product range, resulted in insufficient focus for genuine product innovation. Long product life cycles in CMEA countries—for example, in 1989, the military communication equipment still used radio valves, obsolete in the West for a long time—meant that flexibility, the ability to change technologies and products nimbly, was an unnecessary virtue. Videoton depended on other people's technology, and this dependence accelerated in the 1980s as the entire socialist bloc, because of its inflexible, uninnovative industrial structures, fell farther and farther behind in the microchip revolution. (This failure also had an ideological angle: one Videoton executive recalls being taught at the Budapest Technical University in the 1950s the Stalinist view that the claimed development of computers was a ploy by the capitalists; it was still grimy, proletarian industrial mechanical engineering that really mattered.)

28   Videoton came to rely on a complex web of licenses and, later, joint ventures as technical input for all of its nonmilitary products. This web included arrangements for the manufacture of computer mainframes with the French computer company Bull; printers with Nokia of Finland and Dataproducts Corporation of the US; televisions with the French company Thomson; and several others. Licensing arrangements generally had a number of attractions for the Western grantor of the license: they provided revenue from obsolete products in the form of royalties and access to CMEA markets not otherwise open to them, and did so without threatening home markets; the terms of the licenses permitted sales only to specified countries or to Western markets within defined limits. Moreover, the license often required Videoton to source certain components from companies affiliated with the licensor.

29   Without this influx of Western technology, the company had little chance of producing products that were saleable in the West. Videoton's television sets before the Thomson license had a MTBF ("mean time between failures," a key reliability measure) of around 2,000 hours, unacceptable to Western consumers at almost any price. The license increased the MTBF to over 20,000 hours, which matched Thomson's home performance.

30   For Videoton, exports to the West were a means of earning the hard currency necessary to buy components available in sufficient quantities only in the West—for example, picture tubes. These components were needed to fill the hugely profitable quota of units allocated for sale to the Soviet Union. Thus Videoton was reconciled to making losses on sales of TVs to the West, variously estimated at up to 30 percent of the sales price, because foreign exchange, not profit, was the aim of the transactions. Exhibit 3 provides a breakdown of the costs of a typical TV set; it highlights both the

EXHIBIT 3
The Cost of a Videoton Television Set
1989 Model: a Thomson TS4352 (22″ screen)

	HuF
Imported parts (imported by VFTC)	14,874
Domestic parts (including those from VIRT Chemicals Division, Videoton Component, Ltd., Videoton Audiotechnical, Ltd., and other domestic suppliers)	6,466
Direct labor, including overtime and social security (contracted from Videoton TV Manufacturing, Ltd.)	457
Maintenance and tools	203
Total "direct cost"	22,000
TV factory overhead	798
Administration charge (including general expenses, R&D, and warranty costs)	9,902
Total cost	32,700

1989: 1 US$ = 62 HuF (approximately).
Source: VIRT Television Division.

interdependence among Videoton's operating divisions and the group's inability to produce TVs in a cost-effective manner. Translated at official exchange rates, the cost to manufacture a Videoton TV set was a staggering $500.

31   With the collapse of Communism came the strong possibility that Western companies would find licensing less attractive than before. They would either be permitted to sell directly into Eastern Europe on their own account, or would no longer enjoy favorable access to the former CMEA countries through Hungary (as all trade became dollar denominated). In addition to this undermining of the market-access justification for licensing, the justification that Eastern bloc customers were happy with yesterday's technology had become less relevant. As a result of the liberalization of imports, customers had no difficulty buying up-to-date (imported) technology and the obsolete (domestic) technology lost its appeal. Because new technology tended to deliver the same performance more cheaply than the old, the old technology licensed product, in fact, lost its only possible advantage—price.

32   As noted previously, exports had to be channeled through the government-licensed FTOs. Videoton was privileged in this regard, however; because of its size and importance, it owned and controlled two FTOs—the Videoton Foreign Trade Corporation (VFTC), and Vidimpex. VFTC was chiefly responsible for the sale and implementation of computer projects for foreign customers, most of whom came from CMEA countries. (Its Moscow staff numbered 500.) It also handled the sale of television sets to the West and after-sales service. Vidimpex dealt with above-plan barter activity and what were described as "optional product groups," which were basically *ad hoc* contracts filled using excess capacity.

33   Despite sharing the Videoton name, these FTOs were free-standing organizations located in Budapest, thus geographically removed from the manufacturing and R&D operations centered in Székesfehérvár. Their usefulness as a source of timely market feedback was questionable. One senior Videoton executive claims that new ideas for servicing markets never came from the FTOs. Product innovation was entirely driven by technical factors.

34   Moreover, Videoton management believed that it paid "about 15 percent too much" for Western components even before the FTOs' commission of 3 percent. Various theories were offered to explain this assertion, including alleged conspiracies by Western monopolists, poor negotiators who had no long-term relationships with suppliers, and order quantities that were too small by international standards to obtain the best quotes. Whatever the reason, having to pay 15 percent more than one's competitors for inputs was clearly a burden.

35   As for domestic sales, Videoton's share of the market for television sets was about 30 percent in early 1991, down from 65–70 percent in the 1960s. Until the 1980s, Videoton sales were channeled

entirely through state-owned wholesalers; later, sales were made increasingly through the company's countrywide service shops (up to 30 percent of the total), which had been reorganized into a stand-alone entity, Videoton Electronics, Ltd. A smaller proportion (5 percent) was sold directly to retailers.

GOING TO MARKET: OVERCOMING THE LEGACY OF SOCIALISM

36   The organizational structure of Videoton shown in Exhibits 1 and 2 reveals not only a highly vertically integrated firm, but also one with considerable product diversity. As one of its divisional directors commented, "Videoton did everything a company could do except mining." This tendency toward diversity accelerated in the immediate post-Communist period, as management sought ways, with only minimal industrial logic, to fill the capacity left by the collapse in demand for defense electronics (which in 1989 accounted for 45 percent of the group's employment). The 1989–90 reorganization was the result of management's half-hearted attempts to restructure the 40-year-old monolith they and their predecessors had built.

37   This structure proved unworkable, however, for several reasons. As noted by Western consultants who had personal knowledge of Videoton, first, the prime motivation for the creation of some of the divisional units was tax-driven, not based on an industrial strategy. Second, the company's transfer-pricing mechanism was complex, unreal, and bore little relationship to outside prices. Third, the company lacked an effective profit-center reporting and accountability system, and thus any ability to establish relative competitiveness or success. Finally, with the disappearance of central planning, no effective coordinated managerial control was in place over component and raw-material procurement, production, marketing and sales, or financial expenditure. In short, while the disadvantages of vertical integration were keenly felt, the advantages—opportunities for economies of scale, scope, and coordinated planning—were completely lacking. Thus, Videoton entered a transition period unprepared to accomplish the very task for which its structure had been rigged. In addition, excess capacity existed at almost every level of the production chain, because the 5-year plan for the first half of the 1990s allocated Videoton an even greater quota for sales to the Soviet Union than previously, and much of the necessary investment had already been committed.

38   The process to privatize Videoton began in this troubled environment. Legislation that was important in laying the groundwork for privatization was enacted while the Communists were still in power —for example, the law allowing the formation of privately owned economic associations such as limited liability joint-stock companies. A few privatizations did take place, but all were of the "spontaneous" variety, initiated by management and usually involving the transfer of assets at what the public perceived to be egregiously low prices. With the election of a non-Communist Hungarian government in March 1990, the privatization process began in earnest. Even before the election, public reaction to the sight of the old Communist nomenklatura unfairly enriching themselves in the transition to capitalism compelled the government to establish the State Property Agency (SPA) as a means of controlling the privatization process.

39   The SPA does not have the financial or managerial resources of, say, the Treuhandanstalt (the trust agency responsible for privatizing East German industry), and it was not designed to become a tool of industrial policy channeling government investment into chosen industries. Moreover, unlike the Treuhand, the SPA does not have explicit ownership rights over the enterprises in its charge. Rather, it represents the interests of the Hungarian government in the sell-off of SOEs; its responsibilities extend no further. Therefore, except in very specific circumstances, the SPA is not legally empowered to remove incompetent managers left over from the Communist era; the Treuhand, on the other hand, does have this power because it is the explicit, legally constituted owner of every company assigned to it. As discussed later, the SPA's limited authority has important implications for the restructuring and privatization of Hungarian SOEs such as Videoton.

40   The SPA's principal goal in privatizing Videoton, as with most other Hungarian enterprises, was to promote economic efficiency and thus contribute to a healthy, sustainable private sector. The SPA sought to transfer Videoton's assets into private hands quickly, with due concern for price, in order to initiate a process of enterprise restructuring guided by the needs and requirements of the market. Although unemployment in Hungary was beginning to accelerate, the SPA official in charge of the Videoton case decided in January 1991 that some job losses from the restructuring were politically

acceptable. The assumption was that price had priority over job savings. Nevertheless, many at the agency conceded that this acceptability would not last much longer.

41   The SPA was realistic about Videoton's prospects. By January 1991, the agency's staff thought that the company's chances of survival were less than 50 percent. Because of this fear, the SPA was seeking to remove Videoton from the agency's books as quickly as possible. The official responsible for Videoton was reconciled to the fact that any realistic sale proceeds would barely make a dent in the HuF 40–45 billion budgeted by the Hungarian government for privatization proceeds in 1991. At best, he hoped to sell Videoton for a price high enough to recover costs, including Western advisers' fees.

42   A critical aspect of Videoton's case was that the SPA was only one of those with a say in the group's fate; the creditors, management, and even the Industry Ministry, under whose supervision the company fell because of its earlier strategic significance, also had strong legal or actual power to influence the course of events. The creditors had to play a crucial role in any restructuring of Videoton. Because no conceivable outcome would result in a full, immediate return of the monies owed to them, the agreement of at least some important creditors to any proposed solution was necessary. In addition to trade creditors, other major creditors as of January 1991 included the Hungarian Credit Bank (HCB), Hungary's largest commercial bank, which was owed HuF 7.3 billion (about US$ 100 million) by the group, and three separate departments in the Ministry of Finance —taxation, customs duties, and social security payments. In total, the creditors from the Ministry were owed at least another HuF 5 billion. The HCB inherited the debt when the Central Bank's "assets" were divided up and granted to new commercial banks in order to create a new Western-style banking system.

43   Clearly the creditors' aim was to secure a maximum recovery of their debts. Hungarian banks, because of their exposure to SOEs, were badly undercapitalized, and to write off debts of this size would be extremely damaging to their balance sheets. Similarly, the Hungarian government could ill-afford large-scale non-recovery of taxation debts because of the impact on the budget deficit. Both the taxation and customs authorities sought to strengthen their legal positions by petitioning for the liquidation of the group. The SPA was powerless to stop this process, even though the petitions came from government departments.

44   Meanwhile, the position of Videoton's management, and its ability to obstruct any proposed restructuring of the company, was greatly strengthened by the 1989–90 reorganization, which stripped Videoton Elektronika Vallalat (VEV), the only Videoton entity directly owned by the state, of many of its productive assets, and replaced the assets with shareholdings in subsidiaries. The SPA's legal power covers only state-owned companies; the *Protection of State Property Act 1990* specifically excludes its interference in "economic associations" (such as joint stock companies), which is what these subsidiaries had become.

45   While Videoton's top-management team was hardly unanimous regarding Videoton's future, they shared a general reluctance to see the company for which they had all worked for so many years divided up into small units. A fairly typical response was articulated by the general director of the once-powerful VFTC: "In my 35 years with Videoton I have seen a concentration of human talent and physical assets unmatched in Hungary. Is allowing all this to perish really the best way to take the country into the twenty-first century?" This manager, long experienced in CMEA trade, believed that improved trade relations would reopen the Soviet market: "We cannot compete with Philips in their home market, but we can make televisions five times better than the Soviet Union can. We have a real competitive advantage there." This view was widely held by many of Videoton's managers and workers. Of course, it neglected to consider that the Soviets would have to pay for all imports, whether from Western Europe or Hungary, in hard currency. The Soviets would thus prefer Videoton's product only if it had cost or quality advantages.

46   As a further argument against breaking up the group, some senior managers stressed the indivisibility of the group's infrastructure. Previously, the decision to make instead of buy stretched to power, heating, water, and waste treatment. Other shared facilities included a yacht club on Lake Balaton (the popular Hungarian resort area), and ownership of a local soccer team. Enterprises throughout Eastern Europe, including Videoton, were like "company towns" in that their obligations—housing, day-care centers, sports facilities, and health clinics—made them social as well as economic organizations.

47   Like its managers, many of Videoton's workers seemed to be locked in a socialist time-warp; even in early 1991, a year after Hungary's democratic elections, a bust of Lenin still prominently stood in

the office of the head of Videoton's official trade union. The union leadership strongly supported keeping the Videoton group intact, because it would preserve the alleged benefits of cooperation and synergy between divisions. The union supported its arguments with practical suggestions to the government set out in an open letter to Jozsef Antall, Hungary's prime minister. Suggestions included better relations with the USSR and the revival of a working trade system between the two countries, cancellation of the group's debts, training and retraining programs for workers, and an industrial policy with subsidies, "such as in France," to improve facilities.

48   One important difference between the union's situation and that faced by unions in many other Hungarian SOEs was that Videoton, being under the direct supervision of the Industry Ministry had no "workers' council." This institution was created in SOEs by "industrial democracy" legislation in the early 1980s. The democratic element of the innovation was limited, because the councils were often stuffed with management and party appointees. Nevertheless, the presence of these councils has been known to impede privatization. The practical result of Videoton not having such a council was that its workers had less power than their counterparts elsewhere to hinder the restructuring of their company.

VIDEOTON: THE OPTIONS

49   Videoton's home, Székesfehérvár, one hour from Budapest, is also home to an ailing bus manufacturer, Ikarus, and a large aluminum works. By the beginning of 1991, these two companies had released thousands of workers, and the specter of massive regional unemployment made finding a solution for Videoton's problems politically as well as economically critical.

50   Therefore, in early 1991, KPMG, the international accounting and consulting firm, and James Capel, the London stockbroker and investment bank, were appointed to advise the SPA on the privatization of Videoton. KPMG's responsibility was to prepare full strategic and financial reviews of the company for use by the SPA in assessing options for the business. James Capel's role was to advise on implementation of the restructuring plans that emerged from the review, negotiate with potential purchasers, and manage the privatization of the group's activities. KPMG was not asked to value the business, but it was prepared to confirm whether any offer received was a "fair" price.

51   Among the options normally considered by the SPA for large SOEs, one was rejected outright: a public offering. Videoton was viewed as too unprofitable and debt ridden to justify a share flotation on even the most sophisticated stock markets, let alone the fledgling Budapest exchange. Three privatization approaches remained: trade sale of the entire company to a foreign buyer, break-up and sale of divisions to trade buyers or to divisional management, and an orderly liquidation.

Trade Sale

52   The attraction to senior management of a single sale of the whole group was that they perceived it as offering them a better chance of keeping at least part of their empires intact. For creditors, such a sale would have enabled a one-off (partial) settlement of debts as the price for their acquiescence to the sale, which would be preferable to their uncertain chances of any recovery in a more complex restructuring. On the other hand, a single sale to a single entity was no solution to the fundamental structural problems of the group (although one could argue that the restructuring dilemma would then fall to the buyer). Moreover, the rather unrealistic hope that a white knight would ride in to save the company delayed the taking and implementation of tough decisions.

Break-up and Piecemeal Sale

53   One option was to restructure the group on a unit-by-unit basis. To help provide the necessary information should this option be chosen, KPMG prepared balance sheets and income statements for each key Videoton operation (see Exhibits 4 and 5). Revenue forecasts for 1991 were estimated also, based on both actual revenues for the two months ended 28 February 1991 and unfilled contracts as of that date. These estimates are shown in Exhibit 6.

EXHIBIT 4

VIDEOTON GROUP
Balance Sheets
31 December 1990 (in Fr 000)

	VEV	VIRT 79.84%	Automation 61.51%	Audiotechnical 69.93%	Television Manufacturing 100.00%	Computer 100.00%	Electronics 100.00%	Components 60.00%	Gloria 55.00%	Technical & Contracting 100.00%	Components & Fitting 41.28%
Tangible fixed assets	3,512,220	4,046,735	981,296	382,474	127,084	29,048	107,196	1,303,050	775,118	197,849	185,999
Investments	9,780,604	733,300	4,100	1,00C	0	1,400	1,000	0	0	0	0
	13,292,824	4,780,035	985,396	383,474	127,084	30,448	108,196	1,303,050	775,118	197,849	185,999
Raw materials	8,806	2,440,062	955,262	240,157	80,065	68,535	272,094	73,374	32,579	145,058	91,201
Work in progress	1,593	469,069	136,471	31,951	2,908	0	14,862	5,165	1,720	23,145	17,203
Finished goods	0	491,927	65,671	107,226	0	0	178	3,350	11,203	0	6,729
	10,399	3,401,058	1,157,404	379,334	82,973	68,535	287,134	81,889	45,502	168,203	115,133
Domestic trade debtors	265,693	2,798,843	119,782	205,768	159,318	44,402	159,798	17,964	25,229	275,886	290,832
Overseas trade debtors	543,243	3,103,865	325,211	332,231	0	0	3,764	25,485	44,158	10,414	9,089
Other debtors	1,130,439	148,415	12,255	595	14,047	1,947	2,406	77,739	6,100	9,000	16,021
	1,939,375	6,051,123	457,248	538,594	173,365	46,349	165,968	121,188	75,487	295,300	315,942
Other assets	694,758	1,648,594	118,630	163,402	2	11,309	52,223	136,141	66,133	2,887	156
Cash	153,043	58,469	9,272	11,174	3,481	13,569	88,474	11,689	2,933	3,070	1,597
Total assets	16,090,399	15,939,279	2,727,950	1,475,978	386,905	170,210	701,995	1,653,957	965,173	667,309	618,827
Domestic trade creditors	519,801	1,702,402	154,982	518,503	11,654	17,079	303,576	174,893	13,739	53,465	58,673
Overseas trade creditors	16,259	1,870,614	0	60,089	0	0	1,205	23,097	3,983	1,933	0
	536,060	3,573,016	154,982	578,592	11,654	17,079	304,781	197,990	17,722	55,398	58,673
Short-term loans	324,730	2,164,158	135,115	52,640	0	0	30,000	69,300	0	66,882	29,448
Long-term loans	3,967,298	0	0	0	0	0	0	703,902	589,080	0	0
Taxes payable	114,364	5,618,680	362,880	372,209	3,150	4,791	109,828	148,621	90,874	57,320	79,079
Other liabilities	541,381	475,820	510,792	145,940	19,354	2,472	31,469	302,288	5,542	26,430	13,830
Net assets	10,606,566	4,107,605	1,564,181	326,597	352,747	145,868	225,917	231,856	261,955	461,279	437,797

EXHIBIT 4
(concluded)

Electronical Devices 79.84%	Electro-mechanics 79.84%	Vidtrans 59.88%	Housing & Maintenance 100.00%	Software 50.00%	Walton 50.00%	Foreign Trade Company 53.85%	Vidimpex 50.00%	MFI 51.00%	SEL 47.00%	Total	Adjustments	Total
0	0	2,113	239	10,794	9,050	13,992	61,024	20,900	2,602	11,768,783	0	11,768,783
0	0	0	0	0	0	1,000	23,711	0	0	10,546,115	(10,398,620)	147,495
404,050	0	2,113	239	10,794	9,050	14,992	84,735	20,900	2,602	22,314,898	(10,398,620)	11,916,278
89,775	37,695	17,020	252	3,930	20,920	21,221	266,559	228	558	5,179,626		5,179,626
89,775	23,166	0	0	0	0	0	0	0	0	817,028		817,028
7,307	36,893	0	0	0	3,664	0	0	0	0	734,148		734,148
501,132	97,754	17,020	252	3,930	24,584	21,221	266,559	228	558	6,730,802	(1,535,000)	5,195,802
534,264	28,491	29,806	1,237	6,302	99,089	24,919	458,415	296,824	3,137	5,845,999		5,845,999
67,471	27,460	0	0	7,810	3,769	10,097	403,837	0	2,973	4,920,877		4,920,877
3,273	5,400	35	19	72	21,789	48,511	225,265	0	168	1,723,496		1,723,49
605,008	61,351	29,841	1,256	14,184	124,647	83,527	1,087,517	296,824	6,278	12,490,372	(8,375,832)	4,114,540
8,788	0	326	0	201	9,149	3,437,821	4,777,740	344,274	232	11,472,766	0	11,472,766
129,646	3,985	22,331	1,825	13,794	35,817	364,563	1,804,863	256,151	4,792	2,994,538	0	2,994,538
1,244,574	163,090	71,631	3,572	42,903	203,247	3,922,124	8,021,414	918,377	14,462	56,003,376	(20,309,452)	35,693,924
765,285	38,135	22,095	53	7,115	14,342	56,568	460,353	96,679	6,034	4,995,426		4,995,426
0	0	0	0	559	23,334	2,088	461,685	23,930	0	2,488,776		2,488,776
765,285	38,135	22,095	53	7,674	37,676	58,656	922,038	120,609	6,034	7,484,202	(3,221,356)	4,262,846
50,000	0	2,591	0	0	0	0	0	0	0	2,924,864	0	2,924,864
4,200	0	0	0	0	1,403	0	0	0	0	5,265,883	0	5,265,883
10,957	4,805	1,217	69	602	25,117	8,361	99,773	122,481	2,455	7,237,633	0	7,237,633
43,005	4,451	9,136	2,563	2,809	1,915	3,768,089	6,649,276	36,753	9,105	12,602,420	2,800,000	15,402,420
371,127	115,699	36,592	887	31,818	137,136	87,018	350,327	638,534	(3,132)	20,488,374	(19,888,096)	600,278

Source: KPMG.

14-14

EXHIBIT 5
Videoton Operating Results
For the Year Ended 31 December 1990

	Income (Fm)	Operating Expenditure (Fm)	Profit/(loss) (Fm)
VEV	—	130	(130)
VIRT Television Factory			
VIRT Radio Factory	4,895	4,853	42
VIRT Chemical Factory	644	565	79
VIRT Head Office	697	758	(61)
VIRT Computer Factory	498	540	(42)
Automation	312	604	(292)
Audiotechnical	1,345	1,082	263
Television Limited	2,003	1,804	199
Electronics Limited	594	363	231
Gloria	332	299	33
Computer Limited	20	38	(18)
Components	80	596	(516)
Vidtrans	134	133	1
Housing and Maintenance	7	7	—
Technical & Contracting	291	285	6
Components & Fittings	625	544	81
Electromechanics	72	80	(8)
	12,528	11,732	796
Software	69	61	8
Walton	260	204	56
	13,908	13,915	(7)
Elimination of intra Group trading	(3,355)	(3,355)	—
Operating profit (before depreciation and finance charges)	10,550	10,560	(7)

Source: KPMG.

54   Much of the necessary reorganization of the company into business units had already been accomplished by Videoton's management in 1989–90. Several problems would still have to be dealt with, however, including the complications from assets legally owned by one unit but used by another (a common practice in many Hungarian companies because they had been only halfheartedly broken up into separate legal entities). A break-up strategy would involve one of the following choices: (1) a joint venture or trade sale of units with a long-term future but, in the short term, urgently needing investment capital and marketing expertise; (2) a management/employee buyout (MEBO), particularly for units capable of surviving on jobbing and sub-contracting work; or (3) some combination of the two. Regardless of which approach was chosen, businesses without a long-term future needed to be closed soon to stop the hemorrhaging of Videoton's dwindling resources.

55   While the higher levels of management were reluctant to let units of the group operate under separate ownership, attitudes at the divisional level were different. Not surprisingly, the happiest with the idea of freedom from central control were the managers of the more profitable divisions, and some of them adapted quickly to finding new sources of work for their underemployed workers. For example, the chemicals division of VIRT (see Exhibit 2) improved its sales outside the Videoton

EXHIBIT 6
Videoton Forecasted Revenues for 1991
As of 28 February 1991

	Forecasted Revenues (Fm)
VEV	470
VIRT Head Office	61
VIRT Television Factory	2873
VIRT Computer Factory	1103
VIRT Radio Factory	556
VIRT Chemical Factory	697
Automation	583
Audiotechnics	851
Television Limited	615
Computer Limited	85
Electronics Limited	165
Components	555
Gloria	144
Technical & Contracting	281
Components & Fittings	659
Electronic Devices	222
Electromechanics	74
Vidtrans	*
Housing and maintenance	6
Software	19
Walton	*

Forecasts for each unit are the sum of actual revenues for the first two months of 1991 and unfilled contracts as of 28 February 1991.
*Information not available.
Source: KPMG.

group to 50 percent of output; a year earlier only 5 percent was sold to outsiders. This additional work resulted largely from the efforts of a newly formed divisional marketing department. Videoton Audiotechnical Company Limited (kft) (VACL) moved quickly after the reorganization to terminate the loss-making manufacture of stereos, and restructured the remaining activities (TV cabinets, loudspeakers, and loudspeaker boxes), with 1,400 workers, to make 3 clear operating units. VACL's quality assurance procedures were stringent enough to make its speaker units acceptable to General Motors, and 90 percent of its loudspeaker boxes were exported to the West.

56   By contrast, the Videoton Automatic Joint Enterprise was an example of a division which faced almost certain closure if the break-up option was chosen. This money-losing unit made line printers largely for the Soviet Union, with little chance for improvement. "There are no technical problems with splitting the division off," its director said, "but we could not survive. Our current equipment is highly task-specific and we need time to build up new business." The unit was actively exploring new products, including the use of its software-writing expertise to tailor optical data processing systems to the needs of Hungarian customers. Unfortunately, few of its customers had the money to purchase such technology.

57   Despite Videoton's many problems, the expectation of foreign investment in some business units was not unreasonable. The company offered a number of attractions—the technical skills of its

workforce and R&D departments, experience of CMEA trade and contacts throughout the former CMEA block, well-developed domestic distribution networks, and low-cost labor. The split-off companies would be free from the unsupportable debt burden faced by the Videoton group, although creditors might have to be given equity in these companies as compensation.

58   Nevertheless, while hope existed that foreign investors would acquire equity stakes in some of the units, the SPA and its Western consultants believed that most would have to be sold to their managers and workers. This scenario raised the question of financing the buyout of units and preparing them for market competition with adequate capitalization. Because credit was virtually unobtainable from Hungarian banks, however, any option involving MEBOs would require the creation of a special credit facility. The EC channeled ECU 21 million in 1991 to a Hungarian foundation for the purpose of providing advice, equity, credit, and loan guarantees for small and medium-sized enterprises (SMEs). However, the program defines SMEs as companies with fewer than 150 employees, too few to be of much relevance to Videoton's larger business units.

59   The consultants believed that, if any breakup scheme was to promote the creation of healthy private companies, some sort of strategic overview of the group and the relationships among the units in it was required. The goal might have been a loosely structured partnership among former Videoton units. The now separate businesses would be tied to one another by long-term contracts and a commonality of purpose, but would shed the burdens of common ownership, burdens that could overstretch the scarce resources of financial and human capital. Long-term contracts between entities could make the smaller units more attractive investments than otherwise, because the contracts would represent more secure assets than plant and machinery of uncertain value and vague sale possibilities. Unfortunately, the SPA had no legal position from which to enforce this, or indeed any other, reorganization as it could deal only with VEV, the state-owned holding company. Although fully aware of Videoton's precarious financial position, the SPA lacked both the necessary resources and legal position to enforce a comprehensive restructuring.

Liquidation

60   In the absence of rapid and dramatic action to restructure the business, liquidation was the only alternative. As KPMG bluntly stated in its financial review: "The group's existing operations are not viable given the existing capital structure." Nevertheless, in early 1991, liquidation constituted more of a threat than a reality, as the trauma of insolvency, with the damage to Videoton's credibility and probable interruption in supply, would inevitably damage the value of the separate business units. A liquidator is visibly a forced seller and rarely secures the best price for the sale of a business.

61   On the other hand, the appointment of a liquidator might, in this case, have attractions. It would weaken the position of management and remove the SPA and Industry Ministry from the picture. Both could be desirable outcomes given that these three principal constituencies had conflicting or unclear agendas.

CASE 15

VIDEOTON (B)

1   By the spring of 1991, none of the options had been followed and Videoton was on the verge of collapse. Company management blamed the overnight disappearance of the Soviet market (60 percent of Videoton's sales), the dramatic increase in interest rates (just as a massive investment program was being financed by short-term, floating-rate loans), outdated technology, overdependence on the military, and management mistakes. Mistakes included the failure to cut back on investment until long after it became apparent that anticipated demand would not materialize and the failure to take advantage of opportunities to spin off businesses into joint ventures in 1989 when the outlook was better and Western investors were still interested in Videoton's USSR outlets.

2   Management, however, was still resistant to the break-up option. Indeed, consultants close to the Videoton case confirm that the resistance was very strong. The reasons for this resistance have never been fully understood even by the consultants, but the following explanations have been offered. First, Videoton management may have fraudulently gained from the foreign-currency revenues generated by overseas distribution. In this case, any outcome that left Videoton as only a manufacturing base, with a foreign investor responsible for distribution (as envisaged by James Capel), would have deprived them of their (personal) hard-currency earnings. Second, they may have conspired with a potential French investor that was seeking to buy the entire group. The consultants from James Capel opposed the French buyer, because they doubted the integrity of the company's management (the chief executive officer was facing a criminal investigation at home, and the finance director had been jailed twice). In addition, the French company had no obvious source of funds and had nothing at all to offer in terms of know-how, products, or market access. A third suggested source of group management's hostility to a break-up might have been the prospect that divisional managers (i.e., their former subordinates) would become rich, or at least richer than the group managers. Finally, they may have genuinely believed that Videoton could not rely on its suppliers unless it owned them.

3   The problems caused by management's resistance to the break-up option were aggravated by the SPA's reluctance to fire the general manager it had appointed in 1990. SPA officials were loathe to admit that the appointment had been a mistake.

4   On 16 August 1991, the local Székesfehérvár court appointed a liquidator for six Videoton companies. As the liquidator himself remarked about the group's managers, "They never got around to treating the sore throat, but waited until it developed into pneumonia." Because the six companies to be liquidated included VEV, the state-owned holding company, and VIRT, its main subsidiary, the liquidator had effective control over the entire group. He determined that the interests of creditors would be best served by maintaining parts of the business as a going concern, at least for the short term. In this way, he believed, a few of Videoton's businesses could be sold to investors to generate at least some proceeds for creditors, who would probably receive nothing if all of Videoton's businesses were terminated. To complicate matters, the group's debts were soon revealed to be far greater than previously disclosed by management, although whether disinformation or simply poor accounting procedures were to blame is still not known.

5   When Videoton went into liquidation, neither the SPA nor the Industry Ministry had any further say in the fate of the group. Nothing of consequence could be done regarding Videoton, including the payment of bills, without the liquidator's authorization. The liquidator's initial intent was to define,

This case was written by S. David Young, Associate Professor at INSEAD. It is intended to be used as a basis for class discussion rather than to illustrate either effective or ineffective handling of an administrative situation. Financial support from the INSEAD Alumni Fund European Case Programme is gratefully acknowledged. Reprinted with the permission of INSEAD. Copyright © 1993 INSEAD, Fontainebleau, France.

consolidate, and support a central core business. Within weeks of taking control, however, the liquidator abandoned any hopes of developing a restructuring plan; he chose, instead, to sell the company at auction. The decision to award Videoton to a particular bidder would be based on the liquidator's subjective assessment of the bid price, method of payment, strategy, and employment guarantees.

6   On 5 December 1991, the State Liquidation Agency announced that Videoton had been awarded to a consortium composed of the Hungarian Credit Bank (HCB) (70 percent ownership), a consulting firm (5 percent), and three private investors (25 percent). By this time, the company's acknowledged debts stood at HuF 30 billion, HuF 11 billion of which was owed to the HCB. Assets were said to be worth HuF 5 –7 billion. The HuF 4 billion purchase price, which covered only Videoton's assets and not its debts, was to be shared by Videoton's other creditors. Because the HCB is state-owned, the liquidation resulted in only a partial privatization of Videoton. Bank officials were quoted as saying that the process to privatize the company fully would take at least another two years.

CASE 16

THE 3M COMPANY: INTEGRATING EUROPE (A)

1   Doug Hanson, Vice President of 3M Europe, was very pleased with the recent reorganization which had been orchestrated by the management team in Europe. While 3M, a $14 billion American diversified multinational, had operated with relatively independent country subsidiaries in Europe for the past 40 years, the increasing integration of the European market, in addition to perceived customer and competitive pressures, had led the company to launch a major organizational change in 1991. This new structure created European product line organizations with profit and loss responsibility which were matrixed with regional organizations. The ease with which the reorganization had been accomplished in a short 18 months surprised him:

> I expected there to be concern and turmoil and unease, which there was. I also expected there to be more resistance to change. In fact, I found there was a great deal of buy-in to the change. Everyone believed, as we did, that it was correct. This was not somebody's brainstorm—we got a lot of input before we decided to make the change. The process we used to facilitate the organizational development and implementation was a major factor in helping people get through the period.

3   The structural change of the reorganization having been completed, the new European management teams were moving forward and enthusiastically seizing opportunities to improve their operations in ways which were never possible under the old structure. However, Hanson reflected that perhaps the most difficult time was still to come.

THE 3M COMPANY

4   The Minnesota Mining and Manufacturing Company, better known as the 3M Company, is headquartered in St. Paul, Minnesota. Its first successful product, flexible sandpaper, was launched from there in 1914. Eighty years later, in 1994, one of its most important product lines was still abrasives, but it had diversified into a leadership position in such seemingly unrelated fields as adhesive tapes, medical supplies and equipment, office supplies, traffic and safety signs, and electrical equipment, to name only a few of its market successes. In 1993, 3M yielded a net income of $1.2 billion on its $14 billion in sales through the efforts of its 87,000 employees. (See Exhibit 1 for a financial summary.)

5   3M's array of 60,000 products were organized into four Sectors: Industrial and Consumer; Information, Imaging, and Electronic; Life Sciences; and International. Each Sector (see Exhibit 2 for summary descriptions), except International, contained several Product Groups. Each Group was divided into Divisions for a total of around 50 Divisions for all of 3M. The number changed frequently as new businesses were spawned and evolved, and older businesses were folded into other Divisions. Divisions were further broken down into Business Units.

6   Line management within the Divisions were given ample leeway to pursue their own initiatives as the 3M staff organization was intentionally very small. As one senior staff member noted, "We did a study in the 1960s and 1970s of other organizations that were building up staff and we explicitly decided not to follow their lead." Corporate planning activities relied heavily upon the resources of

This case was written by Mary Ackenhusen, Research Associate, under the supervision and guidance of Associate Professor Daniel Muzyka and Professor Neil Churchill. It is intended to be used as a basis for class discussion rather than to illustrate either effective or ineffective handling of an administrative situation. Funding for this case was provided by the IAF Chair of Entrepreneurship and Digital Equipment Corporation. Reprinted with the permission of INSEAD. Copyright © 1994 INSEAD, Fontainebleau, France.

EXHIBIT 1
3M Consolidated Statement of Income (dollars in millions)

	1993	1992	1991	1990	1989	1988	1987	1986	1985	1984
Net sales	$14,020	$13,883	$13,340	$13,021	$11,990	$11,323	$ 9,429	$ 8,602	$ 7,846	$ 7,705
Cost of goods sold	7,499	7,339	7,144	6,791	6,162	5,830	4,863	4,488	4,226	4,105
Gross margin	6,521	6,544	6,196	6,230	5,828	5,493	4,566	4,114	3,620	3,600
Selling, general, and administrative	3,535	3,543	3,323	3,174	2,894	2,756	2,338	2,118	1,950	1,860
R&D	1,030	1,007	914	865	784	721	650	586	520	454
Operating income	1,956	1,994	1,959	2,191	2,150	2,016	1,578	1,410	1,150	1,286
Other expense	(46)	47	82	56	51	31	13	62	53	33
Income before tax	2,002	1,947	1,877	2,135	2,099	1,985	1,565	1,348	1,097	1,253
Net income	$ 1,263	$ 1,233	$ 1,154	$ 1,308	$ 1,244	$ 1,154	$ 918	$ 779	$ 664	$ 733
Number of employees	86,168	87,015	88,477	89,601	87,584	85,569	85,144	84,498	88,093	89,179

Source: 3M Annual Reports.

line management as did many other staff-type activities. Nevertheless, financial reporting at 3M was tightly controlled at all levels with standard reporting required on a regular basis. Divisional controllers were physically located with the Divisions with whom they were expected to be "business partners," yet they officially reported to the corporate financial function.

The Spirit of Innovation

7   The 3M Company was considered by many companies to be the benchmark for innovation in product development.[1] The company rule until 1992 had been that it required its Divisions to derive 25% of their revenue from products introduced within the previous five-year period, though some flexibility was shown for Divisions with older product lines which had less potential for innovation. The corporation had been able to consistently meet this standard and in 1993, the stakes were raised to 30% in four years. Internally, the importance of this goal was widely respected because historically, 3M's growth had been highly correlated with its rate of product innovation. The assumption that 3M would grow and thus spawn opportunities for individuals was at the core of 3M's culture.

8   One of the most visible drivers of innovation was a rule that was laid down in the company's early days known as "the 15% rule," which gave every technical employee 15% of their working week to pursue whatever project he or she desired. This was seen as the employee's chance to develop an idea which had not been sanctioned by, or often even discussed with, his or her boss and was not any part of a formal new product planning process. In reality, some took advantage of this freedom religiously and others never strayed from their formal workload either by choice or due to the pressures of the business. As one manager explained, "This rule provides a buffer from management because it makes it hard for supervisors to say 'Don't work on that.' In reality, it is usually done between the 40th and 60th hour of the week."

9   The best known product to spring from someone taking advantage of the 15% rule was the Post-It® note product, invented by Art Frye out of a laboratory he constructed in his basement in the early 1980s. This was a note-sized paper which had one edge lined with a light adhesive allowing it to be stuck and restuck several times. After the product was introduced, office workers became addicted to

---

[1] With the increased use of "best in class" benchmarking as a tool for evaluating management processes, 3M staff found that it had to sometimes temporarily refuse requests for benchmarking interviews due to the amount of time being consumed by discussions with companies interested in its innovation process.

EXHIBIT 2
Description of 3M Sectors

Industrial and Consumer	Major Business Units	Principal Products
	Abrasive Technologies Group	Adhesives, coatings and sealers; anti-slip surfacing materials; auto buffing pads; ceramic materials; coated and non-woven abrasives; compounds and glazes; flame-retardant materials; floor-maintenance products; masking tapes; roofing granules; surface conditioning products
	Automotive Systems Group	Acrylic foam tapes; decorative markings; emblems; fastening systems; structural adhesives
	Chemicals, Film and Allied Products Group	Adhesives, coatings and sealers; advanced composite materials; fluorochemicals; specialty films and chemicals
	Commercial and Consumer Markets Group	Coated abrasives; energy control products; masking tapes; O-Cel-O brand sponges; Post-it brand notes; Scotch brand Magic tape; Scotch brand special-purpose tapes; Scotch-Brite brand cleaning pads; Scotchgard brand protectors; tape and note dispensers; wood refinishing products
	Tape Group	Industrial tapes; joining systems; labeling systems; packaging systems; tape application equipment; vibration control products
Information, Imaging and Electronic		
	Electro Products Group	Electrical/electronic connectors; insulating and conductive materials; shielding and protective products; vinyl electrical tapes
	Imaging Systems Group	Camera plate systems; carbonless papers; color proofing systems; digital imaging systems; graphic arts films; lithographic plates; medical laser imaging systems; photographic films; press dampening systems; X-ray films and screens
	Information Systems Group	Dry silver papers; micrographic products; overhead projectors and transparency films
	Memory Technologies Group	Computer tapes and cartridges; consumer video and audio tapes; data cartridges; diskettes; optical recording media; professional video and audio tapes
	Telecom Systems Group	Fiber-optic products and systems; test and measurement products; wiring and cabling products
Life Sciences		
	Medical Products Group	Blood gas monitors; casting and bracing materials; computer software; heart-lung machines; IV systems; monitoring electrodes; orthopedic implants; oxygenators; powered surgical instruments; skin closures and staplers; stethoscopes; surgical drapes, masks and sterilizers; tapes and dressings
	Pharmaceuticals, Dental and Disposable Products Group	Dental materials; diaper closures; drug-delivery systems; encapsulated products; facial cleansing products; orthodontic products; pharmaceuticals; veterinary products
	Traffic and Personal Safety Products Group	Electronically cut sign materials; filtration systems; fleet graphics; garment insulation; music and messaging systems; outdoor advertising; pavement markings; print media advertising; respiratory protection products; security systems; sign materials; spill-control sorbents; traffic control devices

using the little Post-It® pads to the point that, a few years after introduction, it was difficult to find any office in the industrialized world which did not use Post-Its®. By the early 1990s, Post-Its® enjoyed the status of the most profitable product ever after Scotch® tape,[2] within the 3M Commercial Tape Division.

10   In the spirit of innovation, 3M's top management allowed a "healthy disrespect for rules" believing that this attitude encouraged individuals to pursue opportunities without being overly burdened by administrative processes. While many products were supposedly killed in the formal

---

[2] The brand name for 3M's clear adhesive tape used in offices.

new product development review cycle for seemingly logical reasons, such as the market was too small or the technology could not be made to work after a substantial effort, this order to stop development by upper management often motivated researchers to work even harder. Many stories were told in the lore of 3M of employees who believed so strongly in their ideas that they ignored their bosses' directives and continued working on a product, either in their 15% time, at home, or on the side until the effort finally resulted in a successful product. The CEO of 3M in 1994, Livio DeSimone (referred to as Desi), admitted that he tried to terminate the development of the Thinsulate® product line several times before it proved itself worthy of pursuit. Yet, in the 1990s, the lightweight insulating material was widely used by the outerwear clothing industry because it provided warmth without bulk. In further support of employees who had ideas that were not funded through normal channels in the corporation, up to 90 Genesis grants of as much as $50,000 were awarded every year to individuals through a central organization to allow them to pursue projects which their departments had been unable or unwilling to support. A similar program for non-technical employees who wanted to develop new projects or processes existed as well.

11   This tolerance of individuals "going around the system," when necessary, was balanced by detailed policies and procedures which were normally adhered to during the new product development process to ensure that management understood and could control the efforts being expended in the laboratories. Likewise, in the other functions of 3M, operating norms were documented and followed. In the financial function, budgets were closely monitored with the clear expectation that managers would meet their agreed upon targets, barring any unforeseen circumstances. At every level of the corporation, there was a strong sense of self-discipline, which ensured the frugal expenditures of company assets, encouraged a respect for the individual, and, in general, kept the "healthy disrespect for the rules" from resulting in unpredictability.

12   Failure was not only accepted at 3M, it was an expected part of innovation. As one manager said, "Perhaps 40% of the products we work on ever go to market . . . the other 60% are failures." The management consciously tried to develop a risk-taking mentality in its employees and realized that this could only happen if failures did not result in repercussions to the individual. This philosophy stemmed from the early days of 3M under William McKnight, the President and later CEO in the 1950s and 1960s, who laid down many of the beliefs which served as the foundation of the corporate culture. In the 1990s, McKnight was still revered by 3M employees with most of management being able to quote from memory his philosophy of empowering the individual.

> As our business grows, it becomes increasingly necessary to delegate responsibility and to encourage men and women to exercise their initiative. This requires considerable tolerance.
>
> Those men and women to whom we delegate authority and responsibility, if they are good people, are going to want to do their jobs in their own way. These are characteristics we want, and people should be encouraged as long as their way conforms to our general pattern of operations.
>
> Mistakes will be made, but if a person is essentially right, the mistakes he or she makes are not as serious, in the long run, as the mistakes management will make if it's dictatorial and undertakes to tell those under its authority how they must do their job.
>
> Management that is destructively critical when mistakes are made kills initiative, and it is essential that we have many people with initiative if we are to continue to grow.

> *The Challenge of Management*, William McKnight (1948)

17   Rewards and recognition at 3M were showered on those individuals who delivered growth, profits, and innovation. In a general sense, it was the individuals who were associated with successful products who advanced upward through the management ranks or on the equally prestigious technical ladder designed to reward individual contributors who chose not to go into management. In keeping with this philosophy, when a product idea spawned a new business, the business might be spun off as a separate entity and be allowed to prosper under the leadership of its founder, the entrepreneur who had championed its development. Yet, even when this did not happen, the acclaim that the company gave to those individuals who created new businesses was a coveted form of recognition. Additionally, recognition was ongoing for successful new product or technology developments through various award and peer recognition schemes honoring both teams and individuals.

Research and Manufacturing

18 3M valued its research capability very highly but with a practical twist: its culture glorified the economical application of research into marketable products. Researchers within the labs were encouraged to consider issues when developing new products, which in other companies would have been the responsibility of the marketing function such as: How will it add value to the consumer? Is it cost effective? Is the market large enough to support the development of the product? 3M's desire for researchers who, in the words of one manager, "got a thrill out of seeing their product go to market" led the company to most often hire solid "just below the top of the class" scientists and engineers from state universities versus the very bright, but narrowly focused experts from America's top engineering schools.

19 New products were most often developed in response to an identified need in the marketplace, but it could work in the opposite direction as well, with the research labs holding brainstorming sessions to try to find a way to commercialize an interesting development in technology. Applied research to develop products for introduction in the next five-year period absorbed over 85% of the R&D resources at 3M with the balance being allocated to the basic research function to develop longer term technology platforms that would be useful in 5 to 20 years.[3] Research and development spending averaged 6.5% of sales while the average for most industrial companies hovered at about half that level.

20 The key to 3M's wide assortment of products was the creative combination of approximately two dozen core technologies. The bulk of its products stemmed from its long-time expertise in coating technology. Other key technologies included adhesives, ceramics, films, fluorochemicals, nonwoven fibers, and optics. Long before such technologies and their application began to be referred to as "core competencies," 3M's management was highly sensitive to whether new opportunities utilized or built upon existing technologies. New opportunities which did not were given careful consideration to determine if they were worth pursuing.

21 There was a clear understanding among the research labs that all technology belonged to the company, not to the Division or Business Unit. Thus, everyone had free use of the formulas, processes and patents to develop products for their own Business Unit. It was commonplace for an individual to receive a request for information or to be asked to render an opinion on a new product idea by someone from a different Business Unit. As one manager noted, "You can call anyone in the organization, even Desi [the CEO] and get an hour or two of his or her time." Similarly, the borrowing of equipment between labs to run experiments was ongoing. Opportunities were also, to an extent, public property. There were many stories within the company of individuals developing or recognizing opportunities and "shopping around" the organization trying to sell their ideas to a Division.

22 To allow for the free flow of new product ideas and technical information across the company, 3M's scientists spent substantial amounts of time developing and maintaining informal communication networks among themselves. These networks took many forms: technology fairs and poster sessions where the various labs showed off their latest products and technologies, meetings between interest groups, rotations of people between labs and countries, technical audits[4] and sharing of monthly reports between labs. Managers encouraged their teams to communicate regularly. For example, in the 3M-Sumitomo joint venture lab in Japan, a lab scientist might call his or her counterpart in St. Paul every few weeks just to say "How is your work going, any new developments?"

23 Contributing to the ease of sharing was the physical proximity of the labs to each other. Until the mid-80s, nearly all of the new research done by 3M, with the exception of a joint venture in Japan which employed 500 researchers, was done in the company complex in St. Paul. Thus, when a second U.S. nucleus was created of six Divisions in Austin, Texas, in 1986, there was a very real concern that the 2,000-mile separation would create dangerous barriers to the highly interpersonal process of

---

[3] 3M institutionalized the differences in these time horizons by putting very long-run, fundamental research into the Corporate or Central laboratories, medium range work in the Sector laboratories, and short-run application development work in the Division laboratories.

[4] A technical audit was carried out on each lab, worldwide, every few years by a team of both staff and line technical management to give the lab management non-binding feedback on various measures of its effectiveness.

sharing ideas, which was deemed to be so important to the innovation process. These fears, for the most part, did not come true primarily due to a conscious effort by the management to avoid it by providing a corporate plane to shuttle people to and from the two locations on a regular schedule, video conferencing facilities, and many phone calls.

24   Informal networking, in the technical and non-technical arenas, was further leveraged by the longevity of 3M employees. Due to policies of promotion from within and the loyalty of employees to the company, the number of lifetime employees was much higher than in most companies. In 1990, the employee turnover was reported to be less than 4%.

25   By all accounts, this intensive networking by the scientific community at 3M, as well as other functions to a lesser extent, was a key asset of the company. The company relied upon individuals to utilize their personal contacts and to establish new contacts in order to address problems. It was the familiarity of 3Mers with each other, either through actual acquaintance or the strong feeling of family, combined with a trust of each other and the company, that allowed an informal borrowing of resources to support the innovation process. As the company grew to almost 90,000 employees in the 1990s, it worked hard to promote, protect, and leverage this delicate, corporate-wide, people-based network.

26   Manufacturing was an important discipline at 3M with many of the company's successes being attributed to innovations in the manufacturing process. Similar to the sharing of information in the technical function, manufacturing management networked on a formal and informal basis to share best practices. Helping to optimize the manufacturing function, 3M's plants were not associated with any particular Division—placement of products for manufacture was decided primarily on capacity and technical capability. Thus, one plant in Minnesota served 15 different Divisions, which was not atypical. Furthermore, 3M freely subcontracted the manufacture of products which did not fit the company's competencies. For example, overhead transparency projectors, in which 3M had a major market share, were made for the company by outside suppliers because it was more cost effective.

27   Due to the corporate objective of continual innovation, which drove a steady flow of new products and product variations into the plants, the 3M manufacturing function was widely acclaimed for its strong competency in flexibility. As one manager explained, "Sometimes, we feel we are just one big pilot plant." However, at the same time, 3M gave constant attention to minimizing the unit cost of its products. Beginning in 1986, there were two five-year-long, corporate-wide programs to reduce costs in the manufacturing function with specific objectives in areas such as inventory, cycle time, energy consumption, and waste.

Sales and Marketing

28   3M's sales philosophy had always been to "sell at the bottom of the smokestack," meaning sell to the people who actually used the products. In the early days, when 3M was trying to establish itself in the sandpaper business in automobile body repair shops, salespeople often first demonstrated their products to the workers performing the car repairs. After convincing the workers of the value of the product, usually by showing significant labor savings or superior quality, the salesperson would then proceed to the purchasing department to ask for the order. The purchasing agent would be encouraged to call the body shop workers to get direct testimonials and would often find that the workers were no longer willing to accept any substitutes for the 3M product.

29   Though the laboratories were the most common source of innovation, the close customer contact that 3M had maintained since their first ventures in "selling at the bottom of the smokestack" had also been a strong source of ideas and product improvements. For example, the first Scotch® tape dispenser was invented by a regional sales manager who was not satisfied with the dispenser developed by the lab after he saw how frustrated his customers became when they used it. Normally, however, the key players in soliciting customer input were the Technical Service representatives. This group reported organizationally to the research laboratories but maintained a real world perspective by spending most of their days providing advice to customers and servicing products in the field.

30   Lab scientists and marketing people were also frequent visitors to the customer sites. A lab scientist might be called out to a field by a Technical Service representative to witness a problem or to help formulate a product opportunity. Likewise, it would be very typical to see a Marketing manager

EXHIBIT 3
Revenues and Operating Income by Geographic Area (in millions)

	United States		Europe		Asia Pacific*		Rest of World	
	Sales	Operating Income	Sales	Operating Income	Sales	Operating Income	Sales	Operating Income
1993	$7,026	$1,341	$3,646	$205	$2,154	$277	$1,094	$133
1992	7,082	1,317	4,026	321	1,794	228	981	128
1991	6,875	1,169	3,857	409	1,662	243	946	138
1990	6,802	1,268	3,705	463	1,487	232	1,027	228
1989	6,601	1,222	3,023	452	1,834	347	532	129
1988	6,351	1,133	2,911	477	1,834	317	458	89
1987	5,813	929	2,849	405	1,330	245	447	104
1986	5,383	897	2,227	322	†	†	992	191
1985	5,252	818	1,669	177	†	†	925	155
1984	5,190	946	1,599	183	†	†	916	157

*For 1987–1989, Canada is included in Asia Pacific. For other years, it is part of Rest of World.
†For 1984–1986, Asia Pacific region is reported in Rest of World figures.
Source: Company annual reports.

or a scientist from the medical business accompanying doctors and nurses on their hospital rounds for several days, analyzing how they performed one narrow task, such as setting up IVs (intravenous systems) on patients or using a stethoscope. Since nearly all of 3M's products were sold through distributors, the customer contact the company maintained was critical to the product improvement and innovation process.

31　　　3M normally avoided real commodity businesses; rather they tried to produce high margin, high value-added products. Even for items which on the surface appeared to be commodity products, such as Scotch® tape, the company focused on developing a superior quality offering,[5] thus allowing the company to charge a price premium even in a commodity-like market. Furthermore, the company was intentionally conservative when it marketed new products. It would develop a new product to sell in a known market segment or introduce an older, tried product into a new market segment, but generally not attempt to sell a new product into a new market segment. This conservatism extended to its financial management as well. 3M intentionally kept a very low debt level so that its management could keep its focus on the long-term health of the business and maintain a stable level of R&D funding.

3M IN EUROPE

32　　　In 1994, 3M was an expansive multinational which sold its products in nearly every country in the world. It had research labs in 22 different countries and had sited manufacturing plants all over the globe. In 1992, the company had achieved, for the first time, its long-time goal of deriving 50% of its revenues from markets outside the U.S., with 30% of its revenues coming from Europe, 13% from the Asia Pacific region, and 7% coming from other areas, primarily Latin America. (See Exhibit 3 for the historical trend in the European region's contribution to sales.)

The Early Days in International

33　　　In 1929, 3M joined with eight other American abrasive manufacturers to form a company which manufactured and sold sandpaper in England. Over the next 20 years, this company expanded its

---

[5] For example, Scotch® tape did not yellow or lose its adhesive properties with time, and it could be written on.

operations across Europe and into parts of the rest of the world. Supplementing this direct investment in Europe, 3M exported a number of its other products from the U.S. to be sold by local distributors throughout the world. 3M formed a U.S.–based International Division to exploit these overseas opportunities. The sandpaper cooperative flourished until 1950 when an American court ordered that it be disbanded for antitrust reasons. 3M took advantage of the breakup to acquire the key assets in England and France, as well as Brazil and Mexico.

34   In furthering the 3M commitment abroad, two 3M top executives, responsible for the International Division, made a series of marathon "expeditions" in the early 1950s, setting up marketing and wholly-owned sales and manufacturing subsidiaries in many different countries across Europe, Latin America, and Asia. Additionally, a number of "young, up and comers" were identified to dedicate their careers to furthering 3M's international presence, including Em Monteiro who later became the Executive VP of International.

35   As 3M planted its seeds in fertile ground across the world, the philosophy for these many new ventures was one of minimal investment. Monteiro remembered how he helped to build the Latin American presence.

> I had made a study of Columbia. I presented it to the top management of International and basically recommended that we start a plant there. I was asked, "Well, who is going to run it?" I said, "Well, I would like to." Then another executive said, "OK, you run it, but we are not going to give you any help at all. You are going to have to do everything on your own." After that, I went down to Columbia with $10,000 in working capital and some old equipment and started the business.

37   Harry Hammerly, who spent much of his career in International before succeeding Monteiro as the Executive VP of International in 1991, explained the effect that this had:

> The idea was that these companies would grow from what they generated themselves. The people had a sense of ownership of the company. It was not like there was some rich uncle out there that had a lot of money—having a positive cash flow was key.

39   In spite of the low investment strategy in the International Division in the early days, there was always a substantial amount of top management attention and time devoted to the cause. Hammerly explained:

> Our management, since the beginning, has traveled around quite a bit getting into these overseas 3M companies so that we can work with, talk with and know the local people. Since the 1960s, we have had an annual review trip where the executives of 3M split up and visit the different areas of the world. It is kind of "management by walking around" like you see in lots of companies, but we have always kept it active in International too.

Expansion in Europe

41   As 3M expanded its international presence, Europe naturally attracted a great deal of attention as a high potential opportunity. To lead the charge into a European market, 3M would appoint an American as the Managing Director (MD) of a 3M European country subsidiary organization (CSO) with the directive to "simply get out there and sell." The MD would "cherry pick" the 3M products from the U.S. offerings that fit the local European market and then build a 3M company to market and sell them. Thus, the 3M product offerings between countries varied widely based on the product tradeoffs made by the MD. With the exception of the MD, the CSO's employees were nearly always nationals, often hired from the local distributor, which was a "win-win" solution from both the distributor's viewpoint (the distributor got a free salesman) and from 3M's standpoint (it got a locally knowledgeable salesman who knew the 3M product line). The local language and culture prevailed within the CSOs, though each organization discovered its own ways to merge the company customs and culture with their national counterparts. According to Monteiro, this gave 3M a very local image:

> For instance, if someone talks about 3M France, they do not talk about it as an American company. Even when they put up these laws against foreign companies, 3M is never included as a foreigner. It is a local company with foreign shareholders.

EXHIBIT 4
Sample Country Subsidiary Organization

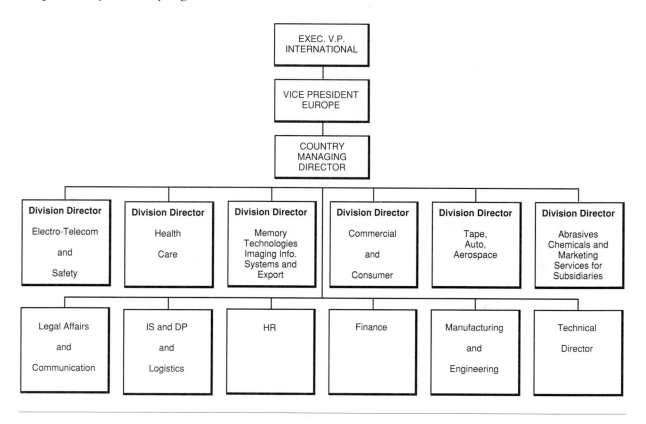

43 Despite the fact that the CSOs maintained a great deal of autonomy, 3M encouraged strong links to headquarters by never appointing a country national to head the operations in a given country. Bill Monahan, past MD for Italy, explained:

> One of the advantages of not having a national as head of the country is that you reduce the departure from the 3M culture that you might get otherwise. The American or third country national is the representative of St. Paul and provides the glue that connects the country subsidiaries to 3M in the U.S.

45 Within each CSO, the product lines sold in that country were managed by a handful of Division Directors who reported to the MD. Each Division Director had responsibility for the products of several of the U.S.–based Product Divisions. These Divisions had an informal link to the Division structure in the U.S. (See Exhibit 4 for CSO organization chart.) For the most part, each Division within the CSO had its own sales and marketing function.

46 Much of the product sold in Europe was imported from the U.S., but when the volume justified the investment, European manufacturing capacity was added to supply product needs on a European-wide basis. Manufacturing plants were owned by the CSO in which they were located and products were sold to the other CSOs in Europe through a transfer pricing scheme. As in the U.S., the manufacturing culture in Europe demanded an ongoing pursuit to lower unit costs. Often, decisions to add or expand capacity in Europe were done on a "space available" basis, independent of marketing and technical strategic decisions. There was only a limited technical capability in Europe in the 1950s and 1960s, and it was primarily focused on making improvements to the manufacturing processes.

47 In keeping with the level of competition in the international markets during the 1950s and 1960s, the international business for 3M was considered somewhat inferior to the American market. Monteiro described the mentality, "We went through an early stage in International when you could

walk through a factory in the U.S. and see a big roll of tape marked "Rejected, OK for International." This attitude toward the international markets sometimes tainted the image of those people who worked for International. Often the managers who were sent overseas found it very difficult to find a domestic position again after their tour was completed. The result was that few high potential managers who were not dedicated to long-term careers in International would voluntarily take an overseas assignment for fear of derailing their careers.

48   However, by the 1970s, the low priority given to the international markets had changed through a sustained, focused effort on the part of 3M management. In the face of the high quality goods being introduced into Europe by the Japanese and others in the 1970s, 3M began to provide products to its overseas markets of equivalent or superior quality to its domestic products. To assure that the proper level of talent was available to support the international thrust, a new rule went into place on overseas assignments. Before managers could be sent abroad, they had to have a sponsor who would monitor their careers during their overseas stay and work to guarantee them a position equivalent to their previous one upon their return. Furthermore, the position of MD of a CSO became a developmental post for promising managers. International experience began to be an important criterion for advancement to the company's top positions.

49   As a part of this international vision, a 3M Europe office was formed in Brussels to coordinate the efforts of the fast growing CSOs across Europe. This new management structure had no direct authority and could only advise the CSOs on how they might strengthen 3M's presence in Europe. Hammerly, who was part of this office, described the reaction of the CSOs to this first attempt at integration: "There was a certain amount of tug and pull between the country MDs and the European office. Sometimes it was quite influential and other times not at all."

50   By the late 1970s, it had become evident that to increase 3M's competitiveness in Europe, it would need to begin developing products specifically for the European market, instead of selling American designs as it had done up to this point. To support this new strategy, the mission of the existing European laboratories, which had been created to address European manufacturing issues, was expanded to include supporting the customization of products for the European market as well as providing Technical Service expertise to customers. Senior technical management, in the role of Technical Directors for the CSOs, were brought over from the U.S. to manage the labs and to instill the historical 3M values considered to be important to the innovation process. According to Manley Johnston, Technical Director of Europe in 1993:

> One of their jobs was to reinforce the 3M R&D culture in the European labs. With this, there was a lot of empowerment. They tried to adhere to the philosophy that everyone had the right to be an entrepreneur.

52   At first, the technical laboratories reported directly to the CSO in which they were located—for example, the Abrasives lab reported to the CSO in the U.K. and the Chemicals lab reported to the German CSO. However, as the European technical organization's importance and size increased, it became very difficult to optimize the lab resources to serve all of Europe as they were continually being pulled to meet their local CSO's needs. Thus, in the early 1980s, the labs' mission to work on a pan-European basis was reinforced by creating a reporting relationship to the appropriate lab head in the U.S., though the day-to-day management was still the responsibility of the CSO management.

53   With the new emphasis on building 3M's European technical capability, the technical function in Europe blossomed to include 1,500 3M scientists, spread among 17 different labs in seven different countries with each lab specializing in a different technology. Factory support activities had shrunk to only 20% of the labs' activities while 60% was technical service/product modifications and 10% was truly new product development. An important role played by the European labs was to work with the U.S. development labs to assure that any product being developed was truly global in nature or could be made to fit European needs with minimal effort. However, if a CSO wanted a product developed specifically for its local market, there was no strong link between the CSO and European lab to drive this unless the lab happened to be located in that country.

54   Europe had by this time developed enough critical mass in the technical function to necessitate fostering a number of processes which would encourage a two-way transfer of knowledge and ideas between the U.S. and Europe, and among the labs in Europe. There were transfers of scientists between the U.S. and Europe for six months to a year. Additionally, individuals switched between

EXHIBIT 5
The Unlikely Development of Door Aperture Tape

The networking between labs in Europe paid off not only in developing products within Divisions but in some cross-divisional technological developments as well, though on a much less frequent scale than in the U.S. The creation of car door aperture refinish tape was one such development that European management liked to use to demonstrate that the European technical development often followed the same circuitous path experienced in the U.S.

In the mid-80s, a Belgian body shop owner "jury-rigged" a system for painting damaged car doors by blocking the aperture with a circular piece of foam tubing to keep paint from spraying on the seats. Normally, when doing this type of work, a tradesman would use masking tape and paper to make a protective frill but this method tended to leave a hard edge of paint that had to be sanded afterwards. The body shop owner showed his method to a 3M salesman who took it to the Tape Division Technical Director (TD), located in Germany, as a potential new product. Though the TD was interested, his lab management vetoed it because they thought that the market for the application was too small. The TD did not give up. He then took it to the Automotive Trades technical service manager who happened to be a qualified body shop painter—he immediately saw potential in the product and called the abrasives lab which was associated with the Automotive Trades Marketing Division and sold 3M product offerings into the auto body shop trade. He explained the opportunity and asked if the lab would back the development effort. Lab management resisted at first, protesting that it was an abrasives lab and thus had expertise in neither the foam nor the adhesive technology which this project would require. They then relented and asked one of the abrasives lab scientists to donate his 15% "free time" to the project as there were no other available resources.

The assigned scientist spent most of his time talking to various technical service representatives about the idea and eventually came to the conclusion that it was a good idea but after reviewing possible methods of fabrication, he was not convinced that 3M could do it cost effectively. Marketing persisted that they were very interested in the product and the development effort became an authorized project which allowed the scientist to work on it full time. He continued his futile search for a cost effective material to use.

The breakthrough came when he asked a lab worker who was working on a completely different project in the next cubicle if he had some leftover foam samples that he could try out. He took one of the samples and cut it with a pair of dull scissors and surprisingly the two sides stuck together, due to the pressure of the scissors, to form the foam tubing he had been searching for. A technical manager in the lab explained, "The irony is that he would never have discovered that it welded if he had been working in the Tape lab because he would have had sharp scissors. Only a guy in the Abrasives lab would have scissors that were dull!"

After the foam was identified, a cross-functional team including the Tape Division and the Automotive Trades lab was formed to develop a manufacturing process. The Tape Division was interested because they thought they would be allowed to manufacture it and then sell it through the Automotive Trades sales force. In the end, the Automotive Trades Division kept the manufacturing capability because the processing equipment was relatively inexpensive and did not share any resources with the rest of the Tape Division processes. The technology was patented and by 1993, sales for the door aperture tape hit $10 million, a 45% increase over the previous year.

---

labs in Europe according to the needs of the business. Technical management of the labs traveled to the U.S. twice per year to see their counterparts, and this visit was reciprocated on the same scale allowing these managers to communicate face-to-face four times a year. On a CSO basis, technical fairs were held in the larger countries (U.K., France, and Germany) to allow all labs in those countries to share their technologies. European-wide fairs were not held due to the cost and the language barriers. Technology fairs in the U.S. were not normally attended by Europeans, though occasionally a European lab would have a booth. However, to encourage global integration of the technical function among the research centers of St. Paul, Austin, Japan, and Europe, annual technical planning meetings were held by some Divisions. Teleconferencing was also strongly encouraged with every major lab in Europe having on-site facilities.

55   The formal and informal networking on the part of the technical community in Europe paid off in the form of product developments which leveraged expertise from more than one Business Unit. Just as was common in the 3M culture in the U.S., a no to a development request by one lab did not necessarily mean the product idea would die. Such was the development of a 3M product called car door aperture tape, which was rejected by the European tape lab, its natural home, and later developed into a multimillion dollar business by the European abrasives lab. (See Exhibit 5 for complete story.)

EXHIBIT 6
European Organization: 1983–1991

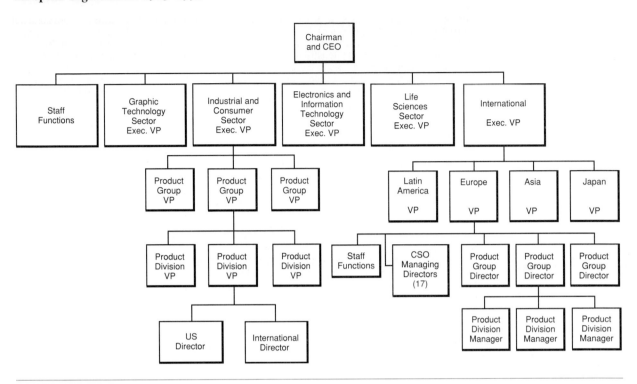

EMATs

56   In the early 1980s, in the face of increasing competition for European sales, it became clear to the VP of 3M Europe, Bent Bjorn, that an improved integration of product line strategies across the countries in Europe could increase 3M's effectiveness. Thus, in 1982, he expanded the European management team to include a European-based Group Director for each Product Group which was active in Europe and a European-based Product Manager for each Division. They functioned in a strictly advisory capacity to the CSOs and became an informal extension of the U.S. Division structure. At the same time, in the corporate structure, international product and business responsibilities were transferred to a newly established International Director position which reported to each U.S. Division VP. (See Exhibit 6 for organization chart.) This change increased the focus upon each Division's international business, but produced varying levels of committed interaction between the U.S. and International business personnel. In the instances when the Division VP took a strong interest and involvement, the new structure improved the planning, marketing, and general resource coordination for the Division's products in overseas markets.

57   Continuing the push to integrate the product strategies across Europe, a number of European Management Action Teams (EMATs) were formed which pulled key Sales and Marketing managers from the larger CSOs into teams responsible for the sales and marketing strategy for each of the major product lines in Europe. The heads of the EMAT teams were the Product Managers from 3M Europe. Secondary to their marketing mission, the groups also worked with the European manufacturing and technical support for their product lines. To support the EMAT mindset, the management in Europe participated in an ongoing training program to help them begin thinking and managing on a European basis to reduce the managerial focus on the country level. The changing political and economic environment in Europe, as it moved towards unification, also helped CSO management to think beyond their own country's borders and internal resource tradeoffs. According to Hammerly:

The external environment [in the 1980s] enabled you to do things which you could have done anyway, but now it was much more acceptable to people. You could say, "This is not 3M, this is something that is happening outside." For example, because the French were driving some of the European unification effort, we found that the French 3M organization was willing to quickly support some of these attempts to better integrate 3M across Europe, such as the EMATs.

59   However, the Achilles heel of the EMAT structure soon emerged when the Sales and Marketing managers went back to their CSO roles to implement the agreed-upon European plans. Often either their boss, the Division Director of the country, or, less often, the Managing Director of the country would not support the implementation of the program in his or her country. When Bill Monahan was the Product Manager for Data Services in Europe in the 1980s, this was the dilemma that he faced:

I would call together a team from the top 6 countries in Europe and we would agree on a strategy, but when they went back to their CSOs, the next level up might say "Now we do not agree with that strategy and we are not going to support the resources." To do my job right, I would have to sell the Division Directors in each country, who each might have 5 or 6 Divisions and did not understand my business very well, on what I wanted to do. Then, I would have to get the Managing Directors behind me and then finally work with the people who were dedicated to my business in each country to get it done.

61   As one manager commented, "The effectiveness of the EMAT structure varied with the amount of time the Product Managers were willing and able to put into the team." According to Monteiro, "The EMATs solidified the conversation and communication between the country organizations."

62   Additionally, the integration along the technical and manufacturing dimensions was not always well managed. Peter Williams, a future EBC head for the abrasives business, explained:

Technology and manufacturing were run by the subsidiaries [CSOs] and the effectiveness of the link between them varied by business from very good to poor. The Manufacturing Director in Europe had a coordinating role mainly, with limited decision making authority. Thus, an investment decision often involved a dialogue between the Group Director [in Europe] and the country Manufacturing Manager and I'm not sure that this led to strategically optimized decisions from a European business perspective.

64   In 1986, 3M management commissioned a task force to determine whether the EMAT structure, in spite of its weaknesses, was still the best organizational structure to encourage the CSOs to operate in a pan-European manner without compromising their local effectiveness. After completion of the study, the task force proposed a more formal pan-European structure organized along product lines, while maintaining the CSOs to support the local needs of the business. This recommendation found favor with many in 3M but the executive team in St. Paul decided not to implement the proposal at that time. Thus, Europe continued to be managed as country organizations, linked by EMAT teams, in spite of the growing recognition of the problems encountered with this approach.

Customer Pressures

65   By 1989, many of 3M's traditional European customers were beginning to work on a pan-European basis, which made it increasingly difficult for the local, autonomous 3M units to respond effectively to their customers' needs. For example, distribution channels were consolidating across Europe, taxing the capability of the CSOs' order entry systems. A large customer like Ford Europe might want to place purchase orders out of its Brussels headquarters for delivery to sites in several different European countries with the bill being sent to yet another site. However, order entry activity involving more than one country was impossible for the CSOs to manage, except manually, because their order systems were independent. Though this new pan-European customer represented only around 20% of 3M's customer base, most of 3M's customers were operating across borders and therefore the company expected that up to 80% of its customers would eventually require some form of pan-European service. Monahan described how stressful the situation became:

The Business Units were screaming that they could not respond to the marketplace the way they had to. Towards the end of the 1980s, you had the development of multinational buyers, companies like HP or Olivetti, who wanted to be treated the same in each country. Large distributors were popping up in Europe that were doing business in many countries and the pan-European distribution had really started to mature. Buyers would say to us, "Well, my price is 10 dollars in France, but in Italy, it is 15 dollars. Wait a minute, what is the deal?" To which we might reply, "Well, we have a rebate program in France but we do not have one in Italy."

67 As pricing was always under the authority of individual CSOs, differentiated pricing prompted a significant amount of cross-border sales as the more sophisticated pan-European customers supplied all of their needs for 3M product in Europe from the CSO with the lowest price.

68 Customers also wanted to have only one contact point with 3M that could speak for all of 3M's operations in Europe. Hanson elaborated:

> Customers wanted decisions immediately. We might have a customer in the Netherlands and our Dutch salesperson would go in and call on them. The customer would say, "Here is what I want done and I want it done in Germany, France and Switzerland." In the past, our man would say "I'm sorry, I can make this deal with you for the Netherlands, but you will have to go to our people in those other countries yourself to work things out." And the customer would ask, "Aren't you a multinational company?"

70 Nevertheless, the need for improved coordination across Europe was quite different for the many businesses on the Continent. For example, in Data Storage products (e.g., floppy diskettes), the European management team had already become very integrated because it was the only way to survive against strong global competitors such as Sony and Verbatim. In contrast, the Visual Systems business, which primarily marketed overhead transparency projectors and supplies, competed against a number of local competitors, which made it difficult to integrate the 3M line across Europe because, "It was smaller and didn't attract much management attention."

Pressures for Growth

71 As the growth of 3M's sales slowed in the U.S. towards the end of the 1980s, 3M management looked to the overseas markets as immediate sources of increased sales to help meet the corporate goal for the 1990s of 10% annual profit growth. Attracting particular attention was the fact that market penetration in Europe was only half of that in the U.S. on many of the company's product lines. However, management knew that there were some important differences between the way products were sold in Europe and the U.S. which would have to be addressed to fully exploit the potential of the European continent.

72 For example, the acceptance of 3M in Europe as a technical company which sold products based on their technological uniqueness was not well-recognized, neither internally by much of the 3M local management, nor externally by customers. Furthermore, the philosophy of "selling at the bottom of the smokestack" which the company had historically used to justify its high margins, was much weaker as well. The European 3M salespeople were less likely to have technical backgrounds than their U.S. counterparts, which meant that many technical explanations or problems which normally could be solved on the spot in the U.S. required the involvement of a Technical Service representative in Europe, and all the expense associated with this extra assistance. In contrast to the U.S., where the Technical Service representatives reported to the technical arm of the business, in Europe this group reported to the sales organization. These field Technical Service representatives were not considered to be as capable as their U.S. counterparts by the laboratory organizations with whom they had limited contact.

73 Because of 3M's lesser reputation in Europe as compared to the U.S., European customers were more sensitive to the pricing of the product. As global competitors began aggressively competing in Europe, the pressure on 3M pricing became even more intense and the costly nature of "supporting 45 product lines 20 times over," as one manager characterized the CSO structure, came increasingly under attack. It was clear that the EMAT structure was not strong enough to solve many seemingly obvious inefficiencies. Stefano Rosselli Del Turco, a new EBC head who had been a Division Director in Italy before the reorganization, gave an example of an inefficient, costly manufacturing arrangement that was never resolvable under the EMAT structure.

> The transparency films [for overhead projectors] that 3M makes in Europe are done in 2 different steps in 2 different countries. First, the polyester is extruded in Italy and then shipped to France for coating and converting. The EMAT was always more marketing oriented and had no power to combine these two operations for better

EXHIBIT 7
European Business Center Organization Model

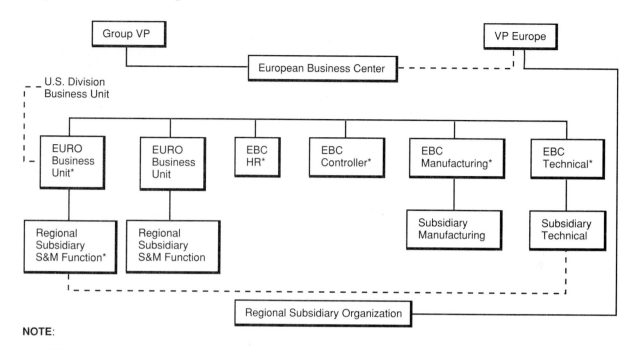

NOTE:

–An EBC may in itself be one or consist of several "Euro Business Units"
–In certain cases the EBC Head & EBU Director Function may be the same
–Finance, Manufacturing & Technical Support depending on need & size
–(*)European Business Operating Committee Members (EBOC)
–Organization structure may vary according to business needs

---

efficiency. The Manufacturing Director for Europe [who primarily had an advisory role] had no power to make this decision. Each of the country heads lobbied to keep their own operations, or even to take it all.

75   These ongoing concerns led to the creation of another task force in 1990, made up of several of the younger MDs from the smaller countries in Europe and two Americans who had a lot of experience in Europe. Their brief was to take another look at the effectiveness of 3M's European organization and its ability to meet the changing needs of customers. The task force solicited opinions from the Group VPs in the U.S., as well as the MDs from the major CSOs and key European staff members. The conclusions of the task force, which were presented to the Executive Committee in the U.S. and the European management team, were very similar to the ones of the task force commissioned four years prior. Specifically, the report recommended a new European organizational structure supported by three management structures: European Business Centers (EBC), Regional Subsidiaries, and a European Operating Committee. The European Business Centers would be formal pan-European product line organizations which would report into the U.S. Group Vice Presidents. Each EBC would be responsible for developing and implementing the Group's European business plan with direct responsibility for Manufacturing, R&D, and Technical Services, as well as profit and loss responsibility. Within the EBC, there might be one or more European Business Units (EBUs) which would be responsible for the sales and marketing of a product line within the EBC (see Exhibit 7 for organization chart of the proposed EBC). For example, the Abrasives EBC might be comprised of several EBUs such as Automotive Trades, Abrasive Systems, and Ceramics. However, all manufacturing and technical resources would be held at the EBC level.

76   The report recommended that the current CSO structure be realigned on a regional basis to "support a continuation of our strong local market presence while facilitating pan-European cooperation." While before there had been 17 different CSOs, the proposed structure would combine them into 10 regional subsidiary organizations (RSOs) of which only 4 (U.K., France, Germany, and Italy) would be one-country regions. These 10 RSOs would provide the resources necessary to carry out the plans of the EBCs, including human resources, financial resources, logistics, manufacturing, and general administration. Importantly, the RSOs would represent 3M externally at the regional level, identify local business opportunities, and manage the legal entity of 3M in each country.

77   An overall management committee called the European Operating Committee (EOC) was proposed to oversee the new European organization. Members of the EOC would include both EBC and RSO heads, as well as various European staff in areas such as technical direction and human resource management. The Vice President of Europe would have "dotted line" authority over the EBCs and direct authority over the RSOs.

78   As in the case of the earlier task force, this second task force's proposal was not immediately accepted with the exception of the move from country organizations to regional organizations which was implemented in May 1991. In the case of the one-country regions, the previous MD of the country organization became the new MD of the regional organization. However, upon the retirement of Monteiro as Executive VP of International in the fall of 1991, his successor, Hammerly, began to implement the organizational change to an EBC pan-European product line structure as his top priority.

REORGANIZING FOR EMERGING OPPORTUNITY

79   Hammerly was a well-known and respected individual within the 3M international community, having spent most of his career in this area. In the early 1970s, he had worked as the European Controller with Bent Bjorn, the Danish head of 3M Europe, and had shared his vision of an integrated product line organization in Europe. Hammerly had then moved on to various assignments in Asia and Latin America before being called back to St. Paul in 1982 to serve as the VP of Finance. In 1986, when Bjorn moved on to another job within 3M, Hammerly had asked to be allowed to return to the international arena as the European VP to continue the work that Bjorn had started. After a period as head of Europe, in 1989, Hammerly had relocated back to the States to run the Industrial and Electronics Sector, which he did for two years, until he was called back to the international side of the business as the Executive VP of International. In his new post, there was no question about what had to be done:

> When I took over International, my mind was made up that I was going to carry out the vision that we had in 1972 which had really been evolving for 20 years, though more aggressively for the last 10 years.

Announcing the Change

81   To help refresh the organizational memory on why a realignment was needed in Europe along product lines, Hammerly orchestrated a discussion of the issue with the heads of the CSOs in October 1991 and then in November, another presentation of the task force report was made to the U.S. top executive group. With the groundwork laid, in January 1992, Hammerly and his European VP, Doug Hanson, embarked on a two-week whirlwind tour of the European CSOs to announce the change. They met with each CSO's Management Operating Committee (the MD, the Division Directors, and staff) to present the customer and competitive reasons that were driving the change. They then introduced the new EBC/EBU organization which was structured as recommended in the task force report. Hammerly remembered:

> After we finished our piece, we told people, "Now we are willing to sit here and talk about it as long as you want to." If people asked questions that we couldn't answer, we said, "We don't know—we're going to have to work together to figure that out."

83   Shortly after the completion of the two-week tour, a brochure entitled, "Managing Business in Europe in the 1990s" was issued describing the new organization in as much detail as was possible at

the time. The publication made clear, strong statements on the changes in responsibility and authority under the new structure. It was perhaps "overly explicit" in some areas to ensure that the deep nature of the change was understood.

84 From the information presented to the CSOs on the new organization, it was clear that it might be "career threatening" to some individuals. Though it was not explicitly stated, it was fairly obvious that the whole first layer of management under the MDs, the Division Directors, was going to be eliminated. In one manager's view:

> These Division Directors had been there forever, in some cases 15–20 years. They were some of our finest, long-term, national employees. On the other hand, this group was a lot more responsible for us not being able to have European-wide programs than the MDs were.

86 Thus, shortly after the initial presentations, Hanson met individually with all 70 Division Directors to openly discuss their endangered positions and future opportunities.

87 In a very short time, the entire European organization seemed very comfortable with the change to come and many even thought it was overdue in coming. Hammerly attributed this acceptance to the history of the top management team in Europe:

> I was a known quantity to those people and they knew that I had been consistent over all the years—when I said something, we followed through on it. Likewise, Hanson had been the Managing Director of Switzerland and Italy for a total of six years so he was also known. One of his strengths is working with people. Together we emphasized open dialogue and visible management.

89 According to one manager:

> Having worked for Hammerly in the past, we trusted him and we trusted 3M. He really represented 3M in this particular change and we bought in.

91 Many of the management team in place at the time attributed the strong buy-in to the participative process used to develop and introduce the change.

Planning the EBCs

92 The implementation of the change was made the responsibility of the European Operating Committee (EOC), which consisted of the MDs of the largest subsidiaries as well as Hanson, the head of Finance in Europe, and the Director who had responsibility for the smaller RSOs. Of the five MDs representing the largest RSOs, three had been recently appointed to their posts in the six months prior to the announcement of the reorganization with the understanding that they were likely to be asked to implement a major reorganization which would significantly change their own and others' roles in Europe. One EBC head reflected on how this facilitated the change:

> There was a big difference between the MDs named before the change and those named after or during the change. The ones named before the change were the leaders of that country and had total authority of what was going on in that country. For them it was not easy to accept that they would lose a lot of power to the EBCs and EBUs. The ones named after or during were briefed that they would have to manage a transition in the right way and fully supported it.

94 The implementation of the new organization at the EBC and EBU level began immediately after the restructuring announcement was completed by Hammerly and Hanson. EBC plans were developed by the key people from the European headquarters operation and subsidiary organizations in collaboration with the Group Vice Presidents and their teams in the U.S. to detail how the labs, plants and other resources were to be split between EBCs. By design, no uniformity in organizational structures was required for the proposed EBCs. Hanson explained:

> We were smart enough to know that a group of us were not going to be able to go into a room and design a structure that would work for each of our businesses, so we allowed each business in 3M to design the structure for itself that would best fit the customer and the business. What we had then was the people who knew the most about the business, and the Europeans who knew the most about Europe, along with the key people from the U.S. together designing the structure.

EXHIBIT 8
3M European Reorganization Timeline

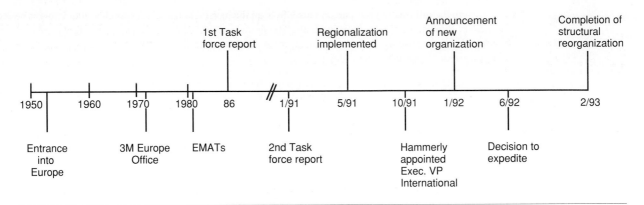

96   The plans for the new EBC/EBU structures were then presented to the European Operating Committee for approval. Karen Welke, the head of the new RSO for France and a part of the committee, described the planning and approval process for the EBC proposals:

> It was all done to the time line of the Group VPs' targets for the EBCs—there were no formal deadlines. The process used to develop the plans varied by business. Some business groups had very open forums and planning processes, and others involved few personnel. European management approved almost all of the EBC structure plans, knowing that any problems would be corrected as the structure evolved.

98   Hammerly felt that the participation of the key players in developing the new EBC structures was critical:

> Many companies put out a new organization chart and say "We have changed the organization." But I do not believe you change an organization by putting out a new organization chart. You have to change the behavior and the thinking of the people and you only do that by their participation in the process.

100   In making the critical choice of the EBC head, Hanson had committed to the organization from the start that he wanted the majority to be Europeans:

> These are very difficult jobs. To run a business across 20 countries in Europe with multiple cultures, at least a dozen languages and different distribution channels, you have to understand Europe. You cannot take inexperienced Americans, even though they may really understand the product, and put them in Europe in the role of running one of the businesses.

102   In parallel with the development of the EBC plans, Hanson and the relevant U.S. Group Vice President developed a list of 3 or 4 candidates for each EBC head position, stating their preferred individual, which went first for approval by a European executive resource committee and then afterwards to the corporate executive resource committee in St. Paul. Hanson commented, "In virtually every case, we received both their approvals for our candidate."

103   Another key decision was where to locate the headquarters for each EBC. Many of the MDs on the EOC were convinced that the EBCs should be sited in close proximity to the manufacturing and technical sites, which were located across Europe. As Bill Monahan, then head of the Italian RSO, explained, "A business unit has to be as close to its technology as possible so that when a manager wants to visit a plant or lab, it does not have to be a special trip." The opposing viewpoint, held mainly by the U.S. Group VPs, was to locate the majority of the EBCs in Brussels, the traditional seat of 3M Europe, which one MD characterized as "a comfortable American ghetto."

104   Between the January announcement and the summer of 1992 (see Exhibit 8 for time line of events), four EBC plans were approved by the EOC out of the potential 19 EBCs planned. However, by this point, though Hanson had originally targeted the reorganization to be completed by the end of

1994, the change was becoming too disruptive to be allowed to drag out. Monahan explained the problems that the organization was facing at that time:

> There was great uncertainty on the part of the people and their jobs. One of their concerns was obviously, what is going to happen to me—are there jobs for all of us? I believe you cannot operate in an environment like that—it freezes people's creativity, innovation, and risk taking. We could not leave some of those Division Directors in place, not knowing when or if they were going to be pulled out of those businesses. And then the people with EBCs that had not formed were saying all the good people were going to be taken by the time theirs came up.

106   Stefano Rosselli Del Turco described his personal experience as a Division Director in Italy as he waited to see if he had a place in the new organization:

> I was a very happy man in Italy. I had a well-respected job. I knew I was not going anywhere because I was reporting to an MD who was always American, but I had one of the biggest groups I could have in Italy. So that was it. And when this change occurred, it was, "Oh, my God! Will I be a candidate for one of those European jobs? Will I have to leave my country?" So after a few years of being happy and secure, now I did not know.

108   Furthermore, the dual organizational structure with some businesses being run under the new EBC structure and others still being run at the regional level added more complexity and it was becoming too confusing. Therefore, the decision was made to expedite the reorganization to be completed by the end of 1993.

109   As the European organization anxiously awaited the completion of the reorganization, trying to guess what it would mean for them personally, daily business still had to be conducted in an increasingly poor economic climate, as the recession in Europe deepened. The new heads of the RSOs played a key role in filling the gaps by taking a much more hands on role than normal. Monahan told how he handled it as MD of Italy:

> As the Division Directors in Italy were disappearing, I began meeting with the Sales and Marketing managers of the businesses on a monthly basis, talking about how to get their sales up, what the issues were and what could the subsidiary do to help them. Still there was no question that the business suffered when we were in this state of flux.

110   Del Turco, after being appointed as the EBC head for the Data Storage and Visual Systems EBC, explained the dependency he had on the RSO management to bridge from the old to the new organization:

> You have to recognize that when I was named it was just me alone, and my secretary. Now you cannot run a business that way. You need to put a team together and help that team become effective. There is quite a lot of time between those two moments. I needed them [the RSOs] because it had to be a gradual taking on of responsibility, step by step.

Recruiting the New Team

112   After the EBC heads were in place, they worked to assemble their own teams. Peter Williams, EBC head for Abrasives, spoke for many EBC heads when he commented, "The biggest difficulties I had when assembling my team was competing for talent and the availability of people with the proper skills." Though all the EBCs wanted to hire managers with pan-European experience, in reality, there were relatively few managers within 3M with that type of background—it was clear that it would have to be learned "on the job."

113   Another concern when hiring was the mobility of the 3M managers in Europe. In many instances, the new heads of the EBCs were asked to leave their home countries to relocate at the predetermined EBC headquarters. Hanson admitted that he expected this to be a problem, but for the most part, they went willingly. Nevertheless, at the next level below EBC head, the EBU heads and staffs, recruiting managers was more difficult. Del Turco explained what he faced when staffing his EBC:

> Most of the people have always worked in the same country, their families have lived in the same place, and not many are willing to move. So you look at your best people, the ones you think can do the European job, then they have to ask their spouse and family if they should accept the European job. So you have that kind of constraint. It has not been easy to form a team—in fact, I have some Americans on the team because I did not have any Europeans willing to take those positions.

EXHIBIT 9
3M's European Business Centers

BRUSSELS
Tapes and adhesives
Commercial & consumer
Traffic, graphic & safety products
Medical products
Electro products
ANTWERP
Chemicals
LOUGHBOROUGH
Pharmaceuticals
BRACKNELL
Abrasive technologies
Personal & environmental protection products
HAMBURG
Telecom systems
NEUSS
Disposable products
Automotive & aerospace
Hardgood & electronic resources
CERGY
Data storage products & visual systems
Audio & video products
MALAKOFF
Dental products
MILAN
Printing systems
Medical imaging systems

115   Many individuals found intermediate solutions to the problem of location. For example, Richard Northrop, the 56-year-old British EBC head of Hardgoods and Electronic Resources, maintained an apartment in Neuss, Germany, the headquarters of the EBC, while his wife divided her time between the U.K. and Germany. As for his people:

> I had the option to relocate them to Germany but because this change is evolutionary, not revolutionary, I said, "We will review it in 2–3 years, but for now, stay where you are." I imagined that if I was 30 years old, I would not want to move. Many are married to professional partners who just could not move. In any case, I was more interested in the person's skills than where he or she lived.

117   The EBC structures were all in place by February 1993, 18 months after Hammerly had taken over International with his agenda to reorganize 3M's activities in Europe and 10 months earlier than the second, expedited deadline. To everyone's satisfaction, 70% of the new heads were Europeans, primarily drawn from the ranks of Division Directors, but also including a few of the MDs from smaller countries. In the final count, there were 18 EBCs comprised of 33 EBUs. Six EBCs were headquartered in Belgium, three in the U.K., three in France, four in Germany, and two were in Italy (see Exhibit 9). Most were located with planned logic such as proximity to lab or manufacturing expertise, or co-location with EBCs which shared the same distribution channels.

118   To the surprise of the European management team, there were only a handful of Division Directors who could not be placed in the new organization. The rest either became EBC or EBU heads or

they became Sales and Marketing regional managers with the responsibility for selling a group of commodities across one or more countries and reported to the EBU head. As for those who did not adapt easily to the new structure, Hanson explained, "We took very good care of them and made sure they left with a good feeling about the company."

119   While the management team of 3M Europe had much apparent success in reorienting the organization, not everyone observing the transition believed it was complete or had taken hold. As one senior manager in 3M's International management team noted:

> I worked in Europe for many years. I am still not completely convinced that this transition is either over or could be declared successful yet. There are still many challenges ahead.

121   This comment was echoed by a senior manager in the European organization who noted:

> We have been through a great deal of change. When I reflect on it, I am not completely sure how we did it all, nor am I sure it is over, or that we know what needs to be changed next.

CASE 17

THE 3M COMPANY: INTEGRATING EUROPE (B)

1   Entering 1994, 3M Europe's transition from a geographic focus to a pan-European focus was pro-
ceeding smoothly, in large part due to the strong efforts of the Managing Directors (MDs) of the
regional subsidiary organizations (RSOs). Doug Hanson, the Vice President of 3M Europe, found an
exciting momentum building within the new organization:

2   We are revitalizing Europe and people are enthusiastic about it. We are unleashing a tremendous amount of
power. We are spreading the wings of these people who were in the second and third layer of management
within the subsidiary managing their product lines. They were constrained, but now these guys see real
opportunity.

3   Nevertheless, in the short term, the organization was hounded by the difficulty of building true
teams across Europe, defining an ongoing, valued role for the RSOs, assuring that the newly formed
EBCs maintained an openness to the regional input and each other, and simply, getting it all done in a
24-hour day.

THE CHALLENGES OF PAN-EUROPEAN MANAGEMENT

4   The 3M Company in Europe had just completed the structural portion of a major reorganization of
the way it conducted business. Due to perceived competitive and customer pressures, in 18 short
months, the company had moved from its historical structure of fairly autonomous country subsidiaries (CSOs) to a new pan-European structure designed to better manage product lines on both a
European and global basis. Under the new organization, the profit and loss responsibility was shifted
to product line structures, called European Business Centers (EBCs), of which there were 18. Each
EBC managed the business strategy, technical development and manufacturing for a product line
across Europe. The head of the EBC reported to the relevant Group Vice President in the U.S. to
create an efficient link between the European strategy and 3M's global strategy for that product line.
Within the EBC structure, there were one or more European Business Units (EBUs) which had
responsibility for sales and marketing for a business within the product line. To assure 3M retained a
responsiveness to local needs, which had been its strength under the old country subsidiary structure,
the EBCs were matrixed with regional subsidiaries (RSOs) which provided the resources to the
EBCs, as well as managing the legal entity of 3M in each country. (See earlier case, "The 3M
Company: Integrating Europe [A].")

Team Building

5   As with any organizational change, it would take time for the new units to begin to work together as a
team to fully leverage the power of the structure. There were several issues which the European
management team recognized could threaten the cohesion of the teams such as the geographical

This case was written by Mary Ackenhusen, Research Associate, under the supervision and guidance of Associate Professor
Daniel Muzyka and Professor Neil Churchill. It is intended to be used as a basis for class discussion rather than to illustrate
either effective or ineffective handling of an administrative situation. Funding for this case was provided by the IAF Chair
of Entrepreneurship and Digital Equipment Corporation.
Reprinted with the permission of INSEAD.
Copyright © 1994 INSEAD, Fontainebleau, France.
Funding for this case was provided by the IAF Chair of Entrepreneurship and Digital Equipment Corporation.

distance between members and the cultural and language barriers. Additionally, some members of the new organization were suffering from what they felt was a lack of senior management attention to guide them in their new positions.

6   The new organization was decentralized in a truly pan-European manner, unlike many multi-national companies which centralize the majority of their headquarters and operations in one location. The geographic dispersement of the research laboratories and manufacturing facilities, combined with a hesitancy to move managers out of their home countries, left most of the EBC heads with management teams physically located in a number of countries across Europe. As a typical example, Peter Williams, head of the Abrasives EBC, which was headquartered in Bracknell, England (near London), had an EBU head in Bracknell, France, and Germany. Furthermore, while his manufacturing head and Controller were in Bracknell, his logistics support was provided from Brussels.

7   On top of the isolation caused by being physically separated, many of the managers in the recently formed EBC organizations did not yet know each other well, though they met as often as possible in order to remedy the situation. When each EBC team was first announced, it had held an offsite meeting to explore the direction of the EBC and develop a sense of common purpose. Since then, on an ongoing basis, most of the EBC top management teams had held regular large-scale meetings at least once per quarter and sometimes as often as once per month. Typically, an EBU manager might talk by phone to his or her Sales and Marketing managers in the regions twice each month and then see them in person at the regular quarterly meeting. EBC travel budgets were rising as managers tried to work together, though this increase in cost was offset by a reduction in travel costs by the European headquarters staff. Telephones and video conferencing were also being used frequently. However, it remained difficult to grow the fledgling relationships between the management team members without regular face-to-face contact. As Richard Northrop, the new EBC head of Hardgoods and Electronic Resources, commented:

8   This is really an experiment but with all the new technology for communicating, I think managing a geographically separated team can work. I want to be open-minded. However, particularly in 3M, we are used to seeing one's boss a lot. The interpersonal relationships can suffer when the team is not together in the same office—we must be careful. Part of the culture here is knowing one's colleague in the next country. It has been part of 3M's success though I do not think it depends on it.

9   Bernard Agis-Garcin was a young Frenchman working as the EBC Brand Marketing Manager for Consumer Tapes in Germany. He had been located in Germany in his previous position before the reorganization and was one of the managers intentionally not relocated to France with the rest of his EBC. Thus, not only was his boss based in France, all of his marketing colleagues with which he needed to work closely were located in a country other than Germany. Both the Trade Marketing Manager and Marketing Communications Manager were located in France, and the Marketing Operations Manager was located in Brussels. Additionally, he worked with the Marketing Operations people who reported to the regional Sales and Marketing Managers and were scattered across five different regions (see Exhibit 1 for organization chart). He found the team building and communication across Europe to be his biggest challenge:

10   We are still trying to set up a strong communications network between our marketing people. We have made good progress but we are not yet to the point that we can share ideas and develop things together. I want this sharing to become spontaneous and not have people wait to present it at the next meeting. I am convinced that our number one priority is to build a European spirit—one organization, one spirit and one resource.

11   To help encourage this European spirit across the EBC, many EBCs were using their local Sales and Marketing managers to drive European projects. As additional benefits, this allowed the EBCs to keep their headquarters staff to a minimal level and gave some relatively young managers immediate pan-European experience. In his own area of responsibility, Garcin had initiated four European task forces to address VHS, headcleaning, audio, and video camcorder products with two teams being run by French Marketing managers and two being run by British Marketing managers.

12   With their boss often in another country, EBU managers had to learn to work independently, or find substitutes where appropriate. The distance between boss and subordinate in the new organization was a very positive experience for the right individual. As Hanson explained:

EXHIBIT 1
Audio & Video Products EBC

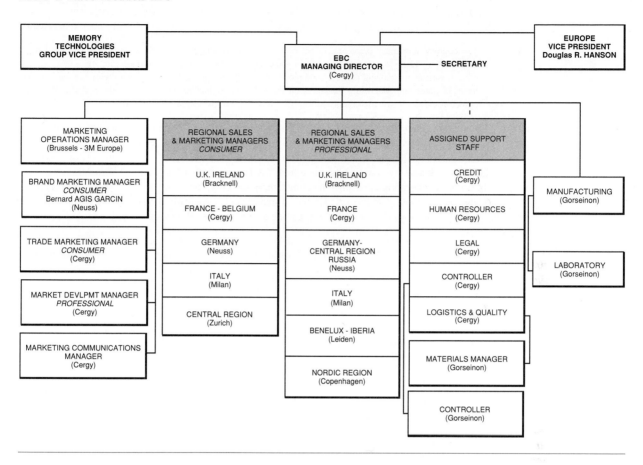

13   It used to be that in the country organizations, the Regional Marketing Manager reported to the Marketing Director whose office was two doors down the hallway. Now this person reports to an EBC head who may or may not be in the same location. Now there are two kinds of managers and they will react differently to this. One has lots of confidence in their ability and loves not having to check everything like they did in the past. They are enthusiastic and exuberant over the change. There is the second kind of manager who likes to check things out with the boss and always get the "okay, go ahead and do it." Making this second kind of person understand that they can take these kind of decisions, and that they must, is important.

14   Before the reorganization, Yves De Royer had been a Division Director in France, reporting to the MD of the country. With the change, he was promoted to EBU head of Abrasive Systems, located in the same building as he had worked in previously. He found that under the new reorganization, he was still caught in the role of mentoring many of the people that used to report to him under the old organization, though his current priority was to manage his new pan-European EBU organization. He commented, "They'll come to me to review a proposal before they present it to the upper management of the French region [RSO]. Unfortunately, I have less and less time for this counseling role."

15   While under the old organization the Technical Service representatives located in the field had been part of the sales organization reporting into the CSO, these individuals now reported into the laboratory structure of the EBC in order to better coordinate the technical effort. Chris Tandy, Technical Manager of the Abrasives EBC, expressed, "Now we can develop European solutions to problems rather than just local solutions." However, Tandy recognized that these often younger, inexperienced employees might need more mentoring than was available with their boss in another

country and, thus, the Sales and Marketing managers in the region were encouraged to support the Technical Service representatives.

16   Stefano Rosselli Del Turco, head of the Data Storage and Visual Products EBC, was concerned that the new EBC heads might not recognize these softer aspects of developing people and teams:

17   The country subsidiary management before the change somehow played the role of the godfather to the organization. There was someone to whom you could refer to for your career, a job rotation, a new opportunity, as well as for sensing the level and motivation of the people and infusing them with energy. Now you have 30 Sales and Marketing managers on the loose, all reporting dotted line to the regional Managing Director and solid line to someone sitting far away. I am a bit nervous about that.

18   Language and cultural differences were a barrier that the EBC teams were working to overcome even though English was the dominant language at 3M. One EBC head commented, "Language is an issue. Nuances and refinements still get lost. I think I underestimated the amount of repetition and clarity I needed in my communication at first." A French mother tongue EBU Director commented, "In our EBC operating committee meetings, there are only one or two without English as a mother tongue. Sometimes, it is too fast for me to understand." At lower levels, the problem was more prevalent. Northrop, EBC head of Hardgoods and Electronic Resources, lamented:

19   All my Sales and Marketing managers speak English but I find it difficult to address groups of sales reps—individually it is okay, but not to groups. I would like to have an integrated sales meeting at all levels, but it does not work with the language issue.

20   Hanson compared the European situation to the U.S.:

21   I think it is a real challenge for the EBU heads to drive the sales forces. They are dealing with 10 regions, they are remote, yet, they have to get to know these people. In the U.S., the National Sales Managers know every salesperson on a first name basis. They know their spouses and kids. Yet in Europe, the EBU head has to drive the sales force recognizing the differences in culture, recognizing the distances—it is difficult.

22   At all levels, 3M employees in Europe were beginning to realize the importance of assuming a pan-European mindset. While a survey taken at 3M Italy in the first year of the reorganization indicated that only 20% were willing to relocate with the company outside Italy, in the same survey taken one year later, the percentage had increased to over 60%. Furthermore, many were now starting to work on their English language skills. Without the language capability and mobility, there was a fear that the new organization could be career limiting.

The Role of Local Management

23   The regional organizations were struggling to clarify how they could most effectively help the businesses. There had been many proclamations by top European management and EBC management concerning how essential the regions were in terms of maintaining the local presence, but the day-to-day execution of how to do this was not always clear. Karen Welke, who had transitioned from being the MD of the French CSO to being the MD of the French RSO, commented:

   3M corporate executives recognized from the start that the new Regional MD roles were more challenging than the independent subsidiary role, not less so. The amount of organizational change together with the EBC matrix would demand leadership effectiveness without the traditional authority lines.

24   As envisioned by the original task force, the primary role of the RSOs was to provide the resources required to support the EBCs' business strategies. EBCs could not own anything,[1] only a RSO could. Thus, an EBC provided the direction on what type and how much product a manufacturing facility should produce, and the RSO implemented the production/engineering steps, equipment acquisition, labor negotiations, and other execution tasks. While an EBC, through its business plan, would establish the cost profile demanded for its business, it was the region's responsibility to assure

---

[1] The EBC was not a legal entity and therefore could neither own assets nor employ people. It was only an internal organizational unit.

that the profile was supported in the areas under RSO control such as manufacturing costs. In the case of employee hiring, the EBC would specify the skill requirements for a particular position and the RSO would recruit to that specification. Hanson commented:

25   It is a very close working relationship but it is the kind that 3M can deal with. Many of the things we are doing in this reorganization are not so different from what we have done in the U.S. For example, in the U.S. we have five Divisions in the Tape Group and we have a Tape Manufacturing Division that manufactures all the products for these Divisions. That is really the same thing as we have in Europe.

26   The MDs of the RSOs maintained the same job grade as they had held as MD of a CSO and the new EBC head was graded at the same level as well. However, many within the European organization saw much of the power being shifted away from the region to the EBC. Bill Monahan, the Italian regional MD until mid-1993, commented on this:

27   People told me the power was taken out of this job with the change, but I have a different view. I think the job is much better now. You can touch what is going on in the country now far better than sitting up above everything. In the past, the Division Directors made most of the business decisions anyway. Now the MDs can really touch the support of all the units. They are not doing it through people, they are doing it personally. For example, I met with every Business Unit head that came through Italy and we would work out the issues that they had in the country. We would figure out how we could support the business better. It was more fun and a lot more hands on.

28   Hanson was well aware of the concern within the organization and emphasized the importance of the local perspective in the regions:

29   The big change here is that the Managing Director and the company within that country has lost its autonomy. It is a big concern. I tell them that it is still in the country that the action is taking place. Only the local Sales and Marketing manager, the local representative, can know the customer. We need that local knowledge, that local input, and that is not going to change. When I talk to the MDs, I tell them that there is no EBC head who can sit several hundred kilometers away and know everything they need to know about that customer's needs.

30   In some cases, the new matrix organization was slowing down the decision making process instead of compressing it as intended. For example, when an EBC manager tried to hire a secretary to the EBC budget, the regional Human Resources manager blocked the hire until it could be checked with the head of the RSO. Similarly, when 3M France put a freeze on buying laptop computers as part of an effort to control expenses, there was confusion about whether an EBC could buy one for an EBC salesman working in France. Stories of this kind were common in the first year of the transition leading one manager to comment, "This new structure has the possibility to create more bureaucracy."

31   To help smooth the transition process, Regional Roundtables were held by each regional MD to work out these issues between the EBC management and the regional management. Hanson described the process:

32   In these meetings, we ask, "What are the problems you are having with the human resources people? What kinds of problems are you having with reporting? Are you getting the right kinds of reports? What about requisitions? What about authority for expenditures?" These are little but irritating things for operational people and they need to be addressed. These roundtables facilitate this.

33   However, at least from one EBC manager's standpoint, taking the time to work out the fine details on lines of authority was a bad use of the limited time available to the new pan-European managers as they worked to get their new businesses coordinated across Europe:

34   I think we spend too much time worrying about whether the matrix will work. We need to just get on with it. We have had a European Management Roundtable, an EBC kickoff meeting, a Sales and Marketing Counsel, and a Regional Roundtable and the output is always the same issues: role of the region, role of the EBCs, lack of policies, key account management, communications to the customers. We need to just do what needs to be done even if we are not sure we have the authority. However, some people hide behind these issues and use them as an excuse for not acting. If we remain customer-focused, it should work itself out.

35   In the short term, the regional MDs were very involved in assuring the transition was as smooth as possible and that the required systems were put in place in a timely manner. For example, as part of

the transition team, each MD of an RSO was leading a European project which related to the general management of all the EBCs. The projects included developing a process to reduce indirect costs in Europe and customer-focused marketing, for example. However, as challenging as the MD role of the RSOs was during the transition, Hanson believed that after the organization stabilized, "The EBC jobs are the more powerful positions. They will be the ones that give the best broadening experience in an international position."

Avoiding Silos

36 There was a very real concern within the European management team that, unless consciously managed, the EBCs would become impenetrable "silos."[2] One manager commented, "We have that in the U.S. because we are Group and Division-oriented. People say this is my business or this is my account—you stay out of it."

37   One of the challenges facing the RSO management was the integration of the EBCs at the local level to avoid "siloing." Some of the regional management teams had developed a number of forums which were designed to help integrate the local workforce with the EBC team and the EBC teams with each other. EBC leaders, while heralding the intent, found that often they had little time for these activities.

38   Another program to help integrate the EBCs was the Customer Focused Marketing program which encouraged EBUs to make deals with each other to collectively serve the needs of a customer. Under this program, if a sales representative from the Tape EBU sold a product from the Abrasives EBU to a common customer, both EBUs would get equal credit for the sale. While 3M had never done much in terms of a key accounts program on a regional basis in Europe, in the new structure, the regional MDs were given explicit responsibility to develop a European key account management program in order to exploit this as a future avenue of increased sales.

39   On the technical side of the house, there was some concern that the focus on resources by EBC would limit the interaction across businesses, discourage the sharing of technology and thus undermine the open system of new product development that 3M prided itself on. Tandy, the Technical Manager for the Abrasives EBC, explained:

40   The only drive to keep the European technical community communicating and working together across Business Units is our members who see a real need for it. I know that any information, technology, whatever I need to do my work in this lab, is within 3M somewhere, but I must find it. I am a great believer in maintaining the network.

41   Several steps were being taken to encourage communication across the European technical labs. For instance, in Germany, a poster session was held at the end of 1993 which included several labs such as Adhesives, Telecom, and Hardgoods and Electronic Resources technology, all from different EBCs, to talk about their new ideas. Additionally, a Technical Operations Committee meeting, including all the technical heads of the EBCs, was held quarterly and an annual meeting was held for all technical managers in Europe. Some countries had appointed an individual as an ad hoc technical head for the country, in addition to being the technical head of an EBC, to facilitate the interaction between EBC labs within the country. Likewise, Manley Johnson, Technical Director of Europe, saw the facilitation of the flow of information between EBCs and countries as one of his principal jobs. Nevertheless, according to at least one manager, 3M was only trading one focus for another, "You could say we have gone from a country silo to an EBC silo."

Support and Loss of Slack

42 It is in the nature of many reorganizations that the managers who are taking on new roles are at first overwhelmed by the challenge of sorting out their responsibilities. In 3M's new EBC management teams, this was also the case, leaving most EBC managers dissatisfied with the amount of time they

---

[2] A reference to a farm silo which will only allow movement up and down within a single silo and not horizontally between silos.

were able to spend with customers. Several elements contributed to the stress, other than just learning a new job. First, the EBCs were leanly staffed in order to guard against poor performance in the first year of an EBC profit and loss statement. The European recession exaggerated the financial concerns. Secondly, the travel required to maintain the team and see customers amounted to 50–60% of the working week for most EBC managers. Lastly, the systems required to give efficient access to customer, financial, market, and employee data were not yet in place.

43   When the transition was accelerated in mid-1992, it became clear that the adjustments to the support systems required by the new organization would not be in place upon the completion of the structural changes. In particular, the information flows needed to support decision making on an EBC basis, rather than a CSO basis, were lacking. For example, even one year after the change, EBC management did not have immediate access to customer information on a consolidated European basis. A major upgrade and rewrite of the order management system was planned for completion by the end of 1994 and was expected to remedy the problem. Financial systems were still being developed as well. As of mid-1993, sales and contribution data was only available by an EBU 20 days after the close of the period. Furthermore, there was no real-time system for product pricing by country, which in at least one instance, had allowed competitors to undersell 3M with the EBC management being unaware of the problem until after the damage had been done.

44   The European management team worked around the lack of systems as well as they could, often manually compiling information so that data for decision making was available. However, this extra task was a burden on an already overstretched organization. Bernard Agis-Garcin, the Brand Marketing Manager for Consumer Tapes, described his own situation:

45   Time management is my biggest challenge. I travel 50–60% of the time and after each trip there is lots of follow-up. I spend a lot of my time collecting figures for management to help them make decisions. I also spend a good amount of time managing the projects we are doing. I have no staff and only 20% of a secretary. But this type of lean management is typical for a low margin business and I certainly expected it when I took the job.

46   Additionally, the Human Resource systems and policies were still vague, which was bothersome, particularly to the lower level managers in the EBCs. Not only did individual situations need to be addressed, the HR policies were not yet harmonized between EBCs, which led to significant amounts of time being spent in both the Regional Roundtables and EBC management meetings trying to sort out these issues.

REAPING THE REWARDS

47   The European management of 3M felt confident that the new organization would go a long way towards making 3M more competitive in Europe. To begin with, the European product line strategy could now be easily linked to the global strategy through the reporting relationship of the EBC heads to the worldwide Group VPs in the U.S. From the viewpoint of a U.S. Product Manager, it would now be much more feasible to coordinate with Europe on a planning, marketing, technical, or operations basis. While before there had been 17 contacts to be made, after the transition, the command channel was dramatically reduced to only 1 contact. The organization was also credited with increasing the responsiveness to customer needs through enhanced flexibility and shortened decision making cycles. As an extra bonus, management expected the new organization to help build 3M's technical prowess in Europe.

Organizational Responsiveness

48   Across the European businesses of 3M, enthusiasm over the bottom line results of the new organization was evident due to the ability to quickly implement programs across Europe as well as the efficiencies made possible from the coordination of the needs of the 10 European regions. Stig Eriksson, the head of the Medical Products EBC, commented:

49   We have already, in our first year as an EBC, showed improved growth versus last year and improved contribution income. So it is working. We have flattened the organization significantly. Now we no longer have decision makers who are too far away from the business to understand it.

50   Eriksson referenced his experience in adding to his EBC's headcount in the U.K. as an example of the new compressed decision making cycle:

51   We can make strategic and resource decisions that we were not able to do before. For example, in February 1993, when we decided to add 7 people to the U.K. organization to take advantage of some growth opportunities there, the U.K. people worked to develop a plan and after it was presented, it only took a week to get the go-ahead. In the old mode, it would have taken several months because it would have impacted the P&L of the U.K. subsidiary and hurt results. The EBC could do it by lowering its investment elsewhere.

52   This increased responsiveness also translated into an ability to better respond to the needs of local markets. Richard Northrop, the Hardgoods and Electronic Resources EBC head, explained why:

53   Before, we actually did not localize much at all. The difference now is the focus. If it is a profitable expansion of the business, we will do it. The local preferences actually get a better hearing now and are more likely to get implemented.

54   Yves De Royer, EBU head for Abrasive Systems, was under heavy pressure to increase market share in abrasives in Europe and felt that the ability to transfer expertise among the previously local operations in Europe would go far in helping him to achieve his growth goal in a recessionary market. He explained:

55   We are now very strong in the distribution channel but to meet the ambitious growth target, we will have to expand our selling network and win a number of large, direct accounts even though some of them have been our competitors' customers for years. We will have to sell them higher value systems, in other words, change the basis of competition or offer some other cost benefits in order to dislodge the competition from these accounts. It will only happen if we are organized to succeed—it will take a cross functional effort to support these accounts because they have very specific requirements.

56   De Royer hoped to leverage the various pockets of expertise found in different countries in Europe to do this. Thus, his German organization would develop a pan-European business planning process for key accounts, the U.K. had the responsibility to develop a sales training package, and France was developing the complementary package for distributor sales. Additionally, he was using the new organization to reduce costs through a dramatic rationalization of the product line and better utilization of existing resources, taking actions which had never been possible before because of each local manager's internal concerns.

Operational Efficiency

57   Many EBCs were experiencing early successes as they implemented marketing and production programs which had been stalled for years. The EBC which sold video cassettes into Germany had been hindered for some time by a customer perception that the quality was inferior to the competition based on the results of testing by a consumer awareness magazine. In reality, the difference in quality was imperceptible to the human eye and did not affect product performance, but the adverse publicity was hurting sales. After the manufacturing operation was put under the EBC structure, it became possible to implement a program to collect all the finished product which fell at the top of the tolerance range for the pertinent coating parameter to sell into the German market. Thus, by 1994, the 3M product sold in Germany was consistently equal or superior in quality to the German competition.

58   Manufacturing and operational efficiencies were now easily accomplished. The decision to combine the Italian extruding operation and the French coating operation for transparency films into one location, which had never been resolved by the EMAT, was quickly made under the new EBC structure. Within the EBC for Hardgoods and Electronic Resources, there were 17 depots stocking spare parts across Europe. By the end of 1993, plans had been put in place to centralize with one depot which would supply overnight delivery of parts throughout Europe and, in turn, save on inventory levels while improving availability.

59 Repair service, such as that done by the Hardgoods and Electronics Resources EBC, was another area that was expected to benefit from the new organization. For example, in the future, the EBC hoped to implement a paging system in some of the smaller countries which would immediately contact the service technician with all the relevant information as each new service call was received, instead of waiting for him or her to call in. Another proposal was to give all the service technicians a keypad which they could download daily with the day's repair activity and the parts consumed in order to provide automatic billing and replenishment of stocks. Northrop, the EBC head, explained:

60 We are trying to be leading edge in terms of service times—we see service response as a significant competitive advantage to 3M. Previously, the size of the business in an individual country like Portugal might not have justified the investment making it difficult to get any kind of uniform service level across Europe. Now the EBC can sanction it if it is important to the harmonization of customer satisfaction across Europe.

Technical Effectiveness

61 The technical side of the business was also experiencing improvements in both efficiency and effectiveness. For example, though the lab was generally proficient in the product development process, according to Tandy, the Technical Manager for the Abrasives EBC, the new organization should give a boost to the product definition phase:

62 With the EMAT structure, the ideas that were coming to us were mainly "me-too" ideas like "a product like the competition's but 10% cheaper." Now, with the new organization, the input can be coordinated between Marketing, the technical function, and Manufacturing and hopefully turn into truly innovative thinking. We can then have Tech Service out testing the competitive offerings while Marketing is looking at the market opportunities. This way we will have real data and spend less time debating.

63 He expected to improve the time-to-market on the back end as well:

64 Before, when a project was completed, it was hard to convince the CSOs to sell it. They all wanted their own modification. Now, with the Euro-organization, it will have been developed so that one product fits everyone's needs. A much neater commercialization process.

65 The organizational link of the Tech Service representatives in the field to the EBC technical organization contributed significantly to a faster testing process of a new product before introduction. While before, a lab representative was sent on a tour of up to six countries to test the product in each region sequentially, now the sample could be sent overnight to the technical representatives in each country to test in parallel. This would cut the testing phase from two months to two weeks. Furthermore, there was now a formal communication channel between the Technical Service function and the laboratories which accelerated the diagnosis of problems found in the field after the product was introduced.

66 Hanson also saw the new structure addressing the problem that European customers did not recognize the added value of the technological content of the 3M product, thus forcing the company to overly rely on price competitiveness in this market:

67 I think the new structure helps because we now have Sales and Marketing, Research and Production all linked together. Also, the technical community, with the Technical Service reps, is all linked together, reporting to the technical head. They can now teach people to sell 3M technology. In the past, the Technical Service person went out and fixed problems but he or she was not a technical leader. Now the sales people know that the technical community is part of their organization. They can get help if they need it, they know who to call. They can bring together the technical resources to meet customer needs.

68 In general, there was the perception in the European 3M technical community that the rest of the European organization did not fully understand its function. Perhaps this was because of the history of the company's development in Europe in which the Sales and Marketing functions initially drove the business. Manley Johnston, the Technical Director for Europe, felt that this needed to change, "We have to establish the laboratories as equal partners at the business level in Europe, as they are in the U.S." Johnston went on to explain the breadth of the opportunity available through a better technical effort:

69   Penetration in Europe for many of our products is only 50% of what it is in the U.S. So there have got to be opportunities that we can identify through more effective technical service activity. In many cases, we have got the products developed now, but if people do not know how to use them or the use is a little different or maybe the product needs to be a little different . . . We need to better focus on this.

70   Externally, he also wanted to enhance the reputation of the company. Currently, when 3M recruited at the *grandes ecoles* in France or other top European schools to attract European technical talent, it found that it was an unknown and often unsuccessful contender. Furthermore, as Johnston commented, "We are not, in my opinion, linked in with the best and the most forward thinking in Europe, not like we are in the U.S. where we know what is going on in the network—the universities and research institutions and such." Though there had been a U.S.–based Technical Director for Europe before the reorganization, under the new structure, Johnston was located in Europe to better coordinate the company's external links.

71   The closer tie of the technical lab to the global business strategy encouraged more global teaming on research. Ideas which were brainstormed in Europe could now be technically supported in the U.S., where the majority of 3M's technical resources were located, because of the direct link between Product Groups in the U.S. and Europe. For example, an innovation of a velcro fastener to attach the abrasive pad on a tool used in automotive body shops was the idea of an European scientist. While before the idea might have stagnated in Europe due to a lack of resources to develop the product, in 1993, this product became the number one global product development project in the abrasives business and was being managed by a multinational team of two U.S.–based scientists and the U.K. scientist who had come up with the original idea.

72   Finally, with the enhanced ties to the global strategy, an ongoing issue with the European labs was likely to be resolved—that is, was their role primarily one of localizing products developed in the U.S. and providing European-specific technical and process support? Or should some of the labs scattered throughout Europe become the primary centers of expertise for Group or Divisional technologies? For the most part, the majority of the truly new product development in Europe came from the imaging technology lab in Italy, which was the only Sector level lab located outside the U.S., and the automotive trades laboratory in the U.K. With the ongoing pressure on resources, it was clear that the company could not continue, in some instances, to duplicate research around the globe.

73   As Hanson reflected on the transition, he noted:

I did not expect this change to be as huge as it is in terms of business process and management style changes—no one did. We knew there would adjustments to be made, but we did not anticipate the hundreds of managers in new jobs and what that really meant. Now they have to reestablish all their networks and relationships and develop new, effective ways of working together. Yet, we know each other, trust each other, and rely on each other. I think we have the kind of willingness to adapt to change as is necessary with new business conditions.

CASE 18

W. L. GORE & ASSOCIATES, INC.

To make money and have fun.
W. L. Gore

THE FIRST DAY ON THE JOB

1   Bursting with resolve, Jack Dougherty, a newly minted M.B.A. from the College of William and Mary, reported to his first day at W. L. Gore & Associates on July 26, 1976. He presented himself to Bill Gore, shook hands firmly, looked him in the eye, and said he was ready for anything.

2   Jack was not ready for what happened next, however. Gore replied, "That's fine, Jack, fine. Why don't you look around and find something you'd like to do?" Three frustrating weeks later he found that something: trading in his dark blue suit for jeans, he loaded fabric into the mouth of a machine that laminated the company's patented GORE-TEX®[1] membrane to fabric. By 1982, Jack had become responsible for all advertising and marketing in the fabrics group. This story is part of the folklore of W. L. Gore & Associates.

3   Today the process is more structured. Regardless of the job for which they are hired, new Associates[2] take a journey through the business before settling into their own positions. A new sales Associate in the fabrics division may spend six weeks rotating through different areas before beginning to concentrate on sales and marketing. Among other things the newcomer learns is how GORE-TEX fabric is made, what it can and cannot do, how Gore handles customer complaints, and how it makes its investment decisions.

4   Anita McBride related her early experience at W. L. Gore & Associates this way:

> Before I came to Gore, I had worked for a structured organization. I came here, and for the first month it was fairly structured because I was going through training and this is what we do and this is how Gore is and all of that. I went to Flagstaff for that training. After a month I came down to Phoenix and my sponsor said, "Well, here's your office; it's a wonderful office" and "Here's your desk," and walked away. And I thought, "Now what do I do?" You know, I was waiting for a memo or something, or a job description. Finally after another month I was so frustrated, I felt, "What have I gotten myself into?" And so I went to my sponsor and I said, "What the heck do you want from me? I need something from you." And he said, "If you don't know what you're supposed to do, examine your commitment, and opportunities."

BACKGROUND

5   W. L. Gore & Associates evolved from the late Wilbert L. Gore's experiences personally, organizationally, and technically. He was born in Meridian, Idaho, near Boise in 1912. By age six, according to his own account, he was an avid hiker in the Wasatch Mountain Range in Utah. In those mountains,

---

This case was prepared by Professor Frank Shipper of Salisbury State University and Professor Charles C. Manz of Arizona State University.

[1] GORE-TEX is a registered trademark of W. L. Gore & Associates.

[2] In this case the word *Associate* is used and capitalized because in W. L. Gore & Associates' literature, the word is always used instead of employees and is capitalized. In fact, case writers were told that Gore "never had employees—always Associates."

at a church camp, he met Genevieve, his future wife. In 1935, they got married—in their eyes, a partnership. He would make breakfast and Vieve, as everyone called her, would make lunch. The partnership lasted a lifetime.

6   He received both a bachelor of science in chemical engineering in 1933 and a master of science in physical chemistry in 1935 from the University of Utah. He began his professional career at American Smelting and Refining in 1936. He moved to Remington Arms Company in 1941 and then to E. I. du Pont de Nemours in 1945. He held positions as research supervisor and head of operations research. While at Du Pont, he worked on a team to develop applications for polytetrafluoroethylene, referred to as PTFE in the scientific community and known as "Teflon" by Du Pont's consumers. (Consumers know it under other names from other companies.) On this team, Wilbert Gore, called Bill by everyone, felt a sense of excited commitment, personal fulfillment, and self-direction. He followed the development of computers and transistors and felt that PTFE had the ideal insulating characteristics for use with such equipment.

7   He tried many ways to make a PTFE-coated ribbon cable without success. A breakthrough came in his home basement laboratory while he was explaining the problem to his 19-year-old son Bob. The young Gore saw some PTFE sealant tape made by 3M and asked his father, "Why don't you try this tape?" Bill then explained that everyone knew that you cannot bond PTFE to itself. Bob went on to bed.

8   Bill Gore remained in his basement lab and proceeded to try what everyone knew would not work. At about 4:00 AM he woke up his son, waving a small piece of cable around and saying excitedly, "It works, it works." The following night father and son returned to the basement lab to make ribbon cable coated with PTFE. Because the breakthrough idea came from Bob, the patent for the cable was issued in Bob's name.

9   For the next four months Bill Gore tried to persuade Du Pont to make a new product—PTFE coated ribbon cable. By this time in his career Bill Gore knew some of the decision makers at Du Pont. After talking to a number of them, he came to realize that Du Pont wanted to remain a supplier of raw materials and not a fabricator.

10   Bill and his wife, Vieve, began discussing the possibility of starting their own insulated wire and cable business. On January 1, 1958, their wedding anniversary, they founded W. L. Gore & Associates. The basement of their home served as their first facility. After finishing dinner that night, Vieve turned to her husband of 23 years and said, "Well, let's clear up the dishes, go downstairs, and get to work."

11   Bill Gore was 45 years old with five children to support when he left Du Pont. He put aside a career of 17 years, and a good, secure salary. To finance the first two years of the business, he and Vieve mortgaged their house and took $4,000 from savings. All their friends told them not to do it.

12   The first few years were rough. In lieu of salary, some of their employees accepted room and board in the Gore home. At one point 11 Associates were living and working under one roof. One afternoon, while sifting PTFE powder, Vieve received a call from the City of Denver's water department. The caller indicated that he was interested in the ribbon cable, but wanted to ask some technical questions. Bill was out running some errands. The caller asked for the product manager. Vieve explained that he was out at the moment. Next he asked for the sales manager and finally, the president. Vieve explained that they were also out. The caller became outraged and hollered, "What kind of company is this anyway?" With a little diplomacy the Gores were able eventually to secure an order for $100,000. This order put the company on a profitable footing and it began to take off.

13   W. L. Gore & Associates continued to grow and develop new products, primarily derived from PTFE. Its best known product would become GORE-TEX fabric. In 1986, Bill Gore died while backpacking in the Wind River Mountains of Wyoming. He was then Chairman of the Board. His son Bob continued to occupy the position of president. Vieve remained as the only other officer, secretary-treasurer.

THE OPERATING COMPANY

14   W. L. Gore & Associates has never had titles, hierarchy, or any of the conventional structures associated with enterprises of its size. The titles of president and secretary-treasurer continue to be used only because they are required by the laws of incorporation. In addition, Gore has never had a corporatewide mission or code of ethics statement; nor has Gore ever required or prohibited business units from developing such statements for themselves. Thus, the Associates of some business units who have felt a need for such statements have developed them on their own. When questioned about this issue, one Associate stated, "The company belief is that (1) its four basic operating principles cover ethical practices required of people in business; (2) it will not tolerate illegal practices." Gore's management style has been referred to as *unmanagement*. The organization has been guided by Bill's experiences on teams at Du Pont and has evolved as needed.

15   For example, in 1965 W. L. Gore & Associates was a thriving company with a facility on Paper Mill Road in Newark, Delaware. One Monday morning in the summer, Bill Gore was taking his usual walk through the plant. All of a sudden he realized that he did not know everyone in the plant. The team had become too big. As a result, he established the practice of limiting plant size to approximately 200 Associates. Thus was born the expansion policy of "Get big by staying small." The purpose of maintaining small plants was to accentuate a close-knit atmosphere and encourage communication among Associates in a facility.

16   In 1995, W. L. Gore & Associates consisted of over 44 plants worldwide with approximately 6,000 Associates. In some cases, the plants are grouped together on the same site (as in Flagstaff, Arizona, with 10 plants). Overseas Gore's facilities are located in Scotland, Germany, France and Italy, and the company has two joint ventures in Japan (see Figure 1). Gore manufactures electronic, medical, industrial, and fabric products. In addition, it has numerous sales offices worldwide, including Eastern Europe and Russia.

17   Gore electronic products have been found in unconventional places where conventional products will not do—in space shuttles, for example, where Gore wire and cable assemblies withstand the heat of ignition and the cold of space. in addition, they have been found in fast computers, transmitting signals at up to 93 percent of the speed of light. Gore cables have even gone underground, in oil drilling operations, and underseas, on submarines that require superior microwave signal equipment and no-fail cables that can survive high pressure. The Gore electronic products division has a history of anticipating future customer needs with innovative products. Gore electronic products have been well received in industry for their ability to last under adverse conditions. For example, Gore has become, according to Sally Gore, leader in human resources and communications, " . . . one of the largest manufacturers of ultrasound cable in the world, the reason being that Gore's electronic cables' signal transmission is very, very accurate and it's very thin and extremely flexible and has a very, very long flex life. That makes it ideal for things like ultrasound and many medical electronic applications."

18   In the medical arena, GORE-TEX–expanded PTFE has been considered an ideal replacement for human tissue in many situations. In patients suffering from cardiovascular disease the diseased portion of arteries has been replaced by tubes of expanded PTFE—strong, biocompatible structures capable of carrying blood at arterial pressures. Gore has a strong position in this product segment. Other Gore medical products have included patches that can literally mend broken hearts by sealing holes, and sutures that allow for tissue attachment and offer the surgeon silk-like handling coupled with extreme strength. In 1985, W. L. Gore & Associates won Britain's Prince Philip Award for Polymers in the Service of Mankind. The award recognized especially the life-saving achievements of the Gore medical products team.

19   Two recently developed products by this division are a new patch material that is intended to incorporate more tissue into the graft more quickly and GORE™ RideOn®[3] Cable System for bicycles. According to Amy LeGere of the medical division, "All the top pro riders in the world are using it. It was introduced just about a year ago and it has become an industry standard." This product had a positive cash flow very soon after its introduction. Some Associates who were also outdoor sports enthusiasts developed the product and realized that Gore could make a great bicycle cable that would have 70 percent less friction and need no lubrication. The Associates maintain that the profitable development, production, and marketing of such specialized niche products are possible because of the lack of bureaucracy and associated overhead, Associate commitment, and the use of product champions.

20   The output of the industrial products division has included sealants, filter bags, cartridges, clothes, and coatings. The specialized and critical applications of these products, along with Gore's reputation

---

[3] GORE RideOn is a registered trademark of W. L. Gore & Associates.

FIGURE 1
International Locations of W. L. Gore & Associates

for quality, have had a strong influence on industrial purchasers. This division has introduced Gore's first consumer product—GLIDE®[4]—a dental floss. "That was a product that people knew about for a while and they went the route of trying to persuade industry leaders to promote the product, but they didn't really pursue it very well. So out of basically default almost, Gore decided, Okay they're not doing it right. Let's go in ourselves. We had a champion, John Spencer, who took that and pushed it forward through the dentist's offices and it just skyrocketed. There were many more people on the team but it was basically getting that one champion who focused on that product and got it out. They told him it 'Couldn't be done,' 'It's never going to work,' and I guess that's all he needed. It was done and it worked," said Ray Wnenchak of the industrial products division. Amy LeGere added, "The champion worked very closely with the medical people to understand the medical market, like claims and labeling, so that when the product came out on the market it would be consistent with our medical products. And that's where, when we cross division, we know whom to work with and with whom we combine forces so that the end result takes the strengths of all of our different teams." Bob Winterling of the Fabrics Division explained, "The product champion is probably the most important resource we have at Gore for the introduction of new products. You look at that bicycle cable. That could have come out of many different divisions of Gore, but it really happened because one or two

---

[4] GLIDE is a registered trademark of W. L. Gore & Associates.

individuals said, 'Look, this can work. I believe in it; I'm passionate about it; and I want it to happen.' And the same thing with GLIDE floss. I think John Spencer in this case—although there was a team that supported John, let's never forget that—John sought the experts out throughout the organization. But without John making it happen on his own, GLIDE floss would never have come to fruition. He started with a little chain of drug stores here, Happy Harry's I think, and we put a few cases in and we just tracked the sales and that's how it all started. Who would have ever believed that you could take what we would have considered a commodity product like that, sell it direct for $3 to $5 apiece. That is so unGorelike it's incredible. So it comes down to people and it comes down to the product champion to make things happen."

21   The Gore fabrics division has supplied laminates to manufacturers of foul weather gear, ski wear, running suits, footwear, gloves, and hunting and fishing garments. Firefighters and U.S. Navy pilots have worn GORE-TEX fabric gear, as have some Olympic athletes. The U.S. Army adopted a total garment system built around a GORE-TEX fabric component.

22   GORE-TEX membrane has 9 billion pores randomly dotting each square inch and is feather light. Each pore is 700 times larger than a water vapor molecule, yet thousands of times smaller than a water droplet. Wind and water cannot penetrate the pores, but perspiration can escape. As a result, fabrics bonded with GORE-TEX membrane are waterproof, windproof, and breathable. The laminated fabrics bring protection from the elements to a variety of products—from survival gear to high-fashion rainwear.

23   Other manufacturers, including 3M, have brought out products to compete with GORE-TEX fabrics. The toughest competition came from firms that violated the patents on GORE-TEX. Gore successfully challenged them in court. In 1993, the basic patent on the process for manufacturing ran out. Nevertheless, as Sally Gore explained, "what happens is you get an initial process patent and then as you begin to create things with this process you get additional patents. For instance we have patents protecting our vascular graft, different patents for protecting GORE-TEX patches, and still other patents protecting GORE-TEX industrial sealants and filtration material. One of our patent attorneys did a talk recently, a year or so ago, when the patent expired and a lot of people who were saying, Oh, golly, are we going to be in trouble! We would be in trouble if we didn't have any patents. Our attorney had this picture with a great big umbrella, sort of a parachute, with Gore under it. Next he showed us lots of little umbrellas scattered all over the sky. So you protect certain niche markets and niche areas, but indeed competition increases as your initial patents expire." Gore, however, has continued to have a commanding position in the active wear market.

24   To meet the needs of a variety of customer needs, Gore introduced a new family of fabrics in the 1990s (Table 1). The introduction posed new challenges. According to Bob Winterling, "we did such a great job with the brand GORE-TEX that we actually have hurt ourselves in many ways. By that I mean it has been very difficult for us to come up with other new brands, because many people didn't even know Gore. We are the GORE-TEX company. One thing we decided to change about Gore four or five years ago was instead of being the GORE-TEX company we wanted to become the Gore company and that underneath the Gore company we had an umbrella of products that fall out of being the great Gore company. So it was a shift in how we positioned GORE-TEX. Today GORE-TEX is stronger than ever as it's turned out, but now we've ventured into such things as WindStopper®[5] fabric that is very big in the golf market. It could be a sweater or a fleece piece or even a knit shirt with the WindStopper behind it or closer to your skin and what it does is it stops the wind. It's not waterproof; it's water resistant. What we've tried to do is position the Gore name and beneath that all of the great products of the company."

25   Bill Gore knew that products alone did not a company make. He wanted to avoid smothering the company in thick layers of formal management. He felt that hierarchy stifled individual creativity. As the company grew, he knew that he had to find a way to assist new people and to follow their progress. This was particularly important when it came to compensation. W. L. Gore & Associates developed its "sponsor" program to meet these needs. When people apply to Gore, they are initially screened by personnel specialists. Those who meet the basic criteria are given interviews with other Associates. Before anyone is hired, an Associate must agree to be his or her sponsor. The sponsor is

---

[5] WindStopper is a registered trademark of W. L. Gore & Associates.

TABLE 1
Gore's Family of Fabrics

Brand Name	Activity/ Conditions	Breathability	Water Protection	Wind Protection
GORE-TEX®	Rain, snow, cold, windy	Very breathable	Waterproof	Windproof
IMMERSION™ TECHNOLOGY	For fishing and paddle sports	Very breathable	Waterproof	Windproof
OCEAN TECHNOLOGY	For offshore and coastal sailing	Very breathable	Waterproof	Windproof
WINDSTOPPER®	Cool/cold, windy	Very breathable	No water resistance	Windproof
GORE DRYLOFT™	Cold, windy, light precipitation	Extremely breathable	Water resistant	Windproof
ACTIVENT™	Cool/cold, windy, light precipitation	Extremely breathable	Water resistant	Windproof

to take a personal interest in the new Associate's contributions, problems, and goals, acting as both a coach and an advocate. The sponsor tracks the new Associate's progress, helping and encouraging, dealing with weaknesses, and concentrating on strengths. Sponsoring is not a short-term commitment. All Associates have sponsors and many have more than one. When individuals are hired initially, they are likely to have a sponsor in their immediate work area. If they move to another area, they may have a sponsor in that work area. As Associates' commitments change or grow, they may acquire additional sponsors.

26   Because the hiring process looks beyond conventional views of what makes a good Associate, some anomalies have occurred. Bill Gore proudly told the story of "a very young man" of 84 who walked in, applied, and spent five very good years with the company. The individual had 30 years of experience in the industry before joining Gore. His other Associates had no problems accepting him, but the personnel computer did. It insisted that his age was 48. The individual success stories at Gore have come from diverse backgrounds.

27   An internal memo by Bill Gore described three roles of sponsors: helping a new Associate get started on a job, seeing that an Associate's accomplishments are recognized, and ensuring that an Associate is fairly paid. A single person can perform any one or all three kinds of sponsorship.

28   In addition to the sponsor program, Bill Gore articulated four guiding principles:

1. Try to be fair.
2. Encourage, help, and allow other Associates to grow in knowledge, skill, and scope of activity and responsibility.
3. Make your own commitments, and keep them.
4. Consult with other Associates before taking actions that may be "below the water line."

29   The four principles have been referred to as *fairness, freedom, commitment,* and *waterline.* The waterline terminology is drawn from an analogy to ships. If someone pokes a hole in a boat above the waterline, the boat will be in relatively little real danger. If someone, however, pokes a hole below the waterline, the boat is in immediate danger of sinking.

30   The operating principles were put to a test in 1978. By this time word about the qualities of GORE-TEX fabric was being spread throughout the recreational and outdoor markets. Production and shipment had begun in volume. At first a few complaints were heard. Next some of the clothing started coming back. Finally, much of the clothing was being returned. The trouble was that the

GORE-TEX fabric was leaking. Waterproofing was one of the major properties responsible for GORE-TEX fabric's success. The company's reputation and credibility were on the line.

31   Peter W. Gilson, who led Gore's fabrics division recalled: "It was an incredible crisis for us at that point. We were really starting to attract attention; we were taking off— and then this." In the next few months, Gilson and a number of his Associates made a number of those below-the-waterline decisions.

32   First, the researchers determined that oils in human sweat were responsible for clogging the pores in the GORE-TEX fabric and altering the surface tension of the membrane. Thus, water could pass through. They also discovered that a good washing could restore the waterproof property. At first this solution, known as the "Ivory Snow solution," was accepted.

33   A single letter from "Butch," a mountain guide in the Sierras, changed the company's position. Butch described what happened while he was leading a group: "My parka leaked and my life was in danger." As Gilson noted, "That scared the hell out of us. Clearly our solution was no solution at all to someone on a mountain top." All the products were recalled. Gilson remembered: "We bought back, at our own expense, a fortune in pipeline material—anything that was in the stores, at the manufacturers, or anywhere else in the pipeline."

34   In the meantime, Bob Gore and other Associates set out to develop a permanent fix. One month later, a second generation GORE-TEX fabric had been developed. Gilson, furthermore, told dealers that if a customer ever returned a leaky parka, they should replace it and bill the company. The replacement program alone cost Gore roughly $4 million.

35   The popularity of GORE-TEX outerwear took-off. Many manufacturers now make numerous pieces of apparel such as parkas, gloves, boots, jogging outfits, and wind shirts from GORE-TEX laminate. Sometimes when customers are dissatisfied with a garment, they return them directly to Gore. Gore has always stood behind any product made of GORE-TEX fabric. Analysis of the returned garments found that the problem was often not the GORE-TEX fabric. The manufacturer, "had created a design flaw so that the water could get in here or get in over the zipper and we found that when there was something negative about it, everyone knew it was GORE-TEX. So we had to make good on products that we were not manufacturing. We now license the manufacturers of all our GORE-TEX fabric products. They pay a fee to obtain a license to manufacture GORE-TEX products. In return we oversee the manufacture and we let them manufacture only designs that we are sure are guaranteed to keep you dry, that really will work. Then it works for them and for us—it's a win-win for them as well as for us," according to Sally Gore.

ORGANIZATIONAL STRUCTURE

36   W. L. Gore & Associates has been described not only as unmanaged, but also as unstructured. Bill Gore referred to the structure as a lattice organization (see Figure 2). The characteristics of this structure are:

1. Direct lines of communication—person to person—with no intermediary
2. No fixed or assigned authority
3. Sponsors, not bosses
4. Natural leadership defined by followership
5. Objectives set by those who must "make them happen"
6. Tasks and functions organized through commitments

37   The structure within the lattice is complex and evolves from interpersonal interactions, self-commitment to group-known responsibilities, natural leadership, and group-imposed discipline.

38   Bill Gore once explained the structure this way: "Every successful organization has an underground lattice. It's where the news spreads like lightning, where people can go around the organization to get things done." An analogy might be drawn to a structure of constant cross-area teams—the equivalent of quality circles going on all the time. When a puzzled interviewer told Bill that he was having trouble understanding how planning and accountability worked, Bill replied with a grin: "So am I. You ask me how it works? Every which way."

FIGURE 2
The Lattice Structure

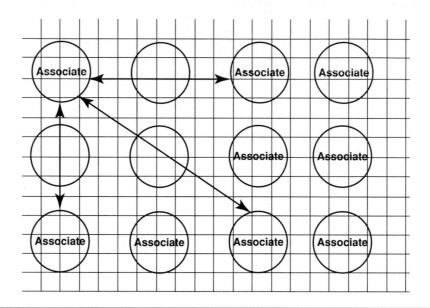

39   Outsiders have been struck by the degree of informality and humor in the Gore organization. Meetings tend to be only as long as necessary. As Trish Hearn, an Associate in Newark, Delaware, said, "No one feels a need to pontificate." Words such as *responsibilities* and *commitments* are commonly heard, whereas words such as *employees, subordinates,* and *managers* are taboo in the Gore culture. This is an organization that has always taken what it does very seriously, without its members taking themselves too seriously.

40   For a company of its size, Gore has always had a very short organizational pyramid. As of 1995 the pyramid consists of Bob Gore, the late Bill Gore's son, as president and Vieve, Bill Gore's widow, as secretary-treasurer. All the other members of the Gore organization were, and continue to be, referred to as *Associates.*

41   Gore has never had any managers, but it has always had many leaders. Bill Gore described in an internal memo the kinds of leadership and the role of leadership as follows:

1. The Associate who is recognized by a team as having a special knowledge, or experience (for example, this could be a chemist, computer expert, machine operator, salesman, engineer, lawyer). This kind of leader gives the team *guidance in a special area.*

2. The Associate the team looks to for coordination of individual activities in order to achieve the agreed-upon objectives of the team. The role of this leader is to persuade team members to *make the commitments* necessary for success (commitment seeker).

3. The Associate who proposes necessary objectives and activities and seeks agreement and team *consensus on objectives.* This leader is perceived by the team members as having a good grasp of how the objectives of the team fit in with the broad objective of the enterprise. This kind of leader is often also the "commitment seeking" leader in 2 above.

4. The leader who evaluates relative contribution of team members (in consultation with other sponsors), and reports these contribution evaluations to a compensation committee. This leader may also participate in the compensation committee on relative contribution and pay and *reports changes in compensation* to individual Associates. This leader is then also a compensation sponsor.

5. The leader who coordinates the research, manufacturing, and marketing of one product type within a business, interacting with team leaders and individual Associates who have commitments regarding the product type. These leaders are usually called *product specialists.* They are respected for their knowledge and dedication to their products.

6. *Plant leaders* who help coordinate activities of people within a plant.
7. *Business leaders* who help coordinate activities of people in a business.
8. *Functional leaders* who help coordinate activities of people in a "functional" area.
9. *Corporate leaders* who help coordinate activities of people in different businesses and functions and who try to promote communication and cooperation among all Associates.
10. *Entrepreneuring Associates* who *organize new teams* for new businesses, new products, new processes, new devices, new marketing efforts, new or better methods of all kinds. These leaders invite other Associates to "sign up" for their project.

It is clear that leadership is widespread in our lattice organization and that it is continually changing and evolving. The situation that leaders are frequently *also* sponsors should not confuse that these are different activities and responsibilities.

Leaders are not authoritarians, managers of people, or supervisors who tell us what to do or forbid us doing things; nor are they "parents" to whom we transfer our own self-responsibility. However, they do often advise us of the consequences of actions we have done or propose to do. Our actions result in contributions, or lack of contribution, to the success of our enterprise. Our pay depends on the magnitude of our contributions. This is the basic discipline of our lattice organization.

42   Many other aspects of the Gore culture have been arranged along egalitarian lines: parking lots with no reserved parking spaces except for customers and disabled workers or visitors; dining areas—only one in each plant—set up as focal points for Associate interaction. As Dave McCarter of Phoenix explained: "The design is no accident. The lunchroom in Flagstaff has a fireplace in the middle. We want people to like to be here." The location of a plant is also no accident. Sites have been selected on the basis of transportation access, a nearby university, beautiful surroundings, and climate appeal. Land cost has never been a primary consideration. McCarter justified the selection by stating: "Expanding is not costly in the long run. The loss of money is what you make happen by stymieing people into a box."

43   Bob Gore is a champion of Gore culture. As Sally Gore related, "We have managed surprisingly to maintain our sense of freedom and our entrepreneurial spirit. I think what we've found is that we had to develop new ways to communicate with Associates because you can't communicate with 6,000 people the way that you can communicate with 500 people. It just can't be done. So we have developed a newsletter that we didn't have before. One of the most important communication mediums that we developed, and this was Bob Gore's idea, is a digital voice exchange we call our Gorecom. Basically everyone has a mailbox and a password. Lots of companies have gone to E mail and we use E-mail, but Bob feels very strongly that we're very much an oral culture and there's a big difference between cultures that are predominantly oral and predominantly written. Oral cultures encourage direct communication, which is, of course, something that we encourage."

44   Not all people function well under such a system, especially initially. For those accustomed to a more structured work environment, there can be adjustment problems. As Bill Gore said: "All our lives most of us have been told what to do, and some people don't know how to respond when asked to do something—and have the very real option of saying no—on their job. It's the new Associate's responsibility to find out what he or she can do for the good of the operation." The vast majority of the new Associates, after some initial floundering, have adapted quickly.

45   Others, especially those who require more structured working conditions, have found that Gore's flexible workplace is not for them. According to Bill, for those few, "It's an unhappy situation, both for the Associate and the sponsor. If there is no contribution, there is no paycheck."

46   As Anita McBride, an Associate in Phoenix, noted: "It's not for everybody. People ask me do we have turnover, and yes we do have turnover. What you're seeing looks like utopia, but it also looks extreme. If you finally figure the system, it can be real exciting. If you can't handle it, you gotta go. Probably by your own choice, because you're going to be so frustrated."

47   In rare cases an Associate "is trying to be unfair," in Bill's own words. In one case the problem was chronic absenteeism and in another, an individual was caught stealing. "When that happens, all hell breaks loose," said Bill Gore. "We can get damned authoritarian when we have to."

48   Over the years, Gore & Associates has faced a number of unionization drives. The company has neither tried to dissuade Associates from attending an organizational meeting nor retaliated when flyers were passed out. As of 1995, none of the plants has been organized. Bill believed that no need

FIGURE 3

W. L. GORE & ASSOCIATES, Inc.

SARAH CLIFTON
SUPREME COMMANDER

1505 NORTH FOURTH STREET
FLAGSTAFF, ARIZONA 86001
PHONE: 602-774-0611
TWX 910-972-0969

existed for third-party representation under the lattice structure. He asked the question, "Why would Associates join a union when they own the company? It seems rather absurd."

49   Overall, the Associates appear to have responded positively to the Gore system of unmanagement and unstructure. Bill estimated the year before he died that "the profit per Associate is double" that of Du Pont.

50   The lattice structure has not been without its critics. As Bill Gore stated, "I'm told from time to time that a lattice organization can't meet a crisis well because it takes too long to reach a consensus when there are no bosses. But this isn't true. Actually, a lattice by its very nature works particularly well in a crisis. A lot of useless effort is avoided because there is no rigid management hierarchy to conquer before you can attack a problem."

51   The lattice has been put to the test on a number of occasions. For example, in 1975, Dr. Charles Campbell of the University of Pittsburgh reported that a GORE-TEX arterial graft had developed an aneurysm. If the bubblelike protrusion continued to expand, it would explode. Obviously, this life-threatening situation had to be resolved quickly and permanently.

52   Within only a few days of Dr. Campbell's first report, he flew to Newark to present his findings to Bill and Bob Gore and a few other Associates. The meeting lasted two hours. Dan Hubis, a former police officer who had joined Gore to develop new production methods, had an idea before the meeting was over. He returned to his work area to try some different production techniques. After only three hours and 12 tries, he had developed a permanent solution. In other words, in three hours a potentially damaging problem to both patients and the company was resolved. Furthermore, Hubis's redesigned graft went on to win widespread acceptance in the medical community.

53   Some outsiders have had problems with the idea of no titles. Sarah Clifton, an Associate at the Flagstaff facility, was being pressed by some outsiders as to what her title was. She made one up and had it printed on some business cards: SUPREME COMMANDER (see Figure 3). When Bill Gore learned what she did, he loved it and recounted the story to others.

54   Eric Reynolds, founder of Marmot Mountain Works Ltd. of Grand Junction, Colorado, and a major Gore customer, raised another issue: "I think the lattice has its problems with the day-to-day nitty-gritty of getting things done on time and out the door. I don't think Bill realizes how the lattice system affects customers. I mean after you've established a relationship with someone about product quality, you can call up one day and suddenly find that someone new to you is handling your problem. It's frustrating to find a lack of continuity." He went on to say: "But I have to admit that I've personally seen at Gore remarkable examples of people coming out of nowhere and excelling."

55   When Bill Gore was asked if the lattice structure could be used by other companies, he answered: "No. For example, established companies would find it very difficult to use the lattice.

Too many hierarchies would be destroyed. When you remove titles and positions and allow people to follow who they want, it may very well be someone other than the person who has been in charge. The lattice works for us, but it's always evolving. You have to expect problems." He maintained that the lattice system worked best when it was put in place in start-up companies by dynamic entrepreneurs.

RESEARCH AND DEVELOPMENT

56   Like everything else at Gore, research and development has always been unstructured. Even without a formal R&D department, the company has been issued many patents, although most inventions have been held as proprietary or trade secrets. Any Associate could ask for a piece of raw PTFE (known as a silly worm) with which to experiment. Bill Gore believed that all people had it within themselves to be creative.

57   One of the best examples of Gore inventiveness occurred in 1969. At the time, the wire and cable division was facing increased competition. Bill Gore began to look for a way to straighten out the PTFE molecules. As he said, "I figured out that if we ever unfold those molecules, get them to stretch out straight, we'd have a tremendous new kind of material." He thought that if PTFE could be stretched, air could be introduced into its molecular structure. The result would be greater volume per pound of raw material with no effect on performance. Thus, fabricating costs would be reduced and profit margins would be increased. Going about this search in a scientific manner, Bob Gore heated rods of PTFE to various temperatures and then slowly stretched them. Regardless of the temperature or how carefully he stretched them, the rods broke.

58   Working alone late one night after countless failures, Bob in frustration stretched one of the rods violently. To his surprise, it did not break. He tried it again and again with the same results. The next morning Bob demonstrated his breakthrough to his father, but not without some drama. As Bill Gore recalled: "Bob wanted to surprise me so he took a rod and stretched it slowly. Naturally, it broke. Then he pretended to get mad. He grabbed another rod and said, 'Oh, the hell with this,' and gave it a pull. It didn't break—he'd done it." The new arrangement of molecules not only changed the wire and cable division, but led to the development of GORE-TEX fabric.

59   Bill and Vieve did the initial field-testing of GORE-TEX fabric the summer of 1970. Vieve made a hand-sewn tent out of patches of GORE-TEX fabric. They took it on their annual camping trip to the Wind River Mountains in Wyoming. The very first night in the wilderness, they encountered a hail storm. The hail tore holes in the top of the tent, and the bottom filled up like a bathtub from the rain. Undaunted, Bill Gore stated: "At least we knew from all the water that the tent was waterproof. We just needed to make it stronger, so it could withstand hail."

60   The medical division began on the ski slopes of Colorado. Bill was skiing with a friend, Dr. Ben Eiseman of Denver General Hospital. As Bill Gore told the story: "We were just to start a run when I absentmindedly pulled a small tubular section of GORE-TEX out of my pocket and looked at it. 'What is that stuff?' Ben asked. So I told him about its properties. 'Feels great,' he said. 'What do you use it for?' 'Got no idea,' I said. 'Well give it to me,' he said, 'and I'll try it in a vascular graft on a pig.' Two weeks later, he called me up. Ben was pretty excited. 'Bill,' he said, 'I put it in a pig and it works. What do I do now?' I told him to get together with Pete Cooper in our Flagstaff plant, and let them figure it out." Not long after, hundreds of thousands of people throughout the world began walking around with GORE-TEX vascular grafts.

61   Gore Associates have always been encouraged to think, experiment, and follow a potentially profitable idea to its conclusion. At a plant in Newark, Delaware, Fred L. Eldreth, an Associate with a third grade education, designed a machine that could wrap thousands of feet of wire a day. The design was completed over a weekend. Many other Associates have contributed their ideas through both product and process breakthroughs.

62   Even without an R&D department, innovations and creativity continued to work very well at Gore & Associates. The year before he died, Bill Gore claimed that "the creativity, the number of patent applications and innovative products is triple" that of Du Pont.

ASSOCIATE DEVELOPMENT

63   Ron Hill, an Associate in Newark, noted that Gore "will work with Associates who want to advance themselves." Associates have been offered many in-house training opportunities, not only in technical and engineering areas but also in leadership development. In addition, the company has established cooperative education programs with universities and other outside providers, picking up most of the costs for the Gore Associates. The emphasis in Associate development, as in many parts of Gore, has always been that the Associate must take the initiative.

PRODUCTS

64   Gore's electronic products division has produced wire and cable for various demanding applications in aerospace, defense, computers, and telecommunications. The wire and cable products have earned a reputation for unequaled reliability. Most of the wire and cable has been used where conventional cables cannot operate. For example, Gore wire and cable assemblies were used in the space shuttle *Columbia* because they could stand the heat of ignition and the cold of space. Gore wire was used in the moon vehicle shuttle that scooped up samples of moon rocks, and Gore's microwave coaxial assemblies opened new horizons in microwave technology. Back on earth, Gore's electrical wire products helped make the world's fastest computers possible because electrical signals could travel through them at up to 93 percent of the speed of light. Because of the physical properties of the GORE-TEX material used in their construction, the electronic products have been used extensively in defense systems, electronic switching for telephone systems, scientific and industrial instrumentation, microwave communications, and industrial robotics. Reliability has always been a watchword for Gore products.

65   In medical products, reliability is literally a matter of life and death. GORE-TEX–expanded PTFE proved to be an ideal material for combating cardiovascular disease. When human arteries have been seriously damaged or plugged with deposits that interrupt the flow of blood, the diseased portions can often be replaced with GORE-TEX artificial arteries. Because the patient's own tissues grow into the graft's open porous spaces, the artificial portions are not rejected by the body. GORE-TEX vascular grafts, produced in many sizes to restore circulation to all areas of the body, have saved limbs from amputation, and saved lives. Some of the tiniest grafts have relieved pulmonary problems in newborns. GORE-TEX–expanded PTFE has been used to help people with kidney disease. Associates have also developed a variety of surgical reinforcing membranes, known as GORE-TEX cardiovascular patches, which can literally mend broken hearts by patching holes and repairing aneurysms.

66   Through the waterproof fabrics division, Gore technology has traveled to the roof of the world on the backs of renowned mountaineers and adventurers facing extremely harsh environments. Because the PTFE membrane blocks wind and water but allows sweat to escape, GORE-TEX fabric has proved ideal for those who work or play hard in foul weather. Backpackers have discovered that a single lightweight GORE-TEX fabric shell will replace a poplin jacket and a rain suit, and dramatically outperform both. Skiers, sailors, runners, bicyclists, hunters, fishermen, and other outdoor enthusiasts have also become big customers of garments made of GORE-TEX fabric. GORE-TEX sportswear, as well as women's fashion footwear and handwear, have proved to be functional as well as attractive. Boots and gloves, for both work and recreation, became waterproof thanks to GORE-TEX liners. GORE-TEX garments have even become standard items issued to military personnel. Wet suits, parkas, pants, headgear, gloves, and boots have kept the troops warm and dry in foul weather missions. Other demanding jobs have also received the protection of GORE-TEX fabric, with its unique combination of chemical and physical properties.

67   The GORE-TEX fibers, like the fabrics, have ended up in some pretty tough places, including the outer protective layer of a NASA spacesuit. In many ways, GORE-TEX fibers have proved to be the ultimate synthetic. They have been impervious to sunlight, chemicals, heat, and cold. They are strong and uniquely resistant to abrasion.

68   Industrial filtration products, such as GORE-TEX filter bags, have reduced air pollution and recovered valuable solids from gases and liquids more completely than alternatives—and they have done so economically. In the future they may make coal-burning plants completely smoke free, contributing to a cleaner environment.

69   Gore's industrial products division has developed a unique joint sealant—a flexible cord of porous PTFE—that can be applied as a gasket to the most complex shapes, sealing them to prevent leakage of corrosive chemicals, even at extreme temperature and pressure. Steam valves packed with GORE-TEX have been sold with a lifetime guarantee, provided the valve is used properly.

COMPENSATION

70   Traditionally, compensation at W. L. Gore & Associates has taken three forms: salary, profit sharing, and an Associates' stock ownership program (ASOP).[6] Entry-level salary has been in the middle for comparable jobs. According to Sally Gore: "We do not feel we need to be the highest paid. We never try to steal people away from other companies with salary. We want them to come here because of the opportunities for growth and the unique work environment." In the past, Associates' salaries have been reviewed at least once a year and more commonly twice a year. The reviews are conducted by a compensation team at each facility, with sponsors for the Associates acting as their advocates during the review process. Prior to meeting with the compensation committee, the sponsor checks with customers or Associates familiar with the person's work to find out what contribution the Associate has made. In addition, the evaluation team considers the Associate's leadership ability and willingness to help others develop to their fullest.

71   Profit sharing follows a formula based on economic value added (EVA). Sally Gore had the following to say about the adoption of a formula, "It's become more formalized and in a way, I think that's unfortunate because it used to be a complete surprise to receive a profit share. The thinking of the people like Bob Gore and other leaders was that maybe we weren't using it in the right way and we could encourage people by helping them know more about it and how we made profit share decisions. The fun of it before was people didn't know when it was coming and all of a sudden you could do something creative about passing out checks. It was great fun and people would have a wonderful time with it. The disadvantage was that Associates then did not focus much on, 'What am I doing to create another profit share?' By using EVA as a method of evaluation for our profit share, we know at the end of every month how much EVA was created that month. When we've created a certain amount of EVA, we then get another profit share. So everybody knows and everyone says, 'We'll do it in January,' so it is done. Now Associates feel more part of the happening to make it work. What have you done? Go make some more sales calls, please! There are lots of things we can do to improve our EVA and everybody has a responsibility to do that." Every month EVA is calculated and every Associate is informed. John Mosko of electronic products commented, "(EVA) lets us know where we are on the path to getting one (a profit share). It's very critical—every Associate knows."

72   Annually, Gore also buys company stock equivalent to a fixed percent of the Associates' annual income, placing it in the ASOP retirement fund. Thus, an Associate can become a stockholder after being at Gore for a year. Gore's ASOP ensures Associates participate in the growth of the company by acquiring ownership in it. Bill Gore wanted Associates to feel that they themselves are owners. One Associate stated, "This is much more important than profit sharing."

73   Commitment has long been considered a two-way street. W. L. Gore & Associates has tried to avoid layoffs. Instead of cutting pay, which in the Gore culture would be disastrous to morale, the company has used a system of temporary transfers within a plant or cluster of plants and voluntary layoffs.

MARKETING STRATEGY

74   Gore's marketing strategy has focused on three assumptions: that it can offer the best-valued products to a marketplace, that people in that marketplace appreciate what it manufactures, and that Gore

---

[6] Similar legally to an ESOP (employee stock ownership plan). Again, Gore simply has never allowed the word *employee* in any of its documentation.

can become a leader in that area of expertise. The operating procedures used to implement the strategy have followed the same principles as other functions at Gore.

1. Marketing a product requires a leader, or *product champion*. According to Dave McCarter: "You marry your technology with the interests of your champions, since you've got to have champions for all these things no matter what. And that's the key element within our company. Without a product champion you can't do much anyway, so it is individually driven. If you get people interested in a particular market or a particular product for the marketplace, then there is no stopping them."

2. *A product champion is responsible for marketing the product through commitments with sales representatives.* Again, according to Dave McCarter:

> We have no quota system. Our marketing and our salespeople make their own commitments as to what their forecasts have been. There is no person sitting around telling them that is not high enough, you have to increase it by 10 percent, or whatever somebody feels is necessary. You are expected to meet your commitment, which is your forecast, but nobody is going to tell you to change it . . . There is no order of command, no chain involved. These are groups of independent people who come together to make unified commitments to do something and sometimes when they can't make those agreements . . . you may pass up a marketplace . . . But that's OK, because there's much more advantage when the team decides to do something.

3. *Sales Associates are on salary, not commission.* They participate in the profit sharing and ASOP plans in which all other Associates participate.

78   As in other areas of Gore, individual success stories have come from diverse backgrounds. Dave McCarter related one of these successes:

> I interviewed Sam one day. I didn't even know why I was interviewing him actually. Sam was retired from AT&T. After 25 years, he took the golden parachute and went down to Sun Lakes to play golf. He played golf a few months and got tired of that. He was selling life insurance.
>
> I sat reading the application; his technical background interested me . . . He had managed an engineering department with 600 people. He'd managed manufacturing plants for AT&T and had a great wealth of experience at AT&T. He said, "I'm retired. I like to play golf but I just can't do it every day so I want to do something else. Do you have something around here I can do?" I was thinking to myself, "This is one of these guys I would sure like to hire but I don't know what I would do with him." The thing that triggered me was the fact that he said he sold insurance and here is a guy with a high degree of technical background selling insurance. He had marketing experience, international marketing experience. So, the bell went off in my head that we were trying to introduce a new product into the marketplace that was a hydrocarbon leak protection cable. You can bury it in the ground and in a matter of seconds it could detect a hydrocarbon-like gasoline. I had a couple of other guys working on the product who hadn't been very successful with marketing it. We were having a hard time finding a customer. Well, I thought that kind of product would be like selling insurance. If you think about it, why should you protect your tanks? It's an insurance policy that things are not leaking into the environment. That has implications, big time monetary. So, actually, I said, "Why don't you come back Monday? I have just the thing for you." He did. We hired him; he went to work, a very energetic guy. Certainly a champion of the product, he picked right up on it, ran with it single handed . . . Now it's a growing business. It certainly is a valuable one too for the environment.

80   In the implementation of its marketing strategy, Gore has relied on cooperative and word-of-mouth advertising. Cooperative advertising has been especially used to promote GORE-TEX fabric products. Those products are sold through a number of clothing manufacturers and distributors, including Apparel Technologies, Lands End, Austin Reed, Timberland, Woolrich, North Face, Grandoe, and Michelle Jaffe. Gore has stressed cooperative advertising because the Associates believe positive experiences with any one product will carry over to purchases of other and more GORE-TEX fabric products. Apparently, this strategy has paid off. When the Grandoe Corporation introduced GORE-TEX gloves, its president, Richard Zuckerwar, noted: "Sports activists have had the benefit of GORE-TEX gloves to protect their hands from the elements . . . With this handsome collection of gloves . . . you can have warm, dry hands without sacrificing style."

81   The power of informal marketing techniques extends beyond consumer products. According to Dave McCarter: "In the technical end of the business, company reputation probably is most important. You have to have a good reputation with your company." He went on to say that without a good reputation, a company's products would not be considered seriously by many industrial customers. In other words, the sale is often made before the representative calls. Using its marketing strategies

Gore has been very successful in securing a market leadership position in a number of areas, ranging from waterproof outdoor clothing to vascular grafts.

ENVIRONMENTAL FORCES

82   Each of Gore's divisions have faced some environmental forces. The fabric division was hit hard when the fad for jogging suits collapsed in the mid-1980s. The fabric division took another hit from the recession of 1989. People simply reduced their purchases of high-end athletic apparel. By 1995, the fabric division was the fastest growing division of Gore again. The electronic division was hit hard when the main frame computer business declined in the early 1990s. By 1995, that division was seeing a resurgence for its products partially because that division had developed some electronic products for the medical industry. As can be seen, not all the forces have been negative. The aging population of America has increased the need for health care. As a result, Gore has invested in the development of additional medical products and the medical division is growing.

FINANCIAL INFORMATION

83   As a closely held private corporation, W. L. Gore has kept its financial information as closely guarded as proprietary information on products and processes. It has been estimated that Associates who work at Gore own 90 percent of the stock. According to Shanti Mehta, an Associate, Gore's returns on assets and sales have consistently ranked it among the top 10 percent of the Fortune 500 companies. According to another source, W. L. Gore & Associates has been doing just fine by any financial measure. For 35 straight years (from 1961 to 1995), the company has enjoyed profitability and positive return on equity. The compounded growth rate for revenues at W. L. Gore & Associates from 1969 to 1989 was more than 18 percent discounted for inflation.[7] In 1969, total sales were about $6 million; by 1989, the figure was $600 million. As should be expected with the increase in size, the percentage increase in sales has slowed over the last five years (Figure 4). Gore financed this growth without long-term debt unless it made sense. For example, "We used to have some industrial revenue bonds where, in essence, to build facilities the government allows banks to lend you money tax free. Up to a couple of years ago we were borrowing money through industrial revenue bonds. Other than that, we are totally debt free. Our money is generated out of the operations of the business, and frankly we're looking for new things to invest in. I know that's a challenge for all of us today," said Bob Winterling. *Forbes* magazine estimates Gore's operating profits for 1993, 1994, and 1995 to be $120, $140, and $192 million, respectively (Figure 5).

84   When asked about cost control, Sally Gore had the following to say:

> You have to pay attention to cost or you're not an effective steward of anyone's money, your own or anyone else's. It's kind of interesting; we started manufacturing medical products in 1974 with the vascular graft and it built from there. The Gore vascular graft is the Cadillac or BMW or the Rolls Royce of the business. There is absolutely no contest, and our medical products division became very successful. People thought this was Mecca. Nothing had ever been manufactured that was so wonderful. Our business expanded enormously, rapidly out there (Flagstaff, Arizona) and we had a lot of young, young leadership. They spent some time thinking they could do no wrong and that everything they touched was going to turn to gold. They have had some hard knocks along the way and discovered it wasn't as easy as they initially thought it was. And that's probably good learning for everyone somewhere along the way. That's not how business works. There's a lot of truth in that old saying that you learn more from your failures than you do your successes. One failure goes a long way toward making you say, Oh, wow!

---

[7] In comparison, only 11 of the 200 largest companies in the Fortune 500 had positive ROE each year from 1970 to 1988 and only 2 other companies missed a year. The revenue growth rate for these 13 companies was 5.4 percent, compared with 2.5 percent for the entire Fortune 500.

FIGURE 4
Growth of Gore's Sales versus Gross Domestic Product

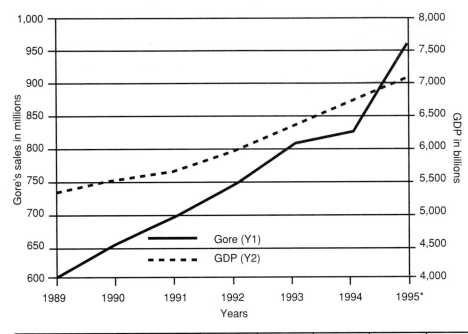

Gore	600	660	700	750	804	828	958
GDP	5,244	5,514	5,673	5,951	6,343.3	6,738.4	7,110

Note: *Estimated GDP for 1995

ACKNOWLEDGMENTS

Many sources were helpful in providing background material for this case. The most important sources of all were the W. L. Gore Associates, who generously shared their time and viewpoints about the company. They provided many resources, including internal documents and added much to this case through sharing their personal experiences as well as ensuring that the case accurately reflected the Gore company and culture.

BIBLIOGRAPHY

Aburdene, Patricia, and John Nasbitt. *Re-inventing the Corporation.* New York: Warner Books, 1985.

Angrist, S. W. "Classless Capitalists." *Forbes,* May 9, 1983, pp. 123–24.

Franlesca, L. "Dry and Cool," *Forbes,* August 27, 1984, p. 126.

Hoerr, J. "A Company Where Everybody Is the Boss." *Business Week,* April 15, 1985, p. 98.

Levering, Robert. *The 100 Best Companies to Work for in America.* New York: Signet, 1985. See the chapter on W. L. Gore & Associates, Inc.

McKendrick, Joseph. "The Employees as Entrepreneur." *Management World,* January 1985, pp. 12–13.

Milne, M. J. "The Gorey Details." *Management Review,* March 1985, pp. 16–17.

Price, Kathy. "Firm Thrives without Boss." *AZ Republic,* February 2, 1986.

Posner, B. G. "The First Day on the Job." *Inc.,* June 1986, pp. 73–75.

Rhodes, Lucien. "The Un-manager." *Inc.,* August 1982, p. 34.

FIGURE 5
Operating and Net Profits of W. L. Gore & Associates

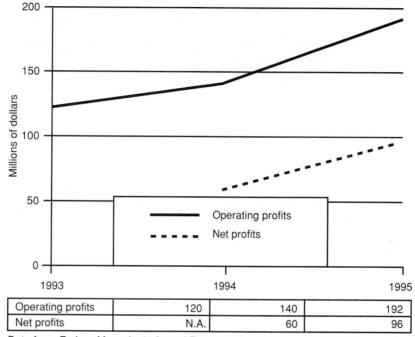

	1993	1994	1995
Operating profits	120	140	192
Net profits	N.A.	60	96

Data from *Forbes* Magazine's Annual Report on the 500 Largest Private Companies in the U.S.

Simmons, J. "People Managing Themselves: Un-management at W. L. Gore Inc." *The Journal for Quality and Participation,* December 1987, pp. 14–19.

"The Future Workplace." *Management Review,* July 1986, pp. 22–23.

Trachtenberg, J. A. "Give Them Stormy Weather." *Forbes* 137, no. 6 (March 24, 1986), pp. 172–74.

Ward, Alex. "An All-Weather Idea." *The New York Times Magazine,* November 10, 1985, Sec. 6.

Weber, Joseph. "No Bosses. And Even 'Leaders' Can't Give Orders." *Business Week,* December 10, 1990, pp. 196–97.

"Wilbert L. Gore." *Industry Week,* October 17, 1983, pp. 48–49.

FIGURE 6
Excerpts from Interviews with Associates

The first excerpt is from an Associate that was formerly with IBM and has been with Gore for two years.

Q. *What is the difference between being with IBM and Gore?*
A. I spent 24 years working for IBM and there's a big difference. I can go 10 times faster here at Gore because of the simplicity of the lattice organization. Let me give you an example. If I wanted to purchase chemicals at IBM (I am an industrial chemist), the first thing I would need to do is get accounting approval, then I would need at least two levels of managers' approval, then a secretary to log in my purchase and the purchase order would go to Purchasing where it would be assigned a buyer. Some time could be saved if you were willing to "walk" the paperwork through the approval process, but even after computerizing the process, it typically would take one month from the time you initiated the purchase requisition till the time the material actually arrived. Here they have one simple form. Usually, I get the chemicals the next day and a copy of the purchase order will arrive a day or two after that. It happens so fast. I wasn't used to that.

Q. *Do you find that a lot more pleasant?*
A. Yeah, you're unshackled here. There's a lot less bureaucracy that allows you to be a lot more productive. Take lab safety for example. In my lab at IBM, we were cited for not having my eyewash taped properly. The first time, we were cited for not having a big enough area taped off. So we taped off a bigger area. The next week the same eyewash was cited again, because the area we taped off was 3 inches too short in one direction. We retaped it and the following week, it got cited again for having the wrong color tape. Keep in mind that the violation was viewed as serious as a pail of gasoline next to a lit Bunsen burner. Another time I had the dubious honor of being selected the functional safety representative in charge of getting the function's labs ready for a corporate safety audit. (The function was a third level in the pyramidal organization—(1) department, (2) project, and (3) function). At the same time I was working on developing a new surface mount package. As it turned out, I had no time to work on development, and the function spent a lot of time and money getting ready for the corporate auditors who in the end never showed. I'm not belittling the importance of safety, but you really don't need all that bureaucracy to be safe.

The second interview is with an Associate who is a recent engineering graduate:

Q. *How did you find the transition coming here?*
A. Although I never would have expected it to be, I found my transition coming to Gore to be rather challenging. What attracted me to the company was the opportunity to "be my own boss" and determine my own commitments. I am very goal oriented, and enjoy taking a project and running with it—all things that you are able to do, and encouraged to do within the Gore culture. Thus, I thought, a perfect fit!

However, as a new Associate, I really struggled with where to focus my efforts—I was ready to make my own commitments, but to what? I felt a strong need to be sure that I was working on something that had value, something that truly needed to be done. While I didn't expect to have the "hottest" project, I did want to make sure that I was helping the company to "make money" in some way.

At the time, though, I was working for a plant that was pretty typical of what Gore was like when it was originally founded. After my first project (which was designed to be a "quick win," a project with meaning, but one that had a definite end point), I was told "Go find something to work on." While I could have found something, I wanted to find something with at least a small degree of priority! Thus, the whole process of finding a project was very frustrating for me. I didn't feel that I had the perspective to make such a choice, and ended up in many conversations with my sponsor about what would be valuable . . .

In the end, of course, I did find that project—and it did actually turn out to be a good investment for Gore. The process to get there, though, was definitely trying for someone as inexperienced as I was. So much ground would have been gained by suggesting a few projects to me and then letting me choose from that smaller pool.

What's really neat about the whole thing, though, is that my experience has truly made a difference. Due in part to my frustrations, my plant now provides college grads with more guidance on their first several projects. (This guidance obviously becomes less and less critical as each Associate grows within Gore.) Associates still are choosing their own commitments, but they're doing so with additional perspective, and the knowledge that they are making a contribution to Gore, which is an important thing within our culture. As I said, though, it was definitely rewarding to see that the company was so responsive, and to feel that I had helped to shape someone else's transition!

CASE 19

HARTMARX CORPORATION

OVERVIEW

1 In his letter to the shareholders of Hartmarx Corporation, Elbert O. Hand, the company's new chairman and chief executive officer, said:

> This is a difficult chapter in the 105 year history of Hartmarx Corporation. 1991 was our worst year since the 1930s depression. And 1992 has been a traumatic year for the company, its shareholders, employees, customers, suppliers, creditors, unions, and the board of directors.[1]

2 Mr. Hand's statement summed up the difficult times Hartmarx experienced in the last few years. After almost half a century of success, Hartmarx, which was composed of such well-known subsidiaries as Hart Schaffner and Marx Clothes, Hickey-Freeman, Kuppenheimer, and others, began to stumble. In 1992, the net sales were $1,054 billion, representing a decline from the net sales of $1,215 billion in 1991 and $1,296 billion in 1990, respectively. The 1992 net loss was $220 million, compared to net losses of $38 million in 1991 and $62 million in 1990. In January 1992, the company suspended paying dividends to stockholders for the first time in its history. And in September 1992, Hartmarx's stock price fell to a 52-week low on rumors that the company's specialty stores were headed for bankruptcy.

HISTORY

3 Hartmarx Corporation, a Chicago-based firm, was incorporated in 1983, succeeding the original firm Hart Schaffner and Marx. The latter dated back to 1872, when two brothers, Harry and Max Hart, opened a clothing store on State Street in Chicago, recognizing that many people had probably lost most of their clothes in the great fire the previous year.[2] The Hart Schaffner and Marx unit remained the link to the past, although it now competed for resources with the company's other strategic business units.

4 Hartmarx did not undergo any significant structural or operational changes until the late 1970s and 1980s when it embarked on a growth strategy that culminated in the acquisition of several companies. Some of the more significant acquisitions are displayed in Exhibit 1.

5 Currently, Hartmarx functions essentially as a holding company, overseeing its various operating units and providing them with resources and services in the areas of finance, administration, legal, human resources, and advertising. Some of Hartmarx's operating units included Hickey-Freeman, Bobby Jones, Hart Schaffner and Marx, and Kuppenheimer. These units operated as separate profit centers. And their respective managements had responsibility for the optimum use of the capital invested in them and for planning their growth and development in coordination with the company's overall corporate strategy.

This case was prepared by A. J. Almaney of DePaul University.

EXHIBIT 1
The Major Companies Acquired by Hartmarx

> Intercontinental Apparel, Inc., the U.S. license for Pierre Cardin men's tailored clothing, 1979.
>
> Intercontinental Appeal, Inc., and Bishop's men's stores, 1980.
>
> The manufacturing and retailing operations of Country Miss, Inc., 1981.
>
> Kuppenheimer Manufacturing Company, Inc., 1982.
>
> Briar, Inc., a men's clothing manufacturer, 1985.
>
> H. Oritsky, Inc. (manufacturing operations), 1986.
>
> Anton's (retailing operations), 1987.
>
> Boyd's men's and women's specialty stores, 1988.
>
> Raleighs men's and women's specialty stores, 1988.
>
> Biltwell Company, Inc. (manufacturing operations), 1989.

Source: Hartmarx Corporation, *Form 10-K*, pp. 1–2.

THE BOARD OF DIRECTORS

6   The board of directors was composed of 12 members. Except for Elbert O. Hand, who was Hartmarx's chairman and chief executive officer, all the other members were outsiders. As shown in Exhibit 2, the outside directors represented a wide variety of business experience, ranging from banking to manufacturing to telecommunications. One director, Donald G. Jacobs, was Dean of J. L. Kellog Graduate School of Management at Northwestern University. Taken as a group, the board members had been directors at Hartmarx for an average of 12 years.

7   The board held four regular meetings annually and conducted its business through several committees. These included audit, compensation and stock option, executive, management operations, nominating, and strategic planning. Each member of the board sat on at least two committees, with some members sitting on as many as five. The committee structure enabled the board to actively participate in Hartmarx's activities, thus providing a balance for important company decisions.

TOP MANAGEMENT

8   In recent years, Hartmarx experienced significant changes in top management. In 1989, John Meinert, a 49-year veteran with the company, stepped down as chairman of the board. Harvey Weinberg, who had been chief executive officer (CEO) since 1987 and a veteran of 25 years with the company, assumed this position. Unlike Meinert, who rose through the manufacturing ranks as a financial specialist, Weinberg hailed from the retailing side. The naming of Weinberg seemed to signal a departure from the traditional manufacturing orientation Hartmarx had followed for decades. However, in 1992 Weinberg resigned, following losses incurred by one of the company's business units [Hartmarx Specialty Stores, Inc. (HSSI)]. Members of the board of directors had pressured Weinberg to close unprofitable stores at a faster pace than he was willing to do.

9   Weinberg was replaced by 54-year-old Elbert O. Hand, a veteran of the manufacturing side of the firm. The move reflected the company's "desire to funnel more resources into its profitable manufacturing division rather than into the unprofitable retail side of the business."[3] The move also signaled the company's intention to close a large number of its 186 specialty stores.

A Profile of Elbert O. Hand

10   Elbert (Bert) O. Hand was chairman and CEO of Hartmarx Corp. and a member of the company's board of directors. After graduating from Hamilton College in Clinton, New York, and holding a

EXHIBIT 2
Board of Directors

A. Robert Abboud
President
A. Robert Abboud and Company
(C,E,N,S)

Letitia Baldrige
President
Letitia Baldrige Enterprises, Inc.
(A,E,N)

Jeffrey A. Cole
Chairman and Chief Executive Officer
Cole National Corporation
(A,E,S)

Reymond F. Farley
Retired President and Chief
Executive Officer
S.C. Johnson Wax
(A,C,E,S)

Elbert O. Hand
Chairman and Chief Executive Officer
Hartmarx Corporation
(E,M,S)

Donald P. Jacobs
Dean, J.L. Kellogg Graduate School
of Management
Northwestern University
(S,C,E,N,S)

Miles L. Marsh
Chairman and Chief Executive Officer
Pet Incorporated
(E,N)

Charles Marshall
Retired Vice Chairman
American Telephone and Telegraph
Company
(C,E,N)

Charles K. Olson
Executive Vice President and
Managing Director
Dearborn Financial, Inc.
(E)

Talat M. Othman
President and Chief Executive
Officer
Dearborn Financial, Inc.
(E)

Sam F. Segnar
Retired Chairman and Chief Executive
Officer
Enron Corp.
(A,C,E)

Director Committees: A:Audit; C:Compensation and Stock Option; E:Executive; M:Management Operations;
N:Nominating; and S: Strategic Planning

Source: Hartmarx Corporation, *1992 Annual Report*, p. 30.

position at a major sportswear company, Hand joined Hart Schaffner and Marx's management training program. In his 28 years with Hartmarx, Hand held marketing and manufacturing positions leading to his appointment as president and chief executive officer of all manufacturing divisions in 1982, president of the corporation in 1985, and chairman and chief executive in 1992.

11   As chairman and chief executive officer of the corporation, Hand led the men's apparel manufacturing and retailing subsidiaries of Hartmarx. Hartmarx manufacturing subsidiaries included Hart Schaffner and Marx Clothes, Hickey-Freeman Co., Intercontinental Branded Apparel, Trans-Apparel Group, Hartmarx Special Markets Group, Universal Design Group, and the Bitwell Company. The Hartmarx women's retail and manufacturing business, Intercontinental Women's Apparel Group, also reported to Hand. The company's retailing unit, Kuppenheimer Men's Clothes, operated 120 menswear specialty stores nationwide.

12   Hand was responsible for all corporate marketing services, which included the in-house advertising agency, Hart Services, Inc., as well as marketing research and public relations.

13   Hand served as chairman of the American Apparel Manufacturers Association. He was also a member of the University of Illinois at Chicago Advisory Council, chairman of the Council's Minority Affairs committee and a member of the University's Chancellor's Advisory Board. In addition, he was a board member of the Better Government Association; a member of Rush Presbyterian–St. Luke's Heart Institute Leadership Committee; and president of the Hamilton College Alumni Association.

14   With the exception of one, all top executives were male, with each holding at least a Bachelor's degree (see Exhibit 3). As a group, the executives' average age was 48 years with an average of 18 years of service with the company. The relatively long executives' tenure was indicative of the company's reliance on a policy of promotion from within.

EXHIBIT 3
Executive Officers

Name	Position	Age	Years of Service with Company	Elected to Present Position
Elbert O. Hand	Chairman and Chief Executive Officer	53	28	1992
Homi B. Patel	President and Chief Operating Officer	43	13	1993
Carey M. Stein	Executive Vice President, Chief Administrative Officer	45	15	1993
Glenn R. Morgan	Senior Vice President and Controller, Chief Accounting Officer	45	13	1993
Frank A. Brenner	Vice President, Marketing Services	63	24	1983
James E. Condon	Vice President and Treasurer	43	15	1986
Linda J. Valentine	Vice President, Compensation and Benefits	42	12	1993
Kenneth A. Hoffman	President—Men's Apparel Group	49	25	1991

Source: Hartmarx Corporation, *10-K Form*, 1992, p. 4.

STRUCTURE

15   Hartmarx operated as a holding company, overseeing several operating subsidiaries organized into four units: Men's Apparel, Women's Apparel, Hartmarx Retail, and International Licensing. The Men's Apparel unit encompassed such companies as Hart Schaffner and Marx, Hickey-Freeman, Austin Reed, Bobby Jones International, Biltwell Company, Intercontinental branded apparel, Trans-Apparel, Universal Design, Henry Grethel Apparel, and Karl Lagerfeld. The Women's Apparel unit consisted of Austin Reed, MM by Krizia line, and Suburbans line. The Hartmarx Retail unit included Kuppenheimer and Barrie Pace Catalog. And the International unit consisted of two operations: licensing and marketing in Europe, the Far East, and Latin America.

16   The subsidiaries functioned as separate profit centers, with their respective managements responsible for determining the best use of their capital and for planning their growth and development. Although they were viewed as profit centers, the subsidiaries were not wholly independent from the parent company. For example, Hartmarx imposed a standard human resource policy on all of its subsidiaries "allowing the parent company to standardize benefits, so that executives could more easily transfer from one company to another."[4]

MISSION

17   Hartmarx stated its mission as follows:

> The company is engaged in the business of merchandising and marketing quality men's and women's apparel to a wide variety of retail channels. The Hartmarx name provides a unifying identity for the many branded men's and women's manufactured apparel lines and for the company's remaining retail operations. The company also licenses certain of its brands to over 40 licensees, principally in 12 foreign countries. Programs are also developed to market directly to retailers in a number of foreign countries.[5]

OBJECTIVES

18   Because of its preoccupation with the immediate task of nursing the company back to health, top management did not formulate long-term objectives. Instead, the following one-year objectives were set for the company:

· To build on our success as an apparel manufacturer and marketer. We will develop brands to fill market voids while repositioning and growing established brands.

· To provide a dynamic mix of apparel products through a broad merchandising strategy.

· To serve a broad range of retail channels, including the finest specialty and department stores, factory direct to consumers, mass merchants, and direct mail.

· To be a leader in technological marketing. We will provide unparalleled service to our customers through such programs as Quick Response and Electronic Data Interchange.

· To expand our presence in the international marketplace. While continuing our licensing efforts, Hartmarx will merchandise, market, and produce branded apparel in markets beyond our borders. Through joint ventures, acquisitions, and selling agencies, we will market our branded products, concepts, and expertise.

STRATEGIES

19   In 1990, Hartmarx launched a restructuring program that reversed the growth-through-acquisitions strategy it had followed in the late 1970s and throughout the 1980s. Instead of growth, the company began to streamline its operations with an eye toward halting, even reversing, its losses.

20   The centerpiece of the restructuring program entailed focusing on the company's profitable manufacturing and wholesale businesses and divesting or closing unprofitable, nonessential, or nonsynergistic retail operations. As a result, the company closed over 70 stores in 1991. In September 1992, the company sold its principal retail unit, Hartmarx Specialty Stores, Inc. (HSSI), for $43 million to a group headed by a Chicago businessman. The sale led to the closing of two-thirds of the chain's 180 stores.

21   The sale got Hartmarx out of the unprofitable apparel retailing business, which was plagued by the sluggish economy and men's tendency to dress less formally today. Some analysts, though, believed that the sale would create some problems for Hartmarx, because the specialty stores accounted for 12 percent of the sales made by Hartmarx's manufacturing operations.[6] The sale of HSSI was followed by the closing of the Old Mill retail stores operated by its Country Miss subsidiary.

MARKETING

22   Hartmarx designed, manufactured, and sold men's suits, sportcoats, slacks, outercoats, sportswear, and golf apparel to affiliated and unaffiliated retailers and end consumers. The company was also engaged in the design, manufacture, merchandising, and sale of women's career apparel and sportwear.

23   The company had over 40 different brands of men's apparel, which were marketed within various fashion segments, including Business Professional, American Contemporary, Italian Fashion, British Fashion, French Fashion, and American Sportsman, at varying retail price points from "popular" (e.g., suits under $300) to "upper" (e.g., $675). This diversification limited the dependence on any one brand or price point. Exhibit 4 displays the prices of selected products.

24   The company sold both apparel that it manufactured and products purchased from unaffiliated sources. Kuppenheimer was a direct-to-consumer manufacturer of value priced men's tailored clothing sold through its 120 retail stores, including 56 in Sears, Roebuck and Co. stores. Eighteen Sansabelt (business professional apparel) shops were operated by Jaymar-Ruby. The Barrie Pace women's catalog features branded products, purchased from both affiliated and unaffiliated sources.

25   As presented in Exhibit 5, of the various distribution channels, the biggest revenue producer was the unaffiliated specialty stores with 34 percent. This was followed by department stores (26%), company stores such as Kuppenheimer (17%), outlet/off-price/mass merchandise (16%), and direct mail (3%).

26   Hartmarx's biggest product revenue producer, as shown in Exhibit 5, was the over-$300 men's suit market. The company had 25 percent share of this market. The next biggest source of revenue

EXHIBIT 4
Prices of Selected Products

| | Price (in dollars) | | | |
Product	Suits	Sportcoats	Slacks	Casual Slacks
Men's Apparel				
Hickey Freeman	675+	450+	125+	90+
Hart Schaffner and Marx	450–675	300–450	75–125	60–90
Henry Grethel	325–450	200–300	50–75	40–60
Women's Apparel				
Austin Reed	450–675	300–450	75–125	60–90
Retail				
Kuppenheimer	Under 325	Under 200	Under 50	Under 40

Source: Hartmarx Corporation, *1992 Annual Reports*, p. 29, and *1991 Annual Report*, p. 5.

was slacks (18%), followed by sportcoats (14%), women's wear (7%), sportwear (6%), and other products (10%).

Wholesale and Retail Operations

27 Hartmarx's business consisted of two broad wholesale and retail segments. The wholesale segment reflected products made by the company and sold to independent retailers for resale to consumers. In 1992, about 90 percent of the products made by the Men's Apparel unit and 50 percent of the Women's Apparel unit were sold to unaffiliated retailers. Wholesale segment sales were $592 million in 1992 and $578 million in 1991. The 2.5 percent increase in 1992 was due to the introduction of new brands by the Women's Apparel group.

28 The retail segment reflected sales to consumers through company-owned retail stores such as Kuppenheimer. About 80 percent of Kuppenheimer's sales represented products manufactured by the company's subsidiaries. The rest was purchased from outside manufacturers. The retail segment sales declined to $462 million in 1992 from $637 million in 1991.

29 Consolidated 1992 sales of $1.054 billion showed a 13.3 percent decline from $1.215 billion in 1991. The decline was caused by the poor performance of the retail segment, the divestiture of Hartmarx Specialty Stores, Inc., and the discontinuance of the Old Mill retail stores. The net loss for 1992 amounted to $221 million, substantially more than the $39 million loss in 1991.

Advertising

30 Hartmarx reduced its advertising expenditures to $33 million (3% of sales) in 1992 from $48 million (4%) in 1991 and $51 million (4%) in 1990. Advertising expenditures for 1993 were expected to decline both in dollars and as a percentage of sales due to the effect of reduced retail operations.

Acceptance of Credit Cards

31 In 1991, Hartmarx refused to make sales on the American Express card because the card would cut into its efforts to return to profitability. Accepting the card meant paying as much as 5 percent of a transaction to American Express to process card bills. However, in 1992, the company reversed its policy by deciding to accept the card even though the company was more financially troubled. "We found there were some people who preferred to use the card, so we decided it was important to serve them,"[7] said Frank Brenner, a spokesman for Hartmarx.

EXHIBIT 5
Revenue Sources in Terms of Distribution Channels and Products

	Percent of Total Revenues
Distribution Channels	
1. Unaffiliated specialty stores	34
2. Department stores	26
3. Company stores	17
4. Outlet/off-price/mass merchandise	16
5. Direct mail	3
6. Miscellaneous	4
Products	
1. Over-$300 men's suits	25
2. Slacks	18
3. Sportcoats	14
4. Women's wear	7
5. Sportwear	6
6. Miscellaneous	30

Source: Hartmarx Corporation, *1992 Annual Report*, p. 3.

International Marketing

32 Hartmarx had an international licensing program in Europe, the Far East, and South America. As the apparel marketplace became increasingly more international, the company planned to shift its focus from licensing to direct marketing of its products. Hartmarx was engaged in discussions with two foreign corporations to form joint ventures that would establish a major presence for its products in China. Currently, the company exports tailored clothing from all its units to Mexico and Canada.

PRODUCTION

33 Hartmarx maintained numerous manufacturing and warehouse facilities to support its retail and wholesale operations. Their locations were scattered throughout the eastern and midwestern sections of the United States. Management believed such locations would enhance the quick movement of goods to market.

34 Apparel production was a batch process with large order sizes taken through three major steps: spreading, marking, and cutting; sewing and assembly; and pressing. This process was very labor intensive, involving numerous repetitive tasks performed by unskilled labor.[8] Recently, Hartmarx made capital investments in automated equipment in order to lower labor costs so that it can compete more efficiently with the high influx of imports from Asian manufacturers.

HUMAN RESOURCES

35 Hartmarx had about 13,000 employees, of whom 85 percent were employed in manufacturing-wholesale and 15 percent in retailing. Most of the Men's Apparel employees engaged in manufacturing and distribution activities were covered by union contracts with the Amalgamated Clothing and Textile Workers Union; a small number of the retail and Women's Apparel employees were covered by other union contracts.

Employee Benefits

36 The company participated with other companies in the apparel industry in making collectively bargained contributions to pension funds covering most of its union employees. Pension costs relating to multi-employer plans were about $12 million in 1992.

37   Hartmarx offered an employee-savings-investment plan (SIP). Eligible participants in SIP could invest from 1 percent to 16 percent of earnings among several investment alternatives, including company stock. Employees participating in this plan automatically participated in the Hartmarx Employee Stock Ownership Plan (ESOP). In addition, certain of the company's subsidiaries made contributions to multi-employer union health and welfare funds pursuant to collective bargaining agreements.

Promotion from Within

38   Hartmarx placed much emphasis on promoting its own employees to higher positions. Lengthy tenure was a prominent element of Hartmarx corporate culture, and led to enhanced employee loyalty. According to Weinberg, the company's former CEO: " . . . that's part of the culture of this company, right down to our second- and third-generation pressers."[9] Addressing the same point, former vice president of human resources, Sherman Rosen, said: "It's not unusual to have people retire after 52 years of service."[10]

Succession Planning

39   Hartmarx used succession planning as a tool of evaluating its employee skills, determining the company's future needs for managers, and grooming subordinates for higher positions. According to Rosen:

> For the first time, we are able to profile our employee population, build a forecasting system and inventory skills in a prompt and timely way. All these are essential to developing and supporting our human resource strategy and their linkage to the company's strategic plan.[11]

SOCIAL RESPONSIBILITY

40   Hartmarx set up the Hartmarx Charitable Foundation to oversee its economic involvements within the community. The Foundation was a million-dollar organization that allocated monies and lent support to programs that were determined to be just and worthy. Hartmarx made all charitable donations through the Foundation. The Foundation's mission stated:

> As a good corporate citizen, Hartmarx recognizes and accepts responsibility to help meet the social, economic, educational, and cultural needs of society and the public we serve. Hartmarx also knows that for our business to grow and prosper we must actively participate in solving the problems and improving the quality of life in communities where we operate."[12]

41   Over the period 1985–1989, the Foundation contributed over $400,000 to worthy charities.[13] The Foundation operated for the benefit of its employees as well. Almost 60 percent of its operating budget was dedicated to educational, matching gift, and general support programs for its employees all over the country.[14]

LEGAL ISSUES

42   Hartmarx Corp. has been involved in two legal suits. In 1989, Hart Schaffner and Marx (HSM), a wholly owned subsidiary of the company, was sued for manufacturing and selling apparel and products bearing Christian Dior's trademarks. Although the lawsuit was settled and dismissed, the settlement agreement was the subject of an unfavorable award against HSM in subsequent arbitration proceedings that became the subject of a new lawsuit.

43   In 1992, David Spillyards, the holder of about 1,800 shares of Hartmarx common stock, filed a class action complaint against the company, its directors, and former director Harvey A. Weinberg.

The complaint claimed that the company's directors breached certain duties owed to the company's shareholders. The complaint alleged that the purpose of the sale of the company's principal retail unit, Hartmarx Specialty Stores, Inc., to HSSA Group, Ltd., was to benefit Mr. Weinberg (who was also alleged to have been a director of HSSA Group at the time of the announcement of the sale). The complaint was dismissed in November 1992, but Mr. Spillyard was given permission by the court to file another amended complaint. Hartmarx filed a motion to dismiss the second amended complaint, believing that the allegations contained in it were without merit.[15]

FINANCE

44   Hartmarx's net loss from operating activities was $62 million in 1990. Although it dropped to $38 million in 1991, it jumped to $220 million in 1992. Its net cash from operating activities dropped from $110 million in 1990 to $11 million in 1991 to $7 million in 1992. As a result, the company stopped payment of dividends in 1992.

45   The company's financial obligations showed a substantial increase. Thus, while its long-term debt in 1991 was $106 million, it increased to $249 million in 1992. In 1992, Hartmarx reached agreements with its lenders requiring it to gradually but substantially reduce its debt by 1995. The agreements included restrictive clauses pertaining to capital expenditures, asset sales, minimum working capital, and current ratio. The agreements also prohibited the company from paying dividends (during the term of the agreements), from purchasing or redeeming its stock, and from making certain acquisitions or investment without specific lender consent.

INDUSTRY

46   The Hartmarx Corporation and all of its subsidiaries operated in the apparel and textile industry. This industry was highly competitive. There were about 2,200 competing firms within the apparel and other finished textile products industry.[16] The industry was composed of three types of apparel companies: manufacturers, contractors, and jobbers. Manufacturers cut and assembled apparel items within their own establishments. Contractors assembled the items only. And jobbers supplied cut material for contractors. Manufacturers, such as Hartmarx, accounted for roughly 60 percent of all industry shipments.[17]

Industry Consolidation

47   Due to stiff competition, the number of competing firms began to fall. As a result, production of goods became increasingly more concentrated. In the last decade, the proportion of value attributed to the four largest firms grew from 17 to 25 percent; the proportion of value attributed to the 20 largest firms increased from 43 to 57 percent during this time period.[18]

Geographic Centers

48   Apparel production facilities were historically centered in New Jersey, New York, and Pennsylvania. In recent years, this changed. Expansion into the Southern and Western states reduced the number of facilities in the Northeast by roughly two-fifths. In 1967, 53 percent of all shipments in the apparel industry came from New Jersey, New York, and Pennsylvania. By the mid 1980s this figure fell to 38 percent.[19]

49   South Carolina emerged as a production center not only for U.S. companies but also for foreign firms. Foreign countries with textile production facilities in South Carolina included Canada, Japan, West Germany, China, France, Great Britain, Italy, Israel, Denmark, Korea, and Switzerland.[20] The relative weakness of the dollar in the 1980s made foreign investment in the U.S. extremely attractive.

Industry Cyclicality

50   The apparel industry was very much tied to economic conditions. In recessionary times, the apparel industry experienced a significant growth slowdown. During such periods, consumers were forced to treat apparel items more as if they were durable goods and had a tendency to put off or delay purchases. Typically, the hardest hit were firms that catered to the high end of the market. On the other hand, apparel companies experienced their most profitable times during periods of sound economic growth and prosperity.

Improved Efficiency

51   Since the early 1980s, the apparel and textile industries suffered due to recessionary conditions and stiff competition from low-cost importers. Collectively, U.S. firms were forced to restructure and streamline their operations. Advanced technology, state-of-the-art manufacturing systems, and automated machinery were introduced. As a result, a textile mill today was capable of achieving efficiency levels many times greater than the same mill would only a few years ago.

52   The push for efficiency was coupled with a significant reduction in the industry's labor force. Employment in the apparel and textile industry decreased by approximately 15 percent between 1980 and 1988 and was expected to decrease by 25 percent in the year 2000. Only the tobacco, metal, and machinery industries experienced greater fall-offs in the number of employees.

Future Industry Outlook

53   The projected future growth rates of the apparel industry was not encouraging. Shipments fell in recent years and inventory levels continued to be a major concern. This resulted not only from poor economic conditions but from continued pressure exerted by foreign manufacturers. Unless the economy improved, the demand for apparel would continue to be weak.

54   However, global changes, specifically the European Community's expected market unification, had the potential to provide the industry with a new stimulus. If barriers to entry broke down and the ease of doing business abroad grew, it would be easier for the U.S. apparel firms to penetrate new international markets.

COMPETITORS

55   Several powerful competitors operated in the apparel industry. Hartmarx, viewed as a whole, occupied the fourth largest position in the apparel and textile market with a 4.4 percent share. The leading manufacturers in these industries were VF Corp. (8.5%), Liz Claiborne Inc. (4.8%), and Fruit of the Loom, Inc. (4.5%).[21] Positioned behind Hartmarx were Crystal Brands, Leslie Fay Companies, Inc., Phillips-Van Heusen, Genesco, and Russell Corp.

56   Of the above apparel manufacturers, only three firms, Crystal Brands, Genesco, and Phillips-Van Heusen compete directly with Hartmarx.

Crystal Brands, Inc.

57   Crystal Brands manufactured, marketed, and sold tailored clothing, dress furnishings, and sportswear for men, women, and children under the names Eagle Shirtmakers, Evan-Picone, Gant, Haspel, Izod, Palm Beach, John Weitz, Polo by Ralph Lauren for Boys, Pierre Cardin for Boys, Turnbury, Hunter Haig, and Austin Hill. These products were sold to consumers through department stores, specialty retail stores, and mass merchandise retail stores. Crystal Brands also operated a chain of factory outlet stores.[22] As shown in Exhibit 6, Crystal Brands' sales and net income declined in both 1991 and 1992.

EXHIBIT 6
Crystal Brands' Five-Year Sales and Income

	1992	1991	1990	1989	1988
Sales ($000)	589,000	651,200	701,000	695,300	390,90
Net income ($000)	−75,300	−71,400	28,900	18,500	14,600
Sales growth rate: 10.7					
Net income growth rate: NA					

Source: Compact Disclosure, *Crystal Brands, Inc., Financial Information*, 1993, p. 1

Genesco, Inc.

58 Genesco operated in two industry segments: footwear and tailored clothing. Genesco manufactured products under the names Chaps by Ralph Lauren, Polo University Club by Ralph Lauren, Perry Ellis, and Perry Ellis Portfolio. Products were sold primarily at wholesale to specialty retail and department stores nationwide through a direct sales force. Suits were sold at the upper retail price points, typically ranging from $350 to $750.[23] The company's five-year sales and net income are presented in Exhibit 7.

Phillips-Van Heusen Corp.

59 Phillips-Van Heusen was primarily engaged in the manufacture and procurement of men's and women's shirts and sweaters. Distribution of such products was on a wholesale basis to major department and specialty stores and, with respect to private label products, to major retail chains and department stores. The company also marketed these products directly to consumers through retail specialty and factory outlet stores and catalog sales.[24] The company's five-year sales and net income are displayed in Exhibit 8.

Foreign Competition

60 Imports from foreign countries played a dominant role in the apparel industry. East Asia (China, Taiwan, South Korea, Hong Kong) was the biggest exporter to the U.S., followed by Canada and Mexico (see Exhibit 9).

61 The Far Eastern countries enjoyed a competitive edge over U.S. companies principally because of their abundant supply of low-cost labor and raw materials. As a result, foreign manufacturers were able to underprice U.S. firms, forcing them to settle for minimum profitability margins.

SUPPLIERS

62 Woolens, polyesters, and blends of wool and polyester were the principal materials used in men's and women's tailored apparel. In other women's apparel, cotton and polyester were largely used, with fleece and denim used to a lesser extent. About three-fourths of the fabrics used were supplied by domestic mills and the remainder was imported. Hartmarx's arrangements with its suppliers did not include long-term contracts. The company maintained that alternative sources of supply were available for its raw material requirements.

63 Wool prices, during the last three years, increased two-fold, while the price of cotton increased 16 percent. However, the price of wool was expected to fall in the future due to anticipated dropping demand.[25]

EXHIBIT 7
Genesco's Five-Year Sales and Net Income

	1992	1991	1990	1989	1988
Sales ($000)	539,867	471,766	476,342	492,248	462,766
Net income ($000)	9,381	461	1,282	18,454	13,720
Sales growth rate: 5.87					
Net income growth rate: −4.46					

Source: Compact Disclosure, *Genesco, Inc., Financial Information*, 1993, p. 1.

LABOR UNIONS

64   The apparel industry was highly labor intensive. About 84 percent of the workforce was in production jobs, compared to the overall manufacturing rate of 68 percent. Women make up 77 percent of the apparel workforce but only 33 percent for total manufacturing.[26] Since 1987 employment within the apparel industry had been falling at roughly 1 percent per year due to automation.

65   About one-half of the production workers in the apparel industry belonged to labor unions who traditionally exhibited a hostile attitude toward management. The major unions were the International Ladies Garment Workers Union (ILGWU) and the Amalgamated Clothing and Textile Workers Union (ACTWU). U.S. apparel workers earned an average wage of $6.35 an hour.[27] This was low when compared with the $10.71 an hour average wage in all other U.S. manufacturing industries.[28] Most of Hartmarx's workers were covered by union contracts with the ACTWU. Due to the workers' low wages and the consequent discontent, serious labor problems might emerge in the future.

GOVERNMENT REGULATIONS

66   Although textile/apparel goods accounted for 24 percent of the U.S. trade deficit, no significant quotas or tariffs were imposed. Historically, U.S. administrations always espoused a free-trade policy. President Bush urged the Congress to grant China, one of the biggest apparel exporters to the United States, "most favored nation" trading partner status.

DEMOGRAPHICS

67   The 35-to-44 and 45-to-54-year-old segments of the population were expected to expand significantly over the next decade. Consumers in these age groups spent the greatest amount of money on apparel purchases. The major target market for quality apparel manufacturers was the 35-50 age group. This group spent more on fashion apparel ($625 million annually) than any other age group. The 25-34 age group spent $380 million annually, and the over 60 age group spent $350 million annually.

CULTURE

68   Foreign cultures were undergoing profound changes as closed societies were opening up and adopting free market systems. Cultural barriers were being broken down as a global economy was taking shape with each passing year. These "new" cultures were readily welcoming Western culture and the vast assortment of goods that accompanies it.

EXHIBIT 8
Phillips-Van Heusen's Five-Year Sales and Net Income

	1992	1991	1990	1989	1988
Sales:	1,042,565	904,100	806,315	732,936	641,038
Net income:	37,881	31,137	26,384	24,192	20,669
Sales growth rate: 12.9					
Income growth rate: 16.3					

Source: Compact Disclosure, *Phillips-Van Heusen, Financial Information*, 1993, p. 1.

ECONOMY

69 After many years of significant expansion in the 1980s, the U.S. economy began to slow down in 1989 with a minimum growth in the GNP. The much anticipated economic recovery in 1991 and 1992 did not materialize. This was due to the depressed real estate market, companies' continuing programs to downsize, and marginal gains in disposable income. Surveys about consumers' future purchasing plans showed that consumers displayed considerable anxiety about jobs and incomes.

PRESSURE GROUPS

70 Numerous groups supported protectionism of American businesses with advertising programs such as "Buy American" or "Crafted with Pride in the U.S.A." This was accompanied by extensive lobbying efforts in Congress to support legislation aimed at imposing trade restrictions on many foreign imports, including apparel.

CONCLUSION

71 Like many other U.S. companies, Hartmarx went on a shopping spree in 1970s and early 1980s. By 1991, however, Hartmarx began losing money and encountering difficulties in managing the new diversified, holding company. Also like many other U.S. companies who began to downsize as a means of stemming their losses, Hartmarx embarked on a divestiture strategy by shedding its losing acquisitions. But will the strategy succeed in restoring this icon of U.S. clothing industry to its former glory days?

NOTES

1. Hartmarx Corporation, *1991 Annual Report*, pp. 1–2.
2. *The Wall Street Journal*, August 27, 1990, p. A5.
3. Nancy Ryan, "Hartmarx Acts to Push Manufacturing," *The Chicago Tribune*, July 15, 1992, Section 3, p. 1.
4. *HRMagazine*, November 1990, p. 55.
5. Hartmarx Corporation, *10-K Form*, 1992, p. 1.
6. Gregory A. Paterson, "Hartmarx Sells Specialty Stores, to Post Charge," *The Wall Street Journal*, September 21, 1992, p. A4.
7. John Schmeltzer, "Hartmarx OKs American Express," *The Chicago Tribune*, August 8, 1992, Section 2, p. 1.
8. *Monthly Labor Review*, November 1988, p. 28.
9. *The Wall Street Journal*, August 27, 1990, p. A5.

EXHIBIT 9
Apparel Imports in 1989

	Value (in $ millions)	Share
Canada & Mexico	1.092	6.8
South America	0.455	2.8
European Community	0.480	3.0
East Asia	8.780	54.5
Japan	0.173	1.1
Other	5.131	31.8
World total	16.111	100.0

Source: Standard and Poor's, *Industry Surveys*, June 1990, p. T90.

10. *HRMagazine*, November 1990, p. 52.
11. Ibid., p. 55.
12. *Corporate 500: The Directory of Corporate Philanthropy, 1990–91 Annual*, p. 353.
13. Ibid., p. 353–54.
14. Ibid., p. 353.
15. Hartmarx Corporation, *10-K Form*, 1992, pp. 304.
16. Dun and Bradstreet, *Key Business Ratios*, 1990, p. 46–48.
17. *Monthly Labor Review*, November 1988, p. 27.
18. Ibid., p. 27.
19. Ibid.
20. Standard and Poor's, *Standard and Poor's Industry Surveys*, June 1990, p. T-80.
21. Ibid., p. T-108.
22. *Moody's Industrial Manual*, 1990, p. 2819.
23. Ibid., p. 1208.
24. Ibid., p. 6093.
25. *U.S. Industrial Outlook—1991*, p. 34-1.
26. Ibid., p. 34-2.
27. Ibid., p. 34-1.
28. *Statistical Abstract of the U.S.—1990*, p. 396.

APPENDIX A

Consolidated Balance Sheet
As of November 30
(in thousands)

	1992	1991
Assets		
Current assets:		
Cash and cash equivalents	$ 22,356	$ 6,571
Accounts receivable, less allowance for doubtful accounts of $16,022 in 1992 and $15153 in 1991	159,772	134,748
Inventories	216,751	404,995
Prepaid expenses	17,179	8,164
Recoverable income taxes	8,158	16,716
Deferred income taxes	5,557	7,438
Total current assets	429,773	578,632
Investments and other assets	15,340	11,560
Properties:		
Land	4,006	3,902
Buildings and building improvement	57,790	58,778
Furniture, fixtures, and equipment	122,482	215,856
Leasehold improvements	39,099	116,719
	223,337	395,255
Accumulated depreciation and amortization	156,531	245,599
Net properties	66,846	149,056
Total assets	$511,959	$739,848
Liabilities and Shareholders' Equity		
Current liabilities:		
Notes payable to banks	$ 65,000	$178,500
Current maturities of long-term debt	889	1,651
Accounts payable	56,016	81,368
Accrued payrolls	18,517	26,838
Other accrued expenses	52,399	58,985
Total current liabilities	$192,821	$347,342
Long-term debt, less current maturities	248,713	105,498
Shareholders' equity:		
Preferred shares, $1 par value; 2,500,000 authorized and unissued	—	—
Common shares, $2.50 par value; authorized 75,000,000; issued 28,106,439 in 1992 and 27,855,802 in 1991	70,266	69,640
Capital surplus	63,810	63,254
Retained earnings (deficit)	(17,758)	207,218
Unearned employee benefits	(12,496)	(13,205)
	103,822	362,907
Common shares in treasury, at cost, 2,198,864 in 1992 and 2,495,357 in 1991	(33,397)	(39,899)
Total shareholders' equity	70,425	287,008
Total liabilities and shareholders' equity	$511,959	$739,848

Source: Hartmarx Corporation, *1992 Annual Report*, p. 14.

APPENDIX B

Consolidated Statement of Cash Flows
As of November 30
(in thousands)

	1992	1991
Increase (decrease) in cash and cash equivalents		
Cash flows from operating activities:		
Net loss	$(220,245)	$ (38,365)
Reconciling items to adjust net loss to net cash provided by operating activities:		
Depreciation and amortization	26,947	33,809
Loss on sale of subsidiary	136,00	—
Changes in:		
Accounts receivable:		
Sales of receivables	(58,000)	(2,000)
Other changes	23,076	(29)
Inventories	68,944	4,604
Prepaid expenses	(10,215)	431
Other assets	(4,280)	243
Accounts payable and accrued expenses	8,541	(6,907)
Taxes on earnings	10,439	(7,305)
Adjustments of properties to net realizable value	11,510	4,493
Net cash provided by (used in) operating activities	(9,456)	(15,488)
Cash flows from investing activities:		
Increase (decrease) in notes payable to banks	30,796	(3,850)
Increase (decrease) in other long-term debt	(1,133)	2,014
Proceeds from issuance of common stock	1,182	38,550
Proceeds from disposition of treasury notes	1,769	7,283
Payment of dividends	—	(13,643)
Net cash provided by (used in) financing activities	32,614	30,354
Cash and cash equivalents at beginning of year	6,571	2,731
Cash and cash equivalents at end of year	$ 22,356	$ 6,571
Supplemental cash flow information:		
Net cash paid (received) during the year for:		
Interest expense	$ 22,200	$ 24,300
Income taxes	(17,000)	(14,300)

Source: Hartmarx Corporation, *1992 Annual Report*, p. 15.

APPENDIX C

Consolidated Statement of Earnings
As of November 30
(in thousands)

	1992	1991	1990
Net sales	$1,053,949	$1,215,310	$1,295,840
Finance charges, interest and other income	9,566	10,761	14,286
	1,063,515	1,226,071	1,310,126
Cost of goods sold	703,645	781,303	806,237
Selling, administrative, and occupancy expenses	374,785	480,970	492,174
Restructuring charges	190,800	—	77,600
Interest expense	21,135	23,796	28,952
	1,290,365	1,286,066	1,404,936
Loss before taxes	(226,850)	(59,995)	(94,810)
Tax benefit	(6,605)	(21,630)	(33,265)
Net loss for the year	$ (220,245)	$ (38,365)	$ (61,545)

Source: Hartmarx Corporation, *1992 Annual Report*, p. 13.

CASE 20

L.A. GEAR, INC.

OVERVIEW

1 In February 1989, Robert Y. Greenberg stood on the floor of the New York Stock Exchange and watched as the letters "LA" flashed across the ticker tape for the very first time after L.A. Gear was listed on the Big Board. "It was my proudest moment. It was my dream," Greenberg said. "You see, I always wanted to be the president of a company on the New York Stock Exchange,"[1] he added.

2 For over 14 years, L.A. Gear promoted the Southern-California lifestyle with attractively-styled shoes designed primarily for women. Later, however, the company altered its focus to include products that appealed to the men's performance athletic market. The company continued to produce fashion shoes for women, but its core business became the performance athletic market where sales were not as dependent on swings in consumer tastes. The company achieved its position as the number three brand maker of footwear products when it surpassed Converse, Inc., in 1989. Greenberg set his sights at the number one position in the industry by challenging Nike and Reebok.

3 However, L.A. Gear began to experience financial difficulties in 1991. Its market share dropped from a high of 12% in 1990, to 8% in 1991, and to 5% in 1992. And its net sales declined from $820 million in 1990, to $619 million in 1991, and to $430 million in 1992. The company incurred losses of $45 million in 1991 and $72 million in 1992. As a result, L.A. Gear was unable to obtain credit from its lenders. To enhance its credit rating, L.A. Gear managed to lure a new investor, Trefoil Capital Investors L.P., who, in September 1991, paid $100 million for a 34% stake in the company.

4 Since the Trefoil deal, L.A. Gear's internal operations underwent major restructuring. As part of the restructuring, the Trefoil team replaced L.A. Gear's top management—including the company's founder, Robert Y. Greenberg. Stanley P. Gold, managing director of Trefoil Capital Investors L.P., and Mark R. Goldston, former Reebok executive, took over. Gold succeeded Greenberg as the company's new chairman and chief executive officer, and Goldston was appointed president and chief operating officer.

5 Gold and Goldston developed a survival strategy to nurse the ailing L.A. Gear back to health. At the core of the turnaround strategy was a new advertising campaign built around the theme, "Get in Gear." In an effort to create a clear identity for L.A. Gear, Goldston reorganized product lines into three groups: athletic, lifestyle, and children. The new management also launched a restructuring program aimed at paring the company's costs.

6 In their letter to the shareholders, Gold and Goldston stated, "We believe that the accomplishments of the past year have laid the groundwork upon which we can build to achieve our ultimate objective—to make L.A. Gear a leader in the footwear industry and one of the most admired companies in America." But, will they be able to accomplish their objective in this highly competitive industry?

HISTORY

7 Robert Y. Greenberg, L.A. Gear's founder, had a knack for selling. First, it was wigs. Later it was roller skates and jeans for the trendy residents of Venice Beach, California. Then it was sneakers. As one analyst described him, "Greenberg is the quintessential salesman."[2]

This case was prepared by A. J. Almaney of DePaul University.

8   Greenberg's story is a 1980s financial fairy tale with a 1990s climax: A street-smart shoemaker who always feared being poor would create a pair of sneakers that brought him fortune. As a kid working in the Brooklyn family's produce business and reading his father's copies of *Forbes* magazine, Greenberg set his sights on starting his own company. He took his first step toward that goal by enrolling in a beauty school. After graduation, he opened a chain of hair salons in Brooklyn in the mid-1960s. Later, he started a wig-importing business. As that venture petered out, Greenberg spotted another trend—fashion jeans—and began importing them from South Korea. By 1979, the jeans business had started to fade, and Greenberg decided to pack up for Southern California.

9   His next inspiration came soon after his arrival in Los Angeles, as he waited three hours at Venice Beach to rent roller skates for his wife and kids. "I figured the guy must be taking in $4,000 to $5,000 a day," he said. So, Greenberg walked out of the skate shop and immediately plunked $40,000 into his own, which soon expanded to nine locations. Not only did he sell skates through the stores, but he established a skate-manufacturing business. The market for skates quickly soured, though. As a result, Greenberg opened a clothing store on Melrose Avenue which he named L.A. Gear. By 1985, the L.A. Gear store was losing money.

10   Greenberg started looking for the next trend to ride. Having watched Reebok storm the market a year earlier with its fashionable aerobics shoes, Greenberg went chasing after Reebok with his own candy-colored sneakers, all aimed at a market he knew: trend-conscious teenage girls. In what proved to be a brilliant marketing strategy, he opted to sell his shoes not just to sporting-goods stores but to big department stores like Nordstrom, May Co., and Bullock's. L.A. Gear's big break came the following year, 1987, when Reebok underestimated the demand for its wildly popular black-and-white athletic shoes. Greenberg stepped in to meet the demand by marketing "The Workout," a simple canvas shoe that became the flagship of the company.

11   During Greenberg's Venice Beach tenure, he had become friends with Sandy Saemann, who was making skating-safety equipment while Greenberg was hawking skates. After Saemann launched his own advertising agency, Greenberg brought him into the company to help craft L.A. Gear's frothy image of sun and sex.

12   The Greenberg-Saemann combination worked. L.A. Gear soon became a highly profitable operation. Sales mushroomed from $200,000 per month at the beginning of 1985 to $1.8 million per month by mid-year. As the company grew to an operation of 51 employees, it needed outside funds for more development and opted for an initial public offering which was completed on July 1, 1986.

13   The company used the $16.5 million in proceeds from the offering to fund its growing working capital requirements and to fund a hefty advertising and promotion budget. The initial single style of footwear developed into 150 styles, and L.A. Gear's preeminence in the youth market expanded to include footwear for customers of all ages. In 1986, L.A. Gear launched lines for men, children, and infants and expanded its women's line to include athletic shoes for basketball, aerobics, and cross-trainers.

14   In 1989, sales rocketed to $617 million from $71 million in 1987, and the company surpassed Converse, Inc., to become the nation's third-largest seller of athletic shoes. In 1989, L.A. Gear's stock switched from trading in the over-the-counter market to the Big Board. L.A. Gear's stock price in 1988 was $10.94 with $224 million in sales. By early December 1989, L.A. Gear's stock had climbed more than 178%, more than any Big Board stock.[3] *The Wall Street Journal, Business Week,* and *Fortune Magazine* named L.A. Gear the best performing stock on the New York Stock Exchange in 1989. Greenberg boasted that he would push L.A. Gear past Reebok and Nike by 1991. Mark R. Goldston, L.A. Gear's current president, described the company's early success as a phenomenon achieved by innovative styling and a unique ability to have their ear to the market and respond quickly.

15   In 1990, however, the company's stock price started to decline, and investors became concerned that L.A. Gear was losing its appeal to fashion-conscious young women. Some analysts marked the beginning of L.A. Gear's troubles with the failure of its Michael Jackson shoes.[4] In 1989, Sandy Saemann, executive vice president, signed a $20 million contract with Michael Jackson for endorsement of a line of black, silver-buckled shoes. But the shoes proved to be a failure. Other signs of trouble included reports of stock selling by insiders as well as the Justice Department's investigation of alleged underpayment of custom duties.[5]

16   In April 1991, L.A. Gear posted a fiscal first-quarter loss of $12.5 million. Sales fell 8.8% to $171 million from 187 million. L.A. Gear posted a tangible net worth of $193 million as of February 28, 1991.[6]

17   In May 1991, L.A. Gear agreed to sell a 30% stake to Roy E. Disney's Trefoil Capital Investors L.P. for $100 million. Under the agreement, Trefoil would also receive three seats on L.A. Gear's board of directors and the opportunity to have first option to buy shares of Greenberg's 3.5 million in common shares should Greenberg decide to sell. L.A. Gear also agreed to hire Disney's Shamrock Capital Advisors, Inc., as consultants for three years, paying fees of $500,000 the first year, $600,000 the second year, and $700,000 the third year.

18   Shortly after the Trefoil agreement was initiated, Sandy Saemann—a flamboyant, gold-chain decked executive vice president—resigned. Saemann was the architect of L.A. Gear's sexy marketing campaign which often featured scantily clad models. He was also credited with gathering celebrity endorsers for L.A. Gear. Saemann agreed to provide consulting services to L.A. Gear for 2.5 years. Analysts said Saemann resigned because his flamboyant personality conflicted with the Trefoil team.[7] Kevin Ventrudo, 32, senior vice president of administration and a board member, also resigned. Mark R. Goldston succeeded Robert Greenberg as president. Greenberg remained chairman and chief executive.

19   On January 27, 1992, Robert Greenberg, L.A. Gear's founder, was eased out as chairman and chief executive and a director, along with Gil N. Schwartzberg, vice chairman. Stanley P. Gold, 50, managing director of Trefoil was appointed as the new chairman and chief executive officer of L.A. Gear.

BOARD OF DIRECTORS

20   As shown in Exhibit 1, the board of directors was composed of eleven members. Three of them were insiders while the others were outsiders. One of the outside directors was a woman, Ann E. Meyers, who worked as a sports commentator. The chairman of the board was Stanley P. Gold, who also served as the chief executive officer (CEO) of the firm. The board carried out its duties through the Executive and Nominating Committees. The Executive Committee consisted of Stanley Gold, R. Rudolph Reinfrank, and Mark Goldston. Reinfrank served as chairman of the Executive Committee. The Nominating Committee consisted of Stephen A. Koffler, Robert G. Moskowitz, and Mark Goldston. Koffler served as the chairman of the Nominating Committee.

TOP MANAGEMENT

21   L.A. Gear's top management underwent major changes since the consummation of Trefoil's $100 million investment in the company. Below is a profile of each of the key executives.

22   **Stanley P. Gold**   Stanley Gold, 50 years old, succeeded Greenberg as chairman and chief executive officer of L.A. Gear, Inc. Formerly, he was president and chief executive officer of Shamrock Holdings, Inc., a Burbank, California–based company wholly owned by the Roy Disney family. Gold was considered to be a turnaround expert. He proved himself by helping revive Walt Disney Co., oil driller Enterra, and soybean processor Central Soyal. Prior to assuming his positions at Shamrock, Gold was a managing partner of Gange, Tyre, Ramer & Brown, Inc., a prominent Los Angeles law firm he joined in 1968. For a number of years, he specialized in corporate acquisitions, sales, and financing. Earlier in his legal career, he served as a trial lawyer in major corporate and civil litigation.[8]

23   A native of Los Angeles, California, Gold first studied at the University of California at Berkeley and subsequently graduated from the University of California at Los Angeles with an A.B. degree in political science. After receiving his J.D. degree from the University of Southern California Law School in 1967, he did postgraduate work at Cambridge University in England.[9] Gold's professional and civic affiliations included the American Bar Association and the Copyright Society. He served as

EXHIBIT 1
L.A. Gear's Board of Directors

Stanley P. Bold
Chairman of the Board and Chief
Executive Officer
L.A. Gear, Inc.
President and Managing Director
Trefoil Investors, Inc., and Shamrock
Capital Advisors, Inc.

Mark R. Goldston
President and Chief Operating
Officer
L.A. Gear, Inc.

Richard W. Schubert
General Counsel and Secretary
L.A. Gear, Inc.

Alan E. Dashling
Chairman of the Board and Chief
Executive Officer
Sterling West Bancorp.

Willie D. Davis
President and Chief Executive
Officer
All-Pro Broadcasting

Stephen A. Koffler
Executive Vice President and
Director of Investment Banking
Sutro & Co., Inc.

Ann E. Meyers
Sports Commentator
KMPC Radio, Prime Ticket, ESPN,
Sportschannel, and ABC

Clifford A. Miller
Chairman
The Clifford Group, Inc.

Robert G. Moskowitz
Managing Director
Trefoil Investors, Inc., and Shamrock
Capital Advisors, Inc.

R. Rudolph Reinfrank
Executive Vice President
Shamrock Holdings, Inc.

Vappalak A. Ravindran
Chief Executive Officer
Paracor Company
President
Elders Finance, Inc.

Source: L.A. Gear, *1992 Annual Report*, p. 29.

a guest lecturer at the Wharton School at the University of Pennsylvania. He was chairman of the board of governors of Hebrew Union College, a trustee of the Center Theater Group in Los Angeles and the George C. Marshall Foundation, and a member of the USC Law Center Board of Councilors.

24   **Mark R. Goldston**   Mark Goldston, 38 years old, succeeded Robert Y. Greenberg, the company's founder, as president and chief operating officer. Greenberg was also eased out as chairman, chief executive, and a director at a board meeting in an apparent effort by the company's largest investor, Trefoil Capital Investors L.P., to bury the "old" L.A. Gear.[10] Despite Greenberg's assertions that "the company is left in great hands," the ouster capped a four-month battle between the laid-back Greenberg and the buttoned-down Trefoil team for the soul of L.A. Gear.[11]

25   Goldston was a principal of Odyssey partners, a leverage buyout and investment firm. At Odyssey, Goldston was part of an internal operating unit that supervised the management of certain portfolio companies. His responsibilities included the development, execution, and management of operating plans and the evaluation of strategic alternatives for those portfolio companies. Prior to joining Odyssey, Goldston was senior and chief marketing officer of Reebok International, Ltd., where he spearheaded the marketing effort for "The Pump," a $500 million line of athletic footwear products. As one of the inventors of the Reebok "Visible Energy Return System Technology," Goldston was on the U.S. patent for that technology. Additionally, Goldston was involved in the development of the Hexalite and Energaire product lines for Reebok. Prior to joining Reebok, Goldston was president of Faberge USA, Inc., a cosmetics and personal care products company. During his tenure there, the company's U.S. sales increased about 50%.

26   Goldston was on the J.L. Kellogg Graduate School of Management Dean's Advisory Board at Northwestern University. In addition, he sat on the board of directors of Revel/Monogram, Inc., ABCO Markets, and Collection Clothing Corp. Goldston's book, entitled *The Turnaround Prescription*, detailing a step-by-step blueprint for effecting a corporate marketing turnaround was published in 1992.[12]

27   In his new position as president and chief operating officer, Goldston brought in fresh talent by hiring former Reebok employees—Gordie Nye, Robert Apatoff, and Christopher Walsh. Gordie Nye,

vice president of marketing athletic footwear, joined the company in December 1991. Previously, he was at Reebok where he was senior director of fitness marketing, with responsibility for marketing men's and women's fitness products.

28   **Christopher Walsh**   Christopher Walsh was 43 years old. He joined L.A. Gear as senior vice president of operations in December 1991. Previously, he was vice president of production at Reebok for three years, where he was in charge of worldwide supply sources. Prior to joining Reebok, he spent two years at Toddler University, a children's shoe manufacturer, as vice president of operations. Prior to that, he worked as a senior consultant for Kurt Satmon Associates for two years, focusing on strategic planning. Earlier in his career, he worked at Nike for 10 years in production and sourcing.[13]

29   **William L. Benford**   William L. Benford, 50 years old, was appointed chief financial officer in September 1991.[14] Prior to that, he was senior vice president and chief financial officer of Central Soya company. Before that he was vice president and treasurer of Dekalb, Inc. He was also affiliated with Shamrock Holdings, Inc., an investment company for the Roy E. Disney family. Shamrock Holdings, Inc., bought Central Soya company in 1985, turned it around, and sold the company two years later at a profit of about $125 million.

MISSION

30   L.A. Gear defined its mission as follows:

> The Company's principal business activity involves the design, development, and marketing of a broad range of quality athletic and casual/lifestyle footwear. Since its inception, the Company has expanded its product line from its original concentration on fashionable women's footwear to diversified collections of footwear for men, women, and children. The Company is organized into two primary marketing divisions: Athletic (including men's and women's basketball, fitness, walking, tennis, and aerobics) and Lifestyle (casual footwear styles intended for non-athletic use). All of the Company's footwear products are manufactured to its specifications by independent producers located primarily in South Korea, Indonesia, Taiwan, and the People's Republic of China.[15]

OBJECTIVES AND STRATEGIES

31   L.A. Gear's short-term objective was to streamline its operations over the next two years. In the long term, the company would attempt to achieve the following objectives:

· To provide a broad range of quality athletic and casual/lifestyle footwear, primarily in the "mid" price range (i.e., $30 to $65 retail).
· To improve relations with, and increase shelf space at, full-margin retailers.
· To improve production and quality control practices.
· To increase international sales and profitability.

32   In attaining these objectives, L.A. Gear adopted a retrenchment/turnaround strategy that involved a comprehensive restructuring of its operations. Thus, in 1992 the company's staff was reduced by 613 employees, or about 45%. In addition, the company reduced its occupancy of about 200,000 square feet of leased office space in five buildings to about 116,000 square feet in two buildings. Further, the general and administrative expenses were reduced in 1992 by $42.7 million, or 21.2%, to $158.7 million from $201.4 million in 1991. The company also discontinued its apparel marketing and design operations, which had a pre-tax operating loss of $14.2 million in 1991.

33   The company's restructuring was augmented with a product development strategy. The product strategy involved developing a broad range of innovative new products for the athletic, lifestyle, and children's line. Grouping products into three well identified divisions was well received by analysts of the footwear industry. Bob McAllister, West Coast market editor for *Footwear News*, said "In the

past, there was no rhyme or reason to L.A. Gear's different styles. Now, the company has introduced new lines that are cleanly divided into athletic, lifestyles, and kids."[16]

34   The company also sought to differentiate its products from its competitors. Goldston was confident that L.A. Gear would increase its market share by using materials in a unique way to carve a specific niche for its products. According to Goldston, "L.A. Gear is committed to designing shoes that do not resemble its competition."[17] While pursuing retrenchment and product development strategies, L.A. Gear launched a marketing campaign that focused on projecting a consistent brand image across varying retail price points and distribution channels.

PRODUCTION

35   L.A. Gear's footwear was manufactured to its specifications by independent producers located primarily in The People's Republic of China, Indonesia, South Korea, and Taiwan. In 1992, manufacturers in these countries supplied 34%, 32%, 30%, and 4% of total pairs of footwear purchased by the company, respectively.

36   The footwear products imported into the U.S. by the company were subject to customs duties, ranging from 6% to 48% of production costs. Duty rates depended on the construction of the shoe and whether the principal component was leather or some other material.

37   The use of foreign manufacturing facilities subjected the company to the customary risks of doing business abroad, including fluctuations in the value of currencies, export duties, import controls, trade barriers, restrictions on the transfer of funds, work stoppage, and political instability. Thus far, these factors, however, did not seem to have an adverse impact on the company's operations.

PRODUCTS

38   L.A. Gear's product lines were organized into three marketing categories: athletic, lifestyle, and children's. Athletic footwear included fitness, walking, tennis, cross-training, and basketball shoes, as well as the recently introduced Light Gear CrossRunner and Dance Training shoes. These products were marketed under two brand names: L.A. Gear, with suggested domestic retail prices under $70; and L.A. Tech, the newly released, higher priced premium brand.

39   The Lifestyle lines included men's and women's casual footwear styles that included the Street Hiker, Vintage Series, and Fashion Athletic and Casual Collections. The children's footwear incorporated features from the athletic and lifestyle lines plus products specifically developed for children. L.A. Lights, lighted shoes for children introduced in June 1992, became one of the largest selling children's shoes in the company's history. The age of the company's target market for the adult products was 14 to 35 years, and for children 5 to 13.[18] Some of L.A. Gear's products and the technologies incorporated in the athletic, lifestyle, and children's lines are described in Exhibit 2.

PRODUCT QUALITY

40   In 1990, L.A. Gear committed a grave marketing blunder in the process of launching its new line of basketball shoes. In a scramble to launch the new shoes, the company outfitted the Marquette University team with handmade pairs, since molds were not completed yet for the large sizes the team members required. As TV cameras zeroed in on one player, the bottom of his sneaker peeled away from the top. This and other cases of poor quality served to seriously tarnish the company's brand image. In an effort to improve quality, L.A. Gear reduced the number of foreign manufacturers from 44 in 1991 to 29 in 1992, retaining only those known for their quality products. The company also engaged a "sourcing" agent with the responsibility of inspecting finished goods prior to shipment by the manufacturer, supervising production management, and facilitating the shipment of goods.

EXHIBIT 2
L.A. Gear's Products and Their Technologies

	Description
Athletic	
Catapult	A midsole system consisting of a carbon graphite spring to provide cushioning and shock absorption
Encapsole Air	A cushioning system which uses air chambers built into the outsole to provide shock absorption
Light Gear	Shoes incorporating battery-powered lights in the outsole that flash upon impact
Lifestyle	
Street Hiker	A light-weight casual hiking shoe
Vintage Series	Footwear based on classic athletic styles
Children's	
L.A. Gear (Galactica for boys; L.A. Twilight for girls; Nightcrawlers for infants)	Shoes incorporating motion-activated battery-powered lights in the outsole that flash with movement
Regulator	Shoes with an adjustable fit and support system using an air inflation device to cushion the foot over the midfoot area
Bendables	Flexible shoes for infants
Clear Gear	Shoes with a clear outsole in flexible plastic with an assortment of designs printed on the midsole

Source: L.A. Gear, *1992 10-K form*, p. 4.

ADVERTISING

41   Sandy Saemann, Greenberg's second in command, was the architect of L.A. Gear's early advertising campaign. His success in signing such celebrities as Paula Abdul and Kareem Abdul-Jabbar was responsible for the phenomenal increase in the company's sales between 1985 and 1990. Saemann fit the image of the laid-back California executive perfectly—right down to the silver necklace. And his flamboyant vision proved perfect for peddling flashy sneakers. Saemann represented L.A. Gear's brash, entrepreneurial roots by producing virtually all of the company's ads and commercials himself without the help of Madison Avenue. However, L.A. Gear's tumble began, ironically, with its biggest advertising deal ever. In 1989, Saemann was able to sign megastar Michael Jackson in what was described as the largest endorsement contract ever: $20 million. L.A. Gear had hoped to time the release of a new line of shoes to an upcoming Michael Jackson greatest-hits album, but the album never materialized. Teenagers everywhere thumbed their noses at the black, buckle-laden shoes. The company was eventually forced to discontinue the entire line, taking a loss of several million dollars.

42   Since the failure of the Michael Jackson advertising campaign, L.A. Gear stopped contracting for the endorsement of its products by entertainment celebrities. Instead, the company chose to contract endorsements with athletic stars such as Karl "The Mailman" Malone of Utah Jazz, Hakeem Olajuwon of the Houston Rockets, and Joe Montana of the San Francisco Forty-Niners. A new slogan, "Get in Gear," was used in the campaign.

43   Under the new management, L.A. Gear changed the focus of many of its advertising campaigns from promoting a fashionable shoe to promoting a performance shoe. Performance was emphasized with the advertisement tag line for the Catapult performance shoe, "It's not just a shoe, it's a machine."[19] L.A. Gear's most successful commercial was the use of the tag line "Anything else is just hot air" to promote the Catapult shoe, with its high-tech, carbon-fiber soles. The ad was an indirect attack at Nike who made the Air Jordan shoes, endorsed by Chicago Bull's star Michael Jordan. NBC refused to run the television ads, and the ensuing exposure received by coverage of NBC's refusal was worth millions to L.A. Gear.[20] In promoting the $110 Catapult shoe, the new

management decided to drop the L.A. Gear logo, believing that the L.A. Gear name was a liability in performance shoes.

44   The new management team subdivided the marketing of the company's products on the basis of price. Shoes costing less than $70 per pair retained the L.A. Gear name and logo, and shoes priced over $70 per pair carried the L.A. Tech name. L.A. Gear's management believed that the L.A. Tech name would help establish the line as a high technology and performance product. The lowest-cost L.A. Gear shoe retailed for approximately $30 per pair, whereas the top of the line L.A. Tech shoe, the Catapult, topped out at about $150 per pair.[21] The L.A. Gear marketing budget amounted to between 10% to 15% of total sales.

RESEARCH AND DEVELOPMENT

45   In designing its products, L.A. Gear conducted comprehensive market research, using a variety of conventional research techniques. Primarily, the company depended on focus groups, product testing, and interviews with consumers and retailers. These methods allowed the company to accurately gauge the image and reputation of L.A. Gear's products and to incorporate changes demanded by the public.

SALES

46   The phenomenal rise in L.A. Gear's sales between 1985 and 1990 was due to Greenberg's ability to create a clear-cut image for the company with brightly colored shoes and sexy ads aimed at teenage girls. The company's spectacular success led Greenberg to set a higher objective for company, $1 billion in sales. To achieve this objective, Greenberg tried to challenge Nike and Reebok directly by adding a line of men's performance shoes. The move was too much, too fast. Venturing into the men's performance shoes blurred L.A. Gear's image. According to one analyst, "When L.A. Gear moved into the performance side, it lost its way." Greenberg, however, was unwilling to lay the company's problems on the men's shoes. Instead, he maintained that "in any battle you're gonna get a little bruised or battered. And we're playing with a couple of billion-dollar companies that don't need us around."

47   The rapid growth also placed an enormous strain on the company. Employees had to push hard to attain the new growth objective. As a result, the company's internal controls got out of hand. A shareholders' class action lawsuit called those controls "chaotic and virtually nonexistent."

48   As a result of the relentless push for fast growth, product-quality problems, and the attendant bad publicity, L.A. Gear saw its share of the overall athletic shoe market drop from a high of 12% in 1990 to 5% in 1992. The company's net sales, as shown in Exhibit 3, declined from $820 in 1990 to $619 in 1991 and to $430 in 1992. The 1992 sales figure represented a 31% decline from 1991. The company incurred losses of $72 million in 1992 and $45 million in 1991. Net international sales, which accounted for about 28% of the company's total net sales, decreased by 6.7% from 1991.

49   According to management, the overall decline in net sales for 1992 was principally due to a drop in the number of pairs sold worldwide resulting from decreased customer demand, and, to a lesser extent, to an average decrease of $1.52 in the selling price per pair. The decline was also due to the continuing effects of the recession and price reductions by the company's principal competitors, which resulted in increased competition at lower prices.

50   Another factor that contributed to the drop in the 1992 sales volume was delivery delays. As part of its restructuring program in 1992, the company changed the manufacturers from which it purchased products. These changes contributed to the company's difficulties in meeting its delivery deadlines on orders for its back-to-school season.

INTERNATIONAL STRATEGY

51   In recent years, sales of athletic and casual/lifestyle footwear in many international markets grew at a faster rate than in the United States. However, L.A. Gear's own sales in the international market declined from $158 million in 1990, to $127 million in 1991, and to $119 million in 1992.

EXHIBIT 3
Net Sales
(dollars in thousands)

	1992		1991		1990	
	Dollars	**Percent**	**Dollars**	**Percent**	**Dollars**	**Percent**
Domestic footwear						
Women's	112,990	26	178,481	29	285,709	35
Men's	104,593	24	176,238	28	196,969	24
Children's	90,997	21	134,485	22	174,486	21
Other	2,688	1	2,517	—	4,217	1
Total domestic Net Sales	311,268	72	491,721	79	661,381	81
International footwear	118,926	28	127,454	21	158,220	19
Total net sales	430,194	100	619,175	100	819,601	100

Source: L.A. Gear, *Form 10-K*, 1992, p. 5.

52   In an effort to stem this decline in sales, L.A. Gear decided to increase its investment in the international market through joint ventures, acquisitions of distributors, and the creation of wholly owned foreign subsidiaries. By selling its products directly abroad (as opposed to the company's historical reliance on independent distributors in those markets), the company sought to increase sales by adopting more competitive marketing and distribution programs. In March 1992, the company established its first foreign subsidiary to conduct direct sales of its products in France.

53   L.A. Gear also began to focus on Asia for its potential as a retail sales market. "We see Asia as a huge market. You have basically got two billion pairs of feet out here," said Goldston. Consequently, the company began investigating promotional alliances and equity partnerships with Asian companies.

DISTRIBUTION

54   L.A. Gear distributed its products out of a 1 million square foot warehouse/distribution center in Ontario, California. The company's products were sold in the U.S. to about 4,000 distributors that included department, sporting goods, athletic footwear, and shoe stores, and wholesale distributors.

55   In recent years, L.A. Gear relied on extensive distribution through wholesale distributors who sold into deep-discount outlets. This policy tarnished the company's image and, as a result, several key retail accounts ceased or reduced their business with the company in 1991. To improve relations with full-margin retailers, the company began to distribute its products through specific channels, using what it called the "Gear Strategy Classification System." In line with this system, distribution channels were grouped in terms of "Image," "Mainstream," "Volume," and "Value." The Image channels were used to market the most technologically advanced and expensive high-performance products such as the L.A. Tech. The Mainstream and Volume channels were used to market "2nd Gear" and "1st Gear" products which incorporated fewer technological and aesthetic features. The Value channels were intended only for the distribution of inventory that could not be sold through the other channels. As part of the Value channels, the company planned to open a limited number of outlet stores.

56   Under Greenberg, the company maintained a next-day (at once) open stock system, where retailers could order products and have them shipped within 24 hours. This system forced inventory expenses to skyrocket. To mitigate this problem, the company also adopted a "futures" ordering system which provided discounts to retailers who ordered products four to six months in advance of shipment. It was hoped that the new program would enable the company to improve inventory management.

57   Internationally, L.A. Gear distributed its product in about 60 countries, primarily through agreements with independent distributors. The distribution agreements were intended to maintain a consistent product offering and brand image throughout the world. However, this arrangement afforded the company little or no control over the ultimate retail price of its footwear. It also restricted both profit and growth potential.

RESEARCH AND DEVELOPMENT

58   L.A. Gear maintained close ties with firms that conducted basic materials research. For example, L.A. Gear had an alliance with U.T.I. Chemicals Corporation of California. U.T.I. developed a new outsole material known as Z-thane, which was a patented plastic compound that outlasted similar materials already in the marketplace.[22] L.A. Gear also applied older materials to their shoe lines, such as the innovative use of carbon fiber heel protectors in its performance shoes. With the Catapult, L.A. Gear hoped to challenge the high performance image of Nike and Reebok by luring the performance-oriented buyer away from these market leaders.

59   L.A. Gear, however, lagged behind its competitors in product innovation. For example, the company introduced a "pump" style shoe almost two years after Nike and Reebok introduced their versions of this technology. Ironically, former CEO Robert Greenberg once boasted that the company spent a fraction of what its competition spent on research and development.[23] The company's "catch-up" R&D practices damaged its relations with retailers. For example, one shoe buyer to a large department-store chain said: "We saw Nike and Reebok 1993 spring lines in May or June of 1992 and started committing for product in July. We didn't see L.A. Gear's product until mid-August."[24]

HUMAN RESOURCES

60   L.A. Gear employs 753 full-time employees. In 1991, the company embarked on a restructuring program to reduce its workforce. By 1992, 613 employees ceased employment with the company, 152 of whom were associated with the company's discontinued apparel design and marketing operations. This represented a 45% reduction in staff and reduced the company's monthly payroll expense from $4.8 million in 1991 to $3.4 million in 1992. The company's employees were not covered by any collective bargaining agreement, but management considered the company's relations with its employees to be satisfactory. The company offered its employees 401(k) retirement savings programs and had an employee stock option plan (ESOP) in place. The ESOP program was instituted as an incentive program for employees and management.

COMMUNICATION AND CORPORATE CULTURE

61   As L.A. Gear grew bigger, it had to hire more employees to handle the new functions. In 1985, 50 people turned out the product; by 1992, that figure swelled to 1,200. As a result, the company, which was characterized by an informal communication system and corporate culture, splintered into departmental fiefdoms scattered in several buildings. The new structure eroded the informal relationships that existed among L.A. Gear's management and employees. In the early days, for instance, Greenberg and Saemann worked just across the hall from each other, and their basic form of communication was to yell back and forth. Greenberg, who had a passion for tropical fish and kept a large tank in his office, would often march across the hall to see Saemann with a dripping net in one hand and a new sneaker design in the other.

62   The new management brought with it buttoned-down seriousness. Coats and ties were now a regular sight at L.A. Gear. Gone were the days when Greenberg would slip each of his employees $100 bills in pink envelopes whenever the company turned a profit. Now, employees carried around black coffee mugs that read ATTACK BUSINESS COSTS.

LEGAL ISSUES

63   In 1990 and 1991, three class action lawsuits were brought against L.A. Gear by shareholders. The shareholders claimed that the company violated the U.S. securities laws by inflating sales by tens of millions of dollars in 1990 when it counted as revenues merchandise that was being stored in L.A. Gear's warehouses and docks. In settling these lawsuits, the company recorded a $23 million pre-tax charge against its 1992 earnings.

64   In October 1992, L.A. Gear reached an agreement with the U.S. Attorney for the District of Massachusetts regarding the resolution of all customs claims arising from the importation of footwear from Taiwan in 1986 and 1987. Accordingly, L.A. Gear entered a guilty plea with respect to two counts charging underpayment of duties on such shipments. A sentencing hearing was scheduled in 1993. In addition, the company paid $1.3 million in settlement of all potential civil claims arising from underpayment of duties on the 1986 and 1987 shipments from Taiwan.

65   In November 1992, L.A. Gear settled a patent infringement lawsuit brought against it by Reebok International Ltd, alleging that certain footwear products marketed by the company infringed on a patent issued to Reebok covering "inflatable bladder" shoe technology. L.A. Gear paid Reebok $1 million to settle the lawsuit. As part of the settlement, L.A. Gear entered into a license agreement under which Reebok granted the company a four-year non-exclusive worldwide license to manufacture, use, and sell footwear utilizing the "inflatable bladder." The license agreement, however, did not grant L.A. Gear access to Reebok's technology.

66   Another legal issue involved L.A. Gear's relationship with entertainer Michael Jackson. In September 1992, the company filed a complaint against Jackson alleging, among other things, fraud, breach of contract, and breach of good faith. The company's claims arose from contracts between the company and the defendant which granted the company the exclusive right to use Jackson's name and likeness in advertising and promoting the company's shoes and apparel as well as the right to develop and market a Michael Jackson athletic shoe line. Michael Jackson countered with a lawsuit, alleging fraud and breach of good faith on the part of the company. No settlement of this dispute has been reached yet.

FINANCE AND ACCOUNTING

67   L.A. Gear's gross profit declined from $286 million in 1990, to $170 million in 1991, and to $109 million in 1992. While the company earned a net income of $31 million in 1990, it lost $66 million and $72 million in 1991 and 1992, respectively.

68   Because of an imbalance between inventory purchases and sales, L.A. Gear accumulated inventory greater than that necessary for its business. The introduction of the company's new product lines also resulted in a greater number of styles being discontinued than would otherwise been the case. As a result, as part of an inventory reduction program, the company sold inventory at significant discounts resulting in lower margins. As was the custom in the footwear industry, substantial changes to the current product lines were made at least twice a year (i.e., for the spring and back-to-school seasons). As a result, a certain number of styles were usually discontinued.

69   In September 1991, Trefoil Capital Investors, L.P., invested $100 million in L.A. Gear in the form of a new issue of Series A Cumulative Convertible Preferred Stock, the net proceeds of which were used to repay indebtedness. In November 1992, the company had cash and cash equivalent balances of $84 million. In addition, the company expected to receive income tax refunds in 1993 of about $25 million.

INDUSTRY

70   The U.S. general footwear market was valued at about $12 billion. The athletic shoe market comprised about $6 billion. According to *Footwear News*, the domestic retail shoe market was expected to continue to grow at a rate of 5.5% at least until the year 2000.[25]

71   A 1987 Census of Manufacturers conducted by the U.S. Bureau of the Census revealed that over 100 companies participated in the men's and women's footwear industries.[26] During 1992 there were two dozen companies competing in the U.S. branded footwear market.[27] Domestically, the two largest athletic shoe makers were Nike and Reebok with a combined share of the market totaling 50%.[28] Although Nike and Reebok, as well as L.A. Gear, were headquartered in the U.S., the majority of their products was manufactured in Asian, European, and South American countries. A shoe that retailed for $100 cost the company between $20 and $25 if manufactured in foreign countries. Markups to the retailer and consumer were nearly 100%.

72   The footwear industry was not cyclical but did show some seasonality with back-to-school sales in August and September. Although profitability and sales for footwear companies fluctuated, these fluctuations were attributable not to economic cycles but to changes in advertising expenditures, price, product quality, and overall market trends such as consumer preferences for fashion versus performance shoes.

73   Entry into the footwear industry was rather difficult. This was due to the fact that success in this industry depended to a great extent on heavy advertising, brand awareness, and intensive research and development. In the high-performance athletic shoe market, advertising was critical to footwear producers as a means of promoting new styles and creating brand awareness. Footwear companies spent vast sums to get popular athletes to endorse certain shoes. Nike and Reebok, for example, spent $200 million on advertising and promotion in 1992. This medium was cost prohibitive to smaller firms whose revenues were often too small to mount an effective marketing campaigns. Another barrier to entry was brand awareness. Consumers purchased shoes based on either how well they perceived a brand to perform or on its fashion characteristics. On the average, when selecting a shoe, men tended to look at sole cushioning and how well an inner structure supported the foot—not fashion or style. Women's purchases, however, were determined more by the design or style of the shoe.[29]

74   An even greater entry barrier in the footwear industry was the excessive capital required for research and development. Nike, Reebok, and L.A. Gear allocated large budgets toward R&D. Each of the top three competitors had a highly advanced technology. Nike had its Air Jordan; Reebok had the Pump and Insta Pump; and L.A. Gear had its Catapult and Regulator shoes that incorporated high-tech carbon fiber soles.

75   In the highly competitive discount-athletic footwear market, barriers to entry were less formidable. Volume companies (mass producers) tended to carve out a niche through brands they licensed or created on their own. According to *Footwear News*, "The mass market usually followed where the better-grade merchandise had already beaten a path. Volume sources capitalized on the consumer appetite for branded-athletic footwear generated by the sophisticated marketing of companies such as Nike, Reebok, and L.A. Gear." According to the Sporting Good Manufacturers Association, discount stores commanded $3.4 billion of the athletic shoe market.[30]

76   The U.S. footwear industry was maturing and analysts expected that consumers would purchase more non-athletic footwear than athletic footwear. With the domestic market maturing, many footwear companies began expanding overseas where the market was expected to grow at a rate of 23% a year in the next decade.[31]

77   The appeal of overseas markets to U.S. footwear companies stemmed not only from their sheer size but also from the cheap advertising common in such markets. Furthermore, a growing number of consumers overseas were becoming increasingly interested in U.S. sports generally and in basketball in particular. Actually, U.S. basketball was now a close second to soccer in worldwide popularity.[32] As a result, footwear companies discovered that their big endorsers, like Michael Jordan for Nike, translated well across borders.

COMPETITORS

78   The athletic and athletic-style footwear industry was highly competitive in the U.S. and on a worldwide basis. L.A. Gear's competitors included both specialized athletic shoe companies and companies with diversified footwear product lines. The company's primary competitors in the domestic athletic and athletic-style markets were Nike and Reebok. These companies were more established

than L.A. Gear and had greater financial, distribution, and marketing resources, as well as greater brand awareness, than the company. Internationally, L.A. Gear's major competitor was Adidas. Below is a brief profile of each of L.A. Gear's major competitors.

Nike

79   Nike was a publicly held sports and fitness company with a 26% share of the domestic market. Nike was the first company in the sports and fitness industry to exceed $2 billion in U.S. revenues and $3 billion worldwide. The company accomplished this in 1991. The diversity of Nike's product lines was far reaching. The company designed and marketed athletic footwear, apparel, and related items for competitive and recreational uses. To promote this breadth of product line, Nike was successful with advertisements that used high-profile athletes. Nike had an impressive stable of endorsers with Michael Jordan, Bo Jackson, David Robinson, and Andre Agassi. The success of these advertising campaigns enabled Nike to command a higher price for its shoes than its competitors.

80   To add to their image as one of the premier athletic footwear companies, Nike began to open a series of high-tech futuristic looking, company-owned outlets around the world called Nike Town. These outlets were a tribute to Nike's innovative flair and marketing genius.[33] The design concept incorporated sports, fitness, entertainment, history, and product innovation.

81   Nike spent more than its competitors on research and development. Nike learned the hard way to push its technology. In 1987, Nike was surpassed by rival Reebok as the number one domestic footwear company. At this time, Nike was concentrating on marketing its apparel and fashion shoes instead of promoting its air-cushioning system. Within 18 months of being surpassed by Reebok, Nike regained the number one spot by marketing its Nike Air Jordan shoes. Now, Nike's engineers began to call the shots—not its fashion designers.

Reebok

82   Reebok International, Ltd., was a designer and marketer of active lifestyle and performance products, including footwear and apparel. Reebok held 24% of the domestic footwear market. According to industry sources, Reebok was the company best positioned to take advantage of the developing worldwide sneaker market.[34] Reebok announced in early 1992 that it had established a new worldwide sports marketing unit and that it would spend 25% more on advertising. Additionally, international sales soared 75% to $832.6 million from $475.2 in 1990. The sports marketing unit worked in conjunction with the fitness and casual units to deliver the best products and programs to consumers and retailers worldwide.

83   In 1988, Reebok acquired Avia and Rockport—two fast-growing companies. Paul Fireman, chairman and chief executive officer, believed that Avia and Rockport exemplified a "sense of aliveness" which was a characteristic of Reebok.[35] In 1991, Avia's sales rose 4.3% to $161 million, and Rockport's sales grew 8.5% to $251.3 million. Rockport produced products primarily for the walking shoe market while Avia competed directly with the Reebok brand for the athletic footwear market.

84   Reebok replaced its ineffective advertising with a cause-related campaign aimed at supporting philanthropic organizations while promoting its own products. In 1990, industry sources noted that Reebok was lacking a winning advertising campaign. In that year, two consecutive advertising campaigns flopped. In 1991 and 1992, Reebok reversed this trend with its cause-related advertising. Practitioners maintained that cause-related advertising could be risky, but when handled carefully, could supply the best of all promotional worlds: higher visibility, a unique image niche resulting from association with worthy projects, and stronger ties to the community.[36] As part of its cause-related marketing, Reebok gave financial support to Amnesty International's Human Rights Now tour. Angel Martinez, vice president of business development at Reebok's Los Angeles office, said that, "the tour was an extension of our value system as a company. We believe in freedom of expression and wanted to do something of importance, beyond selling sneakers".[37] Reebok's president, Joseph LaBonte, added: "We both believe very strongly in the freedom to do what you want."

85   To remain competitive with Nike, Reebok also planned to contract endorsements with high-profile athletes. Even though the Insta-Pump would not be available to consumers until January 1993,

Reebok hoped to get a lot of promotional mileage by putting the shoes on several Olympic track-and-field stars at the 1992 summer games in Barcelona, Spain.

Adidas and Puma

86   A decade ago, most athletic shoes sold in Europe were made by Adidas or its smaller rival, Puma. For years, the two German companies controlled about 75% of Europe's athletic shoe and apparel market, and they were also strong in the U.S. Things changed, however. Now, Nike and Reebok, and to a lesser degree L.A. Gear, made spectacular inroads in Europe. Although Adidas continued to be No. 1 with $1.6 billion in revenues, Nike ranked second with $500 million and Reebok ranked third with $380 million. L.A. Gear's sales were less than $119 million.

87   Both Nike and Reebok profited from long-term problems at Adidas and Puma. In the past five years, both German companies reported steady streams of losses because of unfocused marketing, high costs, and a glut of products. At Adidas, the confusion was acute: In footwear alone, it had 1,200 different variations and styles. "We had everything," said Michel Perrauding, Adidas' manager for logistics, "even shoes for left-handed bowlers."

88   Adidas' poorly coordinated marketing in Europe angered many distributors who started to defect to Nike and Reebok. And in the U.S. where Adidas was once No. 1 in athletic shoes, chronic delivery problems and a failure to spot the trend to more comfortable shoes led to huge losses and a dramatic drop in market share.

89   Nike and Reebok, however, might have to confront the possibility that Adidas and Puma might fight back. A Swedish company took full control of Puma and planned to pump cash into it. At Adidas, a new French owner slashed its product range in shoes and apparel to several hundred from several thousand, retired hundreds of employees, and started a network of more efficient purchasing and production facilities in Asia. Adidas launched a new line, Equipment, featuring no-frills shoes for such sports as soccer, tennis, and track. There was also a new Adidas series of hiking and outdoors shoes. Nevertheless, Adidas and Puma lacked the deep pockets of Nike and Reebok to enable them to spend as much on advertising as the two U.S. companies.

CUSTOMERS

90   L.A. Gear sold to retail stores, specialty shoe stores, and sporting goods stores but their ultimate customer was the individual retail consumer. L.A. Gear's customers historically were young, fashion-minded girls. Under Greenberg, the company promoted the young Southern-California life-style. Its advertisements were of young blondes on the beach in stylish L.A. Gear shoes. Under the new management, the company repositioned itself. Former CEO Robert Greenberg said that they knew that in order to grow they would eventually have to enter the men's market and that meant more technically-oriented footwear.[38] Fashion athletics was now only a part of L.A. Gear.

GOVERNMENT REGULATIONS

91   In 1990, the U.S. Congress passed the Textile, Apparel, and Footwear Trade Act (the "Textile Act") which would have set highly restrictive global quotas on imported textile, apparel, and footwear products. This legislation was vetoed by President Bush, and the veto was sustained by the House of Representatives.

92   There is a possibility that similar legislation will be proposed in the future. If such legislation is enacted into law, L.A. Gear could face restrictions on its ability to import into the U.S. its footwear products manufactured abroad.

93   In 1992, the U.S. placed L.A. Gear's suppliers in Taiwan, China, Indonesia, and South Korea on a "priority watch list" for engaging in unfair trade practices. If such countries wee proved to be engaged in unfair trade practices, the U.S. might retaliate against them, which could result in increases in the cost, or reductions in the supply, of footwear generally and L.A. Gear's footwear in particular.

DEMOGRAPHICS

94   The U.S. population, which totaled 250 million in 1990, was expected to reach 283 million by the year 2010. That was an increase of about 13%. Perhaps more significant to the footwear industry was the rise in the size of the baby boom generation, born between 1946 and 1964. A prime target of footwear companies, this segment, which comprised 18% of the population in 1990, was expected to grow by about 9% by the year 2010.

CULTURE

95   Lifestyle changes in the U.S., as well as in many other countries, were propitious for footwear producers. An increasing segment of the population was becoming more health conscious, engaging in athletic activities such as jogging and walking. Because of the increasing popularity of walking, the walking-shoes market was expected to be the largest growth segment of the footwear industry. According to industry sources, 75% of the walking-shoes market consisted of women in their mid-30s and up.[39]

ECONOMY

96   In 1991 and 1992, the Federal Reserve Board laid the groundwork for an economic recovery by keeping prime interest rates low and gradually expanding the money supply. The Fed was able, at the same time, to keep inflation at less than 4%. Depressed consumer confidence in economic recovery, however, continued to be a major obstacle to increased consumer and business spending. The slow start of President Clinton's economic program served only to slow a long-awaited growth in the nation's economy.

TECHNOLOGY

97   Counterfeiting is the perennial enemy of brand-name producers in Asia. Recognizing the danger to his company's technology, Goldston, L.A. Gear's president said, "The focus of our agreements with new manufacturers is on integrity. Our technology innovation will be protected."[40] However, an L.A. Gear executive said the means available to foreign shoe manufacturers for protecting patents were limited. As a result, athletic-shoe makers could find their most nagging competitors were not each other but the companies who filled their orders. Companies such as L.A. Gear "tend to stumble when faced with competition, and this time it will come from say . . . a factory in Indonesia that has acquired the technology to make a good jogging shoe."[41]

POLITICS

98   With political changes occurring in Eastern Europe and the Soviet Union, markets that were previously closed to Western companies are now fairly wide open.

99   The enactment of NAFTA (North American Free Trade Agreement) among the U.S., Canada, and Mexico, was likely to strengthen U.S. exports. According to estimates made by the U.S. Trade Representative, the tariff reductions alone, if undertaken by all countries, could raise U.S. real GNP by 3% by the year 2000.[42]

CONCLUSION

100   As they implement their turnaround strategy, Gold and Goldston have their work cut out for them. What should they do next? And will their strategic moves be sufficient to restore L.A. Gear's to its heyday or will they cause the company to disappear?

ENDNOTES

1. "L.A. Gear," *Los Angeles Magazine*, December 1991, p. 116.
2. "L.A. Gear Calls in a Cobbler," *Business Week*, September 16, 1991, p. 78.
3. "L.A. Gear +184.6%," *Institutional Investor*, March 1990, pp. 52, 53.
4. "L.A. Gear Co-Founder Saemann Quits in Wake of Firm's Deal with Trefoil," *The Wall Street Journal*, June 13, 1991, p. B1.
5. "The Best and Worst Stocks of 1989," *Fortune*, January 29, 1990, p. 114.
6. "L.A. Gear Inc.," *The Wall Street Journal*, April 4, 1991, p. B1.
7. "L.A. Gear Co-Founder Saemann Quits in Wake of Firm's Deal with Trefoil," *The Wall Street Journal*, June 13, 1991, p. B1.
8. "Stanley P. Gold L.A. Gear Chairman & Chief Executive Officer," L.A. Gear Press Release, January 24, 1992.
9. Ibid.
10. "L.A. Gear Inc. Investor Steps in With New Team," *The Wall Street Journal*, January 27, 1992, pp. B1, B5.
11. Ibid.
12. Ibid.
13. Ibid.
14. "L.A. Gear, Several Changes at Senior Level," *The Wall Street Journal*, September 17, 1991, p. A22.
15. L.A. Gear, Form 10-K, 1991, p. 2.
16. Ibid.
17. Ibid.
18. L.A. Gear, Inc., 1990 Annual Report, p. 7.
19. B. Horivitz, "Some Companies Find They Get More," *Los Angeles Times*, February 5, 1991, p. D6.
20. "L.A. Gear Says High Inventories May Affect 1992 Earnings," *Bloomberg News*, March 3, 1992.
21. Ibid., p. B5.
22. L.A. Gear, Inc., 1990 Annual Report, p. 8.
23. "The Goldston Prescription," *Footwear News*, January 27, 1992, pp. 11–12.
24. "L.A. Gear Still Looks Like an Also-Ran," *Business Week*, December 21, 1992, p. 37.
25. "Footwear (Men's, Women's, Boys' and Girls')," *Fairchild Fact File*, 1990, pp. 5–9.
26. Ibid.
27. F. Meeds, "The Sneaker Game," *Forbes*, October 22, 1990, p. 114.
28. J. Schlax, "The Shoe as Hero," *Forbes*, August 20, 1990, p. 77.
29. Kerwin, "L.A. Gear is Going where the Boys are," *Business Week*, June 19, 1989, p. 54.
30. Ibid., p. 52.
31. M. Grimm, "To Munich and Back With Nike and L.A. Gear," *Adweek's Marketing Week*, February 18, 1991, p. 21.
32. Ibid, p. 22.
33. M. Wilson, "Nike Town Goes Back to the Future," *Chain Store Age Executive*, February, 1991, pp. 82–83.
34. M. Tedeschi, "Reebok Splits U.S. Int'l Setups," *Footwear News*, November 26, 1990, p. 12.

35. S. Gannes, "America's Fastest-Growing Companies," *Fortune*, May 23, 1988, p. 37.

36. A. Shell, "Cause-Related Marketing: Big Risks, Big Potential," *Public Relations Journal*, July, 1989, pp. 8, 13.

37. Ibid., p. 8.

38. M. Rottman, "L.A. Gear Catapults Into Technology," *Footwear News*, February 18, 1991, pp. 12, 14.

39. D. McKay, "Walk This Way," *Footwear News*, September 9, 1991, pp. 14–15.

40. "L.A. Gear President Says Shoe Maker Will Recover and Will Focus on Asia," *The Wall Street Journal*, October 16, 1992, p. B7.

41. Ibid.

42. *OECD Economic Survey* (Washington, DC: United States Government Printing Office, 1990/1991), pp. 60–65.

APPENDIX A

Consolidated Balance Sheet
As of November 30, 1991, and 1992
(in thousands)

	1992	1991
Assets		
Current assets:		
Cash and cash equivalents	$ 55,027	$ 1,422
Collateralized cash	28,955	—
Accounts receivable, net	56,369	111,470
Inventories	61,923	141,115
Prepaid expenses and other current assets	2,557	8,506
Refundable income taxes	25,269	22,795
Deferred income taxes	—	11,763
Total current assets	230,100	297,071
Property and equipment, net	17,667	26,869
Other assets	1,735	1,631
Total assets	**$249,502**	**$325,571**

Liabilities, Mandatorily Redeemable Preferred Stock,
and Shareholders' Equity

	1992	1991
Current liabilities:		
Borrowing under line of credit	$ —	$ 20,000
Accounts payable and accrued liabilities	49,753	55,856
Dividends payable on mandatorily redeemable preferred stock	7,746	—
Costs related to discontinued operations	4,552	18,000
Total current liabilities	**62,051**	**93,856**
Mandatorily redeemable preferred stock: 7.5% Series A cumulative convertible preferred stock, $100 stated value; 1,000,000 shares authorized, issued, and outstanding; redemption value of $100 per share	100,000	100,000
Shareholders' equity:		
Common stock, no par value; 80,000,000 shares authorized; 22,898,182 shares issued and outstanding at November 30, 1992 (19,542,513 shares issued and outstanding at November 30, 1991)	127,714	92,331
Preferred stock, no stated value; 9,000,000 shares authorized; no shares issued	—	—
Retained earnings (accumulated deficit)	(40,263)	39,384
Total shareholders' equity	87,451	131,715
Commitments and contingencies	—	—
	$249,502	**$325,571**

Source: L.A. Gear, *1992 Annual Report*, p. 17.

APPENDIX B

Consolidated Statements of Cash Flows
As of November 30, 1992, 1991, and 1990
(in thousands)

	1992	1991	1990
Operating activities:			
Net income (loss)	$(71,901)	$(66,200)	$ 31,338
Adjustment to reconcile net income (loss) to net cash provided by (used in) operating activities:	17,075	—	—
Shareholders' litigation settlements:			
Depreciation and amortization	7,107	7,182	3,394
Provision for loss on discontinued operations	—	18,000	—
Loss on sale or abandonment of property and equipment	1,871	4,146	—
Issuance of shares to employee stock savings plan	233	382	—
(Increase) decrease in:			
Accounts receivable, net	55,101	44,431	(52,969)
Inventories	79,192	19,553	(21,152)
Prepaids and other assets	6,343	1,565	(998)
Refundable and deferred income taxes	8,791	(26,174)	(3,795)
Increase (decrease) in:			
Accounts payable and accrued liabilities	(6,103)	(8,222)	3,143
Costs related to discontinued operations	(8,343)	—	—
Net cash provided by (used in) operating activities	89,366	(5,337)	(41,039)
Investing activities—capital expenditures	(4,881)	(14,188)	(18,939)
Financing activities:			
Net proceeds from issuance of mandatorily redeemable preferred stock	—	92,511	—
Payment of dividends on mandatorily redeemable preferred stock	—	(1,265)	—
Exercise of stock options and warrants	1,986	414	908
Tax benefits arising from the disposition/exercise of incentive stock options	2,089	356	5,408
Proceeds from issuance of common stock	14,000	—	—
Net borrowing (repayment) under line of credit agreement	(20,000)	(74,000)	56,600
Net cash provided by (used in) financing activities	(1,925)	17,656	62,916
Net increase (decrease) in cash and cash equivalents	82,560	(1,869)	2,938
Cash at beginning of year	1,422	3,291	353
Cash and cash equivalents at end of year, including collateralized cash	$ 83,982	$ 1,422	$ 3,291

Source: L.A. Gear, *1992 Annual Report*, p. 20.

CASE 21

KENTUCKY FRIED CHICKEN AND THE GLOBAL FAST-FOOD INDUSTRY

1   During the 1960s and 1970s, Kentucky Fried Chicken Corporation (KFC) pursued an aggressive strategy of restaurant expansion, quickly establishing itself as one of the largest fast-food restaurant chains in the United States (see Exhibit 1). KFC was also one of the first U.S. fast-food restaurant chains to expand overseas. By 1990, restaurants located outside the United States were generating over 50 percent of KFC's total profits. By the end of 1994, KFC was operating in 68 foreign countries and was one of the three largest fast-food restaurant chains operating outside the United States.

2   Japan, Australia, and the United Kingdom accounted for the greatest share of KFC's international expansion during the 1970s and 1980s. However, as KFC entered the 1990s, a number of other international markets offered significant opportunities for growth. China, with a population of over one billion, and Europe, with a population roughly equal to the United States, offered such opportunities. Latin America also offered a unique opportunity because of the size of its markets, its common language and culture, and its geographical proximity to the United States.

3   By 1995, KFC was operating successful subsidiaries in Mexico and Puerto Rico. A third subsidiary was established in Venezuela in 1993. The majority of KFC's restaurants in Mexico and Puerto Rico were company-owned. However, KFC had established 239 new franchises in Mexico by the end of 1995, following enactment of Mexico's new franchise law in 1990. KFC anticipated that much of its future growth in Mexico would be through franchises rather than company-owned restaurants. KFC was only one of many U S. fast-food, retail, and hotel chains to begin franchising in Mexico following the new franchise law. In addition to Mexico, KFC was operating franchises in 20 other countries throughout the Caribbean, and Central and South America by 1995.

COMPANY HISTORY

4   Fast-food franchising was still in its infancy in 1954 when Harland Sanders began his travels across the United States to speak with prospective franchisees about his "Colonel Sanders Recipe Kentucky Fried Chicken." By 1960, "Colonel" Sanders had granted KFC franchises to over 200 take-home retail outlets and restaurants across the United States. He had also succeeded in establishing a number of franchises in Canada. By 1963, the number of KFC franchises had risen to over 300 and revenues had reached $500,000.

5   By 1964, at the age of 74, the Colonel had tired of running the day-to-day operations of his business and was eager to concentrate on public relations issues. Therefore, he sought out potential buyers, eventually deciding to sell the business to two Louisville businessmen—Jack Massey and John Young Brown Jr.—for $2 million. Massey was named chairman of the board and Brown, who would later become Governor of Kentucky, was named president. The Colonel stayed on as a public relations man and goodwill ambassador for the company.

6   During the next five years, Massey and Brown concentrated on growing KFC's franchise system across the United States. In 1966, they took KFC public and the company was listed on the New York Stock Exchange. By the late 1960s, a strong foothold had been established in the United States, and Massey and Brown turned their attention to international markets. In 1969, a joint venture was signed with Mitsuoishi Shoji Kaisha, Ltd., in Japan, and the rights to operate 14 existing KFC franchises in England were acquired. Subsidiaries were also established in Hong Kong, South Africa, Australia,

This case was prepared by Jeffrey A. Krug of the University of Memphis.

EXHIBIT 1
Leading U.S. Fast-Food Chains

Chain	Parent	U.S. Sales ($M) 1995*	1994	Percent CHG	1995 Units*
McDonald's	McDonald's Corporation	15,800	14,951	5.7%	10,175
Burger King	Grand Metropolitan PLC	7,830	7,250	8.1	6,400
Pizza Hut	PepsiCo, Inc.	5,400	5,000	8.0	8,725
Taco Bell	PepsiCo, Inc.	4,853	4,200	15.5	6,565
Wendy's	Wendy's International, Inc.	4,152	3,821	8.6	4,263
KFC	PepsiCo, Inc.	3,720	3,500	6.3	5,200
Hardee's	Imasco Ltd.	3,520	3,511	0.3	3,405
Subway	Doctor's Associates, Inc.	2,905	2,518	15.4	10,351
Little Caesars	Little Caesar Enterprises	2,050	2,000	2.5	4,720
Domino's Pizza	Domino's Pizza, Inc.	1,973	1,911	3.3	4,245
Red Lobster	Darden Restaurants, Inc.	1,850	1,798	2.9	700
Denny's	Flagstar Cos., Inc.	1,810	1,672	8.3	1,578
Arby's	TriArc Corp.	1,730	1,770	−2.3	2,678
Dunkin' Donuts	Allied Domecq PLC	1,426	1,332	7.0	3,074
Shoney's	Shoney's, Inc.	1,277	1,317	−3.0	907
Olive Garden	Darden Restaurants, Inc.	1,250	1,146	9.1	479
Dairy Queen	International Dairy Queen	1,185	1,160	2.2	4,935
Jack in the Box	Foodmaker, Inc.	1,082	1,036	4.4	1,240
Applebee's	Applebee's International	1,012	881	15.0	551
Big Boy	Elias Bros. Restaurants	1,010	1,050	−3.8	858
Long John Silver's	Long John Silver's Rest.	986	931	5.9	1,564
Cracker Barrel	Cracker Barrel	970	787	23.3	257
Chili's	Brinker International, Inc.	950	885	7.35	446
Sonic Drive-In	Sonic Corp.	880	756	16.45	1,500
T.G.I. Friday's	Carlson Hospitality Worldwide	870	774	12.4	310
Outback Steakhouse	Outback Steakhouse, Inc.	822	549	49.8	279
Ponderosa	Metromedia Co.	741	751	−1.3	680
IHOP Restaurants	IHOP Corp.	729	631	15.5	684
Boston Market	Boston Chicken, Inc.	725	384	88.9	825
Popeye's	America's Favorite Chicken	689	610	13.0	932
Total		74,196	68,872	7.7%	88,526

*1995 sales estimated.
Source: *Nation's Restaurant News.*

New Zealand, and Mexico. By 1971, KFC had 2,450 franchises and 600 company-owned restaurants worldwide, and was operating in 48 countries.

Heublein, Inc.

7   In 1971, KFC entered negotiations with Heublein, Inc., to discuss a possible merger. The decision to seek a merger candidate was partially driven by Brown's desire to pursue other interests, including a political career (Brown was elected Governor of Kentucky in 1977). On April 10, Heublein

announced that an agreement had been reached. Shareholders approved the merger on May 27, and KFC was merged into a subsidiary of Heublein.

8 Heublein was in the business of producing vodka, mixed cocktails, dry gin, cordials, beer, and other alcoholic beverages. It was also the exclusive distributor of a variety of imported alcoholic beverages. Heublein had little experience in the restaurant business. Conflicts quickly erupted between Colonel Sanders, who continued to act in a public relations capacity, and Heublein management. In particular, Colonel Sanders became increasingly distraught over quality control issues and restaurant cleanliness. By 1977, new restaurant openings had slowed to about 20 per year (in 1993, KFC opened a new restaurant on average every two days). Restaurants were not being remodeled and service quality was declining.

9 In 1977, Heublein sent in a new management team to redirect KFC's strategy. Richard P. Mayer, who later became chairman and chief executive officer, was part of this team (Mayer remained with KFC until 1989, when he left to become president of General Foods USA). A "back-to-the-basics" strategy was immediately implemented. New unit construction was discontinued until existing restaurants could be upgraded and operating problems eliminated. Restaurants were refurbished, an emphasis was placed on cleanliness and service, marginal products were eliminated, and product consistency was reestablished. By 1982, KFC had succeeded in establishing a successful strategic focus and was again aggressively building new units.

R.J. Reynolds Industries, Inc.

10 On October 12, 1982, R.J. Reynolds Industries, Inc. (RJR), announced that it would merge Heublein into a wholly-owned subsidiary. The merger with Heublein represented part of RJR's overall corporate strategy of diversifying into unrelated businesses. RJR's objective was to reduce its dependence on the tobacco industry, which had driven RJR sales since its founding in North Carolina in 1875. Sales of cigarettes and tobacco products, while profitable, were declining because of reduced consumption in the United States, due mainly to the increased awareness among Americans regarding the negative health consequences of smoking.

11 RJR's diversification strategy included the acquisition of a variety of companies in the energy, transportation, and food and restaurant industries. RJR had no more experience in the restaurant business than did Heublein when Heublein purchased KFC in 1971. However, RJR decided to take a hands-off approach to managing KFC. Whereas Heublein had installed its own top management at KFC headquarters, RJR left KFC management largely intact, believing that existing KFC managers were better qualified to operate KFC's businesses than were its own managers. By doing so, RJR avoided many of the operating problems that Heublein had experienced during its management of KFC. This strategy paid off for RJR, as KFC continued to expand aggressively and profitably under RJR's ownership.

12 In 1985, RJR acquired Nabisco Corporation for $4.9 billion. Nabisco sold a variety of well-known cookies, crackers, cereals, confectioneries, snacks and other grocery products. In October 1986, Kentucky Fried Chicken was sold to PepsiCo, Inc.

PEPSICO, INC.

Corporate Strategy

13 PepsiCo, Inc. (PepsiCo), was first incorporated in Delaware in 1919 as Loft, Inc. In 1938, Loft acquired the Pepsi-Cola Co., a manufacturer of soft drinks and soft-drink concentrates. Pepsi-Cola's traditional business was the sale of its soft-drink concentrates to licensed independent and company-owned bottlers, which manufactured, sold, and distributed Pepsi-Cola soft drinks. Today, Pepsi-Cola's best known trademarks are Pepsi-Cola, Diet Pepsi, Mountain Dew, and Slice. Shortly after its acquisition of Pepsi-Cola, Loft changed its name to Pepsi-Cola Co. On June 30, 1965, Pepsi-Cola Co. acquired Frito-Lay, Inc., for three million shares, thereby creating one of the largest consumer companies in the United States. At that time, the present name of PepsiCo, Inc., was adopted. Frito-Lay manufactures and sells a variety of snack foods. Its best known trademarks are Fritos brand Corn

EXHIBIT 2
PepsiCo, Inc., 1994 Operation Results ($ in millions)

	Beverages	Snack Foods	Restaurants	Total
Net sales	$9,687.5	$8,264.4	$10,520.5	$28,472.4
Operating profit	1,217.0	1,376.9	730.3	3,324.2
Percent net sales	12.6%	16.7%	6.9%	11.7%
Assets	$9,566.0	$5,043.9	$ 7,202.9	$24,792.0
Capital spending	677.1	532.1	1,072.0	2,288.4

Assets include corporate assets of $2,979.2 million. Capital spending includes corporate allocation of $7.2 million.
Source: PepsiCo, Inc. Annual Report, 1994.

Chips, Lay's and Ruffles brand potato chips, Doritos and Tostitos tortilla chips, and Chee-tos brand cheese flavored snacks. Eight of the top 10 snack chips in the U.S. market during 1995 were Frito-Lay brands. In 1994, 63 percent of PepsiCo's net sales were generated by its soft-drink and snack food businesses (see Exhibit 2).

14   Beginning in the late 1960s, PepsiCo began an aggressive acquisition program. Initially, PepsiCo pursued an acquisition strategy similar to that pursued by RJR during the 1980s, buying a number of companies in areas unrelated to its major businesses. For example, North American Van Lines was acquired in June 1968. Wilson Sporting Goods was merged into the company in 1972 and Lee Way Motor Freight was acquired in 1976. However, success in operating these businesses failed to live up to expectations, mainly because the management skills required to operate these businesses lay outside of PepsiCo's area of expertise.

15   In 1984, then-chairman and chief executive officer Don Kendall decided to restructure PepsiCo's operations. Most importantly, PepsiCo would divest those businesses that did not support PepsiCo's consumer product orientation. PepsiCo sold Lee Way Motor Freight in 1984. In 1985, Wilson Sporting Goods and North American Van Lines were sold. Additionally, PepsiCo's foreign bottling operations were sold to local businesspeople who better understood the cultural and business conditions operating in their respective countries. Lastly, Kendall reorganized PepsiCo along three lines: soft drinks, snack foods, and restaurants (see Exhibit 3). All future investment would be directed at strengthening PepsiCo's performance in these three related areas.

16   When Wayne Calloway became chairman of the board and chief executive officer of PepsiCo in 1986, he expanded PepsiCo's soft-drink segment to include nonsoft-drink beverages such as tea, sports drinks, juices, and bottled water. These included, among others, ready-to-drink Lipton Tea; All Sport, which has become the nation's second best–selling sports drink; and Aquafina Bottled Water. In addition, several new organizations were crated to maximize synergies across PepsiCo's related businesses. These included PepsiCo Foods and Beverages International, designed to coordinate efforts between PepsiCo's beverage and snack food segments, and PepsiCo Worldwide Restaurants, created to maximize synergies across PepsiCo's restaurant companies (see Exhibit 3).

Restaurant Business and Acquisition of Kentucky Fried Chicken

17   PepsiCo first entered the restaurant business in 1977 when it acquired Pizza Hut's 3,200-unit restaurant system. Taco Bell was merged into a division of PepsiCo in 1978. The restaurant business complemented PepsiCo's consumer product orientation. The marketing of fast food followed much of the same patterns as the marketing of soft drinks and snack foods. Therefore, PepsiCo's management skills could easily be transferred among its three business segments. This was compatible with PepsiCo's practice of frequently moving managers among its business units as a way of developing future top executives. PepsiCo's restaurant chains also provided an additional outlet for the sale of Pepsi soft-drink products. In addition, Pepsi soft drinks and fast-food products could be marketed together in the same television and radio segments, thereby providing higher returns for each advertising dollar.

EXHIBIT 3
PepsiCo, Inc., Principal Divisions

Executive Offices: Purchase, New York

Beverage Segment	Snack Food Segment	Restaurants
Pepsi-Cola North America Somers, New York	Frito-Lay, Inc. Plano, Texas	PepsiCo Worldwide Restaurants Dallas, Texas
PepsiCo Food and Beverages International Somers, New York		PepsiCo Restaurants International Dallas, Texas
		Kentucky Fried Chicken Corporation Louisville, Kentucky
		Pizza Hut, Inc. Dallas, Texas
		Taco Bell Corp. Irvine, California
		PepsiCo Food Systems Dallas, Texas

Source: PepsiCo, Inc., Annual Report, 1994.

18   To complete its diversification into the restaurant segment, PepsiCo acquired Kentucky Fried Chicken Corporation from RJR-Nabisco in 1986 for $841 million. The acquisition of KFC gave PepsiCo the leading market share in three of the four largest and fastest growing segments within the U.S. quick-service industry. At the end of 1994, Pizza Hut held a 28 percent share of the $18.5 billion U.S. pizza segment, Taco Bell held 75 percent of the $5.7 billion Mexican food segment, and KFC held 49 percent of the $7.7 billion U.S. chicken segment. (See Exhibits 2 and 4 for business segment financial data and restaurant count.)

19   PepsiCo's success during the late 1980s and early 1990s can be seen by its upward trend in *Fortune* magazine's annual survey of "America's Most Admired Corporations." By 1991, PepsiCo was labeled the fifth most admired corporation overall (of 306 corporations included in the survey). However, PepsiCo's ranking fell to 14th place in 1993, 26th place in 1994, and 72nd place in 1995. PepsiCo's fall in the rankings is partially the result of changes made in *Fortune's* survey methodology in 1994. In particular, it increased the number of industry groups from 32 to 42 (e.g., by adding computer services and entertainment) and divided some industry groups into their components (e.g., by dividing the transportation group into airlines, trucking, and railroads). Home Depot, Microsoft, and Walt Disney, which were added to the survey in 1994, were all ranked in the top 10 most admired corporations in American that year.

20   However, part of PepsiCo's decline in the *Fortune* rankings is the result of a decline in operating profits among its restaurant chains, which declined $48 million in 1994. Much of the decline was the result of increased administrative and support costs, international development costs, and higher store operating costs. In fact, a nearly two-year decline in earnings led PepsiCo to move the international operations of KFC, Pizza Hut, and Taco Bell to the newly formed PepsiCo Restaurants International (PRI) group in Dallas, Texas, in 1994.

PEPSICO RANKING

1995	72
1994	26
1993	14
1992	9
1991	5
1090	6
1989	7
1988	14
1987	24
1986	25

EXHIBIT 4
PepsiCo, Inc., Number of Units Worldwide

	KFC	Pizza Hut*	Taco Bell†	Total
1989	7,948	7,502	3,125	18,575
1990	8,187	8,220	3,349	19,756
1991	8,480	8,837	3,670	20,987
1992	8,729	9,454	4,153	22,336
1993	9,033	10,433	4,921	24,387
1994	9,407	11,546	5,846	26,799
Five-year compounded annual growth rate	3.4%	9.0%	13.3%	7.6%

†Taco Bell data include 178 Hot 'n Now and 53 Chevy's restaurants.
*Pizza Hut data include 25 East Side Mario's restaurants and 197 D'Angelo Sandwich Shops.
Source: PepsiCo, Inc., Annual Report, 1994.

FAST-FOOD INDUSTRY

U.S. Quick-Service Market

21   According to the National Restaurant Association (NRA), 1995 food-service sales will hit $289.7 billion for the approximately 500,000 restaurants and other food outlets making up the U.S. restaurant industry. The NRA estimates that sales in the fast-food segment of the food industry will grow 7.2 percent to approximately $93 billion in the united States in 1995, up from $87 million in 1994. This would mark the second consecutive year that fast-food sales exceeded sales in the full-service segment, which are expected to grow to $87.8 billion in 1995. The growth in fast-food sales reflects the long, gradual change in the restaurant industry from an industry once dominated by independently operated sit-down restaurants to an industry fast becoming dominated by fast-food restaurant chains. The U.S. restaurant industry as a whole is projected to grow by 4.7 percent in 1995.

22   Sales data for the top 30 fast-food restaurant chains are shown in Exhibit 1. Most striking is the dominance of McDonald's. Sales for 1995 are estimated at $15.8 billion, which would represent 17.3 percent of industry sales, or 21.3 percent of sales of the top 30 fast-food chains. McDonald's strong per restaurant sales are more striking given that McDonald's accounts for under 12 percent of the units of the top 30 fast-food chains. U.S. sales for the PepsiCo system, which includes KFC, Pizza Hut, and Taco Bell, are estimated to reach $14.0 billion in 1995, which would represent 15.0 percent of the fast-food industry and 18.8 percent of the top 30 fast-food chains. The PepsiCo system will grow to an estimated 20,490 restaurants in 1995. McDonald's holds the number one spot in the hamburger segment, while PepsiCo holds the leading market share in the chicken (KFC), Mexican (Taco Bell), and pizza (Pizza Hut) segments.

Major Business Segments

23   Six major business segments make up the fast-food market within the food service industry. Exhibit 5 shows sales for the top 64 fast-food chains in the six major segments for the years 1993 through 1995, as compiled by *Nation's Restaurant News*. Sandwich chains make up the largest segment, with estimated sales of $41 billion in 1995. Of the 18 restaurant chains making up the sandwich segment, McDonald's holds a 34 percent market share. Sandwich chains, faced by slowed sales growth, have turned to new menu offerings, lower pricing, improved customer service, and co-branding with other fast-food chains, and have established units in nontraditional locations to beef up sales.

24   Hardee's and McDonald's have successfully introduced fried chicken in many of their restaurants. Burger King has introduced fried clams and shrimp to its dinner menu in some locations, and Jack in

EXHIBIT 5
U.S. Sales of the Top Fast-Food chains by Business Segment ($ billions)

Business Segment	Number of Chains	1993	1994	1995*
Sandwich Chains	18	41.0	44.0	47.2
(McDonald's, Burger King, Taco Bell, Wendy's, Hardee's, Subway, Arby's, Dairy Queen, Jack in the Box, Sonic Drive-In, Carl's Jr., Roy Rogers, Whataburger, Checker's Drive-In, Rally's, Blimpie Subs & Salads, White Castle, Krystal)				
Pizza Chains	8	10.2	10.5	11.2
(Pizza Hut, Little Caesar's, Domino's, Papa John's, Sbarro The Italian Eatery, Round Table Pizza, Chuck E. Cheese's, Godfather's Pizza)				
Family Restaurants	11	7.6	8.0	8.6
(Denny's, Shoney's, Big Boy, Cracker Barrel, IHOP, Perkins, Friendly's, Bob Evans, Waffle House, Coco's, Marie Callender's)				
Dinner Houses	15	7.6	8.7	9.8
(Red Lobster, Olive Garden, Applebee's, Chili's, T.G.I. Friday's, Outback Steakhouse, Ruby Tuesday, Bennigan's, Chi-Chi's, Ground Round, Lone Star, Fuddruckers, Hooters, Red Robin Burger & Spirits, Stuart Anderson's Black Angus)				
Chicken Chains	6	5.0	5.6	6.4
(KFC, Boston Market, Popeyes, Chick-fil-A, Church's, Kenny Rogers Roasters)				
Steak Restaurants	6	3.0	3.0	3.2
(Ponderosa, Golden Corral, Sizzler, Ryan's, Western Sizzlin', Quincy's)				
Total fast-food chains	64	$74.4	$79.8	$86.4

*1995 sales figures estimated.
Source: *Nation's Restaurant News.*

the Box has introduced chicken and teriyaki with rice in several of its California units, in order to appeal to its Asian-American audience. In order to broaden its customer base, McDonald's has installed 400 restaurants in Wal-Mart stores across the country. In addition, it has cut its building costs for its conventional stand-alone units from $1.6 million to $1.1 million in order to counter reduced profit margins resulting from lower pricing. Co-branding is also a potential source of expansion for many fast-food chains. PepsiCo plans to add Taco Bell signs and menus to approximately 800 existing KFC restaurants over the next few years. This would increase Taco Bell's 4,500-unit U.S. system by almost 18 percent.

25   The second largest fast-food segment is pizza, long dominated by Pizza Hut. Pizza Hut expects sales to top $5.4 billion in 1995, which would represent a 53 percent market share among the eight competitors making up the pizza segment. Two years ago, Little Caesar's overtook Domino's as the second largest pizza chain, despite the fact that Domino's operated more outlets. Little Caesar's is the only pizza chain to remain predominately a take-out chain. Home delivery, which has been successfully introduced by Domino's and Pizza Hut, was a driving force for success among the market leaders during the 1970s and 1980s (Little Caesar's has also recently begun home delivery). However, the success of home delivery has driven competitors to look for new methods of increasing their customers' bases. Increased competition within the pizza segment and pressures to appeal to a wider customer base have led pizza chains to diversify into nonpizza menu items, to develop nontraditional units (e.g., airport kiosks), and to offer special promotions. Among the many new product offerings, Domino's has introduced chicken wings, Little Caesar's Italian cheese bread, and Pizza Hut stuffed crust pizza.

26   The highest growth segment in 1995 was the chicken segment. Sales are estimated to increase by 14.3 percent in 1995 over 1994. Dinner houses, which have outgrown the other five segments over the last few years are expected to increase sales by 12.6 percent in 1995. Both the chicken and dinner house segments are growing at almost twice the rate as the sandwich, pizza, and steak restaurant segments. Red Lobster remains the largest dinner house and is expected to surpass $1.8 billion in sales for its fiscal year ending May 1995. This would make Red Lobster the eleventh largest chain among the top 100. Olive Garden is expected to hit the $1.3 billion sales mark for 1995. Olive Garden is currently running a strong second place within the dinner house segment behind Red Lobster.

27   The dinner house segment should continue to outpace most of the other fast-food segments for a variety of reasons. Major chains still have low penetration in this segment, through Darden Restaurants, Inc. (Red Lobster and Olive Garden), and PepsiCo, Inc. (Fresh-Mex), are poised to dominate a large portion of this segment. A maturing population is already increasing demand for full-service, sit-down restaurants. Eight of the fifteen dinner houses in this segment posted growth rates in sales of over 12 percent in 1995. Lone Star Steakhouse & Saloon, Outback Steakhouse, Fuddruckers, Applebee's Neighborhood Grill & Bar, T.G.I. Friday's, Red Robin Burger & Spirits Emporium, Ruby Tuesday, and Hooters grew at rates of 65, 50, 32, 23, 19, 15, 15, and 12 percent in 1995, respectively.

28   KFC continues to dominate the chicken segment, with projected 1995 sales of $3.7 billion. Its nearest competitor, Boston Market (formerly Boston Chicken), is a distant second with projected sales of $725.0 million. Popeye's Famous Fried Chicken and Chick-fil-A follow with projected sales of $689.2 and $507.2 million, respectively. KFC holds a market share of 58 percent in the chicken segment, while Boston Market and Popeyes hold shares of 11.3 and 10.8 percent, respectively. Other competitors within the chicken market include Church's, Kenny Rogers Roasters, Bojangle's, El Pollo Loco, Grandy's, and Pudgie's.

29   Despite KFC's continued dominance within the chicken segment, it has lost market share over the last two years to both Boston Market and Kenny Rogers Roasters, new restaurant chains that have emphasized roasted chicken over the traditional friend chicken offered by other chicken chains. Boston Market has been particularly successful creating an image of an upscale deli offering healthy, "home-style" take-out products. Early in 1995, it changed its name from Boston Chicken to Boston Market. It thereafter quickly broadened its menu beyond rotisserie chicken to include ham, turkey, and meat loaf. KFC has quickly followed by introducing its $14.99 Mega-Meal, which is designed to compete with Boston Market as a home-replacement alternative. It is also aggressively pushing home delivery to support its home-replacement strategy. KFC has also introduced its "Colonel's Kitchen" in Dallas and is testing a full menu of home-meal replacement items.

Industry Consolidation

30   Although the restaurant industry has outpaced the overall economy in recent years, there are indications that the U.S. market is slowly becoming saturated. According to the U.S. Bureau of Labor, sales of U.S. eating and drinking establishments increased by 2.7 percent in 1992. Following a period of rapid expansion and intense restaurant building in the United States during the 1970s and 1980s, the fast-food industry has apparently begun to consolidate. In January 1990, Grand Metropolitan, a British company, purchased Pillsbury Co. for $5.7 billion. Included in the purchase was Pillsbury's Burger King chain. Grand Met has already begun to strengthen the franchise by upgrading existing restaurants and has eliminated several levels of management in order to cut costs. This should give Burger King a long-needed boost in improving its position against McDonald's, its largest competitor in the U.S. market. In 1988, Grand Met purchased Wienerwald, a West German chicken chain, and the Spaghetti Factory, a Swiss chain. In addition, General Mills spun off its Red Lobster, Olive Garden, and China Coast franchises in early 1995 in order to concentrate on its core businesses.

31   Perhaps most important to KFC was Hardee's acquisition of 600 Roy Rogers restaurants from Marriott Corporation in early 1990. Hardee's immediately began to convert these restaurants to Hardee's units and quickly introduced "Roy Rogers" fried chicken to its menu. By the end of 1993, Hardee's had introduced fried chicken into most of its 3,313 domestic restaurants. While Hardee's is

unlikely to destroy the customer loyalty that KFC has long enjoyed, it has cut into KFC's sales as its widened menu selection appeals to a variety of family eating preferences.

32   The effect of these and other recent mergers and acquisitions on the industry has been powerful. The top 10 restaurant chains now control over 55 percent of all fast-food sales in the United States. The consolidation of a number of these firms within larger, financially more powerful firms should give these restaurant chains the financial and managerial resources they need to outgrow their smaller competitors.

Demographic Trends

33   Intense marketing by the leading fast-food chains will likely continue to stimulate demand for fast food in the United States through the year 2000. However, a number of demographic and societal changes are likely to affect the future demand for fast food in different directions. One such change is the rise in single-person households, which has steadily increased from 17 percent of all U.S. households in 1970 to approximately 25 percent today. In addition, disposable household income should continue to increase, mainly because more women are working than ever before. According to Standard & Poor's *Industry Surveys,* Americans will spend 55 percent of their food dollars at restaurants in 1995, up from 34 percent in 1970. In addition to the effect of a greater number of dual-income families and less time for home food preparation, growth of fast-food sales has been stimulated by an increase in the overall number of fast-food chains, easier access to fast-food chains in nontraditional locations such as department stores and airports, and the greater availability of home delivery and take-out service.

34   In addition to these demographic trends, a number of societal changes may also affect future demand for fast food. For example, microwaves have now been introduced into approximately 70 percent of all U.S. homes. This has already resulted in a significant shift in the types of products sold in supermarkets and convenience restaurants, which have introduced a variety of products that can be quickly and easily prepared in microwaves. In addition, the aging of America's baby boomers may change the frequency with which people patronize more upscale restaurants. Therefore, these various demographic and societal trends are likely to affect the future demand for fast food in different ways.

International Quick-Service Market

35   Because of the aggressive pace of new restaurant construction in the United States during the 1970s and 1980s, future growth resulting from new restaurant construction in the United States may be limited. In any case, the cost of finding prime locations is rising, increasing the pressure on restaurant chains to increase per restaurant sales in order to cover higher initial investment costs. One alternative to continued investment in the U.S. market is expansion into international markets, which offers large customer bases and comparatively little competition. However, few U.S. restaurant chains have yet defined aggressive strategies for penetrating international markets.

36   Three restaurant chains that have established aggressive international strategies are McDonald's, Pizza Hut, and KFC. McDonald's currently operates the most units within the U.S. market. McDonald's also operates the largest number of fast-food chains outside of the United States (4,710), recently overtaking KFC, which long dominated the fast-food industry outside the United States. KFC ended 1993 with 3,872 restaurants outside the United States, 838 fewer than McDonald's. However, KFC remains the most internationalized of all fast-food chains, operating 43 percent of its total units outside the United States. In comparison, McDonald's operates 34 percent of its units outside the United States. Pizza Hut presently operates in the most countries (80); however, over 88 percent of its units are still located in the United States.

37   Exhibit 6 shows *Hotels'* 1994 list of the world's 30 largest fast-food restaurant chains. Several important observations may be made from these data. First, 17 of the 30 largest restaurant chains (ranked by number of units) are headquartered in the United States. This may be partially explained by the fact that U.S. firms account for over 25 percent of the world's foreign direct investment. As a result, U.S. firms have historically been more likely to invest assets abroad. However, while both KFC and McDonald's operate over 3,800 units abroad, no other restaurant chain, U.S. or foreign, has

EXHIBIT 6
The World's 30 Largest Fast-Food Chains
(Year-end 1993, ranked by number of countries)

	Franchise	Location	Units	Countries
1	Pizza Hut	Dallas, Texas	9,500	80
2	McDonald's	Oakbrook, Illinois	13,993	70
3	KFC	Louisville, Kentucky	9,000	68
4	Burger King	Miami, Florida	7,121	50
5	Baskin Robbins	Glendale, California	3,557	49
5	Wendy's	Dublin, Ohio	4,168	38
7	Domino's Pizza	Ann Arbor, Michigan	5,238	36
8	TCBY	Little Rock, Arkansas	7,474	22
9	Dairy Queen	Minneapolis, Minnesota	5,471	21
10	Dunkin' Donuts	Randolph, Massachusetts	3,691	21
11	Taco Bell	Irvine, California	4,800	20
12	Arby's	Fort Lauderdale, Florida	2,670	18
13	Subway Sandwiches	Milford, Connecticut	8,477	15
14	Sizzler International	Los Angeles, California	681	14
15	Hardee's	Rocky Mount, North Carolina	4,060	12
16	Little Caesar's	Detroit, Michigan	4,600	12
17	Popeye's Chicken	Atlanta, Georgia	813	12
18	Denny's	Spartanburg, South Carolina	1,515	10
19	A&W Restaurants	Livonia, Michigan	707	9
20	T.G.I. Friday's	Minneapolis, Minnesota	273	8
21	Orange Julius	Minneapolis, Minnesota	480	7
22	Church's Fried Chicken	Atlanta, Georgia	1,079	6
23	Long John Silver's	Lexington, Kentucky	1,464	5
24	Carl's Jr.	Anaheim, California	649	4
25	Loterria	Tokyo, Japan	795	4
26	Mos Burger	Tokyo, Japan	1,263	4
27	Skylark	Tokyo, Japan	1,000	4
28	Jack in the Box	San Diego, California	1,172	3
29	Quick Restaurants	Berchem, Belgium	876	3
30	Taco Time	Eugene, Oregon	300	3

Source: *Hotels*, May 1994.

more than 1,500 units outside the United States. In fact, most chains have fewer than 500 foreign units and operate in less than 22 countries.

38   There are a number of possible explanations for the relative scarcity of fast-food restaurant chains outside the United States. First, the United States represents the largest consumer market in the world, accounting for over one-fifth of the world's gross domestic product (GDP). Therefore, the United States has traditionally been the strategic focus of the largest restaurant chains. In addition, Americans have been quicker to accept the fast-food concept. Many other cultures have strong culinary traditions that have not been easy to break down. The Europeans, for example, have long histories of frequenting more midscale restaurants, where they may spend several hours in a formal setting enjoying native dishes and beverages. While KFC is again building restaurants in Germany, it previously failed to penetrate the German market because Germans were not accustomed to take-out

food or to ordering food over the counter. McDonald's has had greater success penetrating the German market because it has made a number of changes in its menu and operating procedures in order to better appeal to German culture. For example, German beer is served in all of McDonald's German restaurants. KFC has had more success in Asia where chicken is a traditional dish.

39   Aside from cultural factors, international business carries risks not present n the U.S. market. Long distances between headquarters and foreign franchises often make it difficult to control the quality of individual franchises. Large distances can also cause servicing and support problems. Transportation and other resource costs may also be higher than in the domestic market. In addition, time, cultural, and language differences can increase communication and operational problems. Therefore, it is reasonable to expect U.S. restaurant chains to expand domestically as long as they can achieve corporate profit and growth objectives. However, as the U.S. market becomes more saturated, and companies gain additional expertise in international business, we should expect more companies to turn to profitable international markets as a means of expanding restaurant bases and increasing sales, profits, and market share.

KENTUCKY FRIED CHICKEN CORPORATION

Management

40   One of PepsiCo's greatest challenges when it acquired Kentucky Fried Chicken in 1986 was how to mold two distinct corporate cultures. When R.J. Reynolds acquired KFC in 1982, it realized that it knew very little about the fast-food business. Therefore, it relied on existing KFC management to manage the company. As a result, there was little need for mixing the cultures of the two companies. However, one of PepsiCo's major concerns when considering the purchase of KFC was whether it had the management skills required to successfully operate KFC using PepsiCo managers. PepsiCo had already acquired considerable experience managing fast-food businesses through its Pizza Hut and Taco Bell operations. Therefore, it was anxious to pursue strategic changes within KFC which would improve performance. However, replacing KFC with PepsiCo managers could easily cause conflicts between managers in both companies, who were accustomed to different operating procedures and working conditions.

41   PepsiCo's corporate culture has long been based heavily on a "fast-track" New York approach to management. It hires the country's top business and engineering graduates and promotes them based on performance. As a result, top performers expect to move up through the ranks quickly and to be paid well for their efforts. However, this competitive environment often results in intense rivalries among young managers. If one fails to perform, there is always another top performer waiting in the wings. As a result, employee loyalty is sometimes lost and turnover tends to be higher than in other companies.

42   The corporate culture at Kentucky Fried Chicken in 1986 contrasted sharply with that at PepsiCo. KFC's culture was built largely on Colonel Sander's laid-back approach to management. Also, employees enjoyed relatively good employment stability and security. Over the years, a strong loyalty had been created among KFC employees and franchisees, mainly because of the efforts of Colonel Sanders to provide for his employees' benefits, pension, and other non-income needs. In addition, the Southern environment of Louisville resulted in a friendly, relaxed atmosphere at KFC's corporate offices. This corporate culture was left essentially unchanged during the Heublein and RJR years.

43   When PepsiCo acquired KFC, it began to restructure the KFC organization, replacing most of KFC's top managers with its own. By the summer of 1990, all of KFC's top positions were occupied by PepsiCo executives. In July 1989, KFC's president and chief executive officer, Richard P. Mayer, left KFC to become president of General Foods USA. Mayer had been at KFC since 1977 when KFC was still owned by Heublein. PepsiCo replaced Mayer with John Cranor III, the former president of Pepsi-Cola East, a Pepsi-Cola unit. In 1990, PepsiCo named Kyle Craig, a former Pillsbury executive, as president of KFC's USA operations.

EXHIBIT 7
KFC Organizational Chart

KFC Corporation Offices
David Novak
President

John K. Hill Senior V.P. (Finance) & CFO	Colin Moore Senior Vice President, Marketing
Peter Waller Senior V.P. (Franchising)	Olden Lee Senior V.P. (Human Resources)

Source: PepsiCo, Inc., annual report, 1994.

44   Most of PepsiCo's initial management changes in 1987 focused on KFC's corporate offices and USA operations. In 1988, attention was turned to KFC's international division. During 1988, PepsiCo replaced KFC International's top managers with its own. First, it lured Don Pierce away from Burger King and made Pierce president of KFC International. However, Pierce left KFC in early 1990 to become president of Pentagram Corporation, a restaurant operation in Hawaii. Pierce commented that he wished to change jobs partly to decrease the amount of time he spent traveling. PepsiCo replaced Pierce with Allan Huston, who was formerly senior vice president of operations at Pizza Hut. However, by the end of 1995, most of KFC's new top management team had either left the company or moved on to other positions within the PepsiCo organization. John Cranor III resigned in 1994, Kyle Craig resigned in 1994 to join Boston Marketing, Allen Huston (president of KFC International) became president and chief executive of Pizza Hut, and Robert Briggs (vice president of international finance for KFC International) left to become the president of Arby's International.

45   An example of the type of conflict faced by PepsiCo in attempting to implement changes within KFC occurred in August 1989. A month after becoming president and chief executive officer, John Cranor addressed KFC's franchisees in Louisville, in order to explain the details of a new franchise contract. This was the first contract change in 13 years. The new contract gave PepsiCo management greater power to take over weak franchises, to relocate restaurants, and to make changes in existing restaurants. In addition, existing restaurants would no longer be protected from competition from new KFC restaurants. The contract also gave management the right to raise royalty fees on existing restaurants as contracts came up for renewal. After Cranor finished his address, there was an uproar among the attending franchisees, who jumped to their feet to protest the changes. The franchisees had long been accustomed to relatively little interference from management in their day-to-day operations. This type of interference, of course, was a strong part of PepsiCo's philosophy of demanding change.

46   As a result of sluggish performance in its restaurant businesses and a desire to consolidate restaurant operations in order to maximize synergies, PepsiCo created two new divisions to oversee its restaurant business in late 1994: PepsiCo Worldwide Restaurants and PepsiCo Restaurants International. Both are based in Dallas, Texas. David Novak was named president of KFC (see Exhibit 7). Roger Enrico, vice-chairman of PepsiCo and former CEO of Frito-Lay, was named chairman and CEO of PepsiCo Worldwide Restaurants. Laurence Zwain, formerly president of KFC International, was named president and chief operating officer of PepsiCo Restaurants International. Then in October 1995, James H. O'Neal, who had been president of PepsiCo Foods International–Europe, was named to the new position of chairman and CEO of PepsiCo Restaurants International. Zwain retained his title and would report to O'Neal. O'Neal would report directly to Enrico (see Exhibit 3).

OPERATING RESULTS

47   KFC's recent operating results are shown in Exhibit 8. In 1994, worldwide sales, which represent sales of both company-owned and franchised restaurants, reached $7.1 billion. Since 1987, worldwide sales

EXHIBIT 8
KFC Operating Results

	Worldwide Sales ($ billions)	KFC Corp.* Sales ($ billions)	KFC Corp.* Profit ($ millions)	Percent of Sales
1987	$4.1	$1.1	$90.0	8.3%
1988	5.0	1.2	114.9	9.5
1989	5.4	1.3	99.4	7.5
1990	5.8	1.5	126.9	8.3
1991	6.2	1.8	80.5	4.4
1992	6.7	2.2	168.8	7.8
1993	7.1	2.3	152.8	6.6
1994	7.1	2.6	165.2	6.2
7-year growth rate	8.2%	13.6%	9.1%	

*KFC corporate figures include company restaurants and franchise royalties and fees.
Source: PepsiCo., Inc., annual reports for 1988–1994.

have brown at a compounded annual growth rate of 8.2 percent. KFC's domestic market share remained at about one-half of the $7.7 billion U.S. market in 1994. KFC corporate sales, which include company-owned restaurants and royalties from franchised units, reached $2.6 billion, up 14 percent from 1993 sales of $2.3 billion. New restaurants and higher volume contributed $193 and $120 million to corporate sales, respectively.

48   KFC's worldwide profits increased by 8 percent to $165 million in 1994. KFC's operating profits from international operations represented about 40 percent of worldwide profits in both 1993 and 1994. Profits rose as the result of additional units, higher volume, and increased franchise royalties, which were partially offset by a sales mix shift to lower-margin products, lower pricing, and higher administrative and support costs. Growth in international profits were highest in Australia (now KFC's largest international market) and New Zealand. Profits were lowest in Mexico and Canada.

Business-Level Strategies

Marketing

49   As KFC entered 1996, it grappled with a number of important issues. During the 1980s, consumers began to demand healthier foods and KFC was faced with a limited menu consisting mainly of fried foods. In order to reduce KFC's image as a fried chicken chain, it changed its logo from Kentucky Fried Chicken to KFC in 1991. In addition, it responded to consumer demands for greater variety by introducing a variety of new products. Consumers have also become more mobile, demanding fast food in a variety of nontraditional locations such as grocery stores, restaurants, airports, and outdoor events. This has forced fast-food restaurant chains in general to investigate nontraditional distribution channels and restaurant designs. In addition, families continue to seek greater value in the food they buy, further increasing the pressure of fast-food chains to reduce operating costs and prices.

50   Many of KFC's problems during the late 1980s surrounded its limited menu and its inability to quickly bring new products to market. The popularity of its Original Recipe fried chicken allowed KFC to expand through the 1980s without significant competition from other chicken competitors. As a result, new product introductions were never an important part of KFC's overall strategy. However, the introduction of chicken sandwiches and fried chicken by hamburger chains has changed the make-up of KFC's competitors. Most importantly, McDonald's introduced its McChicken sandwich in the U.S. market in 1989 while KFC was still testing its new sandwich. By beating KFC to the market, McDonald's was able to develop a strong consumer awareness for its sandwich. This significantly increased KFC's cost of developing consumer awareness for its chicken sandwich, which was introduced several months later.

51   The increased popularity of healthier foods and consumers' increasing demand for better variety have led to a number of changes in KFC's menu offerings. In 1992, KFC introduced Oriental Wings, Popcorn Chicken, and Honey BBQ Chicken as alternatives to its Original Recipe fried chicken. It also introduced a dessert menu that included a variety of pies and cookies. In 1993, KFC rolled out its Rotisserie Chicken and began to promote its lunch and dinner buffet. The buffet, which includes 30 items, had been introduced into almost 1,600 KFC restaurants in 27 states by the end of 1993.

52   One of KFC's most aggressive strategies was the introduction of its "Neighborhood Program." By mid-1993, almost 500 company-owned restaurants in New York, Chicago, Philadelphia, Washington, D.C., St. Louis, Los Angeles, Houston, and Dallas had been outfitted with special menu offerings to appeal exclusively to the black community. Menus were beefed up with side dishes such as greens, macaroni and cheese, peach cobbler, sweet-potato pie, and red beans and rice. In addition, restaurant employees have been outfitted with African-inspired uniforms. The introduction of the Neighborhood Program has increased sales by 5 to 30 percent in restaurants appealing directly to the black community. KFC is currently testing Hispanic-oriented restaurants in the Miami area, which offer such side dishes as fried plantains, flan, and tres leches.

53   As the growth in sales of traditional, free-standing fast-food restaurants has slowed during the last decade, consumers have demanded fast food in a greater variety of nontraditional locations. As a result, distribution has taken on increasing importance. KFC is relying on nontraditional units to spur much of its future growth. Distribution channels that offer significant growth opportunities are shopping malls and other high-traffic areas that have not traditionally been exploited by fast-food chains. Increasingly, shopping malls are developing food areas where several fast-food restaurant chains compete against each other. Universities and hospitals also offer opportunities for KFC and other chains to improve distribution. KFC is currently testing a variety of nontraditional outlets, including drive-through and carry-out units; snack shops in cafeterias; kiosks in airports, stadiums, amusement parks, and office buildings; mobile units that can be transported to outdoor concerts and fairs; and scaled-down outlets for supermarkets. In order to help its KFC, Taco Bell, and Pizza Hut units more quickly expand into the these nontraditional distribution channels, PepsiCo acquired a partial share of Carts of Colorado, Inc., a manufacturer of mobile merchandising carts, in 1992. Additionally, KFC and Taco Bell plan to add the Taco Bell menu to existing KFC restaurants in 1996 and 1997. This "dual branding" strategy would help PepsiCo improve economies of scale within its restaurant operations and enable KFC restaurants to improve its customer base by widening its menu offerings.

Operating Efficiencies

54   While marketing strategies traditionally improve a firm's profit picture indirectly through increased sales, improved operating efficiencies can directly affect operating profit. As pressure continues to build on fast-food chains to limit price increases in the U.S. market, restaurant chains continue to search for ways of reducing overhead and other operating costs in order to improve profit margins. In 1989, KFC reorganized its U.S. operations in order to eliminate overhead costs and to increase efficiency. Included in this reorganization was a revision of KFC's crew training programs and operating standards. A Renewed emphasis has been placed on improving customer service, cleaner restaurants, faster and friendlier service, and continued high-quality products. In 1992, KFC reorganized its middle management ranks, eliminating 250 of the 1,500 management positions at KFC's corporate headquarters. More responsibility was assigned to restaurant franchisees and marketing managers, and pay was more closely aligned with customer service and restaurant performance.

Restaurant Expansion and International Operations

55   While marketing and operating strategies can improve sales and profitability in existing outlets, an important part of success in the quick-service industry is investment growth. Much of the success of the top 10 competitors within the industry during the late 1980s and early 1990s can be found in aggressive building strategies. In particular, a restaurant chain is often able to discourage competition by being the first to build in a low population area that can only support a single fast-food chain. Additionally, it is equally important to beat a competitor into more populated areas, where location is of prime importance. Internationally, KFC was operating 4,258 restaurants in 68 countries at the end

EXHIBIT 9
KFC (Latin America) Restaurant Count (as of November 30, 1995)

	Company Restaurants	Franchise Restaurants	Total Restaurants	Countries
Mexico	129	29	158	1
Puerto Rico	64	0	64	1
Venezuela	4	0	4	1
Virgin Islands	8	0	8	1
Trinidad and Tobago	0	26	26	1
Franchises	0	118	118	19
Total	205	173	378	24

Source: PepsiCo, Inc.

of 1994. KFC is now the third largest quick-service, and largest chicken, restaurant system in the world. In the future, KFC's international operations will be called on to provide an increasing percentage of KFC's overall sales and profit growth as the U.S. market continues to saturate.

MEXICO AND LATIN AMERICA

56 KFC was one of the first restaurant chains to recognize the importance of international markets. In Latin America, KFC was operating 205 company-owned restaurants in Mexico, Puerto Rico, Venezuela, and Trinidad and Tobago as of November 1995. In addition, KFC had 173 franchisees in 21 countries throughout Latin America, bringing the total number of KFC restaurants in operation in Latin America to 378 (see Exhibit 9).

56 Through 1990, KFC concentrated its company operations in Mexico and Puerto Rico and focused its franchised operations in the Caribbean and Central America. However, by 1994, KFC had altered its Latin American strategy in a number of ways. First, it began franchising in Mexico, mainly as a result of Mexico's new franchise law, which was enacted in 1990. Second, it expanded its company-owned restaurants into the Virgin Islands and Trinidad and Tobago. Third, it reestablished a subsidiary in Venezuela in 1993. KFC had closed its Venezuelan operations in 1989 because of the high fixed costs associated with running the small subsidiary. Last, it decided to expand its franchise operations beyond Central America. In 1990, a franchise was opened in Chile and in 1993, a new franchise was opened in Brazil.

Franchising

57 Through 1989, KFC relied exclusively on the operation of company-owned restaurants in Mexico. While franchising was popular in the United States, it was virtually unknown in Mexico until 1990, mainly because of the absence of a law protecting patents, information, and technology transferred to the Mexican franchise. In addition, royalties were limited. As a result, most fast-food chains opted to invest in Mexico using company-owned restaurants rather than through franchising.

58 In January 1990, Mexico enacted a new law that provided for the protection of technology transferred into Mexico. Under the new legislation, the franchisor and franchisee are free to set their own terms. Royalties are also allowed under the new law. Royalties are currently taxed at a 15 percent rate on technology assistance and know-how and 35 percent for other royalty categories. The advent of the new franchise law has resulted in an explosion of franchises in fast-food, services, hotels, and retail outlets. In 1992, franchises had an estimated $750 million in sales in over 1,200 outlets throughout Mexico.

59 At the end of 1989, KFC was operating company-owned restaurants in three regions: Mexico City, Guadalajara, and Monterrey. By limiting operations to company-owned restaurants in these

EXHIBIT 10
Mexico's Major Trading Partners (% Total Exports and Imports)

	1988		1990		1992	
	Percent Total Exports	Percent Total Imports	Percent Total Exports	Percent Total Imports	Percent Total Exports	Percent Total Imports
USA	72.9%	74.9%	69.3%	68.0%	68.7%	65.2%
Japan	4.9	6.4	5.8	4.5	3.2	6.3
West Germany	1.3	3.5	1.4*	4.2*	N/A	5.1
France	1.8	2.0	3.5	2.3	2.0	2.7
Other	19.1	13.2	20.0	21.0	26.1	20.7
Percent total	100.0%	100.0%	100.0%	100.0%	100.0%	100.0%
Value ($ millions)	20,658	18,903	26,773	29,799	46,196	62,129

*Data include East Germany.
Source: *Business International*, 1994.

three regions, KFC was better able to coordinate operations and minimize costs of distribution to individual restaurants. However, the new franchise legislation gave KFC and other fast-food chains the opportunity to more easily expand their restaurant bases to other regions of Mexico, where responsibility for management could be handled by individual franchisees.

Economic Environment and the Mexican Market

60   Many factors make Mexico a potentially profitable location for U.S. direct investment and trade. Mexico's population of over 91 million people is approximately one-third as large as the United States. This represents a large market for U.S. goods. Because of its geographical proximity to the United States, transportation costs from the United States are minimal. This increases the competitiveness of U.S. goods in comparison with European and Asian goods, which must be transported at substantial cost across the Atlantic or Pacific Ocean. The United States is, in fact, Mexico's largest trading partner. Over 65 percent of Mexico's imports come from the United States, while 69 percent of Mexico's exports are to the U.S. market (see Exhibit 10). In addition, low wage rates make Mexico an attractive location for production. By producing in Mexico, U.S. firms may reduce labor costs and increase the cost competitiveness of their goods in world markets.

61   Despite the importance of the U.S. market to Mexico, Mexico still represents a small percentage of overall U.S. trade and investment. Since the early 1900s, the portion of U.S. exports to Latin America has declined. Instead, U.S. exports to Canada and Asia, where economic growth has outpaced growth in Mexico, have increased more quickly. Canada is the largest importer of U.S. goods. Japan is the largest exporter of goods to the United States, with Canada close behind. While the value of Mexico's exports to the United States has increased during the last two decades, mainly because of the rise in the price of oil, Mexico still represents a small percentage of overall U.S. trade. U.S. investment in Mexico has also been small, mainly because of government restrictions on foreign investment. Instead, most U.S. foreign investment has been in Europe, Canada, and Asia.

62   The lack of U.S. investment in and trade with Mexico during this century is mainly the result of Mexico's long history of restricting trade and foreign direct investment in Mexico. In particular, the Institutional Revolutionary Party (PRI), which came to power in Mexico during the 1930s, had traditionally pursued protectionist economic policies in order to shield its people and economy from foreign firms and goods. Industries have been predominately government-owned or controlled and production has been pursued for the domestic market only. High tariffs and other trade barriers have restricted imports into Mexico and foreign ownership of assets in Mexico has been largely prohibited or heavily restricted.

63   In addition, a dictatorial and entrenched government bureaucracy, corrupt labor unions, and a long tradition of anti-Americanism among many government officials and intellectuals has reduced

EXHIBIT 11
Economic Data for Mexico

	1989	1990	1991	1992	1993
Population (millions)	84.5	86.2	87.8	89.5	91.2
GDP (billions of new pesos)	507.6	686.4	865.2	1,019.2	1,127.6
Real GDP growth rate (%)	3.3	4.4	3.6	2.8	0.6
Exchange rate (New pesos/$)	2.641	2.945	3.071	3.115	3,106
Inflation (%)	20.0	26.6	22.7	15.5	8.6
Current accounting ($ billions)	(5.8)	(7.5)	(14.9)	(24.8)	(23.4)
Reserves (excluding gold, $ billions)	6.3	9.9	17.7	18.9	25.1

Source: *International Financial Statistics,* International Monetary Fund, 1995.

the motivation of U.S. firms for investing in Mexico. Also, the 1982 nationalization of Mexico's banks led to higher real interest rates and lower investor confidence. Since then, the Mexican government has battled high inflation, high interest rates, labor unrest, and lost consumer purchasing power (see Exhibit 11). Total foreign debt, which stood at $125.9 billion at the end of 1993, remains a problem.

64   Investor confidence in Mexico has, however, improved since December 1988, when Carlos Salinas de Gortari was elected President of Mexico. Following his election, Salinas embarked on an ambitious restructuring of the Mexican economy. In particular, Salinas initiated policies to strengthen the free market components of the economy. Top marginal tax rates were lowered to 36 percent in 1990, down from 60 percent in 1986, and new legislation has eliminated many restrictions on foreign investment. Foreign firms are now allowed to buy up to 100 percent of the equity in many Mexico firms. Previously, foreign ownership of Mexican firms was limited to 49 percent. Many government-owned companies have been sold to private investors in order to eliminate government bureaucracy and improve efficiency.

Privatization

65   The privatization of government-owned companies has come to symbolize the restructuring of Mexico's economy. On May 14, 1990, legislation was passed to privatize all government-run banks. By the end of 1992, over 800 of some 1,200 government-owned companies had been sold, including Mexicana and AeroMexico, the two largest airline companies in Mexico, and Mexico's 18 major banks. At least 40 more companies were scheduled to be privatized in 1993. However, more than 350 companies remain under government ownership. These represent a significant portion of the assets owned by the state at the start of 1988. Therefore, the sale of government-owned companies, in terms of asset value, has been moderate. A large percentage of the remaining government-owned assets are controlled by government-run companies in certain strategic industries such as steel, electricity, and petroleum. These industries have long been protected by government ownership. As a result, additional privatization of government-owned enterprises until 1993 was limited. However, in 1993, President Salinas opened up the electricity sector to independent power producers and Petroleos Mexicanos (Pemex), the state-run petrochemical monopoly, initiated a program to sell off many of its nonstrategic assets to private and foreign buyers. This was motivated mainly by a desire by Pemex to concentrate on its basic petrochemical businesses.

North American Free Trade Agreement (NAFTA)

66   Prior to 1989, Mexico levied high tariffs on most imported goods. In addition, many other goods were subjected to quotas, licensing requirements, and other nontariff trade barriers. In 1986, Mexico joined the General Agreement on Tariffs and Trade (GATT), a world trade organization designed to eliminate barriers to trade among member nations. As a member of GATT, Mexico is obligated to apply its system of tariffs to all member nations equally. As a result of its membership in GATT,

Mexico dropped tariff rates on a variety of imported goods. In addition, import license requirements were dropped for all but 300 imported items. During President Salinas's administration, tariffs were reduced from an average of 100 percent on most items to an average of 11 percent.

67   On January 1, 1994, the North American Free Trade Agreement (NAFTA) went into effect. The passage of NAFTA, which included Canada, the United States, and Mexico, created a trading bloc that has a larger population and gross domestic product than the European Union. Over the next several years, all tariffs on goods traded among the three countries will be phased out. Given that Canada is the United States' largest trading partner and Mexico the United States' third largest trading partner, the absence of tariffs and reduced restrictions on investment should result in increased trade and investment among the three countries. In particular, Mexico should benefit from the lower cost of imported goods and increased employment from higher investment from Canada and the United States. Canada and the United States should benefit from lower labor and transportation costs from investing in Mexico.

Foreign Exchange and the Mexican Peso Crisis of 1995

68   Between December 20, 1982, and November 11, 1991, a two-tiered exchange rate system was in force in Mexico. The system consisted of a controlled rate and a free market rate. A controlled rate was used for imports, foreign debt payments, and conversion of export proceeds. An estimated 70 percent of all foreign transactions were covered by the controlled rate. A free market rate was used for other transactions. On January 1, 1989, President Salinas instituted a policy of allowing the peso to depreciate against the dollar by one peso per day. The result was a grossly overvalued peso. This lowered the price of imports and led to an increase in imports of over 23 percent in 1989. At the same time, Mexican exports became less competitive on world markets.

69   Effective November 11, 1991, the controlled rate was abolished and replaced with an official free rate. In order to limit the range of fluctuations in the value of the peso, the government fixed the rate at which it would buy or sell pesos. A floor (the maximum price at which pesos may be purchased) was initially established at Ps 3056.20 and remained fixed. A ceiling (the maximum price at which the peso may be sold) was initially established at Ps 3,056.40 and allowed to move upward by Ps 0.20 per day. This was later revised to Ps 0.40 per day. On January 1, 1993, a new currency was issued— called the *new peso*—with three fewer zeros. The new currency was designed to simplify transactions and to reduce the cost of printing currency.

70   When Ernesto Zedillo became Mexico's president in December 1994, one of his objectives was to continue the stability in prices, wages, and exchange rates achieved by ex-president Carlos Salinas de Gortari during his five-year tenure as president. However, Salinas had achieved stability largely on the basis of price, wage, and foreign exchange controls. While giving the appearance of stability, an overvalued peso continued to encourage imports that exacerbated Mexico's balance of trade deficit. Mexico's government continued to use foreign reserves to finance its balance of trade deficits. According to the Banco de Mexico, foreign currency reserves fell from $24 billion in January 1994 to $5.5 billion in January 1995. Anticipating a devaluation of the peso, investors began to move capital into U.S. dollar investments. In order to relieve some of the pressure placed on the peso, president Zedillo announced on December 19, 1994, that the peso would be allowed to depreciate by an additional 15 percent per year against the dollar compared to the maximum allowable depreciation of 4 percent per year established during the Salinas administration. Within two days, continued pressure on the peso forced the Zedillo administration to allow the peso to float against the dollar. By mid-January 1995, the peso had lost 35 percent of its value against the dollar and the Mexican stock market plunged 20 percent. By November 1995, the peso had depreciated from 3.1 pesos per dollar to 7.3 pesos per dollar.

71   The continued devaluation of the peso resulted in higher import prices, higher inflation, destabilization within the stock market, and the higher interest rates, as Mexico struggled to arrange continued payment of its dollar-based debts. In order to thwart a possible default by Mexico on its dollar-based loans, the U.S. government, International Monetary Fund, and World Bank pledged $12.5, $11.4, and $1.0 billion (a total of $24.9 billion) in emergency loans to Mexico. In addition, president Zedillo announced an emergency economic package called the "pacto," which included reduced government spending, increased sales of government-run businesses, and a freeze on wage increases.

Labor Problems

72   One of KFC's primary concerns is the stability of Mexico's labor markets. Labor is relatively plentiful and cheap in Mexico, though much of the work force is still relatively unskilled. While KFC benefits from lower labor costs, labor unrest, low job retention, absenteeism, and punctuality continue to be significant problems. A good part of the problem with absenteeism and punctuality is cultural. However, problems with worker retention and labor unrest are mainly the result of workers' frustration over the loss of their purchasing power due to inflation and past government controls on wage increases. *Business Latin America* estimated that purchasing power fell by 35 percent in Mexico between January 1988 and June 1990. Though absenteeism is on the decline due to job security fears, it is still high at approximately 8 to 14 percent of the labor force. Turnover also continues to be a problem. Turnover of production line personnel is currently running at 5 to 12 percent per month. Therefore, employee screening and internal training continue to be important issues for foreign firms investing in Mexico.

73   Higher inflation and the government's freeze on wage increases have led to a dramatic decline in disposable income since 1994. Further, a slowdown in business activity brought about by higher interest rates and lower government spending, has led many businesses to lay off workers. By the end of 1995, an estimated one million jobs had been lost as a result of the economic crisis sparked by the peso devaluation. As a result, industry groups within Mexico have called for new labor laws giving them more freedom to hire and fire employees and increased flexibility to hire part-time rather than full-time workers.

Risks and Opportunities

74   The peso crisis of 1995 and resulting recession in Mexico left KFC managers with a great deal of uncertainty regarding Mexico's economic and political future. KFC had benefited greatly from the economic stability brought about by ex-president Salinas's policies during his 1988–1994 tenure. Inflation was brought down, the peso was relatively stable, labor unrest was relatively calm, and Mexico's new franchise law had enabled KFC to expand into rural areas using franchises rather than company-owned restaurants. By the end of 1995, KFC had built 29 franchises in Mexico. KFC planned to continue to expand its franchise base and to rely less heavily on company-owned restaurants as a cornerstone of its strategy to maintain its market share against other fast-food restaurants, such as McDonald's and Arby's, which were pursuing high growth strategies in Mexico.

75   The foreign exchange crisis of 1995 had severe implications for U.S. firms operating in Mexico. In particular, the devaluation of the peso resulted in higher inflation and capital flight out of Mexico. The Bank of Mexico estimated that $7.1 billion fled the country during the first three months of 1995. In order to bring inflation under control, the Mexican government instituted an austerity program in early 1995 that included reduced government spending and a freeze on wage increases. Capital flight reduced the supply of capital and resulted in higher interest rates. Additionally, the government's austerity program resulted in reduced demand for products and services, higher unemployment, and lower disposable income. Imports from the United States dropped dramatically in 1995. About one-third of this decline included the importation of capital goods, such as technology, materials, and updated machinery, which are critical to Mexico's industrialization program.

76   Another problem area has been Mexico's failure to reduce restrictions on U.S. and Canadian investment in Mexico in a timely fashion. While the reduction of trade barriers has resulted in greater U.S. exports to Mexico, U.S. firms have experienced problems getting the required approvals for new ventures in Mexico from the Mexican government. For example, under NAFTA, the United Parcel Service (UPS) was supposed to receive government approval to use large trucks for deliveries in Mexico. As of the end of 1995, UPS had still not received approval. As a result, UPS has been forced to use smaller trucks, which puts it at a competitive disadvantage vis-á-vis Mexican companies, or to subcontract delivery work to Mexican companies that are allowed to use bigger, more cost-efficient trucks. Other U.S. companies such as Bell Atlantic and TRW have faced similar problems. TRW, which signed a joint venture agreement with a Mexican partner, had to wait 15 months longer than anticipated before the Mexican government released rules on how it could receive credit data from

banks. TRW claims that the Mexican government slowed the approval process in order to placate several large Mexican banks.

77   A final area of concern for KFC has been the increased political turmoil in Mexico during the last several years. For example, on January 1, 1994, the day NAFTA went into effect, rebels (descendants of the Mayans) rebelled in the southern Mexican province of Chiapas on the Guatemalan border. After four days of fighting, Mexican troops had driven the rebels out of several towns earlier seized by the rebels. Around 15—mostly rebels—were killed. The uprising symbolized many of the fears of the poor in Mexico. While ex-president Salinas's economic programs had increased economic growth and wealth in Mexico, many of Mexico's poorest felt that they have not benefited. Many of Mexico's farmers, faced with lower tariffs on imported agricultural goods from the United States, felt that they might be driven out of business by the NAFTA agreement. Therefore, social unrest among Mexico's Indians, farmers, and the poor could potentially unravel much of the economic success achieved in Mexico during the last five years.

78   Further, ex-president Salinas's hand-picked successor for president, Luis Donaldo Colosio, was assassinated on March 23, 1994, while campaigning in Tijuana. The assassin—Mario Aburto Martinez, a 23-year-old mechanic and migrant worker—was affiliated with a dissident group upset with the PRI's economic reforms. The possible existence of a dissident group has raised fears of further political violence in the future. The PRI quickly named Ernesto Zedillo, a 42-year-old economist with little political experience or name recognition, as their new presidential candidate. Zedillo was elected president and replaced Salinas in December 1994. However, political unrest is not limited to Mexican officials and companies. In October 1994, between 30 and 40 masked men attacked a McDonald's restaurant in the tourist section of Mexico City to show their opposition to California's Proposition 187, which would have curtailed benefits to illegal aliens (primarily from Mexico). The men threw cash registers to the floor, cracked them open, smashed windows, over-turned tables, and spray-painted slogans on the walls such as "No to Fascism" and "Yankee Go Home."

79   Despite these worries, the passage of NAFTA, the size of the Mexican market, and its proximity to the United States have resulted in a number of opportunities for KFC and other U.S. businesses. During the first five months of 1995, exports from Mexico to the United States jumped 33.5 percent from the previous year as lower tariffs lowered the price of Mexican goods to the American consumer. In fact, during this period, Mexico ran up its highest trade surplus with the United States in Mexico's history.

80   The peso devaluation has also made it less expensive for U.S. and Canadian businesses to buy assets in Mexico. This has enabled businesses to more easily fund expansion in Mexico through new capital at a lower cost. Also, for companies already operating in Mexico, raw materials can be imported from outside of Mexico by converting dollars into pesos at a more favorable rate.

81   For many U.S. companies, the protection of technology and patents is a major concern. In June 1991, a new patent law was passed that replaced the old 1976 law. Patents will now last for 20 years rather than 14. Chemicals, pharmaceuticals, and animal feed will benefit from product patent protection for the first time, opening up the Mexican market to U.S. firms in these fields. Trademarks are now valid for an initial 10 years and are renewable for 10 years, up from the previous five-year terms. Patents on industrial designs are now valid for 15 years, up from 7 years. Additionally, a new copyright law was passed in August 1991. The new law will protect sound recordings and computer software for the first time.

82   KFC's approach to investment in Mexico is to approach it conservatively, until greater economic and political stability is achieved. While resources could be directed at other investment areas with less risk such as Japan, Australia, China, and Europe, the Mexican market is viewed as KFC's most important growth market outside of the United States and second largest international market behind Australia. Also, significant opportunities existed for KFC to expand its franchise base throughout the Caribbean and South America. However, PepsiCo's commitments to these other markets are unlikely to be severely affected by its investment decisions in Mexico, as PepsiCo's large internal cash flows could satisfy the investment needs of KFC's other international subsidiaries regardless of its investments in Mexico. The danger in taking a conservative approach in Mexico was the potential loss of market share in a large market where KFC enjoys enormous popularity.

CASE 22

MATSUSHITA INDUSTRIAL DE BAJA CALIFORNIA (A)

CAN MEXICO COMPETE WITH ASIA?

1   Making his daily crossing from San Diego to Tijuana to the offices of Matsushita Industrial de Baja California (MIBA), Mitsuharu Nakata, Sub-Director Administrativo, was personally concerned about the fate of the Mexican plants since the start of the North American Free Trade Agreement

San Diego and Tijuana Industrial Map

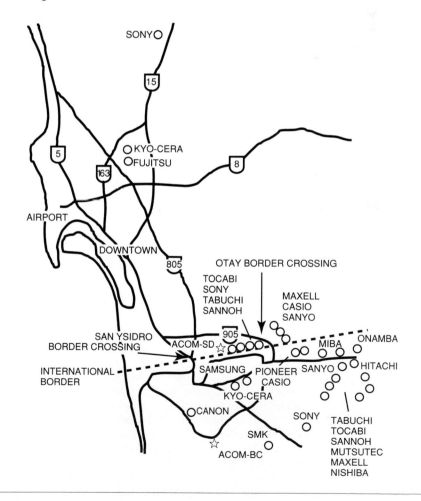

This case was prepared by Stephen Jenner, California State University, Dominguez Hills.

(NAFTA) on January 1, 1994. Before this assignment, Nakata lived in Central America for 6 years working for Matsushita in Guatemala and Costa Rica. After San Diego/Tijuana, he knew that he would move wherever the Company sent him; the idea of leaving Matsushita was unthinkable. As he swung his car to avoid the potholes in the road leading to Ciudad Industrial just across the commercial border crossing from the U.S., he saw the gleaming glass and steel factories belonging to Sanyo, Matsushita's neighbor and worldwide competitor. He had been living in San Diego for 10 years, and he was concerned that after another 5 years, production of televisions in Mexico would no longer be competitive.

Matsushita Group Chart

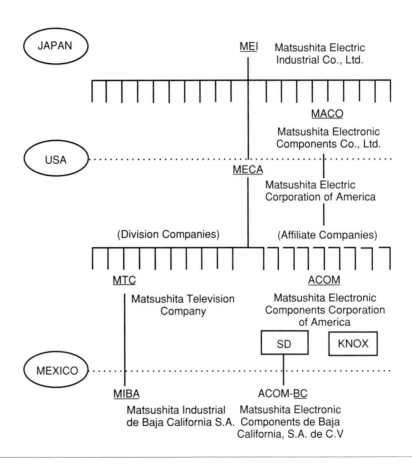

2   Compared to low-cost Asian producers, Mexico in 1994 had offered a 2% savings in transportation as a location supplying the U.S. market. There was also a 5% duty imposed by the U.S. on assembled televisions. Together, these two items represented 7%; if an Asian country such as Malaysia, Indonesia, or China had a 10% labor cost advantage, then they could compete with Mexico. NAFTA's Rules of Origin stipulated that automobiles must be 62.5% North American, but televisions need only a picture tube worth about 33% to qualify as North American products. If the picture tube (or CRT) was made in the U.S., the duty savings were 5% compared to a CRT fixed in a cabinet with a tuner, a TV assembled with its chassis. Importing the CRT alone resulted in a duty of 15%; it was the possibility of importing the CRT duty-free into Mexico via Long Beach, California, and bringing it back to the U.S. as an assembled TV, that brought Japanese producers to Tijuana in the first place. Now it was possible that Matsushita and Sanyo would buy CRTs from Samsung in Tijuana.

3   Nakata wondered why the U.S. government didn't seem to care about the television industry in the same way it nurtured the automobile industry. "I guess the car is closer to what America is all about," he said. "The U.S. Government should assist in the development of TV component manufacturing; it's like a growing tree which needs water and help to reach the size that will allow it to survive a storm. But I guess they don't care about TVs." Any company making TVs has to be concerned with costs and price competition, and production could be moved to the country with the most competitive cost structure.

4   Mexico was special to Japanese producers of TVs because it was close to the U.S. and had good government relations, in addition to low wages, according to Nakata. "But salaries for indirect employees in Mexico are just as high as in the U.S., and there are no sources of transistors, integrated circuits (ICs), registers, or raw materials nearby," complained Nakata. "When the U.S. lost competitiveness, it moved production to Asia, including component manufacturing, which requires 3–5 times the investment of an assembly plant. Now Motorola and Texas Instruments have excellent factories in East Asia, and it makes sense to buy from them. Mexico is very far away from Singapore, Taiwan, Malaysia, Hong Kong, and Japan where Matsushita sources its components."

5   Should Matsushita stay in Baja California and continue to import Asian components while exploring the use of Samsung's picture tubes? Should they locate future plants across the Texas border (in Ciudad Juarez, for example) where they would be closer to the population center of the U.S.? Should they make the decision in 1995 to relocate or add new plants in China or Indonesia where wages were much lower than in Mexico and component plants were close at hand? What about the strategic choice to phase out production of low-end TVs and move up to the higher end of the market, for example, flat panel high definition TVs, multimedia, and semiconductor production?

Historical Background on the Globalization of the Electronics Industry

6   The licensing of the transistor by AT&T (Bell Labs licensed because of U.S. anti-trust legislation), and subsequently General Electric, and RCA led to fierce competition between Fairchild, Sony, and others. Meanwhile, Hong Kong had lost its role as the trade conduit between the U.S., Europe, and China due to the Korean War and China's partnership with the Soviet Union.

7   Sony began to assemble radios in Hong Kong by subcontracting in 1959; in 1960 the local Hong Kong subcontractor and two other local companies began undercutting the Japanese competition. In 1962, the Japanese government banned the export of transistors to Hong Kong, but they were replaced by British and U.S. imports. In the U.S. market, the shift from military to commercial customers demanded lower costs, either through automation or lower wages. Fairchild was the first to invest and locate its own electronic assembly operations anywhere in the Third World; the first plant was located in Hong Kong in 1961, and by 1966 they had 4,500 workers. One of the little-known secrets of Hong Kong's success was providing low-cost housing, food, and clothing—subsidies totaling half of workers' wages.

8   During the period of steady growth of world manufacturing production and exports from 1963–81, Japan's performance was spectacular, followed closely by Hong Kong, Singapore, South Korea, Taiwan, Brazil, and Mexico. In the late 1980s, foreign direct investment really took off, and Japan replaced the UK as the largest country source of investment outflows. The biggest investment flow by far was from Europe to North America (U.S. and Canada), followed by the reverse flow, and a much smaller Japanese flow into North America. The flows from North America to Japan, and from Japan to Europe were much smaller, and the flow from Europe to Japan was the smallest among triad members. The explosion of Japanese foreign direct investment (FDI) in the late 1980s was due to higher production costs because of appreciation of the yen and labor shortages in Japan, and current account surpluses from exports; the more recent slowdown was due to government stimulus for domestic investment, the collapse of the bubble economy, and tighter reserve requirements for Japanese banks.

9   In the case of the electrical and electronic equipment industry, Japanese FDI in the U.S. supported the importation of finished goods and components from Japan and Asia; as of 1992, 99% of purchases by U.S. affiliates of Japanese transnational corporations (TNCs) came from East Asia, and

78% from intra-firm supply networks. For Japanese TNCs, production was centered in Japan with strong upstream linkages to an Asian regionally-integrated supply network. The Southeast Asian countries provided a low cost supply network (including Japanese exports) but did not import from North America or Europe.

THE BIG PICTURE FOR MATSUSHITA

10   Matsushita's long-term response to the appreciation of the yen was to relocate manufacturing outside Japan. In 1994, the Company produced 20% of its goods abroad, and the goal for 1995 was 25%. Nevertheless, many overseas factories rely heavily on imported components from Japan, and there were concerns about Matsushita's ability to maintain quality.

11   Although Matsushita's annual report for 1994 (see Appendix 1) is optimistic, their sale of MCA in April 1995 at a big loss after 5 years was evidence of a strategic disaster. The assumption of hardware makers Matsushita and Sony (Matsushita's main rival) was that they could gain a competitive advantage by controlling audio and video software. According to industry analysts, Hollywood's entertainment products will increasingly be distributed electronically through cable systems and television networks, which are much more strategically important than the boxes that play the music and movies. Due in part to the changes in U.S. regulations that allowed television broadcasters to enter into program production, Matsushita would have to consider strategic alliances with communications companies and cable television if it were to stay in the movie and music production business.

12   Matsushita planned to spend the money from the sale of MCA to focus more on multimedia and manufacturing key components, such as semiconductors. In order to avoid converting the proceeds back into yen at unfavorable exchange rates, Matsushita expected to spend much of the money in the U.S.

OPERATIONS IN TIJUANA, BAJA CALIFORNIA, MEXICO

13   At the end of 1995, MIBA employed 2,600 workers in 6 buildings in Ciudad Industrial (Tijuana, Baja California, Mexico's industrial city on Otay Mesa adjacent to the U.S. border). Another 2,200 workers manufactured tuners and components in two more plants in an industrial park several miles west overlooking the Pacific Ocean. In addition, there were 2,000 workers making components and cellular telephones at another, newer Matsushita plant in Tijuana. The total of 6,800 workers was more than double the number employed a year before.

14   Matsushita's goal for the U.S. market was to expand local content, with 50% to be manufactured locally, and a 70% local content ratio overall. In the low end of the market, the television was Matsushita's loss leader, and the U.S. market was supplied almost entirely by maquiladoras. Tijuana TV producers accounted for 5 million sets annually in 1993, or about half of TVs sold in the U.S. If Toshiba, Thompson-RCA, Zenith, and Philips in Ciudad Juarez (opposite El Paso, Texas) were also included, they accounted for most U.S. TV sales. By the end of 1996, the combined MIBA, Sony, Hitachi, Sanyo, JVC, and Samsung plants were expected churn out 1 million TVs per month, making Tijuana the world's largest TV-producing region. With the passage of NAFTA, these Asian multinationals will face procurement decisions regarding the future location of TV component manufacturing and assembly, which might be done in Mexico or in East Asia.

THE EARLY YEARS: THE NELSON ERA AND THE DECISION TO LOCATE IN TIJUANA

15   Chuck Nelson was "very special" compared to other U.S. managers because he spent 5 years in Japan after World War II and "he knew the culture." He was also married to a Mexican and knew the Spanish language, and he had experience managing a maquiladora/inbond assembly plant before he came to MIBA. Nelson managed what was once the largest maquiladora in Tijuana, Warwick

Electronics, a division of Whirlpool, with 1,500 workers assembling Silverstone TVs sold in Sears stores. In 1973, Matsushita bought a Motorola plant in Franklin, Illinois. It was not profitable, and the Company sent people to all the U.S.-Mexican border cities, because RCA and Zenith already had maquiladoras. Matsushita needed a very competitive price. Tijuana could take material and components from Japan, Malaysia, Taiwan, and Singapore, assemble one standard, high volume model TV in Mexico, and send it to the plant outside Chicago to finish it. Matsushita began in Mexico City with a joint venture, and considered a location in Reynosa, Tamaulipas, Mexico (near McAllen, Texas) before deciding to locate in Tijuana.

16   In 1979, Tijuana was more attractive due to lower transportation costs and proximity to Asian sources of components, although a location along the Texas border was closer to major U.S. markets and distribution centers in the East. According to Nelson, Reynosa also had militant labor unions, and the quality of life for Japanese people living in San Diego, California was considered far superior to the border region of Texas. However, Tijuana had the disadvantages of higher costs of labor, energy, and sites, as well as poor telecommunications infrastructure and delays crossing the border. There was also the problem in Tijuana of extremely high employee turnover of around 6% per month.

17   After locating in Tijuana, Nelson reported in 1985 that "overall MIBA encountered very few problems" and it was expected that there would be expansion. Nelson added that the use of the maquiladora resulted in a net decrease in the total number of Matsushita's U.S. employees during the first 7 years of operations, "but it saved jobs, and perhaps increased jobs in the U.S. in the long run" by allowing Matsushita to be more price competitive.

THE EVOLUTION OF JAPANESE INVESTMENT

18   According to Yasuo Sasaki, a Brazilian of Japanese ancestry who was deeply involved in Sanyo's move to Tijuana, the location decisions by Japanese TV producers began with the oil crisis in the early 1970s. These Japanese multinationals began investing in the U.S. and Mexico as part of a trend toward local manufacturing in foreign markets. This globalization was also due to the appreciation of the Japanese yen from 250 to 200 per U.S. dollar, and a shortage of labor in Japan; college graduates did not want factory assembly jobs. Initially Japanese factories moved to Hokkaido and other more remote islands.

19   The Japanese pattern of entry into Mexican maquiladoras was different than that of U.S. firms. "The Japanese start inside and direct by asking questions, starting with other Japanese companies and Mexican local real estate professionals. They test people's credibility by asking the same questions over and over again," Sasaki noted. In contrast, U.S. companies began "outside and indirect, working through lawyers in Mexico City and New York," according to Sasaki. The Mexican government was unknown to most Japanese corporations, and harder to deal with than the U.S. government.

20   In the case of Sanyo, the original plan was to establish a factory in Mexico City with the involvement of the Mexican government and a Mexican company. Instead, Sanyo decided to go it alone, and originally considered Reynosa just across the Texas border as a location. Zenith was the first TV maker to move to Mexico. Sony established a plant in San Diego, and set up a maquiladora in Tijuana, followed by MIBA in 1979.

21   Sanyo followed Sony and Matsushita to Tijuana, as did Hitachi. "It's part of the Japanese culture and psychology," explained Sasaki, "like the way they play golf together, or go on vacation in Hawaii, always in a group." The fact that the others were there was reason enough—there must be something there," said Sasaki.

22   Japanese companies also chose Tijuana because of its neighbor, San Diego, California, "the only place in the border area with sushi and Japanese schools," he added. "This is important to younger Japanese general managers, production managers, engineers and technicians working in Mexico," noted Sasaki. According to Sasaki, Japanese investment is always "a one-way ticket." There is a long-term commitment, although it may begin very gradually. "For example, Japanese maquiladora buildings were very simple at first, and they could have pulled out easily. Gradually they upgraded." As they became more successful and stronger, Japanese maquiladoras increased their level of technology from "screwdriver" assembly operations to manufacturing, and they brought their other

EXHIBIT 1
New Investments in the San Diego/Tijuana/Mexicali Border Region after NAFTA was Implemented 1/1/94

Name of Firm	Type of Facility
Matsushita	Manufacturing and assembly (200 more workers on car audio, plus 140 more making batteries, in addition to 3,000 in Tijuana) Research and development for hemisphere (140 engineers + administrative/support staff in addition to 150 in San Diego)
Sanyo Electric Co.	TV assembly (200 more workers in addition to 1,300 in Tijuana and 6 purchasing staff in San Diego)
Sony Electronics	Picture tube production (100 more workers in addition to 2,000 in San Diego and 3,000 in Tijuana TV assembly)
Samsung	Picture tube manufacturing ($400 million and 5,000 workers in Tijuana by 1997) Assembly (600 workers in Tijuana)
Goldstar	TV assembly (400 workers in Mexicali)
Daewoo	TV assembly (800 workers near Mexicali)
JVC (announcement expected)	TV assembly (1,000 workers in Tijuana)
Hitachi (existing operation)	TV assembly (1,050 workers in Tijuana and 85 support staff in San Diego)

Source: *San Diego Union-Tribune*, December 31, 1994.

divisions and suppliers. "You must keep pedaling the bicycle," says Sasaki, "It's not just profits, but survival."

23   According to one of the top real estate professionals in Tijuana and landlord for one of Matsushita's factories, Beatrix Sanders, 95% of Japanese companies own the land their maquiladora is built on, while only 50% of U.S. companies own their land. Foreigners may "purchase" Mexican land through a trust held by a Mexican bank and renewable after 30 years. "The Japanese companies want to be around for 200 years," she explained.

THE IMPACT OF NAFTA AND U.S.-MEXICAN RELATIONS IN 1994

24   NAFTA was implemented in January 1, 1994, immediately reducing tariffs and non-tariff barriers on many products, while others would be gradually reduced over 5–10 years. By 1999, two-thirds of U.S. exports were expected to enter Mexico duty-free, up from one-half in 1994. NAFTA's Rules of Origin (which require that 33% goods have North American content, including TV picture tubes) and the restriction of duty drawback (which exempts third-country imports from customs duty) were specific provisions of NAFTA affecting television production (and displays for computers).

25   NAFTA increased trade and led to a modest increase in U.S. foreign direct investment in Mexico in 1994; there were also massive capital flows into the Mexican stock and bond markets. U.S. exports to Mexico increased 25% (including over 50,000 U.S.-made cars and trucks, a 500% increase) as did Mexican exports to the U.S. President Clinton boasted of over 100,000 new U.S. jobs created by NAFTA. Japanese and South Korean television producers made massive investments in Tijuana during 1994 (see Exhibit 1).

26   However, there were also serious concerns about public safety and political stability in Mexico throughout 1994 because of several stunning events. The rebellion in the Mexican State of Chiapas began on January 1, 1994, to coincide with NAFTA's implementation. There were also assassinations of Mexican presidential candidate Luis Donaldo Colosio in Tijuana, and subsequently of a ruling

political party leader in Mexico City. The number of kidnappings of businessmen continued to grow, including a maquiladora owner/manager in Tijuana in November.

27   Most importantly, there was a sudden 40% devaluation of the Mexican peso in December, the "Christmas Crisis" for the Mexican government. The Chiapas rebels were still threatening, and it was their false statement to the media that they had broken out of encirclement by the Mexican Army which precipitated (but did not cause) the devaluation. The greatest challenge of the decade was to restore the confidence of foreign investors, while responding to the growing popular demands within Mexico for human rights and political reform. By late 1995, the peso was down to almost 8 per U.S. dollar from 3.5 a year earlier.

28   On the positive side, the Mexican elections of August 1994 were the cleanest ever, which was attributed in part to the Chiapas rebellion by a small band of Mexican Indians, and also due to the introduction of better voter identification cards with photos. There were still instances of unfair tactics by the ruling party, and the election result in the third largest Mexican city, Monterrey, and for the State of Chiapas were both reversed after an electoral review. Most of the improvements in election processes were at the top or the bottom, with many abuses still prevalent in the middle level of the government apparatus.

29   The issue of border environmental regulation of maquiladoras led to a side agreement to NAFTA and the creation of the Border Environmental Cooperation Commission with $8 billion, and a North American Development Bank (NADBank) to provide additional funding for a deteriorating cross-border infrastructure. However, there was little accomplished in the first year of NAFTA, and critics predicted that increased industrialization on the border would only make things worse. In November of 1994, the U.S. Environmental Protection Agency (EPA) took steps to enforce U.S. environmental laws against 95 U.S.-owned companies operating in Mexicali, Baja California, Mexico. One of the petitions came from a citizens' group in the Chilpancingo neighborhood of Tijuana, which for years had complained about chemical waste dumped on them by maquiladoras above them on Otay Mesa. The EPA issued subpoenas ordering the companies to identify the chemicals that the facilities made, processed, or otherwise used that were likely to be released into water. Along with Mexican sewage and chemical runoff from farms from both sides of the border, these industrial discharges contaminated the New River region in California (immediately north of Mexicali, the "Rio Bravo," flows north from Mexico into the U.S. where it is called the "New River"). The 95 companies included microelectronics firms, and most of the parent firms were based in Southern California; their maquiladoras in Mexico were supposed to return the waste products to their country of origin, although many apparently did not, disposing of the waste in Mexico or simply storing it on site. The EPA also urged the Mexican government to take action against the Mexican companies operating along the border.

30   In the long term, NAFTA was also expected to cause a diversion of U.S. trade and investment to Mexico from China, Thailand, the Philippines, Malaysia, Indonesia, and other low-wage areas. Nevertheless, Asian countries were often more attractive than Mexico to foreign investors, especially Japanese transnational corporations, because they may offer more favorable government investment incentives, trade administration regimes, and networks for supplying components and other production inputs.

APPENDIX 1
Excerpts from Matsushita Electric Annual Report
For the Fiscal Year Ended March 31, 1994

Profile

Matsushita Electric Industrial Co., Ltd., was founded in Osaka in 1918 as a small producer of home electric products. Today, the Company is one of the world's premier manufacturers of electronic products for home, industrial, and commercial uses. Matsushita's products are marketed under such well-known brand names as National, Panasonic, Technics, and Quasar in more than 160 countries.

Financial Highlights (see graphs of Financial Highlights, 1990–94)

In 1994, net sales declined 6%, largely reflecting reduced demand and the impact of yen appreciation on overseas revenues when translated into Japanese currency. Although we worked to minimize manufacturing and overhead costs, earnings were negatively affected by lower sales of audiovisual equipment and seasonal products, a shift in consumer preference toward lower-priced items, and the strong yen. Income before taxes fell 21%, and net income dropped 34%.

There was brisk demand for home facsimile machines and compact read-only (CD-ROM) drives in Japan, and in overseas markets, sales of telephones, hard disc drives, and factory automation equipment were firm. Sales of electronic components achieved a level close to that of 1993 as a result of improved demand, especially for semiconductors.

Ten Principal Business Areas (See "*Matsushita at a Glance*")

To meet the goal of the Revitalization Plan, we have sought to clarify our future direction. To this end, we have identified 10 principal business areas that the Matsushita Group worldwide will develop. These business areas are AV hardware, information and communications, home appliances, housing products, air-conditioning equipment, manufacturing and industrial equipment, components and devices, environmental protection and health-care products, systems and networks, and AV software.

Rapid technological advances have prompted us to target three of these areas—AV hardware, information and communications, and components and devices—for intensive, coordinated development by the entire Matsushita Group.

AV Hardware

The transition from analog to digital technology is changing the nature of AV hardware. In the years ahead, high-definition TV, digital videocassette (DVC), and digital videodisc (DVD) equipment will lead us into a new era of fully developed digitization.

Toward the Multimedia Age

The Company's response to technological and social change will be to build new businesses around imaginative and innovative products that integrate AV, computer, and communications technologies. In the AV field, for example, Matsushita has to date marketed a broad selection of compact disc (CD) and digital compact cassette (DCC) products. The Company is currently employing its advanced technologies to develop next-generation HDTV, DVC, and DVD equipment.

Matsushita capitalized on its accumulated expertise in the AV, computer, and communications fields in fiscal 1994 to market the Panasonic REAL 3DO Interactive Multiplayer, a 32-bit home entertainment machine that has raised the curtain on the multimedia age, and a notebook-sized PC with built-in CD-ROM drive.

As Matsushita seeks new business opportunities, it will make full use of the extensive resources of the Matsushita Group worldwide. In line with its commitment to strengthening its multimedia technologies, the Company has designated software as a key business area to be cultivated and promoted.

Financial Highlights

Matsushita Electric Industrial Co., Ltd. and Subsidiaries
Years ended March 31, 1994 and 1993

	Millions of yen, except per share information		Millions of U.S. dollars, except per share information
	1994	1993	**1994**
Sales	**¥6,623,586**	¥7,055,868	**$64,307**
Percentage of previous year	**93.9%**	94.7%	**93.9%**
Income before income taxes	**¥ 128,223**	¥ 162,207	**$ 1,245**
Percentage of previous year	**79.0%**	45.4%	**79.0%**
Net income	**¥ 24,493**	¥ 37,295	**$ 238**
Percentage of previous year	**65.7%**	27.9%	**65.7%**
Per share of common stock:			
Net income	**¥ 11.67**	¥ 17.66	**$ 0.11**
Cash dividends	**13.50**	12.50	**0.13**
Per American Depositary Share, each representing 10 shares of common stock:			
Net income	**¥ 117**	¥ 177	**$ 1.14**
Cash dividends	**135**	125	**1.31**
Total assets (at end of period)	**¥8,192,632**	¥8,754,979	**$79,540**
Stockholders' equity (at end of period)	**3,288,945**	3,406,303	**31,932**
Capital investment	**¥ 266,522**	¥ 309,097	**$ 2,588**
R&D expenditures	**381,747**	401,817	**3,706**
Employees (at end of period)	**254,059**	252,075	**254,059**

Notes: 1. See note 1 (j) to the consolidated financial statements in respect of the calculation of net income per share amounts. Cash dividends per share are those declared with respect to the income for each fiscal period, and cash dividends charged to retained earnings are those actually paid.
2. U.S. dollar amounts are translated from yen at the rate of ¥103=U.S.$1, the approximate rate on the Tokyo Foreign Exchange Market on March 31, 1994.
3. Beginning with fiscal 1994, the Company adopted SFAS No. 109 (Accounting for Income Taxes), and accordingly, prior year figures have been restated to reflect this change.

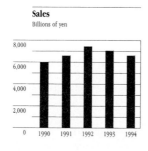

Sales
Billions of yen

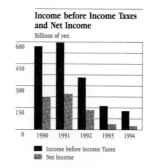

Income before Income Taxes and Net Income
Billions of yen

■ Income before Income Taxes
▨ Net Income

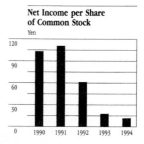

Net Income per Share of Common Stock
Yen

Matsushita at a Glance

Product Category	Percentage of Total Sales	Major Products
Video Equipment	20%	Videocassette recorders, video camcorders and related equipment, color TVs, TV/VCR combination units, projection TVs, liquid crystal display TVs, videodisc players, satellite broadcast receivers, satellite-communications-related equipment
Audio Equipment	8%	Radios, radio/cassette recorders, tape recorders, compact disc players, digital compact cassette players, stereo hi-fi and related equipment, car audio products, electronic musical instruments
Home Appliances	13%	Refrigerators, room air conditioners, home laundry equipment, dishwashers, vacuum cleaners, electric irons, microwave ovens, rice cookers, electric fans, electric and kerosene heaters, infrared-ray warmers, electric blankets, electrically heated rugs
Communication and Industrial Equipment	25%	Facsimile equipment, word processors, personal computers, copying machines, CRT displays, telephones, PBXs, CATV systems, measuring instruments, electronic-parts-mounting machines, industrial robots, welding machines, air-conditioning equipment, compressors, vending machines
Electronic Components	12%	Integrated circuits, discrete devices, charge coupled devices, cathode-ray tubes, image pickup tubes, tuners, capacitors, resistors, speakers, magnetic recording heads, electric motors, electric lamps
Batteries and Kitchen-Related Products	5%	Dry batteries, storage batteries, solar batteries, solar energy equipment, gas hot-water supply systems, gas cooking appliances, kitchen sinks, kitchen fixture systems, bath and sanitary equipment
Other	8%	Bicycles, cameras and flash units, electric pencil sharpeners, water purifiers, imported materials and products such as nonferrous metals, lumber, paper and medical equipment
Entertainment	9%	Filmed entertainment, music entertainment, theme parks, book publishing, gift merchandise, pre-recorded video and audio tapes and discs

APPENDIX 1
(concluded)

Coexistence with the Earth

Matsushita places great importance on environmental protection in its technological and product development activities. Coexistence with the earth and harmony with the natural concerns in the years ahead as the Company strives to adhere to its philosophy of contributing to society through its business activities.

In 1970, Matsushita established the Environmental Control Office, subsequently renamed the Environmental Protection Promotion Office. Since then, we have broadened our environmental protection efforts. In 1991, the Company published the Matsushita Environmental Control Policy, and we have subsequently set forth environmental rules and procedures to be followed at Matsushita Group sites worldwide.

In line with the tenets of the Matsushita Environmental Control Policy, the Company has devoted considerable efforts to developing technologies that are contributing to the fight against environmental deterioration.

In addition, Matsushita has garnered acclaim from all sectors for its revolutionary no-mercury-added alkaline batteries. Since 1990, the Company has manufactured and marketed these cells, which pose fewer disposal hazards than conventional batteries. Matsushita has also made this technology available to overseas battery manufacturers in the belief that the benefits of such technology should be shared.

Matsushita incorporates concern for the environment into all aspects of production, from product development to waste-conscious packaging practices. A particular focus has been the elimination of CFCs and other ozone-depleting substances from manufacturing processes. CFCs have traditionally been used for washing semiconductors and other electronic components, and Matsushita has devoted significant resources to develop production facilities that do not require CFCs. The Company's achievements have earned praise both in Japan and overseas. The United States Environmental Protection Agency selected Matsushita as a winner of the 1993 Stratospheric Ozone Protection Award in recognition of the Company's efforts to eliminate the use of CFCs.

Matsushita will step up efforts to apply new technologies to the development of products that are safe for the environment and people. By doing so, the Company aims to enhance its contribution to tomorrow's society.

Matsushita is manufacturing environmentally conscious products. All of the Company's domestically produced batteries are no-mercury-added cells. Matsushita's overseas subsidiaries are rapidly switching to this type of battery.

Operations in China

In line with its strategy to localize production in the markets where its products are used, Matsushita plans to conclude a formal contract with the government of the People's Republic of China to establish a joint venture to manufacture VCR mechanisms. Production facilities incorporating the newest technology are already in place. Matsushita is also localizing all aspects of its TV operations, from product planning and design to manufacturing and marketing, in selected major markets to enhance the autonomy of its overseas companies.

In September 1993, Matsushita established its first audio equipment production facility in China for mini-component systems, radios, radio/cassette recorders, and portable headphone players. Matsushita will enhance its local presence in the future by having this facility also function as a procurement and supply center for Chinese-manufactured components.

In China, operations progressed smoothly at a joint venture production plant for fully automatic washing machines established in April 1992. Matsushita continues to solidify its operating base in the promising Chinese market. At another joint venture, the Company began manufacturing electric steam irons for the local market in April 1994.

Matsushita is expanding offshore component and material production to bolster overseas procurement and to capitalize on the appreciation of the yen. Following on the success of Beijing Matsushita Color CRT Co., Ltd., Matsushita's first joint venture in China, the Company established two component production joint ventures during the year. One of these companies will manufacture electronic tuners, demodulators, and remote control units for TVs and VCRs, while the other will make feather-touch switches for consumer electronic products.

During the year, Matsushita established a joint venture in Shanghai to produce and market no-mercury-added manganese batteries, primarily for the Chinese market.

International Network: Mexico, China, Indonesia
(as of April 1, 1994)

Mexico   Panasonic de Mexico, S.A. de C.V.
Matsushita Electric de Mexico, S.A. de C.V.
Matsushita Industrial de Baja California, S.A.
Matsushita Electronic Components de Baja California
Kyushu Matsushita Electric de Baja California

China   Beijing-Matsushita Color CRT Co., Ltd.
Hangzhou KIN MATSU Washing Machine Co., Ltd.
Beijing Matsushita Communication Equipment Co., Ltd.
Matsushita-Wanbao (Guangzhou) Electric Iron Co.
Matsushita-Wanbao (Guangzhou) Air-Conditioner Co.
Matsushita-Wanbao (Guangzhou) Compressor Co.
Shunde Matsushita Seiko Co., Ltd.
Beijing Matsushita Electronic Components Co., Ltd.
Shanghai Matsushita Battery Co., Ltd.
Qingdao Matsushita Electronic Components Co., Ltd.
Zhuhai Matsushita Electric Motor Co., Ltd.
Matsushita Audio (Xiamen) Co., Ltd.

Indonesia   P.T. National Gobel
P.T. Matsushita Gobel Battery Industry
P.T. Kotobuki Electronics Indonesia
P.T. Asia Matsushita Battery
P.T. Panasonic Gobel Electronic Components
P.T. National Panasonic Gobel
P.T. MET & Gobel

EXHIBIT 2
China and Indonesia: Regimes for Foreign Direct Investment
by Transnational Manufacturers

The fall of the dollar against the yen has left many Asian Countries wondering if American influence in the region will wane despite President Clinton's moves to shape APEC (Asia Pacific Economic Cooperation forum) into a more powerful regional body . . . Moreover, some Asian countries have seen Mexico as a cautionary tale that free trade, deregulation and economic reform can move too fast, and the result can be a loss of economic control. Their preferred model is Japan, which in the last 40 years has used control over foreign investment as a key element of its effort to protect fledgling industries . . . In their joint declaration, the finance ministers said they would attempt to steer clear of reliance on short-term investments that, as Mexico showed, can leave the country as quickly as they enter. Instead, they said they would seek "flows that generate real economic returns and hence are less susceptible to sudden reversal." That chiefly means direct investment in factories and other facilities that are difficult to uproot if investors get nervous. Indonesia, China and several other large Asian nations have been focused on direct investment for years, and thus are considered less susceptible to what Mr. Rubin [U.S. Treasury secretary] called a Mexico "contagion."*

China

With one-quarter of the world's population and very rapid economic growth in recent years, China is a hugely attractive market. However, key problems in dealing with China include economic inefficiencies, regional inequalities, and environmental degradation. Doing business in China requires dealing with Chinese officials who must deal with multiple bosses, some of whom they obey and some they ignore. Although there is an elaborate Chinese Government, officials follow personalistic norms of behavior and there is widespread corruption. The central authorities issue decrees in the authoritarian imperial tradition, but local officials are often petty dictators who are essentially free to take care of their local interests.

China is seeking to join the World Trade Organization (the successor to the General Agreement on Tariffs and Trade or GATT), but U.S. willingness to support China's entry hinges on improving access to the Chinese market. The issue of human rights has also been raised repeatedly by the U.S.; for example, U.S. Customs agents want to inspect Chinese prisons and "re-education camps."

High-technology product development is a priority in attracting foreign direct investment. Japanese investment tends to be concentrated on East and Northeast China in the form of light industrial production of consumer electronics, although larger scale projects such as cement production and significantly more production of cars and motorcycles are expected. As in other countries taken over by Japan during World War II, there are resentments and unresolved issues which strongly affect bilateral relations with Japan. Poor infrastructure and uncertainty regarding the medium-term political future are expected to moderate foreign investment somewhat. Wage levels for entry-level workers are as low as $50 per month.

(See Exhibit 3, "China's Trade and Investment Environment.")

Indonesia

With over 185 million people, Indonesia has the fifth largest population in the world. As a matter of policy, Indonesia seeks export-oriented, labor-intensive, large-scale investments. Investment incentives include concessions on import duties and value-added tax for equipment and raw materials. The largest government-owned industrial estate is located on Batam Island, 12 miles from Singapore, where foreigners are permitted to invest without a local Indonesian partner if 100% of production is exported. Monthly salaries for unskilled workers can be as low as $50 per month, but investors need to provide training.

The Foreign Investment Law of 1967 opened Indonesia to capital, technology, and management expertise of foreign firms. The President, Major General Suharto, was elected in 1968, following an attempted leftist coup in 1965, and he reversed the anti-foreign policies of his predecessor, Sukarno. However, there are sharp ethnic divisions: ethnic Chinese control Indonesia's economic resources, while indigenous "pribumi" dominate the government. Industrial growth inevitably strengthens the Chinese business sector, contrary to the national goal of redistributing Chinese wealth to other ethnic groups. The 1974 Matari riots were a protest against the domination of both Japanese and Chinese capital. Strengthened by increased oil revenues, Indonesia shifted to a more restrictive foreign direct investment regime in the mid-1970s.

Declining oil revenues and budget deficits since 1982, along with reduced investment flows, led to a moderate loosening. Suharto's latest 5-year plan emphasizes private sector industrial development, and there have been substantial reductions in tariffs and non-tariff barriers. However, large state-owned companies linked to the politico-military regime are resisting reforms. The Indonesian Capital Investment Coordinating Board (BKPM) and the Department of Industry work closely with the Chamber of Commerce and Industry (KADIN).

(See Exhibit 4, "Indonesia's Trade and Investment Environment.")

Japan replaced Western Europe and the U.S. as the leading source of imports, and Japan continues to be the most important market for exports. Indonesia has been the leading site for Japanese investment in East Asia in recent decades. In 1994 alone, Japanese investments in Indonesian assembly lines totaled $1.56 billion, and the U.S. lists Indonesia as one of the 10 "big emerging markets" of the world. However, the surge of Japanese investment is overwhelming Indonesia's infrastructure for electrical power generation and distribution, communications, transportation, and waste management.

---

*Excerpt from "Asians Agree on Disclosure to Halt Crises: Consider Ways to Avoid Mexico-Type Troubles" by David Sanger, *New York Times*, April 17, 1995, p. C1.

EXHIBIT 3
China's Trade and Investment Environment

General

State role in the economy:

Since 1978, China has been introducing market forces in its centrally planned economy. The current 5-year plan (1991–95) continues to emphasize the primacy of state ownership, but promotes reforms toward the Communist Party's stated goal to achieve a "socialist market economy." Instead of the large-scale privatizations in many other nations, an important approach in China is granting greater autonomy in decision making to state-owned enterprises.

The two principal areas of past liberalization efforts are (1) agriculture and (2) foreign trade. China now has a market economy in food as a result of free prices and the replacement of farming communities by family farms. Results have been excellent: in 1992, China was expected to see its 4th straight bumper harvest. With the removal of the central Government's monopoly over foreign trade, and the establishment of 4 "special zones," China benefits from export-led growth. Also, Chinese industry is reducing the dominance of the state. In 1978, state-owned firms accounted for 78 percent of the total; the current comparable share is somewhat above 50 percent.

Exchange rate policy:

China administers a managed, floating official exchange rate linked to a trade-weighted basket of currencies. China also established free adjustment centers (so-called swap centers) in 1986 to accommodate parallel market rates. The Government is apparently following a strategy of incremental devaluations of their currency to eventually unify the official rate and the free market rate.

Intellectual property rights (IPR):

China made some progress in recent years in enacting IPR legislation. Nonetheless, the United States instituted a special Section 301 investigation on China in May 1991 for failing to provide adequate IPR protection. The investigation was resolved in January 1992, when the United States and China reached an agreement and signed a Memorandum of Understanding (MOU) on IPR. In the MOU China pledged to upgrade its IPR regime by amending its patent law, joining the Berne convention, and enacting trade secret legislation.

Foreign Trade

GATT membership:

China's application for GATT membership is under active consideration. Under an October 1992 U.S.-China MOU, China is committed to significantly reducing its multilayered web of import restrictions between 1993 and 1997. The accord was prompted by a huge U.S. trade deficit vis-à-vis China.

Transparency:

Under the MOU with the United States, and in accordance with the GATT, China is committed to making its trade regime transparent by publishing its heretofore unavailable decrees, rules, and regulations, and halting the use of internal directives on foreign trade.

Tariffs:

China adopted the harmonized system for customs classification and statistics, effective January 1, 1992, while at the same time reducing duties on 225 items. In April 1992, China eliminated its import taxes. On January 1, 1993, China's most ambitious tariff cuts to date became effective. The cuts, while generally moderate, covered 3,371 items, over half of the goods in China's tariff schedule.

Import restrictions:

China's import licensing system covers 53 broad categories of goods or about half of China's imports by value. Some 75 percent of all import licensing requirements, quotas, and other restrictions will be eliminated by the end of 1994 under the MOU with the United States. In addition to a variety of U.S. industrial exports, import controls on key U.S. agricultural exports, including wheat, other grains, edible oils, and fruits will be eliminated. China also agreed to discontinue those standards and testing requirements that serve mainly as trade barriers, i.e., those that do not apply to comparable domestic products.

EXHIBIT 3
(concluded)

Foreign Trade

Export subsidies:

China abolished direct subsidies for exports on January 1, 1991. However, manufactured exports receive many forms of indirect subsidies, including guaranteed provision of energy and raw materials, preferential financing, tax rebates, and duty exemptions on imported inputs. China's swap markets allow exporters to exchange foreign exchange at better than official rates.

Foreign investment

General Policy:

China now stresses the role of foreign investment in promoting structural reforms for the economy. China is reportedly considering measures to attract multinational corporations into the infrastructure, new material production, and high-technology product development. In 1991, the United States ranked second in China's overall foreign direct investment, behind Hong Kong.

Presently, China does not provide national treatment to foreign investors who are under strong pressure to export, locate in specified areas, and use domestic versus imported components. Foreign investors may repatriate profits, as long as they have the foreign exchange to cover the funds to be remitted. Some foreign investors have been permitted to set up their own marketing or service organizations, but most must rely on Chinese state-owned operations.

Services:

China generally does not allow foreign firms in the service sector, including banking, insurance, construction, accounting, and legal services. U.S. lawyers and accountants must largely limit their activities to servicing foreign firms. Recently, however, China began allowing some foreign investors, on an experimental basis, to establish joint ventures in accounting, insurance, and legal services.

Source: Office of the United States Trade Representative (USTR), *1993 National Trade Estimate Report on Foreign Trade Barriers,* 1993.

EXHIBIT 4
Indonesia's Trade and Investment Environment

General

State role in the economy:

The Government controls the oil industry through Partamina, the state-run oil and gas company. State enterprises hold dominant positions in oil refining, petrochemicals, fertilizers, steel, aluminum, cement, basic chemicals, capital-goods manufacturing, and ship-building. In most other industries, the Government generally refrains from direct intervention, but has established floor and ceiling prices for certain food items (e.g., rice) and has prohibited exports of goods in short supply.

Exchange rate policy:

Indonesia does not use any foreign exchange restrictions.

Intellectual property rights (IPR):

Though its IPR laws are improving, Indonesia remains on the USTR's Special 301 "watch list" under the provisions of the 1988 Omnibus Trade and Competitiveness Act. An improved trademark law was passed in August 1992 and is expected to provide a legal basis for protection of service and collective marks by April 1, 1993. Indonesia's first patent law came into effect in August 1991. Concerns about the new law remain, including a relatively short term of protection (14 to 16 years), and noncoverage of specific products, such as food and drink products and processes, biotechnology, and integrated circuits.

Foreign Trade

Tariffs:

Tariffs range from 0 percent (raw materials) to 200 percent (sedans and station wagons). Indonesia also imposes 5 to 35 percent surcharges on 255 items (including food, steel, chemical, and pharmaceutical items).

Quotas and licenses

Strict quotas restrict the importation of certain fruits and vegetables, meats, confectionery items, and alcoholic beverages. Licensing requirements remain for some agricultural commodities, alcoholic beverages, and iron and steel products.

Distribution:

While wholesale distribution is permitted by joint ventures, retail distribution is closed to foreign investors. Furthermore, in several industries, foreign companies are allowed to choose only a single agent to cover the entire country.

Government procurement:

International competitive bidding practices are followed for most large projects. However, bidding firms are often required to offer concessional financing. Foreign bidders may also be required to purchase and export Indonesian goods equivalent to the contract amount. Government procurement regulations favor locally produced goods and services by a price margin of 15 percent.

Foreign Investment

Foreign ownership:

A May 1992 Investment Regulation permits 100 percent foreign equity in three types of new investments: (1) projects worth at least $50 million; (2) projects located in one of Indonesia's 14 less developed provinces, with divestiture to a maximum of 80 percent of foreign ownership within 20 years; and (3) projects in bonded zones that will export 100 percent of production, but must be divested to 95 percent within 5 years. For other industries, foreign investment is limited to joint ventures, usually with a minimum foreign investment of $1 million and a maximum foreign state of 80 percent to be divested over 20 years to no more than 49 percent ownership. Foreigners are not allowed to own land. The Capital Investment Coordinating Board is responsible for approving all investment in Indonesia. Its chairman has announced plans to reduce the number of sectors closed to foreign investment.

Repatriation of profits:

Indonesia has a long-standing policy of free repatriation of profits, royalties, fees, loan principal and interest, and costs associated with expatriate workers.

Service barriers:

Service trade barriers exist in most sectors. Indonesia has begun to loosen restrictions in the financial sector, allowing foreign banks security firms, and insurance companies to form joint ventures with local firms. However, these joint ventures are subjected to much higher capitalization requirements than domestic firms. Indonesia strictly limits the practice of foreign lawyers, accountants, advertisers, and express delivery firms. A quota limits the number of foreign firms that can be distributed within Indonesia. In addition, firms can be imported only by a restricted number of local firms. However, a Government decree that will increase the number of companies permitted to import U.S. films and videos is expected to be implemented in early 1993.

Source: Office of the United States Trade Representative (USTR), *1993 National Trade Estimate Report on Foreign Trade Barriers*, 1993.

CASE 23

MATSUSHITA INDUSTRIAL DE BAJA CALIFORNIA (B)

1 Matsushita Industrial de Baja California (MIBA) established in Tijuana, Baja California, Mexico, in 1979 to assemble televisions. The parent company had a commitment to local (Mexican) production and local (U.S.) product development. MIBA had approximately 3,000 Mexican workers in Tijuana in 1994, and about 150 support staff in San Diego, California. Initially there were about 40 Japanese staff working at MIBA, but the number declined steadily. The Company announced additions of 200 more workers to make automobile audio equipment and 140 more to make rechargeable batteries in Tijuana, plus 140 U.S. engineers moving to San Diego from Illinois. Sanyo, Sony, Samsung, Goldstar, Daewoo, JVC, and Hitachi were also established or had announced plans to make TVs in Tijuana and Mexicali.

MATSUSHITA ACCORDING TO THE NEW HIRE

2 A newly hired U.S. manager described Matsushita as "a very vertical organization structure, like the military, and very large, also like the military." (This person had recently retired from the U.S. Navy—San Diego was a very important naval port; he preferred to remain anonymous.) He explained that Matsushita has sales of $65 billion in 133 countries, and sales of "only" $6 billion in North America. He was given a copy of Matsushita's *Velvet Glove, Iron Fist,* which makes many references to the military and political history of Japan and China, and to John Kennedy, former President of the U.S., as the basis for most of its 102 anecdotes. One of the themes is the need for a leader to be both lenient and severe (hence its title). The new hire said that he had been distributing and later testing people on excerpts from this book at staff meetings during his first few weeks on the job.

3 The new hire described the corporate culture of Matsushita in terms of loyalty and globalization. "They have tendencies to operate with much localization, pay relatively poorly, and offer good training opportunities. There are some terminations during the first probationary year, and I do not feel that I have lifetime employment like my Japanese colleagues." There is intense competition between Japanese companies in the same industry, between different divisions within Japanese companies, and among individual rivals for promotion. "The pyramid is growing and there are lots of promotion opportunities for the typical Japanese university graduates who enter Matsushita at age 25," said the U.S. national. "They are typically rotated to MIBA for 3–5 years; there is also an older group of Japanese, and the U.S. employees. The Japanese have tremendous bargaining power with their suppliers, and they are asked to come to Mexico too."

4 His socialization into Matsushita included reading about the Company, and he shared some of the materials with the casewriter. A brochure explained that the U.S. has Matsushita's largest overseas subsidiary, with 1,200 suppliers in North America. The Company's social responsibility was shown by the 0.1% of North American sales allocated to such areas as university relations. Matsushita endowed chairs of management studies at Stanford and Harvard, engineering at MIT, manufacturing and logistics at Wharton, and cross-cultural research at Pacific University. The San Diego branch of the company paid $11,000 for a scoreboard in the Mexican gym used for Olympic training, and has a $30,000 budget for such contributions to the local community.

This case was prepared by Stephen Jenner of California State University, Dominguez Hills.

5   According to the brochure, Matsushita's policy is to have relatively autonomous management, and, when possible, competition between groups within the Company. Matsushita initiated North American production in 1965 in Puerto Rico, and its 19 plants' capacity doubled during the period 1986–91. Matsushita had joint ventures with Kodak, Whirlpool, Tandy, and Solbourne Computers. MIBA was established in Tijuana in 1979, and Kyushu Matsushita Electric Corporation of America was established in Tijuana in 1989 for the manufacture of deflection yokes for TVs. The parent company had a commitment to local production and product development.

6   The new hire also learned the Matsushita story in Japan through a videotape shown on a Panasonic combination TV/VCR. Konosuke Matsushita (Matsushita means "under pine tree") was born into a wealthy family that lost everything speculating on rice. After several of his siblings died, Konosuke became an apprentice at age 9 in a small company which imported bicycles. He was impressed with how expensive the bikes were. Seven years later he joined the Osaka Electric Light Company, and became their youngest inspector at age 22. He suffered with tuberculosis, and his design for a new light socket was rejected. In 1918 at the age of 23, he founded Matsushita on the basic business principles of harmony and industrial development intended to help people. He was profoundly impressed with his visits to a religious shrine in Nara, particularly with the followers' awareness of their mission in life, saving people.

THE COMPANY'S MISSION AND STRATEGY

7   Konosuke Matsushita's industrial mission was to eliminate poverty and improve the lives of people. His vision was to make material wealth available in limitless abundance, like drinking water. Matsushita considered the entire world's population to be his potential customers. On May 5, 1932, he announced a 250-year plan to achieve his vision. The roadmap to the year 2182 consisted of 10 stages of 25 years each, the length of an employee's service. "Unite together in tight solidarity. Work like the President of your own company. Develop yourself. Management is carried out by all employees," according to Matsushita's philosophy.

8   All around the world, Matsushita employees assembled before work in the morning and chanted the Company's 7 objectives. Overseas factories should benefit the host country, and only the Japanese who are really needed must go abroad, said Matsushita.

GETTING ALONG WITH THE JAPANESE IN MEXICO

9   According to Yasuo Sasaki, a Brazilian of Japanese ancestry who was deeply involved in Sanyo's move to Tijuana, there was always cultural conflict. "Relations between Mexicans and Japanese are always a war, although they are closer psychologically than the Mexicans and the Americans. The Mexicans working for Japanese companies first fight with the Americans, until they recognize that the Japanese have the power." U.S. businesspeople tend to be specialists with separate functional area responsibilities, so when they come to work in a maquiladora, "they stay out of the production line and go home at 5 PM; they offer the Mexicans no explanations, no 'why.' They just say 'it's your responsibility, not my area,' " explained Sasaki.

10   In contrast, the Japanese are there at the maquiladora in their company uniform 12 hours every day. The Mexicans perceive that the Japanese are there to work, that the Japanese are less vocal and critical than U.S. managers, and more curious about the production line. They like people to "help each other," and share responsibility, and they are responsive generalists with detailed knowledge of all aspects of company operations. For the Japanese, Mexican workers are easier to understand than workers in the U.S. Midwest. "Mexicans are more emotional and less willing to change; to people in the U.S., personal relationships with your boss and coworkers are most important," said Sasaki.

11   Ideally, the Japanese company would like to create a replica of a Japanese plant, and solve problems by referring to the experience of other Japanese maquiladoras. Initially there were 40 Japanese staff working at MIBA, but the number declined steadily.

12   War stories of Japanese maquiladoras are legend in Tijuana, and they reveal much about the kind of cultural adaptations necessary for effective labor-management relations. In some cases Mexican workers have been known to refuse to keep the factory bathrooms clean, to steal the toilet paper and destroy property and write graffiti on the walls, and to generally spend too much time there instead of working.

13   The traditional Japanese managers' response was to autocratically give orders, and when that didn't work (and it usually didn't) they resorted to attempting to use Japanese-style influence mechanisms such as trying to make people feel ashamed for their behavior. For example, they might call together all the Mexican workers on the factory floor and shout at them telling them that their behavior was wrong. This might be followed by posting a guard in each of the bathrooms, and keeping time records of employee visits.

14   A more successful approach involved explaining to the Mexican workers that it was impossible to make high quality products when the bathrooms were a mess because it sent a negative message to everyone who visited there, threatening the survival of their jobs and even the firm. The Japanese manager then asked the employees to develop their own suggestions for solving the problem, and initiated a contest between employee groups. The best worker suggestions were voted upon and implemented by the workers themselves.

DIFFERENCES IN SOCIAL VALUES, EDUCATION, AND ON-THE-JOB TRAINING

15   When asked what he would say to students attending a U.S. business school, Mitsuhara Nakata, Sub-Director Administrativo, offered a contrast between Japan and the U.S. (Nakata crossed daily from San Diego to Tijuana to the offices of Matsushita Industrial de Baja California [MIBA].) "In Japan, it is the engineer and the technician working in manufacturing who is most respected. In the U.S., people respect lawyers and doctors, and engineers don't want to get their hands dirty or get into the details. We believe that engineers must see their design in process and find the cause of problems on the production line. We say 'the facts remain on the floor, not on papers' and 'the product comes from the floor.' " Nakata also characterized the Japanese educational system as seeking to create a high level group by bringing up people who don't understand. "Students who are doing well can grow by themselves," he explained, "Thomas Edison would have gotten no help in a Japanese school."

16   These differences carry over into training at Matsushita. The traditional apprenticeship approach to on-the-job training is to emphasize self-study and self-development in the process of looking for a better way. "Giving the worker information about the product and asking him to figure out the best way to make it is very typical in Japan," said Nakata. "We also believe that workers should understand all manufacturing operations, including how each component works, and the consequence of making a mistake for the next step in the production process, and for the company's reputation." However, he estimated that MIBA only used about 50% of the Japanese way of training, especially the use of problems or mistakes on the job as "visually strong" opportunities for learning. Training for simple, entry level jobs in the maquiladora lasts 3 days, and is more detailed than in Japan, with more guidance and examples.

THE OPERATIONAL CHALLENGES OF TIJUANA

17   Asked about the high rate of employee turnover, in the range of 7–9% per month for MIBA, Nakata replied that "turnover is not a big problem—in some ways it's good." He went on to explain that people in the key positions remain, while very young people (mostly women in their late teens) are often in their first job after moving to Tijuana from the south of Mexico. "Naturally they want to see 2 or 3 other companies; if they return, they will remain," said Nakata.

18   In working with Mexican managers responsible for Personnel, Accounting, and Materials Control, Nakata talked about the need to listen to their problems and offer guidance. "I spend about one hour per day for the first year to develop understanding, which leads to my winning the confidence and trust of the Mexican manager."

19   One of the biggest problems for the Mexicans was the frustration caused by Japanese managers rotating to another assignment every 5 years. "What can they do, either start again to develop a relationship, or leave. There should be several Japanese who can tell the stories and explain," said Nakata. But only Nakata has stayed at MIBA through the years, and he makes a point of having breakfast or lunch with his Mexican colleagues on a regular basis. "In the evenings we go home to our families," he noted.

APPENDIX 1
Maquiladora Employee Turnover in Tijuana, Baja California, Mexico

Cost of Turnover

There are three published estimates of the cost of turnover: $162, $259, and $400 per person. One study of a Tijuana maquiladora identified several components including time and cost for new workers to get down the learning curve ($300), supervision ($26), administration recruiting ($30), and a total cost of $400 per turnover. Another study in Ciudad Juarez estimated turnover cost at $162, including attaining job proficiency ($130) and training ($14). More recent reports estimate the cost of employee turnover in Ciudad Juarez maquiladoras to be around $259 (1990). Payroll-related turnover costs alone accounted for $52 per month, according to a Tijuana maquiladora association estimate.

The results of a review of the literature can be used to classify causes of maquiladora turnover as follows:

HYPOTHESIZED CAUSES OF TURNOVER IN TIJUANA MAQUILADORAS

External causes (outside the control of management given location):

Labor supply: Characteristics of workforce and workers' situation.
  Age: Workers are more likely to stay if over age 22–25.
  Gender: women more likely to stay.
  Education: 6 years or less schooling more likely to stay.
  Family responsibilities: Workers are more likely to stay if no family in Mexican interior or U.S.; women single with no children or one child; no family problems distracting worker; adequate income.
  Years in city: Longer term more stable.
  Housing adequacy and affordable cost.
  Transportation to and from the plant available at low cost.
Low labor demand: Local economic activity and market conditions.
Seasonality: High turnover at Christmas and summertime.
Mexican labor law and taxation encourage turnover.

Internal Causes (within control of management):

Characteristics of the firm with lower turnover:
  Production technology: Less monotony of work; good job design.
  Perceived security of employment.
  Decentralization of decision making authority to plant level.
  Frequent communication and participation with plant management.
  Opportunities for upward mobility for Mexicans at all levels.
Supervision: Considerate and not authoritarian, Mexican Mother.
Employee characteristics: Longer tenure; expectations consistent.
Human resource management: Careful selection and training; good performance rewarded; job satisfaction and commitment.

"Maquiladora Employee Turnover in Tijuana, Baja California, Mexico," an unpublished preliminary report, co-authored by Stephen Jenner, California State University, Dominguez Hills, and Marco Polo, Universidad de las Americas, Mexico City, 1994.

APPENDIX 2
U.S. and Japanese Managers Working Together in California Banks

In a study of California banks in Los Angeles, San Francisco, and San Diego, U.S. managers working for Japanese supervisors offered comments and suggestions such as the following:

Most Japanese managers treat their employees as an object or a machine. It's not because they feel that we are any bit less human than they are, but because of a communication barrier. They have a hard time expressing themselves so they just keep to themselves.

Many Japanese managers do not understand the cultural differences and cast people off as "difficult" when they do not perceive the Japanese manager's wants, needs, and desires.

Show strong interest in things Japanese, whether honestly held or not. Be an expert in fields they don't understand; this gets respect. In the long run, prepare yourself for a lifetime of never really knowing what management is thinking.

Use upward communication—in writing. Give clear explanations of what is being proposed—always define costs and benefits. Have patience—be prepared to explain until the point is clearly understood. This can take many repetitions. Patience, patience, patience; communication, communication, communication, with emphasis on written.

Understand that decision-making often takes much longer, that change is not readily accepted in the system, and that Japanese managers wish to avoid confrontation, and that they stress cooperation and communication.

There were also frequent complaints about having a Japanese counterpart for each local officer to report to, about the norm of rotating Japanese managers every 3–5 years, and about private meetings relating to important decisions conducted only in Japanese.

On the Japanese side, the following comments were typical:

Local employees must understand that this is probably the first time their managers have ever been outside Japan. These managers are under pressure from not only the upper management of the local subsidiary but also the parent corporation in Japan. Employees should try to make their Japanese managers feel a little bit more comfortable with their new surroundings. In this manner, the managers may feel less tension and stress and will not be so high strung. Employees should also learn a little about the Company they work for so they may understand the operations of the business itself. With some background knowledge, the employee might better appreciate the organization they are working for and try to do a better job.

There is a great deal of underlying loyalty and respect for authority and organizational success among the Japanese. It is felt that in Japan, you do not question authority. There is a great deal of pressure to succeed individually and cooperatively within the organization, for failure is very shameful. It tends to be like a "family" environment, and those adjusting and fitting in tend to be well-liked, understood, and successful.

An American must understand that if he is extremely ambitious to rise to the top, he should consider working elsewhere. It is very difficult for an American to fail in our Japanese organization, and yet it's not too likely any will succeed.

Stephen Jenner, J. Beatty, and A. Omens, "U.S. and Japanese Managers Working Together in California Banks," unpublished preliminary report, San Diego State University, Fall 1984.

CASE 24

GRAND METROPOLITAN PLC

1   Grand Metropolitan PLC is the world's largest wine and spirits seller, and the only one analysts expect will show volume gains this year. Its Burger King hamburger chain, the world's second biggest, has just completed a turnaround. So why is the price of GrandMet shares in New York, compared with its earnings, 10% below the average price/earnings ratio of the companies in the Standard & Poor's 500 index? And more important, why have rumors surfaced that GrandMet, valued at more than $14 billion in the stock market, may be a takeover target?[1]

2   It is our goal to build on GrandMet's strengths and continue to create sustainable competitive advantage in our businesses, which is the bedrock of shareholder value and wealth.[2]

3   By April 1992, senior managers of Grand Metropolitan PLC could look back on a flurry of financial activity. GrandMet had just acquired Cinzano, the Italian vermouth and wines company, for £100 million. In the United States, GrandMet was negotiating a joint venture in which it would receive £39.5 million in exchange for the U.S. flour-milling business it had acquired when it bought Pillsbury in 1989. In 1991, the group sold off about £800 million in businesses in its effort to focus on core activities, food, drink, retailing.

4   In spite of the world recession, Grand Metropolitan beat market forecasts in 1991 with a 4.8 percent increase in pretax profits, which brought the group to a record £963 million. This success was accomplished in what Chairman Sir Allen Sheppard believed was "one of the toughest years in Grand Metropolitan's history." Sheppard emphasized that the positive results demonstrated the validity of GrandMet's strategic intent to focus on its core businesses. While conceding that "1992 will be another tough year," he reiterated the company's goal "to constantly improve on rather than match previous achievements." The 1991 annual report carried the slogan "adding value" imprinted under the company name. Achieving the goal, however, might mean selling off some of the group's poorly performing businesses, such as Pearle Vision. Furthermore, in the previous year, rumors had circulated that GrandMet might be a takeover target.

THE COMPANY

5   With a total 1991 turnover (sales) of £8.75 billion, Grand Metropolitan ranked among Britain's 10 largest companies. It currently acted as a pure holding company for a group of business units that were widely diversified both geographically and in terms of products. Exhibit 1 presents a summary and description of GrandMet's three major operating sectors: foods (30 percent of 1991 trading profit), drinks (46 percent), and retailing (24 percent). The brands it owned and managed ranked among the best known worldwide: Green Giant, Haagen-Dazs, Alpo, and Pillsbury in foods; Smirnoff, Bailey's, J&B, and Cinzano in drinks; Burger King and Pearle Vision in retailing.

This case was prepared by Philippe Demigne, Jean-Christophe Donck, Bertrand George, and Michael Levy under the supervision of Professor Robert F. Bruner. It is intended to be used as a basis for class discussion rather than to illustrate either effective or ineffective handling of an administrative situation. The financial support of the Citicorp Global Scholars Program is gratefully acknowledged. Reprinted with the permission of INSEAD-DARDEN. Copyright © 1992 INSEAD-DARDEN, Fontainebleau, France-Charlottesville, USA. Revised 1993.

[1] Peter Waldman, "Sir Allen Cools the Pace at Grand Met," *European Wall Street Journal,* October 8, 1991.

[2] Grand Metropolitan PLC, "1990 Annual Report to Shareholders."

EXHIBIT 1
Grand Metropolitan PLC's Operating Sectors

Food [Trading profit £300 million (30%)]	Drinks [Trading profit £454 million (46%)]	Retailing [Trading profit £236 million (24%)]	Property Interests
Pillsbury Brands (US) Baked goods (biscuits, sweet foods, pizzas); fresh, frozen, and canned vegetables; milled flour and processed food. Brands included Pillsbury, Janos, Green Giant, Totino's.	**International Distillers and Vintners (worldwide)** Production and distribution of wines and spirits. Owned brands included Smirnoff vodka, J&B Rare Scotch whisky, Bailey's Irish Cream liqueur, Malibu liqueur, Croft Original sherry, La Plat d'Or wines, Metaxa Greek brandy, Popov vodka, Gilbey's gin, Bombay Dry gin, Cinzano vermouth, Ouzo 12, Inglenook, Almaden, and Beaulieu California wines.	**Grand Metropolitan Retailing (UK)** Management and operation of one small restaurant chain, Old Orleans, and around 1,540 managed pubs, both unbranded and under the Chef & Brewer, Clifton Inns, and Country Carvery brand names.	**Grand Metropolitan Estates (UK)** Property management and development.
Pillsbury Food Group (Europe) Prepared meals; baked goods (cookies, cakes, gateaux, pies, savoury pastries); savoury products (meat pies, sausages, burgers and buns). Brands included Erasco, Jokish, Peter's, Hofmann Menu, Fleur de Lys, Memory Lane, Kaysens, Brossard, Goldstein, Jus-rol, Bélin Surgelés, Vinchon Jeanette.	Agency brands included Grand Marnier liqueur, Cointreau, Jose Cuervo Tequila, Absolut vodka, Jack Daniel's bourbon.	**Pearle, Inc. (US, Europe, Far East)** Retailing of eye-care products/services with over 1,100 stores. Brands included Pearle Vision.	**Inntrepreneur Estates (UK)** 50% joint venture with Courage responsible for licensed estate of 7,350 tenanted pubs.
Haagen-Dazs (US, Europe, Far East) Premium ice cream.	Note: This division also previously included Grand Metropolitan Brewing, with owned and licensed beer brands including Webster's, Watney, Foster's, Carlsberg, Budweiser, Holsten. This segment was sold to Courage in February 1991 as part of a pubs-for-breweries swap transaction (Inntrepreneur Estates).	**Burger King (worldwide)** Chain of 6,400 franchised hamburger restaurants in 41 countries.	
Alpo Pet Food (US) Cat and dog food. Brands included Alpo, Jim Dandy, Blue Mountain.			
GrandMet Foodservice (US) Food goods for bakery and catering sectors.			

Source: Annual reports of Grand Metropolitan PLC.

EXHIBIT 2
Distribution of Turnover, Profits, and Assets by Segment and Region
(in £millions except where noted)

	Absolute Performance					As a percentage of Totals				
	1991	1990	1989	1988	1987	1991	1990	1989	1988	1987
Drinks										
Turnover	2,425	3,000	2,784	2,581	2,178	32%	33%	36%	47%	46%
Operating profit	454	473	389	316	257	46	45	45	55	53
Net assets	1,536	1,623	1,626	1,479	1,504	26	26	26	40	49
Operating margin	18.7%	15.8%	14.0%	12.2%	11.8%					
RONA*	**19.2%**	**18.9%**	**15.6%**	**13.9%**	**11.1%**					
Food										
Turnover	3,026	3,506	2,872	1,253	1,047	40	39	37	23	22
Operating profit	300	309	245	84	69	30	29	28	15	14
Net assets	1,997	1,763	2,468	310	260	34	29	39	8	9
Operating margin	9.9%	8.8%	8.5%	6.7%	6.6%					
RONA	**9.8%**	**11.4%**	**6.5%**	**17.6%**	**17.3%**					
Retailing										
Turnover	2,051	2,531	2,040	1,671	1,467	27	28	27	30	31
Operating profit	236	278	230	179	160	24	26	27	31	33
Net assets	2,332	2,785	2,266	1,898	1,290	40	45	36	51	42
Operating margin	11.5%	11.0%	11.3%	10.7%	10.9%					
RONA	**6.6%**	**6.5%**	**6.6%**	**6.1%**	**8.1%**					
U.K. and Ireland										
Turnover	2,940	3,685	4,688	3,836	3,559	34	39	50	64	62
Operating profit	385	451	424	364	331	36	42	44	56	58
Net assets	1,816	2,500	2,626	2,700	1,945	30	40	41	64	62
Continental Europe										
Turnover	862	661	471	221	214	10	7	5	4	4
Operating profit	104	81	66	46	36	10	7	7	7	6
Net assets	557	427	330	384	335	9	7	5	9	11
United States										
Turnover	4,433	4,537	3,720	1,758	1,720	51	48	40	29	30
Operating profit	517	475	395	218	185	48	44	41	33	32
Net assets	3,466	3,149	3,314	1,034	759	57	50	51	25	24
Rest of America										
Turnover	216	216	174	54	58	2	2	2	1	1
Operating profit	20	21	20	14	13	2	2	2	2	2
Net assets	128	148	145	50	61	2	2	2	1	2
Rest of World										
Turnover	2979	295	265	160	155	3	3	3	3	3
Operating profit	45	54	62	12	6	4	5	6	2	1
Net assets	86	91	68	22	24	1	1	1	1	1

*Return on net assets (RONA) is computed as EBIAT (earnings before interest and after taxes) divided by net assets (total assets less current liabilities). A benchmark against which to compare RONA is the weighted-average cost of capital.
Source: Annual reports of Grand Metropolitan PLC.

Geographically, 51 percent of GrandMet's 1991 turnover was generated in the United States, 34 percent came from the United Kingdom, and 10 percent from continental Europe.

6   Exhibit 2 gives GrandMet's historical financial performance broken down by operating sector and by geographical region. Exhibit 3 summarizes the group's consolidated balance sheets and income statements for the past five years.

7   GrandMet was founded in the late 1940s as the Washington Group, a chain of hotels established by Sir Maxwell Joseph. With the acquisition of the Mount Royal Hotel in 1957, the company changed its name to Mount Royal Ltd. to reflect the fact that, with 712 rooms, this new acquisition

EXHIBIT 3
Historical Financial Statements
(in £millions)

	1991	1990	1989	1988	1987
Balance Sheet					
Total assets	9,187	9,420	9,570	5,846	4,577
Fixed assets:					
Intangible assets	2,464	2,317	2,652	588	0
Tangible assets	2,764	3,756	3,839	3,279	2,725
Investments	851	214	144	206	177
Total fixed assets	6,079	6,287	6,635	4,074	2,902
Current assets:					
Stocks	1,286	1,349	1,269	761	734
Debtors	1,561	1,541	1,451	874	828
Cash at bank and in hand	261	243	215	138	113
Total current assets	3,108	3,133	2,935	1,772	1,675
Creditors (less than one year):					
Borrowings	(157)	(206)	(362)	(187)	(330)
Other creditors	(2,135)	(2,343)	(2,316)	(1,301)	(1,166)
Total current liabilities	(2,292)	(2,549)	(2,678)	(1,488)	(1,496)
Current assets – Current liabilities	816	584	257	284	179
Total assets – Current liabilities	6,895	6,871	6,892	4,358	3,081
Creditors (greater than one year):					
Borrowings	(2,703)	(2,925)	(3,494)	(702)	(1,142)
Other creditors	(169)	(191)	(231)	(163)	(103)
Total noncurrent liabilities	(2,872)	(3,116)	(3,725)	(865)	(1,245)
Provisions	(569)	(328)	(325)	(55)	(70)
Total assets – Total liabilities	3,454	3,427	2,842	3,438	1,765
Capital and reserves:					
Capital	515	508	506	443	441
Reserves	2,907	2,893	2,304	2,964	1,296
Minority interests	32	26	32	31	28
Total equity	3,454	3,427	2,842	3,438	1,765
Profit and Loss Account					
Turnover	8,748	9,394	9,298	6,029	5,706
Cost of sales	(7,473)	(8,119)	(8,159)	(5,262)	(5,016)
Depreciation	(204)	(216)	(190)	(125)	(126)
Trading profit	1,071	1,059	949	642	564
Income of related companies	10	23	18	12	8
Other income	18	79	80	39	14
Net interest	(171)	(239)	(280)	(93)	(120)
Exceptional items	35	(3)	(35)	(25)	(9)
Pretax profit	963	919	732	576	456
Taxation	(298)	(279)	(216)	(155)	(120)
Net income	665	640	516	421	336
Minority interests	(7)	(6)	(8)	(8)	(2)
Extraordinary items	(226)	435	560	290	128
Dividends payable	(218)	(198)	(167)	(129)	(104)
Retained earnings	214	871	901	574	358

Source: Annual reports of Grand Metropolitan PLC.

was much larger than the group's existing hotels. In 1961, the company was listed on the London stock exchange, and in 1962, the group changed its name to Grand Metropolitan Hotels.

8   The 1960s saw the first in a series of acquisitions that would move GrandMet into nonhotel businesses. In 1966, the group bought Levy & Franks, owners of the Chef and Brewer pub and restaurant chain. By 1969, GrandMet had expanded into dairy products with the acquisition of Express Dairy (£32 million). During the 1970s, its most important purchases included the Mecca gaming establishments (bought for £33 million, sold in 1985 for £95 million) and Watney (£435 million), the owner of International Distillers and Vintners, which would form the core of GrandMet's drinks division.

EXHIBIT 4
Acquisitions and Divestitures

Acquisitions	Divestitures

1960s and 1970s

1966 Levy & Franks: pub and restaurant chain
1967 Bateman & Midland Catering: contract catering
1969 Express Dairy: distribution of milk products
1970 Berni Inns: hotels in UK; Mecca: gaming, betting, and amusement centers
1971 Truman Hanbury Buxton: brewing, pubs, and hotels
1972 Watney (including International Distillers and Vintners): brewing, distribution of wines and spirits

1980s

1980 Liggett Group (US): cigarettes, wines and spirits, soft-drink bottling, fitness products, pet food (Alpo)	1984	CC Soft drinks: soft-drink manufacturer
1981 Intercontinental Hotels: worldwide luxury hotel chain	1985	Express Dairy (northern area): milk/dairy products; Pinkerton Tobacco (US): chewing tobacco (Liggett); L&M do Brasil: tobacco leaf (Liggett); Mecca Leisure: bingo halls/amusement centers
1983 Children's World (US): early education services		
1985 Cinzano (25%): drinks; Quality Care (US): home health care; Pearle Optical (US): world's largest eye-care products retailing	1986	Dryborough & Co. (UK), Stern Brauerei (D), Brouwerij Maes (B): brewing; Liggett Group (US): cigarettes
1986 G. Ruddle & Co.: brewer	1987	Compass Group: contract and other services; Children's World (US): child care products; Quality Care (US): home health-care products; Diversified Products (US): fitness products (Liggett); McGuinness Distillers: Canadian spirits
1987 Heublein (US): wines and spirits; Almaden Vineyards (US): wines; Saccone & Speed and Roberts & Cooper: wines and spirits; Dairy Produce Packers: dairy products; Martell (10%): cognac; two pet-food manufacturers (US)		
1988 Vision Express and Eye & Tech (US): optical superstores; Kaysens: frozen desserts; Peter's Savoury Products: meat and pastry products; William Hill Org.: retail betting; Wienerwald/Spaghetti Factory: German and Swiss restaurants	1988	Hotel Meurice (F); Atlantic Soft Drink Co./Pepsi-Cola San Joaquin Bottling Co. (US); Intercontinental Hotels
1989 The Pillsbury Company (US) international food group: Burger King, Green Giant, Haagen-Dazs; Metaxa: Greek brandy; Ouzo-Kaloyannis (30%): Greek spirits; Brent Walker: pubs; UB Restaurants: Wimpy, Pizzaland, and Pizza Perfect fast-food chains	1989	Steak & Ale/Bennigans (US): restaurant chain; London Clubs: London casino business; Van De Kamp's: branded frozen foods; Bumble Bee: branded seafood; William Hill: retail betting

1990s

1990 Remy Martini-Cointreau (20%): joint-venture spirits/liqueurs; Anglo Espanola de Distribucion: Spanish wines and spirits distributor; Jus-rol: food manufacturer	1990	Berni Inns: family restaurant chain
1991 Belin Surgelés (France): frozen cakes and pastries; Inntrepreneur Estates (50%) joint venture with Courage: management company for all Courage and 3,750 GrandMet pubs under pubs-for-breweries swap	1991	Pizzaland/Pastificio: pizza/pasta restaurant chains; Perfect Pizza: take-away/delivery pizza chain; Watney Truman, Ruddles Brewery, Samuel Webster and Wilsons: breweries; 4 Pillsbury flour mills (US); 3,570 managed and tenanted pubs to Inntrepreneur Estates; The Dominic group: off-license chain; Express Dairy: liquid milk products; Eden Vale: chilled products
1992 Cinzano: remaining 75%		

Source: Annual reports of Grand Metropolitan PLC; and IBCA report, "Grand Metropolitan," October 1991.

9 GrandMet's pace of acquisition and divestiture accelerated during the 1980s. Its major acquisitions during this decade included the Liggett Group (owner of Alpo pet food, bought for $450 million), Intercontinental Hotels (bought for $500 million, sold in 1988 for $2 billion), Pearle Optical ($385 million), Heublein (US wines and spirits company and owner of Smirnoff vodka, bought for $1.2 billion), and finally, Pillsbury (owner of Burger King and Haagen-Dazs, bought for £3.3 billion).

10 The 1990s started with a flurry of divestitures, as close to £800 million in businesses were sold off. By 1992, GrandMet had divested all of its hotels, breweries, gaming establishments, soft-drink bottling plants, fitness products, and all food brands that were judged not to have international branding potential. The result was a group focused on a "core competence": the management of international brands in food, drinks, and retailing. Exhibit 4 summarizes the transactions that GrandMet undertook from 1960 through 1992.

EXHIBIT 5
Debt Profile

	1991	1990	1989	1988	1987
Debt Maturity					
Current	5%	7%	9%	21%	22%
1 to 2 years	2	58	11	19	25
2 to 5 years	77	30	69	14	28
Over 5 years	16	5	11	46	25
Debt Currency					
US dollar	77	79	11	8	11
Pound sterling	18	15	9	47	33
Deutsche mark (DM)	2	1	1	0	0
Multi-currency	0	0	77	34	47
Various	3	5	3	10	8

Market Value of Equity (as of April 15, 1992):

Common shares prices	£9.48 per share
Shares outstanding	1,005,896,041
Market value of equity	£9,535,894,468

Sources: Annual reports of Grand Metropolitan PLC; and *The Wall Street Journal.*

FINANCIAL STRATEGY

11 In an analysts' briefing given by GrandMet in December 1991, Ian Martin, group managing director and chief operating officer, stated that the group's positive financial results "demonstrate the effectiveness of our operational principles, which can be simplified down to just seven words: build brands, cut costs, develop products, all within the framework of total quality."[3] At this same briefing, David Nash, financial director, outlined the financial strategy that supported these operational principles: capitalize brand value, increase interest coverage, and dispose of products that do not provide an adequate return.

12 **Brand Valuation**   In 1988, GrandMet was the first UK company to begin the practice of assessing the value of recently acquired brands and then capitalizing that value on the balance sheet. As shown in Exhibit 3, the value of the brands (principally, Smirnoff, Pillsbury, Green Giant, and Burger King), consolidated under the label "Intangible assets," constituted 40 percent of 1991 fixed assets and 27 percent of the company's 1991 total assets.

13 **Interest Coverage and Debt Policy**   Senior management was committed to reducing GrandMet's financial gearing (leverage) and noted in announcing the results for 1991 that the ratio of debt/capital had fallen by 9 percentage points in the last year and that the firm's interest-coverage ratio had risen from 4.8 times to 6.6. Exhibit 5 shows the historical evolution of GrandMet's debt structure in terms of its maturity profile and currency profile.

14 **Invest in Projects Meeting Growth Criteria**   At the December 1991 analysts' briefing, CEO Sheppard outlined GrandMet's investment policy as follows: "In addition to Brewing, we have continued to exit those businesses whose future potential earnings do not meet our growth criteria. . . . All these decisions were driven by a thorough analysis of income growth prospects."[4] As Exhibits 2 and 3 indicate, during the 1987–91 fiscal years, GrandMet had generated a compound growth rate in pretax profits of 20.5 percent per year. Implicit in Sheppard's statement was the assumption that only those investments that would not jeopardize this growth trend would be undertaken.

---

[3] GrandMet preliminary-results briefing, December 5, 1991.

[4] GrandMet preliminary-results briefing, December 5, 1991.

EXHIBIT 6
Summary of Percentage Weights of the Various Classes of Capital

	£ Outstandings		£ Weights*		US$ Outstandings		US$ Weights	
	(1) Book Value	(2) Market Value	(3) Book Value	(4) Market Value	(5) Book Value	(6) Market Value	(7) Book Value	(8) Market Value
Specified debts†	1,777.4	1,794.8	33.0%	15.6%	3,107	3,137	33.0%	15.6%
Unspecified debts‡	87.0	87.0	1.6	0.8	152	152	1.6	0.8
Convertible debt	52.0	63.0	1.0	0.5	91	110	1.0	0.5
Preferred stock	12.2	6.3	0.2	0.1	21	11	0.2	0.1
Common stock	3,454.0	9,535.9	64.2	83.0	6,038	16,669	64.2	83.0
Total capital	5,382.6	11,487.1	100.0%	100.0%	9,409	20,079	100.0%	100.0%

*The £ weights are calculated by dividing the £ outstanding in each class of capital by the total amount of £ capital. The US$ weights are estimated the same way.

†The balance sheet listed eight separate classes of debt capital to which costs could be attributed, including bank loans, commercial paper, guaranteed notes, guaranteed debentures, debenture stock, and bonds.

‡The balance sheet listed £87 million of debt outstanding without citing a specific cost. Presumably, this debt consisted of a number of small issues. One way to treat those issues in cost-of-capital estimation is to assume that their average cost is equal to a weighted-average cost of all the other specified debt securities.

Group Cost of Capital

15 Were GrandMet's financial objectives consistent with the creation of value? To approach this question, analysts often used the discounted cash flows of any project as a measure of value creation. This method required knowledge of the opportunity cost of capital for investments of similar risk. One commonly used discount rate was the weighted-average cost of capital (WACC), defined as

$$WACC = (1 - T)i(D/V) + K_e(E/V)$$

where T is the corporate tax rate, i is the pretax cost of debt, D is the market value of debt, E is the market value of equity, K_e is the cost of equity, and V is the market value of the firm's assets ($V = D + nE$).

16 In basic terms, the WACC blends the requirements of the different providers of capital—bondholders and shareholders. A separate WACC could be calculated for each of the three operating sectors as well as for the entire company.

17 **Capital-Structure Weights** Exhibit 6 gives the book-value and market-value weightings for the company's capital structure.

18 **Cost of Debt and Preferred Stock** Exhibit 7 estimates the weighted-average pretax cost of debt for GrandMet in both pounds sterling and U.S. dollars. The 1990 annual report stated,

> The group interest expense is arranged centrally and is not attributable to individual activities or geographical areas . . . The group has arranged interest rate swaps which have the effect of fixing the rate of interest at an average of 8.6 percent on US dollar and Deutschemark borrowings totalling £616 million . . . In addition, the interest rate on borrowings of £1,070 million has been capped for 1 year by the purchase of interest rate caps at a rate of 9 percent. The interest rates shown . . . are those contracted on the underlying borrowings before taking into account any interest rate protection.

19 The firm noted that most of the commercial-paper borrowings were classified as "mid-term" (i.e., longer in maturity than one year but shorter than long term), because the firm intended to roll over the maturing commercial paper indefinitely.

20 The statutory maximum corporate income tax rate prevailing in the United Kingdom in 1992 was 35 percent. In the United States, it was 34 percent.

EXHIBIT 7
Estimation of Average Costs of Debt and Preferred Stock

	Currency	Yield on Book Value	Yield on Market Value	£ Yields Book Value	£ Yields Market Value	US$ Yields Book Value	US$ Yields Market Value
Bank loans and overdrafts	£	9.54%	9.54%	9.54%	9.54%	7.86%	7.86
Commercial paper	US$	5.93	5.93	7.58	7.58	5.93	5.93
Guaranteed notes 1996	US$	8.13	7.97	9.81	9.65	8.13	7.97
Guaranteed notes 2001	US$	8.63	7.87	10.32	9.55	8.63	7.87
Guaranteed debentures 2011	US$	9.00	8.02	10.70	9.70	9.00	8.02
Commercial paper	£	10.80	10.80	10.80	0.80	9.10	9.10
Debenture stock 2008	£	12.13	11.15	12.13	11.15	10.40	9.44
Bonds 1992	DM	6.63	8.57	6.93	8.88	5.29	7.21
Weighted-average cost of debt		7.15	7.13	8.69	8.63	7.03	6.96
Subordinated convertible bonds 2002	£	6.25	9.75	6.25	9.75	4.62	8.07
Preferred stock issues:							
4.75%	£	4.75	10.05	4.75	10.05	3.14	8.36
6.25%	£	6.25	10.15	6.25	10.15	4.62	8.46
5.00%	£	5.00	10.35	5.00	10.35	3.39	8.66
Weighted-average cost of preferred stock		5.31	10.27	5.31	10.27	3.76	8.57

Note: The weighted-average costs are based on the following estimated weightings:

	Securities Outstanding*	Book Value £	Book Value US$	Book Percentage Weights £	Book Percentage Weights US$	Market Value Outstanding	Market Value £	Market Value US$	Market Percentage Weights £	Market Percentage Weights US$
Bank loans and overdrafts	£280	280	489	15.8	15.8	£280	280	489	15.6	15.6
Commercial paper	$1,696	970	1,696	54.6	54.6	$1696	970	1,696	54.1	54.1
Guaranteed notes 1996	$170	97	170	5.5	5.5	$171	98	171	5.5	5.5
Guaranteed notes 2001	$170	97	170	5.5	5.5	$178	102	178	5.7	5.7
Guaranteed debentures 2011	$169	97	169	5.4	5.4	$185	106	185	5.9	5.9
Commercial paper	£139	139	243	7.8	7.8	£139	139	243	7.7	7.7
Debenture stock 2008	£50	50	87	2.8	2.8	£54	54	94	3.0	3.0
Bonds 1992	DM137	47	82	2.6	2.6	DM136	46	80	2.6	2.6
Total specified debts		1,777	3,107	100.0	100.0		1,795	3,137	100.0	100.0
Various unspecified debts	£87	87	152							
Subordinated convertible bonds 2002	£52	52	91			£63	63	110		
Preferred stock issues										
4.75%	£1.2	1.2	2.1	9.8	9.8	£0.56	0.56	1.0	9.0	9.0
6.25%	£3.3	3.3	5.8	27.0	27.0	2.03	2.03	3.5	32.1	32.1
5.00%	£7.7	7.7	13.5	63.1	63.1	3.72	3.72	6.5	58.9	58.9
Total preferred stock	£12.2	12.2	21.3	100.0	100.0	£6.31	6.31	11.0	100.0	100.0

*Currencies were translated to US dollars or pounds sterling at the following rates of exchange prevailing in mid-April 1992: Dollar/Pound=1.748; DM/Pound=2.917; DM/Dollar=1.669.

21   Exhibit 7 also presents the cost of preferred stock (calculated as the annual dividend divided by the market value of the stock) and the cost of convertible debt. Convertible debt was recognized to be a hybrid, a mixture of "straight" debt and equity. Therefore, the cost of the convertible debt, 9.75 percent, was estimated[5] as an average of the cost of equity and cost of debt, weighted by proportions implicit in the convertible; that is, 9.75 percent was not simply the yield on the bond portion of the convertible.

_____

[5] By the casewriters.

22   **Cost of Equity**   Several methods could be used for estimating the cost of equity. One approach was based on the theory that the current stock price was simply the discounted flow of future dividends. In this model, the after-tax cost of equity (K_e) could be approximated by

$$K_e = DIV/P + g$$

where DIV is the current dividend per share, P is the current share price, and g is the expected growth rate of dividends to infinity.

23   Another approach was based on the capital asset pricing model. This model explicitly sets required returns by considering the risk of the investment, where risk is defined with respect to a fully diversified portfolio. This model leads to the following expression for the expected after-tax cost of equity:

$$K_e = R_f + \beta(R_m - R_f)$$

where R_f is the risk-free rate (typically a government-bond rate), β is beta,[6] and $R_m - R_f$ is the stock market risk premium.

24   Exhibit 8 gives information for GrandMet relevant to measuring cost of equity, and Exhibit 9 presents the financial-market conditions in the United States and United Kingdom in April 1992. Which risk-free rate should one use—the U.S. rate (because half the company's revenues were dollar denominated) or the UK rate? How should the decision maker decide on which maturity to use (2 years, 10 years)? What does *risk free* really mean? The same questions arose in the case of the market risk premiums. Should the decision maker use the historical long-term geometric averages or short-term ones? With which market(s) should the decision maker be concerned?

25   The most recent Risk Measurement Service report from the London Business School reported that GrandMet had a beta of 1.14 with respect to the London stock market.[7] *Value Line,* however, the U.S. investment information service, had estimated GrandMet's beta at 0.8 with respect to the New York Stock Exchange.[8] What might account for the difference between these two numbers?

Business-Segment Capital-Cost Estimation

26   How should one estimate the cost of equity for each of GrandMet's individual sectors? Should each segment have a different risk-free rate based on different project lifetimes? How should one determine the beta for each sector? Finally, how should one determine the weights necessary to combine the business segments into an overall WACC for GrandMet? Should one base the weighting factor on revenues, profits, or some other measure?

27   The decision maker knew that he could examine the capital structures of comparable companies to facilitate the evaluation of GrandMet's gearing in each of its segments. Therefore, he collected the information in Exhibit 8 on various companies that competed with GrandMet in each of its operating sectors. Would the fact that this information reflected only book values dramatically affect the

---

[6] In technical terms, beta is the normalized covariance of the asset's return with respect to the market return—basically, a measure of how the company's returns vary with respect to overall market fluctuations. A company with a beta of 1.0 experiences as much volatility as a broad portfolio of stocks, and it varies synchronously with the market. A company with a beta of less than 1.0 is less risky than the market portfolio. A beta greater than 1.0 indicates greater risk than the market portfolio.

[7] Risk Measurement Services (RMS) estimated betas using five years of *monthly* returns. The returns included dividends and capital gains or losses. RMS noted, "Betas may change because the company changes. For example, if a company becomes more highly geared, the beta of its shares will increase. Similarly, if it acquires a less risky firm, the beta of the shares after the merger will be lower than before. You may find it helpful to bear this in mind when interpreting the estimates." London Business School, "Your Questions Answered," *Risk Measurement Services,* October 1991, pp. 63–65.

[8] *Value Line* estimated its betas by regressing *weekly* percentages changes in the price of a stock against the weekly percentage changes in the New York Stock Exchange Composite Index over a period of five years. *Value Line* noted, "There has been a tendency over the years for high Beta stocks to become lower and for low Beta stocks to become higher. This tendency can be measured by studying the Betas of stocks in consecutive five-year intervals. The Betas published in The Value Line Investment Survey are adjusted for this tendency and hence are likely to be a better predictor of future Betas than those based exclusively on the experience of the past five years." ("How to Use the Value Line Investment Survey: A Subscriber's Guide," *Value Line Investment Survey,* 1985, p. 57)

EXHIBIT 8
Information on Comparable Companies

	Sales (in US$ millions)	Dividend Yield	Price/ Earnings Ratio	Interest Coverage	Debt to Capital		Debt to Equity		Average Tax Rate	Beta	Expected Growth Rate in	
					Book Value	Market Value	Book Value	Market Value			Sales	Dividends
Grand Metropolitan	**15,222**	**3.4%**	**13.3**	**6.6**	**35%**	**17%**	**55%**	**21%**	**31%**	**1.14UK .80US**	**6.5%**	**12.0%**
Restaurant/Retailing												
Forte (UK)	4,600	5.7	14.1	2.4	27	30	36	42	16	1.18	12.3	10.6
McDonald's	6,695	0.8	17.3	4.0	42	2	72	2	34	0.95	12.0	13.5
Luby's	328	3.5	14.2	nil	1	0	1	0	34	0.90	10.0	9.0
National Pizza	305	0.0	16.9	3.3	49	37	96	58	36	1.00	15.5	0.0
TCBY Enterprises	129	3.9	26.8	7.8	14	3	16	3	35	1.25	9.0	23.0
Wendy's International	1,060	2.0	20.7	5.9	33	23	49	30	34	1.15	6.0	0.0
Average	**2,186**	**2.7**	**18.3**	**3.9**	**28**	**16**	**45**	**23**	**31**	**1.07**	**10.8**	**9.4**
Food Processing												
Argyll Group (UK)	7,830	4.3	13.5	12.9	32	14	47	16	28	0.72	19.8	18.3
Associated British Foods (UK)	6,110	3.2	9.6	8.3	19	19	23	23	32	0.47	2.3	14.9
Borden	7,235	3.6	14.1	3.9	43	20	75	25	36	1.15	5.5	9.5
Cadbury-Schweppes (UK)	5,475	3.6	17.4	3.8	38	17	62	21	28	0.83	10.9	14.3
Campbell Soup	6,204	1.8	21.1	5.9	30	8	43	9	40	1.00	7.5	15.5
CPC International	6,189	2.7	15.3	6.5	38	12	61	14	40	1.10	8.5	12.5
Dean Foods	2,158	1.9	16.1	9.5	26	10	35	12	42	0.90	8.0	7.0
Dreyer's Grand Ice Cream	355	0.7	31.6	4.2	31	22	45	28	40	1.05	16.5	0.0
Flowers Industries	825	4.1	20.0	5.2	35	14	54	16	40	0.85	5.5	6.5
General Mills	7,153	2.3	23.3	8.6	39	6	64	6	39	1.00	11.0	15.0
Heinz	6,800	2.8	19.4	7.6	10	2	11	2	38	1.00	8.5	11.0
Michael Foods	455	1.3	14.7	4.1	35	26	54	36	36	1.15	9.5	19.0
Quaker Oats	5,491	2.8	17.8	5.6	40	13	67	15	43	0.90	9.0	11.5
Ralston Purina	7,375	2.2	15.8	4.1	70	18	233	23	40	0.90	9.5	11.0
Sara Lee	12,831	1.9	22.0	6.6	29	6	41	7	36	1.00	7.0	13.5
Tate & Lyle (UK)	5,680	3.7	10.1	3.1	52	32	110	47	29	1.10	14.7	14.3
Tesco (UK)	11,050	3.3	13.2	4.0	19	10	23	11	32	0.73	13.6	22.8
Unilever (NL and UK)	42,250	3.2	15.1	4.6	22	31	28	44	35	0.86	8.5	9.5
United Biscuits (UK)	4,225	5.0	13.7	8.5	32	14	48	16	33	0.88	6.1	12.2
Universal Foods	834	2.6	14.7	7.2	34	13	52	15	37	0.90	9.0	12.5
Average	**7,326**	**2.9**	**16.9**	**6.2**	**34**	**15**	**59**	**19**	**36**	**0.92**	**9.5**	**12.5**

EXHIBIT 8
(continued)

Drinks

	Sales (in US$ millions)	Dividend Yield	Price/Earnings Ratio	Interest Coverage	Debt to Capital Book Value	Debt to Capital Market Value	Debt to Equity Book Value	Debt to Equity Market Value	Average Tax Rate	Beta	Expected Growth Rate in Sales	Expected Growth Rate in Dividends
Allied Lyons (UK)	8,940	4.1%	23.4	2.3	43%	30%	75%	44%	29%	0.97	9.2%	14.6%
Anheuser-Busch	10,996	2.0	15.7	8.2	38	15	61	18	38	1.00	7.0	12.0
Bass(UK)	7,630	4.8	10.6	4.3	29	38	40	62	26	0.77	10.1	16.5
Brown-Forman	1,250	2.8	14.7	23.5	14	4	16	4	35	1.20	9.5	11.5
Coors	1,917	2.3	15.2	10.3	13	10	15	11	39	0.85	5.0	0.0
Guinness (UK)	6,110	2.5	15.9	4.7	31	18	44	22	28	1.01	24.2	21.1
Labatt (Canada)	4,400	3.0	14.3	2.9	33	28	49	38	34	0.75	2.0	6.5
Molson (Canada)	2,500	2.1	13.9	3.3	45	37	82	59	34	0.75	5.0	13.0
Scottish & Newcastle (UK)	2,398	5.0	13.5	5.8	23	20	31	25	33	0.59	19.3	16.5
Seagram (Canada)	5,000	1.7	17.2	3.1	29	26	41	35	22	1.10	5.0	12.0
Whitbread (UK)	3,585	5.2	10.7	5.6	15	15	17	17	24	0.70	6.1	15.9
Average	**4,975**	**3.2**	**15.0**	**6.7**	**28**	**22**	**43**	**30**	**31**	**0.88**	**9.3**	**12.7**

Notes:
US and Canadian companies: 1991 and expected annual growth rates until 1997.
UK companies: 1990 and average annual growth rates of the last five years.

EXHIBIT 8
(concluded)

Restaurant

Forte(UK)	Active in contract catering and hotel- and motel-chain management.
Luby's Cafeteria (US)	Operates a chain of cafeterias.
McDonald's (US)	Licenses and operates a fast-food hamburger chain.
National Pizza (US)	Largest franchisee of PepsiCo's Pizza Hut chain.
TCBY Enterprises (US)	Largest franchisor of soft-frozen yogurt stores.
Wendy's International (US)	Licenses and operates a chain of quick-service hamburger restaurants.

Food Processing

Argyll Group (UK)	One of the leading food retailers in the United Kingdom.
Associated British Foods (UK)	Operator of grocery stores, retail bakeries, beauty shops.
Borden (US)	Diversified producer of packaged food (dairy, snacks, pasta, popcorn, jams, potato chips) and adhesives (Elmer's Cement, Crazy Glue).
Cadbury-Schweppes (UK)	Manufacturer of bottled and canned soft drinks, candy and other confectionary products, food preparations.
Campbell Soup (US)	A leading manufacturer of canned soups, spaghetti, fruit and vegetable juices, frozen foods, salads, bakery products, olives, pickles.
CPC International (US)	A leading producer of grocery products (soups, mayonnaise, peanut butter, pasta, baked goods) and a large corn refiner (corn syrups, dextrose, starches).
Dean Foods (US)	Manufacturers and distributes dairy products (fluid milk, ice cream, cheeses), and processes canned and frozen vegetables, sauces, powdered drinks, and creamers.
Dreyer's Grand Ice Cream (US)	Manufacturer and distributor of premium ice cream products.
Flowers Industries (US)	Producer of bakery and snack-food goods.
General Mills (US)	Processes and markets consumer foods (cereals, flour, seafood, yogurt) and operates restaurants.
Heinz (US)	Manufacturers soups, ketchup, baby foods, cat food, frozen potatoes.
Michael Foods (US)	Producer and distributor of egg and egg products, frozen potato products, ice cream products, refrigerator-case products.
Quaker Oats (US)	Produces foods (cereals, breakfast products, beverages) and pet foods, owns Fisher-Price toys.
Ralston Purina (US)	World's largest producer of dry dog and cat foods and dry-cell batteries.
Sara Lee (US)	Diversified, international, packaged consumer goods (Hanes, Dim), with operations in coffee, specialty meats, frozen baked goods, and food-services distribution.
Tate & Lyle (UK)	Producer and distributor of sugar products, beverages, food products.
Tesco (UK)	One of the leading food retailers in the United Kingdom.
Unilever (NL and UK)	One of the world's largest producers and marketers of branded and packaged consumer goods.
United Biscuits (UK)	Maker of biscuits, cookies and crackers, snack foods, and frozen foods, and owner/operator of fast-food restaurant chain.
Universal Foods (US)	International manufacturer and marketer of value-added food products and ingredients for food processing, baking, foodservice, and retail markets.

Drinks

Allied Lyons (UK)	Active in beer and retailing, wines, spirits, eating and drinking places.
Anheuser-Busch (US)	Largest US brewer, also active in baked and snack goods, frozen foods, theme parks.
Bass (UK)	Active in malt beverages, amusement and recreation, hotels and motels, soft drinks.
Brown-Forman (US)	A leading wine and spirits producer and importer, producer of fine china, crystal, and luggage.
Coors (US)	US brewer.
Guinness (UK)	Active in malt beverages, wines, brandy spirits, liquors.
Labatt (CN)	One of Canada's leading brewers, also active in foods, dairy products, fruit juices.
Molson (CN)	Engaged in brewing, cleaning and sanitizing, and retail merchandising.
Scottish & Newcastle (UK)	Active in malt beverages, wine and liquor stores, hotels and motels, soft drinks.
Seagram (CN)	One of the world's largest wine and spirits distillers/producers.
Whitbread (UK)	Maker of malt beverages, operator of hotels and motels, bottler of soft drinks, active in recreation.

Sources: *Value Line; Risk Measurement Services,* London Business School, January–March 1992; Compact Disclosure (Digital Library System, Inc.); casewriters' estimates.

EXHIBIT 9
Capital-Market Conditions, April 1992

Treasury Bond Yields (April 8, 1992)

Term	UK Gilts, Yield to Maturity	US Treasuries, Yield to Maturity
1	10.50%	4.45%
2	20.40	5.29
3	10.30	5.95
5	10.00	6.82
10	9.80	7.45
15	9.60	7.59
20	9.60	7.83

Foreign Exchange Rates

$/£ = 1.748
DM/£ = 2.917
DM/$ = 1.669

Long-Term Expected Rates of Inflation

United Kingdom	4.3% annually
United States	2.7% annually
Germany	4.0% annually

Equity Market Risk Premium

Market	Estimated Current Premium	Geometric Mean Historical Premium	Arithmetic Mean Historical Premium
London	3.9%	4.1%	6.9%
New York	2.7%	5.6%	8.4%

Sources: *Financial Times; The Wall Street Journal;* OECD *Economic Outlook,* June 1992; Banque Degroof, Belgium.

estimation of overall cost of capital? Which tax rate should he use, the U.S. marginal rate, the UK marginal rate, or some effective rate?

Cost of Capital and Currency

28   In evaluating GrandMet's performance, analysts wondered whether the cost of capital should be the same in London as in New York. If differences among local capital markets (such as those induced by country risk) existed, one might be able to diversify the differences away by holding a portfolio of international investments. Using this kind of assumption could free an analyst to work with local costs of capital.

29   The assumption of purchasing-power parity implied the following relationship between home and foreign local costs of capital:

$$\text{Local } K = (1 + \text{Home } K) \left(\frac{1 + \text{Local inflation rate}}{1 + \text{Home inflation rate}} \right) - 1$$

30   This equation implies that real risk-free rates, equity risk premia, and betas are constant across countries. Little evidence either to prove or refute such an assertion existed, although in competitive world capital markets, arbitrage activity would tend to drive the three elements into equilibrium.

Using home capital costs to discount cash flows translated into home currencies would be a conservative response to these uncertainties.

CONCLUSION

31   Analysts noted with interest the circulation of rumors that the company might be the target of a takeover attempt. Had the company performed that badly? Were all segments of the group's business portfolio performing equally well? Might one or two of them be targeted for aggressive restructuring? The decision maker decided to compare the returns on net assets in Exhibit 2 against the segment WACCs.

CASE 25

ROBIN HOOD

---

1   It was in the spring of the second year of his insurrection against the High Sheriff of Nottingham that Robin Hood took a walk in Sherwood Forest. As he walked he pondered the progress of the campaign, the disposition of his forces, the Sheriff's recent moves, and the options that confronted him.

2   The revolt against the Sheriff had begun as a personal crusade. It erupted out of Robin's conflict with the Sheriff and his administration. However, alone, Robin Hood could do little. He therefore sought allies, men with grievances and a deep sense of justice. Later he welcomed all who came, asking few questions and demanding only a willingness to serve. Strength, he believed, lay in numbers.

3   He spent the first year forging the group into a disciplined band, united in enmity against the Sheriff and willing to live outside the law. The band's organization was simple. Robin ruled supreme, making all important decisions. He delegated specific tasks to his lieutenants. Will Scarlett was in charge of intelligence and scouting. His main job was to shadow the Sheriff and his men, always alert to their next move. He also collected information on the travel plans of the rich merchants and tax collectors. Little John kept discipline among the men and saw to it that their archery was at the high peak that their profession demanded. Scarlock took care of the finances, converting loot to cash, paying shares of the take, and finding suitable hiding places for the surplus. Finally, Much the Miller's son had the difficult task of provisioning the ever-increasing band of Merrymen.

4   The increasing size of the band was a source of satisfaction for Robin but also a source of concern. The fame of his Merrymen was spreading and new recruits poured in from every corner of England. As the band grew larger, their small bivouac became a major encampment. Between raids, the men milled about, talking and playing games. Vigilance was in decline and discipline was becoming harder to enforce. "Why," Robin reflected, "I don't know half the men I run into these days."

5   The growing band was also beginning to exceed the food capacity of the forest. Game was becoming scarce and supplies had to be obtained from outlying villages. The cost of buying food was beginning to drain the band's financial reserves at the very moment when revenues were in decline. Travelers, especially those with the most to lose, were now giving the forest a wide berth. This was costly and inconvenient to them but it was preferable to having all their goods confiscated.

6   Robin believed that the time had come for the Merrymen to change their policy of outright confiscation of goods to one of a fixed transit tax. His lieutenants strongly resisted this idea. They were proud of the Merrymen's famous motto: "Rob the rich to give to the poor." "The farmers and the townspeople," they argued, "are our most important allies." "How can we tax them and still hope for their help in our fight against the Sheriff?"

7   Robin wondered how long the Merrymen could keep to the ways and methods of their early days. The Sheriff was growing stronger and becoming better organized. He now had the money and the men and was beginning to harass the band, probing for its weaknesses. The tide of events was beginning to turn against the Merrymen. Robin felt the campaign must be decisively concluded before the Sheriff had a chance to deliver a mortal blow. "But how," he wondered, "could this be done?"

8   Robin had often entertained the possibility of killing the Sheriff but the chances for this seemed increasingly remote. Besides, killing the Sheriff might satisfy his personal thirst for revenge but it would not improve the situation. Robin had hoped that the perpetual state of unrest and the Sheriff's failure to collect taxes would lead to his removal from office. Instead, the Sheriff used his political

Joseph Lampel, New York University. Copyright © 1991, by Joseph Lampel. Reprinted with permission.

connections to obtain reinforcement. He had powerful friends at court and was well regarded by the regent, Prince John.

9   Prince John was vicious and volatile. He was consumed by his unpopularity among the people, who wanted the imprisoned King Richard back. He also lived in constant fear of the barons, who had first given him the regency but were now beginning to dispute his claim to the throne. Several of these barons had set out to collect the ransom that would release King Richard the Lionhearted from his jail in Austria. Robin was invited to join the conspiracy in return for future amnesty. It was a dangerous proposition. Provincial banditry was one thing; court intrigue another. Prince John had spies everywhere and he was known for his vindictiveness. If the conspirators' plan failed, the pursuit would be relentless and retribution swift.

10   The sound of the supper horn startled Robin from his thoughts. There was the smell of roasting venison in the air. Nothing was resolved or settled. Robin headed for camp promising himself that he would give these problems his utmost attention after tomorrow's raid.

CASE 26

PHILIP MORRIS: THE WARNING LABELS ISSUE

1   In 1992, the management of Philip Morris Companies faced a potentially major problem. One of Philip Morris's shareholders, the Midwest Province of the Capuchin Order, planned to present a resolution at the next annual shareholders' meeting. The resolution would require that the company print warnings about the dangers of cigarette smoking on every package of cigarettes produced, including exported cigarettes.

2   While a similar measure had been defeated by stockholders at the 1991 annual meeting, the introduction and discussion of the resolution by the religious order would provide antismoking activists with a highly visible forum for airing their views. The negative publicity could be damaging to the company. Publicity on this issue was particularly unwelcome because there were indications that Congress was turning its attention to warning labels for exported cigarettes.

3   There were several alternatives for dealing with the situation. The company could take a proactive stance by placing the warning labels on all cigarettes before the motion could be made. Other possible responses included seeking procedural methods to inhibit the motion, distributing a position paper describing the views of the company, or simply doing nothing. In any case, a decision was needed prior to the upcoming meeting.

BACKGROUND

4   Philip Morris Companies, Inc., is a diversified, multinational firm that obtains revenues from the manufacture and distribution of tobacco, food, and beer products, from financial services, and from real estate operations. In 1991 Philip Morris had net earnings of $3.9 billion on revenues of $56.4 billion. The company's operating revenues from international tobacco operations ($12.2 billion) had topped operating revenues from U.S. operations ($11.5 billion) for the second consecutive year. Earnings for domestic tobacco operations were $4.7 billion compared to earnings of $1.6 billion for international tobacco. Philip Morris International, Inc. (PMI), is the subsidiary that manufactures and exports cigarettes to a growing number of countries worldwide. During 1991, PMI increased export volume nearly 10 percent over 1990 and contributed $3.6 billion to the U.S. balance of payments.

5   From 1987 to 1991 unit sales of cigarettes in the United States declined while world sales increased. Differences in performance in the domestic and international cigarette businesses may be attributed to a number of factors, not the least of which is antismoking activism. The U.S. Surgeon General, the American Cancer Society, and the American Heart Association are just a few of the individuals and groups who have sought to reduce, if not ban, smoking from American life. A measure of their effectiveness is found in the diminishing percentage of Americans who smoke. Antismoking groups have begun to turn their attention to the export of cigarettes. Former Surgeon General C. Everett Koop has stated:

> At a time when we are pleading with foreign governments to stop the export of cocaine, it is the height of hypocrisy for the United States to export tobacco. Consider these figures. Last year in the United States, 2000 people died from cocaine. In that same year, cigarettes killed 390,000.[1]

This case was written by W. Kent Moore and Phyllis G. Holland, Valdosta State University. This case is intended for classroom discussion only, not to depict effective or ineffective handling of administrative situations. All rights reserved to the authors.

6　　　Antismoking activism was not limited to the United States. The Asian Pacific Association for Control of Tobacco was formed in 1989 with a goal of a smokeless Asia by the year 2000. Another group, the Asian Consultancy on Tobacco Control, representing 14 nations met in Hong Kong in January 1991, to devise a four-year plan to combat smoking in the region. The essence of their plan was to train antismoking activists and to persuade Asian countries to adopt uniform tobacco control regulations. In 1990, Philip Morris shareholders voted down a shareholder proposal that would have required exported cigarettes to carry the same labels in the appropriate language as those marketed domestically.

THE U.S. CIGARETTE INDUSTRY

7　　　With sales in excess of $35 billion in 1990, the United States cigarette industry continues to be a huge enterprise. According to a 1990 survey, 32 percent of American men and 27 percent of American women were smokers. In 1989, U.S. cigarette production was 685 billion, and worldwide, sales of cigarettes ran into the trillions. This sales volume has been achieved with a product that has been linked to cancer and heart disease since the landmark Surgeon General's report in 1964, which has carried health warnings on packs since 1966, and which has been banned from television and radio advertising since 1971. Although Americans have typically started smoking before age 21, by industry agreement, advertisements have not appeared in youth-oriented media or used illustrations or themes aimed at young people.

SMOKING TRENDS IN THE UNITED STATES

8　　　Trends in domestic consumption of cigarettes and percentages of smokers have been of great concern to tobacco companies. Exhibit 1 shows domestic consumption of cigarettes in the 1980s; Exhibits 2 and 3 show percentages of smokers by gender and educational level. If these trends continue, the Centers for Disease Control estimated that by the year 2000, only 22 percent of the adult population in the United States will be smokers. The percentage of female smokers (23 percent) was projected to be slightly higher than the percentage of male smokers (20 percent). By 1987, there were more teenage girl smokers than teenage boy smokers. Also, smoking in the United States is more and more becoming primarily a behavior of the less educated and the socioeconomically disadvantaged.

9　　　Almost half of all adults who ever smoked have quit. Each year, about two million American cigarette customers have been lost, either through death or quitting smoking. A 1991 Gallup poll revealed that 70 percent of smokers would like to quit and 80 percent wished they had never started smoking. For 16 consecutive years, the per capita consumption of cigarettes has decreased, and during the last 5 years, the total national consumption has decreased also.

10　　Exhibit 4 shows the impact of these trends on the major U.S. tobacco companies. From the peak in 1981, cigarette production for the domestic market had dropped by almost 15 percent in 1989. Annual profits were still increasing in 1989, but at modest levels in the 10 percent range rather than at the dramatic rates of previous decades. The industry had been involved in an increasing number of legal and political battles and smoking had been banned from domestic airline flights, many public buildings, portions of restaurants, and some workplaces.

INTERNATIONAL MARKETS

11　　To offset declining sales at home, American cigarette manufacturers, led by Philip Morris, had begun to devote more attention to international markets, with special focus on the Pacific Rim. Exhibit 5 shows the percentages of men and women in various countries in 1990 who smoked and the total population of those countries at the time. Until the mid-1980s, most Asian countries protected their

EXHIBIT 1
Domestic Consumption of Cigarettes

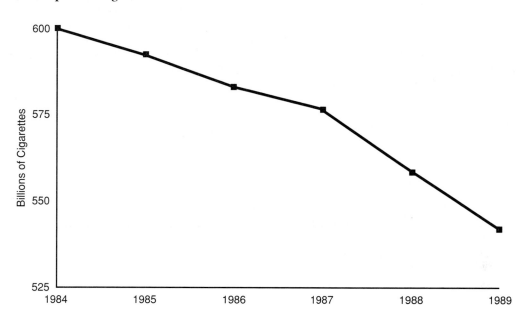

Source: Farmline, March 1990, p. 20.

state-run tobacco monopolies either by banning foreign cigarettes or by imposing high tariffs on imports. For example, quotas and protective tariffs in Taiwan and Korea almost tripled the price of imported tobacco. In 1985, the U.S. Cigarette Export Association, under Section 301 of the 1974 Trade Act, threatened trade sanctions against Asian countries that restricted tobacco imports. The first target was Japan, which was seen as an entry point for the rest of the Pacific Rim. In 1986, the Reagan administration drew up a list of possible retaliatory tariffs on Japanese products, including supercomputers, textiles, and automobile parts. Soon, Japan lifted its tariff on foreign cigarettes, and U.S. cigarette exports to Japan quadrupled.

12   Taiwan's cigarette markets were opened next. Again, Section 301 was used, and lobbying was intense. In 1987, Taiwan agreed to drop its restrictions on foreign cigarettes, including its ban on advertising. Within a year, Philip Morris's Marlboro brand had captured 30 percent of the sales in its price category. The South Korean and Thailand markets were opened in 1988 and 1990, respectively, but unlike the other countries, Thailand continued its ban on advertising.

13   The U.S. government played a crucial role in opening these markets, largely because of its desire to reduce balance of trade deficits. Exhibit 6 shows U.S. merchandise trade balances for 1973 to 1991. Tobacco was one of only four major categories of goods that produced a positive trade balance.

14   The response of Asian markets is reflected in the export data shown in Exhibit 7. U.S. cigarette exports to Japan increased by 56 percent in 1987, and exports to Asia increased by 75 percent in 1988. Total U.S. cigarette exports increased by 17 percent in 1989 and 7 percent in 1990. In 1990, cigarette consumption increased by 5.5 percent in Asia, and the smoking rate in these countries was increasing by 2 percent annually while the smoking rate was decreasing by 1.5 percent annually in industrialized countries.

EXHIBIT 2
Smoking Prevalences for Men and Women with Projections to Year 2000

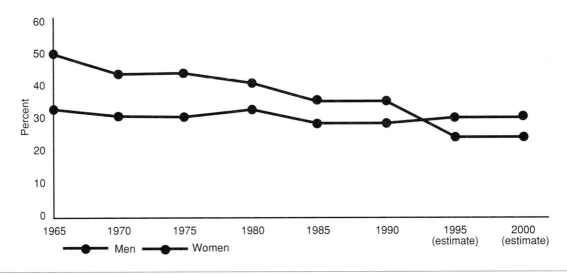

Source: *Editorial Research Reports,* March 24, 1989, p. 153; *Statistical Abstract of the United States,* 1990, p. 123; *The Atlanta Journal and Constitution,* June 27, 1990; *Journal of the American Medical Association,* January 6, 1989, p. 63.

MARKETING CIGARETTES IN THE PACIFIC RIM

15   The presence of U.S. firms in the Asian market has been manifested in both an increase in the number of cigarette ads and a change in the type of ads and promotion used by all cigarette manufacturers. In Japan, from 1986 to 1988, advertising time devoted to cigarettes on prime-time television rose from a rank of fortieth to a rank of second. Before the entry of American firms, Japan had planned to ban cigarette ads on television.

16   With the assistance of the U.S. government, tobacco companies used sophisticated advertisements that included techniques not allowed in the United States. Voluntary agreements not to advertise heavily in ways that target young people or women were dropped. Since 90 percent of smokers began before the age of 21 and a low percentage of Asian women were smokers, promotion to these groups was considered very important. Television commercials were aired during sports events and youth-oriented movies, and American companies sponsored motorcycle races and rock concerts. Young women gave away cigarette samples on Tokyo street corners, and in Taiwan, free samples were handed out at discos. Domestic tobacco companies responded by intensifying their promotional efforts at the same targets. For example, Japan Tobacco introduced a new brand, Dean, capitalizing upon the young, rebellious image of actor James Dean.

17   In countries less affluent than Japan, American cigarettes were promoted as symbols of success, sophistication, and wealth. This was reflected in the practice of disguising cheap local brands in Marlboro or Camel wrappers.

HEALTH ISSUES

18   The primary concerns about smoking, and consequently about cigarette exports, have been health-related. The Advisory Committee to the Surgeon General of the United States concluded that there are causal relationships between smoking and many diseases, including emphysema, cancer of the esophagus, and lung cancer. Exposure to smoke in the environment has been related to lung cancer in nonsmokers. Women who smoke while pregnant are more likely to deliver low-birth-weight babies.

EXHIBIT 3
Smoking Prevalences by Education Level with Projections to the Year 2000

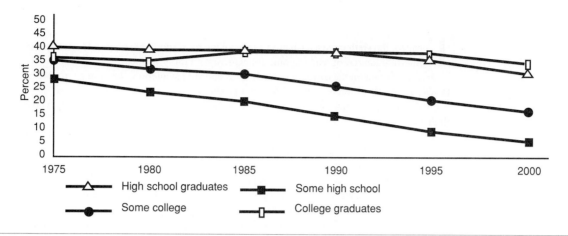

Source: Journal of the American Medical Association, January 6, 1989, p. 64.

Deaths attributable to smoking include 30 percent of cancer deaths, 21 percent of coronary heart disease deaths, 18 percent of stroke deaths, and 82 percent of deaths from chronic obstructive pulmonary disease. Each year in industrialized countries, 1.8 million deaths are linked to smoking; this number exceeds "the combined total of all deaths due to any form of violence, be it accident, homicide, or suicide."[2] Smoking two or more packs of cigarettes a day decreases life expectancy more than eight years, and one pack a day shortens life expectancy more than six years. Smoking has been costing an estimated $23 billion annually in the United states for medical expenses, and another $30 billion has been lost to society each year because of illness and premature death.

19   On the basis of health issues, various spokespersons within the United States have strongly and persistently criticized cigarette sales overseas. A U.S. congressman said: "For the past 100 years, America has been the world's foremost exporter of public health . . . Now the U.S. Trade Representative wants to add a new chapter to that legacy . . . a chapter entitled: America the world's greatest exporter of lung cancer, heart disease, emphysema, and death."[3] Koop stated:

> It's reprehensible for industrial nations to export disease, death, and disability in the way of cigarette smoke to developing countries, putting on their backs a health burden that they will never be able to pay for 20 or 30 years from now.[4]

20   One observer described U.S. policy as "trading the lungs of people who wear ties for those who wear kimonos."[5]

21   In recent years, foreign groups have also become vocal about the perceived evils of cigarettes from the United States. The Asia-Pacific Association for the Control of Tobacco sent a letter to President George Bush in 1989 stating:

> The cigarette issue is not an issue of trade or trade imbalances. It is an issue of human health, and Asian health is as important as American health. Asians want to purchase good American products, not harmful ones.[6]
>
> The Executive Director of the Hong Kong Council on Smoking and Health has noted that smoking-related illnesses, like cancer and heart disease, have overtaken communicable diseases as the leading cause of death in parts of Asia. Health warnings have not been required and have not appeared on cigarette advertisements in Asian countries, and the general level of awareness of the health hazards of smoking has been much lower than in the United States. In the mid-1980s, 95 percent of developed nations had laws pertaining to cigarette marketing and health warnings, but only 24 percent of underdeveloped nations had such regulations. This disparity has continued to exist.

TOBACCO AND THE ECONOMY

Tobacco, the sixth largest cash crop, is one of the most profitable crops a farmer can grow. It is an important source of cash income for America's family farmers.

Tobacco grown on the nation's farms is dried and sold at auction, then transported to manufacturers who make all different types of tobacco products.

Finally, the finished tobacco products are delivered to American consumers by wholesalers and retailers.

All of these businesses that make up the tobacco industry create jobs for over 414,000 people. These same businesses pay their employees more than $6.72 billion.

These jobs and wages are not limited to tobacco growing states. Although industry employment averages 100,000 people in the major tobacco growing states—Kentucky, North Carolina, Tennessee, South Carolina, Virginia, and Georgia—more than 314,000 additional workers are employed by the industry elsewhere around the nation.

At a time when the United States is buying more goods from overseas than it is selling, it is important to note that the world loves America's tobacco and tobacco products. In 1987, the tobacco industry exported $3.4 billion worth of products and only imported $730 million. The result? A $2.7 billion trade surplus in tobacco products.

Jobs, wages, and a positive trade surplus are only a part of the contribution the tobacco industry makes to our economy. (See Exhibit 8.)

TOBACCO SUPPLIER INDUSTRIES

The tobacco industry buys many goods and services from other industries that can be referred to as tobacco supplier industries.

Tobacco farmers purchase farm machinery and fertilizer. Tobacco manufacturers buy equipment and paper. Tobacco retailers buy vending machines and advertising. Examples of the goods and services provided by the tobacco supplier industries could go on and on.

The main point is clear: Tobacco supplier industries produce more than $35 billion worth of goods and services to meet the requirements of the tobacco industry. These same supplier industries employ 296,000 workers and pay out almost $7.4 billion in compensation.

Source: Philip Morris, *The Great American Smoker's Manual*, p. 1–3.

OTHER CONCERNS ABOUT EXPORTS

22   Beyond the health issue has been the concern that the Office of the U.S. Trade Representative's "full-throttle pursuit of profit is fueling an anti-American backlash that could translate into hostility towards other American exports."[7] Many people feel that exporting cigarettes puts the United States in the position of pushing drugs. In 1989 one critic of the industry said: "In a government purportedly concerned with drug abuse, this [exportation and aggressive marketing of American cigarettes] is hypocrisy of the first order."[8]

23   Still another concern has arisen in countries where per-capita income is low. There has been some evidence that cigarettes divert spending from food purchases. In Bangladesh, studies revealed that higher cigarette consumption by adults resulted in reduced caloric intake among children and decreased survival among children.

continued

Add the tobacco industry and tobacco supplier industries together and what do you get? Jobs for 710,000 people and a $31.5 billion contribution to the gross national product (the value of all goods and services) of the United States.

But the story doesn't end here.

THE FULL IMPACT

Workers in the tobacco industry and in the tobacco supplier industries are also consumers. They take vacations and buy houses, cars, groceries, appliances, gas and so on. They also buy services, such as day care, legal help, medical care, and insurance.

When you add up all the money these employees spend on goods and services, the total is surprising. The value of all these goods and services totals $50.6 billion, which is a tremendous contribution to this country's gross national product. To meet the demand for goods and services generated by tobacco industry and tobacco supplier industry employees, more than 1.59 million people are employed by all sorts of companies.

THE TOBACCO INDUSTRY AND TAXES

The big spenders in government who oppose the tobacco industry are biting the hand that feeds them. Why? Because tobacco excise taxes and sales taxes by federal, state, and local governments added up to more than $10 billion in 1987.

The industry's tax liability doesn't end there, however. If you add individual and corporate income taxes paid by the tobacco industry to the more than $10 billion already mentioned, the total tax payment exceeds $13 billion. In fact, tobacco companies are among the largest taxpayers in the world.

In short, government red ink would be a lot redder without the tobacco industry.

Millions of jobs, billions of dollars spent on products and services, a boost to America's family farmers, a trade surplus, and billions of tax dollars—these are the contributions of the tobacco industry to our economy. Keep these contributions in mind as you read the rest of *The Great American Smoker's Manual.*

THE EFFECT OF TOBACCO PRODUCTS UPON THE ECONOMY

24   Philip Morris's view is quite different from the view of the antismoking activists. The box, "Tobacco and the Economy," is taken from the Philip Morris publication *The Great American Smoker's Manual.*

A BRIEF HISTORY OF CIGARETTE WARNING LABELS

25   In 1957, 20 years after the first study of smoking and lung cancer appeared, Senator Wallace Bennett (R-Utah) introduced a bill that would require the following warning label on cigarettes: "Warning: Prolonged use of this product may result in cancer, in lung, heart, and circulatory ailments and in other diseases."

EXHIBIT 4
Domestic Cigarette Producers Market Shares, 1985 to 1992

Company	1992	1991	1990	1989	1988	1987	1986	1985
Philip Morris	42.3	43.4	42.3	42.2	39.4	37.8	36.8	35.9
Reynolds	28.8	27.8	29.6	28.7	31.8	32.5	32.3	31.6
Brown & Williamson	11.9	11.1	10.3	11.4	11.0	11.0	11.7	11.9
Lorillard	7.2	7.3	7.6	7.1	8.3	8.2	8.2	8.1
American	6.8	7.0	6.8	7.0	6.9	6.9	7.2	7.5
Liggett	3.0	3.4	3.4	3.4	2.9	3.6	4.0	5.0
Total	100.0	100.0	100.0	100.0	100.0	100.0	100.0	100.0

Sources: Various issues of *Business Week* and *U. S. Distribution Journal.*

26   When the first warning labels appeared, in 1966, they read: "Warning: The Surgeon General has determined that cigarette smoking is hazardous to your health." In 1971 the label was changed to read "Warning: The Surgeon General has determined that cigarette smoking is dangerous to your health."

27   Beginning in 1986 a new labeling system was mandated. Four labels were required to appear an equal number of times on each brand. The labels read:

Surgeon General's Warning: Cigarette Smoke Contains Carbon Monoxide

Surgeon General's Warning: Smoking by Pregnant Women May Result in Fetal Injury, Premature Birth, and Low Birthweight

Surgeon General's Warning: Quitting Smoking Now Greatly Reduces Serious Risks to Your Health

Surgeon General's Warning: Smoking Causes Lung Cancer, Heart Disease, Emphysema and May Complicate Pregnancy

28   Although the tobacco industry resisted these labeling requirements, it has been suggested that the industry also benefited. Specifically, agreeing to label cigarettes in 1966 was part of a deal that won the industry exemption from the normal federal, state, and local regulatory processes and also made the consumer responsible for the legal risk of cigarette usage. When cigarette ads were banned from radio and television as part of the antismoking campaign in 1971, free air time for antismoking ads also ended. Subsequently, the print media was saturated with cigarette ads, and antitobacco stories began to appear less frequently in magazines, which were the recipient of the advertising revenue bonanza. Finally, the original version of the new warnings in 1986 contained the words *death* and *addiction*. Neither appears in the final version of the warnings.

29   While the United States and Scandinavian countries had the harshest cigarette warnings in 1992, some type of warning labels were mandated in about one hundred countries. Philip Morris estimated that only 10 percent of its exported cigarettes were not labeled for health risks. Countries not

EXHIBIT 5
Percentages of Smokers in Selected Countries (1980–1985)

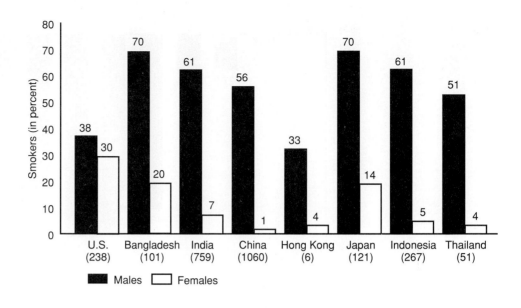

Based on data from the *Journal of the American Medical Association,* June 27, 1990, pp. 3315–16.

requiring labels included Thailand, the Philippines, the Dominican Republic, Morocco, and the former Yugoslavia.

30   The competitive situation for Philip Morris was clouded by the presence of former government tobacco monopolies in many of their overseas markets. Members of Asian Consultancy on Tobacco Control admitted that a strong anti-American sentiment fueled antismoking efforts. Richard L. Snyder, executive vice president of PMI, was more blunt: "It's just covert protectionism."[9] American tobacco interests pointed out that most Asian governments controlled tobacco monopolies and stood to lose from American competition. China's revenues from the state-owned monopoly were approximately $5.2 billion annually, 10 percent of the Korean government's revenues came from the sale of tobacco products, and Japan's government monopoly had an 84 percent share of a market in which 60 percent of all males were smokers. The cigarette warning label mandated by the Japanese government may be translated "For your health, don't smoke too much."

31   It was difficult for Philip Morris to assess the effects of a unilateral labeling of export cigarettes. The effect could be to hurt Philip Morris's market share but not necessarily reduce overall smoking. That is, Asian customers might conclude that Marlboro (a Philip Morris brand) was hazardous to their health but that other American or domestic brands were not dangerous. In some countries, such an unmandated warning label was actually misleading. In Taiwan, for example, the brand with 90 percent market share was the government brand, Long Life. This cigarette had 24 milligrams of tar compared to Marlboro's 16 milligrams of tar, while the Thai government also sold a filterless brand for about 16 cents a pack.

32   Those familiar with the process of marketing cigarettes in underdeveloped countries questioned whether the cigarette warnings would do the good hoped by the antismoking activists or simply cause the competitive problems feared by PMI. Where illiteracy was high, a warning label would have little impact. In some areas, cigarettes were sold individually by street vendors, and the smoker never saw the warning-labeled package. Others pointed out that where per-capita cigarette

EXHIBIT 6
Merchandise Trade Balances

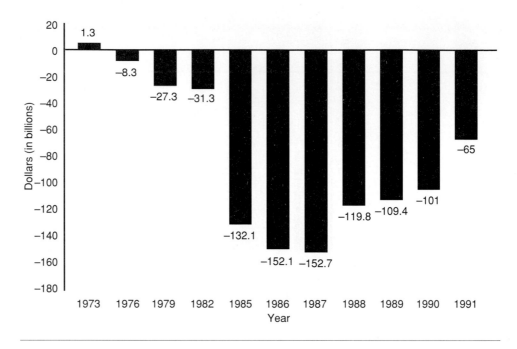

Source: *Statistical Abstract of the United States: 1990; Federal Reserve Bulletin, 1991, 1992.*

consumption was low, there was less likelihood that the majority of smokers would smoke enough to develop smoking-related health problems.[10]

33   A decision to change the warning label policy for exported cigarettes had a number of implications. Politically, a change might be preferable to a policy and wording mandated by Congress. In the United States, 30 members of the House of Representatives sponsored a bill that would require exported cigarettes to meet all domestic standards including warning labels and nicotine and tar labels. This legislation also would make cigarette ads abroad subject to the same restrictions as the United States. Competitively, a change might put Philip Morris at a disadvantage in foreign markets. Philip Morris has been in the forefront of the attacks on studies linking smoking and health. To add a warning label without being required to do so might be viewed as an admission of the health hazards of smoking. On the other hand, a full-blown discussion of the ethics of exporting unlabeled cigarettes was not an attractive agenda item for a stockholders' meeting either.

APPENDIX A: TOBACCO AND THE ECONOMY*

34   The U.S. tobacco industry is a major component of the U.S. economy, providing jobs to many Americans, contributing positively to the U.S. trade balance, and generating substantial tax revenues for federal, state, and local governments. Through a network of suppliers and numerous other industries, the tobacco industry indirectly provides jobs for Americans in virtually every sector of the economy and has a significant economic impact on every state.

*Source: *The Economic Impact of the Tobacco Industry on the U.S. Economy* (Washington, DC: The Tobacco Institute & Price Waterhouse), pp. ES-1–6.

EXHIBIT 7
Domestic Exports of Tobacco, 1982 to 1991 (in millions of $)

	Total Tobacco and Manufacturers	Leaf Tobacco	Cigarettes
1982	2,845	1,547	1,235
1983	2,647	1,462	1,126
1984	2,704	1,511	1,120
1985	2,789	1,521	1,180
1986	2,732	1,209	1,298
1987	3,400	1,090	2,047
1988	4,153	1,252	2,645
1989	3,632	1,340	3,362
1990	5,040	1,445	4,757
1991	4,574	1,428	4,232

Sources: Various issues of the *Statistical Abstract of the United States,* U.S. Census Bureau.

35   The core sector includes tobacco growing, auction warehousing, tobacco manufacturing, wholesale trade, and retail trade activities. In 1990, this sector accounted for an estimated 426,408 jobs for over $7 billion in compensation:

Sector	Employment	Compensation (millions)
Tobacco growing	152,838	859.6
Auction warehousing	9,833	132.8
Tobacco manufacturing	50,527	2,602.7
Wholesale trade	46,419	1,502.4
Retail trade	166,791	2,570.2
Core sector total	426,408	7,667.7

36   The economic contributions of the U.S. tobacco industry reach far beyond the core sector. Each production process of the core sector, from farming to retailing, requires many goods and services as inputs. The industries that supply these goods and services are referred to as the supplier sector. This sector consists of all industries that produce and distribute "intermediate" goods and services for the core sector. Intermediate goods in the tobacco industry are those goods and services that are used as inputs in the production of cigarettes and other tobacco products. The supplier sector accounted for an estimated 254,945 jobs in 1990 for $8,506,200,000 in compensation.

37   Beginning with the core sector and continuing through the supplier sector industries, the economic effects generated by the tobacco industry multiply through the economy in the form of employee wages and spending. Traditionally known as the "ripple" or multiplier effect, the expenditure-induced impacts of the tobacco industry result from the spending of the core and supplier sector employees and their families. The primary and subsequent rounds of expenditures provide corporate profits, tax revenues, investment expenditures, and employee income for a wider range of businesses. Expenditure-induced employment and compensation accounted for an estimated 1,601,164 jobs in 1990 for compensation of $50,538,600,000.

38   Tobacco-related tax revenues are tobacco excise taxes, general sales taxes on tobacco products, personal income and FICA taxes on tobacco industry employees, and corporate income taxes on corporations in the tobacco industry. The estimated total industry impact of tobacco-related tax

EXHIBIT 8
The Tobacco Industry—Employment and Compensation

Sector	Average Annual Employment	Annual Compensation (in millions)
Tobacco growing	100,000	$ 610,700
Auctions	9,240	90,800
Manufacturing	76,900	2,837,000
Wholesale trade	35,357	883,900
Retail trade	192,720	2,303,100
Total	414,217	$6,725,500

revenues in 1990 was $25,956.8 million at the federal level and $12,933.5 million at the state and local levels.

ENDNOTES

1. A. Cockburn, "Getting Opium to the Masses: The Political Economy of Addiction." *The Nation,* 30 October 1989, p. 482.
2. J. Gehorsam and R. Perl, "Smoking Is the No. 1 Killer, World Health Survey Shows." *Atlanta Journal and Constitution,* 26 April 1992, p. E3.
3. T. T. L. Chen and A. E. Winder, "The Opium Wars Revisited as U.S. Forces Tobacco Exports in Asia." *The American Journal of Public Health* 80, no. 6 (June 1990), p. 661.
4. Ibid., p. 659.
5. S. Glazer, "Who Smokes, Who Starts—And Why." *Editorial Research Reports* 1, no. 11 (1989), pp. 150–63.
6. Chen and Winder, "The Opium Wars Revisited as U.S. Forces Tobacco Exports in Asia," p. 661.
7. P. Schmeisser, "Pushing Cigarettes Overseas." *The New York Times Magazine,* July 10, 1988, p. 20.
8. K. E. Warner, "Smoking and Health: A 25-Year Perspective." *The American Journal of Public Health,* 79, no. 2, 1989, p. 143.
9. "Asia: A New Front in the War on Smoking," *Business Week,* February 1991, p. 66.
10. "Should the Activities of the Tobacco Industry in Third World Countries Be Restricted?" in L. H. Newton and M. M. Ford (eds.), *Taking Sides: Clashing Views on Controversial Issues in Business Ethics and Society* (Guilford, CN: The Dushkin Publishing Group, 1990), p. 310.

CASE 27

NINTENDO VERSUS SEGA (A): THE VIDEOGAME INDUSTRY

1   Video and computer games have emerged as a great unforeseen by-product of the electronic age. As technological advances make simulation increasingly more realistic, videogames allow the player to set sail for the New World with a boatload of colonists, to take command of a WWII German U-boat, to fly air-to-air and ground strike missions as a pilot on board the USS Eisenhower, to enter several mystical worlds to untangle an ancient web of treachery and deceit, or to match wits with seven PGA golfers on tour. Half the top 100 games of 1994 (categories included party, family, trivia, word, puzzles, arcade, real-life strategy, abstract strategy, adventure, and war games) were for computers or videogames, up from 37 percent in 1993. For the first time ever, an electronic game ("Myst" by Broderbund) was named 1994 Game of the Year by *Games* magazine.[1]

2   Videogames are a $5 billion a year business in the United States (a $4 billion market in Japan, $15 billion worldwide). Nearly 10 years ago, the industry hit rock bottom with retail videogame sales less than $100 million in 1985 (see Exhibit 1). The rebirth of the industry exceeded everyone's expectations. Since then, Nintendo and SEGA have dominated the industry with over 150 million of their game machines sold worldwide (over 50 million are in U.S. households). Nearly two-thirds of the kids in North America between the ages of 6 and 14 play videogames. Worldwide, Nintendo generated net sales of $4.7 billion and SEGA $4 billion in fiscal year 1994 (ended March 31, 1994).

3   After years of steady growth, videogame industry revenues were expected to decline slightly in 1994 and 1995. Industry analysts attributed the decline to a maturing market, although new game systems were expected to offset some of the decline.

INDUSTRY BACKGROUND[2]

4   The first home videogame system was the Odyssey, released by Magnavox in 1972. The Odyssey required that plastic overlays be attached to the television set. Despite an extensive marketing campaign by Magnavox, the Odyssey never caught on and it died after a year on the market.

5   It took a successful arcade game to build demand for the first home videogame systems. In 1972, Nolan Bushnell created the first electronic arcade videogame, "Pong." Pong was a simple coin-operated table-tennis game that caught on in bars and arcades. With $500, Bushnell and a buddy formed Atari in 1972 to manufacture Pong machines. The success of Pong did not go unnoticed and brought numerous imitators to the newly emerging industry, a trend that characterizes the industry to this day. By 1973, 90 percent of all Pong machines in arcades were clones manufactured by 25 competitors of Atari. Home versions quickly followed.

6   In 1976, Fairfield Camera & Instrument released the "Channel F," the first home system to accept interchangeable cartridges. Previously, home videogame systems played only a limited number of preprogrammed games. Once a player tired of those games the systems were relegated to a back

This case was written by Romuald A. Stone, James Madison University. The generous cooperation of David Cole, president. DFC Intelligence Research, in providing information on the U.S. videogame industry is greatly appreciated. Used with permission.

[1] B. Hochberg, ed., "Games 100," *Games,* December 1994, pp. 67–76.

[2] Extracted from Standard & Poor's *Industry Surveys* (Toys), 1991, pp. L46–47: and DFC Intelligence Research, *The U.S. Market for Video Games and Interactive Electronic Entertainment* (San Diego, 1995).

EXHIBIT 1
Size of the U.S. Market for Videogames: Hardware and Software 1977–1994

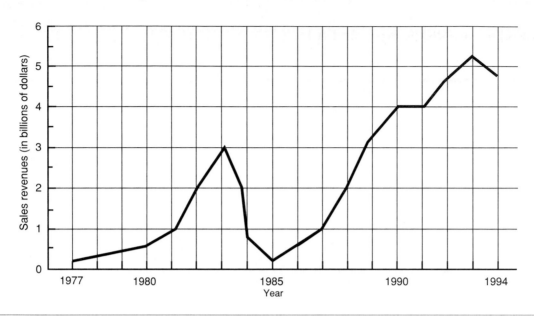

Sources: Nintendo of America and Gerard Klauer Mattison & Co.

closet and forgotten. With interchangeable cartridges, the software became separated from the hardware. By buying a new cartridge, a system played entirely new games.

7   Nolan Bushnell realized that interchangeable cartridges were the wave of the future. Two months after the release of Channel F, he sold Atari to Warner Communications for $27 million for the purpose of raising capital to release a new game system. Warner's Chairman and CEO Steven Ross saw the revolutionary potential of videogames. The company's 1976 annual report observed:

> Toys and games of skill go back to the early history of human life. Stones, bones, and wood were early materials for games, and many of those are still highly salable product today. As technology advanced, games were spring driven, later battery powered, and now they have begun to incorporate electronics. Each new development somewhat eclipsed the past, but virtually every game that was ever enjoyed by a lot of people is still made and sold. Electronic games are a logical step in this historic process.

8   In 1977, Atari released its "video computer system" (VCS) or 2600 home system. Over the next few years, Atari established the 2600 as the dominant videogame system. Industry growth got a booster shot with the introduction in arcades of "Space Invaders" in 1979 and "Pac-Man" in 1981. Atari was the first company to license an arcade game for a home system when it licensed "Space Invaders" for the 2600. The 1980s release of "Space Invaders" on the 2600 was such a smash hit that sales doubled and Atari became the fastest-growing company in the history of American business. Atari followed with the equally successful home version of "Pac-Man" in 1982. Atari remained the undisputed industry leader through 1982, consistently maintaining a 70 to 80 percent share of the home videogame market.

9   While Atari was enjoying its success, competitive rivalry was intensifying. In 1982, 350 new game titles were released by a growing number of competitors. Mattel had joined the fray with Intellivision in late 1979, and Coleco made a splash in early 1983 by introducing ColecoVision (both second-generation systems with improved graphics). Other entrants included Milton Bradley (its Vectrex system flopped) and the toy subsidiaries of Quaker Oats and General Mills.[3]

---

[3] S. P. Schnaars, *Managing Imitation Strategies* (New York: Simon & Schuster, 1994).

10   But by the mid-1980s, the bloom was already fading from the rose. According to Warner Communications' 1983 annual report, in December 1981 there was only one other manufacturer of Atari-compatible cartridges: a year later, there were more than 20. The report observed, "Throughout 1983 and into 1984, unsuccessful software manufacturers liquidated their factory inventories at close-out prices, causing damaging price competition and compounding retailers' inventory problems at a time when demand fell from the peak of 1982." In fact, Warner Communications was ultimately to bury truckloads of videogame cartridges in the Arizona desert. The bottom line for Warner was a $539 million loss on its consumer electronics segment in 1983.

11   In 1984, Warner Communications and Mattel were nearly driven to bankruptcy by the losses of their videogame subsidiaries. Warner sold its Atari division that year, and Mattel and Coleco announced they were leaving the videogame business in 1985. Industry game sales had declined to $100 million in 1985 from its previous high of $3 billion in 1982 (see Exhibit 1). The home videogame market had collapsed; it seemed that the videogame business was dying a rapid death.

Enter Nintendo and SEGA

12   Nintendo proved industry observers wrong when it introduced its Nintendo Entertainment System (NES) in 1985. Encouraged by earlier success with its Famicom game system in Japan, Nintendo ignored analysts who felt that the videogame business was a fad whose time had passed and began selling its NES in New York in the fall of 1985. In 1986, the company sold 1.1 million NES units, largely on the strength of "Super Mario Brothers," a game that eventually sold 40 million copies. Sales of game systems and game cartridges took off. By 1988, Nintendo held an 80 percent share of the $2.3 billion U.S. videogame industry.

13   In his review of the videogame industry, Steven Schnaars noted the position of American competitors regarding Nintendo's entry and early success:

> Domestic observers were skeptical of the market's staying power, and the American sellers were reluctant to commit heavily for fear of being burned again. *Business Week* echoed the timidity of the industry in 1988: The "current video game revival may already be past its prime." An Atari executive acknowledged that "we're not overextending ourselves on a category that might go south again." Nintendo, some seemed to think, was repeating past mistakes. It simply did not know the risks inherent in the American market.[4]

14   However, Nintendo learned a valuable lesson from Warner's failure: it was important to control the supply of game cartridges to ensure quality and prevent fierce price competition. To this end, Nintendo required game developers to follow strict rules. Prior to release, Nintendo had to approve the content of the games. In addition, the agreement required licensees to order games from Nintendo. The licensee developed a game and then placed an order with Nintendo who became the sole manufacturer of cartridges. The minimum order was for 10,000 cartridges, paid in advance. Licensees were charged about twice the cost of manufacturing. This included a royalty to Nintendo, but did not include distribution and marketing costs. Nintendo made money whether or not the game sold. Licensees were also limited to developing five NES games a year, and they could not release a NES game on a competing system for a period of two years.[5]

15   But Nintendo had done more than just manage inventories successfully. The company also established one of the strongest brand names in the industry. The "Official Nintendo Seal of Quality," familiar to children throughout America, was prominently displayed on all of its products. Nintendo also provided "game counselors"—videogame experts available to players by phone, which helped maintain customer loyalty. In 1993, Nintendo's game counselors handled 8 million phone calls and letters, with cumulative contacts surpassing the 30 million mark.[6]

16   SEGA first entered the American videogame market in 1986 with its 8-bit Master System. Although the system was generally considered to have better graphics than Nintendo, it achieved only a

---

[4] Ibid., p. 178.

[5] DFC Intelligence Research.

[6] Extracted from Standard & Poor's *Industry Surveys* (Toys), 1993, pp. L46–47.

15 percent market share. Nintendo's early lead had allowed it to develop a high level of brand awareness and a more extensive library of games. In addition, Nintendo's success gave it the money to fund an aggressive program of game introductions and advertising that SEGA couldn't match with its limited sales. SEGA, however, remained committed to the U.S. market and, in late 1989, introduced its 16-bit Genesis system. While 1989 sales of Genesis were respectable, Nintendo remained the dominant player with a market share of approximately 85 percent, despite the fact that it was competing with the older technology contained in its 8-bit system.[7]

Videogames in the 1990s

17 In the early 1990s, Nintendo lost its grip on the videogame market due to complacency and slow reaction to SEGA's competitive moves. Nintendo, for example, waited 18 months before coming out with its 16-bit system to compete with Genesis.[8] The NES was doing so well that Nintendo did not want to cannibalize sales by introducing a more advanced system. By the time Nintendo did release its Super NES (16-bit), SEGA had even more games available, including the popular "Sonic the Hedgehog." In addition, Nintendo's high fees alienated retailers and software developers; SEGA's license fees were lower. Finally, Nintendo's effort to maintain enthusiasm for its games by limiting supply backfired when retailers lost sales and began looking for other suppliers. SEGA also targeted a broader market than Nintendo, focusing on adults as well as teenagers. Its marketing included TV ads that disparaged Nintendo as a system for ninnies.[9]

18   Helping SEGA's sales was the explosive popularity of its uncensored version of the explicitly violent game, "Mortal Kombat," which Nintendo also released but without the explicit violence.[10] Howard Lincoln, Nintendo's then senior vice president, acknowledged losing tens of thousands of "Mortal Kombat" sales by not releasing the violent version. But he supported the decision by reiterating Nintendo's commitment to social responsibility.

19   By the early 1990s, SEGA's Genesis held a competitive, if not commanding, market share for 16-bit systems, a small but growing segment of the overall market. SEGA's mid-1992 decision to offer its lightning fast "Sonic the Hedgehog" game with the customer's purchase of the company's 16-bit Genesis system further eroded Nintendo's position. When SEGA introduced a CD-ROM attachment for its Genesis machine in November 1992, it gained further momentum. SEGA's strength in the 16-bit market continued to grow throughout 1993, ending with a 51 percent share and the segment leadership (see Exhibit 2). Through the end of fiscal year 1994, SEGA had sold over 17 million Genesis players since its debut in 1989; Nintendo had sold over 18 million Super NES system players. SEGA was projected to be the videogame leader in the 16-bit segment in 1995 with about 52 percent of overall sales. According to one observer. "SEGA has succeeded in positioning itself as the cooler machine . . . The MTV generation plays SEGA and your little brother plays Nintendo."[11]

Beyond 2000[12]

20 Observers believe the outcome of the current videogame wars will determine the future for the next generation of videogames. The long-term outlook for videogame systems is unclear. There is no way to predict how long the next generation game systems will last before they are replaced with still another wave of new products.

---

[7] Ibid.

[8] J. Carlton, "Video Games Sell in Record Numbers This Christmans," *The Wall Street Journal,* December 20, 1993, p. B3.

[9] Ibid.

[10] The potential for licensing titles increased significantly in 1991 after Nintendo ceased requiring its software developers to license titles exclusively to Nintendo.

[11] A. Pollack, "Sega Takes Aim at Disney World." *New York Times,* July 4, 1993, pp. 1, 6.

[12] Extracted largely from DFC Intelligence Research report.

EXHIBIT 2
Estimated Sales and Market Share Summary Data: 16-bit Hardware, Software, and Add-Ons, 1992–1996 (in millions)

	1992	1993	1994	1995	1996
Nintendo Super NES	$1,733	$1,890	$1,728	$1,000	$ 720
EGA Genesis and CD	1,151	1,938	1,710	1,073	719
Total 16-bit	$2,884	$3,828	$3,438	$2,073	$1,439
Percent change		33%	–10%	–40%	–31%
Market Share					
Nintendo Super NES	60%	49%	50%	48%	50%
SEGA Genesis and CD	40	51	50	52	50
Total 16-bit	100%	100%	100%	100%	100%

Source: Gerard Klauer Mattison & Co.

21 Trying to forecast video gaming beyond the next generation is pure speculation: however, analysts have offered several observations. The ideal videogame system should have the power of a computer at an inexpensive price. Most importantly, it should be "plug and play," not only in the ease of installing software but also in the sense that a consumer does not have to worry about whether a given piece of software will play on his or her system. In other words, a given title should play on any machine, whether it is manufactured by SEGA, Nintendo, 3DO, Sony, or another company. Future advances in technology will most likely facilitate releasing titles across multiple platforms.

22 However, the idea of having one common platform excites everyone except the hardware manufacturers. It would make life easier on developers, retailers, and consumers. Despite this, there seems to be little chance of that happening within the next five years. So far, no platform has emerged as dominant. Some experts expect the next generation of games could likely entail three or four relatively popular platforms.

23 It has been also difficult to speculate about the type of machine that will dominate in the future. Would it be a system dedicated solely to entertainment, or would the videogame machine of the future be multipurpose, more like today's computers? Some believe videogame machines could be replaced by an all-purpose electronic device that will deliver not only games but television programs, movies, and computer data. According to Nat Goldhaber, president of Kaleida Labs, "Once they no longer control the box, and once digital distribution of games becomes possible, how then will SEGA and Nintendo continue to be successful?"[13]

THE INTERACTIVE MULTIMEDIA MARKET[14]

24 Consumers have demonstrated a strong interest in interactive multimedia forms of entertainment. In 1991, for example, consumers spent more (approximately $7 billion) on interactive coin-operated arcade games than they spent on tickets to movies (approximately $5.1 billion). Although videogame players and typical personal computers offer only limited graphics performance, over 150 million households worldwide have been consumers of interactive entertainment and education software. In 1991, U.S. consumers spent approximately $3 billion on interactive game software.

25 The potential customers for interactive multimedia systems form a consumer pyramid roughly divided into four tiers, consisting of innovators, early adopters, other current interactive system users, and mass market consumers (see Exhibit 3).

[13] Pollack, "Sega Takes Aim," p. 6.

[14] Extracted from The 3DO Company 10-K, 1993.

EXHIBIT 3
Multimedia Market Pyramid

Innovators have a history of buying new systems that offer significant technological improvements over existing alternatives and are generally insensitive to price, software availability, brand identification, breadth of distribution, and factory support. It is believed that the class of innovators for home interactive media products consists of approximately 500,000 consumers.

Early adopters are similar to innovators except that they consider price/performance and software availability more carefully. Like innovators, they are motivated consumers who learn about a product through word-of-mouth even if it is not advertised heavily. It is believed the class of early adopters consists of several million consumers.

Interactive system users are consumers who currently own at least one interactive system such as a videogame console or a personal computer. These consumers base their purchase decisions on value, software availability, and price. It is believed that there are approximately 50 million households worldwide who are consumers of interactive entertainment and education software.

Mass market consumers are those who have televisions but are not current users of interactive multimedia products.

Source: 3DO 10-K.

26   Products that have penetrated the first three tiers include both personal computers and SEGA and Nintendo videogame consoles. SEGA introduced its 16-bit Genesis system in the United States in 1989. This system offered a significant increase in performance and visual realism over existing 8-bit systems. (Think of the bits as the width of the highway along which game data travels; more bits allow better, faster, more dynamic games.)[15] Prior to Genesis, Nintendo had the dominant market share, brand recognition, broad distribution, and over 60 independent software companies supplying software exclusively for its 8-bit format, while SEGA had limited market share, distribution, or independent software support. Moreover, the price of SEGA's new 16-bit system was approximately twice that of Nintendo's 8-bit system. Despite these considerable obstacles, the superior characteristics of the Genesis system enabled SEGA to rapidly penetrate the first tier, selling an estimated 400,000 systems in the first year alone. By 1992, Genesis had entered the third tier, with an estimated worldwide base of approximately 9 million systems, and captured 40 percent of the U.S. 16-bit market.

27   Although some videogame consoles and personal computers have penetrated the third tier of interactive customers, no interactive multimedia system to date has gained acceptance as a mass market standard equivalent to that of the VCR and audio CD player in the consumer electronics market. To be successful in reaching the mass market, it is believed that any new interactive platform must provide several enhancements over existing systems: (1) a dramatic increase in audiovisual realism to appeal to innovators, (2) the broad-based support of hardware system manufacturers and software developers required to reach early adopters and achieve acceptance as a standard platform, and (3) sufficient value and affordability to reach current interactive system users and address the mass market. Existing interactive multimedia devices have not achieved full mass market penetration because they have not satisfied all of these criteria.

28   Advances in digital processing, storage, graphics, compression, and communication technologies are enabling a new generation of devices to address the home interactive multimedia market. Initial attempts focused on adding CD-ROM drives to exiting videogames and PC-like architectures. Several large Japanese companies developed interactive video devices that utilize a CD-ROM drive. Some of the major computer product manufacturers, including Apple Computer, Inc., Microsoft Corporation, Silicon Graphics, Inc., International Business Machines Corporation, and Sony Corporation, are believed to be developing interactive video products.

29   Several major companies in the cable and telecommunications industry are developing methods to deliver interactive multimedia products and services through existing or planned cable and telephone networks. Additional strategic alliances and partnerships are expected to emerge as this segment of the industry develops further.

---

[15] M. Snider, "Video Market No Longer a 2-Player Game," *USA Today,* November 4, 1993, p. 10.

EXHIBIT 4
Estimated Sales and Market Share Summary by Segment, 1992–1996 (in millions)

	1992	1993	1994	1995	1996
8-bit	$ 720	$ 370	$ 124	$ 62	$ 30
16-bit	2,884	3,828	3,438	2,073	1,439
Portables	967	795	805	645	389
Next generation	49	115	658	2,030	4,014
Total industry	$4,620	$5,108	$5,025	$4,810	$5,872
			Market Share		
8-bit	16%	7%	2%	1%	1%
16-bit	62	75	68	43	25
Portables	21	16	16	13	7
Next generation	1	2	13	42	68
Total industry	100%	100%	100%*	100%*	100%*

*Does not equal 100% due to rounding.
Source: Gerard Klauer Mattison & Co.

VIDEOGAME TECHNOLOGY[16]

30   There are seven principal types of hardware platforms (the systems that drive the videogame software): 8-bit, 16-bit, 32-bit, and 64-bit consoles, portable systems, CD-based systems, and home computers. Videogame machines are actually small computers. For example, the 16-bit chip that powers the SEGA Genesis also ran Apple's first Macintosh. The most popular 8-bit, 16-bit, and portable hardware systems are manufactured and marketed by Nintendo and SEGA. While videogame software has been marketed primarily in cartridge form for 8-, 16-, and 32-bit types of videogame systems, software products in the CD form are expected to replace cartridge-based products as the primary format during the next several years. Companies such as 3DO Company, SEGA, and Atari developed and are currently marketing CD-based delivery systems. In addition, a number of companies have announced the development of 32-bit or 64-bit game systems, collectively referred to as "next generation" players. Currently, there are more than 20 consumer computing and gaming formats available in the United States, all of which are incompatible. Exhibit 4 shows estimated sales and market shares for the 8-bit, 16-bit, portable, and next generation segments.

8-Bit Videogame Systems

31   Home entertainment systems based on 8-bit microprocessors were introduced in the early 1980s. Nintendo introduced the NES in the United States in 1985. It was estimated that at the end of 1993, the installed base of 8-bit videogame systems in the United States was approximately 35 million units, with approximately 700 plus software titles available for use with such videogame systems. Currently, software cartridges available for use on NES are developed by Nintendo as well as approximately 65 authorized Nintendo licensees worldwide.

32   Sales in recent years of 8-bit videogame systems and software cartridges for such systems have declined significantly. It is not expected that significant growth opportunities remain in this segment (see Exhibit 4). Nintendo recently announced it would discontinue manufacture of its NES.

16-Bit Videogame Systems

33   In 1989, SEGA introduced the 16-bit Genesis videogame system in the United States. The Genesis features a more powerful microprocessor, more colors, and superior graphics, animation, and sound

---
[16] Extracted from Activision, Inc., Form 10–K, March 31, 1994.

EXHIBIT 5
Estimated Sales and Market Share Summary: "Next Generation" Hardware and Software,
1993–1996 (in millions)

	1993	1994	1995	1996
3DO-based	$ 29	$370	$ 680	$1,260
Atari Jaguar	7	66	157	118
SEGA 32-X	—	158	218	133
Philips CD-I	78	64	54	171
SEGA Saturn	—	—	230	570
Sony Playstation	—	—	216	570
Nintendo Ultra-64	—	—	475	1,193
Total next generation	$114	$658	$2,030	$4,015
	Market Share			
3DO-based	25%	56%	34%	31%
Atari Jaguar	6%	10%	8%	3%
SEGA 32-X	—	24%	11%	3%
Philips CD-I	68%	10%	3%	4%
SEGA Saturn	—	—	11%	14%
Sony Playstation	—	—	11%	14%
Nintendo Ultra-64	—	—	23%	30%
Total next generation	100%	100%	100%*	100%*

*Does not equal 100% due to rounding.
Source: Gerard Klauer Mattison & Co.

relative to the NES. Nintendo introduced its 16-bit Super NES, with similar capabilities to Genesis, in the United States in September 1991. The 16-bit systems, because of their use of software cartridges, larger memories, and more advanced hardware, offer more realistic video images, natural sounds, and synthesized music. The challenge for software developers and publishers was to produce compelling products that took advantage of the game-playing capacity of the 16-bit systems. Suggested U.S. retail prices for both 16-bit consoles started at less than $100, and prices for the software products to be used on such consoles ranged from $19.95 to $79.95. It has been estimated that the installed base of 16-bit game systems in the United States is approximately 35 million (SEGA had 17 million) and the number of software titles available for use with the Genesis and the Super NES is more than 500 and 350, respectively.

34   Opportunities for 16-bit cartridge-based software are declining, as sales of both 16-bit hardware and software continue to weaken in the United States (see Exhibit 4). Declining 8-bit and 16-bit sales in Japan—which has historically been an early indicator of market changes in the interactive entertainment software industry—have led analysts to predict that strong sales of 16-bit software in the United States would not continue beyond calendar year 1995. It has been anticipated that 32-bit and 64-bit hardware and CD-based systems will displace 16-bit hardware.

32-Bit Videogame Systems

35   In November 1994, SEGA launched its Genesis 32-X adapter, which converts 16-bit Genesis videogame players into a more powerful 32-bit machine. The upgrade was designed to provide the more than 17 million Genesis owners a way to move to the next level in videogames (arcade-quality graphics and speed) at a reasonable cost. Other 32-bit systems include SEGA's Saturn and Sony's Playstation, both released in Japan in 1994 and expected to be released sometime in 1995 in the United States. Nintendo's portable Virtual Boy player was also introduced in the United States in early 1995. Combined sales for the three nonportable 32-bit players (SEGA 32-X, Saturn, and Playstation) were expected to reach $664 million in 1995, or about 33 percent of the market (see Exhibit 5). Both Nintendo and SEGA and their competitors announced plans to introduce 64-bit machines sometime in 1995 that would eclipse the 32-bit players.

EXHIBIT 6
Estimated Sales and Market Share Summary: Portable Game Players, 1992–1996
(in millions)

	1992	1993	1994	1995	1996
Nintendo Game Boy	$770	$563	$415	$298	$220
SEGA Game Gear	162	219	388	348	169
Atari Lynx	35	13	3	—	—
Total portables	$967	$795	$806	$646	$389
Percent change		–18%	1%	–20%	–40%
Market Share					
Nintendo Game Boy	80%	71%	52%	46%	57%
SEGA Game Gear	17	28	48	54	43
Atari Lynx	4	2	0	—	—
Total portables	100%*	100%*	100%	100%	100%

*Does not equal 100% due to rounding.
Source: Gerard Klauer Mattison & Co.

64-Bit Videogame Systems

36 In November 1993, Atari introduced the Atari Jaguar, a 64-bit multimedia entertainment system at a suggested retail price of $249.95. The Jaguar features two proprietary chips (named "Tom" and "Jerry") developed in its own facilities, video with 24-bit graphics with up to 16 million colors, and a 3-D engine that can render 3-D shaded or texture map polygons in real time. The system also supports real-time texture mapping that allows for realistic surfaces to be applied over the 3-D polygons. Atari believed the graphics of the Jaguar video were equal to or superior to any other system currently available. Jaguar incorporates a 16-bit CD quality sound system, which provides realistic sounds in the software and includes human voices. The Jaguar also has a high-speed serial port that would allow for future connection into telephone networks as well as modem-based, two-player games over telephone lines.

37 Both Nintendo and SEGA were expected to introduce 64-bit players for home use in 1995, the Ultra 64 and Saturn. Nintendo's Ultra 64 was being designed by Silicon Graphics, Inc., whose computer workstations had been used to design the 3-D special effects in such movies as *Jurassic Park, Terminator 2,* and *The Abyss.*[17] Estimated sales and market share positions for each of the major next generation machines are shown in Exhibit 5.

Handheld (Portable) Game Systems

38 Nintendo's release in 1989 of the Game Boy, a battery-operated, handheld interactive entertainment system incorporating an 8-bit microprocessor, revolutionized the handheld game machine market. Previously, the only handheld games available were dedicated to a single game. Game Boy offered a portable gaming system—a take-along Nintendo that allows players to insert any number of different game cartridges. SEGA's color Game Gear handheld system, released in 1991, competes directly with the Nintendo Game Boy. Atari offers a color portable handheld game system called the Atari Lynx, released in 1992. The Lynx provides 16-bit color graphics, stereo sound, fast action, and depth of game play, and comes complete with a built-in, eight-directional joypad and a 3.5-inch full color LCD offering up to 16 colors at one time from a palette of over 4,000 colors. At the end of 1993, the purchased base of handheld game systems was approximately 13 million and the numbers of software titles available for use with the Game Boy, the Game Gear, and the Atari Lynx were over 320, 100, and 65, respectively. For 1994, sales of portable systems were expected to peak at $806 million (see Exhibit 6), representing a 16 percent share of the market (see Exhibit 4).

[17] Snider, "Video Market."

CD-Based Systems[18]

39   With the introduction in recent years of computer disk drives that read optical laser disks, or "CDs," the ability to deliver complex entertainment software made significant technological advances. A CD has over 600 times more memory capacity than an 8-bit standard cartridge, enabling CD systems to incorporate large amounts of data, full motion video, and high-quality sound, thus creating vivid multimedia experiences.

40   In addition to personal computer disk drives that read CDs, known as CD-ROM drives, several CD-based videogame systems have been introduced by videogame hardware manufacturers: SEGA introduced its SEGA CD in 1992; 3DO released the 3DO Multiplayer in 1993; and Sony Corporation has a CD-based game system under development. Nintendo's new Ultra 64 does not employ CD capability. As the installed base of CD-ROM drives for personal computers increases and as the videogame industry moves more toward CD-based delivery systems, it is believed that the traditional differentiation between the videogame market and the personal computer market will become less distinct.

41   The market for entertainment software in a CD format is at an early stage of development. As industry standards are developed and prices for CD-based hardware decline, analysts estimate that the 1.4 million CD-ROM-equipped videogame machines in play at the close of 1993 could more than triple to 4.9 million units by the end of 1995. However, the CD-based market presents particular challenges for software developers and publishers. Entertainment software would have to incorporate increasingly sophisticated graphics (video and animation), data, and interactive capabilities, resulting in higher development costs and requiring successful software developers to coordinate talent from a variety of programming and technology disciplines in the development process.

42   CD-based delivery systems do, however, present advantages to software publishers. CDs are less expensive to manufacture ($1 to $2) than videogame cartridges and, unlike floppy disks, cannot yet be readily copied. Publishers could therefore expect to achieve higher profit margins from the sale of CDs than are currently the norm in the cartridge-based videogame or floppy disk–based computer software market. In addition, once a master copy is made, extra copies can be produced in small batch lots as needed. With a cartridge game, the manufacturing process takes about two months and costs from $10 to $20 (not including licensing fees).

43   Despite all the advantages, CD-ROM technology is far from ideal. The biggest problem related to playing videogames is speed. Compared to a cartridge system, it takes longer to access data on a compact disk. Access times are important, as most videogames require fast-paced action. Any slow-down in the access and processing of data negatively affects game play. However, as the technology advances and game developers become more experienced with CD-ROM, speed is expected to become less of a concern. Another related problem with CD-ROM technology is that the hardware is more expensive to manufacture. Currently, there is no standalone CD player under $200. Interviews of consumers have revealed that CDs are easily damaged by users. A single scratch could make a CD unreadable. Finally, there are a number of CD-ROM formats; a title written for one format will not necessarily work on another system.[19]

44   Exhibit 7 compares the major cartridge and CD-based systems.

Home Computers

45   Approximately 36 percent of U.S. households have home computers. In 1994 alone, American consumers spent $9 billion to buy nearly 7 million personal computers. This has presented a new threat for videogame marketers. Industry analysts estimated that the home computer market was already siphoning off nearly 15 percent of videogame sales.

46   Although millions of Americans use home computers for spreadsheets and word processing, home computers are also taking on a different role. Most PCs sold feature multimedia packages that

---

[18] Extracted from Activision Form 10–K, p. 8.

[19] DFC Intelligence Research.

EXHIBIT 7
Comparative Data for Selected Video Game Systems, 1994

	Nintendo NES	SEGA Genesis	Nintendo SNES	Philips CD-I	SEGA CD	3DO	Atari Jaguar	SEGA Genesis 32-X
Release date	10/85	1/90	9/91	1991	10/92	10/93	11/93	11/94
U.S. installed base	35 million	17 million	18 million	250,000	1.5 million	200,000	125,000	500,000
Retail price	No longer manufactured	$90 to $120 (depending on bundled software)	$90 to $120 (depending on bundled software)	$300 (basic system); $500 (full system)	$220	$400	$250	$160
Available titles 1/95	700+	500+	350+	150+	50+	100+	<20	<10
Software unit sales (1994)	4 million (estimated)	23 million (estimated)	22 million (estimated)	<2 million	5 million (estimated)	<2 million	<1 million	NA
System type	Cartridge	Cartridge	Cartridge	Compact disc	CD	CD	Cartridge	Cartridge
System capabilities	8-bit processor, 1.79 MHz, 16 colors Resolution 256 × 240	16-bit processor, 7.6 MHz, 64 colors Resolution 320 × 224	16-bit processor, 3.58 MHz, 256 colors Resolution 512 × 418	16-bit processor, 15.5 MHz, 16.7 million colors	16-bit processor, Genesis processor, 12.7 MHz	32-bit RISC processor, 12.5 MHz, 16.7 million colors, Resolution 640 × 480	64-bit RISC processor, 16.7 million colors, Resolution 720 × 480	32-bit RISC processor (2), 23 MHz, 50,000 polygons/ second, 32,768 colors

Sources: DFC Intelligence estimates based on company reports and various industry sources. 1994 software sales are preliminary estimates and intended to be ballpark figures only.

include faster processors, more memory and storage capacity, CD-ROM drives, and sound cards, all of which serve to make home computers a complete family entertainment center and all-purpose appliance for the Information Age.[20] The number of home computers with multimedia CD-ROMs was predicted to be more than 17 million by the end of 1995. It is expected that most homes in the United States will have home computers by the end of the century.

COIN-OPERATED ARCADE GAMES/THEME PARKS

47   Americans spend approximately $7 billion on arcade games each year. With the $5 billion spent on home versions for videogame hardware and software, the outcome is a combined market nearly two and one-half times the size of the $5 billion movie box office. Arcades have experienced a resurgence in interest in recent years, which may be partly attributed to the image of arcades becoming more "family-friendly." Although many arcades are still dark, smoky, scary dens located in shopping malls, a newer breed of family entertainment centers offers batting cages, bumper cars, fast food, and so on to draw the whole family rather than just teen-aged boys.[21] The video arcade has traditionally been the launching ground for games designed for home use and it has become clear that videogame buyers also like to sharpen their game-playing skills in arcades before buying home versions of the game.

48   SEGA currently operates two miniature theme parks in Japan, featuring both traditional video-games and larger virtual-reality and interactive rides that take players on adventures such as space battles or ghost hunts.[22] The company plans to open as many as 50 high-tech theme parks in the United States by the end of the century and is aggressively looking for partners to help. The first U.S. park has been scheduled to be built in Los Angeles at an estimated cost of $25 million.

SOFTWARE

49   Since 1988, the number of available videogame titles has increased substantially. The increase is attributed to the large number of SEGA and Nintendo licensees. At the end of 1994, for example, Nintendo had a library of 466 titles; SEGA had more than 500 titles for Genesis, 175 CD titles, and more than 200 titles for the Game Gear player.

50   Competitive forces in the entertainment software and videogame marketplace have increased the need for higher quality, distinctive entertainment software concepts. Competition for titles, themes, and characters from television, motion picture, and other media as the basis for "hits" has resulted in higher development costs for software producers. Substantial nonrefundable advance licensing fees and significant advertising expenses also increase the financial risk involved. Moreover, the ability to incorporate compelling story lines or game experiences with full motion video, digital sound, other lifelike technology, and ease of use present artistic as well as technical challenges that add to the cost equation.[23]

51   Software is priced to generate most of the profit; the hardware typically sells for less than $200. Game software for most machines runs between $40 and $60. Software developer costs to develop a new videogame have ranged from $75,000 to $300,000, with some CD titles costing $1 million to develop.[24] The cost to manufacture an interactive CD selling for $40 is approximately $1 to $2. A software publisher could produce a videogame cartridge (including royalties) for between $15 to $25 per unit.[25] To compensate for games that turn out to be duds, companies need some megahits.[26] In 1992,

[20] L. Armstrong et al., "Home Computers," *Business Week,* November 28, 1994, pp. 89–94.

[21] Gerard Klauer Mattison & Co., Inc., *Interactive Electronic Industry: Entertainment Industry Overview* (New York, 1993), p. 9.

[22] D. P. Hamilton, "SEGA Looks Abroad for Partners to Open Theme Parks in U.S.," *The Wall Street Journal,* August 16, 1994, p. B6.

[23] Ibid.

[24] T. Abate, "Atari Wants Back in the Game," *San Francisco Examiner,* February 13, 1994, p. E5.

[25] 3DO Company 10–K, 1993, p. 6.

[26] N. Hutheesing, "Platform Battle," *Forbes,* May 9, 1994, pp. 168–70.

SEGA earned $450 million on worldwide sales on one game, "Sonic 2." In August 1993, the top five videogames accounted for 27 percent of industry sales, with the next five games accounting for about 8.3 percent. Sales are even more concentrated among the top titles during the holiday season.

52   Both SEGA and Nintendo each have more than 65 companies licensed to develop software for use with their respective systems. Typically, the software developer submits a prototype for evaluation and approval from Nintendo or SEGA, including all artwork to be used in packaging and marketing the product. With several kinds of CD players, all incompatible, software developers trying to penetrate the entire market must incur additional expense to recreate their games for each different system.[27]

53   Several motion picture companies have joined the interactive entertainment software segment. Paramount created Paramount Interactive in 1993 to develop products based on Paramount's motion pictures, television, and sports properties. Early game titles included "*Viper:* Assault on the Outfit," a futuristic car adventure based on the television series, and "*Star Trek: Deep Space Nine*—The Hunt," a role-playing adventure. In an exclusive agreement with Paramount, software publishers Spectrum HoloByte released several titles based on *Star Trek: The Next Generation*. Warner Bros. teamed up with game publisher Konami to release *Batman—The Animated Series* for Super NES. Warner also worked with Konami and Virgin Interactive Entertainment (VIE) to feature over 1,500 original animations within game play. According to Martin Alper, CEO of VIE, "This level of collaboration between a major studio and a game company is unique and, no doubt, will become a benchmark for future products of this nature."[28]

54   Capital Cities/ABC Inc. formed a joint venture in December 1994 with Electronic Arts, a pioneer in interactive software, to develop software and videogames based on ABC's children and news TV shows. The new venture was expected to produce about 12 titles a year, starting in December 1995, mostly on CD-ROM, and expand eventually to about 25 titles a year.[29] In December 1994, the Walt Disney Co. also announced formation of a new computer software unit that would produce educational programs and videogames inspired by its movies. The division intended to focus initially on SEGA and Nintendo videogames and CD-ROM educational software linked to its animated musicals, including *Pocahontas*.[30]

55   Earlier attempts to link movies and games had failed, most notably Walt Disney's film based on "Super Mario Bros.," the best-selling videogame series ever. However, more efforts to create movies bringing the best-selling arcade games to the silver screen were underway. *Double Dragon* was released in November 1994; *Street Fighter* (at a cost of $40 million) was released in December 1994;[31] *Mortal Kombat* ($36 million) was released in April 1995. Also on the horizon are movies based on "Doom," "Myst," "King's Quest," and "Leisure Suit Larry."

VIDEOGAME DEVELOPMENT ISSUES

56   Firms must resolve four key considerations in developing a videogame: (1) what development and distribution agreement to arrange, (2) whether to acquire content or create original content, (3) which platform to develop for, and (4) future employment concerns. Each of these issues is discussed in the following sections.[32]

---

[27] Ibid.

[28] Much of this section is extracted from J. Abrams, "Hollywood Comes to Las Vegas," *Dealerscope,* February 1994, pp. 24, 26.

[29] E. Jensen, "Capital Cities and Electronic Arts Plan Venture in Software and Video Games." *The Wall Street Journal.* December 6, 1994, p. B4.

[30] J. Horn, "Disney Forms Interactive Unit Division to Create Computer Software Linked to Its Movies," *San Francisco Chronicle,* December 6, 1994, p. D3.

[31] J. Carlton, "Capcom Bets That Stars and a Story Can Turn a Hot Game into a Hit Film," *The Wall Street Journal.* October 6, 1994, pp. B1, B6.

[32] This section extracted from DFC Intelligence Research.

Development and Distribution Agreements

57   The distribution channels for videogames and other multimedia are constantly evolving. The common method is for a publisher to hire a developer to create a title. The developer is responsible for ensuring the quality of the product. The publisher handles manufacturing, packaging, marketing, and distribution issues. The publisher bears the risk if the product fails. Generally, developers are paid a royalty based on wholesale revenues. This royalty varies greatly, but typically ranges from 5 to 15 percent.

58   Many developers attempt to publish their own titles. Affiliated label and copublishing programs have become a popular means for small companies to publish their own titles and maintain their independence. Under an affiliated label program, a developer handles marketing and publishing, while a copublisher deals with distribution. In return, the developer receives a royalty of up to 75 percent of wholesale revenue. A variation on the affiliated label program is expected to become the distribution method of choice.

Acquiring Content

59   In the past, companies that owned popular intellectual property would license that property for use in videogames in return for a modest royalty. But the vast market potential for games had made content-owners reluctant to license their properties, and acquiring high-potential creative content was becoming difficult and time-consuming. Many large entertainment conglomerates have set up interactive divisions to create titles based on their own intellectual creations and titles. In the future, more publishers will be forced to base their games on original content or else rely on works in the public domain.

Platform Considerations

60   The videogame market is fast reaching the point where it is essential that a software title be released for a number of different hardware platforms. Even worse, the number of hardware platforms is growing. Each platform is incompatible and requires a different set of development tools. The personal computer is the easiest platform to develop for, but personal computer titles so far have had limited revenue potential. Creating titles for the dedicated systems is more time-consuming and difficult. As a general rule, it takes 12 to 18 months to develop a software title for the first platform, and 3 to 6 months for each additional platform.

61   The manufacturers of the dedicated systems (platform providers) control who can develop for their system. A license from the platform provider is required to develop a dedicated system. Licensees pay the platform provider royalty fees based on sales volume. Platform providers often regulate content and limit the number of titles that can be released. Nintendo and SEGA have high licensing fees and are strict about what titles can be released for their systems. 3DO has lower licensing fees and is not as strict about regulating content.

62   Publishers must carefully consider which platforms to develop for. Currently, no CD-ROM platform has a large enough installed base to make it feasible to publish a title for just one platform. In making the decision of which platform to choose, development costs, installed base figures, licensing fees, and player demographics must be studied.

Employment Concerns

63   Top development talent is a rare commodity. In the future, developers are expected to have significant bargaining power. Hollywood guilds and agents are just now starting to organize multimedia developers. As this trend continues, development costs are projected to rise.

EXHIBIT 8
Nintendo SNES U.S. Player Demographics

Age	Percent of Players
Under 6	2%
6–14	48
15–17	11
18+	39

Gender	Percent of SNES Players	Percent of Game Boy Players
Male	82%	59%
Female	18%	41%

Source: Nintendo.

THE VIDEOGAME DEVELOPMENT PROCESS[33]

64 The development of videogames requires a blend of technology and creative talent. Typically, a development team is formed consisting of a producer, designers, programmers, musicians, and graphic artists. The average cartridge game involves the efforts of 10 to 15 individuals, although it is not unusual for many more people to be involved.

65 The producer oversees the project and is responsible for coordinating the efforts of the development team. Designers come up with the basic concepts for the game, draft the script, and are responsible for the characters, plot, and overall objectives of the game. Graphic artists draw the characters and objects in the game. Programmers write the computer code that incorporates all the various elements into a form that can be used on the appropriate hardware platform.

66 Once a workable version of the game has been created, preliminary testing is done to evaluate the computer code and to ensure all the game elements are in place. If all has gone well, the game is play-tested to find any hidden bugs. The next level involves bringing in a group of outside players to test the game's reception with the general public. Only after the completion of all testing can a product be sent off for manufacturing and packaging.

67 Because it takes 10 to 15 months to complete an original game and then another 3 to 6 months to port that game to another platform development, risks are quite high. A lot could change between the time a design was started and the time it is launched in the marketplace. A platform that was popular last year could be out of fashion 12 months later.

DEMOGRAPHICS

68 Videogames are in 69 percent of homes with kids 12 to 17; computers are in 18 percent of homes with kids under 18.[34] Not all videogame customers are teenagers, however. Adults—mostly men—rent sports games like "Bill Walsh College Football" and "NBA Jam." Men in their 20s and 30s represent a growing portion of the videogame market.[35] Nintendo's U.S. player demographics are shown in Exhibit 8. The U.S. population of 10- to 20-year-olds and 30- to 50-year-olds is shown in Exhibit 9.

---

[33] Extracted from DFC Intelligence Research.

[34] "Electronic Games Look to Untapped Girls' Market," *San Jose Mercury News,* November 11, 1994, p. 2D.

[35] D. Wharton, "Video Legions," *Los Angeles Times* (Valley Edition), November 18, 1994, p. 10.

EXHIBIT 9
U.S. Population Data, 1984–2000

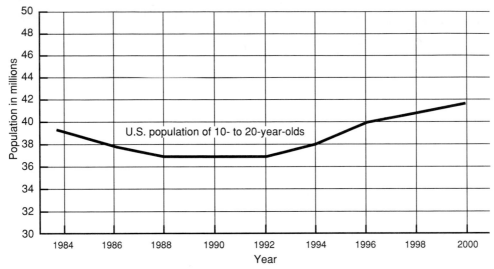

Based on birth rates from U.S. Census Bureau. Does not account for immigration.

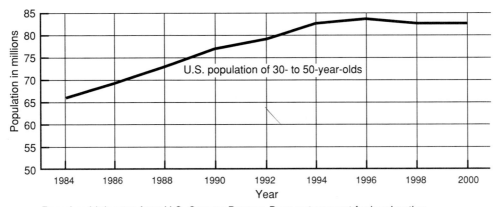

Based on birth rates from U.S. Census Bureau. Does not account for immigration.

Source: Gerard Klauer Mattison & Co.

69   Studies have indicated that many children who grew up playing videogames continue to do so as adults. There are several key differences between adult and younger players. Adolescents are more concerned with what is "in" and "hot." The adult market is composed of numerous niches, each with an interest in a different type of game. Adults like titles that fit in which their life-styles and interests. It is difficult to create one title that appeals to the entire adult market. In addition, the biggest complaint among adults is that most games take too much time to play. Adults prefer to play games in short bursts during the free moments.[36]

70   Generally, videogames have not been popular with women. Many of the most popular games deal with such activities as street fighting, car racing, and football. According to the Software Publishers Association, about 28 percent of computer game and 21 percent of videogame players are female. Only one top videogame, Nintendo's "Super Metroid," has a female lead character. Software

---

[36] DFC Intelligence Research.

developers are slowly responding to this untapped market and rolling out games for girls. SEGA, for example, formed a task force composed of the top female marketers and game developers in the company to develop software products that appeal to female tastes.

71 A clue to what videogames appeal to women comes from Nintendo's experience with its Game Boy handheld players. The company found that women accounted for 40 percent of the 27 million worldwide buyers of Game Boy, a figure double the percentage of women buying its other machines. For some unknown reason, women liked "Tetris," a geometric videogame that was packaged with Game Boy. One 14-year-old boy wrote Nintendo about his mother, saying, "Almost 24 hours a day she plays Tetris . . . I can't hardly play more than one game a day."[37] Nintendo has hired experts to study adult Game Boy habits.

72 In another study of 10,000 children playing video and computer games over two years, Electronic Arts found that girls (1) identify with characters in videogames, (2) like fast action and competitive games less than boys, (3) prefer something they can learn from, and (4) really enjoy puzzle solving and cooperative games that allow them to create and design.

73 The biggest challenge in the videogame industry is to get more adults and females to play videogames. Although numerous studies are underway, no especially successful approaches have emerged.

MARKETING[38]

74 In the past, the marketing of videogames was unsophisticated. Demand was created from the advertising campaigns of platform providers such as Nintendo and SEGA. Demand was so strong that publishers merely had to get their product into the store and it would sell. Advertising was an attempt to gain word-of-mouth publicity and might have consisted of a few pages in the leading videogame consumer magazines and a booth at the Consumer Electronics Show.

75 As of 1994 videogame marketing is big business. As retail space has become crowded, the industry witnessed a marked shift in marketing strategy. The major videogame releases are now marketed much like a release from a major movie studio. Television advertising, promotional tie-ins, merchandising, direct mail, and special launch parties are now commonplace. A well-planned marketing campaign is now a must for a hit game.

76 Many industry observers believe the videogame industry is becoming a "hits"-driven business as marketing costs escalate and access to retail space becomes tighter. Smaller game publishers without the resources of the big players in the industry face an uphill battle. These publishers are likely to be caught in a Catch-22 situation. Retailers only take their product if they have a strong brand name, backed with advertising dollars. But without shelf space, it is hard for small publishers to build a brand image and start generating the revenue necessary to fund large-scale marketing campaigns.

77 Toy stores and computer software stores have been the traditional retailers of videogames. However, as the videogame business has grown, other retailers have begun carrying the high-margin product. In 1994, over 20,000 stores in the United States carried videogames. Toys "Я" Us was the leading retailer with an estimated 20 percent of the U.S. market; mass merchandisers (e.g., Wal-Mart and Kmart) captured about 35 percent of all videogame sales. Exhibit 10 shows estimated market share by retail outlet.

78 Industry growth has created new competitive challenges for retailers. It was only a few years ago that demand for games was so high that a retailer could sell whatever was put on the shelf: Even the bad games sold. The major complaint of retailers was not having enough products. Nintendo went so far as to ration games in 1988 and 1989. All this changed as the market became flooded with product and Nintendo began to face increased competition from SEGA. In 1994, retailers found many of the 16-bit cartridges sitting unsold on the shelf; sales seem to be concentrated in a handful of hit titles. Moreover, most videogames had a shelf life of 30 to 60 days, after which they were sold at a discount.

---

[37] J. Carlton, "Game Makers Study How Tetris Hooks Women," *The Wall Street Journal,* May 10, 1994, p. B1.

[38] Extracted from DFC Intelligence Report.

EXHIBIT 10
Estimated U.S. Retail Outlet Market Share for Videogames, 1994

Toys "Я" Us	20%
Other toy stores (e.g., Kay Bee Toys)	10
Computer software (e.g., Babbages)	15
Video and music stores (e.g., Blockbuster)	15
Consumer electronics (e.g., Best Buy)	5
Mass merchants (e.g., Wal-Mart)	35
	100%

Source: DFC Intelligence estimates based on various industry
sources.

With retailers holding excess inventory, it was not uncommon to see games that originally listed for $60 discounted to the $15 to $20 range. The net effect was a substantial decline in profit margins. DFC Intelligence Research identified that retailers were most concerned about the difficulty of deciding what to buy, the lack of a return policy, and heavy discounting from increased competition. Consequently, retailers became very careful about what they would stock. Retail buyers looked at three things when deciding what product to stock: the quality of the game, the amount of advertising the publisher planned to do, and the reputation of the publisher.

79   Despite overcrowding of traditional distribution channels, analysts expected new channels of distribution to emerge. Technology was making new forms of distribution possible. Several companies are engaging in experiments that could revolutionize distribution. These experiments involve such things as direct marketing, electronic distribution in retail, on demand via cable television, and on-line distribution through networks such as the Internet. Finally, there is the potential that the increased bandwidth of phone and cable systems could make multiplayer networked gaming possible.

SEASONALITY[39]

80   Retail sales for videogames are quite slow between May and August. Analysts attribute the sales slowdown to several factors. First, teenagers spend much more time outside rather than indoors playing videogames. They watch less TV, thus making them less reachable via advertising. In addition, because they are out of school, there is less "I got to level 10, how far did you get?" to spur sales. Finally, sales are slower because the publishers put out fewer games. Two-thirds of the video-game sales occur during the year-end holiday season.

THE INFORMATION SUPERHIGHWAY[40]

81   According to best estimates, there are approximately 25 million people on the Internet, with the number of users growing by about 2.5 million each month. While American media companies scramble to develop strategies to put themselves on the Internet, both Nintendo and SEGA nixed any plan to put their games on-line even though on-line services are one of the fastest-growing segments in the global media market. Companies like America Online, CompuServe, Delphi, and Prodigy have all enjoyed double-digit growth. Microsoft planned to introduce its Marvel on-line service in 1995. On-line services had also taken off in Japan. Most observers believed that games would become an important ingredient in all these services. In fact, one observer predicted that in the not-too-distant

[39] This section was extracted from Gerard Klauer Mattison Industry Overview, 1993.

[40] This section was extracted from M. Schrage, "Why Sonic the Hedgehod Needs to Jump onto the Info Highway," *Los Angeles Times* (Business Section), November 3, 1994, p. 1.

future, people miles apart would play tennis, golf, and perhaps Virtuality Boxing together on global information highways.[41] George Lucas, creator of the *Star Wars* and *Indiana Jones* film trilogies, in an interview in *The Wall Street Journal,* commented on the future interaction of entertainment and technology:

> Well, I have a game company, and I think view-on-demand games will take off pretty quickly. It's a little bit problematical about how it's going to work, but it seems obvious that home delivery of games is a natural . . . Interactive games that involve more than one player . . . will be popular. You're playing with two or three other people at the same time at various places over the phone."[42]

82   Nintendo and SEGA pursued radically different strategies for bringing telecommunications to their game machines, neither of which included the telephone. Nintendo elected to go the satellite route. In 1993, Nintendo paid $8 million for a 20 percent stake in St. Giga, a troubled Japanese satellite broadcaster, for the purpose of downloading games by satellite to Japan's 14 million Nintendo game players. Although considered a novel distribution concept, this approach does not support any opportunity for networked games people can play with or against each other.

83   SEGA began test-marketing its SEGA Channel in the United States in early 1994, and formed SEGA Digital Communications Ltd. in July 1994 to put videogames on cable in Japan. However, the technology is such that the system does not allow for interpersonal interactivity.

84   New services are springing up to deliver games over phone lines. Catapult Entertainment, Inc., is selling Xband Videogame Network, which matches players of similar skill levels to play SEGA with people around the country. The service requires use of a $70 Xband modem available in toy and computer stores. A similar on-line service is available for computer game users from ImagiNation that connects evenly matched players who pay a base fee of $9.95 for five hours of play. Microsoft plans to offer PlayersNet, a software package that also allows PC users to compete against each other over computer networks or telephone lines using a modem.

85   Some industry analysts predicted that videogame companies were well positioned to take advantage of future opportunities related to the "information superhighway." They argued that a videogame machine could evolve into a set-top box that connects to fiber-optic cable networks and delivers interactive services into the home. Companies with the skills to develop and market such hardware at prices well below the cost of home computers could then offer interactive products with the potential to become an important part of the future.[43]

PROFILES OF SELECTED VIDEOGAME COMPETITORS

86   Nintendo and SEGA's key competitors in the videogame industry included Sony, 3DO, Atari, and Philips Electronics NV. Commodore reentered the videogame industry with a CDTV system in 1991, and more recently with the Amiga CD32; however, sales were less than expected, and the company was not considered a significant player. Neither was NEC Corporation. In late 1994, Apple Computer, Inc., formed an alliance with Japan's largest toy maker (Bandai Co., Ltd.) to build a low-cost CD-ROM videogame player, which was expected to be available worldwide for the 1995 holiday season. Exhibit 11 summarizes estimated U.S. videogame industry retail sales and market share statistics for each of the key competitors.

Nintendo Company, Ltd.[44]

87   Nintendo began as a playing card manufacturer in 1889 in Kyoto, Japan. In 1994, the company was headed by the great grandson of Nintendo's founder. Hiroshi Yamauchi. Yamauchi had been in charge since becoming the company's president in 1922 at the age of 22.

---

[41] J. Guyon, "Virtual Center," *The Wall Street Journal* (Entertainment & Technology), March 21, 1994, p. R18.

[42] T. R. King, "Lucasvision," *The Wall Street Journal* (Entertainment & Technology), March 21, 1994, p. R20.

[43] DFC Intelligence Research.

[44] Nintendo's company background provided by DFC Intelligence Research.

EXHIBIT 11
Estimated U.S. Videogame Industry Sales and Market Share Data: Retail Sales of
Hardware and Software, 1992–1996 (in millions)

	1992	Share	1993	Share	1994	Share	1995	Share	1996	Share
Nintendo										
NES hardware	$ 180	4%	$ 120	2%	$ 49	1%	$ 25	1%	$ 10	0%
NES software	540	12	250	5	75	1	38	1	20	0
Game Boy hardware	320	7	263	5	165	3	138	3	100	2
Game Boy software	450	10	300	6	250	5	160	3	120	2
Super NES hardware	743	16	625	12	518	10	250	5	180	3
Super NES software	990	21	1,265	25	1,210	24	750	16	540	9
Ultra 64 hardware	—	—	—	—	—	—	125	3	563	10
Ultra 64 software	—	—	—	—	—	—	350	7	630	11
Total Nintendo	$3,223	70%	$2,823	55%	$2,267	45%	$1,835	38%	$2,162	37%
SEGA										
Genesis hardware	$ 440	10%	$ 550	11%	$ 400	8%	$ 223	5%	$ 170	3%
Genesis software	650	14	1,156	23	1,000	20	675	14	480	8
Game Gear hardware	72	2	99	2	223	4	223	5	89	2
Game Gear software	90	2	120	2	165	3	125	3	80	1
SEGA CD hardware	45	1	150	3	173	3	100	2	36	1
SEGA CD software	17	0	83	2	138	3	75	2	33	1
32-X hardware	—	—	—	—	75	1	94	2	50	1
32-X software	—	—	—	—	83	2	124	3	83	1
Saturn hardware	—	—	—	—	—	—	164	—	350	6
Saturn software	—	—	—	—	—	—	66	—	220	4
Total SEGA	$1,313	28%	$2,157	42%	$2,255	45%	$1,868	39%	$1,591	27%
Atari										
Jaguar hardware	—	—	$ 5	0.1%	$ 42	1%	$ 80	2%	$ 48	1%
Jaguar software	—	—	2	0.0	24	0	60	1	38	1
Lynx hardware	$ 20	0%	9	0.2	2	0	—	—	—	—
Lynx software	15	0	4	0.1	1	0	—	—	—	—
Jaguar CD hardware	—	—	—	—	—	—	10	0	18	0
Jaguar CD software	—	—	—	—	—	—	8	0	15	0
Total Atari	$ 35	1%	$ 20	0.4%	$ 69	1%	$ 157	3%	$ 118	2%
3DO-based										
Hardware	—	—	$ 21	0%	$ 167	3%	$ 350	7%	$ 600	10%
Software	—	—	8	0	204	4	330	7	660	11
Total 3DO-based	—	—	$ 29	1%	$ 370	7%	$ 680	14%	$1,260	21%
Sony										
Playstation hardware	—	—	—	—	—	—	$ 150	3%	$ 350	6%
Playstation software	—	—	—	—	—	—	66	1	220	4
Total Sony	—	—	—	—	—	—	$ 216	4%	$ 570	10%
CD-I										
CD-I hardware	$ 35	1%	$ 50	1%	$ 40	1%	$ 39	1%	$ 105	2%
CD-I software	14	0	28	1	24	0	15	0	66	1
Total CD-I	$ 49	1%	$ 78	2%	$ 64	1%	$ 54	1%	$ 171	3%
Total Industry	$4,619	100%	$5,107	100%	$5,024	100%	$4,809	100%	$5,872	100%
Percent change from prior year			10.6%		−1.6%		−4.3%		22.1%	

88   Under Yamauchi's leadership the company began to expand into the toy business. Nintendo became NCL, Nintendo Company, Ltd., and went public in the early 1960s. In 1975, Nintendo made its first venture into videogames when it got a license to sell Magnavox's videogame system in Japan. Nintendo released its own home videogame system in 1977 and soon began to develop arcade games.

89   Nintendo eventually designed a game system that could use interchangeable cartridges. The machine, called the Famicom (short for Family Computer), was released in Japan in 1983. The 8-bit Famicom sold for about $100, considerably less than the $250 to $300 most game systems cost at that time. Nintendo sold 500,000 units in the Famicom's first two months. The 14 competing systems soon withdrew from the market and Nintendo became the home videogame leader in Japan.

90   In 1980, Nintendo decided to enter the U.S. market and Nintendo of America (NOA) was established as an independent subsidiary. The first president of NOA was Minoru Arakawa, Hiroshi Yamauchi's son-in-law. The original goal of NOA was to break into the $8 billion a year arcade business. Arcade games from Japan were shipped to the United States and distributed by NOA.

91   At first, business for NOA was slow, mainly because Nintendo did not have a hit game. That changed in 1981 with the release of "Donkey Kong," created by legendary Nintendo game developer, Sigeru Miyamota. Donkey Kong was such a success in the United States that NOA ended its second year in business with over $100 million in sales.

92   In 1984, Nintendo began to think about bringing the Famicom to the United States. But, because the U.S. home videogame market had crashed in 1983, no manufacturers, distributors, or retailers would have anything to do with videogames. Nintendo decided to proceed cautiously and began to test the Famicom in New York in 1985. For the U.S. release, the Famicom was renamed the Nintendo Entertainment System (NES). Slowly orders began to come in, and over Christmas 1985, 50,000 units were sold.

93   As noted earlier, the NES went on sale nationwide in 1986. By the end of its first year more than 1 million units had been sold in the United States. Three million units had been sold by the end of 1987, and "The Legend of Zelda" became the first game to sell over a million copies. Nintendo mania had begun.

94   As the NES gained momentum, sales increased from $1 billion in 1987 to over $5 billion in 1992. Game Boy, a portable videogame system released in 1989, sold 40,000 units the first day it was available in the United States. The Super Nintendo Entertainment System (SNES) was released in the United States in 1991. Sales of the SNES took off in 1992 fueled by Nintendo's marketing expertise and the release of Capcoms's "Street Fighter II." The SNES then became Nintendo's top-selling system.

95   As of 1994, Nintendo had been forced to undergo some significant changes. Nintendo had had to deal with increased competition and a declining 16-bit market. Nintendo received a wake-up call in 1993 when SEGA passed Nintendo in sales of 16-bit systems. Nintendo suddenly realized it no longer had the monopoly it once enjoyed. Unhappy with the performance of his U.S. subsidiary, Yamauchi replaced his son-in-law as the leader of NOA and installed Howard Lincoln, a senior vice president, as chairman.

96   Exhibit 12 presents summary financial data on Nintendo. During fiscal year 1994, Nintendo sold more videogame cartridges than in any previous year. However, consolidated net sales fell to $4.714 billion, a 23.5 percent decline from the previous year, and the company's consolidated net income of $511 million decreased by 40 percent from 1993. This represented Nintendo's first decline in sales and net income since it introduced the Famicom in Japan in 1983. Nintendo's stock had fallen from a high of ¥17,500 ($150.86) in 1992 to a low of ¥6,140 ($59.61) in 1994.

97   Sales in Nintendo's home sanctuary were healthy in fiscal 1994, but the strong yen seriously affected the company's performance around the globe. A weak economy in Europe and a soft market in the United States, coupled with increased competition, further hurt export sales. The fact that Nintendo did not introduce any new product categories in 1994 did not help its performance. However, Nintendo's overall financial position remained quite strong. The company had cash and cash equivalents of over $3.334 billion, no debt, and total liabilities of only $1.427 billion. Nintendo's liabilities-to-equity ratio was 0.33 at the end of fiscal year 1994, down from 0.51 the previous year.

98   For the six-month period ending September 30, 1994 (fiscal year 1995), Nintendo reported that earnings slipped 17 percent to $520 million from $623 million in the same period the previous year. Weak demand for its old games coupled with a strong yen against the dollar hurt sales revenue. Nintendo projected selling 6.5 million units of software worldwide in 1995, but later revised its

EXHIBIT 12
Consolidated Financial Summary for Nintendo Co. Ltd., 1992–1994 (in thousands of $)

| | Year Ended March 31 | | |
	1994	1993	1992
Net sales	$4,714,675	$6,161,840	$4,843,475
Cost of goods sold	2,887,106	3,758,376	2,926,885
Gross profit	$1,827,569	$2,403,464	$1,916,590
Selling, general, and administrative expenses	693,507	650,360	483,115
Operating income	$1,134,062	$1,753,104	$1,433,475
Other income/(expenses):			
Interest income	110,392	175,380	206,823
Other	(230,727)	(104,973)	(81,971)
Total	$ (120,335)	$ 70,407	$ 124,852
Income before income taxes	$1,013,727	$1,823,511	$1,558,327
Income taxes	576,497	967,261	807,653
Foreign currency translation adjustments	73,968	4,031	224
Net income	$ 511,198	$ 860,281	$ 750,898
Net income per share	$ 3.61	$ 6.08	$ 5.30
Cash dividend	0.68	0.68	0.52
Cash and cash equivalents	3,334,679	3,425,000	2,549,144
Current assets	5,037,417	4,638,570	3,968,830
Total assets	5,740,070	5,248,012	4,458,664
Current liabilities	1,355,426	1,693,274	1,587,965
Total liabilities	1,427,515	1,762,738	1,626,353
Stockholders' equity	4,312,555	3,485,274	2,832,311

Source: Company annual reports.

estimate to a more realistic 2.5 million. Nintendo counted on Virtual Boy and Ultra 64 to reverse declining profits and help fuel sales growth in 1995.[45]

SEGA Enterprises, Ltd.[46]

99   SEGA Enterprises, Ltd. (SEGA) was one of the few Japanese companies started by Americans. In 1951, two Americans in Tokyo, Raymond Lemaire and Richard Stewart, began importing jukeboxes to supply American military bases in Japan. Their company eventually expanded into amusement game imports and adopted the slogan "service and games."[47] The modern SEGA began to take shape in 1956 when a Brooklyn-born entrepreneur named David Rosen, who had been stationed in Japan with the Air Force, returned to Japan and began importing mechanical coin-operated amusement machines as Rosen Enterprises. In 1965, the "service and games" company merged with Rosen Enterprises. Not happy with the game machines available from U.S. manufacturers, Rosen decided to make his own and acquired a Japanese factory that makes jukeboxes and slot machines. The company stamped SEGA on its games—short for service games—and Rosen adopted the brand name that persists today.[48] The next year it began its transformation from importer to manufacturer, producing a submarine warfare arcade game called "Periscope," which became a worldwide hit.

100   SEGA was acquired by Gulf & Western (G&W) in 1969 and went public in 1974. Hayao Nakayama, a Japanese entrepreneur and former SEGA distributor, was recruited to head SEGA's Japanese operation; Rosen headed the U.S. operation. Through the 1970s and early 1980s, the videogame industry went through a boom period. SEGA's revenues reached $214 million in 1982.

---

[45] "Tough Year Crimps Nintendo Earnings," *USA Today,* November 22, 1994, p. 08B.

[46] Portions of SEGA's company history extracted from DFC Intelligence Research.

[47] Sega's American Roots," *The New York Times,* July 4, 1993, p. 6.

[48] R. Brandt, R. D. Hof, and P. Coy, "SEGA!" *Business Week,* February 21, 1994, pp. 66–74.

EXHIBIT 13
Consolidated Financial Summary for SEGA Enterprises, Ltd., 1993–1994
(in thousands of $)

	Year Ended March 31	
	1994	**1993**
Net sales	$4,038,197	$3,578,968
Cost of goods sold	2,916,161	2,301,496
Gross profit	$1,122,036	$1,277,472
Selling, general, and administrative expenses	831,837	697,988
Operating income	$ 290,199	$ 579,484
Other income/(expenses):		
Interest income	47,561	33,353
Other	(78,865)	(104,024)
Total	$ (31,304)	$ (70,671)
Income before income taxes	$ 258,895	$ 508,813
Income taxes	249,259	267,102
Foreign currency statements translation	99,089	22,752
Net income	$ 108,725	$ 264,463
Net income per share	$ 1.09	$ 2.72
Cash dividend	0.37	0.21
Cash and cash equivalents	1,000,262	963,646
Current assets	2,398,652	2,185,073
Total assets	3,482,821	3,026,354
Current liabilities	1,261,454	1,084,437
Total liabilities	1,973,999	2,001,006
Stockholders' equity	1,508,822	1,025,348
Effective tax rate	0.52	0.52

Source: Company annual reports.

The overall game industry hit $3 billion in 1982, but collapsed three years later with sales of $100 million. G&S became anxious to divest SEGA. Nakayama and Rosen organized a buyout of SEGA's assets for $38 million in 1984 and SEGA Enterprises, Ltd., was formed. The deal was backed by CSK, a large Japanese software company that now owns 20 percent of SEGA. Nakayama became the chief executive and Rosen headed the U.S. subsidiary. SEGA went public in 1986. Rosen was later made a director of SEGA and cochairman of its American subsidiary.

101　　SEGA of America was formed in 1986. Its first task was to market SEGA's first home videogame system, the 8-bit Master System. SEGA had been beaten to the punch in Japan by Nintendo, which got a jump on the market with its 1983 release of the 8-bit Famicom. Unfortunately for SEGA, Nintendo also won the 8-bit war in the United States and the Master System slowly died out. Meanwhile, Nintendo essentially grabbed the entire home videogame market share in the United States and Japan.

102　　Europe was a different story. SEGA systems achieved success in Europe, while Nintendo sales were slow. SEGA of Europe accounted for a large share of SEGA's revenues, and some of SEGA's recent sales declines were due to the slumping European market.

103　　SEGA did not begin to see mass-scale success until the release of its 16-bit Genesis system in 1989. The Genesis system was not an immediate hit. It took the release of "Sonic the Hedgehog" in 1991 for sales to take off. In 1994, the Genesis was challenging Nintendo's SNES as the leading 16-bit system in the United States, and SEGA was considered Nintendo's equal in the videogame industry.

104　　Fiscal 1994 was a lackluster year for SEGA as well as Nintendo. A weak Japanese economy and a dismal consumer market in Europe coupled with an unexpectedly sharp appreciation of the yen against other major currencies resulted in a 12.8 percent increase in net consolidated sales from fiscal 1993 to $4 billion but a 58.9 percent decline in net income to $108.7 million (see Exhibit 13). The sharp decrease in net income was caused by a net loss from SEGA's European operation. From a high of ¥11,000 in 1992, SEGA's stock price declined to a low of ¥7,010 at the end of 1994.

EXHIBIT 14
SEGA Sales by Division (nonconsolidated) (in millions)

	1994	1993
Net sales:	$3,432.2	$2,983.1
Consumer products	2,286.8	1,971.4
Domestic sales	249.7	166.2
Exports	2,037.1	1,805.2
Amusement center operations	598.5	506.6
Amusement machine sales:	505.5	494.9
Domestic sales	377.9	398.4
Exports	127.6	96.5
Royalties on game software	41.4	10.3

Source: Company annual reports.

105   Exhibit 14 depicts SEGA's sales by division (nonconsolidated). Sales of consumer products in 1994 reached $2.3 billion, a 16 percent increase, and accounted for 66.6 percent of net sales. Strong overseas demand for SEGA's products, particularly in the United States, offset the falloff in sales to Europe. Revenues from amusement center operations increased by 18.1 percent to $598.5 million, or about 17.4 percent of net sales. Revenue from amusement machine sales increased by 2.1 percent by $505.5 million, or 14.7 percent of net sales. Royalties on game software were up 302 percent to $41.4 million.

106   In the first six months of fiscal 1995 (ending September 1994), SEGA's unconsolidated pretax profit fell 43 percent to ¥16.33 billion ($166.97 million), down from ¥28.58 billion the previous year. Sales fell 25 percent, to ¥151.07 billion, from ¥200.65 billion. Analysts said the declines were expected due to slumping global demand for videogames and the soaring yen, which made Japanese products less competitive abroad.[49]

107   In its home market of Japan. SEGA was being badly outcompeted by Nintendo (90 percent of all game sales in Japan went to Nintendo), in part because of distribution problems and in part because SEGA's sports-oriented games were not as popular in Japan. SEGA's market strength was in its American and European operations, which had some autonomy from Tokyo. It was reported (unconfirmed) in the press that SEGA of America contributed about 25 percent to the parent company's overall revenue.

Sony Corporation[50]

108   Sony Corporation was established in Japan in May 1946 as Tokyo Tsushin Kogyo Kabushiki Kaisha. In January 1958, it changed its name to Sony Kabushiki Kaisha (Sony Corporation in English). Sony Corporation of America was formed in 1960. Sony engages in the development, manufacture, and sale of various kinds of electronic equipment, instruments, and devices. In addition, Sony has a strong presence in the entertainment industry. Its music group (Sony Music Entertainment, Inc.) includes such companies as Columbia Records Group, Epic Records Group, TriStar Music Group, and others. Sony's Pictures Group includes four motion picture companies: Columbia Pictures, TriStar Pictures, Sony Pictures Classics, and Triumph Releasing Corporation.

109   Eager to claim a stake in the fast-growing videogame business, Sony Corp. set up a new division in May 1994, Sony Computer Entertainment of America, to develop and market a next generation home videogame, called the Sony Playstation (PSX). The PSX had been under development for more than four years and represented an important element in Sony's strategy to dominate the entertainment markets for hardware and software.[51] According to Sony, the game player, powered by a 32-bit

---

[49] "Video-Game Maker's Profit Plunged in Fiscal Fist Half," *The Wall Street Journal,* November 14, 1994. p. B5.

[50] Extracted largely from Sony Corporation Annual Report, 1993.

[51] McGowan and S. Ciccarelli, Interactive Entertainment Industry Overview (New York: Gerard Klauer Mattison & Co., 1994).

microprocessor, provides three-dimensional animated graphics, compact disc–quality sound, and digital full-motion video. The system was released in Japan in December 1994; a U.S. and European release was scheduled for sometime in 1995.

110   As a new entrant in the stable of next generation systems, PSX faced heavy competition from 3DO, the Atari Jaguar, systems planned by Nintendo and SEGA, as well as multimedia PCs. The PSX was not compatible with any existing hardware standard. Sony reported that more than 160 videogame developers and publishers in Japan had agreed to support the Playstation.[52]

111   Despite Sony's lack of history in videogame hardware, and no particular success in software, the company was considered a formidable competitor in areas such as distribution of both hardware and software, a well-known brand name and image with U.S. consumers, and access to Columbia and Tri-Star film libraries.

112   Sony's entrance did not go unnoticed by SEGA Enterprises Ltd. President Hayao Nakayama, who candidly expressed his view that Sony Corp. was likely to become SEGA's biggest adversary in home videogames in the coming year. "Sony is a much stronger company than another company I cannot name [Nintendo] . . . [Sony] has much more experience in the consumer market."[53] It was also rumored that SEGA delayed introducing Saturn from 1994 to 1995 in order to reengineer its system to compete better against Sony's new PSX system.

113   Exhibit 15 presents selected financial data for Sony Corp. For the fiscal year ended March 31, 1994, Sony reported consolidated net income of $148.5 million on total sales of $36.25 billion. Although sales increased by 5.3 percent over the previous year, net income was down by 52.5 percent due to factors including the appreciation of the yen (approximately 16 percent, 24 percent, and 31 percent against the U.S. dollar, the German mark, and the pound sterling, respectively), intensified price competition, and disappointing performance of a number of Sony Pictures Entertainment's motion pictures. Sony estimated that if the value of the yen had remained the same as in the previous fiscal year, corporate sales would have been $4.8 billion over the reported figure.

114   Sony did not anticipate a better year in 1995. The company expected a continued unfavorable operating environment due to uncertainty in the foreign currency market, delayed economic recovery in Japan and Europe, and intensifying price competition in audiovisual equipment markets in Japan and overseas. For the nine months ending December 31, 1994, Sony reported a net loss of $2.8 billion on net sales of $29.8 billion.

115   To counter the unfavorable forces in its environment, Sony's strategy called for aggressively moving forward to develop appealing electronics products and to promote its activities in the entertainment business. Sony also planned to reshape its corporate structure by eliminating product groups and establishing eight new companies within its organization. Finally, the company planned to make every effort to enhance overall performance by reviewing every activity in an effort to reduce costs and streamline company operations.

The 3DO Company[54]

116   3DO has been a relatively new player in the videogame industry. The company was initially formed in 1989 when the principals of NTG Engineering, Inc., launched an effort to create a new home interactive multimedia platform by developing technology that achieved a breakthrough in audiovisual realism. In September 1991, the company was incorporated as SMSG, Inc., in California and changed its name to The 3DO Company in September 1992. In May 1993, 3DO had an initial public offering of $48.6 million. In June 1994, the company raised $37 million through a private placement.

117   The company's initial product design was the 3DO Interactive Multiplayer, which runs interactive entertainment, education, and information applications developed specifically for the 3DO format. It also plays conventional CDs and displays photo CDs, but it is not compatible with other commercially available software formats.

---

[52] DFC Intelligence Research.

[53] "SEGA Now Considers Sony, Not Nintendo, as Top Rival," *The Wall Street Journal,* September 15, 1994, p. B5.

[54] Extracted from The 3DO Company's Form 10-K, 1993 and 1994.

EXHIBIT 15
Selected Financial Data for Sony Corp., 1993–1994 (in millions of $)

	1994	1993
Statement of Operations Data		
Total revenue	$36,250	$34,422
Cost and expenses:		
Cost of sales	26,756	25,249
Selling, general, and administrative expenses	8,526	8,082
	$35,282	$33,331
Operating income	968	1,090
Other income:		
Interest and dividends	373	397
Foreign exchange gain, net	344	193
Other	450	376
	$ 1,167	$ 966
Other expenses:		
Interest	672	788
Other	470	472
	$ 1,142	$ 1,260
Income before taxes	993	796
Income taxes	763	718
Income before minority interest	229	369
Minority interest in consolidated subsidiaries	80	56
Net income	$ 149	$ 313
Net income per depositary share	$ 0.41	$ 0.79
Balance Sheet Data		
Cash and cash equivalents	$ 5,486	$ 4,970
Current assets	19,647	18,189
Working capital	5,982	3,164
Total assets	41,455	39,050
Current liabilities	13,366	15,025
Long-term obligations	13,947	10,974
Total stockholders' equity	12,908	12,312

Source: Annual reports and Form 20-F.

118   3DO's goal was to license its technology to manufacturers of consumer electronics and personal computer systems. Six global electronics companies were licensed to manufacture the 3DO Interactive Multiplayer system. Panasonic Company, a division of Matsushita Electric Corporation of America, had marketed a version of the 3DO system in the United States since October 1993 and introduced a version in Japan in March 1994. More than 500,000 3DO systems had been sold worldwide through 1994. Other companies licensed to use 3DO's technology included AT&T, Sanyo Electric Co., Goldstar and Samsung Electronics Co., Ltd., Creative Technology, Ltd., and Toshiba Corporation. The Goldstar 3DO system was launched in November 1994. 3DO systems were available at over 6,500 retail locations.

119   While early reports indicated videogame sales were flat for other systems, retailers reported 3DO games were selling well during the 1994 holiday season. No doubt contributing to 3DO's success were several recent awards, which included "Best System of 1994" from *DiHard GameFan* magazine and best overall game system from the *Los Angeles Daily News* (December 11, 1994). The 3DO system was also recommended as the game system to buy for the holidays by the *Miami Herald* (December 2, 1994).

120   3DO and its licensees were expanding the available base of software titles (over 135 titles released through 1994) in a variety of application areas, including action/strategy, sports, simulations, interactive movies, information, education, and music/arts. However, 3DO's ability to offer more game titles was hampered by a fracas with software developers over licensing fees. 3DO

EXHIBIT 16
Selected Financial Data for 3DO, 1992–1993 (in thousands except per share data)

	1994	1993	1992*
Statement of Operations Data			
Total revenue	$ 10,295	$ 0	$ 0
Cost of development systems	3,464	0	0
Gross profit	$ 6,831	$ 0	$ 0
Operating expenses:			
Research and development	23,412	11,434	1,146
Sales and marketing	8,248	1,993	64
General and administrative expenses	6,175	2,008	552
Acquisition of NTG royalty rights	21,353	0	0
Total operating expenses	$ 59,188	$ 15,435	$ 2,762
Operating loss	$(52,357)	$(15,435)	$ (2,762)
Interest income	949	50	29
Other income	27	0	0
Loss before provision for income taxes	$(51,381)	$(15,385)	$ (2,733)
Provision for income taxes	50	1	1
Net loss	$(51,431)	$(15,386)	$ (2,734)
Net loss per share	$ (2.60)	$ (1.02)	$ (0.18)
Shares used in per share calculations	19,747	15,018	15,014

	March 31	
	1994	1993
Balance Sheet Data		
Cash, cash equivalents, and short-term investments	$ 14,301	$ 2,827
Current assets	18,333	3,301
Working capital	9,960	(1,175)
Total assets	25,870	6,437
Current liabilities	8,373	4,476
Note payable to stockholder	474	474
Total liabilities	9,991	6,396
Total stockholders' equity (deficit)	15,879	(959)

*Period from October 1, 1991 (inception), to March 31, 1992.
Source: 3DO Form 10-K.

required developers to pay a $3 surcharge on top of the current royalty of $3 a copy for every CD produced. According to Tom Zito, president of Digital Pictures, Inc., a software developer that has created four games for 3DO. "This is going to make me seriously think about investing company resources in developing more titles for their platform."[55] 3DO systems retailed for approximately $399 and were bundled with two free titles through the 1994 holiday season.

121   In an effort to gain a performance edge over its competitors, 3DO planned to introduce in late 1995 a peripheral upgrade, the M2 Accelerator, which promised to introduce movielike graphics and sound to its videogame players. The add-on accessory utilized a new Motorola PowerPC microprocessor and was expected to hit the market just as Nintendo and SEGA introduced their new machines. The company had not disclosed the price.

122   Management expected to incur substantial operating losses as it continued to develop its product, promote growth, and develop and publish software titles. For fiscal years ended March 31, 1994, and 1993. 3DO incurred net losses of $51.4 million and $15.4 million, respectively. Revenue for 1994 totaled $10.3 million. There was no revenue for 1993. Exhibit 16 presents selected financial data for 3DO since start-up operations began.

[55] J. A. Trachtenberg, "Should Santa Bring Nintendo, SEGA, Atari or What?" *The Wall Street Journal*, December 6, 1994, p. B1.

123   For the first nine months of fiscal year 1995 ended December 31, 1994, 3DO generated $22 million in total revenues, or a 262 percent increase over the same period in 1993. The company incurred a loss of $38.3 million as compared to a loss of $44 million in 1993.

124   In December 1994, the company announced a corporate restructuring. The company consolidated its technology, advanced development, product management, licensing, and business development groups into a new business operations department. Analysts said the move signaled the firm's desire to conserve cash and put off another public offering since its stock continued to drift downward.

Atari Corporation[56]

125   Atari Corporation (Atari) designs and markets interactive multimedia entertainment system and related software and peripheral products. Atari's principal products were Jaguar, a 64-bit interactive multimedia entertainment system, along with related game software and peripheral products; Lynx, a 16-bit portable color handheld videogame; and the Falcon 030 series of personal computers. Manufacture of these products was performed by subcontractors. The principal methods of distribution were through mass market retailers, consumer electronic specialty stores, and distributors of electronic products. Atari had approximately 117 employees worldwide.

126   Management recognized in the fall of 1991 that the computer and videogame products it was marketing were rapidly becoming technologically obsolete. Intense competitive rivalry from larger competitors and shrinking margins in computer products profits led Atari to exit this line of products and to refocus itself as an interactive media entertainment company. In an effort to ensure its competitive advantage in this new market, Atari developed a 64-bit videogame system called Jaguar, which it began shipping in the fourth quarter of 1993. jaguar is assembled by IBM in the United States, and currently sells for $249.

127   The Atari Jaguar was named the industry's "Best New Game System" (*VideoGames Magazine*), "Best New Hardware System" (*Game Informer*), and "1993 Technical Achievement of the Year" (*DieHard GameFan*). In April 1994, the Jaguar was given the European Computer Trade Show Award for "Best Hardware of the Year."

128   With the hardware developed (Atari is already working on a second-generation Jaguar system), Atari was busy developing more software titles such as "Alien vs. Predator," "Kasumi Ninja," and "Star Raiders 2000." To ensure a good supply of software titles for Jaguar, Atari licensed more than 125 third-party publishers and developers. By early 1995, Atari was expected to have more than 50 software titles available to users.

129   Atari planned to introduce a peripheral unit in the fall of 1995 that would enable the Jaguar to play CD-ROM games and regular audio CDs. The expected retail price was $149. Also in development was a full motion video cartridge that would enable the CD-ROM to play movies. The company was also funding development of a virtual reality system for Jaguar. In addition, Atari had decided to enter the PC software market, citing economies of scale benefits in developing a title for both the Jaguar and personal computer.

130   Atari's president, Sam Trmiel, was upbeat in his message to shareholders in the company's 1993 annual report: "We have completed our restructuring and consolidation around the world. As the business grows, we will reap the benefits of our streamlined central distribution in Europe and consolidation of U.S. operations." In his 1994 message he ended by saying: "The video game industry is now 20 years old and has provided millions of players with challenging and enjoyable experiences. We are well positioned for the next surge, the 32/64 bit generation."

131   Exhibit 17 presents selected financial data for Atari. In fiscal year 1994, Atari generated net sales of $38.4 million as compared to $28.8 million in 1993, an increase of 33 percent. The increased sales were primarily a result of Atari's national rollout of its new 64-bit Jaguar entertainment system and related software. Sales of Jaguar represented 77 percent of total sales in 1994 as compared to 13 percent in 1993. The Jaguar was launched in two markets in the fall of 1993, and approximately 100,000 units were sold by the end of 1994. Jaguar game players were sold with little or no margin,

---

[56] Extracted from Atari Corporation Annual Report, 1993 and 1994.

EXHIBIT 17
Selected Financial Data for Atari, 1992–1994 (in thousands, except per share data)

	1994	1993	1992
Statement of Operations Data			
Net sales	$ 38,444	$ 28,805	$127,340
Cost of sales	35,093	42,550	132,455
Gross profit	3,351	(13,745)	(5,115)
Operating expenses:			
Research and development	5,775	4,876	9,171
Sales and distribution	14,454	8,895	31,125
General and administrative expenses	7,169	7,558	16,544
Restructuring charges	0	12,425	17,053
Total operating expenses	$ 27,398	$ 33,754	$ 73,893
Operating loss	$(24,047)	$(47,499)	$(79,008)
Settlements of patent litigation	32,062	0	0
Exchange gain (loss)	1,184	(2,234)	(5,589)
Interest income	2,015	2,039	4,039
Other income	484	854	927
Interest expense	(2,304)	(2,290)	(3,522)
Loss before provision for income taxes	$ 9,394	$(49,130)	$(83,153)
Income tax credit	0	264	434
Income (loss) before extraordinary credit	$ 9,394	$(48,866)	$(82,719)
Discontinued operations	0	0	9,000
Income (loss) before extraordinary credit	$ 9,394	$(49,394)	$(73,719)
Extraordinary credit	0	0	104
Income (loss)	$ 9,394	$(49,394)	$(73,615)
Net profit (loss) per share	$ 0.16	$ (0.85)	$ (1.28)
Shares used in per share calculations	58,962	57,148	57,365

	December 31		
	1994	1993	1992
Balance Sheet Data			
Cash, cash equivalents, and short-term investments	$ 22,592	$ 23,059	$ 39,290
Current assets	113,188	50,599	109,551
Working capital	92,670	33,107	75,563
Total assets	131,042	74,833	138,508
Current liabilities	20,518	17,492	33,988
Total long-term obligations	43,454	52,987	53,937
Total stockholders' equity	67,070	4,354	50,583

Source: Atari Corporation 10-K.

but significantly higher margins were achieved on software sales. Sales of Lynx and Falcon 030 computers and other older products represented 23 percent of sales in 1994 as compared to 87 percent in 1993. Atari paid no income taxes in 1994 because of operating loss carryforwards. Overall, Atari reported net income for 1994 of $9.4 million as compared to a net loss of $48.9 million in 1993.

132   Atari's future financial performance hinged on how successful the company's management would be in implementing its turnaround strategy and adapting to future changes in the highly competitive market. Atari's net sales in 1994 were largely dependent on the success of the Jaguar system and related software. Management felt that until such time as Jaguar achieved broad market acceptance and hardware and related software products were sold in substantial volume, the company would not achieve profitability. Margins on Jaguar hardware were expected to be relatively low.

133   In November 1994, Atari announced it completed a deal with SEGA that included a licensing agreement and an equity investment in Atari. The company received $50 million from SEGA in exchange for a license covering the use of a library of patents. SEGA also made an equity investment in Atari of $40 million to acquire common stock equal to a 7 percent interest. Both companies entered into cross-licensing agreements through the year 2001, which allow them to publish on each of their respective game platforms.

EXHIBIT 18
Selected Financial Data for Philips Electronics N.V., 1993–1994 (in millions of $)

	1994	1993
Statement of Operations Data		
Net sales	$33,689	$31,626
Direct costs of sales	(24,461)	(23,154)
Gross income	$ 9,228	$ 8,472
Selling expenses	(6,484)	(6,438)
General and administrative expenses	(815)	(766)
Other business income	148	110
Income from operations	$ 2,077	$ 1,378
Financial income and expenses	(478)	(559)
Income before taxes	$ 1,599	$ 819
Income taxes	(330)	(185)
Income after taxes	$ 1,269	$ 634
Equity in income of unconsolidated companies	72	(24)
Group income	1,341	610
Share of other group equity in group income	(207)	(151)
Net income from normal business operations	$ 1,134	$ 459
Extraordinary items—net	42	596
Net income	$ 1,176	$ 1,055
Balance Sheet Data		
Cash and cash equivalents	$ 1,560	$ 1,248
Current assets	16,517	14,840
Working capital	6,348	5,987
Total assets	26,586	24,884
Current liabilities	10,169	8,853
Long-term obligations	3,316	2,898
Total stockholders' equity	7,007	6,155

Source: Annual reports.

Philips Electronics NV

134   Founded in 1891, Philips Electronics NV (Philips) was Europe's largest consumer electronics company. The Dutch electronics giant also produces semiconductors and PCs and is a world leader in lightbulb manufacturing. Philips owns 79 percent of PolyGram (recordings), 35 percent of Matsushita Electronics (component venture with Matsushita), and 32 percent of Grundig (electronics, Germany). For inventing the digital audio technology used in CD players, Philips and Sony receive royalties on each one sold.

135   The company was number 32 in *Fortune*'s 1994 Global 500 ranking of the world's largest industrial corporations and was listed among the top eight companies in the global electronics industry that included Hitachi, Matsushita Electric, GE, Samsung, Sony, and NEC. In fiscal 1994, Philips earned a net profit of $1.176 billion on total sales of $33.7 billion (see Exhibit 18). By the end of 1994, the company had several hundred subsidiaries in over 60 countries and employed 238,500 people worldwide.

136   Philips is organized into six product divisions, one of which includes "Other Consumer Products." Within this division is Philips Media, which has operations in four key business areas: software development in entertainment and electronic publishing applications, systems development and hardware/software distribution, cable TV, and media-based services. Philips Media is responsible for the CD-I game platform and software.

137   Philips was one of the first companies in the world to market a CD-based interactive entertainment system (called CD-I). The basic machine looks like a simplified VCR; it can play interactive movies and encyclopedias, regular movie videos, videogames, and conventional music CDs.

138   By its own admission Philips's marketing of its CD-I was confused and unfocused before 1993. Until the company decided to stress the machine's ability to play games and movies, consumers didn't know whether it was a video player, a home computer, a game console, or a toy. Limited game

titles left consumers unconvinced that the format would last. Sales were dismal. After several years on the market, the installed base of CD-I machines in the United States at the end of 1994 was estimated at 250,000.

139 Philips tried to build market visibility by improving its marketing effort. A lengthy, high-quality, soft-sell infomercial began running in 1994. Hardware prices were slashed, with some units selling below $300. The company beefed up its software library with top-shelf feature films, music titles (from its Polygram recordings subsidiary), and games; Philips also signed on several leading developers in PC-based CD-ROM games. In 1994, the company introduced over 100 new CD-I software titles; the software catalog now carries close to 300 titles.

140 Analysts projected modest sales of CD-I hardware and software. The CD-I was simply another platform with a chance of carving out a small share of the market for compact disc game players. Moreover, because the CD-I used a 16-bit processor, some perceived the machine as being based on outdated technology. However, Philips seemed to recognize the problems with the CD-I and has been focusing a lot of resources on software development for other platforms as well as the CD-I.

CASE 28

NINTENDO VERSUS SEGA (B): THE VIDEOGAME WARS

Once upon a time (1988, to be exact), Nintendo sat alone atop the mountain, master of its domain. Then came SEGA, scraping and clawing up the slope. The two stood precariously together—plumber vs. hedgehog—each trying to elbow the other off the peak. Today, if they pause and look down, the two will see new videogame challengers approaching on all sides, each promising a higher level of technology . . . Suddenly, the game's wide open again. And Nintendo's—and SEGA's—grip may be slipping . . . This is all-out war.[1]

1 Nintendo and SEGA had been the giants in the videogame industry for the past decade. During this period, the two competitors engaged in an ever increasing rivalry that was labeled the "Videogame Wars." The fight was intensifying, with SEGA winning some crucial engagements in the battle for market share.

2 Despite generally flat sales in 1994, the videogame wars were taking on a new dimension in 1995 as "next generation" game players were being released worldwide by Nintendo, SEGA, and new competitors. The entries included Nintendo's Ultra 64, SEGA's Saturn, and Sony Corp.'s Playstation, joining 3DO's Interactive Multiplayer and Atari Corp.'s Jaguar already on the market. All of these game players were not expected to survive because there was not a big enough market. The challenge for competitors was getting limited shelf space and lining up software developers. One industry observer predicted that consumers would become "very, very confused about what videogame player to buy: Sony versus Atari versus 3DO versus Nintendo versus SEGA? Sixteen-bit versus 32-bit versus 64-bit?"[2] The rapidly growing base of home computers equipped with high-tech entertainment options and CD-ROMs further added to the confusion.

3 Sales were expected to improve significantly once the next generation systems were fully on line in 1996, but profits were expected to be weak. Hardware margins were thin because low retail hardware prices were imperative for building a base to generate software demand. Software sales entailed much higher gross margins. But with the shift to newer game playing systems in 1995–96, margins were expected to be depressed by a rising percent of low-margin hardware sales. For software publishers and developers, increased competition had driven up the cost of securing licenses and developing games for an audience that sought out newer, more action-packed, or more interesting games with better visual graphics.[3] Moreover, software publishers and developers had to decide whether to incur the costs of programming their games to run on all or most of the different types/brands of games players or to gamble on developing software compatible with only one or two game platforms that might fail to win a significant share of the hardware systems purchased by consumers. Consumers, also, were in somewhat of a quandary because if they purchased a new game-playing hardware system that failed to attract many software developers, then the system wouldn't run many of the games on the market.[4]

This case was written by Romuald A. Stone, James Madison University.

[1] M. Snider, "Video Market No Longer a 2-Player Game," *USA Today,* November 4, 1993, p. 1D.

[2] A. Harmon, "What's Coming, When, and Why It's a Big Deal," *Los Angeles Times,* December 18, 1994, p. 6.

[3] S. McGowan and S. Ciccarelli, "Interactive Entertainment Industry Overview" (New York: Gerard Klauer Mattison & Co. 1994).

[4] DFC Intelligence Research. *The U.S. Market for Video Games and Interactive Electronic Entertainment* (San Diego, 1995).

NINTENDO AND SEGA PROFILES

Nintendo Company, Ltd.

Background[5]

4   Nintendo in 1994 was one of the world's largest hardware manufacturers and software developers for interactive entertainment. A profile of Nintendo's first 100 years is presented in Exhibit 1. Exhibit 2 shows a time line of Nintendo's milestones since 1983.

5   Nintendo was credited with singlehandedly reviving the videogame industry after the industry collapsed in the early 1980s due to the weight of too many bad games (such as Atari's ET), poor marketing, and overproduction. In order to get a handle on what kids really wanted, Nintendo sent its representatives to video arcades around the country to learn firsthand why young people went to the arcades rather than playing at home for free. What they discovered set the stage for the eventual Nintendo-led recovery of the videogame industry.

> It wasn't the games themselves or a fickle market, but the arcade-quality, full-animation, imaginative play of the arcade games that the videogame providers—in their gold-rush, sucker-born-every-minute mentality—could not or would not provide for the home player. So Nintendo introduced a game system that was not simply a "player," but a sophisticated device with the power of a personal computer, able to reproduce near arcade-quality games on the home screen.[6]

6   Nintendo's arcade-quality machine was its Nintendo Entertainment System (NES). The NES was far superior to those of the Atari generation. In 1985, when the NES was introduced, 1.1 million units were sold. At the end of 1988, Nintendo accounted for $1.7 billion of the $2.3 billion videogame business. Nintendo sold its game players at cost and made money on the software. Through 1994, Nintendo had sold more than 100 million hardware systems and more than 750 million game packs worldwide. During most of the 1980s, Nintendo was the undisputed leader in the videogame industry, controlling 80 percent of the market at the end of the decade. By 1994, however, Nintendo's market share had declined to about 45 percent and was expected to decline further as SEGA continued its "take no prisoners" strategy.

Financial Performance[7]

7   For the six-month period ending September 30, 1994 (fiscal year 1995), Nintendo's earnings slipped 17 percent to $520 million from $623 million in the same period the previous year. Weak demand for its old games coupled with a strong yen against the dollar hurt sales revenue. Nintendo projected selling 6.5 million units of software worldwide in 1995, but later revised its estimate down to 2.5 million. Nintendo was counting on Virtual Boy and Ultra 64 to reverse declining profits and help fuel sales growth in 1995.[8]

8   During fiscal year 1994 (April 1993–March 1994), Nintendo sold more videogame cartridges than in any previous year. However, consolidated net sales fell to $4.714 billion, a 23.5 percent decline from the previous year, and the company's consolidated net income of $511 million decreased by 40 percent from 1993 (see Exhibit 3). This represented Nintendo's first decline in sales and net income since it introduced the Famicom in Japan in 1983. Nintendo's stock fell from a high of ¥17,500 ($150.86) in 1992 to a low of ¥6,140 ($59.61) in 1994.

9   Sales in Nintendo's home Japanese market sanctuary were strong in fiscal 1994, but the rising value of the yen seriously affected the company's performance around the globe. A weak economy in

---

[5] Additional background information is contained in Case 27, "Nintendo versus SEGA (A)."

[6] S. Wolpin, "How Nintendo Revived a Dying Industry," *Marketing Communications* 14, no. 5 (1989), p. 38.

[7] This section is reprinted from Case 27 "Nintendo versus SEGA (A)," to provide financial data for users of this case who may not have previously reviewed case (A).

[8] "Tough Year Crimps Nintendo Earnings," *USA Today,* November 22, 1994, p. O8B.

EXHIBIT 1
Nintendo's 100-Year History

1989 Fusajiro Yamauchi, great-grandfather of the present president, began manufacturing "Hanafuda," Japanese playing cards, in Kyoto.

1933 Established an unlimited partnership, Yamauchi Nintendo & Co.

1947 Began a distribution company, Marufuku Co. Ltd.

1950 Changed the company name from Marufuku Co. Ltd. to Nintendo Playing Card Co. Ltd. Hiroshi Yamauchi took office as president. Absorbed the manufacturing operation of Yamauchi Nintendo & Co.

1952 Consolidated factories were dispersed in Kyoto.

1953 Became the first to succeed in manufacturing mass-produced plastic playing cards in Japan.

1959 Started selling cards printed with Walt Disney characters, opening a new market in children's playing cards. The card department boomed!

1962 In January, listed stock on the second section of the Osaka Stock Exchange and on the Kyoto Stock Exchange.

1963 Changed company name to Nintendo Co. Ltd. and started manufacturing games in addition to playing cards.

1969 Expanded and reinforced the game department; built a production plant in Uji City, a suburb of Kyoto.

1970 Stock listing was changed to the first section of the Osaka Stock Exchange. Reconstruction and enlargement of corporate headquarters was completed. Started selling the Beam gun series, employing opto-electronics. Introduced electronic technology into the toy industry for the first time in Japan.

1973 Developed laser clay shooting system to succeed bowling as a major pastime.

1974 Developed image projection system employing 16mm film projector for amusement arcades. Began exporting them to America and Europe.

1975 In cooperation with Mitsubishi Electric, developed videogame system using electronic video recording (EVR) player. Introduced the microprocessor into the videogame system the next year.

1977 Developed home-use videogames in cooperation with Mitsubishi Electric.

1978 Created and started selling coin-operated videogames using microcomputers.

1979 Started an operations division for coin-operated games.

1980 Announced a wholly owned subsidiary, Nintendo of America, Inc., in New York. Started selling "GAME & WATCH" product line.

1981 Developed and began distribution of the coin-operated videogame "Donkey Kong." This videogame enjoyed great popularity.

1982 Merged New York subsidiary into Nintendo of America, Inc., a wholly owned subsidiary headquartered in Seattle, Washington, with a capital investment of $600,000.

1983 Built a new plant in Uji City to increase production capacity and to allow for business expansion. Established Nintendo Entertainment Centers Ltd. In Vancouver, B.C., Canada, to operate a family entertainment center. Raised authorized capital of Nintendo of America, Inc., to $10 million. In July, listed stock on the first section of the Tokyo Stock Exchange. Started selling the home videogame console "Family Computer" (Famicom), employing a custom CPU (custom processing unit) and PPU (picture processing unit).

1984 Developed and started selling the unique two-screen interactive coin-operated videogame "VS. System,"

1985 Started to sell the U.S. version of Family Computer "Nintendo Entertainment System" in America. Developed and started selling game software "Super Mario Bros." for the family computer.

1986 Developed and started selling the "Family Computer Disk Drive System" to expand the functions of the Family Computer. Began installation of the "Disk Writer" to rewrite game software.

1987 Sponsored a Family Computer "Golf Tournament" as a communications test using the public telephone network and Disk Faxes to aid in building a Family Computer network.

1988 Nintendo of America, Inc., published the first issue of *Nintendo Power* magazine in July. Researched and developed the Hands Free controller, making the Nintendo Entertainment System accessible to many more Nintendo fans.

1989 Released "The Adventure of Link," sequel to the top-selling game "The Legend of Zelda" in the United States. Started "World of Nintendo" displays in the United States to help market Nintendo products. Studies show that children are as familiar with "Mario" as they are with Mickey Mouse and Bugs Bunny!

1990 Introduced Game Boy, the first portable, handheld game system with interchangeable game paks. Nintendo Power Fest featuring the Nintendo World Championships tours the country. Japan enters the 16-bit market by releasing the Super Famicom in the fall.

1991 Nintendo introduces World Class Service Center locations across the United States. The 16-bit Super NES, along with "Super Mario World," is released in the United States.

1992 The Super NES Super Scope and Mario Paint with the Super NES Mouse Accessory were released. The long-awaited "Zelda" sequel, "The Legend of Zelda: A Link to the Past," arrived for the Super NES.

1993 Nintendo announces the advent of the Super FX Chip, breakthrough technology for home video systems. The first game using the Super FX Chip, "Star Fox," is released in April.

Source: Nintendo of America.

EXHIBIT 2
Nintendo Time Line of Significant Events, 1983–1994

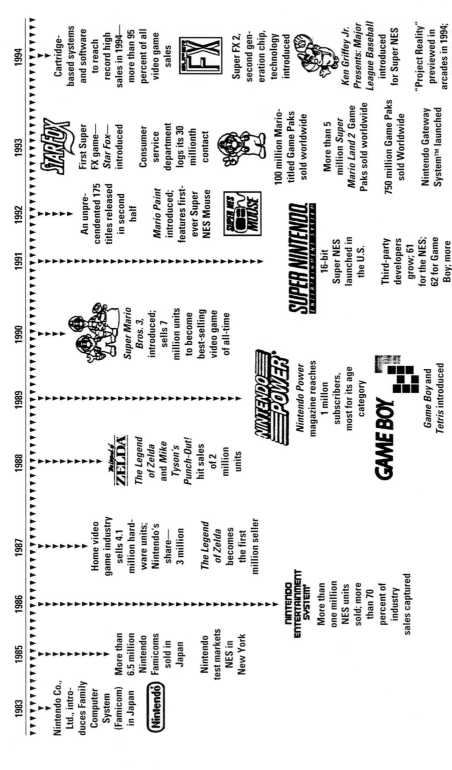

| 1983 | 1985 | 1986 | 1987 | 1988 | 1989 | 1990 | 1991 | 1992 | 1993 | 1994 |

Nintendo Co., Ltd., introduces Family Computer System (Famicom) in Japan

More than 6.5 million Nintendo Famicoms sold in Japan

Home video game industry sells 4.1 million hardware units; Nintendo's share—3 million

The Legend of Zelda becomes the first million seller

The Legend of Zelda and *Mike Tyson's Punch-Out!* hit sales of 2 million units

An unprecendented 175 titles released in second half

Mario Paint introduced; features first-ever Super NES Mouse

First Super FX game—*Star Fox*—introduced

Consumer service department logs its 30 millionth contact

Cartridge-based systems and software to reach record high sales in 1994—more than 95 percent of all video game sales

Super FX 2, second generation chip, technology introduced

Ken Griffey Jr. Presents: Major League Baseball introduced for Super NES

"Project Reality" previewed in arcades in 1994; available for the home in 1995

Nintendo Gateway projected to reach 20 million travelers

Nintendo test markets NES in New York

More than one million NES units sold; more than 70 percent of industry sales captured

Super Mario Bros. 3, introduced; sells 7 million units to become best-selling video game of all-time

Nintendo Power magazine reaches 1 million subscribers, most for its age category

Game Boy and *Tetris* introduced

100 million Mario-titled Game Paks sold worldwide

16-bit Super NES launched in the U.S.

Third-party developers grow; 61 for the NES; 62 for Game Boy; more than 100 for Super NES

More than 5 million *Super Mario Land 2* Game Paks sold worldwide

750 million Game Paks sold Worldwide

Nintendo Gateway System™ launched

"Project Reality," joint venture with Silicon Graphics, Inc., announced

---

EXHIBIT 3
Consolidated Financial Summary for Nintendo Co., Ltd., 1992–1994 (in thousands of $ except per share data)

	Year Ended March 31		
	1994	**1993**	**1992**
Net sales	$4,714,675	$6,161,840	$4,843,475
Cost of goods sold	2,887,106	3,758,376	2,926,885
Gross profit	$1,827,569	$2,403,464	$1,916,590
Selling, general, and administrative expenses	693,507	650,360	483,115
Operating income	$1,134,062	$1,753,104	$1,433,475
Other income/(expenses):			
Interest income	110,392	175,380	206,823
Other	(230,727)	(104,973)	(81,971)
Total	$ (120,335)	$ 70,407	$ 124,852
Income before income taxes	$1,013,727	$1,823,511	$1,558,327
Income taxes	576,497	967,261	807,653
Foreign currency translation adjustments	73,968	4,031	224
Net income	$ 511,198	$ 860,281	$ 750,898
Net income per share	$ 3.61	$ 6.08	$ 5.30
Cash dividend per share	0.68	0.68	0.52
Cash and cash equivalents	3,334,679	3,425,000	2,549,144
Current assets	5,037,417	4,638,570	3,968,830
Total assets	5,740,070	5,248,012	4,458,664
Current liabilities	1,355,426	1,693,274	1,587,965
Total liabilities	1,427,515	1,762,738	1,626,353
Stockholders' equity	4,312,555	3,485,274	2,832,311

Source: Company annual reports.

Europe and a soft market in the United States, coupled with increased competition, eroded export sales. Moreover, Nintendo did not introduce any new product categories in 1994.

Nintendo's Strategy and Product Development

A New Strategy

10   Responding to SEGA's advances, Nintendo appointed Howard Lincoln as head of Nintendo of America and began to make changes in its strategy in 1994. Nintendo historically had demanded that third-party software developers sign exclusive deals and pay 30 percent royalties for the privilege of writing games for its systems. SEGA slowly began taking the top independent software developers away from Nintendo and into its own camp. To counter SEGA's moves, Nintendo started paying companies to write software exclusively for it. Sources reported that Nintendo paid a development fee plus royalties of 2 percent of 12 percent, worth millions of dollars for a hit game.[9] Nintendo also planned to increase the amount spent for inhouse game development and production from its current 35 percent of software sales.

11   While other companies embraced CD-ROM technology. Nintendo elected to stay out of the multimedia end of the business. Its Ultra 64 player plays only cartridges, not CD-ROMs. According to Takashi Kawaguchi, assistant manager at Nintendo's public relations department, "The video game market is a big market that already exists and is still growing, but the multimedia market still remains an illusion that so far has no substance, and we see no point in going into what does not exist."[10] Some observers believed that Nintendo had lost the technological edge to SEGA and the newer, smaller videogame makers offering CD-ROM, virtual reality, and multimedia options.

---

[9] R. Brandt, "It Nintendo a Street Fighter Now?" *Business Week,* August 29, 1994, p. 35.

[10] M. Nashima, "Next-Generation Machines Taking On Sega, Nintendo," *The Japan Times Weekly International Edition* 34, no. 9 (1994), p. 13.

12   When Nintendo saw in early 1994 that it was losing market share to SEGA, the company quickly concluded it needed both a management and an image overhaul. Nintendo President Yamauchi laid part of the blame on his son-in-law, Nintendo of America, Inc., President Minoru Arakawa (whose authority was reduced by the appointment of Howard Lincoln as chairman in early 1994). When SEGA ran comparative ads in 1990, Nintendo did not respond. According to Yamauchi, Arakawa "allowed SEGA to brand our games as children's toys. It was a serious mistake."[11] Arakawa subsequently issued a statement saying that 1994 would be the most aggressive marketing year Nintendo of America had ever seen. Leo Burnett USA, a Chicago ad agency, was selected to design Nintendo's first TV image campaign. Previously, Nintendo had limited advertising to its own magazine, *Nintendo Power,* circulated to 1 million Nintendo owners. Sean McGowan, a toy analyst with Gerard Klauer Mattison, characterized Nintendo's situation:

> Nintendo has a lot of catching up to do, both in advertising and corporate strategy. The next generation of videogames is being decided now, and Nintendo has lost the edge. That will be hard to recapture with newcomers as powerful as Sony entering the game.[12]

13   Nintendo made another about-face in early 1994 when it changed its strategy of not selling videogames directly to video rental dealers. With the videogame rental business representing more than $1 billion a year, Nintendo decided it needed to be a competitor in that segment as well. Nintendo did not plan to require royalties on rental transactions. However, when the law prohibiting rental of computer software expires in 1997, Nintendo hopes to have the law amended to allow the company to collect royalties on game rentals.[13]

14   Nintendo was closely watching development of SEGA's cable TV game channel in the United States and its recent efforts to provide the same service in Japan. In January 1995, Nintendo announced the formation of an alliance with GTE Interactive Media to develop, market, and distribute videogames over telephone lines into interactive television sets. Commenting on the venture, Nintendo's chairman noted, "I think we recognize the market is changing and I don't think it's wise to go it alone in circumstances like that."[14] For Nintendo, the alliance gave the company access to GTE's telephone customer network. For GTE, the alliance provided access to entertainment media that GTE felt would drive initial consumer interest in interactive TV. Initial games were to be developed for Nintendo's Super NES and then later for Ultra 64.

15   Other moves included introducing more (and better) software titles, including the hotly anticipated "Donkey Kong Country." Nintendo also softened its opposition to the depiction of violence in Nintendo-licensed videogames. The company began manufacturing Game Boy systems in the People's Republic of China in order to gain access to that large and new market and opened two new subsidiaries in Spain and Australia.

16   Overall, Nintendo had a substantial customer base, experience in the industry, and was dedicated to providing the consumer with a quality experience. Observers believed Nintendo was positioned to be a major player in the next generation of videogame systems.[15]

New Product Development

17   In August 1993, Nintendo introduced the Nintendo Gateway System, a sophisticated computer designed as an interactive, multimedia information and entertainment system for travelers in airplanes, cruise ships, and hotels. The system was powered by the 16-bit Super NES. At the end of 1994, Nintendo expected to have the systems installed on 170 planes belonging to Northwest Airlines, China Air, Virgin Atlantic, and several other airlines. Nintendo also expanded the system to selected hotels and Holland America cruise ships in 1994. Nintendo expected the Gateway System to

---

[11] N. Gross and R. D. Hof, "Nintendo's Yamauchi: No More Playing Around," *Business Week,* February 21, 1994, p. 71.

[12] Fitzgerald, "Nintendo's Task for Burnett: Image Overhaul," *Advertising Age,* February 28, 1994, pp. 3, 45.

[13] J. Greenstein, "In About-Face, Nintendo Turns to Rental Stores," *Video Business,* April 29, 1994, pp. 1, 12.

[14] J. Carlton, "Nintendo, GTE Unit Offer Games for Interactive TV," *The Wall Street Journal,* January 4, 1995, p. B7.

[15] DFC Intelligence Research.

ultimately provide a full spectrum of entertainment and information services to 20 million travelers worldwide. With 15 million Super NES units in American homes, Nintendo believed it would be doubling its reach and expanding its audience as well.[16]

18   In early 1994, Nintendo introduced an adapter that let users of its Game Boy machines play their games on Nintendo's 16-bit system. The company then took 16-bit game machines to a new level when it launched a turbo-charged chip, the Super FX 2, for its 16-bit NES system. The Super FX 2 was a proprietary custom chip, which Nintendo incorporated into its software game cartridges to enhance graphic and speed capabilities, essentially offering players realistic simulation experiences. The Super NES with the FX 2 chip was the most advanced cartridge-based 16-bit game machine in the industry.

19   Nintendo had recently teamed up with Silicon Graphics, Inc., to design a new game system called Ultra 64. Silicon Graphics had developed the special effects in *Jurassic Park* and *Aladdin*. The technology, called Reality Immersion Technology, allowed videogame players to interact with virtual game environments (a computer-generated 3-D world). This new generation of entertainment created infinitely evolving worlds that instantly and continuously reacted to the commands and whims of individual players. With Reality Immersion Technology, videogame players, for the first time ever, became part of the game itself. Nintendo's strategy was to skip the transition to 32-bit machines (nonportable) and go directly to 64-bit technology. Nintendo planned for the Ultra 64 to be on the market by the end of 1995.

20   In early 1995, Nintendo introduced a new low-priced virtual reality game system in the United States and Japan. The new game system, called "Virtual Boy," is a portable, table-top unit that does not connect to a TV. The game uses 32-bit technology designed to produce a 3-D experience not possible on conventional television or LCD screens. The new system sold for under $200.[17]

Outlook[18]

21   Nintendo's strategy was characterized by industry observers as "slow and steady wins the race." Whereas SEGA was releasing products and expanding into new areas, Nintendo's strategy focused on making quality videogames. While industry observers suspected that Nintendo had ambitions of being a leading provider of services for the interactive age, its present strategic posture was seen as "wait and see."

22   Until the release of Ultra 64, Nintendo was working hard to keep the 16-bit Super NES alive. Still, recent sales were slumping, in part because of slowing demand for 16-bit systems as consumers waited for the next generation systems to come on line in 1995.

SEGA Enterprises, Ltd.

23   SEGA considered itself a leader in interactive digital entertainment media, with operations on five continents competing in three core business segments: consumer products, amusement center operations, and amusement machines. SEGA produced both hardware and software in these areas. Since 1989, SEGA had quadrupled in size from more than $800 million in annual sales to $4 billion in fiscal year 1994. SEGA, which once controlled only 10 percent of the U.S. videogame market, had emerged to contend for market leadership with Nintendo. The two companies in 1994 had approximately equal shares in the U.S. market. In Europe, SEGA had more than a 66 percent share but it trailed Nintendo by a 9 to 1 margin in Japan. A summary of SEGA's company history is presented in Case 27, "Nintendo versus SEGA (A)."

Positioning for the 1990s

24   Some critics questioned whether Hayao Nakayama, SEGA's president and CEO, had the leadership and managerial skills to continue to strengthen SEGA's position in the industry. He had been

---

[16] Nintendo Press Release, "Nintendo Gateway System Takes Off," January 6, 1994.

[17] "Nintendo to Begin Selling 'Virtual Reality' System," *The Wall Street Journal*, November 15, 1994, p. B6.

[18] Extracted from DFC Intelligence Research report.

characterized as an American-style decision-making manager with a good sense of humor. He spoke very rapidly, was opinionated, and impatiently ordered subordinates around. Some said he was obsessed with competing with Nintendo. Like his counterpart at Nintendo, Hiroshi Yamauchi, he did not play videogames.

25   In 1990, SEGA hired a new chief executive, Thomas Kalinski, to run its U.S. subsidiary, SEGA America, Inc. Nakayama specifically hired Kalinske to beat Nintendo and gave Kalinske unprecedented autonomy to do just that. Kalinske was an experienced marketer, with stints as CEO of toymaker Matchbook International, Inc., and 15 years with Mattel, Inc., earlier in his career. To catch Nintendo, Kalinske took decisive and bold steps that included cutting the price of Genesis 25 percent to $149, recruiting software developers to create new games, and accepting lower royalties, sometimes 15 percent below Nintendo's.[19] The strategy worked. SEGA managed to zap Nintendo's 90 percent market share in 1990 to about 50 percent in 1993, increasing its own market position from a meager 7 percent to almost 50 percent in the process. Sales from SEGA's U.S. subsidiary increased from an estimated $280 million in 1990 to more than $1 billion in 1994. Kalinske offered a hint of SEGA's future strategic direction when he said, "I see us as a new form of entertainment company . . . I don't think we should be happy until there are more people using our products than sitting down to watch "Melrose Place" or "Beverly Hills 90210.""[20]

Financial Performance[21]

26   Fiscal 1994 was a lackluster year for SEGA as well as Nintendo. A weak Japanese economy and dismal consumer market in Europe, coupled with an unexpectedly sharp appreciation of the yen against other major currencies, resulted in a 12.8 percent increase in net consolidated sales from fiscal 1993 to $4 billion and a 58.9 percent decline in net income to $108.7 million (see Exhibit 4). The sharp decrease in net income was precipitated by losses in SEGA's European operations. From a high of ¥11,000 in 1992, SEGA's stock price declined to a low of ¥7,010 at the end of 1994. Exhibit 5 depicts SEGA's sales by division.

27   In the first six months of fiscal 1995 (ending September 1994), SEGA's unconsolidated pretax profit fell 43 percent to ¥16.33 billion ($166.97 million), down from ¥28.58 billion the previous year. Sales fell 25 percent, t ¥151.07 billion, from ¥200.65 billion. Analysts said the declines were expected due to slumping global demand for videogames and the soaring yen, which made Japanese products less competitive abroad.[22]

28   In Japan, SEGA was being badly beaten by Nintendo (90 percent of all game sales were Nintendo), in part because of distribution problems and also because SEGA's sports-oriented games were not as popular in Japan. SEGA's performance was helped by its American and European operations, which had some autonomy from Tokyo. SEGA of America contributed about 25 percent to the parent company's overall revenue.

SEGA's Strategy and Product Development

Grand Strategy

29   SEGA's president had made no secret of his strategic intent, to build an entertainment empire. "We'd like to resemble a combination of Sony and Disneyland by the 21st century."[23] To achieve this goal, SEGA had adopted a technology-oriented strategic plan that focused on acquiring and maintaining competitive advantage in such fields as multimedia, computer graphics, virtual reality, and high-tech amusement theme parks. Anticipating the convergence of the worlds of computers, communications,

---

[19] N. Hutheesing, "How a Cool Sega Zapped Nintendo," *Forbes* 15, no. 42 (1993), pp. 72–73.

[20] Brandt, "Is Nintendo a Street Fighter Now?" p. 69.

[21] This section reprinted from Case 27, "Nintendo versus SEGA (A)."

[22] Video-Game Maker's Profit Plunged in Fiscal First Half," *The Wall Street Journal*, November 14, 1994, p. B5.

[23] "The High-Tech Art of Having Fun," *Asia Week* 18, no. 36 (1992), p. 65.

EXHIBIT 4
Consolidated Financial Summary for SEGA Enterprises, Ltd., 1993–1994 (in thousands of $ except per share data)

	Year Ended March 31	
	1994	**1993**
Net sales	$4,038,197	$3,578,968
Cost of goods sold	2,916,161	2,301,496
Gross profit	$1,122,036	$1,277,472
Selling, general, and administrative expenses	831,837	697,988
Operating income	$290,199	$579,484
Other income/(expenses):		
Interest income	47,561	33,353
Other	(78,856)	(104,024)
Total	$ (31,304)	$ (70,671)
Income before income taxes	$258,895	$508,813
Income taxes	249,259	267,102
Foreign currency statements translation	99,089	22,752
Net income	$ 108,725	$ 264,463
Net income per share	$1.09	$2.72
Cash dividend per share	0.37	0.21
Cash and cash equivalents	1,000,262	963,646
Current assets	2,398,652	2,185,073
Total assets	3,482,821	3,026,354
Current liabilities	1,261,454	1,084,437
Total liabilities	1,973,999	2,001,006
Stockholders' equity	1,508,822	1,025,348
Effective tax rate	52%	52%

Source: Company annual reports.

and entertainment. SEGA had stepped up R&D spending in multimedia, "edutainment," and audio-visual products. The company had approximately 850 employees working on interactive amusements for homes, arcade, and theme parks, representing the highest investment in R&D in the industry. SEGA's drive to achieve and maintain its goal of industry dominance led the company to make alliances with AT&T in communications, Hitachi in chips, Yamaha in sound, JVC in game machines, and perhaps Microsoft in future software developments.

30   In an effort to deal with competition from inexpensive multimedia home computers, SEGA has explored the possibility of making some of its popular videogame software available for PCs equipped with CD-ROM drives. According to *The Wall Street Journal:*

> If SEGA does decide to embrace the PC, the company will be making a major break with tradition. Up to now, SEGA has developed its own software mainly for use on its own proprietary game systems. Unlike its archrival Nintendo Co., which relies heavily on outside software developers, SEGA develops roughly 45 percent of the software for its game machines in-house.[24]

31   Since SEGA competes in both home and arcade games (Nintendo is only in home games), it was able to develop expensive technology for arcade machines and then transition the technology to home machines when the price of computer chips fell. Additionally, SEGA planned to move beyond auto racing and action games, at which it excelled, to more general multimedia entertainment featuring full motion video, drama, and characters besides Sonic that could be as popular as Mickey Mouse.[25]

32   One component of SEGA's strategic move into more general multimedia entertainment was its formation in 1994 of the SEGA Club, a vehicle for attracting some of the nearly 32 million kids aged

[24] D. P. Hamilton, "SEGA May Make Some Video Games Available for PCs," *The Wall Street Journal,* May 16, 1994, p. B6.

[25] A. Pollack, "SEGA Takes Aim at Disney World," *New York Times,* July 4, 1993, p. 6.

EXHIBIT 5
SEGA Sales by Division (unconsolidated) (in millions)

	1994	1993
Net sales:	$3,432.2	$2,983.1
Consumer products	2,286.8	1,971.4
Domestic sales	249.7	166.2
Exports	2,037.1	1,805.2
Amusement center operations	598.5	506.6
Amusement machine sales:	505.5	494.9
Domestic sales	377.9	398.4
Exports	127.6	96.5
Royalties on game software	41.4	10.3

Source: Company annual reports.

3 to 11. SEGA's objective was to be an industry leader in bringing good, clean videogame entertainment and educational products to the videogame market for teens and pre-teens.

33 Because domestic sales have been more profitable than its overseas sales, SEGA planned to increase the contribution of its Japanese home sanctuary to overall net sales. Specifically, the company planned to expand sales of new products through heavy advertising and marketing efforts.

34 The company expected to make a complete review of its operations in Europe in order to respond more effectively to the needs of local European markets and to improve sales and gross margins. To stimulate demand for its high-tech entertainment products, SEGA planned to release PICO, Saturn, and the 32-X adapter in Europe.

35 SEGA viewed Asia both as a high-potential market and as a center for manufacturing. The company produced all of its videogame players in Japan in cooperation with a subsidiary of Hitachi Ltd. Localizing production in this part of the world was expected to result in an increased ratio of non-Japan manufacturing, lower costs, and decreased risks associated with fluctuations in the value of the Japanese yen. To lower production costs in Japan, SEGA planned to increase imports of raw materials.

36 SEGA's future strategy aims at capturing some of the $6 billion U.S. theme park industry. Plans call for constructing small theme parks that combine high-tech amusement center machines using state-of-the-art computer graphics with virtual-reality technologies to make customers believe they are somewhere they are not. SEGA's strategy is not to imitate Disney but to reinvent the amusement park:

> Whereas Disney built huge amusement parks with roller coasters and log flume rides, SEGA wants to build small theme parks that will provide the same thrills using computer simulations known as virtual reality—a Disneyland in a box.[26]

37 Noting that Disney has only three huge parks to attract patrons, SEGA said it would build 50 parks in Japan and another 50 in the United States over the next several years. Unlike the Disney attractions that remained fixed for decades, a virtual reality attraction could be changed just by changing the software. The same simulator could be used for a space battle or a police chase.[27] According to Tom Kalinske, "We want consumer to spend their time and money with SEGA entertainment when they're out of the home and when they're inside the home . . . we want to provide entertainment that you'd rather do with us than any of the alternative forms, whether TV, local TV, or whatever."[28]

38 Currently, SEGA derives about one-sixth of its consolidated revenue from amusement center operations. One analyst predicted that SEGA would enjoy gross margins above 30 percent, compared to Disney's 25 percent for its two stateside theme parks. On the downside, SEGA has no experience

---

[26] Ibid.

[27] "Big Plans for Theme Parks," *New York Times,* July 4, 1993, p. 6.

[28] J. Battle and B. Johnstone, "Seizing the Next Level," *Wired,* December 1993, p. 126.

running amusement parks; however, it does know how to provide "experiences"—it has more than 1,200 video arcades in Japan.

New Product Development

39 For the home market, SEGA focused on multimedia, introducing its new $399 CDX player in April 1994. This player uses Genesis cartridges and SEGA CD games in one portable module that also functions as a compact disc player. American Telephone & Telegraph planned to introduce the Edge 16, an under-$150 modem, to permit two Genesis machines to communicate over phone lines.

40 In November 1994, SEGA introduced in Japan its newest entry in the multimedia field, the 32-bit Saturn console; the model was scheduled for release in the United States in the fall of 1995. This game unit has a built-in CD-ROM player (quadruple-speed) and enough processing power to reproduce movielike sound and visual effects.

41 To enhance demand for the firm's 16-bit game players, SEGA developed a hardware booster (Super Genesis 32-X) that enabled 32-bit game cartridges to play on its 16 bit players. SEGA expected to have more than 120 games specifically designed for the 32-X by December 1995.

42 One problem SEGA faced, however, was the numerous game system formats it had on the market. The feeling among some observers was that SEGA was trying to cover too many bases at one time. The result could be consumer confusion, with the various systems cannibalizing each other. SEGA management was aware of this potential.

43 In 1994, SEGA test-marketed its SEGA Channel via cable TV in the United States. Genesis owners could pay $12 to $20 per month for unlimited playing time. Subscribers could choose from a wide selection of popular Genesis games, special versions of soon to be released titles, gameplay tips, news, contexts, and promotions. SEGA hoped to have 1 million subscribers in 1995 and 2 million by the end of 1996. The SEGA Channel was cited by the editors of *Science Magazine* as one of 1994's innovative products and achievements in science and technology in the magazine's seventh annual "Best of What's New" special awards section in its December issue. SEGA was also gearing up to introduce a similar game channel in Japan. However, the number of Japanese homes wired for cable was small at 1.6 million (a 5 percent penetration rate) compared to the United States with more than 60 percent of U.S. homes wired for cable. The diffusion of cable systems in Japan had been hurt by the widespread use of satellite systems.

44 SEGA's strategy included diversification into toy lines that included books that interacted with a TV through an electronic pen. The booklike toy, called "PICO" (about $160), involves touching a pen to a picture in a book that then appears on the TV screen. This product, released in Japan in June 1993, represented SEGA's first entry into the emerging edutainment market.

45 Both Nintendo and SEGA started offering videogame systems that could be attached to exercise equipment in the fall of 1994. SEGA offered add-on units, while Nintendo's product was built into a Life Fitness exercise bike. The systems were designed so that videogame characters reflected the user's speed and effort during the workout, offering entertainment and distraction while motivating exercise. Analysts believed these so-called extertainment systems could become a $2 billion business in a few years.[29]

Outlook[30]

46 Whereas Nintendo's strategy reflected a posture of "slow and steady wins the race," SEGA appeared to operate on the principle of "first at all costs." SEGA had been burned badly by entering the 8-bit market after Nintendo and seemed determined not to let such a delay happen again.

47 The SEGA Genesis was the first 16-bit system on the market, 18 months before Nintendo's 16-bit Super NES. The SEGA CD was released well before any competing systems. Recently, SEGA got the Genesis 32-X out a full year before similar systems from Nintendo and Sony.

48 So far, the strategy of being first had served SEGA well. Nintendo was forced into playing catch-up and SEGA was challenging Nintendo for the lead in the U.S. videogame market. Sales of the

---

[29] K. Fitzgerald, "It's Sonic vs. The Stairmaster," *Advertising Age,* June 13, 1994, p. 26.

[30] Extracted from DFC Intelligence Research report.

SEGA CD had been less than spectacular, but the system had gone a long way toward enhancing SEGA's reputation.

PRICING

49 Price is a key competitive weapon in the battle of the game boxes. 3DO learned a hard lesson when it introduced its interactive player in the United States at an initial price of $699 with disappointing results. According to one Japanese consumer-electronics official, 3DO is "an object lesson in how not to approach the U.S. market . . . For our company we would only enter the U.S. market if we could price our machines at under $200."[31] 3DO eventually dropped the price of its system to $399, but many parents still considered that too expensive for a toy.

50 One sales tactic that had proven successful in the past was getting consumers to buy a new system in installments. This has been SEGA's strategy and one that others appeared to be following. For example, a fully loaded Genesis system contains a $100 game player, a $200 SEGA CD, and a $150 Genesis 32-X. The cost of such a system exceeds the $399 price tag of a 3DO player, even though a 3DO system has superior performance.[32]

51 Widespread emergence of a videogame cartridge rental market has the potential of cannibalizing retail sales of game cartridges and ultimately resulting in a significant increase in competition for retail shelf space and pricing and margin pressures.[33] The shift to a CD-ROM format for games also holds potential for significant reduction in production costs. A CD-ROM game could be pressed and packaged for less than $4, as compared to a cartridge-based system where chip costs and manufacturing expenses could push the cost to make a top-quality cartridge over $20. The cost advantage of the CD-ROM format, coupled with greater ability to match production with demand, offers game marketers a significant improvement in the structure of their value chain systems.

ADVERTISING AND MARKETING

52 Growing advertising budgets for new game titles signalled just how competitive the industry was becoming. Acclaim Entertainment spent $10 million in its marketing campaign to launch "Mortal Kombat II" in September 1994. The original version had sold more than 6 million games since it was introduced in September 1993. The game, in which players rip out the hearts of their enemies, was manufactured for the Nintendo and SEGA home systems. SEGA reportedly spent $45 million on a worldwide marketing blitz to promote its recently introduced game "Sonic & Knuckles;" Nintendo spent $17 million to promote its new game "Donkey Kong Country" for the 1994 holiday season. Good Times Entertainment undertook a $3 million to $5 million campaign for its October 1994 launch of "Doom II," a follow-up to "Doom," one of the industry's most successful computer software titles.[34] Videogame industry analysts predicted that advertising could be the deciding factor in the 1994 race between Nintendo and SEGA to keep their sales pumped up until their newer, more powerful videogame systems came on the market. In 1993 alone, Nintendo spent more than $165 million on marketing support. Despite the big dollars expended on advertising and marketing, word-of-mouth, rental, and borrowing games continued as powerful influences on unit sales volumes. Many game players preferred to try a game before they purchased it.

---

[31] S. Mansfield, "Sony, NEC Video Game Entries No Threat to Sega, Nintendo," *Electronic Business Buyer*, 1994, pp. 30, 32.

[32] DFC Intelligence Research.

[33] Activision's Form 10-K, 1994, p. 15.

[34] J. A. Trachtenberg, "Zap! Smash! Aggressive Ads Plug Game Sequels," *The Wall Street Journal*, August 24, 1994, p. B1.

THE FUTURE

53 The intensifying rivalry between Nintendo and SEGA heightens the need for each company to develop a viable long-term competitive strategy. While it seems clear that videogames have staying power in the entertainment industry, neither company's future success is assured as computers, telecommunications technologies, and entertainment merge to create a vista of new multimedia options—some of which represent opportunities and some of which pose threats. The challenges for Nintendo and SEGA are how to capitalize on their prior successes and market reputations, what directions to pursue, and how to exploit the opportunities before them and win a sustainable competitive advantage. Where will Nintendo and SEGA be in five years? Who will emerge as the dominant provider of videogames?

CASE 29

BANCO COMERCIAL PORTUGUÊS (1993)

INTRODUCTION AND CHALLENGE

1 Banco Comercial Português (BCP) opened on May 6, 1986, with two divisions—one targeted at affluent individuals and the other at medium-sized corporate accounts. A little over half a decade later, by 1992, BCP had grown enormously, claiming to be a truly universal financial group. It established this position by developing a series of "niche" operations, each tightly focused on a market segment. BCP services are now sold through six autonomous banking networks, making it the fifth largest banking group in Portugal in terms of assets. It had 242 locations, 4,000 employees and the equivalent in Portuguese escudos of nearly $9 billion in assets. Loans grew to $3.8 billion at the end of 1991 (up from $282.2 million in 1987). Moreover, from the start, BCP remained solidly profitable.

2 BCP's rapid growth, which in the Portuguese banking context is acknowledged as extraordinary, is closely associated with a series of innovations. From the beginning, BCP's novel approach to banking strategy included: new branches, products, and services; heavy utilisation of careful studies and international management consultants for determination of client needs in each of its target markets; rigorously designed branches to be both efficient and well-appointed; access to the services of a personal Account Manager by each BCP customer; and introduction of high-yield deposit accounts, vigorously promoted with sophisticated and effective advertising.

3 However, by late 1992, BCP faced an increasingly competitive environment. Domestic rivals were improving their capability to meet the demands of a discerning public, partially by imitating many of BCP's innovations. Just as threatening to BCP was the imminent opening of the Portuguese financial markets to foreign European banks.

4 BCP needed to deal with this more dangerous environment. It feared that its demonstrated ability to be a unique product innovator was diminishing. But it still possessed key strengths, such as a vigorous decentralised organisation, a "competitive culture," effective procedures for establishing new distribution channels, a product-line and business-group orientation, an ongoing vision and commitment to an advanced technological infrastructure, and an increasingly comprehensive internal database of relevant customer and market information.

5 At the same time, however, some of these same elements were also worrisome. For example, while BCP's decentralisation was clearly a success, how far should decentralisation go? Already there seemed to be internal competition between BCP subsidiaries for distribution of their respective financial products. How should BCP manage competition for customers between the six business groups, particularly as relevant market segments changed over time?

6 Moreover, having opened 111 new branches and taken on 1,296 new employees in 1991 alone, BCP attempted to maintain control by establishing several new co-ordinating units, including quality teams, audit teams, and a strategic marketing unit. But these initiatives might also adversely affect BCP's entrepreneurial, highly motivated, team-based culture, which had served the bank so well thus far.

7 In short, aiming for sustained high growth, BCP feared becoming distracted by internal concerns. It needed to keep its attention on the market. Therefore, BCP was reaching a turning point by early

This case was written by Carlos de Pommes (Theseus MBA) and Chris Taubman (INSEAD MBA) under the supervision of Yves Doz, Professor at INSEAD, and Mel Horwitch, Professor at Theseus. It is intended to be used as a basis for class discussion rather than to illustrate either effective or ineffective handling of an administrative situation. Reprinted with the permission of INSEAD-THESEUS. Copyright © 1993 INSEAD-THESEUS, Fontainebleau-Sophia Antipolis, France.

1993 and it sought to develop an overall set of policies and key decisions that encompassed such key elements as strategy, organisation, innovation, and information technology.

THE CHANGING PORTUGUESE BANKING ENVIRONMENT (1970S AND EARLY 1980S)

8   The character and evolution of the Portuguese banking system reflect the recent history of the country. Under the dictatorial rule of Antonio de Oliveira Salazar and his successor, Marcelo Caetano, from 1928 to 1974 the banks and the economy were effectively closed to Europe and the remainder of the Western world. Salazar strove to preserve the country as a rural and religious society, protected from the "liberal" and "capitalistic" influences of industrialisation, consumerism, and mass politics. Despite modest attempts at modernising the economy beginning in the 1950s, traditional interests continued to retard economic growth and political freedoms. To the extent that any large-scale industrial and financing activities developed, they were effectively controlled by a small group of families (see Exhibit 1 for an overview of Portuguese banking history and future trends.)

9   Following a bloodless coup in April 1974, the Communist Party acquired power in 1975. Although it was replaced by a democratic constitutional government the following year, the Communist Party had already taken the initiative to nationalise major sectors of the economy, including banking and insurance. Also, the ensuing constitution formally prevented the denationalisation of the Portuguese state-owned banks. (The only banks to escape nationalisation were the established subsidiaries of three foreign banks: Lloyds, Crédit Lyonnais, and Banco do Brazil.) A rather nonchalant attitude toward efficiency and customer satisfaction characterised this sector, which was already protected by a system of regulated interest rates. The combination of highly regulated lending margins and credit ceilings also led to excess bank liquidity, which often found its way into politically motivated and frequently nonperforming loans.

10   Real change only began in 1984 when the government passed legislation enabling individual investors to create private banks in Portugal. The government invited both domestic and foreign applicants to establish private banks with a minimum capital requirement of 1.5 billion escudos ($9.3 million), regardless of the nature of the banking activity to be conducted. Chase Manhattan and Manufacturers Hanover Trust were the first authorised to set up branches in Portugal under the new legislation. They joined the three established foreign banks as the only privately owned banks operating in Portugal.

11   During 1985, a series of additional banking concerns entered the arena. Barclays, Banque Nationale de Paris, Citibank, and Générale de Banque of Belgium were authorised to begin full banking operations in Portugal. Banco Protugês de Investimentos (BPI) was licensed to operate as Portugal's first domestic investment bank. Companhia de Investimentos e Servicos Financeiros (CISF) began operations as a private financial services company, specialising in public and private bond issues and stock exchange brokerage, and was shortly followed by two other domestic Portuguese banks: Banco Comercio e Industria (BCI) and Banco International de Credito (BIC).

THE FOUNDING OF BANCO COMERCIAL PORTUGUÊS (BCP)

12   Spurred on by fast-moving developments in the country during the mid-1980s, two senior bankers from Union Banco Português were approached by a group of investors in the northern city of Oporto with the idea of creating their own private bank to serve specific business needs in northern Portugal.

13   In November 1984, this group invited Jorge Manuel Jardim Gonçalves, then Chairman of Banco Português do Atlântico (BPA) (the largest commercial bank in Portugal), to become Chairman of the proposed new bank.

14   Under Gonçalves's leadership, six key policy decisions provided the foundation of BCP's overall strategy:

   · BCP would not confine itself to one region nor one segment; it would be a nationwide, universal, high-quality bank.

EXHIBIT 1
An Overview of Portuguese Banking Industry, 1974–1993

Year	Political events	Industry developments
1974-5	Revolution	All 22 banks nationalised. Only foreign banks left: Lloyds, Crédit Lyonnais and Banco do Brazil.
1983	Mario Soares (PS) wins election	Enabling legislation for private banks.
1984		Licences given to M. Hanover, Chase and BPI.
1985	Cavaco Silva (PSD) wins election	Licences given to BCP, BCI, BEC, Barclays, BNP, Citicorp and General de Banque.
		First T-Bill issue.
1986	Portugal Joins EC.	BCP starts operation.
1987	Cavaco Silva re-elected with a land-slide victory. Absolute majority	
1988		Caixa Geral de Depositos absorbs Banco Nacional Ultramarino; Banco Fomento e Exterior absorbs Banco Borges e Irmïo.
1989		49% of Banco Totta Accores (BTA) privatised. B Santander and RBS acquire BCI.
		Loan Interest rates liberalised.
		BCP starts its NovaRede operation.
1990		33% of BPA and a further 39% of BTA are privatised. Lloyds bank sells operation to Spain's BBV. BCP makes Portugal's first hostile bid for CISF. Bank of Portugal introduces bad debt swap conditions to open new branches.
1991	Silva (PSD) is re-elected	Credit ceilings lifted from January 1.
		40% of BESCL privatised. BPI acquires Banco Fonsecas & Burnay.
1992		Remaining 60% of BESCL privatised.
		Escudo joins the Exchange Rate mechanism of the European Monetary System.
		International capital movements liberalised.
1993		Deadline for full compliance with EC guidelines.

Source: "Banco Comercial Português (BCP): Portugal's New Wave Bank," UBS Phillips & Drew, March 5, 1992.

· BCP would begin by targeting the "High Net Worth Individuals" (HNWI) and the medium-size corporate market.

· BCP would be run by a professional Board that would be independent of the shareholders.

· BCP would be a "new bank" rather than a copy of anything that existed in Portugal. To achieve this from the beginning the Board would work closely with a highly respected international strategic management consulting firm.

· BCP's initial share capital would be 3.5 billion escudos, more than twice the minimum set by the monetary authorities, which was already considered excessive.

EXHIBIT 1
(concluded)

	1986-89 STAGNATION	1990-94 RESTRUCTURING	1995- STABILITY
Regulation and Supervision	• Administratively set interest rates. • Credit ceilings. • Obstacles to the opening of branches. • Restrictions to the international capital movements. • Bank of Portugal dependent on the Ministry of Finance.	• Lifting of credit ceiling, administrative interest rates and obstacles to the opening of Banks and branches. • Introduction of a new banking law, which takes into account EC directives on banking. • Bank of Portugal regulatory and supervisory capacities strengthen.	• European single financial market-convergence of regulatory and supervisory mechanisms within the EC. • Integration of European financial markets. • Adoption of a common European currency and European Central Bank.
Competition	• State-owned Banks accounted for 90% of banking activity. • No price competition. • Credit ceiling limited the performance of more dynamic institutions.	• Privatisations/mergers/acquisitions • Entry of new aggressive international banks. • Rapid expansion of more efficient bank's branch networks. • Price differentiation. • Increased competition from other financial institutions. • Consolidation of financial groups.	• Stabilisation of the banking structure in terms of number of banks and branches and market share. • Increased convergence of prices. • Competition from non-financial companies.
Market Approach	• No market segmentation. • Scarce promotion of banking products & services. • No specialisation. • Limited personalised treatment.	• Market segmentation developed by several banks. • Intensive advertising. • Use of sales forces, databases and telemarketing. • Personalised services.	• Market segmentation. • Smaller investments in advertising. • Intensive use of sales force to promote several financial products. • Advisory services.
Products and Prices	• Traditional and undifferentiated banking products. • No cross selling. • High inter-mediation margins. • Low commissions. • High operating costs (up to 6% of interest earning assets).	• Innovative products (cash management, composite products, consumer credit). • Increased cross-selling efforts. • Decreasing intermediation margins. • Increasing commissions. • Lower operating costs.	• New products due to technological changes, regulatory trends & market needs. • Stabilisation of interest margins and commissions. • Decrease of operating costs.
Growth Opportunities	• High opportunities to conquer market share easily.	• High opportunities to conquer market share, although increased competition renders it more difficult.	• Low opportunities to conquer market share in a mature market.

· Finally, BCP would employ the latest information technology for delivering high-quality customer services to the target markets.

15   The initial investors, recognising their lack of banking experience, were content to leave management decisions to the professional bankers on the Board. However, it was clear that BCP needed an adequate capital base, so the initial group contacted other potential investors to raise initial capital. In June 1985, BCP was founded with a total of 204 shareholders and 3.5 billion escudos ($25 million).

16   BCP articulated its overall mission:

To become a major Portuguese bank by providing excellent, innovative, and personalised products and services that are designed to meet all financial needs and expectations of the most relevant domestic market segments.

BCP's EXPLICIT SEGMENTATION OF THE MARKET

17   From the outset BCP acted in a professional, rigorous, and thorough manner. With regard to market analysis, traditionally Portuguese banks either monitored the markets themselves or used surveys from an outside service called MARKTEST. Although BCP purchased such reports, it found them too aggregated for use in analysing such key segments as high net worth individuals.

18   BCP firmly believed that market segmentation was the only means to ensure that different customers' needs would be satisfied with high-quality service standards (see Exhibit 2 for details regarding segmentation and marketing).

19   Therefore, BCP launched its own extensive market research effort. BCP established a "market segmentation" task force, supplemented with two consultants, to analyse in-depth target market segments, customer needs, existing products, and business potential. The task force spent 11 months

EXHIBIT 2
Initial Market Segmentation by BCP

Market Research

	Market understanding and positioning	Specific segments understanding	Fine tuning
Types of market research	• Competitors positioning • Ideal positioning • Market Size • Basic behavioural segmentation • Size and wealth of each segment	• Cross-section of behaviour and demographic variables to ensure specific segmentation • Product design and analysis of the different components of the proposal of value	• Behavioural discrimination based upon a few key variables
Objective	• Know ideal positioning • Define a "pull-strategy" • Position the bank's Image	• Define a "push-strategy" for each sub-segment • Design and test products and branches	• Align a comprehensive and integrated "push-strategy"

Market Segmentation

Segment	Size	Wealth	Profile	Lead Products
Sophisticated	10%	High	• University Graduate • Appreciates special attention	• Demand Account • Mortgage credit • Capital market services
Enlightened	6%	Low	• Risk-taker • Younger	• Demand Account • Mortgage credit
Unsatisfied	13%	High	• Very critical • Does not forget mistakes	• Demand Account
Conservative	36%	Average	• Accepts advice • Risk Avoiders	• Demand Account • Time deposits
More than 1 bank- customers	16%	Average High	• Business Owner • Independent Professional	• Demand Account • Mortgage credit
One bank Customers	19%	Average	• Traditional	• Demand Account

reviewing selected market segments, chosen according to such criteria as unfulfilled needs, estimated level of profitability, and BCP's ability to succeed. This task force eventually determined the desired levels of service for each banking activity, as well as the information technology required to support this "greenfield" bank.

20   In deciding to do its own market research, BCP faced an uphill struggle. As one BCP veteran put it:

> Market research companies were just starting in Portugal. Not only did we have to specify precisely what information we needed, but since the market research companies had little statistical capability at this time, we had to work closely with them for the multivariate studies.

EXHIBIT 2
(concluded)

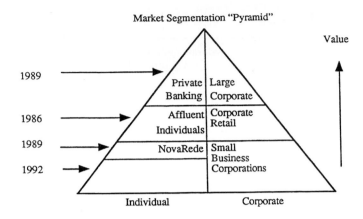

Market Segmentation "Pyramid"

Strategic Concepts

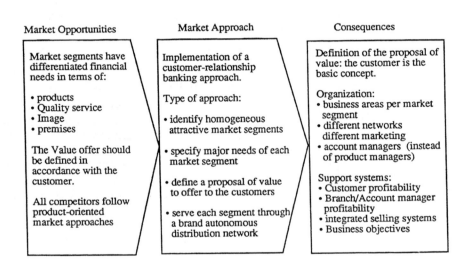

Market Opportunities	Market Approach	Consequences
Market segments have differentiated financial needs in terms of: • products • Quality service • Image • premises The Value offer should be defined in accordance with the customer. All competitors follow product-oriented market approaches	Implementation of a customer-relationship banking approach. Type of approach: • identify homogeneous attractive market segments • specify major needs of each market segment • define a proposal of value to offer to the customers • serve each segment through a brand autonomous distribution network	Definition of the proposal of value: the customer is the basic concept. Organization: • business areas per market segment • different networks different marketing • account managers (instead of product managers) Support systems: • Customer profitability • Branch/Account manager profitability • integrated selling systems • Business objectives

Source: Internal BCP Documents.

21   As a first cut, BCP split the Portuguese market into individual and corporate customers. BCP felt that it could not attract easily very large corporate accounts since it would be competing against well-known international banks. Neither could a new bank compete in lower-income but high-volume segments without a distribution network. This was in part due to regulation restricting a bank from opening new branches[1] and to Portugal's inadequate technological infrastructure, which prevented telephone services from being installed quickly.[2]

---

[1] The government, while allowing competition, recognised that any new bank would have an immediate advantage over existing state-owned banks due to not being hampered by the bad debt provisions on their balance sheet. In 1990, in an effort to level the playing field, the government levied a charge of 20–40 million escudos ($140–280,000) on new branches, which was then used to "write-off" a small proportion of the state-owned banks' nonperforming loans.

[2] For example, data lines from the Portuguese PTT had a backlog of one year. In addition, there was no reliable information available regarding when a line could be installed.

22   The two segments identified as most lucrative for BCP were high net worth individuals (HNWI) and medium-sized companies.

23   BCP's market research allowed it to tailor its studies to specific segments. BCP examined specific behaviour characterising its targeted customers, including:

- How much customers kept in their accounts.
- How many transactions they conducted.
- Customer sophistication (information related to lifestyle).
- Whether customers were net credit or deposit users.

24   This behaviourist/demographic information enabled BCP to classify customers into subsegments (e.g., "sophisticated," "conservatives"—please refer to Exhibit 2 for the complete classification scheme). This information was then stored in a database, which BCP continually upgraded. For example, BCP discovered that "sophisticated" clients were more attracted by special services than "one-bank customers." Still, there always remained grey areas in segmenting the market that were difficult to identify.

EARLY COMMITMENT TO INFORMATION TECHNOLOGY

25   In mid-summer 1985, two months after creating its market segmentation task force, BCP produced an initial document articulating its vision for using information technology (IT) in support of its overall strategy. The document addressed two issues, the hardware platform and software infrastructure.

26   The hardware decision was tied to BCP's aim to be a major Portuguese bank. To achieve this goal BCP felt it needed a large and flexible IT system. If BCP were to opt for a midsize solution, such as the commonly used IBM system 38, the bank's ability to grow quickly might be stifled. In such a case, a painful migration process would be required in the future, distracting BCP from its key growth objectives. BCP, therefore, at the beginning selected a large mainframe in the IBM 43xx series.

27   Even more important than hardware was software. BCP felt software was key for supporting close customer relationships and high service levels. BCP's business strategy almost dictated that its IT system should be built around customers, not around products as was the case for much of traditional banking's software development.

28   Therefore, BCP adopted a customer-information-system (CIS) approach. A CIS consists of a single unified database that contains and links all accounts or products purchased by one customer. Having a CIS allowed BCP from the beginning to obtain a comprehensive view of their client (see Exhibit 3 for a schematic presentation of BCP's software architecture).

29   Using BCP's CIS:

- The Account Manager instantly knew all the BCP products held by a client.
- BCP was able to send a comprehensive bank statement to clients, including information on all of the client's accounts and an aggregated schedule of income earned and payments required for the following month.
- BCP possessed an overall view of its relations with a client. The client might, for example, have insufficient funds in his demand deposit account to cover a cheque. But with the knowledge that this client had a significant balance in a time deposit account, BCP could instantly decide to cover the cheque anyway.

30   Rather than develop a CIS on its own, BCP decided to purchase "off-the-shelf" packages. BCP was advised by its consultants that it could benefit from existing software as long as it conformed to BCP's architectural requirements for providing fast time-to-market and an "error-free" system.[3] After conducting a comprehensive search, Hogan, a UK-based banking software firm, was selected

---

[3] Actually no complex software system is ever "error-free." But a system is usually considered "stable" when the number of outstanding problems does not increase. Most of a system's cost normally occurs after the system goes "live" due to the ongoing maintenance required.

EXHIBIT 3
Software Architecture at BCP

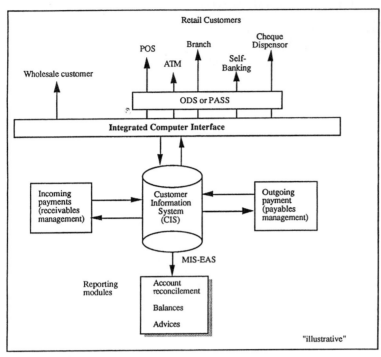

The customer accounts and products supported include: PCS, DDA, TDA, TB, CLIPS, Drafts, Money Market, Foreign Exchange, Cards, Loans, CAD, SEC, etc.

For the retail interface, BCP has two software switches: on-line delivery system (ODS) for financial transactions; and platform automation support system (PASS) for channelling non-financial transactions such as account enquiries.

For international transactions, foreign credit card transactions by BCP customers are passed through a Visa card authorisation centre in the overseas country, and a bank clearing centre in Portugal, before being redirected to BCP's centralised ODS. These international links already enable BCP to process transactions from London and Spain, in Portugal, in real-time.

The software switches also enable BCP to separate presentation from processing. When, for example, BCP decided to integrate videotext into the business group, PASS would translate the videotext transmission to the standard format for processing. In this way, modifications only needed to be made at the videotext level.

With BCP's CIS system, customer data forms the core of the database

for BCP's core system. Buying and outsourcing were established as enduring policies in BCP's EDP department. Only when no acceptable external package existed, such as for securities, drafts, and treasury bills, did BCP consider internal software development.

31   The initial decision to opt for large-scale computer and software systems was painful, absorbing about one-third of BCP's start-up capital. As a Board member described it:

> We invest a lot in technology, but sometimes it is not easy to justify the investment for the future. It is a question of culture. If you spend a lot to buy a building the result is visible. But if you spend a lot to buy a computer then everyone complains—but the computer is more important for the company.

ESTABLISHING A UNIQUE ORGANISATION

32   BCP also felt it needed a fresh approach for control and organisation. The bank knew that firm cost control was required. This meant identifying key costs and key areas of profitability. Traditionally banks had merged costs into a single unifying shared-cost structure, not distinguishing high- and low-cost activities. BCP broke away from this model and created separate semi-autonomous business divisions for its initial two (and later subsequent) lines of businesses. IT centralised only logistical functions. Each stand-alone business had its own cost structure, measurement criteria, and an accounting method (see Exhibit 4 for the internal organisation of businesses and functions).

33   Within each line of business, BCP also decided to depart from the traditional approach by introducing a specifically appointed Account Manager. BCP regarded the Account Manager concept as a major innovation in the Portuguese market. Some banks had Account Managers for some customers; BCP had Account Managers for all customers.

EXHIBIT 3
(concluded)

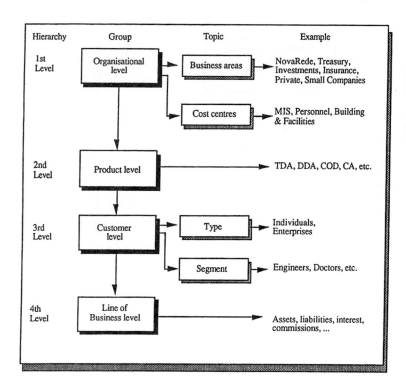

Overview of Levels of Enquiry of the Earnings Analysis System (EAS)

This system has a "hierarchical" presentation organised along "organisation", "product", "customer" and "line of business level" lines. This means that if a report was requested at the lowest level, all information referring to the high level would also be received.

Using this system it is possible to check the profitability of a single Account Manager by customer, line of business, or product.

PREPARATIONS FOR OPENING DAY

34   During the pre-opening period from the latter months of 1985 until May 1986, BCP planned with exceptional care and thoroughness. BCP, offering higher-than-industry-standard salaries, recruited over 100 employees. As one BCP executive recalled, "It was not hard in those early days to attract key staff. Many good IT and banking professionals in state-controlled banks were frustrated and were waiting for just such an exciting opportunity."

35   BCP conveyed a carefully crafted image in its branches by explicitly using design and architecture. The bank initially purchased two buildings, one in Lisbon and one in Oporto. Each location housed a HNWI and a "medium-corporate" branch, but on different floors. The buildings were designed and furnished in a definite "BCP style," which would also come to characterise other BCP business groups. The outside steps and inside floor, for example, were laid with granite tiles—a "noble" stone for the Portuguese; the conference tables had matching granite supports; and clients waited for Account Managers in comfortable, rich red sofas before being escorted to a partitioned space.

36   Behind the scenes, the bank was also vigorously working to install its computer system and to customise its software to BCP's specific needs. This was accomplished in the impossibly short time of four months, though not all functions were ready by opening day in early May 1986. As one software developer said, "We worked 12–14 hours per day, with no weekends, but there was no problem. We were happy to work these hours" (see Exhibit 5 for an overview of BCP's central computer and network structure).

37   But employing such extraordinary preparatory work obviously entailed substantial upfront costs. One Board member commented, "The industry, and some shareholders, thought we were crazy

EXHIBIT 4
Internal Organisation of BCP's Businesses and Functions

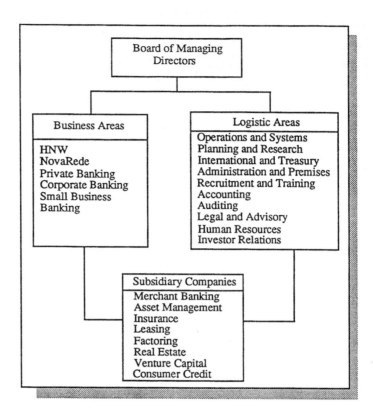

Branches are measured only on the costs they actually incur directly pertaining to their activity, for example, rents, personnel and administration costs. To these are added the costs of using central services which can be directly attributed to the branches through the transactions they generate, such as clearing house costs, central computing resources, etc.

The areas of business profitability contribution also include the costs of a Co-ordinating and Marketing division.

Other costs, such as those of the Audit divisions, and Research and Planning division, are not included in any area of business profitability analysis. These types of central service appear only at the bank level.

Source: BCP internal documents.

putting all that money into a mainframe computer while opening only two branches." Another senior manager remembered that many competitors were confident that BCP would go bankrupt, fueling rumours that BCP might not open at all.

38   But based on its detailed planning and preparation, BCP did open its doors in May 1986 with two business groups. Both business groups were launched with an aggressive marketing campaign featuring, for the first time in Portuguese banking history, a full-page newspaper advertisement. The

EXHIBIT 5
BCP Central Computer and Network Structure

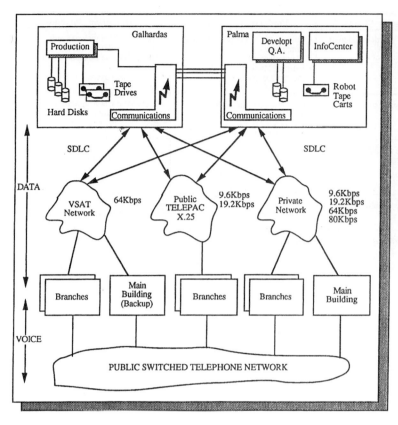

Telecommunications was also a growing element in BCP's strategy. The bank initially had a private communications line between Lisbon and Oporto. It also continued to rely on the public network for linking many new branches. But dependence on the public telephone systems was a major bottleneck. Installing new lines was slow and BCP never had enough lines. BCP responded by being the first Portuguese bank to use a satellite system to link its remote locations - even though such a satellite system was more expensive than normal communications.

BCP maintained two computer sites, one for 'production' (i.e. regular transaction processing) and one for 'development' (both utilising similar configurations - IBM 3090/300). The DP department centralised its staff in the 'production' building, from where it had remote control over the development computer. The 'development' mainframe also served as a backup machine to the 'production' computer.

The 'development' building had a special area dedicated to printing - including client reports and bank statements - which were automatically folded and put into envelopes using optical marks on the paper.

advertisement was a direct message from the five Board members, who signed it personally: "We are starting today," the advertisement read. "We have hundreds of years of experience." The emphasis was on innovation, new products, new services, advanced information technology systems—"exclusively to serve you." These business groups were an instant success.

39   Over the next half decade, BCP swept the Portuguese market—which had suffered with inefficient state-owned banks for more than a decade—with a veritable wave of innovation on a number of fronts, including marketing strategy, customer service, product range, and image definition (see Exhibit 6 for an overview of BCP's banking operations and subsequent growth).

BCP GROWTH AFTER 1986

40   From the beginning, excellence in customer services was explicitly established as BCP's key operating objective. The bank stated in its 1988 Annual Report, "Banco Comercial Português persists in evaluating the level of achievement of its objectives not so much by the numeric expression of the business variables but rather by the level of satisfaction of its clients." The critical decision in assuring high levels of service was to assign primary customer-service responsibility to the Account Managers. The Account Managers acted as personal financial advisors for a designated set of clients and as specialists for all of their client's transactions. As mentioned earlier, the Account Manager was supported in both of these roles by bankwide information systems, which provided data on all of BCP's products, as well as a comprehensive view of a client's financial position and dealings with the BCP.

EXHIBIT 6
Development of BCP's Banking Networks

Operation	Main Phase	Target Clients	Products & Services	Operating Systems
BCP Parent Group	1986-1989	High Net Worth Individuals	• Cash management products (e.g. Conta Mais) • Mortgage credit • Personal loans • Prestige credit cards • Package of insurance	• Autonomous branch network • Decentralised back-office • Global range of flexible financial services • Account Managers • Personalised treatment
		Medium-sized corporations	• Cash management products • Short-term capital financing • Treasury accounts • Investment accounts	• Cross-selling to insurance and leasing • Corporate terminal • Risk assessment system
Corporate banking	1989-1991	Portugal's top 500 corporations	• Off-shore financing & cash management • Swaps • Loan syndication • Capital market services	• Access to dealing rooms • Corporate terminals • Electronic banking • "Tailor-made" products
Private banking	1989-1991	Extremely wealthy customers	• Investment products • Mutual funds • Insurance products	• High level of discretion • Exclusive branches
NovaRede	1989-1993	Urban retail customers	• NovaRede account • NovaConta salary account • Funds transfer • NovaRede Visa credit card • Insurance products	• Fast service, low costs • Low cost branch operations • Monthly combined statements • Automatic cheque dispensing • "Direct Hotline" phone banking • Credit scoring techniques
Merchant banking	Acquired 1990	CISF	• Medium & long-term financing • Valuations and M&A activities • Privatisations • Capital market business	• Complementary business • Separate computing systems
International	June 1991-1993	Portuguese émigrés in France	• Retail banking facilities	• Joint venture with Spain's Banco Popular
Small business	March 1992-1994	Small business	• Hire purchase-type financing • Cheque management service • Loans	• Specialized credit scoring • Revolving line of credit

41   BCP launched lead products for the HNWI and medium-sized corporate segments: "Conta Mais," a demand deposit account paying 6% annually to HNWI customers; and "Conta Gestïo de Tesouraria," a treasury management account paying 5% to corporate customers. (Other Portuguese banks paid zero interest on cheque accounts.) BCP's initial marketing campaigns did not stress credit products because regulatory credit limits restricted lending levels. But BCP introduced a deposit account named "Conta Duplique o Vencimento," which gave HNWI account holders access to automatic credit of up to twice their monthly salary.

42   BCP's technological infrastructure played an important role in introducing such products. Six weeks after BCP's opening, the Portuguese government, responding to lobbying from established retail banks, introduced a regulation limiting interest payments on demand deposit accounts to 4%. However, due to BCP's customer-oriented software structure, BCP was able to develop in two weeks a new product that could "sweep" balances between client accounts. Each evening, checking account balances were swept into overnight treasury bills paying 8% interest and then the balance was re-posted in the checking account the following morning. The market response, as one BCP executive explained, was enthusiastic: "With the fantastic publicity the BCP dual accounts gave us, the fact that no one could copy us allowed us to grow quite nicely."

43   The IT infrastructure generally gave BCP the unique ability to create and handle complex financial products, which consistently appealed to the Portuguese market. For instance, BCP produced an account paying interest at differing rates depending on the average daily outstanding balance.

44   The Account Manager also played a vital innovating role in seeking better ways to satisfy customer requirements by obtaining feedback on products and ideas from clients. Client information was often the basis for many of the new products which were launched by BCP.

EXHIBIT 6
BCP's Growth (concluded)

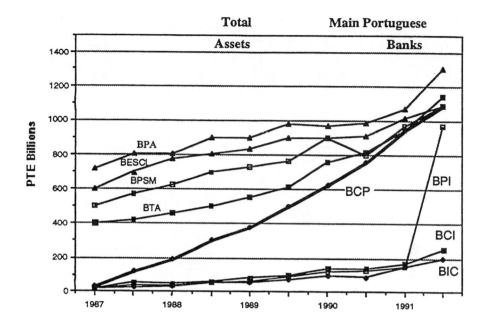

In less than 5 years, BCP has clearly outpaced the 2 other Portuguese commercial banks, which appeared in 1985 (BCI and BIC), and joined the group of Portugal's largest commercial banks.

BCP already accounts for 7% of the overall banking business in Portugal and nearly 13% of the sector's net income.

* BPI merged with BFB in 1991.

Source: BCP internal documents.

45   Necessity also stimulated innovation at BCP. For instance, due to the unreliability of communications lines, BCP installed at each branch a financial branch support system (FBSS), which assumed control over local processing of commonly performed transactions when communication with the overall system was lost. The FBSS kept a log of transactions and forwarded them as soon as a line became available. Therefore, customers never waited to make a transaction at the bank. (See Exhibit 7 for the BCP branch configuration.)

46   BCP also differentiated itself in the area of foreign trade transactions, which often involves large numbers of forms, export documents, and transfers of money. Such procedures could be time-consuming and required great precision. Most Portuguese banks established centralised units and systems for processing overseas documentary credits, which caused delays. BCP decided to move its foreign transactions activity to the branch level. This decentralisation was made possible by a PC-based program called EXIMBILLS, which incorporated all the necessary forms and SWIFT[4] interface for processing import/export transactions locally and which could be used by all personnel.

---

[4] SWIFT is the interbanking network, established by a consortia of international banks to facilitate the movement of funds between them.

EXHIBIT 7
New Vision of Branch Delivery System

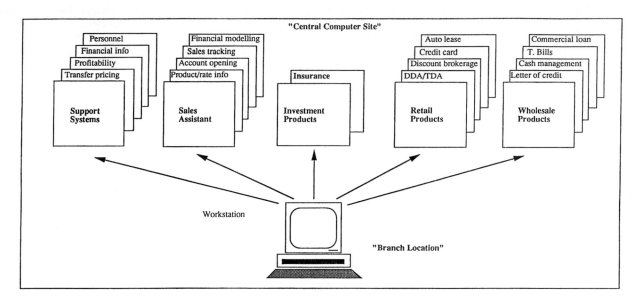

BCP's vision of its integrated computer system was to enable its employees and its customers complete access to the technological infrastructure and through it to BCP's entire range of products. Each terminal connected at the branch locations performed one or several of the following tasks:

- Office Automation functions such as word processing, spread sheets and analysis and increasing inter-office communication with electronic mail.

- Act as "gateways" to other systems, services, or databases, such as Reuters' financial information.

- Local processing and data storage, such as the FBSS/PAB system, which is used whenever there is a communication failure with the central site computer system.

- Act in "dumb terminal mode" in order to access the products and services residing on the central computer.

LAUNCHING THE PRIVATE BANKING BUSINESS GROUP

47   By the end of 1988, BCP was well-established in Portugal with total assets of 296 billion Escudos ($2.02 billion) and a network of 19 individual and corporate branches. This success, together with the expected approval of tax-haven status for the Portuguese island of Madeira, encouraged BCP to create a private banking business group.

48   As in the launch of the first two business groups, BCP reviewed this option systematically. The chairman explained that BCP had a thorough and professional process for considering the opening of a new business group:

> Before launching a new business group we first ask: Is there a market? We do the calculations. There are X customers in the segment. They have an average of Y Escudos. So theoretically we can make money.
>   We then conduct market research . . . We look for the key drivers—what we should focus on . . . Our driving force has not been product pricing; it has been service.

49   This second round of research was conducted by a team comprising experienced bankers and external consultants. This team conducted domestic market research and visited private banks in other countries. Profitability analysis indicated that the key private banking market consisted of individuals with at least $700,000 to $1,000,000 to invest in the bank. But on closer examination the actual market segmentation turned out to be more complex. Some of these people, particularly those from the "old money classes," were already BCP HNWI customers, who welcomed the preferred new special services. Other HNWI members, who were some of BCP's wealthiest customers, chose not to purchase private banking services.

50   BCP believed that success in this area rested on "three pillars":

1. The private banker must be *highly trained* in order to understand fully the major areas of client investment needs. As one team member put it: "Account Managers (for HNWI) in the retail business group have up to 500 clients. A private banker has, at most, 100. You need to know your client very, very well. You learn about the client's hobbies, cars, spouse, and kids. You send cards to your client on important dates. Every time you have a new product you know immediately if it is for your client."
2. The second pillar was to have the private banker act as the client *co-ordinator* of all daily investments. BCP research showed that likely BCP clients preferred that their private banker analyse and oversee a client's overall position daily, drawing on the expertise of specialists in foreign exchange, portfolio, or real estate. Accordingly, BCP private bankers would always be present at meetings arranged between a client and product specialists.
3. The third pillar was to target the appropriate *level of service* analysis for each transaction. BCP market researchers put themselves in the position of the client analysing each banking transaction and specifying an ideal level of service. According to BCP research, level of service really differentiated BCP, as well as determining and supporting the infrastructure down to required operations of, say, stylising and personalising cheque books and credit cards (as instructed by a client during an initial visit).

51   BCP launched its first private banking branches in early 1989. Described by one private banker as a "bank within a bank," each branch had a discrete exterior completely unlike normal BCP branches. Client rooms, for instance, were furnished as elegant lounges. Clients then met with their "private banker" in a closed room (which might or might not contain a computer—depending on the client's particular attitude toward information technology).

52   The private-banking product range proposed to BCP's private banking clientele was also differentiated. It included exclusive access to high-value products like property funds (in contrast to HNWI customers, who were offered only market and equity funds from the asset management subsidiary as part of the portfolio management services).

LAUNCHING THE LARGE CORPORATION BANKING GROUP

53   In January 1989, BCP founded a fourth business group, which focused on large corporations—the 500 largest companies in Portugal (principally private leading industrial groups, state-owned companies and subsidiaries of multinationals). BCP had initially avoided this segment. High profile companies were a natural target for foreign banks entering the Portugese market. Margins on loans to large firms were comparatively small and unattractive for retail banks under the prevailing system of credit ceilings (which remained in place until early 1991). But BCP decided to enter this segment in response to "solicitations of some existing clients."

54   Because practically all deals were done on the phone, the activities for this business group could be based in just two offices, in Lisbon and Oporto. BCP competed on the basis of price, speed of response, and capital market experience. The large corporate business group launched a series of innovative products during 1990 and 1991, including "Guardinvest," a securities custody service, an interactive company terminal for large treasury operations, and "Trade Link—Business Opportunities," a videotext-like message system for corporate customers dealing with business and trade opportunities.

55   BCP's technological infrastructure enabled the bank to develop and launch such products and services quickly. But along with the benefits it also reduced profits. Previously Portuguese banks kept clients' money in non–interest-bearing accounts. With the introduction of corporate terminals, corporate clients were able to move funds easily to increase earnings. Therefore, BCP was forced to examine its fee policy.

THE LAUNCHING OF NOVAREDE

56   A major turning point in BCP's development came in November 1989 with the simultaneous launch of 21 branches (15 in Lisbon and 6 in Oporto) under a new brand, "NovaRede." This fifth business group was targeted at a much larger market segment: individuals in the medium income range. In launching NovaRede, another "bank within a bank," BCP instantly greatly expanded its size. BCP was no longer simply a small and highly profitable niche player.

57   NovaRede was carefully planned throughout 1988 and 1989 in a "BCP-style" project-group mode. This group, which included external consultants, conducted market research studies, determined objectives for serving the target market, and costed out the business. With a population of 6,000 per bank branch, Portugal appeared "underbanked" in comparison with the European average of 4,000 people per branch. NovaRede's challenge was to grow fast and establish a dense branch network in key retail sites, especially Lisbon and Oporto. BCP outlined the principal strategic alternatives facing the NovaRede project group at the time:

> We wanted BCP to be one of the top five banks in Portugal. There were only two ways: buying another branch network or setting up a "NovaRede."
>
> The second alternative was easier. BCP had a strong culture—everyone has the same language. It was a great achievement for the bank to have hired 2,000 people in a short period. Each person quickly absorbed our vision. If we had bought another bank, we would have also bought another culture and may have bought alien styles of management. If we made an acquisition today, we could turn a public bank around. But at that time we did not have the size to carry out such an acquisition effectively.

58   A major concern for BCP, related to NovaRede, was that NovaRede customers might use other BCP branches (such as the branches for the HNWIs) for daily transactions, potentially causing significant HNWI service deterioration. But this never happened, because many NovaRede customers viewed NovaRede as a totally different bank altogether. (See Exhibit 8 for a plan of a typical NovaRede branch.)

59   NovaRede also demonstrated the foresight of BCP's initial decision to purchase a mainframe-based computer system. A mid-range system would not have been able to cope with BCP's growth. BCP would have been forced to "migrate" to a more powerful mainframe system, which could have taken at least two years.

60   BCP's IT infrastructure also enabled NovaRede to maintain a minimum number of staff. NovaRede's maximum of five employees per branch contrasted with an average of 40 for the branches of its competitors. Cost per branch was also low. NovaRede branches took an average of just 18 months to break even. In addition, the IT system made every NovaRede employee a generalist. As one NovaRede manager explained: "At NovaRede, everyone can do everything. Also technology enabled us to use smaller units and smaller teams. In teams of more than five people productivity is lower—there is someone who doesn't work, who just controls."

61   At NovaRede, BCP eliminated the personalised services of an Account Manager. But NovaRede customers had direct access to the IT infrastructure for their transactions. NovaRede branches also offered a convenient, efficient alternative for clients from the other BCP business groups. In fact, to BCP's surprise, 10% of NovaRede's clients also belonged to one of the up-market segments. Therefore, in building a customer base for NovaRede, BCP could build on client relationships developed in the other business groups. NovaRede established its own sales force, which worked closely with the Account Managers of the corporate clients. These firms were then approached and invited to make automatic transfers of participating employee salaries into NovaRede "Salary" accounts. These employees received access to their salaries on the 15th day of the month (instead of the traditional end of the month), an automatic personal line of credit equal to three months of salary, and free personal accident insurance.[5] Also, as a BCP executive pointed out: "The salary account was something completely new for Portugal and relied on some highly specific software products. NovaRede

---

[5] The use of this credit was automatic, bud did imply interest charges. However, the intention of this account was to cope with very temporary situations. The interest paid was designed to be negligible (maximum interest charge being between 1–2% of salary).

EXHIBIT 8
NovaRede Branch Layout

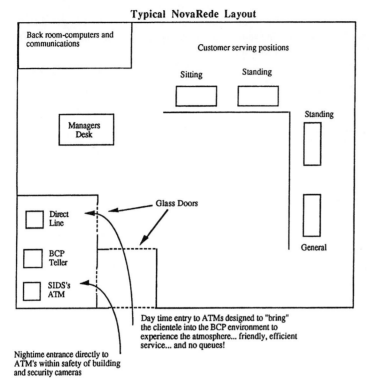

Typical NovaRede Layout

Back room-computers and communications

Customer serving positions

Sitting   Standing

Standing

Managers Desk

Glass Doors

Direct Line

BCP Teller

SIDS's ATM

General

Day time entry to ATMs designed to "bring" the clientele into the BCP environment to experience the atmosphere... friendly, efficient service... and no queues!

Nightime entrance directly to ATM's within safety of building and security cameras

A typical NovaRede branch office was between 100 and 150 square meters.

With NovaRede, BCP possessed the ability to open low-cost branches rapidly and at minimal cost. These branches were small and organised in two rooms (an exterior area with an array of automatic teller machines and an internal office with a counter staffed by a maximum of 5 people). There was no back office. Customers simply conducted their transactions and left. There were no chairs, no Account Managers, and no conference rooms.

Unlike the traditional branch locations, which generally adhered to both the BCP image and the original architecture, NovaRede exhibited uniformity in branch design - so that the customer would feel at home in any branch. Although small, the NovaRede branches were readily identifiable by their bright green and red colour scheme. So identifiable, in fact, that the Lisbon City Council had received protests that they were inconsistent with the traditional architecture of the city.

BCP's IT infrastructure allowed the bank to offer a large range of products unique in the Portuguese market. In addition, numerous incremental IT-oriented innovations also were important, including a system for digitising a customer's signature (so that BCP could have instant verification for payment of cheques), inter-branch electronic mail (so that a teller could send a message to the account's branch manager requesting permission to pay), and a unique system of automatic teller machines (which could, for example, dispense cheques and handle internal BCP banking operations).

Actually, the ATM area was a difficult area for differentiation. BCP did not own its machines. A consortium called SIBS ran an integrated ATM and POS network on behalf of all Portuguese banks. A system called Multi-Banco, while giving the Portuguese banking system competitive advantage over other countries, stripped the subscribing Portuguese banks of the authority to provide extra services. A development done by SIBS on behalf of one bank benefited all. In addition, to propose a differentiated product would be to give all the other banks (competitors) advance warning of planned new services, and rivals, through SIBS, could delay the introduction until they themselves were ready to compete. BCP's own machines did compete head on with SIBS, but did services not provided by SIBS.

had an entire year's head start before anyone else could match it." Furthermore, when other retail banks finally developed the required software and introduced similar products, they failed to support them with a dedicated sales force. (Also, NovaRede's sales force benefited from a long-running advertising campaign on "The Price is Right," a highly popular television program.)

62   NovaRede was a major success. It established 22 branches in 1989, added 77 branches in 1990, and a further 101 in 1991. At the beginning of 1993, BCP had a total of 260 branches.

LAUNCHING THE SMALL BUSINESS GROUP

63   In May 1992, BCP established a sixth business group, housed alongside the corporate branches in the traditional BCP branch locations, to serve small companies and independent businessmen with annual sales of between 30 and 250 million Escudos ($200,000–$1.7 million).

64   BCP had already been serving parts of this customer segment through its corporate and HNWI business groups, as well as through NovaRede. In a sense, by introducing the small business group, BCP was "subsegmenting" its markets. The bank's rationale was that small businesses had special needs that could not be adequately met by the existing business groups. For example, the corporate business group had introduced a credit scoring system which analysed the client's balance sheets for the preceding three years. However, this procedure was not appropriate for smaller businesses, many

of which lacked sophisticated accounting systems. Moreover, the distinction between a small firm and its owner was often blurred, necessitating a joint analysis of the company and the individual.

65   In planning for this new group, the standard BCP-project group, supplemented with external consultants, decided to give Account Managers in the new small business group a large amount of autonomy for making credit decisions. A joint team of users and DP department staff developed a more appropriate system in which the Account Manager could incorporate judgmental factors related to the specific business client into the credit scoring.

66   BCP's small business group relied on the central IT department to develop key software applications to address particular needs, such as processing post-dated cheques.[6]

67   The principal hurdle faced by BCP in this segment concerned customer loyalty. Marketing research showed that approximately 50% of small businesses were unwilling to leave their existing banks, with which on average a small business had a 13-year relationship. BCP countered by offering continuous access to credit because small businesses were intensive users of credit products. BCP did not compete aggressively on price. Ultimately, BCP increased is market share of this small-business segment from 9% to between 10–11% during the first six months of this business group's operations.

INTERNATIONAL ACTIVITY

68   Beginning in 1990, BCP increasingly turned its attention to developments beyond Portugal's borders. As a defensive action against foreign banks entering Portugal, BCP created partnerships rather than opening or acquiring branches abroad. In March 1990, BCP established a strategic alliance with Banco Popular Español (BPE), the most profitable Spanish commercial bank, with a view toward engaging in joint projects. The agreement was accompanied by a "symbolic" exchange of shares: BPE acquired a 1.5% stake in BCP in March 1990. BCP and BPE established the French-based Banco Popular Comercial (BPC), a 50/50 joint venture. BCP also based a sales team at BPC to distribute a range of financial products and services tailored to Portuguese emigrant communities in France. Jardim Gonçalves, BCP's Chairman, explained: "There are nearly 1 million Portuguese in France, with a high savings propensity, increasing financial wealth, and enduring links with Portugal."

69   In the same year, BCP also signed an agreement with Cassa di Risparmio delle Provincie Lombarde (CARIPLO), an Italian mortgage lending company and the world's largest savings bank. Under this agreement, BCP and CARIPLO agreed to support each other's operations in their respective domestic markets. BCP exchanged 1.5% of its shares for an equivalent amount in Mediocredito Lombardo, a merchant banking subsidiary of CARIPLO. In 1991 BCP and CARIPLO founded Imomercado, a Portuguese real estate investment service company, and applied for the formation of a jointly owned mortgage bank to provide financing for home mortgages and real estate developments in Portugal.

70   Again in 1991, BCP formed alliances with Friends Provident (FP), a UK insurance group, and Avero Centraal Beheer (AVCB), a Dutch insurer. These deals were accompanied by share swaps under which the insurers acquired 15% of Ocidental Holding (a holding company for BCP's insurance subsidiaries), 49.9% of Ocidental Seguros (an insurance subsidiary), 49.9% of Ocidental Vida (a life insurance subsidiary), and 49.8% of BCP Investimentos SGPS (a holding company for asset management). These moves increased BCP's insurance and asset management activities. In 1992, BCP was also considering further joint ventures with these partners.

BUSINESS GROUP STRUCTURE AND DECISION MAKING

71   BCP introduced successive new business groups progressively during the 1986–92 period. Each launch took advantage of specific market opportunities and occurred as permitted by BCP's own resource base. (See Exhibit 9 for the growth pattern of various business indicators at BCP.)

---

[6] Portuguese regulations prevented hire-purchase and leasing contracts with retail customers. Therefore, small businesses, such as shopkeepers and car dealers, granted consumer credit by accepting post-dated cheques from their customers. These cheques were typically kept in a drawer then deposited on the agreed dates. BCP developed a complex application package, which enabled the client to deposit all the cheques immediately. BCP would then process the cheques electronically on the pre-agreed dates, granting the customer an overdraft during the interim.

EXHIBIT 9
Key Financial Figures for BCP

Medium-Sized Companies

	1991	1990	1989
Deposits (Esc bn)	212.5	135.7	116.0
Loans and advances (Esc bn)	363.6	255.6	181.1
• Customers	12,262	11,922	9,761
• Branches	38	29	28
• Employees	560	467	410

Private Banking

	1991	1990	1989
Deposits (Esc bn)	69.5	47.3	24.5
Loans and advances (Esc bn)	6.1	5.5	3.2
• Customers	2,199	1,762	1,375
• Branches	6	6	4
• Employees	74	57	32

Individual Retail Customers

	1991	1990	1989
Deposits (Esc bn)	349.4	260.7	172.9
Loans and advances (Esc bn)	28.9	15.4	8.5
• Customers	47,267	44,405	36,639
• Branches	40	30	28
• Employees	495	373	337

Corporate Banking

	1991	1990	1989
Deposits (Esc bn)	72.6	29.3	12
Loans and advances (Esc bn)	99.6	27.2	5.8
• Customers	468	339	123
• Branches	2	2	1
• Employees	27	20	12

NovaRede Network

	1991	1990	1989
Deposits (Esc bn)	177.5	51.3	2.3
Loans and advances (Esc bn)	21.7	3.1	0.1
• Customers	293,230	98,041	8,599
• Branches	200	99	22
• Employees	1,331	608	236

As of 31st December 1991, $1 is approximately 135 Escudos.

Source: "Banco Comercial Português (BCP): Portugal's New Wave Bank," UBS Phillips & Drew, March 5, 1992.

72   With regard to the reporting structure, each board member was responsible for a business group. (Board members were periodically rotated.) Reporting to each board member were the manager of a "Co-ordination Division" (with line responsibility for the business group) and the manager of a "Marketing Division" (who had authority to determine the business group's marketing mix, subject to co-ordination by a central planning division in terms of timing and pricing). (See Exhibit 10 for the typical organisation of a business group.)

73   A BCP manager explained the reasons behind this functional separation: "Although we thought about having a single person in charge of everything, we came back to believing that tension between marketing and line management is good."

EXHIBIT 9
Summary of Indicators
(millions of Escudos) (concluded)

	1991	1990	1989	1988	1987	% increase 1991
Total Assets	1,206,324	801,248	519,223	296,022	129,746	50,6%
Loans	515,885	294,739	139,215	69,397	36,691	75,0%
Funds received from customers	931,272	587,529	404,384	218,106	105,102	58,5%
Shareholders' equity	122,474	109,64	61,653	38,661	12,332	11,7%
Interest income	133,479	80,644	43,152	19,397	7,404	65,5%
Interest expense	90,679	50,018	25,555	11,096	3,495	81,3%
Net interest income	42.8	30,626	17,597	8,301	3,909	39,8%
Cash-Flow	42,399	29,127	15,29	7,192	3,04	45,6%
Amortisation	7,919	4,104	2,185	1,729	930	93,0%
Provisions	12,332	8,32	1,499	400	379	48,2%
Income taxes	3,925	2,96	1,363	405	29	32,6%
Minority interests	2,713	749	15	1		262,2%
Net Banking profit	18,224	13,742	10,243	4,658	1,702	32,6%
Liquidity ratio	10.0%	18.9%	19.8%	23.3%	17.7%	
Return on Assets (ROA)	1.9%	2.2%	2.8%	2.6%	2.7%	
Return on Equity (ROE)	16.9%	14.4%	21.3%	21.5%	25.1%	
Net interest income	5.4%	6.1%	6.0%	6.1%	8.5%	
Number of Branches	242	131	51	19	11	84.7%
Number of Employees	3,499	2,353	1,600	833	479	48.7%
Cash-Flow/Share	642	471	354	263	163	36.3%
Net Profit/Share	276	222	237	170	91	24.2%
Dividend/Share	70	60	67	67	17	16.7%
Share price-Nominal						
Maximum	2,800	3,340	3,535	2,911	4,178	
Minimum	1,940	1,860	1,863	1,878	1,741	
Average	2,479	2.04	3,214	1,972	1,855	
Price / Cash-Flow	3.9	4.7	10.3	11.0	18.0	
Price / Profit (PER)	9.0	9.9	15.4	16.9	32.2	
Price / Book value	1.3	1.2	2.6	2.0	4.4	
Stock market capitalisation (year end)	163,759	136,488	158,100	78,780	54,786	

Source: BCP annual reports.

74   Reporting to the Co-Ordination Manager were the branch managers of the business group, who were in turn responsible for the Account Managers (where they existed) and other officers (such as back office staff providing operations support).

75   The branches themselves were originally designed to operate as autonomously as possible, with separate front and back offices in order to maintain high quality of service. The intention was to decentralise operations and differentiate them by business group. Corporate operations, for example, tended to take longer than transactions by individuals, especially if an employee arrived with a bundle of cheques to be processed. Moreover, by establishing separate front offices at traditional branch locations, inconvenience to HNWI customers could be minimised. Although the front office remained separate in all but a few locations, the back offices at each location were being merged gradually. Quality of service had became easier to monitor and maintain within the highly automated BCP structure, so BCP refocused its emphasis on controlling the cost of operations and particularly on exploiting the synergy between the various areas of the bank.

76   The implied degradation of the principle of autonomous business group management was solved by rotating responsibility for the merged office between the managers of the three business group branches.

EXHIBIT 10
Typical Organisation of a Business Group

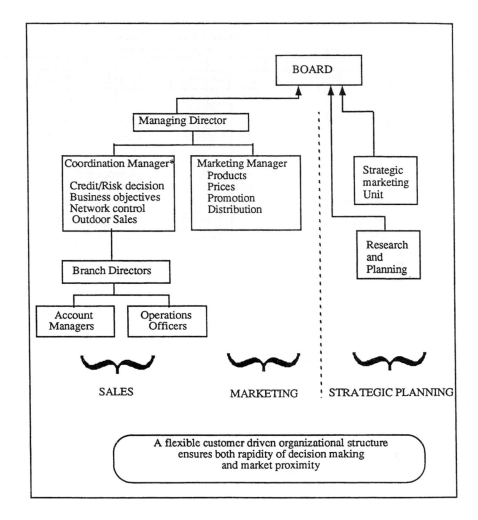

* The Co-ordination Manager supervises and controls the branches and the "selling" effort, along with credit and pricing negotiations, business objectives and personnel management.

Source: BCP internal documents.

77   Fast-growing NovaRede, on the other hand, maintained a separate back office at the level of the business group. It also set up its own sales force, independent from the central sales force that served the traditional business groups. As the General Manager for NovaRede remarked: "We didn't want to de-stabilise the other branches and their back offices. So we went for duplication of banking functions."

78   Each branch also had a "Branch Committee," which met regularly to collect the ideas of the Account Managers and bring them to the attention of the co-ordinating and marketing divisions. For example, the idea behind the sixth business group's post-dated cheque processing program had come from the customers of other business groups. They told their Account Managers, who informed the Branch Manager, who in turn communicated with the co-ordination and marketing divisions.

79   However, the bulk of the information flows in BCP were informal and rapid. BCP attached considerable importance to informal communications and motivating people. As a General Manager

EXHIBIT 11
Group Banco Comercial Português in 1992

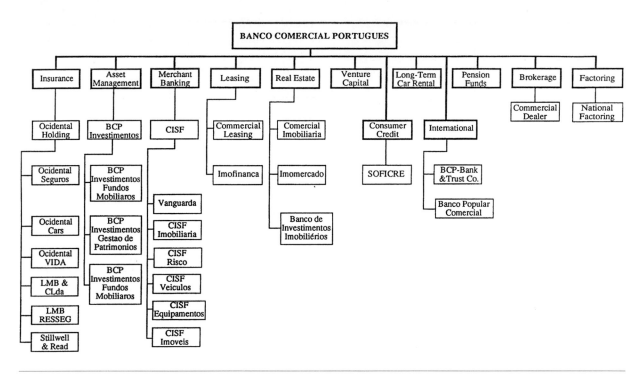

Source: BCP internal documents.

pointed out: "We have over 1,000 employees in this business. But I want to know if any of them has a problem. I talk to them, all of them. This is very important. The people are very attentive. Also, throughout BCP, managers have to deal with their own staff—which creates a good relationship. There is a big emphasis on training managers to manage and motivate people. It is like having many small organisations. There is no personnel department at BCP. People have to do it themselves. It is easy for any employee to talk to me. They can also ask to speak to the Chairman, but it is expected that they should have something important to say!"

CONTINUED GROWTH: SUBSIDIARIES' PRODUCTS

80   By 1992, in addition to expanding its internal banking operations, BCP had also expanded its product range, assisted by the acquisition or establishment of subsidiaries in insurance, leasing, factoring, venture capital, and fund management. (See Exhibit 11 for the overall structure of Group BCP.)

81   BCP's strategy was based on the vision that its success in the Portuguese market was closely associated with the range of ancillary products it could offer. It gave "one-stop-shopping" or "cross-selling" to its clients (see Exhibit 12 for levels of cross-selling). As a high-level executive explained: "Our subsidiary companies enable BCP to provide each customer an integrated and homogenous package of services, which few other banks can achieve. BCP, therefore, possesses technological and marketing edge in cross-selling, which is further enhanced through joint ventures with foreign partners."

82   BCP also introduced the concept of a "Financial Group," which had the specific task of co-ordinating the various financial requirements of BCP customers (e.g., insurance, leasing, factoring). As was common practice in Portugal, many of BCP's customers also held accounts in other banks.

EXHIBIT 12
Present Level of Cross-Selling

Products BCP Subsidiaries	% of Total Subsidiary products sold during 1991				
	Individual retail banking	Private banking	Corporate retail banking	Corporate banking	NovaRede
Life Insurance	15.4%	10.3%	1.7%	0.0%	2.6%
General insurance	38.9%	29.5%	17.2%	6.7%	8.8%
Leasing	1.9%	1.9%	22.5%	4.6%	0.2%
Factoring	---	---	0.7%	1.5%	---

Source: BCP internal presentation for year ending December 31, 1991.

For a customer to be profitable with BCP, the customer's BCP account needed to be the customer's primary one. BCP believed that this Financial Group approach, by providing a high level of service, would foster customer loyalty and thus primary use of the BCP account.

83   As BCP saw it, its sources of innovation were both the various marketing divisions (which remained closely in touch with their respective business groups) and the subsidiaries (as they tried to sell new products to the various marketing divisions and individual Account Managers).

84   The Ocidental Insurance Group, launched by BCP in 1987, illustrates how BCP managed its product subsidiaries and the interface with the business groups. (See Exhibit 13 for the structure of the Ocidental Group in 1991.)

85   Ocidental reflected BCP's overall strategic approach of competing on excellent service. Its products were premium-priced, but supported by a highly trained after-sales staff who provided quick payments on claims. For example, contrary to established industry custom, Ocidental would sometimes pay out on claims that were not covered by the policy. As one manager explained: "Sometimes it isn't worth management time to argue and process." Ocidental was gaining market share in Portugal: ranking 26th in 1988, 12th in 1991, and conceivably among the top ten insurers in 1992.

86   Ocidental was organised into four "Business Areas" based on distribution channels: NovaRede, HNWI (which also covered private banking), Small Business and Corporate, and Large Corporate. As Exhibit 13 shows, each offered a different subset of insurance products, configured for the needs of each segment. There were separate Ocidental back offices for the NovaRede and HNWI business groups and a combined back office for the two corporate groups. Ocidental also had functional departments for marketing, quality control, systems and organisation, planning, and finance and administration.

87   In 1991, the BCP business groups accounted for 62% of Ocidental's business and this percentage was rising, being expected to reach 70% in 1992. The remaining insurance business was sold by brokers. A comparison of how Ocidental marketed its products through the NovaRede and HNWI business groups provides a good illustration of BCP's product differentiation strategy. Ocidental products sold through NovaRede, incorporating the prefix "Nova" in product names to emphasize speed and innovation, reflected a "pull-marketing" strategy with intensive television advertising on the "Price is Right" and posters. Brochures displayed in NovaRede branches incorporated NovaRede's bright red, green, and yellow colour scheme. The "Nova" range of insurance products were only available to NovaRede account holders.

88   A somewhat broader range of essentially identical insurance products which had different names, conservative red and (granite) grey brochures, and higher prices, was distributed through the HNWI business group. Distribution reflected a "push" strategy. There was no independent distribution. According to the head of the Ocidental marketing division: "Insurance managers from the HNWI business group maintained close contact with the HNWI Account Managers. They trained the Account Managers on the insurance products and the features of the promotional campaign."

EXHIBIT 13
Ocidental Holdings

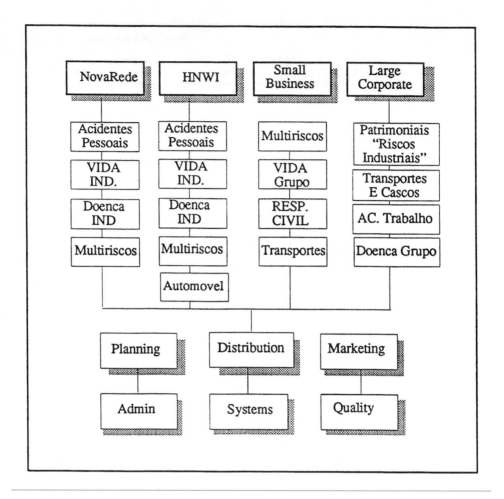

Source: BCP internal documents.

89   In reality, an Account Manager only "opened the door" and would refer a client to an Insurance
      Manager to complete the sale. Insurance Managers were in turn supported by a group of "Insurance
      Consultants," who were responsible for guaranteeing links with a group of Account Managers in a
      region. The Ocidental marketing head went on: "Bank-insurance has not been easy to introduce . . .
      Banks and Insurance companies have different cultures. Bank managers do not like insurance prod-
      ucts. We found that a large state-owned retail bank hated selling insurance. At BCP, the Account
      Manager likes the Insurance Manager because he gives him product support . . . Also, the Insurance
      Manager does not feel that he is kept back from the client because the Account Manager passes the
      client to him after the initial proposal."

DEALING WITH COMPETITION BETWEEN BUSINESS GROUPS

90   Segmentation brought with it the question of possibly excessive internal competition between the
      business groups for clients and products. The general manager of NovaRede explained how BCP
      dealt with client competition: "Everyone asks: 'How do we manage competition for customers
      between the business groups?' The answer is that we define pricing and credit lines for each segment.

For example, if a medium-sized corporate client went to NovaRede, it would be difficult to manage requests for credit of greater than 10 million Escudos ($75,000). NovaRede recognises that it might lose such a client and, thus, would transfer this client to the corporate business group. Another way of dealing with competition between business groups is to rotate staff."

91   However, for the Product Manager in the HNWI marketing division, the issue was not always simple: "In theory, the 'pyramid' sets the clear market boundaries in terms of the annual income of the individual and an ability to maintain a particular balance. But in practice there are grey areas. Some people theoretically belong to one business group but would like to fit into another business group . . . If a customer informs the NovaRede sales force of a desire to be in HNWI, the sales force sets up an appointment with HNWI. But it is harder for NovaRede to give up a good NovaRede customer than for HNWI to transfer a client downwards to NovaRede . . . If the customer definitely decides to have the HNWI service, there is no choice. But if this customer just makes inquires, NovaRede has the option of keeping the account."

92   According to BCP, the issue of which products NovaRede could offer depended on customer needs and price differentiation. It was not necessarily an issue of whether the product or service could be automated. For example, NovaRede clients borrowed according to a fixed repayment schedule. They were not entitled to overdraft limits, which was seen as too costly.[7]

93   On the other hand, managers acknowledged that there was a risk of internal competition between the subsidiaries in marketing products to the Account Managers.

94   Competition also occurred between the business groups for new products, given the limited resources of the DP department. At the beginning of each year, each area of the bank submitted a list of requests to the DP committee, which included the Board, all senior BCP management, and representatives of the DP department. All IT-related disputes were dealt with by the DP committee, which determined priorities for each application. This advance planning was regarded as very important for information system development.

CREATION OF THE STRATEGIC MARKET UNIT

95   By October 1991, BCP grew concerned that it lacked a sufficiently broad vision of its relevant market. The marketing divisions seemed to be focusing exclusively on their respective business groups, raising the likelihood of duplicating market research and marketing targets. These risks were likely to increase over time as BCP pursued a subsegmentation strategy within a high-growth market. At the end of a three-month planning period, BCP established a small "Strategic Marketing Unit" (SMU) to deal with these issues.

96   The SMU was given three principal tasks. First, the SMU was to study BCP's overall competitive position throughout BCP's entire product range and market position. Second, the SMU was to take responsibility for all marketing research. Henceforth, individual marketing divisions would submit requests for further research to the SMU, which would in turn assist them in analysing the results. Finally, the SMU was to organise regular meetings between the marketing divisions of the business groups and to facilitate the resolution of any conflicts they might have. In cases where the marketing divisions of two business groups wished to target the same subsegment, for example, a member of the SMU called a meeting to help resolve the issue. Where appropriate, an SMU opinion would be offered. Unresolved conflicts would be sent to the Board.

INFORMATION TECHNOLOGY AND THE NEED FOR MIS

97   From the very beginning BCP computers and information systems were considered strategic for BCP. The systems kept control of the bank's daily activities through an advanced on-line system whereby senior managers could view the status of the bank's financial position immediately after operations close. In addition, BCP developed a management information system, called STAT, to

---

[7] Actually there are small overdraft limits to holders of salary accounts of approximately $350.

satisfy the legal regulations for reporting to the Portuguese central bank. However, new more demanding IT requirements were emerging. In June 1991, BCP bought the Earnings Analysis System (EAS) from Hogan to replace its in-house systems. EAS gave BCP the capability to measure such key criteria as daily profitability by product, by client, by branch, and by account manager (please refer back to Exhibit 3 for an overview of the Earnings Analysis System). EAS reports are produced on a monthly basis. They are sent out to the requesting manager in both paper and electronic formats.

98   BCP viewed EAS as a strategic asset. Through its use, BCP has the ability to focus quick attention on specific areas that require closer management scrutiny. In addition, EAS helps control areas that have a direct bottom-line impact for BCP. For example, BCP used EAS (along with the credit scoring) to control bad loans. In other Portuguese banks, the Account Manager (or equivalent) alone is responsible for granting loans, whether there is a strong business case or not. Accurate loan information is not usually reported to managers, who traditionally have a broad overview of the loan decision. But in BCP such reporting happens instantly.

99   Based on EAS-reported information, BCP is able to obtain quickly a very clear picture of profitability for each area of a business. The bank uses such data for setting and controlling its objectives. For instance, EAS is proving to be a valuable tool for establishing clear incentive schemes for Account Managers. Based on meeting objectives, Account Managers might receive 30% of their annual base salary as bonus. In other banks, incentives schemes also exist, but are based often on unclear criteria and processes.

100   Unlike its banking divisions, BCP Group subsidiaries have their own computer systems. The factoring subsidiary, for example, installed a Wang system, Commercial Leasing used Digital, and the Insurance Group ran on IBM.

101   The divisions chose the system best suited to their needs, based solely on business criteria. They are then supported by the BCP's DP department (see Exhibit 14 for the structure of the department). Often the central DP department assists in developing software for subsidiaries. Still, the central DP department encourages adopting application packages for an IBM platform. But it is not dogmatic. For example, when BCP's international division felt that its International Money Management System (IMMS) was not offering the required level of performance, it changed the front-office part of the IMMS program from an IBM mainframe to a DEC so that, among other things, it could interface better with the Reuters dealing room system. Jardim Gonçalves, BCP's Chairman explained: "In other banks it is the DP department that defines the information system. In BCP it's the users that decide it."

102   BCP also allows each division to maintain its own DP staff wherever possible, following its general decentralisation policy of keeping key knowledge and decision making as close to the operating units as possible.

TEAM-BASED PROJECTS AND THE BCP CULTURE

103   BCP prided itself on being "a very informal institution." As one manager explained: "We don't have a real organisation chart. We might draw them from time to time. But we never approve one. When you approve something and then you want to change it, you have to make a decision to change it."

104   BCP's process of launching new lines of business reflected BCP's emphasis on team-based projects. Teams members were encouraged to "own" a project and often continued working on it after implementation. Teamwork has been valued since BCP began, when only a few people worked closely. In June 1992, there were 20 to 30 teams at BCP.

105   The team culture was instilled in all new employees when they entered the bank. They went through a three-week training program in teams of mixed background, learning about the bank, use of the bank's systems, etc. However, the main purpose of this training program was to "establish the culture." The BCP culture was never formally defined, but elements of its are reflected in the following comments of BCP people:

> People at BCP battle for their ideas. They work harder and more cohesively than those at the international banks.

EXHIBIT 14
Organisation of the DP Department

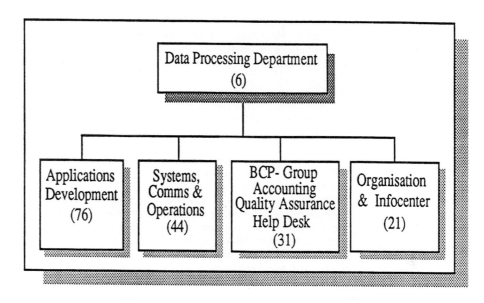

BCP's DP Department is organised into 4 areas, as depicted above:

- Applications Development. This group is responsible for selecting or developing application packages to match user requirements.

- Systems, Communications and Operations. This group is concerned with running of the computer systems, networks and 'production' activities.

- BCP-Group is a support group, responsible for co-ordinating the merging of BCP group's separate systems into a unified and coherent system. Other activities include: accounting systems; analysing the performance of systems; quality assurance; change management i.e. controlling software changes; and a help desk.

- Organisation (i.e. logistics) and Infocentre. The Infocentre managed various projects, including electronic mail evaluations and the DB2-based information system tests.

Source: BCP internal documents.

> There is strong loyalty by the staff to BCP and the Group. The staff feel that they are working in a clear project.

> Working with computers for the first time was a real surprise but now we cannot live without them.

> At BCP people don't keep ideas to themselves. They help each other. The people above understand if we make mistakes. They are enthusiastic if we have ideas . . . we take advantage of our youth.

106   The BCP culture was closely associated with the personality of Jardim Gonçalves, the Chairman himself:

> Mr. Gonçalves has a way of living that is very charismatic. Each incoming group is received by him. He transmits our culture. He also meets with everyone who leaves.

> The 150 Heads of the Departments meet with the Board once a quarter . . . The Chairman can publicly grill a manager, such as: "One of your employees has a problem. What are you doing about it?"

107   On the other hand, the rapid growth in staff since the creation of NovaRede has put a strain on the bank and its culture. In June 1992, part of the training for new recruits was conducted by people with just six months' experience. Some levels of service were going down, including simple things like answering or transferring a phone call. BCP responded by establishing a quality team, which worked closely with the innovative US bank, Banc One. BCP has since introduced quality training based on Banc One training materials.

108   BCP also believed in rotating the managers. One executive explained:

> Staff rotations happen about once a year. We ask the employees about their main interests, and try to accommodate their wishes when we move them. People rotate at all levels—for example, the Number 2 in the DP department left to work in DP at Ocidental (the Group's insurance subsidiary). We also rotate people between areas and between teams—for example, from the demand deposit account team to the time deposit account team. The advantage of these rotations is that they make people more flexible. You also enrich the culture by making people more aware of the issues and difficulties being faced elsewhere. Finally, you build backups for people—by switching personnel between teams there is always someone who can be moved back in the event of an emergency.
>
> The DP department does lose a lot of technical people, who move to other areas of the bank. However, this reinforces mutual understanding and ensures that there are good technicians in user departments like marketing and planning. There is a negative aspect: when the Board decides to move someone, it wants the move done quickly—which has costs for DP. But in general rotation moves are very good for the bank.

109   Rotation of Account Managers posed a particular problem for BCP in terms of client relationships. In the HNWI business group, there had been more customer complaints over rotation of Account Managers than for any other type of complaint. But such a rotation decision served a necessary purpose since BCP wanted the clients to be clients of the bank, not clients of the Account Manager. Rotation also helped reduce the power of these managers vis à vis the bank. However, in the private banking business group rotation was not actively encouraged since the cost was considered to be too great. When a client did have to be transferred to another private banker, the process took at least six months.

BCP's Competitors

110   Since 1985 there has been a gradual liberalisation of the financial sector in Portugal, which has permitted the establishment of private and foreign banks. In 1992, there were 33 banking institutions in Portugal, 12 of which were state-owned banks, 8 domestic private banks, and 13 foreign banks. (See Exhibits 15 and 16 for an overview of BCP's competitors.)

Future Challenges

111   Like its main rivals, BCP faces many challenges in the mid-1990s. (See Exhibit 17 for an overview of BCP's changing challenges.) Firstly, BCP has to deal with the internal directives of the Bank of Portugal (BOP):

- · The BOP established capital adequacy ratios of 4% in 1991, 6% in 1992, and finally 8% in 1993. The imposition of these guidelines will be particularly painful for domestic state-owned banks, which will be forced to raise equity in the short term or reduce assets.
- · A shift from an administered to a market-drive monetary policy, coupled with the squeezing effect of new market entrants, will increase competition and eventually reduce financial margins (the Portuguese spreads have been 7–8% versus 1–3% in Europe).

112   Secondly, challenges are also coming from outside Portugal's border with the EC liberalisation process, such as:

EXHIBIT 15
Listed Banks on the Lisbon Stock Exchange, 1992

Year End 1991	Shares (Mn)	Capital (Esc Bn)	PER	Net Profit (Esc Mn)	Op. expenses (% total inc)	ROE	Nr Branches
BCI	19.06	30.5	16.0	2,670	60.7	19.1	64
BCM	6.50	21.4	--	1,865	54.5	14.8	16
BCP	83.93	165.1	8.7	18,224	50.4	32.8	240
BESCL	40.00	152.0	10.5	15,729	76.6	23.8	220
BIC	11.60	25.5	32.0	1,629	66.6	10.7	14
BPA	35.00	157.5	5.9	25,022	83.3	49.6	187
BPI	21.29	91.6	10.2	9,599	--	--	--
BTA	45.00	146.7	7.2	18,535	80.6	20.7	172
Citibank	6.00	7.1	6.3	1,503	51.7	18.3	2
Credit Lyonnais	1.20	4.9	15.4	1,447	72.1	--	62
Manuf Hanover	16.25	23.1	7.8	3,007	39.2	14.5	16

Privately-held banks have been the most dynamic in the banking industry. Over the last five years they have invested heavily in new information systems and branches in order to improve operational efficiency and broaden their deposit collecting basis. Meanwhile, they have also been introducing new financial products in the "underbanked" Portuguese market. The new products introduced include mortgages, consumer credit, accounts with tailored features and products combining insurance, pension schemes, deposits and access to credit.

Until late August 1986, mortgages were only granted by two state-owned banks, Caixa Geral de Dépositos (CGD) and Crédito Predial Português (CPP), who could grant this type of credit at preferential rates according to the borrower's income. This type of credit was subject to an annual ceiling which did not satisfy demand. In August 1986, mortgage credit was liberalised, but it was only since June 1991 that private banks were able to grant mortgages at the same preferential rates. As far as commercial banks are concerned, this type of credit is still in its infancy and is expected to expand significantly over the next five years given potential demand.

The issue of credit cards was liberalised in May 1986 and has expanded greatly since then. Nevertheless, there is still room for growth.

Meanwhile state-owned banks have taken advantage of high spreads prevalent in Portugal during the late 1980s. These spreads have permitted public banks to clean their balance sheets of unprovisioned bad debt and unfunded pension liabilities and reinforce their capital structure through share capital increases and disposal of non-operational assets. Early retirement schemes and recruitment programs for young graduates have also been introduced.

During the 1992 general recession, BCP has seen its share price suffer along with the Portuguese market. Its prospective PE multiple has contracted from 11x to 9.5x. It has nevertheless outperformed the market and considerably outperformed the other banking stocks which have seen much heavier falls.

BCP does not have the lowest PER of the Portuguese bank stocks, but given its superior outlook, heavy investments in its new areas, superior profitability and strength of capital base many analysts believe that the multiple is undemanding.

BCP is the largest stock on the Portuguese stock market both in terms of market capitalisation and volume traded. As such it represents 20% of the total capitalisation of the market, and one of the few liquid investments in a largely illiquid market.

Source: UBS April 28, 1992.

· The liberalisation of deposit taking in any EC country and easier access to credit and to any financial service provided by institutions operating in the Community.
· The enlargement of the banking system to include all EC-based banks, the expansion of the distribution network, the marketing of new products, and the proliferation and sophistication of services offered by non-monetary financial institutions.

113   Thirdly, Portuguese consumers are being tempted with more choice through stiffer competition:

EXHIBIT 16
BCP's Competitors

New Private Sector Banks

The following are BCP main competitors among the new private sector banks:

Banco de Comércio e Indústria (BCI)	BCI was originally founded by the main share holders of BPI (see below) in 1985 but control was taken over in 1990 by Banco Santander of Spain and The Royal Bank of Scotland of the UK. Plans to expand the branch network were initially hampered by the loss of senior management but 1991 has seen expansion to 82 branches. This has resulted in a doubling of asset size, but it still remains only one quarter the size of BCP.
Banco Português de Investimento (BPI)	Founded in 1984, BPI has been a very successful investment bank. As such it is not a direct competitor of BCP, but in 1991 it acquired an 80% interest in Banco Fonsecas e Burnay (BFB) with 114 branches. Through BFB, BPI is expected to make a significant impact on the market but will take some time to get to grips with this former state-run bank.
Banco Internacional de Crédito (BIC)	Controlled by the Espirito Santo family and Crédit Agricole of France, BIC has been a small and successful operation. It is likely to be integrated into BESCL once the Espirito Santo family and Crédit Agricole take full control of that bank.
Banco Comercial de Macau (BCM)	Established in 1974, BCM merged with Banco de Oriente in 1988 and transferred its headquarters to Oporto. Starting out as a merchant bank it intends to move into retailing. BCM expansion strategy includes acquisitions of other banks and insurance companies. BCM has targeted the urban upper middle class retail segment and the corporate market, with high yielding short term financial instruments.

Major Foreign Banks

At present, foreign interest in the domestic banking sector comes predominately from Spain. Others include:

Banco Bilbao Vizcaya (BBV)	Spain's second largest bank acquired the former Lloyds bank 12 branch network in 1990. After initially losing deposits it has started to expand the branch network.
Barclays	Barclays of the UK has been licensed to operate in Portugal since 1985. An aggressive expansion plan appears to have run into problems after incurring losses in the first half of 1991.
Citibank	Established since 1985, Citibank developed three segments (money market, monetary capital markets and corporate finance), and has capitalised on its parent company in the development of venture capital, back office operations and asset management. Operating out of 2 offices with 78 staff, its strategy is to provide greater personalised customer service and greater coverage of the corporate market.
Crédit Lyonnais	Founded in 1863, Crédit Lyonnais floated capital in 1990. In an effort to gain recognition as an innovative and quality back office financial service company, the bank embarked on a series of acquisitions of asset management, credit card, mutual fund, and leasing companies. The bank also plans to enter into factoring. The Bank's main focus has traditionally been the corporate segment, but now it is attempting to strengthen it's individual banking operations.
Manufacturers Hanover	MH was transformed into a commercial private bank in 1987. The Bank's traditional market segment has been wholesale banking, but is now moving into private banking, specialising in mergers and acquisitions. Pursuing a diversification strategy, MH has launched a Mutual and Bond fund, has attacked the leasing and factoring segments, and has created an offshore subsidiary in Madeira. MH is the largest (in terms of gross profit) of Portugal's foreign banks.

· Portuguese households are increasingly channelling their household savings through alternative savings instruments, such as insurance products, investment funds, and saving funds.

· Eager to broaden the deposit base, commercial banks plan to continue increasing branch networks. Portugal is still underbanked with only 2 branches per 10,000 inhabitants (36 branches per $ billion) versus an average of 9 for other major European economies

EXHIBIT 16
(concluded)

Major Privatised and Public Sector Commercial Banks

The biggest competitive threat to BCP comes mainly from the newly revitalised, formerly nationalised banks. These banks have seen strong improvements in results helped by pre-privatisation capital injections. Healthier profits have in turn allowed them to cover bad debts and pension fund liabilities. The most important of these banks are:

Banco Português do Atlântico (BPA)	Oporto-based BPA is Portugal's largest commercial bank. It has a well-developed financial services group including Banco Comercial de Macau, which it has been developing as an upmarket operation. 33% was privatised in 1990 and the remainder was scheduled for 1992. BPA market leadership was supported by an expansion strategy of increasing its number of retail outlets (including 10 fully automated). Its international focus is on countries that have important "cultural" ties with Portugal.
Banco Espírito Santo & Comercial de Lisboa (BESCL)	The former owners of BESCL, the Espirito Santo family, together with partners Crédit Agricole will have regained control of BESCL when the second tranche of the privatisation issue has been completed. BESCL is Portugal's third largest bank and one of the most profitable of the major banks, servicing mainly small and medium-sized businesses. BESCL has been one of the most aggressive of the larger banks in opening new branches with a total of 220 in 1992 .
Banco Totta e Açores (BTA)	BTA is now fully privatised and, through direct holdings and Portuguese partners, Spain's Banesto has effective control of the bank. The bank is expected to become a more aggressive player in the market place, but as yet Banesto and BTA's management have not agreed a strategy.
Banco Pinto e Sotto Mayor (BPSM)	BPSM is one of the most troubled of the nationalised banks, having been required to lend heavily to Portugal's cement and steel industries. The bank is having to undergo extensive restructuring to be ready for privatisation and may well have to sell off a large part of its 188 branch network in the process.
Caixa Geral de Depósitos (CGD)	The state-controlled savings bank is by far the biggest financial institution in Portugal, operating through post offices as well as its own 414 branches. 80% of its deposits come from retail depositors (a 26% market share). Around 40% of its lending is for house mortgages (60% market share), 22% is to central and local government and much of the remainder is long-term lending to industry. Its cheap deposit base and control of the payment system for the public sector has made it a very profitable operation. CGD acquired 60% of Banco Nacional Ultramarino, formerly the main bank in Portugal's colonies.
Banco de Fomento e Exterior & Banco Borges e Irmão	This Bank consists of a specialised credit institute (BFE) channelling subsidised credits to agriculture and industry, and a small retail bank. BBI originally focused on foreign trade finance, but lacked the ability to move quickly and stay close to its customers and hence has remained a "universal" bank

(50 branches per $ billion). This figure is matched by the number of ATMs (Portugal has 7 ATMs per 1,000 inhabitants versus 15 per 1,000 inhabitants for major European economies). BCP planned a total of 300 branches.

· The domestic financial industry is experiencing further rationalisation. This means that retail banks will increasingly depend on strong brand names and automated branch networks to improve service efficiency and reduce operating costs. Retail banks will also compete to ensure a broader coverage of the targeted markets and diversification of services in order to provide a "one-stop" service.

114   Lastly, BCP's initial growth is now creating its own internal pressures:

· Looking just at IT, BCP's strategy of diversification into other non-financial activities is causing problems due to the co-existence of different systems. The Account Managers are slowly losing a comprehensive view of a client. Multi-vendor inter-connectivity is only partially solved. The computer systems cannot "talk" with each other. For instance,

EXHIBIT 17
Consolidating Market Penetrations

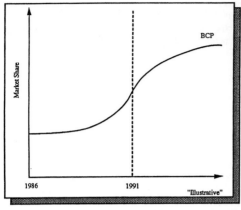

	1986-1991	1992-
Stage	Accelerated Growth	Consolidation
Position	Innovative Outsider	Market-Leader
Differentiation Opportunities	High	Low
Emphasis	Proposal of Value	Value Execution
Market Characteristics	Buyers' Market	Sellers' Market
Strategy	Pull	Push
	Product Innovation	Commercial Efforts
	Communication of Innovation	Customer Relationship
Account Managers Rôle	Capture Nearer Customers	Cross Selling
		Capture Customers Through More Aggressive Commercial Efforts
Marketing	Product Marketing	Customer Marketing
	Launch of New Products	Information Analysis

Account Managers can tell from the overall system that a client owns a certain product from a subsidiary, but they can only obtain limited additional details.

116   Clearly, BCP is a success. But its very growth and expansion raises new and serious problems. Moreover, in 1993 it faced increasing threats from within as Portuguese rivals improved and even imitated. Also foreign banks were eyeing the Portuguese market. The structure of BCP and its culture needs rethinking and reassessment. BCP is also rightfully proud of its IT infrastructure and systems, but were they still as useful, leading edge, and distinctive?

117   BCP needs a fresh look at its overall strategy in order to continue its impressive growth and development during the rest of 1990s and beyond.

EXHIBIT 18
BCP Main Innovations

Product	Category	Description	Date	Competitive Response
Account Managers	New Service	Personal service.	May 1986	1990 Barclays, 1991 BCI (Santander)
Nova Conta Mas	New product	High yield bank account.	Late 1986	1990 Barclays, 1991 BCI (Santander)
Prestice Débico	New product	Visa premier gold debit card (first gold debit card in Portugal).	Late 1986	BCI launched gold card 1987
Conta Fitulos	New service	A more flexible securities account. Supported in BCP central system, it allows any customer access to the Stock exchange at branch level.	May 1986	No one followed.
Direct Marketing	New concept	BCP introduced direct marketing methods such as telemarketing and mailing. The first in the Portuguese banking industry.	May 1986	Others followed late 1988.
Image through premises	New concept	BCP premises designed in order to appeal to the segments they serve.	May 1986	BPA and Barclays followed in 1990, BCI in 1991 and BFB in 1992.
Market Segmentation	New concept	BCP specified the products and service level for each of the tightly defined segments	May 1986	1990 Barclays and 1991 BCI. Others developed products aimed at special market segments. BCP still remains the only bank to follow a full market segmentation strategy.
Financial Group	New concept	In order to serve each customer's global financial needs, BCP established a group to co-ordinate such aspects as insurance, leasing, factoring, etc.	1987	Others have slowly developed a financial group.
Tradelink	New product	An information service to business around the world.	1986	A year later BESCL launched a similar product.
Commercial Bonds	New product	Innovative short/medium term bonds for medium size companies.	Late 1988	No one followed.
Madeira "Off-shore" Branch	New concept	Taking advantage of tax and operating conditions in Madeira's financial "off-shore" status.	Jan. 1989	Others followed in late 1989.
Monthly Income Account	New product	A new financial product combining a high interest rate with flexibility of withdrawal and the payment of monthly income.	Mid 1989	Others followed a year later.

EXHIBIT 18
(concluded)

Product	Category	Description	Date	Competitive Response
Prestige Crédito	New product	Visa Premier (gold) credit card. First ever gold credit card issued in Portugal.	Mid 1989	Barclays launched a gold credit card in 1991.
Short-term Bonds	New product	Securities issued by medium size companies at very competitive interest rates with 1 year maturity.	Late 1989	BPSM followed 2/3 months later.
NovaRede Distribution Network	New concept	Small branches with reduced staff (5 maximum), automated and close to customers. ATM and CAT in all 200 branches (end 91).	Nov. 1989	Other banks opened a few branches of that same size afterwards.
Salary Account	New product	An account based on automatic transfer of monthly salary, enabling early payment of salary from the 15th, an automatic credit line, and free accident insurance.	Nov. 1989	Others followed in 90/91 with similar products.
Hot-Line	New service	A telephone service through which clients may place orders, or request information.	Nov. 19898	BPA launched a hot-line in late 90. Barclays and BFB in 1992.
Monthly Combined Statement	New service	A document which summarizes all financial transactions, and states all the client's assets.	Nov. 1989	No other bank offers such a complete service.
Mortgage Credit	New product	BCP moved into an area that was an "exclusive" of special credit institutions.	1990	Others followed in the same year.
ADR Program	New concept	BCP was the first Portuguese company to have their share capital listed in a foreign market.	Aug. 1990	No other Portuguese bank is listed outside Portugal.
Sponsoring TV Show	New concept	Sponsoring a popular TV show.	Oct. 1990	Others followed in 1992 (BESCL, BFB, etc.)
Personal Credit	New product	BCP launched credit facilities for individuals just after the removal of legal restrictions.	1991	Others followed with 4/5 months lag.
Managing Pre-dated Cheques	New product	A product designed to manage pre-dated checks for small businesses.	Apr. 1992	No other bank offers such a comprehensive product.
Credit Based on Pre-dated Cheques	New product	A credit line based on accounts receivable (as pre-dated checks) held by small businesses.	Apr. 1992	No other bank offers such a comprehensive product.

BCP main competitors became increasingly good at imitating BCP innovations; however, no one bank could follow all of BCP new product introductions. BCP also adopted a policy of "zero-interaction" with other banks in Portugal (for instance on the inter-banking network system, SIBS). This was done in order to reduce the amount of competitive information that was "leaked out" from BCP.

CASE 30

GUINESS PEAT AVIATION: THE FLOTATION

I. INTRODUCTION

1   In June 1992, Dr. Anthony A. Ryan, otherwise known as Tony Ryan, the co-founder, director and chairman of the Guiness Peat Aviation group, GPA, in Shannon, Ireland, prepared to realise his long sought goal of taking his company public in one of the largest international initial public offerings on record. The company he had built with his own two hands and that had grown to become the largest company in Ireland needed a fresh equity injection in order to continue growing according to Ryan's plans.

2   Ryan was agonizing over several issues, large and small, related to the issue. GPA had very nearly approached the public equity markets a year earlier, only to shy away at the last minute. Ryan was convinced that now was the correct time, both for the company and based on the markets. There was evidence, however, that the markets might not be receptive to a new issue from an aircraft leasing company. Most seriously, the global airline industry was suffering its worst recession ever due to the combined effects of the general recession and the Gulf War.

3   In addition, Ryan had to choose a lead manager for the issue. This hinged upon a number of connected issues, the most important being the marketing of the issue. There were several factors which supported a global offering. If this was chosen, the choice of global manager could be critical to the success of the issue. Connected to the choice of lead manager was the negotiation over offer price. The candidates for lead manager with whom Ryan had talked had indicated that Ryan's preferred asking price was too high. Thus, Ryan expected to face tense negotiations with whomever he chose in order to ensure that the issue went to market at a fair price.

II. GPA

4   GPA was the world's leading aircraft leasing and trading company. Based at Ireland's Shannon airport, the company was founded in 1975 by Dr. A. A. Ryan (the chairman and chief executive), Aer Lingus, and the Guinness Peat Group with capital of $50,000 to provide second hand aircraft to airlines on operating leases. In the early 1980s, the company foresaw a significant requirement for new aircraft, then unrecognised by the world's manufacturers or major airlines, and started to order new aircraft, without having leases in place. To that end it had been eminently successful. It became the largest leasing company of new aircraft in the world—with an estimated 37% market share—and was roughly twice the size of its nearest competitor (see Exhibits 1 and 2). In March 1992 it had a fleet of 409 aircraft under management, worth $6.5 billion, and had orders and options outstanding for 528 new aircraft to be delivered over the next decade, worth $21 billion in March 1992 dollars—equivalent to 10% of the anticipated world production over the period.

This case was written by Kevin Kaiser, Assistant Professor at INSEAD, with the help of Research Assistant, Uri Savoray. It is intended to be used as a basis for class discussion rather than to illustrate either effective or ineffective handling of an administrative situation. Partial support for this case was provided by the International Financial Services Programme. Reprinted with the permission of INSEAD. Copyright © 1994 INSEAD, Fontainebleau, France.

EXHIBIT 1
Major Aircraft Operating Lessors and Estimated Market Shares

Lessor	Total Jet Aircraft	Market Share	Pre-85 Aircraft	Market Share	Post-85 Aircraft	Market Share
GPA	352	19.7	230	19.8	230	36.5
Polaris	263	14.7	122	10.5	110	17.4
ILFC	139	7.8	77	6.6	68	10.8
GE Capital	111	6.2	54	4.7	34	5.4
AWAS	84	4.7	50	4.3	33	5.2
UAS	55	3.1	46	4.0	20	3.2
Electra	51	2.8	39	3.4	16	2.5
Aeron Aviation	46	2.6	38	3.3	34	5.4
GATX	40	2.2	36	3.1	13	2.1
International Air Leases	39	2.2	35	3.0	10	1.6
Aviation Sales Co.	38	2.1	31	2.7	7	1.1
Potomac Capital	38	2.1	29	2.5	7	1.1
Pegasus Capital	37	2.1	28	2.4	7	1.1
Caldwell Aircraft Trading	35	2.0	21	1.8	7	1.1
Airbus Leasing	32	1.8	20	1.7	6	1.0
Top 15	1,360	76.0	856	73.9	602	95.4
43 Others	430	24.0	303	26.1	29	4.6
Total	1,790	100.0	1,159	100.0	631	100.0
Percentage of world total	19.0%		19.7%		17.8%	

Source: AISL.

5   Thus far, GPA had financed its impressive growth with privately placed equity issues (Exhibit 3 lists the major shareholders) and debt. Honouring the outstanding orders would require additional financing. While there was a possibility of using new debt, seeking additional equity capital from existing shareholders, or tapping new sources of financing, Ryan felt that the time was right for an initial public offering (IPO).

6   GPA had been instrumental in developing the operating lease as a viable alternative to ownership for the world's airlines, providing larger airlines with much needed flexibility and easing entry into the industry for smaller or start-up carriers. The fact that the world's manufacturers were more than willing to sell such large numbers of aircraft to a company that is not itself an end user represented a structural change in the aviation industry. Its existence itself had removed an element of risk from the industry in providing financial, geographical, and operating flexibility.

7   The company had been consistently profitable. Its management primarily had a financial aim—with internal targets based on return on equity—and over the past eight years, the group had achieved an annual average ROE of 33%. Over that time, revenues had grown 22 times, net income 20-fold, and earnings per share 12-fold. Total assets under management had grown from $230 million to $6,500 million.

8   GPA constantly watched the health of its customers, the industry, and its position within the industry. Consequently it was greatly to its credit that firstly, since foundation, it had lost no more than $30 million in bad debts,[1] and that secondly, in the past financial year—encompassing the worst recession the air transport industry had encountered in its history until that date—it managed to

[1] One of GPA's clients, America West, filed for Chapter 11 bankruptcy protection in June 1991. GPA had 16 A320s on lease to the company at the time. The group, NWA, and Kawasaki had also provided debtor-in-possession financing of $78 million—$35 million of which came from GPA. There remained doubts over the viability of America West's survival, but in

EXHIBIT 2
Estimated Lessor Shares of Jet Orders

Lessor	Jet Orders	Share (%)
GPA	354	49.4%
ILFC	214	29.8
AWAS	29	4.0
Kawasaki	24	3.3
Orix	19	2.6
Lufthansa Lsg	18	2.5
GATX	14	2.0
Top 7	672	93.7
15 Others	45	6.3
Total	717	100.0

Source: AISL.

increase profits, if only marginally, and maintain all but a small amount of its assets on lease. (Exhibit 4 presents recent income statements.)

9   The company was organised into two main operating divisions, GPA Leasing and GPA Capital, but the group should be viewed as a closely co-ordinated single organism that generated cash out of the aircraft assets under management.

10   GPA Leasing was responsible for the acquisition and management of the group's fleet portfolio and global marketing of leases to airlines worldwide. GPA offered its airline clients a physical asset combined with complex financial, legal, and technical services that were tailored to maximise the value to the customer and, thereby, GPA's return on each transaction. Although the component parts of this "product"—the aircraft and money—were essentially commodities, GPA sought to provide added value and, consequently, to sell its product at a premium. The company concentrated on providing its customers with "dry" operating leases, which transferred all the risks and rewards of operation to the lessee while GPA retained substantially all the risks and rewards of ownership.

11   In the ordinary course of business, GPA sold aircraft from its portfolio to realise residual values, to exploit specific opportunities, and to hedge its risks. The company occasionally bought aircraft with the express purpose of resale; in many of these cases, it had identified a purchaser before acquiring the aircraft. In addition, GPA often realised residual value by selling an aircraft and the attached lease as a financial asset to investors (securitisation). Through its technical analysis team and the Trading Floor,[2] GPA monitored the second-hand values of all aircraft types very closely. It had yet to sell an aircraft at a book loss.

12   GPA Capital was the innovative financial services arm of the group, generating liquidity and profits from treating the aircraft as financial packages. In recent years it had pioneered the "securitisation" of aircraft and operating lease streams—separately and together.

13   With the aim of being the world leader in the sale of aircraft as financial assets, GPA Capital offset risk and provided a considerable element of liquidity for the group. Its main products were:

· The packaging of aircraft and lease into a financial asset. This could include any or all of the financial aspects of the aircraft asset—lease receivables, residual values or depreciation and tax benefits.

the meantime, GPA had prior call on moneys due and spent considerable time in monitoring the credit position. If the airline were to cease operations, GPA could suffer further losses arising from the need to remarket the A-320s.

[2] The Trading Floor refers to a group within GPA which monitored and controlled worldwide marketing activities and maintained a sophisticated computerised database containing detailed industry information and the majority of aircraft transactions from around the world.

EXHIBIT 3
GPA Group Major Shareholders

Identity of Shareholder	Number of Ordinary Shares Owned	Percentage of Shares Owned
The Mitsubishi Trust and Banking Corporation	25,611,320	11.29%
Air Canada	21,724,920	9.58
Aer Lingus PLC	19,875,680	8.76
The Prudential Insurance Company of America	15,394,418	6.79
The Long-Term Credit Bank of Japan Ltd.	13,805,158	6.09
Irish Life Assurance PLC	5,366,052	2.37
Kawasaki Enterprises, Inc.	4,197,568	1.85
The Bank of Nova Scotia	3,459,840	1.53
Mitsubishi Corporation	2,937,760	1.30
Nippon Total Finance	2,802,320	1.24
Deutsche Bank Group	2,436,682	1.07
Whirlpool Financial Corporation International	1,935,520	0.85
Allied Irish Banks (Holdings and Investments) Limited	1,640,000	0.72
Bank of Ireland	941,200	0.41
Foreign & Colonial Investment Trust PLC	855,142	0.38

· Management of leases on aircraft sold.

· Remarketing of aircraft from lessees or owners.

14   Its marketing strengths in this esoteric area arose from:

· The group's diversified aircraft portfolio.

· Significant product innovation—it was constantly developing new products.

· Significant marketing experience, range of clients, and penetration into all major world financial areas—in FY 1992, while there were difficulties in doing business in Japan as a result of the credit crunch there, GPA capital arranged financing deals in North America, Mexico, the Gulf States, Ireland, UK, Finland, Norway, Sweden Denmark, and even China.

· Significant financial strength with good investment grade credit rating.

· Strong management and remarketing skills.

15   In addition to the above two divisions, GPA established GPA Technologies in 1990 to manage GPA's investments in related service activities, such as the new maintenance facility being built in Shannon with Lufthansa and Swissair or an aircraft paint shop subsidiary.

III. GPA'S BUSINESS, STRATEGY, AND THE AIRCRAFT LEASING INDUSTRY

16   GPA's business and strategy could be summarized along three main dimensions:

· Very long term financially oriented strategy. Fleet strategy was based on a horizon of 10 years and more while the short to medium horizon was driven by balance sheet and financial structure considerations.

· High level of fundamental research and analysis. GPA's analysts were continuously building and updating 10-year forecasts of world travel, technological and regulatory developments, and the relative merits of different aircraft and engines.

EXHIBIT 4
GPA Profit and Loss Highlights (in $ millions except per share data)

	1988	1989	1990	1991	1992
Revenues:					
Aircraft	197	368	470	582	837
Aircraft sales	422	661	1,480	1,285	1,127
Fees and commissions	31	13	12	22	46
Total	650	1,042	1,962	1,889	2,010
Expenses:					
Cost of aircraft sales			1,355	1,010	952
Depreciation			115	126	179
Net interest expense			128	138	184
Other expenses			142	216	389
Gross profit:					
Aircraft leasing	41	52	80	93	89
Aircraft sales	43	90	125	184	175
Fees and commissions	30	13	2	22	31
Total	123	161	222	308	306
Selling and administrative expenses	19	18	17	63	44
Operating profits	104	143	205	245	262
Share of associates	3	15	42	36	17
Pre-tax profits	107	158	247	281	279
Tax and minorities	(6)	(6)	(5)	(19)	(11)
Preference dividends	(21)	(26)	(36)	(20)	(19)
EPS (fully diluted)	$0.54	$0.70	$1.05	$1.10	$1.15
Dividends per share	$1.70	$0.22	$0.30	$0.30	$0.30

Source: Charterhouse Tilney, 10/6/92; Nomura prospectus.

· Marketing support. As indicated in footnote 2, the Trading Floor along with sales subsidiaries in Stamford, Connecticut, and London ensured that GPA's ability to place aircraft was unparalleled.

Changing Customer Base

17   In 1980, 39% of GPA's leasing profits were derived from customers in the Americas and Europe. In FY 1992, by contrast, North America provided 10%, Europe 26%, South America 30%, and Asia, the Middle East and Africa the remaining 34% of leasing profits. Thus the company had less exposure to country risk and did not depend on any single country or customer. GPA has developed a well-diversified lease portfolio, leasing to 101 customers in 49 countries, with no single country accounting for more than 15% of the group's gross leasing profits.

18   In 1970, the US accounted for a little over 55% of total worldwide revenue passenger miles (RPMs). By 1990, that had dropped to a little over 42% and by the year 2000, it was expected to be 39%. In 1970, Japan, other Asian countries, and the Middle East accounted for only 5.8% of the airline market share or 10% of the US total. By 1990, these three areas had grown to a market share of 16.1%. By the year 2000, those three geographical areas were expected to account for 18.4% of the total airline market share, while by the year 2010, that market share was expected to grow to 20.8%. The European market was expected to remain relatively flat at around 25% of the total. This dramatic shift in market share stemmed from the fact that the US and European domestic markets had become mature, while the economies in the Japan, other Asian countries, and the Middle East had been growing rapidly from an almost nonexistent pre-1970 base.

19   In addition to these observed changes, two markets were emerging that dwarfed all previous new entrants to the world economy, especially in terms of potential aircraft procurement: China and the Commonwealth of Independent States (CIS).

20   Boeing's management had pointed out that if China's economy grew as fast over the next 20 years as it had grown during the previous 14, it would emerge as the largest economy in the world. Boeing estimated that over the next 16½ years the Chinese market needed to absorb 850 new aircraft valued at $47 billion. Most of the airlines operating within China did not exist just 20 years before. Virtually all of western China was still without airline service. Since China was a country with very few good roads and railroads, the cheapest and most efficient way for the country to economically unify itself was through the use of aircraft.

21   Assuming no retrograde political movement in the newly forming countries of the former Soviet Union, an internal Boeing newspaper pointed out that "The market for commercial jetliners there is conservatively estimated at about 1,300 aircraft with value of about $72 billion over the next ten to twelve years." Boeing also pointed out that Aeroflot—the former USSR national airline—had a fleet of approximately 1,600 aircraft. However, most existing Soviet commercial aircraft were less reliable and needed more maintenance than the western-manufactured aircraft, and would be unable to fly within the new regions demanding stricter noise and pollution controls (see below). Moreover, aircraft made in the CIS could not fly to or from many destinations without refueling halfway. Since most Russian airlines did not want to waste hard currency on fuel, the CIS airlines probably would want the more fuel efficient western aircraft rather than those being offered within its borders. In addition, it was already obvious that, given an option, western passengers would choose an airline operating a western aircraft over a Russian aircraft virtually every time. The CIS airlines understood this, and were anxious to close the gap with modern airlines.

Changing Regulatory Environment

22   Noise and pollution standards were expected to dramatically alter the commercial aircraft landscape. In the US, the phasing in of stricter noise and pollution requirements was expected to occur in four stages: by the end of 1994, 25% of each carrier's fleet had to meet Stage 3 requirements, by the end of 1996, 50% had to meet these requirements, by the end of 1998, 75% had to meet the requirements, and 100% compliance was mandated by the end of 1999. For most US domestic carriers, there were expected to be no problems meeting the 1994 requirements, as new aircraft have been glutting the market. At the same time, older aircraft have been sent into retirement in the desert.

23   There were three ways the airlines could meet these new noise and pollution requirements. The first way, offering the greatest longer-term benefit, was for the airlines to buy new equipment and retire their older equipment. The second way was not to buy new equipment, but to retire older equipment and, having one's fleet get smaller, meeting the phase-in requirements. The third way was for airlines to "hush kit" (install silencing kits on existing aircraft engines) and/or put new engines on the older aircraft. This served only a limited market for a limited time. Most of the aircraft flying at the time that needed to meet the new requirements were old. Even with new engines and hush kits, they would have needed ongoing and expensive maintenance.

24   In Europe, the new requirements were more stringent than in the US. After 2002, airlines were not allowed to fly aircraft that were 25 years or older within the confines of the European Community. This requirement (referred to at times as the global village concept) would result in re-aeroplaning the entire world's fleet. If carriers from non-complying nations wished to fly their aircraft into these areas of the world, their aircraft would have to meet these requirements, even though they are not necessary for flying within their own borders.

25   Based on these various observations and GPA's long-term strategy, it was determined that a larger fleet would be necessary over the 10-year horizon to meet demand as the industry rebounded and as the market for leasing became more competitive. In addition, because of significant improvements in operating economics, the newer fourth and fifth generation jet aircraft in production at the time were likely to have longer economic lives and to hold their values better than previous generations of aircraft. GPA therefore had to acquire new aircraft. Exhibit 5 presents historical information on GPA's aircraft portfolio. The reader will note the changing nature of the portfolio over time.

EXHIBIT 5
GPA Group Managed Fleet, 1984–92

Aircraft Type	1984	1985	1986	1987	1988	1989	1990	1991	1992
A-300	2	2	2	2	4	3	4	4	5
A-320	—	—	—	—	—	—	16	16	28
B-727	1	8	5	4	8	3	2	2	nd
B-737-200	18	23	31	21	24	27	25	25	37
B-737-300/400	—	—	1	15	22	44	65	65	108
B-747	1	3	3	2	5	4	3	3	nd
B-757	—	—	—	—	—	—	—	—	2
B-767-200	—	—	—	—	—	—	—	—	1
B-767-300	—	—	—	—	—	—	—	1	7
Other Boeing	—	—	—	—	—	—	—	—	5
L-1011	1	4	5	6	4	4	2	2	nd
DC-8	—	—	—	7	7	2	9	30	30
DC-9	—	—	—	—	—	6	26	26	26
DC-10	—	—	1	1	2	4	5	5	5
MD-80	—	—	—	9	13	32	40	40	50
MD-11	—	—	—	—	—	—	—	—	3
F-100	—	—	—	—	—	—	1	1	26
BAC-111	—	—	—	—	—	12	12	12	nd
Other	—	—	—	4	4	1	—	25	10
Total jet	23	40	48	71	93	142	210	257	343
Turboprops	—	—	—	11	11	28	30	50	66
Total	23	40	48	82	104	170	240	307	409

Source: Hoare Govett Investment Research Ltd., 1/6/92.

The Aircraft Leasing Market

26   The idea of equipment financing (as typified by leasing), particularly where equipment acquisition requires substantial amounts of capital as in large transportation sectors, rests on efficient interaction between the users of the capital and the providers of the capital. The investors providing the capital vary in their views on risk control, capital appreciation, current income, and tax and accounting issues. Thus, there is a role for intermediating between those investors willing to provide capital, and those companies who require the use of the capital. GPA and the new generation of aircraft operating lessors have advanced equipment finance intermediation to its next logical step: the broad, international formation of capital based on the efficient separation of the costs of using and investing in aircraft.

27   There were many types of leases (see Exhibit 6) and within any one lease type, terms and conditions may have varied significantly as to many business and legal issues, including aircraft maintenance, rights of substitution of equipment, return conditions, insurance, and political risk.

28   Unlike some other leasing industries, the operating lease market for new aircraft was characterised by the following:

· Very high capital investment ensuring limited competition and providing considerable barriers to entry.

· Long lead times for equipment delivery.

· Low risk of considerable technical change or obsolescence in the underlying assets.

EXHIBIT 6
Types of Aircraft Leases

There are three major types of leases used in connection with aircraft. Of these the operating lease perhaps constituted the most significant development for the aircraft leasing companies—although these companies may have used finance or leveraged leases to acquire and finance the aircraft that they leased out to airlines.

Operating Leases

An *operating lease* is a short-term lease that allows a lessee to use an asset for a part of its useful life, while the lessor retains virtually all the risks and rewards of ownership. Rental payments are net to the lessor, and the lessee is responsible for all taxes, maintenance, and insurance. Operating leases often permit early cancellation. In accounting terms, an operating lease is one that is not a finance or capital lease, is one where the substantial risks and rewards of ownership are retained by the lessor, and is treated by the lessee as rental payments. Under a "wet" operating lease, the lessor provides other services such as crewing.

The operating lease market for aircraft was young but growing strongly. GPA was a relatively well-developed leader in a fragmented market. Of the 6,000 aircraft in the world fleet in 1980, 360 or 6% were on operating lease. By mid-1991, 20% of all the world's 9,100 aircraft were on operating lease. The majority of these leased aircraft were second-hand, and it was estimated that fewer than 12% were delivered new directly to the lessor for leasing. GPA had a total share of around 20%. Of the new stage 3 equipment, of which 20% were on operating lease, it had a market share closer to 50% (see Exhibit 2).

Finance Leases

A finance or capital lease is one that transfers virtually all the risks and rewards of ownership to the lessee. The lease payments over the life of the lease are sufficient to allow the lessor to recover and make adequate returns on the investment in the asset. The lease agreement normally transfers legal ownership of the asset to the lessee at the end of the lease period for a nominal sum. Finance leases typically cannot be cancelled, meaning that the lessee must make all payments or risk bankruptcy. In accounting, a finance lease is usually treated by the lessee as an on-balance-sheet asset with a matching liability of future rental payments with depreciation and interest being charged to the profit and loss account—although the definition differs somewhat among international accounting bodies.

Leveraged Leases

A leveraged lease is a finance or capital lease that involves at least three parties—a lessee, a lessor, and a long-term creditor. Financing provided by the creditor is substantial to the transaction and non-recourse to the lessor. The lessor's equity portion declines in the early years of the lease and rises in the latter years. In the typical aircraft leveraged lease transaction, the airline or intermediary sells the aircraft into a leveraged lease, which is capitalised by 10%–20% equity and 80%–90% debt. If an aircraft leasing company is involved, it typically assumes the role of lessee/sublessor.

In general, leveraged leases optimise the use of debt and equity through efficient cash flow allocations from the rent of aircraft. The major motivation of the debt participant is a secured, fixed return. The equity participant primarily is seeking tax benefits and a residual stake in the equipment. And the operator's major interest is paying purely rent for the use of the aircraft and having the use of the aircraft at the lowest cost. Cross-border leveraged leases may take advantage of significant additional tax benefits. In a "double-dip" leveraged lease, the lessee may also take capital allowances or investment tax credits in his home jurisdiction as if he had acquired the asset outright.

· Relatively long and historically predictable economic lives of the underlying asset.

· Considerable asset mobility.

· Long-range growth in the underlying market and demand environment.

· Fundamental requirement for the airline operators to re-equip in replacing older aircraft and providing for growth.

29   As a consequence of these relatively high barriers to entry there were many operating lessors of older equipment, but relatively few new equipment lessors. Exhibits 1 and 2 provide some information on GPA's major competitors.

30   GPA concentrated on providing "dry" operating leases to its customers. It leased the aircraft for a relatively long period of time, retaining ownership, and the lessee was responsible for all elements of operation. The company tended to set lease terms at five to seven years (at the time the average was 5.6 years). Lease rentals—averaging in excess of 1.1% of capital value per month—were paid monthly in advance with a significant (typically three-month) deposit to guard against default. All leases were denominated in U.S. dollars, were net to GPA, were non-cancellable, and generally contained interest rate protection.

31   The lessee was responsible for all elements of operation, maintenance, and insurance. In addition, the lessee had to adhere to a stringent security package over and above the advance rental and deposit requirements—in providing maintenance accruals, covenants or guarantees, registration, and sometimes

political risk insurance. The lessee was generally required to pay maintenance accruals on a monthly basis into a reserve held by GPA—in some cases the lease term was shorter than the period remaining to the next major maintenance check. This was an important extra element of GPA's liquidity. Well before the lease was due to expire, GPA would seek to arrange a new lease or, if the circumstances were favourable, to sell the aircraft.

Aircraft Sales and Securitisation

32 GPA has sold some 150 aircraft to investors since 1986, worth more than $5 billion, to 80 customers in 20 countries. In the past three years, revenues from this source have run at a level of $1.1–$1.3 billion a year. In the short run this level of turnover was likely to double. Two years before some 70–75% of the transactions tended to be sale and lease-backs. At the time, some 85% of aircraft sale profits were generated from securitisation.

33 Securitisation of aircraft was one of the principal innovative financing structures that GPA had introduced into the industry. This was in essence the packaging, as a financial asset, of the physical asset of the aircraft with the income stream of a lease in place, which was then sold on to private non-aerospace specialised investors.

34 A typical transaction, such as demonstrated in the table below, would be based on the net present value to the investor of the operating lease income over the period of the lease according to his required return. Each transaction tended to be individual depending on the investor's requirements. GPA tried to ensure that it retained some feature of the rental stream and/or the residual value of the asset. It generally managed the lease for a fee (of around $5,000–$10,000 pcm, for example) and arranged for remarketing of the lease—again for a fee—at the end of the lease term. Usually GPA leased the aircraft back to allow it to retain some element of the lease income stream, in which case it wanted a minimum of 1% capital value for credit risk.

TYPICAL SECURITISATION TRANSACTION OF B-737

In cost of aircraft (15–20% discount)	$25 million
Third party valuation	$28 million
Operating lease rental	$275,000 pcm
Estimated future value after five years	$27 million
Investor's required return	9%
Sale price (PV of above)	$30.5 million
Transaction profit	$5.5 million

35 It is important to emphasise that these deals tended to be non-recourse to GPA—although in some cases the group had provided residual value guarantees or repurchase clauses. The group's contingent liabilities on residual values amounted to $38 million and repurchase commitments $303 million at the end of March 1992.

36 The main benefits of these deals to the group were to:

· Realise the equity invested in the aircraft.
· Realise the value of the manufacturers discount on initial purchase of the aircraft.
· Repay the debt used to buy the aircraft and generate liquidity for the group.
· Realise the value of the available tax benefits.
· Realise the value inherent in the lease income stream.
· Reduce the risk of developing the lease portfolio.

37 The company was at the time taking securitisation one stage further. It was in the process of organising a $500 million global fund intended to cover 14 aircraft leased to 14 customers in 12 countries, which would essentially be an investment fund offering aircraft-backed publicly tradable securities. Industry observers expected the group to use further innovative transactions to double the turnover from this source to at least $3 billion per annum.

IV. FINANCIAL STATE AND NEEDS

38   In the year to March 1992, GPA surprised many—including itself—in maintaining profitability. Net income touched $268 million up from $262 million in the previous year—albeit including the consolidation for the first time of some of the former joint ventures. This was for a period which represented the worst industry recession since Icarus fell to Earth.

Industry Recession Anticipated

39   As part of the group's planning procedures, it maintained a running five-year plan with base case profit and balance sheet forecasts and developed various downside scenarii. The events of the previous 18 months had been very similar to the assumptions in one of the group's more pessimistic cases: a fuel-based industry recession combined with recessionary trends in the world economy. Under the hypotheses of this pessimistic scenario, the group assumed that it would stop selling aircraft—not willing to sell at a book loss—but would still be able to lease out equipment at no worse than holding costs, while fees and commissions would be boosted considerably. As a consequence, within their scenario, profits would dip considerably for a couple of years, but the group—with its superior quality of aircraft product and its relatively strong financial backing—would rebound very strongly out of the recession.

40   What was admirable over the previous year was the speed in which the group management reacted to the changing industry environment and found that it could maintain profitability while working with severe trading conditions. Nonetheless, surviving the continuing recession, and honouring its orders for new aircraft, would require a cash infusion. While the possibilities deriving from its new securitization plans would help, GPA needed to consider additional alternatives for raising the money necessary.

Current Position: Size and Activity (April 1992)

41   GPA carries approximately $4.2 billion in debt on $1.2 billion in shareholder equity, while the JV Companies and other associated businesses have an additional $1.2 billion in debt and $700 million in equity. (Exhibit 7 provides recent balance sheets for the consolidated companies.)

Further Planned Growth: Needs for Financing

42   GPA's strategy had resulted in commitments, outlined above, to purchase $11.9 billion worth of aircraft for GPA and its associate companies over the next decade. While the decision to enter into these purchase contracts was dictated by GPA's long-term strategic goals, there existed the possibility that, in the short term, these commitments could create some financing problems. Of the $11.9 billion committed towards purchases for its own and joint venture fleets over the next decade, $2.2 billion was due in the current year. Over the course of its past operations, as these contracts were negotiated, GPA had placed $957 million on deposit with the aircraft manufacturers. In the event of cancellations of any orders, a portion of this deposit would be forfeited.

43   When the company first started ordering new aircraft from manufacturers, it established a series of specialised joint ventures and associate companies, with outside shareholders, to give it greater credence with the manufacturers and offset some of the risks in the start-up. Each unit was financed with debt that was essentially non-recourse to GPA. These associate companies were now ready to mature, to produce increasingly significant levels of profitability, and to provide the largest source of growth for the group. In addition, GPA's own financing ability had improved substantially. This structure, therefore, was seen no longer to be necessary—even more so with the company's anticipated accession to the world's stock markets. While the total cost of reacquiring these associates was unlikely to exceed $200 million, this was more cash than GPA had at its disposal, and would need to be financed in some way.

EXHIBIT 7
GPA Group PLC and Subsidiaries Consolidated Balance Sheets
(in $ millions)

	1990	1991	March 31, 1992
Assets			
Cash	39	275	387
Accounts receivable	237	406	389
Net investments in finance leases	14	75	76
Investments (principally in associated companies)	260	440	430
Aircraft	1,870	2,656	4,241
Deposits and aircraft predelivery payments	553	626	816
Other assets	89	114	160
Total assets	3,062	4,589	6,499
Liabilities, Share Capital, and Reserves			
Accounts payable	76	102	104
Accrued expenses and other liabilities	355	600	804
Indebtedness	1,637	2,713	4,162
Provision for liabilities and charges	101	127	199
Total liabilities	2,169	3,542	5,269
Share capital outstanding:			
Ordinary shares	4	94	95
A ordinary shares	—	9	9
Convertible redeemable cumulative Preference shares	2	1	1
Convertible cumulative second preference Shares	—	—	100
Deferred shares	8	—	—
Total nominal value	14	104	205
Share premium	546	455	382
Retained earnings	333	487	642
Other reserves	—	1	1
Share capital and reserves	893	1,047	1,230
Total liabilities, share capital, and reserves	3,062	4,589	6,499

Debt as a Possibility

44   As GPA had largely relied on debt to finance its exceptional growth, two issues affected the willingness of GPA to raise further debt. The first concerned the covenants attached to some of the bank debt specifying a maximum debt-to-equity ratio (D/E) of 5:1. GPA currently had a ratio of only 3:1. The second issue concerned the recent announcement (April 1992) that Moody's Investment Service, Inc., had placed GPA's senior debt rating under review for a possible downgrading from its Baa-1 rating. To the press, Moody's said its review reflected GPA's need to fund large numbers of new aircraft deliveries and place them in service with airline lessees during a drop in demand for aircraft. "GPA is committed to a significant firm order capital expenditure program with aircraft manufacturers that extends through the end of the century," according to Moody's.

V. THE FLOTATION

45   While aircraft sales and the new securitization deal would bring in fresh cash, GPA management felt that additional funds would be required. The decision was made to take the company public. It was decided that an issue at this time would succeed, and in so doing would prove to all the strength of GPA.

46   In anticipation of the issue, GPA began teasing the press in February, and in March requested that GPA shares, when eventually made public, be included in the FTSE 100 Index, which the size of the coming issue would appear to warrant. This application (filed jointly with two other Irish firms, Jefferson Smurfit Group PLC, and Allied Irish Banks PLC) to be included in the FTSE 100 was

EXHIBIT 8A
Profit and Loss Accounts Assuming Scenario 1 (existing firm order deliveries only)

Assumed growth in lease rates per year	2.0%
Assumed inflation rate per year[1]	3.0%
Assumed decrease in revenue plane 1993–94 due to recession	10%
Assumed growth in SG&A per year	5.0%
Assumed effective average tax rate	5%

	1992	1993	1994	1995	1996	1997	1998	1999	2000	2001
Revenues from leasing[2]	837	922	973	1,060	1,039	1,005	970	938	882	814
Aircraft sales[3]	1,127	1,240	1,627	1,862	1,726	1,580	1,424	1,467	1,511	1,556
Fees and commissions[4]	46	57	61	60	59	58	57	55	52	49
Total revenue	2,010	2,220	2,661	2,982	2,824	2,644	2,451	2,460	2,446	2,419
Revenue growth		10%	20%	12%	-5%	-6%	-7%	0%	-1%	-1%
Operating costs[4]	389	481	513	507	502	491	478	467	443	413
Cost of aircraft sales[3]	952	1,048	1,374	1,573	1,458	1,335	1,203	1,239	1,276	1,314
Depreciation and amortization[4]	179	215	222	214	205	195	184	175	161	146
Net interest expense[5]	184	203	214	233	228	221	213	206	194	179
SG&A[4,6]	44	46	49	51	53	56	59	62	65	68
Total expenses	1,748	1,993	2,372	2,577	2,447	2,297	2,138	2,148	2,140	2,121
Expense growth	13%	14%	19%	9%	-5%	-6%	-7%	1%	-0%	-1%
Operating margin	13%	10%	11%	14%	13%	13%	13%	13%	13%	12%
Operating profit[7]	262	227	289	404	377	346	313	311	306	299
Taxes[3]	14	11	14	20	19	17	16	16	15	15
Net income	248	216	275	384	358	329	298	296	291	284
Aircraft acquisitions[3]										
Predelivery and deposit payments[9]	322	197	197	197	197	197	197	197	197	197
Cash payments upon delivery	2,152	2,619	2,325	1,171	1,079	831	567	807	349	1,314
Cash flow available for security holders[10]	(911)	(1,135)	(437)	1,035	974	1,051	1,134	912	1,376	411

EXHIBIT 8B
Profit and Loss Accounts Assuming Scenario 2 (Existing firm order and option deliveries only)

Assumed growth in lease rates per year	3.0%
Assumed inflation rate per year[1]	3.0%
Assumed decrease in revenue plane 1993–94 due to recession	10%
Assumed growth in SG&A per year	5.0%
Assumed effective average tax rate	5%

	1992	1993	1994	1995	1996	1997	1998	1999	2000	2001
Revenues from leasing[2]	837	931	1,061	1,324	1,430	1,490	1,515	1,545	1,524	1,477
Aircraft sales[3]	1,127	1,240	1,627	1,862	1,726	1,580	1,424	1,467	1,511	1,556
Fees and commissions[4]	46	57	65	73	79	82	83	85	84	81
Total revenue	2,010	2,229	2,753	3,258	3,235	3,152	3,022	3,097	3,119	3,114
Revenue growth		11%	24%	18%	−1%	−3%	−4%	2%	1%	−0%
Operating costs[4]	389	481	548	615	665	692	704	718	708	686
Cost of aircraft sales[3]	952	1,048	1,374	1,573	1,458	1,335	1,203	1,239	1,276	1,314
Depreciation and amortization[4]	179	215	238	259	272	275	271	269	257	242
Net interest expense[5]	184	205	233	291	314	328	333	340	335	325
SG&A[4,6]	44	46	49	51	53	56	59	62	65	68
Total expenses	1,748	1,995	2,441	2,789	2,762	2,686	2,570	2,628	2,642	2,636
Expense growth		14%	22%	14%	−1%	−3%	−4%	2%	1%	−0%
Operating margin	13%	11%	11%	14%	15%	15%	15%	15%	15%	15%
Operating profit[7]	262	234	311	469	472	466	452	469	477	478
Taxes[8]	14	12	16	23	24	23	23	23	24	24
Net income	248	222	296	446	449	443	429	446	453	454
Aircraft acquisitions[3]										
Predelivery and deposit payments[9]	322	522	490	441	385	342	319	315	305	320
Cash payments upon delivery	2,152	2,619	3,326	3,638	3,091	2,222	1,509	1,712	685	1,314
Cash flow available for security holders[10]	(911)	(1,451)	(1,676)	(1,511)	(983)	(184)	408	267	1,332	701

EXHIBIT 8C
Profit and Loss Accounts Assuming Scenario 3 (Existing firm orders and options + maintain deliveries of 50 aircraft per year)

Assumed growth in lease rates per year	3.0%
Assumed inflation rate per year[1]	3.0%
Assumed decrease in revenue plane 1993–94 due to recession	10%
Assumed growth in SG&A per year	5.0%
Assumed effective average tax rate	5%

	1992	1993	1994	1995	1996	1997	1998	1999	2000	2001
Revenues from leasing[2]	837	931	1,061	1,324	1,430	1,497	1,579	1,664	1,752	1,845
Aircraft sales[3]	1,127	1,240	1,627	1,862	1,726	1,580	1,424	1,467	1,511	1,556
Fees and commissions[4]	46	57	65	73	79	82	87	91	96	101
Total revenue	2,010	2,229	2,753	3,258	3,235	3,159	3,089	3,222	3,360	3,503
Revenue growth		11%	24%	18%	-1%	-2%	-2%	4%	4%	4%
Operating costs[4]	389	481	548	615	665	696	734	773	814	858
Cost of aircraft sales[3]	952	1,048	1,374	1,573	1,458	1,335	1,203	1,239	1,276	1,314
Depreciation and amortization[4]	179	215	238	259	272	276	283	289	296	302
Net interest expense[5]	184	205	233	291	314	329	347	366	385	406
SG&A[4,6]	44	46	49	51	53	56	59	62	65	68
Total expenses	1,748	1,995	2,441	2,789	2,762	2,692	2,625	2,729	2,837	2,948
Expense growth	13%	14%	22%	14%	-1%	-3%	-2%	4%	4%	4%
Operating margin		11%	11%	14%	15%	15%	15%	15%	16%	16%
Operating profit[7]	262	234	311	469	472	467	464	493	523	554
Taxes[8]	14	12	16	23	24	23	23	25	26	28
Net income	248	222	296	446	449	444	441	468	497	527
Aircraft acquisitions[3]										
Predelivery and deposit payments[9]	322	690	697	687	669	665	679	690	698	709
Cash payments upon delivery	2,152	2,619	3,326	3,638	3,091	2,341	2,445	2,592	2,455	2,908
Cash flow available for security holders[10]	(911)	(1,619)	(1,883)	(1,756)	(1,267)	(621)	(850)	(920)	(698)	(1,068)

[1] The inflation rate is applied to fees and commissions, operating costs, and SG&A.

[2] Assumes leasing revenue per plane drops assumed percent per aircraft for 1993 and 1994 (to reflect recession).

[3] From Exhibit 13.

[4] Interest is assumed a constant proportion of revenues (based on 1992). Note this requires an alternative method of financing the negative cash flow in 1992–94.

[5] Driven from 1992 financials as percent of number of aircraft and adjusted upward for inflation each year.

[6] SG&A growth is permitted to be different from inflation for sensitivity analysis.

[7] Revenue less expenses.

[8] Taxes are at assumed rate (base case is 10%) based on 1992 financials (and continuation of Shannon's low-tax status).

[9] This is driven off 1992 amount as a percentage of the next 10 years purchases (as given by cash payments upon delivery).

[10] Depreciation and amortization and cost of aircraft sales are added back to obtain cash flow as it is a sunk cost. The economic cost of maintaining a fleet for sale and lease is captured in the aircraft acquisitions item.

EXHIBIT 9
GPA Consolidated Statement of Cash Flows (in $ millions)

	1990	1991	1992
Cash flows from operating activities:			
Profit before preference dividends	242	262	268
Adjustments to reconcile net profit to net cash provided by operating activities:			
Provision for aircraft maintenance	71	80	134
Depreciation and amortization	115	126	179
Gain on sale of aircraft and property, plant, and equipment	(129)	(189)	(174)
Gain on sale of investment			
Provision for write-down of investments and receivables	—	—	(5)
Share of retained earnings of associated companies	8	—	—
(net of dividends received)	21	(32)	(19)
Changes in operating assets & liabilities (net of acquisitions):			
Accounts receivable and other assets	(206)	(176)	(8)
Accounts payable and other liabilities	156	131	69
Intangible assets	(25)	(20)	(42)
Accrued aircraft maintenance liability	(32)	(57)	(62)
Net proceeds of aircraft sales	1,305	1,217	1,185
Net cash provided by operating activities	1,526	1,342	1,525
Cash flows from investing activities:			
Purchase of aircraft	(1,466)	(1,250)	(2,135)
Investments in and advances to associated companies	(133)	(139)	(124)
Purchase of other tangible fixed assets	(16)	(23)	(7)
Deposits and predelivery payments	(502)	(675)	(322)
Net proceeds of other tangible asset sales	5	1	—
Collections on finance leases	1	2	(1)
Acquisitions net of cash	—	(27)	11
Proceeds from sale of investments	—	—	20
Net cash used by investing activities	(2,111)	(2,111)	(2,558)
Cash flows from financing activities:			
Redemption of preference shares	—	—	(77)
Proceeds from sale of share capital	206	—	101
Dividends paid	(114)	(71)	(97)
Increase in indebtedness	3,378	4,907	4,342
Indebtedness repaid	(2,862)	(3,831)	(3,124)
Net cash provided by financing activities	608	1,005	1,145
Net increase in cash	23	236	112
Cash at beginning of year	16	39	275
Cash at end of year	39	275	387

rejected in late March by the London Stock Exchange on the grounds that stocks in the FTSE 100 had to be of UK-registered companies. This came as a significant disappointment to each of these firms, as being on the FTSE 100 ensured access to the large institutional investors in the UK. It was suggested that these investors would be much less willing to put serious money into a firm which was not included in the FTSE 100.

47   This was not the first hint of trouble, nor would it be the last. On March 16, following numerous reports of difficulties faced by shipping firms in raising capital, Lloyd's List carried the headline "Aviation's Financing Problems are not Dissimilar to Those of Shipping—GPA's Progress Should be Monitored." Also, as mentioned above, in April Moody's put GPA's debt under review for possible downgrading.

48   The problems were not all specific to GPA. The world's markets were looking increasingly nervous as the anticipated issue date approached. The Japanese market in particular was trading close to its lowest level in years. On May 10, the *Independent* carried a story predicting that Japanese institutional support for the issue would be thin, and blaming it on the recent steep decline in the Japanese markets.

EXHIBIT 10
Selected Economic and Airline Traffic Statistics 1986 to 1996

Year	GDP ($ billions)	Revenue Passenger Miles (billions)	Available Seat Miles (billions)	Load Factor (Percent)
1986	4,337	351	582	60.4%
1987	4,683	394	630	62.5
1988	5,045	411	657	62.6
1989	5,345	420	662	63.4
1990	5,561	453	725	62.4
1991	5,753	443	705	62.8
1992*	6,025	472	735	64.1
1993*	6,370	505	760	66.4
1994*	6,750	530	780	67.9
1995*	7,190	553	810	68.3
1996*	7,485	575	845	68.0

*Estimated.

Existing Shareholders

49   In addition to the problems mentioned above, there were problems among the existing shareholders. Hanson had already sold its 2% stake in the firm in March at $20.57 per share, a loss on what it had originally paid for the shares, $21.25, in June 1989. In addition, Hanson announced that the main reason for the sale concerned the anticipated issue and problems with GPA and Ryan's "lock-in" agreement (discussed below). Aer Lingus (which held almost 9%) and Air Canada (holder of almost 10%), among others, were known to be planning to use the issue to sell off at least a portion of their holdings. Exhibit 3 presents some of the major GPA shareholders.

50   In the past several months, Dr. Ryan had talked to a substantial number of shareholders to try to sense whether, in the event of an IPO, they would be willing to sign a "lock-in" agreement. Such an agreement would prevent them from selling their shares for about a year after the issue, thus stabilising the market for GPA's shares. The responses he got were mixed. According to GPA, shareholders holding about 80% of the shares were willing to sign the agreement, which would restrict the number of shares they could sell in the issue to 15% or 20% of their holdings. A further 10% cited technical or legal reasons for them not being able to sign, but stated that they nevertheless intended to keep their shares for the longer run. The remaining 10% were not friendly to the idea of a "lock-in" agreement.

Investor Clienteles

51   To raise the kind of money GPA was considering, it was widely agreed that institutional investors would be crucial. In addition, it was felt that individual investors would not make an ideal clientele for GPA. Any public issue, then, was to be targeted mainly to institutional investors, at least outside Ireland.

52   A second consideration with regard to investor clienteles, was geographic. Some of the largest shareholders were Japanese (Japanese investors currently held 30% of GPA's shares), and it was believed that Japanese investors had the most interest in GPA and its business. Nonetheless, all agreed that U.S. interest in an issue of this size could be critical to its success. Thus, the deal had to attract U.S. (and, of course, UK) investors, but also had to be able to take advantage of potentially more enthusiastic investors in Japan. The advisers expressed some concern that one result of attempting to target these various clientele might be an overly complicated offer structure which would discourage investors.

Pricing

53   GPA's shares had a remarkable history: In 1983 General Electric paid $18 million for a 22.5% stake of GPA. GE sold its shares for $56 million just four years later. A series of equity issues (all private)

EXHIBIT 11
Leasing Rates and Sale Value by Aircraft Type

Aircraft Type	Number Owned	Leasing Information			Sale Value Information			
		Average Monthly Revenue per Aircraft ($000)	Total Revenue ($ millions)	Decline in Rates over 12 Months (%)	Value per Aircraft, January 90 ($ millions)	Value per Aircraft, January 92 ($ millions)	2-year decline (%)	Current Aircraft in World for Sale
A300-B4-200	5	222	13.3	26%	29.5	19	36%	21
B320-200	28	270	90.7	23	35	33	6	8
B737-200	37	50	22.2	25	7.3	5.5	25	57
B737-300	57	175	119.7	22	21	16.5	22	24
B737-400	40	255	122.4	7	25	22	12	5
B737-500	11	230	30.4	8	21	19	10	2
B737-500	2	445	10.7	1	43	42	2	12
B767-200ER	1	400	4.8	20	45	39.5	14	7
B767-300ER	7	550	46.2	8	65	59	9	11
B747-200	3	221	7.9	12	50	37.5	25	28
MD82	8	170	16.3	15	18	17	6	15
MD83	39	245	114.7	11	22	22.5	+1	9
MD87	3	221	7.9	12	25	21	16	9
MD11	3	883	31.8	2	95	91	4	nil
DC10	5	530	31.8	16	37	25	32	27
DC8	30	190	68.4	24	16	11.5	29	21
DC9	26	60	18.7	36	8	4	50	107
F100	26	175	54.6	27	24	17.5	27	5
F28	8	50	4.8	41	3.5	2.4	32	6
BAC111	3	28	1	25	1.8	1.3	28	Not known
L1011	1	150	1.8	18	24	14	42	38
Turboprops/other	66	30	23.8	20	na	na	na	na

Source: Charterhouse Tilney, 10/6/92.

EXHIBIT 12
GPA Group Orders and Options, March 1992

		Year-End December									
		1992	1993	1994	1995	1996	1997	1998	1999	2000	1992–2000
Number of Orders and Options											
GPA	Orders	51	61	43	23	19	16	11	13	4	241
	Options	0	0	31	62	43	27	13	13	3	192
Joint ventures	Orders	15	19	19	7	7	0	0	0	0	67
	Options	0	0	4	7	5	4	3	3	2	28
Group	Orders	66	80	62	30	26	16	11	13	4	308
	Options	0	0	35	69	48	31	16	16	5	220
Total orders and options		66	80	97	99	74	47	27	29	9	528
Orders and Options Cost (1992 $ millions)											
Firm orders		$2,152	$2,619	$2,325	$1,171	$1,079	$ 831	$ 567	$ 807	$349	$11,900
Options		—	—	1,001	2,467	2,012	1,391	942	905	336	9,054
Total orders and options		$2,152	$2,619	$3,326	$3,638	$3,091	$2,222	$1,509	$1,712	$685	$20,954

Source: Hoare Govett Investment Research Ltd., 1/6/92.

followed: in 1986 $125 million, $100 million in 1987, $83.5 million in 1988, and $175 million in two issues in 1989. Despite having to continually tap its shareholders for fresh equity, the GPA share price continually soared skywards. From $13 in 1981 to $650 at its 1990 peak (or from $0.43 to $32.5 if one allows for the 1990 share split). Recent transactions, in particular Hanson's sale mentioned above, placed the value of the GPA shares at $20.57, accounting for a planned 2-for-1 share split to take place prior to the issue; this put the price for the shares in the issue at closer to $10.28 per share. It was widely speculated in the city, however, that Hanson had sold at too low a price, and had bailed out prematurely.[3]

54   In late April, after months of often heated debate between advisers and GPA executives, it was announced that the issue price would likely be set somewhere in the range of $21 to $25 (or $10.50 to $12.50, adjusting for the split).[4] The actual price would be determined at a later date. When the negotiations began in late 1991, it was generally agreed that a reasonable issue price to aim for would be between $24 and $28 ($12 to $14 adjusted for the split). As events of the spring of 1992 occurred, advisers began to consider lowering the issue price below this range. When this was suggested to GPA, however, Ryan was unmoveable. Ryan was fiercely determined that the price not be lowered, and felt that even the range of $24 to $28 was too low. As the negotiations continued, Ryan insisted that the market did not understand the business and that the current range of $24 to $28 was a generous discount to the true value of the shares. He, therefore, considered agreement with the range of $21 to $25 to be a considerable compromise. He apparently believed that the actual issue price would be at the upper end of this range.

[3] Exhibit 8 contains cash flow forecasts based on several assumptions and scenarios. The reader might be interested to know that, while data on comparable publicly traded firms are not available, the average unlevered beta of the major U.S. airlines is approximately .7. The applicable risk-free rate is approximately 3.25%, and the historical market risk premium in the U.S. is approximately 6% (geometric mean from 1926–1991).

[4] Following the offering, there would be 286.3 million shares outstanding. If all existing shareholders sold none of their existing shares, they would hold 226.8 million shares. Thus, the offering was of approximately 60 million new shares and then additional shares which were being sold in the offering by existing shareholders.

EXHIBIT 13
GPA Aircraft Portfolio Forecasts

This exhibit presents 3 scenarios and these numbers drive the cash flow forecasts in Exhibit 8. The first scenario assumes the firm merely satisfies its committed firm orders between 1992 and 2000. The second scenario assumes GPA satisfies both firm orders and its existing options. The third scenario assumes it satisfies its firm orders and options plus new orders necessary to maintain deliveries at 50 aircraft per year.

	1992	1993	1994	1995	1996	1997	1998	1999	2000	2001	1992–2001
Total orders and options	66	80	97	99	74	47	27	29	9	0	528
Assumed new orders (to maintain 50 deliveries per year)[1]	0	0	0	0	0	3	23	21	41	50	138
Assumed aircraft sales[2]	29	35	45	50	45	40	35	35	35	35	384
Ending number of planes											
Existing firm orders only	446	491	508	488	469	445	421	399	368	333	
Existing firm orders and options	446	491	543	592	621	628	620	614	588	553	
Orders to maintain 50 deliveries per year	446	491	543	592	621	631	646	661	676	691	
Cost per aircraft:[3]											
Firm orders	$35	$36	$41	$42	$45	$56	$56	$67	$95	$95	$42
Options			31	39	46	49	64	61	73	73	45
Average of firm orders and options	$35.44	$35.58	$37.27	$39.94	$45.40	$51.39	$60.75	$64.17	$82.73	$83	$43.14
Assumed growth in aircraft prices (for purchase) (1992 base)		0%	2%	3%	3%	3%	3%	3%	3%	3%	
Cost of new orders (to maintain 50 deliveries per year)[4]	$0	$0	$0	$0	$0	$119	$936	$880	$1,770	$2,223	$3,704
Assumed ratio of cost to sale price for aircraft sold[6]	0.84472										
Assumed growth in price per plane (for sales) (1992 base)		0%	2%	3%	3%	3%	3%	3%	3%	3%	
Revenue from assumed aircraft sales[5]	$1,127	$1,240	$1,627	$1,862	$1,726	$1,580	$1,424	$1,467	$1,511	$1,556	$13,563
Cost of assumed aircraft sales[6]	$952	$1,048	$1,374	$1,573	$1,458	$1,335	$1,203	$1,239	$1,276	$1,314	$11,457
Total cost of acquisitions:											
Existing firm orders only[7]	$2,152	$2,619	$2,325	$1,171	$1,079	$831	$56	$807	$349	$1,314	$11,900
Existing firm orders and options[7]	$2,152	$2,619	$3,326	$3,638	$3,091	$2,222	$1,509	$1,712	$685	$1,314	$20,954
Firm orders and options (> = 50)[7]	$2,152	$2,619	$3,326	$3,638	$3,091	$2,341	$2,445	$2,592	$2,455	$2,908	$24,658

[1]This is simply to maintain purchases at the desired level (50) per year starting in 1993.

[2]This is the assumed aircraft sales per year through securitisation or otherwise.

[3]It is assumed that previous deposits average 8% of the purchase price, so that purchase prices reflect only 92% of the cost per aircraft. The costs per aircraft are adjusted upward to reflect 100% of the price.

[4]Because the average cost of each year's existing orders and options per plane rise far faster than inflation, it likely represents a bias in the order sample (the longer maturity orders and options are for larger aircraft). This assumption provides an opportunity to do sensitivity on the assumed increase in prices.

[5]Based on number of planes sold and price, which grows according to the assumed growth based on price per purchase in 1992.

[6]Cost based on assumed ratio of cost to sale price (revenue). (The ratio for 1992 was 84.47% from profit and loss statement.)

[7]To allow for 0% growth interminus, it is assumed that for the terminal year, 2001, purchases are at least the cost of sales.

B INDUSTRY CASE SETS

CASE 31

NOTE ON THE HAZARDOUS WASTE MANAGEMENT INDUSTRY

INTRODUCTION

1 Since the beginning of the Industrial Revolution, the production of hazardous wastes as a by-product of various manufacturing processes had been accepted as an unavoidable consequence. This once-pervasive attitude also considered the disposal of untreated toxic wastes in commercial landfills and waterways as the only practical solution to growing waste management needs. But convenience had its price; by the 1970s the United States had a severe pollution problem. The city of Love Canal, New York, had to be evacuated and Ohio's Cuyahoga River burned out of control. Events such as these enraged the public and led to enactment of several pieces of environmental legislation. These new regulations imposed rigid standards on waste generators and handlers, creating great demand for hazardous waste management professionals.

2 As this vital industry approached maturity, firms had to adapt to the changing competitive environment to survive. For many firms, this meant capitalizing on existing strengths, minimizing weaknesses, and making strategic investments in new markets. The following case analyzes the hazardous waste management industry as it exists in the United States as of 1993. It begins by offering a brief description of the types of services provided by waste management firms. Next, it assesses the influence of the external environment depicted in Exhibit 3, by examining the resulting trends, opportunities, and threats to the industry. From that evaluation, students should be able to determine several critical success factors that relate to this industry.

This industry note was written by Professor John A. Pearce II of Villanova University, and Linda Riesenman.

EXHIBIT 1
Hazardous Waste Generation by Industry, 1990

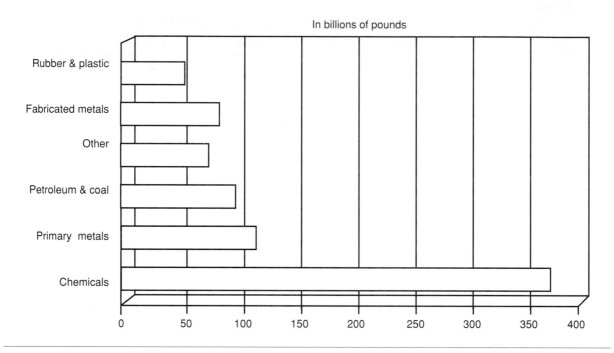

Source: *Chemical & Engineering News*, February 25, 1991, p. 14.

HAZARDOUS WASTE MANAGEMENT SERVICES

3   In general, services provided by the hazardous waste management industry were divided into three broad segments: consulting services; remediation services; and treatment, storage, and disposal services. Consulting services generally included, but were not limited to, environmental audits, permit preparation, compliance audits, risk assessment services, laboratory analysis, and remedial investigations/feasibility studies (RI/FS). Consulting services were characterized as labor intensive and required little in the way of investment capital, fixed assets, or research and development.

4   Based on the findings and recommendations of the consultants, an appropriate remedial action was implemented and supervised by the consultants. Remediation work encompassed a wide variety of activities such as on-site incineration, bioremediation, landfill lining and capping, and chemical stabilization. In contrast to consulting work, remediation work required a moderate investment in vehicles, field equipment, and mobile incinerators.

5   The treatment, storage, and disposal (TSD) segment of the industry provided an invaluable service to both government and private waste generators. For example, the chemical industry produced more than half of the 750 billion pounds of hazardous waste generated in the United States in 1990, but operated only 23 percent of waste treatment facilities. This trend was expected to continue through at least 1995, according to a study conducted by the Environmental Protection Agency. Exhibit 1 provides a representation of hazardous waste generation by industry in 1990. Exhibit 2 contains the EPA projections for 1995 by industry. Compliance with environmental legislation almost single-handedly created the TSD segment since the majority of waste generators were ill-equipped to perform these functions. Heavy investments in property, plant, and equipment were characteristic of those who owned and operated waste incinerators and land disposal facilities. The primary waste treatment alternatives included thermal treatment (incineration), physical treatment (distillation, evaporation, and separation), chemical treatment (oxidation and reduction), precipitation of heavy metals, hydrolysis, and neutralization. The diversity of services offered reflected the nature and abundance of the hazardous wastes themselves.

EXHIBIT 2
Hazardous Waste Generation by Industry, 1995

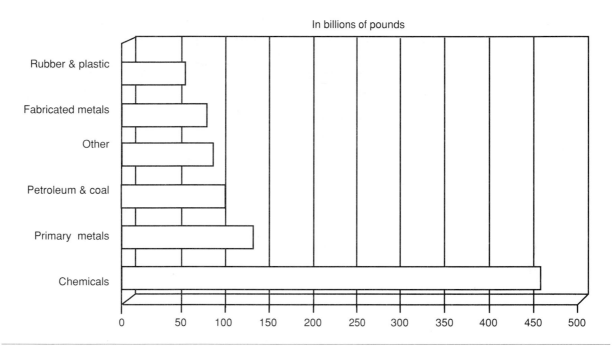

Source: *Chemical & Engineering News*, February 25, 1991, p. 14.

REGULATORY ENVIRONMENT

6   The hazardous waste management industry was driven principally by two pieces of legislation: the Resource Conservation and Recovery Act of 1976 (RCRA) and the Comprehensive Environmental Response, Compensation, and Liability Act of 1980 (CERCLA). Both acts were passed primarily in response to the public's indignation over the contamination of the environment by toxic wastes.

7   Before RCRA, the handling of industrial by-products and hazardous wastes was virtually unregulated. RCRA, however, identified over 450 substances as hazardous wastes and mandated "cradle to grave" responsibility for waste generators, transporters, and persons involved in treatment, storage, or disposal. As of May 8, 1990, RCRA-regulated wastes had to be treated before they were disposed of on land.

8   All companies subject to RCRA were required to first obtain operating permits from the Environmental Protection Agency. Coverage under RCRA extended to any company that generated more than 100 kilograms of waste per month. The emphasis of RCRA was to promote waste treatment and permanent solutions as the number of certified land facilities declined. Waste generators and managers were encouraged to consider alternative and innovative treatment technologies as well.

9   CERCLA was enacted in 1980, but it was strengthened significantly by the Superfund Amendments and Reauthorization Act of 1986 (SARA). The Superfund program provided the EPA with the power to perform long-term cleanups of abandoned hazardous waste sites and immediate removal of life-threatening spills. Like RCRA, SARA emphasized optimal site remediation and detoxification of waste before burial. If the EPA identified the potentially responsible parties (PRPs) of the site contamination, it forced the parties to either perform the remediation or reimburse the Superfund Act trust account for an EPA-contracted cleanup. Under SARA, PRPs were defined as persons who arranged for waste disposal at a site, persons transporting the waste to a site, present owners and operators of waste disposal facilities, and previous owners and operators of waste disposal facilities. If a PRP refused to perform a remedial action, treble damages could be levied.

EXHIBIT 3
Influence of Environmental Variables

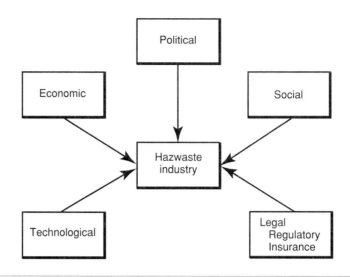

10   In the event that PRPs could not be identified, the cleanup was financed out of the trust account. This account was funded primarily from a feedstock tax on petroleum producers and on manufacturers of certain chemicals. Congress approved an annual Superfund operating budget of $1.8 billion per year through 1995. Although the EPA investigated more than 30,000 hazardous waste sites, only about 1,200 of the most seriously contaminated sites made the EPA's National Priority List.

11   Accountability of PRPs under SARA was promoted by three standards of liability that relieved the EPA of the burden of proof in most cases: strict liability, joint and several liability, and retroactive liability. To charge a PRP with strict liability, the EPA need not prove that the PRP acted negligently in its handling or disposal of waste. There was no defense to the strict liability provisions of SARA. Under joint and separate liability, the PRP could be held responsible for the entire cleanup even though the PRP's contribution to the waste problem was relatively small. Retroactive liability existed for actions that had occurred before CERCLA was enacted if they continued to present a hazard.

12   As of 1986, SARA was extended to cover all federal agencies. In response to this pressure to bring all federal waste dumps and facilities into compliance, both the Department of Defense (DOD) and the Department of Energy (DOE) established special funds. Congress approved the creation of the Defense Environmental Restoration Account to provide an estimated $13 billion for over 3,000 site remediations. In addition, the Environmental Restoration and Waste Management Account was established to provide the DOE with an estimated $100 billion over 30 years. In 1992 alone, it was projected that DOD and DOE expenditures totaled $1.2 billion and $4.2 billion, respectively. However, from 1993 through 1997, the Department of Energy was expected to move into high gear, spending an estimated $41 billion to clean up nuclear weapons facilities across the country.

ECONOMY

13   During the bear market of the 1980s, the hazardous waste industry grew rapidly, leading some to believe the industry was recession-proof. The recession of the early 1990s proved this was not so; growth slowed and stock values flattened. At the beginning of 1993, the recession had moderated, yet the recessionary economic climate continued to affect the industry. The sluggish economy, the discretionary timing element of some environmental expenditures, and decreased manufacturing output kept the industry in a slow-growth mode. A time lag was expected before encouraging

economic statistics resulted in increased discretionary spending by private-sector clients. Remediation efforts, which were closely aligned with certain industries such as petroleum companies and chemical manufacturers, naturally followed the cycle of those industries.

INSURANCE

14   The companies that performed hazardous waste management services came into contact with a wide variety of toxic and often lethal pollutants. This contact might have resulted in an accidental discharge or mishandling, which put the contractor at great risk of environmental damage and personal injury. Additionally, customer contracts sometimes required the waste manager to indemnify the customer for claims, damages, or losses resulting in personal injury or property damage during a cleanup effort. The liability of waste management contractors under SARA was particularly severe, causing insurance premiums to skyrocket and limiting coverage.

15   Three types of pollution insurance were available to firms that qualified and could afford the premiums: comprehensive general liability (CGL), professional errors and omissions, and environmental impairment liability (EIL). CGL insurance covered pollution damage that was sudden and accidental, reimbursing the insured a stated amount per occurrence. Professional errors and omissions insurance covered the insured against damages due to defects in remedial designs and architectural blueprints. EIL insurance protected non-negligent waste managers from liability due to a gradual and accidental release of hazardous waste. Very few insurance companies would underwrite EIL policies, which forced many in the industry to self-insure. Even so, some EIL policies did not transfer risk to the insurer and required the insured to repay claims to the underwriter over a period of years. Such an occurrence could materially affect the earnings and financial condition of the insured. Recognizing the reluctance of many underinsured contractors to pursue Superfund work, the EPA had the authority to grant indemnification for non-negligent acts as long as the contractor could prove that a serious attempt was made to obtain CGL insurance.

SOCIAL ENVIRONMENT

16   Although the seeds for the current grassroots environmental movement were sowed in the early 1970s, a significant increase in public concern over the condition of the environment was documented throughout the 1980s. One primary catalyst for the surge in environmental awareness was the evacuation of Love Canal, New York, in the late 1970s. A large portion of the city had been contaminated by toxic wastes that had leached into the groundwater and soil over 25 years. It was subsequently revealed that a public school and a housing development were constructed over an abandoned landfill. The presence of these hazardous wastes resulted in an unusually high incidence of birth defects and miscarriages in area residents. This event received widespread media coverage, inciting the public and spurring Congress into action. In 1980, the Comprehensive Environmental Response, Compensation, and Liability Act (CERCLA) was passed to provide for cleanups of abandoned toxic waste dumps. In concert with these events, numerous activitist groups, special-interest groups, and lobbyists surfaced and assailed Congress with their often divergent views.

17   The passage of CERCLA, SARA, and RCRA greatly expanded the role and authority of the EPA and cost the taxpayers a substantial amount. Spending on the environment amounted to only 0.9 percent of the gross national product (GNP) in 1972, but in 1992 that amount reached 2.1 percent of GNP. This translated into about $450 per person per year in the United States. Despite this trend, surveys showed the public strongly supported the efforts of the EPA. For example, when asked whether the current environmental laws had gone too far, the majority of those surveyed did not believe regulations were stringent enough. This survey was conducted throughout the 1980s and reflected increasing support for environmental law (Exhibit 4). In similar surveys conducted throughout the 1980s, respondents were asked whether they thought the U.S. government had spent too much on cleaning up the environment. A clear majority answered that too little was currently being spent on environmental restoration (Exhibit 5).

EXHIBIT 4
Views on Environmental Laws and Regulations

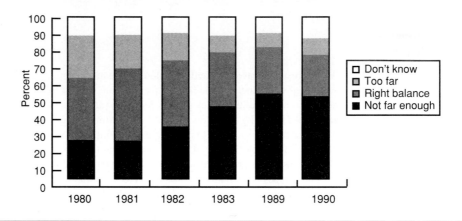

Source: Dunlap, *Environment*, 1991, p. 11.

POLITICAL ENVIRONMENT

18   The Clinton administration seemed to echo the sentiments of the public, positioning itself with an affirmative environmental agent. President Clinton's appointment of Carol Browner to head the U.S. Environmental Protection Agency raised a few eyebrows. Many considered Browner to be somewhat of a radical in terms of her views supporting more stringent environmental legislation. Some concern was voiced that she may regulate the industry to the brink of economic disaster. Browner showed her contempt for the previous EPA administration in a number of ways, but was particularly critical of the progress, or lack thereof, made under the Superfund program. While an estimated $470 million had been spent through 1989, approximately 90 percent of total expenditures were made to cover legal proceedings while only 10 percent went toward actual site cleanups. In retaliation to this inaction, Browner set a goal of performing 200 Superfund remediation projects in fiscal year 1990, with a promise to perform 50 projects per year after that.

19   In recent years, the EPA shifted the responsibility for administering many of its environmental programs to the states. Federal funding for these programs dwindled, forcing many state and local governments to foot the bill for the programs. Although the most burdensome and expensive program for the states to administer had been the Safe Drinking Water Act, RCRA compliance programs were significant as well. The states complained they did not have the staff to implement and monitor these programs. In addition, the majority of state and local governments raised taxes to cover the cost of these programs. Many states claimed they were unable to handle the administration of so many EPA-mandated programs and were pressuring the EPA to return the programs to the federal level. Should the programs remain under state control, progress could become stalled, curtailing revenues for many hazardous waste firms.

LEGAL ENVIRONMENT

20   The annual reports of hazardous waste companies revealed the companies became involved in lawsuits, administrative proceedings, and governmental investigations in the ordinary course of conducting business. Further, they stated that such proceedings might result in fines, penalties, or judgments being assessed against the firm, which might have a material impact on earnings. Investors sought assurance that litigation would not destroy a company and that financial penalties would not

EXHIBIT 5
Views on U.S. Government Spending on the Environment

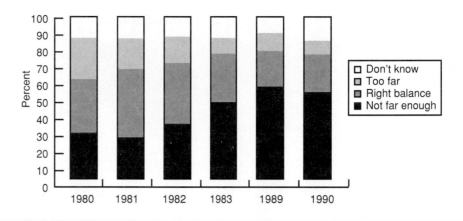

Source: Dunlap, *Environment*, 1991, p. 11.

materially affect a company's overall returns. But the brief history of the hazardous waste industry was a chronicle of court actions and such assurances were hollow.

21   The definition of hazardous waste had been under dispute since the original EPA mandates. The Bush administration sought to weaken the rules defining the parameters of hazardous waste. It sought to repeal a rule that stated any material "derived from" or "mixed with" a hazardous waste must be disposed of or treated as if it were the same concentration of waste. The weakened rules, if adopted, would have enabled manufacturers to decrease disposal costs.

22   In December 1991, a federal appeals court ruled that the EPA violated government procedures in the original issuance of hazardous waste guidelines by not providing for prior public comment. In February 1992, the EPA reissued two rules defining the compounds that it considered hazardous and subject to guidelines for treatment and disposal. The definitions continued to be debated; recent controversy centered on the ash produced by municipal solid waste incinerators. A Chicago municipal court ruled that the incinerator ash must be tested as a hazardous substance; former EPA administrator William Reilly replied that the ash should be managed as nonhazardous, regardless of how it performs on a toxicity testing procedure. Reilly maintained that Congress was unclear on the ash issue and that it was appropriate for the EPA to issue the standard. This incident illustrated the continual series of conflicting decisions by the courts, EPA, and Congress that resulted in a legalistic limbo for the industry.

23   The U.S. Supreme Court ruled in June 1992 that states could not discriminate against other states in providing disposal for waste. Alabama had sought to impose a $72 per ton fee on hazardous waste from other states that was coming into the Chemical Waste Management landfill in Alabama. The Bush administration urged the court ruling, saying Alabama was impeding interstate commerce. Alabama responded with a four-tier tax based on the waste's level of toxicity rather than its state of origin.

TECHNOLOGY AND SERVICE AUTOMATION

24   Legislation was a major driving force behind the increased interest in applying innovative technologies in waste treatment and disposal. Other factors that influenced the rate of technology innovation included scarcity of available commercial disposal sites, significant rise in cost of land disposal, and a growing public opposition to site new land disposal facilities. These factors encouraged a change in regulatory strategies from one focused on disposal to one focused on treatment before disposal.

EXHIBIT 6
Alternative Treatment Technologies (used in 350 remedial actions)

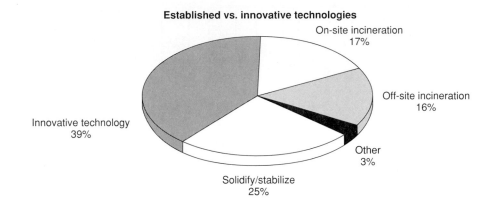

Established vs. innovative technologies

On-site incineration 17%

Off-site incineration 16%

Other 3%

Solidify/stabilize 25%

Innovative technology 39%

Source: U.S. Environmental Protection Agency, 1990.

25   The EPA established two initiatives for encouraging the research and development of treatment technologies. The first was the Hazardous and Solid Waste Amendment of 1984 that allowed the EPA to issue research, development, and demonstration (RD&D) permits. These permits could be issued for any treatment facility that proposed the use of "an innovative and experimental hazardous waste treatment technology or process for which permit standards have not been promulgated" (Valdirio, *Pollution Engineering*, 1990, p. 67). The second program initiated by the EPA was the Superfund Innovative Technology Evaluation (SITE) program. In this program, the EPA participated with the private sector to enhance the availability of these treatment technologies and to evaluate their field performance in the Superfund program. Once technologies were chosen, the EPA then selected the sites by matching the characteristics of a site with those required by the technologies.

26   As of winter 1992, James Kovalick, director of the EPA's Technology Innovation Office (TIO), noted that 132 technologies were under design or construction at Superfund sites, yet only 8 had been used in completed projects. Kovalick stated that much of the future remediation work will fall under RCRA and be performed on active plant sites. He predicted that as cleanup responsibilities begin to take hold, corporate America would be turning to hazardous waste management professionals who possessed expertise in the cheaper innovative technologies.

27   A summary of the distribution of alternative treatment technologies applied on 350 remedial actions through fiscal year 1990 is provided in Exhibit 6. This shows that almost 40 percent of technologies applied were innovative, which made a strong case for investment in research and development. Innovative technologies included any fully developed technology that had insufficient testing to permit its frequent use. The established technologies included the thermal and physical processes of incineration and solidification/stabilization. From the list of established technologies, EPA would give an opinion as to which represented the best available technology.

28   Patented technology was important for overcoming several impediments to developing alternative treatment technologies in the hazardous waste management industry. First, alternative technologies were expensive to use and competed with simple treatment and disposal methods. Second, there was inherent risk in investing in the development of innovative technologies due to the uncertainty of future liabilities. These alternative treatment technologies still generated residues that needed to be treated before final disposal, and companies were not limited from liability in appropriate treatment and disposal. Finally, there was no lessening in the regulation requirements or increasing the speed of the review process, which discouraged many potential high technology innovators from entering this market. Other important benefits of patented technology included helping companies move their technology into international markets, setting barriers to entry for existing companies, and allowing companies appropriate returns on their technology investments while under patent.

EXHIBIT 7
Hazardous Waste Management Hierarchy

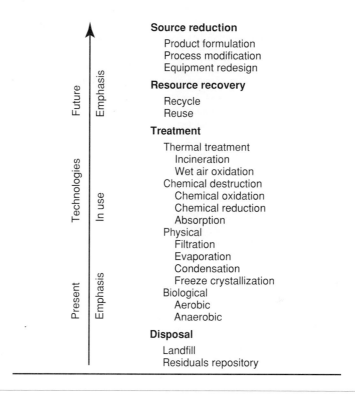

Source reduction
    Product formulation
    Process modification
    Equipment redesign

Resource recovery
    Recycle
    Reuse

Treatment
    Thermal treatment
      Incineration
      Wet air oxidation
    Chemical destruction
      Chemical oxidation
      Chemical reduction
      Absorption
    Physical
      Filtration
      Evaporation
      Condensation
      Freeze crystallization
    Biological
      Aerobic
      Anaerobic

Disposal
    Landfill
    Residuals repository

Source: Waste Management, Inc., "Views on Responsible Environmental Management," Winter 1993, p. 17.

29   Automation of the waste management services became an increasingly important issue in the integration strategy of the larger market players. The industry players consistently expressed their interests in becoming full-service environmental service firms. Project management responsibilities had become a crucial requirement of the full-service environmental management firm, which required more emphasis on development of information systems and tools. In addition, the demand from the customers, both large and small, for on-site services encouraged the development of mobile incinerator units and laboratory analysis capabilities.

INDUSTRY TREND ANALYSIS

30   Following are several trends that surfaced in the hazardous waste management industry. A careful study of these trends should provide insight into the changing competitive environment.

31   The nature and size of the hazardous waste industry was changing. Traditionally money flowed from waste generators to waste management professionals. More recently, high-polluting industries, such as chemicals, primary metals, petroleum and coal, rubber and plastics, and heavy manufacturing, diligently sought to reduce their environmental overheads and their future exposure to more stringent regulations. The Clinton-Gore administration talked of "source reduction" rather than intensifying the traditional collecting and disposal methods. They aimed to link greater national efficiency and productivity with less pollution production. The result was the rapid growth of in-house recycling and resource recovery programs, use of less environmentally destructive raw materials, and changes in the manufacturing cycle. Exhibit 7 provides a hierarchy of treatment

technologies. As the exhibit shows, end-of-the-line disposal was emphasized in 1993, but on the technology continuum greater emphasis will be placed on source reduction and resource recovery in the future. These preventive technologies are designed into production systems to minimize waste generation and facilitate reuse of industrial wastes. This would save private industry a significant amount and reduce exposure under environmental regulations. In doing so, however, the market for traditional remediation and TSD services would shrink. In 1993, these pollution prevention projects were less profitable than the remediation and TSD segments.

32   The hazardous waste industry discovered that, as large companies performed more of their own cleanups internally, some customers turned into competitors. Municipalities became competitors as they began to manage their cleanups. The shift from government cleanup projects to private industry partnerships impacted the bottom line, because private customers were traditionally more cost-conscious. In the early growth stage of the industry, 80 percent of the projects were funded by the federal government. In the current competitive shakeout stage, approximately 50 percent are federally funded. As the industry reaches maturity, it is projected that only 20 percent of revenues will be tied to the federal government, and 80 percent will be from private industry.

33   New entrants were still being attracted to the industry, which increased competition and decreased profit margins. The primary barrier to entry was the permitting process for a hazardous waste disposal facility in the United States. It was far easier to obtain permits for on-site mobile incinerators. The application and approval process for permitting was long and expensive, and ultimate approval was often denied. Other barriers included experience, reputation, insurance, and investment capital. New entrants into the industry were the former defense contractors. They came with the competitive advantages of knowing how to be system integrators, knowing how to develop and rely on technology, and having a network of contacts. Firms such as Lockheed and TRW bid on environmental contracts. Small, regional hazardous waste management firms often lacked the depth of expertise to perform large-scale cleanups. However, there was a niche market for the small firms because of government-mandated small-business set-aside work. Currently, the EPA and DOD must award 8 and 10 percent, respectively, of all contracts to small and disadvantaged businesses. Frequently, large firms sought alliances with these small firms to participate in set-aside work.

34   The domestic waste handling business was becoming increasingly global. The Organization for Economic Cooperation and Development estimated that the U.S. environmental industry in 1990 had a trade surplus of $4 billion. A significant share of international exchanges occurred through technology licensing instead of trade. Large firms developed their own pollution abatement technologies first for home country use and then licensed them to foreign firms to increase market presence abroad. Globalization strategies used to gain entry into foreign markets included direct investment, cross-border mergers, acquisitions, joint ventures, and collaboration with foreign partners.

35   The number of people employed in the environmental industry steadily increased in recent years. In 1985, 5,000 environmental engineers were employed, but by 1995, it was estimated 22,000 would be needed. The growth of firms is constrained by the availability of qualified scientists and professionals with experience in environmental fields. The remediation segment had seen the most rapid expansion as cleanup projects moved into high gear. However, the industry also spawned subspecialties in the legal, regulatory, and insurance industries. Among the larger industry players, employment growth slowed. More remarkable growth was seen in smaller, regional firms and in newly established environmental subsidiaries of larger, private companies.

RESULTING OPPORTUNITIES IN THE INDUSTRY

36   Although growth in more traditional areas slowed, emerging markets provided new opportunities for firms positioned to capitalize on them.

37   An increasing number of U.S. environmental companies penetrated foreign markets. The Organization for Economic Cooperation and Development estimated the world market for environmental equipment and services (including engineering and consulting) in 1990 was $200 billion. Although the United States had lost its worldwide technological advantage in some areas, it retained world leadership in the environmental technologies. The United States exported approximately 10 percent

EXHIBIT 8
Primary Pollution Control Markets for U.S. Exports (in millions)

Country	1990	Estimated 2000
Canada	$700	$1,500
Japan	600	1,200
Former Soviet republics	300	621
Germany	290	400
United Kingdom	200	300
France	171	250
Mexico	116	248
South Korea	108	222
Taiwan	100	208
Australia	94	200

Source: Silverstein, *The Environmental Industry Yearbook and Market Investment Guide*, 1993, p. 88.

of its output of environmental products. The sluggish world economy slowed recent export growth, but the need for international cleanup was acute. Ventures into the international environmental market remind companies that regulatory structures and funding for cleanup were often nonexistent. Exhibit 8 lists the potential international markets for environmental exports in the year 2000 as compared to the market size in 1990.

38   The recently announced closings of many military bases provided markets for environmental cleanup companies. These sites had to be evaluated and declared safe before approval for alternative usage.

39   In addition to the substances the EPA had defined as hazardous wastes, there were special wastes, which included waste streams from mining industries, oil and gas exploration, cement kilns, and coal-fired electric utilities. These special wastes were generated at a rate 25 times greater than the generation of hazardous wastes; the special wastes are exempt from the EPA's RCRA provisions. However, if they are reclassified, the demand for cleanup is expected to increase proportionately.

THREATS TO THE INDUSTRY

40   As market conditions changed, new threats emerged to challenge companies not properly positioned.

41   Because of the uncertainty over pending reauthorization of RCRA and SARA and decreased budget commitments for Superfund, the EPA became a less attractive customer. Reliance on these kinds of contracts might expose the contractor to lengthy delays in contract awards.

42   Private-sector work, which comprised about 50 percent of the customer base, had been slowed by the recession. This created excess capacity for hazardous waste treatment labs and disposal operations, which lowered profit margins.

43   The possibility of more stringent definitions of contractor liability under RCRA and CERCLA existed. The strict liability clause may extend beyond generators to include transporters of hazardous waste.

44   The maturity of the landfill market, and, to a lesser extent, remediation, threatened those companies that were not positioned to compete in the waste minimization strategies. Increasingly, large waste producers were buying or strategically aligning themselves with companies that were able to integrate the cleanup process into the production process.

CASE 32

CHEMICAL WASTE MANAGEMENT

1 As of July 19, 1993, the future of Chemical Waste Management (CWM) could best be described as uncertain. Management regrettably announced the hazardous waste management giant broke even for the first six months of fiscal year 1993. But this trend was not a new one. Earnings in fiscal year 1991 and 1992 were significantly lower than in previous years. Management placed the blame for the poor showing on a continued weak economy, which resulted in a decline in hazardous waste volumes generated and a drop in commercial incineration revenues. But investors thought there might be more to the skid in company profits than management was letting on. For one thing, the Chicago incinerator was still shut down due to allegations that a supervisor intentionally mislabeled drums of toxic waste to avoid inspection. The state regulatory authorities pressed criminal charges in a suit still unresolved. Numerous accidents, some of them unreported to authorities, had also caused CWM to incur heavy fines and penalties. Investors believed that the terrible publicity these events received hurt profitability by driving away customers. And as if that weren't bad enough, industry analysts claimed the industry was nearing maturity, as characterized by increasing competition and falling margins. It was up to senior management to devise a strategy to reposition the company to survive in a market fast approaching maturity.

COMPANY BACKGROUND

2 Waste Management, Inc. (WMI), was founded in 1971 and had grown rapidly to become the world's largest environmental services firm. By 1973, WMI had 93 divisions and over 1 million customers. In 1975, Chemical Waste Management began operations as a division of WMI. At that time, CWM provided treatment and disposal services (T&D) for the chemical wastes of many industrial companies. In particular, CWM operated a disposal facility in Barnwell, South Carolina, that handled low-level radioactive waste. The Resource Conservation and Recovery Act of 1976 (RCRA) and, to a lesser extent, the Toxic Substances Control Act (TSCA), which controls the disposal of harmful PCBs, were the catalysts for the dramatic growth experienced by the CWM division. By 1978, the CWM division had become a wholly owned subsidiary of WMI. After passage of the Comprehensive Environmental Response, Compensation, and Liability Act of 1980 (CERCLA), CWM established an office in Chicago to conduct research in the treatment and disposal of hazardous wastes. The company soon formed its Remedial Services Group and won its first Superfund contract in 1981. In 1983, CWM formed the Environmental Management Department to assist clients in meeting new operating standards. CWM purchased the Brand Companies in 1988, making CWM the nation's largest provider of asbestos abatement services.

3   Until about that time, CWM was a well respected and trusted provider of comprehensive hazardous waste management services. However, a string of accidents, some of them unreported to authorities, damaged the company's reputation. In January 1993, a new WMI subsidiary, Rust International, was set up to house the remediation, engineering, and asbestos abatement groups of the WMI family of companies. Hence CWM's service organization was pared down to refocus on the traditional market of treatment and disposal.

This case was prepared by Professor John A. Pearce II of Villanova University, and Linda Riesenman.

SERVICES

4 Chemical Waste Management was organized around five main service areas:

Waste Reduction, Resource Recovery, and Recycling

5 The company's Waste Reduction Services Group was formed in 1986 to design site-specific waste minimization strategies for industrial customers. Although industrial waste streams were not classified as "hazardous" wastes and therefore subject to minimal regulation, they were generated at a much greater rate than hazardous wastes. During resource recovery, chemical wastes were recycled and either recovered for their original use or converted into liquid fuels for use in cement kilns and blast furnaces. The blended fuels were a good substitute for the more expensive fossil fuels. This was CWM's smallest and newest segment, representing somewhere between 5 and 10 percent of total revenues.

Hazardous Waste Identification, Packaging, and Removal

6 The Technical Services division offered complete on-site management of hazardous wastes for both government agencies and private industry. Drummed wastes were identified, inventoried, and later removed from the customer's site. Complete underground storage tank management was also available. The transportation fleet included approximately 450 tractors and 930 trailers. The company operated 31 transportation centers across the United States and 2 in Mexico.

Hazardous Waste Treatment and Disposal

7 The company's principal treatment technology was thermal destruction, more commonly referred to as incineration. The Thermal Operations Group maintained three RCRA-certified incineration facilities, one in Chicago; one in Sauget, Illinois; and one in Port Arthur, Texas. The Chicago and Port Arthur facilities were authorized to burn cancer-causing PCBs. As of 1992, there were only 18 permitted incineration facilities in the United States, very few of which could burn PCBs. Operations at the Chicago facility had been suspended since the 1991 kiln explosion and whistle-blowing incidents. As land disposal standards became increasingly stringent, incineration became the only viable option for the treatment of certain organic wastes.

8 Other treatment methods utilized included physical treatments and chemical treatments. Distillation, evaporation, and separation were the primary physical treatments CWM used to remove liquids from solid and semi-solid hazardous and toxic wastes. Chemical stabilization was the treatment technology on which many of the inorganic waste performance measures were based. CWM's patented CHEM-MATRIX system neutralized the volatility and toxicity of these wastes, resulting in a stable, solid compound that could be safely buried in secure landfills. Another patented technology, PO*WW*ER, enabled CWM to provide both on-site and off-site wastewater treatment services. Holding treatment technology patents provided CWM with a competitive advantage over companies that relied exclusively on licensing technologies.

9 CWM operated eight RCRA-certified landfills that accepted previously treated solid wastes. The company also utilized deep-well injection, a process in which treated chemical wastewaters are injected into rock formations beneath the base of fresh water.

Engineering and Technology Services

10 CWM operated a national network of analytical chemistry laboratories and regional waste acceptance laboratories. Wastes were analyzed and consolidated before being shipped to an appropriate treatment facility. As of 1992, the company maintained 31 laboratories at its facilities across the country. The labs were instrumental in providing comprehensive site remediation services.

EXHIBIT 1
Chemical Waste Management Treatment and Disposal Facilities

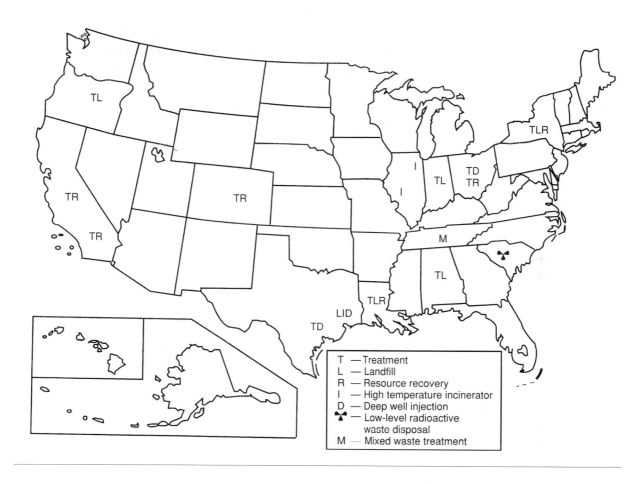

T — Treatment
L — Landfill
R — Resource recovery
I — High temperature incinerator
D — Deep well injection
☢ — Low-level radioactive
      waste disposal
M — Mixed waste treatment

Low-Level Radioactive Waste Services

11   Operating as a wholly owned subsidiary of Chemical Waste Management, Chem-Nuclear Systems, Inc., offered low-level radioactive waste management services. The company's Barnwell, South Carolina, facility was one of two licensed low-level radioactive waste disposal facilities east of the Mississippi. Its primary customers included medical, industrial, research, and government users of radioactive materials as well as operators of nuclear facilities. Chem-Nuclear provided site assessment, licensing, radiological controls, waste processing, decommissioning, volume reduction, transportation, and disposal. Chem-Nuclear Environmental Services, Inc. (CNES), another subsidiary of CWM, offered its federal customers management services for the cleanup and disposal of hazardous and radioactive wastes. Its primary customers were the Department of Energy and the Department of Defense. Exhibit 1 shows a geographical representation of services provided throughout the United States.

FINANCIAL CONDITION

12   During the economic recession of the early 1990s, manufacturing output decreased and customers postponed many discretionary projects. This hurt CWM's profitability in 1991 and 1992. Exhibit 2 summarizes the financial data of CWM from 1988 through 1992. Although revenues had been steadily increasing, the profits, as a percentage of revenues, had been falling since 1988. Exhibit 3

EXHIBIT 2
Chemical Waste Management, Inc., and Subsidiaries Consolidated Selected Financial Data
for the Years Ended December 31 (000s omitted except per share amount)

	1988	1989	1990	1991	1992
Revenues	$662,973	$ 846,778	$1,146,972	$1,358,344	$1,518,603
Costs and expenses	477,535	621,371	868,649	1,184,301	1,378,547
Other expenses (income)	(5,157)	(10,538)	(9,251)	10,450	(38,108)
Income before income taxes	$190,595	$ 235,945	$ 287,574	$ 163,593	$ 178,164
Provision for income taxes	73,700	91,702	111,983	62,787	48,429
Net income	$116,895	$ 144,243	$ 175,591	$ 100,806	$ 129,735
Average shares outstanding	200,292	202,111	207,238	206,917	204,967
Earnings per share	$ 0.58	$ 0.71	$ 0.85	$ 0.49	$ 0.63
Dividends per share	$ 0.07	$ 0.11	$ 0.15	$ 0.19	$ 0.20
Property and equipment, net	431,459	608,649	863,264	1,010,515	1,172,270
Total assets	875,698	1,105,154	1,606,460	2,025,512	2,442,379
Due to Waste Management, Inc.	129,850	104,162	53,230	326,593	626,712
Other long-term debt	3,965	3,515	190,319	373,680	138,338
Stockholders' equity	555,736	794,663	960,642	921,403	1,146,581

Source: *CWM Annual Report*, 1991, 1992.

details the costs and expenses incurred as a percentage of revenues for fiscal years 1989 through 1992. Operating expenses in 1991 and 1992 soared above previous levels, contributing to the decline in profitability. The losses at the Chicago facility were reflected in the jump in operating expenses. Selling and administrative expenses remained relatively unchanged, which was surprising for a company in CWM's predicament. As an industry reaches maturity, marketing expenses increase significantly in an attempt to differentiate a company's services.

13   As compared with an industry average of 1.003, CWM's beta was substantially higher at 1.396. The high beta reflected investors' perceptions regarding the instability and poor investment potential of CWM. The heavy fines and penalties that CWM had incurred in its incineration business had shaken investors' confidence. But what worried investors more was that they did not believe that CWM management perceived the gravity of the situation. Some even speculated that management might have condoned or turned a blind eye to the mismanagement of the incineration facilities so long as it meant good profits for CWM.

14   Before the reorganization, it was estimated that CWM had over 20,000 customers. Significant growth in revenues was attributable to three factors: price increases, acquisitions, and volume increases. As competition increases, price decreases become the norm as competitors try to hold onto market share. In the future, volume increases do not seem likely since the volume of hazardous wastes generated is on the decline. Therefore, the only way to grow revenues in this market is by acquisition. Investors waiting for CWM to boost revenues and earnings may have a long wait.

MARKETING

15   Chemical Waste Management was a decentralized company, with three main regional business units and Chem-Nuclear set up as profit centers. The regional units were responsible for providing all sales and marketing services for their customers. In addition, each regional service center provided a full complement of technical services including hazardous waste management, treatment and disposal, transportation, and analytical laboratory services. In this way, a customer had all needs met at one service location. Under a covenant with the parent WMI and Waste Management International, CWM could not enter the international hazardous waste market until at least July 1, 2000.

16   The new CWM continued to market itself as a full-service waste management company. Through its affiliation with other Waste Management, Inc., companies, CWM drew extensively on the expertise of related companies to bring customers a comprehensive action plan for dealing with their

EXHIBIT 3
Chemical Waste Management, Analysis of Revenue, FY 1989 through 1992

	For the Years Ended December 31			
	1989	1990	1991	1992
Price	7.80%	5.30%	3.20%	1.90%
Business acquisitions	0.00%	19.70%	32.80%	3.60%
Volume	19.90%	10.50%	(17.60%)	6.30%
Percent increase in revenues	27.70%	35.50%	18.40%	11.80%
Treatment, resource recovery, and disposal	57.60%	44.30%	31.90%	34.10%
Specialty services (on-site remediation)	32.20%	37.60%	30.20%	28.90%
Transportation	10.20%	8.70%	7.80%	8.10%
Specialty contracting (brand)	0.00%	9.40%	30.10%	28.90%
Total revenues	100.00%	100.00%	100.00%	100.00%
Costs and expenses:				
Operating	59.00%	62.50%	70.00%	69.80%
Selling and administrative	14.40%	13.30%	14.50%	13.60%
Interest expense	0.00%	0.00%	1.20%	2.10%
Minority interest and sundry expense	(1.20%)	(0.80%)	0.40%	(1.50%)
Percent of revenues	72.20%	75.00%	86.10%	84.00%

Source: *CWM Annual Report*, 1991, 1992.

specific waste management needs (see Exhibit 4). CWM's customer base was quite diverse, with a good mix of industrial clients, the Department of Energy, and the Department of Defense. Environmental restoration was the main focus of CWM's government work. Providing integrated services was becoming increasingly important to industrial customers who desired to form long-term partnerships with one firm for all their waste management needs. However, the new CWM was structured so as to concentrate on its original core business of treatment and disposal.

17   CWM relied on WMI to coordinate marketing efforts across the family of companies. Insurance coverage was secured through policies issued to WMI with the costs shared by all WMI subsidiaries. Although CWM was fortunate to have more insurance needs met in a constricted market, some of the policies did not transfer risk to the insurer and required the insured to repay claims. The company was unable to obtain environmental impairment liability insurance that covered gradual and accidental releases of hazardous wastes. In this respect, the land disposal and incineration facilities were a high risk for CWM due to the volume and toxicity of the wastes they handled. This was of serious concern to investors who feared additional mishaps and lawsuits similar to the Chicago catastrophe. Research and development projects also received some financial backing from WMI. This was particularly important since the EPA strongly encouraged development of innovative technologies. Additionally, it was the EPA that established industry guidelines for the "best available" treatment technologies.

COMPETITION

18   Profit margins varied according to the nature and availability of the services provided. Under the new organizational structure of WMI, the majority of CWM's services were concentrated in hazardous waste treatment and disposal. However, growth in the transportation segment and the resource recovery, waste reduction, and recycling segment had been impressive. Significant capital investment in landfill capacity and state-of-the-art incinerators and the permitting process created high entry barriers in the T&D segment, necessitating the healthy margins. Other barriers included experience, investment capital, insurance, and reputation.

EXHIBIT 4

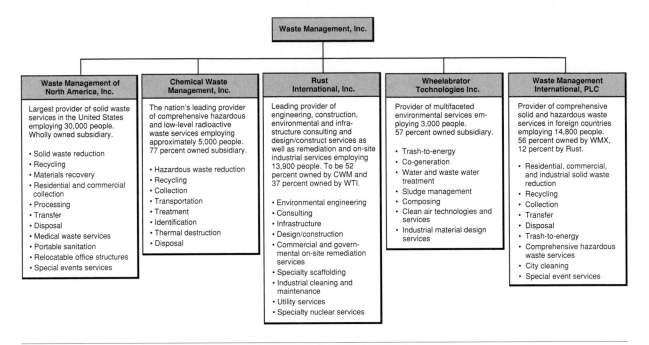

19   The T&D segment was the most profitable for CWM because profits were all based on volume. The landfills' and incinerators' operating costs were generally fixed, and to the extent waste volumes exceeded these costs, margins of up to 40 percent were frequently achieved. Revenues from toxic waste generation grew by 19.9 percent in 1989 and 10.5 percent in 1990, but fell by 17.6 percent in 1991. (See Exhibit 3.) The result was a strong blow to profitability in 1991. Declining sales in this market were attributed to the economic recession and to the increasingly popular strategy of waste minimization and pollution prevention. During the recession, competitors cut prices to attract new customers and cover fixed costs. By 1992, a moderate recovery in waste disposal revenues was recognized. Exhibit 3 provides a comparison of growth factors and services segments.

MAJOR COMPETITORS

20   The U.S. market for hazardous waste services was projected to reach $174 billion in 1995. This industry was comprised of many national, regional, and local environmental management companies. No single firm had a substantial market share. CWM, with 1992 revenues of $1.5 billion, probably serviced about 1 percent of the market. As regulations tightened, many industrial firms found it cheaper to learn to manage their hazardous waste needs internally. Therefore, many former customers of CWM became major competitors, in a sense. Additionally, because CWM is a large company, it might have been less competitive than smaller, low-cost firms for bidding on contracts where technical expertise was not a requirement.

21   A number of large environmental management firms also presented significant competition for CWM in various service segments. Very few firms in the industry, however, offered integrated services. With $240 million in 1992 revenues, Rollins Environmental Services, Inc., was a formidable competitor engaged in transportation, treatment, and disposal nationwide. Incineration was the most frequently utilized treatment technology, although chemical and physical treatment methods were also provided. In fact, in 1970, Rollins began operating the first commercial hazardous waste incinerator in the United States, and throughout the years it had become a highly respected member

of the environmental services industry. Based on this claim to fame, Rollins attempted to differentiate itself from CWM as "the hazardous waste incineration specialist." In 1992, almost 80 percent of revenues were derived from incineration services. Rollins operated three incineration facilities in Baton Rouge, Louisiana; Bridgeport, New Jersey; and Deer Park, Texas. Rollins' history of strong growth and earnings gave it the ability to operate on thin margins. In this way, it competed fiercely with CWM on price.

22 Reaching $795 million in 1992 revenues, Safety-Kleen Corporation competed nationally with CWM in the resource recovery and recycling market. The firm operated solvent recycling centers, waste oil processing plants, and fuel blending facilities. The blended fuels were marketed to cement manufacturers for use in cement kilns. Its primary customers were industrial firms. Due to the nature of its business and the fashionable "greening" of American movement, Safety-Kleen was a well respected pioneer in the field of resource recovery and recycling services. Its reputation, size, and undisputed expertise in the market were its main competitive advantages over CWM.

23 American Ecology Corporation, with $71 million in 1992 revenues, was engaged in the disposal of a variety of lethal wastes across the United States. Almost half of the wastes handled were low-level nuclear wastes, although its chemical waste business had seen steady growth. The company operated a landfill in Nevada that was licensed to accept low-level radioactive wastes. The only other site that accepted low-level radioactive wastes was CWM's Barnwell facility. However, AEC had submitted license applications to construct and operate new facilities in California and Nebraska. This market was not highly competitive and therefore American Ecology competed with CWM geographically.

24 Thermo Instrument Systems, Inc., with $423 million in 1992 revenues, operated a number of analytical laboratories across the country, specializing in hazardous and radioactive waste analysis. However, the company achieved prominence in the industry for developing many state-of-the-art analytical instruments used to monitor the presence of hazardous and radioactive elements in the ground, water, and air. This distinction earned Thermo Instrument Systems an excellent reputation in the industry. Because the laboratory equipment used was also supplied by Thermo Instrument Systems, it could compete very effectively as the industry's low-cost provider of analytical services.

OPPORTUNITIES

25 Through a joint venture, CWM and the Holman Companies, a large cement producer, operated as Cemtech L.P. This relationship was established to promote the sale and distribution of blended fuels to cement manufacturers across the country. Not only did this reduce CWM's disposal costs, but it also helped it increase its customer base. There was the potential to further expand this market for the resource recovery segment by converting paper and plastics into pelletized fuels. In comparison to the T&D business, this was a relatively small niche market for CWM.

26 CWM wished to expand its market geographically into Mexico. Thus far it had established a solvent recycling and processing plant in Tijuana and had broken ground on a land disposal facility in Guadalajara. A joint venture between two Mexican companies and CWM, with Rust International, was formed. Their purpose was to oversee the initial remedial studies of several major oil refineries and to provide restoration services. This was a great opportunity for CWM in the near term. It was estimated that Mexico's pollution market could reach $248 million by the year 2000. If CWM could establish itself while the market was still in the development stage, it would build name brand recognition that would provide CWM with a competitive advantage.

THREATS

27 The Southeast Interstate Low-Level Radioactive Waste Management Compact, which was formed in 1980, was comprised of eight southeastern states. Its purpose was to oversee the disposal of all low-level radioactive waste generated in the southeastern region. It had designated the Barnwell, South Carolina, facility as the only site eligible to receive the region's waste through December 31, 1992. In addition, the

Barnwell facility was permitted to accept waste generated outside the region, although the generators paid an additional surcharge directly to the state. Under the Low-Level Radioactive Waste Policy Amendments Act of 1985, states not part of some regional compact might eventually be denied access to such disposal services if they did not make a serious attempt at constructing their own facilities.

28   While CWM attempted to provide regional compacts with its expertise in site selection and development, progress had been minimal. Furthermore, the southeastern compact designated North Carolina as the future site of the compact's exclusive disposal facility. Due to slow progress by the state of North Carolina, the Barnwell facility had been granted a reprieve by having its exclusive rights guaranteed until December 31, 1995. Several states outside the southeastern compact designed low-level radioactive waste disposal facilities and should begin construction by 1995. Unfortunately, the future of CWM's Barnwell site looks rather bleak. This could mean the permanent closure of the facility in 1995 and substantial site remediation charges for which CWM was uninsured.

29   Landfill capacity peaked about 1986, although many firms continued to increase the size of their facilities. These actions stimulated competition and trimmed margins of those companies providing transportation, treatment, and disposal services. In addition, with waste volumes on the decline and more stringent waste incineration requirements, the demand for space was sure to plunge. CWM owned or leased eight land disposal facilities, and unless management could determine how to prevent facility underutilization, significant losses would mount quickly. Furthermore, any facility that was closed might incur heavy site remediation expenses under CERCLA. CWM was uninsured for such an event.

30   CWM was listed as a potentially responsible party (PRP) on 24 Superfund sites. As such, the company had to determine the extent of its exposure and make adequate provisions for the estimated cleanup costs, fines, and penalties that awaited it. Failure to do so could have hurt the future financial condition of the company. In 1991, CWM established a $36 million reserve for future environmental liabilities related to the remediation of several of its closed landfills.

INDUSTRY TRENDS

31   The supply of hazardous waste professionals had never really caught up with demand; however, employment growth slowed. This was due to the unique blend of education and practical work experience required of employees. A good benefits package, a safe work environment, and a favorable public image all helped to attract and retain quality employees.

32   The volume of hazardous wastes generated in the United States had been steadily declining for the last several years. This was due in part to decreased manufacturing output as seen during the recession and in part to the pollution prevention and waste minimization strategies of many large industrial companies. In addition, toxic waste generators were also painfully aware of environmental regulations and sought to minimize their liabilities. While the current composition of government and private industry customers was roughly equal, projections indicated that private industry clients would comprise 80 percent of the customer base in the coming years.

33   Taken as a whole, the hazardous waste industry was experiencing slowed growth and decreased profitability. However, the industry was really comprised of distinctly different service areas that had their own product life cycles. Of the markets CWM served, only transportation, resource recovery, and recycling were rapidly growing. Analytical laboratory services was a mature market characterized by intense competition, thin margins, and slow growth. All of CWM's other service segments were approaching maturity.

IMAGE PROBLEM

34   The hazardous waste management industry was headed toward a competitive shakeout. This fact was evidenced by falling profits (and in many cases mounting losses), a proliferation of firms entering the industry, and slowing employment. The strategic changes that CWM implemented in the next several years would determine whether or not it survived this transition. A critical issue to be addressed in conjunction with this strategic planning period is that of CWM's poor public image.

35   As a member of the WMI family of companies, CWM's image was influenced by its parent company's activities. The less-than-sterling reputation of WMI had certainly cast doubts on the integrity of CWM management as well. As far back as the 1960s, allegations had been made that WMI companies had connections to organized crime. More recently, WMI and Browning Ferris, Inc., settled a class-action suit in which they were charged with several antitrust violations, including price fixing. Unfortunately, CWM had its share of mishaps, accidents, and bad publicity as well.

36   During 1986 and 1987, pollution monitoring equipment at CWM's Chicago facility was deliberately turned off at least four times when it was believed incinerator emissions had exceeded acceptable levels. There was also at least one incident in which PCBs were incinerated at higher than permitted levels. A shift supervisor who was fired after the incident claims he was fired for whistle-blowing.

37   In 1987, the EPA charged CWM with running its Model City, New York, PCB disposal unit at temperatures exceeding approved levels. Although CWM did not admit guilt, it entered into a consent decree with the EPA and paid a $300,000 civil penalty. In addition, it was instructed by the EPA to make a $730,000 investment in a household hazardous waste collection and disposal project in Niagara, New York.

38   In 1989, the Sauget, Illinois, incineration facility was found to be in noncompliance with several operating standards, which resulted in fines of $250,000. At the same facility the following year, improper testing of tank samples resulted in an unpredicted chemical reaction that produced a dangerous cloud of chlorinated gas. Regulators claimed CWM employees then sprayed water on the plume of gas, increasing its size.

39   Two accidents occurred during 1990 at the Sauget facility. In January, an explosion in a dumpster of incinerated hazardous waste went unreported to local regulators. Further investigation indicated the ash contained unacceptable levels of an explosive material. The next month, a worker used a pole to dislodge molten slag while the incinerator was still operating. The slag fell from the conveyor into a pool of water, creating a scalding cloud of steam. The worker was severely burned and toxic fumes were released. Authorities learned of the accident from an anonymous tip. A civil penalty of $1.9 million was later paid by CWM.

40   In 1991, workers at the Chicago facility mistakenly loaded a volatile compound into the incinerator, causing a large kiln explosion. Total fines and penalties reached $3.5 million.

41   At the same facility the following year, CWM admitted that a supervisor deliberately mislabeled up to 100 drums of hazardous waste to prevent regulators from inspecting them. To keep track of the mislabeled drums, two separate inventory databases were maintained. The supervisor was subsequently fired but claimed that his only crime was whistle-blowing. State authorities launched a lengthy criminal investigation. Plant operations were suspended in May 1992 and several hundred employees were laid off. Under the terms of the Illinois Environmental Protection Agency, CWM was ordered to make severance payments to all terminated plant employees. Management continued negotiating the terms under which the Chicago facility would be allowed to reopen. In addition, CWM applied for a final RCRA Part B operating permit for the facility, which has not yet been granted. Regulators cited over 100 plant deficiencies that needed corrective action in order to receive the permit.

42   Since the market for hazardous waste services had become very competitive, a good reputation provided a firm with a distinct competitive advantage. This was particularly true when bidding on government work, which had traditionally been less price sensitive. Government agencies evaluated bids based on the contractor's technical proficiency, quality, reliability, and cost. The contract was awarded to the bidder who represented the best overall value. In some instances, reputation was the deciding factor.

LOCAL OPPOSITION

43   Local politicians in Illinois petitioned the state EPA to keep the Chicago facility permanently closed. Spearheading this movement was State Representative Clem Balanoff, who engaged the services of a public interest law firm to represent his cause. Representative Balanoff also organized the South East Environmental Task Force as an advisory body to local legislators.

44   Numerous environmental activitist groups had descended on CWM's Chicago facility as well. On one occasion, Greenpeace and Citizens United to Reclaim the Environment (CURE) held a joint civil disobedience demonstration at the embattled incinerator. They blocked all plant entrances and exits with trucks, chaining themselves and the trucks to the gates. The plant was shut down for more than 14 hours. This was a rather shocking example of how pervasive the "not-in-my-backyard" (NIMBY) attitude was concerning hazardous waste incinerators and landfills.

FUTURE CONSIDERATIONS

45   CWM senior management is wondering how the present external environment will influence their future competitive position. In a market fast approaching maturity, management is considering what long-term strategy is best suited to CWM's unique strengths and weaknesses. In developing a strategic plan, management must determine the potential impact of CWM's poor image.

CASE 33

ICF KAISER INTERNATIONAL, INC.

1   ICF Chairman and CEO James Edwards was determined to turn his faltering consulting and engineering company around. Since 1990, ICF had experienced deteriorating profits in the environmental markets it served. The sluggish economy was partially to blame, but other factors contributed to ICF's decline as well. For one thing, the company overdiversified during its acquisition frenzy of the 1980s, venturing into unrelated fields in which it possessed little management expertise. By 1992, President William Stitt and Edwards realized their folly and divested the company of 15 businesses, resulting in a $73 million restructuring charge. Plans to launch a second public offering were indefinitely postponed as ICF stock hit all-time lows. Delays related to the changing U.S. presidential administration and EPA director also softened the market for environmental services. Another unexpected blow came in fiscal year 1993 when longtime President William Stitt resigned for undisclosed reasons. While these events were responsible for short-term losses, investors were more concerned about ICF's long-term viability in a mature and intensely competitive industry. Unless Edwards could come up with a plan to differentiate ICF's services and penetrate new markets, growth prospects looked bleak.

COMPANY BACKGROUND

2   The Inner City Fund (ICF) was established in 1969 by four black World War II fighter pilots to promote investment in Washington, D.C., area businesses. In 1970, William Stitt came on board, followed soon by James Edwards. Both men had strong ties to the Environmental Protection Agency and the Department of Housing and Urban Development and used their influence to expand the consulting business in these areas. In 1973, Stitt was named president of ICF. At that time, ICF's strategy was simple: seek contracts with government agencies that had large program budgets. Initially, urban planning was ICF's main market, but its focus shifted with the government's focus and has led ICF into the health, energy, and environmental markets.

3   In the early 1980s, ICF began adding engineering and design services to its environmental consulting business. In 1988, the failing Kaiser Engineers Group was acquired, more than tripling the size of ICF. Under the guidance of its parent company, ICF Kaiser turned its business around the next year. That success provided the impetus ICF needed to consummate the deal for its initial public offering. Additional acquisitions were made in companies serving the health care, energy, pharmaceuticals, and information technology markets. Many of these new companies were engaged more in product development than in consulting. For a variety of reasons, losses in many of the new acquisitions mounted quickly. ICF was unable to successfully manage product development costs in the new businesses and, as a result, divested itself of 15 businesses in 1992. The financial impact to ICF was enormous—a $44 million loss in fiscal year 1992. The second public offering planned for 1992 was canceled and ICF's stock price plunged. Fiscal 1993 earnings showed moderate improvement, but many investors continued to watch ICF with a wary eye.

SERVICES

4   Through the family of companies that comprised ICF Kaiser International, Inc., the firm was able to provide a wide variety of services for the environmental, infrastructure, industrial, and energy markets.

This case was prepared by Professor John A. Pearce II of Villanova University, and Linda E. Reisenman.

Environmental Consulting and Analytical Services

5   The services offered in this area related primarily to the study and analysis of hazardous wastes and to the environmental concerns associated with operating a manufacturing type business. Many industrial businesses sought the expertise of a company such as ICF in achieving compliance with all environmental regulations. ICF's compliance consulting mainly addressed the Resource Conservation and Recovery Act (RCRA), the Clean Air Act, and the Clean Water Act. In addition to basic compliance issues, ICF endeavored to educate the client concerning cost-effective solutions to unique environmental problems. Guidance also extended to completing the RCRA permitting process.

6   ICF performed risk assessments to determine the extent of contamination and the potential health and environmental risks presented. In conjunction with the risk assessment, analytical laboratories evaluated the content of the soil, air, and water samples. Consulting services also extended to remedial investigations and feasibility studies (RI/FS). From these studies, ICF developed remedial action plans and aided the client in selecting contractors to perform the actual site remediation.

Remedial Services

7   ICF used subcontractors to provide remediation services on Superfund, government agency, and industrial customer sites. Although the company managed a wide range of services in this area, land farming, glassification, and in situ bioremediation were most frequently used. Due to potential conflicts of interest, ICF could not provide both remedial action plans and the remedial management team on government contracts.

Environmental Engineering

8   Pollution prevention was a much cheaper way of dealing with regulatory compliance and minimizing treatment and disposal costs. Therefore, ICF wanted to expand its presence in this market, providing guidance to customers who wished to upgrade their facilities and manufacturing processes. The environmental engineers developed project management systems and designed process control systems that improved operating efficiencies and reduced waste emissions dramatically. ICF, with capabilities in both front-end environmental consulting and engineering, was able to bridge the gap that many hazardous waste management firms without engineering expertise could not. Design, management, and construction of large commercial projects, such as wastewater treatment plants, was made possible by this unique blend of skills.

Traditional Engineering and Construction

9   In this segment, ICF provided comprehensive engineering and construction services primarily related to infrastructure. While progress in infrastructure was once driven by commercial development, it was more frequently prompted by environmental concerns. ICF wished to meet the needs of its public-sector clients in the planning, design, and construction of mass transit systems, airports, highways, bridges, and water resource systems. More specifically, ICF's expertise in this area included master planning, alternative analysis, site development studies, conceptual and preliminary engineering, detail design, specifications development, quality assurance and quality control, construction management, construction, and inspection.

Energy Consulting and Engineering

10   While private industry sought to maximize the value of its energy resources, the federal government employed ICF to evaluate energy policies and program initiatives. ICF conducted research into alternative fuel and energy sources that replaced traditional sources. These alternative sources achieved cost efficiencies and regulatory compliance. The application of new and innovative technologies that generated and stored energy were assessed based on a client's individual needs. In addition,

ICF aided power producers in facility upgrades and modifications, operational support and safety, and capacity utilization. Environmental concerns also impacted this market due to the EPA's emphasis on cleaner burning fuels and air emission standards. Again, ICF's experience in environmental consulting complemented its achievements in the energy market.

MARKETS AND CUSTOMERS

11   The demand for environmental services remained weak during fiscal year 1993. While some of this was attributable to the economic recession, the change in presidential administration and the appointment process had also stalled progress. Consequently, private industry took a cue from this inaction and postponed a significant amount of environmental work. The impact on the bottom line was disastrous for ICF. The 1993 net earnings were a poor 0.5 percent of revenues. ICF expected this market to improve significantly in fiscal year 1994 as the EPA redefined its priorities and commenced work on new projects.

12   In 1993, the company earned about 65 percent of its revenues in the environmental market. The U.S. Department of Energy accounted for approximately 29 percent of total revenues, while the EPA and other government agencies followed up with 11 percent and 7 percent, respectively. These revenues related almost exclusively to the environmental market, with only a minor portion reported in the energy market.

13   The primary focus of the DOE and DOD contracts had been facilities restoration and base closings. Existing military bases and weapons storage facilities had to be brought into compliance with RCRA and CERCLA regulations. In addition to compliance issues, actual site remediation had to be performed to remove unexploded ordnance, chemical weapons, radiological materials, and various hazardous wastes. Since 1987, ICF had been managing the cleanup of the DOE's Hanford nuclear site in Richland, Washington. In 1993, ICF won the recompete of this contract, which was worth $300 million over the next three years. The contract award was under protest from one of the losing bidders, but ICF expected the case to be resolved shortly in the company's favor.

14   Other noteworthy projects in the environmental market related to clean air, water pollution, remediation, analysis, and risk assessment. Clean air services were provided to both public- and private-sector clients. ICF had been awarded a sizable amount of work from the EPA to study global climate change, indoor air quality, and acid rain. Private-sector clients desired services related to reducing pollution emissions through redesigning production processes. Sophisticated computer models had been developed by ICF to simulate various air quality problems experienced by customers. These models assisted ICF in monitoring emissions levels and bringing plants into compliance with permit standards. Additionally, ICF was managing a construction project in Boston Harbor for the country's largest wastewater treatment plant. The contract, awarded in 1990, was with the Massachusetts Water Resources Authority and was worth $140 million over five years. A private client engaged the services of ICF to supervise the demolition and remediation of two steel mills located along the Monongahela River in Pennsylvania. This included managing the disposal of asbestos, PCBs, contaminated groundwater and soils, and toxic storage tanks.

15   The infrastructure market was comprised almost exclusively of public-sector clients. During his campaign, President Clinton spoke of increased spending on infrastructure to rebuild the nation's highways, bridges, and mass transit systems. Therefore, ICF was hopeful that this market would experience robust growth under the direction of the Clinton administration. The Intermodal Surface Transportation Efficiency Act had already authorized $151 billion for federal programs to upgrade national highways and interstate systems. Under this act, ICF had been contracted to provide preliminary design for a light-rail transit line in Chicago. The international market for infrastructure services looked promising as well. As part of a joint venture, ICF provided engineering consulting and design services for an $18 billion, 88-kilometer rapid transit system in Taipei, Taiwan. Other sizable infrastructure projects were being performed in Toronto and London.

16   The industrial market was comprised of private industry, in particular the steel, aluminum, copper, alumina, and tin producers. In recent years, demand for ICF's services in this global market had been very weak due to the low prices worldwide for most metals. With its long history servicing this

market, ICF felt it was in good position to profit from its expertise when the market turned around. In the coal, coke, and coal chemicals area, the company offered services related to cleaning, handling, and environmental controls. ICF also provided engineering services in blast furnace design, construction, and repair for steel and copper manufacturers.

17   The energy market was comprised of various private clients and, to a lesser extent, federal agencies. ICF's private clients, who accounted for about 70 percent of its energy market base, included U.S. electric utilities; oil, natural gas, and coal companies; transportation companies; pipeline companies; and environmental groups. As part of a joint venture, ICF was assisting in the design and construction of an $8 billion liquefied natural gas facility in northwestern Australia. Another significant project involved testing an innovative technology that prevented acid rain by removing pollution emissions. ICF was working with the developer of this process in its installation at the Richmond Power and Light Company in Richmond, Indiana.

COMPETITION

18   The industry was comprised of several different segments, each with its own business life cycle. The consulting and environmental engineering segment was quickly approaching maturity, due to its lower barriers to entry. The industry was comprised of many national, regional, and local companies, so no single firm had a substantial market share. Many new entrants were the waste generators themselves. Many former customers of ICF were now major competitors in a sense. As a large company, ICF might be less competitive than smaller, low-cost firms for bidding on contracts where technical expertise was not a requirement.

19   By far, ICF's largest and most intensely competitive business segment was in the environmental services market. Therefore, the major competitors presented in this case study competed with ICF in this primary market. Approximately one-third of ICF's environmental services were pure consulting, with two-thirds related to engineering and remediation. While infrastructure, industry, and energy were promising markets, ICF had gained prominence as a provider of environmental consulting and engineering services.

20   In the field of pure environmental consulting, the market was teeming with competitors. Competition came from both the small local firms as well as the large international firms. Due to the low capital investment required for consulting businesses, the barriers to entry were low. The only real constraint was attracting and retaining qualified professionals with solid experience. Without experience and a good reputation, government contracts were hard to come by. The presence of so many competitors had decreased the profits of environmental consulting firms as the market matured. Government contracts for consulting and engineering work were usually cost reimbursable plus a fixed fee or an award fee.

21   The market for engineering and construction services was not as intensely competitive, therefore margins on this type of work were slightly higher for firms in general. ICF subcontracted all remediation work to specialty firms with the technical expertise and equipment that ICF lacked. However, this reduced ICF's profit margin on the work since it transferred a significant portion of risk and administrative costs on to the subcontractor. Since ICF never technically took possession of the hazardous waste, its liability under environmental law was minimized. Also, because ICF did not develop or own proprietary technology, it was unbiased in recommending appropriate remedial treatments.

MAJOR COMPETITORS

22   OHM Corporation had been a provider of waste management services since 1969. The company had 30 offices nationwide and in 1992 reported $284 million in annual revenues. Its areas of expertise included comprehensive remediation services and asbestos abatement, with remediation services netting 77 percent of revenues. Related to remediation, OHM provided site assessments, laboratory analysis, regulatory compliance guidance, data management, and treatment evaluation in a consulting

capacity. Environmental engineering services included design, on-site treatment, remedial construction, and resource recovery. OHM's technical proficiency in waste treatment extended to physical, chemical, biological, and thermal treatment. Private industry, which was comprised of petroleum, chemical, transportation, real estate, and manufacturing, accounted for 72 percent of OHM's customer base, with various government agencies picking up the balance. OHM had also established a presence in Canada, South America, Mexico, and the Pacific Rim.

23   OHM offered comprehensive remediation services that ICF, because of its management philosophy, preferred to subcontract. OHM possessed technical expertise in a variety of treatment methods as well. It catered primarily to industrial customers who preferred to deal with one contractor for all their environmental management needs. Because OHM provided integrated remediation services, it was able to achieve higher margins than ICF. Therefore, it could effectively compete on price but it faced greater liability under environmental regulations.

24   In 1992, International Technology Corporation (IT) was named the number one hazardous waste design firm in the United States for the third straight year by the *Engineering News Record*. IT's capabilities in this area included remedial investigations/feasibility studies, RCRA compliance, remedial design, pollution prevention/waste minimization, and thermal process engineering. Although these services represented 55 percent of IT's $420 million in revenues for 1992, the company was also very strong in providing analytical laboratory, construction, and remediation services. IT operated 10 full-service labs through the United States, performing comprehensive technical analysis for a variety of customers, although the DOE was its major customer. Construction and remediation services included thermal treatment, on-site incineration, bioremediation, fixation, stabilization, and decommissioning. IT had a reputation for developing and utilizing innovative treatment technologies. Like ICF, IT targeted the DOE and DOD as major customers in facilities restoration.

25   Like OHM, IT provided integrated remediation services but this feature was not as important when bidding on federal government work. IT and ICF competed head to head in this market. Because of its strong reputation as the industry's number one hazardous waste design firm, IT had a slight competitive advantage over ICF.

26   Roy F. Weston, Inc., provided consulting, environmental engineering, and remediation services to a broad base of clients. Weston had 45 offices and laboratories across the United States and had established a presence in Italy, Ireland, South America, and the Pacific Rim. Sixty-three percent of Weston's business base was comprised of pure consulting and engineering services, with another 22 percent centered in analytical services. The remainder of the business base was classified as construction and remediation. In 1992, over half of Weston's $330 million in revenues was earned on federal government contracts. In business since 1955, Weston was one of the oldest and most respected members of the hazardous waste management community. As such, it was strongly positioned in the federal market with existing contracts and was targeting DOE and DOD base closures for future work. In addition, Weston had established itself as a seasoned veteran of many Superfund projects.

27   Weston, IT, and ICF were all competing for the same federal remediation contracts. Like IT, Weston had earned an excellent reputation in the industry. Unfortunately for ICF, its reputation was not of the caliber of IT's or Weston's. This was partially attributable to its lack of practical, hands-on experience in the physical remediation process.

FINANCIAL CONDITION

28   Since 1990, ICF's profit margin had been very thin. In fiscal year 1993, net income was a mere 0.5 percent of annual revenues. A summary of ICF financial data for 1989 through 1993 is found in Exhibit 1. The small profits were attributable to the recession, delays in federal programs, and increased competition. Additionally, the huge 1992 divestiture resulted in a whopping $76 million restructuring charge. Investors lacked confidence in ICF's long-term investment potential, as seen in ICF's spiraling stock prices. Exhibit 2 provides average quarterly stock prices. ICF's PE ratio of 8 also reflected investors' concerns over ICF's continued viability. The industry average for environmental consulting and engineering companies is 15.4.

29   ICF's debt-to-equity ratio was very high, almost 2:1. Because ICF had not been able to issue additional shares of stock, debt had been its only alternative to financing the heavy loss of 1992. In

EXHIBIT 1
ICF Kaiser International, Inc., and Subsidiaries Consolidated Selected Financial Data for the Years Ended February 29 (000s omitted except per share amount)

	1989	1990	1991	1992	1993
Revenues	$297,866	$503,904	$624,976	$710,873	$678,882
Service revenue	174,328	278,255	363,318	379,826	384,985
Operating expenses	284,021	481,341	591,689	754,836	656,138
Income before income taxes	$ 13,845	$ 22,563	$ 33,287	($ 43,963)	$ 22,744
Provision for income taxes	7,321	13,769	18,996	(3,447)	14,105
Net income	$ 6,524	$ 8,794	$ 14,291	($ 40,516)	$ 8,639
Average shares outstanding	14,389	15,527	20,308	19,085	21,272
Earnings per share	$ 0.45	$ 0.57	$ 0.68	($ 2.25)	$ 0.16
Property and equipment net				23,651	19,680
Total assets	140,571	237,057	357,457	318,947	295,578
Long-term liabilities	40,440	53,019	109,820	85,675	75,602
Stockholders' equity	19,595	58,503	88,839	51,151	58,521

Source: *ICF Annual Report,* 1992, 1993.

1993, $30 million in subordinated debt was carried on ICF's books at an annual percentage rate of 13.5 percent. If ICF could generate sufficient capital through the equity markets, it could retire this debt as early as 1995.

OPPORTUNITIES

30   Over the next 20 to 30 years, the emerging market for pollution prevention and waste minimization services was projected to enjoy steady, solid growth. ICF, with its unique blend of environmental consulting and traditional engineering services, was well positioned to reap the benefits of this market's growth. As many of its industrial clients reinvested in newer manufacturing equipment, it became feasible for them to simultaneously invest in system design and process control with a company like ICF. By designing waste reduction into a manufacturing process, the volume of hazardous wastes could be significantly diminished. Thus, expenditures on traditional treatment and disposal of industrial by-products would be greatly reduced, netting the customer substantial cost savings.

31   The Pacific Rim countries offered a promising young market for experienced waste management professionals. Although environmental regulations were often sorely lacking, many Pacific Rim countries held large sums of U.S. currency. Therefore, they were able to finance the major environmental restoration and infrastructure projects that ICF was qualified to perform. Recognizing this opportunity, ICF established a full-service office in Taipei, Taiwan. Europe, on the other hand, had been a disappointing market so far because many countries lacked U.S. currency to invest in remediation. Most of the work performed in the European community had been funded through the World Bank or the United States Agency for International Development.

32   While competition kept margins low on much of the environmental consulting work, there were exceptions. For example, ICF had several contracts with the EPA to study global climate change, indoor air quality, and acid rain. In 1993 alone, ICF was awarded over $100 million in EPA contracts in these fields. This was a very new area of research and consequently few competitors could provide these specialized services. Therefore, ICF commanded a higher fee on these types of services.

THREATS

33   As much as environmental firms hated to admit it, the market for their services was rapidly approaching maturity. This event was evidenced by several facts. First, the market was saturated with companies providing these services. U.S. firms faced competition locally, regionally, and nationally. Furthermore, the competition was generally as intense for the large firms as it was for the smaller,

EXHIBIT 2
ICF Average Quarterly Stock Price

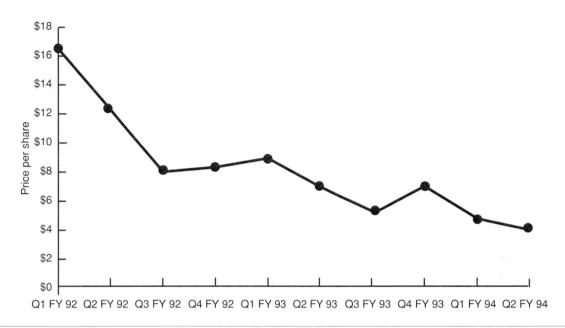

local firms. In fact, larger firms were sometimes at a disadvantage when the job being bid was awarded based on low cost rather than on technical expertise. Many giants in the industry sought firms that qualified for government set-aside work, joining the bidding team as a subcontractor.

34   So many competitors in the market made it very difficult for a company to differentiate its services. Differentiation was especially important for winning work in the government sector where cost might be secondary to technical expertise and reputation. As the market matured, expenditures on advertising and bid and proposal projects soared. Ten years ago, ICF bid on about 5 cents of every dollar spent on environmental projects. In 1993's highly competitive market, ICF felt it had to bid on about 25 cents of every contract dollar. This was a tremendous drain on corporate resources.

FUTURE CONSIDERATIONS

35   Led by CEO James Edwards, ICF's top management was charged with the task of developing a comprehensive, long-term strategic plan that would enhance ICF's competitive posture. Given the rapidly maturing industry environment, Edwards was unsure how to identify and exploit ICF's competitive advantages. He also wished to examine inherent weaknesses in ICF's present strategy and new opportunities for the industry.

CASE 34

NOTE ON THE OIL AND GAS EXPLORATION AND PRODUCTION INDUSTRY

INTRODUCTION

1   In 1993, the oil and gas exploration and production (E&P) industry included a few large companies and thousands of smaller firms. The need for the industry's products and the price it could receive for those products were determined almost solely by factors beyond the influence of companies within the industry. The nature of the risks faced within the industry were also unusual, and it had become one of the country's most regulated mature industries. Technology development had a profound impact, enabling the industry to explore for oil and gas in areas that would never have been possible otherwise.

Industry Definition

2   The oil and gas E&P industry was classified under the Standard Industrial Classification (SIC) system as industry 1311, and defined as follows:

> This industry is made up of establishments primarily engaged in operating oil and gas field properties. Such activities include exploration for crude petroleum and natural gas; drilling, completing, and equipping wells; operation of separators, emulsion breakers, desilting equipment; and all other activities incident to making oil and gas marketable up to the point of shipment from the producing property.[1]

For this industry note, the oil and gas E&P industry was being defined to include some companies that did not have the primary SIC code of 1311. These were the integrated oil companies, which were classified by SIC as industry category 29, reflecting their refining operations. They produced substantial volumes of oil and gas and played an important role in the D&P industry. To omit them from this analysis would not provide an accurate picture of the structure of the industry.

3   Oil and gas E&P is being analyzed as a single industry, which for E&P is appropriate because the methods for discovering and technologies for recovering oil and gas are similar, and when a prospect is being drilled the company cannot be certain whether oil or gas will be found. But some distinctions between oil and gas will be made in this analysis, since on the processing and consumption side, the market forces were quite distinct and growing more so. It is important to recognize these market-based differences, since they could affect producer strategies, even within the E&P segment of the business. While it is still possible to discuss oil and gas E&P as a single industry, the expansion of differences on the market side will increasingly create a separation of the strategies and divergence in the competition within the industry.

4   The focus of this industry analysis is the *domestic* E&P industry in the United States. Many of the companies involved in the industry also have foreign operations, and international activities play a growing role in many corporate strategies. The actions of foreign E&P companies, particularly the government-owned oil companies, play a major role in world petroleum markets and affect the strategic options available to domestic companies, but they have not been a major factor in domestic markets.

This industry note was prepared by Professor John A. Pearce II of Villanova University, and Glenda Smith.

[1] *1987 Census of Mineral Industries, Crude Petroleum and Natural Gas,* Industry 1311, Bureau of the Census, Department of Commerce, 1987.

Unique Nature of E&P Industry

5   Examination of the structure of the oil and gas E&P industry requires consideration of the special nature of the industry. It produced a product that is a commodity, that is exclusively an input to the production of other industries, and that is exhaustible. The major factors that combine to make the oil and gas E&P industry unique include: (1) importance to the national economy, (2) nonrenewable nature of the product, (3) nature of competition in the industry, (4) nature of risks within the industry.

Importance to the National Economy

6   Oil and gas were inextricably linked with domestic economic fortunes. The United States has long relied on access to cheap oil as fuel for its economic growth. Despite becoming a net importer of oil following World War II, demand for oil increased with the economy's growth. Other energy sources made inroads during the 1970s, but in 1992, oil continued to supply 40 percent of total domestic energy consumed. Natural gas contributed another 25 percent. This strong dependence naturally has national security implications. With an economy dependent on oil and gas, secure access to oil and gas resources was a priority for the United States.

7   The strong link between national economic fortunes and petroleum created both advantages and problems for the industry. Cheap oil spurs economic growth by reducing a major input to production. However, low oil and gas prices seriously undermine the long-term stability of the petroleum industry. While higher prices were beneficial for the industry, the impacts of higher prices were felt by all types of consumers throughout the economy. Thus, the industry's pricing policies could appear to be working at cross-purposes to the domestic economic good.

8   In addition to the industry's role as a supplier of energy, the oil and gas E&P industry is a major employer. In 1990, the oil and gas E&P industry accounted for nearly 410,000 jobs. This represented a drop of over 40 percent from a peak during the boom period of 1981 to 1982 of about 700,000. Most of these jobs also paid well, with an average hourly rate of $16.22 in 1990. This added to the importance of these jobs to the economy, since the higher disposable income they generated contributed to local economies and the overall tax base. Few industries could readily replace these jobs at a comparable salary level.

Nonrenewable Nature of the Product

9   Oil and gas, like other mining operations, were among the few industries where the product is exhaustible. No production process, technology, or raw material inputs could create more oil or gas. Once exhausted, more oil and gas must be found. This nonrenewable nature limited a producer's ability to increase production to meet increases in demand for the product, thus increasing vulnerability to alternative suppliers (foreign imports) or substitute products (coal or alternative energy sources). The constant need to renew the sources of production of the industry by making new discoveries also made this a very expensive industry in which to operate. Companies that did not replace the volume of oil or gas they produced became, in essence, self-liquidating.

Nature of Competition in the Industry

10   Oil and gas were commodity products. The only possible way to differentiate was on the basis of quality (gravity, sulfur content), which were not within the control of the producer. A producer could not be certain of the quality of oil or gas in advance of drilling. In marketing their products, oil and gas producers had little option other than to accept the price offered, with no basis (other than price) for enticing a buyer to purchase their product rather than that of another producer.

11   In 1993, oil demand in the United States exceeded supply, as demonstrated by imports that approached 50 percent of total demand. While excess demand had allowed imports to account for a substantial percentage of the market, this inroad had not come at the expense of domestic producers. Although the cost of production in many parts of the world was lower than in the United States, the addition of transportation costs meant domestic oil remained attractive to buyers. Thus, while the product was undifferentiated, a substantial market for the product existed, and domestic producers were able to sell all the oil they could produce. While some competition among producers existed, competition was more limited than in an industry where increases by one producer come largely at the expense of others.

12   In 1987, natural gas began evolving into a highly competitive market. The removal of most price controls and broadening of rules governing access to transportation account for much of this change. Demand for natural gas was increasing; however, unlike oil, the domestic gas market could not take all that could be produced, increasing the competition among producers for access to transportation and to buyers.

13   The most substantial competition in the E&P industry was for access to the best prospects for locating large deposits of oil or gas. Since companies had to replace their production to stay even, and increase reserves to grow, their options were limited. To add to reserves companies could:

· Locate new deposits through exploration (discoveries).
· Further define existing deposits through development (extensions and revisions).
· Employ sophisticated technologies to increase the producibility of existing reserves (improved recovery).
· Purchase reserves from other producers.

Since the largest potential payoffs come through exploration, many of the largest companies had focused efforts there, increasing competition for prospects. But all four methods of replacing reserves played a role in the strategies and competitive stance of companies of all sizes.

14   Larger oil or gas discoveries generally had built-in economies of scale, creating lower production costs. However, even rivalry for these prospects was not generally cutthroat. Since companies spread the risk of the E&P business by taking fractional interests in properties (see below), they found themselves working with another company as often as competing against them. In competing for offshore leases, or acquisition of acreage or properties from another producer, all potential bidders had access to the same information, although they likely would interpret it differently. The difference in bids was generally based on whether the property fit well into the company's portfolio and whether the company believed it had expertise or a technical approach that would allow it to exploit the opportunity better than someone else.

Nature of Industry Risks

15   In most industries, a producer making an investment in increasing productive capacity could be fairly certain what the total investment required would be and what the increase in capacity would be and so could perform a discounted cash flow on the investment to evaluate against alternatives. While some uncertainty might exist, for an established process with substantial demand for the good produced, the risk was quite low. This was not true for the oil and gas E&P industry. Finding oil and gas was sometimes more of an art than a science. While science and technology could increase the probability of finding hydrocarbons, until the well was drilled, the risk remained quite high. Thus, in 1991, 27 percent of all oil or gas wells drilled in the United States were dry holes (not finding commercial quantities of hydrocarbons). For exploratory wells looking for hydrocarbons in new areas, the risks were even higher; 76 percent of wells were dry holes in 1991.

16   Even after oil or gas was discovered, the volume and the producibility[2] were highly uncertain. Subsurface conditions could be encountered (during drilling or production) that required additional measures not anticipated in the initial cash flow analysis; these measures could have a profound effect on project economics. The amount of brine produced with the oil or gas, which must be disposed of as a waste, also depended on subsurface conditions and added to a producer's costs. Stated simply, oil and gas producers making investments to increase capacity could not be certain they would achieve any increase in productive capacity, or how large an increase they would achieve, or what it would cost. The nature of the risks these producers faced affected the strategies pursued by companies within the industry.

---

[2] The porosity and permeability of the rock, the size and shape of the trap, and other factors combine to affect the producer's ability to get the oil or gas out of the ground. Simply finding oil or gas is not enough; unless conditions are favorable, recovering economic quantities may not be feasible.

17   For oil producers, an additional risk also existed in the price of oil. Domestic oil producers had no control over the price of oil; it was established in world petroleum markets, and since the United States did not export, oil produced here had no effect. In addition, the price of oil bore little relationship to the cost of production, so fluctuations might have been unpredictable. Lacking any influence over the price they would receive for their product, domestic oil producers faced additional uncertainties in planning their investments to increase production. Most wells produce over a long time (often decades). Wells in riskier "frontier" areas may require 5 to 10 years from acquiring the lease to commencing production. The uncertainty of oil prices (and volatility since 1979) complicated the evaluation of potential investments and, ultimately, strategy formulation.

18   Most successful companies handled this risk by diversifying their investment over a large number of prospects. Most oil and gas wells had multiple "owners." Although the well was operated by a single partner, many other producers may own a ⅛, 1/16, or even a 1/32 interest. The largest companies had typically taken much larger shares in the wells they participated in, but even with them it was unusual to have 100 percent ownership. By spreading their investment over a larger number of wells, they reduce their potential profits from a really successful well, but they also reduce their risk of a major loss should the well be a dry hole. In 1985, when Phillips Petroleum was trying to reduce the debt incurred to stave off a takeover attempt, it adopted a strategy of spreading risks further by taking a smaller position in many projects. Where it would typically have taken a 50 percent interest, it began taking 25 percent or less, depending on the risk and cost involved.

HISTORY OF THE INDUSTRY

19   Birth of the oil industry in the United States was generally associated with a well drilled by Col. Edwin Drake in Pennsylvania in 1859. While petroleum from oil seeps had been in use for some time, Drake's well proved that oil could be found by drilling through rock. With increasing demand for oil for lamps, an established market and means of supplying it came together to create an industry. Interestingly, Drake's oil sold for $20 per barrel, a price that would not be seen again until 1979.

20   With little technology to assist in locating oil deposits, early exploration was largely a matter of luck. Enough oil was produced to satisfy demand, but the industry was not troubled by excess capacity. That changed in 1901 with the discovery of Spindletop field in Texas. Previous wells had required pumping the oil to the surface. Subsurface pressure at Spindletop forced the oil to the surface, creating the nation's first gusher. The blowout during the drilling of Spindletop left over 800,000 barrels of oil on the ground around the drilling site before it could be capped.[3] With a single well, overcapacity in the industry arrived. The productivity of Spindletop, along with the new techniques and theories tested in its completion, provided incentive for many new entrants to the industry, increasing the overcapacity and pushing the price to a few cents per barrel. Oil production that exceeded demand in the United States would continue until after World War II, when rapid industrial growth would lead to increasing oil imports.

21   For many years, natural gas was perceived as a worthless by-product of oil production and the gas was vented (to the atmosphere) or flared (burned) to get rid of it. Residential and commercial use of natural gas began to grow during the 1950s, quadrupling demand between 1950 and 1970. In the 1970s, as the use of natural gas for electric power generation increased, deliverability problems led to skepticism about the reliability of natural gas as a fuel. As a result, in 1978, Congress prohibited the construction of new generating plants using gas as a fuel, a restriction that was only recently removed. Other regulatory constraints, such as price controls, had kept markets for gas artificial. At some points, these constraints reduced the incentive to produce, while at others they encouraged the development of high-cost resources that would not otherwise have been economic.

---

[3] To provide additional perspective, this volume of oil is nearly three times the amount of oil spilled by the Exxon Valdez accident.

EXHIBIT 1
Technology Development Sustains Domestic Production

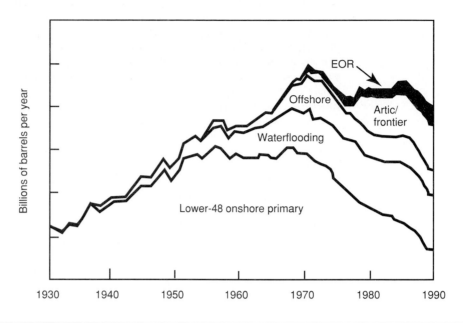

Source: U.S. Department of Energy, Office of Fossil Energy.

Factors Associated with Industry Growth

22   Increased industrialization and economic growth had developed markets for the products of the oil and gas E&P industry. The growth of the industry could be mostly attributed to external factors, not to any actions by the industry itself. With the increased availability of oil signaled by the Spindletop discovery, demand for oil could readily expand from lamp oil to other types of fuel. This was a natural market expansion that was energized by entrepreneurs outside the industry.

23   Although the oil and gas E&P industry had often suffered from boom and bust cycles, most economic conditions contributed to industry growth. Low oil prices spurred economic growth, increasing demand, and allowing producers to increase their capacity. High oil prices, while somewhat limiting to the economy, increased cash flow to the industry, again allowing producers to make the investments needed to increase capacity. Trouble for the industry could arise from low oil prices over a sustained period (as between 1986 and 1993). Since low prices limited the capital available for reinvestment while demand continued to increase, insufficient drilling could occur to replace the oil or gas that was being produced. The most favorable conditions for industry growth include stable, predictable prices at a level sufficient to provide the capital the industry needs for reinvestment without hampering economic growth.

24   Another major factor contributing to the growth of the E&P industry had been technology. Spindletop was the first test of rotary drilling technology, which revolutionized the drilling industry. The concept of injecting water into a reservoir to "push" the remaining oil to a producing well was discovered by accident in the 1920s, and by the 1950s, waterflooding became prevalent and kept many wells producing years longer than would have otherwise been possible. The technology to drill wells offshore expanded the reach of oil companies into the highly productive provinces of the Gulf of Mexico. Alaska's contribution to domestic production could not have occurred without dramatic improvements in technology to allow drilling and production in such hostile environments. Enhanced oil recovery (EOR) techniques had allowed producers to get more oil out of the ground and, in 1991, accounted for 10 percent of domestic production. Exhibit 1 shows the impact of technology development on industry production.

Major Transition Periods for the E&P Industry

25   The first major transition for the industry occurred with the breakup of the Standard Oil Trust. Until then, a substantial portion of domestic oil production was controlled by this enormous company. In antitrust action, the government claimed this high degree of concentration was detrimental to competition (and ultimately prices), so the Standard Oil Trust was broken into several independent entities as a means of increasing competition.[4] This breakup was aimed primarily at the refining aspect of the business, rather than E&P. Competition for properties and employees increased somewhat, but the supply of available, attractive prospects for drilling was sufficient to meet the demand of the new companies. No price impact was felt on the E&P side.

26   Two major transitions in the E&P industry resulted from rapid price increases caused by external forces. The first, the price increase of 1973–74 associated with the Arab oil embargo, caused prices to double (from $3.39 to $6.74 a barrel). In a highly oil dependent economy, this rapid increase was painful. For domestic producers, however, the reaction to dependence on imported oil created incentives to add to productive capacity. Higher prices provided the needed capital, and the number of wells drilled grew by 40 percent from 1973 to 1975. Another change was occurring simultaneously that would also have a profound effect. Until 1973, the United States was the leader in world oil markets and oil prices were largely set by conditions, costs, and actions in the United States. The Arab oil embargo symbolized the emergence of other powers in the world oil markets and the beginning of a shift away from the United States.

27   Less than five years later, turmoil in the Middle East and the rising power of the Organization of Petroleum Exporting Countries (OPEC) led to another dramatic rise in oil prices. In 1978, the average price of a barrel of domestic oil at the wellhead was $8.96. By 1981, the average price had risen to $31.77 a barrel. This dramatic price increase launched an unprecedented drilling boom. Not only could producers obtain prices three- to four-fold higher than a couple of years earlier, but the tax code also added to the attractiveness of oil industry investments. The financial incentives led to an enormous number of new entrants, many financed by individuals or companies from outside the industry. Many of these new entrants were ill-equipped to deal with the special nature of the risks in the E&P industry and were not very successful despite high prices. Others bid the prices for acreage, drilling rigs, drill pipe, and other supplies to astronomical highs. Banks lent money freely on projections of even higher prices, and much of the new investment was financed by debt. After prices peaked and began to return to more realistic levels, the transition continued as overcapacity by suppliers, changes to the tax code, and the need to service substantial debt continued to affect industry operations. Moreover, the transition to a truly international market for oil was complete. Domestic producers could no longer exercise any influence over the price of oil. While they were pleased to accept prices set by others when prices were high, inability to affect the free fall in prices forced producers to accept that prices were now being set in world markets.

28   The fallout from the bust led to a huge number of bankruptcies and a wave of merger and acquisition activity from 1982 to 1984. A fundamental shift had occurred; for many companies it was now cheaper to replace reserves by buying them from a financially troubled, smaller company than to explore for them. The actions of T. Boone Pickens and other corporate raiders contributed to the forced restructuring, industry megamergers, and consolidation among the industry's largest producers that occurred in 1984, when Chevron bought Gulf, Texaco bought Getty, and Mobil bought Superior.

29   The rapid downward spiral of oil prices in 1986 and changes in financial markets led many companies to a much shorter-term perspective, emphasizing the need to satisfy shareholders with a quick return on investment. While trying to recover from its own forced restructuring, Phillips Petroleum emphasized taking the shortest path from the wellhead to cash flow, by reducing risk. Total spending also fell due to the need to service debt. In this respect, Phillips was not alone. A survey of the capital spending by companies involved in mergers or restructuring found that capital spending (investment) by those companies dropped by four times as much as for companies that had remained essentially intact.

---

[4] Several of 1993's largest oil companies, including Exxon, Chevron, Mobil, Amoco, and BP America (formerly Sohio), were formed from the former Standard Oil Trust.

30   While this short-term perspective for shareholder enrichment had abated slightly between 1990 and 1993, producers clearly examined potential investments with much different criteria than they did before 1979. Price uncertainty, especially for natural gas, continued to affect business strategies. Some speculated that a continuation of low oil and gas prices could spur another round of merger and acquisition activity.

CHARACTERIZATION OF INDUSTRY STRUCTURE

31   The structure of the oil and gas E&P industry was characterized by a large number of companies, widely diverse in size. The industry was highly concentrated, but could be segmented into six major strategic groups, based on their level of vertical integration and the size of domestic oil and gas reserves. Companies had several ways of developing and maintaining a competitive advantage, and several key success factors applied to the companies within this industry. Each of these industry characteristics is discussed in more detail below.

Number of Companies

32   The number of companies in the oil and gas E&P industry was difficult to determine with precision. While the large operators were well known, they comprised only a small portion of all operators. The small operators were not well known and were difficult to identify because they went in and out of business, altered their corporate identities, and changed addresses frequently. In 1987, as part of its annual production and reserves survey, the Energy Information Administration (EIA) counted 27,329 operators that operated at least one well. In its 1987 census of the mineral industries, the Bureau of Census found 10,203 "establishments" in SIC code 1311, over 94 percent of which had fewer than 10 employees.

33   Approximately 95 percent of the companies within the industry were privately held. The *Oil & Gas Journal* annually compiled the OGJ400 report of the largest publicly traded oil and gas companies. Bankruptcies, mergers, and acquisitions had substantially reduced the number of companies of all sizes and types active in the industry. Comparing the first OGJ400 listing from 1983 with the 1990 listing indicated that 252 of the 400 companies had left the E&P industry by 1990. Many of these companies went out of business or were sold, and many others sold their producing properties and undeveloped acreage, exiting the E&P industry. In 1991, *Oil & Gas Journal* had to convert its annual compilation to the OGJ300, since industry consolidation had reduced the number of publicly traded firms.

Concentration Ratios

34   The oil and gas E&P industry was highly concentrated, as measured by (1) production of oil and gas on a barrel of oil equivalent (BOE)[5] basis, to measure market concentration, and (2) reserves of oil and gas on a BOE basis, to indicate future market potential. Exhibit 2 shows the concentration ratios for the top eight firms in the E&P industry for selected years from 1981 to 1991.

35   With nearly 40 percent of production controlled by the eight largest firms, the E&P industry was highly concentrated, and substantial market power rested with these firms. The top eight firms were selected as a measure of concentration because the volume of reserves held fell off quickly after the eighth largest firm in the industry.[6] Between 1981 and 1991, concentration of production in the top firms within the industry increased by about 3 percentage points. Nearly all of this growth was due to the megamergers that occurred in 1984, when 3 of the largest companies purchased other companies within the top 15 in the industry. An examination of concentration ratios based on BOE reserves

---

[5] Natural gas is converted to oil equivalent on a heating value basis. The approximate value of 6,000 cubic feet of natural gas per barrel of oil was used.

[6] The BOE reserves of the 9th largest firm are less than 53 percent of the total for the 8th largest company.

EXHIBIT 2
Domestic E&P Industry Concentration Ratios (eight largest firms)*

Year	Production†	Reserves†
1981	34.0%	39.7%
1984	36.9	45.8
1985	39.0	42.7
1987	38.9	39.6
1988	39.2	41.0
1989	38.9	42.3
1990	37.8	42.3
1991	37.4	41.4

Note: Decline in concentration ratio for reserves between 1984 and 1987 is largely due to the write-down of Alaskan North Slope gas reserves by ARCO, BP America, and Exxon before their removal from U.S. reserve totals by the Energy Information Administration.
*Amoco, ARCO, BP America, Chevron, Exxon, Mobil, Shell, and Texaco.
†Oil and gas represented on a barrel of oil equivalent (BOE) basis.

disclosed a similar picture. Reserves represent the industry's backlog of productive capacity, providing insight into the companies that may wield market power in the future. The ratios imply that the industry could be expected to continue to be highly concentrated.

Strategic Groups

36   Common usage within the E&P industry divided industry participants into two groups—the majors and the independents. Most companies clearly fall into one group or the other, with 10 to 20 companies potentially switching groups depending on who was defining *major*. In general, the major companies were considered to be the integrated oil companies. For income tax purposes, this definition was used to determine eligibility for certain deductions.

37   But to the extent that strategic groups were considered to follow similar strategies, two broad classifications were inadequate. The number of potential dimensions for classifying companies within the industry was large—onshore versus offshore, domestic versus foreign, giant fields versus stripper wells, and oil versus gas, among others. While all of these distinctions were relevant, for the purpose of this analysis, two alternative dimensions had been used for classifying companies—level of vertical integration and size (based on BOE domestic reserves). Since companies could be vertically integrated on either the oil side (refining and marketing operations) or the gas side (pipelines and gas distribution utilities), this separation had been considered among integrated companies in forming strategic groups. Since the size of a company's reserve base indicated future production capability (and the ability to generate cash flow for reinvestment), size of reserves was determined to be an appropriate determinant of strategic groups. However, since the industry was so highly concentrated, alternative classification schemes would probably result in little realignment of companies between groups.

38   Using available data for more than 60 large publicly traded oil and gas E&P companies, the industry had been divided into six strategic groups along the dimensions of integration and size of reserves as mapped in Exhibit 3. Group 1 was comprised of the 11 largest vertically integrated oil companies. Group 2 companies were also large, integrated oil companies, but these companies had larger interests in gas and were quite a bit smaller than the Group 1 companies. Group 3 was the integrated gas companies, with a substantial portion of their revenues received from gas pipeline or local distribution utility operations. Group 4 was comprised of contract drilling companies with substantial oil and gas operations; most would not be included, but their reserves placed them in the Top 100, and for many, future success depends on profitable E&P operations. Group 5 was a broadly defined group that included numerous medium to large nonintegrated companies; many were niche

EXHIBIT 3
Map of Strategic Groups in the E&P Industry

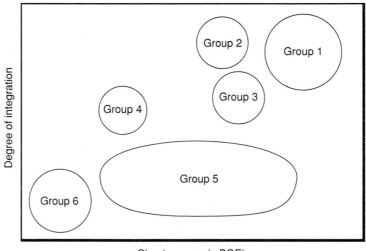

players. Group 6 included all the remaining companies within the industry—the thousands of small independent operators. Exhibit 4 summarizes the primary characteristics and general competencies associated with each of the strategic groups.

39   The first strategic group was comprised of 11 very large integrated oil companies. These companies all were active both in the United States and abroad, although ARCO, Shell (the U.S. subsidiary of Royal/Dutch Shell), and BP America (the U.S. subsidiary of British Petroleum) concentrated their operations more in the United States, while some others were increasingly moving overseas. Their substantial refining operations provided these companies with a cushion against the cyclical nature of the industry and oil price fluctuations. When oil prices were high, the E&P side of the business profited while refining suffered. When oil prices were low, the opposite was true. This cushion assured that these companies would have the cash flow available to pursue attractive opportunities, even in a down market.

40   The companies in strategic Group 1 all had R&D departments and made extensive use of advanced technology. These companies were more likely than the rest of the industry to replace production through enhanced recovery techniques. Traditionally, as technology was developed it was generally held proprietary for a period, then licensed to others as appropriate. New technologies assisted in creating competitive advantages for these companies.

41   With advanced technologies and substantial capital, the companies in Group 1 pursued the opportunities that represented the largest potential deposits of oil or gas. As the domestic onshore resource base matured (the big deposits had already been found), these companies shifted their focus to the offshore, frontier areas (such as Alaska), and, increasingly, overseas, where the potential for a large find was much higher. Although these companies had substantial gas production, most of them concentrated their activities in oil, since they needed oil to supply their refineries.

Potential Competitive Advantages

42   Companies in the domestic oil and gas E&P industry created and maintained competitive advantages in four primary ways:

· Attaining economies of scale.
· Establishing expertise in a particular area.

EXHIBIT 4
Characteristics of the Strategic Groups in the Domestic E&P Industry

Group	General Characteristics	Vertically Integrated?	Conduct R&D?	Domestic/ International	Areas of Expertise	Concerns/Areas Improvement	Key Success Factors/Outlook
1	Largest companies; largest portion of reserves were oil	Yes—oil	Yes	International operations account for around 40% for group as whole	Use of advanced technology; financial capacity; offshore, Arctic, other technical plays	Finding costs highest in industry; many not replacing reserves	Reserve replacement; access to large prospects; lowering finding costs; application of technology to improve recovery
2	Quite a bit smaller than Group 1, but still sizable companies; reserves a mix of oil and gas but slanted to oil	Yes—oil, but much smaller portion of operations	Limited—Conoco only one with major R&D	Some international, but primary focus domestic	Good at replacing production; good success with technology	Maintaining baseload supply of domestic crude to supply their refineries	Gaining access to latest technology; finding areas where competition with Group 1 unnecessary
3	Substantial portion of revenue from gas pipeline and local gas distribution utility operations	Yes—gas	No—but do contribute to Gas Research Institute	Domestic focus	Well-positioned to exploit growth in gas markets	With changes in regulation, pipeline operations could be less profitable	Must keep finding costs low, especially if prices remain low
4	Primarily contract drilling companies, but maintain reserves that would place them in top 100 companies	Yes—suppliers	No	Domestic focus for E&P operations; contract drilling international	Varies, but no clear expertise in E&P	Cash from E&P reinvested to keep drilling operations going; not replacing reserves	E&P potential source of revenue to balance poor performance in drilling; must keep finding costs low; must replace reserves
5	Broadly defined group that includes numerous medium-to-large non-integrated companies; reserves fairly balanced between oil and gas	No	Very limited	Domestic	Most were niche players; many were low-cost producers; most good at replacing production	With no integration, price fluctuations hit hard	Continue to increase technological sophistication; need strong balance sheet as best hedge to price swings; property sales by large companies provide opportunity
6	Thousands of small companies—generally 2 groups: (1) explore, then sell properties to larger companies; (2) explore, then develop properties themselves	No	No—little use of advanced technology	Domestic; smallest companies focus on limited regions	Develop small deposits that are uneconomic for others; produce properties others cannot profitably	Lack of capital limits options; increased operating costs (due to environmental regulations, price, etc.) could cause abandonment	Property sales by large companies provide opportunities; manage finances well; limit risks; build technical capabilities

· Applying advanced technologies.
· Developing new technologies through R&D.

Each of these potential areas of competitive advantage are discussed below.

Economies of Scale

43   Economies of scale in the oil and gas E&P industry did not necessarily equate to lower costs of production like they did in other industries. The economy of scale example within the E&P industry that would be comparable to that of a large manufacturing plant would be a well with a high rate of production. This high well productivity was what allowed Middle East oil to be produced at much lower cost than most wells in the United States. While well productivity could create economies of scale, it was not a factor within the control of the producer. However, it was one of the many reasons producers preferred to explore for the largest potential discovery opportunities.

44   Economies of scale could also result from attaining a larger presence in a single field or basin. The ability to use common supply facilities or centralized waste disposal facilities could reduce the total costs of finding or producing. This was one motivation for selective divestitures and acquisitions, building a portfolio of properties to create or take advantage of this type of economy of scale.

45   In an industry as concentrated as E&P, it was reasonable to assume that substantial economies of scale accrue to the largest producers. Since the industry required substantial reinvestment to replace the oil and gas produced, larger companies generated greater cash flow and had greater access to debt or equity financing for investment opportunities. The smaller, privately held companies did not have as many resources available to take advantage of investment opportunities. The larger companies also had the resources to outbid the smaller companies for the best leases, properties, and prospects. When supplies were tight, as they were in 1980–81, the largest companies could also get better deals from drilling contractors and other suppliers, by making multiwell deals and buying in quantity.

Expertise in a Particular Area

46   Subsurface conditions were a major determinant in the ability to locate and economically produce oil or gas. Expertise in the geology, drilling processes, or recovery technologies required in a particular area could allow a company to successfully exploit opportunities that other companies could not. Since reservoirs with a similar geologic deposition were believed to have similar recovery factors, operations in a particular area could provide a producer with expertise in anticipating and solving the problems unique to that environment. This expertise could translate to lower costs than may be faced by another producer less familiar with that area. While expertise could benefit producers throughout the nation, these benefits were most pronounced in the unconventional, higher-cost, and frontier areas such as Alaska and offshore.

Application of Advanced Technologies

47   As discussed previously, development and application of technology had made substantial contributions to the growth of the E&P industry. Application of advanced technologies could allow companies to:

· Better define their drilling prospects, thereby lowering the risk of a dry hole (e.g., 3-D seismic technology).
· Drill a well faster or less expensively (e.g., improved drilling mud, measurement-while-drilling technology).
· Increase the volume of oil produced from a reservoir (e.g., fracturing technologies, horizontal drilling, enhanced oil recovery techniques).
· Exploit oil and gas deposits in difficult environments (e.g., subsea completions for deep water, ice islands for Arctic sea, directional drilling under wetlands).
· Reduce environmental compliance costs (e.g., closed drilling systems to recycle and reduce waste volume).

Companies that mastered the application of these types of advanced technologies were more successful than their competitors. This advantage derived from developing resources for which other companies lacked capabilities or being able to develop resources more cost-effectively.

48   For example, although initially more costly than conventional techniques, advanced secondary and enhanced oil recovery technologies could be employed profitably, as demonstrated by the South Belridge field in California. Shell purchased South Belridge in 1979 for nearly 2.5 times the estimated reserves value. It immediately implemented a technology-driven development plan that tripled production. By 1989, Shell had already produced more oil than was estimated to remain when the field was purchased and had raised estimates of ultimate recovery by 250 percent.

R&D to Develop New Techniques

49   In most industries, R&D serves as a source of new product development or product differentiation. While R&D expenditures do not serve that purpose in the E&P industry, they could provide important sources of competitive advantage. Technology had allowed the industry to operate in environments where it was not previously possible and to prolong production. A 1965 study by the National Petroleum Council (NPC) determined that advances in technology after WW II had reduced costs by between $0.85 and $1.00 per barrel produced (oil sold for around $3 per barrel in 1965). A 1990 NPC analysis confirms continuation of this trend, estimating that technology advances had resulted in a 3 percent per year decline in drilling costs since 1970.

50   Only the largest companies within the industry engage in E&P-related R&D. While the exact number of companies was not known, it was likely less than 50, out of the 10,000-plus total companies within the industry. Thus, to the extent that advances in technology create competitive advantages, they were not well diffused throughout the industry. Even as technologies began to mature and the major companies no longer held them as proprietary, technology transfer to the smaller oil companies was poor.

51   In 1985, as ARCO was restructuring, it began to redirect resources toward R&D. With a large inventory of prospects, particularly on the North Slope of Alaska, its strategy involved developing those properties as economically as possible, with production research a key to reducing development costs. ARCO estimated that the development of its West Sak field in Alaska would take 8,000 to 10,000 wells. If drilling costs could be reduced by $100,000 per well, ARCO would save $1 billion—far more than it was spending on research. Ultimately, ARCO wanted to reduce drilling costs from roughly $1 million per well to $500,000 to $600,000 per well on the North Slope.[7]

52   The competitive advantage associated with having an R&D group was twofold: (1) new technologies or practices developed in the lab could be applied in the field to provide a cost or technological advantage, and (2) R&D personnel could serve a consulting function, applying their expertise to assist with problem-solving in the field. In the first case, the new technology could be held proprietary until the advantage began to erode, then licensed for use by other companies, generating additional revenue. In the latter, the availability of experts from various disciplines that could apply their knowledge to field-specific solutions could create a cost advantage within a particular area. In both cases, companies that engage in R&D were likely to hold advantages over those who do not, even companies that generally employ advanced techniques.

Key Success Factors for the Industry

53   To be successful, all E&P companies must replace their production with new reserves; if production was not replaced, the company became self-liquidating. For the largest companies, who had some of the highest finding costs in the industry, identifying ways to lower the costs of finding and producing oil and gas was key to continued success. Although these large companies tended to operate in the highest-cost areas (offshore, Alaska), the resources developed received the same price as any other,

---

[7] Low oil prices since 1986 sabotaged ARCO's West Sak development plans. In 1993, the project remained on hold until economics improved.

making cost-efficiencies key to profitability. The largest companies were also most successful when they concentrated on the opportunities that only they were capable of pursuing—opportunities that required sophisticated technology, substantial capital, and experienced personnel.

54   Certain key factors of success applied across all companies in the domestic oil and gas E&P industry. The industry was mature to declining in the United States, with industry growth potential limited. Companies that wanted to remain active in the domestic E&P industry had to do several things:

· Replace production each year with new reserves—for an individual company this could be through discoveries, improved recovery, or purchase.
· Focus on cost containment; keep finding and operating costs low.
· Access and employ technology to exploit opportunities, including greater production from existing properties and niche opportunities such as coal-bed methane recovery.
· Maintain a strong financial position so that capital was available to pursue attractive opportunities.

These key success factors provided a yardstick against which the performance and strategies of companies within the industry could be evaluated.

CHARACTERIZATION OF INDUSTRY TRENDS

55   The petroleum industry had always been dynamic, with regulatory and external forces shaping the industry's future to a great extent. The strategies of the companies within the industry reflected the threats and opportunities presented by industry trends, which were likely to affect their ability to replace reserves and generate profits. Forces shaping the domestic oil and gas E&P industry included:

· Continuing price instability.
· Restructuring of natural gas markets.
· Increasing environmental regulatory requirements.
· Expanding exploration and development opportunities overseas.
· Growing importance of technology.

Continuing Price Instability

56   In the last two decades, the oil and gas industry experienced unprecedented volatility. After hovering near $3 a barrel (bbl) for decades, two price shocks brought oil prices to a peak of over $30/bbl in early 1981. Forecasts of $100/bbl oil by 1995 were common. Prices began dropping in 1982 and plummeted in 1986 to as low as $12/bbl. Since then, oil prices had continued to fluctuate, and in early 1993 hovered around $20/bbl. Many investments barely pass corporate hurdle criteria at this price; if prices fall below that threshold, domestic E&P would become even less attractive. Price controls on natural gas created a complex structure within which some gas sold for $0.35/thousand cubic feet (mcf), while other gas earned as much as $10/mcf. As price controls were removed, gas prices generally fell, reaching a low (on average) of $1/mcf in early 1992, and rising slowly into 1993.

57   Several factors influenced price instability. Continuing conflict with OPEC concerning production levels was one factor. OPEC member states' political stability also increased the uncertainty of supply. Additionally, improved market information concerning petroleum stocks, production quotas, and world and industry events had increased the trading activity in petroleum futures markets and had increased the price volatility. Domestic producers were price takers in the oil market; the lack of price stability increases the risk associated with exploration and production.

58   Despite the short-term price uncertainty, the overall prices of oil and gas were expected to rise moderately through 2010. World oil prices were expected to rise at approximately 2 percent annually, and domestic natural gas prices were expected to increase by about 5 percent per year.

But in neither case were these likely to be steady increases; continual upward and downward swings were more likely.

Restructuring of Natural Gas Markets

59 Natural gas markets were quite different from oil markets. Natural gas cannot be readily stored and could be transported (in its gaseous state) only by pipeline. Traditionally, pipeline companies had been the only potential purchasers of natural gas, just as refiners were for oil. However, the gradual deregulation of the gas industry and recent actions by the Federal Energy Regulatory Commission (FERC) were dramatically transforming the nature of natural gas markets. FERC had recently ordered (Order 646) the "unbundling" of pipeline services, allowing natural gas producers to purchase transportation services only. This allowed producers to sell directly to end users, even in other parts of the country. In some cases, producers and large end users (industrial or utility) had the option of bypassing local gas distribution utilities. The full impact of these changes on the market for natural gas was as yet unclear, however, producers would have substantially increased power within the market than had traditionally been the case.

60 An additional factor in future natural gas markets was greater potential for international movement of natural gas in liquefied form (liquefied natural gas or LNG). While the technology for liquefying natural gas and transporting it had existed for decades, it had not been economical in most situations. Some LNG does move in international markets, and the United States had previously imported small volumes of LNG from countries such as Algeria where gas production costs were very low. The United States had four terminals built for LNG imports, although only two were operating. As the technology improved and domestic gas prices rose, competition from LNG imports was increasingly likely.

Increasing Environmental Regulatory Requirements

61 The domestic oil and gas E&P industry was subject to numerous environmental regulatory requirements at both the state and federal levels. This industry was spending an estimated $1.5 to $2 billion per year to comply with environmental regulatory requirements, and these costs were increasing at a rate of 3 to 5 percent per year. At the federal level, requirements stemmed from four primary environmental statutes—Resource Conservation and Recovery Act (RCRA), Safe Drinking Water Act (SDWA), Clean Water Act (CWA), and Clean Air Act (CAA). The CAA was reauthorized in 1990, resulting in substantial, stringent new requirements on air emissions that would take effect over the next several years. All three of the other statutes were due for reauthorization during the 1993 congressional session, and stringent new requirements were possible.

62 Producing oil and gas resulted in substantial volumes of wastes and by-products that must be disposed. Over 98 percent of these wastes, however, were produced water (subsurface brine or brackish water brought to the surface with oil or gas). Unlike many other industries, as a well matured and its production of oil or gas declined, the volume of waste (produced water) increased. The average well in the United States produced 6 to 7 barrels of water for every barrel of oil; for low-productivity wells in certain areas of the country, as many as 100 barrels of water were produced for each barrel of oil. Obviously, waste disposal costs were a major component of operating costs for the industry.

63 Oil and gas E&P wastes were not considered hazardous under RCRA. The justification for this exemption was the high volume, but relatively low toxicity of these wastes. Another factor in granting the exemption was the potential severe economic impacts to the industry of regulating these wastes as hazardous. Although generally low in toxicity, some of these wastes do exhibit hazardous characteristics (primarily due to benzene content), which environmental groups continue to argue pose unacceptable human health risks. These concerns could lead to reconsideration of the exemption and tend to guarantee escalating compliance requirements (and costs) even if the exemption were retained.

64 Regulatory initiatives likely to be considered under the four primary federal environmental statutes could raise operating costs for a "typical" oil or gas well by 10 to 50 percent. This could translate to as much as a 12 percent loss of oil production and a 10 percent loss of gas production. Between 7 and 19 percent of the oil that was a target for advanced recovery technologies could also be lost, and up to 25 percent of undiscovered oil resources could become uneconomical to develop. Although the production losses would be disproportionately borne by the smaller companies, the large companies would also be affected by the increased costs of compliance and reduced economics of exploration and improved recovery. Clearly, increased environmental regulatory requirements had the potential to have profound impacts on project economics.

Attractive Overseas Investment Opportunities

65   The major domestic oil and gas producers were continuing to shift their investment focus overseas. The process began in earnest after the 1986 oil price collapse. The shift was a reflection of the maturity of the domestic resource base and the lack of freedom to explore in frontier areas offshore and in Alaska. For example, during 1986 to 1990, Mobil Oil invested approximately 60 percent of its E&P budget domestically. By 1992, this ratio was reversed, with 60 percent going overseas. Chevron likewise spent over 60 percent of its exploration budget outside the United States and had indicated that it would continue to do so until U.S. government policies changed.

66   The potential for large discoveries existed primarily in frontier areas where relatively little exploration had been conducted. With the best possible areas in the United States off-limits (the Arctic National Wildlife Refuge [ANWR] and most of the Outer Continental Shelf), the available frontier areas existed overseas. Deepwater areas of the Gulf of Mexico held the greatest potential of available domestic prospects, and leasing of these areas was becoming increasingly competitive. A large discovery could generate substantial economies of scale. The typical new Oklahoma well, for example, produced a maximum of around 300 bbl/day, compared to 5,000 bbl/day or more at wells in many other parts of the world. Developing nations, eager to attract investment capital and hoping to locate large deposits of oil or gas, were offering very attractive terms to companies willing to explore within their country. These factors were also contributing to the shift away from domestic exploration.

67   In addition to the exploration areas being offered throughout Southeast Asia, Africa, South America, and areas of the Middle East, the countries of the former Soviet Union represented a substantial foreign investment opportunity. Many of these countries needed to restore production levels (which were falling) both to meet internal energy needs and to generate export revenue. Numerous giant oil and gas fields existed in the former Soviet Union; many of them had been inadequately explored or developed and represented huge potential. However, political instability and the specification of clear contract rights and obligations remained a concern of companies investing in these countries.

68   To finance their overseas investment, the major domestic producers initiated a divestment of domestic properties, assessing leases and wells for their strategic fit, and selling the nonstrategic properties. Generally, these were the smaller, less-productive properties in the company's portfolio. For example, since 1987 Chevron had sold or traded about 2,300 U.S. fields, including more than 450 in 1992. The 1992 sales accounted for about 13 percent of Chevron's domestic production. When its divestments were complete, Chevron would focus on around 360 properties in California, Texas, and the Gulf of Mexico, down from 3,500 in 1985. With other major companies doing likewise, an unprecedented number of domestic producing properties were for sale; most would be purchased by midsize to small companies that could operate them more cost-effectively (e.g., lower overhead rates) or who sought to exploit a particular niche in the market, but were generally less technologically sophisticated.

Growing Role of Technology Development

69   While the maturity of the domestic resource base made overseas investment attractive, substantial volumes of oil remained in domestic reservoirs. Conventional oil recovery technologies allowed producers to recover only about one-third of the oil in a reservoir. The remaining two-thirds was a target for advanced recovery technologies. Over 340 billion barrels of oil remained in known reservoirs in the United States, which could potentially be recovered via advanced technology. This

compared with slightly less than 25 billion barrels of oil considered economically recoverable. This remaining resource represented a substantial target; however, generally only the largest companies in the industry possessed the technological sophistication and financial resources to apply advanced technologies successfully.

70   Producers who developed and employed advanced recovery techniques could obtain properties that others were willing to abandon because production had reached its economic limit. Since technology in a mature industry has the potential to rejuvenate the industry, advanced recovery technologies could rejuvenate an old field, and producers with appropriate expertise could benefit. The tax laws also provided an incentive for employing enhanced oil recovery techniques, providing producers with an added bonus and helping to reduce the total cost of the investment.

71   As exploration increasingly focused on deeper water areas offshore, the Arctic, and other frontier areas, technology grew in importance. Production in these areas would not be possible without the technological advances of the past 20 years, and future success was keyed to technology as well. Technological advances could help to reduce drilling and production costs, increasing profit margins and lowering finding costs. They could also develop new environmental techniques to reduce potential risks or increase the level of protection. Even companies exploring overseas would find technology crucial, as many unexplored areas may be in harsh (jungle, permafrost) or sensitive (rain forest, wetlands) environments, where known techniques could not provide sufficient protection. Technology and the R&D expenditures that develop new technologies would be increasingly important to achieving and maintaining a competitive advantage.

CASE 35

ATLANTIC RICHFIELD CORPORATION

OVERVIEW

1   Atlantic Richfield Company (ARCO) was a worldwide, vertically integrated hydrocarbons company that traced its history back to July 1, 1866, the beginning of Atlantic Refining Company, its principal predecessor. Another ARCO predecessor, Richfield Oil Co., was responsible for the first discovery of oil in Northern Alaska. In 1993, ARCO's operations encompassed all aspects of the oil and gas business: exploration and production of crude oil, natural gas, and natural gas liquids, plus refining, marketing, and transporting petroleum products. ARCO also mined and marketed coal and had interests in two petrochemical companies. ARCO had three subsidiaries engaged in oil and gas exploration and production in separate geographic areas: ARCO Alaska, ARCO Oil and Gas (lower-48 states), and ARCO International.

2   In 1985, ARCO's return on equity had fallen below its cost of equity capital and the stock price reflected its poor performance. Merger-mania was rampant in the industry, and ARCO feared a takeover attempt. Consequently, ARCO undertook a major restructuring to improve shareholder value and reduce the chance of being taken over. The company continued to follow the basic business strategies crafted at that time, which it felt were sufficiently flexible to respond to short-term economic conditions.

3   However, in 1991 the company undertook another restructuring of its lower-48 oil and gas operations. Concern over continued low natural gas prices led the company to carefully review operations, resulting in steps to reduce operating costs and refocus the company's exploration program so that it could compete more effectively. This process continued throughout 1992 as the company sought to identify its strategic properties and carry out programs of consolidation, cost reduction, and divestiture of nonstrategic properties. During 1992, ARCO divested nearly 1,100 oil and gas properties, totaling approximately 6 percent of the company's 1991 lower-48 production. In early 1993, ARCO sold its interests in another 146 fields (36 percent of the 1993 total) that comprised an additional 4 percent of 1991 production. In total, ARCO sold over $1 billion in properties between 1985 and early 1993.

4   ARCO was generally recognized as one of the best performers in the oil and gas industry, often generating one of the highest rates of return. For example, in 1990, return on stockholders' equity was 29.3 percent. Despite somewhat difficult years, ARCO continued to increase its dividend payments and generated a 10.1 percent and 11.8 percent return on stockholders' equity in 1991 and 1992, respectively. In 1992, ARCO had the highest return to stockholders of any large publicly traded domestic exploration and production (E&P) company. This financial strength resulted from generally sound management and prudent investment policies. Similarly, ARCO's yields on its E&P investments were among the highest in the industry.

5   Application of technology was one of ARCO's strengths. In 1991, over 55 percent of total reserve additions resulted from the application of improved recovery techniques; however, this ratio fell somewhat during 1992. ARCO's major efforts were focused on areas that required sophisticated technology for success. When needed, ARCO's R&D department had been able to respond with the technologies required to support and consolidate ARCO's competitive advantage. As technology became increasingly important to increase the recovery from known reservoirs or to explore frontier environments, ARCO was well positioned to take advantage of any opportunities. With its expertise

This case was prepared by Professor John A. Pearce II of Villanova University, and Glenda Smith.

in technology development and application, ARCO was able to gain a competitive edge in pursuit of any opportunities. However, cost-cutting measures at ARCO led to a sizable reduction in its research staff. In 1992, the company's R&D expenditures fell by 25 percent to $89 million (including refining, chemicals, and E&P). These factors could begin to erode ARCO's technological advantage over some competitors by the late 1990s.

FOCUS IN 1993

6   Of the large U.S.-based oil companies that were not subsidiaries of a foreign company, ARCO had traditionally maintained the greatest domestic focus. In 1993, ARCO still maintained 92 percent of its oil reserves and 62 percent of its gas reserves in the United States. Over 70 percent of the company's domestic oil reserves and 44 percent of its domestic natural gas reserves were located in Alaska. The remainder of ARCO's reserves were primarily in Southern California, along the Gulf Coast, and in the Gulf of Mexico.

7   Oil comprised over 74 percent of ARCO's domestic oil and gas reserves. Much of this was Alaskan North Slope (ANS) crude oil. ARCO operated two of the country's most efficient refineries—in Carson, California (near Los Angeles), and Cherry Point, Washington; both operated exclusively on ANS crude oil. Together, these refineries required 425,000 barrels of oil per day, or around 36 percent of ARCO's total oil production in the United States. The other oil produced by ARCO was sold to other refiners. ARCO also had a 21.3 percent interest in the Trans-Alaska Pipeline System (TAPS), which transported crude oil over 800 miles from Alaska's North Slope to the marine terminal at Valdez, Alaska.

Alaska

8   ARCO's long-term success in Alaska continued during the early 1990s, as four new oil fields were discovered—two of them potentially giant fields. These included the Sunfish discovery in Cook Inlet, in an area that had not yielded a discovery since 1965 and that most companies had written off. In the eastern Beaufort Sea, ARCO discovered Kuvlum, which was about 60 miles east of Prudhoe Bay. The other two discoveries were also in the Beaufort Sea, about 10 miles west of the Kuparuk River field. While further drilling would be required to determine the extent of these discoveries and generate development plans, their proximity to existing operations held out the potential for economies of scale from sharing staging and some production facilities. During 1992, ARCO also worked out a property trade with Unocal Corp., swapping properties that would strengthen ARCO's position on the North Slope and Unocal's in the Cook Inlet Basin. ARCO had perfected the drilling techniques and operating practices that allowed it to cost-effectively exploit the large discoveries that were possible in the still largely unexplored areas of Alaska's North Slope.

9   Prudhoe Bay, the nation's largest oil field, was co-operated by ARCO and BP America. This field produced its 8 billionth barrel of oil during 1992 and daily production from the field was in natural decline. ARCO was focusing efforts in two areas: (1) capital investment in an expanded gas handling system (which would help to mitigate the decline rate somewhat), and (2) decreasing operating costs. Operating costs were reduced by 17 percent in 1992, largely due to consolidating many facilities and services with the field's co-operator. ARCO's Kuparuk River field near Prudhoe Bay was also one of the nation's largest oil fields. Production at Kuparuk continued to increase, but ARCO reduced operating costs by 4 percent in 1992. Development of the Point McIntyre field, discovered in 1989, was initiated during 1992 using ARCO's facilities at the nearby Lisburne field, creating substantial cost savings.

Lower-48 States

10   The second area where ARCO had concentrated a sizable portion of its domestic operations was in application of thermal enhanced oil recovery (EOR) techniques to improve recovery from heavy oil reservoirs, particularly in Southern California. ARCO's 1991 acquisition of Oryx's properties in Midway-Sunset allowed the company to use its existing operating structure to improve its competitive position in the field. In 1992, ARCO expanded two existing steamflood operations in Midway-Sunset, which were expected to produce an additional 4,000 barrels of oil per day at peak production.

11   Although the heavy oil recovered from ARCO's California EOR projects yielded a lower price than most lower-48 crude oils, ARCO had developed the technologies and operating practices that allowed it to produce from these properties profitably. In 1991, ARCO made two major acquisitions to add to its strong reserve base in California. As a result of these two acquisitions, two fields in Southern California, Midway-Sunset and Wilmington, accounted for 21 percent of ARCO's oil production in 1991, compared to only 11 percent in 1990.

12   However, environmental regulations had the potential to restrict ARCO's expansion of its EOR operations. New requirements under the Clean Air Act Amendments of 1990 and increasingly stringent California air quality standards (which exceeded federal requirements) had a disproportionate impact on operations in Southern California, where over one-quarter of ARCO's domestic operations were located. The ability to install new facilities to recover more oil was severely constrained by regulations that prohibited new sources of air emissions without corresponding offsets elsewhere in a producer's operations in the area. Having already installed stringent emission controls, offsets might be impossible to locate within ARCO's operations, effectively curtailing expansion. These regulations could represent an impediment to ARCO's exploitation of its reserves in this area to generate capital to pursue other opportunities (or for reinvestment). The purchase of properties that had offset potential from other companies was one possible strategy for addressing this limitation. However, the costs associated with increased environmental regulations would continue to squeeze profit margins, perhaps eroding ARCO's competitive advantage.

13   ARCO recently confronted a major environmental problem through the innovative use of a trade-off. ARCO held the lease on nearly 4,000 acres in the Coal Point area offshore California near Santa Barbara. Oil was discovered, but the state, at the urging of environmental groups, had denied ARCO the right to develop these resources, which ARCO expected to yield 80,000 to 85,000 barrels of oil per day. ARCO had filed suit to force the state to either allow development or pay damages of about $793 million to compensate for lost value. At the same time, ARCO also wanted to implement an advanced technology waterflood project to increase recovery from its leases in the Long Beach oil field, which was controlled by the state of California. In an innovative move, ARCO suggested a trade-off—for approval to install the planned project at Long Beach, it would drop the lawsuit and file a quitclaim deed to the Coal Point leases. The state accepted ARCO's offer.

14   ARCO continued to make substantial investments in the Gulf of Mexico, including development drilling in the prolific South Pass 90 field designed to exploit the complex underlying geology. The drilling program replaced 90 percent of the volume produced from this field, which had been in operation since 1972. Spurred by the Section 29 tax credit, ARCO completed an extensive drilling program for coalbed methane (gas) reserves in New Mexico's San Juan basin, adding over 550 billion cubic feet of gas reserves between 1988 and 1992. (The Section 29 tax credit expired in 1992, but the company would continue to gain tax benefits on the wells drilled for another 10 years.) Other promising lower-48 activities included application of horizontal drilling technology to develop oil reserves in Texas's Austin Chalk play and gas at North Dauphin Island offshore Alabama, improving the economics of these fields. ARCO was also active in EOR projects involving the injection of CO_2 in West Texas' Permian Basin.

15   A major focus of lower-48 operations was cost containment and finding more cost-effective operating procedures. One effort that had begun to pay dividends was expanding the role of automation at oil and gas facilities, including the use of computerized field data gathering and operations monitoring. Other cost-reduction measures implemented during 1993 included establishing longer-term alliances with service companies, consolidating certain field office and shore base activities for the Gulf of Mexico, a more cost-effective approach to offshore transportation (using boats instead of helicopters where possible), and increased "outsourcing" of various functions to contractors.

International

16   Outside the United States, over 71 percent of ARCO's reserves were natural gas, but 65 percent of 1993 foreign production was oil. ARCO's principal foreign operations were in the North Sea, Indonesia, and Dubai. Exploration areas include Algeria, China, the Congo, Dubai, Ecuador (where a discovery was announced in 1992), Egypt, Ethiopia, the North Sea, New Zealand, Romania, Syria,

EXHIBIT 1
Wells Drilled and Success Ratios

	1992	1991	1990	1989	1988	1987	1986
United States							
Exploratory wells drilled*	86	68	75	66	70	47	56
Exploratory success ratio†	18.6%	38.2%	36.0%	37.9%	40.0%	40.4%	19.6%
Development wells drilled‡	183	606	406	351	392	225	266
Development success ratio	89.6%	71.5%	89.2%	90.9%	90.8%	92.9%	94.0%
Total wells drilled	269	674	481	417	462	272	322
Total success ratio	66.9%	68.1%	80.9%	82.5%	83.1%	83.8%	81.1%
Foreign							
Exploratory wells drilled	24	25	24	18	20	15	9
Exploratory success ratio	37.5%	24.0%	25.0%	16.7%	15.0%	46.7%	44.4%
Development wells drilled	23	29	25	25	14	18	40
Development success ratio	95.7%	100.0%	96.0%	100.0%	100.0%	100.0%	97.5%
Total wells drilled	47	54	49	43	34	33	49
Total success ratio	67.0%	64.8%	61.2%	65.1%	50.0%	75.8%	87.8%

*Exploratory wells are seeking oil or gas in areas where no current production or proved reserves exist (discoveries).

†Success ratios are calculated as the wells that are successful (find commercial quantities of hydrocarbons) divided by the total number of wells drilled.

‡Development wells are seeking oil or gas in areas near current production or proved reserves (extensions, infill drilling [improved recovery and revisions]).

Turkey, and Yemen. In 1993, the greatest concentration of foreign operations was in the North Sea, where increased use of natural gas and the privatization of power generation in the United Kingdom opened new market opportunities for North Sea natural gas.

17   Development of the giant Yacheng natural gas field offshore China began in 1992 with ARCO as operator, holding a 34.3 percent working interest. This field alone added nearly 700 billion cubic feet of natural gas to ARCO's international reserve base during 1992. Production from the field was expected to begin in 1996, and long-term delivery contracts had already been obtained. Much of the gas would be transported via pipeline to a gas utility in Hong Kong.

PERFORMANCE IN 1992–93

18   Exploration had long been one of ARCO's strengths. The company generally achieved success ratios that exceeded industry averages by a substantial margin. Exhibit 1 presents ARCO's recent exploration and development well drilling performance. ARCO held leases on over 6 million undeveloped acres in the United States and 32 million undeveloped acres worldwide in 1993. During 1992 and early 1993, ARCO was the successful bidder on exploration acreage throughout Alaska, including nearly 130,000 acres near its recent Sunfish discovery. ARCO held over 1.2 million developed and undeveloped acres in Alaska.

19   Despite its exploration success, ARCO's reserves had been declining since 1988. While nonstrategic property divestitures accounted for much of the decline, incomplete replacement of oil and gas produced were also major factors. Exhibit 2 illustrates ARCO's reserves and replacement performance on a barrel of oil equivalent basis since 1986. ARCO's domestic reserve replacement ratio was quite low, but it improved when the effect of property sales was removed. However, ARCO still had not replaced 100 percent of its production since 1988, liquidating a portion of its domestic asset base. Given the early stages of development for most of ARCO's foreign properties, reserve replacement well in excess of 100 percent was expected.

20   Exhibit 3 presents ARCO's oil and gas E&P performance. ARCO's efforts to reduce production costs per barrel during 1992 were successful, yielding an increased return on E&P revenues. The reinvestment of the revenues from oil and gas production in E&P activities are presented in Exhibit 4. ARCO's reinvestment in E&P was generally lower than its primary competitors. The portion of

EXHIBIT 2
Barrel of Oil Equivalent Reserves and Replacement Ratios (thousands of barrels of oil equivalent)

	1992	1991	1990	1989	1988	1987	1986
United States							
Total reserves—January 1	3,608,333	3,762,667	3,840,333	3,891,167	3,793,667	3,715,167	3,768,333
Revisions	43,667	(1,000)	43,333	72,000	87,167	175,333	62,333
Extensions and discoveries	124,167	70,500	102,167	163,500	135,333	137,667	30,667
Improved recovery	47,000	89,500	115,333	33,000	104,833	141,000	238,500
Purchases of minerals in place	41,167	141,500	32,167	39,833	124,500	9,167	4,167
Sales of minerals in place	(155,833)	(112,667)	(30,833)	(13,833)	(11,167)	(52,667)	(61,000)
Other changes	(12,000)	—	—	—	—	—	—
Total production	(315,333)	(342,167)	(339,833)	(345,333)	(343,167)	(332,000)	(327,833)
Total reserves—December 31	3,381,167	3,608,333	3,762,667	3,840,333	3,891,167	3,793,667	3,715,167
Reserve replacement*	28%	55%	77%	85%	128%	124%	84%
Reserve replacement (excluding sales)	77%	88%	86%	89%	132%	140%	102%
Foreign							
Total reserves—January 1	589,833	509,333	438,000	472,167	372,500	361,000	340,167
Revisions	29,333	14,500	19,667	167	13,333	(40,000)	20,667
Extensions and discoveries	155,833	67,333	119,000	3,000	17,000	77,167	35,167
Improved recovery	0	0	16,000	0	0	0	0
Purchases of minerals in place	0	43,167	10,000	0	101,667	7,167	0
Sales of minerals in place	(1,000)	0	(57,500)	(1,000)	0	0	0
Other changes	833	0	0	0	0	0	0
Total production	(42,667)	(44,500)	(35,833)	(36,333)	(32,333)	(32,833)	(35,000)
Total reserves—December 31	730,500	589,833	509,333	438,000	472,167	372,500	361,000
Reserves replacement	434%	281%	299%	6%	408%	135%	160%

*Calculated by dividing revisions + extensions and discoveries + improved recovery + purchases + sales + other changes by the total volume of production.

35-5

EXHIBIT 3
Oil and Gas Revenue Accounting (thousands of dollars)

	1992	1991	1990	1989	1988	1987	1986
United States							
Total oil and gas revenues	4,070,000	4,189,000	5,184,000	4,322,000	3,600,000	4,065,000	3,404,000
Production costs	1,584,000	1,868,000	1,626,000	1,392,000	1,220,000	1,237,000	1,255,000
Exploration expenses	381,000	326,000	404,000	283,000	277,000	194,000	393,000
Depreciation, depletion, and amortization	914,000	1,046,000	1,002,000	1,094,000	1,024,000	1,050,000	1,080,000
Income tax expense	350,000	215,000	732,000	533,000	359,000	604,000	263,000
Other income (expense)	170,000	(305,000)	(167,000)	(134,000)	(136,000)	(175,000)	(104,000)
Results of operations	671,000	429,000	1,253,000	886,000	584,000	805,000	309,000
Return on E&P revenues (%)*	16.5	10.2	24.2	20.5	16.2	19.8	9.1
Foreign							
Total oil and gas revenues	844,000	915,000	805,000	592,000	501,000	573,000	456,000
Production costs	291,000	307,000	240,000	211,000	172,000	192,000	173,000
Exploration expenses	243,000	233,000	244,000	157,000	192,000	141,000	90,000
Depreciation, depletion, and amortization	236,000	244,000	215,000	192,000	141,000	90,000	188,000
Income tax expenses	32,000	52,000	30,000	40,000	42,000	77,000	29,000
Other income (expense)	(129,000)	0	0	0	(71,000)	0	(18,000)
Results of operations	171,000	79,000	76,000	(8,000)	(71,000)	13,000	14,000
Return on E&P revenues (%)*	20.3	8.6	9.4	−1.4	−14.2	2.3	3.1

*Excludes corporate G&A and overhead expenses.

EXHIBIT 4
E&P Costs Incurred and Reinvestment Ratio (thousands of dollars)

	1992	1991	1990	1989	1988	1987	1986
United States							
Exploration costs incurred	385,000	416,000	483,000	384,000	323,000	232,000	341,000
Development costs incurred	393,000	776,000	657,000	625,000	734,000	395,000	703,000
Property acquisition costs	54,000	4C1,000	151,000	128,000	600,000	49,000	18,000
Total costs incurred	832,000	1,593,000	1,291,000	1,137,000	1,657,000	676,000	1,062,000
Reinvestment ratio (%)*	33.5	68.6	36.3	38.8	69.6	23.9	49.4
Foreign							
Exploration costs incurred	270,000	275,000	232,000	173,000	232,000	163,000	120,000
Development costs incurred	388,000	258,000	233,000	216,000	209,000	90,000	293,000
Property acquisition costs	7,000	64,000	69,000	6,000	702,000	0	0
Total costs incurred	665,000	597,000	534,000	395,000	1,143,000	253,000	413,000
Foreign/worldwide costs incurred (%)	44.4	27.3	29.3	25.8	40.8	27.2	28.0
Reinvestment ratio (%)*	120.2	98.2	94.5	103.6	347.4	66.4	145.9

*Calculated as total costs incurred/(oil & gas revenues – production costs).

ARCO's E&P budget invested outside the United States grew dramatically in 1992 to over 44 percent, although many of ARCO's closest competitors invested 60 percent or more of their E&P budgets on foreign activities.

E&P INVESTMENT DECISIONS

21   In expanding its international operations, ARCO employed a careful strategy of concentrated growth. Recognizing that technology was one of the company's strengths, and that this could be utilized effectively in foreign operations, ARCO relocated its international E&P company next door to its research laboratory and began inviting research staff to operating meetings. This involvement led to an increase in the use of 3-D seismic technology, which improved ARCO's understanding of the resource potential associated with each project. ARCO's management process incorporated "postmortems" of all unsuccessful exploratory wells. A review was made to determine whether the dry hole could have been anticipated on the basis of the information available before drilling. Frequently, this process indicated the decision to drill was appropriate based on available information, but occasionally a mistake was identified and additional evaluation for similar problems was incorporated in future predrill analyses.

22   In selecting its international investment opportunities, ARCO International reviewed around 200 internally generated, competitor, and competitive sales offerings annually. Most of these opportunities could be justified in economic terms, but the risks and geologic uncertainties were so great that ARCO generally elected to invest in only the top five or six each year. In selecting its investments, ARCO had determined it had the capabilities to pursue the best opportunities anywhere in the world, without focusing on particular countries or basins. ARCO's strategy had expanded its inventory of quality foreign acreage (which had significant potential and would be explored as funds were available). ARCO regularly conducted country reviews to understand the political risks associated with its investments, and, other things begin equal, ARCO preferred to invest where its technology and risk capital were needed for the long term, rather than merely being an incremental supplier of capital to a country.

23   Another technique being used by ARCO involved spreading the risks associated with its lower-48 oil and gas E&P operations. Traditionally, ARCO had taken a major, often 100 percent working interest in the properties it operated. This was in contrast to most other domestic operators and was possible due to capital availability. However, as capital became constrained, ARCO began to reduce its working interest percentage. This allowed ARCO to participate in a greater number of wells for the same amount of capital, expanding its portfolio of opportunities, thereby spreading the risks.

24   As ARCO had responded to various external pressures such as low prices, its capital budget had been reduced. In 1991, ARCO announced a five-year capital budget of $18.6 billion for 1991–95, with $11.3 billion (61 percent) earmarked for E&P. This budget was to be distributed among the E&P subsidiaries as follows: ARCO Oil and Gas, 48 percent; ARCO International, 28 percent; ARCO Alaska, 24 percent. By early 1993, this budget had been cut substantially. Corporate spending for the subsequent five years was planned as $13.5 billion, of which 60 percent would be devoted to E&P.

25   For 1993, ARCO established a capital budget of $1.5 billion for E&P investments. While individual project investment decisions would be made by the company's three E&P operating subsidiaries (ARCO Alaska, ARCO Oil and Gas, ARCO International), corporate officials had yet to determine how to divide this total budget among the three companies, especially the amount to be invested on domestic versus foreign projects. Management's decision would be based on the threats and opportunities provided by the external environment, as well as its assessment of its ability to respond to those challenges. The operations and performance of each E&P subsidiary are summarized in Exhibit 5.

26   Questions facing management include: Should the company follow its competitors by increasing its focus overseas? If so, how quickly should it refocus? What domestic opportunities could ARCO exploit better than its competitors? Given the company's recent performance in domestic and international markets and price, economic, and political considerations, what allocation of funds was most likely to generate solid corporate performance?

EXHIBIT 5
Recent Earnings and Expenditures of ARCO's E&P Subsidiaries

	1992	1991	1990	1989	1988
ARCO Alaska, Inc.					
Earnings (millions)	$ 453	$ 413	$ 700	$ 546	$ 382
Total assets (millions)	3,542	3,700	3,724	3,850	3,977
Additions to fixed assets (millions)	294	343	298	243	214
Exploration expenses (millions)	112	76	147	69	56
Average crude oil price (per barrel)	11.41	11.23	14.84	11.71	8.51
Crude oil production (thousand barrels per day)	438.9	440.6	433.8	459.4	487.3
Oil and gas revenues (millions)*	1,828	1,806	2,350	1,964	1,514
Return on oil and gas revenues (%)†	24.8%	22.9%	29.8%	27.8%	25.2%
ARCO Oil & Gas Company (Lower-48 operations)					
Earnings (millions)	$ 192	$ 57	$ 588	$ 349	$ 231
Total assets (millions)	4,405	5,185	5,040	5,068	5,174
Additions to fixed assets (millions)	404	1,083	808	703	1,285
Exploration expenses (millions)	289	339	334	312	297
Average crude oil price (per barrel)	16.34	16.72	20.85	16.92	14.20
Average natural gas price (per thousand cubic feet)	1.66	1.54	1.67	1.68	1.69
Crude oil production (thousand barrels per day)	221.6	227.9	204.5	200.6	186.9
Natural gas production (millions cubic feet per day)	1,161	1,358	1,515	1,497	1,359
Oil and gas revenues (millions)	2,025	2,154	2,480	2,157	1,807
Return on oil and gas revenues (%)	9.5%	2.7%	23.7%	16.2%	12.8%
ARCO International Oil & Gas Company					
Earnings (millions)	$ 171‡	$ 79	$ 76	$ (8)	$ (71)
Total assets (millions)	2,415	2,466	2,205	1,902	1,895
Additions to fixed assets (millions)	551	464	454	363	1,056
Exploration expenses (millions)	185	178	170	98	132
Average crude oil price (per barrel)	18.17	18.67	20.15	16.25	14.20
Average natural gas price (per thousand cubic feet)	2.96	3.16	3.08	2.71	2.64
Crude oil production (thousands of barrels per day)	77.7	75.7	67.1	70.1	63.6
Natural gas production (million cubic feet per day)	239.7	261.2	193.5	169.2	154.1
Oil and gas revenues (millions)	774.3	817.1	711.0	583.1	478.1
Return on oil and gas revenues (%)	22.1%	9.7%	10.7%	(1.4%)	(14.9%)

*Calculated by multiplying production volumes and price.

†Calculated by dividing earnings by oil and gas revenues.

‡Includes gain from settlement on assets nationalized by Iran in the late 1970s.

CASE 36

ICF RESOURCES INCORPORATED

BACKGROUND

1   ICF Resources Incorporated (ICFR) was an energy and environmental consulting firm based in Fairfax, Virginia. A subsidiary of ICF Kaiser International, Inc. (NASDAQ-ICFI), an international engineering, construction, and consulting firm, ICFR covered all aspects of the energy business—crude oil, natural gas, coal, electric utilities, and related environmental issues. Approximately half of the company's business was from the public sector (U.S. Department of Energy, Environmental Protection Agency), while the remainder was from private-sector organizations such as oil companies, gas transmission companies, electric utilities, and banks. ICFR was often selected by the private sector to provide objective analyses of various issues and competitive situations.

COMPETITIVE ANALYSIS OBJECTIVE

2   Andrew Tejiro joined ICFR in 1993 as an associate following completion of his M.B.A. He had yet to receive a major assignment when Gloria Lynch, a project manager with the firm, called to ask him to meet with her. At the meeting, Gloria explained that the company had recently received a contract from a large oil and gas company that needed to be completed in a relatively short time frame. She was counting on him to provide extensive analytical assistance to the effort. She indicated she understood that his knowledge of the oil and gas industry was limited, but she would be available as necessary to answer questions. However, she felt that his M.B.A. studies should have provided all the skills he needed to perform the analysis and that he was fully capable of taking on this assignment.

3   Gloria outlined the assignment to Andrew as a competitive analysis of the 11 largest companies within the oil and gas exploration and production (E&P) industry as ranked by their reserves on a barrel of oil equivalent (BOE) basis. ICFR had been retained by one of these companies to look at its competitive situation and performance within the domestic E&P segment of the industry versus its closest competitors. Gloria indicated that for this phase of the analysis she preferred not to tell Andrew which company had retained the firm, freeing him to provide his unbiased, objective analysis of the relative positions of all the companies.

4   Gloria explained that the final product would be a report with tables and graphs evaluating the performance of each of the 11 companies relative to the performance of the group as a whole and to each other. This report would also summarize the outlook for each company relative to both its performance and its ability to deal with threats in the external environment. The final report would also include a section focusing on the particular company for which the work was being prepared, but that section would be added later. Gloria indicated she would assist with the final report, but she needed Andrew to analyze all the data. After reviewing his analysis, she would be asking Andrew to prepare a first draft of the early sections of the report.

5   Under Gloria's direction, a research assistant had already collected and preprocessed much of the data needed to perform the analysis (shown in Exhibits 3 through 37). He inquired whether he needed to be concerned about data inconsistencies due to different account systems or interpretation of data

This case was prepared by Professor John A. Pearce II of Villanova University, and Glenda Smith.

items. Gloria indicated he need not be overly concerned about the comparability of the data because the Securities and Exchange Commission (SEC) required standardized filings of all companies engaged in the E&P business in the United States. These filings, called Reserve Recognition Accounting, were designed to assure that all companies accounted for their E&P activities similarly so that investors could readily compare performance. However, she conceded that in some cases the accounting requirements resulted in reports that did not accurately reflect the companies' true costs because they did not allow for the allocation of corporate overhead and G&A (such as with results of operations). Nevertheless, she was confident the data would at least provide Andrew with a common basis for analysis.

6   In briefly discussing each of the 11 companies to be analyzed—Amoco, AROC, BP America, Chevron, Exxon, Mobil, Phillips Petroleum, Shell, Texaco, Unocal, and USC (Oil & Gas Segment)—Gloria indicated it was important for Andrew to remember that despite their size and competitor relationships, and distinctive strategies, these companies often work together. BP America and Shell, for example, were U.S. subsidiaries of foreign oil companies, so it was reasonable to expect them to have a domestic focus. Exxon, Chevron, Mobil, and Texaco were the partners of ARAMCO, the company responsible for the development of the extensive oil resources in Saudi Arabia, so a larger international focus would be expected. USX's Oil & Gas Segment was comprised of Marathon Oil Company and Texas Oil and Gas Company, which operate separately but were consolidated for accounting purposes in USX's annual report.

7   Gloria indicated there was one company for which data could require some interpretation—BP America. Until 1987, the company was known as Standard Oil Co. of Ohio (Sohio) and was 45 percent owned by British Petroleum (BP). In 1987, BP purchased the remaining portion of Sohio and created BP America by combining Sohio and another subsidiary, BP North America. BP North America included operations in Canada as well as the United States, which were maintained as part of BP America. In 1988 and 1989, annual reports continued to be released separately for BP America, but beginning in 1990, the only data available were taken from BP's annual reports and reflected U.S. operations only. As one of the largest producers in the United States, BP included Reserve Recognition Accounting data, but it was more difficult to know that other data were directly comparable. When Andrew inquired whether Shell posed similar problems, Gloria indicated that Royal Dutch Shell had always issued a separate annual report for Shell Oil, the U.S. subsidiary. Gloria assured Andrew that the person who had collected the data tried to use only data that were comparable, so he would find some missing data items.

8   With this brief introduction, Gloria and Andrew agreed he would go back to his office, look over the data, and formulate a plan for the analysis, including a description of the tables that would be part of the first phase of the analysis. Then they would meet again so that Gloria could approve of his approach and indicate any problems she would anticipate from his description.

OUTLINING ASSIGNMENTS

9   Back in his office, Andrew looked in the file of data tables and found that Gloria had included a list of the key success factors for companies in the E&P industry. After surveying the information included in the data tables, Andrew began to think he had sufficient information to evaluate the performance of each company against those key success factors. Andrew set up a matrix that would include a brief discussion of each company's performance by key success factors and called it Exhibit 1. Andrew knew this discussion of corporate performance would be useful, but it would not provide a ranking of the companies relative to each other. Therefore, Andrew set up Exhibit 2 to convert the data from Exhibit 1 into numerical scores that could be totaled to get an overall idea of each company's performance. Gloria had also mentioned that an outlook for each company in responding to external factors and industry trends was part of the analysis, but he thought he needed to complete the initial data analysis before trying to consider these factors.

10   Feeling pleased with his assessment of what was required, Andrew met with Gloria again to formalize his initial assignment. Gloria was pleased with the exhibits he had prepared, and complimented him on his ability to organize the information in a way that would be easy to understand and

useful. Looking at Exhibit 1, Gloria cautioned Andrew that he may not be able to fully evaluate application of technology from the data he had available. They agreed he would complete it on the basis of the data he had and that Gloria would add her perspectives to his analysis before the report was drafted. Gloria also cautioned him not to think of the key success factors, such as reserve replacement, too narrowly. A wide range of factors other than just the percentage of reserves replaced reflected a company's ability to succeed in this area. Gloria also cautioned Andrew that some of the data, such as reserves found or the cost of finding new reserves, tended to fluctuate from year to year and that he should concentrate more on trends than year-to-year variations. Measures such as finding costs were also approximate, since investments made this year may not result in an addition to reserves until several years later. However, everyone recognized that the data were of this nature and the measures still provided a reasonable basis for comparing companies.

11   For Exhibit 2, Gloria indicated she thought ranking the companies only against each other would be most useful, since most were well above average when compared with other companies in the industry. Andrew clarified that she wanted him to focus primarily on the companies' domestic operations. Gloria agreed, but indicated that when he began to identify strategy or strategic changes, it would be necessary to consider foreign performance also, since for many of these companies, pursuing foreign opportunities was a valid strategic option.

12   As their meeting came to a close, Gloria and Andrew agreed he would complete the following analyses in two ways:

- Complete Exhibit 1 with a brief discussion of performance based on relevant data items.
- Complete Exhibit 2 by evaluating the performance of each company relative to each other on a scale of 1 to 10 based on Exhibit 1.

After these items were complete, Andrew could assess what additional data he felt necessary to complete a more thorough analysis of each company's position relative to current trends in the industry. Realizing that he had a lot to do, but feeling confident of his ability to complete these assignments, Andrew went back to his office to begin the analyses.

EXHIBIT 1
Domestic performance of top companies against key industry success factors

| Company | Reserve Replacement | Cost Containment | | Application of Technology | Financial Strength/ Performance |
		Finding Costs	Production Costs		
Amoco					
ARCO					
BP America					
Chevron					
Exxon					
Mobil					
Phillips Petroleum					
Shell					
Texaco					
Unocal					
USX Corp., Oil & Gas					

EXHIBIT 2
Comparison of Companies against Key Success Factors (relative ranking on scale of 1 to 10)

Company	Reserve Replacement	Cost Containment	Application of Technology	Financial Strength	Total Score
Amoco					
ARCO					
BP America					
Chevron					
Exxon					
Mobil					
Phillips Petroleum					
Shell					
Texaco					
Unocal					
USX Corp., Oil & Gas					

EXHIBIT 3
Net Income (millions $)

	1992	1991	1990	1989	1988	1987	1986
Amoco	$ (74)	$ 1,484	$ 1,913	$ 1,610	$ 2,063	$ 1,360	$ 747
ARCO	801	709	2,011	1,953	1,583	1,224	615
BP America*	467	1,043	1,470	2,041	2,129	564	(345)
Chevron	1,569	1,293	2,157	251	1,768	1,250	(1,411)
Exxon	4,770	5,600	5,010	3,510	5,260	4,840	5,360
Mobil	862	1,920	1,929	1,809	2,087	1,348	(354)
Phillips Petroleum	180	258	779	219	650	35	228
Shell	(190)	20	1,036	1,405	1,239	1,230	883
Texaco	712	1,294	1,450	2,413	1,304	(4,135)	(1,425)
Unocal	220	73	401	260	480	181	176
USX, Oil & Gas	(222)	(71)	508	425	53	20	50
Total	9,095	13,623	18,664	15,896	18,616	7,917	4,524

*Replacement cost operating profit, before interest expense.

EXHIBIT 4
Return on Revenues

	1992	1991	1990	1989	1988	1987	1986
Amoco	(0.3%)	5.2%	6.1%	6.0%	8.6%	6.1%	3.7%
ARCO	4.2	3.7	10.1	11.6	8.4	7.0	3.9
BP America	4.7	11.4	14.1	11.6	13.8	3.6	(3.4)
Chevron	3.7	3.2	5.1	0.8	6.1	4.3	(5.2)
Exxon	4.1	4.8	4.3	3.6	5.9	5.8	7.0
Mobil	1.3	3.0	3.0	3.2	3.8	2.6	(0.8)
Phillips Petroleum	1.5	1.9	5.6	1.8	5.7	0.3	2.3
Shell	(0.9)	0.1	4.2	6.4	5.8	5.8	5.1
Texaco	1.9	3.4	3.5	6.8	3.7	(11.7)	(4.4)
Unocal	2.2	0.7	3.4	2.3	4.7	1.9	2.1
USX, Oil & Gas	(1.7)	(0.5)	3.5	3.4	0.5	0.2	—
Composite	2.4	3.6	4.8	4.7	5.8	2.6	1.7

EXHIBIT 5
Return on Stockholders' Equity

	1992	1991	1990	1989	1988	1987	1986
Amoco	(0.6%)	10.5%	13.6%	11.8%	15.5%	11.2%	6.6%
ARCO	11.9	10.4	28.1	19.8	25.3	20.8	11.7
BP America	—	—	—	—	—	10.1	(4.9)
Chevron	11.4	8.8	14.5	1.8	12.0	9.0	(9.1)
Exxon	14.1	16.0	15.2	11.6	16.6	14.4	16.7
Mobil	5.2	11.0	11.3	11.1	13.3	9.0	(2.3)
Phillips Petroleum	6.7.	9.4	28.7	10.3	30.8	2.2	13.2
Shell	(1.3)	0.1	6.3	8.8	8.1	8.3	6.2
Texaco	7.1	13.2	15.5	26.3	16.1	(56.7)	(10.4)
Unocal	7.0	3.0	15.7	11.3	22.2	10.2	10.5
USX, Oil & Gas	(6.7)	(2.2)	14.0	11.5	1.3	0.5	—
Composite	7.7	11.2	14.2	13.9	16.4	6.8	3.5

EXHIBIT 6
Results of Domestic E&P Operations* (millions $)

	1992	1991	1990	1989	1988	1987	1986
Amoco	$ 778	$ 595	$ 861	$ 521	$ 468	$ 483	$ 93
ARCO	671	429	1,253	886	584	805	309
BP America	312	342	440	1,008	200	597	(389)
Chevron	1,047	408	988	(97)	129	425	(45)
Exxon	672	415	1,202	822	494	1,006	230
Mobil	348	189	189	117	132	509	86
Phillips Petroleum	230	(45)	185	(57)	35	(25)	(68)
Shell	476	226	572	400	230	652	393
Texaco	648	717	939	592	96	279	16
Unocal	219	217	420	278	175	213	131
USX, Oil & Gas	160	74	86	168	25	132	44
Total	5,561	3,567	7,135	4,638	2,568	5,076	800

*Results of operations are after taxes, but exclude corporate overhead and G&A.

EXHIBIT 7
Return on Domestic E&P Operations

	1992	1991	1990	1989	1988	1987	1986
Amoco	23.3%	17.5%	21.2%	14.2%	12.5%	13.0%	2.6%
ARCO	16.5	10.2	24.2	20.5	16.2	19.8	9.1
BP America	18.0	17.1	18.3	28.7	7.2	16.7	(19.6)
Chevron	27.1	10.3	20.1	(2.3)	3.9	10.9	(1.2)
Exxon	15.5	9.5	21.8	16.7	11.5	20.7	5.3
Mobil	13.0	6.7	5.8	4.0	4.8	16.4	3.3
Phillips Petroleum	19.4	(3.9)	14.5	(4.9)	3.3	(2.2)	(5.9)
Shell	14.9	6.8	14.6	11.7	7.2	16.1	10.3
Texaco	18.1	19.0	21.3	15.1	2.6	7.1	0.4
Unocal	14.4	13.9	25.2	19.0	14.5	16.4	10.4
USX, Oil & Gas	14.8	6.2	6.0	11.5	2.0	9.6	3.1
Composite	18.2	11.2	18.8	13.3	8.3	14.5	2.5

EXHIBIT 8
Foreign Results of Operations (millions $)

	1992	1991	1990	1989	1988	1987	1986
Amoco	$ 95	$ 215	$ 860	$ 365	$ 314	$ 453	$ 251
ARCO	171	79	76	(8)	(71)	13	14
BP America	—	—	—	(26)	(31)	(14)	389
Chevron	430	339	498	331	561	567	245
Exxon	1,832	1,546	1,925	1,426	1,238	1,752	1,419
Mobil	966	1,062	1,365	913	752	1,019	841
Phillips Petroleum	109	231	363	150	161	143	(8)
Shell	94	64	140	110	21	2	(36)
Texaco	104	103	184	46	162	302	(27)
Unocal	243	206	291	172	150	171	86
USX, Oil & Gas	1	73	133	50	(4)	59	(72)
Total	4,045	3,918	5,835	3,529	3,253	4,467	2,647

EXHIBIT 9
Return on Foreign E&P Investment

	1992	1991	1990	1989	1988	1987	1986
Amoco	2.6%	6.1%	18.1%	10.3%	11.4%	16.0%	9.1%
ARCO	20.3	8.6	9.4	(1.4)	(14.2)	2.3	3.1
BP America	—	—	—	(28.6)	(51.7)	(28.6)	(19.6)
Chevron	15.0	11.8	16.3	13.1	25.9	21.7	11.3
Exxon	21.9	18.8	21.1	19.2	18.3	23.9	22.3
Mobil	18.1	19.8	24.8	21.7	20.2	25.1	23.4
Phillips Petroleum	8.5	15.5	24.3	13.6	16.7	13.9	(0.7)
Shell	20.7	11.0	21.5	21.4	5.8	1.0	(29.5)
Texaco	8.2	7.2	10.8	3.3	8.5	11.1	(1.2)
Unocal	23.7	19.8	26.7	21.1	19.9	22.7	11.8
USX, Oil & Gas	0.2	10.2	16.4	8.9	(0.8)	11.5	(17.3)
Composite	15.8	15.0	20.0	15.5	15.9	19.5	13.3

EXHIBIT 10
Domestic BOE Production (millions BOE)

	1992	1991	1990	1989	1988	1987	1986
Amoco	247.8	247.8	244.8	260.3	249.8	244.2	243.0
ARCO	327.3	342.2	339.8	345.3	343.2	332.0	327.8
BP America	267.3	290.3	296.5	307.5	332.7	326.5	306.0
Chevron	299.2	309.5	328.2	322.8	300.3	303.0	318.8
Exxon	324.2	339.7	354.7	377.0	403.2	398.5	414.3
Mobil	214.0	224.7	202.0	214.3	220.7	213.7	207.0
Phillips Petroleum	108.3	101.5	102.2	101.5	102.0	97.8	105.2
Shell	251.7	250.5	254.2	268.7	289.8	313.3	317.8
Texaco	270.0	286.3	290.5	296.5	322.0	321.7	337.3
Unocal	106.8	115.5	106.0	105.7	103.0	110.2	105.5
USX, Oil & Gas	79.3	87.8	94.3	107.5	108.7	103.7	115.1
Total	2,496.0	2,595.8	2,613.2	2,707.2	2,775.3	2,765.2	2,797.9

EXHIBIT 11
U.S. as Portion of Worldwide BOE Production

	1992	1991	1990	1989	1988	1987	1986
Amoco	50.9%	51.3%	50.3%	51.1%	53.1%	53.1%	52.7%
ARCO	88.3	88.5	90.5	90.5	91.4	91.0	90.4
BP America	100.0	100.0	100.0	98.1	98.6	98.8	99.2
Chevron	63.9	65.5	66.9	67.7	65.2	65.2	66.1
Exxon	38.9	40.7	42.6	42.7	44.2	45.5	47.8
Mobil	38.5	40.7	39.1	41.6	45.0	45.9	46.1
Phillips Petroleum	59.5	58.0	58.2	59.0	60.1	61.6	62.7
Shell	91.1	88.8	89.3	89.8	91.6	96.5	97.4
Texaco	75.7	74.5	73.1	73.6	66.9	64.0	64.2
Unocal	57.5	60.5	61.0	63.2	62.9	65.4	66.6
USX, Oil & Gas	67.6	67.3	69.0	72.1	72.4	74.4	74.5
Composite	60.9	62.1	62.7	63.4	64.1	65.0	65.6

EXHIBIT 12
Liquids as Portion of Total U.S. BOE Production

	1992	1991	1990	1989	1988	1987	1986
Amoco	43.2%	46.8%	51.9%	54.5%	59.6%	58.0%	58.4%
ARCO	73.9	71.3	68.6	69.8	71.7	73.2	73.2
BP America	93.9	92.7	90.7	93.0	94.4	94.6	95.1
Chevron	52.8	53.6	50.9	54.5	58.9	61.1	62.4
Exxon	66.6	66.5	66.0	67.1	69.0	69.3	67.1
Mobil	53.3	53.9	50.5	49.9	50.3	52.4	55.1
Phillips Petroleum	46.2	46.3	48.0	47.3	49.0	52.1	55.2
Shell	64.8	66.7	66.1	67.0	66.6	65.1	65.8
Texaco	58.5	58.0	57.5	59.0	59.6	61.2	63.7
Unocal	44.0	49.4	49.1	52.1	55.3	57.2	59.7
USX, Oil & Gas	52.9	52.4	48.8	48.4	51.9	55.9	55.4
Composite	62.0	62.6	61.8	63.4	65.7	66.5	66.9

EXHIBIT 13
Domestic BOE Reserves (million BOE)

	1992	1991	1990	1989	1988	1987	1986
Amoco	3,262	3,372	3,639	3,728	3,798	3,452	3,272
ARCO	3,381	3,608	3,763	3,840	3,891	3,794	3,715
BP America	2,925	2,957	2,980	2,941	3,057	3,275	3,122
Chevron	2,285	2,663	2,834	3,053	3,185	2,989	3,132
Exxon	4,015	4,141	4,027	4,048	4,187	4,261	5,622
Mobil	2,163	2,272	2,399	2,427	2,393	2,314	2,323
Phillips Petroleum	1,096	1,120	1,141	1,507	1,009	1,019	1,035
Shell	3,084	3,470	3,889	3,898	3,892	3,872	3,763
Texaco	2,254	2,330	2,408	2,371	2,399	2,400	2,509
Unocal	1,145	1,203	1,271	1,219	1,249	1,277	1,411
USX, Oil & Gas	926	975	971	1,051	1,105	1,167	1,201
Total	26,536	28,109	29,322	29,633	30,165	28,819	31,105

EXHIBIT 14
U.S. as Portion of Worldwide BOE Reserves

	1992	1991	1990	1989	1988	1987	1986
Amoco	62.4%	60.6%	62.4%	63.3%	62.8%	67.1%	65.6%
ARCO	82.2	86.0	88.1	89.8	89.2	91.1	91.1
BP America	100.0	100.0	100.0	89.2	88.5	89.1	89.2
Chevron	60.3	62.7	65.2	67.5	67.8	65.6	65.2
Exxon	39.6	39.6	38.4	37.0	40.5	41.1	49.2
Mobil	37.4	37.9	40.2	41.6	41.1	40.1	39.6
Phillips Petroleum	53.7	56.1	55.5	55.5	54.2	56.9	58.8
Shell	90.3	90.3	92.7	93.3	93.7	95.2	95.7
Texaco	69.4	70.0	71.9	72.6	63.1	59.4	59.9
Unocal	59.7	61.9	66.2	66.7	69.9	71.5	74.5
USX, Oil & Gas	62.0	63.0	62.3	71.2	71.7	73.4	74.8
Composite	60.2	61.0	62.4	62.5	63.0	63.5	64.8

EXHIBIT 15
Liquids as Portion of Domestic BOE Reserves

	1992	1991	1990	1989	1988	1987	1986
Amoco	40.6%	42.4%	42.8%	45.2%	45.7%	48.4%	47.7%
ARCO	74.4	73.2	72.3	72.0	72.7	74.3	73.4
BP America	83.8	83.8	83.0	87.7	87.6	90.2	90.2
Chevron	59.9	58.9	58.3	57.7	56.7	60.5	60.0
Exxon	59.6	59.1	60.5	61.4	62.8	61.8	46.7
Mobil	54.0	54.2	50.3	49.5	47.6	44.2	43.6
Phillips Petroleum	42.7	43.2	44.4	43.4	44.4	44.9	47.9
Shell	71.7	71.3	72.6	73.4	73.2	71.8	69.9
Texaco	66.5	66.4	66.4	66.0	67.7	66.8	65.9
Unocal	44.2	44.0	44.1	43.5	42.4	42.6	46.8
USX, Oil & Gas	62.2	61.2	58.9	55.7	54.1	53.2	52.3
Composite	62.1	62.0	61.8	62.4	62.5	63.4	60.1

EXHIBIT 16
Total U.S. Reserve Additions from Drilling* (millions BOE)

	1992	1991	1990	1989	1988	1987	1986
Amoco	145.3	134.8	221.8	219.7	229.8	386.5	(6.2)
ARCO	214.8	159.0	260.8	268.5	327.3	454.0	331.5
BP America	232.0	331.1	505.3	196.5	131.0	479.2	49.3
Chevron	183.3	189.8	209.2	217.0	225.0	168.5	71.8
Exxon	218.0	461.8	336.7	162.7	270.3	217.8	299.0
Mobil	138.5	144.0	188.5	269.2	310.3	210.0	228.7
Phillips Petroleum	89.5	80.7	184.0	147.2	95.8	83.0	20.7
Shell	(79.0)	(149.7)	236.5	291.3	240.0	317.7	221.8
Texaco	220.5	228.7	333.8	251.5	355.8	228.0	114.8
Unocal	54.2	57.7	113.5	93.5	56.5	(30.7)	57.3
USX, Oil & Gas	47.3	98.8	62.0	51.3	45.7	60.2	87.5
Total	1,464.5	1,736.8	2,656.2	2,168.3	2,287.7	2,574.2	1,476.3

*Includes revisions, extensions and discoveries, and improved recovery.

EXHIBIT 17
Total U.S. Reserve Additions* (millions BOE)

	1992	1991	1990	1989	1988	1987	1986
Amoco	137.3	(18.7)	155.5	190.8	596.0	424.8	82.3
ARCO	100.2	187.8	262.2	294.5	440.7	410.5	274.7
BP America	232.0	267.3	504.5	191.5	114.5	479.2	50.6
Chevron	(79.2)	138.3	109.3	190.7	496.7	160.2	70.3
Exxon	198.7	452.8	334.2	238.0	329.2	335.3	320.7
Mobil	105.7	97.7	174.0	248.3	299.0	204.7	227.5
Phillips Petroleum	84.3	80.3	187.0	149.2	92.3	81.7	(32.8)
Shell	(134.3)	(169.3)	245.3	274.5	310.0	422.2	378.0
Texaco	194.5	208.0	328.0	268.3	320.7	212.5	113.5
Unocal	48.5	47.3	157.7	76.0	74.8	(23.7)	62.5
USX, Oil & Gas	30.3	92.2	13.5	52.8	47.4	69.7	78.4
Total	918.0	1,383.8	2,471.2	2,174.7	3,121.2	2,777.1	1,625.7

*Includes revisions, extensions and discoveries, improved recovery, and net sales and purchases.

EXHIBIT 18
U.S. BOE Reserve Replacement from Drilling*

	1992	1991	1990	1989	1988	1987	1986
Amoco	58.6%	54.4%	90.6%	84.4%	92.0%	157.9%	(2.5%)
ARCO	65.6	46.5	76.8	77.8	95.4	136.7	101.1
BP America	86.8	114.1	170.4	63.9	39.4	146.8	17.8
Chevron	61.3	61.3	63.7	67.2	74.9	55.6	22.5
Exxon	67.2	136.0	94.9	43.1	67.1	54.7	72.2
Mobil	64.7	64.1	93.3	125.6	140.6	98.3	110.5
Phillips Petroleum	82.6	79.5	180.1	145.0	94.0	84.8	19.7
Shell	(31.4)	(59.7)	93.0	108.4	82.8	101.4	69.8
Texaco	81.7	79.9	114.9	84.8	110.5	70.9	34.0
Unocal	50.7	49.9	107.1	88.5	54.9	(27.8)	54.3
USX, Oil & Gas	59.7	112.5	65.7	47.8	42.1	58.0	76.0
Composite	58.7	66.9	101.5	80.1	82.4	93.1	53.3

*Includes revisions, extensions and discoveries, and improved recovery.

EXHIBIT 19
U.S. BOE Reserve Replacement*

	1992	1991	1990	1989	1988	1987	1986
Amoco	55.4%	(7.5%)	63.5%	73.3%	238.6%	173.5%	33.9%
ARCO	30.6	54.9	77.1	85.3	128.4	123.6	83.8
BP America	86.8	92.1	170.2	62.3	34.4	146.8	18.2
Chevron	(26.5)	44.7	33.3	59.1	165.4	52.9	22.1
Exxon	61.3	133.3	94.2	63.1	81.6	84.1	77.4
Mobil	49.4	43.5	86.1	115.9	135.5	95.8	109.9
Phillips Petroleum	77.8	79.1	183.0	147.0	90.5	83.5	(31.2)
Shell	(53.4)	(67.6)	96.5	102.2	107.0	134.7	118.9
Texaco	72.0	72.6	112.9	90.5	99.6	66.1	33.6
Unocal	45.4	41.0	148.7	71.9	72.7	(21.5)	59.2
USX, Oil & Gas	38.2	104.9	14.3	49.1	43.6	67.2	68.1
Composite	36.8	53.3	94.6	80.3	112.5	100.4	58.7

*Includes revisions, extensions and discoveries, improved recovery, and net sales and purchases.

EXHIBIT 20
Foreign Reserve Replacement from Drilling*

	1992	1991	1990	1989	1988	1987	1986
Amoco	46.1%	109.0%	141.7%	65.1%	43.6%	81.5%	34.4%
ARCO	425.7	183.9	431.6	8.7	93.8	113.2	159.5
BP America	—	—	—	—	—	—	—
Chevron	62.9	156.5	122.7	70.7	99.9	86.9	36.8
Exxon	73.6	84.6	23.4	135.1	93.8	115.7	59.0
Mobil	78.6	147.0	135.3	97.0	109.5	66.2	121.8
Phillips Petroleum	193.0	97.1	186.4	89.8	221.2	174.9	307.2
Shell	324.3	311.6	174.3	160.9	136.5	330.4	235.3
Texaco	88.7	149.4	137.2	142.2	70.1	77.8	71.1
Unocal	171.1	222.3	221.1	215.7	146.4	148.1	137.9
USX, Oil & Gas	83.8	68.0	478.3	96.0	132.8	149.3	20.7
Composite	94.2	126.5	123.7	107.9	96.7	100.5	80.7

*Includes revisions, extensions and discoveries, and improved recovery.

EXHIBIT 21
Foreign BOE Reserve Replacement*

	1992	1991	1990	1989	1988	1987	1986
Amoco	5.0%	99.4%	112.6%	65.0%	350.4%	90.8%	33.7%
ARCO	423.4	280.9	299.1	6.0	408.2	135.0	159.5
BP America	—	—	—	—	—	—	—
Chevron	54.5	145.2	123.0	75.2	64.2	38.3	36.9
Exxon	63.2	70.9	11.8	241.1	112.4	164.0	61.
Mobil	71.9	143.1	120.7	91.2	88.6	65.8	116.0
Phillips Petroleum	194.1	44.4	195.9	89.8	221.2	174.9	134.3
Shell	(60.8)	311.6	174.3	160.9	136.5	330.4	235.3
Texaco	91.4	159.3	142.8	(376.8)	(47.8)	76.0	69.5
Unocal	142.0	221.5	157.5	215.2	147.0	145.0	135.3
USX, Oil & Gas	83.8	68.0	478.3	76.8	132.8	149.3	(753.7)
Composite	75.3	119.7	107.7	105.8	133.6	112.1	51.7

*Includes revisions, extensions and discoveries, improved recovery, and net sales and purchases.

EXHIBIT 22
U.S. Net Exploratory Wells Drilled*

	1992	1991	1990	1989	1988	1987	1986
Amoco	79	154	355	197	201	205	286
ARCO	86	68	75	66	70	47	56
BP America	—	—	—	—	—	39	51
Chevron	58	64	92	72	73	64	82
Exxon	16	36	44	77	82	56	87
Mobil	49	104	105	80	88	98	173
Phillips Petroleum	14	14	26	24	19	31	32
Shell	21	32	27	34	43	72	100
Texaco	60	81	93	44	85	38	65
Unocal	16	22	25	29	29	29	—
USX, Oil & Gas	41	67	62	79	71	59	43
Total	440	642	904	702	761	738	975

*Represents sum of company's fractional interest in all exploratory wells drilled.

EXHIBIT 23
U.S. Exploratory Success Ratio

	1992	1991	1990	1989	1988	1987	1986
Amoco	34.2%	76.6%	92.4%	87.8%	62.7%	63.9%	65.0%
ARCO	18.6	38.2	36.0	37.9	40.0	40.4	19.6
BP America	—	—	—	—	—	10.0	18.4
Chevron	72.4	60.9	51.1	58.3	47.9	57.8	56.1
Exxon	31.3	36.1	29.5	31.2	26.8	16.1	16.1
Mobil	67.3	56.7	59.0	40.0	48.9	70.4	47.4
Phillips Petroleum	50.0	50.0	38.5	33.3	36.8	54.8	31.3
Shell	38.1	56.3	18.5	29.4	34.9	25.0	29.0
Texaco	66.7	77.8	52.7	43.2	30.6	26.3	36.9
Unocal	31.3	31.8	36.0	31.0	13.8	24.1	—
USX, Oil & Gas	70.7	62.7	33.9	38.0	40.8	49.2	23.3
Composite	48.4	61.1	63.2	53.0	44.3	47.4	43.4

EXHIBIT 24
U.S. Net Development Wells Drilled*

	1992	1991	1990	1989	1988	1987	1986
Amoco	324	348	344	178	406	424	317
ARCO	183	606	406	351	392	225	266
BP America	—	—	—	—	—	83	105
Chevron	222	451	426	181	269	219	270
Exxon	126	247	281	374	420	318	544
Mobil	260	462	425	531	443	548	581
Phillips Petroleum	107	161	196	110	150	128	92
Shell	198	523	735	508	840	1,194	1,397
Texaco	243	334	662	362	447	661	335
Unocal	163	146	249	194	226	237	—
USX, Oil & Gas	29	109	271	318	326.	369	400
Total	1,855	3,387	3,995	3,107	3,919	4,406	4,307

*Represents sum of company's fractional interest in all exploratory wells drilled.

EXHIBIT 25
U.S. Development Well Success Ratio

	1992	1991	1990	1989	1988	1987	1986
Amoco	96.6%	96.3%	98.3%	95.5%	95.6%	95.5%	88.6%
ARCO	89.6	71.5	89.2	90.9	90.8	92.9	94.0
BP America	—	—	—	—	—	87.1	85.6
Chevron	97.7	98.7	97.9	94.5	98.5	97.7	96.3
Exxon	86.5	90.7	90.4	87.7	85.0	87.1	79.6
Mobil	96.2	97.8	97.9	94.9	95.0	96.4	94.3
Phillips Petroleum	91.6	96.3	89.8	92.7	92.0	91.4	88.0
Shell	97.5	97.9	98.8	98.0	98.5	98.7	97.1
Texaco	96.7	95.8	96.7	96.1	97.1	96.2	94.9
Unocal	95.1	95.9	96.8	97.9	98.7	97.5	—
USX, Oil & Gas	96.6	94.5	84.5	78.9	79.8	79.4	80.0
Composite	95.0	92.1	95.1	92.7	93.6	94.4	95.1

EXHIBIT 26
U.S. BOE Discovered per Well Drilled* (thousands BOE)

	1992	1991	1990	1989	1988	1987	1986
Amoco	341	(37)	222	509	982	675	137
ARCO	372	279	545	706	954	1,509	853
BP America	—	—	—	—	—	3,928	325
Chevron	(283)	269	211	754	1,452	566	200
Exxon	1,399	1,600	1,028	528	656	897	508
Mobil	342	173	328	406	563	317	302
Phillips Petroleum	697	459	842	1,113	546	514	(265)
Shell	(613)	(305)	322	506	351	333	253
Texaco	642	501	434	661	603	304	284
Unocal	271	282	575	341	293	(89)	345
USX, Oil & Gas	433	524	41	133	119	163	177
Composite	400	343	504	571	667	540	298

*Total reserve additions from drilling divided by total net wells drilled (exploratory + development).

EXHIBIT 27
Foreign BOE Discovered per Well Drilled* (thousands BOE)

	1992	1991	1990	1989	1988	1987	1986
Amoco	463	968	1,262	806	398	1,096	212
ARCO	3,940	1,515	3,156	74	892	1,126	1,139
BP America	—	—	—	—	—	2,393	—
Chevron	1,119	1,581	1,915	878	1,069	1,394	424
Exxon	1,718	1,938	465	2,611	758	818	557
Mobil	3,535	4,822	3,197	3,243	2,122	1,173	1,433
Phillips Petroleum	5,481	2,853	8,039	2,533	3,650	5,614	12,833
Shell	2,581	3,289	2,127	1,897	2,009	1,520	1,176
Texaco	2,406	2,118	1,722	1,821	444	832	704
Unocal	1,338	2,018	1,875	1,579	888	957	971
USX, Oil & Gas	1,326	4,143	10,658	3,077	4,995	6,672	511
Composite	1,702	1,970	1,876	1,735	931	1,062	765

*Total reserve additions from drilling divided by total net wells drilled (exploratory + development).

EXHIBIT 28
U.S. Total Costs Incurred for E&P* (million $)

	1992	1991	1990	1989	1988	1987	1986
Amoco	$ 646	$ 1,125	1,235	1,222	2,648	1,815	1,830
ARCO	832	1,593	1,291	1,137	1,657	676	1,062
BP America	432	516	525	791	831	714	1,258
Chevron	707	1,045	1,123	970	3,530	911	962
Exxon	1,423	1,834	1,442	2,055	1,948	1,691	1,947
Mobil	439	872	981	850	968	789	1,054
Phillips Petroleum	242	389	444	326	292	299	309
Shell	869	1,387	1,365	1,188	2,130	1,685	2,014
Texaco	821	1,006	1,222	1,403	1,119	1,056	1,140
Unocal	427	570	1,080	511	510	436	483
USX, Oil & Gas	258	371	484	492	485	521	430
Total	7,096	10,708	11,192	10,945	16,118	10,593	12,489

*Includes exploratory, development, and property acquisition costs incurred. Part of reserve recognition accounting requirements, these data are roughly equivalent to capital investment in E&P (although not all costs are capitalized).

EXHIBIT 29
Foreign Total Costs Incurred for E&P* (million $)

	1992	1991	1990	1989	1988	1987	1986
Amoco	$ 1,342	$ 1,763	$ 1,550	$1,318	$ 4,144	$ 823	$ 893
ARCO	665	597	534	395	1,143	253	413
BP America	0	0	0	610	243	217	1,482
Chevron	1,267	1,201	936	979	801	697	662
Exxon	2,899	2,694	2,677	6,366	2,417	2,923	1,845
Mobil	1,542	1,614	1,219	872	839	708	746
Phillips Petroleum	410	367	333	270	195	198	176
Shell	315	404	340	331	218	159	156
Texaco	875	967	699	384	694	488	563
Unocal	376	466	434	413	372	272	225
USX, Oil & Gas	606	468	375	245	298	354	361
Total	10,297	10,541	9,097	12,183	11,364	7,092	7,522

*Includes exploratory, development, and property acquisition costs incurred. Part of reserve recognition accounting requirements, these data are roughly equivalent to capital investment in E&P (although not all costs are capitalized).

EXHIBIT 30
U.S. as Portion of Total Worldwide Costs Incurred

	1992	1991	1990	1989	1988	1987	1986
Amoco	32.5%	339.0%	44.3%	48.1%	39.0%	68.8%	67.2%
ARCO	55.6	72.7	70.7	74.2	59.2	72.8	72.0
BP America	100.0	100.0	100.0	56.5	77.4	76.7	100.0
Chevron	35.8	46.5	54.5	49.8	81.5	56.7	59.2
Exxon	32.9	40.5	35.0	24.4	44.6	36.6	51.3
Mobil	22.2	35.1	44.6	49.4	53.6	52.7	58.6
Phillips Petroleum	37.1	51.5	57.1	54.7	60.0	60.2	63.7
Shell	73.4	77.4	80.1	78.2	90.7	91.4	92.8
Texaco	48.4	51.0	63.6	78.5	61.7	68.4	66.9
Unocal	53.2	55.0	71.3	55.3	57.8	61.6	68.2
USX, Oil & Gas	29.9	44.2	56.3	66.8	61.9	59.5	54.4
Composite	40.8	50.4	55.2	47.3	58.6	59.9	62.4

EXHIBIT 31
U.S. Reinvestment Ratio*

	1992	1991	1990	1989	1988	1987	1986
Amoco	31.3%	54.8%	45.8%	50.8%	106.8%	72.5%	80.0%
ARCO	33.5	68.6	36.3	38.8	69.6	23.9	49.4
BP America	38.3	40.2	37.4	37.9	50.1	30.0	109.2
Chevron	29.7	49.7	36.6	45.3	224.1	44.3	50.7
Exxon	54.6	74.6	39.3	63.5	70.0	50.8	71.6
Mobil	26.6	54.6	50.0	49.0	62.9	38.4	70.4
Phillips Petroleum	34.1	60.4	53.2	41.9	42.7	42.8	44.6
Shell	49.7	81.9	58.0	60.8	115.9	63.6	85.4
Texaco	35.8	42.4	41.4	57.0	56.4	44.5	51.1
Unocal	39.8	54.5	90.6	49.4	60.8	46.0	54.5
USX, Oil & Gas	33.9	52.3	49.3	47.9	59.6	54.8	44.8
Composite	37.5	58.6	45.4	50.2	86.8	46.5	66.3

*Calculated as total costs incurred/(Oil and gas revenues – Production costs).

EXHIBIT 32
Foreign Reinvestment Ratio*

	1992	1991	1990	1989	1988	1987	1986
Amoco	75.2%	78.1%	44.5%	55.0%	228.1%	39.9%	80.0%
ARCO	120.3	94.8	91.1	103.7	247.4	66.4	145.9
BP America	—	—	—	—	—	—	—
Chevron	58.8	52.4	34.0	47.1	46.4	31.6	38.4
Exxon	54.4	53.3	43.9	127.2	55.0	58.0	44.2
Mobil	41.0	41.8	29.7	28.4	33.6	25.2	32.0
Phillips Petroleum	50.3	33.7	27.7	37.3	30.8	34.8	24.6
Shell	99.4	98.8	72.8	89.5	96.9	148.6	339.1
Texaco	117.0	102.9	57.9	42.6	55.5	23.8	33.7
Unocal	46.0	55.8	48.2	63.1	62.1	44.4	40.5
USX, Oil & Gas	183.1	104.9	65.1	68.4	112.5	107.9	157.6
Composite	62.0	59.2	42.6	76.1	82.5	43.8	55.6

*Calculated as total costs incurred/(Oil and gas revenues – Production costs).

EXHIBIT 33
U.S. Estimated Production Costs per BOE produced ($/BOE)

	1992	1991	1990	1989	1988	1987	1986
Amoco	$5.12	$5.47	$5.56	$4.86	$5.02	$4.89	$5.15
ARCO	4.84	5.46	4.78	4.03	3.56	3.73	3.83
BP America	2.25	2.48	3.36	4.66	3.34	3.67	3.01
Chevron	5.94	6.04	5.66	6.20	5.89	6.07	6.30
Exxon	5.32	5.60	5.23	4.46	3.80	3.84	3.91
Mobil	4.76	5.37	6.30	5.55	5.53	4.89	5.29
Phillips Petroleum	4.38	4.98	4.33	3.85	3.82	4.28	4.37
Shell	5.72	6.42	6.20	5.45	4.75	4.46	4.60
Texaco	4.74	4.91	5.04	4.88	5.17	4.76	5.21
Unocal	4.17	4.43	4.47	4.09	3.53	3.17	3.50
USX, Oil & Gas	4.01	5.51	4.88	4.04	4.11	4.13	3.88
Composite	4.66	5.18	5.12	4.85	4.45	4.40	4.54

EXHIBIT 34
Foreign Estimated Production Costs per BOE Produced ($/BOE)

	1992	1991	1990	1989	1988	1987	1986
Amoco	$7.78	$5.47	$5.29	$4.58	$4.25	$4.41	$4.29
ARCO	6.69	6.40	6.11	5.81	5.32	5.85	4.94
BP America	—	—	—	3.33	4.14	5.50	—
Chevron	4.15	3.61	3.06	2.95	2.72	2.54	2.68
Exxon	5.94	6.44	6.36	4.78	4.66	4.77	4.84
Mobil	4.60	4.55	4.47	3.76	4.57	4.96	5.20
Phillips Petroleum	6.30	5.54	4.02	5.43	4.91	7.56	5.79
Shell	5.55	5.43	6.03	4.73	5.06	7.48	8.94
Texaco	6.00	4.96	4.64	4.59	4.09	3.75	3.60
Unocal	2.65	2.71	2.77	2.59	2.52	2.42	3.33
USX, Oil & Gas	6.50	6.33	5.55	4.92	5.73	5.23	4.77
Composite	5.62	5.28	5.05	4.32	4.30	4.47	4.43

EXHIBIT 35
U.S. Estimated Finding Costs* ($/BOE)

	1992	1991	1990	1989	1988	1987	1986
Amoco	$4.33	$8.16	$ 5.35	$5.05	$6.65	$3.77†	†
ARCO	3.62	6.51	4.37	3.76	3.23	1.38	3.15
BP America	1.86	1.54	0.91	3.63	5.85	1.45	24.93
Chevron	3.67	5.19	5.12	4.35	4.06	5.16	13.09
Exxon	6.36	3.76	4.09	10.25	5.14	†	6.16
Mobil	3.06	5.74	4.92	2.94	2.49	3.45	4.34
Phillips Petroleum	2.61	4.45	2.24	1.97	2.85	3.27	14.32
Shell	†	†	5.41	3.53	5.37	4.29	6.84
Texaco	3.63	4.26	3.39	3.53	2.83	4.18	9.41
Unocal	7.55	9.03	5.40	5.07	7.54	†	8.01
USX, Oil & Gas	5.22	3.56	6.79	8.16	9.89	6.45	4.60
Composite	4.69	5.61	3.78	4.30	4.32	6.85	7.65

*Calculated as exploration and development costs incurred/reserve additions from drilling.

†Data not meaningful since reserve additions were negative due to downward revisions following additional drilling. Composite values do consider these negative revisions.

EXHIBIT 36
Foreign Estimated Finding Costs* ($/BOE)

	1992	1991	1990	1989	1988	1987	1986
Amoco	$12.02	$ 6.82	$ 4.43	$ 7.59	$11.01	$ 4.40	$11.44
ARCO	3.55	6.51	3.01	122.84	14.54	6.81	7.40
BP America	—	—	—	†	51.56	8.69	—
Chevron	11.47	4.54	4.38	7.13	4.41	4.64	10.84
Exxon	7.65	6.38	23.44	4.85	4.53	3.97	6.51
Mobil	5.63	3.32	2.79	2.79	2.66	4.16	2.51
Phillips Petroleum	2.82	5.12	1.97	4.11	1.25	1.79	0.90
Shell	3.86	4.06	6.19	6.57	6.00	3.97	7.70
Texaco	11.23	6.31	4.65	2.54	5.44	3.34	4.10
Unocal	2.67	2.70	2.57	3.00	4.06	30.01	3.03
USX, Oil & Gas	18.38	15.66	1.80	6.03	5.13	6.61	42.53
Composite	6.68	5.14	4.53	5.02	4.68	4.07	4.95

*Calculated as exploration and development costs incurred/reserve additions from drilling.

†Data not meaningful since reserve additions were negative due to downward revisions following additional drilling. Composite values do consider these negative revisions.

EXHIBIT 37
U.S. Improved Recovery as Portion of Total BOE Reserve Additions from Drilling

	1992	1991	1990	1989	1988	1987	1986
Amoco	1.4%	10.8%	0.0%	11.0%	14.8%	15.0%	*
ARCO	21.9	56.3	44.2	12.3	32.0	31.1	7.19%
BP America	54.2	35.7	17.0	15.4	9.8	0.6	4.1
Chevron	12.6	19.8	33.9	33.5	7.6	23.3	65.4
Exxon	4.1	3.8	4.0	11.0	7.3	*	10.1
Mobil	10.1	50.0	46.9	57.2	63.2	42.7	23.6
Phillips Petroleum	24.4	28.5	10.4	3.6	7.3	4.8	4.8
Shell	*	*	25.7	10.6	68.7	16.5	38.4
Texaco	17.2	23.7	31.0	13.9	18.3	2.3	0.0
Unocal	5.5	10.4	14.1	19.3	7.1	*	10.5
USX, Oil & Gas	27.5	28.3	10.2	21.8	23.5	21.5	44.0
Composite	20.5	27.9	21.9	19.9	27.8	37.1	35.1

*Data not meaningful since total reserve additions from drilling were negative. Composite values do consider these negative revisions.

C INDIVIDUAL INDUSTRY NOTES

CASE 37

NOTE ON THE AIRLINE INDUSTRY

---

1   The U.S. airline industry, with approximately $450 billion in revenue passenger miles (a revenue passenger mile represents one fare-paying passenger transported one mile), accounted for 1 percent of the 1994 U.S. gross domestic product. The industry continues to be in a state of turbulence characterized by price wars, layoffs, fleet cutbacks, and bankruptcies. Pounded by overcapacity, the recent recession, and volatile fuel prices, the industry has sustained $8 billion in losses since 1990. Air traffic has not grown at the forecasted rate as corporate America tries to hold costs and scrutinize its travel needs, electing for substitutes such as videoconferences. The load factor, or the percentage of seating utilized, has been at 63 percent in the past few years. Traffic on U.S. airlines has been forecasted to increase 4.7 percent annually from 1993 to 2002.

THE EFFECTS OF DEREGULATION

2   The Airline Deregulation Act of 1978 eliminated most domestic economic regulation of passenger and freight services. However, the U.S. Department of Transportation (DOT) is responsible for protecting consumer rights such as baggage liability and denied boarding compensation. The DOT also has jurisdiction over international routes and international tariffs and pricing. The Federal Aviation Administration (FAA) has jurisdiction over air safety, including control of navigable space, flight personnel, and aircraft certification and maintenance. Economic deregulation allows unfettered competition with respect to domestic routes, services, fares, and rates. Any air carrier the DOT finds "fit" to operate can begin competing in the airline industry. On most of the principal routes, companies compete with at least one other major airline, in addition to the regional carriers. The fruits of deregulation have been enjoyed by the traveling public. Since 1979, passenger enplanements have

This case was prepared by James Almeida and Richard Robinson, University of South Carolina.

increased by more than 70 percent, revenue has tripled from $27 billion to more than $77 billion, and nearly all passengers during the 1980s traveled on discounted fares.

THE HUB-AND-SPOKE CONCEPT

3   A potential entrant to the airline industry experiences high capital requirements for investing in planes, routes, airport gates, and an assorted support infrastructure. For example, access to four major U.S. airports (JFK and LaGuardia in New York, O'Hare in Chicago, and National in Washington, D.C.) is through ''slots'' allocated by the FAA, which authorizes airlines to land or take off from the particular airports during a specified time period.

4   The hub-and-spoke system, a product of airline deregulation, provides the larger carriers a significant competitive edge at the expense of smaller airlines. A simple hub-and-spoke system is illustrated below:

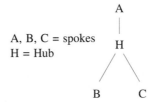

A, B, C = spokes
H = Hub

The argument made for this system is that increases in the traffic volume on the spokes contribute to economies of density on the spokes and thus reduce the fares in the markets served by the system. Thus, the larger the size (in terms of the *number of cities* connected) of the system, and/or the larger the *size of the cities*, the lower the fares in the individual markets served. The hub-and-spoke system was initially a great success. It enabled the major airlines to develop huge geographical regions like giant spiderwebs in which to snare passing traffic and expand market share. Hubs also integrated remote cities into a national and international route network. Exhibits 1A and 1B illustrate the location of different hubs used by major carriers including American Airlines, Delta Air Lines, Northwest Airlines, United Airlines, and USAir.

Advantage or Liability

5   As seen in Exhibits 1A and 1B, the major carriers established their respective hubs across the country and eventually this myriad of hubs grew too close to each other, vying for the same customer. The deployment of employees and assets at the hubs is usually not efficient. Work activity increases when the flights arrive in a series of banks at various times in the day. Thus, the hubs have to manage anywhere between 20 and 60 flights simultaneously. The activity then drops off when these flights leave for other destinations, until the next bank of flights arrives. Larger airports that can generate sufficient traffic for continuous flight operations can exploit the economies of the hub system. The top 10 U.S. airports in 1993 as well as the top 10 airports (excluding U.S.) in the world, in terms of revenue passengers enplaned, are shown in Exhibit 2. The 20 top airline routes in the United States are shown in Exhibit 3.

6   The recession during the early 1990s hurt air travel, and the hubs were unable to generate the heavy traffic volume that is required to offset the soaring costs of the large fleet of planes flying in and out of the hubs. During their expansion years following deregulation, the airlines overestimated the growth in future air traffic. This excess capacity has served as a drag on the fortunes of the airline industry. One of the few airlines to earn a profit during the early 1990s was one that opted for the point-to-point service system as opposed to the hub-and-spoke one, Southwest Airlines. A number of smaller carriers have also followed in Southwest's footsteps and shunned the hub system, avoiding the burdensome fixed costs in an attempt to gain a cost advantage over the larger carriers. Exhibit 4

EXHIBIT 1A
Hubs of Major U.S. Airlines

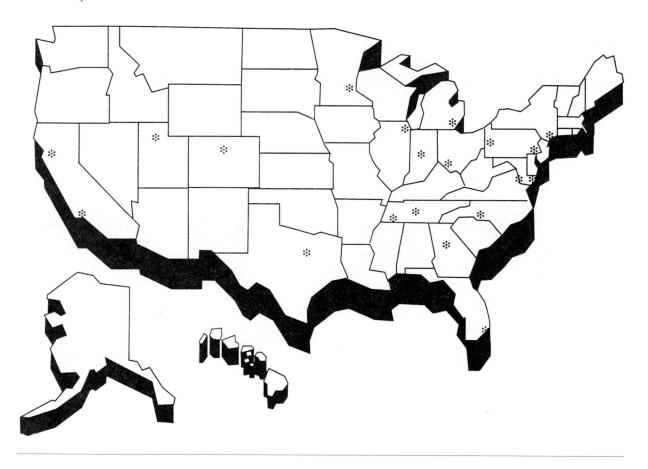

provides a break down of the costs incurred by a typical airline in 1993. Exhibit 5 compares the cost structure among the major carriers during 1994.

BATTLING THE LOW-COST PLAYERS

7   Airlines have begun to reexamine the concept of the hub-and-spoke. Some of these hubs are being eliminated or their operations curtailed. As the larger airlines try to overcome the threat posed by the smaller carriers, they have eliminated some routes, replaced commodious jets at smaller fields with crammed turboprops, and entered into alliance agreements with smaller operators to service more remote locations. The larger carriers also have restructured their schedules by dumping the short-hop competitive routes where they lose money and concentrating instead on long-haul domestic and inter-national routes where they can charge a premium. The larger airlines attract customers with the enticement of earning frequent flyer miles to fly with their regional partners. Thus, these majors maintain their brand recognition in the smaller markets without having to operate an unprofitable route.

8   Nonetheless, some of them have decided to battle the low-cost carriers head-on. Continental Airlines has initiated new, low-fare flights called CALite up and down the East Coast in the mold of Southwest, the paragon of low-price, no-frills flying. Unlike Southwest, however, CALite provides

EXHIBIT 1B
U.S. Hubs Operated by Major Carriers

American Airlines	Dallas/Fort Worth, TX; Chicago, IL; Miami, FL; Nashville, TN
Delta Air Lines	Atlanta, GA; Dallas/Fort Worth, TX; Salt Lake City, UT; Cincinnati, OH; Los Angeles, CA; New York City, NY
Northwest Airlines	Minneapolis/St. Paul, MN; Detroit, MI; Memphis, TN
United Airlines	Chicago, IL; Denver, CO; San Francisco, CA; Washington, DC
USAir	Charlotte, NC; Pittsburgh, PA; Philadelphia, PA; Baltimore, MD; Indianapolis, IN

assigned seats. Similarly, in 1994 United Airlines launched its United Shuttle in the West Coast markets where Southwest has made its fortune. Southwest Airlines itself has sought to beef up its East Coast beachhead in Baltimore as it expands its operations. America West, another low-price competitor, also seeks to establish its presence on the East Coast out of Philadelphia. It's still too early to evaluate the mixed results of these efforts. Besides these established players, as many as 28 start-up carriers have been formed in the past two years, targeting Eastern cities from Boston to Miami. However, these start-ups will continue to face barriers such as getting takeoff and landing slots at congested airports and gaining access to airport facilities such as boarding gates.

9   According to a report that examined 1992 yields in various markets in the United States, market share is the major determinant of a carrier's yield. Thus, in the Boston—New York market, Continental, which controlled the routes, enjoyed yields of 60.46 cents per RPM versus Delta's 53.17 cents. Similarly, in the New York—Orlando market, Continental had a 12.52 cent yield compared to 11.66 cents for Delta and 11.27 cents for USAir. Carriers that dominate a market also enjoy superior yields on flights originating from those markets. Carriers that are third or fourth in a market suffer poor yields. Experts estimate that hubs will continue to dominate airline operations with almost 80 percent of traffic being routed through them. Thus, carriers that control hubs should be able to enjoy better yields, following their ongoing attempts at restructuring their hubs.

A STRUCTURAL SHIFT

10   The larger airlines have historically targeted the "high-yield" first-class and business travelers to boost revenues. These passengers occupy one-fifth of an aircraft's capacity, but they contribute two-thirds of the revenue. A round-trip, first-class ticket from New York to London was $6,410 as opposed to $500 for an economy ticket on a representative flight from JFK to Heathrow airport. Guided by cost austerity measures, companies are forcing their executives into the economy section as opposed to the business section. A study by the European manufacturer Airbus Industrie predicts that by early 2000 only about one in five air travelers will be making a journey for business. In the past few years, passenger growth has been primarily in the leisure segment, a market that is especially sensitive to prices. In addition, 95 percent of passengers use discounted tickets that average more than 60 percent off the published full fare. Airline executives in 1994 were seeking to determine what these trends would mean for future competition.

THE BATTLE FOR THE EAST

11   The pricing blitzkrieg is being witnessed primarily on the East Coast as these new, small, nimble carriers make strafing runs in the region. The East Coast represents 37 percent of U.S. air travel and encompasses many of the nation's important business cities. The increase in the activities of their competitors has made Delta Air lines and USAir extremely nervous, because the bulk of their

EXHIBIT 2

Top 10 U.S. Airports in 1993 (in revenue passengers enplaned)

	Revenue Passengers (in thousands)	Percent Change over Previous Year
1. Chicago, O'Hare	65,077	1.0%
2. Dallas/Fort Worth International	49,970	−3.6
3. Los Angeles International	47,845	1.9
4. Atlanta, Hartsfield International	47,088	12.0
5. San Francisco International	32,737	0.4
6. Denver, Stapleton*	32,623	5.7
7. Miami International	28,660	8.2
8. New York, Kennedy International	26,790	−3.5
9. Newark International	25,612	5.5
10. Boston, Logan International	24,215	4.3

*Replaced by Denver International in February 1995.

Top 10 Airports outside the United States in 1993 (in passengers enplaned)

	Passengers (in thousands)	Percent Change over Previous Year
1. London, Heathrow	47,899	5.9%
2. Tokyo, Haneda	41,562	−2.6
3. Frankfurt	32,536	5.8
4. Paris, Charles de Gaulle	26,115	3.6
5. Paris, Orly	25,368	0.8
6. Hong Kong, Kai Tak	25,156	11.0
7. Osaka	23,361	−0.7
8. Seoul	22,634	6.1
9. Tokyo, Narita	22,141	0.5
10. Amsterdam, Schiphol	21,275	10.9

Source: Airports Council International.

earnings are generated on their East Coast flights—salespeople packing shuttle flights between Boston and Washington, D.C.; executives flying to Pittsburgh from New York; and Northeastern families seeking the sun in Orlando. The low-cost aggressors see the incumbent carriers as vulnerable and also believe the vast East Coast market will yield more benefits if fares are substantially lowered.

12   Southwest's entry into Baltimore is indicative of competitive forces in the future. USAir had a dominant presence in Baltimore, controlling almost 55 percent of the daily departures. Baltimore's lower landing fees as compared to nearby airports, reasonably priced gate rentals, and close proximity to Washington and southern Pennsylvania make it a huge travel market and hence attracted Southwest's attention. The company sent a planning team to the city to research the local demographic and economic data. Southwest entered the Baltimore market in mid-1994 offering its rock-bottom fares. By the end of 1994, Southwest had grabbed travelers while USAir saw its flyer base decrease.

A Significant Price Differential

13   Airline travelers on the East Coast have welcomed these new carriers with open arms, cheering the low-price fares they offer. Traditionally, East Coast travelers pay much more than their counterparts on the West Coast to fly the same distance. For example, flights of 300 miles or less cost Easterners double the average fare charged Westerners. According to a study by ATX, Inc., a potential new airline, between 1982 and 1992, short-haul fares in the eastern United States more

EXHIBIT 3
Top 20 Domestic Routes in the United States (includes all commercial airports in the area; excludes connecting passengers)

Market	Passengers
1. New York—Los Angeles	2,904,060
2. New York—Boston	2,350,240
3. New York—Chicago	2,330,750
4. New York—Washington	2,282,480
5. Los Angeles—San Francisco	2,153,360
6. New York—Miami	2,142,690
7. Dallas/Fort Worth—Houston	2,090,390
8. Honolulu—Kahului, Maui	2,035,100
9. New York—San Francisco	2,010,350
10. New York—Orlando	1,727,260
11. New York—Fort Lauderdale	1,547,970
12. New York—San Juan	1,524,400
13. Los Angeles—Phoenix	1,402,160
14. Chicago—Detroit	1,339,600
15. New York—Atlanta	1,330,730
16. Honolulu—Lihue, Kauai	1,273,460
17. Los Angeles—Las Vegas	1,217,420
18. Chicago—Los Angeles	1,188,980
19. New York—West Palm Beach	1,187,110
20. Los Angeles—Honolulu	1,165,470

than doubled while passenger traffic dropped 12 percent. By contrast, the western United States, populated by the low-cost carriers such as Southwest, saw a 75 percent increase in traffic during the same period while fares rose by only 5 percent. According to aviation consultants, lower fares on the East Coast should provide cost savings and incentives to the traditional airline traveler while also luring more discretionary travelers away from cars and trains. Some experts predict air traffic could jump by as much as 50 percent for some cities. However, some experts caution that this price cutting could lead to hostile conditions, especially for the smaller operators, resulting in a severe industry shakeout.

CRS: A VITAL ASSET

14 Since their introduction almost three decades ago primarily to manage the ticketing process, customer reservation systems (CRSs) have evolved into a critical competitive weapon. the SA-BRE™ system, introduced by American Airlines in 1962, can today predict whether a flight is going to be full. An airline seat on a flight is a perishable product. On any flight, the objective is to carry as many passengers as possible at as high a fare as the airline can demand so as to maximize revenue. Seeking to get the greatest revenue, some airlines want to save some seats for last-minute business travelers willing to pay the full fare. However, as departure approaches, carriers prefer to get a few dollars for a seat that would otherwise remain empty and generate nothing. The trick then is to use real-time information on reservations to adjust fares at the last possible moment to fill the planes.

15 The CRSs let airlines and travel agents see which flights are available. Using proprietary revenue management systems (RMSs), airlines can make regular checks on the CRS to see how the seats are filling up. The RMS keeps an eye on rivals' fares and checks travel patterns from historic databases kept for every flight. The RMS then calculates how to pitch the fares. If it looks like there will be many empty seats, the airline can increase the number of low-priced seats available on the flight.

16 Recently, aircraft manufacturers have sought to incorporate these changing dynamics in the design of their aircrafts. Boeing uses quick-change sliding bulkheads in its new 777 airplanes so the mix of classes can be changed rapidly according to bookings.

EXHIBIT 4
Airline Industry Expenses (1993)

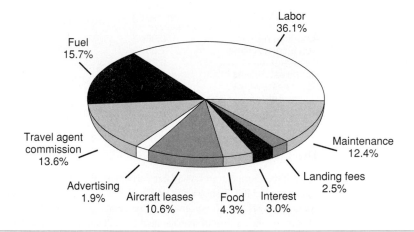

A POLICY TO PROTECT THE CONSUMER, OR REWARD INEFFICIENCY?

17   The big three airlines—American, Delta, and United—complain that weaker carriers have unfairly benefited from existing bankruptcy regulation. They claim that current bankruptcy laws allow insolvent airlines to continue operating for long periods with protection from creditors. The bigger airlines contend that carriers operating under bankruptcy protection are relieved of the need to make payments on pre-petition liabilities, thus giving them lower cost structures than their solvent competitors as long as they remain under Chapter 11. Also, the Chapter 11 carriers are able to borrow money only at extremely high costs and consequently are forced to concentrate on pricing as a means of generating their cash flow. Finally, the large airlines claim most of these carriers do not enjoy a favorable image among consumers and hence are compelled to offer price discounts to entice customers. These conditions have led these carriers to initiate the fratricidal wars that break out every few months, according to the big three. A recent study estimated that the bankrupt carriers have directly cost the rest of the scheduled airline industry at least $3 billion over the past three years.

18   The proponents of the bankruptcy legislation claim that they are ensuring competition in the industry and thus protecting the consumer. The weaker carriers argue that the real culprit of the price wars is the capacity expansion decisions made by the big three when they added 430 jets and 108.2 billion available seat miles to the system between 1989 and 1992. An increasing number of these Chapter 11 carriers have emerged from bankruptcy protection in 1994, possibly signaling a turn-around in the industry.

THE INTERNATIONAL ENVIRONMENT

19   As the U.S.-based carriers turn their attention to international routes, the waters become murkier. Commercial aviation across national borders has operated since 1944 on the premise that all interna-tional markets are closed until the governments involved agree to open them. Foreign routes must also conform with national defense and foreign policy objectives. Although the United States has sought to minimize the regulation of routes, schedules, fares, aircraft type, and the like, there are more than 1,200 bilateral agreements worldwide. Exhibit 6 shows that 6 of the top 10 airlines in the world, in terms of the number of passengers carried, are based in the United States.

EXHIBIT 5
Unit Costs Incurred by Major U.S. Airlines in 1994 (per available seat mile)

Airline	Cost (in cents)
American Airlines	8.36¢
Continental Airlines	7.85
Delta Air Lines	9.26
Northwest Airlines	9.56
Southwest Airlines	7.18
United Airlines	8.77
USAir	10.87

The Competition

20   Most of the European and Asian flag carriers are top heavy, inefficient, and hurting from the recent global recession. Exhibit 7 shows the cost and revenue figures for some of Europe's major carriers. Their operating costs are 30 percent to 50 percent higher than those of their American rivals. A study by McKinsey, Inc., a firm of management consultants, reveals that there is a 28 percent difference in labor productivity between the American and European airlines. This is critical because labor constitutes the major component in the airlines' cost structure (see Exhibit 4). Consequently, foreign carriers don't relish the thought of having to compete with their deregulation-hardened U.S. counterparts who have a huge domestic feed, good global networks, popular frequent-flyer programs, sophisticated yield-management techniques, and a great deal of marketing prowess. Some of those that operate in a large domestic market such as Germany's flagship, Lufthansa, have attempted to imitate some of these strategies.

21   Although the U.S. airline industry has been incurring losses during the past few years, the picture is not as bleak as the numbers would imply. Two-thirds of the losses in 1990 and 1991 were accounted for by Eastern, Pan Am, and Continental. In 1993, the losses of the 10 largest U.S. carriers were primarily the result of large, one-time, off-balance-sheet, noncash charges to comply with a new accounting standard for retirement and health benefits. Most of the foreign airlines have lobbied their respective governments to adopt protectionist measures designed to keep the U.S.-based carriers from expanding their international operations. Some of the European carriers, apprehensive about the diversion of excess U.S. capacity, have adopted a model of managed competition. In 1993, for example, KLM Royal Dutch Airlines, Swissair, Scandinavian Airlines System, and Austrian Airlines teamed up on purchasing, marketing, route planning, and other activities with a view to quadruple their earnings.

The Trans-Atlantic Market

22   The trans-Atlantic routes have been a sore point for a number of airlines. The U.S.-based carriers had collective operating losses of $845.3 million for the year 1992–93. These problems stem primarily from overcapacity that has plagued this market since 1989 when U.S. and foreign airlines added routes indiscriminately in a bid for rapid global expansion. Although U.S.-based carriers since 1980 have seen their international passenger traffic increase by 100 percent, international cargo freight by 158 percent, and international revenue by 184 percent, many are suspending service on some trans-Atlantic routes. However, recognizing the emergence of Asian countries as current and potentially future of economic power, the U.S.-based carriers are expanding their presence in those markets. Northwest is one of the biggest operators in the Pacific Rim market, for example, controlling 24 percent of the U.S.-Japan market. By 2010 Asia's share of world air travel is expected to rise from 25 percent now to more than 40 percent. Over the same period, American domestic air travel, currently about 30 percent of the world market, will shrink to 20 percent. Exhibit 8 shows the forecasted growth in various international markets for 1995 and 1996.

Globalization Trends

23   As carriers seek to penetrate the restricted international markets, transnational alliances appear to be the vehicle of choice. In 1993, British Airways bought a controlling interest in USAir and gained a critical foothold in the domestic American market. According to Sir Collin Marshall, the chairman of

EXHIBIT 6
The Global Airline Industry

Airlines	Rank	Passenger Kilometers* (in billions)	Passengers (in millions)	Fleet (aircraft)
American	1	156.7	86.0	672
United	2	149.1	66.7	536
Delta	3	129.5	83.1	551
Aeroflot	4	117.4	62.6	437
Northwest	5	93.7	43.0	359
Continental	6	70.0	38.8	319
British Airways	7	69.7	25.4	229
USAir	8	56.5	54.7	445
Air France	9	55.5	32.7	220
Japan Airlines	10	55.1	24.0	103
Deutsche Lufthansa	11	48.1	27.9	219
TWA	12	46.9	22.4	172

*Revenue passenger kilometers.
Source: *Air Transport World.*

British Airways, "Consolidation and globalization of the airline industry will leave no more than a score or so airlines dominating the world." KLM has a minority stake in Northwest Airlines, Air Canada has invested in Continental Airlines, Air France is teamed with Sabena and the Czech carrier CSA, and Swissair, Delta Air Lines, and Singapore Airlines have each taken small stakes in one another in a tripartite alliance.

24   Ownership of foreign landing rights is a controversy currently brewing in the airline industry. The Clinton administration is debating whether these foreign routes are owned by the United States or are the property of the airline that operates them. Traditionally, these routes have been treated as the property of the airline and are reflected as assets on the company's balance sheet. A reversal of this policy would adversely affect the financial health of some of the troubled carriers, which would not only be unable to sell these routes but would also see them disappear from their balance sheets.

25   American, Delta, and United Airlines are also negotiating bilateral "open skies" agreements with various European Community (EC) countries. In 1992, an agreement was negotiated with the Dutch, while negotiations with the Germans and French continue. However, the freedom to provide *cabotage* services in Europe—the right of an airline from one state to operate on a domestic route in another state—is banned until April 1997, even for airlines belonging to the EC.

26   Another blip on the international radar is the emergence of the *charter* airlines in Europe, some of which are low-cost subsidiaries of big airlines. These companies operate on the basis of full plane sales. For example, a ticket wholesaler will purchase the total aircraft capacity and then resell it in the form of incentive travel packages. These charters typically operate in a niche market, conducting services to tourist destinations within Europe and also to American, African, and Asian sites. The tickets for a charter flight are supposed to be sold only as part of a packaged tour, that is, one including hotels, meals, and transfers. As most of the larger airlines directed their efforts at business travelers, this segment was typically ignored. McKinsey estimates that charter airlines now account for about 30 percent of all passenger miles flown by European airlines.

27   The U.S. Department of Transportation estimates total charter flights represent less than 3 percent of all available seat miles (ASMs) flown within the United States annually. Of the 13.7 billion ASMs logged by U.S.-based charter airlines, almost 60 percent involved international services. Charters usually operate on a load factor of about 74 percent compared to 65 percent for the major airlines. Consequently, they can offer much deeper discounts to the customers. However, consumers typically have a negative perception of charters, associating them with "owning rusty planes, offering lousy in-flight service, and entailing long delays." Some of these charters are now selling tickets for flights only and thus are making inroads into the traditional domain of the scheduled airlines. The larger airlines have begun to take notice and offer their own versions of packaged tours, exemplified by Delta Air Lines' "Dream Vacations."

EXHIBIT 7
Unit Costs and Revenue Incurred by Major European Airlines (per available ton miles)

Airline	Costs (in cents)	Revenue (in cents)
Air France	0.50	0.45
Alitalia	0.87	0.85
British Airways	0.72	0.76
KLM	0.61	0.65
Lufthansa	0.55	0.49
Sabena	0.75	0.80
SAS	1.08	1.15
Swissair	0.92	0.92

EXHIBIT 8
ICAO* Scheduled Passenger Traffic Forecast
ICAO* Scheduled Passenger Traffic Forecast for 1995–96 (revenue passenger kilometer)

Market	1995 Forecast (billions of passengers)	Growth (%)	1996 Forecast (billions of passengers)	Growth (%)
Africa	46	4.8%	48	5.1%
Asia/Pacific	544	10.0	600	10.3
Europe	546	4.5	582	6.6
Middle East	67	6.5	71	6.7
North America	901	5.5	952	5.7
Latin America/Caribbean	103	5.5	110	6.3

*ICAO is a trade organization for international carriers.
Source: *Air Transport World*, September 1994.

ALTERNATIVES TO FLYING

28   Domestically, the U.S. airlines face stiff competition from alternate means of transportation, especially for the short-hop flights such as the Boston–New York–Washington, D.C., sector. Amtrak's Metroliner service completes the journey from New York to Washington, D.C., in 2 hours and 40 minutes, which is not much longer than flying when travel time to and from airports is considered. The competition from this source is likely to intensify when Amtrak introduces high-speed trains on these busy corridors. Airlines are faced with perennial delays at some of the larger airports in the country, further exacerbating this problem. Therefore, some airlines have opted to bypass these larger airports in favor of satellite airports, usually older, neglected airports. Southwest Air operates from Love Field in Dallas instead of DFW International and from Midway in Chicago instead of from O'Hare International.

29   Organizations are also exploiting advanced communication technologies such as videoconferences to minimize employee travel and thus hold down their operating costs. Further improvements in communication technologies may reduce the demand for air travel. Since businesses are using integrated computer networks, in addition to electronic aids such as facsimiles and modems, to interact with their counterparts on the information superhighways, teleconferencing may become a routine means of business communication. In 1992, more than 1,000 U.S. organizations, including more than half of the Fortune 1000 companies, had purchased videoconferencing systems.

30   As technology improves and prices fall as a result of increased competition among the teleconferencing hardware vendors, the technology is well within the reach of even medium and small-scale companies. Systems costs are within the $20,000 to $40,000 range with per hour network costs around $10. In a recent survey of information systems professionals of Fortune 1000 companies, 16 percent responded that videoconferencing had replaced travel "a lot" while 51 percent said that it replaced travel "somewhat." In the words of Herb Kelleher, the CEO of Southwest Airlines, "If you had telecommunications with a real-time, commercial-quality picture, it would be very competitive with business travel, especially if the alternative is a $3,000 ticket and 30 hours in the air."

CASE 38

NOTE ON THE PERSONAL COMPUTER INDUSTRY

1   Although the ability to monitor and adapt to changes in the general environment are important in every industry, firms in the personal computer industry are especially challenged by the technological forces that constantly alter the competitive landscape. As indicated in Exhibit 1, in 1992 the computer industry invested $14.2 billion in research and development (R&D). As a whole, the industry spent more than any other industry in R&D and is second only to the health care industry in R&D spending as a percentage of sales. The survival of the industry depends on the ability to convert these investments into innovations with commercial applications.

2   Since the development of microprocessor chips in the mid-1970s paved the way for personal computers, mainframes have been all but displaced by personal computers and workstations or a new generation of supercomputers. Personal computers (PCs) are defined as general application computers based on microprocessor chips with a resident operating system and local programming capability. PCs, which can be stationary or portable, consist of the hardware (equipment) and the software that makes the computer function. Three operating systems dominate the market, Microsoft's DOS, IBM's OS/2, and Apple's Macintosh OS. Although the distinction between PCs and workstations are blurring, workstations are generally more powerful and operate on a Unix operating system. Supercomputers are even more powerful than workstations, utilizing "enabling" technology that is capable of processing the most advanced scientific and commercial applications such as weather forecasting.

3   Within the person computer segment of the computer industry, rapid improvements in technological sophistication keep today's market leaders scrambling to retain a strong market position. The estimated PC life cycle has shrunk from five years in 1981 to six months in 1993. For example, while computers using the 80386 DX and SX chips accounted for 50 percent of PC unit sales in 1992, this number fell to 19 percent in 1993 as the 386 chips were replaced by the 80486 chip, which captured 66 percent of the market. In May 1993, however, Intel introduced a new generation of chips that is two times faster than the 486-based PCs, the Pentium chip. Further, competition from Motorola's 680X0 microprocessor as well as the PowerPC, Alpha, and MIPs chips challenge the longevity of the 80486 technology. By the year 2000, main memory size is expected to expand to one gigabyte and access time could fall to four nanoseconds.

4   Another big area of growth for PCs is in portable technology. In 1992, portables constituted about 20 percent of the market. The quest for the thinner, more compact computer has led to a proliferation of portables ranging from A/C and battery-powered laptops to notebooks, subnotebooks, handheld, and pen-based models. Consumers want convenience but balk at "cramped keyboards, diminutive screens and the absence of a built-in floppy disk drive."[1] In response, Digital developed a 4-pound subnotebook that is only 1.2 inches thick and is as long and wide as a letter-size sheet of paper. Pen-operating systems are also expected to take off as this technology develops. Experts expect an annual sales increase of 45 percent between 1995 and 1997. The market share of traditional desktop PCs is forecast to drop from 80 percent to under 65 percent by 1997.

5   Technological advances that increase the integrative ability of PCs may have the biggest impact on the industry's future. Computer, communication, and consumer electronic technologies are expected to converge, providing access to interactive information and services. Multimedia, the general label for this convergence, is broadly defined as a full range of technologies designed to combine video, animation, still pictures, voice, graphics, and text into a fully integrated and interactive

---

This industry note was prepared by Amy Beekman and Richard Robinson, University of South Carolina.

[1] Walter S. Mossberg, "Computer Notebooks Get Smaller, Lighter, and Costlier," *The Wall Street Journal*, February 2, 1995.

EXHIBIT 1
U.S. R&D Spending, 1992 (in billions of dollars, percent)

Industry	R&D Spending	Percent of Sales
Computer equipment	14.2	8.3
Automotive	12.3	4.0
Health care	11.8	9.7
Electrical and electronics	8.0	6.0
Chemicals	5.6	4.3
Aerospace	4.6	4.4
Telecommunications	3.7	3.1

Source: *Business Week*, August 9, 1993.

system. Multimedia has also been referred to as "infotainment." As shown in Exhibit 2, potential uses include training, education, publishing, entertainment, voice and video mail, teleconferencing, public information, and document-imaging and archival systems.

6   Although multimedia technology and products are still developing, industry sources estimated a $13 billion market by 1995. This market should provide many opportunities to computer companies but at the same time create significant challenges by inviting competition from firms with greater experience in consumer electronics and communications technologies. The use of strategic alliances to develop and share technologies may become critical to keep pace with the rate and range of change. Some alliances that have already formed between computer, communications, and entertainment companies include: IBM, Apple, and Toshiba; Time Warner and US West; Time Warner and Telecommunications, Inc. (TCI); and IBM, NBC-TV, and NuMedia Corporation.

7   Technological change is not the only driving force in the general environment affecting the industry. The industry continues to rebound from the recent economic recession. Corporations uncertain about the economy have actually boosted PCs sales in an effort to improve per worker productivity through increased computer usage while downsizing the total work force. In addition, companies continue to shift from mainframes into more cost-effective PC networks and upgrade existing operating systems.

8   Another factor influencing the growth of the computer industry is the internationalization of markets. Compared to the rest of the world, the U.S. market is approaching saturation. Although growth opportunities exist within the United States, dramatic growth is expected in developing markets. Even within developed countries, significant opportunities exist. For example, the combined population of EC markets exceeds the U.S. market by more than 80 million, but the estimated installed base of computers is barely half of the U.S. total. Commodore is the leading supplier to Europe followed by IBM, Apple, Compaq, and Olivetti.

9   In addition to Europe, Japan is another market opportunity. The installed base of computers in Japan is one-fifth the size of the U.S. base, reflecting the still limited use of computers in Japan. Japanese markets are forecast to expand. Not only has the Japanese government started promoting PC use in the education system, but also acceptance of PCs by consumers has increased as prices have decreased. In 1993, the release of a Japanese version of Windows™ has also stimulated the market. Before this release, proprietary versions of DOS were utilized, which limited the use of software applications. The majority of Japanese PCs utilize the DOS/V operating system, which is IBM compatible. Apple has approximately 8 percent of the market. In 1994, unit shipment growth to countries outside the United States was expected to increase 16 percent, with revenue approaching $45 billion.

10   Legislation has also affected the PC industry. Within the United States, the Clinton administration has demonstrated its commitment to maintaining the competitiveness of U.S. high-technology firms by initiating the National Information Infrastructure (NII) which creates the information superhighway. The NII is intended to create a partnership between government and industry to facilitate industry development. Although the government supports growth, it also seeks to encourage environmentally friendly growth. According to a study, PCs are the U.S. government's biggest energy consumers among the computer and business equipment. Based on the recommendations of the

EXHIBIT 2
Competing Industries and Growth Opportunities in the Evolving "Infotainment" Market

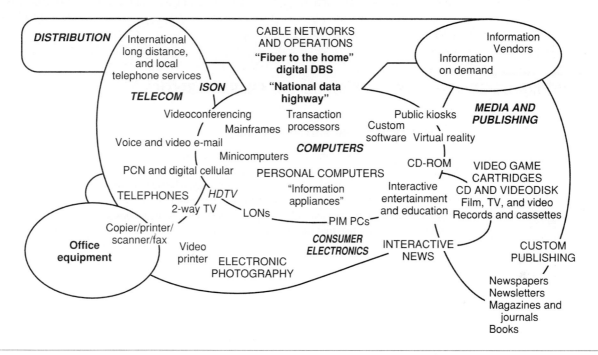

Source: Apple Computer, Inc.

Department of Energy and the Environmental Protection Agency (EPA), the president issued an executive order that limits the purchase of computer equipment to those computers that meet the criteria of the EPA's Energy Star program. In response to the legislation, about 70 computer manufacturers have agreed to develop energy-efficient products. The EPA projects that these products will cut electricity consumption by 25 billion kilowatt hours by the year 2000.

11   Another legal issue affecting the industry is software protection. Traditionally, copyright law has been the primary form of protection from infringement, but the courts are increasingly recognizing the use of contracts such as licensing agreements as well as the legal concepts of trade secrets and patents. For example, in a suit filed by Apple Computer, Inc., against Microsoft Corp. and Hewlett-Packard Co. alleging copyright violations, the court denied Apple's claim. Instead, the court validated the argument by Microsoft and Hewlett-Packard that the material at issue was covered by a license agreement signed by Apple and thus barred from broad claims of copyright protection.[2]

12   The government is supporting the computer industry by pursuing violations of intellectual property rights worldwide. In February 1995, the U.S. government threatened to levy 100 percent tariffs on $1.08 billion of Chinese exports for China's failure to enforce laws protecting patents, copyrights, and other intellectual property.[3] At the last hour, the United States and China reached "the single most comprehensive and detailed (intellectual property rights) enforcement agreement" ever negotiated.[4] As part of the deal, China agreed to establish at least 22 task forces to monitor the preservation

---

[2] Paul M. Barrett, "Justices Refuse to Hear Apple's Appeal in Copyright Suit against Microsoft, H-P," *The Wall Street Journal*, February 22, 1995.

[3] Craig S. Smith and Marcus W. Brauchli, "The Long March: To Invest in China, Foreigners Find Patience Crucial," *The Wall Street Journal*, February 23, 1995.

[4] Helen Cooper and Kathy Chen, "China Averts Trade War with U.S., Agrees to Combat Piracy of Various Items." *The Wall Street Journal*, February 27, 1995.

of intellectual property rights. This includes planned inspections of factories, raids on retail establishments, and severe penalties for violations.

13   Although most of these trends have affected all aspects of the PC industry, some differences exist in the hardware and software segments of the industry. Consequently, the next section will address industry-level factors by segment.

THE PC EQUIPMENT INDUSTRY STRUCTURE AND CHARACTERISTICS

Industry Structure and Barriers to Entry

14   The rapid growth of the PC in the 1980s led to a proliferation of companies vying for market share in the PC equipment industry. Because of standardized technologies and the availability of off-the-shelf components, entry into the market has been relatively easy. The number of competitors is estimated to be about 3,000. Despite this large number, the top 10 vendors have between 50 and 60 percent of the market. Consequently, entry may be fairly easy but strong financial resources and manufacturing economies of scale are required to acquire market share.

Competitive Rivalry

15   Although a few firms dominate the industry, some evidence of an industry shakeout exists. In 1993, the top three companies, IBM, Apple, and Compaq, had about 30 percent of market sales. These market shares are down from 50 percent of the market in 1987, and market positions continue to fluctuate. In 1994, Compaq Computer Corp. surpassed IBM in worldwide PC shipments for the first time. In the U.S. market, IBM dropped to fourth place behind Compaq, Apple, and Packard-Bell.[5] Although IBM's PC division had $10 billion in sales, the division also lost $1 billion. Much of this loss represents a write-down of PCs the company was unable to sell in 1993 because of obsolescence. In 1994, the company came out with well-accepted new products at competitive prices, but it still struggled due to an inability to keep up with demand. IBM's dilemma reflects the dual nature of a key success factor in the industry—not only does a firm have to keep pace with technological change or risk writing down unsold inventory, but a firm also has to accurately anticipate market demand or else it risks lost sales.

16   The total PC equipment market for 1993 was approximately $25 billion. Although this is a slight increase from 1992, market growth has slowed considerably from the rate of increases in the 1980s. In addition to reduced sales volume, increasing competition has led to price cutting, which has reduced profit margins. Intense price discounting began in 1991, and the industry set price reduction records in 1992 with average prices being cut by one-third. Prices are expected to continue to fall by more than 20 percent a year.[6] Falling profits have hurt many firms, forcing employee layoffs, bankruptcies, lower stock prices, and restructurings. For example, IBM and Digital Equipment Corporation (DEC) announced cutbacks totaling 70,000 employees worldwide. The slow rate of growth, especially in the largest segments of the market—government and business—coupled with the intense level of price rivalry suggests the market is approaching maturity.

17   Because of the volatile market dynamics, a continued industry shakeout is expected among current market leaders, especially with new firms such as Dell Computer Corp., Gateway 2000, and AST Research gaining momentum. Fourth-quarter sales in 1994 of Dell, a direct marketer with strong sales in Pentium-based computers and notebook computers, were triple the previous year's. For the 1994 fiscal year, sales rose 21 percent to $3.48 billion.[7]

---

[5] Bart Ziegler, "IBM Tries and Fails to Fix PC Business," *The Wall Street Journal*, February 22, 1995.

[6] Scott McCartney, "Dell's Profits More than Tripled to $60.3 Million in 4th Quarter," *The Wall Street Journal*, February 22, 1995.

[7] Scott McCartney, "Dell's Profits More than Tripled to $60.3 Million in 4th Quarter," *The Wall Street Journal*, February 22, 1994.

Buyers

18   As this industry shakeout continues and the industry matures, current PC users will become a replacement market and companies will target new customers to foster growth. Consequently, the market is expected to break into two distinct segments: a low and high end. The low end will concentrate on selling portable and desktop PCs to buyers who want powerful but competitively priced computers. The primary customer will be the currently less-developed markets such as home, education, and small business. Although PC utilization by home users has never reached predicted levels, this market is expected to grow quickly as acceptance and familiarity with PCs increases. Similarly, small businesses with less than 10 employees are a growth opportunity. In 1993, this market grew 20 percent and was expected to continue expanding. The high end will focus on workstations and powerful network servers required by the current largest buyers in the PC industry—business and government.

19   That this shift is already in progress is evidenced by the changes in distribution channels. In 1990, 66 percent of PC sales were through dealers and direct sales, but by 1997, this percentage is projected to decline to 41 percent. Instead of the traditional channels, companies are increasingly relying on computer superstores, mail-order catalogs, telemarketing operations, consumer electronics stores, and large retail chains. Successful innovations like the direct-response channel pioneered by Dell Computer have already encouraged new marketing techniques by other companies. In 1993, 36 percent of PC sales were through retail channels. Dealers and direct sales will probably remain the chief sales vehicle at the high end of the market. At the low end, however, mass market and retail outlets will be the major means to reach consumers.

Suppliers

20   In 1993, prices and profit margins were also hurt by the availability and cost of PC components. The increase in the demand for notebook computers created a shortage in LEDs, memory, and I/O chips. The cost of these delays was exacerbated by the increased cost of components, mainly due to the appreciation of the yen against the dollar.

21   Even within the United States, however, suppliers have considerable power. Microsoft supplies over 80 percent of PC operating systems. Intel is a major microprocessor chip supplier but is facing competition from other suppliers such as Motorola. To minimize competition from other chip manufacturers, Intel expanded and stepped up product introductions in 1993. For example, Intel introduced the Pentium chip in May 1993. Although the success of the Pentium chip was tainted by an operating defect discovered in late 1994 which resulted in Intel replacing defective chips with updated versions, the introduction was nevertheless influential in shortening the product life cycle of microprocessors. Product life cycles have shortened to as little as six months. Increasing competition between microprocessors should help keep prices competitive in the future, but the power of suppliers, coupled with the slow growth and decreasing profitability in the hardware segment, is causing many PC manufacturers to integrate backward into the software segment. For example, Apple, IBM, and Motorola formed a joint venture to develop the PowerPC, a chip to compete with Intel chips.

THE PC SOFTWARE INDUSTRY STRUCTURE AND CHARACTERISTICS

Industry Structure and Barriers to Entry

22   Although PC manufacturers are integrating backward into the software segment to decrease reliance on suppliers, another equally viable justification for such a move is the large growth potential of software systems and applications. The software industry is one of the fastest growing sectors of the U.S. economy, becoming a $32 billion industry in 1993. By 1997, the market is projected to reach $52 billion as the bulk of growth associated with the emerging multimedia market will benefit software developers. The strong performance of this market is also reflected in the 44.7 percent of the world market share held by U.S. firms. According to *Business Week* , sales of 19 major software firms increased 15 percent and profits increased 44 percent in 1993. As in the hardware segment of the industry, entry is fairly easy but strong financial resources and manufacturing economies of scale are required to achieve market share.

Competitive Rivalry

23   In contrast to the hardware segment, fewer competitors exist and two firms, Microsoft and Electronic Data Systems (EDS), account for 40 percent of total sales and 54 percent of total profits. Microsoft sells operating systems and application software, and EDS focuses more on information programming design and services. Microsoft has dominated the operating systems segment, but backward integration is increasing the level of competitive rivalry. Where the main choices used to be between Microsoft's DOS-based operating systems and Apple, IBM introduced its own operating system, OS/2, in May 1993.

24   It is still too early to assess the success of IBM and Apple versus Microsoft, but Microsoft controls 80 percent of the operating systems market and continues to innovate.[8] In August 1993, Microsoft released Windows NT™, which is a sophisticated 32 bit multitasking operating system that can compete with Unix, the powerful operating system for workstations. In response to this system, some firms have formed alliances to counter the threat of domination by Microsoft. For example, Sun Microsystems, Novell, Santa Cruz Operations, IBM, and Hewlett-Packard are working together to develop UNIX software that can compete with Windows NT. Microsoft released a new, powerful version of Windows, Windows 95, in 1995.

25   While Microsoft dominates the market in operating system sales, competition in the software application segment is more vigorous. Price competition is especially prevalent among companies selling software applications. For example, three leading companies, Microsoft, Lotus, and Borland, are using aggressive pricing strategies, such as low introductory prices and special upgrade deals, in an effort to grab a bigger portion of Windows-based application sales. These price wars are diminishing profit margins and will eventually have to be reevaluated but are expected to continue for the next few years. Backward integration is also evident in this segment, as Apple Computer is a software developer.

26   Another example of the increasing level of rivalry is the amount of litigation between industry competitors. Lotus Development Corp. filed a claim against Borland International Inc. seeking at least $100 million in damages for alleged copyright violations.[9] As the market leader, Microsoft Corp. is often the target of legal action. Currently the focus in an ongoing antitrust investigation, Apple also filed a suit against Microsoft for monopolistic behavior. This is in addition to the suit Apple previously filed against Microsoft for software copyright violations. In the latest suit, Apple claims Microsoft's failure to share advance copies or prototypes of its new operating system with rivals amounts to the company exerting monopoly power over industry competitors. The advance copies are called beta versions.

27   Although Microsoft maintains it has no legal obligation to provide beta versions and the legal requirements on this matter are not clear-cut, many believe Microsoft's strong market position creates a unique obligation. According to David Bradford, corporate counsel for Novell Inc., a chief rival, "They're so big they can control the pipeline, so they ought to be required to play by rules that others aren't."[10] The beta versions are sought by everyone from hardware manufacturers to software application developers in order to avoid incompatibility with Microsoft's operating system. In an industry where the latest in technology is demanded and the product life cycle is increasingly shorter, the sales lost in the time it would take to develop Microsoft-compatible PCs or software would have disastrous consequences.

---

[8] G. Pascal Zachary, "Microsoft on Power: If You've Got It, Flaunt It," *The Wall Street Journal*, February 24, 1995.

[9] John R. Wilke, "Borland's Cash Shrinks as Lotus Seeks Damages," *The Wall Street Journal*, February 27, 1995.

[10] G. Pascal Zachary, "Microsoft on Power: If You've Got It, Flaunt It," *The Wall Street Journal*, February 24, 1995.

Suppliers

28 In 1993, significant component and peripheral shortages caused production delays. For example, an explosion at a chemical plant in Japan limited the supply of epoxy resins used in the production of semiconductors. Further, the appreciation of the yen against the dollar increased costs.

Buyers

29 As in the PC equipment segment, buyers consist of home users, corporate applications, and governments. Computer equipment companies that sell assembled PCs also purchase operating systems and software.

30   In both the software and hardware segments, substitutes are not a major force.

CASE 39

NOTE ON THE BIOPHARMACEUTICAL INDUSTRY

1   Biotechnology refers to the use of living organisms to make commercial products, including foods, beverages, and pharmaceuticals. Although the use of biotechnology to manufacture pharmaceuticals is a new process, biotechnology has been used for foods and beverages for hundreds of years.

2   There are three major technologies under the biotechnology umbrella: recombinant DNA technology, monoclonal antibody technology, and bioprocess technology. The newest biotechnology is recombinant DNA technology or genetic engineering. Use of this technology began after scientists determined that strands of DNA could be cut, the genes rearranged or new genes inserted, and then pasted back together to make a new and different strand of DNA. This area of biotechnology is being used to treat genetic defects and diseases in humans, for agricultural products such as tomatoes with a longer shelf life or strawberries that are frost resistant, and for pesticides made from bacteria inserted into a plant to cause immunity or toxicity to certain insects.

EVOLUTION OF THE BIOTECHNOLOGY INDUSTRY

3   The biotechnology industry is evolving. This evolution also changes the focus and challenges for firms in the industry. The industry has changed dramatically since the early 1980s, and it will be far different in the future (see Exhibit 1).

The Early Years

4   The biotechnology industry broke away from traditional biological industries in the early 1970s and experienced a period of rapid growth through the mid-1980s. There are five market segments within the biotech industry: diagnostics, therapeutics (or pharmaceutical), agricultural-biotechnology, chemical and environmental services, and supplier firms. In the early 1980s, an average of 75 new companies entered the industry each year. These start-ups represented a significant portion of the industry, and they focused on research and development (R&D), product definition, and plans for clinical trials (testing).

5   Sources of funding included venture capital, private investment, and alliances with traditional industries. With heavy expenditures for R&D and no revenue-generating products, most segments of the industry operated in the red. Biotech suppliers were the only participants in the industry who had meaningful sales or profits. Management's primary task was to find the funding and scientific expertise for the firm's R&D efforts.

The Industry in 1993

6   In the late 1980s and early 1990s, the industry began to show signs of a transition from the laboratory to the marketplace. There are now a significant number of products on the market or in the latter

This industry note was prepared by Professor John A. Pearce II of Villanova University with the assistance of Paul Downey, Chris Kopang, Don Sinclair, and Terri Stewart.

EXHIBIT 1
Biotechnology Industry Life Cycle

	Early Phase	Current Phase	Future Phase
Demographics			
Start-ups	Many—varying quality; high percent of industry	Decreasing percent of industry	Fewer—higher quality; lower percent of industry
Source of managers	Traditional industries; academia	Large companies from traditional industries and large biotech companies	Large biotech companies
Consolidation	Little	Increasing (mostly by traditional industry)	Significant (biotech/biotech consolidation)
Number of firms	Growing rapidly	Slower growth	Decreasing
Profitability			
Products	Few products	Significant product approvals	Constant product pipeline pressure to maintain R&D efficiency
Infrastructure	Little sales, marketing, or manufacturing	Begin to build sales, marketing, and manufacturing	Infrastructure in place
Expenditures:			
R&D	Primary expenditure	Decreasing amount	Constant amount
Infrastructure	Very little	Increasing amount	Primary expenditure
Profits	None	Some profitable companies	Overall industry profitability
Financings			
Strategic alliances:			
Strategic partners	Traditional industry	Traditional industry and biotech/biotech	Increasing biotech/biotech
Motivation	Capital	Capital and marketing	Marketing and R&D
Financings:			
Venture capital	High proportion	Decreasing proportion	Small proportion
Public equity	Hard to obtain	More available	Easily available
Market capitalization	Low	Rapidly increasing	Increase more slowly

Source: Adapted from G. Steven Burrill and Kenneth Lee Jr., *Biotech '92: Promost to Reality* (Ernst & Young, 1991), p. 3.

stages of development. A few industry participants are even profitable. The industry has seen record merger and acquisition activity, expansion of financing alternatives, and growth in manufacturing, sales, and marketing abilities. Market capitalization reached $50 billion in 1992, a 70 percent increase from the previous year. Approximately $5 billion was raised via initial public offerings ($2 billion) and secondary public offerings ($3 billion) in 1992. The amount raised was a record for the industry. Overall, however, the industry continues to lose money. R&D is no longer the only focus of managers. They now must make many more strategic decisions (e.g., pricing policies and capital management).

Future Challenges

7   The complexity of manager decisions will continue to increase. The environment will become more competitive. Resource allocation decisions will be of greater strategic importance. The firm will be subject to greater regulations. The increase of public funding will increase public scrutiny of the firm's operations. It is during this phase that science and business are truly integrated.

EXHIBIT 2
Profile of Total Biotech Industry by Market Segment

Industry Segment	Percent of Market
Therapeutic	38%
Ag-bio	28
Supplier	16
Diagnostic	10
Chemical and environmental services	8

BIOTECHNOLOGY PHARMACEUTICAL

8   According to Ernst & Young's annual reports on the biotech industry, total sales for the industry as a whole are expected to reach $20.3 billion and $58 billion by 1995 and 2010, respectively. The following chart demonstrates historic and projected sales revenues for the industry as a whole:

Sales Revenues (in $ billions)

1990	1991	Percent change	1992	Percent Change	1995	Percent Change	2010	Percent Change
2.9	4.4	38%	5.9	35%	20.3	244%	58.0	300%

9   The 1990s will be a decade of dramatic sales growth in all segments of the industry. Currently, the therapeutic segment accounts for 38 percent of the entire market and 66 percent of the larger publicly traded companies (see Exhibit 2). The therapeutic (or pharmaceutical) segment is anticipated to experience the most growth, to more than 50 times the 1991 level of sales by the year 2000. The reasons for this large growth will be the introduction of blockbuster products and the small revenue base from which development-stage companies start.

KEY SUCCESS FACTORS

10   Biotechnology pharmaceutical companies seek to transform biological processes into beneficial, competitively priced products for enhanced human health improvement. This transformation process requires focusing R&D productively, managing clinical trials/field tests and regulatory relations effectively, negotiating supportive partnerships and strategic relationships, and maintaining access to capital.

11   The factors that are paramount for success in biopharmaceuticals can be grouped in three categories: product management, research/development, and financial management. Some of the contributing factors include:

· Lengthy FDA product approval process.
· High start-up capital requirements, with long horizons to payback.
· R&D expenditures represent majority of budget, as industry is based upon new technology breakthroughs.

12   The successful firm will be able to manage each of these success factors to its advantage. These key success factors are discussed below.

Product Management

13   Since the industry is still in its early stages, biotech products are primarily serving as substitutes for traditional products or procedures. As such, they must meet or exceed the performance (as measured

EXHIBIT 3
Top Factors Influencing Pricing in the Health Care Market

Efficacy relative to existing treatments	39%
Price of competing products or treatments	30
Product novelty	29
Manufacturing costs	28
R&D costs	13

by price, quality, etc.) of existing products and procedures to support entry into the market. In 1992, the total market for biotech health care products approached $2.5 billion. Market size for the turn of the century is projected to be $50 billion.

14   The development cycle for a biotech product can take from 7 to 10 years at costs that on average run from $100 million to $230 million. The traditional pharmaceutical industry has a similar time-span for product development, but its costs tend to run toward the high end of the range, whereas the biotech industry's costs tend to run closer to the low end of the range. Much of this advantage is attributable to the lack of overhead associated with biotech companies. As biotech companies build their infrastructures to become production companies, it is unclear if they can maintain this edge. The time spans are similar because both industries must go through the multiyear regulatory approval process. Because of this development cycle, managers must not only make traditional decisions about the products that they sell, but also decisions about the products in the pipeline are of critical importance. A misjudgment about a product that is in the pipeline can severely harm the biotech company.

15   The factors that most affect management of biopharmaceutical products include: (1) pricing policies, (2) distribution abilities, (3) product mix, (4) product pipelines, and (5) regulation. Each of these factors is discussed below.

1. Pricing Policies

16   The most significant marketing factor for companies in the biotechnology industry today is the increased pricing pressure being placed by the public. Price competition is a growing market reality. Discounts, promotions, and pure marketing muscle are becoming critical determinants of success (see Exhibit 3). It is becoming more difficult for companies to cover product development costs and generate capital for future product development.

17   In the past, an ethical drug proven safe and effective was reasonably sure to win a share of the market, namely, prescribing physicians. Price competition was a nonissue. Today, Medicare/Medicaid, hospital formularies, and managed care organizations represent much of the market, and they have made pricing a key issue. Products that are viewed as expensive without adding identifiable value will be rejected in the cost-conscious marketplace.

18   Since the market is more active in setting prices, managers must now have a reasonable sense of how much a product will cost to develop. This cost information will determine what the company will have to charge for the product. In many cases, development costs may become prohibitively expensive when compared to the market price for the product.

2. Distribution

19   Some biotech firms in the health care market have extensive sales forces that market directly to physicians and pharmacists primarily in hospitals and clinics. Others use major wholesale distributors of pharmaceutical products as the principal means of distribution. To reduce costs, biotech firms will frequently enter into strategic alliances with large pharmaceutical companies that have established distribution channels.

20   Any one of these distribution strategies can be appropriate. The proper strategy depends on the type of products that are being sold and the amount of control the company needs over its distribution.

EXHIBIT 4
Federal Food, Drug, and Cosmetic Act and Major Amendments

Federal Food, Drug, and Cosmetic Act of 1938—authorized the FDA to establish rules setting various requirements that the food, drug, device, and cosmetic industries would be obligated to meet for products administered to humans and animals.

1951 The Durham-Humphrey Amendment—provided guidance for distinguishing between prescription drugs and over-the-counter (OTC) drugs.

1956 The Hale Amendment—made formal evidentiary hearings nonmandatory for specific proposals to issue, modify, or repeal regulations.

1958 The Food Additives Amendment—established preclearance scheme for substances directly added to formulated foods or used in processing and packaging food.

1960 The Color Additive Amendment—provided the agency jurisdiction over all substances imparting color to food, drugs, and cosmetics. The Delaney Clause deems an additive unsafe if found to cause cancer in man or animal.

1962 The Drug Amendments—required the FDA to deny or withdraw approval of a new drug if it finds a lack of substantial evidence that the drug is effective. (The 1938 act based such action on safety only.) Tightened control on new investigative drugs.

1968 The Animal Drug Amendments—intended to consolidate regulatory authority related to evaluation of foods and new drugs administered to animals.

1976 The Medical Device Amendments—made all medical devices subject to different levels of regulation based upon their classifications by the FDA into one of three escalating categories under criteria defined in the statute.

1984 The Drug Price Competition and Patent Term Restoration Act—allowed an abbreviated application for the approval of generic drugs, and authorized the extension of the patents for certain regulated products.

3. Product Mix

21   The product mix refers to the variety and growth potential of the products a company is selling. If all a company's products have similar uses, company earnings could be subject to volatile swings because of cyclical demand or competitive pressure in the segment. Products with limited growth potential put a cap on company profitability.

22   A company must work toward diversifying its product line and selecting products that have great growth potential. In an industry that has so few approved products, this is a great challenge for managers. Development efforts must be coordinated with the other products in development and products on the market.

4. Product Pipelines

23   It is as important to have products in development as it is to have products in the market. Firms that can get new products through the pipeline to market quickly have a great competitive advantage. Due to regulatory and legal protection, a firm can get protected market share for a drug if it is the first to get approval. Since many companies have similar products in development, it is not inconsequential to be the first firm in the market with a new drug.

5. Regulation

24   The biotechnology pharmaceutical industry is regulated by the U.S. Food and Drug Administration (FDA). If a company decides to conduct business overseas, it will also have to comply with foreign agency regulation. Regulation covers all stages of development including research and development, field testing, and the final marketing of the product. Federal regulatory agencies review data from laboratory experiments to determine whether test organisms are toxic to humans. The agencies use the same laws as those that govern products made from other technologies, but may develop new procedures to deal with biotechnology products.

25   The FDA is responsible for the regulation of the safety of most pharmaceuticals and uses the provisions of the Food, Drug, and Cosmetic Act (Exhibit 4). The law enables the FDA to ensure the safety of pharmaceuticals by setting standards, testing new pharmaceutical products before letting them into the market, and establishing enforcement tools that can be used by the FDA if the need arises.

EXHIBIT 5
FDA Product Approval Process

Submission of investigational new drug notice (IND)

Contains information on the:

—Composition of the drug

—Manufacturing process

—Results of animal testing

—Plans for clinical trials in humans

—Consent forms to be used with human subjects

—Background of the investigators

—Data required to demonstrate that the drug will be safe for human testing.

Clinical trials begin upon approval of IND

Submission of new drug application (NDA)

Contains:

—Full report of the results of clinical trials in humans

—Statement of the drug's quantitative composition

—Description of the methods and controls used to manufacture, process, and package the drug

Product approval

26   Before the advent of biotechnology products, the FDA allowed companies to use abbreviated approval processes for products that were identical to already approved products or existing substances that were manufactured by identical techniques. For biotechnology products, the FDA has decided to require any product made by the recombinant DNA process to be treated as a new product and to be subject to the entire approval process. Getting approval on a new drug is a long and costly process (Exhibit 5). FDA approval of a new drug application takes between six and eight years and costs tens of millions of dollars. However, the FDA has been making some changes.

27   The FDA User Fee Bill passed in October 1992 levies three different fees (Exhibit 6):

1. Application fees will be assessed on new drug applications (NDA) and product license applications (PLA), as well as NDA supplements and PLA amendments for new indications, submitted on or after September 1, 1992. (Half of the fee is due upon submission of the application and half within 30 days of the company's receipt of an action letter.)

2. Establishment fees will be assessed annually on each foreign and domestic manufacturing plant at which at least one FDA-approved drug is manufactured. A single fee covers all buildings within a five-mile radius. No fee is assessed if the company does not have an application pending before the FDA or if a generic form of the drug is approved for sale.

3. Product fees will be assessed annually on each specific potency of an FDA-approved drug. No fee is assessed if the company does not have an application pending before the FDA or if a generic form of the drug is approved for sale.

28   The extra revenue generated by these fees enabled the FDA to hire 300 new reviewers for the Center for Biologics Evaluation and Review and Center for Drug Evaluation and Review. These centers are working to decrease the time it takes to get a new product through the agency approval process. *Science* magazine estimates that the new biological product applications already submitted would have taken nearly 13 years to move through the FDA process. Once the new centers are fully staffed, the time for approval should be cut in half.

29   One provision of the FDC Act empowers the FDA to oversee the export of products to foreign countries. The FDA has interpreted it to mean that products not approved in the United States cannot be exported for commercial purposes. While this provision is used to prevent companies from "dumping" drugs into foreign countries, it has hurt the U.S. biotechnology industry.

EXHIBIT 6
FDA User Fee Schedule

Fiscal Year Ended September 30	Fees
1993:	
NDA/PLA applications fee*	$100,000
Supplemental applications fees	50,000
Annual establishment fees	60,000
Annual product fees	6,000
Total fee revenues	36,000,000
1994:	
NDA/PLA application fees*	150,000
Supplemental applications fees	75,000
Annual establishment fees	88,000
Annual product fees	9,000
Total fee revenues	54,000,000
1995:	
NDA/PLA application fees*	208,000
Supplemental applications fees	104,000
Annual establishment fees	126,000
Annual product fees	12,500
Total fee revenues	75,000,000
1996:	
NDA/PLA application fees*	217,000
Supplemental applications fees	108,000
Annual establishment fees	131,000
Annual product fees	13,000
Total fee revenues	78,000,000
1997:	
NDA/PLA application fees*	233,000
Supplemental applications fees	116,000
Annual establishment fees	138,000
Annual product fees	14,000
Total fee revenues	84,000,000

*Small companies eligible for reduced rates and deferred payment. The program will expire on October 1, 1998, unless renewed by Congress.

30 Once a product is approved overseas, a company can build production facilities in the foreign country. This option is usually open only to larger companies with the resources. Smaller companies usually choose to enter into joint ventures with foreign firms. This latter option strains U.S. competitiveness because the U.S. company must transfer the technology to its foreign partner while it awaits approval for its product in the United States. Once the foreign production facility is established, manufacture of the product usually does not return to the United States once FDA approval is received.

The Orphan Drug Act

31 In 1983, Congress enacted the Orphan Drug Act to provide additional incentives for the commercial development of drugs for rare diseases, defined as a disease that afflicts fewer than 200,000 people. As many as 20 million Americans suffer from one of 5,000 rare diseases, including cystic fibrosis, hepatitis B, and multiple sclerosis. Under the provisions of the act, the first company to receive FDA approval for a therapeutic designated with orphan status is entitled to the exclusive right to market that product for that disease for seven years.

32 The Orphan Drug Act has encouraged the development of drugs for the treatment of rare disease when market forces, by themselves, would have been inadequate. In the 10 years preceding the 1983 act, only 10 orphan drugs were marketed; since enactment, more than 50 have received FDA approval and another 330 are in development.

The Clinton Administration

33   The Clinton administration made health care reform one of its major initiatives in 1994. The cost of health care has grown 9 percent annually and in 1993 composed 14 percent of the U.S. gross domestic product.

34   Two of the reform issues developing from this reform are drug price controls and the R&D tax credit. The government wanted to regulate the amount of annual increase to which drug prices can rise. They believed this would help the cost of health care stay at a reasonable level. The administration also discussed eliminating the R&D tax credit. The total R&D expenditure was $4.9 billion in 1992. Small companies have been reported spending as much as 119 percent of revenue on R&D, with an industry average of 68 percent. This tax credit was believed by industry leaders as vital for the continued growth of the industry.

Research and Development Management

Expenses

35   R&D expenses represent the largest single component of costs and expenses for the biotech companies. R&D expenditures for the biotechnology industry as a whole, including both public and private companies, were $4.9 million in 1992, an increase of 42 percent over 1991. Public companies reinvested almost 68 percent of product sales and revenue into research activities, including the scale-up of manufacturing facilities.

36   On average, small public companies (1 to 50 employees) report spending 119 percent of revenue on R&D expenses, compared with 43 percent and 42 percent for the large and top-tier companies.

Patents

37   Patents coming from a company's R&D are a key component in companies' valuation and access to capital. The fact that the patent environment was not well prepared to deal with the range of issues raised by biotechnology contributed to the industry's unpredictability. Through 1993, there was a 15 percent annual growth rate in biotechnology patent filings. In 1990, the most recent year for which data are available, 3,378 patents were issued and 9,385 new patent applications were filed. To support the growth of biotechnology activity, the U.S. Patent and Trademark Office more than doubled its staff in 1991. However, the review time for biotechnology patents is currently 25 months, versus 18 months for all patents.

38   There are signs that the relative importance of patent approval is decreasing. As the market matures and companies develop competing products in the same categories, the duration and extent of any market exclusivity is decreasing. Companies are competing less on proprietary science and more on product benefits, pricing, and marketing/distribution. However, the value of a company's patents still remains a critical factor in the success of any biotech firm.

Financial Management

39   The biopharmaceutical industry lost over $8 billion in 1992. Financial management is very critical to many of the industry's firms. Proper financial management allows the firm to have access to the funding that is necessary for development of products. Since many firms do not currently market a product, access to funding is the only way the company can survive. For this reason, biotech companies manage their financial condition very carefully.

40   R&D and acquisition costs have the biggest impact on the company's financial condition. Managers must take the necessary steps to ensure the company can make these expenditures.

Sources of Funding

41   The biotechnology industry must have inexpensive and abundant access to capital in order to finance the development of new technologies. Ernst & Young estimated in 1992 that it would require an

aggregate of over $40 billion in capital if each of 225 existing public companies brought just one product to market.

42   In its early phase, the biotechnology industry was driven by access to private capital, mostly venture financing and private placements. In the early 1990s, the most economical and accessible financing was public capital, while venture capital remained in relatively short supply. Companies have developed creative financing vehicles such as R&D partnerships and strategic alliances for particular development objectives.

43   From July 1991 through June 1992, public capital was biotechnology's strong suit. Biotech companies completed more initial public offerings (IPOs) than any other industry. However, the IPO market has cooled since the spring of 1992.

44   Biotech companies raised over $3 billion in public equity in 1991, compared to the same amount of public equity being raised in the entire decade of the 1980s. Additionally, in the first six months of 1992, biotech companies raised almost $2 billion.

45   Several factors led to the success of public offerings for biotech firms through early 1992. Investors went to the equity markets seeking higher yields compared to the low bond and money market rates that resulted from the economic recession. Recession-resilient health care stocks became particularly attractive, as it was one of the few expanding sectors during 1990–91. The biotechnology firms represented a growth play in this market. Finally, the success of biotechnology firms such as Amgen encouraged investment in biotech stocks.

46   However, conditions turned around in the equity markets in 1992. The economy began to improve, leading investors back into cyclical stocks. Public concern over rising health care and pharmaceutical costs led to concerns of future pricing constraints. Regulatory disappointments for major firms such as XOMA, Centocor, and U.S. Bioscience increased the unpredictability of returns on stocks in the biotech market.

47   The number of initial public offerings and secondaries being filled to access public capital seemed beyond the capacity of the market for such high-risk equities. Although investors had received extraordinary returns in biotech stocks, there were signs by early 1992 that valuations, in terms of fundamentals, had gone beyond reason. The decline in market value for biotech stocks was so substantial that the timing for recovery was longer than previous corrections and more fundamental developments to restore optimism and appetite for biotech equities. Offerings in 1993–94 demonstrated that investors were cautious, based on the fact that for virtually every IPO completed, the offering prices and number of shares sold were less than originally filed.

48   The availability of venture capital funding has been more a factor of the fortunes of the venture industry than of biotechnology. The U.S. venture industry hit its peak fund-raising year in 1987, at nearly $5 billion. Only $1.3 billion was raised in 1991. However, biotechnology firms continued to receive a sizable share of venture financing compared to other industries, receiving more than 8 percent of total disbursements.

49   In addition to a reduction in total availability of funds, venture capital is increasingly concentrated in the hands of a few major players. The IPO slowdown created an opportunity for start-up firms, financed by these venture capitalists. According to Ernst & Young's 1993 report on the industry, the leading venture funds had over $500 million of capital earmarked for investment in biotechnology.

50   Although private placement financing is desirable because it tends to be less subject to the valuation pressures associated with venture or public markets, it is rarely used by the industry. The primary reason for its lack of use is that, in general, biotechnology does not have the investment banking muscle in private placements that it has at the IPO and secondary placement levels.

INDUSTRY PARTICIPANTS

51   The more than 1,200 biotech firms in the United States can be classified by size and function: small, single-product entrepreneurial firms and larger multiproduct firms. Both types have contributed to the U.S. lead in the industry.

52   Although many companies have had an impact in the biopharmaceutical segment of the biotechnology industry, this industry note will discuss only the top six first-tier companies that have products

EXHIBIT 7
Profile of Total Biotech Industry by Company Size

Size Category	Percent of Industry
Top tier	2%
Large	6
Midsize	16
Small	76

in the market. A "top-tier" firm is defined as a company that has more than 300 employees. Only 2 percent of the companies in the entire biotechnology industry are top-tier companies (see Exhibit 7). These six companies account for 45 percent of the industry sales revenue. The six firms in order of rank are Amgen, Genentech, Chiron, Genzyme, Biogen, and Immunex.

Amgen

53   Amgen, headquartered in Thousand Oaks, California, is a leading biopharmaceutical company developing human therapeutics based on cellular and molecular biology. The company markets two important human therapeutics in the United States, Epogen, a hormone that stimulates red blood cell production, and Neupogen®, a recombinant granulocyte colony-stimulating factor. Amgen's therapeutic product pipeline includes additional hematopoietic growth factors, tissue growth factors, and most recently, neurotrophic growth factors. The total number of employees exceeds 1,000. Sales for Amgen in 1992 were $1.05 billion with net profit as $357.6 million. Amgen has marketing rights in the United States, Canada, and Australia and jointly shares rights with F. Hoffmann-LaRoche Ltd. in the European Community. Hoffmann-LaRoche has the rights to market products throughout the rest of the world except for Japan, Taiwan, and Korea where rights are held by Kirin Brewery.

Genentech

54   Genentech, based in San Francisco, is a leading biotechnology company with 2,100 employees that discovers, develops, manufactures, and markets human pharmaceuticals for significant medical needs. Genentech's products include Protropin®, its first marketed product, which is a human growth hormone. Another main product is t-PA, or Activase. This drug helps to quickly open clogged arteries of heart attack victims. This drug is also approved for sale in Japan as well as in the United States. Actimmune® interferon gamma is Genentech's third marketed product and is used for patients with chronic granulomatous disease. All of these products are being tested for expanded uses. Hoffmann-LaRoche purchased 62 percent of Genentech in September 1990. Genentech's sales in 1992 were $391 million and net income was reported as $20.8 million.

Chiron Corporation

55   Chiron Corporation applies genetic engineering and other tools of biotechnology to develop products that diagnose, prevent, and treat human disease. Chiron is building a health care business to address needs in four markets: diagnostics, vaccines, biopharmaceuticals, and ophthalmics. Chiron is best known for its work in infectious diseases, and in particular for its discovery of hepatitis C virus (HCV), the cause of what was formerly non-A, non-B hepatitis, and development of an HCV antibody test now being used for universal screening of donated blood. The company developed the first genetically engineered vaccine for hepatitis B, now manufactured and marketed by Merck, as by Novo Nordisk. For the year ending December 31, 1992, Chiron had sales of $174 million, but with a net loss of $102 million. Chiron acquired Cetus Corporation, a freestanding biotechnology company, in 1991. Chiron employs 1,440 people in four buildings in Emeryville, California, and at Chiron Ophthalmics, a fully integrated subsidiary, in Irvine, California.

Genzyme

56   Genzyme Corporation is a diversified health care products company that has a distinctive position in the industry based on its development of three strategic businesses: biotherapeutics, diagnostic products and services, and pharmaceuticals and fine chemicals. Genzyme's achievements to date are based on its innovative use and integration of key technologies, specifically carbohydrate engineering, protein chemistry, enzymology, and molecular biology. Ceradase® is the first product in Genzyme's emerging biotherapeutic business and is used for treating Gaucher's disease. Genzyme is the leading independent producer of diagnostic enzymes and substrates for use in clinical diagnostic kits in the United States and also a major supplier of research biological products for use by researchers in studying the underlying mechanisms of the body's immune system. The company has 1,275 employees worldwide. Its sales were $219.1 million in 1992, but its net loss was $30.3 million.

Biogen

57   Biogen, with 330 employees and headquartered in Cambridge, Massachusetts, is a biopharmaceutical company principally engaged in developing and manufacturing drugs for human health care through genetic engineering. The company's revenues are generated from worldwide sales by licenses of five products, including alpha interferon, hepatitis vaccines, and hepatitis diagnostic products. Biogen is focused primarily on developing and testing products used for the treatment of cardiovascular disease, inflammatory diseases, AIDS, and certain cancers. Sales were $121.7 million in 1992, and net income was $38.3 million.

Immunex

58   Immunex Corporation is a biopharmaceutical company focused on the discovery, development, manufacture, and marketing of products to treat cancer and autoimmune disease employing 525 people. The company received approval on its first product, Leukine®, in March 1991. Leukine® is used to stimulate the growth of two types of white blood cells in the human body. Three products that are in clinical trials but have been pinpointed as high priorities are PIXY321, Interleukin-1 receptor, and TNF receptor. The company also just opened a manufacturing plant for its products, both marketed ones and those in clinical trials. Sales figures for the company in 1992 were $51.9 million, but its net loss was $77.6 million.

STRATEGIC CHOICES

59   Even after companies overcome the regulatory, financial, and R&D obstacles, they find that the market penetration and manufacturing/distribution processes are long, costly, and fairly unpredictable. Early-stage companies are turning to accelerated commercialization strategies so that they can spread their infrastructure investment risk over the more stable foundation of a diversified product portfolio.

60   The methods of accelerated commercialization are diverse. Besides traditional methods such as strategic alliances and acquisitions, product swaps and license arrangements have also been used.

61   In the early to mid-1980s, most biotechnology companies pursued a business strategy of a straightforward progression from start-up to a fully integrated company. Influential investors favored "linear thinking," supporting companies with a pure focus on developing a few flagship products with tremendous sales potential. The extreme optimism of the industry's youth in the 1980s has given way to more mature strategies. Instead of pursuing the one-dimensional, long-shot, "bet-the-company" strategy, investors are supporting firms with accelerated, well-planned commercialization strategies. The top-tier firms still generally follow a full integration approach, but they have adapted their strategies to put more emphasis on commercialization. Through a variety of approaches, companies engaged in developing their flagship products are generating revenues,

EXHIBIT 8
Key Success Factors by Company

Company	Products		R&D	Financial
	Sold	In Pipeline		
Amgen	Neupogen Epogen PROCRIT	Stem-Cell Factor PDGF Consensus Interferon	% sales: 17.4% % revenues: 16.7%	Net income: $357.60 EPS: .67 Net burn rate: −46.93 Working capital: 562.42
	• Strong sales • Growth potential	• Early stages of development	• Fast development • Future increases • Low % of sales • Educational ties	• Very strong • Watch expenses • Debt rating
Biogen	Intron A Engerix-B Recombivax	Hirulog Beta Interferon	% sales: 49.6% % revenues: 48.8%	Net income: $38.31 EPS: 1.12 Net burn rate: −3.33 Working capital: 242.25
	• Uses licensees • Narrow product line	• Future increases • Very competitive markets	• Future increases • R&D contracts	• Limited control • 100% equity • Transition costs
Chiron	Proleukin IL-2	Betaseron Macrolin M-CSF Various cancer treatments	% sales: 128.1% % revenues: 82.1%	Net income: −$102.61 EPS: −3.40 Net burn rate: 7.70 Working capital: 243.69
	• Strong sales • Growth potential • Diversified business	• Mature pipeline • Competitive markets	• Buy technology • Partnership • High % of sales	• Volatile earnings • Strong capitalization

Note: As of December 31, 1992; dollars in millions except per share data.

developing manufacturing, sales, and distribution infrastructures, and buying time before the more well-thought-out arrangements pass them by.

62   Some strengths and weaknesses of the six leading firms in the industry are described below and summarized in Exhibit 8.

Amgen

63   Based on the strength of its product line, Amgen was the first biotech company to top $1 billion in annual revenues. The sales of its two main drugs Neupogen and Epogen, have a strong base of sales, good growth potential, and very limited competition. In the future, both products could gain regulatory approval for other purposes. Currently, Amgen has no products in the latter stages of development. Without a constant supply of new products in the market, company performance is at risk to seasonal, technological, and operational risks.

64   Amgen's research and development effort has a history of developing new products twice as quickly as the industry average. This is a key competitive advantage for the firm and testimony to the quality of its R&D staff. In part to offset the pipeline gap, Amgen intends to increase its expenditures on R&D by at least 50 percent this year. As of 1993, its R&D budget was significantly below the other leaders in the industry (see Exhibit 9). Instead of R&D, Amgen has allocated its resources toward building its manufacturing and marketing abilities. Amgen uses many sources to get its R&D breakthroughs. In addition to strong internal abilities, Amgen uses partnerships, acquisitions, and educational affiliations.

EXHIBIT 8
(concluded)

Company	Products Sold	In Pipeline	R&D	Financial
Genentech	Activase Protropin Actimmune Roferon Humulin	Pulmozyme HER2	% sales: 71.3% % revenues: 51.2%	Net income: $20.84 EPS: .18 Net burn rate: −1.83 Working capital: 446.96
	• Diverse products • Strong sales • Growth potential	• Balanced pipeline	• Internal focus • Strong firm commitment • Good abilities	• Very strong • Capitalization • Low margins • Increasing costs
Genzyme	Ceradase	Cystic Fibrosis Therapy GCR	% sales: 22.0% % revenues: 18.1%	Net income: −$30.32 EPS: −1.41 Net burn rate: −4.86 Working capital: 292.55
	• Limited growth • Diversified business	• Early stages of development	• Buy technology • Low % of sales • Low firm priority	• Acquisition costs • High selling and admin. costs
Immunex	Leukine Prokine	PIXY321 Interleukin-1 TNF receptor	% sales: 71.5% % revenues: 60.1%	Net income: −$77.60 EPS: −5.21 Net burn rate: −1.57 Working capital: 40.62
	• Narrow product line • Growth potential • Agreements	• Middle stages of development	• Partnerships • Mergers • Acquisition • New internal push	• Weak cash position • Vulnerable earnings

Note: As of December 31, 1992; dollars in millions per share data.

65   Amgen has by far the strongest financial condition. With net income of over $350 million in 1992, it dwarfs all other companies in the industry. In fact, Standard & Poor's rating agency has given Amgen's commercial paper an A-1 rating and its senior debt a single-A rating—the strongest ratings of any of the biotech firms. This means that the public debt markets are very much available as a means of funding. The biggest concern with Amgen's financials is the company's high general and administrative costs.

Biogen

66   Biogen's current product line is very narrow. Engerix-B and Recombivax are both hepatitis B vaccines. Intron A is used for hepatitis B, hepatitis C, and a few other uses. Instead of developing marketing abilities, Biogen has licensed its products. Engerix-B is sold by SmithKline Beecham. Recombivax is sold by Merck. Schering-Plough markets Intron A. Sales for Biogen's products have been very good. Engerix-B and Recombivax sales increased because of a vaccination program for workers covered by OSHA regulations and the growth in childhood vaccinations in the United States. The increase in Intron A sales is due largely to sales in Japan for the treatment of hepatitis C.

67   The major product in Biogen's pipeline is Hirulog. Hirulog is an anticoagulant used with cardiovascular patients. The potential sales in this market are very high. However, a number of other firms have similar products in clinical trials. There is a race to see whether Biogen can get its product to market before other firms. The company is also working on a beta interferon that will be used to treat hepatitis, certain cancers, and multiple sclerosis.

EXHIBIT 9
Comparative Balance Sheets as of December 31, 1992 (in millions except share data)

	Amgen	Chiron	Genentech	Biogen	Genzyme	Immunex
Assets						
Current assets:						
Cash and securities	$ 555.41	$ 256.78	$ 391.90	$227.89	$ 248.33	$ 118.73
Trade receivables	156.04	29.77	93.91	33.42	0.00	0.00
Inventories	56.80	21.73	65.32	0.00	0.00	0.00
Other current assets	104.84	40.83	29.38	7.14	80.85	0.00
Total current assets	873.09	349.10	580.50	268.45	329.18	118.73
Property, plant, and equipment	425.96	89.59	432.53	32.30	87.93	96.99
Other noncurrent assets	75.28	273.67	292.11	10.40	63.58	20.07
Total assets	$1,374.33	$ 712.37	$ 1,305.13	$311.15	$ 480.69	$ 235.79
Liabilities and Equity						
Current liabilities	$ 310.67	$ 105.42	$ 133.54	$ 26.20	$ 36.62	$ 78.11
Long-term debt	129.93	107.19	152.02	0.00	0.00	23.69
Other noncurrent liabilities	0.00	6.83	12.24	0.00	121.12	0.00
Total liabilities	440.60	219.43	297.81	26.20	157.74	101.80
Stockholders' equity	933.73	492.93	1,007.32	285.00	322.95	133.99
Total liabilities and equity	$1,374.33	$ 712.37	$ 1,305.13	$311.20	$ 480.69	$ 235.79
Shares outstanding	136.32	31.71	113.99	31.70	21.57	14.90
Income:						
Sales	$1,050.65	$ 111.58	$ 390.98	$121.71	$ 179.97	$ 51.92
Corporate partner	29.62	40.50	0.00	2.04	39.11	9.85
Other revenue	12.77	21.94	153.29	0.00	0.00	0.00
Total revenues	$1,093.04	$ 174.03	$ 544.27	$123.75	$ 219.08	$ 61.76
Operating Expenses:						
Cost of sales	$ 184.74	$ 56.34	$ 66.82	$ 9.38	$ 80.09	$ 15.74
R&D	182.30	142.93	278.62	60.40	39.68	37.13
Selling, general, and administrative	299.89	101.16	172.49	16.99	57.58	39.93
Other operating expenses	0.00	47.54	0.00	8.42	0.00	0.00
Total operating expenses	$ 666.93	$ 347.97	$ 517.93	$ 95.18	$ 177.35	$ 89.80
Other Income (expense):						
Interest income—net	$ 35.25	$ 7.46	$ (4.41)	$ 11.37	$ 14.88	$ 9.15
Equity in affiliated companies	24.70	74.12	0.00	0.00	1.68	0.00
Misc. income (expense)	77.08	0.00	0.00	0.00	0.00	0.00
Total other income (expense)	$ 137.02	$ 81.58	$ (4.41)	$ 11.37	$ 16.56	$ 9.15
Gross income	$ 563.13	$ (92.36)	$ 21.93	$ 39.93	$ 58.29	$ (18.88)
Taxes	205.53	3.60	1.10	1.62	18.80	0.00
Extraordinary items	0.00	(6.66)	0.00	0.00	(69.81)	(58.72)
Net income	$ 357.60	$(102.61)	$ 20.84	$ 38.31	$ (30.32)	$ (77.60)
Earnings/share	0.67	(3.40)	0.18	1.12	(1.41)	(5.21)

68   Biogen spends 50 percent of product revenue on R&D and is committed to future increases in R&D spending. Besides doing R&D for themselves, Biogen also contracts out its R&D resources. In particular, it has been involved with an insurance company in AIDS research.

69   The financial condition of Biogen is strong and unique to the industry. The company is financed almost completely with equity and thus has no interest expenses. Since biotech stocks do not pay dividends, Biogen has minimized its funding costs. As the company grows, Biogen may have to tap other sources of funding. Earnings for Biogen have been volatile from quarter to quarter. This is because the license agreements and narrow product line really give Biogen's management limited control over earnings.

EXHIBIT 9
Ratios and working capital (concluded)

	Amgen	Chiron	Genentech	Biogen	Genzyme	Immunex	6-Company Average
Liquidity:							
Current ratio	2.81	3.31	4.35	10.25	8.99	1.52	4.46
Burn rates:							
Overall rate	55.58	29.00	43.16	7.93	14.78	7.48	22.56
Net burn rate	(46.93)	7.70	(1.83)	(3.33)	(4.86)	1.57	(6.81)
Survival index	(0.85)	0.31	(0.05)	(0.17)	(0.18)	0.16	(0.11)
Leverage:							
Debt/assets	0.09	0.15	0.12	0.00	0.00	0.10	0.07
Debt/equity	0.14	0.22	0.15	0.00	0.00	0.18	0.10
Activity:							
Sales turnover	0.76	0.16	0.30	0.39	0.37	0.22	0.32
Profitability:							
Gross margin	0.82	0.50	0.83	0.92	0.55	0.70	0.62
Operating margin	0.50	(0.95)	0.07	0.23	(0.15)	(1.67)	(0.28)
Net margin	0.34	(0.92)	0.05	0.31	(0.17)	(1.49)	(0.27)
ROA	0.26	(0.14)	0.02	0.12	(0.06)	(0.33)	(0.02)
ROS	0.34	(0.92)	0.05	0.31	(0.17)	(1.49)	(0.27)
ROE	0.38	(0.21)	0.02	0.13	(0.09)	(0.58)	(0.05)
Working capital	562.42	243.69	446.96	242.25	292.55	40.62	261.21

70   In 1993, the company's management announced that it intends to become a fully integrated firm. For Biogen this meant that considerable resources would be put into building its marketing abilities. The transition from vertically integrated to fully integrated may depress earnings.

Chiron

71   Chiron has taken a portfolio approach to its business. In addition to therapeutics, Chiron is active in diagnostics, vaccines, and ophthalmics surgical products. Chiron has expanded its business through a series of acquisitions and joint venture agreements. Chiron's strategy for building a health care business includes the optimization of its financial participation by marketing products from its technology through its own and other sales forces. Chiron's goal is to increase its selling activities in key markets, consistent with its corporate strengths, resources, and focus. Frequently, products are developed by collaboration with other, generally more mature health care companies.

72   Chiron's main product is Proleukin IL-2, a treatment for kidney cancer. Clinical trials are being conducted to get approval for its use on a number of other cancers and infectious diseases. The product has only been on the market since May 1992, but sales potential is very high. Proleukin IL-2 is sold through Chiron's two subsidiaries: Cetus Oncology in the United States and EuroCetus in Europe.

73   Betaseron, used in the treatment of multiple sclerosis, received approval in 1993. Chiron manufactures Betaseron for Belix Laboratories, which markets the product. Chiron will get 15 percent of worldwide net sales of Betaseron. Biogen is developing a similar drug to Betaseron. If Biogen is successful, Betaseron sales could decline sharply, but Biogen was not expected to have a product to market until 1996.

74   Chiron has a variety of new products in the pipeline. The products in its pipeline have great potential; however, they are in markets that are very competitive. Chiron will need to harvest these products as quickly as possible.

75   Rather than rely on internal R&D, Chiron tends to acquire a lot of its R&D. For example, Proleukin IL-2 was being developed by Cetus. Cetus ran into delays in the approval process and could not afford to continue the process. Chiron bought Cetus and now runs it as a subsidiary. In addition to acquisition, Chiron has several R&D partnerships designed to minimize developmental risks.

76   Chiron has only had one profitable year since it was founded in 1981. Recent earnings have been greatly hurt as a result of expenses associated with its acquisition activity; however, Chiron's financial condition remains fairly good.

Genentech

77   In the late 1980s, Genentech's investors began to see some success at making the company profitable. The company had a number of products in development and in the market, but Genentech's performance was below expectations. Since management was committed to reinvesting 40 percent of revenues back into product development, earnings were not expected to rise a lot. However, this strategy began to impair Genentech's ability to raise capital.

78   The solution to this problem came in 1990 when Genentech sold controlling interest of the firm to Hoffmann-LaRoche, a giant pharmaceutical company. Under the terms of the deal, Hoffmann-La-Roche received 60 percent of the company (LaRoche can increase its stake in the company up to 75 percent). Hoffmann-LaRoche has allowed Genentech to remain independent in culture. It holds only two seats on Genentech's board. Strategic decisions are the responsibility of Genentech's management. In addition to the increased resources, Genentech also gained access to the marketing channels of Hoffmann-LaRoche.

79   Genentech developed four of the first six biopharmaceutical products on the market. It directly markets three products (Activase, Actimmune, and Protropin) and licenses two (Humulin and Roferon). Its product line is very diverse. Activase is used with heart attack patients. Protropin is a human growth hormone. Actimmune is used with patients that have chronic granulomatous. The sales of one of these products does not affect the sales of any others.

80   Genentech's pipeline is full and balanced. Genentech is about to file for FDA approval of Pulmozyme for the treatment of cystic fibrosis. It has also started Phase II trials of Pulmozyme for chronic bronchitis. Genentech also has a number of cancer and AIDS related products in Phase I.

81   R&D remains as the firm's number one priority, and Genentech spends more than half of its revenue on R&D (see Exhibit 9). Genentech's biggest problem is to decide how R&D money should be spent. As discussed earlier, it has a great number of products in development.

82   Genentech's financial position is very strong although it has lower operating margins than most of the industry, and it is very well capitalized.

Genzyme

83   Similar to its larger competitor Chiron, Genzyme has fashioned itself as a diversified human health care company. In addition to therapeutics, Genzyme has diagnostic and traditional pharmaceutical business units. Genzyme's only biotech pharmaceutical is Ceradase. Ceradase is used in the treatment of Type I Gaucher's disease. The sales growth for Ceradase is limited because Gaucher's disease is fairly rare. Many of the patients that can use the drug are already doing so.

84   The products in Genzyme's pipeline are all in the early stages of development and none are near the key clinical testing and approval phases.

85   Although the company has internal abilities, Genzyme's R&D efforts have been done primarily through partnerships. The amount spent on R&D is very low by industry standards. However, many of Genzyme's partnership arrangements give Genzyme the right to buy out the technology. Doing so has been a great drain on the company's cash and earnings. Genzyme's selling and administrative costs are much higher than the other five companies, straining Genzyme's profitability.

Immunex

86   Immunex is a fully integrated biopharmaceutical company. The primary focus of the company is on large cancer and autoimmune disease markets. Currently, Immunex has two products on the market: Leukine and Prokine. Leukine is a white blood cell stimulant used with bone marrow patients. Given that Leukine is likely to get FDA approval for other applications, the growth prospects for Leukine are good. Prokine is also used with bone marrow patients and sold through Hoechst-Roussel Pharmaceuticals. Prokine and Leukine compete with each other and have a great deal of outside competition.

87   Immunex has a number of products that are in the early and middle stages of clinical testing. None has yet to reach the critical Phase III testing.

88   Although the company initially used partnerships and other collaborative projects, Immunex has moved away from these efforts. Proprietary projects allow Immunex to have greater control over the marketing rights on any resulting products. In the middle of 1992, Immunex made the strategic decision to accelerate spending levels for the development of its key new products.

89   Immunex's financial condition is very weak. The shift to proprietary projects and the acceleration of spending levels for development has left the company with little working capital. Immunex has used up its cash position without actually getting any new products into the market.

CONCLUSION

90   Biotechnology as an industry will continue to bring new products forward for approval. As the industry develops, firms will face an increasingly challenging environment. Regulatory pressures will increase. Pricing policy will be under intense scrutiny. There will be heavier emphasis on speeding commercialization of new products. Competition for financial resources will increase. In this environment, only firms that cultivate the ability to adapt to the changing competitive environment will prosper.

CASE 40

NOTE ON THE LIFE INSURANCE INDUSTRY

THE NATURE OF THE INDUSTRY

1   Life insurance was the main product of the life insurance industry until the 1970s. The industry always received some investment money for its pension and annuity products, but in the early 1970s, life insurers became investment providers and margin lenders. As a consequence, life insurers were in direct competition with other types of financial institutions. Increased competition had put a squeeze on profit margins in the industry.

2   The industry's traditional products were term life and whole life. Term insurance promises to pay the beneficiary if the insured dies within a specified time period. The firm selling term insurance faces mortality and lapse risks. Whole life promises to pay the beneficiary whenever death occurs, or to pay the insured in the event that he or she reaches a predetermined age (e.g., 90 years). Typically, the premiums paid on whole life insurance remain the same throughout the term of the policy. In the early years, when the risk of mortality is low, that portion of the premium in excess of the amount needed to cover the insurance company's mortality claims creates a cash value for the insured. Throughout the life of the policy, the cash value earns interest for the insured at a rate stipulated in the policy. This offsets what would otherwise be increasing premiums from rising mortality risk as the insured ages.

3   During the 1970s and early 1980s, rising interest rates forced the insurance industry to introduce new investment-oriented products in order to compete with products offered by other financial institutions. The following products were sold by the life insurance industry as a result: universal life, variable life, guaranteed investment contracts (GICs), and single premium deferred annuities (SPDAs).

4   A 1979 Federal Trade Commission study explored the vulnerability of traditional life insurance products to rising interest rates. The study noted that the interest rates being paid to policyholders by the industry on the cash value of consumers' whole life policies lagged market interest rates. This study was the basis for the recommendations of some financial advisors to buy term and invest the difference. Insurers responded by developing new products that allowed consumers to buy term insurance and invest the difference with an insurer.

5   A universal life policy allows the insured to determine, within a range, both the amount and the frequency of premium payments. The policy separately tracks the term insurance death benefit and the cash value. The minimum premium allowed was the amount required to keep the term insurance in force; anything above that up to a maximum determined by formula is accumulated into the case value. A guaranteed minimum interest rate on the cash value is specified by the contract. An addition to this rate, called the excess interest rate, is credited if certain policy conditions are met. The excess interest rate may be declared by the company or by a formula based on current market interest rates.

6   Variable life policies are similar to whole life policies because they have cash values. The cash value earns a return based on the performance of one or more funds selected by the insured. A minimum death benefit is guaranteed, but the cash value is not. The early 1980s saw a significant rise in annuity business from the growth of group annuities and the development of SPDAs and GICs.

This industry note was prepared by Professor John A. Pearce II of Villanova University with the assistance of Keith Bankston, Stefan Becker, Robin Lee, and Joanne Szuminski.

Allocated group annuity contracts were purchased by pension plans to distribute benefits but were owned by individual plan recipients of retirement benefits. Since allocated group annuities were immediate annuities, which means they pay benefits from inception, they create mortality, credit quality, and reinvestment risks for the underwriting insurer.

7   The industry's life insurance product mix stabilized in the 1980s, and experts expect it to stay roughly the same throughout the 1990s. Unless major legislative changes occur, life insurers may be hard pressed to create products more versatile than variable life policies. Product developments in the near future may be limited to minor additions and modifications to basic products for specific circumstances and needs. In other words, life insurers do not compete based on product differentiation.

8   The life insurance industry is a mature industry as defined by the following characteristics. First, a 1980s shakeout phase brought about the insolvency of several smaller competitors due to poor reserve investments in risky securities. First Executive Corporation was the largest of the life insurance firms not to survive. Second, industry segments were expanding due to new distribution channels. Third, slow technical growth occurred in product design due to the generic nature of life insurance products. Every company competes with essentially the same product lines. Finally, increased efficiency in the industry has arisen in response to the need to sell at lower profit margins.

9   Forecasting industry growth is vital to the sales estimates needed for investment strategies employed by the treasury function of a firm. A mis-estimation can cause investing that may extend operating cash flows for the firm to its limits. A "times interest earned ratio" for the firm that is too low is detrimental to the firm's industry ratings. Conversely, a firm does not want to underutilize its resources. Investment income is a large source of revenue for life insurance companies.

10   Despite a 5.6 percent increase in benefits and 6.4 percent increase in expenses, the life insurance industry enjoyed a 5.2 percent rise in pretax operating income in 1992 (to $18.3 billion, up from $17.4 billion). However, taxes took a bigger bite out of insurers' profits. After paying out taxes at a 28.0 percent rate, versus 21.8 percent the previous year, the industry's net operating profits eroded 2.9 percent to $13.2 billion in 1992, from $13.6 billion in 1991.

11   Premiums from "ordinary" life products, which are sold to individuals rather than to group representatives, accounted for 23 percent of 1992 premium income or about $60 billion. Accident and health premiums accounted for 25 percent ($65 billion) of 1992 premiums. Group annuities equaled 27 percent of premiums ($71 billion); while individual annuities accounted for 20 percent ($51 billion). Group life equaled a little over five percent ($14 billion). Credit life (term insurance designated to cover the repayment of a loan, installment purchase, or other obligations) accounted for less than 1 percent of premiums ($1.7 billion) as did industrial life ($510 million).

12   Life insurance sales (or new business issued) rose 0.2 percent during 1992, to $1.688 trillion from $1.685 trillion in 1991. Ordinary life sales, which accounted for almost 61 percent of total sales, declined 6 percent during 1992. Within the ordinary life sector, sales of term policies were off 3 percent, while whole and endowment life (traditional and interest-sensitive) policy sales fell almost 9 percent. This slowdown in ordinary life sales was largely attributable to the general decline in interest rates.

13   Life insurance in force in the United States at the end of 1992 equaled $11.6 trillion, up 5.5 percent from the $11 trillion of life insurance in force at year-end 1991. Of the 1992 total, whole and endowment life accounted for $3.8 trillion (33 percent); group life equaled $3.8 trillion (33 percent); term life, $3.1 trillion (28 percent); credit life, $278.5 billion (2 percent); and industrial and other, $639.5 billion (6 percent).

MAINTAINING A LOW LEVEL OF RISK

14   Insurers who subject themselves to a high degree of risk are unable to explore new distribution channels. Banks, for example, may not establish partnerships with firms whose riskiness may directly affect consumer perception of the bank's creditworthiness. Furthermore, life insurers that are perceived to be risky may be unable to attract middle- and upper-income investors. Instead, these riskier firms are forced to cater to lower-income customers and commodity-like insurance sales.

15   When insurance companies sell life insurance and annuity policies, they incur risk. Insurance firms are subject to three types of risk. The first type is asset default risk, which occurs when an insurance company's assets are subject to credit risk. When a firm invests in volatile assets, such as mortgage loans, that may go into default, the insurance firm's assets depreciate.

16   The second type of risk is insurance pricing risk. This class of risk has two components:

1. The risk that arises in the pricing of a line of businesses, which is a result of mis-estimating the frequency and severity of claims. Life insurance frequency mis-estimation risk arises when insured persons die earlier than anticipated. Annuity frequency mis-estimation risk arises when insured persons live longer than anticipated.
2. The risk that arises from less favorable persistency (policyholder lapses) that results in policies that do not stay in force long enough for the company to get back the high expenses incurred when a policy is issued.

17   The third type of risk, interest rate risk (which is also called disintermediation and reinvestment risk), arises from fluctuations in interest rates. Fluctuations in interest rates lead to policyholder surrenders (lapses) of investment products and changes in the rates that can be earned on investments used to pay policyholder claims. Furthermore, insurance companies are forced to compete with other investment products. Low interest rates make it difficult for firms to compete with higher-rate investment products.

EFFICIENCY MANAGEMENT OF THE RISKS OF CYCLICALITY

18   The 1991 economic recession threatened consumer confidence regarding the solvency of many life insurers. As interest rates fell, so did the rates of interest credited to interest-sensitive policies. Credit life sales in 1992, representing slightly more than 6 percent of all sales, were off 22 percent from 1991 levels. Industrial life sales, which accounted for a fractional part of overall sales, declined 36 percent, year to year. The only area of growth was the group life area (33 percent of sales), which produced a 22 percent rise in new business issued.

19   A life insurance firm must hedge against recessionary pressures. Firms that invested in highly cyclical products, such as real estate and mortgage loans, were still working to regain financial credibility in 1993. Life insurance firms that secured capital reserves through low-risk investments were better equipped to compete in the postrecessionary environment. Many firms in the industry suffered heavy losses due to poor forecasting (Aetna, Signa, and Traveler's, which all had real estate exposure equal to more than one-third invested assets, all had heavy losses during the recession) and some became insolvent (First Executive Corp.).

DEVELOPING NEW DISTRIBUTION CHANNELS

20   The life insurance industry's channels of distribution include brokers (both company and independent), employee deduction programs, banks, and other financial intermediaries selling small proportions of life insurance products such as investment banks.

21   Life insurance distribution channels were growing and changing due to continued pressure for profitability. As insurance companies compete with each other and investment banks for product, sales price competition had increased. Profit margins eroded 0.4 percent between 1990 and 1992 and stood at 4.8 percent in 1992. As a consequence of the shrinking profits, successful life insurance firms were seeking the optimal means of bringing a certain product to a specific market rather than relying on one system for all markets.

22   Mutual funds and annuities were being established in commercial bank branches around the country at an accelerating rate. In addition, banks were starting to push their way into the life insurance business. Federal and state laws impede a bank's ability to write insurance policies (due to the strict capital requirements already in place for banks), but there are fewer restrictions on the sales of insurance products. In 1993, banks only accounted for 1 percent of the market of written insurance policies. However, 77 percent of banks surveyed in 1992 by the Independent Bankers Association stated they were selling or intend to sell insurance products. In 1993, nearly one-half of the states permit state-chartered banks to sell most insurance products. Eugene Ludwig, the U.S. comptroller of the currency, endorsed the notion that banks would be stronger and safer if allowed to sell insurance as well as other financial products.

23   Some life insurers were entering into joint ventures with banks to step up marketing efforts for their products. About 7 percent of the products were sold through joint venture operations since agents principally pursue only the most affluent customers because the majority of an agent's compensation is commission based. Banks may reach a market segment that the agents ignore, which benefits both banks and insurers.

24   Life insurers can view banks as competitors or allies. Sales of life products through banks could provide customers with a less expensive product and offer a convenient outlet for buying insurance. A 1993 survey indicated that insurers felt that the customer may benefit from the existence of multiple outlets for insurance products.

25   One factor that determines a firm's need to explore new distribution channels is management risk. This risk involves the expense of maintaining policies, including state premium taxes, administrative costs, or salaries. Management risk was playing an increasingly important role in a firm's ability to sell life insurance products through agencies. The costs of running an agency office were as high as $700,000 a year. Additionally, the industry's average agent retention rate was 13 percent to 20 percent. Decreasing margins in the life insurance industry do not support these high management costs. If a firm wishes to maintain a single distribution strategy, management must be able to keep overhead low and to retain agents in order to hold down training and recruiting costs. Firms that are unable to limit management risk may have to seek alternative channels of distribution such as banks, independent agents, and brokerage firms.

26   Companies that maintain strong agent networks may continue to be successful without using new channels of distribution. However, firms that are unable to control the costs of the agent approach may be forced to seek new opportunities. Insurers that do not take advantage of these new distribution channels may be missing out on important industry opportunities.

BALANCING SALES OF TRADITIONAL LIFE AND ANNUITY PRODUCTS

27   Due to industry requirements, some life insurance premiums that are received by the issuing firm can be invested for longer periods of time and at a higher rate of return than others. The products that warrant the higher rate of return for the firm are not necessarily the products that the public is more interested in purchasing. Balancing the sales of the different products allows a life insurance company to have a wider range of investment opportunities and a more stable premium income.

28   Premium income provides a better gauge of a life underwriter's volume of business than does insurance in force. While the latter measures the potential maximum liability an insurer could face, premium income is proportionate to the actuarial risk assumed by the insurer. Also, the kind of policy written determines the level of premium income, as well as the amount of reserves that must be established for future policyholder benefits. These additions to reserves, in turn, determine the amount of investment income that can be generated.

29   Whole life and industrial life warrant the highest premiums because these policies remain in force until a policyholder dies. As a consequence, whole and industrial life policies have the largest reserve requirements and have the potential to produce the highest level of investment income. On the other hand, term, group, and credit life insurance are all in force for limited time periods, reducing the likelihood of a claim, which leads to lower premiums, reserves, and investment income vis-à-vis other life insurance products. Companies that are able to successfully balance sales of these products can diversify risk and stabilize returns.

30   The sale of annuities has a greater impact on an insurer's premiums than on earnings. Earnings from a typical annuity come largely from loan fees and other charges. A large inflow of annuity business distorts the income statement of an insurer. While this business increases invested assets and liability reserves, annuities provide lower profit contributions and reduce the overall return on assets. Moreover, since

margins tend to be very narrow, achieving a critical mass of assets is key to long-term profit growth. Stated simply, annuities bring in a smaller contribution margin than do traditional life products, and too many annuity sales as a proportion of total sales can be detrimental to a firm if not managed properly.

MATCHING COMPANY STRATEGY WITH DEMOGRAPHIC TRENDS

31   Several demographic trends in the United States have ramifications for the life insurance industry. First, the continued aging of the general population is leading to an increase in the market for estate and retirement planning, making life insurance-related products more attractive. Second, the increasing percentage of living older Americans is fueling the continued growth and evolution of the market for long-term care and financial planning. Third, the maturity of the baby boom generation is increasing the demand for estate, investment, and inheritance planning. Fourth, the continued growth of ethnic markets (especially Asian and Hispanic) is providing opportunities in all markets for those companies that were able to practice multiculturalism. Finally, the continued decline of the traditional husband-wife family household (the divorce rate in the United States is approximately 50 percent) increases the number of policies demanded. As a result of these trends, new distribution channels may have to be created to reach new customer groups. The increasing heterogeneity and complexity of the marketplace force life insurance firms to use innovative target marketing techniques to gain market share or just to hold on to the present percentage of market share in an expanding market.

32   The overriding factor contributing to the growth in estate planning is the huge wave of post-World War II baby boomers, approximating 70 million, approaching retirement age. Nearly one-third of the total U.S. population, and almost one of every two adults in the nation, belong to this demographic group. From 1994 to the year 2000, an additional 17 million people will enter the 40-to-60 age bracket, which is typically the period when individuals have the highest propensity to save and accumulate assets, funneling an estimated $500 billion into retirement savings and other investment areas.

33   One important result of these demographic trends is the increasing demand for annuities. According to information compiled by the Life Insurance Marketing and Research Association (LIMRA), sales of individual annuities grew 10 percent during 1993, to over $60 billion, continuing a trend of double-digit sales growth that began in 1984. Annuities provide protection against the possibility of outliving one's financial resources. Most were intended to provide a predetermined amount of guaranteed retirement income, often for life. The onset of strong growth in the annuity area coincided with the adoption of the Employee Retirement Income Security Act (ERISA) in 1974, which extended individual retirement account (IRA) eligibility to persons covered by employer pension plans. While the Economic Reform Act of 1981 raised contribution levels on IRAs, the Tax Reform Act of 1986 subsequently limited IRA contributions for many individuals. This heightened the need to shelter income for retirement.

34   These demographic trends provide opportunities for firms that have strong annuity products because the aging of the population means that there may be more net-savers in the economy. In addition, lower income and ethnic markets provide profitable opportunities for volume and niche marketers. Life insurance firms that create distribution channels and hybrid products that meet the demands of these demographic groups may enjoy success in the industry.

MAINTAINING FINANCIAL SOUNDNESS

35   Maintenance of a top company rating from Best's and an excellent bond rating from Moody's is essential for life insurance companies. For a life insurance company to become a pension manager, trust manager, or asset manager of any large stakeholder, the firm must have a top financial rating. Pensions, bonds, and other financial agreements have covenants that require the portfolio managers to have credible resources and this is directly tied to the company's ratings on its financial strength. A poor reputation and rating may therefore lead to a substantial loss in management fees for asset management. Life insurance companies must manage assets in such a way as to get the highest rating possible.

36   Total admitted assets for the life insurance industry topped $1.5 trillion by the end of 1993, up more than 7 percent from year-end 1991. Of the total, bonds accounted for 51 percent; common equities accounted for 4 percent; preferred stock accounted for less than 1 percent; and separate account assets, which were used to fund certain annuity and investment-oriented life policies, accounted for 14 percent; miscellaneous other assets were 11 percent. The most troublesome asset class for life insurers was mortgage loans and real estate, which accounted for a combined 19 percent of admitted assets.

37   The buildup of real estate and mortgage bond assets during the 1980s was largely a result of the popularity of annuities. Since annuities do not possess the mortality and morbidity risks inherent in traditional life and health insurance products, insurers view the annuity market as a relatively low-risk means of growing their asset base. As a result, many insurers made aggressive forays into this market during the 1980s, often promising imprudently high rates of return (or credited rates) on the contracts as a means of attracting new business. However, as competition heated up and interest rates headed down, many companies were forced into making speculative, theoretically higher-yielding investments in real estate and junk bonds. Their goal was to cover the spread between the high rates that life insurance companies were promising to pay investors and the low rates that they could earn on firm investments.

38   While pricing and competitive pressures were realigned following the collapse of the junk bond and commercial real estate markets in the late 1980s, many insurers continue to be troubled with concerns about asset quality and liquidity because their balance sheets were loaded with nonperforming real estate and commercial mortgages. Despite aggressive write-downs and reversing actions taken in the early 1990s, the burden of nonperforming or underperforming real estate and commercial mortgages was one that may remain with the insurers to the turn of the century.

39   Companies that were unable to divest risky real estate assets faced difficulties in appealing to risk-averse investors and distribution channels.

AWARENESS OF AND REACTION TO REGULATORY ISSUES

40   Lingering concerns over asset quality and potential changes in the tax code that would abolish the tax-deferred status of certain annuity products cloud the long-term outlook for annuities. Firms that rely too heavily on sales of annuities may face review if annuities lose their tax-deferred status.

41   Arguing that tax-deferred annuities had become more a means of dodging taxes than a way of saving for one's retirement, the Bush administration proposed eliminating the tax-deferred status of individual annuities that did not distribute proceeds over the course of an annuitant's lifetime. Although Bush backed away from this proposal amid a torrent of negative response from Republicans, the likelihood of similar proposals reemerging seemed great with Democrat Clinton in the White House.

42   Other attempts had been made to undercut annuities' most attractive feature. Unable to legislate a similar proposal as a part of a broad-based tax overhaul plan in 1986, Congress compromised by implementing a 10 percent tax penalty on annuity withdrawals made before the age of 59 1/2.

43   Congress had also been directing its efforts at avoiding a solvency crisis in the insurance industry as a whole. Several years of research on the industry resulted in the 1992 introduction of the Federal Insurance Solvency Act. Following derisive testimony on the inefficiency of the state-controlled regulatory system, the bill's sponsor, Rep. John Dingell (D-Mich.), used the federal regulatory system that governs the securities industry as a model for his legislative proposal to more closely regulate the insurance industry. Although this bill did not pass, it was seen as a harbinger of possible future regulation.

44   The NAIC was the most vocal opponent of legislation like Dingell's. Amid fears that the financial health of the insurance industry was headed down the same insolvent path taken by the savings and loan institutions, the Dingell-led House Energy and Commerce Subcommittee on Oversight and Investigations studied the cause of four insurer insolvencies. The study named the lack of uniformity in capital and surplus requirements among the various state regulatory bodies and the ineffectiveness of the NAIC as the most prominent weaknesses of the present system.

45   The most controversial issue tackled by the NAIC was that of risk-based capital (RBC). In 1993, capital requirements were relatively low and varied widely from state to state. In general, they required an insurer to maintain minimum capital levels of several million dollars regardless of its size or mix of assets. Taking its cue from the banking industry, which implemented risk-based capital requirements during the 1980s, the NAIC formed working groups to deal specifically with the life insurance industry in an attempt to formulate a risk-based capital model. The life insurance model was unveiled in mid-1992 and was approved in 1993. It established required amounts of capital that an insurer must maintain in relation to four risk components: asset default risk, insurance risk, interest rate risk, and business risk.

46   In addition to prescribing minimum capital levels using the above four risk variables as a guide, the new system also dictated when and to what degree regulators should intervene. A company that failed to meet at least 75 percent of its risk-based capital level would be required to file a plan with regulators outlining steps it plans to take to boost its capital to required levels. Companies with 50 to 75 percent of the required capital would be issued a regulatory mandate ordering certain corrective actions; those achieving only 35 to 50 percent of the required capital levels could be placed under regulatory control. Regulators would be required to take over the operations of those companies with capital levels of 35 percent or less of the required amount. Industry analysts worried that this system threatened the long-run viability of insurance firms. At minimum, a life insurance firm's profitability could be negatively impacted by these requirements.

INDUSTRY LEADERS

47   Lincoln National Corporation, Equitable Corporation, and American General Corporation were the three largest in the life insurance industry in 1993, based on total assets and total revenues. American General Corporation, the smallest of these three companies, was twice the size of the next largest company in the industry. The following is an analysis of each company, detailing its position in terms of seven factors that appear to have driven success in the life insurance industry.

The Equitable Companies

Assets:	$70 billion
Best's rating:	A– (Excellent)
Target markets:	Small businesses
	Affluent individuals
	Professionals
	Nonprofit organizations and public schools
	Emerging affluent households and individuals
	Existing customers
Mission:	To be one of the world's premier providers of insurance and asset management products for financial security and retirement plans.

48   Equitable was a diversified financial services organization offering a broad spectrum of insurance, investment banking, and investment management services to its customers.

49   In its 135-year history, 1992 ranked as one of the more significant years for Equitable because the firm completed the largest demutualization in U.S. history, a conversion from a mutual life insurance company to a publicly owned corporation. It formed a global partnership with AXA, a European-based insurance company that became Equitable's largest shareholder after the initial public offering.

1. Maintaining a Low Level of Risk

50   Historically, Equitable had difficulty in managing interest rate risk. It was still carrying unprofitable GICs on its books in 1993. GICs guarantee a rate of interest for a specified time. In order to attract new customers during the 1980s, Equitable promised high rates of return on these contracts.

However, as interest rates fell, the company attempted to cover the difference between the interest expense it was paying on the GICs and what it was earning on its own investments (negative spread) by buying risky, high yield securities like junk bonds and real estate.

51   In 1991, the range of credited interest rates on outstanding GIC contracts was 7.20 percent to 17.35 percent. The firm treated GICs as a discontinued operation; however, the remaining contracts were valued at approximately $2.7 billion in 1991 and pretax losses of $24.7 million for 1991 were incurred on the GIC segment. Continuing to reduce these holdings even further remained a priority for Equitable.

52   Accordingly, the junk bonds it purchased to hedge against its GIC losses continued to be a drag on earnings. However, the firm had taken great strides in reducing its holdings on these risky assets. In 1992, the amount outstanding was reduced to $1.8 billion. At the end of 1993, Equitable completed a $700 million collateralized bond obligation, which cleared most of the remaining junk bond exposure off its books. Overall, the company reduced its total below-investment-grade portfolio to less than 4 percent of its assets. The CBO pool was backed both by bonds and floating rate bank participations that the insurer had bought in private placement securities.

2. Managing the Risks of Financial Cyclicality

53   Liquidity is a key factor in the ability to weather financial downturns. A company that is highly liquid may not have to use reserves to finance policyholder benefits during times of financial hardships. Best's Insurance Reports gave Equitable a liquidity rating of 60.7, which was relatively poor compared to American General and Lincoln National, which earned ratings of 90.6 and 152.1, respectively. Equitable's poor rating was partly due to its earnings loss in 1992.

3. Developing New Distribution Channels

54   Equitable utilized a single distribution channel for its insurance products, a network of approximately 8,200 field agents. Although banks seemed reluctant to form strategic alliances with Equitable because they did not want to form partnerships with firms that could adversely affect their own level of risk, banks would sell their products. Banks could reach a market segment that the insurance firm was unable to reach through its agent network.

4. Balancing Sales of Traditional Products and Annuities

55   Equitable was the industry leader in variable annuity products. Group and annuity sales accounted for 80 percent of its revenue for 1992. Reliance on annuity sales was dangerous because annuities generally provided lower profit contributions than other products. In addition, annuities would become much less appealing to consumers if they lost their tax-deferred status. However, it would have been imprudent for Equitable to shift its focus from the annuity-type products to more traditional products and relinquish its corner on the annuity market, especially with the expected growth in the retirement savings market due to the aging population.

56   Equitable repriced its various life products with the objective of improving profitability while maintaining a strong competitive position. Among the changes, it restructured cash value buildup (rewarding customers who stayed with Equitable) and increased the duration and amount of surrender charges to discourage early surrenders.

5. Matching Company Strategy with Demographic Trends

57   Equitable, the industry leader in variable life and variable annuity products, was well positioned to take advantage of the growth in the retirement savings market from the aging of the baby boom population. Increased demand was expected for variable life insurance, variable annuities, and other products that provided for the accumulation of financial assets.

58   Equitable was also known for its excellent asset management capabilities. To the extent that the risk-based capital guidelines resulted in highly conservative investing, Equitable felt that future policyholders would turn to variable life and variable annuity products as a means of obtaining higher returns. Through these products, policyholders would have a choice of funding alternatives, including equities. The firm's strategy was to emphasize these products, as reflected in their mission statement: "Equitable, together with its global partner AXA, seeks to be one of the world's premier providers of insurance and asset management products for financial security and retirement savings."

59   Tailoring products to customer needs resulting from the changing demographic nature of the life insurance industry was a goal of Equitable. For example, Momentum was developed to focus on the small pension market. This product was introduced in 1993 to improve customer service and enhance growth in this market area. In addition, several enhancements were added to the EQUI-VEST variable annuity product, including a dollar cost averaging feature and a mechanism that automatically swept interest from the general account to the separate account chosen by the customer.

6. Maintaining Financial Soundness

60   Before the conversion, Equitable was perceived to be a capital-short mutual life insurance company, afflicted by asset quality problems and high-cost liabilities that were draining profitability. The firm took several measures to reverse this condition, including converting to stock ownership, which helped double capital, upgrading asset quality, reducing expenses, and obtaining an upgrade by major credit rating agencies in 1992.

61   Best's Insurance Reports gave Equitable a rating of A– (excellent) in 1993. The rating reflected the successful demutualization, its global affiliation with AXA, the quality and national presence of its career agent distribution, and its improved capitalization, operating results, and liquidity.

62   The demutualization and the capital raised from the IPO in 1992 greatly improved Equitable's operating performance. Its pretax loss from continuing operations was reduced from $506.3 million to $16.1 million. In 1993, Equitable had a profit of $343.4 million. After-tax effects resulted in a loss of $32.2 million in 1992 from continuing operations, down from $307.8 million in the prior year, not including extraordinary expenses (primarily demutualization expenses). For 1993, the after-tax effects yielded a gain of $234.5 million.

7. Reacting to Regulatory Issues

63   The risk-based capital guidelines are a measure of regulatory capital, based on a complex series of formulas. The most important aspect of these guidelines for Equitable was the measure of general account investment risk, which relates asset risk to the size of the capital base. The general account included all of Equitable's assets, other than those allocated to separate accounts by policyholders. Funds of the general account were invested to support benefit guarantees to policyholders. The RBC guidelines assessed severe capital charges for all assets other than investment-grade bonds (i.e., common stocks, junk bonds, equity real estate, and commercial mortgages).

64   Equitable's general account had approximately $32.70 billion of investment assets as of the start of 1993, which were comprised of the following categories: fixed maturities, including both investment-grade and below-investment-grade public and private debt securities; mortgages, principally on commercial properties; equity real estate, which included significant investments in office properties and regional malls; and equity interests, which consisted principally of limited partnership investments in funds that invested in below-investment-grade debt and equity securities. A 30 percent capital charge was placed on real estate and equity holdings in investment subsidiaries, areas in which Equitable had substantial holdings, thereby adversely affecting the firm's profitability. Equitable was also highly reliant on annuity sales. This strategy put the company at risk because of the potential for loss of the tax-deferred status of annuities.

Lincoln National Corporation

Assets:	$40 billion
Best's rating:	A (excellent)
Target markets:	401K plans
	Nonprofit organizations
	Individual retirement accounts
	Government-deferred compensation plans
Mission:	To be the company that other life insurance firms compare themselves against.

65   From 1989 to 1993, Lincoln National Life underwent a dramatic strategic overhaul. The strategic change was implemented with one major objective in mind: to facilitate an increase in sales volume by improving service quality and reducing unit costs to the company. Fortunately, Lincoln National was well positioned for this change.

1. Maintaining a Low Level of Risk

66   Lincoln National's greatest strength was its ability to maintain a low level of interest rate risk and policy writing risk. Lincoln received an A in this category by engaging in four major activities. First, the company increased its level of capital and surplus funds by 184 percent from 1989 to 1993. This action left Lincoln with a buffer of funds to offset interest rate fluctuations. Second, the firm was highly effective at matching the duration of the firm's assets with the duration of its liabilities. This approach allowed the firm to hedge against shifts in the yield curve or interest rate risk. Third, the company had a high retention rate of existing customers because of high returns on investments and low risk. Finally, the company underwrote low-risk policyholders to maintain a predictable mortality rate.

2. Ability to Endure Financial Cyclicality

67   Lincoln National received a Best's index rating of 150.2 for its highly liquid nature in 1993. In fact, 72 percent of the company's assets were liquid.

3. Developing New Distribution Channels

68   Lincoln National sold 96 percent of its products through agents. The agent network was very strong due to the high income characteristics of customers and the modern information system designed to facilitate agent services. Lincoln National Corporation also had low management risk and stream-lined agency sales and underwriting processes. Lincoln National made an investment in information systems technology that improved the process time and sales time required for agents. However, Lincoln was a low-risk insurer, a characteristic that afforded opportunities in alternative channels of distribution such as banks and employers. Nonetheless, Lincoln chose to emphasize sales of annuities through agents rather than pursuing potential life annuity product customers that were buying from new channels of distribution.

4. Balancing Sales of Traditional Products and Annuities

69   A full 80 percent of the company's revenues in 1992 came from annuity premiums, a 30 percent increase from the year before. Lincoln's increasing commitment to annuity business could cause problems for the company. The firm was accepting business with lower profit margins than traditional life projects; the firm's 1992 pretax profit margin was 4.2 percent lower than the industry average.

5. Matching Company Strategy with Demographic Trends

70   Lincoln National was positioned well to meet the demands of the aging baby boomer generation. In 1989, its management decided to overhaul the firm's marketing strategy. It wanted Lincoln's products to be viewed as investment opportunities. A decision was made to target three different markets with its annuities: nonprofits; individual retirement accounts and government-deferred compensation plans; and 401K plans. Lincoln decided to ignore high-volume and high-margin opportunities in the traditional life markets.

6. Maintaining Financial Soundness

71   Lincoln National was financially sound. However, the company held some fairly risky assets. Real estate assets and mortgage loans continued to be a thorn in Lincoln's side. The company had over $500 million in problem loans on the books in 1993. The company was unable to divest itself of real estate assets that have an average market value of 94 percent of book value. Best's Insurance reports gave Lincoln National an A rating (excellent) for financial soundness, stating that underperforming real estate and mortgage loans prevented the company from achieving "superior" status.

7. Reacting to Regulatory Issues

72   Lincoln National had $16 billion in invested assets as of December 31, 1993, which was comprised of the following categories: Fixed income including government agency, corporate, and public utility bonds; mortgage loans on office buildings, retail establishments, and apartment complexes; equity securities; and real estate assets. Lincoln was highly subject to the risks of the elimination of the tax-deferred status of annuities.

American General Corporation

Assets:	$40 billion
Best's rating:	A++ (superior)
Target markets:	Low- to middle-income households
	Federal and state employees
	Hospital employees
	Employer-sponsored programs
	Business owners
	Credit union members
Mission:	To be a leader in American General principal markets and sell more life insurance policies than any other shareholder-owned life insurance organization in the United States.

1. Maintaining a Low Level of Risk

73   American General wrote policies in volume. This strategy diminished the negative effects of individual policy lapses and mortality. Because a large volume of American General's sales came from lower-income, commodity life policyholders, the firm was subject to less interest rate risk. Commonly, these lower-income policyholders thought of their costs in terms of the amount deducted from their paychecks, not the total amount of coverage. They did not view life as an investment, therefore, they were less concerned with fluctuations in interest rates.

2. Efficient Management of the Risks of Cyclicality

74   Although American General was a high-volume insurer, a significant number of people give up insurance policies during a recession or business downturn, especially lower-income investors. American General's average level of liquidity (Best's rating of 90.6) provided the company with an ability to avoid the use of capital reserves to pay out policies commitments in case of recession or business downturns.

3. Developing New Distribution Channels

75   This key success factor was one of American General's greatest strengths. Until 1983, American General relied heavily on independent agents and on company-managed distribution channels. Managing two channels of distribution led to inefficiencies. As a result, American General moved to utilize only company-managed distribution. The property-casualty business, which relied almost exclusively on independent agents, was exited. In 1993, American General offered products that were consistent with its target markets by using a combination of direct sales, employee deduction plans, credit unions, and banks to distribute life insurance and annuity products. The company had a very high bond rating, making it a reliable partner to financial institutions and employers.

4. Balancing Sales of Traditional Life Products and Annuities

76   Eight percent of the company's sales were of traditional life insurance products. Only 20 percent of the company's products were annuities. This provided American General with a competitive edge over Equitable and Lincoln National. American General's profit margins were larger than its competitors because margins from traditional life products were higher than for annuities. In addition,

American General was exposed to less risk from the potential loss of the tax-deferred status of annuities.

5. Matching Company Strategy with Demographic Trends

77   American General had a highly focused strategy to target niche markets. It was actively taking advantage of the market niches that many other life insurance companies ignored due to the apparent lack of revenue-producing potential of these niches. American General made this strategy successful by selling policies in volume. The company was especially successful at targeting the lower-income group of policyholders.

6. Maintaining Financial Soundness

78   American General was the only one of the big three firms that was not plagued by investments in risky assets. Its holding of invested real estate, for example, was less than 4 percent of total investments. The consequence of this condition was that the company could guarantee long-term obligations to policyholders while fulfilling shareholder expectations for competitive returns.

7. Reacting to Regulatory Issues

79   Because of low investment in real estate, risky mortgage loans, and equity securities, American General was subject to low capital charges relating to risk-based capital requirements. The company was heavily invested in fixed maturity securities and policy loans.

80   Because only 20 percent of American General's revenues came from annuity sales, the company had a low-level exposure to changes in this product's tax-deferred status.

CHALLENGE OF THE DECADE

81   A major challenge from the remote environment of the life insurance industry had been met successfully by the majority of major competitors. By the end of 1993, the 1990–91 recession and its record 15-month recovery period were bitter but fading memories. The issue facing the survivors was how to position their firms in a somewhat newly reconstituted competitive arena.

GLOSSARY

Annuity.   A contract that pays a periodic income benefit for the life of a person (the annuitant), or the lives of two or more persons, for a specific time period.

Asset Valuation Reserve (AVR).   The asset valuation reserve establishes statutory reserves for virtually all types of investments except policy loans. AVR generally captures all realized and unrealized gains and losses on such assets, other than those resulting from changes in interest rates.

Deposits.   All payments and other considerations received during the year on certain contracts, principally universal life and investment-type contracts. These amounts were not included in insurance group revenues under GAAP but were included directly in policyholders' account balances.

Equity Real Estate.   An investment asset category comprised of the general account portion of real estate and equity in real estate joint ventures and consisting primarily of a diversified group of office, retail, hotel, industrial, and other properties (discussed in conjunction with Equitable).

GAAP.   United States Generally Accepted Accounting Principles, including those applicable to stock life insurance companies.

General Account.   All an insurer's assets other than those allocated to a separate account.

Guaranteed Investment Contract (GIC).   A security that pays a guaranteed rate of interest for a specified period of time on invested funds. They were generally purchased by institutional investors and were unallocated group annuity contracts because the purchasing group jointly owns the contract.

Premiums. Payments and considerations received during the year on policies and contracts, other than universal life and investment-type contracts, issued or reissued (assumed less ceded) by an insurance company and accounted for as revenues under GAAP.

Risk-Based Capital (RBC). Beginning with the 1993 year-end statutory financial statements, the New York Insurance Law imposed risk-based capital (RBC) requirements on life insurers, based on the model adopted by the National Association of Insurance Commissioners (NAIC) in December 1992. The RBC requirements provide a method to measure the minimum amount of adjusted capital (statutory surplus and capital stock plus AVR and other adjustments) that a life insurance company should have, taking into account the risk characteristics of the company's investments and products. The formula is to be used by regulatory authorities as an early warning tool to identify possible weakly capitalized companies for purposes of initiating further regulatory action. The New York Insurance Law gives the insurance superintendent explicit regulatory authority to require various actions by, or take various actions against, insurance companies whose adjusted capital does not meet the minimum level.

Separate Account. Investment accounts maintained by an insurer to which funds have been allocated for certain policies under provisions of relevant state insurance law. The investments in each separate account were maintained separately from those in other separate accounts and the general account. The investment results of the separate account assets were passed through directly to the separate account policyholders, so that an insurer derives management and other fees from, but bears no investment risk on, these assets.

Single Premium Deferred Annuity (SPDA). Entitles the purchaser to repayment of the single premium with interest after a period of 5 to 10 years, much like a certificate of deposit. The interest rate can either be fixed or derived based on a formula using market rates. The life insurance component of an SPDA consists of a death benefit payable in the early years of the contract, which typically covers the penalty for early contract termination.

Statutory Reserves. Amounts established by state insurance law that an insurer must have available to provide for future obligations with respect to all policies. Reserves were liabilities on the balance sheet of financial statements prepared in conformity with statutory accounting practices.

Surrenders and Withdrawals. Surrenders of life insurance policies and annuity contracts for their entire net cash surrender values and withdrawals of a portion of such values.

Universal Life Insurance. Life insurance under which (1) premiums were generally flexible, (2) the level of death benefits may be adjusted, and (3) expenses and other changes were specifically disclosed to a purchaser. This policy is sometimes referred to as unbundled life insurance because its three basic elements (investment earnings, cost of protection, and expense charges) were separately identified both in the policy and in an annual report to the policyholder.

Variable Life Insurance. Life insurance under which the benefits payable upon death or surrender vary to reflect the investment experience of a separate account supporting such policies; variable life insurance policies typically include a general account guaranteed interest investment option.

Whole Life Insurance. Permanent life insurance offering guaranteed death benefits and guaranteed cash values.

CASE 41

NOTE ON THE MOTION PICTURE INDUSTRY

INTRODUCTION

1   In 1994, U.S. consumers spent over $6 billion on movie tickets and another $34 billion on cable TV and video purchases and rentals. These figures were only a fraction of total filmed entertainment outlays worldwide, spent mostly on American-made movies.

2   The movie business had a record year in 1994. Domestic box office gross revenues had increased to $5.8 billion, a full 7.8 percent higher than 1993, and the holiday season alone earned movie studios $192 million, just $5 million off the record set in 1989. Buena Vista Studios, Disney's motion picture house, also became the first major studio to gross over $1 billion ($1.234 billion), a 53 percent improvement from 1993. Yet, despite the strong industry growth, other major movie studios did not fare as well. Columbia-Tristar (owned by Sony) had suffered its worst year since 1983, grossing just over $500 million (a 53 percent drop from 1993), and Twentieth Century-Fox had its fourth consecutive year of declining box office earnings.

3   The most significant event of the year was the announcement on October 15 of the first new movie studio to open in Hollywood in over 60 years. The new partnership would combine the artistic talent of director Steven Spielberg, the production skills of David Geffen, and the studio management expertise of Jeffrey Katzenberg, the longtime Disney studio chief. Despite their lack of infrastructure and film libraries, the "dream team" was not short on ego and reputation. Many of Hollywood's biggest stars and directors had already called, eager to work for the new studio that would be the only one not owned by a large conglomerate. How would this announcement impact the industry and how would the other movie studios position themselves to compete against Hollywood's newest entry?

4   This industry note will describe the characteristics of the motion picture industry and identify the key participants and their relative strengths and weaknesses. The industry note is intended to allow the reader to identify the unique choices facing the largest competitors and define key strategies the selected companies would employ to take advantage of growth opportunities and to safeguard against potential risks.

HISTORY OF THE MOTION PICTURE INDUSTRY

5   In 1908, the Motion Pictures Patents Company had formed a natural monopoly by buying most of the major film exchanges (distributors) and organizing them into a massive rental exchange, the General Film Company. However, total control of the industry was undermined by many "independent" film producers who would use the Patents Company equipment without authorization. These independents (Universal, Fox, and Paramount) later became the founding giants of the silver screen, joining Disney, Columbia, and Warner as major movie studios. They have now been competing against one another for over 60 years.

This industry note was prepared by Eric Brown under the direction of Professor John A. Pearce II of Villanova University and with the assistance of James Denora.

EXHIBIT 1
Major Film Studios and Parent Companies, 1993

Film Studio	Parent Company
Buena Vista Studios	Walt Disney Co.
Warner Brothers	Time Warner
Paramount Pictures	Viacom
Twentieth Century-Fox	News Corp.
Universal Studios	Matsushita Ltd.
Sony Pictures Entertainment	Sony Ltd.

INDUSTRY PROFILE

6 Theatrical film production and distribution (SIC code 7812) includes organizations of two different sizes, participating in some or all parts of the project development and marketing processes. The first group, the "majors," are companies with important and long-standing presence in both production and distribution, with substantial film libraries and studio production facilities. Exhibit 1 lists the major studios as of 1994 and their parent companies. These companies produced, financed, and distributed their own films, but also financed and distributed movies initiated by independent filmmakers working either directly for them or picking up their projects after progress toward completion had already been achieved. This note will focus on this group of companies, hereafter referred to as major studios.

7 Of lesser size and scope in production and distribution activities are "mini-majors" such as Orion Pictures and numerous independent producers ("indies"). These companies do not have the distribution capabilities of the majors. Instead, they feed their productions through established distribution pipelines or through their own smaller distribution organizations. For example, of the top 300 movies released since 1986, all but 8 were distributed by companies other than the top eight producers, including Orion Pictures and MGM/United Artists. This group also differs from majors in that their product lines are not as broad and their access to capital is limited. However, these small companies have been part of Hollywood since the industry began and have contributed a considerable amount of variety to the filmmaking process.

MARKET SHARE

8 As shown in Exhibit 2, the releases of the major studios accounted for approximately 86 percent of domestic box office receipts in 1994. This figure had been growing steadily, peaking in 1992 at 94 percent and reflecting a higher level of concentration in the industry.

9 Because consumers have little brand identification with movie distributors or producers, and because market share tends to fluctuate considerably from year to year, these data have limited relevance for short-term analysis. Market share analysis is more applicable to measuring long-term market performance or for comparing a film's short-term performance in one region against another.

10 The impact of blockbusters is an important factor in determining market share growth and profitability. For example, the top 10 grossing films in 1993—only 2 percent of total films released—accounted for over 27 percent of the total box office gross. Moreover, as only 70 percent (±10 percent) of the production costs are recovered from theatrical revenues, a film's profit potential depends on a solid run at the box office. Not surprisingly, those companies that released the most blockbuster hits found themselves atop the rankings of domestic box office market share.

DISTRIBUTION POWER

11 That major studio enterprises could remain profitable throughout the years given that 93 percent of movies fail to make a profit at the box office is surprising. Part of the apparent mystery is explained by the fact that the heart of a studio's business is distribution, and that studio profits are highly dependent on distribution income. A major studio could charge its distribution wing a distribution fee

EXHIBIT 2
Domestic Box Office Market Share of Industry Leaders

Studio	1988	1989	1990	1991	1992	1993	1994	Average
Disney	19.4	13.9	15.5	13.7	19.4	16.3	23.1	17.4
Columbia/TriStar	9.3	16.0	13.9	20.0	19.1	17.5	9.4	15.1
Warner Bros.	11.2	17.4	13.1	13.9	19.8	18.5	16.2	15.8
Universal	9.8	16.6	13.1	11.0	11.7	13.9	14.1	12.9
Paramount	15.2	13.8	14.9	12.0	9.9	9.3	13.8	12.7
Fox	11.6	6.5	13.1	11.6	14.2	10.7	9.4	11.0
Totals	76.5	84.2	83.6	82.2	94.1	86.2	86.0	84.5

Source: S&P Industry Surveys, 1994.

of 15 to 20 percent of the film's profits. As a result, a film could report a loss of 20 percent, but because the studio paid its distribution arm a distribution fee of 20 percent, the movie actually broke even. This distribution fee is used to support the studio's distribution arm, as well as to function as a revenue pool from which future films can be financed. Such creative accounting came under scrutiny following a much celebrated 1990 lawsuit brought by syndicated columnist Art Buchwald against Paramount, in which Paramount was accused of stealing his idea for the movie *Coming to America*. Despite the fact that the film grossed over $250 million, Paramount Productions claimed it actually lost $15 million and could therefore pay the plaintiff no more than $150,000 in compensatory damages. In reality, profits from the film were $27 million because Paramount had paid its distribution arm a fee of $42 million.

12   The major studios have traditionally derived their power from their ability to control and expand distribution channels. By maintaining distribution networks across the country and in major foreign cities, these companies can ensure that their films, and those of independent producers they agree to distribute, get to theaters and television screens. However, in order to reach the audience, a film passes through a complicated and dispersed system of distribution that includes many different firms employing a wide array of technologies. Distribution outlets in the motion pictures industry can be broken down into two areas: theaters and ancillary markets, which include video sales, network and cable TV, and direct-access channels.

Theaters

13   Before the 1950s, many theaters—and most of the important ones—were owned by the major studios. This strategy was extremely popular in the early years of the industry because a company could produce many films, betting that while most would flop, the others would produce enough revenue to make the whole enterprise profitable. The very collection of functions that gave a vertically integrated company commercial protection, however, aroused the suspicion that Hollywood was attempting to concentrate the marketplace of ideas. This situation came to a head in an antitrust suit against Paramount in 1948 that resulted in the studios being forced to relinquish their ownership of theaters. Under the Reagan administration, however, the Justice Department relaxed its enforcement of the 1948 decree, allowing Universal, Paramount, and Columbia to acquire interests in various theater chains. While the major studios controlled only 10 percent of America's 23,000 movie screens by the end of 1993, a clearly visible trend toward vertical integration had emerged. This risk-reduction strategy combines the production, distribution, and exhibition functions under the studios' control.

14   There were several benefits associated with vertical integration into theaters. First, the studio had the freedom to exhibit its own movies. While the larger theater chains retained some bargaining power with the distributors, the 90 percent nonaffiliated theaters individually would bargain with the major distributors for access to the product of each; by owning their own theaters, the balance of power shifted from the exhibitor to the producer/distributor. Second, not only could a studio guarantee extended runs for its blockbuster movie, but it also would not have to negotiate bargain prices with theater chains for the lesser productions. Finally, owning theaters provided significant profits from concessions, which could be nearly equal to box office profits.

EXHIBIT 3
Market Windows from Release Date, 1990

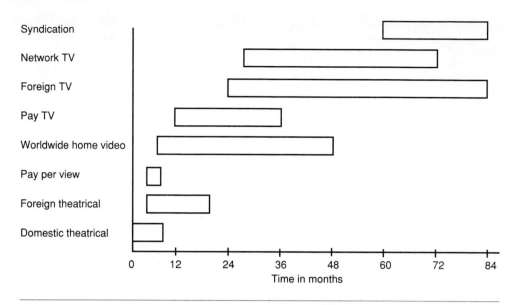

Source: *Entertainment Industry Economics.*

Ancillary Markets

15   Beginning in the late 1980s, ancillary markets (video, TV, cable, or pay per view) began to emerge as the high-growth segment in the industry. Except for the biggest blockbusters, movie companies would rarely profit from the box office, hoping instead that a film could break even and recover the cost of producing, distributing, and marketing it. If successful in recovering their costs, the profit margins from ancillary markets greatly improved. For example, during the 1987 holiday season, Disney sold 3 million copies of the 32-year-old animated classic *Lady and the Tramp,* bringing the studio $60 million of almost pure profit. Also, as illustrated in Exhibit 3, ancillary markets can extend the revenue-earning life of a movie by three to eight years.

16   The basic distribution pattern seen in theaters was reproduced in ancillary markets, where a complex system functioned to deliver videocassettes to video rental stores and consumers and movies to home video receivers through network television and a dizzying array of cable channels. As with theater exhibition, firms in the motion picture industry began to vertically integrate into these media, owning cable stations, TV networks, and video chains.

17   Integration into video distribution most closely resembled theater integration in terms of its cost and its function. However, the convergence of movie studios with cable and network TV was more gradual, and the balance of power between these two distribution wings was historically evenly shared. Movie companies relied on TV and cable networks to exhibit their products, and networks remained dependent on programming that would attract millions of viewers, having nowhere to turn but to the movie studios who own the film libraries.

18   This relationship remained an integral part of the industry, but developments in 1992–93 shifted the balance of power in favor of the studios. Examples included 20th Century-Fox combining its movie *Seduction* and distribution with several television stations and its own network, and Time Warner's HBO fully stocking the cable network with Warner Studios products. The most recent entry into the movie business was Turner Broadcasting, which had acquired the MGM film library and New Line Cinema (a small film production company) in 1992. Because of its size, cash flow surplus, and clear advantage in distributing its products through its vast cable empire, Turner was eager to break into the Hollywood ranks.

EXHIBIT 4
Film Industry Sources of Revenue, 1980 and 1990

	1980		1990	
Source of Revenue	$ millions	Percent of total	$ millions	Percent of total
Theatrical:				
Domestic	$1,183	29.6%	$2,100	15.9%
Foreign	911	22.8	1,200	9.1
Home video	280	7.0	5,100	38.6
Pay cable	240	6.0	1,100	8.3
Network TV	430	10.8	100	0.8
Syndication	150	3.8	600	4.6
Foreign TV	100	2.5	1,000	7.6
Made for TV movies	700	17.5	2,000	15.2
Total	3,994	100.0	13,200	100.0

Source: *Entertainment Industry Economics.*

19   Pay per view (PPV), whereby consumers elect to pay for a specific movie, remained a relatively small and uncertain distribution channel in filmed entertainment. Demand for PPV was constrained by restrictive scheduling and by the fact that popular home movies were generally available in video format before they come to PPV. While video and cable media were relatively mature, PPV was in its infancy. However, as telephone companies continued developing the necessary technologies to make the information superhighway a reality, PPV would be further refined as a delivery system.

20   In summary, new technology provided the viewer with unprecedented access to and control over entertainment. This technology also helped lower the price per view and established important new sources of revenue. However, the assumption that new viewing options could lead to increased profitability would not always hold true for two reasons: (1) new viewing options almost invariably displaced old ones, and (2) marketing costs rose as both old and new media competed for the attention of increasingly demanding audiences. Nevertheless, movie companies appeared eager to take advantage of all available technology as a way of enriching their marginal revenue streams.

SOURCES AND GROWTH OF REVENUE

21   Industry growth had come mainly from improved channels of distribution for films. The challenge for film producers was to deliver the products to consumers economically and conveniently, and the growth of the cable television and home video industries had fueled much of the recent growth. According to the Motion Picture Association of America (MPAA), in 1993 nearly 63 percent of households (59 million) subscribed to cable television, an increase of 200 percent from 1980, while 77 percent of all households (72 million) owned at least one VCR in 1993, up from 2.4 percent of households in 1980.

22   The growth of cable television and home video, however, had a negative impact on box office sales as ticket growth was limited by the relatively inexpensive availability of movies outside the traditional theater. In 1993, admissions to theaters totaled 1.24 billion. By contrast, in the 1950s, before the advent of television, theater attendance routinely topped 4 billion.

23   In 1993, Americans spent over twice as much on home video, including sales and rentals, than at the box office. Exhibit 4 shows that as recently as 1980, theatrical sources accounted for over half of all industry rentals. Ten years later, theatrical sources accounted for only one-fourth of all such revenues. With more channels of distribution available to film distributors, a smaller portion of total revenues originated from the box office, although box office appeal was still an important factor as it would determine a film's future success in the ancillary markets. In addition, theatrical releases (as opposed to licensing home video, pay cable, and network TV) remained the only area of distribution carrying the possibility of negative cash flow, when the cost of releasing the movie exceeded the income it generated.

EXHIBIT 5
Average Production and Marketing Costs, 1983–93 (in $ million)

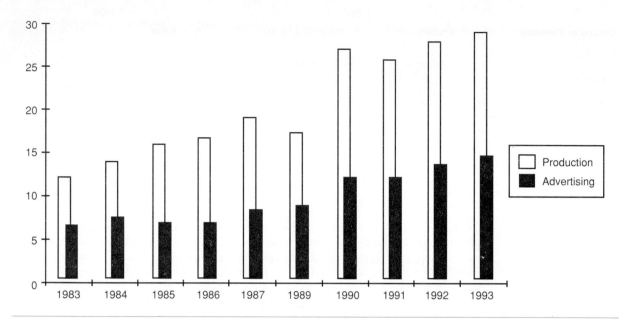

Source: MPAA.

24   By 1993, video had become the highest growing source of revenue for movie distributors. Disney was the leading domestic supplier of videos and derived much of its $5.8 billion in 1993 video revenues from previously released animation classics. Disney's strength in the video segment of the industry was a result of high consumer demand for its products. The company further boosted demand by rereleasing animated classics at the box office for a limited time as a precursor to a wide release in the video format, as it did in 1994 with its classic, *Snow White*. In addition, households with children were more likely to buy rather than rent Disney animated videos, figuring they could save money in the long term because children do not tire of watching the same video repeatedly.

FILM PROFIT POTENTIAL

25   Film profits were not only rare, but had traditionally been difficult to measure. The time between idea generation and box office release sometimes took as long as five years and overall costs varied greatly, depending on the star performers and the complexity involved in completing the film. The MPAA reported that film production costs of feature films grew to $29.9 million in 1993, and advertising and print marketing costs averaged another $14.1 million. As illustrated in Exhibit 5, these costs rose steeply between 1983 and 1993, at a rate 17 percent over inflation. The reason for the growth in *negative costs* (industry term referring to overall cost of production) stemmed from the fact that major studios would find it less risky to pay a high salary to a star actor, whose ability to attract large audiences was proven, than to pay a relatively unknown actor or director a small salary. The presence of the star easily increased the value of the film by an amount that was several times the negative costs incurred through increased sales in the ancillary markets. Thus, there appeared to be few incentives to contain costs in the movie industry.

26   The figure in Exhibit 6 shows a typical cost scenario for a box office dollar. Assuming that the film is a major release and thus commands a 90:10 split with the exhibitor, the producer would be left with only 31 cents of every box office dollar from which to recover production costs. This remainder could

EXHIBIT 6
Splitting the Box Office Dollar

Box office	$1.00
Less:	
Distribution fee	0.24
House expenses	0.10
Ads and print costs	0.20
Exhibitors' fee	0.09
Miscellaneous	0.06
Available to cover production costs	0.31

Source: *Entertainment Industry Economics*, 1990.

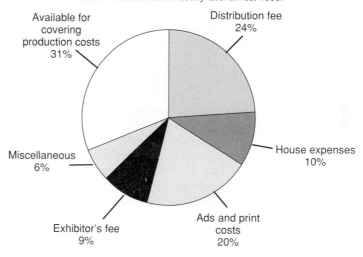

shrink even further because of interest expenses if the film was not fully financed by the studio or if a major actor was due a participation fee from the studio. It was, therefore, not surprising that so many firms, large and small, would find production to be more difficult and less profitable than originally thought. Some of the most notable failures included Columbia's *Ishtar*, which grossed only $7.5 million of an investment of $45 million. The pendulum, however, could swing both ways: *Jaws* grossed over $130 million in domestic rentals alone on a film budget of $8.0 million.

DEMOGRAPHICS, MOVIE RATINGS, AND FILM GENRES

27   In 1993, the motion picture industry was suffering from the shrinking population of 13-to-25-year-olds who would traditionally see as many as 12 films per year. Besides being heavily influenced by television advertising, this group also tended to go to the movies on impulse and was rarely swayed by recommendations and word of mouth. While many studios continued to target the teen market, the real growth audiences were becoming both younger and older, specifically the age groups that bracketed those teens. While the older group (40–49) appreciated mature themes, those with children were also attracted to family-oriented movies.

28   In general, films rated G and PG earned more than R-rated films. Between 1984 and 1991, family films rated G or PG grossed an average of $35 million, whereas R-rated movies grossed only $19 million. Furthermore, PG films were three times more likely to gross over $100 million than were R-rated movies, and they represented over 70 percent of the top-grossing films of the 1990s. In striking contrast, however, only 2 percent of the movies released between 1986 and 1993 were rated G, while over 61 percent were rated R.

29   In the early 1990s, several important trends in movie genres emerged. First, there was an increase in crossover movies from popular TV series aimed at children. Examples included *The Flintstones, Dennis the Menace,* and *The Addams Family.* Second, there was a growth in movies based on best-selling novels, such as the Tom Clancy series (*Hunt for Red October, Patriot Games, Clear and Present Danger*) and the John Grisham legal thrillers (*The Firm, The Client, The Pelican Brief*). The advantage of these tie-ins was immediate name recognition to a film and introduction to a wider audience.

30   Lastly, movies began showing less sex and violence, reflecting a change in consumer tastes and values. In a *USA Today* poll taken in 1993, an overwhelming majority of readers agreed with the statement: "Hollywood no longer reflects, nor respects, the values of American families." Movie companies were quick to respond and cleaned up films to reverse the long decline in movie attendance. This trend was also reflected in the fact that between 1991 and 1993 the number of G-rated movies increased from 14 to 22, a 57 percent increase. By contrast, there was no growth in the number of R-rated movies released during this time period, and the number of NC-17 movies dropped nearly 80 percent. The figures in Exhibit 7 illustrate the growth in movie releases by film rating; Exhibit 8 shows the trends in the ages of moviegoers.

FOREIGN MARKETS

31   Foreign demand for U.S. movies increased rapidly between 1989 and 1993 due to the construction of large multiplex theaters and the growth in the number of broadcast outlets in various countries, including satellite to home dish services in the United Kingdom and Japan and commercial stations in France, Germany, and Spain. One of the most attractive markets, according to industry observers, was the Far East, and many 1993 movies centered around Asian themes (*The Joy Luck Club, Farewell My Concubine,* and *M. Butterfly* among others) clearly reflected this trend. In addition to their international appeal, these films benefited from an Asian-American audience perhaps not numerous, but well represented geographically on both coasts.

32   With per capita income rising faster overseas than in the United States, foreign markets provided a major source of revenue for U.S. movie companies. The share of domestic box office receipts to total revenue for U.S. movie companies has dwindled from 80 percent in 1983 to just over 30 percent in 1993, while foreign box office receipts nearly doubled over the same period. Moreover, theater revenues were up 29 percent, television revenues up 29 percent, and video sales up 39 percent in foreign markets.

33   Exhibit 9 shows a breakdown of foreign versus domestic box office revenues. Of the 25 highest-grossing films in 1993, foreign box office receipts accounted for about 59 percent of total receipts for the major studios. Because of its worldwide appeal and the success of its film *Aladdin,* Disney derived nearly 70 percent of its filmed entertainment income from overseas markets. In total, the 100 highest-grossing films in 1993 (of which 88 were U.S. theatrical releases) had box office sales of $8.05 billion, 52 percent of which came from foreign markets. The biggest hit among non-U.S. movies was a French film (*Les Visiteurs*) which earned over $90 million, all of which came from outside the United States.

34   A blockbuster hit in the United States was more than likely to win instant appeal in foreign markets; however, a growing number of films generated more revenue overseas than in the U.S. market. For example, *Last Action Hero* generated over 65 percent of its sales in foreign theaters, while *Cliffhanger* and *The Bodyguard* received 62 percent.

35   Hollywood's long dominance of the international market had raised the specter of trade quotas from Europe, particularly France. While Hollywood had captured over 90 percent of the local markets in Italy, Germany, and the United Kingdom, France still had a worthwhile national film industry with over 40 percent of its local market that it was seeking to protect against U.S. competition. The issue came to the fore during world trade negotiations in 1993, when the European Commission delayed a decision on whether to allow UIP (a joint venture between Universal, Paramount, and MGM) to continue distributing U.S. films under a 1989 exemption that expired in 1993. In an attempt to soothe the French film industry's complaints of the spread of American culture in France, Disney and Miramax announced in October 1994 the creation of a company to promote the distribution of French films in the United States and increased funding to French filmmakers.

36   Because of the importance of foreign markets to U.S. movie companies, the Motion Picture Association of America (the major studios' trade organization) spent between $40 and $50 million in

EXHIBIT 7
Growth in Movies by Ratings, 1991–93

Rating	Number of Movies		Percent change
	1991	1993	
G	14	22	57.14%
PG	86	98	13.95
PG-13	119	111	−6.72
R	374	370	−1.06
NC-17/X	21	4	−80.95

Source: MPAA, *US Economic Review.*

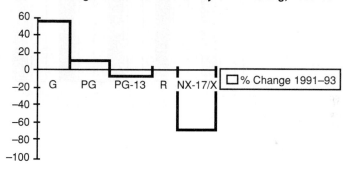

Percent Change in Movies Released by CARA Rating, 1991–93

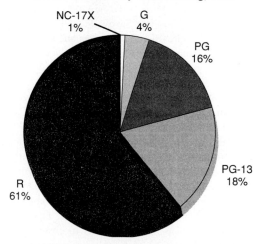

Movies Released by CARA Rating, 1993

1993 to combat the unauthorized duplication and sales of movies without royalty fees and millions more to lobby foreign governments to loosen their import restrictions.

ENTRY BARRIERS

37   The last successful major studio was 20th Century-Fox, formed in 1935. Along the way, many small studios have tried, but the majority have failed. The most notable victims include Frank Capra's Liberty Studios in the 1940s, Francis Coppola's bankruptcy in the 1980s, and the collapse of Carolco Pictures in September 1994. Those few small independent studios that had succeeded in producing

EXHIBIT 8
The Aging of Moviegoers

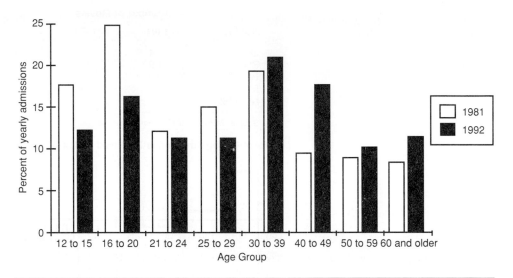

Source: *Entertainment Industry Economics,* MPAA.

enough profitable film ventures to prosper in the short term were vulnerable to being acquired by any of the major studios, as Disney did with Miramax films. Still trying to break in on their own were Gramercy Films and Savoy Pictures, two independent studios based in New York, which were growing impressive film libraries and showing an increased ability to attract above-par talent. And not to be outdone, media giant Turner Broadcasting's acquisition of New Line Cinema and Castle Rock Entertainment in 1993 would help redefine the industry profile.

38   There were many reasons for the high entry barriers to the motion picture industry. The most obvious was the high cost of acquisition, which limited entry to huge conglomerates with ample resources. For example, Sony's purchase of Columbia Pictures in 1989 cost $4.4 billion and Matsushita's acquisition of Universal/MCA in 1990 cost $6.6 billion. Deep pockets allowed the larger studios to survive box office disasters, to finance the next film slate irrespective of the last slate's performance, and to spend larger sums in marketing their movies. Small studios, on the other hand, could be crushed by a bad run at the ticket window and were usually forced to raise their own capital for new projects. However, if an independent could convince a major studio that its project had commercial potential, it could obtain financing from that studio.

39   Another reason was the fact that major studios maintained distribution networks across the country and in foreign markets to ensure that their films got to theaters and television screens. Independents did not have this distribution power and had to rely on the major studios to handle their films. In rare cases, they attempted to distribute their own films, but this strategy usually met with less than favorable results. Before the 1950s, the majority of theaters were owned by the major studios, but by 1993, only 10 percent of theaters were part of studio systems. As a result, the large distributors had better leverage than smaller companies in bargaining with theater chains for the access to their products.

40   Finally, entry barriers were higher for foreign entries than for national ones. Viacom's purchase of Paramount in 1993 was valued at about 12 times cash flow, whereas Sony's acquisition of Columbia was estimated at 25 times cash flow. Exhibit 10 shows that the foreign companies that invested in Hollywood between 1989 and 1993 had lost close to $3.3 billion, with Credit Lyonnais the biggest loser ($1.2 billion) resulting from its ill-fated investment in MGM/United Artists. The losses stemmed from the foreign companies' desire to disassociate themselves from the Hollywood

EXHIBIT 9
Industry Domestic and Foreign Box Office Hits, 1993

Distributor*	Number of Releases	Domestic Box Office ($ millions)	Foreign Box Office ($ millions)	Total Box Office ($ millions)	Percent Foreign to Total
Warner Bros.	8	497	792	1,290	61%
Universal	2	400	586	986	59
Disney	2	118	277	395	70
Sony	7	513	570	1,083	53
Paramount	3	301	325	626	52
Fox	3	138	228	367	62
Totals	25	1,967	2,780	4,747	59%

*Does not include 1992 box office receipts.
Source: *Salomon Brothers Industry Report, 1994.*

establishment and "go it alone." Companies that had invested directly with established studios (such as Itochu/Toshiba's 12.5 percent stake in Time-Warner) fared much better, realizing a 22.5 percent appreciation in their investments. By comparison, the leading French entertainment giant Canal Plus invested $320 million to acquire independents New Regency and Carolco in the early 1990s, but stood to lose more than 20 percent of their investment, possibly much more following Carolco's collapse in 1994.

TECHNOLOGICAL INNOVATIONS

41   The technology that had gone into producing movies had made quantum leaps over the past 20 years, from the innovation of Technicolor to the advancement of Dolby Surround Sound. The *Star Wars* trilogy showed that special effects, if done properly, could greatly improve the profit potential of a movie. Although most film studios outsourced their special effects to specialized firms in Hollywood, Warner Brothers had recently brought this function back in house with its Wabbit special effects division.

42   In terms of film viewing, not much had changed over the years. Editing a movie was still a tedious process and the final products were shipped in the same film canisters that were used 30 years ago. However, IMAX was a company that was breaking new ground by developing a new technology that, if successful, could revolutionize theater viewing. Commonly seen in museums across the country, IMAX used a system of screen magnifiers and enhancers on six-minute loops, creating giant pictures and giving the viewer the impression of being in the middle of the action. IMAX used this technology to produce famous museum attractions like the film *To Fly.* In the summer of 1994, IMAX filmed the Rolling Stones U.S. concert tour where adoring audiences in packed stadiums were entertained by six-story tall moving projections of the band. The film footage was edited and compiled into a full-length feature film that was shown in six IMAX theaters around the country. The main drawback to this technology was that it could not be transferred to video or home-use formats; this would make the company reliant on the box office as the primary source of revenue.

43   The latest technological frontier for motion picture companies was in direct-access TV through telephone lines. While still in its embryonic stage, telecommunication companies were joining together to install fiber optic cables in households in order to deliver movies through the information superhighway. In October 1994, Bell Atlantic, Nynex, and PacTel teamed up with Hollywood super-agent Michael Ovitz to produce television shows and interactive entertainment. Stargazer, Bell Atlantic's interactive multimedia television service, was expected to be launched in 1995, serving the Washington, D.C., market on a test pilot basis.

EXHIBIT 10
How Foreign Companies Have Fared in Hollywood

Company	U.S. Investment*	Year of Investment	Outlay ($ millions)	Gain/(Loss) ($ millions)
Matsushita	MCA	1990	$ 6,600	$(1,400)
Sony	Columbia	1989	5,400	(800)
Credit Lyonnais	MGM/UA	1990	2,100	(1,100)
Yamaichi Securities	Disney	1991	600	0
Itochu	Time Warner	1992	500	125
Toshiba	Time Warner	1992	500	125
PolyGram	Various	1992–93	235	(35)
Canal Plus	New Regency	1991	105	0
	Carolco	1992	90	(25)
Pioneer	Carolco	1992	125	(40)
JVC	Largo Entertainment	1989	100	10
Berlucsoni	Pent/America	1990	100	(60)
Others†	Various	1989–93	450	(100)
Total			$16,905	$(3,300)

*Investments over $100 million.

†Investments under $100 million.

Source: *Forbes,* June 7, 1993.

COMPANY PROFILES

44   The following section describes the six major motion picture companies. The parent companies are mentioned only in their function as distributors of motion pictures.

Walt Disney Company

45   The Walt Disney Company was founded in 1923 by Walt and Roy Disney when they set up an animation studio in the back of a real estate office in Hollywood, California. In 1928, Disney introduced its most famous character, Mickey Mouse. All early Disney movies were animated features: *Snow White* in 1937; *Pinocchio* in 1939; *Cinderella* in 1950; and *Peter Pan* in 1953. However, the enormous rise in production costs of animated films led Disney to diversify into live-action feature films. In 1954, *20,000 Leagues under the Sea* was released and became a box office hit. Ten years later, *Mary Poppins* was released and grossed $45 million at the box office.

46   Walt Disney died in 1966 and the company's fortunes began to falter. The studio released a number of mediocre movies that did not live up to the high standards Disney had set. The only financial highlight of the late 60s and early 70s for the company was the successful performance of the company's amusement parks in California and Florida. In 1983, the company launched its Touchstone Pictures subsidiary, which was designed to make films appealing to adults, without tarnishing the company's image of making family-oriented movies. One hit movie, *Splash* in 1984, however, was not enough to improve the company's faltering financial performance.

47   With Michael Eisner taking over leadership of Disney in 1984, the company's performance began to improve. The company released a number of hit movies and television series in the late 1980s and attendance at the amusement parks continued to grow. Hollywood Pictures, another new motion picture subsidiary, also released a number of hit movies, including *Beauty and the Beast,* which grossed $145 million and became the first animated feature to receive an Oscar nomination for best picture.

48   Nevertheless, Disney still depended on animation for its blockbuster draw, as evidenced by its performance at the box office in 1993 when no G-rated animation film was released in theaters (*Nightmare Before Christmas* was rated PG-13). As a result, its most profitable movies averaged only $53 million, compared to $126 million in 1992. The success of *Lion King* in 1994, which was expected to gross over $300 million at the box office and another $150 million at the video store, would help correct this anomaly, but it underscored Disney's need to continually attract artistic talent for its animation portfolio. The company planned to double its animated film production and deliver two full-length animation features each year starting in 1996.

49   Disney's theatrical production costs had traditionally been the lowest in the industry thanks to the cost-cutting penchant of its ex-studio chief Jeffrey Katzenberg. The company relied on its visibility and name recognition for marketing advantages. Although the estimated operating margin on filmed entertainment of 19.6 percent in 1994 was the highest in the industry, it was still lower than the 22.3 percent margin for theme parks or 24.6 percent for consumer products.

50   Animation remained Disney's engine for box office growth, but its live-action films amply complemented its film portfolio. Its three subsidiaries offered perhaps the most diversified mix of movie themes in the industry. Miramax concentrated on R-rated thrillers (*Pulp Fiction*), Touchstone focused on comedy (*Ed Wood*) and drama (*When a Man Loves a Woman*), and Hollywood Pictures offered a general mix of themes, including action and science fiction. More importantly, these subsidiaries were increasingly able to attract high-profile directors (Robert Redford and Jane Campion) and actors (Geena Davis and Bruce Willis). Disney's planned expansion to 60 live-action films in 1994 was thought to be overly optimistic, possibly saturating the market and driving down profits. Nevertheless, any losses would be overshadowed by consistent revenues from its animation films, both at the box office and when they hit the video stores.

51   Disney was the leading domestic supplier of videos in 1993 with a 21 percent share of the industry's total video revenues of $5.8 billion. Moreover, Disney videos were consistently among the top selling, mainly because of their appeal among children. Nine of the 12 highest-selling videos of all time (and 5 of the top 6) were Disney productions. The home video business continued to be the most profitable with margins exceeding 50 percent, and the continued development of the international sell-through market could allow Disney to double or triple its foreign video revenues by the year 2000.

52   The company licensed its feature films for pay television in several geographic markets, including the United Kingdom and other parts of Europe. In addition to owning its own cable service (The Disney Channel), its arrangement with Showtime would run through 1996, and new licensing agreements were reached with Encore (a division of TCI) to distribute Miramax films in 1994 and Touchstone and Hollywood Pictures releases in 1997.

53   As of 1993, Disney's film library consisted of 257 full-length live-action features, 32 full-length animated color features, and approximately 550 cartoon shorts. The company would increase the demand for its films by withdrawing its successful releases from the market early and rereleasing them at a later date. For example, Disney announced it would release *Snow White* on video for a limited time during the 1994 holiday season and would not release it again for another 50 years. The acquisition of Miramax added instant value to the library, thanks to the gender-bending thriller *The Crying Game* and the Oscar-winning drama *The Piano*.

Warner Brothers

54   Warner Brothers Pictures began in 1905 with a small theater in Pennsylvania and soon branched out into film distribution. By the 1920s, the company had acquired numerous theaters in the United States and Canada. In 1925, Warner Brothers began experimenting with sound movies, producing a sound-on-disc program called Vitaphone for synchronized film-sound recording. These films contained only synchronized songs and fragments of dialogue. In 1928, the company released the first full talking movie, *Lights of New York,* a one-hour feature that broke all box office records. This advancement into sound thrust Warner Brothers into the forefront of the industry and resulted in further expansion of its theater acquisitions and studio development.

55   Along with other motion picture companies, Warner suffered from lost revenues and profits brought on by the Depression in the early 1930s. The company sold theaters and cut production costs and was able to return to profitability in the boom years of the 1940s. In the late 1950s and throughout the 1960s, the company was acquired and sold by numerous conglomerates. The conglomerate that owned Warner Brothers in 1971 was Warner Communications, which was headed by Stephen J.

Ross. By 1984, Warner Communications had divested its poor performing businesses to concentrate on motion picture and television production and music recording and publishing.

56   In 1989, Warner Communications was acquired by Time for $18 billion after a bitter takeover battle with Paramount Communications. The Time–Warner merger created one of the largest communications and entertainment companies in the world. The Time Warner empire included Home Box Office, Cinemax, and HBO Video, which are all outlets for Warner Brothers products in ancillary markets.

57   Warner was the market share leader for the third consecutive year in 1993 with 7 of the top 25 hits, 6 of which grossed more than $50 million each. The company's consistent track record and ability to avoid costly bombs were notable in this volatile business. On a worldwide basis, Warner Brothers' lead was even more evident as *The Fugitive* grossed about as much overseas as it did domestically in 1993 for a total of $350 million, second only to *Jurassic Park.*

58   Warner led off the summer of 1994 with an impressive lineup that included *Maverick* (James Garner, $92 million), *The Client* (Susan Sarandon, $100 million), and *Natural Born Killers* (Oliver Stone, $80 million). Releases planned for the remainder of the year, including *Interview with a Vampire* (Tom Cruise) and *Free Willy II,* were expected to do quite well. However, Warner Brothers was unable to retain the top market share position it had held for three consecutive years, yielding the top spot to Disney.

59   Except for animation, Warner releases covered a wide variety of film genres that appealed to viewers of all age groups. Warner was also the only studio that had released Western hits over the last few years. Moviegoers had rediscovered a taste for Westerns like *Wyatt Earp, Maverick,* and *Unforgiven,* the latter perhaps aided by a mildly surprising Oscar-winning role for Clint Eastwood. The studio's ability to consistently attract top acting talent and directors accounted for its superior performance at the box office. Its 15 biggest hits between 1992 and summer of 1994 averaged $91.7 million, $15.3 million more than its nearest competitor, Universal. Even its movies that did not succeed in the United States often became blockbusters overseas. For example, foreign revenues for *The Specialist* were more than twice domestic revenues.

60   Warner was also well known in the industry for its ability to put together production deals with independent production companies. In addition, it also co-produced movies with Geffen Films through a joint venture and had entered into a distribution service arrangement with the up-and-coming studio Morgan Creek. In an effort to contain production costs, Warner had entered into an innovative agreement with three producers (Monarchy, Canal Plus, and Alcor Films) for the financing, production, and distribution of 10 major motion pictures for $200 million. Under the terms of the agreement, Warner would advance (and have the right to recoup, together with a distribution fee) part of the production budget of each film and all necessary marketing and distribution of the films, in return for all international theatrical and home video rights to these motion pictures. Through these agreements, Warner would duplicate its performance in 1993 when more film revenues were generated overseas (52 percent) than in the United States and Canada (48 percent).

61   Benefiting from warehousing and distribution advantages with its music division, the home video segment generated about $1.2 billion in worldwide revenues, second only to Disney. The company also launched the Family Entertainment Label in 1993 with the affordably priced video releases of *Free Willy* and *Dennis the Menace,* which generated video sales of over 7 million and 3 million units, respectively. Based on this experience, the company was contemplating the video release of certain blockbuster hits on a direct sell-through basis.

62   Warner's film library was comprised of films produced by Warner Brothers since 1949, as well as films produced by others and licensed to them for television exhibition in either selected markets or on a worldwide basis. These films in turn were licensed under exclusive rights to Warner's growing cable empire (HBO and Cinemax). The company also planned two major launches in 1995: the Warner Brothers Network and the Full Services Network (FSN). The first would compete directly with Paramount to obtain broadcast stations as network affiliates. The latter, made possible through the US West investment in Time Warner, would offer about 60 movies-on-demand, HBO on-demand (e.g., for a night, weekend), home shopping through specialty stores, and video games to 4,000 homes in Orlando. Capital expenditures on the FSN were estimated at more than $1.5 billion, and the need to fund filmed entertainment from operating cash flow could result in the company assuming more debt.

Paramount Pictures

63   Paramount Pictures can trace its origins to 1914 with the merger of the General Film Company and the Jesse L. Lasky Feature Play Company. In 1919, the company began acquiring theaters around the country and by the late 1920s owned over 300 theaters throughout the United States.

64   In December 1949, as a result of a consent decree reached with the federal government, Paramount split into two companies. Paramount Pictures Corporation produced and distributed movies, and United Paramount Theaters owned and operated movie theaters. Paramount continues to hold interest in U.S. theaters and has also entered into the theme park business with its 1992 purchase of Kings Entertainment Co.

65   Paramount merged with Gulf+Western in 1966, with Paramount becoming a subsidiary of the newly formed organization. Under the management of Charles Bluhdorn, Paramount expanded its theatrical film production and increased the company's investment in television production. The company had great success with the films *Love Story* and *The Godfather* in the early 1970s. Barry Diller became head of Paramount in 1975, and the company continued to have many hit movies in the 1980s, including the *Star Trek* and *Indiana Jones* series and *Fatal Attraction*. Paramount Pictures Corporation was acquired by Viacom in 1994.

66   Paramount had become the unquestionable blockbuster king: Among films released between 1986 and 1993, 15 Paramount releases grossed more than $100 million, 6 more than its nearest competitor. However, the protracted battle that led to Viacom's successful acquisition in 1994 disrupted film production plans, and filmmakers and stars became more hesitant about committing to new projects at the studio. Nevertheless, state-of-the-art studios in both New York and Hollywood would continue to churn out products that the company could exploit as new distribution opportunities presented themselves.

67   Filmed entertainment revenue in 1993 was up 32 percent to $358 million versus $271 million last year, and film production business continued to be hit-driven. In 1993, Paramount released only 15 films, lowest among the major studios, but 2 of these (*Indecent Proposal* and *The Firm*) went on to gross over $250 million each worldwide. As a result, Paramount's average film in 1993 grossed $30.8 million in the domestic market, second only to Universal. The 1994 film slate promised more of the same: Of the 14 releases planned in 1994, two (*Clear and Present Danger* and *Forrest Gump*) were the second and third highest grossing movies of the year and the much-anticipated release of *Star Trek VII* would give the company its third blockbuster of the year and impressive growth in market share.

68   The new Viacom-Paramount combination created a premier media company with an enticing mix of cable programming and TV broadcasting opportunities for its film library of 880 full-length movies. Viacom also owned Showtime and the Movie Channel, and The Paramount Stations Group owned three Fox affiliates, three independent stations in the United States, and had a 50 percent interest with Universal/MCA in two advertiser-supported cable television networks. Viacom's acquisition of Blockbuster Video also provided increased growth in this segment, along with international growth through its licensing arrangement with Cinema International BV, a joint venture with MCA. Viacom was a partner with Time Warner in the Cinamerica theater chain, which operated 382 screens in 73 theaters in the United States. Internationally, the company owned 474 screens in 120 theaters in Canada through Famous Players and an additional 369 screens in 69 theaters in Europe through its 50 percent interest in a joint venture with MCA (United Pictures International). Industry analysts believed that Viacom was among the most well-positioned companies to benefit from the development of multimedia services around the globe.

Twentieth Century-Fox

69   Twentieth Century-Fox Film Corporation is a combination of a number of businesses that began in the nickelodeon days of show business. In 1915, the Fox Film Corporation was founded with the intention of combining the production, exhibition, and distribution of films under one name. Fox was one of the first companies to incorporate sound into its pictures with the invention of Movietone, a sound-on-film process, in 1926. In 1935, the Fox Film Corporation merged with Twentieth Century

Pictures, a major movie producing company. During the 1940s and 1950s, Twentieth Century-Fox was an industry also-ran; it wasn't until the appointment of Darryl F. Zanuck as president and Richard D. Zanuck as executive vice president in charge of worldwide productions in the 1960s that the company gained prestige and became an industry leader.

70   Fox merged with a company owned by the Marvin Davis family in 1981, and Davis sold the company in 1985 to News Corporation, headed by Australian media mogul Rupert Murdoch. In October 1985, Fox was formed by consolidating Twentieth Century-Fox Film Corporation, Fox Television Stations, and Fox Broadcasting. In 1989, another corporate reorganization resulted in a greater emphasis being placed on motion pictures. Movie releases were to be increased to 30 films per year as compared to the 12 films released in 1989.

71   Fox released 21 films in 1993, averaging about $26.2 million per film for a 10.9 percent market share. *Home Alone II* grossed over $340 million worldwide in box office sales alone, with another $21 million added in video sales. Its other blockbuster, *Mrs. Doubtfire* starring Robin Williams, provided substantial revenues in the international market. In the six weeks preceding the 1993 holiday season, the film had already made $124 million in the United States alone. Altogether, it was expected to earn as much as $420 million in worldwide theater and video. In 1994, Fox hoped to cash in on the film *True Lies,*which was estimated to gross over $150 million in theater sales and an additional $75 million in video sales in the domestic market alone. Beyond this film, however, the outlook was bleak.

72   Although the success of *Mrs. Doubtfire* had stolen most of the attention (as indeed a film that was likely to gross close to $200 million in the United States alone should), a lot of work had been done in the background to make Fox Film a much more consistent studio. In terms of earnings, the combination of seven successful films and video rentals of *Home Alone II* resulted in a lift in Fox Film FY94 earnings from $36 to $150 million. It would also establish a much more solid base for FY95, and the changes implemented in 1994 implied that this business segment could consistently make a $150 to $200 million profit.

73   In an attempt to control the rising costs of production, Fox had on certain occasions reduced its financial risk by sharing film production costs and distribution costs with other parties in exchange for specified percentages of certain revenues through the disposition of certain rights. Fox also had varying production and development arrangements with directors, producers, writers, and actors. Typically under such arrangements, the creative talent would submit the project to Fox on a first-look basis, and the company then provided office support and development funding for the completion of the project.

74   Between 1988 and 1993, Fox's revenues from distribution of motion pictures in television markets (home video and pay television) often exceeded its revenues from releases of motion pictures in theaters. The company benefited from an exclusive arrangement with HBO providing for the licensing of the first 80 films released after 1991. In the international market, Fox licensed its motion pictures to British Sky Broadcasting and to Star Television, the Asian TV broadcasting system in which News Corporation holds a 64 percent interest. The company had also signed licensing agreements with pay-per-view systems in the United States, where consumers would pay for each viewing of a movie and Fox would obtain a percentage of the revenues received. For also owned 140 television station affiliates across the United States and had launched a cable programming service in Latin America.

75   The Fox film library consisted of varying rights to approximately 2,000 previously released films, of which approximately 250 had been released since 1980.

Universal Pictures

76   Universal Pictures began in the earliest days of the movie industry. Universal was the first movie company to employ the star system when it hired Florence Lawrence for $1,000 per week and billed her as the "Queen of the Screen." In the 1930s, Universal embarked upon the policy of developing star values and was the most successful studio during this time. In 1946, the studio underwent a second transformation by eliminating the production of "B" movies, Westerns and serials. The company also completed a distribution deal with J. Arthur Rank and became the American distributor

NOTE ON THE MOTION PICTURE INDUSTRY

for British movies produced by the Rank organization. Also in 1946, Universal established United World Pictures, a wholly owned subsidiary that produced and distributed non-theatrical films. United World amassed a film library of over 6,000 titles.

77   In 1956, the company established Universal City Studios with separate motion picture and television production operations. In 1966, Universal became a subsidiary of MCA. In 1982, Universal released Steven Spielberg's *E.T.*, which grossed $228 million at domestic box offices, the highest grossing movie at that time. In November 1990, MCA, along with Universal Pictures, was purchased by Matsushita Electrical Industrial Company for $6.6 billion, the most expensive purchase of an American company by the Japanese in history.

78   The one-hit wonder of 1993, *Jurassic Park,* had surpassed all major box office sales records (previously held by *E.T.*) and was well on its way to becoming the biggest blockbuster movie ever in the movie industry. Total revenues from the film, including videotape sales were expected to top $8 billion and would help keep the film studio in the black for the next two to four years. More importantly, the success of *Jurassic Park* provided Matsushita with an opportunity to enter the growing videogame market. Except for the success of *The Flintstones* and *Schindler's List,* the outlook for 1994 was not promising. The two most notable flops were *The Shadow* and *The Little Rascals.* Not surprisingly these films were targeted to children who were unaware that the ideas for these films originated from popular TV series in the 1950s.

79   The film production company had benefited from a long-standing relationship between its CEO (Mr. Sheinberg) and the movie industry's leading director Mr. Spielberg who had said he wants to maintain a relationship with Universal as long as Sheinberg was there. The announcement in 1994 of a new film studio headed by Spielberg had hastened a dispute between Matsushita and Universal/ MCA executives who were unhappy with the parent's attempt to control spending as a result of the Japanese economic recession. In 1993, Matsushita declined MCA's proposals to purchase Virgin Records and a share in a television network and to expand theme park operations.

Sony Pictures Entertainment (Columbia-Tristar)

80   Columbia Pictures began in 1920 by producing a series of short films called Screen Snapshots. These films showed the off-screen activities of movie stars and were intended to help publicize the star's current movies. The company expanded quickly and began producing short comedy and Western films. In 1922, the company produced its first feature film, *More To Be Pitied Than Scorned.* In the early 1930s, the company produced mainly low-budget "B" films and it was not until 1934 that Columbia produced its first artistic success, *It Happened One Night,* which was the top box office draw of the year and won five Academy Awards, including best picture.

81   Columbia prospered and by the end of the 1940s it was one of the most powerful studios in the industry. Unlike the other major studios, Columbia did not own theaters and, therefore, was not subject to the consent decree that forced those studios to divest their theaters. In 1951, Columbia diversified into television with the formation of Screen Gems, a wholly owned subsidiary that made TV programs and commercials. Columbia was the first major studio to make "telefilms," movies produced specifically for television viewing.

82   The company entered into a period of decline in the late 1950s with the death of studio head Harry Cohn. Columbia underwent numerous management changes over the next two decades. In 1982, Columbia was purchased by the Coca-Cola Company for $750 million and in 1989 Sony Corporation purchased Columbia for almost $5 billion.

83   Sony's purchase of Columbia in 1989 for $3.4 billion, plus assumption of another $1.3 billion in debt, looked expensive at the time. But using the price-to-sales ratio from the Paramount-Viacom deal, Columbia would sell for $7.4 billion in 1994 terms. The strategic value would be even higher due to the opening of the Japanese cable TV market and the GATT agreement to honor intellectual property rights worldwide.

84   Earnings from films were depressed in 1993 due to the year's biggest flop, *The Last Action Hero,* which cost over $80 million to produce and market, but grossed little over $30 million at the box office. Sony's production costs were consistently higher than the industry average and the company was known for its excessive spending. The bulk of the $8 billion Sony had spent over the past eight

years had not been on making movies, but rather on buying the company, hiring executives, and funding bonus pools and company perks. Heavy spending in the early days was viewed as necessary to attract star powers such as Tom Cruise and Arnold Schwarzenegger. But a string of big-budget flops in 1993 and a dim outlook for film releases in 1994 cut Columbia's market share in half. Traditional allies Carolco and Castle Rock Entertainment had left Columbia for MGM and Turner, and because management had been slow in developing new projects and making decisions, high-profile directors such as Penny Marshall and James Brooks had left to direct their future films for Disney. Sony was burdened with nearly $13 billion in debt, making new acquisitions nearly impossible. In 1994, it was shopping a 25 percent interest in Columbia to telephone or cable companies for $3 billion, but Wall Street analysts believed this figure to be overinflated given the studio's lackluster performance and cable companies' reduced interest in acquiring film companies.

85   Through Loews Theater Management and its affiliates, all of which are subsidiaries of Sony Pictures Entertainment, the company operated 869 motion picture screens in 179 locations in 1993. The company had no interests in cable programmers.

INDUSTRY SCORECARD

86   Three factors would determine sustained success in the motion picture industry: (1) "blockbuster-ability," or the ability to consistently produce a wide variety of popular films at a profit; (2) expanding distribution channels into the ancillary markets where profit margins are higher; and (3) the value and depth of film libraries, which extend a film's life cycle and generate revenues far into the future.

Blockbuster-ability

87   Hollywood used the star system for many years as a business strategy in order to differentiate entertainment programs and products and provide increasing returns on investment. In the earlier days of show business, theater operators began to realize the tremendous disparity in drawing power the most popular stars commanded over films featuring less well-known actors and actresses. These stars became commodities to movie production companies in the 1930s and 1940s and were often signed to long-term movie contracts to guarantee success at the box office. In the modern era, employment relationships between star actors and motion picture companies have changed to more of a free-lance basis. However, star appeal remained the same. A study by Audience Research concluded that 27 percent of the variation in movie box office success can be attributed to the marquee value of the star system. In addition, star directors joined star actors and actresses as critical to determining a movie's success. The ability to attract quality acting and directing talent on a free-lance basis would depend not only on the quality of the studio and its management, but also on their ability to develop or preserve relationships with actors and directors.

88   Blockbuster-ability also hinges on the need to produce a wide variety of film genres. Changing demographics and consumer tastes and values had compelled movie companies to diversify their product offerings to appeal to a wider audience. A company's ability to consistently produce popular movies across generational and cultural lines would give a movie *legs,* a Hollywood term that represents the additional revenues movie hits generate as they pass through the various distribution channels and ancillary markets.

89   As shown in Exhibit 11, blockbusters (films generating in excess of $50 million) released between 1993 and 1994 accounted for only 10 percent of total films released, but grossed nearly five times more than the average film. Exhibit 12 breaks down blockbusters released between 1992 and 1994 by film genre and their associated box office revenues. During this period, the average blockbuster movie grossed $100.7 million.

90   Because of the phenomenal success of *Mrs. Doubtfire,* Fox scored the second-highest average revenue per blockbuster between 1993 and 1994. However, this result was undermined by the fact that its film output was the lowest in the industry. Warner, on the other hand, with a much higher film output generated $81.2 million per blockbuster, again showing its strength in consistently releasing

EXHIBIT 11
Films and Blockbusters* Released and Box Office Gross, 1993–94

	Disney		Warner		Universal		Paramount		Fox		Sony	
	1993	1994	1993	1994	1993	1994	1993	1994	1993	1994	1993	1994
Number of films released	60	63	37	43	22	33	15	19	21	18	60	47
Average B/O per film ($ million)	$16.3	$19.6	$25.2	$20.1	$31.7	$22.9	$30.8	$38.7	$26.2	$27.9	$14.6	$10.7
Number of blockbusters released	4	3	7	6	2	3	4	3	3	2	5	2
Average B/O per blockbuster ($ million)	$53.5	$167.3	$80.3	$82.2	$202.2	$79.3	$89.2	$164.0	$111.5	$132.5	$78.9	$71.0
Blockbuster multiple†	3.3	8.5	3.2	4.1	6.4	3.5	2.9	4.2	4.3	4.7	5.4	6.6
Blockbusters/films released	6.7%	4.8%	18.9%	14.0%	9.1%	9.1%	26.7%	15.8%	14.3%	11.1%	8.3%	4.3%

*Blockbusters are defined as movies grossing in excess of $50 million at the box office.

†Blockbuster multiple = Average box office gross per blockbuster/Average box office gross per film.

Source: Paul Kagan and Associates, S&P Industry Surveys 1994.

EXHIBIT 12
Blockbusters Released and Box Office Revenue by Film Genre, 1992–94 (in $ million)

Studio	Year	Romance/Drama Released	Gross	Comedy/ Comedrama Released	Gross	Action/Thriller Released	Gross	Family Released	Gross	Western/Sci-Fi Released	Gross	Animation Released	Gross	Total Blockbusters Released	Gross
Warner	1994	1	$ 102.0	2	$ 142.0	3	$ 249.0							6	$ 493.0
	1993	1	50.1	1	63.3	2	262.3	2	$129.0	1	$ 57.6			7	562.3
	1992	1	121.9			3	391.0			1	101.2			5	614.1
Total		3	274.0	3	205.3	8	902.3	2	129.0	2	158.8			18	1,669.4
Universal	1994	1	96.0					2	142.0					3	238.0
	1993	1	63.1			1	341.3							2	404.4
	1992	1	58.9	1	58.4			2	115.5					4	232.8
Total		3	218.0	1	58.4	1	341.3	4	257.5					9	875.2
Fox	1994					2	265.0							2	265.0
	1993			1	219.0	1	62.5	1	53.1					3	334.6
	1992	1	72.2	1	72.0			1	172.7					3	316.9
Total		1	72.2	2	291.0	3	327.5	2	225.8					8	916.5
Paramount	1994	1	299.0			1	122.0			1	71.0			3	492.0
	1993			1	45.5	2	265.3	1	46.0					4	356.8
	1992			2	188.3	1	82.9							3	271.2
Total		1	299.0	3	233.8	4	470.2	1	46.0	1	71.0			10	1,120.0
Sony	1994	1	77.0			1	65.0							2	142.0
	1993	1	126.6	1	70.8	2	147.9	1	49.6					5	394.9
	1992	1	82.5	1	107.4	2	258.5							4	448.4
Total		3	286.1	2	178.2	5	471.4	1	49.6					11	985.3
Disney	1994					1	64.0	1	138.0			1	$300.0	3	502.0
	1993	1	50.4	2	113.9							1	49.6	4	213.9
	1992			1	139.6	2	150.0	1	58.7			1	217.0	5	565.3
Total		1	50.4	3	253.5	3	214.0	2	196.7			3	566.6	12	1,281.2
Totals		12	$1,199.7	14	$1,220.2	24	$2,726.7	12	$904.6	3	$229.8	3	$566.6	68	$6,847.6

Blockbusters are defined as movies grossing in excess of $50 million at the box office. Movies are grouped based on the year in which they first appeared in theaters; all receipts were not necessarily collected in the year that a movie was released.

Source: *S&P Industry Surveys 1994; Salomon Brothers Industry Report*, February 7, 1994; Paul Kagan and Associates.

EXHIBIT 13
Operating Margin of Parent Company's Filmed Entertainment Segment

Studio	Operating Margin
Disney	16.30%
Paramount	10.52
Universal	8.13
Warner	6.27
Fox	4.84
Sony	0.00

Source: *Financial Reports,* 1992–94.

profitable films. Disney ranked last, a surprising result given that its three animated releases averaged $188.8 million each. This result, though, underscored Disney's reliance on animation as the principal source of revenue generation, and with plans to continue increasing film releases to over 60 per year, this figure would potentially drop even further. Finally, because of the box office advantage of *Jurassic Park,* Universal was able to generate $140.75 million per blockbuster.

91   Because production and marketing costs per film are generally unavailable, the operating margin of the filmed entertainment segments of the studios' parent companies, as reported in various financial reports and shown in Exhibit 13, represents the closest measure of film profitability.

Distribution Channels

92   While good product is an important factor, its benefit would be negated without an adequate delivery system to theaters, video stores, and cable/network stations. This fact would explain why small film production companies with no delivery systems remained small and dependent on their large competitors who operated their own distribution networks. Those small firms that grew sufficiently large to begin distributing their own films were frequently acquired by the larger firms in the industry.

93   Strengthening the power of distribution for the large firms would hinge on their ability to further integrate distribution to ancillary markets, through acquisition of video outlets and interests in cable and TV companies. Because the costs of production are "sunk," it made sense for a producer/distributor to expose a film to as many windows of exhibition as possible, from home video to pay cable and free TV. Similarly, integrating vertically into theater exhibition allowed companies to increase the profit margin at the box office.

94   The matrix in Exhibit 14 shows each company's relative advantage in the (*a*) theater integration, (*b*) video market, and (*c*) cable and television networks.

Film Libraries

95   Film libraries are invaluable assets to major motion picture companies. The value of a film library can be measured by its contribution toward covering overhead and providing future cash flows. If a big studio had a weak film slate, as Fox did in 1992, the library could carry the studio. By the same token, the easiest way for a major studio to commit suicide would be to sell its film library, as MGM did in 1985.

96   The overall value of a film library, however, can be quite difficult to determine and can vary according to interest rates and inflation (if valuation were done on a net present value basis), or according to subjective assessments of a film's artistic worth; indeed, some Disney classics are considered priceless. Furthermore, except for some older films that have withstood the test of time and continue to generate revenues for the major studios (e.g., *Gone with the Wind, Ten Commandments*), the best measure of a film library's worth would come from the more recent major releases, which arouse the greatest audience interest and thus garner the greatest amount of marginal revenue.

97   In his book, *Entertainment Industry Economics,* Harold Voges estimated the probable minimum values of film libraries as of 1983. Starting with these values as the basis for the analysis, the figures

EXHIBIT 14
Advantages in Motion Picture Distribution

Studio	Theater Exhibition	Video Market	Cable and Network TV
Paramount	850 screens (Cinamerica, Famous Players, UPI)	Blockbuster video	United Paramount Network Cable interests (USA network, Sci-Fi Channel, Showtime, The Movie Channel)
Warner	191 screens (Cinamerica)	Blockbuster-ability drives video sales	HBO and other cable interests Full Service Network and planned Warner network
Disney	None	Animation and "classics" give major advantage	Disney Channel Venture with 3 baby Bells to develop viewing option via telephone lines
Fox	None	None	Fox TV network British Sky Broadcasting Star TV (42 million viewers in Asia)
Universal	185 screens (UPI)	Jurassic Park in the short term	Shared interest in USA network with Paramount
Sony	869 screens (Loews)	None	None

EXHIBIT 15
Estimated Probable Minimum Film Library Values, 1993

Studio	Approximate Number of Titles as of 1993	Approximate Value of Film Library as of 1993	Average Value per Title
Columbia	2,700	$1,950,000,000	$ 722,222
Universal	3,100	1,880,000,000	604,452
Disney	289	1,556,000,000	5,384,083
Warner	1,800	1,312,000,000	728,889
Fox	2,000	1,296,000,000	648,000
Paramount	800	817,000,000	1,021,250

Source: *Entertainment Industry Economics.*

were first adjusted to take into account the increase in the number of titles up to 1993, and future values were then determined using an interest rate of 10 percent. The results are shown in Exhibit 15.

CONCLUSION

98   The motion picture industry, like most other entertainment segments, is unusual in that success depends on bridging the gap between producing art and profiting from it. Moviemaking is still truly entrepreneurial, but magical elements aside, it is a very risky business. With movie appeal steadily growing among audiences worldwide, and with movies moving out of theaters and into homes where they can be seen on demand, the studios capable of integrating their production and distribution to realize this potential would enjoy a competitive advantage in the industry.

CASE INDEX

A

Airline industry, 37:1–10
Atlantic Richfield Corporation, 35:1–9

B

Banco Comercial Português, 29:1–34
Ben and Jerry's Homemade, Inc., 8:1–14
Biopharmaceutical industry, 39:1–17

C

Chemical Waste Management, 32:1–10
Coca-Cola Company, 22–25, 57–60, 99–102, 131–135, 164–167, 203–209, 244–246, 273–275, 297–299, 228–237, 370–378, 400–405

D

Diesel Technology Company, 11:1–15

E

Eastman Kodak Company, 10:1–15

F

Fast food industry, 21:1–20
Friends Provident, 4:1–21

G

Grand Metropolitan PLC, 24:1–14
Guiness Peat Aviation, 30:1–19

H

Hartmarx Corporation, 19:1–17
Hazardous waste management industry, 31:1–11

I

ICF Kaiser International, Inc., 33:1–7
ICF Resources Incorporated, 36:1–23

K

Kentucky Fried Chicken, 21:1–20

L

L. A. Gear, Inc., 20:1–19
Life insurance industry, 40:1–13
Liz Claiborne, 2:1–12

M

Matsushita Industrial de Baja California (A), 22:1–16
Matsushita Industrial de Baja California (B), 23:1–5
Merrill Electronics Corporation (A), 12:1 8
Merrill Electronics Corporation (B), 13:1–12
Mobil Chemical, 5:1–11
Mobil Chemical's Washington, New Jersey, Facility, 6:1–8
Motion picture industry, 41:1–22

N

Nintendo versus SEGA (A), 27:1–31
Nintendo versus SEGA (B), 28:1–13
NTN Communications, Inc., 1:1–11

O

Oil and gas exploration amd production industry, 34:1–16

P

Perdue Farms, Inc., 3:1–17
Perrigo Company, 7:1–14
Personal computer industry, 38:1–7
Philip Morris Companies, Inc., 26:1–12

R

Robin Hood, 25:1–2

S

SEGA (A), 27:1–31
SEGA (B), 28:1–13
Snapple Beverage Corporation, 9:1–13

T

3M Company: Integrating Europe (A), 16:1–21
3M Company: Integrating Europe (B), 17:1–10

V

Videogame industry, 27:1–31
Videogame wars, 28:1–13
Videoton (A), 14:1–17
Videoton (B), 15:1–2

W

W. L. Gore and Associates, Inc., 18:1–18

SUBJECT INDEX

A

ABC/Capital Cities, 173
Acceptable objectives, 214
Acceptable quality level, 43
Accountability, 16
Accounting, 315–316
Accounts receivable turnover, 195
Achievable objectives, 215
Acquisition strategy, 232–233
Action plans, 16
    elements of, 304–305
    EnergyCo, 305–306
    value-added benefits, 308
Activity-based cost accounting,
    179, 315
Activity ratios, 195–196
Adaptive mode, 9
Age distribution, 65
AIDS, 53
Airborne Express, 5
Aircraft industry, 84
Air pollution, 67
    laws, 72
Air Quality Act, 72
Albert, Kenneth J., 294
Alcoa, 7
Allied Signal, 354, 355, 396
American Express, 64, 88
    customer segmentation, 91
America OnLine, 172
Ameritech, 349
Amoco, 228
Andreessen, Marc, 261
Andrews, K. R., 45 n
Anfuso, Dawn, 118
Apple Computer, 152, 175, 222
Apple Macintosh, 85
ARCO, 39
Arthur D. Little Company,
    148–149, 285 n
Ashley, Laura, 169
Asset reduction, 231
Asset turnover, 195
AT&T, 64, 124, 225, 277
    downsizing, 361
Austin, Paul, 372
Auto emissions, 68
Avery Denison, benchmarking at,
    185

B

Backward vertical integration, 228
Baeder, Robert W., 109
Bama Pies, 292
Bare bones posture, 263
Barnard, Chester, 173
Barrier, M., 393 n
Barriers to entry, 76–77
    experience curve, 78
    industry concentration, 84
    and industry structure, 85–86
Bartlett, Christopher A., 212,
    351 n
BCG growth-share matrix,
    283–285
Becker, Dan, 68
Begley, S., 68
Benchmarking, 43, 162
    at Avery Denison, 185
    for cost leadership opportunities,
    249
    for differentiation, 252–253
    in internal analysis, 185–188
    at Kmart, 188
    at SAS, 186–187
Bethlehem Steel, 237
Bice restaurant, 6–7
Bleackley, Mark, 230 n
BMW, 85, 253
Boards of directors
    and company mission, 42–45
    empowerment, 11
    and stakeholders, 46
Boeing Corporation, 85, 383–384
Bonoma, Thomas V., 93
Booz Allen and Hamilton, 226
Bossidy, Larry, 354, 355
Boston Consulting Group, 283
Boulton, W., 45 n
Bracker, J. S., 48 n, 162
Brainstorming, 145, 151
Brand loyalty, and new entrants,
    253
Broad-line global competition, 264
Brown, Paul, 316
Brownstein, Andrew R., 365 n
Buckley, J. T., 238
Budgets, 389
Buffet, Warren, 373
Burrows, Peter, 174

Bush administration, 68
Business-level decisions, 6, 8
Business processes, 395
    reengineering, 347–349
Business Week, 313
Buyer behavior, 92
Buyer group, 79–80

C

CACI, Inc., 215
Cadillac Motor Company, 44
Calloway, Wayne, 269
Camillus, J. C., 12 n, 13, 19, 95
Campbell, A., 9 n
Campbell Soup Company, 11
Capabilities sharing, 278–280
Capital budget, 389
Capitalizing on supporting brands,
    404, 405
Capital requirements, 76
Carter, Jimmy, 100
Cash cows, 284
Cash flow budget, 389
Cassano, J. S., 351 n
Caterpillar Tractor, 39, 212, 213
CBS, Inc., 235
Central America, 154
CEOs; *see* Chief executive officers
Chaebol, 240
Champy, James, 347
Chancellor, Andrea, 109
Chandler, Alfred D., 351
Chapter 11 bankruptcy, 235
    Wang Laboratories, 236
Chase Econometric, 145
Chemlawn, 218–219
Chesebrough-Ponds, 224
Chief executive officers
    compensation issues, 365 n
    in strategic management, 10
Chrysler Corporation, 237
Citicorp, 172, 386–387
Clark, Kim, 389 n
Clean Air Act, 68, 72
Clean Air Act Amendments, 72
Clean Water Act, 73
Clearly Canadian, 102
Cleary, M. J., 158
Cleland, David I., 12 n, 13, 19,
    29 n, 47, 95

Clymer, Roy, 360
Coalitions, 293
*Coca-Cola, a Business System
    toward 2000,* 57–60, 244
Coca-Cola Company, 281, 347,
    353
    acquisitions, 23
    company mission, 57–60
    competitive advantage, 273–275
    continuous improvement,
    404–405
    corporate culture and reward
    system, 373–378
    differentiation at, 336–337
    external environment, 99–102
    financial reformation, 334–335
    forecasting, 164–167
    geographical expansion,
    328–332
    global corporation, 373–378
    in global environment, 131–135
    grand strategies, 245–246
    history, 22–25
    in Hungary, 135
    infrastructure fortification, 333
    internal analysis, 203–209
    in Japan, 134
    leadership at, 372–373
    long-term objectives, 24–245
    shareholder value, 297–299
    strategic controls, 400–404
    strategy implementation,
    328–337
    structure, 370–372
Cohen, Jonathan, 261
Cohen, Richard, 254
Colgate-Palmolive Company,
    118–119
Commerce Department Export
    Now Program, 123
Communications revolution, 314
Community and economic
    development, 52
Companies; *see* Firms
Company creed, 34–35
Company goals, 32–34, 121
Company mission, 13–14
    at Coca-Cola, 57–60
    and company responsibility,
    45–51
    core competencies, 120–121
    customer orientation, 39–40
    definition, 29

Company mission—*Cont.*
  excerpts from, 31–32, 33–42, 119
  formulating, 29–42
  at General Electric, 106
  globalization, 118–122
  goals, 32–34, 121
  inputs, 48
  newest trends in, 39–42
  Nicor, Inc., 30
  and organizational culture, 359–360
  philosophy, 34–35, 121–122
  public image, 35–37, 122
  purpose, 29
  and quality, 41–42
  responsibility for, 42–45
  self-concept, 37–39, 122
  and social responsibility, 47–49
  statement components, 31
Company philosophy, 34–35, 121–122
Company policies, 16; *see also* Policies
Company profile, 14–15
Company responsibility, 45–51
Company self-concept, 37–39
Comparative benchmarking, 162
Compensation; *see* Reward systems
Competencies; *see* Core competencies
Competition
  broad-line global, 264
  for Coca-Cola Company, 99–100
  generic strategies, 216–217
  global industries, 115–116
  identifying, 86–88
  multidomestic industries, 113–114
  profile of, 88
Competitive advantage
  at Coca-Cola, 273–275
  core competencies, 281–282
  cost leadership, 249–251
  differentiation opportunities, 251–254
  through diversification or integration, 277–291
  early achievement of strategy-structure, 352
  in emerging industries, 259–260
  in global industries, 263–264
  market focus, 257–258
  in mature and declining industries, 260
  Netscape, 260–261
  at Scania, 258
  seeking, 248–259
  speed as, 254–257
  transition to industry maturity, 260–262
Competitive analysis, 86–88
Competitive benchmarking, 43
Competitive environment; *see* Operating environment
Competitive forces, 75–81
  jockeying for position, 80–81
  powerful buyers, 79–80
  powerful suppliers, 77–79
  substitute products, 80
  threats of entry, 76–77
Competitiveness
  environmental costs, 70

Competitiveness—*Cont.*
  and operating environment, 88–89
  and strategy, 74–75
Competitive position, 212
Competitive reaction, 294–295
Competitive strategies
  contract manufacturing, 123–124
  foreign branching, 125
  foreign subsidiaries, 125
  joint ventures, 124–125
  licensing, 123–124
  niche market exporting, 123
  for US firms in foreign markets, 122–125
Competitive Strategy (Porter), 73
Comprehensive Environmental Response, Compensation, and Liability Act, 73
Computer industry; *see also* Personal computer industry
  boundaries, 81–82
  product segments, 83
Concentrated growth, 218–222, 266
  at Coca-Cola, 246
Concentration of industry, 84
Concentration strategy, 219
Concentric diversification, 266
  as grand strategy, 229–230
Concorde airplane, 383–384
Conglomerate diversification, 266
  as grand strategy, 230–231
Consolidated Foods, 32
Consortia, 239
Consulting firms, 147–148
Contingency plans, 392
Continuous improvement, 380
  at Coca-Cola, 404–405
  process, 43
  quality imperative, 393–397
Contract manufacturing, 123–124
Control; *see also* Operational controls *and* Strategic controls
  definition, 390
  of global firm, 112–113
Control charts, 43
Cooper, Donald K., 109
Coors Brewery, 389
Core competencies
  capitalizing on, 281–282
  in company mission, 120–121
  and stages of industrial evolution, 184
Core values, 357
Corman, Joel, 108
Corporate combinations, 235–240
  consortia, *keiretsu*, and *chaebol*, 239–240
  joint ventures, 236–237
  strategic alliances, 237–238
Corporate Leadership Council, 324, 325
Corporate-level decisions, 7
Corporate-level strategic managers, 5
Corporate philanthropy
  by Exxon, 50
  by General Motors, 51
  types of, 52–53
Corvette, 35
Cost accounting, 179, 315
Cost cutting, obsessive, 251
Cost differences, decline in, 251
Cost disadvantages, 76–77

Cost leadership opportunities, 249–251
Cost of capital, 320–321
Cott Corporation, 99, 203–206, 403
Cox, Tom, 257
Creditors, in operating environment, 93
Critical success factors/strategy issues analysis, 162
Cross Pens, 35
Crouse, William, 40–41
Crown, Cork, and Seal Company, research and development, 326
Cultural diversity, 358 n
Current deviation, 390
Customer orientation, 393–394
Customer profiles, 89–92
Customers
  for Coca-Cola, 100–101
  in company mission, 39–40
  dangerous assumptions about, 92
Customer segmentation
  at American Express, 91
  variables, 90–92
Customer-service-driven organizations, 42
Customer surveys, 145, 146
Customer value, 393
Czinkota, M. R., 109

D

D. M. Offray and Son, 66
Daft, Douglas, 376
Daihatsu Mira, 213
Daimler Benz, 277, 280
Dalton, D. R., 45 n
Darlin, Damon, 185
Data Resources, 145
Days Inn, 383, 386
Dayton Hudson Corporation, 32
  board empowerment, 11
  management philosophy, 34, 36
  mission statement, 33–34
Decentralization, 263
Decisions; *see* Strategic decisions
Declining industries, competitive advantage, 262
DeDee, J. Kim, 122 n
Delite fast foods, 250
Delivery speed, 256
Delphi method, 145, 151, 162
Delta Air Lines, 186–187, 321, 357
Demand forecasting, 138
Deming, W. Edwards, 393
  approach to quality, 41–42
Demographics, 65
  and forecasting, 138–140
  variables, 91
Dess, G. G., 248 n, 249 n, 319 n, 394, 396
Deviations, 390–393
Devlin, Godfrey, 230 n
Dialectical inquiry, 162
Diamond-Star Motors, 237
Dicken, Peter, 114
Dickinson, Becton, 355
Differentiation strategy, 251–254
Dillard Department Stores, 8

Direct foreign investment, 104–105
Directory of National Trade Associations, 198
Disney World, 248
Distribution channels, 77
Diversification
  to build value, 264–271
  at Coca-Cola, 297–299
  concentric, 229–230
  conglomerate, 230–231
  at Daimler Benz, 280
  grand strategy selection matrix, 265–266
  versus integration, 270–271
  model of grand strategy clusters, 267–270
  of products, 351
  rationalizing, 277–291
  Walt Disney Company, 282–283
Diversity
  benefits of, 351–352
  of markets, 314–315
Divestiture, 266
  as grand strategy, 234–235
Divisional structure, 342, 344
Dogs, 284–285
Dominant coalitions, 293
Dominant values, 357
Domino's Pizza, 109
Donance, R. G., 158
Donovan, Andrew, 225
Doug Suk Foods Corporation, 107
Dow Chemical, 36
Downsizing, 349–351
  at IBM, 137
Doyle, Peter, 184
Doz, Yves, 115 n
Drexler, Mickey, 182–183
Dun and Bradstreet, 198
Du Pont, 223
  financial analysis, 197
Dynamic system, 18

E

Early warning system, 155
Eckhouse, R. H., 112
Ecological issues
  auto emissions, 68
  benefits of eco-efficiency, 70–73
  costs and competitiveness, 70
  federal legislation, 72–73
  packaging and, 69
  pollution, 67–70
  premise control, 382
  scenario, 148–149
Ecology, 67–73
Econometric models, 144–146
Economic environment, 62–64
Economic forecasts, 143
Economic value added, 316; *see also* Value added
  power of, 320–321
Economies of scale, 76, 84–85
Education, 358
Eisner, Michael, 365 n
Electromagnetic wave engine, 227
Emerging industries, 259–260
Employee development, 213
Employee relations, 213
Employment rates, 94
Empowering personnel, 320–325

Encyclopedia of Associations, 198
EnergyCo, 305–306
Entrenched cost leader, 250
Entrenchment, 221–222
Entrepreneurial mode, 9
Environment; *see* External
    environment; Forecasting;
    Global environment; *and*
    Industry environment
Environmentalism, 53; *see also*
    Ecological issues
Environmental Protection Agency,
    67, 68
    on costs and competitiveness, 70
Environmental scanning, 163
Epps, Howard, 358 n
Equal employment opportunity, 50
Ernst and Young, 393 n, 397
Error-free attitude, 396
Ethiopian Airlines, 66
Etienne Aigner, 35
European Community, 62–64
Executives; *see also* Chief
    executive officers *and*
    Management
    and external environment, 3
    general opinions and attitudes,
        13
    views of strategic management,
        12
Experience curve, 78, 163
External assessment, 110
External environment
    Coca-Cola, 99–102
    definition, 15
    difficulty of assessing, 94–95
    impact of strategic decisions, 5
    industry, 73–74
    makeup of, 3, 62
    operating, 88–94
    remote, 62–73
Exxon, 50

F

Factories of the future, 313
Fahey, Liam, 294
Federal ecological legislation,
    72–73
Federal Environmental Pesticide
    Control Act Amendments, 73
Federal Express, 64, 321
Federal Insecticide, Fungicide, and
    Rodenticide Act, 73
Federal Water Pollution Control
    Act, 73
Federal Water Pollution Control
    Act Amendments, 73
Feedback, 18
Finance, 315–316
Financial analysis, 191–202
    activity ratios, 195–196
    definition, 191
    at Du Pont, 197
    leverage ratios, 194
    liquidity ratios, 191–194
    profitability ratios, 196–198
    sources and uses of funds,
        198–199
Financial ratios, 192, 201–202
Firms; *see also* Global
    corporations

Firms—*Cont.*
    BCG growth-share matrix,
        283–285
    benefits of diversity, 351–352
    consideration of structure, 339
    divisional structure, 342, 344
    downsizing, outsourcing, and
        self-management, 349–351
    effective structure, 339–352
    evolution of strategy and
        structure, 351–352
    external dependence, 292–293
    foreign manufacturing, 110–111
    functional structure, 341–342
    geographic structure, 342, 343
    internal political considerations,
        293–294
    key internal factors, 176
    leadership in, 352–356
    levels of strategy, 5–7
    long-term prosperity, 4–5
    major activities, 177–178
    matching strategy and structure,
        346–352
    matrix organization, 344–346
    maximizing synergy, 360
    organizational culture, 356–361
    portfolio management, 282–291
    primary structure, 340–346
    production/operations
        management, 311–313
    reengineering, 347–349
    resource allocation, 4
    restructuring, 346–347
    reward systems, 361–366
    steps to globalization, 109–111
    strategic business units,
        342–344, 345
Fischer, Donald, 182–183
Fischer, Istvan, 135
Flexible objectives, 214
Focus groups, 162
Focus on business processes, 395
Focus strategy, 216–217, 257–258
Ford Escort, 114
Ford Explorer, 253
Ford Motor Company, 41, 222,
    396
Forecasting
    by brainstorming, 151
    at Coca-Cola, 164–167
    critical aspects of managing,
        153–155
    data use, 144
    Delphi method, 151, 162
    demand, 138
    early warning system, 155
    econometric models, 144–146
    economic, 143
    importance of, 137
    information sources, 141,
        158–161
    key variables, 137–141
    political, 147–149
    popular approaches, 145
    social forecasts, 146–147
    strategic issues, 142–143
    and strategic management,
        151–153
    techniques, 141–151
    technological, 150–151
    technological change, 67
    tools and techniques, 162–163
Foreign branching, 125

Foreign manufacturing site,
    110–111
Foreign subsidiaries, 125
Formality of systems, 9–12
Formula facilities, 263
Forrester Research, 174
Forward vertical integration, 228,
    246
Fox, Harold, 184
Fragmented industries, 262–263
Franchises, 237
Frankenberg, Bob, 279–280
Frenette, Charles, 245
Frito-Lay, 357
Frost and Sullivan's World
    Political Risk Forecasts, 148
Functional analysis, 169
Functional approach to internal
    analysis, 173–176
Functional-level decisions, 6–8
Functional structure, 341–342
Functional tactics, 16
    in accounting and finance,
        315–316
    compared to strategies, 310–311
    empowering personnel, 320–325
    at General Cinema, 309
    in human resources
        management, 318–319, 323
    in marketing, 313–315
    participants, 311
    in production/operations,
        311–313
    in research and development,
        316–318, 322
    specificity, 310
    time horizon, 310
Future-oriented decisions, 5
Future studies, 162

G

Galbraith, V. R., 352 n
Gap, The, 180, 182–183
Gates, William, 354
Gatewood, Elizabeth, 191
General Cinema, 189, 281
    functional tactics, 309
    policies, 326
General Electric, 12, 39, 124–125,
    186–187, 320–321
    downsizing, 349
    on globalization, 106
General Electric Appliances, 33
General Motors, 216, 219–220
    board empowerment, 11
    environmental principles, 34, 38
    philanthropic activities, 51
Generic strategies, 15, 216–217
    for competitive advantage, 249
    risks, 218
Geographic expansion, 351
Geographic market segment, 90–91
Geographic organizational
    structure, 342, 343
Georgia Power Company, 147, 150
Gerber, 35
Germany, Coca-Cola in, 373–374
Gerstner, Louis V., Jr., 349, 353,
    384, 388
Ghoshal, Sumantra, 212, 351 n
Giant Foods, 220–221

Global corporations
    control problems, 112–113
    development of, 106–107
    factors driving, 108
    global industries, 115–116
    multidomestic industries,
        113–115
    multinational challenge,
        116–117
    organizational culture, 358–359
Global environment, 104–135
    and Coca-Cola, 131–135
    complexity, 111–113
    components, 129–130
    location and coordination issues,
        116–117
    strategic planning, 113–118
Global focus strategy, 264
Global industries, 115–116
    competitive advantage, 263–264
Globalites, 118
Globalization
    basic options, 264
    of Coca-Cola, 24–25, 373–378
    at Colgate, 118–119
    of company mission, 118–122
    competitive strategies, 264
    competitive strategies for US
        firms, 122–125
    conditions prior to, 109–111
    Domino's Pizza, 109
    nature of, 104–105
    Philip Morris Kraft Foods,
        106–107
    pricing services, 316–317
    reasons for, 107–108
    at Yamanouchi, 104
Global strategic planning, 113–118
Goeldner, C. R., 158
Goizueta, Roberto C., 206, 353,
    365 n, 375, 377, 400
    as company CEO, 372–373
    on company mission, 57–60
    on company structure, 370–372
    on competitive advantage,
        273–274
    on external environment, 99
    on forecasting, 164
    on geographic expansion, 328
    on global environment, 131
    on global perspective, 24–25
    on portfolio analysis, 298
Goldberg, L. D., 45 n
Goldfarb, D. L., 150
Goodyear Tire and Rubber
    Company, 234
Goold, M., 9 n
Government
    barrier to entry, 77
    customer function of, 66
    ecological legislation, 72–73
    innovation-friendly regulation,
        86–87
    supplier function of, 66
Grand strategies, 15, 217–235
    at Coca-Cola, 245–246
    concentrated growth, 218–222
    concentric diversification,
        229–230
    conglomerate diversification,
        230–231
    corporate combinations,
        235–240
    divestiture, 234–235
    horizontal integration, 227

Grand strategies—*Cont.*
  innovation, 226–227
  liquidation, 235
  market development, 222–225
  options under, 223
  at PepsiCo, 268–269
  product development, 225–226
  selection of, 240
  sequence of selection, 241
  turnaround, 231–234
  vertical integration, 228–229
Grand strategy clusters, 267–270
Grand strategy selection matrix, 265–266
Graniteville Company, 221
Gray, Harry J., 362
Green economics, 68
Greenhouse effect, 67
Greyhound, 173
Growth
  company goal, 32–34, 121
  concentrated, 218–222
  scenario, 150
  strategies, 351
GTE, 254–255
Guccione, Bob, 254
Gulf and Western Americas Corporation, 121
Gulf Oil, 212
Guyette, James M., 387

H

Hager, M., 68
Hall, R. H., 38 n
Haloid Company, 138
Hamel, Gary, 281 n
Hammer, Michael, 347
Haner's Business Environment Risk Index, 147
Harrison, J. R., 45 n
Harvel, G., 116 n
Harvey, J., 218 n
Head Ski, 229–230
Hechinger, John W., Jr., 220
Hechinger store concept, 220
Henke, J. W., Jr., 45 n
Herbert, Ira, 372
Hewlett-Packard
  company mission, 120–121
  mission statement, 33
Hofer, Charles W., 88 n, 184, 285 n
Holiday Inns, 121, 342, 360
  portfolio management, 288–290
Holmelius, Kaj, 258
Home Depot, 220
Honda, 281
Horizontal integration, 265
  as grand strategy, 227
Hout, T., 104 n
Hrebiniak, Laurence G., 307
Human resource management
  functional tactics in, 318–319, 323
  future of, 324–325
  at The Gap, 183
Human resources
  at Colgate, 118–119
  in operating environment, 93–94
  in strategic alliances, 238–239
Hungary, 135

Hunger appeals, 52
Huss, W. R., 150

I

Iacocca, Lee, 365 n
IBM, 12, 107, 108, 175, 183
  downsizing, 137
  and Internet, 360
  in Japan, 181
  network-centric computing, 339, 353
  policies, 326
  premise control, 384–385
  PS/2 computer, 85
  strategic business units, 344
Iglesias-Solomon, Teresa, 65
Ikeda, Hajime, 181
Imitation, and differentiation, 253
Implementation controls, 383–386
Incentives, 363
Industrial markets, segmentation variables, 93
Industry analysis, 81–88; *see also* Internal analysis
Industry attractiveness-business strength matrix, 285, 286, 287
Industry boundaries, 81–84
Industry definition, 83–85
Industry environment, 62, 73–88
  competitive analysis, 86–88
  competitive forces and strategies, 74–75
  experience curve, 78
  forces driving competition, 75–81
  global, 104–135
  industry analysis, 81–88
  industry boundaries, 81–84
  industry structure, 84–86
  information sources, 158–161
  jockeying for position, 80–81
  overview, 74
  powerful buyers, 79–80
  strategic analysis and choice, 259–264
  substitute products, 80
  threats of entry, 76–77
Industry evaluation, stages, 181–185
Industry factors, in premise control, 382
Industry maturity, transition to, 260–262
Industry shakeout, 183
Industry structure
  barriers to entry, 85–86
  concentration, 84
  economies of scale, 84–85
  product differentiation, 85
Information explosion, 115
Information sharing, 256–257
Information sources
  forecasting, 141
  industry and operating environments, 160–161
  remote and industry environments, 158–159
Infrastructure sharing, 278–280
Innovation, 266
  as grand strategy, 226–227

Innovation-friendly regulation, 86–87
Integration
  versus diversification, 270–271
  rationalizing, 277–291
Intel Corporation, 36–37, 39, 226
Internal analysis
  benchmarking, 184–185
  at Coca-Cola, 203–209
  comparison with past performance, 181
  financial analysis, 191–202
  functional approach, 173–176
  at Laura Ashley, 170
  potential strengths and weaknesses, 176
  stages of industry evolution, 181–185
  success factor comparisons, 188–189
  SWOT analysis, 170–173
  traditional approaches, 169–181
  value chain analysis, 176–181
Internal assessment, 110
Internal political considerations, 293–294
Internet, 384–385
  and IBM, 360
  Netscape, 260–261
  and Penthouse magazine, 254
Inventory turnover ratio, 195
Isdell, Neville, 374–375
ITT Barton, company mission, 31–32
Iverson, Ann, 169, 170
Ivester, Douglas, 375–377
Izod Lacoste, 35

J

J. C. Penney Company, company mission, 40
Jacobs, Melvin, 182
Jain, Chaman L., 144
Jamieson, David, 358 n
Japan
  Coca-Cola in, 134, 403
  IBM in, 181
  keiretsu, 239
Job skills, 94
Jockeying for position, 80–81
John Deere & Company, 220, 222
Johnson & Johnson, 35, 39
Joint ownership, 236–237
Joint ventures, 124–125, 265
  as grand strategy, 236–237
  in Siberia, 238
Jones, Charles, 91
Jones, T. M., 45 n
Joyce, William F., 307
Judgmental models, 145
Juliussen, Egil, 83
Juliussen, Karen, 83
Jupfer, Andrew, 225
Juran, Joseph M., 41, 393
Juries of executive opinion, 145, 146
Just-in-time delivery, 43, 312

K

Kamata, Hiroki, 181
Kanter, Rosabeth Moss, 358 n
Kao, John, 376
Kaplan, Neal, 220
Katada, Tetsuya, 212–213
Kawai, Ryoichi, 212
Kazanjian, R. K., 352 n
Keiretsu, 239
Kelley, E. J., 39 n
Kelly, J., 38 n
Kelly-Moore, 180
Kendall, Donald, 268
Kennell, J. D., 141 n
Keough, Don, 373–374
Kesner, I. F., 45 n
Kevlar, 223
Key managers, 355–356
Key success factors, 390
Key themes, 357
King, William R., 12 n, 13, 19, 29 n, 47, 95
Kinicki, A. J., 48 n
Kirkpatrick, David, 260
Kirks, L. M., 158
Kmart, 188, 361
Knight-Ridder, 254
Komatsu, remaking, 212–213
Korea, 105, 240
Kotler, Philip, 184, 223
Kotter, John P., 352–353
Kraft General Foods International, 106–107
Kramer, R., 109 n
Kroger, 102

L

L. L. Bean, 357
Labor market
  globalites, 118
  new labor force, 139
  in operating environment, 93–94
Land's End, 221
Landford, H. W., 158
Land pollution, 68
Land pollution laws, 72
Langley, A., 10 n
Laura Ashley Holdings, 169, 170
Leadership
  at Coca Cola, 372–373
  creating organizational culture, 357–358
  embracing change, 353–355
  existing versus outsiders, 356
  key managers, 355–356
  Kotter on, 352–353
  rebuilding organizations, 354
  shaping organizational culture, 354–355
Lee, Chuck, 254
Lee Hun-Hee, 13
Lenz, R. C., Jr., 158
Leverage, 194
Leverage ratios, 194
Levine, J., 6
Levitt, Theodore, 104 n
Licensing, 123–124, 237

Life cycle-competitive strength
    matrix, 285–286, 291
Lifestyle variables, 91–92
Linneman, R. E., 141 n
Liquidation, 266
    as grand strategy, 235
Liquidity ratios, 191–194
Literacy programs, 52–53
Long-term objectives, 15, 211–216
    at CACI, Inc., 215
    at Coca-Cola, 244–245
    competitive position, 212
    employee development, 213
    employee relations, 213
    linked to short-term objectives,
        307–308
    productivity, 212
    profitability, 211
    public responsibility, 214
    qualities of, 214–216
    selection of, 240
    sequence of, 241
    technological leadership, 213
Long-term strategies, 4–5
Lorsch, Jay W., 11, 52
Lotus Development Corporation,
    261
    key success factors, 390
Low cost advantages, 249–251
Low-cost leadership, 216
Lussier, Robert N., 108

M

MacMillan, Ian C., 92
Mahendroo, Vikesh, 325
Malcolm Baldrige Quality Award,
    42, 394
Mallinckrodt, 11
Management; see also Chief
        executive officers
    decision makers, 9–10
    focus on execution, 339
    and forecasting, 153–154
    and functional tactics, 311
    globalites, 118
    key managers, 355–356
    portfolio approach, 5
    production/operations, 311
    and restructuring, 347
    seeking competitive advantage,
        248–259
    and strategic control, 380
Management process, 3
Managerial accounting, 315
Managerial confidence, 115
Manufacturing
    choosing foreign site, 110–111
    contractual, 123–124
    globalization for Ford Escort,
        114
Mark, Reuben, 118–119
Market development, 266
    as grand strategy, 222–225
Market focus, as competitive
        advantage, 257–258
Marketing, 313–315
Marketing for sale, 234
Market niches, 314–315
Market opportunity analysis, 162
Market penetration, 219

Markets
    in company mission, 31–32
    customer profiles, 88–92
    diversity of, 314–315
    geographic, 90–91
    globalization, 104–105
Market segmentation
    variables in consumer market,
        90–92
    variables in industrial markets,
        93
Marlow, Raymond, 394–395
Marlow Industries, 393, 394–395
Marshak, David, 261
Mason, Julie Cohen, 71
Matrix organization, 344–346
Matsumoto, Junichiro, 104–105
Mature industries, 262
McDonald's, 264, 267–268, 357
McGrath, Rita Gunther, 92
MCI Communications, 225, 277,
    354–355
McKinsey 7–S Framework, 339,
    340, 352
McKinsey and Company, 258,
    285
McMillan, John D., 365 n
Measurable objectives, 214,
    306–307
Medtronic, board empowerment,
    11
Mercury One-2-One, 225
Merrill Lynch, 171, 319, 361
Metagame analysis, 163
Microsoft Corporation, 171,
    260–261
Milestone reviews, 383–386
Miller, A., 236, 248 n, 249 n,
    319 n, 394, 396
Miller, Annetta, 224
Miller, Richard W., 236
Miller Brewing Company,
    294–295
Milliken, 357
Mintzberg, Henry, 9
MIPS Computer System, 237
Mission statement; see Company
        mission
Mitsubishi Motors, 237
Mizuchi, M. S., 45 n
Molz, R., 45 n
Monsanto Company, 11, 100
Moody's Manual, 198
Moor, R. C., 112
Morioka, Shigeo, 104
Morrison's Cafeteria, 278–279
Motivating objectives, 214
Motivational payoff, 308
Motorola, 42, 44, 347
Muller, Horst, 374
Multibusiness companies
    building value, 278–279
    Coca-Cola, 297–299
    rationalizing diversification and
        integration, 277–291
    strategic analysis and choice,
        277–299
Multidomestic industries, 113–115
Multinational challenge, 116–117
Multinational corporations, 106
    components of global
        environment, 129–130
Multiple scenarios, 163
Murayama, Tomiichi, 134
Murdick, R. G., 112

N

Nabisco Brands, 226
Nader, Ralph, 45 n
Nakauchi, Isao, 134
Naroyanan, V. K., 294
Nathanson, D. A., 351 n
National Environmental Policy
    Act, 72
National focus strategy, 264
NationsBank, operating policy, 326
Nayyar, Seema, 224
NEC, 181
Netscape, 260–261
Network-centric computing, 339,
    353
New Age beverages, 102
New entrants, 250
    and brand loyalty, 253
New products
    ideas, 228
    forecasting demand for, 138
Niche market exporting, 123
Nicor, Inc., company mission, 30
Night Owl Security, 221
Niños (Iglesias-Solomon), 65
Nippondenso microcar, 226–227
Nissan Motor Manufacturing, Ltd.,
    34, 37
No-frills posture, 263
Noise Control Act, 73
Nominal group technique, 162
Nordstrom, 8
North American Free Trade
    Agreement, 154
Novell, 279–280
Nucor Corporation, reward system,
    364–365
Nun, A. B., 158
NutraSweet Company, 100

O

Oak, Brian, 254
O'Brien, Louise, 91
O'Daniell, Robert F., 361, 362–363
O'Mara, Julie, 358 n
O'Neill, Paul, 7
Onoda, Masayoshi, 104
Operating environment, 62
    competitive position, 88–89
    creditors, 93
    customer profiles, 89–92
    and firm's reputation, 94
    human resources, 93–94
    information sources, 160–161
    suppliers, 92
Operational controls
    budgets, 389
    evaluating deviations, 390–393
    key success factors, 390
    monitoring performance,
        390–393
    scheduling, 389
    steps, 388
Opportunity, 171
Organizational culture
    at Coca-Cola, 373–377
    definition, 356–357
    in global corporations, 358–359

Organizational culture—Cont.
    role of leadership, 354–355
    strategy relationship, 359–361
    at United Technologies, 362–363
    ways of creating, 357–358
Organizational leadership, 352–356
Organizational politics, 293–294
Organizational renewal, 40–41
Organization of Petroleum
    Exporting Countries, 64
Ortha Diagnostic Systems, Inc.,
    40–41
Ostling, Leif, 258
Ouchi, William, 32
Outsourcing, 238–239, 312–313,
    349–351
Overlay structure, 345–346

P

Packaging, 69
Panner, Morris J., 365 n
Paré, Terence P., 315
Pareto chart, 43
Parker-Pope, Tara, 170
Past performance, 181
Patricia Seybold Group, 261
Pearce, John A., II, 29, 31, 44 n,
    45 n, 218 n, 231 n, 233,
    248 n
Pearson, Andrall, 268
Penthouse magazine, 254
PepsiCo, 135, 203–206, 268–269
Pepsi-Cola, 91–92, 100, 264
Perfectly competitive industry, 74
Performance
    monitoring, 390–393
    past, 181
    and rewards, 364
    superior, 219
Personal computer industry, SWOT
    analysis, 174–175
Pesticide Control Act, 73
Philip Morris, 106–107
Pilko, George, 71
Pilko and Associates, 71
PIMS analysis, 33, 162
Planning
    forecasting tools and techniques,
        162–163
    global, 113–118
    key issues, 95
    mode, 9
Poka-yoke, 43
Polaroid, 226
Policies, 16
    definition, 322
    for empowerment, 322–325
    examples of, 326
Political Agenda Worksheet,
    152–153
Political environment, 76–77
Political forecasts, 147–149
Pollution, 67–70
Pollution credits, 68
Population changes, 65
    and forecasting, 138–140
Porter, Michael E., 73–74, 85, 87,
    104 n, 113, 117, 120, 178,
    216–217, 218, 250, 252, 255,
    259, 279, 281 n

Portfolio classification analysis, 163
Portfolio management, 5
  BCG growth-share matrix, 283–285
  at Coca-Cola, 297–298, 334–335
  and core competencies, 281
  and financial resources, 282–290
  Holiday Inns, 288–290
  industry attractiveness-business strength matrix, 285, 286, 287
  levels of risk and growth, 291
  life cycle-competitive strength matrix, 285–286, 291
  limitations, 296–290
Prahalad, C. K., 115 n, 116 n, 281 n
PremierFoods Corporation, 107
Premise control, 381–383
  at IBM, 384–385
Preventive approach, 396
Pricing services, 316–317
Primary activities, 177–178
Primary organizational structure, 340–346
Priorities, 307
  in company mission, 46–47
Private labels, 99
Probe International, 148
Process, 12–13, 17–18
Procter & Gamble, 12, 357
Product development, 266
  at Coca-Cola, 246
  cycles, 256
  as grand strategy, 225–226
Product differentiation, 76, 85, 216
  at Coca-Cola, 336–337
  for competitive advantage, 248–249
  evaluating opportunities, 251–254
Product diversification, 246, 351
Product improvement, 256
Production, deviations, 390–393
Production/operations management, 311–313
Productivity, 212
Product life cycle analysis, 162
Products, in company mission, 31–32, 120–121; *see also* Substitutes
Profitability
  goal, 32–34, 121
  long-term objective, 211
Profitability ratios, 196–198
Profit and loss budgets, 389
Profit margin, 177
Promus Companies, 288–290
Protected niche strategy, 264
Prudential Insurance Company, 380–381
Psychographic variables, 91–92
Public image, 35–37
  in company mission, 122
Public responsibility, 214
Purchasing, 178 n

Qualitative forecasting models, 145
Quality
  in company mission, 41–42

Quality—*Cont.*
  definition, 393
  terminology about, 43
Quality function deployment, 43
Quality imperative/continuous improvement, 380, 393–397
Quality-of-life issues, 65
Quantitative-causal forecasting models, 145
Question marks, 285

Radio Shack, 182
Ramanujam, V., 12 n, 13, 19, 95
Ranges of deviation, 392
Ranking priorities, 307
Rapid response, 255
Ratio of sales to fixed assets, 195
Rechner, P. L., 45 n
Recovery response, 234
Reengineering, 16–17, 347–349
Refocusing, 16–17
Refuse Act, 72
Regulation
  environmental laws, 72–73
  innovation-friendly, 86–87
Rehder, Robert R., 35, 37
Reif, W., 162
Related diversified businesses, 351, 352
Religion, 358
Remote environment, 62–73, 156
  components, 3, 62
  ecological factors, 67–73
  economic factors, 62–64
  in industry, 73–78
  information sources, 158–159
  political factors, 65–66
  social factors, 64–65
  technological factors, 66–67
Reputation of firm, 94
Research and development, 316–318, 322
Resource allocation, 4
Resource Conservation and Recovery Act, 72
Resource Recovery Act, 72
Restructuring, 16–17, 346–347
  strategic priorities, 348
Retrenchment, 233–234, 266
Return on equity, 196–197
Return on investment, 196–197
Reuter, Edzard, 277, 280
Reward systems
  CEO compensation, 365 n
  at Coca-Cola, 373–377
  guidelines, 362–366
  and motivation, 361–362
  at Nucor Corporation, 364–365
Rich's, 361
Richway, 361
Risk
  attitudes toward, 293
  portfolio management, 291
  in strategic management, 11–12
Rivoli, P., 109
RJR Nabisco, 226
Roach, John, 224
Robbins, D. K., 231 n, 233
Robert Morris Associates, 198
Roberts, Bert, 354–355

Robinson, Richard B., Jr., 248 n
Robust design, 43
Ronkainen, I. A., 109
Ronstadt, R., 109 n
Rose, Mike, 288–290
Rosenberg, D., 236
Ross, Steve, 365 n
Rubbermaid, 382
Rudden, E., 104 n
Ruggeri, Roberto, 6–7
Rumelt, Richard, 351
Rutledge, Sam, 308

Safe Drinking Water Act, 73
Sager, Ira, 384
Sales force estimates, 145, 146
Sam's Choice, 99, 102
Samsung Group, 13–14
San Luis Sourdough Company, 314, 316–317
Saturn Motors, 34, 35, 253
Saudi Arabian Oil, 5
Sawyer, G. E., 51 n
Scandinavian Airline system, 186–187
Scania, 248, 258
Scarborough, N., 316
Scenario development, 145, 147
  Georgia power Company, 150
  for 21st, 148–149
Scheduling, 389
Schendel, D., 88 n
School reform, 53
Schrempp, Jurgen E., 277, 280
Schreyogg, G., 381, 386 n, 388
Schroeer, Will, 68
Sears, Roebuck & Company, 8, 186–187
Self-concept, 37–39, 122
Self-management, 349–351
Semon, Thomas T., 138
Service
  in company mission, 31–32, 120–121
  pricing, 316–317
Shapiro, Benson P., 93
Shareholder value, 297–299
Shirouzi, Norihiko, 403 n
Short-term objectives, 16
  and action plans, 304–305
  linked to long-term objectives, 307–308
  qualities of, 306–308
  value-added benefits, 308
Shulman, L. E., 393 n
Siemens, 123, 124
Simulation techniques, 162
Single dominant businesses, 351, 352
Single/multiple regression, 145
Single-product businesses, 351, 352
  strategic analysis and choice, 248–275
Situational analysis, 162
Situation severity, 232–233
Sivak, Anatoly, 238
Six-sigma quality, 43
Smith, Adam, 68
Snapple, 102

Social environment, 64–65
Social forecasts, 146–147
Social index, 49
Social norms, 358
Social responsibility, 47–49
  ecological issues, 71
  guidelines, 49–51
Soho Beverages, 257
Solid Waste Disposal Act, 72
Sorrentino, Gianfranco, 6
Sources and uses of funds analysis, 198–199
South America, 154
Southwest Airlines, 171
Special alert control, 387–388
Specialization, 263
Specificity
  of functional tactics, 310
  of short-term objectives, 304
Speed, as competitive advantage, 254–257
Spindler, Michael, 175
SPIRE (Systematic Procedure for Identification of Relevant Environment), 163
Sprout, Alison, 354 n
Stahl, Jack, 245
Stakeholder activism, 113
Stakeholders, 17
  and company mission, 45–51
  types of, 47
Stalk, G., 393 n
Standard and Poor's, 198
Standard operating procedures, 322
Stanhome, 11
Stars, 284
Statement of means, 15
Statistical process control, 43, 313
Statistical quality control, 43
Steade, R., 64 n
Steering control, 380
Steinmann, H., 381, 386 n, 388
Stephenson, Robert, 175
Stewart, Tom, 324
Stilwell, E. J., 69
Strategic alliances, 266
  as grand strategy, 237–239
Strategic analysis, 15
Strategic analysis and choice, 248–275
  basic issues, 248
  behavioral considerations, 292–295
  at Coca-Cola, 273–275
  diversifying to build value, 264–271
  grand strategy clusters, 267–270
  grand strategy selection matrix, 265–266
  industry environments, 259–264
  in multibusiness companies, 277–299
  rationalizing diversification and integration, 277–291
  strategies for competitive advantage, 248–259
Strategic business units, 342–344, 345
Strategic choice, 15
  options, 240
Strategic controls, 17, 308
  characteristics, 388
  at Coca-Cola, 400–404
  definition, 380
  establishing, 380–388

Q

R

S

Strategic controls—*Cont.*
  examples of, 386–387
  implementation control, 383–386
  premise control, 381–383
  special alert control, 3873–88
  strategic surveillance, 386–387
  types of, 381
Strategic decisions
  characteristics, 7–8
  decision makers, 9–10
  dimensions of, 4–5
  levels of, 5–7
Strategic gap analysis, 163
Strategic intent, 353–354
Strategic management
  alternative structures, 8
  benefits, 10–11
  and competitive forces, 74–75
  components of model, 13–17
  definition and tasks, 3–4
  and forecasting, 151–153
  formality of systems, 9–12
  general trends, 19
  key planning issues, 95
  process, 12–13, 17–18
  risks, 11–12
  strategic decisions, 4–8
Strategic management teams, 9–10
Strategic surveillance control,
    386–387
Strategic thrusts, 383
Strategy; *see also* Generic
    strategies *and* Grand strategies
  attitudes toward risk, 293
  competitive reaction to, 294–295
  critical ingredients, 169
  current, 292
  definition, 4
  for emerging industries, 259–260
  and firm's external dependence,
    292–293
  internal politics, 293–294
  levels of, 5–7
  linking rewards to, 362–363
  matching structure to, 346–352
  seeking sustained competitive
    advantage, 248–259
  timing of, 294
  types, 15
  for US firms' competitiveness,
    122–125
Strategy acquisition, 232–233
Strategy implementation
  action plans, 304–308
  at Coca-Cola, 328–337
  empowering operating personnel,
    320–325
  examples, 326
  functional tactics for, 309–319
  major concerns, 304
  operational controls, 388–393
  quality imperative, 393–397
  short-term objectives, 304–308
  strategic controls, 380–388
Strength, 171
  potential, 176–177
Strickland, A., 178
Structure, 84; *see also* Industry
    structure
  of Coca-Cola, 370–372

Structure—*Cont.*
  effective, 339–352
  matching strategy to, 346–352
Substitutes, 80, 102
  lessening attractiveness of, 250
Success factor comparisons,
    188–189
Suitable objectives, 215
Sun Oil Company, 140
Suppliers
  for Coca-Cola, 100
  as competitive force, 77–79
  cost increases, 250–251
  loyalty, 250–251
  in operating environment, 92
  partnerships with, 396
Support activities, 177–178
Supporting brands, 404, 405
Surface Mining and Reclamation
    Act, 72
Survival
  in company mission, 121
  goal, 32–34
Sustainable growth model, 163
Sustained competitive advantage;
    see Competitive advantage
SWOT analysis, 162, 169
  computer industry, 174–175
  definition, 170–173
Synergy, 360

T

Taguchi, Genichi, 43
Taguchi methods, 43
Tandy Corporation, 224
Tanner, D. A., 232
Target market, 88–92
Tashakori, A., 45 n
Task environment, 156; *see also*
    Operating environment
Technological environment, 66–67
Technological forecasts, 150–151
Technological leadership, 213
Technology
  in company mission, 31–32,
    120–121
  and differentiation, 253
  economies of scale, 84–85
  and information sharing,
    256–257
  innovation, 226–227
  rapid development, 115
  scenario for 21st Century,
    148–149
Teitelbaum, R. S., 254
Telecommunications industry,
    225–226, 254–255
Teplitz, Paul V., 155
Thomas, R. R., 358 n
Thompson, A. A., 178
Thompson, Judith Kenner, 37
Threats, 171
3M, 69, 185, 282
  strategy implementation, 326
Tibbs, H. B. C., 69

Time frame/horizon
  for competition, 16
  for completion, 304
  of functional tactics, 310
Time series models, 145
Times Mirror, 254
Timing, 294
Top-management decisions, 4
Total quality control, 43
Total quality management,
    393–394
  at Marlow Industries, 393,
    394–395
TOWS; *see* SWOT analysis
Toxic Substances Control Act, 73
Toyota Model AA, 227
Trachtenberg, Jeff, 174
Travellers Insurance, 353–354, 355
Treaty of Rome, 64
Trend analysis, 163
Trend analysis models, 145–146
Trend extrapolation, 145
Trigger point level of deviation,
    392
Trogen, Karl-Erling, 4
Tropicana Twisters, 102
Truck industry, 258
Turnaround, 266
  as grand strategy, 231–234
  responses, 233–234
  situation, 231

U

Understandable objectives, 215
United Airlines, 387
United Technologies, 362–363
Unrelated diversified businesses,
    351, 352
USX Corporation, 137

V

Value added, 263, 316
  power of, 320–321
Value chain, 169
Value chain analysis, 176–191
  at The Gap, 180, 182–183
Values
  core, 357
  cultural, 358
  dominant, 357
  reinforced, 357–358
ValuJet Airlines, 312–313
Van der Linde, Claas, 87
Velsical Chemical Company, 382
Venkatraman, N., 12 n, 13, 19, 95
Vertical integration, 266, 351
  at Coca-Cola, 246
  as grand strategy, 228–229
Volume expansion, 351
Volvo, 248, 258

Volvo General Motors Heavy
    Truck Corporation, 4

W

Wade, Judy, 348 n
Wall Street Journal, 386
Wal-Mart, 99, 102, 179–180, 188,
    248, 307–308, 347, 361, 382
Walston, Gerald, 238
Walt Disney Company, 173,
    282–283
Walton, Mary, 393 n
Wang, An, 236
Wang Laboratories, bankruptcy,
    236
Wasson, Charles, 184
Water pollution, 67
Water pollution laws, 72–73
Water Quality Act, 73
Water Quality Improvement Act,
    73
Weaknesses, 171
  potential, 176–177
Webster, J., 162
Weil, Sanford, 353–354
Weiner, Benjamin, 152
Weizorek, Heinz, 374
Welch, Jack, 256, 280, 315
Wendy's, purchasing policy, 326
West, David, 316–317
West, Linda, 316–317
Wharton Econometric Forecasting
    Associates, 145
Wheelwright, Steven C., 389 n
Whirlpool Corporation, Quality
    Express delivery program, 4
White Nights Joint Enterprise, 238
Wilson, Kemmons, 288
Winegardner, Roy, 288
Witzke, Chris, 394–395
Wloszezyna, Chris, 49
Wolf, Clark, 7
Women, in work force, 65
Woodward, D., 110 n
WordPerfect, 279–280
Worldwide Web, 384–385
Wrigley, Larry, 351

X–Z

Xerox Corporation, 40, 357
Yamanouchi Pharmaceuticals
    Company, globalization,
    104–105
Yearout, Stephen, 397
Zahra, Shaker A., 44 n, 122 n
Zale Corporation, 119
Ziegler, Bart, 174
Zimmerer, T. W., 112, 316
Zytec, 44